**Hoover's Online** is your source for business information that works.

Millions of businesspeople use Hoover's Online every day for research, analysis, and prospecting. Hoover's updates information daily on thousands of companies and hundreds of industries worldwide.

### USE HOOVER'S ONLINE FOR:

- COMPANY RESEARCH
  - Overview
  - History
  - Competitors
  - News
  - Products
  - Location(s)
  - Financials
  - Stock data

- INDUSTRY RESEARCH
  - Quick synopsis
  - Leading companies
  - Analysis of trends
  - Associations
  - Glossary of terms
  - Research reports

- PROSPECTING
  - Search by industry,
  - location, sales, keyword
  - Full officer lists
  - Company history
  - Financials

"You simply can't find more information on corporate America in any other single source." —*Business Week*

For accurate online business information, visit us at www.hoovers.com

# Hoover's
# Handbook of
# Private
# Companies

## 2 0 0 2

**BUSINESS PRESS**

Austin, Texas

*Hoover's Handbook of Private Companies 2002* is intended to provide readers with accurate and authoritative information about the enterprises covered in it. Hoover's asked all companies and organizations profiled to provide information. Many did so; some did not. The information contained herein is as accurate as we could reasonably make it. In many cases we have relied on third-party material that we believe to be trustworthy, but were unable to independently verify. We do not warrant that the book is absolutely accurate or without error. Readers should not rely on any information contained herein in instances where such reliance might cause loss or damage. The publisher, the editors, and their data suppliers specifically disclaim all warranties, including the implied warranties of merchantability and fitness for a specific purpose. This book is sold with the understanding that neither the publisher, the editors, nor any content contributors are engaged in providing investment, financial, accounting, legal, or other professional advice.

The financial data in this book are from the companies profiled or from trade sources deemed to be reliable. Hoover's, Inc., is solely responsible for the presentation of all data.

Many of the names of products and services mentioned in this book are the trademarks or service marks of the companies manufacturing or selling them and are subject to protection under US law. Space has not permitted us to indicate which names are subject to such protection, and readers are advised to consult with the owners of such marks regarding their use. Hoover's is a trademark of Hoover's, Inc.

**BUSINESS PRESS**

10 9 8 7 6 5 4 3 2 1

Publishers Cataloging-in-Publication Data

Hoover's Handbook of Private Companies 2002     *864 p.*

Includes indexes.

1. Business enterprises — Directories. 2. Corporations — Directories.

HF3010 338.7

Hoover's Company Information is also available on America Online, Bloomberg Financial Network, CNBC on MSN Money, EBSCO, Factiva, FORTUNE, Hoover's Online, LexisNexis, NewsEdge, ProQuest, The Washington Post, and other Web sites.

A catalog of Hoover's products is available on the World Wide Web at www.hoovers.com.

ISBN 1-57311-075-2

ISSN 1073-6433

The Hoover's Handbook series is edited by George Sutton and produced for Hoover's Business Press by Sycamore Productions, Inc., Austin, Texas, using Quark, Inc.'s QuarkXPress 4.04; EM Software, Inc.'s Xtags 4.1; and fonts from Adobe's Clearface, Futura, and Myriad families. Cover design is by Shawn Harrington. Electronic prepress and printing were done by Edwards Brothers Incorporated, Ann Arbor, Michigan. Text paper is 50# Arbor.

**US AND WORLD DIRECT SALES**

Hoover's, Inc.
5800 Airport Blvd.
Austin, TX 78752
Phone: 512-374-4500
Fax: 512-374-4501
e-mail: orders@hoovers.com

**EUROPE**

William Snyder Publishing Associates
5 Five Mile Drive
Oxford OX2 8HT
England
Phone & fax: +44-186-551-3186
e-mail: snyderpub@cs.com

# HOOVER'S, INC.

**Founder:** Gary Hoover
**Chairman:** Patrick J. Spain
**President and CEO:** Jeffrey Tarr
**EVP Corporate Strategy and Development:** Carl G. Shepherd
**SVP Product Management:** Russell Seeker

## EDITORIAL

**Managing Editor:** Nancy Regent
**Assistant Managing Editor:** Valerie Pearcy
**Editorial Operations Manager:** Ashley Schrump
**Director, Financial Information:** Dennis Sutton
**Senior Editors:** Rachel Brush, Margaret Claughton, Paul Geary, Joe Grey, Kathleen Kelly, Mary Mickle Morales
**Assistant Senior Editors:** Larry Bills, Angela Boeckman, Joe Bramhall, Michaela Drapes, Chris Huston, Joe Simonetta
**Associate Editors:** Joy Aiken, Sally Alt, Graham Baker, Jason Cother, Bobby Duncan, Carrie Geis, Todd Gernert, Allan Gill, Gregg Gordon, Melanie Hall, Matt Saucedo, Vanita Trippe, Randy Williams, David Woodruff
**Contributing Editor:** Travis Brown
**Senior Writers:** David Hamerly, Stuart Hampton, Guy Holland, Josh Lower
**Writers:** Linnea Anderson, James Bryant, Ryan Caione, Jason Cella, Danny Cummings, Tom Elia, Laura Ivy, Andreas Knutsen, Julie Krippel, Anne Law, Diane Lee, John MacAyeal, Nell Newton, Sheri Olander, Amanda Palm, Elizabeth Paukstis, Rob Reynolds, Amy Schein, Seth Shafer, Tim Walker, Chris Zappone
**Financial Editors:** Adi Anand, Troy Bryant, John Flynn, Joel Sensat
**Chief Copyeditor:** Emily Weida Domaschk
**QA Editors:** Anthony Staats, John Willis
**Assistant Editors:** Tommy Ates, Lesley Epperson Dings, Jeanette Herman, Michael McLellan, David Ramirez, Christopher Sovine, Daysha Taylor
**Editorial Assistants:** Daniel Croll, Jana Cummings, Jay Koenig, Michelle Medina, Anna Porlas, Kcevin Rob
**Research Coordinator:** Jim Harris
**Library Coordinator:** Kris Stephenson

## PRINT PRODUCTS DIVISION

**Director, Print Products:** Dana Smith
**Distribution Manager:** Rhonda Mitchell
**Fulfillment and Shipping Manager:** Michael Febonio
**Shipping Clerk:** James H. Taylor IV

## ABOUT HOOVER'S, INC.

Hoover's, Inc. (Nasdaq: HOOV) provides online business information and tools to help business-people get their jobs done. Hoover's information is available through its destination site Hoover's Online (http://www.hoovers.com), through co-branding agreements with other online services, and through customized applications developed for enterprise information portals. Hoover's investors include AOL Time Warner (NYSE: AOL), Media General (AMEX: MEGA), and Knowledge Universe, through its Knowledge Net Holdings and Nextera Enterprises (Nasdaq: NXRA) units. Hoover's is head-quartered in Austin, Texas, and has offices in New York City and San Francisco.

# Abbreviations

**AFL-CIO** – American Federation of Labor and Congress of Industrial Organizations
**AMA** – American Medical Association
**AMEX** – American Stock Exchange
**ARM** – adjustable-rate mortgage
**ATM** – asynchronous transfer mode
**ATM** – automated teller machine
**CAD/CAM** – computer-aided design/computer-aided manufacturing
**CASE** – computer-aided software engineering
**CD-ROM** – compact disc – read-only memory
**CEO** – chief executive officer
**CFO** – chief financial officer
**CISC** – complex instruction set computer
**CMOS** – complementary metal-oxide semiconductor
**COO** – chief operating officer
**DAT** – digital audiotape
**DOD** – Department of Defense
**DOE** – Department of Energy
**DOS** – disc operating system
**DOT** – Department of Transportation
**DRAM** – dynamic random access memory
**DVD** – digital versatile disk/digital videodisk
**EPA** – Environmental Protection Agency
**EPROM** – erasable programmable read-only memory
**EPS** – earnings per share
**ESOP** – employee stock ownership plan
**EU** – European Union
**EVP** – executive vice president
**FCC** – Federal Communications Commission
**FDA** – Food and Drug Administration
**FDIC** – Federal Deposit Insurance Corporation
**FTC** – Federal Trade Commission
**FTP** – file transfer protocol
**GATT** – General Agreement on Tariffs and Trade
**GDP** – gross domestic product
**GUI** – graphical user interface
**HMO** – health maintenance organization
**HR** – human resources
**HTML** – hypertext markup language
**ICC** – Interstate Commerce Commission
**IPO** – initial public offering
**IRS** – Internal Revenue Service
**ISDN** – integrated services digital network
**kWh** – kilowatt-hour
**LAN** – local-area network

**LBO** – leveraged buyout
**LCD** – liquid crystal display
**LNG** – liquefied natural gas
**LP** – limited partnership
**Ltd.** – limited
**mips** – millions of instructions per second
**MW** – megawatt
**NAFTA** – North American Free Trade Agreement
**NASA** – National Aeronautics and Space Administration
**Nasdaq** – National Association of Securities Dealers Automated Quotations
**NATO** – North Atlantic Treaty Organization
**NYSE** – New York Stock Exchange
**OCR** – optical character recognition
**OECD** – Organization for Economic Cooperation and Development
**OEM** – original equipment manufacturer
**OPEC** – Organization of Petroleum Exporting Countries
**OS** – operating system
**OSHA** – Occupational Safety and Health Administration
**OTC** – over-the-counter
**PBX** – private branch exchange
**PCMCIA** – Personal Computer Memory Card International Association
**P/E** – price-to-earnings ratio
**RAM** – random access memory
**R&D** – research and development
**RBOC** – regional Bell operating company
**RISC** – reduced instruction set computer
**REIT** – real estate investment trust
**ROA** – return on assets
**ROE** – return on equity
**ROI** – return on investment
**ROM** – read-only memory
**S&L** – savings and loan
**SEC** – Securities and Exchange Commission
**SEVP** – senior executive vice president
**SIC** – Standard Industrial Classification
**SPARC** – scalable processor architecture
**SVP** – senior vice president
**VAR** – value-added reseller
**VAT** – value-added tax
**VC** – venture capitalist
**VP** – vice president
**WAN** – wide-area network
**WWW** – World Wide Web

# Contents

# Companies Profiled

# Companies Profiled

# ABOUT *HOOVER'S HANDBOOK* OF *PRIVATE COMPANIES 2002*

Privately held enterprises are major players in the US economy (giant food processor Cargill or insurer State Farm, for example) and their activities affect our daily lives. Publishing current, relevant information about these companies can be a challenge, as many of them see secrecy as a competitve strategy. Our mission with this volume is to fill the information gap that exists.

In this seventh edition of *Hoover's Handbook of Private Companies*, we have compiled the hard-to-find facts on 750 of the largest and most influential enterprises in the US.

This book contains two-page, in-depth profiles on 250 of these enterprises, mostly larger companies, but we've included several smaller but equally interesting ones as well. In addition, we provide basic information, including officers, sales, and top competitors for 500 other key private enterprises with revenues of $800 million or more. We believe no other guide provides the comprehensive information contained in *Hoover's Handbook of Private Companies 2002*.

If you are interested in finding out more about other companies, we encourage you to visit Hoover's Online (www.hoovers.com), which provides coverage of some 12 million business enterprises. Our goal with our Web site is to provide one location that addresses all the needs of business professionals. Hoover's has partnered with other prestigious business information and service providers to bring you all the right business information, services, and links in one place. Additionally, Hoover's Company Information is available on other sites on the Internet, including The Washington Post, LexisNexis, and online services Bloomberg Financial Network, Factiva, and America Online.

*Hoover's Handbook of Private Companies* is one of a four-title series that is available as an indexed set. The other three titles are *Hoover's Handbook of American Business* (two volumes), *Hoover's Handbook of Emerging Companies*, and *Hoover's Handbook of World Business*.

We believe anyone who buys from, sells to, invests in, lends to, competes with, interviews with, or works for a company should know about that enterprise. This book and our other Hoover's products and resources represent the most complete source of basic corporate information readily available to the general public.

This book consists of five sections:

1. Using the Profiles describes the contents of our profiles and explains the ways in which we gather and compile our data.

2. A List-Lover's Compendium contains lists of the largest private companies. The lists are based on the information in our profiles, or compiled from well-known sources.

3. Profiles of 250 major private enterprises, arranged alphabetically, make up the largest and the most important part of the book.

4. Capsule summaries of 750 private companies (including summaries for companies with in-depth profiles in the book) follow the profiles. The page number of the full profile is listed on the capsule page for quick reference.

5. Three indexes complete the book. The companies are indexed by industry group and headquarters location, and there is a main index of all the brand names, companies, and people mentioned in the profiles in the book.

We hope you find our books useful. We invite your comments by phone (512-374-4500), fax (512-374-4501), mail (5800 Airport Blvd., Austin, TX 78752), or e-mail (comments@hoovers.com).

The Editors
Austin, Texas
February 2002

# USING THE PROFILES

## COMPANIES PROFILED

The 750 enterprises profiled in this book include the largest and most influential private enterprises in America. Among them are:

- private companies, from the giants (Cargill and Koch) to the colorful and prominent (King Ranch and Skidmore, Owings & Merrill)
- mutuals and cooperative organizations owned by their customers (State Farm Insurance, Ace Hardware, Ocean Spray Cranberries)
- not-for-profits (American Red Cross, Kaiser Foundation Health Plan, Smithsonian Institution)
- joint ventures (Motiva Enterprises, Dow Corning)
- partnerships (Baker & McKenzie, Kohlberg Kravis Roberts & Co.)
- universities (Columbia, Harvard, University of California)
- government-owned corporations (US Postal Service, New York City's Metropolitan Transportation Authority)
- and a selection of other enterprises (National Basketball Association, AFL-CIO, Texas Lottery Commission).

## ORGANIZATION

The profiles are presented in alphabetical order. We have shown the full legal name of the enterprise at the top of the page, unless it is too long, in which case you will find it above the address in the Where section of the profile. If a company name is also a person's name, such as Edward J. DeBartolo or Mary Kay, it will be alphabetized under the first name; if the company name starts with initials, for example, L.L. Bean or S.C. Johnson, look for it under the combined initials (in the above examples, LL and SC, respectively). All company names (past and present) used in the profiles are indexed in the main index in the book. Basic financial data are listed under the heading Historical Financials & Employees.

The annual financial information contained in the profiles is as current as possible through fiscal year-ends as late as September 2001. We have included certain nonfinancial developments, such as officer changes, through January 2002.

## OVERVIEW

In the first section of the profile, we have tried to give a thumbnail description of the company and what it does. The description will usually include information on the company's strategy, reputation, and ownership. We recommend that you read this section first.

## HISTORY

This extended section reflects our belief that every enterprise is the sum of its history, and that you have to know where you came from in order to know where you are going. While some companies have limited historical awareness and were unable to help us much and other companies are just plain boring, we think the vast majority of the enterprises in this book have colorful backgrounds. We have tried to focus on the people who made the enterprises what they are today. We have found these histories to be full of twists and ironies; they make fascinating reading.

## OFFICERS

Here we list the names of the people who run the company, insofar as space allows.

While companies are free to structure their management titles any way they please, most modern corporations follow standard practices. The chief officer, the person on whose desk the buck stops, is usually called the chief executive officer (CEO). Often, he or she is also the chairman of the board.

Because corporate management has become more complex, it is common for the CEO to have a right-hand person who oversees the day-to-day operations of the company, allowing the CEO plenty of time to focus on strategy and long-term issues. This right-hand person is usually designated the chief operating officer (COO) and is often the president of the company. In other cases one person is both chairman and president.

A multitude of other titles exists, including chief financial officer (CFO), chief administrative officer, and vice chairman. We have always tried to include the CFO, the chief legal officer, and the chief human resources or personnel officer (HR). The Officers section also includes the name of the company's auditing (accounting) firm, where available.

The people named in the profiles are also included in the main index.

## LOCATIONS

Here we include the company's headquarters, street address, telephone and fax numbers, and Web site, as available. An index of companies listed by headquarters location is located in the back of the book.

In some cases we have also included information on the geographical distribution of the company's business, including sales and profit data. Note that these profit numbers, like those in the Products/Operations section below, are usually operating or pretax profits rather than net profits. Operating profits are generally those before financing costs (interest income and payments) and before taxes, which are considered costs attributable to the whole company rather than to one division or part of the world. For this reason the net income figures (in the Historical Financials & Employees section) are usually much lower, since they are after interest and taxes. Pretax profits are after interest but before taxes.

## PRODUCTS/OPERATIONS

This section lists as many of the company's products, services, brand names, divisions, subsidiaries, and joint ventures as we could fit. We have tried to include all its major lines and all familiar brand names. The nature of this section varies by company and amount of information available. If the company publishes sales and profit information by type of business, we have included it. The brand, division, and subsidiary names are listed in the main index in the book.

## COMPETITORS

In this section we have listed companies that compete with the profiled company. This feature is included as a quick way to locate similar companies and compare them.

## HISTORICAL FINANCIALS & EMPLOYEES

Here we have tried to present as much data about each enterprise's financial performance as we could compile. Many private companies don't readily give out information about themselves, but we have tried to provide annual sales and employment figures (although in some cases they are estimates based on statistics from numerous sources). The following information is generally present:

A 10-year table, with relevant annualized compound growth rates, covering:
- **Sales** — fiscal year sales (year-end assets for most financial companies)

- **Net Income** (where available) — fiscal year net income (before accounting changes)
- **Income as a Percent of Sales** (where available) — fiscal year net income as a percent of sales (as a percent of assets for most financial firms)
- **Employees** — fiscal year-end or average number of employees

The information on employees is intended to aid the reader interested in knowing whether a company has a long-term trend of increasing or decreasing employment. As far as we know, we are the only company that publishes this information in print form.

The year at the top of each column in the Historical Financials & Employees section is the year in which the company's fiscal year actually ends. Thus a company with a September 30, 2001, year-end is shown as 2001. Generally, for private companies, we have graphed net income or, where that is unavailable, sales.

Key year-end statistics are included in this section for insurance companies and companies required to file reports with the SEC. They generally show the financial strength of the enterprise, including:
- Debt ratio (total debt as a percent of combined total debt and shareholders' equity)
- Return on equity (net income divided by the average of beginning and ending common shareholders' equity)
- Cash, marketable securities, and short-term investments on hand
- Current ratio (ratio of current assets to current liabilities)
- Total long-term debt (including capital lease obligations)

## KEY PRIVATE COMPANIES

Each of the 500 shorter capsule summaries contains the company's name, headquarters address, phone and fax numbers, and Web address (where available); the names of the chief executive officer (CEO), chief financial officer (CFO), and chief human resources officer (HR); the company's fiscal year-end; the most recent annual sales figure available; the sales change over the prior year; and the number of employees. It also includes an overview of the company's operations and ownership and a list of key competitors. Since some entities (associations, foundations, universities) do not compete against one another in the traditional sense, for them we have omitted the list of key competitors.

# Hoover's Handbook of Private Companies

## A List-Lover's Compendium

# The 300 Largest Companies by Sales in
## *Hoover's Handbook of Private Companies 2002*

| Rank | Company | Sales ($ mil.) |
|---|---|---|
| 1 | Blue Cross and Blue Shield | 126,000 |
| 2 | United States Postal Service | 65,919 |
| 3 | Equilon Enterprises LLC | 50,010 |
| 4 | Cargill, Incorporated | 49,400 |
| 5 | State Farm Insurance | 47,863 |
| 6 | Koch Industries, Inc. | 40,000 |
| 7 | TIAA-CREF | 37,273 |
| 8 | Nationwide | 32,834 |
| 9 | Marathon Ashland Petroleum | 28,885 |
| 10 | PricewaterhouseCoopers | 24,000 |
| 11 | New York Life Insurance | 21,996 |
| 12 | IGA, INC. | 21,000 |
| 13 | Motiva Enterprises LLC | 19,446 |
| 14 | CalPERS | 18,845 |
| 15 | Kaiser Foundation Health Plan | 17,700 |
| 16 | University of California | 16,156 |
| 17 | Northwestern Mutual | 15,382 |
| 18 | Massachusetts Mutual Life | 15,340 |
| 19 | Bechtel Group, Inc. | 15,108 |
| 20 | Mars, Incorporated | 15,000 |
| 21 | Publix Super Markets, Inc. | 14,724 |
| 22 | Verizon Wireless Inc. | 14,236 |
| 23 | Liberty Mutual Insurance | 13,470 |
| 24 | Federal Reserve Bank of New York | 13,456 |
| 25 | Cingular Wireless | 12,647 |
| 26 | Deloitte Touche Tohmatsu | 12,400 |
| 27 | Carlson Wagonlit Travel | 12,000 |
| 28 | Farmland Industries, Inc. | 11,763 |
| 29 | KPMG International | 11,700 |
| 30 | FMR Corp. | 11,096 |
| 31 | Health Care Service Corporation | 10,430 |
| 32 | Meijer, Inc. | 10,000 |
| 33 | Ernst & Young International | 10,000 |
| 34 | Penske Corporation | 10,000 |
| 35 | Carlson Companies, Inc. | 9,800 |
| 36 | Blue Cross Blue Shield of Michigan | 9,487 |
| 37 | Andersen | 9,340 |
| 38 | The ASCII Group, Inc. | 9,200 |
| 39 | Duke Energy Field Services Corporation | 9,093 |
| 40 | Highmark Inc. | 9,000 |
| 41 | H. E. Butt Grocery Company | 8,965 |
| 42 | Cenex Harvest States Cooperatives | 8,571 |
| 43 | USAA | 8,551 |
| 44 | C&S Wholesale Grocers, Inc. | 8,500 |
| 45 | Huntsman Corporation | 8,000 |
| 46 | The Trump Organization | 8,000 |
| 47 | Cox Enterprises, Inc. | 7,824 |
| 48 | Equistar Chemicals, LP | 7,495 |
| 49 | Chevron Phillips Chemical Company LP | 7,470 |
| 50 | Army and Air Force Exchange | 7,369 |
| 51 | Premcor Inc. | 7,302 |
| 52 | JM Family Enterprises, Inc. | 7,100 |
| 53 | Concert Communications | 7,000 |
| 54 | Tennessee Valley Authority | 6,999 |
| 55 | The Marmon Group, Inc. | 6,786 |
| 56 | Dairy Farmers of America | 6,700 |
| 57 | CFM International, Inc. | 6,700 |
| 58 | Seagate Technology, Inc. | 6,448 |
| 59 | Ascension Health | 6,400 |
| 60 | Enterprise Rent-A-Car | 6,300 |
| 61 | Guardian Life Insurance | 6,283 |
| 62 | The University of Texas System | 5,943 |
| 63 | Science Applications International | 5,896 |
| 64 | Wakefern Food Corporation | 5,800 |
| 65 | Land O'Lakes, Inc. | 5,756 |
| 66 | Catholic Health Initiatives | 5,742 |
| 67 | MacAndrews & Forbes | 5,500 |
| 68 | Rosenbluth International | 5,500 |
| 69 | Graybar Electric Company, Inc. | 5,227 |
| 70 | MidAmerican Energy Holdings | 5,103 |
| 71 | State University of New York | 5,076 |
| 72 | Menard, Inc. | 5,000 |
| 73 | Cardone Industries Inc. | 4,900 |
| 74 | Catholic Healthcare West | 4,800 |
| 75 | Doctor's Associates Inc. | 4,720 |
| 76 | New United Motor Manufacturing | 4,699 |
| 77 | Levi Strauss & Co. | 4,645 |
| 78 | Advance Publications, Inc. | 4,542 |
| 79 | Catholic Healthcare Network | 4,523 |
| 80 | S.C. Johnson & Son, Inc. | 4,500 |
| 81 | Trinity Health | 4,500 |
| 82 | Peter Kiewit Sons', Inc. | 4,463 |
| 83 | Giant Eagle Inc. | 4,435 |
| 84 | Flying J Inc. | 4,349 |
| 85 | VT Inc. | 4,300 |
| 86 | Catholic Health East | 4,300 |
| 87 | Holberg Industries, Inc. | 4,250 |
| 88 | Empire HealthChoice | 4,240 |
| 89 | The Mutual of Omaha Companies | 4,240 |
| 90 | Hallmark Cards, Inc. | 4,200 |
| 91 | American Family Insurance | 4,127 |
| 92 | New York City Health and Hospitals Corporation | 4,100 |
| 93 | California State University | 4,050 |
| 94 | Metropolitan Transportation Authority | 4,033 |
| 95 | ContiGroup Companies, Inc. | 4,000 |
| 96 | Asbury Automotive Group, Inc. | 4,000 |
| 97 | Hy-Vee, Inc. | 4,000 |
| 98 | Guardian Industries Corp. | 4,000 |
| 99 | Milliken & Company Inc. | 4,000 |
| 100 | National Football League | 4,000 |

Source: Hoover's, Inc., Database, January 2002

# The 300 Largest Companies by Sales in
## Hoover's Handbook of Private Companies 2002 (continued)

| Rank | Company | Sales ($ mil.) | Rank | Company | Sales ($ mil.) |
|------|---------|---------------|------|---------|----------------|
| 101 | TruServ Corporation | 3,994 | 151 | Wegmans Food Markets, Inc. | 2,800 |
| 102 | Hyatt Corporation | 3,950 | 152 | University of Florida | 2,782 |
| 103 | Texas Lottery Commission | 3,940 | 153 | Dow Corning Corporation | 2,751 |
| 104 | Massachusetts State Lottery | 3,936 | 154 | University of Illinois | 2,722 |
| 105 | United Way of America | 3,910 | 155 | MBM Corporation | 2,700 |
| 106 | YMCA of the USA | 3,907 | 156 | Perdue Farms Incorporated | 2,700 |
| 107 | Reyes Holdings LLC | 3,900 | 157 | Blue Cross and Blue Shield of Massachusetts, Inc. | 2,700 |
| 108 | The Lefrak Organization | 3,800 | | | |
| 109 | WorldTravel BTI | 3,800 | 158 | Kohler Co. | 2,700 |
| 110 | Mayo Foundation | 3,710 | 159 | University of Washington | 2,696 |
| 111 | SYNNEX Information Technologies, Inc. | 3,700 | 160 | The University of Michigan | 2,696 |
| 112 | New York State Lottery | 3,674 | 161 | Keystone Foods LLC | 2,650 |
| 113 | Los Angeles Department of Water and Power | 3,628 | 162 | Port Authority of New York | 2,648 |
| | | | 163 | ESPN, Inc. | 2,600 |
| 114 | TAP Pharmaceutical Products Inc. | 3,539 | 164 | Micro Warehouse, Inc. | 2,600 |
| 115 | Alticor Inc. | 3,500 | 165 | Allina Health System | 2,600 |
| 116 | Southern Wine & Spirits | 3,500 | 166 | Gordon Food Service | 2,600 |
| 117 | Sutter Health | 3,500 | 167 | A-Mark Financial Corporation | 2,600 |
| 118 | Penske Truck Leasing | 3,477 | 168 | Clark Retail Group, Inc. | 2,600 |
| 119 | Eby-Brown Company | 3,400 | 169 | Stater Bros. Holdings Inc. | 2,574 |
| 120 | McKinsey & Company | 3,400 | 170 | Intermountain Health Care | 2,552 |
| 121 | The Hearst Corporation | 3,400 | 171 | The American Red Cross | 2,529 |
| 122 | Associated Wholesale Grocers, Inc. | 3,370 | 172 | Adventist Health | 2,510 |
| 123 | Partners HealthCare System, Inc. | 3,317 | 173 | The Martin-Brower Company | 2,500 |
| 124 | Pension Benefit Guaranty Corporation | 3,298 | 174 | California State Lottery | 2,500 |
| | | | 175 | Brown Automotive Group Ltd. | 2,500 |
| 125 | Gulf States Toyota, Inc. | 3,250 | 176 | Consolidated Electrical | 2,500 |
| 126 | Providence Health System | 3,229 | 177 | Quality Chekd Dairies, Inc. | 2,500 |
| 127 | Major League Baseball | 3,178 | 178 | Hendrick Automotive Group | 2,483 |
| 128 | Topco Associates, Inc. | 3,150 | 179 | Transammonia, Inc. | 2,447 |
| 129 | Carpet Co-op Association of America | 3,140 | 180 | The Connell Company | 2,425 |
| 130 | Schwan's Sales Enterprises, Inc. | 3,100 | 181 | Health Insurance Plan of Greater New York | 2,410 |
| 131 | Pacific Mutual Holding Company | 3,092 | 182 | Quality King Distributors Inc. | 2,400 |
| 132 | Schneider National, Inc. | 3,089 | 183 | Clark Enterprises, Inc. | 2,400 |
| 133 | Bonneville Power Administration | 3,041 | 184 | Venture Industries | 2,400 |
| 134 | Core-Mark International, Inc. | 3,035 | 185 | Parsons Corporation | 2,400 |
| 135 | SRP | 3,027 | 186 | Gilbane, Inc. | 2,388 |
| 136 | International Data Group | 3,010 | 187 | Catholic Healthcare Partners | 2,373 |
| 137 | The University of Pennsylvania | 3,007 | 188 | Allied Worldwide, Inc. | 2,372 |
| 138 | J.R. Simplot Company | 3,000 | 189 | Black & Veatch | 2,358 |
| 139 | Raley's Inc. | 3,000 | 190 | Georgia Lottery Corporation | 2,310 |
| 140 | Visa International | 3,000 | 191 | North Shore-Long Island Jewish Health System | 2,310 |
| 141 | Roundy's, Inc. | 2,991 | 192 | University of Minnesota | 2,301 |
| 142 | Ace Hardware Corporation | 2,945 | 193 | Sisters of Mercy Health System-St. Louis | 2,298 |
| 143 | Unified Western Grocers, Inc. | 2,929 | | | |
| 144 | QuikTrip Corporation | 2,929 | 194 | University System of Maryland | 2,291 |
| 145 | National Amusements Inc. | 2,918 | 195 | University of Wisconsin System | 2,279 |
| 146 | Kemper Insurance Companies | 2,913 | 196 | Springs Industries, Inc. | 2,275 |
| 147 | Bloomberg L.P. | 2,800 | 197 | Belk, Inc. | 2,270 |
| 148 | Delta Dental Plan of California | 2,800 | 198 | State of Florida Lottery | 2,256 |
| 149 | NRT Incorporated | 2,800 | 199 | Washington Group International | 2,248 |
| 150 | AAA | 2,800 | 200 | Do it Best Corp. | 2,215 |

# The 300 Largest Companies by Sales in
## Hoover's Handbook of Private Companies 2002 (continued)

| Rank | Company | Sales ($ mil.) | Rank | Company | Sales ($ mil.) |
|---|---|---|---|---|---|
| 201 | Jones Financial Companies | 2,212 | 251 | Schnuck Markets, Inc. | 1,969 |
| 202 | Holman Enterprises | 2,200 | 252 | Ag Processing Inc | 1,962 |
| 203 | CHRISTUS Health | 2,200 | 253 | Crown Central Petroleum | 1,961 |
| 204 | Alcoa Fujikura Ltd. | 2,200 | 254 | DPR Construction, Inc. | 1,958 |
| 205 | Duke University | 2,200 | 255 | Stanford University | 1,957 |
| 206 | Kinko's, Inc. | 2,200 | 256 | Westcon Group, Inc. | 1,939 |
| 207 | Massachusetts Institute of Technology | 2,191 | 257 | Sammons Enterprises, Inc. | 1,934 |
|  |  |  | 258 | The City University of New York | 1,927 |
| 208 | National Basketball Association | 2,164 | 259 | The Ohio State University | 1,923 |
| 209 | Sunoco Logistics Partners L.P. | 2,161 | 260 | American United Life Insurance | 1,907 |
| 210 | Ohio Lottery Commission | 2,156 | 261 | Ergon, Inc. | 1,900 |
| 211 | The Pennsylvania State University | 2,150 | 262 | Sinclair Oil Corporation | 1,900 |
| 212 | Renco Group Inc. | 2,150 | 263 | Global Companies LLC | 1,900 |
| 213 | Johns Hopkins Medicine | 2,121 | 264 | California Dairies Inc. | 1,900 |
| 214 | Amtrak | 2,111 | 265 | Henry Ford Health System | 1,900 |
| 215 | BJC Health System | 2,100 | 266 | Dr Pepper/Seven Up Bottling Group, Inc. | 1,900 |
| 216 | The Johns Hopkins University | 2,100 |  |  |  |
| 217 | Lumbermens Merchandising | 2,100 | 267 | Sheetz, Inc. | 1,900 |
| 218 | The Structure Tone Organization | 2,100 | 268 | Alex Lee, Inc. | 1,890 |
| 219 | Harvard Pilgrim Health Care, Inc. | 2,100 | 269 | DreamWorks SKG | 1,873 |
| 220 | The Scoular Company | 2,098 | 270 | J. F. Shea Co., Inc. | 1,863 |
| 221 | University of Alabama System | 2,090 | 271 | Goodwill Industries International | 1,850 |
| 222 | Ingram Industries Inc. | 2,075 | 272 | RaceTrac Petroleum, Inc. | 1,846 |
| 223 | TravelCenters of America, Inc. | 2,060 | 273 | Bcom3 Group, Inc. | 1,834 |
| 224 | Haworth Inc. | 2,060 | 274 | Central National-Gottesman Inc. | 1,825 |
| 225 | Jitney-Jungle Stores | 2,054 | 275 | Gold Kist Inc. | 1,811 |
| 226 | Air Wisconsin Airlines | 2,052 | 276 | DynCorp | 1,809 |
| 227 | Power Authority of the State of New York | 2,034 | 277 | Salvation Army USA | 1,803 |
|  |  |  | 278 | Demoulas Super Markets Inc. | 1,800 |
| 228 | Cerulean Companies, Inc. | 2,034 | 279 | New Jersey State Lottery | 1,800 |
| 229 | Harvard University | 2,023 | 280 | Beaulieu Of America, LLC | 1,800 |
| 230 | UniGroup, Inc. | 2,009 | 281 | DFS Group Limited | 1,800 |
| 231 | K-B Toys | 2,000 | 282 | Emory University | 1,800 |
| 232 | The Golub Corporation | 2,000 | 283 | Quad/Graphics, Inc. | 1,800 |
| 233 | Mark IV Industries, Inc. | 2,000 | 284 | Tauber Oil Company | 1,800 |
| 234 | Vertis Inc. | 2,000 | 285 | Bill Heard Enterprises | 1,796 |
| 235 | LifeStyle Furnishings | 2,000 | 286 | The Texas A&M University System | 1,792 |
| 236 | Minnesota Mutual Companies | 2,000 |  |  |  |
| 237 | Hunt Consolidated Inc. | 2,000 | 287 | Indiana University | 1,782 |
| 238 | Apex Oil Company, Inc. | 2,000 | 288 | BE&K Inc. | 1,776 |
| 239 | Tufts Associated Health Plans | 2,000 | 289 | 84 Lumber Company | 1,775 |
| 240 | H.T. Hackney Co. | 2,000 | 290 | AgriBank, FCB | 1,774 |
| 241 | UJC of North America | 2,000 | 291 | Pilot Corporation | 1,768 |
| 242 | Trammell Crow Residential | 2,000 | 292 | Golden State Foods | 1,764 |
| 243 | NASCAR | 2,000 | 293 | Morse Operations, Inc. | 1,762 |
| 244 | JELD-WEN, inc. | 2,000 | 294 | Southern States Cooperative | 1,739 |
| 245 | Quexco Incorporated | 2,000 | 295 | Banner Health System | 1,735 |
| 246 | CARQUEST Corporation | 2,000 | 296 | Discovery Communications, Inc. | 1,730 |
| 247 | Booz-Allen & Hamilton Inc. | 2,000 | 297 | Sentry Insurance | 1,716 |
| 248 | Jordan Automotive Group | 2,000 | 298 | Kinray, Inc. | 1,710 |
| 249 | Puerto Rico Electric Power | 1,987 | 299 | Builders FirstSource, Inc. | 1,710 |
| 250 | Gulf Oil, L.P. | 1,970 | 300 | The Pennsylvania Lottery | 1,707 |

# The 300 Largest Companies by Employees in
## Hoover's Handbook of Private Companies 2002

| Rank | Company | Number of Employees |
|------|---------|--------------------:|
| 1 | Express Personnel Services | 262,000 |
| 2 | Carlson Companies, Inc. | 192,000 |
| 3 | PricewaterhouseCoopers | 160,000 |
| 4 | Blue Cross and Blue Shield | 150,000 |
| 5 | Publix Super Markets, Inc. | 126,000 |
| 6 | University of California | 108,827 |
| 7 | Deloitte Touche Tohmatsu | 95,000 |
| 8 | KPMG International | 92,800 |
| 9 | IGA, INC. | 92,000 |
| 10 | Kaiser Foundation Health Plan | 90,000 |
| 11 | Cargill, Incorporated | 90,000 |
| 12 | Ernst & Young International | 88,000 |
| 13 | Andersen | 85,000 |
| 14 | Hyatt Corporation | 80,000 |
| 15 | Meijer, Inc. | 80,000 |
| 16 | The University of Texas System | 79,430 |
| 17 | State Farm Insurance | 79,300 |
| 18 | Goodwill Industries International | 77,895 |
| 19 | Cox Enterprises, Inc. | 74,000 |
| 20 | Ascension Health | 67,000 |
| 21 | Catholic Health Initiatives | 66,000 |
| 22 | Metropolitan Transportation Authority | 62,800 |
| 23 | H. E. Butt Grocery Company | 60,000 |
| 24 | Seagate Technology, Inc. | 60,000 |
| 25 | Army and Air Force Exchange | 52,400 |
| 26 | Enterprise Rent-A-Car | 50,000 |
| 27 | Hy-Vee, Inc. | 46,000 |
| 28 | Trinity Health | 45,700 |
| 29 | Salvation Army USA | 45,096 |
| 30 | Mayo Foundation | 44,000 |
| 31 | Catholic Health East | 44,000 |
| 32 | Science Applications International | 41,500 |
| 33 | Chick-fil-A Inc. | 40,000 |
| 34 | Bechtel Group, Inc. | 40,000 |
| 35 | The Marmon Group, Inc. | 40,000 |
| 36 | Catholic Healthcare West | 40,000 |
| 37 | California State University | 40,000 |
| 38 | Verizon Wireless Inc. | 38,000 |
| 39 | NRT Incorporated | 37,000 |
| 40 | Liberty Mutual Insurance | 37,000 |
| 41 | AAA | 37,000 |
| 42 | Alcoa Fujikura Ltd. | 36,000 |
| 43 | CARQUEST Corporation | 36,000 |
| 44 | Nationwide | 35,000 |
| 45 | The American Red Cross | 35,000 |
| 46 | Sutter Health | 35,000 |
| 47 | North Shore-Long Island Jewish Health System | 35,000 |
| 48 | Penske Corporation | 34,000 |
| 49 | The Freeman Companies | 34,000 |
| 50 | New York City Health and Hospitals Corporation | 33,500 |

| Rank | Company | Number of Employees |
|------|---------|--------------------:|
| 51 | FMR Corp. | 33,186 |
| 52 | Providence Health System | 32,238 |
| 53 | University of Minnesota | 30,823 |
| 54 | Mars, Incorporated | 30,000 |
| 55 | LifeStyle Furnishings International Ltd. | 30,000 |
| 56 | Partners HealthCare System | 30,000 |
| 57 | Wegmans Food Markets, Inc. | 29,826 |
| 58 | The Ohio State University | 29,502 |
| 59 | Metromedia Company | 29,500 |
| 60 | Life Care Centers of America | 29,350 |
| 61 | Marathon Ashland Petroleum | 28,000 |
| 62 | The Johns Hopkins University | 28,000 |
| 63 | Catholic Healthcare Partners | 27,941 |
| 64 | University of Missouri System | 27,914 |
| 65 | Pennsylvania State University | 27,112 |
| 66 | Bon Secours Health System | 27,000 |
| 67 | 24 Hour Fitness Worldwide Inc. | 26,794 |
| 68 | BJC Health System | 26,038 |
| 69 | Sisters of Mercy Health System-St. Louis | 26,000 |
| 70 | Day & Zimmermann Group | 26,000 |
| 71 | Louisiana State University System | 26,000 |
| 72 | TTC Illinois, Inc. | 26,000 |
| 73 | University of Washington | 25,917 |
| 74 | Giant Eagle Inc. | 25,600 |
| 75 | Asplundh Tree Expert Co. | 25,500 |
| 76 | Buffets, Inc. | 25,200 |
| 77 | Delaware North Companies Inc. | 25,000 |
| 78 | AMTRAK | 25,000 |
| 79 | Kinko's, Inc. | 25,000 |
| 80 | YMCA of the USA | 25,000 |
| 81 | Banner Health System | 24,500 |
| 82 | Advocate Health Care | 24,500 |
| 83 | Hallmark Cards, Inc. | 24,500 |
| 84 | ClubCorp, Inc. | 24,000 |
| 85 | University of Wisconsin System | 23,981 |
| 86 | Johns Hopkins Medicine | 23,550 |
| 87 | University of Florida | 23,500 |
| 88 | Jones Financial Companies | 23,432 |
| 89 | Federal Reserve System | 23,056 |
| 90 | Intermountain Health Care | 23,000 |
| 91 | Advance Publications, Inc. | 23,000 |
| 92 | Texas A&M University System | 23,000 |
| 93 | Washington Group International | 22,000 |
| 94 | The Trump Organization | 22,000 |
| 95 | USAA | 22,000 |
| 96 | Allina Health System | 21,500 |
| 97 | Belk, Inc. | 21,000 |
| 98 | MedStar Health | 21,000 |
| 99 | DynCorp | 20,842 |
| 100 | SSM Health Care System Inc. | 20,500 |

Source: Hoover's, Inc., Database, January 2002

## The 300 Largest Companies by Employees in
## *Hoover's Handbook of Private Companies 2002* (continued)

| Rank | Company | Number of Employees | Rank | Company | Number of Employees |
|------|---------|---------------------|------|---------|---------------------|
| 101 | Grant Thornton International | 20,300 | 151 | MSX International, Inc. | 14,000 |
| 102 | Carlson Wagonlit Travel | 20,100 | 152 | Taylor Corporation | 14,000 |
| 103 | Duke University | 20,020 | 153 | Hobby Lobby Stores, Inc. | 13,500 |
| 104 | Kohler Co. | 20,000 | 154 | Parsons Corporation | 13,500 |
| 105 | Milliken & Company Inc. | 20,000 | 155 | International Data Group | 13,200 |
| 106 | JELD-WEN, inc. | 20,000 | 156 | K-B Toys | 13,000 |
| 107 | Guardian Industries Corp. | 20,000 | 157 | CareGroup, Inc. | 13,000 |
| 108 | University of Alabama System | 20,000 | 158 | Wawa Inc. | 13,000 |
| 109 | Penske Truck Leasing | 19,562 | 159 | Inova Health System | 13,000 |
| 110 | The Golub Corporation | 19,500 | 160 | Equilon Enterprises LLC | 13,000 |
| 111 | MacAndrews & Forbes | 19,500 | 161 | J.R. Simplot Company | 13,000 |
| 112 | Perdue Farms Incorporated | 19,500 | 162 | McKinsey & Company | 13,000 |
| 113 | Emory University | 19,000 | 163 | The University of Kentucky | 13,000 |
| 114 | Schneider National, Inc. | 18,775 | 164 | Hewitt Associates LLC | 12,933 |
| 115 | The Hearst Corporation | 18,300 | 165 | Cornell University | 12,866 |
| 116 | Holberg Industries, Inc. | 18,300 | 166 | AECOM Technology Corporation | 12,800 |
| 117 | Springs Industries, Inc. | 18,200 | 167 | Petco Animal Supplies, Inc. | 12,800 |
| 118 | Singer N.V. | 18,000 | 168 | New York University | 12,790 |
| 119 | Venture Industries | 18,000 | 169 | Stater Bros. Holdings Inc. | 12,600 |
| 120 | Gold Kist Inc. | 18,000 | 170 | University of Rochester | 12,242 |
| 121 | Levi Strauss & Co. | 17,300 | 171 | Memorial Hermann Healthcare System | 12,000 |
| 122 | Bcom3 Group, Inc. | 17,000 | | | |
| 123 | Jitney-Jungle Stores of America | 17,000 | 172 | Baylor Health Care System | 12,000 |
| 124 | University of Southern California | 17,000 | 173 | Health Midwest | 12,000 |
| 125 | Raley's Inc. | 17,000 | 174 | Novant Health, Inc. | 12,000 |
| 126 | Adventist Health | 16,500 | 175 | General Parts, Inc. | 12,000 |
| 127 | Detroit Medical Center | 16,500 | 176 | The University of Chicago | 11,900 |
| 128 | BREED Technologies, Inc. | 16,300 | 177 | New York Life Insurance | 11,800 |
| 129 | The Lefrak Organization | 16,200 | 178 | University of Virginia | 11,608 |
| 130 | The University of Iowa | 16,006 | 179 | Metaldyne Corporation | 11,600 |
| 131 | Huntsman Corporation | 16,000 | 180 | William Beaumont Hospital | 11,500 |
| 132 | Texas Health Resources | 16,000 | 181 | Koch Industries, Inc. | 11,500 |
| 133 | Henry Ford Health System | 16,000 | 182 | Cushman & Wakefield Inc. | 11,500 |
| 134 | Navy Exchange Service Command | 16,000 | 183 | Provena Health | 11,400 |
| 135 | Schnuck Markets, Inc. | 16,000 | 184 | Harvard University | 11,360 |
| | | | 185 | University of Massachusetts | 11,256 |
| 136 | Investors Management Corp. | 16,000 | 186 | MediaNews Group, Inc. | 11,200 |
| 137 | Carondelet Health System | 16,000 | 187 | Peter Kiewit Sons', Inc. | 11,146 |
| 138 | Mark IV Industries, Inc. | 15,500 | 188 | Demoulas Super Markets Inc. | 11,000 |
| 139 | Vanderbilt University | 15,427 | 189 | Knowledge Universe, Inc. | 11,000 |
| 140 | Regal Cinemas, Inc. | 15,159 | 190 | Highmark Inc. | 11,000 |
| 141 | OhioHealth | 15,000 | 191 | UniHealth Foundation | 11,000 |
| 142 | Domino's Inc. | 14,600 | 192 | Beaulieu Of America, LLC | 11,000 |
| 143 | ContiGroup Companies, Inc. | 14,500 | 193 | Flying J Inc. | 11,000 |
| 144 | Farmland Industries, Inc. | 14,500 | 194 | Booz-Allen & Hamilton Inc. | 11,000 |
| 145 | Haworth Inc. | 14,500 | 195 | American Retail Group Inc. | 11,000 |
| 146 | University of Tennessee | 14,004 | 196 | The Vanguard Group, Inc. | 11,000 |
| 147 | H. B. Zachry Company | 14,000 | 197 | Yale University | 10,800 |
| 148 | Sentara Healthcare | 14,000 | 198 | BE&K Inc. | 10,799 |
| 149 | Renco Group Inc. | 14,000 | 199 | Brookshire Grocery Company | 10,750 |
| 150 | Quad/Graphics, Inc. | 14,000 | 200 | TravelCenters of America, Inc. | 10,635 |

# The 300 Largest Companies by Employees in
## Hoover's Handbook of Private Companies 2002 (continued)

| Rank | Company | Number of Employees | Rank | Company | Number of Employees |
|---|---|---|---|---|---|
| 201 | CH2M Hill Companies, Ltd. | 10,600 | 251 | Colliers International Property Consultants Inc. | 8,000 |
| 202 | Graybar Electric Company, Inc. | 10,500 | 252 | CHRISTUS Health | 8,000 |
| 203 | Alticor Inc. | 10,500 | 253 | Baker & McKenzie | 8,000 |
| 204 | AMSTED Industries Incorporated | 10,300 | 254 | Washington University in St. Louis | 7,963 |
| 205 | NESCO, Inc. | 10,250 | 255 | Montefiore Medical Center | 7,935 |
| 206 | Puerto Rico Electric Power | 10,200 | 256 | Big Y Foods, Inc. | 7,800 |
| 207 | Sisters of Charity of Leavenworth Health Services Corporation | 10,000 | 257 | Boston University | 7,750 |
| 208 | White Castle System, Inc. | 10,000 | 258 | Delco Remy International, Inc. | 7,707 |
| 209 | Vertis Inc. | 10,000 | 259 | Battelle Memorial Institute | 7,607 |
| 210 | United Way of America | 10,000 | 260 | Menard, Inc. | 7,600 |
| 211 | Boscov's Department Stores | 10,000 | 261 | R. B. Pamplin Corp. | 7,584 |
| 212 | Platinum Equity Holdings | 10,000 | 262 | Dade Behring Inc. | 7,500 |
| 213 | Carilion Health System | 10,000 | 263 | Presbyterian Healthcare Services | 7,500 |
| 214 | Harbour Group Industries, Inc. | 10,000 | 264 | Sheetz, Inc. | 7,500 |
| 215 | Retail Brand Alliance, Inc. | 10,000 | 265 | Oxford Automotive, Inc. | 7,400 |
| 216 | Watkins Associated Industries | 10,000 | 266 | Journal Communications Inc. | 7,300 |
| 217 | Group Health Cooperative of Puget Sound | 9,873 | 267 | Memorial Sloan-Kettering Cancer Center | 7,296 |
| 218 | Horseshoe Gaming Holding Corp. | 9,699 | 268 | Crown Equipment Corporation | 7,290 |
| 219 | Wake Forest University Baptist Medical Center | 9,600 | 269 | American Family Insurance Group | 7,247 |
| 220 | CB Richard Ellis Services, Inc. | 9,600 | 270 | Pilot Corporation | 7,209 |
| 221 | MidAmerican Energy Holdings | 9,550 | 271 | Save Mart Supermarkets | 7,200 |
| 222 | Foster Farms | 9,500 | 272 | Bloomberg L.P. | 7,200 |
| 223 | S.C. Johnson & Son, Inc. | 9,500 | 273 | Columbia University | 7,072 |
| 224 | Parsons Brinckerhoff Inc. | 9,289 | 274 | Ritz Camera Centers, Inc. | 7,000 |
| 225 | Dick's Sporting Goods, Inc. | 9,100 | 275 | Rich Products Corporation | 7,000 |
| 226 | Roundy's, Inc. | 9,071 | 276 | Duchossois Industries, Inc. | 7,000 |
| 227 | Contran Corporation | 9,000 | 277 | Port Authority of New York | 7,000 |
| 228 | Barnes & Noble College Bookstores | 9,000 | 278 | Allied Worldwide, Inc. | 7,000 |
| 229 | Dow Corning Corporation | 9,000 | 279 | Los Angeles Department of Water and Power | 7,000 |
| 230 | DFS Group Limited | 9,000 | 280 | Recreational Equipment, Inc. | 7,000 |
| 231 | Discount Tire Co. | 8,987 | 281 | Lane Industries, Inc. | 7,000 |
| 232 | Towers Perrin | 8,919 | 282 | C&S Wholesale Grocers, Inc. | 7,000 |
| 233 | UIS, Inc. | 8,910 | 283 | Bose Corporation | 7,000 |
| 234 | Rush System for Health | 8,896 | 284 | Quexco Incorporated | 7,000 |
| 235 | Bashas' Inc. | 8,800 | 285 | Klaussner Furniture Industries | 7,000 |
| 236 | K-VA-T Food Stores, Inc. | 8,690 | 286 | Jordan Industries, Inc. | 6,967 |
| 237 | SAS Institute Inc. | 8,500 | 287 | Builders FirstSource, Inc. | 6,800 |
| 238 | Alex Lee, Inc. | 8,500 | 288 | MTS, Incorporated | 6,795 |
| 239 | Black & Veatch | 8,500 | 289 | Jostens, Inc. | 6,700 |
| 240 | Massachusetts Institute of Technology | 8,400 | 290 | Keystone Foods LLC | 6,700 |
| 241 | The SF Holdings Group, Inc. | 8,234 | 291 | Minyard Food Stores, Inc. | 6,700 |
| 242 | Bass Pro Shops, Inc. | 8,200 | 292 | Anderson News Company | 6,600 |
| 243 | IASIS Healthcare Corporation | 8,100 | 293 | Cumberland Farms, Inc. | 6,545 |
| 244 | Massachusetts Mutual Life | 8,000 | 294 | MTD Products Inc. | 6,500 |
| 245 | The Longaberger Company | 8,000 | 295 | Land O'Lakes, Inc. | 6,500 |
| 246 | Motiva Enterprises LLC | 8,000 | 296 | Genmar Holdings, Inc. | 6,500 |
| 247 | Cinemark USA, Inc. | 8,000 | 297 | Dillingham Construction Corporation | 6,500 |
| 248 | Freedom Communications, Inc. | 8,000 | 298 | Sinclair Oil Corporation | 6,500 |
| 249 | Follett Corporation | 8,000 | 299 | Ingram Industries Inc. | 6,494 |
| 250 | Dr Pepper/Seven Up Bottling Group, Inc. | 8,000 | 300 | Smithsonian Institution | 6,400 |

# The *Inc.* 500 Fastest-Growing Private Companies in America

| Rank | Company | Headquarters | 1996–2000 Sales Growth Increase (%) |
|------|---------|--------------|-------------------------------------|
| 1 | High Point Solutions | Sparta, NJ | 29,902 |
| 2 | VistaRMS | Herndon, VA | 21,869 |
| 3 | First American Equipment Finance | Chicago | 15,247 |
| 4 | EYT | Chantilly, VA | 13,542 |
| 5 | Jefferson Wells International | Milwaukee | 13,023 |
| 6 | Group Management Services | Valley View, OH | 10,938 |
| 7 | Job Strategies | Raleigh, NC | 10,837 |
| 8 | Yash Technologies | East Moline, IL | 10,393 |
| 9 | Caliber Collision Centers | Irvine, CA | 10,029 |
| 10 | Orange Glo International | Greenwood Village, CO | 9,907 |
| 11 | Administerve | Greenwood, IN | 9,341 |
| 12 | Jules and Associates | Los Angeles | 8,932 |
| 13 | Access Group | Atlanta | 8,695 |
| 14 | Active Services | Birmingham, AL | 8,307 |
| 15 | Clarity Visual Systems | Wilsonville, OR | 8,046 |
| 16 | J. Calnan & Associates | Braintree, MA | 7,409 |
| 17 | Silicon Valley Staffing Group | Emeryville, CA | 7,384 |
| 18 | Lighthouse Computer Services | Lincoln, RI | 7,282 |
| 19 | National Heritage Academies | Grand Rapids, MI | 7,094 |
| 20 | Universal Solutions | Ridgeland, MS | 6,832 |
| 21 | Burst Media | Burlington, MA | 6,820 |
| 22 | Vesta | Portland, OR | 6,575 |
| 23 | SigmaTel | Austin, TX | 6,318 |
| 24 | Intermedia Group | New York City | 6,238 |
| 25 | Oakleaf Waste Management | East Hartford, CT | 6,178 |
| 26 | Morinda | Orem, UT | 6,137 |
| 27 | Ready Staffing Services | Louisville, KY | 6,070 |
| 28 | ICR Services | Livonia, MI | 5,938 |
| 29 | Professional Staffing Group | Boston | 5,780 |
| 30 | Sanvision Technology | New York City | 5,571 |
| 31 | ComGlobal Systems | San Diego | 5,202 |
| 32 | Destiny WebSolutions | Conshohocken, PA | 5,040 |
| 33 | Micro Solutions Enterprises | Chatsworth, CA | 5,033 |
| 34 | HealthScribe | Sterling, VA | 5,022 |
| 35 | Zaiq Technologies | Woburn, MA | 5,013 |
| 36 | ePartners | Irving, TX | 4,704 |
| 37 | NewRoads | Greenwich, CT | 4,639 |
| 38 | Interactive Futures | New York City | 4,612 |
| 39 | Office Resources | Boston | 4,382 |
| 40 | Tastefully Simple | Alexandria, MN | 4,334 |
| 41 | Mercom Systems | Lyndhurst, NJ | 4,276 |
| 42 | SupplyCore.com | Rockford, IL | 4,260 |
| 43 | Youngsoft | Livonia, MI | 4,214 |
| 44 | GCI | Parsippany, NJ | 4,123 |
| 45 | Noodles & Co. | Boulder, CO | 4,093 |
| 46 | American Capital Group | Orange, CA | 4,084 |
| 47 | Boldtech Systems | Denver | 4,075 |
| 48 | LexJet | Sarasota, FL | 4,049 |
| 49 | ThinkFast Consulting | Chicago | 3,993 |
| 50 | CLT Meetings International | Orlando, FL | 3,978 |
| 51 | Apex Systems | Richmond, VA | 3,919 |
| 52 | Cargo Express | Yardley, PA | 3,899 |
| 53 | Foreshock | Irvine, CA | 3,850 |
| 54 | Door to Door Storage | Kent, WA | 3,726 |
| 55 | Blue Ocean Software | Tampa | 3,558 |

Source: *Inc.* 500; October 2001

# The *Inc.* 500 Fastest-Growing Private Companies in America (continued)

| Rank | Company | Headquarters | 1996–2000 Sales Growth Increase (%) |
|---|---|---|---|
| 56 | AssembleTech | Sugar Land, TX | 3,541 |
| 57 | Trinity HomeCare | College Point, NY | 3,430 |
| 58 | Random Walk Computing | New York City | 3,413 |
| 59 | Wolcott Systems Group | Fairlawn, OH | 3,286 |
| 60 | Ventera | McLean, VA | 3,197 |
| 61 | Exinom Technologies | Iselin, NJ | 3,196 |
| 62 | Spirian Technologies | Chicago | 3,177 |
| 63 | Info Directions | Victor, NY | 3,151 |
| 64 | Terra Firma | Denver | 3,131 |
| 65 | Magnet Communications | Atlanta | 3,118 |
| 66 | College Kit | West Lebanon, NH | 3,053 |
| 67 | Scooter Store | New Braunfels, TX | 3,038 |
| 68 | Fiber Network Solutions | Columbus, OH | 2,995 |
| 69 | Meritage Technologies | Columbus, OH | 2,961 |
| 70 | Professional Placement Resources | Jacksonville Beach, FL | 2,851 |
| 71 | Iron Hill Brewery & Restaurant | Wilmington, DE | 2,845 |
| 72 | Employer Services | Amherst, NY | 2,823 |
| 73 | ATP Oil & Gas | Houston | 2,814 |
| 74 | SM Consulting | Linthicum, MD | 2,786 |
| 75 | Iris Software | Metuchen, NJ | 2,774 |
| 76 | AlphaSoft Services | Walnut Creek, CA | 2,761 |
| 77 | SDG | Norwalk, CT | 2,755 |
| 78 | Pro2Serve Professional Project Services | Oak Ridge, TN | 2,748 |
| 79 | Portage Environmental | Idaho Falls, ID | 2,701 |
| 80 | Tactica | Dallas | 2,680 |
| 81 | IVCi | Hauppauge, NY | 2,652 |
| 82 | TW Medical Vet Supply | Leander, TX | 2,638 |
| 83 | QSS Group | Lanham, MD | 2,622 |
| 84 | OPM Services | Louisville, KY | 2,615 |
| 85 | Envision Telephony | Seattle | 2,591 |
| 86 | Visionary Integration Professionals | Folsom, CA | 2,583 |
| 87 | Youcentric | Charlotte, NC | 2,573 |
| 88 | Technology Professionals | Grand Rapids, MI | 2,568 |
| 89 | Technica | Dulles, VA | 2,561 |
| 90 | Cyber Dialogue | New York City | 2,527 |
| 91 | Security Check | Oxford, MS | 2,501 |
| 92 | BeaverHome.com | Niagara Falls, NY | 2,492 |
| 93 | ScriptSave | Tucson, AZ | 2,479 |
| 94 | Thaumaturgix | New York City | 2,455 |
| 95 | Pangea Group | Chesterfield, MO | 2,428 |
| 96 | MedSpan | Hartford, CT | 2,414 |
| 97 | Goliath Networks | Madison, WI | 2,381 |
| 98 | Softworld | Waltham, MA | 2,374 |
| 99 | Software Technology Group | Salt Lake City | 2,362 |
| 100 | Virtual Financial Services | Indianapolis | 2,353 |
| 101 | ADT | Huntsville, AL | 2,330 |
| 102 | Intraforce | Columbia, MD | 2,316 |
| 103 | Alliance Consulting | Philadelphia | 2,315 |
| 104 | College Financial Aid Services | Albany, NY | 2,296 |
| 105 | Prosoft Technology Group | Downers Grove, IL | 2,272 |
| 106 | GRT | Stamford, CT | 2,239 |
| 107 | Midwest Media Group | Schaumburg, IL | 2,215 |
| 108 | Laser Welding International | Fraser, MI | 2,198 |
| 109 | Worknet | Naperville, IL | 2,174 |
| 110 | PharmaFab | Grand Prairie, TX | 2,164 |

# The *Inc.* 500 Fastest-Growing Private Companies in America (continued)

| Rank | Company | Headquarters | 1996–2000 Sales Growth Increase (%) |
|------|---------|--------------|-------------------------------------|
| 111 | Integra Telecom | Beaverton, OR | 2,154 |
| 112 | Pragmatech Software | Amherst, NH | 2,127 |
| 113 | Case Engineered Lumber | Suwanee, GA | 2,125 |
| 114 | Demark | Joliet, IL | 2,122 |
| 115 | Granite Systems | Manchester, NH | 2,103 |
| 116 | Systech Solutions | Glendale, CA | 2,091 |
| 117 | Lenel Systems International | Pittsford, NY | 2,075 |
| 118 | Flash Electronics | Fremont, CA | 2,060 |
| 119 | Radiant Systems | South Plainfield, NJ | 2,058 |
| 120 | STI Knowledge | Atlanta | 2,048 |
| 121 | GDI Infotech | Ann Arbor, MI | 2,036 |
| 122 | TRX | Atlanta | 2,030 |
| 123 | Flake-Wilkerson Market Insights | Little Rock, AR | 2,010 |
| 124 | Florida Family Insurance Services | Naples, FL | 1,987 |
| 125 | NovaSoft Information Technology | Lawrenceville, NJ | 1,986 |
| 126 | Keystone RV | Goshen, IN | 1,961 |
| 127 | MHF Logistical Solutions | Zelienople, PA | 1,932 |
| 128 | Painted Word | Cambridge, MA | 1,921 |
| 129 | Carteret Mortgage | Centreville, VA | 1,915 |
| 130 | Techmar Communications | Canton, MA | 1,904 |
| 131 | Alternative Business Systems | Lincoln, NE | 1,893 |
| 132 | Cardtronics | Houston | 1,874 |
| 133 | TechBooks | Fairfax, VA | 1,871 |
| 134 | Pacific Consultants | Mountain View, CA | 1,871 |
| 135 | Personnel Consultants | Tulsa, OK | 1,863 |
| 136 | Socket Internet | Columbia, MO | 1,852 |
| 137 | Unica | Lincoln, MA | 1,847 |
| 138 | Process Plus | Cincinnati | 1,847 |
| 139 | Peak Industries | Longmont, CO | 1,842 |
| 140 | Aurora Electric | Jamaica, NY | 1,829 |
| 141 | KSJ & Associates | Falls Church, VA | 1,817 |
| 142 | Imports By Four Hands | Austin, TX | 1,801 |
| 143 | Cherokee Information Services | Arlington, VA | 1,801 |
| 144 | Computer Source | Lenexa, KS | 1,796 |
| 145 | NexTec Group | Houston | 1,790 |
| 146 | Rosen Group | Cherry Hill, NJ | 1,790 |
| 147 | Fusion Staffing Services | Walnut Creek, CA | 1,789 |
| 148 | MTI Home Video | Miami | 1,770 |
| 149 | Advanced Technologies & Services | Wayne, NJ | 1,758 |
| 150 | Hold Brothers On-Line Investment Services | Jersey City, NJ | 1,747 |
| 151 | Scientific & Engineering Solutions | Annapolis Junction, MD | 1,741 |
| 152 | Coventor | Cary, NC | 1,739 |
| 153 | Calence | Tempe, AZ | 1,736 |
| 154 | York Enterprise Solutions | Westchester, IL | 1,735 |
| 155 | Bit Group | Boston | 1,712 |
| 156 | PGR Media | Providence, RI | 1,698 |
| 157 | Natural Data | Phoenix | 1,696 |
| 158 | Network Hardware Resale | Santa Barbara, CA | 1,660 |
| 159 | Spectrum Communications Cabling Services | Corona, CA | 1,652 |
| 160 | Line 6 | Thousand Oaks, CA | 1,651 |
| 161 | Multimedia Live | Petaluma, CA | 1,650 |
| 162 | Tucker Technology | Oakland, CA | 1,644 |
| 163 | Sea Fox Boat | Charleston, SC | 1,639 |
| 164 | VMS | Richmond, VA | 1,634 |
| 165 | InfoPros | Citrus Heights, CA | 1,629 |

# The *Inc.* 500 Fastest-Growing Private Companies in America (continued)

| Rank | Company | Headquarters | 1996–2000 Sales Growth Increase (%) |
|------|---------|--------------|-------------------------------------|
| 166 | Integral Strategies | Pittsburgh, PA | 1,628 |
| 167 | Ardus Medical | Cincinnati | 1,624 |
| 168 | Optomec | Albuquerque, NM | 1,622 |
| 169 | Solipsys | Laurel, MD | 1,611 |
| 170 | Magi Realty | San Antonio | 1,611 |
| 171 | E Commerce Group Products | New York City | 1,596 |
| 172 | Conseva Learning Center of Kansas City | Kansas City, MO | 1,588 |
| 173 | Speck Product Design | Palo Alto, CA | 1,586 |
| 174 | Corporate Technologies | Burlington, MA | 1,574 |
| 175 | Elite Show Services | San Diego | 1,570 |
| 176 | Indigo Investment Systems | Sarasota, FL | 1,569 |
| 177 | Profit Logic | Cambridge, MA | 1,564 |
| 178 | U.S. Energy Services | Wayzata, MN | 1,560 |
| 179 | Osprey Imaging | Englewood, CO | 1,557 |
| 180 | TDS | Houston | 1,542 |
| 181 | XOR | Boulder, CO | 1,538 |
| 182 | Interactive Solutions | Memphis | 1,535 |
| 183 | Virtual Meeting Strategies | Indianapolis | 1,529 |
| 184 | Timberlane Woodcrafters | North Wales, PA | 1,523 |
| 185 | Cherokee Staffing | Houston | 1,508 |
| 186 | Pulse | Walpole, MA | 1,501 |
| 187 | Super Smokers BBQ | O'Fallon, MO | 1,497 |
| 188 | Molecular | Watertown, MA | 1,493 |
| 189 | Martin Progressive | New York City | 1,487 |
| 190 | V-Span | King of Prussia, PA | 1,487 |
| 191 | Client Network Services | Gaithersburg, MD | 1,479 |
| 192 | Pyramid Digital Solutions | Birmingham, AL | 1,476 |
| 193 | Auragen Communications | Rochester, NY | 1,476 |
| 194 | Derivatech Consulting | Chicago | 1,469 |
| 195 | Venoco | Carpinteria, CA | 1,468 |
| 196 | Diaspark | New York City | 1,454 |
| 197 | NLX | Sterling, VA | 1,448 |
| 198 | USA Instruments | Aurora, OH | 1,437 |
| 199 | C & G Moving and Storage | Chantilly, VA | 1,423 |
| 200 | Access US | St. Louis | 1,419 |
| 201 | ProdEx Technologies | Saratoga, CA | 1,407 |
| 202 | Advanced Vending Systems | Ringgold, GA | 1,393 |
| 203 | James River Technical | Glen Allen, VA | 1,393 |
| 204 | Legal Network | Pittsburgh, PA | 1,392 |
| 205 | Capella Education | Minneapolis | 1,391 |
| 206 | Memories & More | Centerville, UT | 1,384 |
| 207 | Ved Software Services | Farmington Hills, MI | 1,380 |
| 208 | Telecommunications Analysis Group | Menands, NY | 1,370 |
| 209 | Telecom Labs | Seattle | 1,365 |
| 210 | Technology Resource Center | West Dundee, IL | 1,356 |
| 211 | Bertech-Kelex | Torrance, CA | 1,356 |
| 212 | Nature's Cure | Oakland, CA | 1,354 |
| 213 | Van Dyke Technologies | Albuquerque, NM | 1,352 |
| 214 | Pioneer Credit Recovery | Arcade, NY | 1,352 |
| 215 | Curtis-Straus | Littleton, MA | 1,333 |
| 216 | Parson Group | Chicago | 1,326 |
| 217 | Teklution | Salt Lake City | 1,323 |
| 218 | Strategy Associates | Foster City, CA | 1,313 |
| 219 | Portosan | El Monte, CA | 1,306 |
| 220 | 3t Systems | Denver | 1,301 |

| Rank | Company | Headquarters | 1996–2000 Sales Growth Increase (%) |
|------|---------|--------------|-------------------------------------|
| 221 | Tilia | San Francisco | 1,297 |
| 222 | ACC Staffing | Raleigh, NC | 1,293 |
| 223 | Atlantic.Net | Gainesville, FL | 1,275 |
| 224 | Monitronics International | Dallas | 1,273 |
| 225 | Presenting Solutions | San Clemente, CA | 1,270 |
| 226 | New View Gifts & Accessories | Media, PA | 1,264 |
| 227 | Perfect Order | Mechanicsburg, PA | 1,262 |
| 228 | Solutions-II | Littleton, CO | 1,257 |
| 229 | Integrated Decisions and Systems | Eagan, MN | 1,254 |
| 230 | Aquascape Designs | Batavia, IL | 1,249 |
| 231 | Parker Compound Bows | Staunton, VA | 1,249 |
| 232 | StarNet | Palatine, IL | 1,248 |
| 233 | PepperCom | New York City | 1,243 |
| 234 | SALT Group | Kerrville, TX | 1,242 |
| 235 | Computer World Services | Washington, DC | 1,236 |
| 236 | Northwoods Software Development | Brown Deer, WI | 1,232 |
| 237 | Rose International | Chesterfield, MO | 1,231 |
| 238 | Unique Computing Solutions | Framingham, MA | 1,229 |
| 239 | ACS International Resources | Newark, DE | 1,227 |
| 240 | T. Williams Consulting | Collegeville, PA | 1,204 |
| 241 | Extreme Pizza | San Francisco | 1,203 |
| 242 | Heartlab | Westerly, RI | 1,191 |
| 243 | AI Signal Research | Huntsville, AL | 1,188 |
| 244 | Quest Marketing | Eugene, OR | 1,186 |
| 245 | SimStar Internet Solutions | Princeton, NJ | 1,184 |
| 246 | Authoria | Waltham, MA | 1,180 |
| 247 | WellMed | Portland, OR | 1,179 |
| 248 | Financial Technologies | Jackson, MS | 1,175 |
| 249 | Advantage Credit International | Pensacola, FL | 1,173 |
| 250 | Hesta | Wayne, PA | 1,168 |
| 251 | Space Hardware Optimization Technology | Greenville, IN | 1,162 |
| 252 | Magenic Technologies | Minneapolis | 1,157 |
| 253 | Genex | Los Angeles | 1,152 |
| 254 | North Highland | Atlanta | 1,144 |
| 255 | Techniki Informatica | Dallas | 1,129 |
| 256 | Smithgall Enterprises | Louisville, KY | 1,127 |
| 257 | Bird Brain | Ypsilanti, MI | 1,123 |
| 258 | Astute | Columbus, OH | 1,122 |
| 259 | Pan Ocean | Woodland, CA | 1,121 |
| 260 | Adtron | Phoenix | 1,121 |
| 261 | Studio B Productions | Indianapolis | 1,117 |
| 262 | Maus Haus | San Mateo, CA | 1,114 |
| 263 | One Web Systems | Atlanta | 1,107 |
| 264 | Brian's Toys | Fountain City, WI | 1,106 |
| 265 | Your Employment Solutions | North Salt Lake, UT | 1,105 |
| 266 | SafeHome Security | Provo, UT | 1,104 |
| 267 | Maryville Technologies | St. Louis | 1,099 |
| 268 | Alternative Technology | Denver | 1,096 |
| 269 | Transition Products | Columbus, OH | 1,085 |
| 270 | Chatham Systems Group | Madison, NJ | 1,083 |
| 271 | Appriss | Louisville, KY | 1,082 |
| 272 | Bowdoin Group | Wellesley, MA | 1,079 |
| 273 | Teamsoft | Middleton, WI | 1,079 |
| 274 | Infiniti Systems Group | Brecksville, OH | 1,078 |
| 275 | John Keeler & Co. | Miami | 1,078 |

# The *Inc.* 500 Fastest-Growing Private Companies in America (continued)

| Rank | Company | Headquarters | 1996–2000 Sales Growth Increase (%) |
|---|---|---|---|
| 276 | MarketLab | Kentwood, MI | 1,078 |
| 277 | Gray Hawk Systems | Alexandria, VA | 1,074 |
| 278 | SYS-CON Media | Montvale, NJ | 1,072 |
| 279 | gomembers | Lombard, IL | 1,069 |
| 280 | Lakeshore Staffing | Chicago | 1,069 |
| 281 | Meridian Project Systems | Folsom, CA | 1,062 |
| 282 | Strafford Technology | Windham, NH | 1,057 |
| 283 | Promotions by Design | Trevose, PA | 1,054 |
| 284 | Vertex Engineering Services | Weymouth, MA | 1,052 |
| 285 | BASE Consulting Group | Oakland, CA | 1,051 |
| 286 | Go-e-biz.com | Eagan, MN | 1,034 |
| 287 | Elite Computers & Software | Cupertino, CA | 1,034 |
| 288 | Suntech Systems | Marietta, GA | 1,032 |
| 289 | Enterprise Events Group | San Rafael, CA | 1,029 |
| 290 | Aegis Software | New York City | 1,025 |
| 291 | Schoff & Baxter | Burlington, IA | 1,022 |
| 292 | T.I.M.S. | Highland Heights, OH | 1,022 |
| 293 | Lighthouse Financial Group | Tampa | 1,020 |
| 294 | SCI | Depew, NY | 1,015 |
| 295 | Andrew General Contractors | Orlando, FL | 1,012 |
| 296 | Lloyd Group | New York City | 1,009 |
| 297 | Yam's Choice Plus Autos | Little Rock, AR | 1,008 |
| 298 | TriNet Systems | Sharon, MA | 1,005 |
| 299 | Comnet International | Lisle, IL | 983 |
| 300 | Component Graphics | Roseville, CA | 983 |
| 301 | Encore Software | Gardena, CA | 974 |
| 302 | Connect Direct | Redwood City, CA | 974 |
| 303 | Professional Cutlery Direct | North Branford, CT | 972 |
| 304 | Transpower Technologies | Reno, NV | 971 |
| 305 | Travel Excellence | Schaumburg, IL | 969 |
| 306 | Peris Cos. | Falls Church, VA | 968 |
| 307 | BuildingStars | St. Louis | 968 |
| 308 | Pacific Trade International | Rockville, MD | 964 |
| 309 | Univance Telecommunications | Denver | 964 |
| 310 | Product Development Technologies | Lincolnshire, IL | 962 |
| 311 | Springbok Technologies | Richardson, TX | 957 |
| 312 | C & A Industries | Omaha, NE | 952 |
| 313 | Educational Services | Washington, DC | 949 |
| 314 | Mister Sparky | Marietta, GA | 948 |
| 315 | Lumber Liquidators | Boston | 948 |
| 316 | eCopy | Nashua, NH | 945 |
| 317 | Diversified Computer Consultants | New Orleans | 945 |
| 318 | Infrasoft | Beverly, MA | 941 |
| 319 | Adaytum Software | Minneapolis | 940 |
| 320 | ClearOrbit | Austin, TX | 939 |
| 321 | IQ Systems | Sparks, NV | 937 |
| 322 | Computer & Hi-Tech Management | Virginia Beach, VA | 933 |
| 323 | Dynamix Group | Roswell, GA | 928 |
| 324 | Lynk Systems | Atlanta | 926 |
| 325 | Compri Consulting | Denver | 910 |
| 326 | Abacus Travel | Peabody, MA | 910 |
| 327 | Thompson Brooks | San Francisco | 909 |
| 328 | ThoughtWorks | Chicago | 909 |
| 329 | Total Waste Systems | Norman, OK | 904 |
| 330 | Terradigm | Albuquerque, NM | 902 |

# The *Inc.* 500 Fastest-Growing Private Companies in America (continued)

| Rank | Company | Headquarters | 1996–2000 Sales Growth Increase (%) |
|---|---|---|---|
| 331 | Oxygen Generating Systems | Niagara Falls, NY | 901 |
| 332 | Turner Consulting Group | Washington, DC | 899 |
| 333 | Integrated Electrical and Datacom | Nicholasville, KY | 898 |
| 334 | Madison Group | Memphis | 896 |
| 335 | RS Information Systems | McLean, VA | 888 |
| 336 | ProTec Building Services | San Diego | 887 |
| 337 | Majac Steel | East Chicago, IN | 878 |
| 338 | Ahead Headgear | New Bedford, MA | 876 |
| 339 | NetForce Technologies | Austin, TX | 871 |
| 340 | ZT Group International | Secaucus, NJ | 871 |
| 341 | MRE Consulting | Houston | 870 |
| 342 | CrossLink | Boulder, CO | 869 |
| 343 | TNCI | Boston | 867 |
| 344 | New Age Electronics | Carson, CA | 861 |
| 345 | Vitacost.com | Boynton Beach, FL | 861 |
| 346 | Global Filtration | Houston | 860 |
| 347 | Sonnet Technologies | Irvine, CA | 856 |
| 348 | Diamond Systems | Newark, CA | 856 |
| 349 | Sigma Systems | Shrewsbury, MA | 853 |
| 350 | Northern Lights Post | New York City | 853 |
| 351 | White Wave | Boulder, CO | 850 |
| 352 | Linksys | Irvine, CA | 850 |
| 353 | Ascend HR Solutions | Salt Lake City | 848 |
| 354 | Navigator Systems | Addison, TX | 845 |
| 355 | Afterburner Seminars | Atlanta | 845 |
| 356 | TestChip Technologies | Plano, TX | 844 |
| 357 | Lisa Adelle Design | Dallas | 843 |
| 358 | REI Systems | Annandale, VA | 836 |
| 359 | Backtrack | Mentor, OH | 835 |
| 360 | PK Controls | Worthington, OH | 834 |
| 361 | Veri-Tek International | Farmington Hills, MI | 834 |
| 362 | Solix Systems | Santa Clara, CA | 830 |
| 363 | America's Media Marketing | Spring Hill, FL | 828 |
| 364 | American Minority Business Forms | Glenwood, MN | 825 |
| 365 | Ascent Computing Group | White Plains, NY | 823 |
| 366 | Advanced Technologies Group | West Des Moines, IA | 819 |
| 367 | Street Glow | Wayne, NJ | 819 |
| 368 | Corporate Electric Services | Winter Park, FL | 814 |
| 369 | Cello Development | San Francisco | 811 |
| 370 | InDyne | McLean, VA | 804 |
| 371 | SSCI | West Lafayette, IN | 800 |
| 372 | Food Concepts | Middleton, WI | 796 |
| 373 | Pro-Tech Welding and Fabrication | Rochester, NY | 789 |
| 374 | PowerLight | Berkeley, CA | 789 |
| 375 | Hsu Development | Rockville, MD | 789 |
| 376 | Engineering Services Unlimited | Huntsville, AL | 785 |
| 377 | Inforonics | Littleton, MA | 767 |
| 378 | Universal Software | Chelmsford, MA | 765 |
| 379 | ATX Forms | Caribou, ME | 765 |
| 380 | Accurate Autobody | Tulsa, OK | 764 |
| 381 | Elite Flooring & Design | Norcross, GA | 755 |
| 382 | Security Solutions | Raleigh, NC | 755 |
| 383 | PayMaxx | Franklin, TN | 754 |
| 384 | Jamba Juice | San Francisco | 748 |
| 385 | Thermagon | Cleveland, OH | 746 |

| Rank | Company | Headquarters | 1996–2000 Sales Growth Increase (%) |
|------|---------|--------------|-------------------------------------|
| 386 | Qestrel Companies | Pasadena, CA | 744 |
| 387 | ProLaw Software | Albuquerque, NM | 743 |
| 388 | Enterprise Development Services | Atlanta | 742 |
| 389 | Precision Metal Fabricating | Beaver Dam, WI | 742 |
| 390 | Teammates Commerical Interiors | Denver | 740 |
| 391 | NuWare Technology | Iselin, NJ | 738 |
| 392 | CCX | Lafayette, CO | 737 |
| 393 | Multi-Media Solutions | Alcoa, TN | 736 |
| 394 | Apollo Design Technology | Fort Wayne, IN | 736 |
| 395 | Arena Communications | Salt Lake City | 734 |
| 396 | Progressive Medical | Westerville, OH | 731 |
| 397 | Glyphics Communications | Draper, UT | 731 |
| 398 | Bowman Consulting Group | Chantilly, VA | 731 |
| 399 | Cody-Kramer Imports | Blauvelt, NY | 728 |
| 400 | Talking Book World | Oak Park, MI | 727 |
| 401 | Lee Technologies Group | Fairfax, VA | 726 |
| 402 | America's Choice Healthplans | King of Prussia, PA | 724 |
| 403 | MBI | De Land, FL | 720 |
| 404 | Security Leasing Partners | St. Louis | 718 |
| 405 | Laschober Construction | Cocoa, FL | 718 |
| 406 | Payne, Lynch & Associates | Sartell, MN | 715 |
| 407 | Fiber Science | Palm Bay, FL | 715 |
| 408 | Joe Lombardo Plumbing + Heating of Rockland | Suffern, NY | 713 |
| 409 | Sunbelt Software | Clearwater, FL | 711 |
| 410 | MicroTek | Oakbrook Terrace, IL | 711 |
| 411 | Bennett & Curran | Englewood, CO | 710 |
| 412 | ProfitLine | San Diego | 710 |
| 413 | EIMS | Dripping Springs, TX | 710 |
| 414 | Distribution Planning | Grandville, MI | 709 |
| 415 | ELMCO | Huntsville, AL | 708 |
| 416 | Career T.E.A.M. | Hamden, CT | 705 |
| 417 | PSC Info Group | Valley Forge, PA | 703 |
| 418 | Accounting Connections | Portland, OR | 703 |
| 419 | DC Group | Minneapolis | 700 |
| 420 | Open Software Solutions | Greensboro, NC | 698 |
| 421 | AnviCom | Vienna, VA | 695 |
| 422 | One Source Printing | Franklin, TN | 695 |
| 423 | Arrow Financial Services | Lincolnwood, IL | 689 |
| 424 | Thompson Technologies | Kennesaw, GA | 686 |
| 425 | EuroSoft | Austin, TX | 686 |
| 426 | Protis Executive Innovations | Avon, IN | 683 |
| 427 | Winemiller Communications | Carlisle, PA | 683 |
| 428 | United Systems Integrators | Stamford, CT | 683 |
| 429 | Safespan Platform Systems | Tonawanda, NY | 681 |
| 430 | Parks & Co. | Charlotte, NC | 679 |
| 431 | Atlantic Corporate Interiors | Beltsville, MD | 679 |
| 432 | Beacon Institute for Learning | Plantation, FL | 679 |
| 433 | Garrett & Associates | Danville, CA | 677 |
| 434 | Metzger Associates | Boulder, CO | 677 |
| 435 | Guy Chemical | Berlin, PA | 675 |
| 436 | Franklin American Mortgage | Franklin, TN | 674 |
| 437 | Spectrum Astro | Gilbert, AZ | 673 |
| 438 | Crown Products | Mobile, AL | 672 |
| 439 | Knightsbridge Solutions | Chicago | 669 |
| 440 | Joseph Sheairs Associates | Medford, NJ | 668 |

| Rank | Company | Headquarters | 1996–2000 Sales Growth Increase (%) |
|------|---------|--------------|-------------------------------------|
| 441 | Vision 1 | Bozeman, MT | 667 |
| 442 | Vistronix | McLean, VA | 666 |
| 443 | Triple Point Technology | Westport, CT | 666 |
| 444 | CWS Corporate Leasing | Austin, TX | 662 |
| 445 | Medical Data Processing | Atlanta | 659 |
| 446 | Tech Superpowers | Boston | 658 |
| 447 | InfoStreet | Tarzana, CA | 655 |
| 448 | Bills Khakis | Reading, PA | 655 |
| 449 | Software Methods | Valley Forge, PA | 655 |
| 450 | Insurance Consulting Associates | Petaluma, CA | 655 |
| 451 | Priority Express Courier | Boothwyn, PA | 652 |
| 452 | Infinity Software Development | Tallahassee, FL | 651 |
| 453 | On-Site Financial Solutions | Portland, OR | 651 |
| 454 | Extra Mile Transportation | Buffalo, NY | 650 |
| 455 | AMC Technology | Richmond, VA | 646 |
| 456 | Newton Interactive | Pennington, NJ | 644 |
| 457 | S.E. Cline Construction | Palm Coast, FL | 643 |
| 458 | Stone Technologies | Fenton, MO | 643 |
| 459 | HTC Global Services | Southfield, MI | 643 |
| 460 | Power-Glide Foreign Language Course | Provo, UT | 641 |
| 461 | Meridian Technology Group | Lake Oswego, OR | 641 |
| 462 | Research Data Design | Portland, OR | 640 |
| 463 | BOWA Builders | McLean, VA | 631 |
| 464 | Westover Scientific | Mill Creek, WA | 631 |
| 465 | Advanced Composites Technology | Huntsville, AL | 628 |
| 466 | PPM Consultants | Monroe, LA | 627 |
| 467 | Pierpont Communications | Houston | 627 |
| 468 | BenchmarkQA | Bloomington, MN | 627 |
| 469 | Chocoholics Divine Desserts | Stockton, CA | 626 |
| 470 | Intelligent Information Systems | Durham, NC | 623 |
| 471 | Synygy | Conshohocken, PA | 623 |
| 472 | Power On Software | New Albany, OH | 621 |
| 473 | ASAP Staffing | Norcross, GA | 619 |
| 474 | U.S. Medical | Denver | 618 |
| 475 | Elysium Power Solutions | Gulf Breeze, FL | 617 |
| 476 | Mercedes Medical | Sarasota, FL | 616 |
| 477 | PB Systems | Irvine, CA | 614 |
| 478 | Swiss Watch International | Hollywood, FL | 610 |
| 479 | Crown E.S.A. | Portage, IN | 610 |
| 480 | CEI | Pittsburgh, PA | 609 |
| 481 | Scott Pipitone Design | Pittsburgh, PA | 607 |
| 482 | Orbital Research | Cleveland, OH | 600 |
| 483 | Tele-Servicing Innovations | Englewood, CO | 600 |
| 484 | Kelmoore Investment | Palo Alto, CA | 599 |
| 485 | Presentation Group | Orlando, FL | 599 |
| 486 | Elite Systems | Salt Lake City | 599 |
| 487 | Legacy South | Atlanta | 597 |
| 488 | Roth Staffing | Orange, CA | 595 |
| 489 | Southern Diversified Technologies | Brookhaven, MS | 595 |
| 490 | Advanced Video | Columbia, SC | 595 |
| 491 | Advanced Financial Solutions | Oklahoma City | 595 |
| 492 | MasterMind Technologies | Washington, DC | 593 |
| 493 | Cavanaugh | Pittsburgh, PA | 593 |
| 494 | Yesterday's Business Computers | Bridgewater, NJ | 592 |
| 495 | CurrentMarketing | Louisville, KY | 589 |
| 496 | Portable Church Industries | Madison Heights, MI | 588 |
| 497 | CMA Evaluation Consultants | Wyomissing, PA | 588 |
| 498 | Prime Office Products | Nashville, TN | 585 |
| 499 | QCI | Louisville, KY | 585 |
| 500 | Intrepid Lighting Manufacturing | Bohemia, NY | 584 |

# The *Forbes* 500 Largest Private Companies in the US

| Rank | Company | Revenues ($ mil.) | Rank | Company | Revenues ($ mil.) |
|------|---------|-------------------|------|---------|-------------------|
| 1 | Cargill | 49,408 | 51 | International Data Group | 3,010 |
| 2 | Koch Industries | 40,700 | 52 | Allegis Group | 3,000 |
| 3 | PricewaterhouseCoopers | 23,100 | 53 | Raley's | 3,000 |
| 4 | Mars | 15,500 | 54 | Schwan's Sales Enterprises | 3,000 |
| 5 | Publix Super Markets | 14,575 | 55 | JR Simplot | 3,000 |
| 6 | Bechtel | 14,300 | 56 | QuikTrip | 2,929 |
| 7 | Deloitte Touche Tohmatsu | 12,200 | 57 | Bloomberg | 2,850 |
| 8 | KPMG International | 11,800 | 58 | RaceTrac Petroleum | 2,811 |
| 9 | Fidelity Investments | 11,096 | 59 | Wegmans Food Markets | 2,800 |
| 10 | Ernst & Young | 10,000 | 60 | Perdue Farms | 2,700 |
| 11 | Meijer | 10,000 | 61 | Keystone Foods | 2,650 |
| 12 | Andersen | 9,340 | 62 | A-Mark Financial | 2,600 |
| 13 | HE Butt Grocery | 8,965 | 63 | Clark Retail Enterprises | 2,600 |
| 14 | C&S Wholesale Grocers | 8,500 | 64 | Consolidated Electrical Distributors | 2,600 |
| 15 | Huntsman | 8,500 | 65 | Gordon Food Service | 2,600 |
| 16 | Aramark | 7,745 | 66 | Kohler | 2,600 |
| 17 | Premcor | 7,312 | 67 | Sinclair Oil | 2,600 |
| 18 | JM Family Enterprises | 7,100 | 68 | Pilot | 2,586 |
| 19 | Marmon Group | 6,786 | 69 | Micro Warehouse | 2,565 |
| 20 | Alliant Exchange | 6,600 | 70 | Stater Bros Markets | 2,550 |
| 21 | Seagate Technology | 6,387 | 71 | Transammonia | 2,447 |
| 22 | Enterprise Rent-A-Car | 6,300 | 72 | Clark Enterprises | 2,445 |
| 23 | Science Applications Intl | 5,896 | 73 | Connell | 2,425 |
| 24 | Graybar Electric | 5,214 | 74 | Parsons | 2,400 |
| 25 | Menard | 4,850 | 75 | Platinum Equity | 2,400 |
| 26 | Levi Strauss & Co | 4,645 | 76 | Quality King Distributors | 2,400 |
| 27 | SC Johnson & Son | 4,500 | 77 | Venture Industries | 2,400 |
| 28 | Peter Kiewit Sons' | 4,463 | 78 | Gilbane | 2,388 |
| 29 | Giant Eagle | 4,435 | 79 | Allied Worldwide | 2,372 |
| 30 | Advance Publications | 4,400 | 80 | Black & Veatch | 2,358 |
| 31 | Hallmark Cards | 4,233 | 81 | H Group Holding | 2,300 |
| 32 | ContiGroup Cos | 4,000 | 82 | HT Hackney | 2,300 |
| 33 | InterTech Group | 4,000 | 83 | Metaldyne | 2,300 |
| 34 | Cox Enterprises | 3,925 | 84 | Advance Stores | 2,288 |
| 35 | Hy-Vee | 3,900 | 85 | Springs Industries | 2,275 |
| 36 | Milliken & Co | 3,900 | 86 | Belk | 2,270 |
| 37 | Reyes Holding | 3,900 | 87 | Edward Jones | 2,212 |
| 38 | MBM | 3,823 | 88 | Kinko's | 2,184 |
| 39 | Guardian Industries | 3,800 | 89 | Renco Group | 2,150 |
| 40 | Synnex Information Technologies | 3,700 | 90 | BDO International | 2,135 |
| 41 | Alticor | 3,525 | 91 | Structure Tone | 2,100 |
| 42 | Southern Wine & Spirits | 3,500 | 92 | Scoular | 2,098 |
| 43 | Hearst | 3,413 | 93 | Carlson Cos | 2,083 |
| 44 | Eby-Brown | 3,400 | 94 | Ingram Industries | 2,075 |
| 45 | McKinsey & Co | 3,400 | 95 | Haworth | 2,060 |
| 46 | Flying J | 3,330 | 96 | TravelCenters of America | 2,060 |
| 47 | Capital Group of Companies | 3,300 | 97 | UniGroup | 2,009 |
| 48 | Gulf States Toyota | 3,200 | 98 | Apex Oil | 2,000 |
| 49 | Schneider National | 3,089 | 99 | Booz, Allen & Hamilton | 2,000 |
| 50 | Core-Mark International | 3,035 | 100 | Golub | 2,000 |

Source: *Forbes;* November 26, 2001

# The *Forbes* 500 Largest Private Companies in the US (continued)

| Rank | Company | Revenues ($ mil.) | Rank | Company | Revenues ($ mil.) |
|---|---|---|---|---|---|
| 101 | Hunt Consolidated/Hunt Oil | 2,000 | 151 | Save Mart Supermarkets | 1,524 |
| 102 | JELD-WEN Holding | 2,000 | 152 | Cumberland Farms | 1,500 |
| 103 | KB Toys | 2,000 | 153 | Delaware North Cos | 1,500 |
| 104 | LifeStyle Furnishings Intl | 2,000 | 154 | Grocers Supply | 1,500 |
| 105 | Vertis | 1,994 | 155 | Hewitt Associates | 1,500 |
| 106 | Gulf Oil | 1,970 | 156 | National Gypsum | 1,500 |
| 107 | Schnuck Markets | 1,969 | 157 | Southwire | 1,500 |
| 108 | Crown Central Petroleum | 1,961 | 158 | Wawa | 1,500 |
| 109 | DPR Construction | 1,958 | 159 | DHL Airways | 1,497 |
| 110 | Sammons Enterprises | 1,934 | 160 | DiGiorgio | 1,496 |
| 111 | Ergon | 1,905 | 161 | Glazer's Wholesale Drug | 1,480 |
| 112 | Dr Pepper Bottling/Seven-Up Bottling Group | 1,900 | 162 | Services Group of America | 1,480 |
| 113 | HR Logic | 1,900 | 163 | Asplundh Tree Expert | 1,473 |
| 114 | Sheetz | 1,900 | 164 | General Parts | 1,459 |
| 115 | BCom3 Group | 1,894 | 165 | Metromedia | 1,450 |
| 116 | Alex Lee | 1,890 | 166 | Purity Wholesale Grocers | 1,450 |
| 117 | DreamWorks SKG | 1,873 | 167 | Sierra Pacific Industries | 1,450 |
| 118 | JF Shea | 1,863 | 168 | Towers Perrin | 1,448 |
| 119 | DeMoulas Super Markets | 1,850 | 169 | Frank Consolidated Enterprises | 1,431 |
| 120 | Central National-Gottesman | 1,825 | 170 | Heico Companies | 1,425 |
| 121 | DynCorp | 1,809 | 171 | Breed Technologies | 1,422 |
| 122 | Heafner Tire Group | 1,807 | 172 | Hunt Construction Group | 1,418 |
| 123 | Beaulieu of America Group | 1,803 | 173 | Flint Ink | 1,400 |
| 124 | Quad/Graphics | 1,800 | 174 | WL Gore & Associates | 1,400 |
| 125 | 84 Lumber | 1,775 | 175 | Software House International | 1,400 |
| 126 | Golden State Foods | 1,764 | 176 | HB Zachry | 1,400 |
| 127 | BE&K | 1,756 | 177 | Walsh Group | 1,388 |
| 128 | Leprino Foods | 1,714 | 178 | AEI Resources | 1,380 |
| 129 | Builders FirstSource | 1,710 | 179 | EBSCO Industries | 1,375 |
| 130 | Kinray | 1,710 | 180 | ViewSonic | 1,371 |
| 131 | CH2M Hill Companies | 1,707 | 181 | Hensel Phelps Construction | 1,368 |
| 132 | Andersen | 1,700 | 182 | Schreiber Foods | 1,352 |
| 133 | Brookshire Grocery | 1,694 | 183 | Devcon Construction | 1,351 |
| 134 | Grant Thornton | 1,690 | 184 | IMG | 1,350 |
| 135 | Amsted Industries | 1,650 | 185 | EPIX Holdings | 1,331 |
| 136 | Bruno's Supermarkets | 1,650 | 186 | Maritz | 1,318 |
| 137 | Whiting-Turner Contracting | 1,646 | 187 | Dunn Industries | 1,311 |
| 138 | Tishman Realty & Construction | 1,640 | 188 | Young's Market | 1,310 |
| 139 | National Distributing | 1,630 | 189 | Ritz Camera Centers | 1,305 |
| 140 | Rich Products | 1,620 | 190 | CC Industries | 1,300 |
| 141 | E&J Gallo Winery | 1,600 | 191 | SC Johnson Commercial Markets | 1,300 |
| 142 | Kingston Technology | 1,600 | 192 | Lanoga | 1,300 |
| 143 | Aecom Technology | 1,575 | 193 | Taylor | 1,300 |
| 144 | Comark | 1,560 | 194 | WinCo Foods | 1,300 |
| 145 | AG Spanos Cos. | 1,560 | 195 | SF Holdings Group | 1,282 |
| 146 | Follett | 1,554 | 196 | Tang Industries | 1,270 |
| 147 | Day & Zimmermann Group | 1,554 | 197 | Life Care Centers of America | 1,265 |
| 148 | Swinerton | 1,550 | 198 | Republic Technologies Intl. | 1,265 |
| 149 | Fry's Electronics | 1,530 | 199 | ICC Industries | 1,260 |
| 150 | Borden | 1,524 | 200 | Dillingham Construction | 1,258 |

# The *Forbes* 500 Largest Private Companies in the US (continued)

| Rank | Company | Revenues ($ mil.) | Rank | Company | Revenues ($ mil.) |
|---|---|---|---|---|---|
| 201 | Bose | 1,250 | 251 | Delco Remy International | 1,087 |
| 202 | Meridian Automotive Systems | 1,250 | 252 | UIS | 1,087 |
| 203 | ABC Supply | 1,239 | 253 | GSC Enterprises | 1,082 |
| 204 | Holiday Cos | 1,225 | 254 | Conair | 1,082 |
| 205 | G-I Holdings | 1,208 | 255 | Michael Foods | 1,081 |
| 206 | McCarthy Building Companies | 1,205 | 256 | MA Mortenson | 1,080 |
| 207 | DeBruce Grain | 1,201 | 257 | MTS | 1,080 |
| 208 | Austin Industries | 1,200 | 258 | Watkins Associated Industries | 1,076 |
| 209 | Barnes & Noble College Bookstores | 1,200 | 259 | Parsons & Whittemore | 1,075 |
| 210 | Mary Kay | 1,200 | 260 | ClubCorp | 1,069 |
| 211 | Purdue Pharma | 1,200 | 261 | Ben E Keith | 1,068 |
| 212 | Swagelok | 1,200 | 262 | Anderson News | 1,063 |
| 213 | Parsons Brinckerhoff | 1,193 | 263 | Earle M Jorgensen | 1,060 |
| 214 | Discount Tire | 1,192 | 264 | Ingram Entertainment Holdings | 1,057 |
| 215 | Connell Limited Partnership | 1,185 | 265 | Rooney Brothers | 1,053 |
| 216 | Dade Behring | 1,184 | 266 | Carpenter | 1,050 |
| 217 | United Defense | 1,184 | 267 | Dick Corp | 1,050 |
| 218 | Bashas' | 1,170 | 268 | MediaNews Group | 1,042 |
| 219 | Dart Container | 1,170 | 269 | Primus | 1,040 |
| 220 | Noveon | 1,168 | 270 | Rooms to Go | 1,040 |
| 221 | Domino's Pizza | 1,167 | 271 | Arctic Slope Regional | 1,038 |
| 222 | Knoll | 1,163 | 272 | MSX International | 1,035 |
| 223 | Barton Malow | 1,160 | 273 | Dunavant Enterprises | 1,030 |
| 224 | Skadden, Arps, Slate, Meagher & Flom | 1,154 | 274 | Battelle Memorial Institute | 1,029 |
| 225 | LL Bean | 1,150 | 275 | Printpack | 1,027 |
| 226 | Big Y Foods | 1,150 | 276 | New Age Electronics | 1,024 |
| 227 | NESCO | 1,150 | 277 | JM Huber | 1,022 |
| 228 | North Pacific Group | 1,150 | 278 | Buffets | 1,021 |
| 229 | Petco Animal Supplies | 1,150 | 279 | Medline Industries | 1,016 |
| 230 | TTI | 1,146 | 280 | Horseshoe Gaming Holding | 1,013 |
| 231 | Regal Cinemas | 1,131 | 281 | Parkdale Mills | 1,001 |
| 232 | Wilbur-Ellis | 1,131 | 282 | Baker & McKenzie | 1,000 |
| 233 | Riverwood International | 1,129 | 283 | Baker & Taylor | 1,000 |
| 234 | Crown Equipment | 1,127 | 284 | Bass Pro | 1,000 |
| 235 | Foster Farms | 1,127 | 285 | Boscov's | 1,000 |
| 236 | Quality Stores | 1,126 | 286 | Cantor Fitzgerald Securities | 1,000 |
| 237 | SAS Institute | 1,120 | 287 | Genmar Holdings | 1,000 |
| 238 | Truman Arnold Cos | 1,120 | 288 | Longaberger | 1,000 |
| 239 | Modern Continental Cos | 1,118 | 289 | TIC-The Industrial Co | 998 |
| 240 | Goodman Manufacturing | 1,115 | 290 | VarTec Telecom | 995 |
| 241 | Menasha | 1,112 | 291 | Beck Group | 990 |
| 242 | Shamrock Foods | 1,109 | 292 | Big V Supermarkets | 990 |
| 243 | Dot Foods | 1,107 | 293 | Stevedoring Services of America | 989 |
| 244 | Sealy | 1,102 | 294 | Warren Equities | 984 |
| 245 | American Century Investments | 1,100 | 295 | Honickman Affiliates | 983 |
| 246 | Boston Consulting Group | 1,100 | 296 | K-VA-T Food Stores | 963 |
| 247 | Swifty Serve | 1,100 | 297 | Hoffman | 954 |
| 248 | TAC Worldwide Cos | 1,100 | 298 | Ashley Furniture Industries | 952 |
| 249 | Duchossois Industries | 1,090 | 299 | O'Neal Steel | 941 |
| 250 | Red Apple Group | 1,090 | 300 | M Fabrikant & Sons | 930 |

# The *Forbes* 500 Largest Private Companies in the US (continued)

| Rank | Company | Revenues ($ mil.) | Rank | Company | Revenues ($ mil.) |
|---|---|---|---|---|---|
| 301 | Chemcentral | 917 | 351 | ASI | 818 |
| 302 | Micro Electronics | 916 | 352 | Plastipak Packaging | 812 |
| 303 | Sunbelt Beverage | 915 | 353 | Bartlett and Co | 810 |
| 304 | Pella | 914 | 354 | Gould Paper | 810 |
| 305 | Royster-Clark | 913 | 355 | Journal Communications | 810 |
| 306 | 24 Hour Fitness Worldwide | 911 | 356 | MTD Products | 810 |
| 307 | Hobby Lobby Stores | 905 | 357 | US Can | 810 |
| 308 | New Balance Athletic Shoe | 901 | 358 | TTC Illinois | 809 |
| 309 | Colfax | 900 | 359 | Jordan Industries | 807 |
| 310 | McKee Foods | 900 | 360 | Landmark Communications | 805 |
| 311 | Minyard Food Stores | 900 | 361 | Linsco/Private Ledger | 801 |
| 312 | Love's Travel Stops & Country Stores | 894 | 362 | Bain & Co | 800 |
| 313 | Dick's Sporting Goods | 893 | 363 | Columbia Forest Products | 800 |
| 314 | Iasis Healthcare | 892 | 364 | MicronPC | 800 |
| 315 | Doane Pet Care | 892 | 365 | National Textiles | 800 |
| 316 | RB Pamplin | 890 | 366 | Rosen's Diversified | 800 |
| 317 | Oxford Automotive | 885 | 367 | Crowley Maritime | 790 |
| 318 | Newark Group | 883 | 368 | Les Schwab Tire Centers | 790 |
| 319 | Freeman Cos | 878 | 369 | Turner Industries Group | 788 |
| 320 | Soave Enterprises | 878 | 370 | Cinemark USA | 786 |
| 321 | PC Richard & Son | 875 | 371 | Charmer Industries | 785 |
| 322 | Topa Equities | 865 | 372 | PMC Global | 784 |
| 323 | Wirtz | 865 | 373 | Simpson Investment | 780 |
| 324 | Berwind Group | 860 | 374 | Deseret Management | 778 |
| 325 | Hale-Halsell | 859 | 375 | Ilitch Holdings | 777 |
| 326 | Texas Petrochemicals | 859 | 376 | S Abraham & Sons | 776 |
| 327 | Freedom Communications | 855 | 377 | Feld Entertainment | 776 |
| 328 | MA Laboratories | 855 | 378 | Findlay Industries | 776 |
| 329 | Fisher Development | 854 | 379 | Bellco Health | 775 |
| 330 | Rudolph and Sletten | 852 | 380 | Cabela's | 775 |
| 331 | Brasfield & Gorrie | 849 | 381 | Formica | 774 |
| 332 | Pliant | 844 | 382 | Avondale | 773 |
| 333 | Alberici | 837 | 383 | Miller & Hartman | 773 |
| 334 | Inserra Supermarkets | 834 | 384 | King Kullen Grocery | 770 |
| 335 | Pepper Construction Group | 834 | 385 | S&P Co | 770 |
| 336 | Solo Cup | 833 | 386 | Fiesta Mart | 769 |
| 337 | Bozzuto's | 830 | 387 | Horsehead Industries | 765 |
| 338 | Goya Foods | 830 | 388 | Sigma Plastics Group | 765 |
| 339 | Icon Health & Fitness | 830 | 389 | US Oil | 760 |
| 340 | Roll International | 830 | 390 | Webcor Builders | 760 |
| 341 | Sutherland Lumber | 830 | 391 | Ty | 758 |
| 342 | Golden Rule Financial | 829 | 392 | Concentra | 752 |
| 343 | David Weekley Homes | 828 | 393 | Brookshire Brothers | 750 |
| 344 | World Kitchen | 828 | 394 | Lifetouch | 750 |
| 345 | Green Bay Packaging | 826 | 395 | McWane | 750 |
| 346 | J Crew Group | 826 | 396 | RTM Restaurant Group | 750 |
| 347 | CenTra | 825 | 397 | Superior Group | 750 |
| 348 | Graham Packaging Holdings | 825 | 398 | Walbridge, Aldinger | 750 |
| 349 | Houchens Industries | 820 | 399 | Petro Stopping Centers | 749 |
| 350 | OmniSource | 820 | 400 | F Dohmen | 748 |

# The *Forbes* 500 Largest Private Companies in the US (continued)

| Rank | Company | Revenues ($ mil.) | Rank | Company | Revenues ($ mil.) |
|------|---------|-------------------|------|---------|-------------------|
| 401 | Holiday Retirement/Colson & Colson | 747 | 451 | Jones, Day, Reavis & Pogue | 675 |
| 402 | Cupertino Electric | 746 | 452 | Angelo Iafrate Companies | 674 |
| 403 | RAB Holdings | 745 | 453 | Kimball Hill Homes | 673 |
| 404 | Wintec Industries | 745 | 454 | Darby Group Cos | 670 |
| 405 | KinderCare Learning Centers | 743 | 455 | Sidley Austin Brown & Wood | 670 |
| 406 | WG Yates & Sons Construction | 743 | 456 | Haggen | 666 |
| 407 | McJunkin | 741 | 457 | Schottenstein Stores | 665 |
| 408 | Express Services | 741 | 458 | Suffolk Construction | 663 |
| 409 | Colorado Boxed Beef | 740 | 459 | National Wine & Spirits | 661 |
| 410 | Marc Glassman | 740 | 460 | American Golf | 660 |
| 411 | Pinnacle Foods | 740 | 461 | Everett Smith Group | 660 |
| 412 | Inductotherm Industries | 735 | 462 | Amerigroup | 660 |
| 413 | Orius | 735 | 463 | HBE | 658 |
| 414 | American Commercial Lines | 734 | 464 | Northern Tool & Equipment | 655 |
| 415 | Washington Cos | 734 | 465 | E-Z Mart Stores | 654 |
| 416 | Cigarettes Cheaper | 730 | 466 | Electek Group | 651 |
| 417 | Georgia Crown Distributing | 730 | 467 | Dawn Food Products | 650 |
| 418 | Harold Levinson Associates | 730 | 468 | Fellowes | 650 |
| 419 | WWF Paper | 730 | 469 | National Envelope | 650 |
| 420 | Simmons | 727 | 470 | Ukrop's Super Markets | 650 |
| 421 | Pacific Coast Building Products | 725 | 471 | Veridian | 650 |
| 422 | Roseburg Forest Products | 725 | 472 | Weitz | 650 |
| 423 | Safelite Glass | 725 | 473 | Merrill | 649 |
| 424 | Koppers Industries | 724 | 474 | AppleOne Employment Services | 648 |
| 425 | MWH | 722 | 475 | Stewart's Shops | 648 |
| 426 | Hampton Affiliates | 721 | 476 | TNP Enterprises | 644 |
| 427 | Academy Sports & Outdoors | 719 | 477 | API Group | 643 |
| 428 | Great Lakes Cheese | 717 | 478 | Latham & Watkins | 643 |
| 429 | Chas Levy | 717 | 479 | Tutor-Saliba | 642 |
| 430 | Steiner | 712 | 480 | Grove Worldwide | 640 |
| 431 | Kraus-Anderson | 710 | 481 | Kerr Drug | 640 |
| 432 | CIC International | 709 | 482 | WorkPlaceUSA | 640 |
| 433 | Interactive Brokers Group | 707 | 483 | Grede Foundries | 633 |
| 434 | Wherehouse Entertainment | 706 | 484 | KI | 631 |
| 435 | Bradco Supply | 700 | 485 | Forsythe Technology | 631 |
| 436 | Fairchild Dornier | 700 | 486 | Crescent Electric Supply | 630 |
| 437 | GS Industries | 700 | 487 | Fareway Stores | 630 |
| 438 | HP Hood | 700 | 488 | Cactus Feeders | 625 |
| 439 | Ormet | 700 | 489 | Goss Graphic | 623 |
| 440 | Sauder Woodworking | 700 | 490 | ACF Industries | 623 |
| 441 | Wells' Dairy | 700 | 491 | Koch Enterprises | 617 |
| 442 | Motor Coach Industries Intl | 692 | 492 | Drummond | 615 |
| 443 | Estes Express Lines | 691 | 493 | Gate Petroleum | 615 |
| 444 | Variety Wholesalers | 691 | 494 | Leiner Health Products Group | 612 |
| 445 | Peerless Importers | 690 | 495 | Schonfeld Securities | 612 |
| 446 | Empire Beef | 682 | 496 | Hudson Group | 610 |
| 447 | Modus Media International | 682 | 497 | Telcobuy.com | 609 |
| 448 | Forever Living Products Intl | 680 | 498 | Atlas World Group | 607 |
| 449 | TRT Holdings | 680 | 499 | Marathon Cheese | 605 |
| 450 | Henkels & McCoy | 675 | 500 | Jockey International | 604 |

## American Lawyer's Top 25 US Law Firms

| Rank | Firm | Number of Lawyers | Gross Revenues ($ mil.) |
|---|---|---|---|
| 1 | Skadden, Arps, Slate, Meagher & Flom | 1,154.0 | 1,441 |
| 2 | Baker & McKenzie | 940.0 | 2,721 |
| 3 | Jones, Day, Reavis & Pogue | 675.0 | 1,298 |
| 4 | Latham & Watkins | 642.5 | 951 |
| 5 | Shearman & Sterling | 590.0 | 805 |
| 6 | Mayer, Brown & Platt | 533.5 | 853 |
| 7 | Davis Polk & Wardwell | 525.0 | 535 |
| 8 | Sullivan & Cromwell | 516.5 | 495 |
| 9 | Morgan, Lewis & Bockius | 515.5 | 999 |
| 10 | Weil, Gotshal & Manges | 505.5 | 750 |
| 11 | McDermott, Will & Emery | 503.0 | 840 |
| 12 | Simpson Thacher & Bartlett | 500.0 | 533 |
| 13 | White & Case | 491.0 | 1,008 |
| 14 | Brobeck, Phleger & Harrison | 476.0 | 724 |
| 15 | Sidley & Austin | 473.0 | 797 |
| 16 | Kirkland & Ellis | 470.0 | 662 |
| 17 | Gibson, Dunn & Crutcher | 469.0 | 647 |
| 18 | Cleary, Gottlieb, Steen & Hamilton | 460.0 | 550 |
| 19 | Wilson Sonsini Goodrich & Rosati | 450.0 | 812 |
| 20 | Morrison & Foerster | 437.0 | 809 |
| 21 | Akin, Gump, Strauss, Hauer & Feld | 430.0 | 889 |
| 22 | O'Melveny & Myers | 400.5 | 708 |
| 23 | Paul, Hastings, Janofsky & Walker | 388.5 | 654 |
| 24 | Vinson & Elkins | 386.5 | 690 |
| 25 | Cravath, Swaine & Moore | 380.0 | 344 |

Source: *American Lawyer;* July 2001

## America's Top 25 Tax & Accounting Firms Ranked by US Revenues

| Rank | Firm | Headquarters | 2000 US Revenues ($ mil.) |
|---|---|---|---|
| 1 | PricewaterhouseCoopers | New York | 8,878.0 |
| 2 | Deloitte & Touche | New York | 5,838.0 |
| 3 | KPMG | New York | 5,400.0 |
| 4 | Ernst & Young | New York | 4,270.0 |
| 5 | Anderson | Chicago | 3,600.0 |
| 6 | H&R Block Tax Services Inc. | Kansas City, MO | 1,431.0 |
| 7 | Century Business Services | Cleveland | 436.1 |
| 8 | Grant Thorton | New York | 416.0 |
| 9 | BDO Seidman | Chicago | 408.0 |
| 10 | RSM McGladrey | Bloomington, MN | 338.1 |
| 11 | American Express | New York | 325.0 |
| 12 | Jackson Hewitt Tax Service | Parsippany, NJ | 192.8 |
| 13 | Crowe, Chizek and Co. | Indianapolis | 150.3 |
| 14 | Moss Adams | Seattle | 143.0 |
| 15 | Plante & Moran | Southfield, MI | 142.7 |
| 16 | Centerprise Advisors Inc. | Chicago | 140.8 |
| 17 | Baird Kurtz & Dobson | Springfield, MO | 117.8 |
| 18 | Clifton Gunderson | Peoria, IL | 113.3 |
| 19 | Fiducial Triple Check Inc. | Montrose, CA | 112.3 |
| 20 | Gilman + Ciocia | White Plains, NY | 89.6 |
| 21 | Constantin Associates | New York | 88.6 |
| 22 | Eisner | New York | 76.0 |
| 23 | Larson, Allen, Weishair & Co. | Minneapolis | 75.7 |
| 24 | Virchow, Krause & Co. | Madison, WI | 72.7 |
| 25 | Olive | Indianapolis | 65.5 |

Source: *Accounting Today;* March 19–April 1, 2001

# Top 25 Universities

| Rank | School |
|------|--------|
| 1 | Princeton University |
| 2 | Harvard University |
| 2 | Yale University |
| 4 | California Institute of Technology |
| 5 | Massachusetts Institute of Technology |
| 5 | Stanford University |
| 5 | University of Pennsylvania |
| 8 | Duke University |
| 9 | Columbia University |
| 9 | Dartmouth College |
| 9 | University of Chicago |
| 12 | Northwestern University |
| 12 | Rice University |
| 14 | Cornell University |
| 14 | Washington University in St. Louis |
| 16 | Brown University |
| 16 | Johns Hopkins University |
| 18 | Emory University |
| 19 | University of Notre Dame |
| 20 | University of California – Berkeley |
| 21 | University of Virginia |
| 21 | Vanderbilt University |
| 23 | Carnegie Mellon University |
| 23 | Georgetown University |
| 25 | University of Michigan – Ann Arbor |

Ranked by composite score, including such factors as graduation and retention rates, faculty resources, and student-to-faculty ratio.

Source: *U.S. News and World Report;* September 17, 2001

# Top 25 Public Universities

| Rank | School |
|------|--------|
| 1 | University of California – Berkeley |
| 2 | University of Virginia |
| 3 | University of Michigan – Ann Arbor |
| 4 | University of California – Los Angeles |
| 5 | University of North Carolina – Chapel Hill |
| 6 | College of William and Mary |
| 7 | University of California – San Diego |
| 8 | University of Wisconsin – Madison |
| 9 | University of Illinois – Urbana-Champaign |
| 10 | Georgia Institute of Technology |
| 10 | University of California – Davis |
| 10 | University of California – Irvine |
| 13 | University of Washington |
| 14 | Pennsylvania State University – University Park |
| 15 | Texas A&M University – College Station |
| 15 | University of California – Santa Barbara |
| 15 | University of Texas – Austin |
| 18 | University of Georgia |
| 19 | University of Florida |
| 19 | University of Minnesota – Twin Cities |
| 21 | Ohio State University – Columbus |
| 21 | Purdue University – West Lafayette |
| 21 | University of Maryland – College Park |
| 24 | Rutgers – New Brunswick |
| 24 | University of Delaware |

Ranked by composite score, including such factors as graduation and retention rates, faculty resources, and student-to-faculty ratio.

Source: *U.S. News and World Report;* September 17, 2001

# Top 10 Health Care Systems by Net Patient Revenues

| Rank | System | 2000 Revenues ($ mil.) |
|------|--------|------------------------|
| 1 | U.S. Department of Veterans Affairs | 22,382.9 |
| 2 | HCA–The Healthcare Company | 16,700.0 |
| 3 | Tenet Healthcare Corporation | 10,666.0 |
| 4 | Ascension Health | 5,800.1 |
| 5 | Catholic Health Initiatives | 5,016.2 |
| 6 | Catholic Healthcare West | 4,502.2 |
| 7 | New York City Health and Hospitals Corp. | 3,480.9 |
| 8 | Trinity Health | 3,436.2 |
| 9 | Mayo Foundation | 3,053.6 |
| 10 | New York Presbyterian Healthcare System | 3,029.7 |

Source: *Modern Healthcare;* June 4, 2001

# Top 25 US Foundations

| Rank | Name | State | Assets ($ mil.) |
|---|---|---|---|
| 1 | Bill & Melinda Gates Foundation | WA | 21,149.1 |
| 2 | Lilly Endowment Inc. | IN | 15,591.7 |
| 3 | The Ford Foundation | NY | 14,659.7 |
| 4 | J. Paul Getty Trust | CA | 10,929.8 |
| 5 | The David and Lucile Packard Foundation | CA | 9,793.2 |
| 6 | The Robert Wood Johnson Foundation | NJ | 8,793.8 |
| 7 | The Andrew W. Mellon Foundation | NY | 4,888.2 |
| 8 | W. K. Kellogg Foundation | MI | 4,853.4 |
| 9 | The Pew Charitable Trusts | PA | 4,800.8 |
| 10 | The Starr Foundation | NY | 4,486.5 |
| 11 | John D. and Catherine T. MacArthur Foundation | IL | 4,479.2 |
| 12 | The William and Flora Hewlett Foundation | CA | 3,930.4 |
| 13 | The Rockefeller Foundation | NY | 3,619.0 |
| 14 | The California Endowment | CA | 3,490.3 |
| 15 | Robert W. Woodruff Foundation, Inc. | GA | 3,139.7 |
| 16 | The Annie E. Casey Foundation | MD | 3,001.9 |
| 17 | Charles Stewart Mott Foundation | MI | 2,881.8 |
| 18 | The Duke Endowment | NC | 2,874.0 |
| 19 | Casey Family Programs | WA | 2,810.5 |
| 20 | The Kresge Foundation | MI | 2,770.5 |
| 21 | The Annenberg Foundation | PA | 2,755.8 |
| 22 | Ewing Marion Kauffman Foundation | MO | 2,473.7 |
| 23 | John S. and James L. Knight Foundation | FL | 2,199.0 |
| 24 | The Freeman Foundation | NY | 2,113.7 |
| 25 | The Harry and Jeanette Weinberg Foundation, Inc. | MD | 2,063.3 |

Source: The Foundation Center; http://www.fdncenter.org; December 28, 2001

# Hoover's Handbook of Private Companies

## THE COMPANY PROFILES

# 84 LUMBER COMPANY

84 = 2x4s. Based in Eighty Four, Pennsylvania, 84 Lumber Company sells lumber and do-it-yourself (DIY) kits for kitchens, garages, decks, and even entire homes through about 415 locations. The stores (or lumberyards, depending on your view) are located mostly in the East, the Southeast, and the Midwest; products are also sold internationally.

Founded to serve professionals, 84 Lumber expanded its product offering to attract more DIY consumers. It has since re-shifted its focus to professional builders, which account for about three-fourths of sales. (The company is testing nearly a dozen component factories —

roof and floor trusses — that serve builders in North and South Carolina.) While the professional market is less profitable and more cyclic than the DIY segment, it has the advantage of being less crowded than heavy competitors such as The Home Depot and Lowe's.

84 Lumber is also reconfiguring stores for individual markets; this includes adding more lumber inventory and specialty services, as well as expanding its 84-Plus store format (lumberyard *plus* hardware store). President Maggie Hardy Magerko, daughter of CEO and founder Joseph Hardy Sr., owns about 80% of the company.

## HISTORY

In 1956 Joseph Hardy Sr. opened the first 84 Lumber store in Eighty Four, Pennsylvania, a town near Pittsburgh. Hardy had a bare-bones approach and kept a tight rein on his company (he once ordered the office staff to weed the company headquarters lawn), paying cash for new building sites (he was known to lowball landowners by dressing like a simple country hick) and driving to work in an old car.

The strategy was successful, and for the next two decades 84 Lumber prospered, growing steadily to more than 350 stores in the early 1980s under Hardy's reign.

But the 1980s brought trouble, not only for 84 Lumber but also within the Hardy family. Paul Hardy, the second-eldest son, left the company after continued sparring with Joe. Another son, Joe Hardy Jr., seemed to be his father's handpicked successor: He had worked for 84 Lumber since 1967, rising to the level of COO. However, Joe Jr. and Joe Sr. clashed and under pressure from his father, Joe Jr. resigned in 1988 and went on to run a real estate development company near Pittsburgh.

Joe Sr. also underwent a transformation during this time, opening his once-tight purse strings to buy himself an honorary English title — lord of the manor of Henley-in-Arden — for about $170,000. In 1987 he paid $3.1 million to purchase a retreat in southwestern Pennsylvania, the Nemacolin Woodlands. He placed the renovation of the resort (at the cost of some $100 million) in the hands of his daughter Maggie, who was in her early 20s at the time.

While Hardy was transforming, so was 84 Lumber. The company started moving away from its traditional approach in an attempt to gain a piece of the budding yuppie market. This approach, along with an ill-timed expansion,

led to a loss of customers and falling profits. Earnings fell from $52 million in 1987 to $22 million in 1989.

84 Lumber started to right itself in 1991. Hardy transferred stock to Maggie, his heir apparent. While running Nemacolin Woodlands, Maggie strove to emulate her father's business style, which included holding obscenity-laced staff meetings. 84 Lumber shut stores and returned to its basic operating scheme as a low-cost provider of lumber in small towns.

Under new president Maggie, 84 Lumber's sales topped the $1 billion mark in 1993 and the company refocused on its professional contractor customers. The company first shipped its building materials internationally in 1996 (to New Zealand) and added customers in Australia, China, Korea, and Switzerland, in the late 1990s. In 1997, 84 Lumber opened Maggie's Building Solutions Showroom, a 7,500-sq.-ft. remodeling center featuring upscale home products. By 1997 the company was the US's largest dealer of building supplies to professional contractors.

In a further effort to attract contractors' business, 84 Lumber introduced a builder financing program in 1999 and began converting some of its stores to the 84-Plus store format, in which its traditional lumberyard setup is matched with a 10,000-sq.-ft. hardware store. In 2000, 84 Lumber opened 35 new stores. In an effort to reach more professionals, it increased its outside sales staff by 25%.

Each year the company hosts a 10-year reunion for employees who've been with the company for a decade. Founder and CEO Joe Hardy was surprised for his 78th birthday at the 2001 reunion with a birthday cake rolled out by comedian Bill Cosby.

**CEO:** Joseph A. Hardy Sr.
**President:** Maggie Hardy Magerko
**COO:** Bill Myrick
**CFO:** Dan Wallach
**VP Marketing and Advertising:** Randy Vankirk
**VP:** Mark Mollico
**Director of Human Resources:** Nicole Madden

## LOCATIONS

**HQ:** Route 519, Eighty Four, PA 15330
**Phone:** 724-228-8820        **Fax:** 724-228-4145
**Web:** www.84lumber.com

84 Lumber operates stores in over 30 states and also
sells its products in Australia, China, New Zealand,
South Korea, and Switzerland.

## PRODUCTS/OPERATIONS

**Selected Products**
Doors
Drywall
Flooring
Insulation
Lumber
Plywood
Project kits
  Barns (pole and storage)
  Decks
  Garages
  Houses
  Kitchens
  Playsets
Roofing
Room additions
Siding
Skylights
Trim
Trusses
Ventilation
Windows

## COMPETITORS

Ace Hardware
BMA
Builders FirstSource
Building Materials
  Holding
Carolina Holdings
Carter Lumber
Contractors' Warehouse
Do it Best
Foxworth-Galbraith
  Lumber

Grossman's
Home Depot
Lanoga
Lowe's
McCoy
Menard
Payless Cashways
Sutherland Lumber
TruServ
Wickes
Wolohan Lumber

## HISTORICAL FINANCIALS & EMPLOYEES

| Private<br>FYE: December 31 | Annual<br>Growth | 12/91 | 12/92 | 12/93 | 12/94 | 12/95 | 12/96 | 12/97 | 12/98 | 12/99 | 12/00 |
|---|---|---|---|---|---|---|---|---|---|---|---|
| Sales ($ mil.) | 8.9% | — | 898 | 1,060 | 1,275 | 1,275 | 1,590 | 1,600 | 1,625 | 1,800 | 1,775 |
| Employees | 5.7% | — | 3,200 | 3,500 | 3,500 | 3,500 | 4,500 | 4,815 | 4,400 | 4,500 | 5,000 |

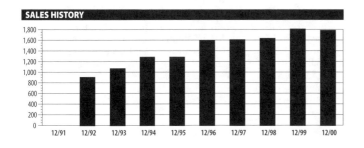

### SALES HISTORY

# AARP

AARP: It's not just for retired people anymore. The Washington, DC-based association is the nation's largest organization for the improvement of life for older Americans. The association has about 34 million members, both working and retired. Anyone 50 years or older can be a member (the annual dues are $10) and receive services from or contribute to the not-for-profit organization's four main areas of activity: information and education, community service, advocacy, and member services. AARP disseminates information in a variety of formats (a Web site, public policy agendas, radio and TV spots, *Modern Maturity* magazine) and pursues educational and research efforts through the AARP Andrus Foundation, the Research Information Center, and the Public Policy Institute.

AARP may not be the most exclusive club around, but it is one of the most powerful. One of the largest lobbying groups in the US, the organization spends more than $50 million a year on lobbying and related activities. AARP is attempting to transform itself by adapting to its changing demographics. The organization has initiated a $100 million, five-year marketing plan to attract aging baby boomers who are becoming eligible for membership. The campaign includes the launch of a new magazine called *My Generation*.

AARP members are eligible for such services as savings on prescription drugs, travel, investment opportunities, and health, life, and auto insurance. Retired educators who join the National Retired Teachers Association (a division of AARP) can receive both AARP services and other benefits designed specifically for them.

Ethel Andrus, a retired Los Angeles high school principal, founded the National Retired Teachers Association (NRTA) in 1947. In 1958 she founded the American Association of Retired Persons (AARP) with the help of Leonard Davis, a New York insurance salesman who had helped her find an underwriter for the NRTA. The new organization's goal: to "enhance the quality of life" for older Americans and "improve the image of aging."

Andrus offered members the same low rates for health and accident insurance provided to NRTA members. She also started publishing AARP's bimonthly magazine, *Modern Maturity*, in 1958. The organization's first local chapter opened in Youngstown, Arizona, in 1960. Still an insurance man, Davis formed Colonial Penn Insurance in 1963 to take over the AARP account. Andrus led AARP and its increasingly powerful lobby for the elderly until her death in 1967.

With criticism of Colonial Penn mounting in the 1970s (critics charged the organization was little more than a front for the insurance company), Prudential won AARP's insurance business in 1979. The NRTA merged with AARP in 1982, and the following year it lowered the membership eligibility age from 55 to 50. The organization continued to expand its offerings, adding an auto club and financial products such as mutual funds and expanded insurance policies. The organization also started a federal credit union for members in 1988, but despite rosy projections, it ceased operations two years later.

AARP forked over $135 million to the IRS in 1993 as part of a settlement regarding the tax status of profits from some of its activities, but the dispute remained unresolved. AARP switched insurance providers again in 1996 (this time to New York Life) and started offering discounted legal services. Also that year, AARP said it would let HMOs offer managed-care services to members. Objections over the plan's potential violation of Medicare anti-kickback laws led AARP to develop a revised payment plan in 1997.

AARP's image was bruised in 1998 when Dale Van Atta wrote a scathing account of the organization, *Trust Betrayed: Inside the AARP.* The book accused the organization of operating out of lavish accommodations, acting as a shill for businesses to hawk their wares, and concealing a drop in membership. Also in 1998, recognizing that nearly a third of its members were working, the organization dropped the American Association of Retired Persons moniker and began to refer to itself by the AARP abbreviation.

To end its long-running dispute with the IRS, AARP reached a settlement over its alleged profit-making enterprises by creating a new taxable subsidiary called AARP Services in 1999. The following year AARP announced a five-year plan to attract aging baby boomers and the launch of its new *My Generation* magazine.

## OFFICERS

**Chairman:** C. Keith Campbell
**President:** Esther Canja
**Executive Director and CEO:** William D. Novelli, age 60
**CFO:** Jocelyn Davis
**VP, Secretary, Treasurer, and Director:**
J. Kenneth Huff Sr.
**VP Membership and Member Services and Director:**
Beatrice Braun
**Associate Executive Director, Operations:**
Richard Henry
**Associate Executive Director, Field Operations:**
Thomas C. Nelson
**Associate Executive Director, Membership:**
Dawn Sweeney
**Chief of Staff:** Cheryl Cooper
**General Counsel:** Joan Wise
**Director Human Resources:** J. Robert Carr
**Auditors:** Arthur Andersen LLP

## LOCATIONS

**HQ:** 601 E St. NW, Washington, DC 20049
**Phone:** 202-434-2277      **Fax:** 202-434-2525
**Web:** www.aarp.org

AARP has offices in 32 states, with plans to have them in all 50 states, the District of Columbia, Puerto Rico, and the Virgin Islands.

## PRODUCTS/OPERATIONS

**2000 Sales**

|                    | $ mil. | % of total |
|--------------------|--------|-----------|
| Membership dues    | 145    | 29        |
| Programs & royalties | 106  | 21        |
| Health care options | 98    | 19        |
| Investment income  | 78     | 16        |
| Advertising        | 74     | 15        |
| Other              | 1      | —         |
| **Total**          | **502** | **100**  |

**Selected Operations and Programs**
55 ALIVE/Mature Driving
AARP Andrus Foundation (gerontology research)
*AARP Bulletin* (monthly news update)
AARP Services (taxable product management,
    marketing, and e-commerce subsidiary)
Connections for Independent Living
Mature Focus Radio (daily news program)
Maturity Broadcast News (weekly video news clips)
*Modern Maturity* (bimonthly magazine)
Money After 50
National Legal Assistance Training Program
National Retired Teachers Association
Public Policy Institute
Research Information Center
Senior Community Service Employment Program
Tax-Aide
Widowed Persons Service
Women's Financial Information Program

## HISTORICAL FINANCIALS & EMPLOYEES

| Association<br>FYE: December 31 | Annual<br>Growth | 12/91 | 12/92 | 12/93 | 12/94 | 12/95 | 12/96 | 12/97 | 12/98 | 12/99 | 12/00 |
|---|---|---|---|---|---|---|---|---|---|---|---|
| Sales ($ mil.) | 6.4% | — | 305 | 369 | 469 | 506 | 475 | 529 | 471 | 485 | 502 |
| Employees | 1.9% | — | 1,718 | 1,793 | 1,752 | 1,800 | 1,850 | 1,900 | 2,000 | 2,000 | 2,000 |

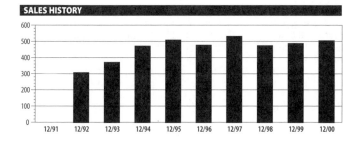

SALES HISTORY

# ACE HARDWARE CORPORATION

## OVERVIEW

Luckily, Ace has John Madden up its sleeve. Despite the growth of warehouse-style competitors, Ace Hardware has remained a household name, thanks to ads featuring Madden, a former Oakland Raiders football coach and TV commentator. The Oak Brook, Illinois-based company is the #2 hardware cooperative in the US, behind TruServ (operator of True Value and several other hardware chains). Ace dealer-owners operate about 5,000 Ace Hardware stores throughout the US and in about 65 other countries. TruServ supplies almost twice as many stores as Ace, but TruServ's sales are only about 40% greater.

Ace distributes products such as electrical and plumbing supplies, power tools, hand tools, garden equipment, and housewares to its members through about 20 warehouses nationwide. It also makes its own brand of paint and offers thousands of other Ace-brand products. Subsidiary Ace Insurance Agency offers dealers insurance for their stores and employees. Ace also provides training programs and advertising campaigns.

Challenged by big-box chains such as The Home Depot and Lowe's, Ace is remodeling stores and polishing its image. Ace dealers own the company and receive dividends from Ace's profits.

## HISTORY

A group of Chicago-area hardware dealers — William Stauber, Richard Hesse, Gern Lindquist, and Oscar Fisher — decided in 1924 to pool their hardware buying and promotional costs. In 1928 the group incorporated as Ace Stores, named in honor of the superior WWI fliers dubbed aces. Hesse became president the following year, retaining that position for the next 44 years. The company also opened its first warehouse in 1929, and by 1933 it had 38 dealers.

The organization had 133 dealers in seven states by 1949. In 1953 Ace began to allow dealers to buy stock in the company through the Ace Perpetuation Plan. In the 1960s Ace expanded into the South and West, and by 1969 it had opened distribution centers in Georgia and California — its first such facilities outside Chicago. In 1968 it opened its first overseas store in Guam.

By the early 1970s the do-it-yourself market began to surge as inflation pushed up plumber and electrician fees. As the market grew, large home center chains gobbled up market share from independent dealers such as those franchised through Ace. In response, Ace and its dealers became a part of a growing trend in the hardware industry — cooperatives.

Hesse sold the company to its dealers in 1973 for $6 million (less than half its book value), and the following year Ace began operating as a cooperative. Hesse stepped down that year. In 1976 the dealers took full control when the company's first Board of Dealer-Directors was elected.

After signing up a number of dealers in the eastern US, Ace had dealers in all 50 states by 1979. The co-op opened a plant to make paint in Matteson, Illinois, in 1984. By the following year Ace had reached $1 billion in sales and had initiated its Store of the Future Program, allowing dealers to borrow up to $200,000 to upgrade their stores and conduct market analyses. Former head coach John Madden of the National Football League's Oakland Raiders signed on as Ace's mouthpiece in 1988.

A year later the co-op began to test ACENET, a computer network that allowed Ace dealers to check inventory, send and receive e-mail, make special purchase requests, and keep up with prices on commodity items such as lumber. In 1990 Ace established an International Division to handle its overseas stores. (It had been exporting products since 1975.) EVP and COO David Hodnik became president in 1995. That year the co-op added a net of 67 stores, including a three-store chain in Russia. Expanding further internationally, Ace signed a five-year joint-supply agreement in 1996 with Canadian lumber and hardware retailer Beaver Lumber. Hodnik added CEO to his title that year.

Ace fell further behind its old rival, True Value, in 1997 when ServiStar Coast to Coast and True Value merged to form TruServ, a hardware giant that operated more than 10,000 outlets at the completion of the merger.

Late in 1997 Ace launched an expansion program in Canada. (The co-op already operated distribution centers in Ontario and Calgary.) In 1999 Ace merged its lumber and building materials division with Builder Marts of America to form a dealer-owned buying group to supply about 2,700 retailers. In 2000 Ace gained 208 member outlet stores but saw 279 member outlets terminated.

## OFFICERS

**Chairman:** Howard J. Jung, age 53
**President and CEO:** David F. Hodnik, age 53,
$686,700 pay
**EVP:** Rita D. Kahle, age 44, $401,704 pay
**EVP, Retail:** Ray A. Griffith, age 47
**SVP, International and Technology:**
Paul M. Ingevaldson, age 55, $380,550 pay
**SVP, Retail Support and Logistics:** David F. Myer,
age 55, $343,215 pay
**VP, Human Resources:** Fred J. Neer, age 61
**VP, Marketing, Advertising, Retail Development, and
Company Stores:** Michael C. Bodzewski, age 51,
$358,070 pay
**VP, Merchandising:** Lori L. Bossmann, age 40
**VP, Retail Operations:** Ken L. Nichols, age 52
**Auditors:** KPMG LLP

## LOCATIONS

**HQ:** 2200 Kensington Ct., Oak Brook, IL 60523
**Phone:** 630-990-6600      **Fax:** 630-990-6838
**Web:** www.acehardware.com

Ace Hardware wholesales products to dealers with retail
operations in the US and about 65 other countries.

## PRODUCTS/OPERATIONS

**2000 Sales**

|  | % of total |
|---|---|
| Paint, cleaning & related supplies | 20 |
| Plumbing & heating supplies | 15 |
| Hand & power tools | 14 |
| Garden, rural equipment & related supplies | 14 |
| Electrical supplies | 12 |
| General hardware | 12 |
| Sundries | 7 |
| Housewares & appliances | 6 |
| **Total** | **100** |

**Subsidiaries**
Ace Corporate Stores (operation of company-owned
stores)
Ace Hardware Canada
Ace Hardware de México, S.A. de C.V.
Ace Insurance Agency (dealer insurance program)
AHC Realty Corporation (broker services to dealers
buying and selling stores)
A.H.C. Store Development Corp.
Loss Prevention Services (security training and loss
prevention services for dealers)
National Hardlines Supply (supply sales to retailers
outside the Ace dealer network)

## COMPETITORS

| | |
|---|---|
| 84 Lumber | Lowe's |
| Akzo Nobel | McCoy |
| Benjamin Moore | Menard |
| Building Materials | Payless Cashways |
| Holding | Pergament Home |
| Carolina Holdings | Réno-Dépôt |
| Costco Wholesale | Sears |
| D.I.Y. Home Warehouse | Sherwin-Williams |
| Do it Best | Sutherland Lumber |
| Fastenal | TruServ |
| Grossman's | United Hardware |
| Home Depot | Distributing Co. |
| House2Home | Wal-Mart |
| ICI Americas | Wickes |
| Kmart | Wolohan Lumber |
| Lanoga | |

## HISTORICAL FINANCIALS & EMPLOYEES

| Cooperative FYE: December 31 | Annual Growth | 12/91 | 12/92 | 12/93 | 12/94 | 12/95 | 12/96 | 12/97 | 12/98 | 12/99 | 12/00 |
|---|---|---|---|---|---|---|---|---|---|---|---|
| Sales ($ mil.) | 5.8% | — | 1,871 | 2,018 | 2,326 | 2,436 | 2,742 | 2,907 | 3,120 | 3,182 | 2,945 |
| Net income ($ mil.) | 3.6% | — | 61 | 57 | 65 | 64 | 72 | 76 | 88 | 93 | 80 |
| Income as % of sales | — | — | 3.2% | 2.8% | 2.8% | 2.6% | 2.6% | 2.6% | 2.8% | 2.9% | 2.7% |
| Employees | 6.8% | — | 3,256 | 3,405 | 3,664 | 3,917 | 4,352 | 4,685 | 4,672 | 5,180 | 5,513 |

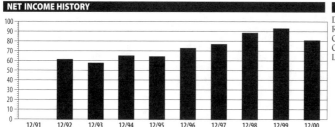

**NET INCOME HISTORY**

**2000 FISCAL YEAR-END**
Debt ratio: 27.1%
Return on equity: 4.5%
Cash ($ mil.): 25
Current ratio: 1.29
Long-term debt ($ mil.): 106

# ADVANCE PUBLICATIONS, INC.

## OVERVIEW

This company is propelled forward by magazine and newspaper publishing. Based in Staten Island, New York, Advance Publications is one of the top periodical publishers in the US. Its newspaper operations include 26 titles such as *The Cleveland Plain Dealer, The Star-Ledger* (New Jersey), and its namesake *Staten Island Advance.* Its American City Business Journals unit produces 40 weekly papers and niche publications, including Street & Smith's *SportsBusiness Journal.* Advance is also the #2 magazine publisher in the US (behind Time, Inc.), with subsidiaries such as Condé Nast Publications (*Vogue, Glamour, The New Yorker, Vanity Fair*) and trade journal publisher Fairchild Publications (*Women's Wear Daily*). In addition, Advance owns Parade Publications (*Parade Magazine* Sunday newspaper insert).

Advance is not only a traditional print publisher but also has a significant Internet presence with nearly a dozen news Web sites. Its CondéNet unit runs Web versions of Condé Nast's magazines and other Internet properties, including Epicurious (food and dining) and Concierge.com (travel). The company also has stakes in cable TV systems (33% with AOL Time Warner), broadband ISP Road Runner (9%), and cable broadcaster Discovery Communications (25%).

Perhaps late to the Internet party, Advance launched online versions of its Condé Nast magazine titles in 2000 to increase their reach. It also took steps to increase its magazine portfolio by acquiring The New York Times Company's Golf Properties unit (*Golf Digest*) for about $430 million and Miami-based Ideas Publishing Group, which produces Spanish language versions of US magazines. Chairman Samuel "Si" Newhouse and his brother Donald (president) control the very closely held company.

## HISTORY

Solomon Neuhaus (later Samuel I. Newhouse) got started in the newspaper business after dropping out of school at age 13. He went to work at the *Bayonne Times* in New Jersey and was put in charge of the failing newspaper in 1911; he managed to turn the paper around within a year. In 1922 he bought the *Staten Island Advance* and formed the Staten Island Advance Company in 1924. After buying up more papers, he changed the name of the company to Advance Publications in 1949. By the 1950s the company had local papers in New York, New Jersey, and Alabama.

In 1959 Newhouse bought magazine publisher Condé Nast as an anniversary gift for his wife. (He joked that she had asked for a fashion magazine, so he bought her *Vogue.*) His publishing empire continued to grow with the addition of the *Times-Picayune* (New Orleans) in 1962 and *The Cleveland Plain Dealer* in 1967. In 1976 the company paid more than $300 million for Booth Newspapers, publisher of eight Michigan papers and *Parade Magazine.*

Newhouse died in 1979, leaving his sons Si and Donald to run the company, which encompassed more than 30 newspapers, a half-dozen magazines, and 15 cable systems. The next year Advance bought book publishing giant Random House from RCA. Si resurrected the Roaring Twenties standard *Vanity Fair* in 1983 and added *The New Yorker* under the Condé Nast banner in 1985. The Newhouses scored a victory over the IRS in 1990 after a long-running court battle involving inheritance taxes. Condé Nast bought Knapp Publications (*Architectural Digest*) in 1993 and Advance later acquired American City Business Journals in 1995.

In 1998 the company sold its increasingly unprofitable Random House to Bertelsmann for about $1.2 billion. Advance later bought hallmark Internet magazine *Wired* (though it passed on Wired Ventures' Internet operations). That year revered *New Yorker* editor Tina Brown, credited with jazzing up the publication's content and increasing its circulation, left the magazine; staff writer and Pulitzer Prize winner David Remnick was named as Brown's replacement.

In 1999 Advance joined Donrey Media Group, E.W. Scripps, Hearst Corporation, and MediaNews Group to purchase the online classified advertising network AdOne (later named PowerOne Media). It also bought Walt Disney's trade publishing unit, Fairchild Publications, for $650 million. In 2000 the company shifted *Details* from Condé Nast to Fairchild and relaunched the magazine as a fashion publication. Later that year the company announced it would begin creating Web versions of its popular magazine titles.

In 2001 Condé Nast bought a majority stake in Miami-based Ideas Publishing Group (Spanish language versions of US magazines). Also that year Advance bought four golf magazines, including *Golf Digest,* from the New York Times Company for $430 million.

## OFFICERS

**Chairman and CEO; Chairman, Condé Nast Publications:** Samuel I. Newhouse Jr.
**President:** Donald E. Newhouse
**COO, Advance Magazine Publishers; COO, Condé Nast:** Charles H. Townsend
**VP Data Processing:** Nick Guido
**VP Finance and Human Resources; Comptroller, Staten Island Advance:** Arthur Silverstein
**VP Investor Services:** George Fries
**VP Marketing:** Jack Furnari
**VP Sales:** Gary Cognetta
**Chairman, CEO, and Publisher, Parade Publications:** Walter Anderson
**Chairman and Editorial Director, Golf Digest Companies:** Jerry Tarde
**Chairman, American City Business Journals:** Ray Shaw
**President and CEO, Condé Nast Publications:** Steven T. Florio
**President and CEO, Golf Digest Companies:** Mitchell Fox
**President and CEO, Fairchild Publications:** Mary G. Berner, age 40
**President and Creative Director, Advance.net:** Jeff Jarvis
**President, Advance Internet:** Peter Wienberger
**Publisher, Staten Island Advance:** Richard Diamond

## LOCATIONS

**HQ:** 950 Fingerboard Rd., Staten Island, NY 10305
**Phone:** 718-981-1234   **Fax:** 718-981-1456
**Web:** www.advance.net

Advance Publications publishes 26 newspapers in more than 20 cities and 40 business weeklies in 22 states.

## PRODUCTS/OPERATIONS

**2000 Sales**

|  | $ mil. | % of total |
|---|---|---|
| Newspapers | 2,753 | 61 |
| Magazines | 1,789 | 39 |
| **Total** | **4,542** | **100** |

### Selected Operations

**Broadcasting and Communications**
Cartoonbank.com
Discovery Communications (25%, cable TV channels)
Newhouse Broadcasting (33% of cable TV joint venture with AOL Time Warner)
Newhouse News Service
Religion News Service
Road Runner (9%, broadband Internet service)

**Magazine Publishing**

| Condé Nast Publications | · Vogue |
|---|---|
| Allure | Wired |
| Architectural Digest | Fairchild Publications |
| Bride's | Details |
| Condé Nast Traveler | Jane |
| Glamour | W |
| Gourmet | Women's Wear Daily |
| GQ | The Golf Digest |
| House & Garden | Companies |
| The New Yorker | Golf Digest |
| Self | Golf Digest Woman |
| Vanity Fair | Golf World |

**Newspaper Publishing**
American City Business Journals (40 weekly titles in 22 states)
Newhouse Newspapers (26 papers in over 20 cities)
Parade Publications

**Online Publishing**
Advance Internet
CondéNet

**Selected Newspapers**
*The Birmingham News* (Alabama)
*The Oregonian* (Portland)
*The Plain Dealer* (Cleveland)
*The Star-Ledger* (Newark, NJ)
*The Times-Picayune* (New Orleans)

## COMPETITORS

| American Express | Hachette Filipacchi | New York Times |
|---|---|---|
| Crain Communications | Médias | PRIMEDIA |
| Dow Jones | Hearst | Reader's Digest |
| E. W. Scripps | Knight Ridder | Reed Elsevier |
| Gannett | McClatchy | Time |
| Gruner + Jahr | Company | Tribune |
|  | Meredith | Washington Post |

## HISTORICAL FINANCIALS & EMPLOYEES

| Private<br>FYE: December 31 | Annual<br>Growth | 12/91 | 12/92 | 12/93 | 12/94 | 12/95 | 12/96 | 12/97 | 12/98 | 12/99 | 12/00 |
|---|---|---|---|---|---|---|---|---|---|---|---|
| Sales ($ mil.) | 0.4% | — | 4,416 | 4,690 | 4,855 | 5,349 | 4,250 | 3,669 | 3,859 | 4,228 | 4,542 |
| Employees | 2.4% | — | 19,000 | 19,000 | 19,000 | 24,000 | 24,000 | 24,000 | 24,000 | 26,300 | 23,000 |

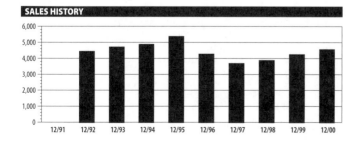

SALES HISTORY

# AFL-CIO

Talk about spending a long time in labor: The AFL-CIO (American Federation of Labor and Congress of Industrial Organizations) has been at it for more than a century. Based in Washington, DC, the AFL-CIO is an umbrella organization for 66 autonomous unions representing more than 13 million workers — ranging from actors and airline pilots to teachers and Teamsters — and works to improve wages and working conditions. Union members generally receive about 28% higher pay and more benefits than do nonmembers.

The organization's membership has been decreasing because of the decline in manufacturing jobs and the increased use of temporary workers and automation. However, the AFL-CIO is reviving under the leadership of John Sweeney, primarily because of his aggressive emphasis on recruiting. It also is restructuring for the first time in almost 45 years; the plan calls for consolidating some of the AFL-CIO's nearly 600 local labor councils and giving the national office greater power to set the agenda for the more autonomous state affiliates.

## HISTORY

The American Federation of Labor (AFL) was formed in 1886 in Columbus, Ohio, by the merger of six craft unions and a renegade craft section of the Marxist-oriented Knights of Labor. Samuel Gompers, a New York cigar factory worker who headed the AFL until his death in 1924, initiated the AFL's pragmatic focus: to work within the economic system to increase wages, improve working conditions, and abolish child labor.

Gompers' successes incensed employers, whose arsenal, supported by the US courts and public opinion, included injunctions, government-backed police forces to crush strikes, and the Sherman Anti-Trust Act (used to assail union monopoly powers.)

WWI's production needs boosted AFL membership to four million by 1919. Labor clashes with management were widespread in the 1920s amid the fear of Bolsheviks. As part of open-shop drives, employers replaced strikers with southern African-Americans and Mexican workers.

The Great Depression brought more supportive public and pro-labor laws, including the National Industrial Recovery Act (NIRA, 1933), which allowed union organizing and collective bargaining. After NIRA was declared unconstitutional, the Wagner Act (1936) restated many of NIRA's provisions and established the legal basis for unions.

Union power split in 1935 when AFL coal miner John L. Lewis began organizing unskilled workers. Lewis and his allies, expelled from the AFL, formed the Congress of Industrial Organizations (CIO, 1938) and enjoyed success in unionizing the auto, steel, textile, and other industries. By 1946 the AFL and CIO had 9 million and 5 million members, respectively.

Amid postwar concern over rising prices, communist infiltration, and union corruption, Congress passed the Taft-Hartley Act in 1947 (which outlawed closed shops). The new climate

of hostility led the AFL (headed by plumber George Meany) and the CIO (headed by autoworker Walter Reuther) to merge in 1955. The AFL-CIO soon expelled the Teamsters and other unions on charges of corruption. (The Teamsters reaffiliated in 1987.)

AFL-CIO membership jumped after President John F. Kennedy gave federal employees the right to unionize (1962); state, county, and municipal workers soon followed.

Union membership, which peaked in the mid-1940s with more than a third of the US labor force, was particularly hurt by a jump in imported goods in the 1970s and automation's triumph over manual labor in the 1980s. Legislation supported by the AFL-CIO included a law requiring 60 days' notice for plant closings (1988) and the Family Leave Act (1993). But labor lost its battle against NAFTA (North American Free Trade Agreement), which it feared would export jobs to Mexico.

In 1995 John Sweeney, former head of the Service Employees International Union, became president of the AFL-CIO in its first contested election. Under Sweeney the union spent $35 million in advertising in 1996 to draw attention to issues. After years with little focus on organizing, in 1997 the AFL-CIO launched a massive campaign to organize construction, hospital, and hotel workers in Las Vegas, and committed a third of its budget to recruiting and reorganizing. It supported the Teamsters' successful strike against UPS in 1997 and in 1998 threw its weight behind the Air Line Pilots Association's walkout on Northwest Airlines. It approved a restructuring plan in 1999 and the next year spent significant time and money rallying members all across the US in support of losing presidential candidate Al Gore.

**President:** John J. Sweeney, age 66
**EVP:** Linda Chavez-Thompson, age 56
**Secretary and Treasurer:** Richard L. Trumka, age 51
**VP; President, American Federation of State, County, and Municipal Employees:** Gerald W. McEntee
**VP; President, American Federation of Teachers:** Sandra Feldman
**VP; President, International Association of Machinists and Aerospace Workers:** R. Thomas Buffenbarger
**VP; President, International Brotherhood of Electrical Workers:** John J. Barry
**VP; President, International Brotherhood of Teamsters:** James P. Hoffa
**VP; President Sheet Metal Workers Union:** Mike Sullivan
**VP; President, U.A.W.:** Stephen P. Yokich
**Director Corporate Affairs:** Ron Blackwell
**Director International Affairs:** Barbara Shailor
**Director Human Resources:** Carl Garland
**Director Legislative:** Peggy Taylor
**General Counsel:** Jonathan Hiatt

## LOCATIONS

**HQ:** 815 16th St. NW, Washington, DC 20006
**Phone:** 202-637-5000     **Fax:** 202-637-5058
**Web:** www.aflcio.org

The AFL-CIO encompasses 66 national and international unions.

## PRODUCTS/OPERATIONS

**Selected Trades and Workers Represented**
Acting
Airline pilots
Broadcasting
Building trades
Education
Electrical trades
Engineering
Farm workers
Firefighters
Flight attendants
Food trades
Government workers
Hotel employees
Industrial trades
Maritime trades
Metal trades
Mining
Music
Office employees
Police
Postal employees
Restaurant employees
Teachers
Transportation trades
Utility workers
Writers

# AG PROCESSING INC

## OVERVIEW

Ag Processing (AGP) could be called Soys "R" Us. The Omaha, Nebraska-based cooperative, one of the largest soybean refiners in the US, processes more than 15,000 acres of soybeans every day. AGP coaxes oil, flour, grits, meal, hulls, and other products from soybeans and helps turn these products into livestock feeds and food ingredients, including meat extenders for ground beef. Valuable by-products include lecithin and bio-fuels.

Member-owned, AGP includes nearly 300 local co-ops and 10 regional co-ops representing some 300,000 farmers. Members come from 16 states in the US and Canada; most are in Iowa, Kansas, Minnesota, Missouri, Nebraska, and South Dakota. Internationally, AGP is involved in feed manufacturing through joint ventures in Hungary and Venezuela.

To capitalize on new Environmental Protection Agency emission limits and mandates, the co-op is lobbying to increase retail demand for ethanol, which it produces from corn. Additionally, AGP is promoting methyl ester, a by-product of soy oil refining, for use as a clean fuel and fuel additive, agricultural spray, and non-toxic solvent to replace petroleum-based products.

## HISTORY

Seeking strength in numbers, Ag Processing (AGP) was formed in 1983 when agricultural cooperatives Land O' Lakes and Farmland Industries merged their money-losing soybean operations into similarly struggling Boone Valley Cooperative.

Separately, AGP's six soybean mills had been unable to compete successfully against each other and larger corporations. The entire industry had been hampered by the Soviet grain embargoes imposed by the US in 1973 and 1979, and US government policies had contributed to increased competition from heavily subsidized soy producers in Argentina and Brazil. Soy exports from the US had fallen dramatically, leading to a production capacity surplus.

Collectively, AGP was able to attract a stronger management staff than its predecessors had; it hired 21-year Archer Daniels Midland (ADM) veteran James Lindsay as CEO and general manager. With operations scattered over four states, AGP placed its headquarters in Omaha, Nebraska — chosen for its central location and close proximity to the co-op's main bank.

In its first two years, AGP cut employee rolls by 20% and scaled back production, thus trimming costs and squeezing higher prices for finished products. A turnaround came quickly, and in 1985 members received a dividend from the co-op's $8 million pretax profit.

AGP dismantled two plants in 1987. By the next year the co-op witnessed an increase in domestic demand and had resumed selling to the Soviet Union. It generated additional sales by further processing soybean oil into food-grade products like hydrogenated oil and lecithin.

With an eye on diversification and value-added products, by 1991 AGP had expanded to eight soybean plants and two vegetable oil refineries; it also acquired the feed and grain business of International Multifoods that year through an 80%-owned joint venture with ADM. The acquisition included 29 feed plants in the US and Canada, 26 retail centers, 18 grain elevators, and the brands Supersweet and Masterfeeds. In 1994 AGP formed feed manufacturer Consolidated Nutrition, a 50-50 joint-venture with ADM.

Consolidated Nutrition introduced a Swine Operations program in 1996. The program quickly grew through the development of PORK PACT, a partnership to serve pork producers. The next year AGP's grain division sold nine grain elevators in Ohio and Indiana to Cargill. That year the co-op gained control of Venezuelan feed manufacturer Proagro.

By 1998 passage of the Freedom to Farm Act and growing demand had spurred soybean planting. The co-op in 1998 opened an additional processing plant in Emmetsburg, Iowa, followed by another in Eagle Grove, Iowa. AGP sold off its pet food operations in 1998. Also that year Consolidated Nutrition combined its Master Mix and Supersweet feed brands into the Consolidated Nutrition label.

In 1999 the company added the Garner-Klemme-Meservey cooperative to its grain operations. It opened a new plant late that year in St. Joseph, Missouri, to make value-added products such as hardfat (used in emulsifiers).

Fire shut down the co-op's soybean crusher in Mason City, Iowa in February 2001. Customers were routed to crushing facilities in Eagle Grove and Emmetsburg, Iowa while repairs were made. In June of that year the company announced that ADM would acquire the US and Caribbean operations of Consolidated Nutrition.

**Chairman:** Denis E. Leiting
**CEO:** Martin P. Reagan
**SVP Member Relations:** Mike Maranell
**SVP Human Resources:** Judy Ford
**SVP Food Group:** George L. Hoover
**SVP Transportation:** Terry J. Voss
**Group VP Finance and CFO:** Kenneth S. Grubbe
**VP Government Relations:** John B. Campbell
**VP Technical Operations:** Richard P. Copeland
**VP Hedging:** Daryl D. Dahl
**VP Administration:** William K. Hahn
**VP Grain Operations and Marketing:** Michael J. Knobbe
**VP Soybean/Corn Operations:** Gary L. Olsen
**VP Research and Technology:** Wayne L. Stockland
**VP and Corporate Controller:** Tim E. Witty

## LOCATIONS

**HQ:** 12700 W. Dodge Rd., Omaha, NE 68103
**Phone:** 402-496-7809     **Fax:** 402-498-5548
**Web:** www.agp.com

Ag Processing has operations in 16 states and in Canada, as well as subsidiary ventures in Hungary and Venezuela.

## PRODUCTS/OPERATIONS

**Selected Brands**
Consolidated Nutrition (feeds)
Masterfeeds (feeds, Canada)
SOYGOLD (bio-diesel, solvents, fuel additives)
Tindle Mills (feeds)

**Selected Operations**
Commercial feeds
Food (lecithin, soybean oil, vegetable oil)
Grain
Industrial products (ethanol, methyl ester)
Soybean processing
Transportation (barge, rail, truck)

**Selected Subsidiaries**
Ag Environmental Products (soybean methyl ester
  products)
AGP Grain Cooperative
AGP Grain, Ltd.
Consolidated Nutrition (50%, commercial feed)

## COMPETITORS

| | |
|---|---|
| Agway | DeBruce Grain |
| Andersons | Farmland Industries |
| ADM | High Plains |
| Bunge Limited | JR Simplot |
| Cargill | MFA |
| Cenex Harvest States | Riceland Foods |
| ConAgra | Southern States |
| ContiGroup | Stake Technology |
| Corn Products | Tate & Lyle |
| International | |

## HISTORICAL FINANCIALS & EMPLOYEES

| Cooperative FYE: August 31 | Annual Growth | 8/91 | 8/92 | 8/93 | 8/94 | 8/95 | 8/96 | 8/97 | 8/98 | 8/99 | 8/00 |
|---|---|---|---|---|---|---|---|---|---|---|---|
| Sales ($ mil.) | 7.2% | — | 1,127 | 1,219 | 1,377 | 2,132 | 2,765 | 2,948 | 2,615 | 2,095 | 1,962 |
| Employees | (4.8%) | — | — | — | — | — | 3,050 | 3,000 | 2,550 | 2,500 | 2,500 |

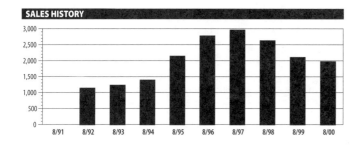

SALES HISTORY

Ag Processing Inc

# AGWAY INC.

Agway knows the way to help farmers. The DeWitt, New York-based agricultural cooperative sells farm supplies to its 69,000 members, who operate mostly in the Northeast and Ohio. It also markets its members' produce to distributors and retailers.

Its Agway Agricultural Group offers feed for livestock and poultry and seed, fertilizers, herbicides, and soil preparation products for crops. It primarily sells directly to farmers through its own sales force. The co-op's Country Products Group processes, packages, and markets fresh produce to the East Coast (mostly under the Country Best label), and sunflower seeds, bird food, and edible beans. That group also makes bags and oversees the co-op's investments in pet food manufacturer ProPet and companies that develop agricultural technology. Agway also finances buildings, equipment, and vehicles for its rural customers and insures farms, homes, autos, and businesses in the agricultural sector.

Another unit, Agway Energy Products LLC, sells and services heating and air-conditioning equipment; it also sells heating oil, propane, and diesel fuel to farms, homes, and small businesses. Agway has begun marketing electricity and natural gas in states that have deregulated those businesses.

Long an operator of farm supply stores in the Northeast, Agway has exited that money-losing business by selling the stores and the consumer wholesale business that supplied them. It is also selling its bean and soybean operations.

Agway was formed in 1964 by the merger of three large northeastern agricultural cooperatives: Eastern States Farmers Exchange, founded in 1918; Cooperative Grange League Federation Exchange, founded in 1920; and Pennsylvania Farm Bureau Cooperative Association, founded in 1934.

About the time of the merger, Agway indirectly acquired voting control of Curtice Burns Foods through a co-op that a group of Agway's members owned. Between 1971 and 1981 the subsidiary acquired at least eight other food companies, including Nalley's Fine Foods, National Brands Beverage, and National Oats. Excited by the success of Curtice Burns, Agway purchased a leading dairy processor, H.P. Hood, in 1980.

In the early 1990s chairman Ralph Heffner, owner of a large farm in Pennsylvania, set his sights on re-engineering Agway. He had listened to the grim reports from industry experts: More than 20,000 northeastern farms had closed down since 1990. Slimming down and stockpiling cash were two of his early goals. More than 400 employees took early retirement in 1992. Agway Energy Products, the energy group, was trimmed considerably: Eight fuel distribution businesses were sold, and the group turned its focus from low-margin commercial accounts to higher-profit homeowner accounts.

Also in 1992 Agway took a $75 million hit related to restructuring costs. That year the co-op launched a program designed to secure a strong financial standing for the organization and to provide efficient delivery of products and services.

The co-op's biggest move in this direction was the sale of the two food operations that had been providing almost 50% of overall revenues. In 1994 Agway sold its share of Curtice Burns (which had sales of $829 million that year) to Pro-Fac Cooperative. The next year it sold its H.P. Hood dairy food processing business to Catamount Dairy Holdings, and in 1996 it sold its lawn care business, Pro-Lawn, to turf care products company LESCO.

Taking advantage of deregulation of energy markets, in 1997 the firm began offering natural gas to customers, and later that year it began a pilot program supplying electricity to farmers in New York.

The following year Agway tested a new store format aimed primarily at suburban women interested in gardening and home decor, but later yanked that concept. In a massive restructuring beginning in 1999, the co-op hitched its retail unit with its agricultural unit and cut about 2% of its workforce. Agway then sold its company-owned stores to independently owned dealers in 2000 (the stores retained the Agway name), and sold to Virginia-based Southern States Cooperative the wholesale business that supported the Agway dealer system. Agway also sold its flour mill operation that year.

In December 2000 the co-op announced that it was realigning its agriculture business into a feed and nutrition division and an agronomy division. As part of the realignment about 60 facilities are being sold, closed, or converted to dealer operations. Agway announced in 2001 that it was selling its bean and soybean operations.

**Chairman:** Gary K. Van Slyke, age 58, $60,000 pay
**Vice Chairman:** Andrew J. Gilbert, age 42, $45,000 pay
**President and CEO:** Donald P. Cardarelli, age 45,
$879,529 pay
**SVP and Chief Administrative Officer; Chairman and
President, Agway Insurance Group:** Gerald R. Seeber,
age 54
**SVP, Finance and Control:** Peter J. O'Neill, age 54,
$494,008 pay
**SVP, General Counsel, and Secretary:**
Christopher W. Fox, age 53
**SVP, Public Affairs:** Stephen H. Hoefer, age 46
**VP and Chief Information Officer:** William L. Parker,
age 54
**VP and Chief Investment Officer:** G. Leslie Smith,
age 58
**President, Agriculture Group:** Robert A. Fischer Jr.,
age 53, $784,616 pay
**President, Agway Energy Products:**
Michael R. Hopsicker, age 36, $465,758 pay
**President, Country Products Group:** Roy S. Lubetkin,
age 44
**President, Telmark:** Daniel J. Edinger, age 50,
$409,587 pay
**Treasurer:** Karen J. Ohliger, age 39
**Corporate Controller:** John F. Feeney, age 40
**Director, Human Resources:** Richard Opdyke
**Auditors:** PricewaterhouseCoopers LLP

## LOCATIONS

**HQ:** 333 Butternut Dr., DeWitt, NY 13214
**Phone:** 315-449-7061  **Fax:** 315-449-6008
**Web:** www.agway.com

Agway's Agricultural Group has operations in Delaware,
Connecticut, Maine, Maryland, Massachusetts, New
Hampshire, New Jersey, New York, Pennsylvania, and
Vermont. Country Products Group has facilities in
California, Florida, Georgia, Idaho, Maine, New York,
North Dakota, Ohio, Oklahoma, Pennsylvania, and Texas.
Agway Energy Products distributes petroleum products
to customers in New Jersey, New York, Pennsylvania,
and Vermont. Agway Insurance Group has operations in
the Northeast, as well as Kentucky and Virginia. Telmark
provides financing nationwide.

## PRODUCTS/OPERATIONS

**2001 Sales**

|  | $ mil. | % of total |
|---|---|---|
| Energy | 723 | 47 |
| Agriculture | 514 | 33 |
| Country Products Group | 198 | 13 |
| Leasing | 85 | 5 |
| Insurance | 28 | 2 |
| **Total** | **1,548** | **100** |

**Major Operating Units**

**Agriculture**
Agway Agricultural Group (animal feeds, crop seeds,
fertilizers, crop protectants, and farm supplies)

**Country Products Group**
The Produce Group (packaging and marketing of fresh
produce)
The Business Group (commodity processing and distri-
bution, bag manufacturing, pet food investing)
The Investment Group (CPG Nutrients; LifeRights Foods
LLC, 45%; Planet Polymer Technologies Inc., 33%)

**Energy**
Agway Energy Products LLC (fuel oil, kerosene, propane,
and motor vehicle fuel; heating and air-conditioning
equipment; gas and electricity in some markets)

**Insurance**
Agway Insurance Group (property, auto, and liability
insurance to farm, home, and small businesses)

**Leasing**
Telmark Inc. (lease financing for buildings, equipment,
and vehicles)

## COMPETITORS

| | |
|---|---|
| Able Energy | Energy East |
| Ag Processing | Farmland Industries |
| Ag Services | GROWMARK |
| AmeriGas Partners | Niagara Mohawk |
| ADM | Purina Mills |
| Cenex Harvest States | Quality Stores |
| CH Energy Group, Inc. | RGS Energy Group |
| ConAgra | Southern States |
| ContiGroup | Star Gas Partners |
| DeBruce Grain | Wilbur-Ellis |

## HISTORICAL FINANCIALS & EMPLOYEES

| Cooperative FYE: Last Saturday in June | Annual Growth | 6/92 | 6/93 | 6/94 | 6/95 | 6/96 | 6/97 | 6/98 | 6/99 | 6/00 | 6/01 |
|---|---|---|---|---|---|---|---|---|---|---|---|
| Sales ($ mil.) | (1.7%) | 1,801 | 1,720 | 1,695 | 1,592 | 1,663 | 1,671 | 1,563 | 1,484 | 1,427 | 1,548 |
| Net income ($ mil.) | — | (59) | 20 | (3) | (16) | 13 | 11 | 13 | 2 | (9) | 9 |
| Income as % of sales | — | — | 1.1% | — | — | 0.8% | 0.6% | 0.8% | 0.1% | — | 0.6% |
| Employees | (6.2%) | 8,400 | 6,600 | 7,900 | 9,000 | 7,500 | 7,100 | 7,000 | 7,200 | 5,600 | 4,700 |

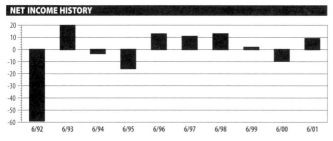

**NET INCOME HISTORY**

**2001 FISCAL YEAR-END**
Debt ratio: 61.5%
Return on equity: —
Cash ($ mil.): 0
Current ratio: 0.92
Long-term debt ($ mil.): 271

# AMERICAN CANCER SOCIETY, INC.

## OVERVIEW

Fighting one of the deadliest of diseases, the American Cancer Society (ACS) has more than 3,400 local units nationwide. The Atlanta-based organization is staffed by professionals as well as 2 million volunteers. It is the largest source of private cancer research funds in the US, providing more than $2.2 billion since its inception. Recipients of the society's funding include 30 Nobel prize laureates. Patient services include moral support; transportation; assistance in obtaining hairpieces, swimwear, and prostheses; and camps for children who have or have had cancer.

The ACS has generated considerable income by marketing its name for antismoking nicotine patches and orange juice, and is contemplating even more lucrative deals. Programs account for about 71% of expenses; 29% goes to administration and fund raising.

## HISTORY

Concerned over the lack of progress in detecting and treating cancer, a group of 10 physicians and five laymen met in New York City in 1913 to form the American Society for the Control of Cancer (ASCC). Because public discussion of cancer was taboo, the group struggled with how to educate people without raising unnecessary fears. Some physicians even preferred keeping knowledge of the disease from the public. In the 1920s the ASCC began sponsoring cancer clinics and collecting statistics on the disease. By 1923 some states reported improvements in early diagnosis and treatment. In 1937 the ASCC started its first nationwide public education program, with the help of volunteers known as the Women's Field Army. President Franklin Roosevelt named April National Cancer Control Month, a practice since followed by every president.

By 1944 some cancer rates were rising but the word "cancer" still couldn't be mentioned on radio. Mary Lasker, wife of prominent ad executive Albert Lasker, was instrumental in getting information about cancer broadcast. At her insistence, in 1945 the newly renamed American Cancer Society began donating at least 25% of its budget to research. The society raised $4 million in its first major national fund-raising campaign.

The link between smoking and lung cancer became known after a study in the early 1950s by ACS medical director Charles Cameron. That information became part of the Surgeon General's Report of 1964. In 1973 an ACS branch in Minnesota held the first Great American Smokeout to encourage people to quit smoking.

The ACS backed the 1971 congressional bill that inaugurated the War on Cancer. The society was attacked in the 1970s for emphasizing cures rather than prevention because, critics claimed, research would reveal environmental causes from industrial products made by companies with connections to ACS directors. In the 1970s and 1980s, the ACS backed tougher restrictions on tobacco and, in response to earlier criticism, directed research toward prevention as well as treatment. The society played a major role in the 1989 airline smoking ban.

John Seffrin, a former Indiana University professor, was named CEO of ACS in 1992. The first of several genetic breakthroughs came in the 1990s when ACS grantees isolated genes believed to be responsible for triggering various types of cancer. In 1995 the ACS accused the tobacco industry of infiltrating its offices in the 1970s and using its papers to aid in the early marketing of low-tar cigarettes.

In 1996 the ACS announced that new data showed a drop in the US cancer death rate for the first time ever. The ACS entered agreements with SmithKline Beecham (NicoDerm antismoking patches) and the Florida Department of Citrus in 1996 to allow the use of the American Cancer Society name in marketing.

The proposed $369 billion settlement between the attorneys general of 40 states and the tobacco industry was big news in 1997. The ACS had wanted more concessions, such as a $2-per-pack tax increase, more power for industry regulation by the FDA, and underage use rate-reduction targets for smokeless tobacco products as stringent as those for cigarettes.

In 1998 the ACS launched a $5 million national advertising campaign to combat what it sees as "misleading" information spread by the tobacco industry. It argued in Supreme Court in 1999 to help the FDA gain control over cigarette production and distribution. In 2000 ACS restructured its $50 million-a-year research program to increase the size of individual grants; it also awarded its largest-ever award, $1.7 million, to study the side effects of cancer treatment.

## PRODUCTS/OPERATIONS

**Selected Patient Services Programs**
Children's Camps (for children and teens with cancer; some for siblings)
Hope Lodge (housing assistance)
I Can Cope (education and support classes on living with cancer)
Look Good ... Feel Better (cosmetics and beauty techniques for women experiencing side effects of cancer treatment)
Man To Man Prostate Cancer Support
Reach to Recovery (support for women with breast cancer and their families)
Road to Recovery (transportation services)

**Selected Public Education Programs and Publications**
Great American Smokeout (national stop-smoking-for-a-day event)
Making Strides Against Breast Cancer (fund raiser)
Relay for Life (fund raiser)

**Selected Research Grants and Awards**
Clinical Research Professorships
Clinical Research Training Grants
Institutional research grants
Postdoctoral fellowships
Research Opportunity Grants
Research Professorships

## HISTORICAL FINANCIALS & EMPLOYEES

| Not-for-profit FYE: August 31 | Annual Growth | 8/91 | 8/92 | 8/93 | 8/94 | 8/95 | 8/96 | 8/97 | 8/98 | 8/99 | 8/00 |
|---|---|---|---|---|---|---|---|---|---|---|---|
| Sales ($ mil.) | 10.8% | — | 358 | 388 | 392 | 420 | 458 | 602 | 677 | 672 | 812 |
| Employees | 0.9% | — | 4,650 | 4,200 | 4,100 | 4,656 | 4,500 | 4,418 | 4,500 | 4,500 | 5,000 |

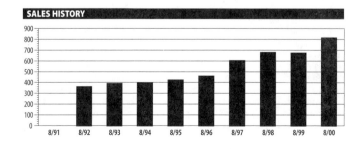

SALES HISTORY

# AMERICAN FAMILY INSURANCE

## OVERVIEW

Straight from the heartland, it's American Family Insurance Group. The Madison, Wisconsin-based company offers commercial and personal property/casualty, life, and health insurance, as well as investment and retirement-planning products. It is one of the largest US mutual companies specializing in auto insurance (State Farm is #1).

American Family offers reduced-rate auto insurance for its homeowners' policy holders. Other lines include such consumer finance

products as home equity and personal lines of credit. American Family also offers specialized coverage for businesses such as apartments, restaurants, and auto repair shops. It also provides coverage for motorcycles, snowmobiles, and boats.

The company has about 4,000 agents operating in some 15 states in the Midwest and the West. Unlike many of its competitors, American Family has said it has no plans to demutualize.

## HISTORY

In 1927 Herman Wittwer founded Farmers Mutual Automobile Insurance to sell coverage to Wisconsin farmers. As farms became mechanized in the 1920s, the insurance market grew. Low-density rural traffic reduced the potential for accidents, a fact that attracted Wittwer and others, such as State Farm (founded in 1922) to serve the similar markets. Wittwer also noted that rural Wisconsin's severe winters made cars unusable for a good part of the year, further reducing risk.

Farmers Mutual grew despite the Depression and WWII, spreading to Minnesota (1933); Missouri (1939); Nebraska and the Dakotas (1940); and Indiana, Iowa, and Kansas (1943). The war years were generous to insurers: Rising incomes allowed people to insure their cars, but rationing programs limited use of them. The postwar suburban boom — when cars became a necessity rather than a luxury — also helped auto insurers.

Growing prosperity for single-earner households in the 1950s helped boost the demand for life insurance. In 1958 Farmers Mutual formed American Family Life Insurance. The company wrote $1.6 million in insurance on its first day in the life insurance business. During that decade, Farmers Mutual moved into Illinois.

The 1960s brought growth and change to the company. To capture more auto business, it founded American Standard Insurance to write nonstandard auto insurance. The firm also launched consumer finance operations for insurance customers and noncustomers alike, departing from standard industry practice by selling through agents rather than offices. In 1963, in recognition of its growing diversification, Farmers Mutual changed its name to American Family Mutual Insurance.

During the 1970s and 1980s, the firm strengthened its infrastructure and added regional offices. It moved into Arizona and later formed American Family Brokerage to fill in

gaps in its own coverage by obtaining insurance for clients through other insurers.

During this period American Family suffered cultural pains. It moved beyond its traditional rural clientele and into the urban unknown as it sought to increase its market share. In 1981 community groups questioned whether the company was adequately serving racially mixed neighborhoods. In 1988 the US Justice Department began investigating allegations that the firm engaged in redlining (offering inferior or no service for minority neighborhoods); a class-action suit based on similar claims was filed in 1990. The suit went all the way to the Supreme Court, which ruled that insurance sales must comply with the Fair Housing Act.

The company had begun rectifying its practices before the case was decided. Nevertheless, when American Family settled the case in 1995, it agreed to pay a $14.5 million settlement plus about $2 million in court costs. Part of the settlement was to compensate people who had suffered from the company's discrimination, but most of the money went to fund community programs begun in 1996 to promote home ownership among minorities. In 1997 trouble came from within and without: One lawsuit claimed the company falsely promised to shrink premiums as policies earned dividends, and two dissident agents filed a civil complaint for wrongful termination (the latter case was settled the next year).

The company's profits tumbled in 1998 because of severe storms in Minnesota and Wisconsin. The next year American Family expanded its operations in Colorado and moved into Cleveland.

In 2000 Wisconsin was again pounded by hail, high winds, and floods. American Family Insurance announced $100 million in expected losses from the event. Streamlining claims processing, the company closed nine of its offices in 2001.

## OFFICERS

**Chairman and CEO:** Harvey R. Pierce
**President, COO, and Director:** David R. Anderson
**EVP, Administration:** Darnell Moore
**EVP, Corporate Legal and Secretary:** James F. Eldridge
**EVP, Finance and Treasurer:** J. Brent Johnson
**EVP, Sales:** Daniel R. DeSalvo
**VP and Controller:** Daniel R. Schultz
**VP, Actuarial:** Bradley J. Gleason
**VP, Claims:** Terese A. Taarud
**VP, Commercial, Farm/Ranch:** Jerry G. Rekowski
**VP, Education:** Nancy M. Johnson
**VP, Government Affairs and Compliance:** Mark V. Afable
**VP, Human Resources:** Vicki L. Chvala
**VP, Information Services:** Byrne W. Chapman
**VP, Investments:** Thomas S. King
**VP, Legal:** Christopher S. Spencer
**VP, Marketing:** Alan E. Meyer
**VP, Office Administration:** Richard J. Haas
**VP, Public Relations:** Richard A. Fetherston
**VP, Sales, Great Lakes Region:** David N. Krueger
**Auditors:** PricewaterhouseCoopers LLP

## LOCATIONS

**HQ:** 6000 American Pkwy., Madison, WI 53783
**Phone:** 608-249-2111          **Fax:** 608-243-4921
**Web:** www.amfam.com

American Family Insurance Group operates in 15 states
in the Midwest and West.

## PRODUCTS/OPERATIONS

**2000 Assets**

|  | $ mil. | % of total |
|---|---|---|
| Cash | 22 | — |
| Bonds | 5,277 | 53 |
| Stocks | 1,973 | 20 |
| Mortgage loans | 175 | 2 |
| Real estate | 248 | 2 |
| Policy loans | 150 | 2 |
| Receivables | 810 | 8 |
| Other | 1,315 | 13 |
| **Total** | **9,970** | **100** |

**Selected Subsidiaries**
American Family Mutual Insurance Co.
    American Family Financial Services, Inc.
    American Family Insurance Co.
    American Family Life Insurance Co.
    American Standard Insurance Company of Ohio
    American Standard Insurance Company of Wisconsin

## COMPETITORS

| | |
|---|---|
| 21st Century | Liberty Mutual |
| Allstate | Lincoln National |
| American Financial | Loews |
| American General | Mutual of Omaha |
| AIG | Nationwide |
| Berkshire Hathaway | Ohio Casualty |
| Chubb | Old Republic |
| CIGNA | Progressive Corporation |
| Cincinnati Financial | Prudential |
| Citigroup | SAFECO |
| CNA Financial | St. Paul Companies |
| GeneralCologne Re | State Farm |
| The Hartford | USAA |
| Kemper Insurance | |

## HISTORICAL FINANCIALS & EMPLOYEES

| Mutual company FYE: December 31 | Annual Growth | 12/91 | 12/92 | 12/93 | 12/94 | 12/95 | 12/96 | 12/97 | 12/98 | 12/99 | 12/00 |
|---|---|---|---|---|---|---|---|---|---|---|---|
| Assets ($ mil.) | 9.9% | — | 4,698 | 5,228 | 5,706 | 6,256 | 6,836 | 8,348 | 8,949 | 9,569 | 9,970 |
| Net income ($ mil.) | 6.4% | — | 144 | 159 | 163 | 218 | 55 | 252 | 40 | 282 | 237 |
| Income as % of assets | — | — | 3.1% | 3.0% | 2.9% | 3.5% | 0.8% | 3.0% | 0.4% | 2.9% | 2.3% |
| Employees | 1.6% | — | 6,436 | 6,373 | 6,365 | 6,411 | 6,506 | 6,800 | 6,940 | 7,247 | 7,300 |

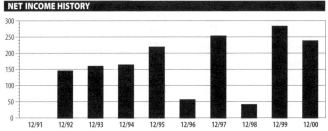

**NET INCOME HISTORY**

**2000 FISCAL YEAR-END**
Equity as % of assets: 34.8%
Return on assets: 2.4%
Return on equity: 6.7%
Long-term debt ($ mil.): —
Sales ($ mil.): 4,388

# THE AMERICAN RED CROSS

When it comes to disaster, the American Red Cross is the master. The American Red Cross is a member of the International Red Cross and Red Crescent Movement, a not-for-profit organization committed to helping those in need. Based in Washington, DC, the American Red Cross is chartered by Congress to provide relief services, but it isn't a government agency. It has more than 1.3 million volunteers — about 40 for every paid staffer.

Aside from providing relief to victims of more than 60,000 natural and man-made disasters nationwide each year, the American Red Cross teaches CPR and AIDS awareness courses, provides counseling and emergency message transmission for US military personnel, and is

guardian of the nation's largest blood, plasma, and tissue banks. The American Red Cross played a major role after the terrorist assaults on New York City and Washington, DC, in 2001. As the Red Cross gained praise immediately after the attacks, it soon drew fire from critics. Dr. Bernadine Healy, who was appointed as president and CEO of the organization in 1999 to succeed Elizabeth Dole, was pushed out after many board members disagreed with a plan to use some proceeds from donations made toward victims of the September 11 attacks for a blood bank reserve. A public outcry resulted, as some felt the donations should only be used to benefit the families of the terrorist attack victims.

## HISTORY

In 1863 a five-member committee (including Swiss businessman Jean-Henri Dunant) formed the International Committee of the Red Cross in Geneva. A red cross on a white background (the reverse of the Swiss flag) was chosen as the organization's symbol; the Red Crescent symbol was added in 1876 by Muslim relief workers during the Russo-Turkish War.

Clara Barton, famous for her aid to soldiers during the US Civil War, learned about the Red Cross when she assisted with relief efforts during the Franco-Prussian War (1870-71). In 1881 she and some friends founded the American Association of the Red Cross, with the first chapter in Dansville, New York.

Barton soon expanded the Red Cross' mission to include aiding victims of natural disasters. The group received a congressional charter in 1905, making it responsible for providing assistance to the US military and disaster relief in the US and overseas.

Membership soared during WWI as the number of chapters jumped from 107 to 3,864, and volunteers from the US and other nations served with the armed forces in Europe. After the war, the American Red Cross helped refugees in Europe, recruited thousands of nurses to improve the health and hygiene of rural Americans, and provided food and shelter to millions during the Depression.

The Red Cross established its first blood center, in New York's Presbyterian Hospital, in 1941. During WWII the American Red Cross again mobilized massive relief efforts. At home, volunteers taught nutrition courses, served in hospitals, and collected blood.

In 1956 the Red Cross began research to increase the safety of its blood supply. It also

continued to provide assistance during natural disasters, as well as during the Korean and Vietnam Wars and other US military conflicts.

During the 1980s the Red Cross was criticized for moving too slowly to improve testing of its blood supply for the HIV virus. Elizabeth Dole, named the organization's president in 1991, reorganized the blood collection program. (Dole took a leave of absence in 1996 to help her husband, Bob Dole, in his unsuccessful bid for the US presidency.)

In 1996 *Money* magazine reported that the Red Cross spent more than 91 cents of every dollar on programs, the best ratio of any major charity. In 1998 the organization ran up against its costliest year ever, spending more than $162 million to fight some 240 disasters across the US. The next year Dole resigned from the Red Cross and followed in her husband's footsteps by making her own bid for the US presidency in 2000 (she later dropped out of the race).

Dole was succeeded by Dr. Bernadine Healy, a former dean of the Ohio State University College of Medicine and the first physician to head the association. In 2001 the American Red Cross' mission was spotlighted following the terrorist attacks on New York City and Washington, DC. Healy was given her walking papers less than two months after the September 11 attacks amid disagreements with the Red Cross board and ire from critics. General Counsel Harold Decker was tapped to replace Healy at the end of 2001. That same year the FDA announced that the Red Cross has failed to be in compliance with safety laws in its blood collection program, despite being under a consent decree since 1993.

**Chairman:** David T. McLaughlin
**President and CEO:** Harold Decker
**EVP and CEO, Biomedical Services:** Rames Thadani
**EVP Corporate Operations and Interim Chief
  Information Officer:** Joanne O'Rourke Lindman
**SVP Development:** Jennifer Dunlap
**SVP Chapter Services Network:** James Krueger
**VP Finance and CFO:** John D. Campbell
**VP Disaster Services:** John Clizbe
**VP Human Resources:** Nancy Breseke
**Chief Diversity Officer:** Anthony J. Polk
**Corporate Secretary:** Andrea Morici

## LOCATIONS

**HQ:** 430 17th St. NW, Washington, DC 20006
**Phone:** 703-737-8300          **Fax:** 703-248-4256
**Web:** www.redcross.org

The American Red Cross has some 1,500 chapters and military outposts, as well as 15 tissue centers and 38 regional blood centers worldwide.

## PRODUCTS/OPERATIONS

### Selected Activities

**Armed Forces Emergency Services**
Counseling
Emergency assistance
Veterans assistance

**Biomedical Services**
Blood
Dental programs
Plasma operations
Research and development
Stem cell
Tissue

**Disaster Services**
Disaster mitigation
Emergency assistance
Long-term assistance
Mass care

**Health and Safety Education**
Babysitting courses
CPR courses
First aid courses
HIV/AIDS education
Nurse assistant training

## COMPETITORS

America's Blood Centers
Daxor
Ellis & Associates
HemaCare
Tissue Banks

## HISTORICAL FINANCIALS & EMPLOYEES

| Not-for-profit FYE: June 30 | Annual Growth | 6/91 | 6/92 | 6/93 | 6/94 | 6/95 | 6/96 | 6/97 | 6/98 | 6/99 | 6/00 |
|---|---|---|---|---|---|---|---|---|---|---|---|
| Sales ($ mil.) | 6.2% | — | 1,568 | 1,796 | 1,740 | 1,724 | 1,814 | 1,940 | 2,080 | 2,421 | 2,529 |
| Employees | 4.3% | — | 25,000 | 25,000 | 32,169 | 31,000 | 30,021 | 29,850 | 30,000 | 35,000 | 35,000 |

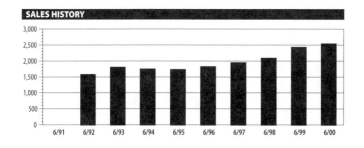

SALES HISTORY

American Red Cross

# AMERICAN STOCK EXCHANGE, INC.

## OVERVIEW

The American Stock Exchange (AMEX) is rallying back against the big kids.

A subsidiary of the National Association of Securities Dealers (NASD), New York-based AMEX lists small and midsized companies, derivatives, foreign issues, American depositary shares, and options.

Its most popular issues sound more like the contents of Grandma's attic than an investor's portfolio: SPDRS or spiders (S&P 500 depository receipts), WEBS (World Equity Benchmark Shares), and Diamonds (unit investment trusts that track the Dow Jones Industrial Average). Such exchange-traded funds (ETFs)

have represented a growth area for AMEX, whose listed companies have declined to about 600 even while those on the New York Stock Exchange and Nasdaq have soared. AMEX looks to lure overlooked companies with market caps from $50 million to $1 billion, promising more personalized services.

The exchange hopes to reap some financial spoils from the planned spinoff of Nasdaq from the NASD and has earmarked the funds to continue its growth and eventually topple its chief options exchange rival, the Chicago Board Options Exchange.

## HISTORY

For 128 years after the 1792 formation of what is now known as the New York Stock Exchange (NYSE), a gypsy crew of traders continued to deal in stocks on the streets of New York. The trade was risky, as both the traders and their stocks were unfettered by listing or dealing standards, and pricing and volume reporting was impossible.

In 1911 some of these traders formed the New York Curb Market Association to set trading rules. It moved indoors as the New York Curb Market (later the New York Curb Exchange) 10 years later, which allowed it to begin reporting trades. "The Curb" grew in the 1920s.

Renamed the American Stock Exchange, or AMEX, in 1953, it suffered scandals over price manipulation and the trading of unregistered stocks during the 1950s. Always less an old-boys preserve than the NYSE, AMEX appointed its first woman governor, Mary Roebling, in 1958. Though women were soon granted regular membership, they did not trade on the floor until 1977.

In the 1960s AMEX began to automate, offering computerized telephone quotations and, later, computerized ticker, clearing, and surveillance systems. In 1972 it joined with the NYSE to form the Securities Industry Automation Corporation. That year NYSE and AMEX had nearly equal listings. But then Nasdaq, a new electronic marketplace without a trading floor, began grabbing listings, particularly of high-tech companies that would ordinarily have gone to AMEX, whose market share began a decade-long decline.

In response, the exchange added Treasury instruments, options, and derivatives and sought foreign listings and alliances. After 1987's stock crash, AMEX raised margin limits

and established circuit-breaker procedures to control price declines.

Having fallen to a distant third in the securities market, AMEX sought new blood, appointing Wall Street outsider and former congressman James Jones chairman in 1989. But his tenure was marked by dissension. After Jones was named ambassador to Mexico in 1993, the chairmanship remained open for nearly a year.

AMEX continued to seek niche markets. It formed the Emerging Companies Market (ECM), a micro-cap market. But inadequate vetting of listees resulted in embarrassment when officers of several companies were found to have had prior problems with the SEC. Despite the ECM's tendency to attract risky, even shady, ventures, AMEX proposed creating an index of even smaller companies.

In the 1990s AMEX upgraded its technical systems, becoming the first exchange to feature an electronic system of recording trades with wireless, handheld terminals.

Richard Syron, a former president of the Boston Federal Reserve Bank, came on as chairman and CEO in 1994. He upgraded AMEX's image, shuttered the ECM in 1995, and increased promotional efforts. AMEX began restructuring the next year to cut costs and further emphasize customer service.

In 1997 AMEX lost one of its biggest listings, The New York Times, to the NYSE. The next year the NASD acquired AMEX. In 1999 Syron departed and Salvatore Sodano took his place. AMEX announced plans in 2000 to create mutual fund stocks to let investors track popular mutual funds. To leverage its position in the ETF market, which it had pioneered, AMEX in 2001 launched an ETF services unit.

## OFFICERS

**Chairman and CEO:** Salvatore F. Sodano
**President:** Peter Quick
**Vice Chairman:** Anthony J. Boglioli
**SVP Capital Markets:** Richard A. Mikaliunas
**SVP Derivatives Marketing and Research:**
  Michael T. Bickford
**SVP Derivative Securities:** Lawrence Larkin
**SVP Finance and CFO:** Raqui Selwanes
**SVP Market Operations and Trading Floor Systems:**
  Ralph R. Rafaniello
**SVP Member Liaison:** Steven Lesser
**VP Listing Qualification:** Michael S. Emen
**Director of Human Resources:** Katie Casey
**Auditors:** KPMG LLP

## LOCATIONS

**HQ:** 86 Trinity Place, New York, NY 10006
**Phone:** 212-306-1000     **Fax:** 212-306-1218
**Web:** www.amex.com

## PRODUCTS/OPERATIONS

**Selected Products and Services**
Diamonds (Dow Jones Industrial Average unit trusts)
HOLDRS (Holding company depository receipts)
Index options
Long-term Equity Anticipation Securities
SPDRS (Depository Receipts)
World Equity Benchmark Shares

## COMPETITORS

Archipelago
Bloomberg TRADEBOOK
CBOT
CBOE
Instinet
Island ECN
NYSE
Reuters

## HISTORICAL FINANCIALS & EMPLOYEES

| Subsidiary<br>FYE: December 31 | Annual<br>Growth | 12/91 | 12/92 | 12/93 | 12/94 | 12/95 | 12/96 | 12/97 | 12/98 | 12/99 | 12/00 |
|---|---|---|---|---|---|---|---|---|---|---|---|
| Sales ($ mil.) | 11.4% | — | 114 | 131 | 144 | 153 | 170 | 198 | 210 | 231 | 270 |
| Employees | (5.7%) | — | — | 850 | 708 | 690 | 676 | 671 | — | — | — |

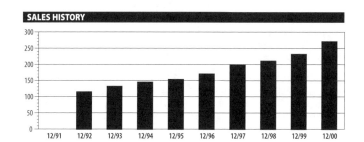

SALES HISTORY

# ANDERSEN

## OVERVIEW

Where's the rest of me? Once THE accounting/consulting powerhouse, Chicago-based Andersen (formerly Andersen Worldwide) lost its 11-year battle to prevent its Andersen Consulting unit (which accounted for 60% of revenues) from leaving the fold. As the audit business became subject to pricing pressure (in part because the Big Five accounting firms priced their audit services to attract consulting clients), the consultants flourished and finally tired of sharing their profits with the auditors who had formerly subsidized them. Andersen Consulting renamed itself Accenture.

Although still a Big Five stalwart, Andersen has ceded its top-dog accountant status to PricewaterhouseCoopers. Andersen offers traditional and ourtsourced auditing and tax services, legal services, human resources services, and risk consulting services. The company has some 390 offices in more than 80 countries.

Andersen's growing legal network faces legal restrictions on the business association between lawyers and nonlawyers. Its remaining consulting operations face growing pressure from the SEC's campaign against potential conflicts of interest arising from the provision of both consulting and auditing services to the same company. A 2001 brouhaha over the collapse of Andersen's Australian client HIH Insurance Limited, has been overshadowed by Andersen's entanglement in the implosion of energy giant Enron, for which it served as auditor.

## HISTORY

Arthur Andersen went to work in Price Waterhouse's Chicago office in 1907. In 1913 he and Clarence DeLany formed Andersen, DeLany & Company. The establishment of both the Federal Reserve System and the federal income tax that year increased the demand for accounting services. After DeLany's departure in 1918, the firm became Arthur Andersen & Co.

The company grew rapidly in the 1920s and began performing financial investigations — the basis for its consulting practice. When Samuel Insull's utility empire collapsed in 1932, Andersen was appointed the bankruptcy trustee. The firm contined to expand during the 1930s and 1940s.

Andersen dominated the firm until his death in 1947. His successor, Leonard Spacek, who headed the firm until 1963, continued to expand in the US and also began foreign expansion. The consulting business became a separate unit in 1954, but it grew slowly; by 1979 it accounted for just over one-fifth of revenues. Nine years later, after a flood of corporate reorganizations, fees had risen to 40% of sales.

The rise of the consultants and the accompanying power struggle resulted in the 1989 formation of Andersen Worldwide as an umbrella for both units. But it did not solve the issue of financial dominance, and the formation of another consulting unit by the accounting unit in 1990 (to serve smaller companies) only increased tensions.

The consultancy in the 1990s built its information technology business through alliances for client service and implementation with major technology companies like Microsoft and Sun Microsystems. Its share of the business grew too, to more than half of sales. During the same period the accountancy was hit by legal fallout from the failure of Savings & Loans whose books it had audited (it made a financial settlement with the US government in 1993) and by an evolving standard that held accountants increasingly liable for detecting fiscal misdeeds by its clients.

The rift between the audit and consulting sides widened in 1997 when CEO Lawrence Weinbach announced his retirement. When voting deadlocked, the board appointed accounting partner W. Robert Grafton as CEO. Soon thereafter, Andersen Consulting's partners voted to break away.

In 1998 a migration of workers between the units brought rumors that the split was at hand, but the dispute went into arbitration in 1999. A Colombian arbitrator for the International Chamber of Commerce eventually awarded Andersen Worldwide $1 billion in compensation from Andersen Consulting (far less than the nearly $15 billion it hoped for) and awarded the accountants rights to the Andersen name. Andersen Consulting was subsequently renamed Accenture.

In 2001 Andersen Worldwide renamed itself Andersen. The same year the company's Australian client HIH Insurance collapsed, prompting the Australian government to form a Royal Commission to investigate, among other things, how HIH's dangerous financial position eluded Andersen's attention.

In 2001 Andersen acquired a French management consulting unit that had been part of rival PricewaterhouseCoopers. Late that year, Andersen came under scrutiny for its involvement in the collapse of its client Enron.

Managing Partner and CEO; CEO, Andersen:
Joseph Berardino, age 50
Managing Partner, Markets and Solutions, Andersen:
Thomas L. Elliott III, age 43
Managing Partner and CFO, Andersen:
Barbara J. Duganier
Managing Partner, People, Andersen: Kay G. Priestly,
age 44
Managing Partner, Global Operations, Andersen:
Phillip A. Randall, age 48
Managing Partner and General Counsel, Andersen:
Daniel D. Beckel
Managing Partner, Global Risk Management, Andersen:
Robert G. Kutsenda
Managing Partner, Human Resources and Partner
Matters: Peter Pesce
Managing Partner, Western Europe, Andersen:
Alberto E. Terol
Area Managing Partner, Asia/Pacific, Andersen:
John Prasetio
Area Managing Partner, U.S. and North America,
Andersen: Terry E. Hatchett
Area Managing Partner, Latin America, Andersen:
José Luis Vázquez
Area Managing Partner, Central and Eastern Europe,
the Middle East, India and Africa, Andersen:
Roman W. McAlindon
Managing Partner, Marketing: Daniel A. Archabal

## LOCATIONS

**HQ:** 33 W. Monroe St., Chicago, IL 60603
**Phone:** 312-580-0033          **Fax:** 312-507-6748
**Web:** www.andersen.com

Andersen Worldwide operates in more than 80
countries.

### 2001 Sales

|  | $ mil. | % of total |
|---|---|---|
| North America | 4,490 | 48 |
| Western Europe | 2,870 | 31 |
| Asia/Pacific | 1,200 | 13 |
| Central Europe, Middle | | |
| East, India & Africa | 390 | 4 |
| Latin America | 390 | 4 |
| **Total** | **9,340** | **100** |

## PRODUCTS/OPERATIONS

### 2001 Sales

|  | % mil. | % of total |
|---|---|---|
| Assurance & business advisory | 4,260 | 46 |
| Tax, legal & business advisory | 2,980 | 32 |
| Business consulting | 1,710 | 18 |
| Global corporate finance | 390 | 4 |
| **Total** | **9,340** | **100** |

### Services

Assurance and process assessment services (financial
audit assurance and process assessment; internal
audit, regulatory compliance, information used in
strategic transactions)
Business consulting
  Claims and disputes
  Corporate finance
  Digital markets and supply chain
  Intellectual asset management
eBusiness (Web site design, strategy, and
  implementation)
Human resources (design and monitoring of pension
  and employee benefits plans)
Legal services
Outsourcing
  Enterprise resource planning and application services
  Finance operations management
  High-volume transaction processing
Risk consulting (management of risks related to
  business process, technology, regulatory compliance,
  government contracting, fraud, and treasury and
  trading operations)
Tax services (local, national, and international tax
  strategies for corporations and the wealthy)

## COMPETITORS

American Management
Arthur D. Little
Bain & Company
BDO International
Booz-Allen
Boston Consulting
Deloitte Touche Tohmatsu
Ernst & Young

Grant Thornton
  International
KPMG
Marsh & McLennan
McKinsey & Company
PricewaterhouseCoopers
Towers Perrin
WorldCom

## HISTORICAL FINANCIALS & EMPLOYEES

| Partnership FYE: August 31 | Annual Growth | 8/92 | 8/93 | 8/94 | 8/95 | 8/96 | 8/97 | 8/98 | 8/99 | 8/00 | 8/01 |
|---|---|---|---|---|---|---|---|---|---|---|---|
| Sales ($ mil.) | 5.9% | 5,577 | 6,017 | 6,738 | 8,134 | 9,499 | 11,300 | 13,900 | 16,300 | 8,400 | 9,340 |
| Employees | 3.5% | 62,134 | 66,478 | 72,722 | 82,121 | 91,572 | 104,933 | 123,791 | 135,000 | 77,000 | 85,000 |

### SALES HISTORY

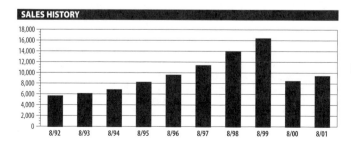

# ANDERSEN CORPORATION

## OVERVIEW

A room with a view is always in style with Andersen, one of the world's largest manufacturers of wooden windows and patio doors. Based in Bayport, Minnesota, Andersen products range from a wide variety of windows, including skylights, to hinged patio doors. The Andersen brand is one of the most-recognized brands in the industry. The company sells its products through independent and company-owned distributorships to architects, general contractors, and building owners in the Americas, Europe, Asia, and the Middle East.

Andersen competes in the marketplace by building strong brand recognition for its products. Acquisitions also play an important role in the company's growth strategy, and Andersen has been buying many of the independent distributorships that carry its products.

Members of the Andersen family are major shareholders in the company.

## HISTORY

Danish immigrant Hans Andersen and his two sons, Fred and Herbert, founded Andersen in 1903. Andersen's first words in English, "All together, boys," became the company motto. Andersen had arrived in Portland, Maine, in 1870 and worked as a lumber dealer and manufacturer. In the 1880s he bought a sawmill in St. Cloud, Minnesota, and later managed one in Hudson, Wisconsin. When the Hudson mill owners asked him to let workers go during the off season, Andersen refused and then resigned. He subsequently launched his own lumber business — Andersen Lumber Company — and hired some of the men who were laid off. He opened a second lumberyard, in Afton, Minnesota, in 1904. Andersen and his sons revolutionized the window industry in the early 1900s by introducing a standardized window frame with interchangeable parts. Buoyed by success, the Andersens sold their lumberyards in 1908 to focus on the window-frame business. (Andersen purchased lumberyards again in 1916 before exiting the lumberyard business for good in the 1930s.)

Thrifty Hans launched the company's first (and the US's third) profit-sharing plan shortly before his death in 1914. Herbert became VP, secretary, treasurer, and factory manager, and Fred became president. Herbert died in 1921 (at age 36), but Fred proved to be a versatile and capable successor. Among his accomplishments, Fred came up with the tag line "Only the rich can afford poor windows."

In 1929 the company changed its name to Andersen Frame Corporation. In the following decade Andersen introduced a number of innovations, including Master Frame (a frame with a locked sill joint, 1930); a casement window, the industry's first complete factory-made window unit (1932); and a basement window (1934). The company adopted its current name in 1937.

Andersen introduced the gliding window concept in the early 1940s. It also launched the Home Planners Scrap Book consumer ad campaign in 1943. During the 1950s Andersen's new products included the Flexivent awning window, which featured welded insulating glass that served as an alternative to traditional storm windows. In the 1960s the company produced a gliding door and introduced the Perma-Shield system. The system featured easy-to-maintain vinyl cladding to protect wood frames from weathering. By 1978 Perma-Shield products accounted for three-quarters of sales. Fred, who had run the company as president until 1960 and had subsequently held the positions of chairman and chairman emeritus, died in 1979 at age 92.

Between 1984 and 1994 the company increased its sales threefold by introducing additional customized and state-of-the-art products, including patio doors. In 1995 it launched Renewal by Andersen, a retail window-replacement business that has expanded to about 40 US locations.

Andersen acquired former long-term strategic partner Aspen Research (materials testing, research, and product development) in 1997. Among its jointly developed products is Fibrex, a composite material used in replacement windows. Also in 1997 the company moved its international division office from Bayport, Minnesota, to the Minnesota World Trade Center in St. Paul to help boost its export drive.

In 1998 company veteran Donald Garofalo succeeded Andersen's president and CEO Jerold Wulf, who retired after 39 years with the company. Andersen reinforced its company-owned distributorships in 1999 when it bought millwork distributors Morgan Products and Independent Millwork.

Looking to expand its product offerings, Andersen purchased EMCO Enterprises, a private manufacturer of storm doors and accessories, in 2001.

**Chairwoman:** Sarah J. Andersen
**President and CEO:** Donald Garofalo
**SVP, Corporate Business Services and CFO:**
  Michael O. Johnson
**Manager, Human Resources:** Jan Grose

## LOCATIONS

**HQ:** 100 4th Ave. North, Bayport, MN 55003
**Phone:** 651-264-5150      **Fax:** 651-264-5107
**Web:** www.andersencorp.com

Andersen markets its products throughout the Americas,
Asia, Europe, and the Middle East.

## PRODUCTS/OPERATIONS

**Selected Products**
Patio doors (Frenchwood brand)
Windows
  Art glass
  Awning
  Basement
  Bay and bow
  Casement
  Double-hung
  Fixed
  Horizontal sliding
  Picture
  Skylights and roof windows
  Transom
  Utility

## COMPETITORS

Anglian Group
JELD-WEN
Overhead Door
Pella
Royal Group Technologies
Sierra Pacific Industries
Thermal Industries
Weru

## HISTORICAL FINANCIALS & EMPLOYEES

| Private<br>FYE: December 31 | Annual<br>Growth | 12/91 | 12/92 | 12/93 | 12/94 | 12/95 | 12/96 | 12/97 | 12/98 | 12/99 | 12/00 |
|---|---|---|---|---|---|---|---|---|---|---|---|
| Estimated sales ($ mil.) | 6.9% | — | 1,000 | 1,000 | 1,100 | 1,200 | 1,250 | 1,300 | 1,400 | 1,500 | 1,700 |
| Employees | 8.4% | — | — | — | 3,700 | 3,700 | 3,700 | 3,700 | 3,700 | 6,000 | 6,000 |

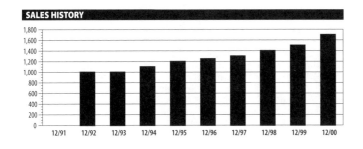

**SALES HISTORY**

# ARMY AND AIR FORCE EXCHANGE

## OVERVIEW

Armies of shoppers — armed with wallets instead of weapons — march through the doors of the Army and Air Force Exchange Service (AAFES). The Dallas-based AAFES has deployed more than 12,000 facilities at Post Exchanges (PXs) and Base Exchanges (BXs) on Army and Air Force bases, respectively, around the world. Its operations include military clothing stores, fast-food outlets, movie theaters, gas stations, catalog services, and beauty shops. AAFES facilities serve soldiers, airmen, guardsmen, reservists, retirees, and their family members.

AAFES is a government agency under the Department of Defense (DoD). It receives no funding from the DoD but pays neither taxes nor rent for US government property. More than 70% of AAFES's profits go into Morale, Welfare, and Recreation Programs for amenities such as libraries and youth centers. Other profits are used to renovate or build stores. Active military personnel head AAFES, but its staff consists mostly of military family members and other civilians.

## HISTORY

During the American Revolution, peddlers known as sutlers followed the Army, selling items such as soap, razors, and tobacco. The practice lasted until after the Civil War, when post traders replaced sutlers. This system was replaced in 1889 when the War Department authorized canteens at military bases.

The first US military exchanges were established in 1895, creating a system to supply military personnel with personal items on US Army bases around the world. The exchanges were run independently, with each division creating a Post Exchange (PX) to serve its unit. The post commander would assign an officer to run the PX (usually along with other duties) and would decide how profits were spent.

In 1941 the Army Exchange Service was created, and the system was reorganized. A five-member advisory committee made up of civilian merchandisers was created to provide recommendations for the reorganization. The restructuring made the system more like a chain store business. The independent PXs were bought by the War Department from the individual military organizations that ran them. Civilian personnel were brought in to staff the PXs, and a brigadier general was named to head an executive staff made up of Army officers and civilians that provided centralized control of the system. The Army also created a special school to train officers to run the PXs.

Sales at the PXs skyrocketed during WWII; a catalog business was added so soldiers could order gifts to send home to their families. The Department of the Air Force was established in 1947, and the exchange system organization was renamed the Army and Air Force Exchange Service (AAFES) the next year.

In 1960 the government allowed the overseas exchanges to provide more luxury items in an effort to keep soldiers from buying foreign-made goods. By the time the military had been cranked up again for the Vietnam War, big-ticket items such as TVs, cameras, and tape recorders were among the exchanges' best-sellers. In 1967 AAFES moved its headquarters from New York City to Dallas.

By 1991 the exchanges were open to the National Guard and the Reserve; AAFES's customer base had grown to 14 million. When the military began downsizing during the 1990s following the end of the Cold War, AAFES's customer base shrank by 35%.

AAFES stores sold more than $12 million worth of pornographic materials in 1995. The US House of Representatives passed the Military Honor and Decency Act the next year prohibiting the sale of pornography on US military property, including AAFES stores; this ban was struck down as unconstitutional in 1997. That year AAFES was approved as a provider of medical equipment covered by federal CHAMPUS/TRICARE insurance. It also created a Web site to offer online shopping in 1997.

The Supreme Court upheld the 1996 porn ban in 1998; the Pentagon banned the sale of more than 150 sexually explicit magazines (such as *Penthouse*), while a military board permitted the continued sale of certain publications (including *Playboy*).

Maj. Gen. Barry Bates took over as AAFES's commander and CEO in 1998. To better battle other retailers, that year AAFES announced its stores would offer best-price guarantees, matching prices of local stores and refunding price differences if customers found lower prices within 30 days of buying products.

In 1999 AAFES expanded to Macedonia and Kosovo, providing its services to military personnel in Operation Joint Guardian. In 2000 Bates was replaced as AAFES commander and CEO by Maj. Gen. Charles J. Wax.

**Chairman:** Lt. Gen. Michael E. Zettler, USAF
**Commander and CEO:** Maj. Gen. Charles J. Wax, USAF
**Deputy Commander:**
  Brig. Gen. Velma L. Richardson, USA
**COO:** W. Michael Beverly
**CFO:** Terry B. Corley
**SVP Human Resources Directorate:** James K. Winters
**SVP Sales Directorate:** Robert D. Bohn
**General Counsel:** Col. Alfred L. Faustino, USA
**Auditors:** Ernst & Young LLP

## LOCATIONS

**HQ:** Army and Air Force Exchange Service,
  3911 S. Walton Walker Blvd., Dallas, TX 75236
**Phone:** 214-312-2011     **Fax:** 214-312-3000
**Web:** www.aafes.com

The Army and Air Force Exchange Service has
operations in all 50 states and in 25 countries and
overseas areas.

## PRODUCTS/OPERATIONS

**Selected Merchandise and Services**
Barber and beauty shops
Books, newspapers, and magazines
Catalog services
Class Six stores
Concessions
Food facilities (mobile units, snack bars, name-brand
  fast-food franchises, and concession operations)
Gas stations and auto repair
Military clothing stores
Movie theaters
Retail stores
Vending centers

## COMPETITORS

7-Eleven
Best Buy
Circuit City
Costco Wholesale
J. C. Penney
Kmart
Kroger
METRO AG
Sears
Target
Wal-Mart

## HISTORICAL FINANCIALS & EMPLOYEES

| Government agency FYE: January 31 | Annual Growth | 1/92 | 1/93 | 1/94 | 1/95 | 1/96 | 1/97 | 1/98 | 1/99 | 1/00 | 1/01 |
|---|---|---|---|---|---|---|---|---|---|---|---|
| Sales ($ mil.) | 0.7% | 6,908 | 6,763 | 7,276 | 6,746 | 6,710 | 6,874 | 6,620 | 6,783 | 6,992 | 7,369 |
| Net income ($ mil.) | 2.8% | 297 | 301 | 315 | 269 | 228 | 348 | 337 | 343 | 361 | 381 |
| Income as % of sales | — | 4.3% | 4.5% | 4.3% | 4.0% | 3.4% | 5.1% | 5.1% | 5.1% | 5.2% | 5.2% |
| Employees | (4.0%) | 75,584 | 72,562 | 60,000 | 58,556 | 56,495 | 57,583 | 53,946 | 54,000 | 54,000 | 52,400 |

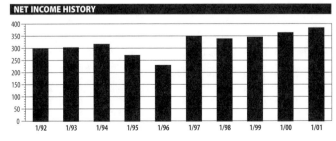

**NET INCOME HISTORY**

**2001 FISCAL YEAR-END**
Debt ratio: 0.0%
Return on equity: 13.1%
Cash ($ mil.): 172
Current ratio: 2.18
Long-term debt ($ mil.): 0

# ARTHUR D. LITTLE, INC.

## OVERVIEW

While it's not nearly as big as some of its competitors, there's nothing small about Arthur D. Little (ADL). From its base in Cambridge, Massachusetts, ADL's staff of more than 3,000 provides consulting services to *FORTUNE* 100 corporations and governments as well as emerging companies.

The world's first consulting firm, ADL operates about 50 offices and laboratories in more than 30 countries around the globe. Its strong point is technology and product development, helping clients refine their manufacturing, research, and systems operations, and developing products for in-house commercialization.

ADL also offers a graduate program in management through its Arthur D. Little School of Management. ADL's international operations have grown dramatically over the past decade and account for more than 60% of revenue.

ADL found itself in dire financial straits after plans for an IPO were canceled. It came close to securing a deal with Safeguard International Fund and Whitney & Co that would have ended the company's worries but the two firms eventually left Arthur D. Little at the altar. Cerberus Capital Management is picking up ADL on the rebound in a plan that involves ADL's filing for Chapter 11 bankruptcy.

## HISTORY

Former Massachusetts Institute of Technology chemistry student Arthur D. Little and chemist Roger Griffin opened their Boston office of Griffin & Little, Chemical Engineers in 1886, a time when chemists and their science were held in low regard. The firm had developed a reputation for expertise in papermaking before Griffin was killed in a laboratory accident in 1893. Little persevered and picked up William Walker as a partner in 1900, and the firm was renamed Little & Walker. Walker left for a teaching post at MIT five years later, and the firm was permanently renamed Arthur D. Little, Inc. (ADL) in 1909.

Through the years leading up to WWII, ADL was instrumental in a number of new developments, including an odor classification system (to aid in the development of consumer products such as food and cosmetics), glass fibers (the basis for fiberglass), and a sea-to-fresh water converter. Little died in 1935, but ADL continued to thrive after WWII and played a significant role in the industrialization of Puerto Rico by developing a technical-economic plan for the island in 1946.

In the meantime, Arthur Little's nephew, Royal Little (who is credited with creating the modern conglomerate and who served on ADL's board of directors), devised a scheme to buy back the 55% of the company that MIT had come to own through a trust that Royal controlled. He created the Memorial Drive Trust in 1953, a profit-sharing trust for the company's employees, and transferred the shares into it.

The 1950s brought on a new concept at ADL called operations research (business operations analysis); John Magee (who eventually would become CEO) was brought on board to help run the department. The company picked up several prominent industrial clients. In the 1960s ADL helped develop the Sabre reservations system with IBM for American Airlines. It also started a management education program.

As the world economy slowed in the 1970s, other consulting firms moved into ADL's technical territory, but ADL resisted moving into management consulting. And while the rest of the consulting industry charged into business reengineering (in response to the economic upheavals of the 1970s), ADL poked along with small contracts.

By the mid-1980s ADL had become a takeover target (which it successfully resisted), its laboratories were sliding into obsolescence, and it was losing its best and brightest because of low pay. Magee brought in Charles LaMantia, an ADL alum then working for Koch Industries, as CEO. LaMantia pruned the firm to its current organization and moved ADL more solidly into strategic consulting.

Results started improving in the 1990s, and LaMantia began increasing the company's international presence. LaMantia became chairman in 1998. He announced his retirement in 1999 and was replaced as chairman by Gerhard Schulmeyer. (Lorenzo Lamadrid came in as CEO, but was replaced two years later by Pamela McNamara.) In 2000 ADL launched Pyxsys Corporation to produce high-speed network storage capabilities, and SciRox to help entrepreneurs market hard sciences products.

In 2001 takeover talks between ADL and UK-based PA Consulting broke down as did later negotiations with Whitney & Co and Safeguard International Fund. Cerberus Capital Management took the plunge in early 2002 and agreed to buy the company as part of ADL's Chapter 11 reorganization. McNamara also resigned as CEO that year.

**Chairman:** Gerhard Schulmeyer
**SVP and COO:** Ladd Greeno
**SVP Human Resources:** Michael Eisenbud
**CEO, Cambridge Consultants Limited:** Brian Moon
**Managing Director, Global Management Consulting:**
Eulogio Naz
**Managing Director, Technology and Innovation:**
John Collins

## LOCATIONS

**HQ:** 25 Acorn Park, Cambridge, MA 02140
**Phone:** 617-498-5000       **Fax:** 617-498-7200
**Web:** www.arthurdlittle.com

## PRODUCTS/OPERATIONS

**Selected Subsidiaries and Affiliates**
Arthur D. Little Enterprises (commercialization of
company and client technologies)
Arthur D. Little School of Management
Cambridge Consultants Limited (technology center, UK)
Cambridge Silicon Radio (single-chip radio devices
design and marketing)
Cataligent (Internet business consulting)
Innovation Associates (training programs)
Nuvera Fuel Cells (fuel processors)
Pyxsys (high-speed data storage)
SciRox (non-Internet technology product development)

## COMPETITORS

Accenture
A.T. Kearney
Bain & Company
Booz-Allen
Boston Consulting
Cap Gemini
CH2M Hill
Deloitte Touche Tohmatsu
KPMG
McKinsey & Company
PricewaterhouseCoopers
Towers Perrin

## HISTORICAL FINANCIALS & EMPLOYEES

| Private<br>FYE: December 31 | Annual<br>Growth | 12/91 | 12/92 | 12/93 | 12/94 | 12/95 | 12/96 | 12/97 | 12/98 | 12/99 | 12/00 |
|---|---|---|---|---|---|---|---|---|---|---|---|
| Sales ($ mil.) | 7.4% | — | 367 | 385 | 433 | 514 | 574 | 589 | 608 | 629 | 650 |
| Employees | 3.4% | — | 2,300 | 2,400 | 2,600 | 3,039 | 3,200 | 3,300 | 3,500 | 3,500 | 3,000 |

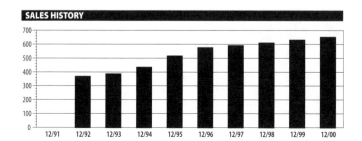

SALES HISTORY

**Arthur D Little**

# ASCENSION HEALTH

Ascension Health rises to the occasion. The US's largest Roman Catholic health care system was formed by the 1999 merger of two religious order-sponsored systems — the Daughters of Charity National Health System and the Sisters of St. Joseph Health System. The St. Louis-based company is a network of about 60 hospitals, as well as residential centers and other health care facilities in some 15 states and Washington, DC. Ascension is also the US's largest not-for-profit health care provider. The system takes to heart the words of St. Vincent de Paul, co-founder of the Daughters of Charity, who advised the order to serve "the poor sick bodily, ministering to them in all their needs, and spiritually also so that they will live and die well."

Nuns from Ascension's sponsoring religious orders sit on its governing board, which is led by non-clergy CEO Douglas French. Prior to the merger, Daughters of Charity National Health System stirred controversy with talk of mergers with non-Catholic hospitals, since church doctrine forbids abortion, most birth control, and artificial conception; the merger with Sisters of St. Joseph Health System put concerns to rest.

In this age of high-cost health care, Ascension realizes the need for fiscal health. The company is selling money-losing hospitals and has reorganized its facilities by geographic regions to cut costs.

## HISTORY

The Daughters of Charity order was formed in France in 1633 when St. Vincent de Paul recruited a rich widow (St. Louise de Marillac) to care for the sick on battlefields and in their homes.

Elizabeth Ann Seton, America's first saint (canonized 1974), brought the order to the US. In 1809 Seton earned the title of Mother and started the Sisters of Charity. The Sisters adopted the vows of the Daughters of Charity, adding "service" to them in 1812.

The Sisters officially became part of the Daughters of Charity in 1850. The Daughters cared for soldiers during the Civil War and were responsible for training Florence Nightingale. In the late 1800s the Daughters pioneered exclusive provider arrangements (similar to today's managed care contracts) with railroads, lumber camps, and the like. During the next 100 years, the order furthered its mission of caring for the sick and the poor. To support their efforts, the nuns founded hospitals (44 by 1911), schools, and other charity centers.

In 1969 the charity association formed a health care services cooperative, which became the Daughters of Charity National Health System (DCNHS).

DCNHS operated as two regional institutions (one based in Maryland, the other in Missouri) until 1986, when the systems merged. The first task was to balance their holy mission with the need to make money. With competition from managed care companies increasing, DCNHS responded by cutting staff and diversifying into nursing homes and retirement centers.

The Daughters of Charity's western unit combined its six hospitals in California with Mullikin Centers (a physician-owned medical group) in 1993 to form one of the largest health care associations in the state.

DCNHS expanded its network in 1995 by merging its hospitals with and becoming a co-sponsor of San Francisco-based Catholic Healthcare West. That year it joined with Catholic Relief Services to operate a hospital in war-torn Angola.

In 1996 DCNHS dropped a proposed merger of its struggling 221-bed Carney Hospital in Boston with Quincy Hospital because the municipally owned Quincy facility was required by law to provide abortions. Instead, DCNHS sold Carney Hospital to Caritas Christi Health Care System (owned by the Boston Roman Catholic archdiocese), one of about a dozen hospital sales by DCNHS in the mid-1990s.

DCNHS reorganized its leadership in 1997, creating SVP positions for system direction and policy and for program development to strengthen and update its programs. In 1998 Sister Irene Kraus, who had founded DCNHS and led it through its expansion, died.

In 1999 DCNHS merged with fellow Catholic caregiver Sisters of St. Joseph Health System, then Michigan's largest health care system.

In 2000 Ascension saw the collapse of a five-hospital merger in Florida between subsidiary St. Vincent's Health System and Baptist Health System. The organization also launched the Voice for the Voiceless initiative, which combines private monies and federal grants to fund programs for the uninsured in Detroit, New Orleans, and Austin, Texas.

## OFFICERS

**President and CEO:** Douglas D. French, age 46
**EVP and COO:** Anthony R. Tersigni, age 51
**SVP Central and Southern States Operating Group:** Charles J. Barnett
**SVP Strategic Business Development and Innovation:** John D. Doyle
**SVP Great Lakes and Mid-Atlantic States Operating Group:** Robert J. Henkel
**SVP Legal Services and General Counsel:** Rex P. Killian
**SVP Clinical Excellence:** Marsha A. Ladenburger
**SVP Advocacy and External Relations:** Susan Nestor Levy
**SVP Mergers and Acquisitions:** Matthias D. Maguire
**SVP Operations Improvement:** Robert E. Pezzoli
**SVP Organizational Effectiveness:** Deborah A. Proctor
**VP Communications:** Synetta S. Armstrong
**VP Financial Services:** Anthony J. Filer
**VP Risk Management:** Steve Gillen
**VP Ethics:** Dan O'Brien
**VP and Associate General Counsel:** Steven H. Pratt
**VP Human Resources:** David A. Smith, age 41
**VP Leadership Development:** Tom Thibault
**CEO Supply Chain Initiative:** Arnie Kimmel
**Executive Director Shared Services/Operations Support and Corporate Responsibility Officer:** John Nusbaum

## LOCATIONS

**HQ:** 4600 Edmundson Rd., St. Louis, MO 63134
**Phone:** 314-253-6700      **Fax:** 314-253-6807
**Web:** www.ascensionhealth.org

## PRODUCTS/OPERATIONS

**Facilities**
Acute care hospitals
Adult residential facilities
Community health centers
Long-term acute care
Long-term care
Psychiatric hospitals
Rehabilitation facilities

## COMPETITORS

Beverly Enterprises
Catholic Health East
Catholic Health Initiatives
Catholic Healthcare Partners
HCA
HMA
HEALTHSOUTH
Kindred
Life Care Centers
Tenet Healthcare
Triad Hospitals
Trinity Health
Universal Health Services

## HISTORICAL FINANCIALS & EMPLOYEES

| Not-for-profit FYE: June 30 | Annual Growth | 6/91 | 6/92 | 6/93 | 6/94 | 6/95 | 6/96 | 6/97 | 6/98 | 6/99 | 6/00 |
|---|---|---|---|---|---|---|---|---|---|---|---|
| Sales ($ mil.) | 1.0% | — | 5,900 | 6,500 | 7,000 | 6,200 | 5,700 | 5,700 | 6,170 | 6,400 | 6,400 |
| Employees | (0.1%) | — | — | — | 67,400 | 62,300 | 61,100 | 60,000 | 65,000 | 67,000 | 67,000 |

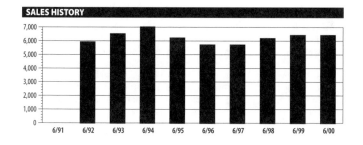

SALES HISTORY

ASCENSION HEALTH

# ASSOCIATED MILK PRODUCERS

Associated Milk Producers Incorporated (AMPI) might wear a cheesy grin, but it churns up solid sales. The farmers in the New Ulm, Minnesota-based regional dairy cooperative start with milk, but then concentrate on solid dairy products, such as cheese, butter, and dry milk.

AMPI has 4,800 member farms in Iowa, Minnesota, Missouri, Nebraska, North Dakota, South Dakota, and Wisconsin. It markets nearly five billion pounds of dairy products each year, and it has upgraded its 14 plants to produce additional value-added dairy products such as shredded cheese, aseptic-packaged cheese sauces (coated cardboard containers for stable shelf life), and individually wrapped butter pats. Only one plant produces fluid milk. AMPI produces 60% of all instant milk sold in the US, and it is a major cheddar producer.

In addition, AMPI's 93,000-sq-ft plant in New Ulm, Minnesota is the biggest butter barn in the US. It whips up nearly 20,000 pounds of butter per hour.

The co-op is primarily a private-label producer for retailers and food service customers. However, AMPI also produces State brand cheese and butter, which are distributed nationally.

In 1969, faced with a decline in US milk consumption and a subsequent drop in income, about 100 dairy cooperatives in the Midwest and the South merged to form Associated Milk Producers Incorporated (AMPI). AMPI elected John Butterbrodt, from a Wisconsin co-op, as the first president. Co-ops throughout the central US clamored to join, and AMPI became the largest US dairy co-op within two years of its formation.

Almost from the beginning, AMPI became embroiled in the two main controversies involving dairy co-ops: monopolistic practices and political contributions. In 1972 consumer advocate Ralph Nader alleged that the three main dairy co-ops — AMPI, Dairymen, and Mid-America Dairymen — had illegally contributed $422,000 to President Nixon's reelection campaign in an attempt to obtain higher price supports (enacted in 1971) and an agreement that the administration would drop antitrust suits against the co-ops. Watergate investigators subpoenaed Nixon's tapes, and AMPI was accused of bribery, destruction of evidence, and attempting to achieve "complete market dominance." In 1974 it pleaded guilty to making illegal political contributions in 1968, 1970, and 1972. By 1975 three former AMPI employees had been convicted of various charges and Butterbrodt had resigned.

The co-op spent the last half of the 1970s quietly reorganizing. In 1982 a suit for monopolistic practices, originally filed in 1971 by the National Farmers Organization (NFO), finally reached the federal courts. The case was decided in favor of AMPI and two other large co-ops, but before the year was out an appeals court reversed the decision, saying AMPI and its co-defendants had conspired to eliminate competitive sellers of milk. (The US Supreme Court subsequently upheld the appeals court ruling.)

AMPI extended its dominance of the industry in 1985 by merging its central region with 2,200 members of Wisconsin-based co-op Morning Glory Farms. (It sold Morning Glory to dairy co-op Foremost Farms USA in 1995.)

Business soured in the early 1990s, and despite successfully lobbying the Department of Agriculture to strengthen dairy price supports, AMPI posted losses. Although Congress spent heavily, AMPI watched decades of government support to dairy farmers fall away as the 1996 Farm Bill established free-market agriculture.

Faced with falling prices, deregulation, and foreign competition, in 1997 AMPI entered into consolidation talks with three of its dairy co-op brethren: Mid-America Dairymen, Milk Marketing, and Western Dairymen Cooperative. AMPI's Southern Region, which primarily produced fluid milk, decided to join the new co-op, Dairy Farmers of America; members of its Northern Region, which focused on hard products, stayed put, renaming itself North Central AMPI to reduce confusion during the transition. However, the co-op officially readopted the original name in 1999.

High butterfat prices in 1998 helped the co-op post record earnings during its first year after the separation. Amid wild consolidations within the dairy industry, in mid-1999 AMPI made a modest merger with the Glencoe Butter & Produce Association. The small regional cooperative based in Glencoe, Minnesota, brought a cheese production plant and 1,000 new members to AMPI. In 2000 a Minnesota cooperative, the Fremont Cooperative Creamery Association, sold its plant and added its 40 members to AMPI rolls.

**President:** Paul Toft
**General Manager:** Mark Furth
**CFO:** Steve Sorenson
**Human Resources Manager:** Leigh Heilman

## LOCATIONS

**HQ:** Associated Milk Producers Incorporated,
315 N. Broadway, New Ulm, MN 56073
**Phone:** 507-354-8295     **Fax:** 507-359-8651
**Web:** www.ampi.com

Associated Milk Producers has more than 4,800 members and 14 milk processing plants in Iowa, Minnesota, Missouri, Nebraska, North Dakota, South Dakota, and Wisconsin.

## PRODUCTS/OPERATIONS

**Selected Products**
Butter
Cheese
Dry milk
Fluid milk
Ice cream mixes
Lactose
Sauces
Whey

## COMPETITORS

Dairy Farmers of America
Dairylea
Dean Foods
Foremost Farms
Great Lakes Cheese
Land O'Lakes
Leprino Foods
Marathon Cheese
MMPA
Parmalat Finanziaria
Prairie Farms Dairy
Saputo
Schreiber Foods

## HISTORICAL FINANCIALS & EMPLOYEES

| Cooperative<br>FYE: December 31 | Annual<br>Growth | 12/91 | 12/92 | 12/93 | 12/94 | 12/95 | 12/96 | 12/97 | 12/98 | 12/99 | 12/00 |
|---|---|---|---|---|---|---|---|---|---|---|---|
| Sales ($ mil.) | (12.2%) | — | 2,835 | 2,692 | 2,629 | 2,554 | 2,189 | 928 | 1,100 | 1,100 | 1,000 |
| Employees | (11.8%) | — | 4,364 | 4,199 | 4,500 | 4,500 | 4,500 | 1,600 | 1,600 | 1,600 | 1,600 |

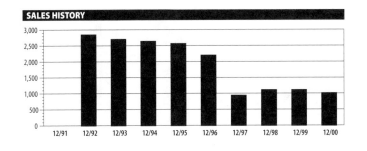

**SALES HISTORY**

# THE ASSOCIATED PRESS

This just in: The Associated Press (AP) is reporting tonight and every night wherever news is breaking. The world's largest newsgathering organization, New York-based AP provides news, photos, graphics, and audiovisual services to print, radio, and television media in more than 120 countries through about 240 news bureaus. Its reports are translated into five languages (Dutch, English, French, German, and Spanish) and reach more than 1 billion people daily.

AP also maintains photo archives, a continuous online news service, an international television division, an ad placement and billing service, and a digital ad delivery service. The company has created a new division to sell news to Internet markets.

A not-for-profit cooperative owned by 1,550 US member newspapers, the group is governed by a board of directors elected by its members. To ensure widespread representation, according to the AP's charter at least three of its directors must be from independent newspapers published in cities with fewer than 50,000 people.

The Associated Press was formed in 1848 when six New York City newspapers joined to share news that arrived by telegraph wire. A year later the organization established its first foreign bureau in Halifax, Nova Scotia. Halifax was the first North American port of call for Cunard's ocean liners coming from Europe, and when each ship arrived, the latest news from Europe was telegraphed to AP's New York office. In 1850 the AP began selling wire reports to other papers and before long started creating regional associations.

By the turn of the century, the AP began to expand its services internationally. In 1902 the group created a cable service to serve Cuba, the Philippines, and Central America, and in 1919 it began service to 22 newspapers in South America. In 1933 the AP began service to Japan's Ringgo news agency.

In 1927 the company began offering news pictures along with its stories. Originally, the photos were delivered by an air, sea, and rail system, but in 1935 the company introduced the AP WirePhoto network, transmitting pictures to all AP affiliates simultaneously via telephone wires.

Meanwhile the AP was adapting to changing tastes and interests, by expanding its offerings. It began covering sports, financial, and public interest stories in the 1920s. The company also adapted to new technologies, adding a service to create news reports for radio stations in 1941.

In the late 1960s AP and Dow Jones introduced services to improve business and financial reporting. AP improved photo delivery, reception, and storage in the 1970s with the advent of Laserphoto and the Electronic Darkroom. In 1974 the company launched the AP Radio Network to provide hourly newscasts, sportscasts, and business programs to member radio stations.

The company began transmitting news by satellite and offering color photographs to newspapers in the 1980s. In 1985 Louis Boccardi took over the job as president and CEO of AP.

AP adjusted to the media-heavy culture of the 1990s by launching the APTV international news video service and the All News Radio network in 1994. In 1996 the company formed a joint venture with Trans World International (TWI) to launch sports news video service SNTV. Also in 1996 the AP moved onto the Internet when it launched The WIRE. The next year it began offering online access to its Photo Archive. The group bought Worldwide Television News in 1998, combining it with APTV to form APTN (Associated Press Television News). The following year it purchased the radio news contracts of UPI after the rival organization announced it was getting out of broadcast news.

In 2000 AP created an Internet division, AP Digital, to focus on marketing news to online providers. The cooperative continued its Internet focus the following year, launching AP Online en Español (news for Spanish-language Web sites) and AP Entertainment Online (multimedia entertainment news for Web sites).

In 2001 AP bought the Newspaper Industry Communication Center from the Newspaper Association of America.

## OFFICERS

**Chairman:** Donald E. Newhouse
**Vice Chairman:** Burl Osborne, age 63
**President and CEO:** Louis D. Boccardi
**SVP and CFO:** Patrick T. O'Brien
**VP, Secretary, and Director Human Resources:**
James M. Donna
**Treasurer:** Daniel M. Boruch
**Assistant Treasurer:** Ann Randolph
**Assistant Secretary:** Lilo Jedelhauser
**Assistant Secretary:** Greg Groce

## LOCATIONS

**HQ:** 50 Rockefeller Plaza, New York, NY 10020
**Phone:** 212-621-1500    **Fax:** 212-621-5447
**Web:** www.ap.org

The Associated Press has about 240 news bureaus
serving 121 countries.

## PRODUCTS/OPERATIONS

**Selected Products and Services**
AP AdSEND (digital transmission of advertisements)
AP Digital (news for Internet and wireless markets)
AP Information Services (news products for
corporations, government, and online distributors)
AP Photo Archive (more than 700,000 online photos)
AP Telecommunications (land-based and satellite
information networks)
AP Wide World Photos (20th-century historical photos
for professional photographers)
APTN (Associated Press Television Network,
international television news service)
ENPS (electronic news production system)
The WIRE (24-hour news service for the Internet)
NICC (Newpaper Industry Communication Center; ad
placement, billing and tear sheet processing)

## COMPETITORS

Agence France-Presse
Bloomberg
Business Wire
COMTEX
Corbis
Dow Jones
Gannett
Getty Images
Knight Ridder
New York Times
PR Newswire
Reuters
Tribune
UPI

## HISTORICAL FINANCIALS & EMPLOYEES

| Cooperative FYE: December 31 | Annual Growth | 12/91 | 12/92 | 12/93 | 12/94 | 12/95 | 12/96 | 12/97 | 12/98 | 12/99 | 12/00 |
|---|---|---|---|---|---|---|---|---|---|---|---|
| Sales ($ mil.) | 5.8% | — | 365 | 382 | 406 | 390 | 418 | 441 | 495 | 572 | 574 |
| Employees | 2.2% | — | 3,100 | 3,150 | 3,150 | 3,150 | 3,000 | 3,500 | 3,500 | 3,500 | 3,700 |

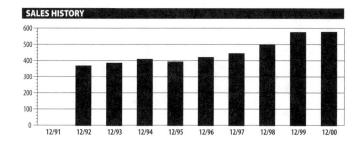

SALES HISTORY

# ASSOCIATED WHOLESALE GROCERS

## OVERVIEW

Associated Wholesale Grocers, Inc. (AWG) helps people in the Midwest fill up their shopping baskets. The Kansas City, Kansas-based co-op is owned by more than 350 members (independent retailers) who operate about 850 grocery stores, primarily in the Midwest (Illinois, Iowa, Kansas, Missouri, Nebraska, Oklahoma), but also in the South (Arkansas, Kentucky, Tennessee, Texas). Its grocers operate under a variety of banners: supermarket chains Apple Market, Cash Saver, and Thriftway; the upscale Sun Fresh chain; and warehouse chains Country Mart, Price Chopper, and Price Mart.

AWG supplies members with brand-name and private-label food (Always Save and Best Choice) and nonfood items; it also provides services such as advertising and marketing support, property/casualty insurance, employee benefits packages, store design, loan programs, and real estate lease assistance.

The cooperative moved into food retailing in 1998 with its acquisition of more than 30 Falley's and Food 4 Less stores in Kansas and Missouri.

## HISTORY

About 20 Kansas City, Kansas-area grocers met in a local grocery in 1924 and organized the Associated Grocers Company to get better deals on purchases and advertising. They elected J. C. Harline president, and each chipped in a few hundred dollars to make their first purchases. It took a while to find a manufacturer who would sell directly to them; a local soap maker was finally convinced, and others gradually followed.

In 1926 the group was incorporated as Associated Wholesale Grocers (AWG). It outgrew two warehouses in four years, finally moving to a 16,000-sq.-ft. facility big enough to add new lines and more products. Membership doubled between 1930 and 1932 as grocers moved from ordering products a year ahead to the new wholesale concept, and members took seriously the slogan: "Buy, Sell, Buy Some More." They met every week to plan how to sell their products, and buyer and advertising manager Harry Small gave sales presentations and advertising ideas (his trade-in plan for old brooms sold more than two traincarloads of brooms in two weeks). Heavy newspaper advertising also paid off; AWG topped $1 million in sales in 1933.

The cooperative made its first acquisition in 1936, buying Progressive Grocers, a warehouse in Joplin, Missouri; a second such warehouse named Associated Grocers was acquired the next year in Springfield, Missouri. AWG continued building and expanding warehouses, and annual sales were at $11 million by 1951.

Louis Fox became CEO in 1956. Fox maximized year-end rebates for members, led several acquisitions, and formed a new subsidiary for financing stores and small shopping centers where AWG members had a presence (Supermarket Developers). Sales increased nearly fifteenfold to over $200 million in his

first 15 years. James Basha succeeded Fox, who retired in 1984, and saw sales reach $2.4 billion by his own retirement in 1992. Basha was followed by former COO Mike DeFabis, once a deputy mayor of Indianapolis.

DeFabis orchestrated several acquisitions, including 41 Kansas City-area stores — most of which were quickly bought by members — from bankrupt Food Barn Stores in 1994 and 29 Oklahoma stores and a warehouse from Safeway spinoff Homeland Stores in 1995 (members bought all the stores).

The group's nonfood subsidiary, Valu Merchandisers Co., was established in 1995; its new Kansas warehouse began shipping health and beauty aids and housewares the following year to help members battle big discounters. Members narrowly defeated a proposal in late 1996 to convert the cooperative into a public company. Proponents promptly petitioned for a second vote, which was defeated early the next year.

AWG veteran Doug Carolan succeeded DeFabis in 1998, becoming only the fifth CEO in the cooperative's history. The company bought five Falley's and 33 Food 4 Less stores in Kansas and Missouri from Fred Meyer in 1998 for $300 million.

In 2000 after a months-long labor dispute with the Teamsters was resolved, Carolan left AWG. The company's CFO, Gary Phillips, was named president and CEO later that year. In 2001 the company debuted a new format, ALPS (Always Low Price Stores) — small stores that carry a limited selection of grocery top-sellers. Also that year AWG's Kansas City division began distributing to more than 10 new stores that had formerly been served by Fleming, the #2 US wholesale food distributor after SUPERVALU.

## OFFICERS

**Chairman:** J. Fred Ball
**President and CEO:** Gary Phillips
**EVP and CFO:** Robert C. Walker
**EVP, Marketing:** Jerry Garland
**SVP and General Manager, KC Division:** Mike Rand
**SVP, Real Estate:** Scott Wilmoski
**VP and General Counsel:** Chi Chi Puhl
**VP, Secretary, and Treasurer:** Joe Campbell
**VP, Corporate Sales:** Bill Lancaster
**VP, Human Resources:** Frank Tricamo
**VP, Procurement:** Dennis Kinser
**President and CEO, Benchmark Insurance Companies:**
William R. Morrison
**President, Valu Merchandisers:** Ken Nemeth
**Executive Director, AWG Brands:** Marc Mullins

## LOCATIONS

**HQ:** Associated Wholesale Grocers, Inc.,
5000 Kansas Ave., Kansas City, KS 66106
**Phone:** 913-288-1000      **Fax:** 913-288-1508
**Web:** www.awginc.com

Associated Wholesale Grocers serves grocers in
Arkansas, Illinois, Iowa, Kansas, Kentucky, Missouri,
Nebraska, Oklahoma, Tennessee, and Texas. The
cooperative has four distribution centers in Kansas,
Missouri, and Oklahoma.

## PRODUCTS/OPERATIONS

**Selected Private-Label Brands**
Always Save
Best Choice

**Selected Services**

| | |
|---|---|
| Advertising | Private-label products |
| Employee training | Real estate lease assistance |
| Financial planning | Site acquisition |
| In-store marketing | Store engineering and |
| Insurance | construction |
| Market research and | Store financing |
| analysis | Store franchise formats |
| Merchandising advice | Store remodeling |

**Selected Store Formats**
Apple Market (15,000 to 25,000-sq.-ft. grocery stores
designed for neighborhood locations in both rural and
metropolitan areas)
Cash Saver (designed with fewer perishables to serve
rural areas)
Country Mart (25,000 to 45,000-sq.-ft. value-priced
stores designed for county-seat and medium-sized
towns)
Falley's (conventional supermarkets)
Food 4 Less (warehouse stores)
Price Chopper and Price Mart (50,000 to 92,000-sq.-ft.
value-priced warehouse stores designed for high-
volume areas)
Sun Fresh (40,000 to 63,000-sq.-ft. stores designed to
serve medium-to-upper-income customers)
Thriftway (neighborhood locations)

**Selected Operations/Subsidiaries**
Benchmark Insurance Co.
Supermarket Developers, Inc. (financing for stores and
supermarkets)
Supermarket Insurance Agency Inc.
Valu Merchandisers Company (health and beauty
supplies, general merchandise, and pharmacy
products)

## COMPETITORS

| | |
|---|---|
| Affiliated Foods | Nash Finch |
| Albertson's | Roundy's |
| Delhaize America | S. Abraham & Sons |
| Fleming Companies | Schnuck Markets |
| GSC Enterprises | Shurfine International |
| H.T. Hackney | Spartan Stores |
| Hy-Vee | SUPERVALU |
| IGA | Topco Associates |
| Kroger | Wal-Mart |

## HISTORICAL FINANCIALS & EMPLOYEES

| Cooperative<br>FYE: December 31 | Annual<br>Growth | 12/91 | 12/92 | 12/93 | 12/94 | 12/95 | 12/96 | 12/97 | 12/98 | 12/99 | 12/00 |
|---|---|---|---|---|---|---|---|---|---|---|---|
| Sales ($ mil.) | 3.6% | — | 2,404 | 2,540 | 2,600 | 2,970 | 3,096 | 3,129 | 3,180 | 3,370 | 3,200 |
| Employees | 4.2% | — | — | — | — | — | 2,797 | 3,000 | 3,100 | 3,300 | 3,300 |

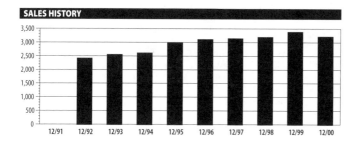

SALES HISTORY

# BAIN & COMPANY

## OVERVIEW

More than 2,000 companies have picked the brains of Bain's "Bainies." Boston-based Bain & Company, whose consultants are known as Bainies, is one of the world's leading strategic consulting firms offering a variety of consulting services, including business unit, organizational, and corporate strategy; distribution and logistics advice; merger, acquisition, and divestiture consulting; and sales and marketing strategy. Bain's clients hail from industries such as media and communications, consumer products and services, financial services, and high tech. The firm has 26 offices in nearly 20 countries. Although founded by the same individuals, Bain & Company and investment firm Bain Capital are separate entities.

Bain was one of the many consulting firms riding high on the wave of Internet mania, helping both startups and established companies develop business strategies for the New Economy. While the post-dot-com boom world might not be as exciting, a softening economy has created an increased demand for efficiency and cost analysis services. Bain's bainlab incubator unit has also shifted its focus to performing due diligence for other VCs. Bain is also facing increased competition from consulting units spawned by the Big 5 accounting firms.

## HISTORY

Although he had no formal business training, Bill Bain got a job through a friend at the Boston Consulting Group (BCG) in 1967. Bain and a group of colleagues later defected from BCG and founded Bain & Company in 1973. The new firm strove to set itself apart from its rivals by establishing long-term relationships with its clients: it wouldn't take on other clients in the same industry (a policy that was later relaxed), and it would help clients implement its recommendations. By 1979 Bain had opened an office in London to serve US clients in Europe.

The firm's strategy of establishing relationships with clients seemed to attract executives looking for a crutch, a quality Bain exploited with spectacular results in the 1970s and 1980s. Until 1985 Bill Bain retained total control of the firm (even the other partners did not know how much the firm was making). In 1985 and 1986 he and several partners contributed 30% of the firm to an employee stock option plan (ESOP) and had the ESOP borrow money to pay for the stock. The loans burdened the firm with debt, however, and strained its financial health.

In the midst of its financial crisis, Bain's tendency to become intimately involved in its clients' affairs backfired during a 1987 UK investigation of client Guinness PLC. It was revealed that Bain VP Olivier Roux had continued to draw his Bain salary while employed by Guinness. Though the episode exposed a serious conflict of interest, Bain was not formally charged with wrongdoing. More trouble came from an economic downturn late in the decade, which led to a sharp decline in Bain's business. The debt-ridden firm continued to expand, however, becoming one of the first Western consulting firms to open an office in Russia (1990).

By 1991 Bain's employee count had fallen from 1,000 (in 1989) to 550. Bill Bain was ousted, and Mitt Romney (head of Bain Capital, which had been founded with money from the 1985 ESOP deal) was brought in to revive the firm. Romney recapitalized Bain by pressing the original partners to return most of their holdings and redistributing ownership: About 40% went to the ESOP and 60% to a group of 75 partners. Bill Bain was left with no ownership save a small share of the ESOP.

In 1993 the flashy Orit Gadiesh was appointed chairman of the firm. The 16-year Bain veteran and former Israeli military intelligence officer helped turn the firm around by prodding its partners to question Bain's purpose and find its "true north." By 1994 the number of Bain consultants had risen to 800, and the firm's financial health had improved.

Trouble reared its head again in 1998 when the firm was hit with a lawsuit from Value Partners, an Italian consulting firm that accused Bain of raiding its Brazilian office and stealing confidential information. The suit was dismissed, but Value Partners refiled the case in a different court that year; Bain's attempt to have the case dismissed failed in 1999. That year it promoted e-commerce expert John Donahoe to worldwide managing director (CEO), and in 2000 formed eVolution Global Partners, a joint venture with Kleiner Perkins Caufield & Byers and Texas Pacific Group to help international companies develop their own e-commerce sites.

## OFFICERS

**Chairman:** Orit Gadiesh, age 50
**Worldwide Managing Director:** John Donahoe
**CFO:** Len Banos
**VP:** Kim Ogden
**VP:** David Bechhofer
**VP:** Louis Amory
**VP:** Neil Cherry
**VP:** Norbert Hultenschmidt
**VP:** Ugo Loser
**VP:** Giorgio Marchegiani
**VP:** Henrik Naujoks
**VP:** Jean-Christophe Pettinotti
**VP:** Teresa Martin-Retortillo
**VP:** Vincenzo Santelia
**VP:** Heidi Locke Simon
**VP:** Miwa Suto
**VP:** Ravi Vijayaraghavan
**VP:** Fredrik Wilhelmsson
**Director of Human Resources:** Elizabeth Corcoran

## LOCATIONS

**HQ:** 2 Copley Place, Boston, MA 02116
**Phone:** 617-572-2000　　**Fax:** 617-572-2427
**Web:** www.bain.com

Bain & Company has operations in Australia, Belgium, Brazil, Canada, China, France, Germany, Italy, Japan, Mexico, the Netherlands, Singapore, South Africa, South Korea, Spain, Sweden, Switzerland, the UK, and the US.

## PRODUCTS/OPERATIONS

**Selected Consulting Services**
Business unit strategy
Corporate strategy
Distribution and logistics
Organizational strategy
Post-merger integration
Marketing strategy

**Selected Industries Served**
Aerospace and defense
Business services
Consumer products
Financial services
Government agencies
Healthcare and medical services
Media and entertainment
Natural resources
Not-for-profits
Retail
Technology
Telecommunications
Utilities

## COMPETITORS

Accenture
Arthur D. Little
A.T. Kearney
Booz-Allen
Boston Consulting
Cap Gemini
Deloitte Touche Tohmatsu
Grant Thornton
　International
KPMG Consulting
Marsh & McLennan
McKinsey & Company
PricewaterhouseCoopers
Towers Perrin
Watson Wyatt

## HISTORICAL FINANCIALS & EMPLOYEES

| Partnership FYE: December 31 | Annual Growth | 12/91 | 12/92 | 12/93 | 12/94 | 12/95 | 12/96 | 12/97 | 12/98 | 12/99 | 12/00 |
|---|---|---|---|---|---|---|---|---|---|---|---|
| Sales ($ mil.) | 21.0% | — | — | 213 | 300 | 375 | 450 | 480 | 499 | 700 | 810 |
| Employees | 17.0% | — | — | 900 | 1,000 | 1,200 | 1,500 | 1,700 | 2,100 | 2,400 | 2,700 |

## SALES HISTORY

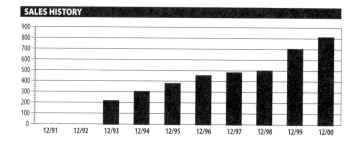

BAIN & COMPANY

# BAKER & MCKENZIE

How many lawyers does it take to break through a glass ceiling? Whatever the answer, Baker & McKenzie has more than enough. The Chicago-based law firm is the world's second largest (the UK's Clifford Chance is #1), with more than 3,000 lawyers and another 1,000 fee earners spread across more than 60 offices in about 35 countries. It also became one of the first major partnerships to elect a woman to manage the firm when Christine Lagarde was chosen in 1999 to replace outgoing chairman John Klotsche. In addition to closing the gender gap, Lagarde is also one of the youngest partners (age 43 when she was elected) to lead the firm.

Baker is a global firm offering legal services in areas such as banking, securities, labor, international trade, and tax. The half-century-old firm has handled the legal affairs of such heavy-duty clients as Chase Manhattan (now J.P. Morgan Chase), Honeywell, and Ingersoll-Rand. Although its size has helped attract clients and employees, Baker has also had to struggle with the image of being more concerned with size (some have dubbed it McFirm) than with quality legal work.

The firm is beginning to face new competition on the global scene. Clifford Chance merged with two other practices in 2000 to create a network larger than Baker's. Meanwhile, the Big Five multinational accounting firms (such as Andersen Worldwide and Ernst & Young) are becoming more active in offering legal advice and have lured away several of Baker's top tax partners.

## HISTORY

Russell Baker traveled from his native New Mexico to Chicago on a railroad freight car to attend law school. Upon graduation in 1925 he started practicing law with his classmate Dana Simpson under the name Simpson & Baker. Inspired by Chicago's role as a manufacturing and agricultural center for the world and influenced by the international focus of his alma mater, the University of Chicago, Baker dreamed of creating an international law practice. He developed an expertise in international law, and in 1934 Abbott Laboratories retained him to handle its worldwide legal affairs. Baker was on his way to fulfilling his dream.

Baker joined forces with Chicago litigator John McKenzie in 1949, forming Baker & McKenzie. In 1955 the firm opened its first foreign office in Caracas, Venezuela, to meet the needs of its expanding US client base. Over the next 10 years it branched out into Asia, Australia, and Europe, with offices in London, Manila, Paris, and Tokyo. Baker's death in 1979 neither slowed the firm's growth nor changed its international character. The next year it expanded into the Middle East and opened its 30th office in 1982 (Melbourne). To manage the sprawling law firm, Baker & McKenzie created the position of chairman of the executive committee in 1984.

In late 1991 the firm dropped the Church of Scientology as a client, losing an estimated $2 million in business. It was speculated that pressure from client Eli Lilly (maker of the drug Prozac, which Scientologists actively oppose) influenced the decision. In 1992 Baker & McKenzie was ordered to pay $1 million for wrongfully firing an employee who later died of AIDS. (The case became the basis for the 1993 film *Philadelphia*.) The firm fought the verdict but eventually settled for an undisclosed amount in 1995.

In 1994 Baker & McKenzie closed its Los Angeles office (the former MacDonald, Halsted & Laybourne; acquired 1988) amid considerable rancor. Also that year a former secretary at the firm received a $7.1 million judgment for sexual harassment by a partner. (A San Francisco Superior Court judge later reduced the award to $3.5 million.)

John Klotsche, a senior partner from the firm's Palo Alto, California, office was appointed chairman in 1995. The following year the firm began a major expansion into California's Silicon Valley as part of an initiative to serve technology companies around the world. It also expanded its Warsaw, Poland, office through a merger with the Warsaw office of Dickinson, Wright, Moon, Van Dusen & Freman.

In 1998 Baker & McKenzie formed a special unit in Singapore to deal with business generated by the financial troubles in Asia. The opening of offices in Taiwan and Azerbaijan in 1998 brought the firm's total number of offices to 59. Klotsche stepped down in 1999 as the firm celebrated its 50th anniversary; Christine Lagarde replaced him. In early 2001 Baker & McKenzie created a joint venture practice with Singapore-based associate firm Wong & Leow. Also that year it merged with Madrid-based Briones Alonso y Martin to create the largest independent law firm in Spain.

## OFFICERS

**Chairman Executive Committee:** Christine Lagarde,
age 45
**COO:** Peter F. Smith
**CFO:** Robert S. Spencer
**Chief Technology Officer:** Craig Courter
**General Counsel:** Edward J. Zulkey
**Director Special Projects:** Suzanne M. Clough
**Director, Professional Development:** Anne Waldron
**Manager, Human Resources:** Wilbert Williams
**Auditors:** Arthur Andersen LLP

## LOCATIONS

**HQ:** 1 Prudential Plaza, 130 E. Randolph Dr., Ste. 2500,
Chicago, IL 60601
**Phone:** 312-861-8800          **Fax:** 312-861-2899
**Web:** www.bakerinfo.com

Baker & McKenzie has more than 60 offices throughout
Asia, Australia, Europe, Latin America, and North
America.

## PRODUCTS/OPERATIONS

**Selected Practice Areas**
Banking and finance
Corporate and securities
E-commerce
International commercial arbitration
International trade
Information technology and communications
Labor and employment
Tax
US Litigation

## COMPETITORS

| | |
|---|---|
| Andersen | Mayer, Brown & Platt |
| Clifford Chance | McDermott, Will |
| Deloitte Touche Tohmatsu | PricewaterhouseCoopers |
| Ernst & Young | Sidley Austin Brown & |
| Jones, Day | Wood |
| Kirkland & Ellis | Skadden, Arps |
| KPMG | |

## HISTORICAL FINANCIALS & EMPLOYEES

| Partnership FYE: June 30 | Annual Growth | 6/92 | 6/93 | 6/94 | 6/95 | 6/96 | 6/97 | 6/98 | 6/99 | 6/00 | 6/01 |
|---|---|---|---|---|---|---|---|---|---|---|---|
| Sales ($ mil.) | 7.9% | 504 | 512 | 546 | 594 | 646 | 697 | 785 | 818 | 940 | 1,000 |
| Employees | 5.6% | 4,919 | 5,054 | 5,114 | 5,248 | 5,680 | 6,100 | 6,700 | 6,900 | 8,000 | 8,000 |

## SALES HISTORY

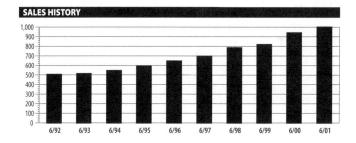

BAKER & MᶜKENZIE

# BAKER & TAYLOR CORPORATION

## OVERVIEW

Although Baker & Taylor (B&T) is at the top of its industry, it's very quiet about it. The Charlotte, North Carolina-based company is the largest US wholesaler of books to libraries and the nation's #2 book wholesaler overall (after Ingram Industries' Ingram Book Group). It offers some 3.5 million English-language book titles, plus about 240,000 music titles and more than 135,000 video, DVD and CD titles.

B&T's institutional unit supplies books, audio books, calendars, and audio-video and other information services to about 28,000 school, public, and specialty libraries. The unit also offers acquisition and collection management support services to libraries through its YBP Library Services subsidiary. Baker & Taylor Retail handles stores, Internet sales (providing fulfillment for companies such as Amazon.com and barnesandnoble.com), and international operations. The company's business-to-business e-commerce arm, Informata.com, distributes electronic content, licenses database services and applications, and creates Internet portals such as theLibraryPlace.com.

B&T also offers automatic shipping of books by popular authors (mailed as soon as they are published), and its Replica Books publishes out-of-print and paperback titles on demand.

Investment firm The Carlyle Group and its affiliates own nearly 85% of B&T. Management, employees, and other private investors own the rest.

## HISTORY

Baker & Taylor (B&T) traces its roots back to a bindery and subscription publisher founded by David Robinson and B. B. Barber in Hartford, Connecticut, in 1828. A few years later it opened a bookstore that sold books by other publishers in addition to its own titles; in 1835 it moved to New York. James Baker and Nelson Taylor bought the business 50 years later and renamed it Baker & Taylor. After Taylor died in 1912, the company stopped publishing in order to concentrate on wholesaling.

B&T moved to New Jersey in 1950. It was acquired by the Parents' Institute, publisher of *Parents Magazine,* in 1958, but was sold to W. R. Grace in 1970 during the period when Grace was assembling an eclectic collection of unrelated companies. Under Grace, B&T's hard-won reputation suffered. Customers complained about incomplete orders, insufficient stock, and poor communications.

Nevertheless, Grace continued to build its media distribution business, buying two video distributors (Sound Video Unlimited and VTR) and software distributor SoftKat in 1986. Those operations (renamed Baker & Taylor Video and Baker & Taylor Software) remained independent. However, customer problems continued, which B&T management attributed to Grace and its overemphasis on short-term financial performance.

Grace had its own problems in the late 1980s and early 1990s. Overinvestment in energy and the firm's purchase of a large block of its own stock took it deeply into debt. In 1992 Grace sold B&T to company management and The Carlyle Group. Video and software units were combined into Baker & Taylor Entertainment.

After the buyout, B&T began focusing on global markets. UK library supplier T.C. Farries and Co. agreed to supply its books, and B&T released a world edition of its Title Source CD, which combined the firm's B&T Link title database with new ordering capabilities.

The Carlyle Group's unsuccessful 1994 attempt to sell B&T to college bookstore leader Follett led to a management shakeup that included the resignation of longtime chairman Gerald Garbacz; Craig Richards became CEO. A restructuring included the formation of the Electronic Business and Information and Library Services units.

B&T's first big contract to perform library purchasing was with the State of Hawaii in 1996. The next year, however, Hawaii slapped the company with a lawsuit, which the US Justice Department later joined, accusing B&T of overcharging public schools, libraries, and federal agencies by $100 million to $200 million from 1983 to 1993. In 1998, 17 states joined the federal government, filing their own lawsuit alleging book overcharges. The federal suit was settled in 1999, with B&T paying $3 million but admitting no wrongdoing.

To expand its institutional reach, B&T bought Yankee Book Peddler, a supplier of books and information services to libraries, in 1999. Also that year B&T filed to go public, reorganized into retailer and institutional divisions, and began allowing customers to order online. The company withdrew its filing in 2000 and formed Informata.com. Later that year B&T and Grace agreed to pay $12.5 million to settle the state book overcharge lawsuits.

**Chairman:** Daniel A. D'Aniello
**President, CEO, and COO:** Gary M. Rautenstrauch
**EVP and CFO:** Edward H. Gross
**EVP; General Manager, Baker & Taylor Entertainment:** Richard S. Czuba
**EVP, Distribution:** Marshall A. Wight
**SVP and General Counsel:** Bradley D. Murchison
**SVP, A/V Library Services:** William Hartman
**SVP, Customized Library Services:** Livia Bitner
**SVP, Finance and Corporate VP:** David Finlon
**SVP, Human Resources:** Claudette Hampton
**SVP, Information Technology:** Matt Carroll
**SVP, Operations:** James Benjamin
**SVP, Retail Sales and Marketing:** William Preston
**President, Baker & Taylor Institutional:** George Coe
**President, Baker & Taylor Retail:** James S. Ulsamer, age 50
**CEO, YBP Library Services:** John Secor
**President and COO, YBP Library Services:** Gary Shirk
**Chief Marketing Officer:** Pamela Smith
**Auditors:** Arthur Andersen LLP

## LOCATIONS

**HQ:** 2709 Water Ridge Pkwy., Charlotte, NC 28217
**Phone:** 704-357-3500     **Fax:** 704-329-8989
**Web:** www.btol.com

Baker & Taylor has operations in Colorado, Georgia, Illinois, Nevada, New Hampshire, New Jersey, and North Carolina, and sales offices in Australia and Japan. The company supplies books and services to libraries and retailers worldwide.

## PRODUCTS/OPERATIONS

**Selected Products and Services**
Accessories
Audiocassettes
Calendars
Cataloging database (B&T MARC)
CD-ROM and Internet database and ordering software (Title Source II)
CDs
DVDs
Hardcover and paperback books
Library automation system (Libris 2020)
On-demand printing (Replica Books)
Online prepublication information (B&T Express Wired)
Spoken-word audiocassettes
Standing-order service (Compass)
Videos

**Operating Units and Subsidiaries**
Baker & Taylor Institutional
   Professional Media Services Corp.
   YBP Library Services
Baker & Taylor Retail
Informata.com

## COMPETITORS

| | |
|---|---|
| Advanced Marketing | Ingram Entertainment |
| Alliance Entertainment | Ingram Industries |
| BH Blackwell Ltd. | LDI |
| Book Wholesalers | Ludington News |
| Brodart | Major Video Concepts |
| Chas. Levy | Midwest Library Service |
| Dawson Holdings | Navarre |
| East Texas Distributing | Publishers Group West |
| Educational Development | Rentrak |
| Follett | Valley Media |
| Handleman | |

## HISTORICAL FINANCIALS & EMPLOYEES

| Private<br>FYE: Last Friday in June | Annual<br>Growth | 6/92 | 6/93 | 6/94 | 6/95 | 6/96 | 6/97 | 6/98 | 6/99 | 6/00 | 6/01 |
|---|---|---|---|---|---|---|---|---|---|---|---|
| Sales ($ mil.) | 4.1% | — | — | — | 784 | 751 | 829 | 883 | 1,021 | 1,130 | 1,000 |
| Employees | 0.0% | — | — | — | — | — | — | — | 2,500 | 2,700 | 2,500 |

### SALES HISTORY

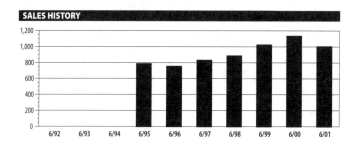

# BATTELLE MEMORIAL INSTITUTE

## OVERVIEW

Battelle Memorial Institute is one of the world's largest contract research enterprises. The Columbus, Ohio-based not-for-profit trust was established to perform metallurgy research. However, it has diversified into chemicals, agrochemicals, energy, medical products, pharmaceuticals, software, and other areas.

The institute, which works with corporations and governments in nearly 30 countries, was instrumental in developing the photocopy machine, optical digital recording (used with compact discs), and bar codes. Battelle is also a major source of research and development expertise for the US government. It serves the departments of Energy, Defense, and Health and Human Services; the Environmental Protection Agency; and nearly 800 other government organizations.

Battelle is spinning off for-profit companies to benefit its not-for-profit cause; it has shed its medical, flat-panel display, and software units as subsidiaries. Current development projects include cancer prevention, crude oil extraction, and paper mill waste recycling.

## HISTORY

Battelle Memorial Institute was founded with a $1.5 million trust willed by Gordon Battelle, who died in 1923. Battelle was a champion of research for the advancement of humankind, and before taking his father's place as president of several Ohio steel mills, he had funded a former university professor's successful work to extract useful chemicals from mine waste. Battelle's mother, upon her death in 1925, left the institute an additional $2.1 million. The institute opened in 1929.

The institute took on perhaps the most important project in its history in 1944 when it helped an electronics company's patent lawyer, Chester Carlson, find practical uses for his invention, called xerography. Eventually Battelle developed the first photocopy machine, and in 1955 it sold the patent rights for the machine to Haloid (now Xerox) in exchange for royalties.

During WWII Battelle worked on uranium refining for the Manhattan Project, and in the early 1950s it established the world's first private nuclear research facility. The company also set up operations in Germany and Switzerland.

The tax man came knocking in 1961, questioning the tax-free status of some of Battelle's activities. The organization eventually had to pay $47 million. In 1965 Battelle developed a coin with a copper core and a copper-and-nickel-alloy cladding for the US Treasury.

As the result of a ruling that reinterpreted a clause in Gordon Battelle's will, in 1975 the institute gave $80 million to philanthropic enterprises. This ruling, coupled with the taxes that the organization was still unaccustomed to paying, forced Battelle to reexamine its strategy.

Battelle co-developed the Universal Product Code (the bar code symbol found today on nearly all consumer goods packaging) in the 1970s. The institute also landed a lucrative contract from the US Department of Energy (DOE) to manage its commercial nuclear waste isolation program.

In 1987 Battelle chose Douglas Olesen — a 20-year veteran of the institute — to replace retiring CEO Ronald Paul. The company signed an extension with the DOE in 1992 to run its Pacific Northwest Laboratory (which it has operated since 1965).

An Ohio court in 1997 approved a seven-page agreement with the institute outlining the key principles that must be followed according to Gordon Battelle's will. This agreement replaced the 1975 decree and ended more than 20 years of scrutiny by the state Attorney General's Office.

In 1998 the DOE contracted Brookhaven Science Associates — a partnership between the State University of New York and Battelle — to operate Brookhaven National Laboratory. That year a Battelle contract to dispose of Vietnam War-era napalm drew national attention when subcontractor Pollution Control Industries backed out of the project, citing safety concerns. Under Battelle's direction, Houston-based GNI Group took the 3.4 million gallons of napalm off the US Navy's hands.

Battelle and the University of Tennessee in 1999 won a five-year contract to operate the US government's Oak Ridge National Laboratory. That year the institute made several breakthroughs in cancer research, including FDA approval to test an inhalation delivery system for treating lung cancer.

In 2000 the company spun off OmniViz (data mining software) and Battelle Pulmonary Therapeutics (pulmonary and drug delivery technology) as wholly owned subsidiaries. In 2001 Battelle chose former Kodak EVP and chief technology officer Carl Kohrt to replace Olesen that October.

**Chairman:** John B. McCoy Jr.
**First Vice Chairman:** John J. Hopfield
**Second Vice Chairman:** W. George Meredith
**President and CEO:** Carl F. Kohrt, age 57
**EVP, Department of Energy Market Sector; Director, Oak Ridge National Laboratory:** William J. Madia
**EVP, Government Market Sectors:**
Merwyn R. VanderLind
**SVP and Chief Technology Officer, Core Technology Development:** Richard C. Adams
**SVP, CFO, and Treasurer:** Mark W. Kontos
**SVP; Director, Pacific Northwest Laboratory:**
Lura J. Powell
**SVP; General Manager, Automotive Technology Market Sector:** Donald P. McConnell
**SVP; General Manager, Chemical Products Market Sector:** Benjamin G. Maiden
**SVP; General Manager, Energy Products Market Sector:**
Henry J. Cialone
**SVP; General Manager, Pharmaceutical and Medical Products Market Sector:** Richard D. Rosen
**SVP, Administration, General Counsel, and Secretary:**
Jerome R. Bahlmann
**SVP, Organizational Development:** Robert W. Smith Jr.
**President and CEO, Battelle Pulmonary Therapeutics:**
Dennis Cearlock
**VP; General Manager, AgriFood Market Sector:**
Corazon A. Steginsky
**VP; General Manager, Air Force Market Sector:**
Charles E. Lucius
**VP; General Manager, Army/Marines/Office of Secretary of Defense Market Sector:** Stephen E. Kelly
**VP; General Manager, Environment Market Sector:**
Gabor J. Kovacs

## LOCATIONS

**HQ:** 505 King Ave., Columbus, OH 43201
**Phone:** 614-424-6424 **Fax:** 614-424-5263
**Web:** www.battelle.org

Battelle Memorial Institute manages programs in nearly 30 countries. It has major technology centers in Columbus, Ohio; Richland, Washington; Long Island, New York; Oak Ridge, Tennessee; Golden, Colorado; and Geneva.

## PRODUCTS/OPERATIONS

**Selected Inventions**
Automobile cruise control (1960s)
Exploded-tip paintbrush (nylon brush for Wooster Brush Co., 1950)
Golf ball coatings (1965)
Heat Seat (microwaveable heated stadium cushion, 1990s)
Holograms (work began in the 1970s)
Insulin injection pen (for Eli Lilly, 1990s)
Oil spill outline monitor (1992)
PCB-cleaning chemical process (1992)
Photocopy machine (with Haloid, 1940s)
Plastic breakdown process (1990s)
"Sandwich" coins (copper/copper and nickel alloy cladding design for US Treasury, 1965)
SenSonic toothbrush (with Teledyne/WaterPik, 1990s)
Smart cards (cards embedded with tiny computer chips that store information, 1980s)
SnoPake (correction fluid, 1955)
Universal Product Code (co-creator; bar code, 1970s)

**Subsidiaries**
Battelle Pulmonary Therapeutics, Inc.
Geosafe Corporation
Gloabl Transaction Company, Inc.
OmniViz, Inc.
Research Insurance Company Ltd.
Scientific Advances, Inc.
State Science and Technology Institute
Vitex Systems, Inc.

## COMPETITORS

Altran Technologies
The Charles Stark Draper Laboratory
ClinTrials Research
Kendle
MIT
MITRE
PAREXEL
Quintiles Transnational
Research Triangle Institute
SAIC
Southwest Research Institute
SRI International
University of California

## HISTORICAL FINANCIALS & EMPLOYEES

| Not-for-profit FYE: September 30 | Annual Growth | 9/92 | 9/93 | 9/94 | 9/95 | 9/96 | 9/97 | 9/98 | 9/99 | 9/00 | 9/01 |
|---|---|---|---|---|---|---|---|---|---|---|---|
| Sales ($ mil.) | 2.0% | 859 | 869 | 958 | 974 | 945 | 946 | 710 | 901 | 950 | 1,029 |
| Employees | (1.3%) | 8,553 | 8,400 | 8,583 | 7,500 | 7,163 | 7,060 | 7,250 | 7,060 | 7,100 | 7,607 |

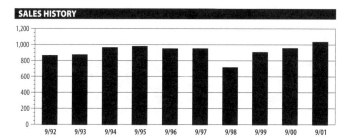

### SALES HISTORY

# BCOM3 GROUP, INC.

## OVERVIEW

As sometimes happens in a marriage, two have become three. Formerly BDM, Chicago-based Bcom3 was formed through the combination of The MacManus Group and The Leo Group in 2000, a merger that created one of the world's largest advertising agencies.

Through its more than 520 operating companies in about 90 countries, Bcom3 provides its clients with advertising, marketing, media planning and buying, and public relations services. Its ad agencies include global networks such as Leo Burnett Worldwide and D'Arcy Masius Benton & Bowles (which does business under the shortened moniker D'Arcy), as well as domestic agencies, including N.W. Ayer and the Kaplan Thaler Group.

The company's Starcom MediaVest unit is one of the largest media buying and planning agencies in the world. Bcom3's clients include Burger King, General Motors, Kellogg's, and Procter & Gamble.

When The Leo Group and The MacManus Group combined to form Bcom3, executives hoped the merged companies could challenge larger rivals like WPP Group and Interpublic for market dominance. The new company also announced plans for an IPO to raise capital for acquisitions to strengthen its position. However, investor uncertainty and a weakening economy forced Bcom3 to delay its public offering. In the interim, the company has been cutting costs and staff to weather a slowdown in ad spending.

Bcom3's top executives and directors, including chairman Roger Haupt, president Craig Brown, and former chairman Roy Bostock, control 78% of the company through a voting trust; Japan's top ad agency Dentsu owns the remaining 22% of Bcom3.

## HISTORY

Bcom3 was formed in 2000 through the merger of The MacManus Group and The Leo Group, bringing together two venerable brands in US advertising: D'Arcy Masius Benton & Bowles and Leo Burnett Worldwide.

D'Arcy traces its roots back to D'Arcy Advertising, an agency formed by William D'Arcy in 1906. With Coca-Cola as an early client, the firm's success attracted other major accounts, including Anheuser-Busch in 1914 and General Tire in 1916. In 1931 D'Arcy launched its signature Christmas campaign for Coca-Cola, featuring Santa with a Coke. It also came up with the slogan "The Pause That Refreshes" in the 1930s. (Coke dropped D'Arcy in the 1950s in favor of McCann-Erickson.) D'Arcy later launched the iconic red and white Budweiser label in 1965 and represented McDonald's in the 1960s until 1970.

In 1971 D'Arcy merged with Detroit's MacManus, John & Adams (MacManus had been founded in 1911 by image advertising pioneer Theodore MacManus) and in 1973 joined UK-based Masius, Wynn-Williams (founded as Masius & Ferguson in 1943). In 1985 D'Arcy-MacManus, Masius (DM&M) merged with New York City's Benton & Bowles (founded in 1929 by William Benton and Chester Bowles) to form D'Arcy Masius Benton & Bowles (DMB&B). After a decade of acquisitions, the agency eventually reorganized under a holding company called The MacManus Group in 1996.

Leo Burnett Worldwide had its beginnings in 1935 when Leo Burnett left Erwin Wasey & Company, one of the top US ad agencies at the time, to start his own firm. He opened his office in Chicago with eight staffers, three clients (Minnesota Valley Canning, Hoover, and Realsilk Hosiery), and a bowl of red apples on the receptionist's desk as a gesture of hospitality. Some said Burnett would soon be selling his apples rather than giving them away, but the agency landed Pillsbury Mill's Farina account in 1944, an assignment that quickly grew to other baking products. Billings surpassed $10 million in 1947. The agency later represented the Oldsmobile brand in the late 1960s and stole the McDonald's account from rival Needham in the 1980s. Leo Burnett reorganized under a holding company called The Leo Group in 1999.

To better compete with mammoth rivals like Interpublic and WPP Group, MacManus and The Leo Group began merger talks in 1999. Those negotiations stalled but later resumed and in 2000 the two companies merged to form BDM. MacManus chairman Roy Bostock and incoming Leo Group CEO Roger Haupt retained those positions in the new company. BDM later sold a 20% stake to top Japanese ad firm Dentsu and changed its name to Bcom3. Executives also announced plans for an IPO. That year the company's Starcom MediaVest unit landed General Motors' $2.9 billion consolidated media buying account.

With a slowing economy and the collapse of the capital funding markets late in 2000, the company eventually shelved its IPO plans in 2001. Haupt later added chairman to his title when Bostock stepped down that year.

**Chairman and CEO:** Roger A. Haupt, age 53,
$2,002,976 pay
**Vice Chairman:** Reiner Erfert
**Vice Chairman and Chief Client Officer:**
Arthur Selkowitz
**President, COO, and Director:** Craig D. Brown,
$1,544,583 pay
**Chief Administrative Officer and Chief Legal Officer:**
Christian E. Kimball, age 45, $673,809 pay
**Chief Information Officer:** William W. Jenks
**EVP and Director Print Development; CEO, Capps
Digital:** Rick Capps, age 47
**EVP Global Corporate Communications:**
Elizabeth Krupnick
**EVP Global Human Resources Director:** Beth Reeves
**Chairman and CEO, Bromley Communications:**
Ernest Bromley
**Chairman and CEO, Leo Burnett Worldwide:**
Linda S. Wolf, age 53
**Chairman and CEO, Manning, Selvage & Lee:**
Lou Capozzi
**Chairman and CEO, NOVO Group:** Kelly A. Rodriques
**Chairman, President, and Chief Branding Officer;
D'Arcy Masius Benton & Bowles:**
Susan McManama Gianinno, age 52
**Chairman, Bartle Bogle Hegarty:** Nigel Bogle
**Chairman, Moroch & Associates:** Tom Moroch
**Vice Chairman and Chief Creative Officer, Leo Burnett
Worldwide:** Michael B. Conrad, age 55
**President and CEO, D'Arcy Masius Benton & Bowles:**
John Farrell, age 43
**President and CEO, Kaplan Thaler Group:**
Linda Kaplan Thaler
**President and CEO, N. W. Ayer & Partners:**
Mary Beth Casey
**Auditors:** Arthur Andersen LLP

**Selected Operations and Operating Units**
Advertising
  Buhler & Partners
  D'Arcy Masius Benton & Bowles
  The Kaplan Thaler Group
  Leo Burnett Worldwide
  N. W. Ayer & Partners
Digital media
  Capps Digital
  Highway One
  NOVO Group
Direct marketing and database services
  Cartwright Williams
  Clarion Marketing & Communications
Ethnic marketing
  Bromley Communications
  Vigilante
Health care marketing
  Medicus Group International
  Williams-Labadie Advertising
Media services
  Starcom MediVest Group
Public relations
  Manning, Selvage & Lee

Grey Global
Hakuhodo
Havas Advertising
Interpublic Group
Omnicom
Publicis
WPP Group

**HQ:** 35 W. Wacker Dr., Chicago, IL 60601
**Phone:** 312-220-1000    **Fax:** 312-220-3299
**Web:** www.bcom3group.com

Bcom3 has more than 520 operating units in about 90
countries.

| Private<br>FYE: December 31 | Annual<br>Growth | 12/91 | 12/92 | 12/93 | 12/94 | 12/95 | 12/96 | 12/97 | 12/98 | 12/99 | 12/00 |
|---|---|---|---|---|---|---|---|---|---|---|---|
| Sales ($ mil.) | — | — | — | — | — | — | — | — | — | — | 1,834 |
| Net income ($ mil.) | — | — | — | — | — | — | — | — | — | — | (66) |
| Income as % of sales | — | — | — | — | — | — | — | — | — | — | — |
| Employees | — | — | — | — | — | — | — | — | — | — | 17,000 |

Debt ratio: 26.9%
Return on equity: —
Cash ($ mil.): 598
Current ratio: 1.12
Long-term debt ($ mil.): 389

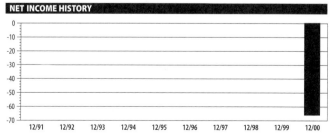

# BECHTEL GROUP, INC.

## OVERVIEW

Whether it's raising an entire city or razing a nuclear power plant, you can bet the Bechtel Group will be there to bid on the business. The engineering, construction, and project management firm, based in San Francisco, is #1 in the US heavy construction industry (ahead of Fluor).

Bechtel builds facilities for diverse industries, ranging from aerospace to civil infrastructure to mining and metals to waste management. The company has made a name for itself on huge projects such as the Hoover Dam and the San Francisco-Oakland Bay Bridge; and on difficult ones, such as the cleanup of the Chernobyl nuclear plant. It completes more than 1,000 projects a year, operating in 66 countries.

In addition to project management and construction, Bechtel offers such services as environmental restoration and remediation, telecommunications (installing cable-optic networks and constructing data centers), and e-business infrastructure (including design, systems integration, and commissioning). Jumping on the international broadband wagon, Bechtel is expanding its telecommunications services into overseas markets. Through Bechtel Enterprises, the company invests in infrastructure projects and arranges financing for its clients.

Chairman and CEO Riley Bechtel is the fourth generation of Bechtels to lead the firm. The Bechtel family still controls the private company.

## HISTORY

In 1898, 25-year-old Warren Bechtel left his Kansas farm to grade railroads in the Oklahoma Indian territories, then followed the rails west. Settling in Oakland, California, he founded his own contracting firm. Foreseeing the importance of roads, oil, and power, he won big projects such as the Northern California Highway and the Bowman Dam. By 1925, when he incorporated his company as W.A. Bechtel & Co., it ranked as the West's largest construction company. In 1931 Bechtel helped found the consortium that built the Hoover Dam.

Steve Bechtel (president after his father's death in 1933) won projects such as the San Francisco Bay Bridge and WWII defense contracts. Noted for his friendships with influential people, including Dwight Eisenhower, Adlai Stevenson, and Saudi Arabia's King Faisal, Steve developed projects that spanned nations and industries, such as pipelines in Saudi Arabia, and numerous power projects. By 1960, when Steve Bechtel Jr. took over, the company operated on six continents.

In the next two decades, Bechtel worked on transportation projects — such as San Francisco's Bay Area Rapid Transit (BART) system and the Washington, DC, subway system — and power projects, including nuclear plants. After the 1979 Three Mile Island accident, Bechtel tried its hand at nuclear cleanup. With nuclear power no longer in vogue, it focused on other markets, such as mining in New Guinea (gold and copper, 1981-84) and China (coal, 1984). Bechtel's Jubail project in Saudi Arabia, begun in 1976, raised an entire industrial port city on the Persian Gulf.

The US recession and the debt of developing countries in the early 1980s sent Bechtel reeling. It cut its workforce by 22,000 and stemmed losses by piling up small projects. One disaster was Bechtel's good fortune. When the Chernobyl nuclear plant exploded in 1986, Bechtel became part of the cleanup team.

Riley Bechtel, great-grandson of Warren, became CEO in 1990. He soon profited from another disaster: After the 1991 Gulf War, Bechtel extinguished Kuwait's flaming oil wells and worked on the oil-spill cleanup. That decade it also worked on such projects as the Channel tunnel (Chunnel) between England and France, the new airport in Hong Kong, and pipelines in the former Soviet Union.

Bechtel was part of the consortium contracted in 1996 to build a high-speed passenger rail line between London and the Chunnel.

That year Bechtel began a venture, Netcon (Thailand), with Lucent to build telecom systems abroad. Bechtel also joined with other companies to buy interests in energy projects in developing regions. In 1998 it won a major contract to construct a gas production plant with Technip in Abu Dhabi.

In 1999 Bechtel was hired to decommission the Connecticut Yankee nuclear plant. The next year Bechtel teamed up with Shell Oil to build a $400 million power plant in Baja California to meet the high demands of the US-Mexico border region. It also formed Nexant, an energy consulting service for the oil and gas industry and utilities.

Bechtel expanded its telecommunications operations in 2001 to provide turnkey network implementation services in Europe, the Middle East, and Asia.

## OFFICERS

**Chairman Emeritus:** Steve Bechtel Jr.
**Chairman and CEO:** Riley P. Bechtel, age 49
**President, COO, and Director:** Adrian Zaccaria
**EVP and Director:** John Carter
**EVP and Director; President and COO, Bechtel Enterprises Holdings:** Paul Unruh
**EVP and Director; President, Bechtel Systems and Infrastructure:** Jude Laspa
**EVP and Director; President, Civil:** Lee McIntire
**EVP and Director; President, Pipeline:** Mike Thiele
**SVP, CFO, and Director:** Georganne Proctor
**SVP, General Counsel, and Director:** Foster Wollen
**SVP and Director:** Tim Statton
**SVP and Manager of Procurement:** Jack Futcher
**President, Bechtel Infrastructure:** John McDonald
**President, Bechtel National:** Tom Hash
**President, Fossil Power:** Scott Ogilvie
**President, Mining and Metals:** Andy Greig
**President, Nuclear Power:** Jim Reinsch
**President, Petroleum and Chemical:** Bill Dudley
**President, Telecommunications and Industrial:** George Conniff
**President, Asia Pacific:** Bob Baxter
**Auditors:** PricewaterhouseCoopers LLP

## LOCATIONS

**HQ:** 50 Beale St., San Francisco, CA 94105
**Phone:** 415-768-1234     **Fax:** 415-768-9038
**Web:** www.bechtel.com

Bechtel Group has offices in 10 states and in Argentina, Australia, Brazil, Canada, Chile, China, Egypt, France, India, Indonesia, Japan, Korea, Malaysia, Mexico, Oman, Peru, the Philippines, Russia, Saudi Arabia, Singapore, Spain, Taiwan, Thailand, Turkey, United Arab Emirates, the UK, and Venezuela.

### 2000 Sales

|  | % of total |
|---|---|
| North America | 53 |
| Europe, Africa, Middle East & Southwest Asia | 23 |
| Asia/Pacific | 15 |
| Latin America | 9 |
| **Total** | **100** |

## PRODUCTS/OPERATIONS

**Selected Services**
Automation technology
Community relations
Environmental health and safety
Equipment operations
International consulting
Labor relations
Project management, engineering, and financing
Worldwide procurement

**Selected Industries Served**
Civil infrastructure
Defense and space
e-Business
Environmental
Government services
Hazardous waste cleanup
Hotels, resorts, and theme parks
Manufacturing
Mining and metals
Petroleum and chemicals
Pipelines
Ports and harbors
Power (fossil and nuclear)
Surface transportation
Telecommunications
Water and wastewater treatment

## COMPETITORS

| | | |
|---|---|---|
| ABB | Hyundai | Philipp |
| AMEC | Engineering | Holzmann |
| Black & Veatch | and | PowerGen |
| Bouygues | Construction | Roy F. Weston |
| CH2M Hill | IT Group | RWE |
| Chicago Bridge | ITOCHU | Safety-Kleen |
| and Iron | Jacobs | Samsung |
| Chiyoda Corp. | Engineering | Schneider |
| Eiffage | Kværner | Shaw Group |
| EllisDon | Marubeni | Siemens |
| Construction | NKK | Skanska |
| Enron | Parsons | Technip-Coflexip |
| Fluor | Perini | URS |
| Foster Wheeler | Peter Kiewit | VINCI |
| Halliburton | Sons' | Washington |
| HOCHTIEF | | Group |

## HISTORICAL FINANCIALS & EMPLOYEES

| Private FYE: December 31 | Annual Growth | 12/91 | 12/92 | 12/93 | 12/94 | 12/95 | 12/96 | 12/97 | 12/98 | 12/99 | 12/00 |
|---|---|---|---|---|---|---|---|---|---|---|---|
| Sales ($ mil.) | 8.7% | — | 7,774 | 7,337 | 7,885 | 8,504 | 8,157 | 11,329 | 12,645 | 12,600 | 15,108 |
| Employees | 3.3% | — | 30,900 | 29,400 | 29,200 | 29,400 | 30,000 | 30,000 | 30,000 | 40,000 | 40,000 |

### SALES HISTORY

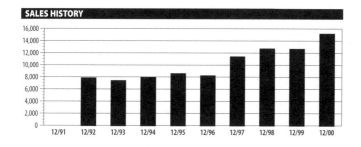

# BELK, INC.

## OVERVIEW

No need to call in Richard Dawson to settle the Belk family feud. The Belk brood, which has not always brimmed with brotherly love, runs the largest privately owned department store chain in the US. With about 210 stores located in 13 southeastern and mid-Atlantic states, Charlotte, North Carolina-based Belk sells moderately priced brand-name and private-label clothing, cosmetics, gifts, and housewares. Some larger Belk stores also have hair salons, restaurants, and optical centers.

In 1998 the firm streamlined its operations by consolidating its gangly network of 112 separate companies, formed over the past century,

into Belk. While some might say a public offering is the logical next step, chairman John Belk has vowed that will not happen while he is alive. The Belk family owns most of the company.

Family feuding nearly toppled the company back in 1952, when founder William Henry Belk died. His six children squabbled over the direction of the company, even suing each other, before making peace. When president Tom Belk died in 1997, the transition went a little more smoothly: His three sons became co-presidents, the third generation of Belk brothers to run the company.

## HISTORY

William Henry Belk didn't mind being known as a cheapskate. At 26 he opened his first store, New York Racket, in 1888 in Monroe, North Carolina. He nicknamed the tiny shop "The Cheapest Store on Earth" and created the slogan "Cheap Goods Sell Themselves." In 1891 Belk convinced his brother John to give up a career as a doctor and join him in the retail business.

The new company, Belk Brothers, opened stores in North and South Carolina, often with partners who were family members or former employees, resulting in many two-family store names such as Belk-Harry and Hudson-Belk.

The Belks formed a partnership with the Leggett family (John's in-laws) in 1920. But feuding between the two families led to a split in 1927. The Leggetts agreed that the Belk family could keep a 20% share of the Leggett stores. John died the next year.

A strict no-credit policy worked in William's favor during the Depression, when he was able to buy out his more lenient competitors for rock-bottom prices. The shrewd businessman grew the chain from 29 stores in 1929 to about 220 stores by 1945, employing concepts such as a no-haggling policy and easy returns. William died in 1952.

That year one of his six children, William Henry Jr., opened a Belk-Lindsey store in Florida using a new format that featured, among other things, an Oriental design. Most of his siblings balked at the store's new look, but William Jr. opened another store in 1953 following the same format.

Two years later four of William Jr.'s siblings — John, Irwin, Tom, and Sarah — cut ties with the Florida stores and formed Belk Stores Services to organize their other stores. Angry at the rebuke, William Jr. and another brother,

Henderson, sued the rest of the family, but they later dropped the lawsuit. In 1956 Belk Stores, with John at the helm, bought out 50-store rival chain Effird.

John had political ambitions and was elected mayor of Charlotte, North Carolina, in 1969, despite attempts by his brother William Jr. to foil the campaign. He remained mayor until 1977. Tom became the company's president in 1980.

Belk Stores continued to hold its own in the 1980s against larger department store chains on the prowl for acquisitions, but the company was stung by family discord and a loose ownership structure. Some relatives sold Belk stores to competitors such as Proffitt's (now Saks Inc.) and Dillard's. Irwin and his family, discouraged about the company's direction, sold their stock to John. In 1996 the Leggetts came back into the fold when Belk Stores bought out their 30-store chain.

Tom died in 1997 after complications from gall bladder surgery. His three sons, Tim, Johnny, and McKay, stepped up as co-presidents but continued to answer to their uncle John, the CEO. Also in 1997 Belk Stores closed its struggling 13-store Tags off-price outlet chain.

A year later the firm reorganized its brood and brought all 112 separate corporations under one company, a move to save money by streamlining the company's accounting (previously it had to fill out tax forms for all 112 businesses) and other operations. Soon after, Belk consolidated its 13 divisional offices into four regional units. Also in 1998 it traded several store locations with Dillard's.

In 1999 Belk formed Belk National Bank in Georgia to manage its credit card operations. In 2001 the company closed four of its distribution centers, consolidating their operations into its new Blythewood, South Carolina center.

## OFFICERS

**Chairman and CEO:** John M. Belk, age 81, $728,000 pay
**Vice Chairman:** B. Frank Matthews II, age 73
**President, Finance, Systems and Operations, and
Director:** John R. Belk, age 42, $535,000 pay
**President, Merchandising and Marketing, and Director:**
H. W. McKay Belk, age 44, $535,000 pay
**President, Store Divisions and Real Estate, and
Director:** Thomas M. Belk Jr., age 46, $535,000 pay
**EVP, Systems:** Robert K. Kerr Jr., age 52
**EVP, Finance:** Brian T. Marley, age 44
**EVP, Secretary, and General Counsel:** Ralph A. Pitts,
age 47, $468,000 pay
**EVP, Real Estate and Store Planning:**
William L. Wilson, age 53
**SVP, Treasurer, and Controller:** Bill R. Walton, age 52
**VP, Human Resources:** Carolyn McGinnis
**Auditors:** KPMG LLP

## LOCATIONS

**HQ:** 2801 W. Tyvola Rd., Charlotte, NC 28217
**Phone:** 704-357-1000        **Fax:** 704-357-1876
**Web:** www.belk.com

| 2001 Stores | No. |
|---|---|
| North Carolina | 74 |
| Georgia | 39 |
| South Carolina | 38 |
| Virginia | 19 |
| Florida | 18 |
| Kentucky | 4 |
| Alabama | 3 |
| Tennessee | 3 |
| Arkansas | 2 |
| Maryland | 2 |
| Texas | 2 |
| West Virginia | 2 |
| Mississippi | 1 |
| **Total** | **207** |

## PRODUCTS/OPERATIONS

**Private Labels**
Andhurst

Home Accents
J.Khakis
Kim Rogers
Madison Studio
Meeting Street
Nursery Rhyme
Saddlebred

## COMPETITORS

Dillard's
Dunlap
Elder-Beerman Stores
Federated
Jacobson Stores
J. C. Penney
Kohl's
May
Saks Inc.
Sears
Stein Mart
Target
TJX
Wal-Mart

## HISTORICAL FINANCIALS & EMPLOYEES

| Private<br>FYE: January 31 | Annual<br>Growth | 1/92 | 1/93 | 1/94 | 1/95 | 1/96 | 1/97 | 1/98 | 1/99 | 1/00 | 1/01 |
|---|---|---|---|---|---|---|---|---|---|---|---|
| Sales ($ mil.) | 4.0% | — | 1,662 | 1,674 | 1,694 | 1,685 | 1,773 | 1,974 | 2,091 | 2,145 | 2,270 |
| Net income ($ mil.) | 0.3% | — | 56 | 54 | 49 | 44 | 101 | 54 | 57 | 57 | 57 |
| Income as % of sales | — | — | 3.4% | 3.2% | 2.9% | 2.6% | 5.7% | 2.8% | 2.7% | 3.3% | 2.5% |
| Employees | (4.3%) | — | — | — | — | — | 25,000 | 29,000 | 22,000 | 21,000 | 21,000 |

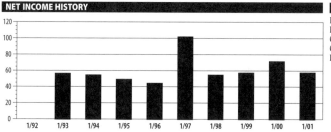

**NET INCOME HISTORY**

**2001 FISCAL YEAR-END**
Debt ratio: 33.8%
Return on equity: 6.7%
Cash ($ mil.): 28
Current ratio: 3.01
Long-term debt ($ mil.): 442

# BILL & MELINDA GATES FOUNDATION

Microsoft founder and chairman Bill Gates doesn't mind spreading his billions around. Through their Seattle-based charitable trust — the Bill & Melinda Gates Foundation — one of the world's richest couples helps a variety of selected causes. Gates' foundation is the largest in the world with an endowment of $24 billion. Gates has said he would like to give away most of his fortune while he is still living. According to federal law, tax-exempt foundations must give away at least 5% of their total assets every year.

The foundation was formed in 1999 when the William H. Gates Foundation (created in 1994) and the Gates Learning Foundation were consolidated. The foundation donates money toward a number of different areas: world health issues (including vaccination of the world's poorest children), library computer programs, and projects in the Pacific Northwest.

Some of the foundation's beneficiaries have included the Global Health Council, Helen Keller International, International Planned Parenthood, the International Vaccine Institute, the National Institute of Child Health and Human Development, the Pacific Institute for Women's Health, and the United Negro College Fund. The foundation also has the Gates Millennium Scholars Program, which plans to provide scholarships to 20,000 minority students over the next 20 years.

Bill Gates created the William H. Gates Foundation in 1994 with $106 million. During the next four years, he added about $2 billion to the charity. He appointed his father the head of the foundation, which at first was housed in Bill Gates Sr.'s basement.

In 1997 Gates established the Gates Learning Foundation (originally called the Gates Library Foundation), a philanthropic effort to improve technology and Internet access at libraries. Some of Gates' critics saw the effort as a way for him to plant Microsoft software at libraries nationwide. Patty Stonesifer, a former executive at Microsoft, ran the organization from an office above a pizza parlor.

During 1998 the Gates Learning Foundation provided funding and computers for approximately 1,000 libraries. Also that year the Gateses donated $20 million to Duke University, Melinda Gates' alma mater. At the end of 1998 the couple established the Bill and Melinda Gates Children's Vaccine program with an initial grant of $100 million.

In 1999 Gates decided to merge his two charity programs into one entity: the Bill & Melinda Gates Foundation, to be run by the elder Gates and Stonesifer. Bill and his wife Melinda contributed some $16 billion to the foundation that year, making it the largest philanthropic foundation in the world.

In early 2000 Gates made another $5 billion gift of stock to the foundation. That year a federal judge ordered that Microsoft be split up. That ruling was eventually struck down, and Microsoft reached a settlement with the US Justice Department. What effect, if any, Microsoft's legal wranglings will have on the foundation is unclear. (Most of its donations come in the form of stock that is then converted to cash.) In 2000 the foundation pledged $10 million toward construction of an underground visitors center at Capitol Hill in Washington, DC.

The Bill & Melinda Gates Foundation donated another $10 million in 2001 to be awarded over three years to the Hope for African Children Initiative, which will help African children affected by AIDS. Also in 2001 the foundation gave a five-year, $1 million grant to Smith College to support a residency program for five African scholars. The program will provide fellowships for faculty members from universities in Africa at Amherst, Hampshire, Mount Holyoke, and Smith, and the University of Massachusetts. Also that year Bill and Melinda Gates donated another $2 billion to the foundation, boosting its endowment to nearly $24 billion.

In 2002 the foundation gave a grant of $7.5 million to The Alan Guttmacher Institute to develop a five-year research program to study youth attitudes toward sex and to improve programs designed to prevent HIV/AIDS in Sub-Saharan Africa as well as worldwide.

**Co-Founder and Trustee:** William H. Gates III, age 45
**Co-Founder:** Melinda French Gates, age 35
**Co-Chairman and CEO:** William H. Gates Sr.
**Co-Chairman and President:** Patricia Q. Stonesifer,
age 44
**CFO and Administrative Officer:** Allan C. Golston
**Executive Director, Education:** Tom Vander Ark
**Executive Director, Libraries and Public Access to
Information:** Richard Akeroyd
**EVP:** Sylvia Mathews
**Director, Global Health Program:** Gordon W. Perkin
**Director, Human Resources:** Julie Olson
**Senior Program Officer, Pacific Northwest Giving:**
Jaime Garcia

## LOCATIONS

**HQ:** 1551 Eastlake Ave. East, Seattle, WA 98102
**Phone:** 206-709-3100      **Fax:** 206-709-3180
**Web:** www.gatesfoundation.org

## PRODUCTS/OPERATIONS

**2000 Grant Distribution**

|  | % of total |
|---|---|
| Global health | 48 |
| Education | 28 |
| Special projects | 17 |
| Libraries & public access to information | 5 |
| Pacific Northwest | 2 |
| **Total** | **100** |

**Selected Beneficiaries**

Alliance for Cervical Cancer Prevention ($3.9 million
over two years)
Gay City Health Project ($30,000 over three years)
Global Health Council ($4.8 million over three years)
Helen Keller International ($5 million over five years)
International Planned Parenthood Federation
($8.8 million over five years)
International Tuberculosis Foundation ($1.9 million
over five years)
International Vaccine Institute ($40 million over five
years)
Library and Information Commission ($4.2 million over
one year)
National Institute of Child Health and Human
Development ($15 million over five years)
Oxfam ($2.9 million over four years)
Pacific Institute for Women's Health ($1 million over
three years)
Population Council ($4 million over two years)
Portland Children's Museum ($600,000 over three years)
United Negro College Fund ($1 billion over 20 years)
US Fund for UNICEF ($15 million over five years)

## HISTORICAL FINANCIALS & EMPLOYEES

| Foundation<br>FYE: December 31 | Annual<br>Growth | 3/91 | 3/92 | 3/93 | 3/94 | 3/95 | 3/96 | 3/97 | 3/98 | *12/99 | 12/00 |
|---|---|---|---|---|---|---|---|---|---|---|---|
| Sales ($ mil.) | 54.2% | — | — | — | — | — | — | — | 128 | 276 | 304 |
| Employees | 73.2% | — | — | — | — | — | — | — | 2 | 4 | 6 |

\* Fiscal year change

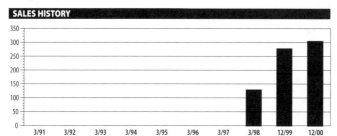

### SALES HISTORY

BILL & MELINDA
GATES *foundation*

# BLOOMBERG L.P.

## OVERVIEW

Spreading the lowdown on the financial world through virtually every aspect of modern media, Bloomberg is brimming with business information. Foremost among the New York City-based company's products are its Bloomberg proprietary terminals, which provide institutional investors and other users with real-time, around-the-clock news, market data, and analysis. With more than 156,000 terminals installed (at a monthly rate of $1,285 each), Bloomberg ranks as one of the world's largest providers of such devices. It serves more than 400,000 customers in 126 countries.

Although terminals generate most of the company's sales, Bloomberg distributes financial news and information through many other channels in an effort to build its brand and keep up with the intense competition. It provides a syndicated news service (Bloomberg News); publishes books and magazines; and broadcasts business information via TV, radio, and the Internet.

In addition to the company's media products, Bloomberg also offers the Bloomberg Tradebook (an order-matching system) and the Bloomberg Trading and Bloomberg Portfolio Trading systems.

Founder Michael Bloomberg left the company in 2001 before taking office as the mayor of New York City. Bloomberg controls the company. Merrill Lynch holds a 20% interest.

## HISTORY

By the mid-1970s Michael Bloomberg had worked his way up to head of equity trading and sales at New York investment powerhouse Salomon Brothers. He left Salomon in 1981, just after the firm went private, cashing out with $10 million for his partnership interest.

Bloomberg founded Innovative Marketing Systems and spent the next year developing the Bloomberg terminal, which allowed users to manipulate bond data. In 1982 he pitched it to Merrill Lynch, which bought 20 machines. Regular production of the terminals began in 1984, and in 1985, Merrill Lynch invested $39 million in the company to gain a 30% stake. The company prospered during the 1980s boom, and over time the data, not the machines, became the heart of the business. It was renamed Bloomberg L.P. in 1986.

The company weathered the stock market crash of 1987, opening offices in London and Tokyo. Bloomberg made its entry into newsgathering and delivery in 1990 when Bloomberg News began broadcasting on its terminals. The company built its news organization from scratch, hiring away reporters from such publications as *The Wall Street Journal* and *Forbes*. Bloomberg bought a New York radio station in 1992 and converted it to an all-news format. The next year it built an in-house TV studio and created a business news show for PBS. A satellite TV station followed in 1994, along with a personal finance magazine.

In 1995 Bloomberg began offering business information via its Web site. The company also introduced the Bloomberg Tradebook, an electronic securities-trading venue designed to compete with Reuters' Instinet. (In 1997 Tradebook was approved by the SEC for use in connection with some Nasdaq-listed stocks.) Bloomberg also started offering its services to subscribers in a PC-compatible format and selling its data to other news purveyors, such as LexisNexis (an online information service).

In 1996 Michael Bloomberg bought back 10% of the company from Merrill Lynch for $200 million, giving Bloomberg L.P. an estimated market value of $2 billion. The company agreed in 1997 to supply the daytime programming for Paxson Communications' New York TV station WPXN. When Bridge Information Systems bought Dow Jones Markets from Dow Jones in 1998, Bridge surpassed Bloomberg in number of financial information terminals installed. But Bloomberg continued expanding its offerings through strategic agreements with Internet companies such as America Online (now AOL Time Warner) and CNET Networks, and through the introduction of *Bloomberg Money*, a personal finance magazine.

In 1999 Bloomberg secured a deal with the Australian stock exchange that would allow its terminals to facilitate international order routing into the Australian market. The company also expanded its presence in the Spanish-language market through its agreement with CBS Telenoticias to produce a TV news program Lynch's institutional e-commerce portal available to Bloomberg customers.

The company established Bloomberg Index License in 2001, which creates and licenses indices to fund managers, stock exchanges, and other clients. Also that year Michael Bloomberg was elected mayor of New York City. He left his namesake company before taking office.

## OFFICERS

**Founder:** Michael R. Bloomberg, age 59
**Chairman:** Peter T. Grauer, age 55
**COO:** Lex Fenwick
**Human Resources:** Linda Norris
**Head of Affiliate Relations & Marketing:** Michael Rosen

## LOCATIONS

**HQ:** 499 Park Ave., New York, NY 10022
**Phone:** 212-318-2000 **Fax:** 212-893-5999
**Web:** www.bloomberg.com

Bloomberg has offices in New York City; Princeton, New Jersey; and San Francisco; as well as Frankfurt; Hong Kong; Sao Paulo; Singapore; Sydney; and Tokyo.

## PRODUCTS/OPERATIONS

**Selected Products and Services**
Bloomberg Data License (financial database service)
Bloomberg Energy (Web site focusing on energy)
Bloomberg Index License (indices creation and licensing)
*Bloomberg Investimenti* (financial publication focusing on Italian finance)
*Bloomberg Magazine* (financial magazine)
*Bloomberg Money* (financial magazine for European investors)
Bloomberg News (syndicated news service)
*Bloomberg Personal Finance* (personal finance magazine)
Bloomberg Portfolio Trading System (asset management tool)
Bloomberg Press (book publishing)
Bloomberg Pro (wireless access to news and information)
Bloomberg Professional Service (24-hour, real-time financial information system)
Bloomberg Radio (syndicated radio news service)
Bloomberg Television (24-hour news channel and syndicated reports)
Bloomberg Tradebook (equities trading technology)
Bloomberg Trading System (Bloomberg information combined with trading technology)
*Bloomberg Wealth Manager* (magazine for financial planners and investment advisers)
Bloomberg.com (Web site)

## COMPETITORS

| | |
|---|---|
| Agence France-Presse | MarketWatch.com |
| Associated Press | Media General |
| Dow Jones | Multex.com |
| FactSet | Reuters |
| Forbes | TheStreet.com |
| Interactive Data | Thomson Corporation |
| Intuit | |

## HISTORICAL FINANCIALS & EMPLOYEES

| Private<br>FYE: December 31 | Annual<br>Growth | 12/91 | 12/92 | 12/93 | 12/94 | 12/95 | 12/96 | 12/97 | 12/98 | 12/99 | 12/00 |
|---|---|---|---|---|---|---|---|---|---|---|---|
| Estimated sales ($ mil.) | 32.8% | — | 290 | 370 | 550 | 650 | 760 | 1,300 | 1,500 | 2,300 | 2,800 |
| Employees | 26.5% | — | 1,100 | 1,800 | 2,000 | 2,500 | 3,000 | 4,000 | 4,900 | 5,150 | 7,200 |

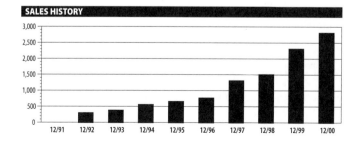

**SALES HISTORY**

**Bloomberg**

# BLUE CROSS AND BLUE SHIELD

## OVERVIEW

The rise of managed health care has had some of its members singing the blues, but Blue Cross and Blue Shield Association still has major market power. The Chicago-based association governs some 45 chapters that offer health care coverage to more than 80 million Americans via indemnity insurance, HMOs, PPOs, point-of-service (POS) plans, and Medicare plans.

While some Blues always faced competition head-on, most received tax benefits for taking all comers. But as lower-cost plans attracted the hale and hearty, the Blues' customers became older, sicker, and more expensive.

With their quasi-charitable status and outdated rate structures, many Blues lost market share.

They have fought back by merging among themselves, creating for-profit subsidiaries, forming alliances with for-profit enterprises, or dropping their not-for-profit status and going public — while still using the Blue Cross Blue Shield name. A history of tax breaks complicates these efforts and usually requires the creation of charitable foundations. As a result, the umbrella association is becoming a licensing and brand-marketing entity. The conversion of the Blues to for-profit status is sparking a backlash by consumer organizations.

## HISTORY

Blue Cross was born in 1929, when Baylor University official Justin Kimball offered schoolteachers 21 days of hospital care for $6 a year. A major plan feature was a community rating system that based premiums on the community claims experience rather than members' conditions.

The Blue Cross symbol was devised in 1933 by Minnesota plan executive E. A. van Steenwyck. By 1935 many of the 15 plans in 11 states used the symbol. Many states gave the plans non-profit status, and in 1936 the American Hospital Association formed the Committee on Hospital Service (renamed the Blue Cross Association in 1948) to coordinate them.

As Blue Cross grew, state medical societies sponsored prepaid plans to cover doctors' fees. In 1946 they united under the aegis of the American Medical Association (AMA) as the Associated Medical Care Plans (later the Association of Blue Shield Plans).

In 1948 the AMA thwarted a Blue Cross attempt to merge with Blue Shield. But the Blues increasingly cooperated on public policy matters while competing for members, and each Blue formed a not-for-profit corporation to coordinate its plan's activities.

By 1960 Blue Cross insured about a third of the US. Over the next decade the Blues started administering Medicare and other government health plans, and by 1970 half of Blue Cross' premiums came from government entities.

In the 1970s the Blues adopted such cost-control measures as a review of hospital admissions; many plans even abandoned the community rating system. Most began emphasizing preventive care in HMOs or PPOs. The two Blues finally merged in 1982, but this had little effect on the associations' bottom lines as losses grew.

By the 1990s the Blues were big business. Some of the state associations offered officers high salaries and perks but still insisted on special regulatory treatment.

Blue Cross of California became the first chapter to give up its tax-free status when it was bought by WellPoint Health Networks, a managed care subsidiary it had founded in 1992. In a 1996 deal, WellPoint became the chapter's parent and converted it to for-profit status, assigning all of the stock to a public charitable foundation which received the proceeds of its subsequent IPO. WellPoint also bought the group life and health division of Massachusetts Mutual Life Insurance.

The for-profit switches picked up in 1997. Blue Cross of Connecticut merged with insurance provider Anthem, and other mergers followed. Half the nation's Blues formed an alliance called BluesCONNECT, competing with national health plans by offering employers one nationwide benefits organization. The association also pursued overseas licensing agreements in Europe, South America, and Asia, assembling a network of Blue Cross-friendly caregivers aiming for worldwide coverage.

In 1998 Blues in more than 35 states sued the nation's big cigarette companies to recoup the costs of treating smoking-related illnesses. In a separate lawsuit, Blue Cross and Blue Shield of Minnesota received nearly $300 million from the tobacco industry. In 1999 Anthem moved to acquire or affiliate with Blues in Colorado, Maine, and New Hampshire.

In 2000, after years of discussions, the New York State Attorney General permitted Empire Blue Cross and Blue Shield to convert to for-profit status.

## OFFICERS

**Chairman:** Michael B. Unhjem
**President and CEO:** Scott P. Serota
**SVP, Corporate Secretary, and General Counsel:**
Roger G. Wilson
**SVP, Policy, Representation, and Membership Services:**
Mary Nell Lehnhard
**VP, Finance and Administration:** Ralph Rambach
**VP, Human Resources:** Bill Colbourne
**Auditors:** PricewaterhouseCoopers LLP

## LOCATIONS

**HQ:** Blue Cross and Blue Shield Association
225 N. Michigan Ave., Chicago, IL 60601
**Phone:** 312-297-6000    **Fax:** 312-297-6609
**Web:** www.bcbs.com

The Blue Cross and Blue Shield Association has offices
in Chicago and Washington, DC, with licensees
operating throughout the US as well as in Africa,
Australia, Asia, Canada, Latin America, the Middle East,
and western Europe.

## PRODUCTS/OPERATIONS

**Selected Operations**
BlueCard Worldwide (care of US members in foreign
countries)
BluesCONNECT (nationwide alliance)
Federal Employee Health Benefits Program (federal
employees and retirees)
Health maintenance organizations
Medicare management
Point-of-service programs
Preferred provider organizations

## COMPETITORS

Aetna
CIGNA
Health Net
Humana
Kaiser Foundation
Oxford Health Plans
PacifiCare
Prudential
UniHealth
UnitedHealth Group

## HISTORICAL FINANCIALS & EMPLOYEES

| Association<br>FYE: December 31 | Annual<br>Growth | 12/91 | 12/92 | 12/93 | 12/94 | 12/95 | 12/96 | 12/97 | 12/98 | 12/99 | 12/00 |
|---|---|---|---|---|---|---|---|---|---|---|---|
| Sales ($ mil.) | 7.4% | — | 70,913 | 71,161 | 71,414 | 74,400 | 75,200 | 76,500 | 94,700 | 93,700 | 126,000 |
| Employees | 0.6% | — | 143,000 | 135,883 | 146,352 | 146,000 | 150,000 | 150,000 | 150,000 | 150,000 | 150,000 |

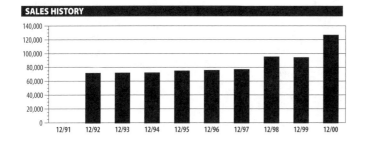

### SALES HISTORY

**Blue Cross
Blue Shield**

# BLUE CROSS MASSACHUSETTS

## OVERVIEW

Back to black, Blue Cross and Blue Shield of Massachusetts (BCBSMA) is feeling in the pink. The Boston-based health insurer is battling its way back to financial health (selling noncore businesses and reducing staff) after spending recent years in the red.

BCBSMA offers groups and individuals traditional indemnity insurance, HMOs, and medical PPO coverage. It also teams up with other regional Blues to offer plans HMO Blue New England and Blue Choice New England, which feature discounts at some health clubs.

Like Blues nationwide, BCBSMA has been hit hard by competition. It is now refocusing on its core business (health insurance) through divestitures and new products. BCBSMA is also keen to form a regional alliance with other New England Blues.

## HISTORY

The predecessor of the Blue Cross Association was founded in Dallas in 1929 to allow teachers to prepay for hospitalization. The idea spread quickly during the Depression. By 1937, when its 26th affiliate was founded in Massachusetts, the organization had become associated with the Blue Cross logo. Fairly priced by Depression standards, Blue Cross pegged its premiums to care costs in each region rather than underwriting each policyholder or group individually.

Seeing the success of Blue Cross, doctors joined up to offer similar prepayment plans known together as the Blue Shield Association. Doctor participation in Massachusetts was so widespread that members had a nearly unlimited choice of physicians.

Blue Cross and Blue Shield worked almost as one unit in Massachusetts but remained legally separate. At first they limited memberships to groups, but during the 1940s they began accepting individuals. In the 1960s the groups became co-administrators of the state's Medicare program. The Medex program was started in 1966 to supplement Medicare, but later evolved to encompass a state-mandated program for the medically indigent elderly. During the 1970s the companies began creating HMOs, but mostly for rural areas.

The groups continued to dominate Massachusetts health care in the 1980s. By the decade's end, however, the Massachusetts Blues had hit hard times, suffering lost market share, bloated management, and antiquated systems. As Blues in other states merged, competitors repeatedly blocked efforts to join the two Massachusetts organizations. Both Blues lost money from 1986 to 1988.

Efforts to help the situation only made matters worse (a failed upgrade of Blue Cross' information systems was abandoned in 1992 after six years and $100 million). The groups' efforts to drive harder bargains with hospitals led to cries that the plans were trying to force rejected hospitals out of business.

In 1988 the organizations were at last allowed to merge. William Van Faasen became CEO in 1990, charged with reengineering BCBSMA. For five years his efforts seemed to work. But the Medex segment was an earnings vacuum, and the new management drew criticism for hefty pay raises.

Blaming Medex, BCBSMA lost $90 million in 1996, which led the state insurance commissioner to step in and oversee its operations.

To make money like a regular health care company, BCBSMA started acting like a regular health care company — it slashed 16% of its workforce, enforced 10% pay cuts for those executives who survived a year-long purge, sold 10 clinics (to what is now Caremark Rx), and attempted to cancel 7,000 policies.

In 1998 BCBSMA agreed to pay $9.5 million to settle lawsuits that it overcharged Massachusetts subscribers for medical care. It also agreed in 1999 to pay $4.75 million to reimburse the US government for claims paid on people who were actually covered by BCBSMA. In the meantime, it created a new health insurance plan, Access Blue (launched in 2000), that lets patients see specialists without referrals. The plan has met resistance from hospitals and doctors, who consider its premiums too low to be financially viable.

BCBSMA filed to divide its operations into three companies, a move shot down by state legislators in 1998. Meanwhile, for-profit Blues licensees like Anthem continue to buy Blues (including those in Connecticut and New Hampshire). BCBSMA is pursuing affiliation with other not-for-profit regional Blues, although its attempt to do so in Rhode Island was rejected by the state's attorney general. In 2000, BCBSMA put its dental insurance product up for sale and got state permission to enter the reinsurance business.

## OFFICERS

**Chairman:** Milton L. Glass
**Vice Chairman:** Robert J. Haynes
**President and CEO:** William C. Van Faasen, age 53
**COO:** Arthur E. Banks
**VP, Human Resources:** Robert Martin
**Chief Actuary:** Bruce W. Butler
**EVP and Chief Legal Officer:** Sandra J. Carter
**SVP, Corporate Relations:** Fredi Shonkoff
**CFO:** Allen P. Maltz
**EVP, Healthcare Services:** Sharon L. Smith
**SVP, Corporate Planning and Development:**
  Phyllis L. Baron
**EVP, Sales, Marketing, and Services:** Stephen R. Booma
**EVP, Corporate Affairs:** Peter G. Meade
**Auditors:** Ernst & Young LLP

## LOCATIONS

**HQ:** Blue Cross and Blue Shield of Massachusetts, Inc.
  LandMark Center 401 Park Dr., Boston, MA 02215
**Phone:** 617-246-5000      **Fax:** 617-246-4347
**Web:** www.bcbsma.com

## PRODUCTS/OPERATIONS

**Selected Services**
Access Blue (managed care plan)
Blue Care Elect Preferred (managed care plan)
Blue Choice (managed care plan)
Blue Choice New England (regional managed care)
Comprehensive Major Medical (traditional plan)
Dental Blue
Dental Blue PPO
Direct Blue (nongroup plans)
HMO Blue (statewide managed care)
HMO Blue New England (regional managed care)
Medex (Medicare supplement)

## COMPETITORS

Aetna
Anthem
CIGNA
Harvard Pilgrim
Prudential
Tufts Health Plan

## HISTORICAL FINANCIALS & EMPLOYEES

| Not-for-profit<br>FYE: December 31 | Annual<br>Growth | 12/91 | 12/92 | 12/93 | 12/94 | 12/95 | 12/96 | 12/97 | 12/98 | 12/99 | 12/00 |
|---|---|---|---|---|---|---|---|---|---|---|---|
| Sales ($ mil.) | (2.8%) | — | 3,397 | 3,792 | 3,595 | 3,575 | 3,504 | 2,123 | 2,041 | 2,120 | 2,700 |
| Employees | (10.9%) | — | 6,559 | 6,171 | 5,865 | 5,630 | 5,500 | 2,756 | 2,579 | 2,601 | 2,601 |

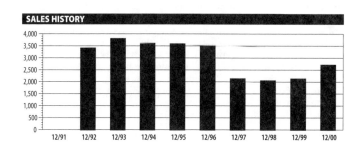

SALES HISTORY

Blue Cross
Blue Shield

# BLUE CROSS OF MICHIGAN

## OVERVIEW

For Detroit-based Blue Cross Blue Shield of Michigan (BCBSM, also known as Michigan Blues), operating a "profitable" not-for-profit is a constant struggle. BCBSM is one of the nation's top Blue Cross Blue Shield health insurance associations, serving more than 4.7 million members, including workers at automakers General Motors and Ford.

BCBSM offerings include Blue Traditional (fee for service), Preferred and Community Blue PPOs, and Blue Care Network (HMO). It also owns Preferred Provider Organization of Michigan, a for-profit subsidiary that provides private health care management services.

While other Blues have converted to for-profit status or have teamed up with for-profit companies to become more competitive, BCBSM is committed to remaining not-for-profit. Rate hikes have helped get the company's insurance operations back into the black, and it plans to continue raising rates to keep up with the skyrocketing costs of health care.

## HISTORY

The history of prepaid medical care began in 1929, when Baylor University Hospital administrator Justin Kimball developed a plan to offer schoolteachers 21 days of hospital care for $6 a year. Fundamental to the plan was a community rating system, which based premiums on the community's claims experience rather than subscribers' conditions.

A similar program was started in Michigan in 1938 when a group of hospitals formed the Michigan Society for Group Hospitalization, which became the Michigan Hospital Service and later became a chapter of the national Blue Cross association. The health care plan was funded by local hospitals and private grants. (A group of private donors, including Oldsmobile automotive founder Ransom Olds, loaned the group $5,000.)

The state insurance commission approved tax-exempt status for the Michigan Blue Cross in 1939. Nine days after opening a three-person office in Detroit, Blue Cross landed its first customer, insurance company John Hancock Mutual Life. John Hancock's Detroit branch manager became the first subscriber, paying $1.90 per month for 21 days of hospitalization coverage for his family of eight.

Due in part to the addition of Chrysler, Ford, and General Motors to its health plans, Blue Cross grew from less than 1 million members in the 1940s to more than 3 million in the 1950s. In 1945 it began to offer coverage for individuals; 14 years later the association started to offer policies to seniors who were ineligible for group coverage. Blue Cross took over operation of Michigan's Medicare program in 1966.

Michigan's Blue Cross merged with longtime partner Blue Shield in 1975 to create Blue Cross Blue Shield of Michigan, with a total of 5 million subscribers. Blue Shield, a prepayment plan that covered doctors' services, had been started in 1939 by the Michigan State Medical Society (a group of Michigan physicians).

As overseas competition forced automakers to cut their employment rolls, Blue Cross Blue Shield of Michigan's membership contracted. BCBSM chairman John McCabe, realizing the need to generate additional revenue, pushed for an end to the company's not-for-profit status in the 1980s but was rejected by the Michigan legislature. This failure was at least partially behind McCabe's resignation in 1987.

The struggling Michigan Blues moved towards profitability in 1994 when the state legislature specially authorized its $291 million purchase of the for-profit State Accident Fund, the state's workers' compensation program. It also lost its large, but hard-to-manage state Medicare contract to Blue Cross Blue Shield of Illinois (now Health Care Service Corporation). In 1996 the company reorganized, with a division for Michigan residents and one for nationwide accounts. In 1997 BCBSM continued its efforts to increase revenue by acquiring private health management company Preferred Provider Organization of Michigan, which operates in Michigan and nearby states. BCBSM president and CEO Richard Whitmer announced that he was willing to compete with other Blues in bordering states.

In 1998 Blue Cross Blue Shield of Michigan consolidated four regional HMOs into a single statewide HMO, the Blue Care Network. Costs of the merger and growing losses in drug coverage constrained earnings, but were counterweighted by returns on assets invested in the stock market. In 1999 and 2000 the company rankled Detroit's small business owners with double-digit premium hikes.

## OFFICERS

**Chairman:** Charles L. Burkett
**President and CEO:** Richard E. Whitmer
**SVP and CFO:** Mark R. Bartlett
**SVP and Chief Information Officer:** Raymond R. Khan
**SVP, General Counsel, and Secretary:** Steven C. Hess
**SVP, Auto/National Business Unit:** Leslie A. Viegas
**SVP, Health Care Products and Provider Services:**
Marianne Udow
**SVP, Human Resources, and Chief Administration**
**Officer:** George F. Francis III
**SVP, Michigan Sales and Services:** J. Paul Austin
**SVP, Corporate Communications:** Richard T. Cole
**Auditors:** Deloitte & Touche LLP

## LOCATIONS

**HQ:** Blue Cross Blue Shield of Michigan
600 E. Lafayette Blvd., Detroit, MI 48226
**Phone:** 313-225-8000     **Fax:** 313-225-5629
**Web:** www.bcbsm.com

## PRODUCTS/OPERATIONS

**Selected Health Care Plans**
Blue Care Network (health maintenance)
Blue Choice (point of service)
Blue MedSave (prescription plan)
Blue Preferred PPO (preferred provider for auto industry
workers)
Blue Traditional (prepayment)
Blue Vision PPO
Community Blue PPO
Community Dental
Medicare Blue HMO
Personal Plus HMO
Preferred Rx (prescription plan)
Traditional Dental
Traditional Rx (prescription plan)
Traditional Vision Coverage

## COMPETITORS

Aetna
Anthem
CIGNA
Henry Ford Health System
Humana
United American
 Healthcare
UnitedHealth Group

## HISTORICAL FINANCIALS & EMPLOYEES

| Not-for-profit FYE: December 31 | Annual Growth | 12/91 | 12/92 | 12/93 | 12/94 | 12/95 | 12/96 | 12/97 | 12/98 | 12/99 | 12/00 |
|---|---|---|---|---|---|---|---|---|---|---|---|
| Sales ($ mil.) | 6.9% | — | 6,177 | 6,193 | 6,411 | 6,926 | 7,001 | 7,731 | 8,432 | 9,487 | 10,507 |
| Net income ($ mil.) | (8.4%) | — | — | 120 | 71 | 154 | 101 | 43 | 83 | 89 | 65 |
| Income as % of sales | — | — | — | 1.9% | 1.1% | 2.2% | 1.4% | 0.6% | 1.0% | 0.9% | 0.6% |
| Employees | 1.2% | — | — | 8,417 | 8,415 | 6,500 | 7,980 | 8,827 | — | — | — |

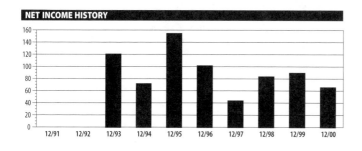

NET INCOME HISTORY

Blue Cross
Blue Shield

# BOOZ-ALLEN & HAMILTON INC.

## OVERVIEW

Governments all over the world use plenty of Booz. McLean, Virginia-based Booz-Allen & Hamilton provides government agencies and *FORTUNE* 500 companies with international management and technology consulting expertise. The firm operates in two segments: worldwide technology business and worldwide commercial business. Its technology business unit covers such areas as defense and national security, the environment, transportation, and space. The commercial unit includes consumer and engineered products;

communications, media, and technology; energy; and financial services.

Booz-Allen's gargantuan staff of more than 11,000 covers the US and more than 30 other countries through more than 100 offices. The rising tide of privatization in many foreign governments has provided an increasing source of consulting work for the company, and Booz has plenty of experience working with governments. The US government is the company's largest customer, accounting for about 60% of revenue.

## HISTORY

Edwin Booz graduated from Northwestern University in 1914 with degrees in economics and psychology and started a statistical analysis firm in Chicago. After serving in the army during WWI, he returned to his firm, renamed Edwin Booz Surveys. In 1925 Booz hired his first full-time assistant, George Fry, and in 1929 he hired a second, James Allen. By then the company had a long list of clients, including U.S. Gypsum, the *Chicago Tribune,* and Montgomery Ward, which was losing a retail battle with Sears, Roebuck and Co.

In 1935 Carl Hamilton joined the partnership, and a year later it was renamed Booz, Fry, Allen & Hamilton. The firm prospered well into the next decade by providing advice based on "independence that enables us to say plainly from the outside what cannot always be said safely from within," according to a company brochure.

During WWII the firm worked increasingly on government and military contracts. Fry opposed the pursuit of such work for consultants and left in 1942. The firm was renamed Booz, Allen & Hamilton. Hamilton died in 1946, and the following year Booz retired (he died in 1951), leaving Allen as chairman. He successfully steered the firm into lucrative postwar work for clients such as Johnson Wax, RCA, and the US Air Force.

A separate company, Booz, Allen Applied Research, Inc. (BAARINC) was formed in 1955 for technical and government consulting, including missile and weaponry work, as well as consulting with NASA. By the end of the decade, *Time* had dubbed Booz, Allen "the world's largest, most prestigious management consultant firm." The partnership was incorporated as a private company in 1962, and in 1967 Commissioner Pete Rozelle requested its services for the merger of the National Football League and American Football League.

When Allen retired in 1970, Charlie Bowen became the new chairman, and the company went public. However, as the economy stalled during the energy crisis, spending for consultants plunged. Jim Farley replaced Bowen in 1975, and the company was taken private again in 1976. A turnaround was engineered, and the firm was soon helping Chrysler through its historic bailout and developing strategies for the breakup of AT&T.

Booz-Allen again experienced troubles in the 1980s as Farley set up a competition to select his successor. In 1984 Michael McCullough was chosen, but the selection process had taken a toll on morale. McCullough began restructuring the firm along industry lines, creating a department store of services in an industry characterized by boutique houses. The turmoil was too much, and by 1988 nearly a third of the partners had quit.

William Stasior became chairman in 1991 and reorganized Booz-Allen yet again, splitting it down public and private sector lines. James Allen died in 1992, the same year the firm moved to McLean, Virginia. The company began privatization work in the former Soviet Union and in eastern Europe in 1992 and continued to emphasize government business, including contracts with the IRS (1995) for technology modernization and with the General Services Administration (1996) to provide technical and management support for all federal telecommunications users.

In 1998 the company won a 10-year, $200 million contract with the US Defense Department to establish a scientific and technical data warehouse. Ralph Shrader was appointed CEO in early 1999; Stasior retired as chairman later that year. Booz-Allen formed a venture capital firm with Lehman Brothers in 2000. Also that year Booz-Allen announced it would spin off Aestix, its e-commerce business.

**Chairman and CEO; President, Worldwide Technology Business:** Ralph W. Shrader
**CFO:** Doug Swenson
**President, Worldwide Commercial Business:** Daniel C. Lewis
**VP:** Eduardo M. Alvarez, age 37
**VP Communications Media and Technology:** Adam Klein, age 50
**Chief Personnel Officer:** DeeAnne Aguirre
**Senior Director Public Relations:** Marie Lerch

## LOCATIONS

**HQ:** 8283 Greensboro Dr., McLean, VA 22102
**Phone:** 703-902-5000          **Fax:** 703-902-3333
**Web:** www.bah.com

Booz-Allen & Hamilton has more than 100 offices in the US and more than 30 other countries.

**Foreign Offices**

| | |
|---|---|
| Abu Dhabi, United Arab Emirates | Malmo, Sweden |
| Amsterdam | Melbourne |
| Bangkok | Mexico City |
| Beirut | Milan, Italy |
| Bogotá, Colombia | Moscow |
| Brisbane, Australia | Munich, Germany |
| Buenos Aires | Oslo |
| Caracas, Venezuela | Paris |
| Copenhagen | Rio de Janeiro |
| Düsseldorf, Germany | Rome |
| Frankfurt | Santiago, Chile |
| Gothenburg, Sweden | São Paulo |
| Helsinki, Finland | Seoul |
| Hong Kong | Stockholm |
| Jakarta, Indonesia | Sydney |
| London | Tokyo |
| Madrid | Wellington, New Zealand |
| | Zurich |

## PRODUCTS/OPERATIONS

**Selected Consulting Services**

**Commercial Services**
Corporate strategy
E-business strategy
Innovation
Knowledge management
Productivity improvement

**Technology Business Services**
Engineering
Information technology
Management consulting (systems development/systems integration)

## COMPETITORS

Accenture
American Management
Arthur D. Little
A.T. Kearney
Bain & Company
Boston Consulting
Cap Gemini
Computer Sciences
Day & Zimmermann
Deloitte Consulting
IBM
KPMG Consulting
McKinsey & Company
PricewaterhouseCoopers
SRI International
Towers Perrin

## HISTORICAL FINANCIALS & EMPLOYEES

| Private FYE: March 31 | Annual Growth | 3/92 | 3/93 | 3/94 | 3/95 | 3/96 | 3/97 | 3/98 | 3/99 | 3/00 | 3/01 |
|---|---|---|---|---|---|---|---|---|---|---|---|
| Sales ($ mil.) | 15.9% | 530 | 700 | 804 | 989 | 1,100 | 1,300 | 1,400 | 1,600 | 1,800 | 2,000 |
| Employees | 14.7% | 3,200 | 5,000 | 5,481 | 6,000 | 6,700 | 7,500 | 8,000 | 9,000 | 9,800 | 11,000 |

### SALES HISTORY

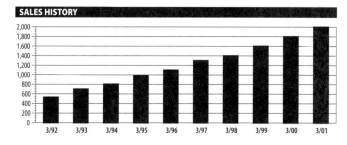

BOOZ·ALLEN & HAMILTON

# BORDEN, INC.

## OVERVIEW

After giving Elsie the cow and the Cracker Jack boy their pink slips, Borden has reinvented itself as a specialty chemicals manufacturer. The Columbus, Ohio-based company, controlled by Kohlberg Kravis Roberts & Co. (KKR), has sold its dairy division and its decorative products unit, as well as its Cracker Jack snack food and Eagle Brand condensed milk divisions. Borden's decentralized operations include Borden Chemical (resins, coatings, adhesives, melamine crystal, and specialty inks) and Elmer's Products (consumer adhesives), one of the largest producers of household and school glues (Elmer's and Krazy Glue) in the US.

Although the company's Borden Foods unit has been sold to KKR affiliate BW Holdings, Borden won't go hungry. The company still manages Borden Foods, which makes Creamette and Prince pasta brands, Classico pasta sauces, and Wyler's bouillon and dry soups. It also manages housewares maker World Kitchen (Pyrex, Corelle, and Corning; formerly Corning Consumer Products).

Nearly half its size before the selloffs, Borden bought the suffering formaldehyde business of PVC resin maker Borden Chemicals & Plastics, a supplier to Borden subsidiary Borden Chemicals.

## HISTORY

Galveston, Texas, resident Gail Borden Jr. founded one of Texas' first newspapers, the *Telegraph and Texas Register*. He was also an inventor and by 1853 had developed a process to preserve milk by condensing it in a vacuum.

Borden located his business in Burrville, Connecticut, in 1857 and called it Gail Borden, Jr., and Company. He formed New York Condensed Milk with grocer Jeremiah Milbank the next year. A big break came with the Civil War, when the US Army ordered condensed milk. When Borden died in 1874, the company was the leading US milk condenser.

The company incorporated in 1899 and took the name Borden Company in 1919. Between 1928 and 1929 Borden doubled in size and added ice cream, cheese, and powdered milk to its product list. By 1929 it had diversified by buying glue maker Casein.

By the end of WWII, Borden had expanded internationally. To reduce dependence on dairy revenues, Borden increased its chemicals business by buying Columbus Coated Fabrics (1961) and Smith-Douglass (1964). Expansion into snacks began in 1964 with the purchase of Wise Foods and Cracker Jack. In 1979 Borden bought Buckeye and Guy's Food potato chip makers.

In the 1980s Borden spent $1.9 billion on 91 acquisitions, mainly regional makers of snack foods and pasta, but the lack of a centralized manufacturing and selling network slowed growth and resulted in lost market share for many of the company's best-known products. At that time, Borden was the world's largest pasta maker.

Borden axed CEO Anthony D'Amato in 1993, under whose leadership the company's market value had dropped 50% in two years to $2.4 billion. In 1994 Borden sold its food service unit (to Heinz) and several other small food divisions. Later that year Kohlberg Kravis Roberts & Co. (KKR) bought 64% of Borden, paying for it with $2 billion in RJR Nabisco stock, which had been a disappointment to KKR. Eventually, affiliates of KKR owned virtually all of Borden.

Still saddled with debt, in 1996 Borden sold its Global Packaging business to AEP Industries. Borden sold its Borden Foods Corporation and Wise salty-snacks business to other branches of KKR, which kept them affiliated with Borden.

PepsiCo's Frito-Lay bought Cracker Jack from Borden in 1997. The Borden/Meadow Gold Dairies division was sold to a group led by giant dairy co-op Mid-America Dairymen (now part of Dairy Farmers of America). Also that year the company's Borden Chemical subsidiary acquired Melamine Chemicals, which makes melamine crystals used in adhesives and coatings.

Borden bought the chemicals unit of Sun Coast Industries (specialty resins and compounds) in 1998. That year KKR affiliate BW Holdings, Borden's parent, acquired 92% of Corning Consumer Products to be managed by Borden. Borden sold its decorative products business to buyout firm American Capital Strategies and its Eagle Brand, Cremora, ReaLemon, Kava, and None Such grocery brands to startup Eagle Family Foods.

In 1999 Borden bought two makers of formaldehyde and resins — Spurlock Industries and the chemicals unit of Blagden PLC (UK). The next year, through subsidiary Borden Chemicals, Borden bought the formaldehyde unit and other assets of Borden Chemicals & Plastics, a PVC resin maker and supplier of formaldehyde to Borden Chemicals.

In October 2000 KKR sold Wise Holdings to Palladium Equity Partners.

**Chairman, President, and CEO:** C. Robert Kidder, age 56, $1,194,063 pay
**EVP and CFO:** William H. Carter, age 47, $662,538 pay
**EVP, Strategy and Development:** Kevin M. Kelley, age 43, $587,500 pay
**EVP; Chairman and CEO, Elmer's Products:** Ronald C. Kesselman, age 57
**EVP, Human Resources and Corporate Affairs:** Nancy A. Reardon, age 48, $437,795 pay
**EVP and General Counsel:** William F. Stoll Jr., age 52, $477,425 pay
**SVP and Treasurer:** Ronald P. Starkman, age 46
**President and CEO, World Kitchen:** Steven G. Lamb, age 44
**SVP and CFO, World Kitchen:** Joseph W. McGarr, age 49
**Auditors:** Deloitte & Touche LLP

## LOCATIONS

**HQ:** 180 E. Broad St., Columbus, OH 43215
**Phone:** 614-225-4000
**Web:** www.bordenfamily.com

Borden has about 15 chemical plants in Australia, Canada, Europe, the Far East, and South America and nearly 30 chemical plants in the US.

### 2000 Sales

|  | $ mil. | % of total |
|---|---|---|
| US | 1,043 | 68 |
| Canada | 166 | 11 |
| Other countries | 315 | 21 |
| **Total** | **1,524** | **100** |

## PRODUCTS/OPERATIONS

### 2000 Sales

|  | $ mil. | % of total |
|---|---|---|
| Chemicals | 1,336 | 88 |
| Other | 188 | 12 |
| **Total** | **1,524** | **100** |

### Selected Operations

**Borden Chemical, Inc.**
Forest product resins
Formaldehyde
Foundry resins
Industrial resins
Melamine and derivatives
Oilfield products (resin-coated sand and resin proppant systems)
UV coatings

**Borden Foods Corporation**
Bouillon (Wyler's)
Pasta (Anthony's, Creamette, Catelli, Prince, R&F, Ronco)
Pasta sauces (Classico)
Soup mixes (Mrs. Grass)
Soup starter (Wyler's)

**Elmer's Products, Inc.**
Consumer adhesives (Elmer's, Crazy Glue)

**World Kitchen, Inc.**
Bakeware (Baker's Secret, EKCO, Farberware)
Barbecue tools and accessories (Grilla Gear)
Cookware (Revere, Visions)
Cutlery (Chicago Cutlery, OXO, Regent Sheffield)
Dinnerware (Corelle, CorningWare)
Glass and glass-ceramic products (CorningWare, Pyrex)
Kitchen tools (Cuisinart, OXO)

## COMPETITORS

| | | |
|---|---|---|
| Akzo Nobel | Georgia Gulf | New World Pasta |
| American Italian | Georgia-Pacific | Newell |
| Pasta | Corporation | Rubbermaid |
| Ashland | Georgia-Pacific | Procter & |
| Barilla | Group | Gamble |
| BASF AG | Hormel | R.J. Reynolds |
| Campbell Soup | Huntsman | Tobacco |
| Celanese | ICI | Rohm and Haas |
| ConAgra | Kraft Foods | Sara Lee |
| Dainippon Ink | Lancaster Colony | TOTAL FINA |
| and Chemicals | Lawter | ELF |
| Dow Chemical | International | Unilever PLC |
| DuPont | McWhorter | Valspar |
| General Mills | Technologies | |

## HISTORICAL FINANCIALS & EMPLOYEES

| Private FYE: December 31 | Annual Growth | 12/91 | 12/92 | 12/93 | 12/94 | 12/95 | 12/96 | 12/97 | 12/98 | 12/99 | 12/00 |
|---|---|---|---|---|---|---|---|---|---|---|---|
| Sales ($ mil.) | (15.5%) | — | 5,872 | 5,506 | 5,626 | 5,944 | 5,765 | 3,482 | 1,400 | 1,360 | 1,524 |
| Net income ($ mil.) | — | — | (364) | (631) | (598) | (366) | 82 | 278 | 63 | 53 | 34 |
| Income as % of sales | — | — | — | — | — | — | 1.4% | 8.0% | 4.5% | 3.9% | 2.2% |
| Employees | (25.4%) | — | 41,900 | 41,900 | 32,300 | 27,500 | 20,000 | 15,000 | 4,200 | 4,000 | 4,000 |

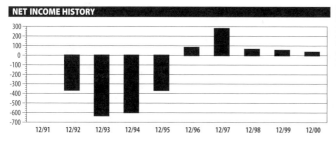

**NET INCOME HISTORY**

**2000 FISCAL YEAR-END**
Debt ratio: 97.4%
Return on equity: 86.7%
Cash ($ mil.): 27.8
Current ratio: 0.61
Long-term debt ($ mil.): 530.5

# BOSE CORPORATION

## OVERVIEW

The opposite of a rigid parent, Amar Bose wants his speakers to be heard but not seen. Framingham, Massachusetts-based Bose (rhymes with rose) is one of the world's leading speaker makers. Bose specializes in high-end audio products used everywhere from homes, cars, and computers to stadiums and chapels.

Founder and owner Bose, a professor at MIT, keeps his company sharp with unconventional products and methods. The firm stands out by offering such small, yet technologically advanced products as palm-sized cube speakers and compact radios with rich sound; its most famous product is the compact Wave radio with a sound that belies its size. To stay on the cutting edge, Bose invests much of its profits in research and development. Bose sells its products through retailers and 90 of its own stores.

## HISTORY

Music and electronics struck a chord in Amar Bose, the son of an Indian emigrant from Calcutta. As a youngster he studied violin and liked fixing electronic gadgets. A teenaged Bose started a radio repair shop in his basement during WWII that turned out to be the family's main source of income when his father's import business faltered during the war. Bose's interest in electronics led him to college at MIT in 1947.

His quest to develop a better sound system began nearly a decade later when the hi-fi stereo he bought as a reward for doing well in his graduate studies made his violin record sound shrill. MIT allowed Bose to research the topic while he taught there. He formed his namesake company in 1964 and hired as its first employee Sherwin Greenblatt, a former student who later became company president.

Bose discovered that most speaker systems funneled sound directly at the listener, while live concerts sent sound directly and indirectly by bouncing it off walls, floors, and ceilings. He designed a system in which only some speakers are aimed at the listener while others reflect the sounds around the room. Calling the concept "reflected sound," Bose began selling his 901 stereo speakers in 1968.

A feud with *Consumer Reports* showed the arrogant side of the self-made entrepreneur. After the magazine concluded in a 1970 review that Bose speakers created a sound that tended to "wander around the room," Bose sued, claiming product disparagement. (The lawsuit was settled 13 years later when the Supreme Court ruled in favor of *Consumer Reports*.) Bose began making professional loudspeakers in 1972.

After trying and failing to gain market share in Japan throughout the 1970s, in 1978 Bose hired sales executive Sumi Sakura, who convinced 400 Japanese dealers to find space in their jam-packed stores for Bose products. Sales jumped within months. Bose also turned his attention to car stereos in the 1970s.

After promising talks with General Motors in 1979, he risked $13 million and four years developing a stereo that could be custom-designed for cars. The first one was offered in 1983 in a Cadillac Seville. Contracts with other major carmakers followed, usually for their top-of-the-line models.

In the 1980s the company took its technology to TV sets. With an agreeable guinea pig in Zenith, Bose developed a speaker tube that could coil inside the set without adding much bulk. The set was a hit, even with a price tag of more than $1,400 (in 1987). The firm's speakers were also used in several space shuttle flights, beginning in 1992 with *Endeavour*.

The critically acclaimed Wave radio was introduced in 1993 and has been a huge success, even though it is primarily offered through direct mail. A year later Bose acquired professional loudspeaker maker US Sound from Carver. In 1996 it teamed up with satellite TV firm PRIMESTAR to offer the home theater Companion systems. (The systems were discontinued in 1999, dissolving the partnership.) The next year Bose and IBM paired up to upgrade the quality of PC sound systems.

Bose upped the ante on its retail operations in 1997 when it began opening more upscale showcase stores where audiophiles can test sound systems at in-store music theaters. The company began making its sound systems for more mainstream cars, such as the Chevrolet Blazer, the following year. In 1999 Bose began selling its products online and introduced a new version of its popular Wave radio (with a CD player).

In 2001 Bose introduced the Bose Wave/PC interactive system that provides one-touch access to Internet radio, digital audio files, AM/FM radio, and compact discs through a personal computer.

## OFFICERS

**Chairman and CEO:** Amar G. Bose, age 72
**President:** John Coleman
**VP of Finance and CFO:** Daniel A. Grady, age 65
**VP of Engineering:** Joseph Veranth
**VP of Europe:** Nic A. Merks
**VP of Human Resources:** John Ferrie
**VP of Manufacturing:** Thomas Beeson
**VP of Research:** Thomas Froeschle
**VP of Sales:** David Wood
**VP:** Sumiyoshi Sakura
**Secretary:** Alexander Bernhard
**Treasurer:** William R. Swanson
**Assistant Secretary:** Mark E. Sullivan
**Auditors:** PricewaterhouseCoopers LLP

## LOCATIONS

**HQ:** The Mountain, Framingham, MA 01701
**Phone:** 508-879-7330 **Fax:** 508-766-7543
**Web:** www.bose.com

Bose has plants in Canada, Ireland, Mexico, and the US.

## PRODUCTS/OPERATIONS

**Selected Products**
Aircraft entertainment systems
Auto sound systems and speakers
Aviation headsets
Custom home audio systems
Home stereo speakers
Marine speakers
Multimedia speakers
Music systems
Outdoor audio systems
PC sound systems
Professional loudspeakers
Radios
Speaker accessories

**Selected Brands**
131 (marine speakers)
141 (speakers)
151 (environmental speakers)
201, 301, 501, 701, 901 Series (direct/reflecting
    speakers)
Acoustic Wave (music systems)
Acoustimass (speaker systems)
Auditioner (computer system used to analyze building
    acoustics based on architectural blueprints)
Jewel Cube (speakers)
Lifestyle (music systems)
Wave radio (compact radio with full stereo sound)
Wave radio with CD player

## COMPETITORS

| | |
|---|---|
| Aiwa | Philips Electronics |
| Bang & Olufsen | Phoenix Gold |
| Boston Acoustics | Pioneer |
| Cambridge SoundWorks | Polk Audio |
| Cerwin-Vega | Recoton |
| Creative Technology | Rockford |
| Emerson Radio | Ruark Acoustics |
| Harman International | Sharp |
| Jamo | Snell Acoustics |
| Kenwood | Sony |
| Koss | Telex Communications |
| Matsushita | Victor Company of Japan |
| Paradigm Electronics | Yamaha |

## HISTORICAL FINANCIALS & EMPLOYEES

| Private<br>FYE: March 31 | Annual<br>Growth | 3/92 | 3/93 | 3/94 | 3/95 | 3/96 | 3/97 | 3/98 | 3/99 | 3/00 | 3/01 |
|---|---|---|---|---|---|---|---|---|---|---|---|
| Sales ($ mil.) | 13.6% | — | 450 | 500 | 600 | 700 | 750 | 850 | 950 | 1,100 | 1,250 |
| Employees | 11.2% | — | 3,000 | 3,100 | 3,100 | 3,500 | 4,000 | 4,000 | 4,000 | 6,000 | 7,000 |

## SALES HISTORY

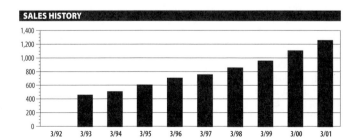

# THE BOSTON CONSULTING GROUP

## OVERVIEW

Some of the world's largest corporations turn to Beantown brainpower for advice and guidance. The Boston Consulting Group (BCG) is one of the top ranked consulting practices in the world, serving the leading firms in such industries as consumer goods, financial services, and telecommunications. Its 2,000 consultants assist clients in developing and implementing corporate strategies, improving efficiencies, and integrating new technologies. The firm is noted for developing and applying its own original consulting concepts, such as "time-based competition" (rapid response to change) and "deconstruction" (an end to vertical integration). BCG has about 50 offices in more than 30 countries worldwide.

While the employee-owned firm is nearly 40 years old, BCG remains on the cutting edge of the technology-fueled economy and is regarded as one of the premier e-commerce consultancies. About 20% of its North American sales come from e-commerce consulting. BCG has established several "Web labs" to create e-commerce sites and other online products for its clients.

## HISTORY

Bruce Henderson, a Harvard Business School graduate, began his career at Westinghouse, and in 1953 was named by *Time* as one of Pittsburgh's "newsmakers of tomorrow." After a stint at consulting firm Arthur D. Little, Henderson opened his own one-man consulting boutique in 1963. The business operated as part of Boston Safe Deposit and Trust, whose CEO had encouraged Henderson to strike out on his own. The firm was one of the first consultancies to specialize purely in strategy. It was also ahead of the curve when it opened an office in Japan in 1965.

During the 1970s BCG helped popularize the consulting field in part by its willingness to pay large salaries to top business school graduates. Henderson and BCG developed such concepts as the experience curve (the longer a company makes a product, the more cost-efficient its production becomes) and the growth and market-share matrix (a strategy for managing a group of products based on their growth potential). In 1974 Henderson took his company independent as Boston Consulting Group, vesting ownership in the firm to his employees. (It was among the first to utilize new retirement income laws to do this.)

BCG's influence waned during the 1980s, when corporate reengineering and operations-focused planning replaced strategic initiatives. By then many of the firm's innovative concepts had become core subjects at leading business schools, and Henderson retired in 1985 to teach at Vanderbilt, where he continued to develop new ideas. A prolific business writer, he published "The Origin of Strategy" in 1989; the article compared theories of business with Darwin's theories on competition and survival.

Also impacting BCG's business, the then-Big-Eight accounting firms became more active in the consulting field (especially in the area of systems integration). As a result BCG avoided areas that would lead it into direct battle with the bigger firms and instead focused its energies on helping its clients get products to market more expeditiously. During the 1990s, however, BCG saw business increase as companies that had streamlined during the 1980s returned their focus to strategy. Henderson died in 1992 at the age of 77.

In 1994 Ohio's Figgie International filed suit against BCG, claiming that the company was responsible for designing and implementing "flawed programs" and consistently overbilling for its services. The suit was settled out of court the next year. In 1997 surveys of American and European business and engineering school graduates named BCG the second-most desirable firm to work for (after rival McKinsey). That year 23-year BCG veteran Carl Stern was elected CEO by a vote of the firm's 200 worldwide partners.

As the rest of the world braced against the Asian economic crisis in 1998, Stern saw the crisis as a boon for the company. BCG shored up its relations with its Asian clients and continued its international expansion. The company furthered this strategy in 1999 with a contract to consult for the Indonesian government on the eventual privatization of more than 150 state-owned companies. In 2000 BCG launched initiatives to build e-commerce Web sites and was engaged to develop Orbitz.com, a travel and ticketing site for a consortium of several airlines, including United and Delta. In 2001 *Consulting Magazine* named the company as "the best consulting company to work for."

## OFFICERS

**Chairman:** John S. Clarkeson
**President and CEO:** Carl Stern, age 55
**CFO:** Hugh Simon

## LOCATIONS

**HQ:** Exchange Place, 31st Fl., Boston, MA 02109
**Phone:** 617-973-1200 **Fax:** 617-973-1399
**Web:** www.bcg.com

Boston Consulting Group has 50 offices in more than 30 countries.

## PRODUCTS/OPERATIONS

**Selected Practice Areas**
Branding
Consumer
Corporate development
Deconstruction
E-commerce
Energy
Financial services
Globalization
Health care
Industrial goods
Information technology
Operational effectiveness
Organization
Pricing
Technology communications
Travel and tourism

## COMPETITORS

Accenture
Arthur D. Little
A.T. Kearney
Bain & Company
Booz-Allen
Deloitte Consulting
KPMG Consulting
Marsh & McLennan
McKinsey & Company
PricewaterhouseCoopers
Towers Perrin

## HISTORICAL FINANCIALS & EMPLOYEES

| Private<br>FYE: December 31 | Annual<br>Growth | 12/91 | 12/92 | 12/93 | 12/94 | 12/95 | 12/96 | 12/97 | 12/98 | 12/99 | 12/00 |
|---|---|---|---|---|---|---|---|---|---|---|---|
| Sales ($ mil.) | 18.3% | — | — | 340 | 430 | 550 | 600 | 655 | 730 | 948 | 1,100 |
| Employees | 22.9% | — | — | — | 1,246 | 1,320 | 1,550 | 2,000 | 3,000 | 4,334 | 4,300 |

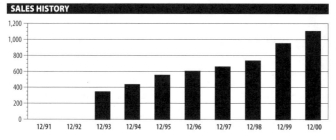

**SALES HISTORY**

THE BOSTON CONSULTING GROUP

# CALPERS

OVERVIEW

California's public sector retirees already have a place in the sun; CalPERS gives them the money to enjoy it.

The Sacramento-based California Public Employees' Retirement System (CalPERS) is one of the largest public pension systems in the US, with more than $140 billion in assets. It manages retirement and health plans for some 1.2 million beneficiaries from nearly 2,500 government agencies. CalPERS' board consists of six elected, three appointed, and four designated members (the director of the state's Department of Personnel Administration, the state controller, the state treasurer, and a member of the State Personnel Board).

Most of its revenue comes from its enormous investment program: It has interests in US and foreign securities, real estate development and investment, and even hedge funds and venture capital activities. CalPERS has steadily increased its investments in private equity, looking to take ownership stakes in more firms (it already owns 10% of investment bank Thomas Weisel). In addition, the system is spending about $2 billion to acquire Cabot Industrial Trust, which owns some 350 industrial properties in 20 states. CalPERS uses its size to influence such corporate governance issues as company performance, executive compensation, and sometimes social policy. It is also a powerful negotiator for such services as insurance; rates established by the system serve as benchmarks for other employers.

Over the next few years CalPERS may be forced to sell assets, as it is expected to be hit with a wave of early retirements by middle-aged workers. The system is eyeing more short-term investments with higher returns.

## HISTORY

The state of California founded CalPERS in 1931 to administer a pension fund for state employees. By the 1940s the system was serving other public agencies and educational institutions on a contract basis.

When the Public Employees' Medical and Hospital Care Act was passed in 1962, CalPERS added health coverage. The fund was conservatively managed in-house, with little exposure to stocks. Despite slow growth, the state used the system's funds to meet its own cash shortfalls.

CalPERS became involved in corporate governance issues in the mid-1980s, when California treasurer Jesse Unruh became outraged by corporate greenmail schemes. In 1987 he hired as CEO Wisconsin pension board veteran Dale Hanson, who led the movement for corporate accountability to institutional investors.

In the late 1980s CalPERS moved into real estate and Japanese stocks. When both crashed around 1990, Hanson came under pressure. CalPERS was twice forced to take major writedowns for its real estate holdings and turned to expensive outside fund managers, but its investment performance deteriorated and member services suffered.

Legislation in 1990 enabled CalPERS to offer long-term health insurance. Governor Pete Wilson's 1991 attempt to use $1.6 billion from CalPERS to help meet a state budget shortfall resulted in legislation banning future raids. CalPERS made its first direct investment in 1993, an energy-related infrastructure partnership with Enron.

CalPERS suffered in the 1994 bond crash.

That year Hanson resigned amid criticism that his focus on corporate governance had depressed fund performance. The system moved to an indexing strategy.

CalPERS eased its corporate relations stance, creating a separate office to handle investor issues and launching an International Corporate Governance Program. In 1996 it teamed with the Asian Development Bank to invest in the Asia/Pacific region; it took a major hit in the Asian financial crisis the next year, but used the downturn as an opportunity to expand its position there in undervalued stocks. In 1998 CalPERS pressured foreign firms to adopt more transparent financial reporting methods.

In 2000 the system raised health care premiums almost 10% to keep up with rising care costs. It widened the scope of its direct investments with stakes in investment bank Thomas Weisel Partners (10%) and asset manager Arrowstreet Capital (15%); it also moved into real estate development, buying Genstar Land Co. with Newland Communities, and announcing plans to invest in high-tech firms focused on B2B online real estate services. CalPERS said that year it would sell off more than $500 million in tobacco holdings.

In 2001 state controller and CalPERS board member Kathleen Connell sued the system for not following state-sanctioned rules regarding pay increases. CalPERS was forced to cut salaries for investment managers, a move that prompted chief investment officer Daniel Szente to resign.

## OFFICERS

**CEO:** James E. Burton
**Deputy Executive Officer:** James H. Gomez
**Assistant Executive Officer, Financial and Administration Services:** Vincent P. Brown
**Assistant Executive Officer, Governmental Affairs, Planning, and Research:** Robert D. Walton
**Assistant Executive Officer, Investment Operations:** Robert Aguallo
**Assistant Executive Officer, Health Benefit Services:** Allen D. Feezor
**Assistant Executive Officer, Member and Benefit Services:** Barbara D. Hegdal
**Chief, Human Resources:** Tom Pettey
**Chief, Information Technology Services Division:** Jack Corrie
**Chief Investment Officer:** Mark Anson
**Chief, Office of Public Affairs:** Patricia K. Macht
**Chief Actuary:** Ronald L. Seeling
**General Counsel:** Kayla J. Gillan
**Senior Investment Officer, Alternative Investment Management:** Richard J. Hayes
**Auditors:** PricewaterhouseCoopers LLP

## LOCATIONS

**HQ:** California Public Employees' Retirement System
Lincoln Plaza, 400 P St., Sacramento, CA 95814
**Phone:** 916-326-3000       **Fax:** 916-558-4001
**Web:** www.calpers.ca.gov

## PRODUCTS/OPERATIONS

**2000 Assets**

|  | $ mil. | % of total |
|---|---|---|
| Cash & equivalents | 17 | — |
| Treasury & agency securities | 5,899 | 3 |
| Corporate bonds | 14,242 | 7 |
| International bonds | 6,292 | 3 |
| Stocks | 109,744 | 57 |
| Mortgage loans | 17,534 | 9 |
| Real estate equities | 9,095 | 5 |
| Other investments | 25,771 | 14 |
| Receivables | 3,009 | 2 |
| **Total** | **191,603** | **100** |

**Selected Retirement Plans**
Defined Benefit Plans
  Judges' Retirement Fund
  Judges' Retirement Fund II
  Legislators' Retirement System
  Public Employees' Retirement Fund
  Volunteer Firefighters' Length of Service Award System
Defined Contribution Plans
  State Peace Officers' and Firefighters' Defined Contribution Plan Fund
Health Care Plans
  Public Employees' Health Care Fund
  Public Employees' Contingency Reserve Fund
Others
  Old Age & Survivors' Insurance Revolving Fund
  Public Employees' Deferred Compensation Fund
  Public Employees Long-Term Care Fund
  Replacement Benefit Fund

## COMPETITORS

AXA Financial
Charles Schwab
FMR
Janus Capital Corp.
Merrill Lynch
Morgan Stanley Dean Witter
Putnam Investments
Salomon Smith Barney Holdings
T. Rowe Price
TIAA-CREF
UBS PaineWebber
Vanguard Group

## HISTORICAL FINANCIALS & EMPLOYEES

| Government-owned FYE: June 30 | Annual Growth | 6/91 | 6/92 | 6/93 | 6/94 | 6/95 | 6/96 | 6/97 | 6/98 | 6/99 | 6/00 |
|---|---|---|---|---|---|---|---|---|---|---|---|
| Sales ($ mil.) | 5.4% | — | — | 13,027 | 4,986 | 16,174 | 17,179 | 23,918 | 27,514 | 20,889 | 18,845 |
| Employees | 10.0% | — | — | — | 900 | 1,000 | 1,037 | 1,089 | 1,247 | 1,500 | 1,594 |

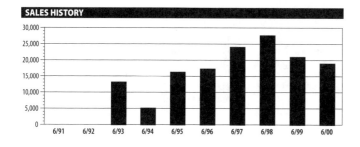

SALES HISTORY

# CALIFORNIA STATE UNIVERSITY

## OVERVIEW

California State University (CSU) turns students into teachers. Long Beach-based CSU traces its roots to the state's teaching colleges and trains some 60% of California's teachers. It runs neck and neck with the State University of New York (SUNY) as the nation's largest university system in terms of enrollment (around 390,000), and has campuses in 23 cities, including Bakersfield, Los Angeles, San Francisco, and San Jose. The university primarily awards bachelor's and master's degrees in about 240 subject areas, leaving higher levels of study to the University of California (UC) system.

CSU is developing strategies to cope with an expected enrollment increase of about 40% between 1998 and 2010 — what it calls Tidal Wave II. The first waves are starting already, with more than 20,000 additional students flooding the system in the fall of 2001. To battle the crippling influx of new students, CSU has begun offering distance-education programs in which students are taught via teleconferencing and the Internet. Other strategies involve adding a summer semester to create year-long schooling, and expanding the use of off-campus centers.

## HISTORY

In 1862 San Francisco's Normal School, a training center for elementary teachers, became California's first state-founded school for higher education. Six students attended its first classes, but there were 384 by 1866. It later moved to San Jose to escape the bustle of San Francisco.

In the late 1880s State Normal Schools opened in Chico, San Diego, and San Francisco, followed in 1901 by California State Polytechnic Institute, which offered studies in agriculture, business, and engineering. Other new colleges included Fresno State (1911) and Humboldt State (1913). Most of the schools offered four-year programs and admitted any student with eight years of grammar school education.

The Normal Schools were renamed Teachers Colleges in 1921 to reflect their role in teacher education. Two years later the colleges began awarding bachelor of arts degrees in education.

In 1935 the schools were renamed State Colleges and expanded into liberal arts. In 1947 they were authorized to confer master's degrees in education.

After WWII, students on the GI Bill helped increase enrollment, and campuses opened in Los Angeles, Sacramento, and Long Beach. The prospect of the first baby boomers reaching college age prompted the founding of more campuses in the late 1950s. Russia's 1957 launch of Sputnik spurred additional focus on science and math at all education levels. The next year the colleges began awarding master's degrees in subjects unrelated to teacher education.

During the Red Scare, the system's first chancellor, Buell Gallagher, was accused by the press of being soft on communism. Other faculty were subpoenaed to appear before the House Committee on Un-American Activities.

In 1961 the system became the California State Colleges (CSC) and the board of trustees

was created, giving the schools more independence from state government. In 1969 student and faculty groups seeking ethnic studies departments went on strike in San Francisco; the unrest closed the campus.

In 1972 CSC became known as the California State University and Colleges. Ten years later, it became California State University.

Barry Munitz became chancellor in 1991, taking over a system that had become oppressive because of its heavy-handed administration. Munitz, who came from corporate America, brought his business sense to the university and increased private fund-raising, among other activities. Munitz also increased tuition, which caused enrollments to drop from 1991 to 1995.

CSU added two new campuses in 1995, including CSU Monterey Bay, the first military base to be converted into a university since the end of the Cold War. In 1997 Charles Reed was named to replace Munitz as chancellor, effective the following year. In 1999, after lengthy contract negotiations between Reed and faculty members failed to produce accord over teacher salaries and employment conditions, Reed imposed his own merit-based plan. The faculty responded with official rebukes and a vote of no confidence in Reed. The two sides eventually settled on a new three-year contract with provisions that salary and benefits may be negotiated annually.

The rancor over pay continued in 2000 when the California Faculty Association issued a report claiming women were discriminated against and the merit system was inherently unfair; CSU issued its own report denying the charges. In 2001 Reed, stirring up more controversy, began a quest to allow CSU to offer doctorate degrees. The move is bitterly opposed by the competing University of California system.

## OFFICERS

**Chairman:** William Hauck
**Chancellor:** Charles B. Reed, age 60
**Executive Vice Chancellor and Chief Academic Officer:** David S. Spence
**Executive Vice Chancellor and CFO:** Richard P. West
**Vice Chancellor Human Resources:** Jackie McClain
**Vice Chancellor University Advancement; President, CSU Foundation:** Louis E. Caldera, age 45
**General Counsel:** Christine Helwick, age 54
**President, California Maritime Academy:** William B. Eisenhardt
**President, California State Polytechnic University, Pomona:** Bob Suzuki, age 65
**President, California Polytechnic State University, San Luis Obispo:** Warren J. Baker, age 63
**President, CSU, Bakersfield:** Tomas A. Arciniega, age 64
**President, CSU, Channel Islands:** Richard Rush
**President, CSU, Chico:** Manuel A. Esteban
**President, CSU, Dominguez Hills:** James E. Lyons Sr.
**President, CSU, Fresno:** John D. Welty, age 57
**President, CSU, Fullerton:** Milton A. Gordon
**President, CSU, Haywood:** Norma S. Rees
**President, CSU, Long Beach:** Robert C. Maxson
**President, CSU, Los Angeles:** James M. Rosser
**President, CSU, Monterey Bay:** Peter P. Smith
**Auditors:** KPMG LLP

## LOCATIONS

**HQ:** Trustees of the California State University
401 Golden Shore, Long Beach, CA 90802
**Phone:** 562-951-4000
**Web:** www.calstate.edu

California State University has campuses in 23 cities.

**California State University Campuses**
California Maritime Academy
California Polytechnic State University, San Luis Obispo
California State Polytechnic University, Pomona
California State University
  Bakersfield
  Channel Islands
  Chico
  Dominguez Hills
  Fresno
  Fullerton
  Hayward
  Long Beach
  Los Angeles
  Monterey Bay
  Northridge
  Sacramento
  San Bernardino
  San Marcos
  Stanislaus
Humboldt State University
San Diego State University
San Francisco State University
San Jose State University
Sonoma State University

## HISTORICAL FINANCIALS & EMPLOYEES

| School<br>FYE: June 30 | Annual<br>Growth | 6/92 | 6/93 | 6/94 | 6/95 | 6/96 | 6/97 | 6/98 | 6/99 | 6/00 | 6/01 |
|---|---|---|---|---|---|---|---|---|---|---|---|
| Sales ($ mil.) | 7.4% | 2,131 | 2,085 | 2,121 | 3,121 | 3,889 | 2,522 | 2,612 | 3,272 | 3,803 | 4,050 |
| Employees | 2.1% | — | 33,859 | 34,779 | 33,000 | 37,360 | 38,512 | 39,000 | 40,323 | 40,000 | 40,000 |

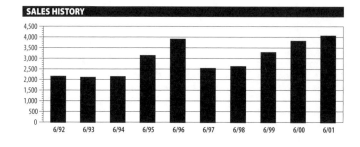

SALES HISTORY

# CALVIN KLEIN, INC.

Mark Wahlberg's underwear and Brooke Shields' implied lack thereof made everyone aware of their Calvins. New York City-based Calvin Klein designs men's, women's, and children's clothing and accessories. Aside from its flagship ready-to-wear collection of women's clothing, most of the company's revenues come from licensing royalties.

Calvin Klein licenses its brand to manufacturers of shoes, coats, fragrances, handbags, coats, jeans, underwear, men's clothing and furnishings, women's clothing, hosiery, watches, eyewear, socks, bedding, and tabletop products. Among its licensees are Warnaco (underwear and jeans), Unilever (fragrances), and Jones Apparel (shoes and handbags). Calvin Klein also licenses more than 40 outlet stores worldwide.

Almost as well known as the clothes are Calvin Klein's advertisements, created in-house by CRK Advertising. The company's erotic campaigns continue to remain controversial: In 1999 it canceled two multimillion-dollar ad campaigns for children's underwear after being blasted for promoting pedophilia.

Calvin Klein has begun a companywide restructuring effort; it has cut jobs from its headquarters and is shutting down its mid-priced sportswear division in the US (the company's last self-manufacturing division). Calvin Klein also plans to consolidate some overseas operations, but says it will continue to open about 20 stores over the next few years.

VC Calvin Klein and CEO Barry Schwartz own the company.

After five years designing for other Seventh Avenue fashion houses, Calvin Klein went out on his own in 1968, bankrolled with $10,000 from childhood friend Barry Schwartz, who handled the business. That year a Bonwit Teller executive stumbled into Klein's small showroom, leading to a $50,000 order. Klein expanded from coats into sportswear in 1970. Schwartz, realizing that coats only sold during one season, sped the move into the more lucrative sportswear market by only selling coats to buyers who also bought the other line.

Nurturing the aura of exclusivity, Calvin Klein kept his outlets few. The designer's look became so influential by 1975 that *Vogue* was calling it "a definitive picture of the American look." Klein introduced his designer jeans in a self-directed commercial in 1980. He paid 15-year-old Brooke Shields $500,000 to suggest that she was pantiless beneath her Calvins. Sales of designer jeans peaked in 1982. In the early 1980s Klein introduced gender-bending boxer shorts for women, complete with a fly. In an effort to increase profits, Calvin Klein purchased its jeanswear licensee, Puritan Fashions, for $60 million in 1983. Two years later Klein touted his first fragrance, Obsession, with a slew of ads featuring nude models.

The company signed a pact with Marchon Eyewear in 1991 to make Calvin Klein eyewear (rolled out in 1992). Pal David Geffen bailed the company out of $62 million in junk bond debt (stemming from the Puritan purchase) in 1992 and helped Klein license his underwear business to Warnaco. The company also licensed apparel manufacturer Designer Holdings for jeans. In the early 1990s Klein benefited

when the youth market suddenly turned on to his clothes. The youthful resurgence also led the designer to shift down from the kind of exclusive fashions sold at Bergdorf Goodman to a more casual, universal look.

Calvin Klein hired Armani veteran Gabriella Forte as president and COO in 1994; she was instrumental in giving the Calvin Klein name a strong global licensing presence. In the mid-1990s Calvin Klein drew criticism for using models who looked anorexic, underaged, and drugged. New advertising in 1998 focused on a more wholesome lifestyle, with healthier looking models in outdoor settings. But it didn't take the firm long to wind up back in the hot seat when it used children in an underwear campaign, which was withdrawn in 1999.

Also in 1999, after Forte announced she was leaving, Calvin Klein began shopping for a merger or buyout, but it took itself off the market in 2000. Calvin Klein later filed suit against Warnaco, accusing it of selling full-price merchandise in discount outlets, selling unauthorized designs, and selling other Warnaco products at Calvin Klein outlets. Warnaco fired back with a lawsuit of its own. The companies announced a settlement moments before their trial was due to begin in 2001.

In Spring 2001 Calvin Klein launched a companywide restructuring effort. Its first moves were to cut 10% of its headquarters staff and begin shutting down its CK mid-priced sportswear division in the US (the last business manufactured by the company itself). Overseas, Calvin Klein said it would merge its CK Calvin Klein apparel division with CK Calvin Klein Jeans.

## OFFICERS

**Chairman and CEO:** Barry Schwartz
**Vice Chairman:** Calvin Klein
**President and COO:** Tom Murry
**CFO:** Len LaSalandra
**SVP Marketing:** Harlan Bratcher, age 43
**SVP CK Men and CK Women North America:**
  Dennis L. Trites
**Creative Director of Design:** Tim Gardner, age 52

## LOCATIONS

**HQ:** 205 W. 39th St., 4th Fl., New York, NY 10018
**Phone:** 212-719-2600      **Fax:** 212-730-4818

Calvin Klein has offices in Asia, Europe, and the US; it
licenses more than 40 retail stores worldwide.

## PRODUCTS/OPERATIONS

**Brands**
Calvin Klein Collections (upscale women's and men's
  apparel and home furnishings)
Calvin Klein Cosmetics (cK One, Eternity, Obsession)
Calvin Klein Tabletop
Calvin Klein Underwear
cK (apparel for men and women)
cK Calvin Klein Jeans (jeans for women, men, juniors,
  and kids)

**Licensed Products**
Accessories
Apparel
Bedding
Coats
Eyewear
Fragrances
Home furnishings
Hosiery
Shoes
Sleepwear
Socks
Swimwear
Tabletop products
Underwear
Watches

## COMPETITORS

| | |
|---|---|
| Benetton | Joe Boxer |
| Diesel | Jones Apparel |
| Donna Karan | Levi Strauss |
| Estée Lauder | Liz Claiborne |
| The Gap | LVMH |
| Gianni Versace | Marzotto |
| Armani | Nautica Enterprises |
| Gucci | Perry Ellis International |
| Prada | Polo |
| Jil Sander | Tommy Hilfiger |

## HISTORICAL FINANCIALS & EMPLOYEES

| Private<br>FYE: Sat. nearest Dec. 31 | Annual<br>Growth | 12/91 | 12/92 | 12/93 | 12/94 | 12/95 | 12/96 | 12/97 | 12/98 | 12/99 | 12/00 |
|---|---|---|---|---|---|---|---|---|---|---|---|
| Estimated sales ($ mil.) | (3.2%) | — | 220 | 280 | 177 | 127 | 141 | 150 | 160 | 175 | 170 |
| Employees | 0.0% | — | — | — | — | — | 900 | 900 | 1,000 | 900 | — |

### SALES HISTORY

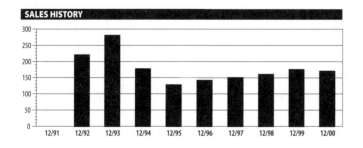

# C&S WHOLESALE GROCERS, INC.

## OVERVIEW

C&S Wholesale Grocers is working its way up the food chain. Based in Brattleboro, Vermont, the company is one of the largest food wholesalers in the nation. C&S Wholesale sells more than 53,000 products — ranging from dairy products and locally grown produce to groceries and nonfood items — to about 4,000 independent supermarkets, major supermarket chains, mass marketers such as Wal-Mart, and wholesale clubs. It has distribution facilities in Connecticut, Maryland, Massachusetts, New Jersey, New York, Pennsylvania, and Vermont.

C&S Wholesale targets medium-sized and large chains that most wholesalers ignore.

The company handles inventory tracking, warehouse, and distribution operations and can offer better prices because of high-volume buying. Independent stores benefit because the wholesaler carries a much wider selection of products than these stores would have access to otherwise.

To avoid losing one of its top customers, the company, through affiliate GU Markets, bought bankrupt supermarket chain The Grand Union Company's assets, which will expand C&S Wholesale into retailing. C&S Wholesale is owned by chairman and CEO Richard Cohen, grandson of the founder.

## HISTORY

Israel Cohen and Abraham Siegel began C&S Wholesale Grocers in 1918 in Worcester, Massachusetts. Cohen ran the company for more than 50 years after buying out Siegel in 1921. It became a family concern in 1972 when Cohen turned the company over to his son Lester, who soon brought in his sons, Jim and Rick.

C&S Wholesale expanded over the years, growing along with its customers. It had $98 million in sales in 1981, the year its skyrocketing growth began. Also in 1981 Rick, now the company's chairman, president, and CEO, engineered a move to Brattleboro, in southern Vermont, where it had better access to interstate highways and a larger workforce.

After attending a seminar hosted by management whiz Tom Peters, in 1987 Cohen set up self-managed teams of three to eight employees who would act as small business units responsible for a customer's order from the time it was received to when it was delivered. Team members were paid for the amount of time they worked and were given bonuses for error-free operations and penalties for errors or damaged goods. His plan saw an immediate response in terms of increased sales, and by 1992 C&S Wholesale had more than $1 billion in sales. Rick bought out his father in 1989 and the next year became the company's single shareholder when he bought out his brother.

C&S Wholesale started its produce business in 1990 (by 1994 it was the major purchaser of locally grown fruits and vegetables) and began making plans to build an 800,000-sq.-ft. refrigerated warehouse near a scenic highway in Brattleboro. However, it ran up against environmentalists and Vermont's Act 250 environmental impact law, and eventually dropped its original plan, opting instead to expand at its headquarters.

In 1992 the wholesaler offered plans for a smaller, revised warehouse, but again met opposition. After a two-year battle, C&S Wholesale gave up and said it would build elsewhere. (Most of its employees and warehouses are now in Massachusetts and New Jersey.)

The following year C&S Wholesale welcomed 127 Grand Union stores and several East Coast Wal-Mart stores as customers. The next year the company picked up another 103 Grand Union stores; Grand Union said it was closing two distribution centers and shifting distribution to C&S Wholesale in a deal worth $500 million a year. A $650 million-per-year contract with Edwards stores was inked in 1996, the year C&S Wholesale's sales topped $3 billion.

The company acquired ice-cream distributor New England Frozen Foods in 1997. Continuing its move toward the Mid-Atlantic, C&S Wholesale took over the distribution and supply operations of New Jersey-based grocery chain Pathmark Stores in 1998 for $60 million. In 1999 C&S Wholesale purchased the wholesale division of Shaw's Supermarkets' Star Markets and moved into Pennsylvania with a facility in York.

In 2001 the company, through affiliate GU Markets, bought most of the assets of one of its biggest customers, bankrupt The Grand Union Company. C&S acquired about 170 of Grand Union's 197 stores in the purchase. It transferred most of the stores to third-party purchasers, but will continue operating about 20 of them. Also in 2001 news reports claimed that C&S Wholesale is among the bidders seeking to buy Kings Super Markets from Marks and Spencer.

**Chairman, CEO:** Richard B. Cohen
**CFO:** Mark Gross
**Chief Operating Officer:** Edward Albertian
**SVP Strategic Planning:** William Hamlin
**SVP Human Resources:** Charlotte Edwards

## LOCATIONS

**HQ:** Old Ferry Rd., Brattleboro, VT 05301
**Phone:** 802-257-4371    **Fax:** 802-257-6727
**Web:** www.cswg.com

C&S Wholesale Grocers services more than 4,000 stores from Maine to Maryland. It has warehouses and distribution facilities in Aberdeen and Collingwood, MD; Brattleboro, VT; Hatfield and Westfield, MA; Montgomery and Newburgh, NY; Windsor Locks, CT; Woodbridge, New Brunswick, North Brunswick, and Dayton, NJ; and York, PA.

## PRODUCTS/OPERATIONS

**Selected Customers**
A&P
Big Y Foods
BJ's Wholesale Club
Foodtown
Giant-Carlisle (owned by Royal Ahold)
Giant-Landover (owned by Royal Ahold)
Pathmark
Safeway
Shaw's
Stop & Shop
Wal-Mart

## COMPETITORS

| | |
|---|---|
| Associated Wholesalers | McLane |
| Bozzuto's | Nash Finch |
| Di Giorgio | Richfood |
| Fleming Companies | SUPERVALU |
| IGA | Wakefern Food |
| Krasdale Foods | |

## HISTORICAL FINANCIALS & EMPLOYEES

| Private<br>FYE: September 30 | Annual<br>Growth | 9/92 | 9/93 | 9/94 | 9/95 | 9/96 | 9/97 | 9/98 | 9/99 | 9/00 | 9/01 |
|---|---|---|---|---|---|---|---|---|---|---|---|
| Sales ($ mil.) | 22.8% | 1,335 | 1,867 | 1,837 | 2,650 | 3,348 | 3,665 | 5,120 | 6,050 | 7,000 | 8,500 |
| Employees | 24.1% | 1,000 | 1,300 | 1,500 | 2,000 | 2,850 | 3,000 | 3,800 | 4,000 | 5,000 | 7,000 |

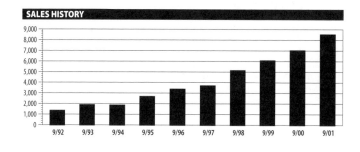

SALES HISTORY

# CARGILL, INCORPORATED

## OVERVIEW

Being private doesn't mean Cargill is cut off from the world. The Wayzata, Minnesota-based agribusiness giant — the US's largest private corporation — operates from more than 1,000 locations in over 70 countries. Cargill is the US's #1 grain exporter, the #3 meat and poultry processor (its Excel unit trails ConAgra and IBP), a commodity trader, and a producer of animal feed and crop fertilizers. A global supplier of oils, syrups, flour, and other products used in food processing, Cargill's own retail brands include Honeysuckle White and Riverside (poultry), Sterling Silver (beef), and Gerkens (cocoa).

Cargill also is involved in petroleum trading, financial trading, futures brokering, shipping, and steelmaking (subsidiary North Star is major minimill steelmaker in the US). To focus on processing, Cargill has sold its seed operations and coffee trading business and is selling part of its steel business.

Descendants of the founding Cargill and MacMillan families own about 85% of Cargill.

## HISTORY

William W. Cargill founded Cargill in 1865 when he bought his first grain elevator, in Conover, Iowa. He and his brother Sam bought grain elevators all along the Southern Minnesota Railroad in 1870, just as Minnesota was becoming an important shipping route. Sam and a third brother, James, expanded the elevator operations while William worked with the railroads to monopolize transport of grain to markets and coal to farmers.

Around the turn of the century, William's son William S. invested in a number of ill-fated projects. William W. found that his name had been used to finance the projects; shortly afterward, he died of pneumonia. Cargill's creditors pressed for repayment, which threatened to bankrupt the company. John MacMillan, William W.'s son-in-law, took control and rebuilt Cargill. It had recovered by 1916 but lost its holdings in Mexico and Canada. MacMillan opened offices in New York (1922) and Argentina (1929), expanding grain trading and transport operations.

In 1945 Cargill bought Nutrena Mills (animal feed) and entered soybean processing; corn processing began soon after and grew with the demand for corn sweeteners. In 1954 Cargill benefited when the US began making loans to help developing countries buy American grain. Subsidiary Tradax, established in 1955, became one of the largest grain traders in Europe. A decade later Cargill began trading sugar by purchasing sugar and molasses in the Philippines and selling them abroad.

Cargill made its finances public in 1973 (as a requirement for its unsuccessful takeover bid of Missouri Portland Cement), revealing it to be one of the US's largest companies, with $5.2 billion in sales. In the 1970s it expanded into coal, steel, and waste disposal and became a major force in metals processing, beef, and salt production.

In the early 1990s Cargill began selling branded meats and packaged foods directly to supermarkets. To placate family heirs who wanted to take Cargill public, CEO Whitney MacMillan, grandson of John, created an employee stock plan in 1991 that allowed shareholders to cash in their shares. He also boosted dividends and reorganized the board, reducing the family's control. MacMillan retired in 1995 and nonfamily member Ernest Micek became CEO and chairman.

The firm bought Akzo Nobel's North American salt operations in 1997, becoming the #2 US salt company. Cargill bulked up its grain trading business by acquiring the grain export operations of Continental Grain in 1999. Micek resigned as CEO that year and was replaced by Warren Staley. Also in 1999 Cargill fessed up to misappropriating some genetic seed material from rival Pioneer Hi-Bred, killing the $650 million sale of its North American seed assets to Germany's AgrEvo.

Cargill sold its coffee trading unit in 2000 and sought buyers for its rubber business. Also, Cargill sold its North American hybrid seed business to Dow Chemical (Cargill had sold its foreign seed operations to Monsanto in 1998) and bought Agribrands International (Purina and Checkerboard animal feeds sold outside the US).

In 2001 the company bought family-held turkey and chicken processor Rocco Enterprises. That year the North Star Steel subsidiary agreed to sell off its tubing business and laid off employees in other divisions, citing high energy costs and lower demands for steel. In late 2001, Cargill announced that it had agreed to purchase Cerestar (starches, syrups, feeds) from Montedison, and Taylor Packing Co. (beef) to enrich its Excel unit.

## OFFICERS

**Chairman and CEO:** Warren R. Staley
**Vice Chairman and CFO:** Robert L. Lumpkins
**Vice Chairman:** F. Guillaume Bastiaens, age 58
**Vice Chairman:** David W. Raisbeck
**President and COO:** Gregory R. Page
**EVP:** Fredric W. Corrigan
**EVP:** David M. Larson
**EVP:** Hubertus P. Spierings
**SVP, Director of Corporate Affairs:** Robbin S. Johnson
**SVP:** David W. Rogers
**Corporate VP:** William A. Buckner
**Corporate VP and Chief Technology Officer:**
Ronald L. Christenson
**Corporate VP, Deputy General Counsel:** Steven C. Euller
**Corporate VP:** John E. Geisler
**Corporate VP:** James N. Haymaker
**Corporate VP and Controller:** Galen G. Johnson
**Corporate VP:** John D. March
**Corporate VP, Public Affairs:** Bonnie E. Raquet
**Corporate VP, Transportation:** Frank L. Sims, age 50
**Corporate VP, Human Resources:** Nancy P. Siska

## LOCATIONS

**HQ:** 15407 McGinty Rd. West, Wayzata, MN 55391
**Phone:** 952-742-7575    **Fax:** 952-742-7393
**Web:** www.cargill.com

## PRODUCTS/OPERATIONS

**Selected Divisions and Products**

**Agriculture**
Animal feed
Biosciences
Fertilizer
Pet food

**Financial Markets**
Asset Investment &
  Finance Group
Cargill Technical Services
Financial Markets Group

**Food Processing**
Apples
Bulk and packaged oils
Cargill Malts
Citric acid
Corn and corn products
Cottonseed
Ethanol
Flaxseed
Hazelnuts
High fructose corn syrups
Masa flour (tortillas)
Oranges
Palm oil
Peanuts
Poultry
Progressive Baker

Riverside (turkey)
Soybeans
Sunflower seeds
Sunny Fresh (processed
  egg products)
Wilbur Chocolate
  Company

**Industrial**
Cargill Corn Milling
Cargill Industrial Oils &
  Lubricants
Cargill Steel and Wire
North Star Recycling
North Star Steel
Phosphate mining and
  fertilizer manufacturing
Salt

**Trading**
Cargill Investor Services
Cargill Marine and
  Terminal
Cargo Carriers
G&M Stevedoring
Greenwich Marine (ocean
  shipping)
Hohenberg Bros (cotton
  trading)

## COMPETITORS

Ag Processing
André
ADM
BASF AG
Bethlehem Steel
Bunge Limited
Cenex Harvest
  States
Cereol
COFCO
ConAgra

ContiGroup
Corn Products
  International
Dow Chemical
DuPont
Farmland
  Industries
General Mills
Hormel
IBP
Koch

Nippon Steel
Nucor
Perdue
Rohm and Haas
Saskatchewan
  Wheat Pool
Smithfield Foods
Tate & Lyle
Tyson Foods
United States
  Steel

## HISTORICAL FINANCIALS & EMPLOYEES

| Private<br>FYE: May 31 | Annual<br>Growth | 5/92 | 5/93 | 5/94 | 5/95 | 5/96 | 5/97 | 5/98 | 5/99 | 5/00 | 5/01 |
|---|---|---|---|---|---|---|---|---|---|---|---|
| Sales ($ mil.) | 0.6% | 46,800 | 47,100 | 47,135 | 51,000 | 56,000 | 56,000 | 51,400 | 50,000 | 47,602 | 49,400 |
| Net income ($ mil.) | (2.5%) | 450 | 358 | 571 | 671 | 902 | 814 | 468 | 597 | 480 | 358 |
| Income as % of sales | — | 1.0% | 0.8% | 1.2% | 1.3% | 1.6% | 1.5% | 0.9% | 1.2% | 1.0% | 0.7% |
| Employees | 4.0% | 63,500 | 70,000 | 70,700 | 73,300 | 76,000 | 79,000 | 80,600 | 84,000 | 84,000 | 90,000 |

**NET INCOME HISTORY**

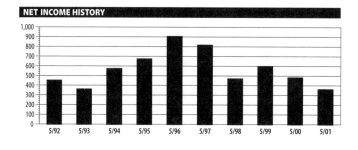

# CARLSON COMPANIES, INC.

## OVERVIEW

One of the largest private enterprises in the US, Minneapolis-based Carlson Companies has evolved from its humble origins as the creator of the Gold Bond trading stamps program to embrace travel, hotels, restaurants, and marketing services.

Carlson Companies' travel operations include Carlson Wagonlit Travel, its 50-50 joint venture with Accor. One of the largest business travel firms in the world, Carlson Wagonlit has more than 3,000 locations worldwide and counts AT&T, General Electric, and IBM among its clients. It sold its 22% stake in UK travel firm Thomas Cook Holdings to C&N, a German tour company, in 2001.

Operating more than 745 hotels worldwide, Carlson's lodging empire includes the 420-unit Radisson chain, as well as the Country Inns & Suites By Carlson (270 hotels) and Regent International (12 hotels) brands. Carlson also is active in cruise operations through its Radisson Seven Seas Cruises, which offers one all-suite and five deluxe ships sailing to about 485 destinations.

Carlson's most familiar brand may be its T.G.I. Friday's restaurant chain, which spans 670 units (about two-thirds are franchised) across more than 50 countries. Friday's is housed within the company's Carlson Restaurants Worldwide subsidiary, which also operates eateries under the Fishbowl, Italianni's, Mignon, Samba Room, Star Canyon, Taqueria Canonita, Pick Up Stix, and Timpano Italian Chophouse names.

The company's Carlson Marketing Group specializes in relationship marketing and offers services such as sales promotion; event and sports, employee, and direct marketing; and customer loyalty programs.

CEO Marilyn Carlson Nelson and director Barbara Carlson Gage, the daughters of the company's late founder Curtis Carlson, own the company.

## HISTORY

Curtis Carlson, the son of Swedish immigrants, graduated from the University of Minnesota in 1937 and went to work selling soap for Procter & Gamble in the Minneapolis area. In 1938 he borrowed $55 and formed Gold Bond Stamp Company to sell trading stamps. His wife, Arleen, dressed as a drum majorette and twirled a baton to promote the concept. By 1941 the company had 200 accounts. Business was slowed by WWII but took off in the 1950s. During the 1960s the company began diversifying into other enterprises such as travel, marketing, hotels, and real estate.

In 1962 Gold Bond Stamp bought the Radisson Hotel in Minneapolis and began expanding the chain. The company adopted the Carlson Companies name in 1973. Carlson Companies continued expanding its holdings during the 1970s, buying the 11-unit T.G.I. Friday's chain, as well as Country Kitchen International, a string of family restaurants.

In 1979 Carlson bought First Travel Corp., which owned travel agency Ask Mr. Foster and Colony Hotels. Carlson Companies slowed the pace of its acquisitions in the 1980s. Hired in 1984, Juergen Bartels changed the hospitality division's strategy from building and owning hotels to franchising and managing them. This enabled Carlson to weather the crash that followed the 1980s hotel building boom.

The company took T.G.I. Friday's public to fund expansion in 1983, but it reacquired all outstanding shares in 1989. Carlson launched its cruise ship business in 1992, when the luxury liner SSC *Radisson Diamond* set sail.

The company made a major international advance in 1994 when it formed joint venture Carlson Wagonlit Travel, with France's Accor. In 1997 Carlson expanded into the luxury hotel business when it bought Regent International from Four Seasons. Nodding its roots, the company also unveiled the Gold Points Reward guest loyalty system to reward customers who frequent its hotels and restaurants.

In 1998 Curtis Carlson appointed his daughter, Marilyn Carlson Nelson, as the company's chief executive (he remained chairman). The following year, Carlson Companies merged its UK leisure travel business with UK-based travel and financial services firm Thomas Cook. Founder Curtis Carlson died that year and Nelson became chair. The company later filed to spin off its T.G.I. Friday's unit as Carlson Restaurants Worldwide, but decided to put that offering on hold until market conditions improved.

In 2001 Carlson Companies sold its 22% stake in Thomas Cook Holdings to German tour company C&N. In mid-2001 the company bought 52-unit Asian restaurant chain Pick Up Stix. That year it also added a sixth ship to its cruise line.

## OFFICERS

**Chairman and CEO:** Marilyn Carlson Nelson
**EVP and CFO:** Martyn R. Redgrave, age 49
**SVP and General Counsel:** William Van Brunt
**SVP Human Resources:** Rosalyn Mallet
**SVP and Chief Information Officer:** Stephen Brown
**VP Public Relations and Communications:**
Douglas R. Cody
**VP and Treasurer:** John M. Diracles Jr.
**VP Tax:** Darrel M. Hamann
**VP Corporate Strategic Development and Acquisitions:**
Richard F. Hamm Jr.
**VP Corporate Financial Services and Business Risk
Management:** Anita Phillips
**VP Business Development for Corporate Customers:**
Robbin M. Rouillard
**VP Legal & Corporate Secretary:** Ralph Beha
**COO, Carlson Consumer Group:** Curtis C. Nelson
**COO, Carlson Corporate Solutions:** James J. Ryan
**President and CEO, Carlson Wagonlit Travel:**
Hervé Gourio
**President and CEO, Carlson Leisure Group:**
Michael Batt
**EVP and General Manager, Gold Points Rewards:**
Harold Schrum

## LOCATIONS

**HQ:** PO Box 59159, Minneapolis, MN 55459
**Phone:** 763-212-5000       **Fax:** 763-212-2219
**Web:** www.carlson.com

Carlson Companies has operations in more than 140
countries.

## PRODUCTS/OPERATIONS

**Selected Operations**

Cruises
  Radisson Seven Seas
    Cruises
Hotels
  Country Inns & Suites
    By Carlson
  Park Inn and Park Plaza
    hotels
  Radisson Hotels &
    Resorts
  Regent International
    Hotels
Marketing
  Carson Employee
    Marketing
  Carlson Marketing
    Group
Restaurants
  Fishbowl
  Italianni's
  Pick up Stix
  Samba Room
  Star Canyon
  Taqueria Canonita
  T.G.I. Friday's
  Timpano Italian
    Chophouse

Travel
  Carlson Destination
    Marketing Services
  Carlson Leisure
    Fulfillment Services
  Carlson Wagonlit Travel
    (50%)
  CarlsonTravel.com
  Neiman Marcus Travel
    Services
  Travel Agents
    International
Other
  Carlson Leasing Group
    (equipment lease
    financing)
  Carlson Vacation
    Ownership (vacation
    ownership properties)
  Gold Points Rewards
    (consumer loyalty
    program)
  Provisions (food and
    beverage distribution)

## COMPETITORS

Advantica
  Restaurant
  Group
American
  Express
Applebee's
Brinker
Carnival
Darden
  Restaurants
Fairmont Hotels
Four Seasons
  Hotels
Gage Marketing

Hilton
Hyatt
Interpublic
  Group
Maritz
Marriott
  International
Metromedia
O'Charley's
Omnicom
Outback
  Steakhouse
Ritz Carlton

Rosenbluth
  International
Royal Caribbean
  Cruises
Six Continents
Starwood Hotels
  & Resorts
Sunterra
TRT Holdings
WorldTravel
WPP Group
Wyndham
  International

## HISTORICAL FINANCIALS & EMPLOYEES

| Private<br>FYE: December 31 | Annual<br>Growth | 12/91 | 12/92 | 12/93 | 12/94 | 12/95 | 12/96 | 12/97 | 12/98 | 12/99 | 12/00 |
|---|---|---|---|---|---|---|---|---|---|---|---|
| Estimated sales ($ mil.) | 15.0% | — | 3,200 | 3,500 | 3,900 | 4,500 | 4,900 | 6,600 | 7,800 | 9,800 | 9,800 |
| Employees | 18.5% | — | 49,350 | 41,000 | 65,000 | 69,000 | 65,462 | 68,530 | 147,000 | 188,000 | 192,000 |

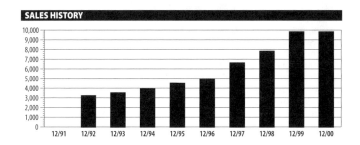

SALES HISTORY

# CARLSON WAGONLIT TRAVEL

## OVERVIEW

History was bunk for Henry Ford, but for Carlson Wagonlit Travel it was a bunk bed. Plymouth, Minnesota-based Carlson Wagonlit (pronounced Vah-gon-LEE) Travel descends from Europe's Wagons-Lits (literally, sleeping cars) company, which was founded by the creator of the Orient Express, and from the US's oldest travel agency chain (Ask Mr. Foster). Carlson Wagonlit Travel is the second-largest travel company in the world behind American Express. The company manages business travel from about 3,000 locations in more than 140 countries.

Carlson Wagonlit Travel is co-owned by France's Accor Group (motel and hotel franchises, travel and tourism services) and the US's Carlson Companies. Carlson Companies is a service conglomerate with nonbusiness travel operations such as hospitality (it franchises Radisson Hotels, T.G.I. Friday's and Italianni's restaurants, and luxury cruise lines) and marketing services (motivational and incentive programs for businesses).

The company's two parents have invested €100 million to get Carlson Wagonlit Travel online with business-to-consumer and business-to-business sites. Accor also is reaping the benefits of training the company's travel agents in booking Accor hotel rooms.

## HISTORY

Belgian inventor Georges Nagelmackers' first enterprise was adding sleeping compartments to European trains in 1872. Nagelmackers later created the Orient Express. Over the years his Wagons-Lits company expanded its mission to become Wagonlit Travel.

While Nagelmackers was establishing his business in Europe, Ward G. Foster was giving out steamship and train schedules from his gift shop facing the stately Ponce de Leon Hotel in St. Augustine, Florida. As legend has it, hotel patrons with travel questions were directed to Foster's shop with: "Ask Mr. Foster. He'll know." In 1888 he founded Ask Mr. Foster Travel (it became the oldest travel agency in the US). By 1913 the company had offices located in pricey department stores and in the lobbies of upscale hotels and resorts throughout the country. After 50 years at the helm, Foster sold his business in 1937, three years before his death.

After suffering hard times during WWII and into the 1950s, the company changed hands again in 1957 when Donald Fisher and Thomas Orr, two Ask Mr. Foster shareholders, bought controlling interests for $157,000. In 1972 Peter Ueberroth (Major League Baseball commissioner and Los Angeles Olympic Organizing Committee president) bought the company, then sold it in 1979 to Carlson Companies, Inc., Carlson Wagonlit's parent. In 1990 Ask Mr. Foster became Carlson Travel Network. Also that year Carlson Companies acquired the UK's A.T. Mays, the Travel Agents — a leading UK seller of vacation and tour packages. By 1992 Carlson Companies, besides adding a travel agency a day to the 2,000-plus it already owned, was adding a new hotel every 10 days.

Europe's Wagonlit Travel and the US's Carlson Travel Network joined forces in 1994 to pursue expansion efforts. Under a dual-president ownership, the parent companies owned operations in specific world regions. The two companies began developing new business technology and expanded into new global business markets. In 1994 the venture acquired Germany's Brune Reiseburo travel agency and opened a branch office in Moscow. Acquisitions in 1995 and 1996 targeted the Asia/Pacific region, including Hong Kong's and Japan's Dodwell Travel and the corporate travel business of Singapore's Jetset Travel. It also formed a partnership with Traveland, an Australian travel agency.

In 1997 Wagonlit Travel and Carlson Travel Network finalized the merger of their business activities operations, renamed Carlson Wagonlit Travel. The following year the new company acquired Florida's Travel Agents International, with more than 300 franchised operations and $600 million in annual sales. In 1999 three travel agencies in eastern Canada consolidated under the Carlson Wagonlit Travel brand, creating the largest travel network in that region. Also, Carlson Companies founder and Carlson Wagonlit Travel chairman Curtis Carlson died. In 2000 the company agreed to form a Japan-based joint venture with Japan Travel Bureau (now JTB Corp.). The arrangement will increase Carlson Wagonlit's presence in Asia while increasing the number of JTB locations in North America.

In 2001 Carlson Wagonlit cut jobs because of a slowdown in business travel.

CEO and President; President, Europe, Middle East,
and Africa: Hervé Gourio
President, Asia Pacific: Geoffrey Marshall
President, North America: Robin Schleien
CFO: Tim Hennessy
EVP Global Sales and Account Management:
Liliana Frigerio
EVP Europe, Middle East, and Africa: Richard Lovell
EVP Client Service Industry Relations and Solutions
Group, North America: Robert Deliberto
EVP North American Operations: Dan Miles
Chief Information Officer: Loren Brown
CFO, Europe, Middle East, and Africa:
Nicholas Francou
VP Human Resources North America: Cindy Rodahl
VP Information Technology, Europe, Middle East, and
Africa: Len Blackwood

## COMPETITORS

American Express
JTB
Kuoni Travel
Maritz
Preussag
Rosenbluth International
Thomas Cook AG
WorldTravel

## LOCATIONS

HQ: 1405 Xenium Ln., Plymouth, MN 55441
Phone: 763-212-4000
Web: www.carlsonwagonlit.com

## HISTORICAL FINANCIALS & EMPLOYEES

| Joint venture FYE: December 31 | Annual Growth | 12/91 | 12/92 | 12/93 | 12/94 | 12/95 | 12/96 | 12/97 | 12/98 | 12/99 | 12/00 |
|---|---|---|---|---|---|---|---|---|---|---|---|
| Sales ($ mil.) | 6.0% | — | — | — | — | — | 9,500 | 10,600 | 11,000 | 11,000 | 12,000 |
| Employees | 0.1% | — | — | — | — | — | 20,000 | 20,000 | 20,100 | 20,100 | 20,100 |

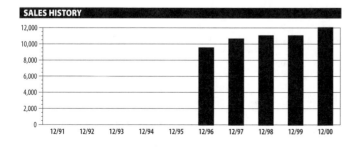

SALES HISTORY

# THE CARLYLE GROUP

Can you say military-industrial complex? The Carlyle Group can. With former Defense Secretary Frank Carlucci leading the charge, the Washington, DC-based investment firm made a name for itself in the 1990s by snatching up defense industry remnants.

Carlyle's directorship reads like George W. Bush's inaugural ball invite list. Reagan Secretary of the Treasury James Baker serves as a senior counselor, and Richard Darman, former director of the Office of Management and Budget under George Bush (the elder), is a managing director. Former President Bush has served as well, and Secretary of State Colin Powell, before joining the current Cabinet, made an appearance on behalf of the firm.

The firm takes part in management-led buyouts (MBOs), acquires minority stakes, and provides other investment capital for companies in aerospace and defense (United Defense Industries), consumer products (Dr Pepper/Seven Up Bottling Group), energy, health care (MedPointe), information technology, real estate, and telecommunications. MBOs make up the bulk of Carlyle's investments. Although the majority of the firm's money is in North America, it is also pushing more intensely overseas, launching funds aimed at Asia, Europe, Latin America, and Russia. In a sign of slowing times, The Carlyle Group signaled it may return some uninvested funds to investors.

In 1987 T. Rowe Price director Edward Mathias brought together David Rubenstein, a former President Carter aide; Stephen Norris and Daniel D'Aniello, both executives with Marriott Corp.; William Conway Jr., the CFO of MCI; and Greg Rosenbaum, a VP with a New York investment firm. They pooled their experience along with a load of money from T. Rowe Price Associates, Alex. Brown & Sons (now Deutsche Banc Alex. Brown), First Interstate (now part of Wells Fargo), and Pittsburgh's Mellon family to form a buyout firm.

Named after the Carlyle Hotel in New York, the firm opted to make Washington, DC, its headquarters so it wouldn't get lost in the crowd of New York investment firms. The company spent its first years investing in a mish-mash of companies, using Norris' and D'Aniello's Marriott experience to focus primarily on restaurant and food service companies (including Mexican restaurant chain Chi-Chi's).

In 1989 it wooed the well-connected Frank Carlucci, who had served as President Reagan's secretary of defense, to join the group. Soon Carlyle began making more high-profile deals. That year it acquired Coldwell Banker's commercial real estate operations (sold 1996) and Caterair International, Marriott's airline food services (sold 1995).

Carlucci helped redirect the firm's focus to the downsizing defense industry. Among its targets were Harsco Corp. (1990), BDM International (1991), and LTV Corp.'s missile and aircraft units (1992). Carlyle helped overhaul their operations and make them attractive (for the right price) to the industry's elite, including Boeing and Lockheed Martin.

As the company's reputation grew, so did its cast of players. Among its new backers were James Baker and Richard Darman (both Reagan and Bush administration alums) and investor George Soros, who chipped in some $100 million into the Carlyle Partners L.P. buyout fund. With the help of its "access capitalists" such as Baker and Saudi Prince al-Waleed bin Talal (whom the firm helped add to his fortune in a 1991 Citicorp stock transaction), Carlyle made deals in the Middle East and western Europe (including a bailout of Euro Disney) in the mid-1990s.

While the firm continued to invest in the defense industry, acquiring such defense companies as aircraft castings maker Howmet in 1995, it picked up a grab bag of holdings, such as natural food grocer Fresh Fields Markets (1994; sold 1996); the quick turnaround helped build Carlyle's war chest. The firm also began investing in industrial-cleanup companies, seeing increased government spending as a major opportunity for profit.

As Carlyle's esteem rose, so did the number of its investors. In the late 1990s the firm launched buyout funds targeting Asia, Europe, Russia, and Latin America. At home, it faced a dwindling number of opportunities as the long-running bull market drove up prices and more investors chased fewer deals. Among those was its partnership with Cadbury Schweppes to buy the Dr Pepper Bottling Co. of Texas and merge it with its own American Bottling Co.

In 2000 the company inked a deal for Ssangyong Information & Communications Corp., a computer network integration firm in South Korea, but the deal was called off the next year. Also in 2001 Carlyle launched Carlyle Asset Management Group.

## OFFICERS

**Chairman and Managing Director:** Frank C. Carlucci, age 71
**Senior Counselor:** James A. Baker III
**CEO, Carlyle Management Group:** B. Edward Ewing
**Chairman of Carlyle Europe:** Rt. Hon. John Major, CH, age 57
**Founder and Managing Director:** William E. Conway Jr.
**Founder and Managing Director:** Daniel A. D'Aniello
**Founder and Managing Director:** David M. Rubenstein
**Senior Advisor:** Arthur Levitt
**Managing Director and CFO:** John F. Harris
**Managing Director, US Buyouts:** Leslie L. Armitage
**Managing Director US Buyouts, Global Telecommunications and Media Group:** James A. Attwood Jr.
**Managing Director, US Buyouts:** Peter J. Clare
**Managing Director US Buyouts, Global Telecommunications and Media Group:** Francis B. Barker
**Managing Director, US Buyouts:** Daniel Cummings
**Managing Director, US Buyouts Healthcare Group:** W. Robert Dahl
**Managing Director, US Buyouts:** Allan M. Holt, age 49
**Managing Director, US High Yield Group:** Jack S. Mann
**Managing Director, US Buyouts Global Telecommunications and Media Group:** William E. Kennard
**Managing Director, US Buyouts, Global Telecommunications and Media Group:** Bruce Rosenblum
**Managing Director, US Buyouts, Consumer and Industrial Group:** Jerome H. Powell

## LOCATIONS

**HQ:** 1001 Pennsylvania Ave. NW, Ste. 220 South, Washington, DC 20004
**Phone:** 202-347-2626          **Fax:** 202-347-1818
**Web:** www.thecarlylegroup.com

The Carlyle Group has about 20 offices in more than a dozen countries around the world.

## COMPETITORS

| | |
|---|---|
| ABN AMRO | Investcorp |
| Bain Capital | J.P. Morgan Partners |
| Blackstone Group | KKR |
| Credit Suisse First Boston (USA), Inc. | Lehman Brothers |
| | Texas Pacific Group |
| Forstmann Little | Thomas Lee |
| Goldman Sachs | UBS Warburg |
| Hicks, Muse | |

# CARQUEST CORPORATION

## OVERVIEW

Searching for a sensor, solenoid, or switches? CARQUEST can steer you in the right direction. The auto parts distribution group, based in Raleigh, North Carolina, sells its own line of auto parts (made by Moog Automotive, Gabriel, and Dana, among others) to jobbers and wholesalers for eventual resale to professional repair centers, service stations, dealerships, and, to a lesser degree, do-it-yourself (DIY) customers. CARQUEST is owned by seven warehouse distributors.

The company's more than 60 warehouse distribution centers (DCs) service more than 4,000 distributor-owned and independent jobbers in the US and Canada. General Parts, its largest distributor, owns about 1,200 stores across the US and Canada. The average CARQUEST store carries about 15,000 parts, while a DC carries some 150,000 items.

To strengthen ties with service shops, CARQUEST offers the Tech-Net Professional Service program. The program, available for an annual fee, includes 20 minutes of diagnostic hotline service per month (additional time is available), as well as a full guarantee on parts; signage and other marketing tools are also included.

Consolidation in the aftermarket industry has blurred the lines of distribution between wholesalers and retailers, causing all segments of the industry to scramble for ways to gain or maintain market share. CARQUEST focuses on professional mechanics, but it is being squeezed as retailers such as AutoZone look beyond their regular DIY customers for a piece of the commercial pie. At the same time, chains such as The Pep Boys - Manny, Moe & Jack are chipping away at service stations' business by offering parts and service.

## HISTORY

Even though he didn't know the auto parts business, Temple Sloan recognized America's infatuation with the automobile and started distributor General Parts in 1961 at age 21. By 1972 he had acquired enough warehouse space to supply the entire state of North Carolina. Determined to get bigger faster, Sloan studied auto parts kingpin Genuine Parts, digging through its annual reports and uncovering tricks of the trade, while working on a few of his own. To compete in what was then a fast-growing industry, Genuine Parts had created a marketing alliance, NAPA, that used mass buying power to garner better pricing and service from manufacturers that often wouldn't recognize individual companies.

Sloan recruited friends and fellow distributors Dan Bock, president of Bobro Products, and Joe Hughes, president of Indiana Parts Warehouse, and together they formed CARQUEST in 1974. The company was designed to help jobbers (middlemen between distributors and mechanics) being threatened by retailers attempting to get a piece of the commercial business market traditionally served by jobbers. CARQUEST began recruiting other distributors and achieved first-year sales of $29 million. In the first five years, almost 1,500 jobbers committed to CARQUEST. Leadership rotated among distributor members until Bock became president in 1984.

As CARQUEST grew, the need for a unifying private-label line became apparent. In the 1970s it developed the Proven Value line of do-it-yourself-oriented products such as oils and filters. The establishment of the CARQUEST brand in the mid-1980s gave the company complete control over quality, coverage, price, and promotions, giving CARQUEST jobbers an advantage in the marketplace. Private-label sales grew from 20%-25% of business to 70% by 1996.

That year CARQUEST relocated its national headquarters from Tarrytown, New York, to Lakewood, Colorado, and Peter Kornafel became president and CEO, replacing Bock. Kornafel had been president of Hatch Grinding, a Denver distributor that merged with General Parts in 1996. The next year the firm moved into Canada, as General Parts bought half of the McKerlie-Millen subsidiary of Acklands (more than 400 parts stores). In 1998 CARQUEST launched its Tech-Net Professional Service program.

Also in 1998 CARQUEST added about 150 new stores to its network when General Parts bought bankrupt APS Holding; it also added 75 stores and eight DCs from Republic Auto. In 1999 General Parts bought The Parts Source, which included 41 Ace Auto Parts stores in Florida.

In January 2000 General Parts bought Acktion Corp's 50% interest in CARQUEST Canada, giving them complete ownership. Later in the year, General Parts also bought St. Louis-based distributor A.E. Lottes Co. In 2001 CARQUEST moved its headquarters to Raleigh, North Carolina, and Art Lottes III succeeded Kornafel as president.

## OFFICERS

**Chairman:** Neil Stockel
**President**: A.E. Lottes III
**EVP:** Daniel M. Bock
**Human Resources, Administration and Marketing Department:** Louise Veasman

## LOCATIONS

**HQ:** 2635 Millbrook Road, Raleigh, NC 27604
**Phone:** 919-573-2500        **Fax:** 919-573-2501
**Web:** www.carquest.com

CARQUEST operates more than 60 warehouse distribution centers serving more than 4,000 stores in the US and Canada.

## PRODUCTS/OPERATIONS

**Member Warehouse Distributors**
Auto Parts Wholesale
Automotive Warehouse, Inc.
BWP Distributor, Inc.
CAP Warehouse
CARQUEST CANADA, Ltd. (owned by General Parts)
General Parts, Inc.
Muffler Warehouse
Strafo, Inc.

**Selected Manufacturers of CARQUEST Products**
Airtex
American Driveline
Autoline Industries
Cardone Industries
Dana
Federal
Federal Mogul Corporation
Gates
Maremont/Gabriel
Melling
Moog Automotive
NEAPCO
Standard Motor Products
Wells Manufacturing Corp.
WIX

## COMPETITORS

AutoZone
CSK Auto
Genuine Parts
Hahn Automotive
  Warehouse
Pep Boys
Sears
Target
Wal-Mart

## HISTORICAL FINANCIALS & EMPLOYEES

| Private<br>FYE: December 31 | Annual<br>Growth | 12/91 | 12/92 | 12/93 | 12/94 | 12/95 | 12/96 | 12/97 | 12/98 | 12/99 | 12/00 |
|---|---|---|---|---|---|---|---|---|---|---|---|
| Sales ($ mil.) | 13.3% | — | 734 | 860 | 860 | 940 | 1,200 | 1,300 | 1,400 | 2,000 | 2,000 |
| Employees | 6.7% | — | — | — | — | 26,000 | 26,000 | 35,000 | 35,000 | 36,000 | 36,000 |

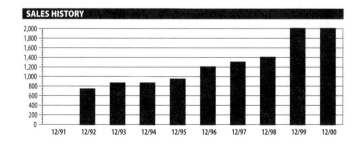

SALES HISTORY

# CATHOLIC HEALTH EAST

Catholic Health East doesn't believe prayers to St. Jude are necessary to continue providing health care to any person in need. Based in Newtown Square, Pennsylvania, the company is one of the top religious health systems in the US.

The company carries out its mission of serving the poor and the old through more than 30 hospitals, some 30 nursing homes, about 20 independent- and assisted-living facilities, and three behavioral health facilities. Its services for the elderly include hospice care, adult day care, and home health services. Catholic Health East is governed by a board composed of 10 sisters, eight secular health care professionals, and one reverend.

Like many religious health care systems, Catholic Health East continues to struggle with the problem of keeping both the faith and the bottom line intact. Providing indigent care is becoming increasingly difficult thanks to the ever-rising costs of health care coupled with cuts in reimbursements that have hurt not only the system's hospital services but also nursing home and outpatient services.

## HISTORY

It was three easy pieces that made up Catholic Health East in 1997. Allegany Health System, Eastern Mercy Health System, and Sisters of Providence Health System operated almost entirely in separate, but adjacent, geographic areas on the East Coast, overlapping only in Florida.

Catholic Health East's history goes as far back as 1831, when the Sisters of Mercy was founded in Dublin, Ireland, by Catherine McAuley, who established a poorhouse using her inheritance. Some of the sisters hopped the Pond in 1843, establishing the first Catholic hospital in the US, the Mercy Hospital of Pittsburgh, four years later. Over the years the Sisters of Mercy expanded throughout the US. By 1991 there were 25 Sisters of Mercy congregations; they united that year under the newly formed Institute of the Sisters of Mercy of the Americas.

The Sisters of Providence came from Kingston, Ontario, to found the first hospital in Holyoke, Massachusetts. Having established their own ministry, the sisters in Holyoke became a separate congregation in 1892. The congregation expanded slowly, moving into North Carolina in 1956, eventually forming the Sisters of Providence Health System.

A Polish nun, Mother Colette Hilbert, formed a new congregation in Pittsburgh in 1897 after the other members of her former parish were recalled to Poland. The new congregation entered health care in 1926, establishing a home for the elderly in New York. In honor of Hilbert's favorite saint, the order became the Franciscan Sisters of St. Joseph in 1934.

The Franciscan Sisters of St. Joseph and the Sisters of Mercy united to form the ministry that became Pittsburgh Mercy Health System in 1983. In 1986 the congregations formed Eastern Mercy Health System as a holding company for the health concern. The consolidation served to cut costs, as well as to preserve the organization's religious mission.

The Franciscan Sisters of Allegany congregation got its start in 1859 teaching children in Buffalo, New York. In 1883 the order took over St. Elizabeth Hospital in Boston, expanding its health care services ministry throughout New York, New Jersey, and Florida by the 1930s. In 1986 the sisters organized the operations as Allegany Health System.

In the early 1990s Catholic health care systems underwent a round of consolidation. Allegany Health Systems and Eastern Mercy Health Systems combined services, aiming to lower costs through economies of scale.

The mid-1990s also brought consolidation, but this time operational costs weren't the major problem; Catholic health systems across the nation were facing a shortage of sisters. To have a sufficient number of sisters to keep the "Catholic" in Catholic health care, the three health systems merged in 1997, becoming Catholic Health East.

After the merger, the company continued to build its network through acquisitions, including Mercy Health in Miami (1998) and a suffering, secular Cooper Health System in Camden, New Jersey (1999). In 2000 it gained control of two troubled hospitals in Palm Beach, Florida, only to sell them the following year. It also announced plans to buy five Philadelphia-area hospitals from Catholic Health Initiatives.

**President and CEO:** Daniel F. Russell
**EVP and CFO:** C. Kent Russell
**EVP, Long Term and Continuing Care:**
Robert H. Morrow
**EVP, Mission Integration:** Sister Juliana Casey
**EVP, System Integration and Development:**
Stanley T. Urban
**SVP and Chief Medical Officer:** Richard F. Afable
**VP, Advocacy and Government Relations:**
Kenneth A. Becker
**VP, Communications:** Salvatore C. Foti
**VP, Corporate Compliance and Legal Services:**
Michael C. Hemsley
**VP, Financial Services:** Randal Schultz
**VP, Information Technology and Chief Information
Officer:** John Hueter
**VP, Leadership Formation and Human Resources:**
George F. Longshore
**VP, Mission Services:** Mary Ann Carter
**VP, Quality Services:** Diane S. Denny
**VP, Risk Management Services and Chief Risk Officer:**
Theodore Schlert
**VP, Strategy Development:** Elaine Bauer
**VP, Treasury Services:** Paul Klinck
**EVP, Mid-Atlantic Division:** Robert V. Stanek
**EVP, Northeast Division:** Sister Kathleen Popko
**EVP, Southeast Division:** Howard Watts

## LOCATIONS

**HQ:** 14 Campus Blvd., Ste. 300,
Newtown Square, PA 19073
**Phone:** 610-355-2000    **Fax:** 610-355-2050
**Web:** www.che.org

## PRODUCTS/OPERATIONS

**Divisions**

**Northeast**
Catholic Health System (Buffalo, NY)
Mercy Health System of Maine (Portland)
Mercycare Corporation (Albany, NY)
Sisters of Providence Health System (Springfield, MA)
St. James Mercy Health System (Hornell, NY)

**Mid-Atlantic**
Lourdes Health System (Camden, NJ)
Mercy Health System (Conshohocken, PA)
Pittsburgh Mercy Health System

**Southeast**
BayCare Health Systems (Clearwater, FL)
Holy Cross Health Ministries (Fort Lauderdale, FL)
Intracoastal Health System (West Palm Beach, FL)
Mercy Hospital (Miami)
Saint Joseph's Health System (Atlanta)
St. Mary's Health Care System, Inc. (Athens, GA)

**Long-Term Care**
Mercy Community Health (West Hartford, CT)
Mercy Medical (Daphne, AL)
Mercy Uihlein Health Corporation (Lake Placid, NY)
St. Joseph of the Pines (Pinehurst, NC)

**Other**
Franciscan Health Foundation (Tampa, FL)
Catholic Managed Care Consortium (St. Louis)
Catholic Health Association (St. Louis)
Children's Health Matters (Alexandria, VA)
Mercy Resource Management, Inc. (Naperville, IL)
NewCap Insurance Company, Limited (Cayman
Islands)
Premier (California, Illinois, and North Carolina)

## COMPETITORS

Ascension
Bon Secours Health
Catholic Health Initiatives
HCA
Triad Hospitals

## HISTORICAL FINANCIALS & EMPLOYEES

| Not-for-profit FYE: December 31 | Annual Growth | 12/91 | 12/92 | 12/93 | 12/94 | 12/95 | 12/96 | 12/97 | 12/98 | 12/99 | 12/00 |
|---|---|---|---|---|---|---|---|---|---|---|---|
| Sales ($ mil.) | 12.3% | — | — | — | — | — | 2,700 | 3,000 | 3,800 | 4,300 | 4,300 |
| Employees | 11.4% | — | — | — | — | — | — | 31,838 | 45,000 | 45,000 | 44,000 |

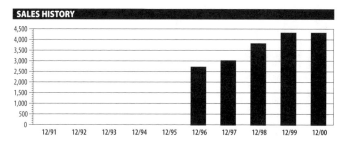

**SALES HISTORY**

CATHOLIC HEALTH EAST

# CATHOLIC HEALTH INITIATIVES

## OVERVIEW

"And he sent them out to preach the Kingdom of God and to heal the sick" (Luke 9:2). Denver-based Catholic Health Initiatives (CHI) hopes to make those words the driving force behind its initiative. CHI is one of the top Roman Catholic health care systems in the US. Sponsored by 12 congregations, the not-for-profit organization serves residents in about 20 states. It operates more than 60 hospitals and more than 40 long-term care, assisted-living, and residential facilities.

CHI has to deal with the conundrum facing many Catholic health systems: Their religious mission — to care for the "unserved and

underserved" (and underinsured) members of its communities — is financially uncompetitive. CHI offsets the expense of its mission by also providing health care to the general public and by making business decisions more often associated with secular business (cutting staff, centralizing functions, and joining with other Catholic health care institutions to drive harder bargains with medical suppliers).

As a reflection of its divine purpose in a mundane health care market, the company's governing board is made up of both religious and lay officers.

## HISTORY

In 1860 the Sisters of St. Francis established a hospital in Philadelphia, laying the foundation for a larger health care organization. In 1981 Franciscan Health System was formally established to be a national holding company for Catholic hospitals and related organizations. By the mid-1990s the system consisted of 12 member and two affiliate hospitals and 11 long-term-care facilities located in the mid-Atlantic states and the Pacific Northwest.

Sisters of Charity of Cincinnati and the Sisters of St. Francis Perpetual Adoration of Colorado Springs co-sponsored The Sisters of Charity Health Care Systems, incorporated in 1979 as a multi-institutional health care network. By the mid-1990s the system included 20 hospitals in Colorado, Kentucky, Nebraska, New Mexico, and Ohio.

Three congregations collaborated to form Catholic Health Corporation in 1980, one of the first such health care partnerships between religious communities within the Roman Catholic Church in the US. By 1996 this coalition operated 100 health care facilities in 12 states.

The development of modern managed care systems put pressure on the smaller Catholic hospital operations, so the three systems established Catholic Health Initiatives (CHI) in 1996 as a national entity serving five geographic regions. Patricia Cahill, a lay health care veteran who previously served the Archdiocese of New York, was appointed president and CEO of CHI. The following year CHI absorbed the 10-hospital Sisters of Charity of Nazareth Health Care System, based in Bardstown, Kentucky (founded in a log cabin in 1812).

That year CHI continued to seek new partnerships to improve efficiency. With Alegent Health it formed provider network Midwest

Select with nearly 200 hospitals, marketing discounted rates to businesses. CHI allied with the Daughters of Charity to form for-profit joint venture Catholic Healthcare Audit Network to provide operational, financial, compliance, and information systems audits, as well as due diligence reviews. CHI also joined insurance joint venture NewCap Insurance with the Daughters of Charity and Catholic Health East; the firm allowed CHI to operate independently of commercial insurers.

CHI made a secular tie-in with the University of Pennsylvania Health System in 1998, whereby the university's system would offer care through five Catholic hospitals (CHI made plans to transfer these hospitals to Catholic Health East in 2001). The next year CHI announced its first loss, due to lackluster performance in the Midwest. In 2000 the company responded by streamlining operations and changing management, resulting in a positive bottom line. The next year it sold three hospitals in Pennsylvania and one in Delaware to Catholic Health East; it also made plans to sell facilities in New Jersey.

Late in 2001 CHI announced it was seeking a buyer for St. Joseph's Healthcare System located in Albuquerque, New Mexico. The system includes three acute care hospitals, a rehabilitation hospital, and physician practices.

## OFFICERS

**Chairman:** Maryanna Coyle
**President and CEO:** Patricia A. Cahill
**EVP and COO:** Kevin Lofton
**SVP, Finance and Treasury:** Sister Geraldine Hoyler
**SVP and Chief Medical Officer:** Harold E. Ray
**SVP, Human Resources, and Chief Administrative
    Officer:** Michael Fordyce
**Chief Information Officer:** Christopher Macmanus
**Auditors:** Ernst & Young LLP

## LOCATIONS

**HQ:** 1999 Broadway, Ste. 2605, Denver, CO 80202
**Phone:** 303-298-9100    **Fax:** 303-298-9690
**Web:** www.catholichealthinit.org

Catholic Health Initiatives has facilities in 21 states.

## PRODUCTS/OPERATIONS

### 2001 Sales

|  | $ mil. | % of total |
|---|---|---|
| Patient services |  |  |
| Acute inpatient | 2,752 | 48 |
| Outpatient care | 1,892 | 33 |
| Physician | 259 | 4 |
| Long-term care | 189 | 3 |
| Home-based & residential | 156 | 3 |
| Premiums & other | 107 | 2 |
| Non-patient |  |  |
| Investment income | 91 | 2 |
| Other | 296 | 5 |
| **Total** | **5,742** | **100** |

**Sponsoring Congregations**
Benedictine Sisters of Mother of God Monastery
    (Watertown, SD)
Congregation of the Dominican Sisters of St. Catherine
    of Siena (Kenosha, WI)
Franciscan Sisters of Little Falls (Little Falls, MN)
Nuns of the Third Order of St. Dominic (Great Bend,
    KS)
Sisters of Charity of Cincinnati
Sisters of Charity of Nazareth (Bardstown, KY)
Sisters of the Holy Family of Nazareth (Philadelphia, PA)
Sisters of Mercy of the Americas, Regional Community
    of Omaha (Omaha, NE)
Sisters of the Presentation of the Blessed Virgin Mary
    (Fargo, ND)
Sisters of St. Francis of Colorado Springs
Sisters of St. Francis of the Immaculate Heart of Mary
    (Hankinson, ND)
Sisters of St. Francis of Philadelphia

## COMPETITORS

| | |
|---|---|
| Allina Health | Health Midwest |
| Ascension | Life Care Centers |
| Beverly Enterprises | Mayo Foundation |
| BJC Health | OhioHealth |
| Catholic Healthcare | Presbyterian Healthcare |
| Partners | Services |
| HCA | Tenet Healthcare |
| HMA | |

## HISTORICAL FINANCIALS & EMPLOYEES

| Not-for-profit FYE: June 30 | Annual Growth | 6/92 | 6/93 | 6/94 | 6/95 | 6/96 | 6/97 | 6/98 | 6/99 | 6/00 | 6/01 |
|---|---|---|---|---|---|---|---|---|---|---|---|
| Sales ($ mil.) | 24.7% | — | 985 | 1,116 | 3,800 | 3,755 | 4,002 | 4,500 | 5,000 | 5,551 | 5,742 |
| Employees | 14.5% | — | — | — | — | — | — | 44,000 | — | 56,100 | 66,000 |

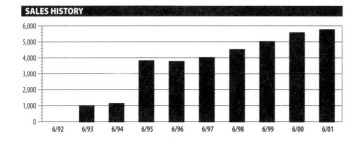

SALES HISTORY

CATHOLIC HEALTH INITIATIVES

# CATHOLIC HEALTHCARE WEST

Faced with skyrocketing health care costs, diminishing health care spending, and a host of problems related to its growth, Catholic Healthcare West (CHW) is operating on a wing and a prayer. The organization is one of the Golden State's largest private, not-for-profit health care systems.

San Francisco-based CHW has a network of more than 45 facilities in California, Arizona, and Nevada; these include hospitals, medical centers, and skilled nursing facilities. CHW also has an alliance with Scripps, a large San Diego-based provider. With both clergy and laity on its governing board, CHW has grown by consolidating hospitals owned by Roman Catholic women's religious orders. Additional affiliations with non-Catholic institutions have raised some hackles because Catholic doctrine opposes abortion, most forms of birth control, and *in vitro* fertilization.

The rapid expansion that made CHW a name in the California health care industry also left it bloated. Rising health care costs and trouble with its physician management groups have cut deeply into earnings. Management casualties occurred as CHW tried to regain profitability by reorganizing.

## HISTORY

Catholic Healthcare West traces its roots to 1857, when the Sisters of Mercy founded St. Mary's Hospital in San Francisco. The order expanded in that area, and in 1986 two different communities of the Sisters of Mercy merged their hospitals into an organization with one retirement home and 10 hospitals from the Bay Area to San Diego. Declining membership in Roman Catholic religious orders, combined with consolidation in the field, led the orders to see merger as their only route to survival.

Rising medical costs, slow payers, and merger expenses dropped the organization's combined net income to $20 million in 1988 (from nearly $58 million in 1986). One of the hardest-hit CHW affiliates was Mercy Healthcare Sacramento, which lost $4.2 million between 1986 and 1987. In 1988 Mercy Healthcare restructured along regional lines.

The next year the Sisters of St. Dominic brought two hospitals into the alliance. CHW launched the Community Economic Assistance program, which provided $220,000 in grants to 16 human service and health care agencies in its first year.

CHW continued to add facilities, including AMI Community Hospital in Santa Cruz, California, in 1990. Since CHW already owned the area's only other acute care hospital, Dominican Santa Cruz Hospital, CHW in 1993 was ordered not to acquire any more acute care hospitals in Santa Cruz County without FTC approval.

As the trend to managed care became a stampede in the 1990s, CHW moved more into preventive care and began reining in costs through productivity improvement plans. It continued to add hospitals, including tax-supported institutions trying to compete with national for-profit systems.

The network increased its medical clout in 1994 by allying with San Diego-based Scripps, one of the state's largest HMO systems. In 1995 the Daughters of Charity Province of the West realigned its six-hospital operation with CHW. The next year the Dominican Sisters (California), the Dominican Sisters of St. Catherine of Siena (Wisconsin), and the Sisters of Charity of the Incarnate Word allied their California hospitals with CHW. New community hospitals included Bakersfield Memorial, Sierra Nevada Memorial (Grass Valley), Sequoia Hospital (Redwood City), and Woodland Healthcare.

Charity and cost-consciousness clashed in 1996 when union members staged a walkout to protest nonunion outsourcing of vocational nursing, housekeeping, and kitchen jobs. This dispute was settled, but CHW continued to be a target for union organizers, with a bitter battle against the Service Employees International Union (SEIU) starting in 1998.

CHW agreed in 1996 to merge with Samaritan Health Systems (now Banner Health System) in a move that would have made CHW one of the US's top five providers, but the deal fell apart in 1997. In 1998 CHW merged with UniHealth, a group with eight facilities in Los Angeles and Orange counties. Mounting costs forced CHW to post a loss, and in 1999 it cut some managerial positions and reorganized to recover.

The year 2000 brought CHW more problems with labor relations: SEIU argued that the organization was resistant to unionization. Continued losses led the organization to implement major restructuring the following year, as its 10 regional divisions were consolidated into four.

## OFFICERS

**Chairperson:** Diane Grassilli
**President and CEO:** Lloyd H. Dean
**EVP and CFO:** Michael Blaszyk
**SVP and Chief Medical Officer:** George Bo-Linn
**SVP Legal Services and General Counsel:**
Robert Johnson
**SVP Mission Services:** Bernita McTernan
**VP Finance:** Mary Connick
**VP Home Health Services:** Meg Piscitelli
**VP Human Resources:** Ernie Urquhart
**VP Information Systems and Technology Services:**
Gayle Simpkin
**Chief Administrative Officer:** Elizabeth Shih
**Division President, Arizona/Nevada Region:**
Michael Erne
**Division President, Greater Bay Area Region:**
Anna Mullins
**Division President, Northern California Region:**
Edward G. Schroeder
**Division President, Southern California Region:**
Beth O' Brien
**Auditors:** Arthur Andersen LLP

## LOCATIONS

**HQ:** 1700 Montgomery St., Ste. 300,
San Francisco, CA 94111
**Phone:** 415-438-5500     **Fax:** 415-438-5724
**Web:** www.chw.edu

Catholic Healthcare West operates hospitals in Arizona,
California, and Nevada.

## PRODUCTS/OPERATIONS

**Sponsoring Organizations**
Daughters of Charity, Province of the West
Dominican Sisters of San Rafael
Franciscan Sisters of the Sacred Heart of Frankfort,
Illinois
Sisters of Charity of the Incarnate Word of Houston,
Texas
Sisters of Mercy, Auburn and Burlingame Regional
Communities
Sisters of St. Catherine of Siena of Kenosha, Wisconsin
Sisters of St. Dominic of Adrian, Michigan
Sisters of St. Francis of Penance and Christian Charity
of Redwood City

## COMPETITORS

Adventist Health
Carondelet Health
Catholic Health Initiatives
HCA
Los Angeles County
Department of Health
Memorial Health Services
Sutter Health
Tenet Healthcare
Triad Hospitals

## HISTORICAL FINANCIALS & EMPLOYEES

| Not-for-profit FYE: June 30 | Annual Growth | 6/91 | 6/92 | 6/93 | 6/94 | 6/95 | 6/96 | 6/97 | 6/98 | 6/99 | 6/00 |
|---|---|---|---|---|---|---|---|---|---|---|---|
| Sales ($ mil.) | 16.0% | — | 1,464 | 1,633 | 2,584 | 2,674 | 2,688 | 2,749 | 3,301 | 4,200 | 4,800 |
| Employees | 9.9% | — | 18,806 | 17,451 | 17,618 | 20,000 | 21,495 | 17,451 | 20,000 | 38,000 | 40,000 |

**SALES HISTORY**

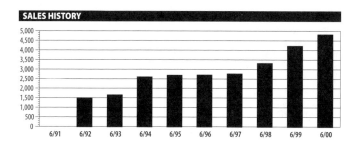

Catholic Healthcare West

# CB RICHARD ELLIS SERVICES, INC.

## OVERVIEW

CB Richard Ellis Services believes the most important things in real estate are location, *ubicacion,* and *l'emplacement* — not to mention *posizione* and *Standort.* El Segundo-based CB Richard Ellis is the largest commercial real estate services company in the US and a powerhouse throughout the world, with offerings ranging from real estate brokerage to property management (it manages hundreds of millions of square feet of commercial space) to asset services. The company also offers mortgage banking through its L.J. Melody subsidiary and advisory and management services for private pension funds and large investors through CB Richard Ellis Investors L.L.C.

CB Richard Ellis has expanded to about 250 offices, about half of which are in more than 40 countries in Africa, Asia, Europe, and South America. The company has moved strongly into construction in Japan, where it hopes land values have hit rock bottom. However, the vast majority of sales still come from the US, where the company is streamlining its operations and investing in Internet real estate services. A group of investors led by director Richard Blum's BLUM Capital Partners and CEO Ray Wirta have bought the 60% of CB Richard Ellis that they did not already own and taken the company private.

## HISTORY

Colbert Coldwell and Albert Tucker started real estate brokerage Tucker, Lynch, & Coldwell in 1906 in San Francisco. In 1922 the company expanded to Los Angeles, where it began developing real estate in 1933 with a 60-acre subdivision in the burgeoning city.

Having profited from California's rapid growth in the 1950s and 1960s, the firm expanded out of state. The partnership incorporated in 1962 as Coldwell Banker, which went public in 1968. Sears, Roebuck & Co. bought the company in 1981 for 80% above its market price. But by 1991 Sears had abandoned aims to become a financial services giant and sold Coldwell Banker's commercial operations to The Carlyle Group as CB Commercial Real Estate Services Group.

Free of Sears but $56 million in the red, the company didn't return to profitability until 1993. Two years later it embarked on a shopping spree in real estate services, buying tenant representatives Langon Rieder and Westmark Realty. In 1996 the company went public and bought mortgage banker L.J. Melody & Co., followed by the purchase of Koll Real Estate Services in 1997.

In 1998 the company widened its global scope with the acquisition of REI Limited, the non-UK operations of Richard Ellis; and was renamed CB Richard Ellis Services. CB Richard Ellis also bought Hillier Parker May & Rowden (now operating in the UK as CB Hillier), a London-based provider of commercial property services.

CB Richard Ellis experienced a revenue crunch in 1999 and responded by restructuring its North American operations into three divisions (transaction, financial, and management

services) and cutting management ranks by 30%. Growth continued in 1999 with the purchase of Pittsburgh-based Gold & Co., the addition of an office in Venezuela, and a fat contract to manage more than 1,100 locations for Prudential.

In 2000 the company committed significant resources to the Internet, inking a deal to offer the lease management services of MyContracts.com, investing in Canadian real estate transaction tracker RealNet Canada and partnering with Jones Lang LaSalle, Trammell Crow, and Insignia Financial to create a Web-based real estate transaction services platform.

The following year CB Richard Ellis created a new subsidiary, CB Richard Ellis Sports, to provide facility maintenance for sporting venues. That year the company won a contract to provide facility maintenance services at PNC Park, home of Major League Baseball's Pittsburgh Pirates.

A group of investors including CEO Ray Wirta, director Richard Blum (and his BLUM Capital Partners), and Freeman Spogli took the company private in 2001. Also that year the California Public Employees' Retirement System (CalPERS) selected the firm to manage its $500 million Joint Real Estate and Alternative Investment Management Technology Program.

**Chairman:** James J. Didion, age 61, $506,308 pay
**CEO:** Raymond E. Wirta, age 57, $1,472,000 pay
**COO, Americas:** Calvin Frese
**CFO:** James H. Leonetti, $154,615 pay
**Chairman, The Americas:** W. Brett White, age 41, $1,089,601 pay
**Chairman, Asia/Pacific:** David Runciman
**Chairman, Europe, Middle East, and Africa:** James A. Reid
**Chairman, Latin America and the Caribbean:** Francis Pons
**President, Transaction Management:** Christopher R. Ludeman
**President, Corporate Services:** Gary J. Beban
**President, CBRE Investors:** Robert Zerbst
**President, Investment Properties:** Gregory Vorwaller
**President, Management Services:** Jana L. Turner
**President, Valuation and Advisory Services:** Douglas W. Haney
**SEVP, General Counsel, and Secretary:** Walter V. Stafford, age 60, $544,375 pay
**SEVP, Human Resources:** Pam Perry
**SVP:** David R. Lind, age 51
**SVP, Investment Properties:** John Norjen
**Chief Information Officer:** Steve Sutherland
**Executive Managing Director, Organizational Development:** Skip Beebe
**Auditors:** Arthur Andersen LLP

**HQ:** 200 N. Sepulveda Blvd., Ste. 300, El Segundo, CA 90245
**Phone:** 310-563-8600    **Fax:** 310-563-8670
**Web:** www.cbrichardellis.com

CB Richard Ellis operates worldwide.

**2000 Sales**

|  | $ mil. | % of total |
|---|---|---|
| US | 1,027 | 78 |
| Europe, Middle East & Africa | 165 | 12 |
| Asia/Pacific | 85 | 6 |
| Canada, South & Central America | 47 | 4 |
| **Total** | **1,324** | **100** |

**2000 Sales**

|  | $ mil. | % of total |
|---|---|---|
| Transaction Management |  |  |
| Leases | 510 | 38 |
| Sales | 379 | 29 |
| Other | 62 | 5 |
| Financial Services |  |  |
| Appraisal fees | 73 | 6 |
| Loan fees | 58 | 4 |
| Investment management | 40 | 3 |
| Other | 43 | 3 |
| Management Services |  |  |
| Property management | 83 | 6 |
| Facilities management | 23 | 2 |
| Other | 53 | 4 |
| **Total** | **1,324** | **100** |

**Selected Subsidiaries**
CB Commercial Ltd. (UK)
CB Richard Ellis, Inc.
CB Richard Ellis Investors KK (Japan)
CB Richard Ellis Investors, L.L.C.
CBRE Stewardship (UK)
L.J. Melody & Company

Cadillac Fairview
Cendant
Cushman & Wakefield
FirstService
Forest City Enterprises
Grubb & Ellis
Hines Interests
Inland Group
Insignia Financial Group
JMB Realty
Jones Lang LaSalle
Lincoln Property
Mitsui Fudosan
Tishman Realty
Trammell Crow

| Private FYE: December 31 | Annual Growth | 12/91 | 12/92 | 12/93 | 12/94 | 12/95 | 12/96 | 12/97 | 12/98 | 12/99 | 12/00 |
|---|---|---|---|---|---|---|---|---|---|---|---|
| Sales ($ mil.) | 17.7% | — | 360 | 392 | 429 | 469 | 583 | 730 | 1,035 | 1,213 | 1,324 |
| Net income ($ mil.) | — | — | (37) | 9 | 7 | 7 | 71 | 26 | 25 | 23 | 33 |
| Income as % of sales | — | — | — | 2.3% | 1.7% | 1.6% | 12.1% | 3.6% | 2.4% | 1.9% | 2.5% |
| Employees | 16.2% | — | — | — | 3,899 | 4,000 | 4,100 | 6,700 | 9,400 | 9,853 | 9,600 |

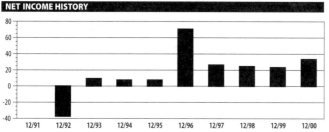

Debt ratio: 56.3%
Return on equity: 15.0%
Cash ($ mil.): 21
Current ratio: 0.72
Long-term debt ($ mil.): 304

# CENEX HARVEST STATES

## OVERVIEW

Why can't we all just get along? Cenex Harvest States Cooperatives (CHS) thinks grain producers can. The Inver Grove Heights, Minnesota-based co-op is a network of grain marketing, farming supply, energy, and processing operations. CHS is owned by about 325,000 farmers and ranchers who are members of some 1,200 local co-ops, located primarily in the Midwest and Northwest. CHS is the nation's #2 agricultural co-op (behind Farmland Industries).

CHS's grain trading activities include buying, selling, and arranging for transport. The co-op operates wheat mills to produce flour for pasta and bread, and it provides farm supplies at 330 stores; CHS also processes soybeans for use in margarine, salad dressings, and animal feed. The energy division operates two oil refineries, and the Country Energy subsidiary sells wholesale propane and other petroleum products and operates more than 700 convenience stores. Joint ventures with Farmland, Land O'Lakes, Mitsui, and Cargill supply farmers with crop products, market grain, and produce and export feed.

In addition to forming joint ventures to reduce costs of some operations, CHS is expanding its soybean processing and food production operations (subsidiary Sparta Foods makes tortillas) to reduce its reliance on the relatively weak commodity prices.

## HISTORY

To help farmers through the Great Depression, the Farmers Union Terminal Association (a grain marketing association formed in 1926) created the Farmers Union Grain Terminal Association (GTA) in 1938. With loans from the Farmers Union Central Exchange (later known as CENEX) and the Farm Credit Association, the organization operated a grain elevator in St. Paul, Minnesota. By 1939 GTA had 250 grain-producing associations as members.

GTA leased terminals in Minneapolis and Washington and built others in Wisconsin and Montana in the early 1940s. It then took over a Minnesota flour mill and created Amber Milling. GTA also began managing farming insurance provider Terminal Agency. In 1958 the association bought 57 elevators and feed plants from the McCabe Company.

Adding to its operations in 1960, GTA bought the Honeymead soybean plant. The next year the co-op acquired Minnesota Linseed Oil. In 1977 it acquired Jewett & Sherman (later Holsum Foods), which helped transform the company into a provider of jams, jellies, salad dressings, and syrups.

In 1983 GTA combined with North Pacific Grain Growers, a Pacific Northwest co-op incorporated in 1929, to form Harvest States Cooperatives. Harvest States grew in the early and mid-1990s by acquiring salad dressing makers Albert's Foods, Great American Foods, and Saffola Quality Foods; soup stock producer Private Brands; and margarine and dressings manufacturer and distributor Gregg Foods.

The company started a joint venture to operate the Ag States Agency agricultural insurance company in 1995. The next year the co-op's Holsum Foods division and Mitsui & Co.'s edible oils unit, Wilsey Foods, merged to form Ventura Foods, a distributor of margarines, oils, spreads, and other food products.

Harvest States merged in 1998 with the Minnesota-based CENEX, a 16-state agricultural supply co-op that had been founded in 1931 as Farmers Union Central Exchange. (Among CENEX's major operations was a farm inputs, services, marketing, and processing joint venture with dairy cooperative Land O'Lakes formed in 1987.) CENEX CEO Noel Estenson took the helm of the resulting co-op, Cenex Harvest States Cooperatives, which soon formed a petroleum joint venture called Country Energy with Farmland Industries.

CHS members rejected a proposed merger with Farmland Industries in 1999. Also that year Cenex/Land O'Lakes Agronomy (it became Agriliance in 2000 when Farmland Industries joined the joint venture) bought Terra Industries' $1.7 billion distribution business (400 farm supply stores, seed and chemical distribution operations, partial ownership of two chemical plants).

CHS bought the wholesale propane marketing operations of Williams Companies in 2000. Estenson retired that year and company president John Johnson took over as CEO. Also in 2000 CHS launched an agricultural e-commerce site (Rooster.com) in conjunction with Cargill and DuPont. The site was shut down the next year, however, because of a lack of funds. Also in 2001 the cooperative became the full owner of Country Energy by purchasing Farmland Industries' share and announced that it would form a wheat-milling joint venture with Archer Daniels Midland.

## OFFICERS

**President and CEO:** John D. Johnson, age 53, $1,534,838 pay
**EVP and CFO:** John Schmitz, age 51, $507,500 pay
**EVP, Consumer Foods:** James D. Tibbetts, age 50
**EVP and COO, Energy and Crop Inputs:**
Leon E. Westbrock, age 54, $707,400 pay
**EVP and COO, Grains and Foods:** Mark Palmquist, age 44, $607,680 pay
**EVP, Corporate Planning:** Patrick Kluempke, age 53, $362,675 pay
**EVP, Public Affairs:** Tom Larson, age 53, $367,850 pay
**VP, Human Resources:** Dick Baldwin
**Auditors:** PricewaterhouseCoopers LLP

## LOCATIONS

**HQ:** Cenex Harvest States Cooperatives
5500 Cenex Dr., Inver Grove Heights, MN 55077
**Phone:** 651-451-5151     **Fax:** 651-451-5073
**Web:** www.cenexharveststates.com

## PRODUCTS/OPERATIONS

**Selected Joint Ventures**
Ag States Benefits, LLC (between Ag States Agency and the Insurance Cooperative Association of Wisconsin; dental, disability, health, long-term care, and life insurance)
Agriliance, LLC (with Land O'Lakes and Farmland Industries to supply crop nutrients and protection products to farmers)
Rocky Mountain Milling, LLC (with Farmland Industries, Bay State Milling, and other local co-ops)
TEMCO (with Cargill to produce and export feed grains for overseas customers)
Triton TBS (with Farmland Industries and Universal Cooperatives to supply farm equipment)
United Harvest (with Mitsui & Co. to market grain and operate terminal elevators that move grain)
Ventura Foods, LLC (with the Wilsey Foods subsidiary of Mitsui & Co. to produce vegetable-oil based products for consumers)

**Selected Operations**
Farm financing (Fin-Ag, Inc.)
Farm supplies (Agri-Service Centers)
  Crop-protection products
  Fertilizer
  Grain purchasing
  Seeds
Feed manufacturing
Futures and options services (Country Hedging, Inc.)
Grain merchandising (grain purchasing, transportation, and sales)
Petroleum marketing (Country Energy, LLC)
Soybean crushing (soybean conversion into animal feed and crude soybean oil)
Soybean refining (soybean oil conversion into margarine, salad dressings, and baked goods)
Wheat milling (semolina and durum wheat milling for flour)

## COMPETITORS

| | |
|---|---|
| 7-Eleven | Equilon Enterprises |
| Ag Processing | Farmland Industries |
| Agway | Ferrellgas Partners |
| Andersons | Frito-Lay |
| ADM | General Mills |
| Barilla | George Warren |
| Bartlett and Company | GROWMARK |
| Bunge Limited | King Arthur Flour |
| Cargill | Louis Dreyfus |
| Central Soya | Riceland Foods |
| ConAgra | Scoular |
| ContiGroup | Wilbur-Ellis |
| Dakota Growers | |

## HISTORICAL FINANCIALS & EMPLOYEES

| Cooperative<br>FYE: August 31 | Annual<br>Growth | 8/91 | 8/92 | 8/93 | 8/94 | 8/95 | 8/96 | 8/97 | 8/98 | 8/99 | 8/00 |
|---|---|---|---|---|---|---|---|---|---|---|---|
| Sales ($ mil.) | 11.9% | — | 3,482 | 3,482 | 3,898 | 5,121 | 8,236 | 7,109 | 5,607 | 6,435 | 8,571 |
| Net income ($ mil.) | 13.8% | — | 31 | 32 | 35 | 45 | 51 | 53 | 57 | 86 | 87 |
| Income as % of sales | — | — | 0.9% | 0.9% | 0.9% | 0.9% | 0.6% | 0.7% | 1.0% | 1.3% | 1.0% |
| Employees | 21.6% | — | — | — | — | — | 2,428 | 2,178 | 2,404 | 2,576 | 5,308 |

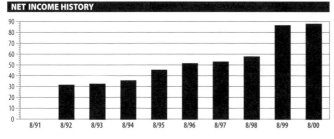

**NET INCOME HISTORY**

**2000 FISCAL YEAR-END**
Debt ratio: 27.1%
Return on equity: —
Cash ($ mil.): 56
Current ratio: 1.16
Long-term debt ($ mil.): 480

# CHICK-FIL-A INC.

## OVERVIEW

Which came first, the chicken or the sandwich? Atlanta-based Chick-fil-A is too busy to wonder. The nation's #2 quick-service chicken restaurant chain (behind TRICON's KFC and just ahead of AFC's Popeyes/Church's) has some 980 locations (nearly 45% in shopping malls) in about 35 states and in South Africa.

One of the largest private resturant companies in the US, the company has been helped by its popular "Eat Mor Chikin" advertising campaign, featuring black and white Holstein cows that ask consumers to eat chicken rather than beef. The ads are featured on billboards, radio, television, and in print and have been so successful the company now offers clothing, calendars, and other merchandise featuring the cows.

Chick-fil-A is focused on increasing its number of freestanding stores, as well as its nontraditional licensed outlets in hospitals, schools, airports, and other locations.

S. Truett Cathy, the company's founder and owner, is a devout Baptist and requires all stores to close on Sundays. Cathy also emphasizes employee care; the company claims a relatively low management turnover rate for its industry.

## HISTORY

S. Truett Cathy began his restaurant career after returning from WWII. In 1946 he and his brother, Ben, raised $10,000 by pooling their savings and getting a bank loan in order to open a 24-hour diner called the Dwarf Grill in the Atlanta suburb of Hapeville. So named because it only had 10 stools and four tables, it was later renamed Dwarf House. It was there that Cathy perfected a quick-cooking boneless chicken sandwich.

Cathy ventured into the rapidly growing fast-food industry more than 20 years later, when in 1967 he convinced a local shopping mall to make room for the first Chick-fil-A unit. There he found a successful niche, and for nearly 20 years the company placed its units exclusively inside malls, primarily in the southern US.

Chick-fil-A moved slowly at first, opening just six stores from 1968 to 1970. The company launched an employee scholarship program, the first of its kind in the fast-food industry, in 1973. In 1974 Chick-fil-A opened 14 new restaurants.

The company really hit its stride in the early 1980s, opening 101 units during the first two years of the decade. Chick-fil-A Dwarf House, the chain's first full-service restaurant, opened in 1985. By 1990 the company had reached $300 million in annual sales.

As mall construction slowed and competition increased, the company began looking at alternatives. Chick-fil-A began licensing its restaurants in 1992, entering into agreements with Georgia Tech and Clemson University. The following year Chick-fil-A established its first drive-through-only outlet in Greenville, South Carolina, and its first hospital restaurant, in Georgia Baptist Medical Center in Atlanta. By 1995 the company had reached $500 million in annual sales.

In an effort to extend its brand name, Chick-fil-A signed on as a sponsor for the Ladies Professional Golf Association in 1995. Also in 1995 the company launched its "cow" advertising campaign, featuring two life-size Holstein cows painting a billboard with the words, "Eat Mor Chikin."

In 1996 the company signed on as the sponsor of college football's Peach Bowl, played every year in Atlanta. Also that year Chik-fil-A opened its first airport store (at Atlanta's Hartsfield International) and expanded internationally with a unit in Durban, South Africa. Also in 1996 the company opened a Truett's Grill in suburban Atlanta. The restaurant featured a 1950s' retro-style decor and had an expanded menu, serving breakfast, lunch, and dinner.

In 1999 the company continued aggressive expansion, opening 88 new restaurants (56 of them stand-alone units). Chick-fil-A opened about 100 new outlets in 2000.

In 2000 the company reached $1 billion in annual sales for the first time. Also that year Chick-fil-A sued Burger King, claiming the hamburger chain's "Save the Chickens: Eat More Beef" ad campaign, associated with the movie *Chicken Run*, too closely resembled Chick-fil-A's "Eat Mor Chikin" campaign.

Dan Cathy, son of the founder, was named president and COO of Chick-fil-A in 2001.

## OFFICERS

**Chairman, CEO, and Founder:** S. Truett Cathy
**President and COO:** Dan T. Cathy
**SVP; President, Dwarf House:** Donald M. Cathy
**SVP, Design and Construction:** Perry A. Ragsdale
**SVP, Finance and CFO:** James B. McCabe
**SVP, Marketing:** Steve A. Robinson
**SVP, Operations:** Timothy P. Tassopoulos
**SVP, Real Estate and General Counsel:**
Bureon E. Ledbetter Jr.
**Human Resources Administrator:** Renea Boozer

## LOCATIONS

**HQ:** 5200 Buffington Rd., Atlanta, GA 30349
**Phone:** 404-765-8000        **Fax:** 404-765-8971
**Web:** www.chick-fil-a.com

Chick-fil-A has about 980 units in 34 US states and
South Africa.

## PRODUCTS/OPERATIONS

### 2000 Stores

| | |
|---|---|
| Mall stores | 422 |
| Freestanding stores | 314 |
| Licensed stores | 166 |
| Drive-through only | 29 |
| Satellite counters | 25 |
| Dwarf House restaurants | 11 |
| Other countries | 3 |
| Truett's Grill | 1 |
| **Total** | **971** |

## COMPETITORS

Advantica Restaurant
  Group
AFC Enterprises
American Restaurant
  Group
Boston Market
Burger King
CKE Restaurants
Subway
Jack in the Box
KFC
McDonald's
Morgan's Foods
Nathan's Famous
Pollo Tropical, Inc.
Wendy's

## HISTORICAL FINANCIALS & EMPLOYEES

| Private<br>FYE: December 31 | Annual<br>Growth | 12/91 | 12/92 | 12/93 | 12/94 | 12/95 | 12/96 | 12/97 | 12/98 | 12/99 | 12/00 |
|---|---|---|---|---|---|---|---|---|---|---|---|
| Sales ($ mil.) | 15.8% | — | — | — | 451 | 502 | 570 | 672 | 799 | 935 | 1,086 |
| Employees | 12.5% | — | — | — | — | — | 25,000 | 28,500 | 30,000 | 35,000 | 40,000 |

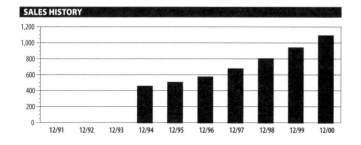

SALES HISTORY

# CINEMARK USA, INC.

## OVERVIEW

Thanks to Cinemark, you can see the movie stars of Tinsel Town at a Tinseltown. Plano, Texas-based Cinemark USA operates more than 270 theaters with more than 2,900 screens (some larger theaters go by the Tinseltown moniker). About 15% of its theaters are discount cinemas and nearly 20% offer online ticketing. All of Cinemark's theaters are multiplexes (89% have eight or more screens), many of which sport neon color schemes not found in nature.

The company prefers to build new theaters in midsized markets or in suburbs of major cities where the Cinemark theater is the only game in town. The company now focuses almost exclusively on building stadium-seating-style theaters.

Cinemark's theaters can be found in 33 states and 12 other countries, primarily in Latin America. Despite signs of improvement, the company continues to struggle along with the rest of its industry, which has faced a downturn due to a glut of theaters and competiton from other entertainment sources, including cable and satellite television.

Chairman and CEO Lee Roy Mitchell owns 24% of the company's stock and controls all of its voting shares. Invesment firm Cypress Merchant Banking Partners owns 42% and CGI Equities owns 18%.

## HISTORY

Lee Roy Mitchell and partner Paul Broadhead founded Cinemark in 1985; by the end of 1989, Cinemark had about 660 screens in 18 states. Mitchell set a company goal of 1,000 screens by 1992 and, in addition to constructing its own theaters, Cinemark made acquisitions to achieve its goal.

In 1992 Cinemark built its first megaplex, Hollywood USA — featuring 15 movie screens, a pizzeria, and an arcade. As the multiplex became one of its most profitable theaters, the company added more to its portfolio. Cinemark also started developing a Latin American presence in 1992, building theaters in Mexico and Chile. It formed a joint venture in 1995 to build theaters in Argentina, and in 1996 created three more joint ventures for theaters in Brazil, Ecuador, and Peru.

Meanwhile, Cinemark continued to add megaplexes; it opened 12 theaters with 165 screens (an average of about 14 screens per theater) in 1997. That year Cinemark signed a deal with high-tech theater developer IMAX to build 12 IMAX 3-D movies theaters as part of Cinemark multiplexes in the US, Mexico, and South America.

Also in 1997 the company formed a joint venture with Japan's Shochiku Co. Ltd. to develop multiplex theaters in Japan. The company continued its Asian expansion in 1998 when it signed a joint venture deal with Core Pacific Development Co., Ltd., one of Taiwan's largest real estate development companies to develop multiplex cinemas in that country.

In the first half of 1998, the company added 223 more screens, including 64 in Latin America. Later that year a group of wheelchair users sued the company, claiming the front-row spaces reserved for them in Cinemark's stadium-seating theaters were uncomfortably close to screens. (A US Court of Appeals sided with the theater chain in 2000 and the US Supreme Court refused to hear the plaintiffs' appeal.) At the end of 1998 the company moved its headquarters from Dallas to suburban Plano, Texas.

Cinemark entered the world of online sales in early 2000 when it teamed with Dallas-based e-commerce software company Vectrix.com to sell movie tickets in real time over the Internet at Cinemark's Web site.

In 2001 the company announced it would build a 4-screen, stadium-seating theater in Park City, Utah. In conjunction with that announcement the company said it had signed an agreement with the Sundance Film Festival to make the Park City multiplex the official "Home of the Sundance Film Festival." The agreement runs through 2006.

Also in 2001 the company acquired 42 screens in San Antonio from Regal Cinemas. Later that year Cinemark announced plans to build a 15-screen multiplex at the South Center Mall in South Dallas. The announcement came after several years of delays due to financial setbacks at the mall. The theater is scheduled to open in 2003.

**Chairman and CEO:** Lee Roy Mitchell, age 64,
$431,378 pay
**Vice Chairman, EVP, and Secretary:** Tandy Mitchell,
age 50
**President and COO:** Alan W. Stock, age 40, $422,179 pay
**SVP, Director of Operations:** Robert F. Carmony, age 43
**SVP, Treasurer, CFO, and Assistant Secretary:**
Robert D. Copple, age 42, $308,272 pay
**VP General Counsel:** Michael Cavalier, age 34
**VP Construction:** Don Harton, age 43
**VP Purchasing:** Walter Hebert, age 55
**VP Marketing:** Randy Hester, age 48
**VP Film Licensing:** John Lundin, age 51
**VP Real Estate and Assistant Secretary:**
Margaret E. Richards, age 42
**VP Information Systems:** Philip Wood, age 37
**President, Cinemark International:** Tim Warner,
$342,355 pay
**Director Human Resources:** Brad Smith
**Auditors:** Deloitte & Touche LLP

## LOCATIONS

**HQ:** 3900 Dallas Pkwy., Ste. 500, Plano, TX 75093
**Phone:** 972-665-1000          **Fax:** 972-665-1004
**Web:** www.cinemark.com

Cinemark USA has theaters in Argentina, Brazil, Canada,
Chile, Colombia, Costa Rica, Ecuador, El Salvador,
Honduras, Nicaragua, Mexico, Peru, and the US.

**2000 Sales**

|  | $ mil. | % of total |
|---|---|---|
| US | 599 | 76 |
| Mexico | 62 | 8 |
| Brazil | 61 | 8 |
| Other countries | 67 | 8 |
| Adjustments | (3) | — |
| **Total** | **786** | **100** |

## PRODUCTS/OPERATIONS

**2000 Sales**

|  | $ mil. | % of total |
|---|---|---|
| Admissions | 511 | 65 |
| Concessions | 236 | 30 |
| Other | 39 | 5 |
| **Total** | **786** | **100** |

## COMPETITORS

AMC Entertainment
Carmike Cinemas
GC Companies
Loews Cineplex
 Entertainment
National Amusements
Regal Cinemas
United Artists Theatre

## HISTORICAL FINANCIALS & EMPLOYEES

| Private<br>FYE: December 31 | Annual<br>Growth | 12/91 | 12/92 | 12/93 | 12/94 | 12/95 | 12/96 | 12/97 | 12/98 | 12/99 | 12/00 |
|---|---|---|---|---|---|---|---|---|---|---|---|
| Sales ($ mil.) | 19.1% | — | 195 | 240 | 283 | 299 | 342 | 435 | 571 | 713 | 786 |
| Net income ($ mil.) | — | — | 6 | 10 | 7 | 13 | 15 | 15 | 11 | 1 | (10) |
| Income as % of sales | — | — | 2.9% | 4.1% | 2.5% | 4.4% | 4.3% | 3.5% | 1.9% | 0.1% | — |
| Employees | 6.6% | — | — | 5,100 | 5,500 | 7,000 | 6,500 | 7,000 | 8,000 | 8,000 | 8,000 |

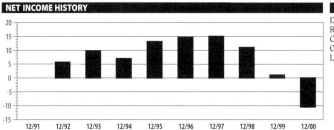

**NET INCOME HISTORY**

**2000 FISCAL YEAR-END**
Debt ratio: 94.1%
Return on equity: —
Cash ($ mil.): 20
Current ratio: 0.25
Long-term debt ($ mil.): 778

# THE CITY UNIVERSITY OF NEW YORK

OVERVIEW

CUNY is the big "U" in the Big Apple. The sizable City University of New York (CUNY) has about 200,000 undergraduate and graduate students; the university also teaches some 150,000 students in adult and continuing education programs. CUNY's 20 campuses span New York City's five boroughs. The public university has 10 senior colleges, six community colleges, a doctoral-level graduate school, a four-year technical college, and law and medical schools. It offers more than 900 programs, from traditional liberal arts curricula to specialized, career-oriented courses. CUNY's 12,000-person faculty is split almost evenly between full- and part-time members. Tuition and fees account for about 30% of funds for the university, which once provided free tuition to New York City residents.

CUNY, the nation's biggest urban university system, has made some big changes, including tougher admission standards that critics feared would hurt the university's ethnic diversity, a hallmark of the school (enrollment numbers have proven otherwise). Continuing a tradition of immigrant enrollment, the university has students from 145 countries. Notable CUNY alumni include novelist Oscar Hijuelos, US Secretary of State Colin Powell, comedian Jerry Seinfeld, and 11 Nobel laureates.

## HISTORY

The New York State Legislature first created a municipal college system in New York City in 1926, forming the New York City Board of Higher Education to manage the operations of the City College of New York and Hunter College. City College's roots were established in 1847 when New York passed a referendum creating the Free Academy, a tuition-free school. Hunter College was founded in 1870 as a women's college, and it was the first free teacher's college in the US.

The Board of Higher Education authorized City College to create the Brooklyn Collegiate Center (a two-year men's college) in 1926; Hunter established a similar two-year women's branch in Brooklyn. Four years later the schools merged to create the Brooklyn College of the City of New York, the city's first public, coed liberal arts college. Other schools added to the municipal system included Queens College (1937) and the New York City (1947), Staten Island (1955), Bronx (1957), and Queensborough (1958) community colleges.

The state legislature renamed New York City's municipal college system The City University of New York (CUNY) in 1961 and ordered its board of trustees to expand the system's facilities and scope. One of the first actions was to create a graduate school. CUNY chartered a number of new schools during the 1960s, including Richmond College (1965), York College (1966), Medgar Evers College (1968), and several community colleges. CUNY took over management of the New York State Institute of Applied Arts and Sciences (renamed New York City Technical College) in 1964 and established the John Jay College of Criminal Justice. CUNY became affiliated with Mount Sinai School of Medicine in 1967.

Despite its expansion, the university system had difficulty keeping up with demand, particularly after 1970, when it established an open admissions policy for all New York City high school graduates. Richmond College and Staten Island Community College became the College of Staten Island in 1976. Both CUNY and the City of New York ran into serious financial problems in the mid-1970s, spelling the end of CUNY's tradition of free undergrad tuition for New York City residents. To increase state financial support for CUNY, the legislature signed the City University Governance and Financing Act in 1979.

The City University School of Law held its first classes in 1983. The following year the state board of regents authorized CUNY to offer a doctor of medicine degree. CUNY's law school received accreditation from the American Bar Association in 1992.

After several years of budget cuts and steadily increasing enrollment, CUNY declared a state of financial emergency in 1995. The following year New York's Governor George Pataki proposed new budget cuts, and in 1997 he called for tuition hikes. CUNY's board of trustees introduced a resolution calling for the elimination of remedial education programs at the senior college level in 1998. The state Board of Regents approved the plan in 1999 (most remedial classes were to be phased out by 2001). Matthew Goldstein was appointed chancellor in 1999 and has worked to increase CUNY's budget to hire more full-time faculty.

## OFFICERS

**Chancellor:** Matthew Goldstein
**Vice Chancellor for Budget, Finance, and Administrative Computing:** Sherry F. Brabham
**Executive Vice Chancellor for Academic Affairs:** Lousie Mirrer
**Vice Chancellor for Facilities Planning, Construction, and Management:** Emma Espino Macari
**Vice Chancellor for Faculty and Staff Relations:** Brenda Richardson Malone
**Vice Chancellor for University Relations:** Jay Hershenson
**University Dean for Academic Affairs:** Russell K. Hotzler
**University Dean for Student Services and Enrollment Management:** Otis Hill
**University Dean for Academic Computing:** Michael Ribaudo
**University Dean for Research:** Alvin Halpern
**Acting University Dean for the Executive Office:** Robert Ptachik
**Special Counsel to the Chancellor:** Dave Fields
**General Counsel and Vice Chancellor for Legal Affairs:** Frederick P. Schaffer
**Auditors:** KPMG LLP

## LOCATIONS

**HQ:** 535 E. 80th St., New York, NY 10021
**Phone:** 212-794-5555      **Fax:** 212-794-5590
**Web:** www.cuny.edu

The City University of New York has schools serving the Bronx, Brooklyn, Manhattan, Queens, and Staten Island boroughs of New York City.

## PRODUCTS/OPERATIONS

**2001 Sales**

|  | $ mil. | % of total |
|---|---|---|
| Government appropriations | 830 | 43 |
| Tuition & fees | 597 | 31 |
| Government grants & contracts | 332 | 17 |
| Private gifts & grants | 71 | 4 |
| Investment income | 37 | 2 |
| Sales & services | 17 | 1 |
| Student activity fees | 15 | — |
| Other | 29 | 2 |
| Adjustment | (1) | — |
| **Total** | **1,927** | **100** |

**Senior Colleges**
Bernard M. Baruch College
Brooklyn College
City College
City University School of Law at Queens College
The College of Staten Island
The Graduate School and University Center
Herbert H. Lehman College
Hunter College
John Jay College of Criminal Justice
Medgar Evers College
New York City Technical College
Queens College
York College

**Community Colleges**
Borough of Manhattan Community College
Bronx Community College
Eugenio Maria de Hostos Community College
Fiorello H. LaGuardia Community College
Kingsborough Community College
Queensborough Community College

## HISTORICAL FINANCIALS & EMPLOYEES

| School FYE: June 30 | Annual Growth | 6/92 | 6/93 | 6/94 | 6/95 | 6/96 | 6/97 | 6/98 | 6/99 | 6/00 | 6/01 |
|---|---|---|---|---|---|---|---|---|---|---|---|
| Sales ($ mil.) | 2.2% | — | — | 1,655 | 1,722 | 1,756 | 1,729 | 1,784 | 1,873 | 1,900 | 1,927 |
| Employees | 3.1% | — | — | — | 25,800 | 25,800 | 27,900 | 28,000 | 28,000 | 30,000 | — |

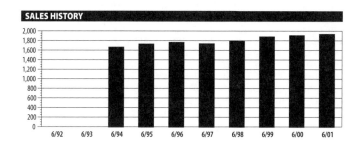

SALES HISTORY

# CLUBCORP, INC.

## OVERVIEW

It's always tee time at ClubCorp. The Dallas-based holding company is the world's largest operator of golf courses, private clubs, and resorts. The company owns or manages a collection of about 220 resorts, country club and golf facilities, and city clubs spanning nearly a dozen countries. Under the leadership of billionaire founder and chairman Robert Dedman (named by *Forbes* magazine as one of the 400 wealthiest Americans), ClubCorp's properties have grown to include Mission Hills Country Club near Palm Springs, California, and North Carolina's Pinehurst Resort and Country Club

(site of the 1999 US Open). ClubCorp also owns 26% of ClubLink, a leading Canadian developer and operator of golf courses.

In addition, ClubCorp has a 30% stake in PGA European Tour Courses, an operator of tournament golf courses across Europe. Striving to stay on top of the game, the company has been acquiring and building new properties in a joint venture with golf legend Jack Nicklaus. Dedman and his family own about 75% of ClubCorp; investment firm The Cypress Group, nearly 15%.

## HISTORY

Though his childhood in Depression-era Arkansas was dominated by intense poverty, ClubCorp founder Robert Dedman knew how to dream big. At a young age he vowed to become "very, very rich," and the scrappy Dedman embarked on achieving that goal by earning a college scholarship, obtaining a law degree, and eventually launching a Dallas law practice that flourished.

Dedman's law firm was successful, but he realized that it wouldn't bring him the $50 million he wanted to earn by age 50. In 1957 he formed Country Clubs, Inc., to venture into the country club business. At that time, doctors and lawyers working on a volunteer basis were managing most clubs, and Dedman believed his new company could bring professional management expertise to these facilities. The company opened its first country club, Dallas' Brookhaven Country Club, in 1957. Through the subsequent purchase of 20 more clubs, Country Clubs refined its management style, implementing unique practices such as reducing playing time on the golf course and developing specialized training for club staff.

In 1965 the company expanded into city and athletic clubs and assumed the Club Corporation of America name. The expansion drive that followed fueled a 30% growth rate that the company maintained from the 1960s through the 1980s. In 1985 the company was restructured and divided into a handful of separate companies owned by the newly formed Club Corporation International holding company.

In 1988 the company bought an 80% interest in Franklin Federal Bancorp. The bank's club properties had initially caught his eye, but Dedman also believed that the 400,000 members of his clubs might prove to be fertile ground for the marketing of financial services.

In 1996, however, Club Corporation International sold the financial institution to Norwest. Although Franklin Federal was turning a profit, losses from investment in derivatives, coupled with the bank's inability to compete with larger competitors, prompted the company to sell the bank and refocus on its core club and resort business.

In 1996 Japanese cookie-maker Tohato sued the company, claiming that it intentionally mismanaged the Pinewild Country Club. Pinewild was owned by Tohato, managed by Club Corporation International, and located next door to Club Corporation International's Pinehurst Resort and Country Club. Tohato alleged that the company's mismanagement was part of a scheme to eventually buy Pinewild at a reduced price. The case was eventually settled, but the nasty legal wrangling that ensued cast a pall over the impending 1999 US Open at Pinehurst.

In 1998 the company was reincorporated as ClubCorp International, Inc. It expanded its international base that year by purchasing nearly 30% of PGA European Tour Courses. The company also entered into a joint venture with Jack Nicklaus to develop three dozen new golf courses.

The company shortened its moniker to Club-Corp in 1999. Among the additions ClubCorp made to its holdings that year were 22 properties acquired from The Meditrust Companies. The company also increased its ownership of Canadian club developer ClubLink to 25%. An influx of funds for further expansion came in 1999 after investment firm The Cypress Group took a 15% stake. In 2000 the company took a 9% stake in Lifecast.com, which develops members-only Web sites for ClubCorp's properties.

**Chairman:** Robert H. Dedman Sr., age 75, $342,689 pay
**President and CEO:** Robert H. Dedman Jr., age 43, $535,600 pay
**COO:** James M. Hinckley, age 45, $370,200 pay
**CFO:** Jeffrey P. Mayer, age 44
**SVP People Strategy Department:** Kim Besse
**EVP Strategic Operations:** Albert E. Chew III
**EVP:** Mark W. Dietz, age 47
**EVP:** James E. Maser, age 63
**EVP, Secretary and General Counsel:** Terry A. Taylor, age 45
**EVP ClubCorp Resorts, Inc:** Patrick A. Corso, age 50, $363,548 pay
**EVP Sales ClubCorp USA, Inc:** Frank C. Gore, age 51, $343,755 pay
**EVP Domestic Club Operations; ClubCorp USA Inc.:** Douglas T. Howe
**EVP Development:** Murray S. Siegel
**Chief Information Officer:** Colby H. Springer
**Auditors:** KPMG LLP

## LOCATIONS

**HQ:** 3030 LBJ Fwy., Ste. 700, Dallas, TX 75234
**Phone:** 972-243-6191 **Fax:** 972-888-7338
**Web:** www.clubcorp.com

ClubCorp has operations worldwide.

## PRODUCTS/OPERATIONS

### 2000 Sales

|  | % of total |
|---|---|
| Country club & golf facilities | 47 |
| Business & sports clubs | 24 |
| Resorts | 21 |
| Real estate & international operations | 8 |
| **Total** | **100** |

### Selected Clubs

The Athletic and Swim Club at Equitable Center (New York)
Barton Creek Resort and Country Club (Texas)
Columbia Tower Club (Washington)
Drift Golf Club (UK)
Firestone Country Club (Ohio)
Golden Bear Golf Club (South Carolina)
Inverrary Country Club (Florida)
Kingwood Cove Golf Club (Texas)
Lakelands Gold Club (Australia)
Metropolitan Club (Illinois)
Mission Hills Country Club (California)
Pinehurst Resort and Country Club (North Carolina)
Teal Bend Golf Club (California)

## COMPETITORS

| | |
|---|---|
| American Golf | National Golf Properties |
| Club Med | ResortQuest International |
| Golf Trust of America | Sandals Resorts |
| Hillman | Silverleaf Resorts |
| Hilton | Starwood Hotels & Resorts |
| Hyatt | |

## HISTORICAL FINANCIALS & EMPLOYEES

| Private<br>FYE: Last Wed. in Dec. | Annual<br>Growth | 12/91 | 12/92 | 12/93 | 12/94 | 12/95 | 12/96 | 12/97 | 12/98 | 12/99 | 12/00 |
|---|---|---|---|---|---|---|---|---|---|---|---|
| Sales ($ mil.) | 2.4% | — | 884 | 1,200 | 773 | 761 | 784 | 840 | 851 | 1,028 | 1,069 |
| Net income ($ mil.) | — | — | 19 | 41 | 15 | (11) | 29 | 122 | 38 | 12 | (16) |
| Income as % of sales | — | — | 2.1% | 3.4% | 1.9% | — | 3.7% | 14.5% | 4.5% | 1.1% | — |
| Employees | 9.1% | — | 12,000 | 13,000 | 19,200 | 19,800 | 19,000 | 20,000 | 21,000 | 23,000 | 24,000 |

### NET INCOME HISTORY

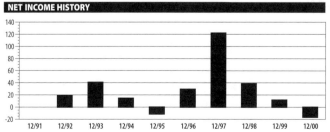

### 2000 FISCAL YEAR-END

Debt ratio: 54.2%
Return on equity: —
Cash ($ mil.): 25
Current ratio: 0.78
Long-term debt ($ mil.): 643

# COLT'S MANUFACTURING COMPANY

The Colt .45 may have won the West, but it took a New York investment firm to save Colt's Manufacturing from a post-Cold War decline in weapons sales and tough foreign competition. The West Hartford, Connecticut-based company makes the direct descendent of the Colt .45, along with other handguns, semiautomatic rifles, and military weapons, through subsidiaries. Its products are sold to the US and international governments and to commercial distributors. Colt's licenses its name to a variety of other companies, such as Encore Software (for Encore's Wild West Shootout game).

With the firearms industry taking cover from safety and health care expense-related lawsuits filed by cities and counties across the US, Colt's is discontinuing a number of handguns it makes for the consumer market. It is also focusing on its "smart gun" technology that makes it impossible for anyone other than a weapon's owner to fire it. The company spun off its smart gun division as iColt but the division soon closed.

Investment firm Zilkha & Co., which owns about 83% of Colt's, has been reviving the company since 1994 when it bought the firm out of bankruptcy.

## HISTORY

After waiting four years for a patent, Samuel Colt started the Patent Arms Manufacturing Company in 1836 to make his revolutionary handgun, a revolver. The newfangled gun was slow to catch on (the company went bankrupt in 1842), but it gained fame after being adopted by the Texas Rangers. The US Army delegated Captain Samuel Walker to work with Colt to improve the design, and sales of the resulting "Walker Colt" enabled Colt to set up a factory in Hartford, Connecticut.

In 1851 the company was the first American manufacturer to open a plant in England. Patent Arms Manufacturing was renamed Colt's Patent Fire Arms Manufacturing Co. four years later. Colt was a millionaire when he died in 1862 at age 47.

Colt's introduced the six-shot Colt .45 Army Model, "the gun that won the West," in 1873. More products followed, including machine guns and automatic pistols designed by inventor John Browning. Colt's widow sold the firm to an investor group in 1901.

Business boomed during both world wars, but by the 1940s labor strife and outmoded equipment began to take a toll, and Colt's lost money during the last years of WWII. In 1955 the struggling firm was acquired by conglomerate Penn-Texas. In 1959 Colt's patented the M-16 rifle; in 10 years it sold a million units to the US military.

During the Vietnam War the company flourished, but the 1980s brought low-end competition and shrinking defense orders. Colt's sales were hurt when the US government replaced the Colt .45 as the standard-issue sidearm for the armed forces. A three-year strike prompted the Army to shift its M-16 contract to Belgium's FN Herstal in 1988.

Two years later Colt's was acquired by private investors and a Connecticut state pension fund and was renamed Colt's Manufacturing. Sales remained flat, however, forcing the company to seek bankruptcy protection in 1992. There Colt's remained until New York investment firm Zilkha & Co. bailed it out in 1994, reorganizing the company. The new management made an offer for rival FN Herstal in 1997, but the deal was blocked by the Belgian government and fell through. Late that year the company won a contract to supply M-4 rifles to the Army.

Colt's bought military weapons specialist Saco Defense, maker of MK 19 and Striker grenade launchers, in 1998. Also that year Steven Sliwa succeeded retiring CEO Ronald Stewart. As US cities began suing Colt's and other makers of firearms in attempts to recover safety and health expenses attributed to gun violence, the company stepped up lobbying in 1999 and said it would increase gun safety efforts, including development of its "smart gun" technology.

A restructuring in 1999 ended most of Colt's consumer handgun business. It also spun off its smart gun technology as a separate company, iColt. Sliwa left to head iColt, and retired US Marine Lieutenant General William Keys was named president and CEO of Colt's. Also in 1999 Colt's bought Ultra-Light Arms, a maker of upscale hunting rifles, and said it would buy Heckler & Koch, a small arms manufacturer based in Germany.

By 2000 the company had withdrawn iColt (investors didn't seem interested in a lawsuit-laden industry) and stepped away from the Heckler & Koch deal. The company continued to focus on weapons for the military and police, but in 2001 it lost out to CAPCO Inc. on a contract to upgrade the Air Force's M16 rifles.

**Chairman:** Donald Zilkha
**President and CEO:** William M. Keys
**CFO:** Tom Siegel
**Human Resources Manager:** Mike Magouirk

## LOCATIONS

**HQ:** Colt's Manufacturing Company, Inc.
   545 New Park Ave., West Hartford, CT 06110
**Phone:** 860-236-6311     **Fax:** 860-244-1442
**Web:** www.colt.com

## PRODUCTS/OPERATIONS

**Selected Products and Brands**
Commercial rifles
   Colt accurized rifles
   Match target rifles
Law enforcement
   AR15
   Carbine
   Colt accurized rifles
   Commando
   M-16
   M203 Grenade Launchers
   M-4 Carbine
   Match target rifles
   Submachine guns
Performance products
   Colt XS Series
   Gold Cup Trophy
   Special Combat Government Competition
Personal protection
   Colt Defender
   M1991A1
Western
   Colt Cowboy
   Model Ps

## COMPETITORS

| | |
|---|---|
| Action Arms | Navegar |
| BAE SYSTEMS | Remington Arms |
| Browning | Saf T Lok |
| Crosman | Saf-T-Hammer |
| Beretta | SIG |
| FN Manufacturing | Springfield Inc. |
| Glock | Sturm, Ruger |
| Magnum Research | U.S. Repeating Arms |
| Mauser-Werke | |

## HISTORICAL FINANCIALS & EMPLOYEES

| Private<br>FYE: December 31 | Annual<br>Growth | 12/91 | 12/92 | 12/93 | 12/94 | 12/95 | 12/96 | 12/97 | 12/98 | 12/99 | 12/00 |
|---|---|---|---|---|---|---|---|---|---|---|---|
| Sales ($ mil.) | 2.8% | — | — | — | — | — | — | 92 | 96 | 100 | 100 |
| Employees | 0.0% | — | — | — | — | — | — | 700 | 700 | 700 | 700 |

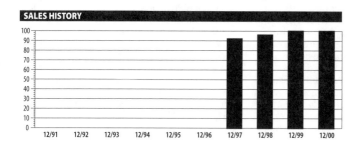

SALES HISTORY

# COLUMBIA UNIVERSITY

## OVERVIEW

Central Park isn't the only place you'll find ivy in New York City. Located on 36 acres in the Morningside Heights neighborhood of Manhattan, Columbia University represents the Ivy League in the city of New York. The private university is the oldest university in New York and the fifth oldest in the country. While best known for its top-notch programs in journalism, law, and medicine, almost 22,000 students seek graduate and undergraduate degrees in about 70 fields of study. Among Columbia's 7,000 faculty members are four Nobel laureates and former vice president Al Gore.

With a strong reputation for research, Columbia earns more money through patents and royalties than any other university.

Columbia has also forged affiliations with nearby institutions such as Barnard College, Teachers College, and Union Theological Seminary. Columbia-Presbyterian Medical Center, the result of more than 70 years of partnership between Columbia and The Presbyterian Hospital, helped pioneer the concept of academic medical centers.

Columbia's list of alumni includes such luminaries as Yankee great Lou Gehrig, Supreme Court Justice Ruth Bader Ginsberg, and President Franklin Roosevelt. Columbia has gone to the alumni well (and others sources) often over the past 10 years, collecting a record $2.8 billion in fund-raising.

## HISTORY

Created by royal charter of King George II of England, the university was founded in 1754 as King's College. Its first class of eight students met in a schoolhouse adjacent to Trinity Church (in what is now Manhattan). Some of the university's earliest students included Alexander Hamilton and John Jay. King's College was renamed Columbia College in 1784, a name that symbolized the patriotic mind-set of the age.

The college moved to 49th Street and Madison Avenue in 1849. The School of Law was founded in 1858, followed by the predecessor to the School of Engineering and Applied Science in 1864. The Graduate School of Arts and Sciences was established in 1880, and Columbia became affiliated with Barnard College in 1889.

Columbia College became Columbia University in 1896, and the following year it moved to its present location, the former site of the Bloomingdale Insane Asylum. (Columbia retained its original site, on which Rockefeller Center was built, until selling it in 1985.) Columbia continued to expand during the early 20th century. It added the School of Journalism in 1912 with funding from publishing magnate Joseph Pulitzer. Other additions included the School of Business (1916), the School of Public Health (1921), and the School of International and Public Affairs (1946).

Dwight Eisenhower became president of Columbia in 1948, retaining the position until becoming President of the United States in 1953. During the late 1960s Columbia gained a reputation for student political action, and in 1968 students closed down the university for several days in protest of the Vietnam War.

Facing financial woes, an escalating New York City crime rate, and contention among its faculty, Columbia struggled to maintain its reputation during the 1970s and 1980s. With this challenge as a backdrop, the university continued to evolve, welcoming its first coed freshman class in 1983.

Still facing economic pressures and reductions in government research spending, Columbia was forced to cut costs, eliminating its linguistics and geography departments in 1991. George Rupp became Columbia's president in 1993.

By the late 1990s Columbia had begun to recover from its financial and academic decline. Under the leadership of president Rupp, the university improved its fund-raising efforts and became more selective in student admissions. Microsoft founder Bill Gates donated $150 million to Columbia's School of Public Health in 1999 for research into the prevention of death and disability from childbirth in developing countries. That year Columbia created Morningside Ventures, a for-profit company focused on producing educational materials.

The university partnered with the British Library, Cambridge University Press, the London School of Economics, the New York Public Library, and the Smithsonian to form Fathom.com in 2000, another for-profit venture that will provide online access to various scholarly resources from each institution. The next year, the National Science Foundation awarded Columbia a $90,000 grant to gather personal accounts and create an oral history piece on the World Trade Center attacks of September 11.

**Chairman:** David J. Stern, age 58
**President:** George Rupp
**President Designate:** Lee C. Bollinger
**Provost and Dean Faculties:** Jonathan R. Cole
**Executive Vice Provost:** Michael M. Crow
**EVP Administration:** Emily Lloyd
**EVP Finance:** John Masten
**VP and Dean Arts and Sciences:** David Cohen
**VP Human Resources:** Colleen M. Crooker
**Secretary:** R. Keith Walton
**Treasurer and Controller:** Patricia L. Francy
**Vice Provost for Academic Administration:**
  Stephen Rittenberg
**Auditors:** Deloitte & Touche LLP

## LOCATIONS

**HQ:** Columbia University in the City of New York
  2690 Broadway, New York, NY 10027
**Phone:** 212-854-1754     **Fax:** 212-749-0397
**Web:** www.columbia.edu

Columbia University is located in the Morningside
Heights section of Manhattan.

## PRODUCTS/OPERATIONS

**Selected Schools, Colleges, and Programs**
Continuing Education
Graduate and Professional Schools
  College of Physicians and Surgeons
    Human Nutrition
    Occupational Therapy
    Physical Therapy
  The Fu Foundation School of Engineering & Applied
    Science
  Mailman School of Public Health
  School of Architecture, Planning & Preservation
  School of the Arts
  School of Arts and Sciences
  School of Business
    Executive Education Program
    Executive MBA Program
  School of Dental & Oral Surgery
  School of International and Public Affairs
  School of Journalism
  School of Law
  School of Nursing
  School of Social Work
Undergraduate Schools
  Columbia College
  The Fu Foundation School of Engineering and Applied
    Science
  School of General Studies

## HISTORICAL FINANCIALS & EMPLOYEES

| School FYE: June 30 | Annual Growth | 6/92 | 6/93 | 6/94 | 6/95 | 6/96 | 6/97 | 6/98 | 6/99 | 6/00 | 6/01 |
|---|---|---|---|---|---|---|---|---|---|---|---|
| Sales ($ mil.) | 6.6% | 953 | 1,032 | 1,103 | 1,160 | 1,234 | 1,339 | 1,448 | 1,574 | 1,789 | 1,700 |
| Employees | (9.9%) | — | — | 14,639 | 16,565 | 16,300 | 17,930 | 15,300 | — | — | 7,072 |

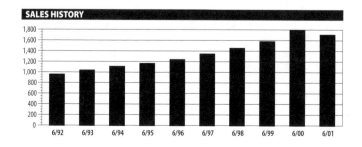

SALES HISTORY

# COMARK, INC.

Comark believes that the key to sales is service. The Bloomingdale, Illinois-based company resells some 40,000 products, including computers, software, peripherals, communications devices, networking gear, and backup storage devices. Among its suppliers are top hardware manufacturers such as Hewlett-Packard, IBM, and Compaq, and software leaders such as Lotus, Microsoft, and Novell.

Known for keeping close ties to its customers, Comark supports its sales with system design and maintenance, networking, help desk, staffing, Internet and e-commerce consulting, and other services. The company caters to the largest corporations in the US, but it also counts on government agencies and schools for a significant portion of sales. To better serve its government and education customers, Comark has consolidated the divisions that serve those markets, streamlining their operations.

Comark also continues to increase its focus on information technology (IT) services (the company describes itself as an IT solutions provider, not a reseller). It has expanded its partnerships with leading hardware and software manufacturers to include consulting and support services for the products it sells.

Co-founders Philip Corcoran and Chuck Wolande (chairman and president, respectively) own the company.

## HISTORY

Comark, originally called Communications Marketing, was founded in 1977 by former St. Mary's College (Minnesota) fraternity brothers Philip Corcoran and Chuck Wolande. After college Corcoran took a job at Memorex, where he was in charge of finding small companies to distribute Memorex products. Wolande, unable to get into medical school, went to work for Jefferson Electric as a gopher. Corcoran developed a plan to form his own distribution company and talked Wolande into sharing the project. The pair quit their jobs and began operations from a spare room in a neighbor's warehouse that stored corrugated cardboard boxes.

Starting with a single supplier (Memorex) and working 12-hour days (each had a goal of 30 calls a day), Corcoran and Wolande sold about $100,000 worth of products by the end of their first year. Soon they added employees, and by 1979 sales topped $1 million.

The company's turning point came in 1981, when IBM debuted the PC. Comark quickly added computers to its product list, getting in on the ground floor of an industry that was on the verge of explosive growth. The following year Comark began selling Hewlett-Packard printers and printing supplies. Epson joined the Comark lineup in 1985, and IBM products were added in 1989.

Comark's business continued to expand with the information technology tidal wave. The company added Compaq and Toshiba as suppliers in 1990. Comark formed its Corporate Services Division in 1992 as sales topped $170 million.

In 1992 Compaq chose several companies, including Comark affiliate USA FLEX, to sell PCs by mail. Comark opened its first satellite office, in Minneapolis, in 1994. The next year it added an office in Miami.

In 1996 the company sold USA FLEX to computer catalog retailer Micro Warehouse for $100 million. That year Comark opened a 175,000-sq.-ft. distribution center in Hanover Park, Illinois (near Chicago), where it stocks more than $100 million in products.

Comark celebrated its 20th anniversary in 1997 by topping $1 billion in sales and keeping its 20-year profitability streak intact. That year the company was chosen to participate in IBM's authorized assembler program. Also in 1997 Comark added offices in Georgia, New Jersey (serving the New York City area), Oregon, Tennessee, and Virginia.

The company opened its Milwaukee office in 1998. Industry trade magazine *Computer Reseller News* ranked Comark #1 among general business value-added resellers that year. Also in 1998 Comark was one of three firms chosen by the US Army for a blanket purchase agreement for computer products.

In 1999 Comark increasingly focused on services, expanding its partnerships with companies such as Computer Associates, Cisco, and Microsoft to include service and support.

Comark merged its education and government divisions to form a streamlined unit in 2000. The next year the company signed distribution agreements with MicronPC and Interactive Intelligence.

## OFFICERS

**Chairman:** Philip E. Corcoran
**President:** Chuck Wolande
**CFO:** Gary D. Kovanda
**Chief Information Officer:** Rick Goddard
**EVP:** David W. Keilman
**EVP, Sales and Marketing:** Tim McGrath
**SVP and COO:** Michael V. Wise
**VP, Corporate Sales:** John Thomas
**VP, Human Resources:** Larry Fazzini

## LOCATIONS

**HQ:** 444 Scott Dr., Bloomingdale, IL 60108
**Phone:** 630-888-5390    **Fax:** 630-351-7497
**Web:** www.comark.com

Comark has offices in Florida, Georgia, Illinois,
Massachusetts, Minnesota, Virginia, and Wisconsin.

## PRODUCTS/OPERATIONS

**Products**

| Hardware and Accessories | Hubs |
|---|---|
| Desktops and workstations | Network adapters |
| Digital cameras | Network software |
| LCD projectors | Routers |
| Monitors | Servers and accessories |
| Notebooks | Switches |
| Office products | Thin clients |
| PC accessories | Transceivers |
| Personal digital assistants | Utilities |
| Printers and printing | |
| supplies | **Software** |
| Scanners | Business |
| Servers | Consumer |
| Terminals | Graphics and design |
| Video cards | Internet |
| | Network |
| **Networking** | Operating systems |
| Accessories | Utilities |
| Communication print | |
| storage servers | |

**Services**

| | |
|---|---|
| Asset management | Internet and e-commerce |
| Custom system | Leasing and remarketing |
| configuration | Network design |
| Hardware maintenance | Platform migration |
| Help desks | Software installation |
| Integration | Staff augmentation |

**Selected Suppliers**

| | |
|---|---|
| 3Com | Microsoft |
| Adaptec | NEC |
| Canon | Nikon |
| Cisco Systems | Novell |
| Compaq | Samsung |
| Hewlett-Packard | Sony |
| IBM | Toshiba |
| Interactive Intelligence | Xerox |
| MicronPC | |

## COMPETITORS

| | |
|---|---|
| Accenture | IBM |
| CDW Computer Centers | Merisel |
| CompuCom | Micro Electronics |
| CompUSA | Micro Warehouse |
| Computer Sciences | Pomeroy Computer |
| EDS | Sayers Group |
| En Pointe | Systemax |
| Hartford Computer | Tech Data |
| Ingram Micro | Technica |

## HISTORICAL FINANCIALS & EMPLOYEES

| Private<br>FYE: March 31 | Annual<br>Growth | 12/91 | 12/92 | 12/93 | 12/94 | 12/95 | 12/96 | 12/97 | 12/98 | 12/99 | *3/01 |
|---|---|---|---|---|---|---|---|---|---|---|---|
| Sales ($ mil.) | 26.7% | — | — | 297 | 411 | 563 | 782 | 1,100 | 1,478 | 1,550 | 1,560 |
| Employees | 19.3% | — | — | — | 472 | 605 | 670 | 900 | 1,320 | 1,383 | 1,364 |

\* Fiscal year change

### SALES HISTORY

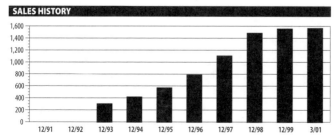

# CONSUMERS UNION

## OVERVIEW

Consumers Union of United States (CU) can make or break new products almost as fast as the average eight-year-old. The Yonkers, New York-based not-for-profit organization publishes the monthly *Consumer Reports* magazine (4.1 million subscribers) and a subscriber Web site (500,000 paid subscribers), which rates products ranging from candy bars to cars. CU also reaches consumers through its newsletters, books and videos, car and insurance pricing services, TV and radio programs, and its children's magazine, *Zillions*. The organization testifies before legislative and regulatory entities and files lawsuits on behalf of consumers. CU is governed by an 18-member board, and the organization's Consumer Policy

Institute conducts research and education projects on issues such as air pollution, biotechnology, food safety, and right-to-know laws.

CU derives revenue from sales of its publications, from car and insurance pricing services, and from contributions, grants, and fees. In 2001 it added online licensing to the mix when CU agreed to distribute its content on Yahoo! To preserve its independence, CU does not accept advertising, nor does it permit its ratings or comments to be used commercially. It maintains 50 laboratories within its National Testing and Research Center in Yonkers. In addition to conducting its own product testing, CU gathers product information by surveying the readers of its publications.

## HISTORY

In 1926 engineer Frederick Schlink organized a "consumer club" (in White Plains, New York), which distributed lists of recommended and non-recommended products. The lists led to the founding of Consumers' Research and a magazine devoted to testing products.

Schlink moved the group to Washington, New Jersey, in 1933. In 1935 three employees formed a union. Schlink fired them. Faced with another strike that year, Schlink accused the strikers of being "Red" and responded with strikebreakers and armed detectives. The next year the strikers set up their own organization, the Consumers Union of United States (CU).

CU's first magazine, *Consumers Union Reports*, came out three months later and rated products that the fledgling organization could afford to test, such as soap and breakfast cereals. Subsequent issues focused on food and drug regulation and working conditions for women in textile mills.

The organization drew the wrath of both *Reader's Digest* and *Good Housekeeping* (which accused it in 1939 of prolonging the Depression). The next year the House Un-American Activities Committee put CU on its list of suspect organizations. CU cut staff and dropped "Union" from its magazine title, but circulation remained low until after WWII.

By 1950, however, Americans began consuming again, helping to boost circulation to almost 400,000. During the 1950s CU published a series of reports on the health hazards of smoking.

In 1960 CU helped found the International Organization of Consumers Unions (now Consumers International) to foster the consumer movement worldwide. Rhoda Karpatkin was

hired as publisher in 1974. During the 1970s CU established consumer advocacy offices in California, Texas, and Washington, DC.

Recession and an increase in not-for-profit mailing rates caused the organization to lose money in the early 1980s. CU looked to its readers, who donated more than $3 million. The organization was hit by a 13-week strike in 1984 by union members calling for more say in management.

In 1996 CU slapped "not acceptable" ratings on the Isuzu Trooper and the Acura SLX. The next year the National Highway Traffic Safety Administration declared that CU's testing procedure of the Trooper was flawed, but CU stood by its tests of the vehicle.

CU hit another bump in 1998 when it was compelled to retract a story on the nutritional value of Iams and Eukanuba pet food. Admitting its test results were incorrect, CU's retraction of the story was something of a rarity — its last retraction had occurred almost 20 years earlier.

In 1999 the company defended itself in court against allegations by Isuzu and Suzuki that their companies were defamed through negative reviews by Consumer Reports. The following year a jury found CU guilty of falsely reporting on the Isuzu but declined to impose fines on the publisher. Also in 2000 a district court upheld the dismissal of Suzuki's suit against CU (based on CU's 1988 rating of the Suzuki Samurai as "not acceptable" because of its high rollover risks); Suzuki is appealing. Karpatkin stepped down as president in 2001, to be replaced by James Guest, CU's chairman since 1980. Also that year CU agreed to license its content to Internet portal Yahoo!

**Chairman, President:** James Guest, age 59
**CFO:** Conrad Harris
**VP, Marketing and Circulation:** Peter Chidsey
**VP, Technical Director:** David Pittle
**Director, Consumer Policy Institute:** Jean Halloran
**Human Resources:** Rick Lustig
**Auditors:** KPMG LLP

## LOCATIONS

**HQ:** Consumers Union of United States, Inc.
101 Truman Ave., Yonkers, NY 10703
**Phone:** 914-378-2000    **Fax:** 914-378-2900
**Web:** www.consumersunion.org

Consumers Union of United States performs most
product tests at a renovated warehouse in Yonkers, New
York. It tests cars and trucks in East Haddam,
Connecticut, and has consumer advocacy offices in
Austin, Texas; San Francisco; and Washington, DC.

## PRODUCTS/OPERATIONS

**Selected Products and Services**

**Auto Services**
CR New Car Price Service
CR Used Car Price Service

**Books and Buying Guides**
Auto Books
*New Car Buying Guide*
*New Car Preview*
*Sport Utility Special*
*Used Car Buying Guide*
*Used Car Yearbook*
House and Home
*Best Buys for Your Home*
*Buying Guide*
*Guide to Online Shopping*
*Home Computer Buying Guide*
Money
*Consumer Reports Money Book*
*How to Plan for a Secure Retirement*
Personal and Leisure
*Best Travel Deals*
*Complete Drug Reference*
*Guide to Baby Products*
*Guide to Health Care for Seniors*

**Educational Videos**
*The 30-Second Seduction*
*America At Risk: A History Of Consumer Protest*
*Buy Me That! A Kid's Survival Guide To TV*
  *Advertising*
*Buy Me That Too! A Kid's Survival Guide To TV*
  *Advertising*
*Buy Me That 3! A Kid's Guide To Food Advertising*
*Earth To Kids: A Guide to Parents for a Healthy*
  *Planet*
*Kids and Lead Hazards: What Every Family Should*
  *Know*
*Smoke Alarm: The Unfiltered Truth About Cigarettes*
*Staying Alive: A Consumer Reports Car Safety Special*
*To Care: A Portrait of Three Older Caregivers*
*Warning: Dieting May Be Hazardous To Your Health*
*Zillions TV: A Kid's Guide to the Best Toys and Games*

**Magazines and Newsletters**
*Consumer Reports Magazine*
*Consumer Reports on Health*
*Consumer Reports Travel Letter*
*Zillions*

**TV and Radio**
*Consumer Reports TV News*
*Report to Consumer Radio*

## COMPETITORS

Consumers' Research
eBay
Epinions
Hearst
International Data Group
J.D. Power
Microsoft
National Technical
 Systems
PRIMEDIA
Productopia
Reader's Digest
Reed Elsevier
Underwriters Labs

## HISTORICAL FINANCIALS & EMPLOYEES

| Not-for-profit FYE: May 31 | Annual Growth | 5/91 | 5/92 | 5/93 | 5/94 | 5/95 | 5/96 | 5/97 | 5/98 | 5/99 | 5/00 |
|---|---|---|---|---|---|---|---|---|---|---|---|
| Sales ($ mil.) | 2.1% | — | — | — | 124 | 129 | 136 | 135 | 140 | 140 | 140 |
| Employees | (0.0%) | — | — | — | 451 | 453 | 451 | 461 | 475 | 482 | 450 |

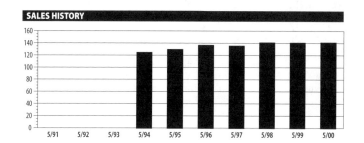

**SALES HISTORY**

Consumers Union

# CONTIGROUP COMPANIES, INC.

## OVERVIEW

Talk about going against the grain. New York City-based ContiGroup Companies (CGC, formerly Continental Grain) has gotten out of the business in which it literally made its name. CGC was once the US's #2 grain exporter before it sold its commodities marketing business to Cargill to move a bit farther up the food chain.

CGC's largest businesses include ContiBeef LLC, one of the nation's largest cattle feeders; Premium Standard Farms, the #2 pork producer in the US (after Smithfield Foods); and Wayne Farms, a major poultry producer. In China, the Caribbean, and Latin America, CGC has interests in flour milling, animal feed, and aquaculture. CGC owns about 78% of publicly traded ContiFinancial, a finance company that specializes in home equity loans but is currently under bankruptcy. CGC's investment arm, ContiInvestments, maintains interest in real estate and other investments.

Chairman Paul Fribourg (the great-great-great-grandson of ContiGroup's founder) and his family own the company.

## HISTORY

Simon Fribourg founded a commodity trading business in Belgium in 1813. It operated domestically until 1848, when a drought in Belgium caused it to buy large stocks in Russian wheat.

As the Industrial Revolution swept across Europe and populations shifted to cities, people consumed more traded grain. In the midst of such rapid changes, the company prospered. After WWI, Russia, which had been Europe's primary grain supplier, ceased to be a major player in the trading game, and Western countries picked up the slack. Sensing the shift, Jules and Rene Fribourg reorganized the business as Continental Grain and opened its first US office in Chicago in 1921.

Throughout the Depression the company bought US grain elevators, often at low prices. Through its purchases, Continental Grain built a North American grain network that included major locations like Kansas City, Missouri; Nashville, Tennessee; and Toledo, Ohio.

In Europe, meanwhile, the Fribourgs were forced to endure constant political and economic upheaval, often profiting from it (they supplied food to Republican forces during the Spanish Civil War). When Nazis invaded Belgium in 1940, the Fribourgs were forced to flee, but they reorganized the business in New York City after the war.

Following the war, Continental Grain pioneered US grain trade with the Soviets. The company went on a buying spree in the 1960s and 1970s, acquiring Allied Mills (feed milling, 1965) and absorbing many agricultural and transport businesses, including Texas feedlots, a bakery, and the Quaker Oats agricultural products unit.

In the 1980s Continental Grain sold its baking units (Oroweat and Arnold) and its commodities brokerage house. Amid an agricultural bust, it formed ContiFinancial and other financial units.

Michel Fribourg stepped down as CEO in 1988 and was succeeded by Donald Staheli, the first nonfamily-member CEO. The company entered a grain-handling and selling joint venture with Scoular in 1991. In 1994 Staheli added the title of chairman, and Michel's son Paul became president. Continental Grain sold a stake in ContiFinancial (home equity loans and investment banking) to the public in 1996. Also in 1996 the firm formed ContiInvestments, an investment arm geared toward the parent company's areas of expertise.

That year Continental Grain and an overseas affiliate (Arab Finagrain) agreed to pay the US government $35 million, which included a $10 million fine against Arab Finagrain, to settle a fraud case involving commodity sales to Iraq.

Paul succeeded Staheli as CEO in 1997. The company bought Campbell Soup's poultry processing units that year, and in 1998 it bought a 51% stake in pork producer/processor Premium Standard Farms. Meanwhile, ContiFinancial diversified into retail home mortgage and home equity lending. Continental Grain sold its commodities marketing business in 1999 to #1 grain exporter Cargill. With its grain operations gone, in 1999 the company renamed itself ContiGroup Companies.

In 2000 ContiFinancial declared bankruptcy, and ContiGroup sold its Animal Nutrition Division (Wayne Foods) to feed manufacturer Ridley Inc. In mid-2000, Premium Standard Farms doubled its processing capacity with the purchase of Lundy Packing Company. Chairman emeritus Michel Fribourg, the founder's great-great-grandson, died in 2001. Also that year ContiSea, the salmon and seafood processing joint venture between ContiGroup and Seaboard, was sold to Fjord Seafood.

## OFFICERS

**Chairman, President, and CEO:** Paul J. Fribourg
**EVP and COO:** Vart K. Adjemian
**EVP, Investments and Strategy and CFO; President, ContiInvestments:** Michael J. Zimmerman, age 50
**EVP, Human Resources and Information Systems:** Teresa E. McCaslin
**CEO, ContiBeef:** John Rakestraw
**CEO, Premium Standard Farms:** John M. Meyer
**CEO, Wayne Farms:** Elton Maddox
**SVP and Managing Director, Asian Industries Division:** Michael A. Hoer
**VP and General Manager, ContiLatin:** Brian Anderson

## LOCATIONS

**HQ:** 277 Park Ave., New York, NY 10172
**Phone:** 212-207-5100   **Fax:** 212-207-2910
**Web:** www.contigroup.com

ContiGroup Companies operates in the Caribbean, China, Latin America, and the US.

## PRODUCTS/OPERATIONS

**Major Business Units**

**Asian Industries**
Feed milling (China)
Pork production (China)
Poultry production (China)

**ContiBeef, LLC**
Cattle feedlots

**ContiInvestments, LLC**
Investment management

**ContiLatin**
Feed and flour milling
Poultry operations
Salmon farming
Seafood processing
Shrimp farming

**Premium Standard Farms (51%)**
Pork production

**Wayne Farms, LLC**
Poultry production

## COMPETITORS

| | |
|---|---|
| ADM | JR Simplot |
| Bartlett and Company | Koch |
| Cactus Feeders | Perdue |
| Cargill | Pilgrim's Pride |
| Cenex Harvest States | Salomon Smith Barney |
| ConAgra | Holdings |
| Farmland Industries | Smithfield Foods |
| Gold Kist | Tyson Foods |
| IBP | |

## HISTORICAL FINANCIALS & EMPLOYEES

| Private<br>FYE: March 31 | Annual<br>Growth | 3/92 | 3/93 | 3/94 | 3/95 | 3/96 | 3/97 | 3/98 | 3/99 | 3/00 | 3/01 |
|---|---|---|---|---|---|---|---|---|---|---|---|
| Estimated sales ($ mil.) | (13.7%) | 15,000 | 15,000 | 15,000 | 14,000 | 15,000 | 16,000 | 15,000 | 10,500 | 10,000 | 4,000 |
| Employees | (0.2%) | 14,750 | 14,700 | 15,500 | 16,000 | 16,000 | 16,800 | 17,500 | 14,000 | 13,500 | 14,500 |

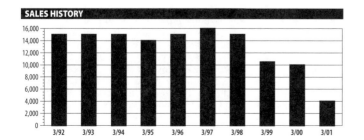

SALES HISTORY

# CONVERSE INC.

## OVERVIEW

As Converse has shown, even teams full of All Stars can find themselves in a slump. The North Reading, Massachusetts-based maker of athletic and leisure footwear — including the classic Chuck Taylor All Star canvas basketball sneaker — has been struggling with an industrywide downturn in demand for traditional athletic shoes.

The company has sold nearly 575 million pairs of Chuck Taylor All Stars in its 93-year-history, and while popular with rock-n-rollers, fashion designers, and other celebrities going for the basic look, the American classic's popularity has dipped with youths favoring fancier footwear. The company is increasingly interested in other categories: new athletic models, children's shoes, and action sports (footwear for skateboarding, climbing, and mountain biking). It has also designed sporty shoes targeted to women.

Converse's products are sold through about 5,500 athletic specialty, sporting goods, department, and shoe stores. The company itself operates nearly 25 retail outlets, and Converse also licenses its name to other companies for sports apparel and accessories such as caps and clothing.

Refusing to let the brand die, management-led buyout firm Footwear Acquisition bought the company's assets after Converse filed for Chapter 11 bankruptcy and liquidated in 2001. It closed the company's remaining US and Mexican plants and turned over all production to Far East and Indonesian manufacturers.

## HISTORY

With a capital investment of $250,000, in 1908 Marquis Converse established the Converse Rubber Co. in Malden, Massachusetts, with 15 employees. The company got its big break shortly after its Converse canvas All Star shoe was launched in 1917. The shoe was chosen by young basketball star Chuck Taylor as his favorite basketball sneaker. Taylor joined the Converse sales team in 1921 and — in one of the first examples of sports endorsement — peddled the shoes at basketball clinics he hosted at schools and colleges. In 1923 Taylor's signature was added to the brand.

Converse fell into bankruptcy in 1929 and was acquired by Hodgman Rubber. The Depression and reduced profits led to another takeover in 1933, when the Stone family of Boston began its lucrative 39-year period of ownership. WWII provided a boost to the firm as it supplied the US military with protective footwear, parkas and other equipment.

The company expanded after WWII, establishing plants in New Hampshire (1946) and a subsidiary in Puerto Rico (1953). It then acquired Tyler Rubber (1961) and the Hodgman line of sporting goods (1964). Taylor retired from Converse in 1968.

In 1972 Converse was acquired by Eltra, which made electrical and typesetting equipment. Within a year Converse expanded with the purchase of B.F. Goodrich's footwear division. Eltra was acquired by conglomerate Allied Corp. in 1979. Converse executives led a buyout of the division in 1982 before taking it public in 1983. The rise of the retro look in fashion starting in the mid-1980s made the old Chuck Taylor sneaker hot with models, film stars, and the fashion-conscious.

Furniture, footwear, and apparel firm INTERCO bought Converse in 1986. After being financially overstretched in fighting off a 1988 hostile takeover by the Rales brothers of Washington, DC, INTERCO filed for bankruptcy in 1991 — one of the largest bankruptcy cases in US history.

As part of INTERCO's reorganization, Converse emerged in 1994 as a public company controlled by financial adviser Leon Black. The next year it dumped its outdoor, running, walking, tennis, and football lines. Converse, hurt particularly by weak sales of basketball sneakers and restructuring charges, posted losses and saw revenue fall in 1995 and 1996.

Sporting goods veteran Glenn Rupp was hired as chairman and CEO in 1996. Converse had record sales in 1997, but still finished in the red, due in part to a slowdown in retail demand in the last half of the year. The company laid off 5% of its workforce in 1998 and another 20% in 1999.

In 2000 Converse slipped close to NYSE delisting because of its low stock price and market cap. The company filed for Chapter 11 bankruptcy protection in January 2001.

Footwear Acquisition, Inc. stepped in that spring, however, and bought the rights to the names and property of Converse. Former Converse employee Jack Boys was named CEO. Converse closed its factories in North America (two in the US and one in Mexico) and sent all production to its suppliers in the Far East and Indonesia.

**Co-Chairman:** Marsden Cason
**Co-Chairman:** William Simon
**CEO:** Jack Boys
**VP Distribution:** Lloyd Wallsten
**VP Finance:** Lisa Kempa
**VP Legal:** Laura Kelley
**VP Licensing:** Tim Ouellette
**VP Marketing and Product Development:**
David Maddocks
**VP Sales:** Jim Stroesser
**Managing Director, Far East Operations:** Jerry Lan
**Director of Information Technology:** Ellen Garvey
**Human Resources Manager:** Susan Rogato
**Auditors:** PricewaterhouseCoopers LLP

## COMPETITORS

adidas-Salomon
ASICS
Deckers Outdoor
Fila
K-Swiss
New Balance
NIKE
PUMA
R. Griggs
Reebok
Saucony
Skechers U.S.A.
Stride Rite
Timberland
Vans

## LOCATIONS

**HQ:** One Fordham Rd., North Reading, MA 01864
**Phone:** 978-664-1100 **Fax:** 978-664-7472
**Web:** www.converse.com

Converse distributes its products in 110 countries
through 5,500 athletic specialty, sporting goods,
department, and shoe stores and in 23 company-owned
retail outlet stores.

**2000 Sales**

|  | % of total |
|---|---|
| US | 69 |
| Other countries | 31 |
| **Total** | **100** |

## HISTORICAL FINANCIALS & EMPLOYEES

| Private<br>FYE: Sat nearest Dec 31 | Annual<br>Growth | 12/91 | 12/92 | 12/93 | 12/94 | 12/95 | 12/96 | 12/97 | 12/98 | 12/99 | 12/00 |
|---|---|---|---|---|---|---|---|---|---|---|---|
| Sales ($ mil.) | (5.0%) | — | 316 | 380 | 437 | 408 | 349 | 450 | 308 | 232 | 209 |
| Net income ($ mil.) | — | — | (11) | 12 | 18 | (72) | (18) | (5) | (23) | (44) | (27) |
| Income as % of sales | — | — | — | 3.2% | 4.0% | — | — | — | — | — | — |
| Employees | (9.5%) | — | — | 3,042 | 3,053 | 2,459 | 2,249 | 2,956 | 2,658 | 2,024 | 1,510 |

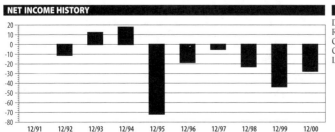

**NET INCOME HISTORY**

**2000 FISCAL YEAR-END**
Debt ratio: 0.0%
Return on equity: —
Cash ($ mil.): 3
Current ratio: 0.38
Long-term debt ($ mil.): 0

# CPB

This organization is made possible by a grant from the federal government and by support from viewers like you.

The Washington, DC-based Corporation for Public Broadcasting (CPB) is an independent, not-for-profit government organization (not a government agency) that receives appropriations from Congress to help fund programming for more than 1,000 member-owned stations of the Public Broadcasting Service, National Public Radio, Public Radio International, and other organizations.

A political hot potato (often a target of Republicans who are opposed to government funding of educational, informational, and cultural programming), CPB's funding has been approved at $340 million for 2001, $350 million for 2002, and $365 million for 2003.

## HISTORY

As commercial radio began to fill the radio dial, the FCC in 1945 reserved 20 channels from 88 FM to 92 FM for noncommercial, educational broadcasts. The FCC reserved television channels for similar purposes in 1952, and the first public television station started broadcasting in Houston in 1953. In 1962 the Federal government began funding public broadcasting through passage of the Education Television Facilities Act. By 1965 there were 124 public TV stations across the country. To help allocate government funds to these public TV and radio stations, Congress created the Corporation for Public Broadcasting (CPB) in 1967.

CPB was officially formed in 1968. That same year one of public television's most popular programs, *Mister Rogers' Neighborhood*, debuted. *Sesame Street* debuted the following year. Also in 1969 CPB formed the Public Broadcasting Service (PBS) to handle its television operations. PBS began distributing television programming five nights a week that year.

CPB formed National Public Radio (NPR) in 1970, with 90 public radio member stations. A year later NPR debuted its long-running news program *All Things Considered*. PBS's popular nightly news program, the *Robert MacNeil Report* (later the *MacNeil/Lehrer NewsHour*) made its debut in 1975. PBS began distributing its programming by satellite in 1978. In 1980 NPR also began distributing programming via satellite. That same year author Garrison Keillor's *A Prairie Home Companion* debuted on public radio.

In 1981 Walter Annenberg, a publisher who made his fortune with *TV Guide* and the *Daily Racing Form*, teamed with CPB to create the Annenberg/CPB Project to provide educational videos and other materials to public schools. PBS began to look to "event programming" as a way to attract more viewers with big hits including *Eye on the Prize* (1987) and Ken Burns' *Civil War* documentary (1990).

CPB has always been politically controversial; critics have often charged it with elitism, cultural bias, and liberalism. When Republicans gained control of Congress in 1994, their laundry list of grievances included government cultural spending. They were foiled in their effort to eliminate funding for CPB, however, in part because of public support for public television. Congress still cut funding by $100 million, forcing CPB to reduce its staff by almost 25% and introduce performance criteria for stations seeking grant money, including listenership and community financial support minimums.

To help make up the loss in funding, in 1995 the CPB introduced its Future Funds program, which provides financial incentives to television and radio stations that find innovative ways to raise money or to streamline their operations. Those ideas are then passed on to other member stations.

In 1996 the Annenberg/CPB Project launched a satellite TV channel providing schools, public libraries, and other community agencies with teacher development and instructional programming free of charge.

Robert Coonrod was promoted to CEO in 1997. The following year Congress approved additional funding to help public television's transition from analog to digital broadcasting. Frank Cruz was appointed chairman of CPB in 1999. In 2000 the Annenberg/CPB channel expanded to 24 hour-a-day, seven day-a-week programming.

Increased funding for 2003 (funding is approved two years in advance) was threatened when it was discovered that some PBS stations were giving their mailing lists to the Democratic party for fundraising purposes. Nevertheless, funding for CPB was increased in the 2001 budget.

## OFFICERS

**Chairman:** Frank H. Cruz
**President and CEO:** Robert T. Coonrod
**EVP and COO:** Frederick L. DeMarco
**SVP Policy, General Counsel and Corporate Secretary:** Kathleen Cox
**VP Communications:** Carole Florman
**VP Finance and Administration, Treasurer:** Elizabeth A. Griffith
**VP Government Relations:** David Guhse
**VP Program Operations:** Yoko Arthur
**VP Radio:** Richard H. Madden
**VP Strategic Development:** Douglas A. Weiss
**VP Television Operations:** Constance Foster
**President and CEO, Public Broadcasting Service:** Pat Mitchell
**Executive Director, Special Projects:** Edward Coltman
**Inspector General:** Ken Konz
**Director Human Resources and Assistant to the President for EEO:** Alicia Schoshinski

## LOCATIONS

**HQ:** Corporation for Public Broadcasting
901 E St. NW, Washington, DC 20004
**Phone:** 202-879-9600     **Fax:** 202-879-9768
**Web:** www.cpb.org

## PRODUCTS/OPERATIONS

**Selected Affiliations**
American Public Television (programs for public television)
The Annenberg/CPB Projects (telecourses and education programs)
Association of America's Public Television Stations (organization of public TV stations)
Independent Television Service (independent creative programming for public TV)
National Public Radio (radio programming distribution)
Public Broadcasting Service (TV distribution)
Public Radio International (international radio distribution)

## COMPETITORS

A&E Networks
BBC
Discovery Communications
Fox Entertainment
NBC
Time Warner Entertainment
Viacom
Walt Disney
Westwood One

## HISTORICAL FINANCIALS & EMPLOYEES

| Not-for-profit FYE: September 30 | Annual Growth | 9/91 | 9/92 | 9/93 | 9/94 | 9/95 | 9/96 | 9/97 | 9/98 | 9/99 | 9/00 |
|---|---|---|---|---|---|---|---|---|---|---|---|
| Sales ($ mil.) | 1.5% | — | 341 | 339 | 275 | 286 | 296 | 282 | 285 | 283 | 384 |
| Net income ($ mil.) | — | — | 10 | 35 | (12) | (6) | 21 | (1) | (8) | (2) | (1) |
| Income as % of sales | — | — | 3.0% | 10.2% | — | — | 7.0% | — | — | — | — |
| Employees | (0.1%) | — | 101 | 900 | 100 | 95 | 85 | 90 | 90 | 90 | 100 |

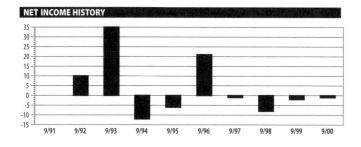

NET INCOME HISTORY

# COX ENTERPRISES, INC.

## OVERVIEW

Cox Enterprises is well beyond the printed word. The Atlanta-based company is one of the largest media firms in the US, with interests in newspapers, radio, and broadcast and cable TV. Cox publishes 18 daily newspapers (including its flagship, *The Atlanta Journal-Constitution*) and about 30 weeklies and shoppers in nine states and Washington, DC. It owns 15 TV stations through Cox Television and more than 80 radio stations through its stake in Cox Radio (63%). The company also owns 68% of Cox Communications, one of the largest cable systems in the US with more than 6 million subscribers in 23 states.

Cox is online as well, operating more than 20 city information Web sites (such as AccessAtlanta.com) and other sites such as AutoTrader.com, which it operates in conjunction with its Manheim Auctions subsidiary. Manheim is the world's largest used-car auctioneer, with more than 100 automobile auctions worldwide. Other operations include publishing newsletters and shopping circulars, TV ad sales, and direct mail advertising. Barbara Cox Anthony (mother of chairman and CEO James Kennedy) and Anne Cox Chambers, daughters of founder James Cox, own the company.

## HISTORY

James Middleton Cox, who dropped out of school in 1886 at 16, had worked as a teacher, reporter, and congressional secretary before buying the *Dayton Daily News* in 1898. After acquiring the nearby *Springfield Press-Republican* in 1905, he took up politics, serving two terms in the US Congress (1909-1913) and three terms as Ohio governor (1913-1915; 1917-1921). He even ran for president in 1920 (his running mate was future President Franklin Roosevelt) but lost to rival Ohio publisher Warren G. Harding.

Once out of politics, Cox began building his media empire. He bought the *Miami Daily News* in 1923 and founded WHIO (Dayton, Ohio's first radio station). He bought Atlanta's WSB ("Welcome South, Brother"), the South's first radio station, in 1939 and added WSB-FM and WSB-TV, the South's first FM and TV stations, in 1948. Cox founded Dayton's first FM and TV stations (WHIO-FM and WHIO-TV) the next year, and *The Atlanta Constitution* joined his collection in 1950. Cox died in 1957.

The company continued to expand its broadcasting interests in the late 1950s and early 1960s. It was one of the first major broadcasting companies to expand into cable TV when it purchased a system in Lewistown, Pennsylvania, in 1962. The Cox family's broadcast properties were placed in publicly held Cox Broadcasting in 1964. Two years later its newspapers were placed into privately held Cox Enterprises, and the cable holdings became publicly held Cox Cable Communications. The broadcasting arm diversified, buying Manheim Services (auto auctions, 1968), Kansas City Automobile Auction (1969), and TeleRep (TV ad sales, 1972).

Cox Cable had 500,000 subscribers in nine states when it rejoined Cox Broadcasting in 1977. Cox Broadcasting was renamed Cox

Communications in 1982, and the Cox family took the company private again in 1985, combining it with Cox Enterprises. James Kennedy, grandson of founder James Cox, became chairman and CEO in 1987.

Expansion became the keyword for Cox in the 1990s. The company merged its Manheim unit with the auto auction business of Ford Motor Credit and GE Capital in 1991. It also formed Sprint Spectrum in 1994, a partnership with Sprint, TCI (now part of AT&T), and Comcast to bundle telephone, cable TV, and other communications services (Sprint bought out Cox in 1999). Then, in one of its biggest transactions, Cox bought Times Mirror's cable TV operations for $2.3 billion in 1995 and combined them with its own cable system into a new, publicly traded company called Cox Communications. The following year it spun off its radio holdings into a public company called Cox Radio.

To expand its online presence, the company formed Cox Interactive Media in 1996, establishing a series of city Web sites and making a host of investments in various Internet companies, including CareerPath, Excite@Home, iVillage, MP3.com, and Tickets.com. Cox also applied the online strategy to its automobile auction businesses, establishing AutoTrader.com in 1998 and placing the Internet operations of Manheim Auctions into a new company, Manheim Interactive, in 2000. Manheim spent $1 billion in acquiring ADT Automotive from Tyco International in 2000 and plans on spending another $1 billion over the next five years improving and expanding its operations. Plans for an AutoTrader.com IPO in 2000 were scrapped.

## OFFICERS

**Chairman and CEO:** James C. Kennedy, age 53
**Vice Chairman:** David E. Easterly, age 58
**President and COO:** G. Dennis Berry
**EVP and CFO:** Robert C. O'Leary, age 62
**SVP Administration:** Timothy W. Hughes
**VP and Chief Information Officer:** Scott A. Hatfield
**VP and Treasurer:** Richard J. Jacobson
**VP Human Resources:** Marybeth H. Leamer
**VP Legal Affairs and Secretary:** Andrew A. Merdek
**VP Marketing and Communication:** John C. Williams
**VP Materials Management:** Michael J. Mannheimer
**VP Public Policy:** Alexander V. Netchvolodoff
**VP Tax:** Preston B. Barnett
**President and CEO, Cox Communications, Inc.:**
James O. Robbins, age 58
**President and CEO, Manheim Auctions:** Dean H. Eisner
**President, Cox Interactive Media:** Peter M. Winter
**President, Cox Television:** Andrew S. Fisher
**President, Cox Newspapers Inc.:** Jay R. Smith
**VP Sales, Cox Interactive Media:** Neil Helms

## LOCATIONS

**HQ:** 1400 Lake Hearn Dr., Atlanta, GA 30319
**Phone:** 404-843-5000    **Fax:** 404-843-5109
**Web:** www.coxenterprises.com

Cox Enterprises has operations in Australia, Canada,
France, New Zealand, Puerto Rico, the UK, and the US.

## PRODUCTS/OPERATIONS

**2000 Sales**

|  | % of total |
| --- | --- |
| Cable TV | 45 |
| Auctions | 22 |
| Newspapers | 19 |
| TV stations | 9 |
| Radio stations | 5 |
| **Total** | **100** |

### Selected Operations

Atlanta Beat (women's professional soccer)
Cox Communications (68%, cable system)
Cox Interactive Media (city Web sites)
Cox Newspapers
  Cox Target Media (direct-mail advertising)
  Daily Newspapers
    *The Atlanta Journal-Constitution*
    *Austin American-Statesman* (Texas)
    *Palm Beach Daily News* (Florida)
    *The Palm Beach Post* (Florida)
    *Springfield News Sun* (Ohio)
  Trader Publishing (50%, classified advertising)
Cox Radio (63%)
  Atlanta (WBTS-FM, WSB-AM, WSB-FM)
  Honolulu (KRTR-FM, KXME-FM)
  Houston (KLDE-FM)
  Jacksonville (WAPE-FM, WFYV-FM, WKQL-FM)
  Long Island, NY (WBAB-FM, WBLI-FM)
  Miami (WEDR-FM, WHQT-FM)
  Orlando, FL (WHTQ-FM, WWKA-FM)
  San Antonio (KCYY-FM, KISS-FM, KONO-FM)
  Tampa (WDUV-FM, WWRM-FM)
Cox Television
  TV stations
    KICU (San Francisco/San Jose, CA)
    KIRO (Seattle)
    KRXI (Reno, NV)
    KTVU (Oakland/San Francisco, CA)
    WAXN (Charlotte, NC)
    WFTV (Orlando, FL)
    WHIO (Dayton, OH)
    WPXI (Pittsburgh)
    WRDQ (Orlando, FL)
    WSB-TV (Atlanta)
    WSOC (Charlotte, NC)
  TeleRep (TV ad sales)
Manheim Auctions
  Manheim Interactive (online auto auctions)
  AutoTrader.com (majority owned, online auto sales)

## COMPETITORS

| | | |
| --- | --- | --- |
| Advance | E. W. Scripps | Time Warner |
| Publications | Gannett | Cable |
| AT&T Broadband | Hearst | Tribune |
| Belo | Knight Ridder | Viacom |
| Clear Channel | New York Times | Walt Disney |
| Comcast | News Corp. | Washington Post |
| Dow Jones | | |

## HISTORICAL FINANCIALS & EMPLOYEES

| Private<br>FYE: December 31 | Annual<br>Growth | 12/91 | 12/92 | 12/93 | 12/94 | 12/95 | 12/96 | 12/97 | 12/98 | 12/99 | 12/00 |
| --- | --- | --- | --- | --- | --- | --- | --- | --- | --- | --- | --- |
| Sales ($ mil.) | 15.4% | — | 2,495 | 2,675 | 2,939 | 3,806 | 4,591 | 4,936 | 5,355 | 6,097 | 7,824 |
| Employees | 11.6% | — | 30,865 | 31,000 | 37,000 | 38,000 | 43,000 | 50,000 | 55,500 | 61,000 | 74,000 |

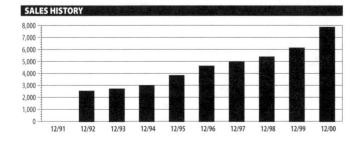

**SALES HISTORY**

# DAIRY FARMERS OF AMERICA

## OVERVIEW

Dairy Farmers of America (DFA) seeks strength in numbers — big numbers. As the world's largest dairy cooperative, Kansas City, Missouri-based DFA rides herd on about 27,000 members in 45 states, and it controls 27% of the US milk supply or an annual pool nearing 45 billion pounds of milk.

These partners in cream sell fluid milk, cheese, butter, and other dairy products to grocery, food service, and manufacturing customers. DFA also holds the license to produce Borden cheeses, and it bottles up Starbucks' Frappuccino coffee drink. In addition, the co-op provides marketing, research and development, and legislative lobbying on behalf of its members.

American dairy farmers face an uncertain future due to consolidation in the retail industry, dissolving government milk price supports, and increased foreign competition. DFA itself was formed by the 1997 merger of four large regional co-ops. To better compete with other dairy processors, DFA has invested heavily in facilities and joint ventures to process its fluid milk into value-added products and high-end ingredients.

## HISTORY

Mid-America Dairymen (Mid-Am), the largest of the cooperatives that merged to form Dairy Farmers of America (DFA), was born in 1968. At that time, several midwestern dairy co-ops banded together to attack common economic problems, such as reduced government subsidies, price drops resulting from a rising milk surplus, dealer consolidation, and improvements in production, processing, and packaging. The merging organizations — representing 15,000 dairy farmers — were Producers Creamery Company (Springfield, Missouri), Sanitary Milk Producers (St. Louis), Square Deal Milk Producers (Highland, Illinois), Mid-Am (Kansas City, Missouri), and Producers Creamery Company of Chillicothe (north central Missouri).

In the early 1970s Mid-Am struggled with internal restructuring. Most dairy farmers and co-ops were hit hard by the energy crisis and the government's decision to allow increased dairy imports in 1973, the same year the US Justice Department filed an antitrust suit against Mid-Am. (A judge cleared the co-op 12 years later.)

In 1974 Mid-Am lost almost $8 million on revenues of $625 million, chalked up to record-high feed prices, a weakened economy, a milk surplus, and a massive inventory loss. Co-op veteran Gary Hanman was named CEO that year. Over the next two years, Mid-Am cut costs, sold corporate frills, downsized management, and began marketing more of its own products under the Mid-America Farms label, thus reducing dependency on commodity sales.

Mid-Am expanded its research and development efforts throughout the 1980s. After 20 years of fighting, in 1991 Mid-Am, along with two other co-ops, reached a $21.4 million settlement of an antitrust suit filed by the National Farmers Organization.

The co-op opened its services to farmers in California and New Mexico in 1993, and a series of mergers in 1994 and 1995 nearly doubled its size. In 1997 it purchased some of Borden's dairy operations, including rights to the valuable Elsie the Cow and Borden's trademarks.

Wary of falling milk prices, Mid-Am merged with Western Dairymen Cooperative, Milk Marketing, and the Southern Region of Associated Milk Producers at the end of 1997 to form DFA. Hanman moved into the seat of CEO at the new co-op. DFA began a series of joint ventures with with the #1 US dairy processor, Suiza Foods.

DFA added California Gold (more than 330 farmers, 1998) and Independent Cooperative Milk Producers Association (730 dairy farmer members in Michigan and parts of Ohio and Indiana, 1999). In another joint venture with Suiza, in early 2000 DFA sold its 50% stake in the US's #3 fluid milk processor, Southern Foods, in exchange for 34% of a new company named Suiza Dairy Group.

After mollifying the government's antitrust fears, DFA acquired the butter operations of Sodial North America in 2000. It then molded all its butter businesses into a new entity, Keller's Creamery, LLC.

In 2001 the cooperative went in with Land O'Lakes 50-50 to purchase a cheese plant from Kraft, and it sold back its stake in Suiza Dairy Group to Dean Foods (a new company formed by the acquisition of Dean Foods by Suiza, which then took on the Dean Foods name). DFA also teamed with a group of dairy investors to form a new joint venture, National Dairy Holdings, which received 11 processing plants from the new Dean Foods as part of the exchange for Suiza Dairy.

President and CEO: Gary E. Hanman
EVP: Don Schriver
CFO: Jerry Bos
VP, Marketing and Economic Analysis: John Wilson
VP, Human Resources and Administration:
  Harold Papen
COO, Mideast Area: Jim Carroll
COO, Northeast Area: Rick Smith
COO, Western Area: Dave Parrish
COO, Southwest Area: David Jones
COO, Southeast Area: John Collins
COO, Central Area: Randy McGinnis
COO, Mountain Area: Greg Yandoo
Auditors: Deloitte & Touche LLP

## LOCATIONS

HQ: 10220 N. Executive Hills Blvd.,
  Kansas City, MO 64153
Phone: 816-801-6455      Fax: 816-801-6456
Web: www.dfamilk.com

Dairy Farmers of America includes 27,000 members
from 45 states.

## PRODUCTS/OPERATIONS

Selected Products
Butter (Breakstone's, Hotel Bar, Keller's, Plugra)
Cheese dips
Cheeses (Borden)
Coffee creamer
Condensed milk
Cream
Dehydrated dairy products
Infant formula
Nonfat dry milk powder
Shelf-stable nutritional beverages (Sport Shake)
Whey products

## COMPETITORS

AMPI
California Dairies Inc.
Dairylea
Danone
Dean Foods
Foremost Farms
Galaxy Nutritional Foods
Kraft Foods North America
Lactalis
Land O'Lakes

Leprino Foods
Nestlé
Parmalat Finanziaria
Prairie Farms Dairy
Saputo
Schreiber Foods
Suprema Specialties
Unilever
WestFarm Foods

## HISTORICAL FINANCIALS & EMPLOYEES

| Cooperative<br>FYE: December 31 | Annual<br>Growth | 12/91 | 12/92 | 12/93 | 12/94 | 12/95 | 12/96 | 12/97 | 12/98 | 12/99 | 12/00 |
|---|---|---|---|---|---|---|---|---|---|---|---|
| Sales ($ mil.) | 17.3% | — | 1,868 | 1,826 | 2,491 | 3,681 | 4,085 | 3,818 | 7,325 | 7,600 | 6,700 |
| Employees | 6.7% | — | 3,600 | 3,500 | 3,000 | 3,100 | 3,200 | 5,300 | 5,300 | — | — |

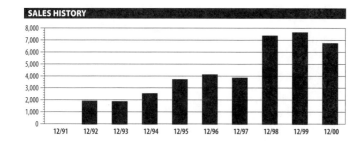

SALES HISTORY

# DART CONTAINER CORPORATION

Dart Container's cups runneth over and over and over. The world's #1 maker of foam cups and food containers, Dart Container is the money machine of the secretive and contentious Dart family. Based in Mason, Michigan, the company has four recycling centers, as well as manufacturing operations in Argentina, Australia, Canada, Mexico, the UK, and the US. To undercut competition, the company makes its own feedstocks and machines and uses its own trucks for distribution.

Dart Container makes foam cups and cup lids, disposable dinnerware, and disposable cutlery for hospitals, schools, and restaurants.

The firm sells its recycled polystyrene to companies that make such items as insulation material and egg cartons.

The king of cups has a simple strategy — secrecy. The cup-making machine developed by the Darts was never patented; this has allowed the Dart family to avoid revealing how it works. Most of the company's factory workers have never seen the machines, and Dart's salespeople are not allowed inside the plants. After years of legal battles, the Darts have reached an agreement regarding alleged discrepancies in the family inheritance. The terms of the settlement are, naturally, secret.

## HISTORY

William F. Dart founded a Michigan firm to make steel tape measures in 1937. Dart's son William A. started experimenting with plastics in 1953, and in the late 1950s the two devised a cheap way to mold expandable polystyrene and built a cup-making machine. Dart Container was incorporated in Mason, Michigan, in 1960 and shipped its first cups that year. By the late 1960s the rising demand for plastic-foam products sparked an increase in R&D. In 1970 the company built a plant in Corona, California.

It was a family feud in the making in 1974, as William F. divided the business among his grandsons — Tom, Ken, and Robert — in separate trusts that named William A. trustee for all. Tom branched out in 1975 and founded oil and gas company Dart Energy, which was later absorbed into Dart Container. William F. died the next year. Following the oil market crash of the early 1980s, Tom went through a sticky divorce and admitted to cocaine abuse. His father temporarily removed him as head of Dart Energy in 1982, and the next year the entire family underwent group psychiatric counseling.

The family reorganized its assets in 1986, giving Ken and Robert the cup business and Tom the energy business plus $58 million in cash. In 1987 Ken began to swell the family fortune with a series of successful investments. Better tax rates motivated Dart family members to move to Sarasota, Florida, in 1989. They set up shop in an unmarked building behind a sporting-goods store. By the late 1980s Dart Container commanded more than 50% of the worldwide market for foam cups.

In 1990 the company paid $250,000 to settle a factory worker's minority discrimination lawsuit. The next year Ken bought 11% of the Federal Home Loan Mortgage Corp. (Freddie Mac), as well as portions of Salomon and

Brazil's foreign debt. According to Tom, that year Ken also financed brain research in hopes of finding a way to keep his brain alive after the death of his body in an attempt to avoid future estate taxes.

Tom sued his brothers and father in 1992 for allegedly cheating him out of millions of dollars in trust money in the 1986 reorganization. Ken turned a $300 million investment into $1 billion by selling the Freddie Mac shares. The next year he and Robert renounced their US citizenship to avoid paying taxes. Ken also made a failed attempt to block the restructuring of Brazil's debt (of which Dart owned 4%). That year Ken's new $1 million Sarasota home was firebombed (the case remains unsolved), and Robert moved to the UK, where he soon filed for divorce.

Ken began hiring bodyguards, and he moved his family to the Cayman Islands in 1994. Dart shelled out $230,000 to settle yet another discrimination case. In 1995 Tom was fired from Dart Energy, and Ken tried — and failed — to return to the US as a diplomat of Belize. In 1996 Tom accused Judge Donald Owens of being biased in favor of William A. The judge succumbed to the pressure in 1997 and removed himself from the proceedings, only to be ordered back on the case by Michigan's Court of Appeals. The lawsuit was settled in 1998 before going to trial, but the terms were kept secret. The following year saw yet another series of lawsuits for the container company. In 1999 Dart Container filed an appeal to an IRS demand to pay $31 million in back taxes and late penalties. The legal wrangling continued through 2001.

**Chairman:** William A. Dart
**President:** Kenneth B. Dart
**VP:** Robert C. Dart
**CFO and Treasurer:** William Myer
**VP, Administration:** Jim Lammers
**Director, Human Resources:** Mark Franks

## LOCATIONS

**HQ:** 500 Hogsback Rd., Mason, MI 48854
**Phone:** 517-676-3800        **Fax:** 517-676-3883
**Web:** www.dartcontainer.com

Dart Container has four recycling centers in Canada and the US, and manufacturing operations in Argentina, Australia, Canada, Mexico, the UK, and the US.

## PRODUCTS/OPERATIONS

**Selected Products**
Clear containers
Container lids
Deli containers and lids
Dinnerware
Foam cups
Hinged containers
Paper cups and lids
Plastic cups and lids
Plastic cutlery

**Selected Services**
CARE (Cups Are REcyclable) Program (provides densifier to larger customers to compact their polystyrene, which Dart then picks up)
Foam-Recycling (four plants in Canada, Florida, Michigan, and Pennsylvania and a drop-off site in Georgia)
Recycla-Pak (provides small-volume businesses with cup-shipping containers that double as recycling bins)

## COMPETITORS

EarthShell
Huhtamäki
Huntsman
Jim Pattison Group
NOVA Chemicals
Pactiv
sf holdings
Smurfit-Stone Container
Sonoco Products
Temple-Inland
Tetra Laval

## HISTORICAL FINANCIALS & EMPLOYEES

| Private<br>FYE: December 31 | Annual<br>Growth | 12/91 | 12/92 | 12/93 | 12/94 | 12/95 | 12/96 | 12/97 | 12/98 | 12/99 | 12/00 |
|---|---|---|---|---|---|---|---|---|---|---|---|
| Estimated sales ($ mil.) | 12.3% | — | 475 | 600 | 800 | 1,000 | 1,000 | 1,000 | 1,150 | 1,100 | 1,200 |
| Employees | 6.6% | — | 3,000 | 3,750 | 3,600 | 4,300 | 4,300 | 5,000 | 5,000 | 5,000 | 5,000 |

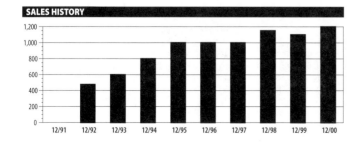

SALES HISTORY

# DELCO REMY INTERNATIONAL, INC.

## OVERVIEW

Delco Remy International is the legacy of Charles "Boss" Kettering, who invented the electric starter in 1911. The Anderson, Indiana-based company manufactures, remanufactures, and distributes electrical, power train, and drivetrain components for cars, trucks, and heavy-duty vehicles. Sold primarily under the Delco Remy name, its products include starters, alternators, engines, transmissions, fuel systems, and traction control systems. Now owned by Citigroup Citicorp Venture Capital, Delco

Remy sells to vehicle and equipment makers, including General Motors (30% of sales), Navistar (13% of sales), Ford, and Freightliner. The company also sells to warehouse distributors and retail auto parts chains such as Pep Boys and AutoZone.

Acquisitions boosted Delco Remy's sales, but they failed to do much for the company's stock price, which consistently traded below its IPO price. The company was finally acquired by Citicorp Venture Capital in 2001.

## HISTORY

Charles Kettering, a cofounder of Dayton Engineering Laboratories (known as "Delco"), was one of the most famous inventors of the early 20th century, his creations including "no-knock" gasoline, the refrigerant Freon, and four-wheel brakes.

Kettering also solved one of the main problems that had kept the automobile from becoming a mass market product when he invented the electric starter. Prior to his invention, starting an automobile was a difficult and hazardous proposition. The driver had to hand crank the engine to get it started, and backfires during cranking could break the user's arm.

In 1910, after a Detroit man was killed when a crank handle hit his face, a friend of the deceased, Cadillac president Henry Leland, promised an end to hand cranks in his cars. Hearing of Leland's promise, Kettering began tinkering with one of his inventions, an electric motor that opened a cash register drawer. After a few months, he created the electric starter, which first appeared in the 1912 Cadillac. By the early 1920s Delco was building millions of starters a year.

In 1927 Delco merged with Remy Electric to form Delco Remy, and became a division of General Motors. Remy Electric had been founded in 1896 by brothers Frank and Perry Remy to wire homes for electricty. The company moved into developing electrical products for automobiles in the early 1900s, and as the auto industry grew, Remy turned its focus away from homes and toward automobiles.

Kettering became head of GM's research division, where he served for more than a quarter century, while royalties from his inventions made him a wealthy man. (In 1945 he helped fund the Sloan-Kettering Institute cancer research center.)

Delco Remy remained a unit of General Motors until its partial spinoff in 1994. It was then privately held primarily by GM and Citicorp Venture Capital.

In 1995 Delco Remy bought The A&B Group (starters and alternators), followed in 1996 and 1997 by the respective purchases of about 80% each of Power Investments (remanufactured engines) and World Wide (starters and alternators). The company recorded a fiscal 1996 loss related to restructuring charges and acquisitions. It went public in late 1997 to raise funds.

In 1998 Delco Remy sold its marine engine and stern-drive propulsion businesses to focus on vehicle parts. GM's strike that year dropped Delco Remy's GM sales from an expected 39% to 27% and continued the company's losses. To recover, Delco Remy closed two former GM plants and opened three new focus factories (plants that make one product line in order to increase efficiency and cut costs).

To establish a strong international presence, Delco Remy bought Belgium-based automotive starter and alternator remanufacturer Electro Diesel Rebuild and the starter and alternator remanufacturing operations of UK-based LucasVarity (now part of TRW).

Global expansion continued in 1999 with Delco Remy increasing its stake in Remy Korea Ltd. (heavy-duty starters and alternators) from 50% to 80%. The company boosted distribution and marketing efforts targeting aftermarket sales.

In 2000 Delco Remy took a controlling stake in M&M Knopf, the world's largest automotive component recovery and exchange company. It also bought Elmot, a Polish starter and alternator maker. The same year — after the company announced a restructuring that would cut about 860 jobs — Citicorp Venture Capital agreed to acquire the company in a deal that valued Delco Remy at about $247 million. Citicorp completed the deal in 2001.

## OFFICERS

**Chairman:** Harold K. Sperlich, age 69, $587,400 pay
**Vice Chairman:** E. H. Billig, age 72
**President and COO:** Thomas J. Snyder, age 55,
$587,400 pay
**CFO:** David E. Stoll, age 57
**SVP Business Development:** J. Timothy Gargaro, age 46
**SVP and General Manager, Aftermarket Division, Delco
Remy America:** Thomas R. Jennett
**SVP, Human Resources and Communications:**
Roderick English, age 47
**Group VP, Aftermarket:** Joseph P. Felicelli, age 53,
$327,400 pay
**VP and General Counsel:** Susan E. Goldy, age 45,
$366,700 pay
**VP; Managing Director, Europe:** Patrick C. Mobouck,
age 45
**VP, Sales, Automotive Systems Division:** Denise M. Lee
**President, A&B Group, Inc.:** John M. Mayfield
**President, Delco Remy America:** Richard L. Stanley,
age 43
**President, Power Investments, Inc.:** J. Michael Jarvis
**President, TracTech, Inc.:** Ralph F. McGee
**President, World Wide Automotive, Inc.:**
Richard L. Keister
**Auditors:** Ernst & Young LLP

## LOCATIONS

**HQ:** 2902 Enterprise Dr., Anderson, IN 46013
**Phone:** 765-778-6499      **Fax:** 765-778-6404
**Web:** www.delcoremy.com

Delco Remy International has manufacturing facilities
in Belgium, Canada, Hungary, Ireland, Mexico, Poland,
South Korea, Tunisia, the UK, and the US.

### 2000 Sales

|  | $ mil. | % of total |
|---|---|---|
| North America |  |  |
| US | 937 | 86 |
| Canada | 44 | 4 |
| Europe | 62 | 6 |
| Asia | 34 | 3 |
| Other regions | 14 | 1 |
| **Total** | **1,091** | **100** |

## PRODUCTS/OPERATIONS

### 2000 Sales

|  | $ mil. | % of total |
|---|---|---|
| Electrical systems | 859 | 79 |
| Power train/drivetrain | 194 | 18 |
| Other | 38 | 3 |
| **Total** | **1,091** | **100** |

### Selected Products

Alternators
Engines
Fuel systems
Starter motors
Torque converters
Traction control systems
Transmissions

## COMPETITORS

| | |
|---|---|
| Champion Parts | Mitsubishi Motors |
| Dana | Motorcar Parts |
| Federal-Mogul | Robert Bosch |
| General Parts | Valeo |
| Genuine Parts | |
| Hahn Automotive | |
| Warehouse | |

## HISTORICAL FINANCIALS & EMPLOYEES

| Private<br>FYE: July 31 | Annual<br>Growth | 7/91 | 7/92 | 7/93 | 7/94 | 7/95 | 7/96 | 7/97 | 7/98 | 7/99 | 7/00 |
|---|---|---|---|---|---|---|---|---|---|---|---|
| Sales ($ mil.) | 13.7% | — | — | — | — | 573 | 637 | 690 | 815 | 954 | 1,091 |
| Net income ($ mil.) | 12.2% | — | — | — | — | 7 | (5) | (14) | (4) | 28 | 12 |
| Income as % of sales | — | — | — | — | — | 1.2% | — | — | — | 3.0% | 1.1% |
| Employees | 18.4% | — | — | — | 2,800 | 3,000 | 3,000 | 4,949 | 4,833 | 6,845 | 7,707 |

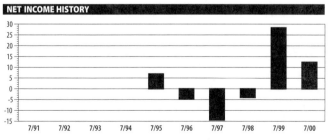

### NET INCOME HISTORY

### 2000 FISCAL YEAR-END

Debt ratio: 80.4%
Return on equity: 10.9%
Cash ($ mil.): 18
Current ratio: 2.21
Long-term debt ($ mil.): 484

# DELOITTE TOUCHE TOHMATSU

## OVERVIEW

This company isn't "deloitted" by the changes in the accounting/consulting industry. New York-based Deloitte Touche Tohmatsu (DTT, which operates as Deloitte & Touche in the US) is swimming against the tide that is breaking up the combined operations built up during the 1980s and 1990s.

Operating some 700 offices in more than 130 countries, DTT has pursued a strategy of using accountants and consultants in concert to provide seamless service in auditing, accounting, strategic planning, information technology,

financial management, and productivity. This made DTT vulnerable to the drive by the SEC to force audit firms to divest their consultants because of a perceived conflict of interest between obtaining consulting clients and offering impartial fiscal assurance. The SEC has imposed stricter revenue disclosure rules for accountancies, increasing the scrutiny they face.

DTT also provides human resources and tax consulting services, as well as services to governments and international lending agencies working in emerging markets.

## HISTORY

In 1845 William Deloitte opened an accounting office in London, at first soliciting business from bankrupts. The growth of joint stock companies and the development of stock markets in the mid-19th century created a need for standardized financial reporting and fueled the rise of auditing, and Deloitte moved into the new field. The Great Western Railway appointed him as its independent auditor (the first anywhere) in 1849.

In 1890 John Griffiths, who had become a partner in 1869, opened the company's first US office in New York City. Four decades later branches had opened throughout the US. In 1952 the firm partnered with Haskins & Sells, which operated 34 US offices.

Deloitte aimed to be "the Cadillac, not the Ford" of accounting. The firm, which became Deloitte Haskins & Sells in 1978, began shedding its conservatism as competition heated up; it was the first of the major accountancy firms to use aggressive ads.

In 1984 Deloitte Haskins & Sells tried to merge with Price Waterhouse, but the deal was dropped after Price Waterhouse's UK partners objected.

In 1989 Deloitte Haskins & Sells joined the flamboyant Touche Ross (founded in 1899) to become Deloitte & Touche. Touche Ross's Japanese affiliate, Ross Tohmatsu (founded in 1968) rounded out the current name. The merger was engineered by Deloitte's Michael Cook and Touche's Edward Kangas, in part to unite the former firm's US and European strengths with the latter's Asian presence. Cook continued to oversee US operations with Kangas presiding over international operations. Many affiliates, particularly in the UK, rejected the merger and defected to competing firms.

As auditors were increasingly held accountable for the financial results of their clients, legal action soared. In the 1990s Deloitte was

sued because of its actions relating to Drexel Burnham Lambert junk bond king Michael Milken, the failure of several savings and loans, and clients' bankruptcies.

Nevertheless, in 1995 the SEC chose Michael Sutton, the firm's national director of auditing and accounting practice, as its chief accountant. That year DTT formed Deloitte & Touche Consulting to consolidate its US and UK consulting operations; its Asian consulting operations were later added to the group to facilitate regional expansion.

In 1996 the firm formed a corporate fraud unit (with special emphasis on the Internet) and bought PHH Fantus, the leading corporate relocation consulting company. In 1997, amid a new round of mergers in the industry, rumors swirled that a merger of DTT and Ernst & Young had been scrapped because the firms could not agree on ownership among the two firms' partners. DTT disavowed plans to merge and launched an ad campaign directly targeted against its rivals.

In 1998 the firm's overseas expansion was hit by the Asian economic crisis, but a rise in restructuring consulting was the silver lining to this cloudy time. In 1999 the firm sold its accounting staffing service unit to its managers and Evercore Partners, citing possible conflicts of interest with its core audit business. Also that year Kangas stepped down as CEO to be succeeded by James Copeland, and Deloitte Consulting decided to sell its computer programming subsidiary to CGI Group.

In 2000 Deloitte Consulting announced it would start a business-to-business e-commerce venture with Chase Manhattan (now J.P. Morgan Chase & Co.) The following year the SEC forced Deloitte & Touche to restate Pre-Paid Legal Services' financial results. In an unusual move, Deloitte & Touche publicly disagreed with the SEC's findings.

**Chairman Emeritus:** Edward Kangas
**Chairman:** Piet Hoogendoorn
**CEO:** James E. Copeland Jr.
**COO:** J. Thomas Presby
**CFO:** William A. Fowler
**Chairman and CEO, Deloitte Consulting:**
Douglas M. McCracken
**Chief Executive and Senior Partner, Deloitte & Touche (UK):** John P. Connolly
**Global Managing Partner, Tax and Legal:** Jerry Leamon
**National Director, US International Operations:**
Tom Schiro
**Director, Communications:** David Read
**Director, Human Resources:** Martyn Fisher
**National Director, Human Capital and Actuary Practice:**
Ainar D. Aijala Jr.
**National Director, Human Resources:** James H. Wall
**National Director, Operations:** William H. Stanton
**International Counsel:** Joseph J. Lambert
**General Counsel:** Philip R. Rotner
**Director, Finance:** Ashish Bali
**National Director, Marketing, Communications, and Public Relations:** Paul Marinaccio

## LOCATIONS

**HQ:** 1633 Broadway, New York, NY 10019
**Phone:** 212-492-4000 **Fax:** 212-492-4111
**Web:** www.deloitte.com

Deloitte Touche Tohmatsu operates through about 700 offices in more than 130 countries.

## PRODUCTS/OPERATIONS

**Selected Services**
Accounting and auditing
Corporate finance
Emerging markets consulting
Human resource, actuarial, insurance, and managed care consulting
Information technology consulting
Management consulting
Mergers and acquisitions consulting
Reorganization services
Tax advice and planning
Transaction services

**Industry Specializations**
Communications
Consumer business
Financial services
Health Care
Manufacturing
Mining
Utilities

## COMPETITORS

Accenture
Andersen
Arthur D. Little
BDO International
Booz-Allen
Boston Consulting
Cap Gemini
Cap Gemini Ernst & Young U.K.
EDS
Ernst & Young
Grant Thornton International
H&R Block
KPMG
Marsh & McLennan
McKinsey & Company
PricewaterhouseCoopers
Towers Perrin
Watson Wyatt

## HISTORICAL FINANCIALS & EMPLOYEES

| Partnership<br>FYE: May 31 | Annual<br>Growth | 8/92 | 8/93 | 8/94 | 8/95 | 8/96 | 8/97 | 8/98 | 8/99 | *5/00 | 5/01 |
|---|---|---|---|---|---|---|---|---|---|---|---|
| Sales ($ mil.) | 11.1% | 4,800 | 5,000 | 5,200 | 5,950 | 6,500 | 7,400 | 9,000 | 10,600 | 11,200 | 12,400 |
| Employees | 6.0% | 56,000 | 56,000 | 56,600 | 59,000 | 63,440 | 65,000 | 82,000 | 90,000 | 90,000 | 95,000 |

* Fiscal year change

### SALES HISTORY

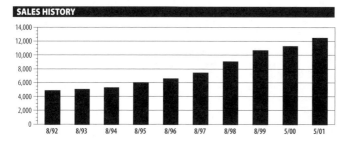

# DFS GROUP LIMITED

## OVERVIEW

DFS Group would have been wise to heed the old Japanese proverb, "Even monkeys fall from trees." Based in San Francisco, DFS (Duty Free Shoppers) Group has been the dexterous 900-lb. gorilla of duty-free retailing, with more than 150 stores in airports, hotels, and downtown locales, mostly along the Pacific Rim. It sells high-quality, brand-name clothing, liquor, perfume, tobacco, jewelry, and other goods.

The company's reliance on the Japanese, who were grounded by the Asian currency crisis, has hurt sales and forced it to shift focus to non-airport stores. To reduce its dependence on duty-free retailing, DFS has opened new store formats in resort and downtown locations with cheaper rents. These Galleria centers contain upscale specialty stores, designer boutiques, and entertainment complexes. The company also operates Miami Cruiseline Services, a shipboard duty-free retailer.

LVMH Moët Hennessy Louis Vuitton owns 61% of DFS and supplies it with Christian Dior perfumes and clothing, among other luxury goods; co-founder Robert Miller owns 38% of the company.

## HISTORY

Charles Feeney and Robert Miller were classmates at Cornell University's School of Hotel Administration in the mid-1950s. They started a business in Europe in the late 1950s selling duty-free liquor and foreign cars to tourists and US servicemen. By 1960 the business had moved to Asia, where Feeney and Miller opened offices near US Air Force and Navy bases.

By the early 1960s the company, by then known as Duty Free Shoppers (DFS), opened its first duty-free stores at the Hong Kong and Honolulu international airports, where sales boomed. But DFS was in dire financial straits by 1965 after the US government eased restrictions on duty-free liquor (DFS's main merchandise) and allowed US car manufacturers to sell on military bases. To salvage the operation, Feeney and Miller in 1966 sold lawyer Anthony Pilaro and British accountant Alan Parker each 10% of the company.

Overseas travel from Japan skyrocketed after the 1964 Tokyo Olympics, when travel restrictions on the Japanese were lifted. DFS targeted Japanese tourists because of the huge amounts they spent while traveling and their penchant for expensive designer goods. In 1968 it opened its first non-airport location in downtown Hong Kong.

Feeney and Miller had handed over day-to-day operations to others by the early 1980s, and DFS had opened airport stores in Alaska, Guam, Los Angeles, Saipan, San Francisco, and Singapore. In 1983 Adrian Bellamy was appointed chairman and CEO.

In 1987 and 1988 the company opened new stores in Australia and New Zealand after learning that Japanese newlyweds were going there instead of Hawaii. Also in the late 1980s, DFS opened new stores at airports in major cities in the US as well as in the UK. In 1989 the company tried to renew its contract at the San Francisco airport but was outbid by rival Allders International. DFS switched to selling general merchandise there and opened one of its first department stores in downtown San Francisco.

DFS entered Canada in 1990 with a five-year contract at Toronto's Pearson International Airport. The Persian Gulf War curtailed international travel in 1991 and sales dropped about 15%. The sales slump halted plans for European expansion and led DFS to close its London stores. In 1994 the company opened its first multi-department Galleria store in Guam.

Myron Ullman, former chairman and CEO of Macy's, replaced Bellamy as chairman and CEO of DFS in 1995. That year, despite Miller's protests, Feeney, Parker, and Pilaro sold their stakes in DFS (totaling 61%) to luxury goods conglomerate LVMH Moët Hennessy Louis Vuitton. (The sale of Feeney's stake revealed that he had secretly donated $600 million to charity and had created two foundations holding $3.5 billion more.) After rejecting the aid of an outside arbitrator, Miller said in 1997 that he would not only hold onto his share of DFS but would also return to more active duty with the company.

Saks Holdings' COO, Brian Kendrick, succeeded Ullman as CEO in 1998. The next year Edward Brennan took the helm from Kendrick, who left to join Asbury Automotive Group. DFS also furthered its duty-free position with the 2000 acquisition of Miami Cruiseline Services' onboard cruise ship shops. DFS announced plans to open six Galleria stores in 2001 in Guam, Hong Kong, Singapore, and the US.

**Chairman, President, and CEO:** Edward J. Brennan, age 44
**CFO:** Caden Wang
**EVP Human Resources and Merchandise Planning:** James Wiggett
**SVP Human Resources:** Peggy Tate

## LOCATIONS

**HQ:** First Market Tower, 525 Market St., 33rd Fl., San Francisco, CA 94105
**Phone:** 415-977-2700     **Fax:** 415-977-4289
**Web:** www.dfsgroup.com

DFS Group operates more than 150 duty-free and general merchandise stores in airport terminals, hotel lobbies, and downtown locations, primarily in North America and the Pacific Rim.

## PRODUCTS/OPERATIONS

**Stores and Services**
Airport concessions (duty-free shops)
Galleria (designer boutiques, entertainment complexes, and upscale specialty stores)
Miami Cruiseline Services (duty-free onboard retailers)

## COMPETITORS

Aldeasa
BAA
Federated
Hermès
King Power
Little Switzerland
Neiman Marcus
Nordstrom
Richemont
Saks Inc.
Shiseido
Tiffany

## HISTORICAL FINANCIALS & EMPLOYEES

| Private<br>FYE: December 31 | Annual<br>Growth | 12/91 | 12/92 | 12/93 | 12/94 | 12/95 | 12/96 | 12/97 | 12/98 | 12/99 | 12/00 |
|---|---|---|---|---|---|---|---|---|---|---|---|
| Estimated sales ($ mil.) | (2.2%) | — | 2,150 | 2,600 | 2,600 | 3,000 | 2,689 | 2,240 | 1,574 | 1,300 | 1,800 |
| Employees | (6.5%) | — | — | — | 13,500 | 10,000 | 9,300 | 8,600 | 8,500 | 8,000 | 9,000 |

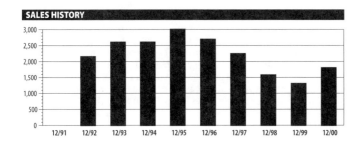

SALES HISTORY

# DISCOVERY COMMUNICATIONS, INC.

## OVERVIEW

With shows such as *Walking With Dinosaurs* and *Raising the Mammoth* (the two highest-rated documentaries ever shown on cable), Discovery Communications, Inc. (DCI) knows that documentaries should be anything but boring. The Bethesda, Maryland-based company owns and operates about 33 cable networks that reach more than 500 million homes in about 150 countries. DCI's most popular networks are Discovery Channel (more than 75 million households in the US), The Learning Channel (science, history, and human behavior, more than 77 million homes), Animal Planet (more than 67 million homes), and

Travel Channel (more than 51 million homes). It also operates six digital Discovery cable channels focused on specific topics such as science and home and leisure.

Building on its name brand, DCI creates original programming, games, and activities for a series of science and nature Web sites under the Discovery.com name (it may take its Internet unit public), and publishes videos, books, and CD-ROMs. It also operates about 170 Discovery Channel retail stores. Liberty Media Corp. owns 49% of DCI; Cox Communications and Advance/Newhouse Communications own 25% each DCI.

## HISTORY

John Hendricks, a history graduate who wanted to expand the presence of educational programming on TV, founded Cable Educational Network in 1982. Three years later he introduced the Discovery Channel. Devoted entirely to documentaries and nature shows, the channel premiered in 156,000 US homes. After dodging bankruptcy (it had $5,000 cash and $1 million in debt to the BBC), within a year the Discovery Channel had 7 million subscribers and a host of new investors, including Cox Cable Communications and TCI (now AT&T Broadband). It expanded its programming from 12 hours to 18 hours a day in 1987.

Discovery continued to attract subscribers, reaching more than 32 million by 1988. The next year it launched Discovery Channel Europe to more than 200,000 homes in the UK and Scandinavia. The company began selling home videos in 1990 and entered the Israeli market. The following year Discovery Communications, Inc. (DCI) was formed to house the company's operations, and it bought The Learning Channel (TLC, founded in 1980). The company revamped TLC's programming, and in 1992 introduced a daily, six-hour, commercial-free block of children's programs. The next year it introduced its first CD-ROM title, *In the Company of Whales,* based on the Discovery Channel documentary.

DCI increased its focus on international expansion in 1994, moving into Asia, Latin America, the Middle East, North Africa, Portugal, and Spain. The next year the company introduced its Web site and began selling company merchandise such as CD-ROMs and videos. DCI solidified its move into the retail sector in 1996 with the acquisition of The Nature Company and Scientific Revolution chains (renamed Discovery Channel Store).

Also that year it launched its third major cable channel, Animal Planet.

The company continued expanding internationally throughout the mid-1990s, establishing operations in Australia, Canada, India, New Zealand, and South Korea (1995); Africa, Brazil, Germany, and Italy (1996); and Japan and Turkey (1997). DCI also added to its stable of cable channels with the purchase of 70% of Paxson Communications' Travel Channel in 1997 (it acquired the rest in 1999). The company's 1997 original production *Titanic: Anatomy of a Disaster* attracted 3.2 million US households, setting a network ratings record.

The following year DCI and the British Broadcasting Corporation launched Animal Planet in Asia through a joint venture and agreed to market and distribute new cable channel BBC America. DCI spent $330 million launching its new health and fitness channel, Discovery Health, in 1999 and formed partnerships with high-speed online service Road Runner (to provide interactive information and services to Road Runner customers) and Rosenbluth Travel (to provide vacation packages based on DCI programming).

In 2000 DCI reorganized its Internet activities into one unit called Discovery.com with plans to eventually take it public. Later that year the Discovery Channel set back-to-back records with the two highest-rated documentaries ever on cable, *Raising the Mammoth* (10.1 million people) and *Walking With Dinosaurs* (10.7 million people). In 2001 the company cut about 50 jobs as part of a restructuring. Later that year DCI struck a three-year deal to lease time from NBC on Saturday mornings (paying $6 million per season) to show its Discovery Kids programs.

**Chairman and CEO, Discovery Communications and Discovery.com:** John S. Hendricks, age 49
**President and COO:** Judith A. McHale, age 54
**EVP and CFO:** Gregory B. Durig
**EVP Strategy & Development:** Donald A. Baer
**EVP Human Resources and Administration:** Pandit Wright
**President, Discovery Health Media:** John Ford
**President, Discovery Networks International:** Dawn McCall
**President, Discovery Networks US:** Johnathan A. Rodgers, age 55
**President Discovery Consumer Products:** Michela English
**EVP and General Manager, Animal Planet:** W. Clark Bunting
**EVP and General Manager, TLC:** Jana Bennett
**EVP and General Manager, Travel Channel:** Steve Cheskin
**SVP and General Manager, Discovery Digital Network:** Charley Humbard
**SVP and General Manager, Discovery Online Networks:** Bill Allman
**EVP Corporate Operations and General Counsel:** Mark Hollinger
**Director Human Resources:** Eric Hawkins

## LOCATIONS

**HQ:** 7700 Wisconsin Ave., Bethesda, MD 20814
**Phone:** 301-986-0444      **Fax:** 301-771-4064
**Web:** www.discovery.com

**Selected International Networks**
Animal Planet América Latina
Animal Planet Brasil
Discovery América Latina
Discovery Asia
Discovery Australia/New Zealand
Discovery Canada
Discovery Channel Middle East
Discovery Español
Discovery Europe
Discovery Germany
Discovery India
Discovery Japan
Discovery Southeast Asia
Home and Leisure Channel UK

## PRODUCTS/OPERATIONS

**Selected Operations**
Discovery Enterprises Worldwide
  Discovery Channel Education (educational materials)
  Discovery Channel Interactive Media (CD-ROM)
  Discovery Channel Publishing (books)
  Discovery Channel Retail (170 Discovery Channel stores)
  Discovery Channel Video
  Discovery.com
Discovery Networks International (24 languages, 149 countries)
Discovery Networks US
  Animal Planet (61 million households)
  BBC America (markets and distributes for the BBC)
  Discovery Channel (78.6 million)
  Discovery Civilization Channel (digital)
  Discovery en Español (digital)
  Discovery Health Channel (12 million)
  Discovery Home & Leisure Channel (digital)
  Discovery Kids Channel (digital)
  Discovery Science Channel (digital)
  Discovery Wings Channel (digital)
  The Learning Channel (74 million)
  Travel Channel (41.4 million)

## COMPETITORS

A&E Networks
AOL Time Warner
CPB
NBC
National Geographic
News Corp.
USA Networks
Viacom
Walt Disney

## HISTORICAL FINANCIALS & EMPLOYEES

| Joint venture<br>FYE: December 31 | Annual<br>Growth | 12/91 | 12/92 | 12/93 | 12/94 | 12/95 | 12/96 | 12/97 | 12/98 | 12/99 | 12/00 |
|---|---|---|---|---|---|---|---|---|---|---|---|
| Sales ($ mil.) | 65.0% | — | — | 52 | 200 | 452 | 662 | 860 | 1,100 | 1,400 | 1,730 |
| Employees | 46.8% | — | — | — | 400 | 500 | 1,900 | 3,000 | 3,000 | 3,500 | 4,000 |

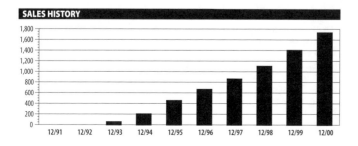

SALES HISTORY

# DOCTOR'S ASSOCIATES INC.

## OVERVIEW

They're called heros, hoagies, and po-boys, but co-founder Fred DeLuca calls his foot-long submarine sandwiches easy money. Milford, Connecticut-based Doctor's Associates owns the Subway chain of sandwich shops, which has more than 15,000 restaurants in 75 countries — more units than any other restaurant company except McDonald's.

Subway fare includes hot and cold sandwiches featuring classic items such as meatballs, turkey breast, and roast beef. The restaurants also offer chicken, steak, and turkey wraps, as well as salads, breakfast sandwiches, and cookies. Virtually all Subway restaurants are franchises and can be found in freestanding buildings, airports, colleges,

convenience stores, hospitals, military bases, and sports facilities.

With a low initial franchise cost and simple operations (minimum space requirements and little on-premises cooking), Subway has been one of the fastest-growing franchises in the world. But the company's heavy reliance on franchising hasn't been without controversy. Disgruntled franchisees have involved Subway in a number of legal skirmishes. However, the company continues to expand and is placing emphasis on growth in international markets. President and CEO Fred DeLuca and chairman Peter Buck own the company they founded in 1965.

## HISTORY

In 1965, 17-year-old Fred DeLuca dreamed of becoming a doctor and worked as a stockboy in a Bridgeport, Connecticut, hardware store to earn college tuition. It wasn't enough, so he cornered family friend Peter Buck at a backyard barbecue and asked for advice. Buck, a nuclear physicist, suggested DeLuca open a submarine sandwich shop; Buck put up $1,000 to get him started.

As the summer of 1965 was coming to an end, DeLuca rented a small location in a remote area of Bridgeport, opened Pete's Super Submarines, and began selling foot-long sandwiches. On the first day the sandwiches were so popular that DeLuca hired customers to work behind the counter; by the end of the day, he had sold out of all his supplies. The sandwiches continued to be popular for a while, but within a few months the shop started losing money — DeLuca and Buck found that selling submarine sandwiches was a seasonal business. They decided they could create an illusion of success by opening a second location and then a third. The third store was finally successful, partly because of its more visible location and increased marketing and partly because of a new name — Subway.

DeLuca and Buck had set a goal to open 32 shops by 1975, but they had only 16 by 1974. They realized that the only way they could reach their goal in one year was to license the Subway name. The first franchise opened that year, in Wallingford, Connecticut, and there were 32 by the end of 1975. The partners hit 100 by 1978 and 200 by 1983, and DeLuca set a new goal: 5,000 Subway shops by 1994. The first international Subway opened in Bahrain in 1984, and DeLuca hit his goal of 5,000 shops by 1990.

During the 1990s, DeLuca experimented with several other franchise concepts, including We Care Hair (budget styling salons), Cajun Joe's (spicy fried chicken), and Q Burgers. But none of these ventures fared as well as his sandwich empire. As Subway grew, however, controversy surrounding its treatment of franchisees began to surface. A Federal Trade Commission investigation of the company was dropped in 1993, but Subway continued to battle franchisees complaining about broken contracts, market over-saturation (and, therefore, too much competition), and what the franchisees viewed as unreasonably high royalty fees.

In spite of its franchising troubles, Subway kept growing. The company expanded into Russia and China in the mid-1990s, and opened its 11,000th restaurant in 1995. In 1997 Subway inked deals with the Army, Navy, and Air Force exchange services to bring Subway units to military bases. Two years later the company reached its 14,000-restaurant mark in Mount Gambier, Australia, an event that coincided with Subway's renewed push to expand internationally.

The company got some unexpected publicity in 1999 when 22-year-old Jared Fogle claimed that he dropped 245 pounds from his 425-pound frame by subsisting on a diet of Subway turkey sandwiches. Subway helped Fogle extend his 15 minutes of fame by featuring him and his oversized pants in a TV commercial. Subway introduced its largest menu initiative ever in 2000 when it unveiled its Subway Selects Gourmet Sandwiches, adding 13 items to the menu. Subway reached the 15,000-store mark in April 2001.

**Chairman:** Peter Buck
**President and CEO:** Frederick A. DeLuca
**Treasurer:** Carmela DeLuca
**Controller:** David Worroll
**Director Human Resources:** Wendy Kopazna
**Director Franchise Sales:** Don Fertman
**Public Relations Coordinator:** Les Winograd

## LOCATIONS

**HQ:** 325 Bic Dr., Milford, CT 06460
**Phone:** 203-877-4281    **Fax:** 203-876-6695
**Web:** www.subway.com

Doctor's Associates has Subway restaurants in 75 countries.

## PRODUCTS/OPERATIONS

**Selected Menu Items**
Breakfast sandwiches
  Bacon and egg
  Cheese and egg
  Ham and egg
  Western egg
Chips
Cookies
Salads
  Tuna
  Turkey breast
  Veggie
Sandwiches
  Club
  Cold cut trio
  Italian B.M.T.
  Meatball
  Roast beef
  Roasted chicken breast
  Seafood and crab
  Steak and cheese
  Tuna
  Turkey breast
  Veggie
Wraps
  Chicken parmesan
  Steak and cheese
  Turkey breast and bacon

## COMPETITORS

| | |
|---|---|
| 7-Eleven | Miami Subs |
| Blimpie | Papa John's |
| Burger King | Pret A Manger |
| Chick-fil-A | Quizno's |
| CKE Restaurants | Schlotzsky's |
| Domino's Pizza | Triarc |
| Dairy Queen | TRICON |
| Jack in the Box | Wall Street Deli |
| Little Caesar | Wawa |
| McDonald's | Wendy's |

## HISTORICAL FINANCIALS & EMPLOYEES

| Private FYE: December 31 | Annual Growth | 12/91 | 12/92 | 12/93 | 12/94 | 12/95 | 12/96 | 12/97 | 12/98 | 12/99 | 12/00 |
|---|---|---|---|---|---|---|---|---|---|---|---|
| Estimated sales ($ mil.) | 11.5% | — | — | 2,200 | 2,400 | 2,600 | 2,700 | 3,300 | 3,100 | 3,200 | 4,720 |
| Employees | — | — | — | — | — | — | — | — | — | — | 730 |

## SALES HISTORY

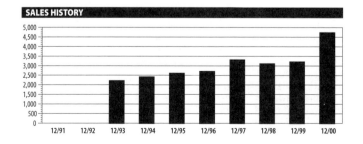

# DOMINO'S INC.

## OVERVIEW

Creating its own definition of the domino effect, Domino's Pizza has spread a craving for pizza across the globe. Ann Arbor, Michigan-based Domino's is the world's #1 pizza delivery company and the #2 pizza chain overall (behind TRICON's Pizza Hut). The company boasts more than 7,100 stores (most are franchised) in nearly 65 countries. Toppings vary from location to location — refried beans are popular in Mexico, while pie-lovers elsewhere favor pickled ginger (India), green peas (Brazil), canned tuna and corn (UK), and squid (Japan).

Domino's has built its reputation on speedy delivery, but the company also has begun to emphasize the quality of its fare. In the hard-fought war for pizza market share, the company also restructured and closed some underperforming units and has moved aggressively into e-commerce territory by offering online ordering at many locations. Domino's founder Thomas Monaghan, a devout Catholic, retired from the company in 1998 to concentrate on his religious activities. He sold 93% of his company to Boston-based investment firm Bain Capital.

## HISTORY

Thomas Monaghan's early life was one of hardship. After growing up in an orphanage and numerous foster homes, Monaghan spent his young adult life experimenting, trying everything from a Catholic seminary to a stint in the Marine Corps.

In 1960 Monaghan borrowed $500 and bought DomiNick's, a failed pizza parlor in Ypsilanti, Michigan, which he operated with the help of his brother James. In 1961 James traded his share in the restaurant to his brother for a Volkswagen Beetle, but Thomas pressed on, learning the pizza business largely by trial and error. After a brief partnership with an experienced restaurateur with whom he later had a falling out, Monaghan developed a strategy to sell only pizza and to locate stores near colleges and military bases. In 1965 the company changed its name to Domino's.

In the 1960s and 1970s, Monaghan endured setbacks that brought the company to the brink of bankruptcy. Among these were a 1968 fire that destroyed the Domino's headquarters and a 1975 lawsuit from Domino Sugar maker Amstar (now Tate & Lyle) for trademark infringement. But the company won the ensuing legal battles, and by 1978 it was operating 200 stores.

In the 1980s Domino's grew phenomenally. Between 1981 and 1983 the company doubled its number of US stores to 1,000; it went international in 1983, opening a store in Canada. The company's growth brought Monaghan a personal fortune. In 1983 he bought the Detroit Tigers baseball team and amassed one of the world's largest collections of Frank Lloyd Wright objects.

Domino's expansion continued in the mid-1980s. With sales figures mounting, the company introduced pan pizza (its first new product) in 1989. That year Monaghan put Domino's up for sale, but his practice of linking his personal and professional finances had gotten both the founder and company into such dire fiscal straits that no one wanted to buy the chain. Monaghan removed himself from direct management in 1989 and installed a new management group.

When company performance began to slide, Monaghan returned in 1991, having experienced a religious rebirth. He sold off many of his private holdings (including his resort island and his baseball team, which went to cross-town pizza rival Michael Ilitch of Little Caesar) to reinvigorate the company and reorganize company management.

In 1989 a Domino's driver, trying to fulfill the company's 30-minute delivery guarantee, ran a red light and collided with another car. The $79 million judgment against the company in 1993 prompted Domino's to drop its famous 30-minute policy and replace it with a satisfaction guarantee.

The company revamped its logo and store interiors with a new look in 1997. The following year, prompted by his decision to devote more time to religious pursuits, Monaghan retired from the business he had guided for nearly 40 years. He sold 93% of his company to investment firm Bain Capital. David Brandon, former CEO of sales promotion company Valassis Communications, replaced Monaghan as chairman and CEO in 1999. He initiated a restructuring that year that involved eliminating 100 managers; he closed or sold 142 stores to franchisees. Also that year the company introduced the first in its line of Italian Originals — specialty pizzas featuring Italian spices.

In 2001 Domino's bought a majority stake in Dutch Pizza Beheer B.V., an operator of 52 Domino's restaurants in the Netherlands. With the buy, the company is establishing a base to manage future expansion in Europe.

**Chairman and CEO:** David A. Brandon, age 48,
$1,405,000 pay
**EVP Finance and CFO:** Harry J. Silverman, age 42,
$654,818 pay
**EVP Distribution:** Michael D. Soignet, age 41,
$584,877 pay
**EVP Franchise Operations:** Hoyt D. Jones III, age 43
**EVP Flawless Execution:** Patrick W. Knotts, age 46
**EVP, General Counsel, and Secretary:** Elisa D. Garcia,
age 43
**EVP International:** J. Patrick Doyle, age 37,
$517,358 pay
**EVP PeopleFirst:** Patricia A. Wilmot, age 52
**VP Corporate Communications:** Tim McIntyre
**Special Assistant to Chairman and CEO:**
James G. Stansik, $425,498 pay
**Chief Information Officer:** Timothy Monteith, age 48
**Manager, Public Relations:** Holly Ryan
**Auditors:** Arthur Andersen LLP

## LOCATIONS

**HQ:** 30 Frank Lloyd Wright Dr., Ann Arbor, MI 48106
**Phone:** 734-930-3030    **Fax:** 734-668-1946
**Web:** www.dominos.com

Domino's Pizza has operations in about 65 countries.

## PRODUCTS/OPERATIONS

**Menu Items**
Pizzas
    Classic Hand Tossed
    Crunchy Thin Crust
    Italian Originals
    Ultimate Deep Dish
Sides
    Breadsticks
    Buffalo Wings
    Cheesy Bread

## COMPETITORS

Bertucci's                McDonald's
Burger King               Papa John's
CEC Entertainment         Pizza Hut
CKE Restaurants           Pizza Inn
Subway                    Round Table Pizza
Godfather's Pizza         Sbarro
KFC                       Uno Restaurant
LDB Corp                  Wendy's
Little Caesar             Whataburger

## HISTORICAL FINANCIALS & EMPLOYEES

| Private<br>FYE: Sun. nearest Dec. 31 | Annual<br>Growth | 12/91 | 12/92 | 12/93 | 12/94 | 12/95 | 12/96 | 12/97 | 12/98 | 12/99 | 12/00 |
|---|---|---|---|---|---|---|---|---|---|---|---|
| Sales ($ mil.) | 4.9% | — | — | — | 875 | 905 | 970 | 1,045 | 1,177 | 1,157 | 1,166 |
| Net income ($ mil.) | 137.1% | — | — | — | 0 | 25 | 20 | 61 | 77 | 2 | 25 |
| Income as % of sales | — | — | — | — | 0.0% | 2.8% | 2.0% | 5.8% | 6.5% | 0.2% | 2.2% |
| Employees | 1.4% | — | — | — | — | — | — | — | 14,200 | 14,400 | 14,600 |

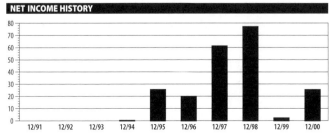

**NET INCOME HISTORY**

**2000 FISCAL YEAR-END**
Debt ratio: 100.0%
Return on equity: —
Cash ($ mil.): 25
Current ratio: 0.90
Long-term debt ($ mil.): 665

# DOW CORNING CORPORATION

## OVERVIEW

With health consequences of silicone-gel breast implants still under debate, Dow Corning is experiencing its own side effects. Midland, Michigan-based Dow Corning is facing thousands of claims made by women who reported injuries due to its breast implants. Dow Corning, a 50-50 joint venture between chemical titan Dow Chemical and glass giant Corning, is operating under bankruptcy protection.

The company makes more than 7,000 products from silicone, a polymer that combines the chemical- and temperature-resistant properties of glass with the versatility of plastic. It is used in such products as adhesives, insulating materials, and lubricants for aerospace, automotive, and electrical applications. Semiconductor makers also use the company's silicon-based products in chip fabrication.

Although the breast-implant case has dragged on for nearly a decade, Dow Corning appeared close to a settlement that would help it emerge from bankruptcy protection. The deal was stymied, however, when the bankruptcy judge ruled that women who did not agree to the settlement could still sue Dow Corning's corporate parents. Dow Corning and about 94% of the women who have sued it appealed the judge's ruling.

## HISTORY

Dow Corning was founded in 1943 as a joint venture between Dow Chemical and Corning Glass Works. Corning, founded by Amory Houghton in 1875, provided Thomas Edison with glass for the first lightbulbs. It developed Pyrex heat-resistant glass in 1915.

Corning made its first silicone resin samples in 1938. It teamed with a group of Dow Chemical scientists who were also working on silicone products in 1940. Dow Chemical president Willard Dow and Corning Glass Works president Glen Cole shook hands on the idea of a joint venture in 1942, and 10 months later Dow Corning was formed. Its first product, the engine grease DOW CORNING 4, enabled B-17s to fly at 35,000 feet (a major contribution to the Allied war effort). In 1945 DOW CORNING 35 (an emulsifier used in tire molds) and Pan Glaze (which made baking pans stick-proof and easier to clean) were instant successes on the home front.

Dow Corning expanded rapidly in international markets and in 1960 set up Dow Corning International to handle sales and technical service in markets outside North America. By 1969 the company had operations worldwide.

Dow Corning's first breast implants went on the market in 1964. Since then Dow Corning and other silicone makers have sold silicone breast implants to more than a million women in the US. In the early 1980s breast-implant recipients began suing Dow Corning and other implant makers, claiming that the silicone gel in the implants leaked and caused health problems. Dow Corning, the leading implant maker, defended the devices as safe. Dow Corning stopped making implants in 1992, after the Food and Drug Administration called for a moratorium on silicone-gel implants.

In 1993 Baxter International, Bristol-Myers Squibb, and Dow Corning offered $4.2 billion to settle thousands of claims. The corporation declared bankruptcy in 1995 to buy time for financial reorganization. A federal judge stripped Dow Chemical of its protection from direct liability, and the company was later ordered to pay a Nevada couple $4.1 million in damages (other jurisdictions did not follow suit). Dow Corning sold its Polytrap polymer technology to Advanced Polymer, maker of polymer-based pharmaceutical delivery systems, in 1996. The following year the company sold Bisco Products, its silicone-foam business, to Rogers Corporation for $12 million.

Dow Corning's $3.7 billion bankruptcy reorganization plan, offered in 1997, allowed for $2.4 billion to be set aside to settle most implant lawsuits against the corporation. However, a federal bankruptcy judge found legal flaws in the proposal and refused to allow claimants to vote on it. In 1998 Dow Corning upped the ante to $4.4 billion — $3 billion to the silicone claimants and the rest to creditors.

Both sides later agreed to a $3.2 billion compensation package, and in 1999 the plan received approval from a bankruptcy judge and creditors. However, the settlement stalled when the judge ruled that women who disagreed with the settlement could sue Dow Corporation and Corning (Dow Corning is appealing). Despite its court battles, in 2000 the company acquired the 51% of Universal Silicones & Lubricants (high-tech lubricants and silicone sealants) it did not own and renamed the company Dow Corning India.

**Chairman, President, and CEO:** Gary E. Anderson,
$564,585 pay (prior to promotion)
**Vice Chairman:** Peter F. Volanakis, age 45
**EVP:** Stephanie Burns
**SVP; General Manager, Geographic Development
Business Unit:** Richard Hoover
**SVP; General Manager, Paper and Process Industries
and Specialty Chemicals Industry Business Unit
(IBU):** Jere Marciniak
**SVP, Mergers and Acquisitions and Special Projects:**
John W. Churchfield
**Global VP, Planning and Finance, and CFO:**
Gifford E. Brown
**VP, Secretary, and General Counsel:** John Rothhaar
**VP and Chief Human Resources Officer:**
Burnett S. Kelly
**VP; General Manager, Construction Industry and Core
Products Business Unit:** Chris Bowyer
**VP; General Manager, Electronics Industry and
Advanced Materials Business IBU:** Ian Thackwray
**VP; General Manager, Life Sciences Industry and Life
Sciences Product Business IBU:** Endvar Rossi
**VP; General Manager, New Ventures Business Unit:**
Jean-Marc Gilson
**VP; General Manager, Service Enterprise Unit:**
Alan Ludgate
**VP; General Manager, Transportation, Energy and
Fabrication Industries and Engineered Elastomers
and Lubricants Business IBU:** Bruno Sulmon
**President, Hemlock Semiconductor Corporation:**
Donald Pfuehler

## LOCATIONS

**HQ:** 2200 W. Salzburg Rd., Midland, MI 48686
**Phone:** 989-496-4000          **Fax:** 989-496-4393
**Web:** www.dowcorning.com

Dow Corning has about 25 manufacturing sites
worldwide.

### 2000 Sales

| | % of total |
|---|---|
| US | 38 |
| Other countries | 62 |
| **Total** | **100** |

## PRODUCTS/OPERATIONS

**Selected Products**

**Aerospace**
Adhesives
Exotic composite materials
Greases
Protective coatings
Sealants

**Automotive**
Body components
Brake systems
Chassis
Electrical components
Electronic components
Engine/drivetrain
Fuel systems

**Chemical and Material Manufacturing**
Agrochemicals
Auto appearance chemicals
Oil and gas
Pulp manufacturing

**Cleaning Products**
Hand cleaners
Janitorial floor waxes
Laundry detergents

**Electrical/Electronics**
Adhesives and sealants
High-voltage insulators
Hyperpure polycrystalline silicon
Silicone rubber insulators
Thermally conductive adhesives

**Food and Beverage**
Packaging

## COMPETITORS

| | |
|---|---|
| Aventis | ICI |
| BASF AG | Lexington Precision |
| Baxter | 3M |
| Bristol-Myers Squibb | Shin-Etsu Chemical |
| Crompton | Th. Goldschmidt |
| Degussa | Wacker-Chemie |
| Exxon Mobil | Witco Corporation |

## HISTORICAL FINANCIALS & EMPLOYEES

| Joint venture<br>FYE: December 31 | Annual<br>Growth | 12/91 | 12/92 | 12/93 | 12/94 | 12/95 | 12/96 | 12/97 | 12/98 | 12/99 | 12/00 |
|---|---|---|---|---|---|---|---|---|---|---|---|
| Sales ($ mil.) | 4.4% | — | 1,956 | 2,044 | 2,205 | 2,493 | 2,532 | 2,644 | 2,568 | 2,603 | 2,751 |
| Net income ($ mil.) | — | — | (72) | (287) | (7) | (31) | 222 | 238 | 207 | 110 | 105 |
| Income as % of sales | — | — | — | — | — | — | 8.8% | 9.0% | 8.0% | 4.2% | 3.8% |
| Employees | 0.6% | — | 8,600 | 8,000 | 8,300 | 8,500 | 8,900 | 9,100 | 9,000 | 9,000 | 9,000 |

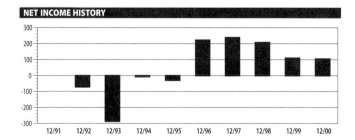

### NET INCOME HISTORY

DOW CORNING

# DREAMWORKS SKG

## OVERVIEW

Steven Spielberg, Jeffrey Katzenberg, and David Geffen had a Dream and now it Works. Glendale, California-based DreamWorks SKG is the brainchild of the three Hollywood moguls who formed the multimedia company in 1994, along with Microsoft co-founder Paul Allen. Spielberg oversees the live-action movies, which include box-office smashes *Gladiator* (the 2000 winner for Best Picture) and *What Lies Beneath.* Katzenberg heads up the animation division, responsible for such films as *Chicken Run* and *Shrek* (one of 2001's highest

grossing films) while Geffen runs DreamWorks Records, producing the soundtracks to all DreamWorks films and albums for popular artists such as Henry Rollins. The company also produces TV shows (*Spin City, The Job, Undeclared*).

A former production head at Disney, Katzenberg is essentially DreamWorks' CEO, handling the day-to-day operations. The company's bid to build a new studio failed, and its current offices remain at Universal Pictures, where Spielberg hangs his hat.

## HISTORY

Before pooling their collective talents in 1994, Steven Spielberg, Jeffrey Katzenberg, and David Geffen had each established an impressive track record. Spielberg had spawned such blockbusters as *Jaws,* the *Indiana Jones* trilogy, and *Jurassic Park.* Katzenberg had guided Walt Disney's return to animation (*The Lion King, Aladdin*) before a falling out with Disney CEO Michael Eisner. Music guru Geffen had helped make superstars of the Eagles and Nirvana.

A high-tech who's who embraced the SKG dream. Microsoft invested around $30 million to develop video games, while Microsoft co-founder Paul Allen shelled out nearly $500 million for a stake in the new company. Soon DreamWorks had arranged a $100 million programming deal with ABC and a 10-year HBO licensing agreement worth an estimated $1 billion, and had co-founded a $50 million animation studio with Silicon Graphics. DreamWorks then announced plans in 1995 to build the first new studio since the 1930s, just outside of Los Angeles in Playa Vista.

DreamWorks produced a string of TV flops before finding success with the Michael J. Fox comedy *Spin City* in 1996. Later that year the company released the first record under its new label, a dud from pop star George Michael, and it announced its partnership with SEGA and MCA (now Universal Studios) to develop SEGA GameWorks (video arcade super-centers featuring SEGA titles and games designed by Spielberg). The company finally released its first three movies in 1997 (*The Peacemaker, Amistad,* and *Mouse Hunt*) to mixed critical acclaim and mediocre box office performance. Combined with DreamWorks' less-than-stellar offerings in TV and music, buzz circulated that the meeting of the minds at DreamWorks wasn't all it was cracked up to be.

But DreamWorks started showing signs of

life in 1998 with the comet disaster film *Deep Impact* and Spielberg's Oscar-winning *Saving Private Ryan,* the highest grossing film of the year. It also introduced its first two animated films in 1998, *Antz* and *The Prince of Egypt,* both of which were successful. DreamWorks finished the year with the highest average gross per film of all the major studios.

After facing a multitude of environmental protests, cost overruns, and construction delays, DreamWorks scrapped its Playa Vista studio plans in 1999. Around the same time, Katzenberg settled his high-profile lawsuit against Disney over a bonus owed him when he resigned. Later in 1999 DreamWorks joined with Imagine Entertainment and Paul Allen's Vulcan Ventures to create POP.com, a Web site offering digital short films and streaming video features. It also announced a five-picture deal with Academy Award-winning animation firm Aardman Animations, with which it coproduced *Chicken Run* (released in 2000).

DreamWorks and Microsoft sold DreamWorks Interactive, their video game joint venture, to Electronic Arts in 2000. Later that year *American Beauty* took home the Oscar for Best Picture of 1999, and the studio continued its successful box-office run with three films that grossed more than $100 million (*Gladiator,* which scored the studio its second Best Picture Oscar; *Chicken Run;* and *What Lies Beneath*). After Allen failed to merge the struggling, unlaunched POP.com with IFILM.com (in which he is also a major investor), DreamWorks and Imagine shut down the netcaster.

The studio scored an early summer hit in 2001 with *Shrek,* which became one of that year's highest grossing films with more than $265 million at the box office. Also that year the company exited the GameWorks venture when the arcades failed to catch on quickly.

## OFFICERS

**Partner:** David Geffen, age 58
**Partner:** Jeffrey Katzenberg, age 50
**Partner:** Steven Spielberg, age 53
**CFO:** Ronald L. Nelson, age 48
**COO:** Helene Hahn
**President, DreamWorks Consumer Products:** Brad Globe
**President, DreamWorks Records:** Mo Ostin
**President, Feature Animation:** Ann Daly
**Head of Production:** Michael De Luca
**Senior Executive, Strategic Marketing, Public Relations, and Special Projects:** Terry Press
**Feature Executive:** Laurie MacDonald
**Feature Executive:** Walter Parkes
**Director, Human Resources:** Heidi Gonggryp

## LOCATIONS

**HQ:** 1000 Flower St., Glendale, CA 91201
**Phone:** 818-733-7000        **Fax:** 818-733-9918
**Web:** www.dreamworks.com

DreamWorks SKG has offices in Glendale, Los Angeles, and Universal City, California.

## PRODUCTS/OPERATIONS

**Selected Films, Recording Artists, and Television Shows**

**DreamWorks Pictures**
*American Beauty* (1999)
*Amistad* (1997)
*Antz* (1998)
*Chicken Run* (2000, co-produced with Aardman Animations)
*Deep Impact* (1998, co-produced with Paramount Pictures)
*Galaxy Quest* (1999)
*Gladiator* (2000, co-produced with Universal Studios)
*The Legend of Bagger Vance* (2000)
*Mouse Hunt* (1997)
*The Peacemaker* (1997)
*The Prince of Egypt* (1998)
*Road Trip* (2000)
*Saving Private Ryan* (1998, co-produced with Paramount Pictures)
*Shrek* (2001)
*Small Time Crooks* (2000)
*What Lies Beneath* (2000, co-produced with 20th Century Fox)

**DreamWorks Records**
Asleep At The Wheel
Buckcherry
Morphine
Papa Roach
Chris Rock
Henry Rollins
Elliott Smith

**DreamWorks Television**
*The Job*
*Spin City*
*Undeclared*

## COMPETITORS

| | |
|---|---|
| Alliance Atlantis Communications | Lucasfilm |
| | MGM |
| AOL Time Warner | Pixar |
| Artisan Entertainment | Sony |
| Carsey-Werner-Mandabach | Universal Studios |
| Fox Entertainment | Viacom |
| Lions Gate Entertainment | Walt Disney |

## HISTORICAL FINANCIALS & EMPLOYEES

| Private<br>FYE: December 31 | Annual<br>Growth | 12/91 | 12/92 | 12/93 | 12/94 | 12/95 | 12/96 | 12/97 | 12/98 | 12/99 | 12/00 |
|---|---|---|---|---|---|---|---|---|---|---|---|
| Sales ($ mil.) | 36.9% | — | — | — | — | — | — | — | 1,000 | 1,242 | 1,873 |
| Employees | (3.2%) | — | — | — | — | — | — | — | 1,600 | 1,500 | 1,500 |

SALES HISTORY

# E. & J. GALLO WINERY

## OVERVIEW

"We don't want most of the business," E. & J. Gallo Winery chairman Ernest Gallo has said. "We want it all." Once known primarily as the maker of cheap jug wine such as Carlo Rossi and Gallo and fortified favorites such as Thunderbird, the world's largest winemaker has also siphoned market share from upscale rivals by branching into more profitable middle- and premium-priced wines, including Gallo Sonoma. The Modesto, California-based winery also sells premium wines such as Turning Leaf and Gossamer Bay without the Gallo name on the label.

Already the leader in US table wines, with about 25% of the market, Gallo sells wine worldwide and is the leading US wine exporter. The vintner's strong affiliation with Wal-Mart has boosted wine sales in new Wal-Mart markets such as Germany and the UK. Gallo cultivates more than 3,000 acres in prestigious Sonoma County, California, and buys grapes from other area growers. Gallo sells nearly 35 brands over a wide price range, from fortified wines and wine coolers to upscale varietals that fetch more than $50 a bottle.

The founding Gallo family owns the firm.

## HISTORY

Giuseppe Gallo, the father of Ernest and Julio Gallo, was born in 1882 in the wine country of northwest Italy. Around 1900 he and his brother, Michelo (they called themselves Joe and Mike), traveled to America seeking their fame and fortune in the San Francisco area. Both brothers became wealthy by growing grapes and anticipating the growth of the market during Prohibition. (Home winemaking was legal and popular.)

Giuseppe's eldest sons, Ernest and Julio, worked with their father from the beginning. Their relationship was strained, and the father was reluctant to help his sons, particularly Ernest, in business. However, the mysterious murder-suicide that ended the lives of Giuseppe and his wife in 1933 eliminated that problem: The sons inherited the business their father had been unwilling to share.

From then on Ernest ran the business end, assembling a large distribution network and building a national brand, while Julio made the wine and Joe Jr., the third, much younger, brother, worked for them. In the early 1940s Gallo opened bottling plants in Los Angeles and New Orleans, using screw-cap bottles, which then seemed more hygienic and modern than corks. Gallo lagged during WWII, when alcohol was diverted for the military. Under Julio's supervision, it upgraded its planting stock and refined its technology.

In an attempt to capitalize on the sweet wines popular in the 1950s, Gallo introduced Thunderbird, a fortified wine (its alcohol content boosted to 20%), in 1957. In the 1960s Gallo spurred its growth by advertising heavily and keeping prices low. It introduced Hearty Burgundy, a jug wine, in 1964, along with Ripple. Gallo introduced the carbonated, fruit-flavored Boone's Farm Apple Wine in 1969,

creating an interest in "pop" wines that lasted for a few years.

The company introduced its first varietal wines in 1974. In the 1970s Gallo field workers switched unions, from the United Farm Workers to the Teamsters. Repercussions included protests and boycotts, but sales were largely unaffected. From 1976 to 1982 Gallo operated under an FTC order limiting its control over wholesalers. The order was lifted after the industry's competitive balance changed.

Through the 1970s and 1980s, Gallo expanded its production of varietals; in 1988 it began adding vintage dates to the wines' labels. But it also kept a hand in the lower levels of the market, introducing Bartles & Jaymes wine coolers.

Gallo began a legal battle in 1986 with Joe, who had been eased out of the business, over the use of the Gallo name. In 1992 Joe lost the use of his name for commercial purposes. Julio died the next year when his jeep overturned on a family ranch.

In 1996 rival Kendall-Jackson sued Gallo for trademark infringement over Gallo's new wine brand, Turning Leaf, claiming Gallo copied its Vintner's Reserve bottle and label. A jury ruled in Gallo's favor in 1997; a federal appeals court supported that decision in 1998.

Gina Gallo, Julio's granddaughter and a company winemaker, broke the firm's publicity-shy tradition in 1999 by appearing in national advertising to promote its more expensive wines.

In May 2000 Gallo announced plans to promote wine-cooler market leader Bartles & Jaymes with a new advertising campaign, although the category continues to wane.

**Chairman:** Ernest Gallo
**Co-President:** James E. Coleman
**Co-President:** Joseph E. Gallo
**Co-President:** Robert J. Gallo
**EVP and General Counsel:** Jack B. Owens
**EVP, Marketing:** Albion Fenderson
**VP, Controller, and Assistant Treasurer:** Tony Youga
**VP, Human Resources:** Mike Chase
**VP, Information Systems:** Kent Kushar
**VP, Media:** Sue McClelland
**VP, National Sales:** Gary Ippolito

## LOCATIONS

**HQ:** 600 Yosemite Blvd., Modesto, CA 95354
**Phone:** 209-341-3111    **Fax:** 209-341-3569
**Web:** www.gallo.com

E. & J. Gallo Winery has four wineries in the California
counties of Fresno, Livingston, Modesto, and Sonoma,
and vineyards throughout the region. Its wine is sold
throughout the US and in more than 85 countries.

## PRODUCTS/OPERATIONS

**Selected Products and Labels**
Bargain generic and varietals (Carlo Rossi, Livingston
    Cellars, Peter Vella, Wild Vines)
Brandy (E & J Brandy, E&J Cask & Cream, E&J VSOP)
Dessert (Fairbanks, Gallo, Sheffield Cellars)
Flagship (Ernest & Julio Gallo Vineyards, Gallo of
    Sonoma)
Fortified and jug (Gallo, Hearty Burgundy, Night Train,
    Ripple, Thunderbird)
Hospitality industry (Burlwood, Copperidge by E&J
    Gallo, William Wycliff Vineyards)
Imported varietals (Ecco Domani)
Mid-priced varietals (Garnet Point, Gossamer Bay,
    Turning Leaf)
Sparkling (André, Ballatore, Indigo Hills, Tott's)
Ultra-premium (Anapamu, Indigo Hills, Marcelina,
    Rancho Zabaco)
Wine-based and other beverages (Bartles & Jaymes,
    Boone's Farm, Hornsby's Pub Draft Cider)

## COMPETITORS

| | |
|---|---|
| Allied Domecq | Pernod Ricard |
| Asahi Breweries | Ravenswood Winery |
| Bacardi USA | R.H. Phillips |
| Beringer Blass | Robert Mondavi |
| Brown-Forman | Sebastiani Vineyards |
| Chalone Wine | Taittinger |
| Constellation Brands | Terlato Wine |
| Foster's | Trinchero Family Estates |
| Heaven Hill Distilleries | UST |
| GIV | Concha y Toro |
| Kendall-Jackson | Wine Group |
| LVMH | |

## HISTORICAL FINANCIALS & EMPLOYEES

| Private<br>FYE: December 31 | Annual<br>Growth | 12/91 | 12/92 | 12/93 | 12/94 | 12/95 | 12/96 | 12/97 | 12/98 | 12/99 | 12/00 |
|---|---|---|---|---|---|---|---|---|---|---|---|
| Estimated sales ($ mil.) | 6.5% | — | 1,000 | 1,100 | 980 | 1,100 | 1,200 | 1,300 | 1,500 | 1,515 | 1,650 |
| Employees | 2.3% | — | 3,000 | 4,000 | 4,000 | 4,000 | 5,000 | 5,000 | 5,000 | 5,000 | 3,600 |

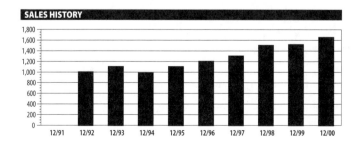

SALES HISTORY

# EBSCO INDUSTRIES INC.

## OVERVIEW

Few portfolios are more diverse than that of EBSCO Industries (short for Elton B. Stephens Company). Among the conglomerate's 80 sales, service, and manufacturing subsidiaries are magazine subscription and fulfillment firms, a fishing lure manufacturer, a rifle manufacturer, a specialty office and computer furniture retailer, and a real estate company. Birmingham, Alabama-based EBSCO's main businesses revolve around the publishing industry: EBSCO operates a subscription management agency and is one of the largest publishers of information online and on CD-ROM. It also provides such services as sales, promotion, telemarketing, and fulfillment to other publishers.

EBSCO provides bulk subscription services for print and electronic journals, technical reports, books, and other publications to schools, libraries, and professional offices. It also owns commercial printers and supplies bindery and packaging products.

Among EBSCO's eclectic subsidiaries are promotional products manufacturers Four Seasons and Vitronic; PRADCO, which makes fishing tackle; Valley Joist, which produces steel construction materials; Vulcan Industries, which makes point-of-purchase displays; Knight & Hale, which makes hunting accessories; specialty furniture makers H. Wilson and Luxor; and EBSCO Development, a community development company.

Founder and chairman Elton Stephens and his family own EBSCO.

## HISTORY

During the 1930s Elton Stephens put himself through college selling magazine subscriptions. Although he later earned a law degree, Stephens thought he could make more money selling magazines. Stephens and his wife, Alys, formed Military Service Co. in 1944 to sell magazines, binders, and display racks to the US military.

Early in his career Stephens suggested that he'd like to own five companies so that he'd have a fallback if one failed. He set about fulfilling his wish, forming Metal Fabricators and Finishers (now Vulcan Industries) in 1946, Vulcan Binder & Cover (now Vulcan Information Packaging) in 1947, and Vulcan Enterprises (now Directional Advertising Services) in 1954. In 1958 the Stephens' businesses were combined under the name EBSCO Industries, Inc. (the name is an acronym for Elton B. Stephens Company). In 1960 EBSCO acquired Chicago's Hanson-Bennett Magazine Agency, and in 1967 it bought Los Angeles' National Publications and binder manufacturer The Burkhardt Co. of Detroit.

Stephens retired as president of the company in 1971, and his son, James, took the job. The following year EBSCO bought the Franklin Square Agency and Ziff-Davis' subscription service, doubling the volume of EBSCO Subscription Services. EBSCO started its Publisher Promotion and Fulfillment service and added operations in Europe in 1975.

EBSCO acquired Valley Joist (metal construction products) in 1976 and H. Wilson Co. (audiovisual and computer furniture) in 1977. EBSCO Curriculum Materials and EBSCO Reception Room Subscription Services were formed in 1979 and 1980, respectively. Purchases in 1980 included Metro Press (now EBSCO Graphics), National Billiard, and PRADCO (fishing lures).

In 1981 Elton began a second career at age 70 when he founded Alabama Bancorp.

Under James's direction, EBSCO continued to grow through acquisitions and startups. It bought Four Seasons (promotional clothing and other items, 1983) and NSC International (binding and laminating products, 1984). The company formed electronic database publisher EBSCO Electronic Information (now EBSCO Publishing, 1986) and bought Bomber Bait (1988).

After a short breather, the company acquired Luxor (school and library furniture) in 1992. That year the various Vulcan operations were combined in a new facility in Moody, Alabama. In 1995 it bought Northeast Looseleaf (now part of Vulcan Information Packaging), and in 1996 it formed EBSCO Magazine Express.

The next year EBSCO bought Fred Arbogast, maker of the Jitterbug and Hula Popper fishing lures, and hunting game-call maker Knight & Hale. In 1998 EBSCO Development Company was formed, beginning plans for Mt. Laurel, a traditional neighborhood development. The next year EBSCO Publishing revealed Searchasaurus, an online search engine for children. In 2000 EBSCO formed EBSCOPrint.com to sell promotional products via the Internet.

In order to handle all its insurance needs in-house, in 2001 EBSCO acquired insurance firm S.S. Nesbitt & Co.

**Chairman:** Elton B. Stephens
**President and CEO:** James T. Stephens
**VP and CFO:** Richard L. Bozzelli
**VP and Chief Accounting Officer:**
Carol Matthews Johnson
**VP Administration:** Jean S. Mallette
**VP; General Manager, EBSCO Curriculum Materials:**
John R. Fitts
**VP; General Manager, EBSCO Publishing:**
Timothy R. Collins
**VP; General Manager, EBSCO Realty:**
Elton B. Stephens Jr.
**VP; General Manager, EBSCO Subscription Services Division:** F. Dixon Brooke Jr.
**VP; General Manager, EBSCO Telemarketing Service:**
Robert Prosise
**VP; General Manager, Publisher Promotion and Fulfillment:** Mark Williams
**VP; General Manager, Publisher's Warehouse:**
William F. Haver
**VP Marketing; General Manager, EBSCO Reception Room Subscription Services:** Jack H. Breard Jr.
**VP Corporate Communications:** Joe K. Weed
**VP Human Resources:** Pat R. Sisbarro
**VP Personnel:** John Thompson

## LOCATIONS

**HQ:** 5724 Hwy. 280 East, Birmingham, AL 35242
**Phone:** 205-991-6600        **Fax:** 205-995-1636
**Web:** www.ebscoind.com

EBSCO Industries has operations in more than 20 countries.

## PRODUCTS/OPERATIONS

**Selected Operations**

**Manufacturing**
EBSCO Media (commercial printer)
Four Seasons (promotional products)
H. Wilson Co. (audiovisual and computer products and furniture)
Knight & Hale (hunting accessories)
Knight Rifles
Luxor (specialty furniture for offices, schools, libraries, and health care facilities)
PRADCO (fishing lures, fishing line, and related products)
Valley Joist (steel joists, girders, and metal decks for the construction industry)
Vulcan Industries (point-of-purchase displays)

**Sales and Information Services**
Directional Advertising Services (marketing in reception rooms and other reading areas)
EBSCO Furniture Pavilion (office furniture and fixtures)
EBSCO Information Services (reference databases, online journals, and subscription services)
EBSCO Magazine Express (direct-marketing subscription agency)
EBSCO Realty (real estate broker)
EBSCOPrint.com (Internet sales of promotional products)
Kinescope Interactive (multimedia marketing services)
Military Service Company (producer and manufacturers' representative serving military base exchanges)
Publishers' Warehouse (publishers' warehousing and shipping service)
Relais International (interlibrary loan management)
Vulcan Service/Periodical Sales (magazine subscriptions)

## COMPETITORS

| | | |
|---|---|---|
| ACI Telecentrics | HA-LO | RoweCom |
| AMREP | Industries | R. R. Donnelley |
| APAC Customer | Johnson | Scholastic |
| Services | Outdoors | Simon |
| Black Dot Group | McGraw-Hill | Worldwide |
| Bowne | Moore | SITEL |
| Brunswick | Corporation | TeleSpectrum |
| Dai Nippon | Quebecor | Thomson |
| Printing | Reed Elsevier | Corporation |
| General Binding | Roanoke Electric | |
| | Steel | |

## HISTORICAL FINANCIALS & EMPLOYEES

| Private<br>FYE: June 30 | Annual<br>Growth | 6/92 | 6/93 | 6/94 | 6/95 | 6/96 | 6/97 | 6/98 | 6/99 | 6/00 | 6/01 |
|---|---|---|---|---|---|---|---|---|---|---|---|
| Estimated sales ($ mil.) | 8.8% | — | — | — | — | 900 | 1,000 | 1,000 | 1,210 | 1,375 | 1,375 |
| Employees | 2.4% | — | — | — | — | 4,000 | 4,000 | 4,000 | 4,200 | 4,200 | 4,500 |

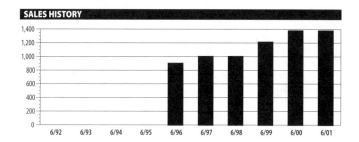

SALES HISTORY

EBSCO Industries, Inc.

# EDWARD J. DEBARTOLO

## OVERVIEW

Real estate holdings, gambling, horse racing, a felony conviction, and warring siblings surrounded by a storied NFL franchise — sounds like an old episode of *Dallas*. But the story of The Edward J. DeBartolo Corporation takes place in Youngstown, Ohio (where the company is based), via San Francisco (where the company owns the 49ers football team). The company also owns the Louisiana Downs racetrack in Bossier City.

The saga of the DeBartolo family concerns chairman and CEO Denise DeBartolo York and her brother, former CEO Eddie DeBartolo Jr.,
children of the company's eponymous founder. Eddie's guilty plea in 1998 to charges of failing to report a felony led to his ouster and a lawsuit from his sister to recover a $94 million debt from him. Eddie countersued, and after much wrangling, the siblings reached an agreement whereby Denise DeBartolo York took the company name, the 49ers, and the racetrack, and Eddie DeBartolo received real estate and the firm's 11% of Simon Property Group (SPG), North America's largest public real estate company.

## HISTORY

Edward J. DeBartolo left his stepfather's paving business in 1944 and established the company that bears his name. DeBartolo's foresight about the growth of the suburbs led him to build one of the first strip-style malls outside California, the Belmont Plaza near Youngstown, Ohio, in 1949. Over the next 15 years, the company built 45 more strip centers throughout the US. In the 1960s DeBartolo became one of the first to develop large, covered regional malls in many parts of the nation. DeBartolo opened the Louisiana Downs racetrack in 1974 and moved the company into the sports business in 1977 when he helped his son, Edward Jr. (Eddie), buy the San Francisco 49ers.

When the management of Allied Stores asked DeBartolo to help fend off a bid by real estate developer Robert Campeau, DeBartolo thought that control of Allied's department store chains would provide anchor stores for his mall developments and loaned Campeau $150 million for the takeover instead. Two years later DeBartolo borrowed $480 million and lent it to Campeau for his acquisition of Federated Department Stores.

The company reached its zenith in the late 1980s (opening the Rivercenter in San Antonio and Lakeland Square in Florida), but Campeau was in trouble — the highly leveraged Allied and Federated went bankrupt and threatened to take DeBartolo with them. As part of the bankruptcy settlement, DeBartolo took a 60% interest in California-based Ralphs supermarket (since sold) and started selling off assets in 1991 to cover the loan he made to Campeau and the company's own $4 billion debt. The fire sale included his private jet, three malls, two office buildings, a 50% stake in Higbee's department stores, and the Rivercenter.

Edward DeBartolo died in 1994. His daughter, Denise DeBartolo York, became chairman,
and his son, Eddie (who was also chairman and CEO of the 49ers) became president and CEO. Eddie reshuffled the company's assets with most of its real estate holdings turned into DeBartolo Realty, a real estate investment trust that went public that year, raising $575 million. Mounting tensions between the siblings intensified in 1995 when Eddie formed DeBartolo Entertainment, his own separate company in the gaming business (Denise tried to distance the family business from Eddie's new company in a press release). DeBartolo Realty merged with Simon Property Group the following year.

Eddie ran into trouble in 1997 when an investigation revealed that he had paid former Louisiana governor Edwin Edwards $400,000 in an effort to obtain a riverboat gambling license for DeBartolo Entertainment. (Before the gambling fraud probe became public, San Francisco voters approved a $100 million bond issue to help finance a $525 million stadium/shopping mall for the 49ers. Those plans were put on ice.) Eddie pleaded guilty to felony charges of concealing wrongdoing the next year, was fined $2 million, and stepped down from DeBartolo Corp. (His later testimony against Edwards helped lead to the government official's conviction on extortion charges.) The NFL then fined Eddie another $1 million and banned him from the 49ers in 1999. Later that year Denise sued Eddie for debt owed to the company, and he countersued. DeBartolo Corp. also sold two of its racetracks (Thistledown and Remington Park) in 1999. In 2001 the DeBartolos completed the division of the company's assets between them.

## OFFICERS

**Chairman and CEO:** Marie Denise DeBartolo York, age 50
**EVP; VP, San Francisco 49ers:** John C. York II, age 52
**SVP and CFO:** Lynn E. Davenport
**President and CEO, 49ers:** Peter Harris
**VP and General Manager, San Francisco 49ers:** Bill Walsh
**Head Coach, San Francisco 49ers:** Steve Mariucci
**Executive Secretary (HR):** Linda Pearce

## LOCATIONS

**HQ:** The Edward J. DeBartolo Corporation
7620 Market St., Youngstown, OH 44512
**Phone:** 330-965-2000 **Fax:** 330-965-2077

The Edward J. DeBartolo Corporation has operations in California, Louisiana, and Ohio.

## PRODUCTS/OPERATIONS

**Selected Holdings**
Louisiana Downs (horse racetrack, Bossier City)
San Francisco 49ers (NFL franchise)

## COMPETITORS

Atlanta Falcons
Carolina Panthers
Fair Grounds
Harrah's Entertainment
JMB Realty
New Orleans Saints
St. Louis Rams

## HISTORICAL FINANCIALS & EMPLOYEES

| Private<br>FYE: June 30 | Annual<br>Growth | 6/91 | 6/92 | 6/93 | 6/94 | 6/95 | 6/96 | 6/97 | 6/98 | 6/99 | 6/00 |
|---|---|---|---|---|---|---|---|---|---|---|---|
| Estimated sales ($ mil.) | (8.3%) | — | 500 | 525 | 550 | 230 | 220 | 250 | 250 | 254 | 250 |
| Employees | 0.9% | — | — | — | 3,800 | 3,000 | 3,000 | 3,000 | 4,000 | 4,000 | 4,000 |

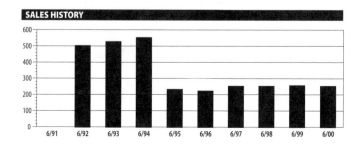

SALES HISTORY

# EMPIRE HEALTHCHOICE, INC.

## OVERVIEW

Empire Blue is slowly turning shades of green. Empire HealthChoice, known as Empire Blue Cross and Blue Shield, serves more than 4 million customers in eastern New York and is the largest health care provider in its market. The company offers traditional indemnity, HMO, PPO, and EPO (exclusive provider organization) plans for individuals and groups. It also has dental, pharmacy, and vision care plans.

A licensee of the Blue Cross and Blue Shield Association, New York City-based Empire was traditionally an insurer of last resort. In exchange for covering otherwise uninsurable people, Empire received quasi-charitable status and generous state tax breaks. But increased competition through consolidation has reduced its market share, and Empire now wants to convert to for-profit status to be more competitive.

The conversion plan has to contend with state legislation that appears to block such a move, as well as with consumer advocates' concerns about the fate of Empire's less-profitable clientele (and about the use of public funds to build the value of a for-profit company). In response, Empire plans to set up a charitable foundation — which would initially own the company's stock — to provide health care for New York's uninsured population.

## HISTORY

Prepaid medical care was born in 1929 when Baylor University Hospital administrator Justin Kimball began offering hospital care coverage to teachers for $6 a year. Kimball's plan — to stabilize hospital costs while encouraging people to insure themselves — eventually developed into the national Blue Cross and Blue Shield Association.

Empire's story began in 1934 when the Associated Hospital Service (AHS Blue Cross) was created to provide hospital insurance in New York. It had more than 40,000 members at the end of its first year, and 2.2 million members by 1945. In 1936 the organization that would later become Blue Cross of Northeastern New York was founded as the Associated Hospital Service Capital District (AHSCD).

In 1940 not-for-profit Medical Expense Fund began providing payment for doctors' services. Four years later it merged with AHS affiliate Community Medical Care to create United Medical Service (UMS). UMS signed up 1.5 million members in just four years. It joined the national Blue Shield Association in 1949 and became New York Blue Shield.

AHSCD became a contractor with the US military's CHAMPUS insurance program in 1956 and began using the name Blue Cross of Northeastern New York in 1965. In 1966 the federal government selected AHS Blue Cross to help manage New York State's Medicare program. In the early 1970s the association created an HMO to challenge the managed care companies that were crowding into its territory.

AHS Blue Cross and New York Blue Shield merged to form the Blues of Greater New York in 1974. Finally, in 1985 the Blues of Greater New York and Blue Cross of Northeastern New York merged to form Empire.

The 1990s were rocky, as Empire lost younger, healthier members to managed care companies offering lower rates. In 1992 and again in 1995, the US Senate investigated Empire, uncovering mismanagement and fraud. In 1997 former CFO Jerry Weissman (fired in 1993) was convicted of lying to the Senate in 1992 about Empire's financial problems. His successor, Michael Stocker, cut costs and boosted managed care membership.

In 1996 Empire created for-profit subsidiaries Family HealthChoice (an HMO, now Empire HealthChoice) and Family Health Assurance (an accident and health insurer, now Empire HealthChoice Assurance), then announced plans to convert to for-profit status. That year New York ended Empire's preferred status and deregulated hospital rates (Empire had been exempt from a 13% hospital surcharge), forcing all insurers to compete on equal footing.

In 1997 it bought Central National Life Insurance Co. of New Jersey, giving Empire a foothold in that state and a license to sell health insurance in seven more states. Empire posted a loss that year because of rising claims against its HMOs and startup costs for its Medicare supplement. To offset the loss, it applied in 1998 to raise its HMO rates by almost 21%. In 1999 the firm started a cost-containment program and returned to profitability. The next year, the state's attorney general gave his approval to Empire's plan to convert to for-profit status; the state legislature is still considering the application.

## OFFICERS

**Chairman:** Philip Briggs
**President and CEO:** Michael A. Stocker
**President and COO:** David B. Snow Jr.
**SVP and CFO:** John W. Remshard
**SVP and Chief Sales Officer:** Bryan Birch
**SVP, Business Technology Development:**
William B. O'Loughlin
**SVP and General Counsel:** Linda V. Tiano
**SVP, Systems, Technology, and Infrastructure:**
Kenneth O. Klepper
**SVP, Human Resources and Services:** Ronald Mason
**SVP, Operations, Managed Care, and Medicare Services:**
Gloria M. McCarthy
**SVP and Chief Marketing Officer:** Jack A. Smith
**Chief Medical Officer:** Alan E. Sokolow
**VP and Chief Actuary:** Michael W. Fedyna
**VP, Public Affairs:** Deborah L. Bohren
**VP and Chief Information Officer, Core Processing**
**Systems:** Grace Messina
**VP Human Resources:** Pam Adams
**Corporate Secretary:** Peter Liria Jr.
**Auditor:** Ernst & Young LLP

## LOCATIONS

**HQ:** 11 W. 42nd St., New York, NY 10036
**Phone:** 212-476-1000     **Fax:** 212-476-1281
**Web:** www.empirehealthcare.com

Empire operates in 28 counties in eastern and
southeastern New York.

## PRODUCTS/OPERATIONS

**Selected Products and Services**
Direct HMO
EPO
HMO
Managed dental care
Managed pharmacy plan
Managed vision care
PPO
Traditional indemnity plans

## COMPETITORS

Aetna
Anthem
CIGNA
Health Insurance of New
York
Health Net
Oxford Health Plans
Prudential
Travelers
UnitedHealth Group
WellCare Management

## HISTORICAL FINANCIALS & EMPLOYEES

| Not-for-profit FYE: December 31 | Annual Growth | 12/91 | 12/92 | 12/93 | 12/94 | 12/95 | 12/96 | 12/97 | 12/98 | 12/99 | 12/00 |
|---|---|---|---|---|---|---|---|---|---|---|---|
| Sales ($ mil.) | (3.2%) | — | — | 5,338 | 4,798 | 4,088 | 3,401 | 3,329 | 3,277 | 3,367 | 4,240 |
| Employees | (3.3%) | — | — | 8,215 | 7,900 | 6,821 | 6,099 | 6,000 | 6,000 | 6,000 | 6,500 |

### SALES HISTORY

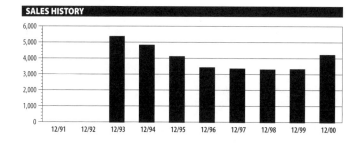

Blue Cross
Blue Shield

# ENCYCLOPAEDIA BRITANNICA, INC.

## OVERVIEW

Would any of us have escaped grade school without Encyclopaedia Britannica? The Chicago-based company publishes reference works such as its 32-volume flagship *Encyclopaedia Britannica* and numerous titles through its Merriam-Webster subsidiary, including *Merriam Webster's Collegiate Dictionary*. Other reference works include *The Annals of America* and *Great Books of the Western World*.

Most of the company's titles are available online and on CD-ROM and DVD through sister firm Britannica.com. The Britannica.com Web site offers free access to its entire collection of encyclopedia articles, an editorially reviewed Web site directory, and third-party content from *The Washington Post, Newsweek,* and other providers. Advertising supports the site, but Britannica also operates subscription-based Britannica Online Web site, which targets students and institutions allowing full access to its 72,000 encyclopedia articles unencumbered by advertising.

Although they are separate companies, Encyclopaedia Britannica and Britannica.com are both owned by Swiss financier Jacob Safra (a nephew of the late banking king Edmond Safra). With the launch of Britannica.com, Safra has begun the painful (and expensive) process of transforming his empire from old media to new, a transformation made more difficult by the firm's late entry into the online fray. (Safra has announced plans to eventually integrate the two firms into a single company.)

## HISTORY

Engraver Andrew Bell and printer and bookseller Colin Macfarquhar created the first edition of the *Encyclopaedia Britannica* in Scotland, releasing the three-volume set in weekly installments between 1768 and 1771. Benjamin Franklin and John Locke were among early contributors. The second edition, completed in 1784, expanded to 10 volumes; the fourth (1809) contained 20. The ninth edition (1889) captured the scientific spirit of the age with articles by Thomas Henry Huxley and James Clerk Maxwell.

American businessmen Horace Hooper and Walter Jackson purchased the *Encyclopaedia* in 1901 and established the Encyclopaedia Britannica Company in the US. It published the first *Britannica Book of the Year* in 1913. Sears chairman Julius Rosenwald bought the company in 1920 and tried to market *Britannica* through Sears' retail operations, as well as with door-to-door sales. William Benton (of Benton & Bowles Advertising) bought the business from Sears in 1941 and built a nationwide sales force with a hard-sell reputation. Britannica released its first foreign-language encyclopedia, *Enciclopedia Barsa,* in 1957 and acquired dictionary publisher G. & C. Merriam in 1964.

When Benton died in 1974, he bequeathed the operation to the University of Chicago, which ran it through the not-for-profit William Benton Foundation. Britannica later bought out rival Compton's Encyclopedia in the mid-1970s. The 1989 CD-ROM release of *Compton's MultiMedia Encyclopedia* was a first for the industry, but Britannica sold Compton's NewMedia division to Chicago's Tribune Company in 1993 just before the CD-ROM market exploded. The company launched its subscription-based Britannica Online the same year.

Jacob Safra, a *Britannica* lover since childhood, led a group that paid $135 million for the struggling company in 1996. With book sales dwindling and heavy competition from Microsoft's CD-ROM *Encarta,* Britannica cut its prices and ceased its door-to-door marketing that year. It agreed to sell both its CD-ROM and print encyclopedias in retail stores in 1997, and lured publisher Paul Hoffman away from Walt Disney's successful *Discover* magazine. Britannica Internet Guide (BIG), a free Internet search engine, launched that year. Britannica added guest columns and other features to BIG in 1998.

Encyclopaedia Britannica Holdings (Safra's umbrella firm for the publisher) launched a sister firm, Britannica.com, in 1999 to oversee the company's electronic and Internet products and services. CEO Don Yannias resigned his post with the print company and took the reins of the new digital firm, allowing Hoffman to take over as the publisher's president. Britannica.com struggled with the rest of the Internet industry in 2000, laying off almost 25% of its staff.

In 2001 Yannias resigned as CEO from both firms and was replaced by Ilan Yeshua. The move was made as part of a strategy to eventually integrate Encyclopaedia Britannica and Britannica.com into a single company. Also that year the company announced its plans to sell Merriam-Webster in an effort to raise capital.

## OFFICERS

**Chairman:** Jacob E. Safra
**CEO:** Ilan Yeshua
**EVP, Secretary, and General Counsel (HR):**
William J. Bowe
**VP Operations and Finance:** Richard Anderson
**VP and Controller:** Helen Townsend
**VP and Editor:** Dale Hoiberg
**Director Strategic Marketing and Planning:**
Diana Simeon Spadoni
**Publisher, Merriam-Webster:** John Morse
**COO, Britannica.com:** Jorge Cauz
**SVP Operations, Britannica.com:** Tony Bingham
**Director Human Resources, Britannica.com:**
Carman Weatheringon
**Auditors:** PricewaterhouseCoopers

## LOCATIONS

**HQ:** 310 S. Michigan Ave., Chicago, IL 60604
**Phone:** 312-347-7000      **Fax:** 312-347-7399
**Web:** corporate.britannica.com

## PRODUCTS/OPERATIONS

**Selected Products**
Dictionaries
   *Merriam Webster's Biographical Dictionary*
   *Merriam Webster's Collegiate Dictionary*
   *Merriam Webster's Collegiate Thesaurus*
   *Merriam Webster's Dictionary of Law*
Encyclopedias
   *Britannica First Edition Replica Set*
   *Encyclopaedia Britannica*
   *The Encyclopedia of Popular Music*
Other Reference Works
   *The Annals of America*
   *Gray's Anatomy*
   *Great Books of the Western World*

## COMPETITORS

Berkshire Hathaway
Franklin Electronic Publishers
Grolier
Harcourt General
McGraw-Hill
Microsoft
Pearson
Random House
Thomson Corporation
Time
Vivendi Universal Publishing

## HISTORICAL FINANCIALS & EMPLOYEES

| Private<br>FYE: September 30 | Annual<br>Growth | 9/91 | 9/92 | 9/93 | 9/94 | 9/95 | 9/96 | 9/97 | 9/98 | 9/99 | 9/00 |
|---|---|---|---|---|---|---|---|---|---|---|---|
| Sales ($ mil.) | (9.0%) | — | 586 | 540 | 453 | 400 | 375 | 325 | 300 | 279 | 275 |
| Employees | (15.0%) | — | 1,100 | 1,000 | 900 | 800 | 700 | 400 | 400 | 350 | 300 |

### SALES HISTORY

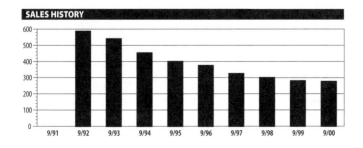

# ENTERPRISE RENT-A-CAR

This Enterprise is boldly going where it hasn't gone before — the airport. St. Louis-based Enterprise Rent-A-Car is the largest car rental firm in the US. Enterprise offers free customer pickup and has about 430,000 cars and almost 4,000 offices in North America and Europe.

Most of Enterprise's business comes from customers who need rentals because their own vehicles are in the repair shop. However, Enterprise has begun serving vacationers and small-business customers passing through more than 90 of the nation's top 100 airports. The company's sites in and near airports offer rates that are up to 20% lower than those of most major competitors.

Enterprise also leases vehicles and manages fleets for other companies (Enterprise Fleet Services), and it sells cars (Enterprise Car Sales). The company has split off its non-automotive operations (formerly known as Enterprise Capital Group) as a separate company, Centric Group.

Founder Jack Taylor and his family control the company. Taylor's son Andrew is Enterprise's president and CEO.

In 1957 Jack Taylor, the sales manager for a Cadillac dealership in St. Louis, hit on the idea that leasing cars might be an easier way to make money than selling them. Taylor's idea sounded good to his boss, Arthur Lindburg, who agreed to set Taylor up in the leasing business. In return for a 50% pay cut, Taylor received 25% of the new enterprise, called Executive Leasing, which began in the walled-off body shop of a car dealership.

In the early 1960s Taylor started renting cars for short periods as well as leasing them. When his leasing agents expressed annoyance with the rental operation, Taylor turned that business over to Don Holtzman. Holtzman realized that his 17-car rental operation was too little to take on industry giants like Hertz and Avis; instead, he concentrated on the "home city" or replacement market. He offered competitive rates to insurance adjusters who needed to find cars for policyholders whose cars were damaged or stolen. Propelled by court decisions that required casualty companies to pay for loss of transportation, Taylor expanded from his St. Louis base in 1969 with a branch office in Atlanta. Since another car leasing outfit in Georgia was already named Executive, Taylor changed the name of his company to Enterprise Rent-A-Car.

The company expanded into Florida and Texas in the early 1970s, targeting garages and body shops that performed repairs for insured drivers. Oil price shocks of that period compelled Taylor to diversify his operations. In 1974 Enterprise acquired Keefe Coffee and Supply, a supplier of coffee, packaged foods, and beverages to prison commissaries. To service *FORTUNE* 1000 companies wanting to lease or buy more than 50 vehicles, the company started Enterprise Fleet Services in 1976. Enterprise acquired Courtesy Products (coffee and tea for hotel guests) in 1980, and the following year sales reached the $100 million mark. It acquired ELCO Chevrolet in 1986, the same year it formed Crawford Supply (hygiene products for prisons). Taylor bought out the Lindburg family's interest in Enterprise the next year. In 1989 Enterprise raised its brand recognition with a national TV campaign that focused on an older and higher-income audience by showing its commercials exclusively on CBS. Also in the late 1980s, the company began targeting "discretionary rentals" to families with visiting relatives or with children home for the holidays.

Taylor's son, Andrew, became CEO of Enterprise in 1991, and sales topped $1 billion for the first time. By 1994 sales had passed $2 billion, and the company had expanded into Canada and the UK. By 1996 Enterprise had a fleet of more than 300,000 vehicles. That year it opened several locations in the UK. In 1997 the company opened locations in Ireland, Germany, Scotland, and Wales.

In 1998 Enterprise battled other rental firms over use of the advertising tagline, "We'll pick you up," which it had trademarked. Rent-A-Wreck lost a court case over the matter; Hertz settled with Enterprise over use of the phrase.

In 1999 the company more than doubled the number of its airport locations in an attempt to woo occasional travelers (rather than hard-core corporate fliers). That year the Taylor family split off their non-automotive operations (including companies involved in prison supplies, hotel amenities, a golf course, mylar balloons, and athletic shoes) as Centric Group.

**Chairman:** Jack C. Taylor
**President and CEO:** Andrew C. Taylor, age 53
**SEVP and COO:** Donald L. Ross
**EVP and CFO:** John T. O'Connell
**SVP and Chief Information Officer:** William W. Snyder
**SVP North American Operations:** Pam Nicholson
**VP Fleet Services:** Steven E. Bloom
**VP Human Resources:** Ed Adams
**VP Rental:** Jim Runnels
**VP Marketing:** Callaway Ludington
**Chevrolet:** Mark S. Hadfield
**Manager Media Relations:** Christy Conrad
**Auditors:** Ernst & Young LLP

## LOCATIONS

**HQ:** 600 Corporate Park Dr., St. Louis, MO 63105
**Phone:** 314-512-5000      **Fax:** 314-512-4706
**Web:** www.enterprise.com

Enterprise Rent-A-Car has about 4,000 offices in Canada, Germany, Ireland, the UK and the US.

## PRODUCTS/OPERATIONS

**Operations**
ELCO Chevrolet Inc. (car dealership, St. Louis)
Enterprise Car Sales (used car sales)
Enterprise Fleet Services (vehicle leasing)
Enterprise Rent-A-Car

## COMPETITORS

Airways Transportation
 Group
AMERCO
AutoNation
Budget Group
Cendant
Dollar Thrifty Automotive
 Group
Hertz
Penske
Rent-A-Wreck
Ryder
Sixt

## HISTORICAL FINANCIALS & EMPLOYEES

| Private<br>FYE: July 31 | Annual<br>Growth | 7/92 | 7/93 | 7/94 | 7/95 | 7/96 | 7/97 | 7/98 | 7/99 | 7/00 | 7/01 |
|---|---|---|---|---|---|---|---|---|---|---|---|
| Sales ($ mil.) | 21.1% | 1,124 | 1,659 | 2,108 | 2,464 | 3,127 | 3,680 | 4,180 | 4,730 | 5,600 | 6,300 |
| Employees | 21.8% | 8,500 | 14,000 | 18,500 | 21,703 | 28,806 | 35,182 | 37,000 | 40,000 | 45,000 | 50,000 |

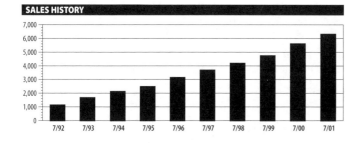

SALES HISTORY

# EQUITY GROUP INVESTMENTS

## OVERVIEW

Equity Group Investments is the apex of financier Sam Zell's pyramid of business holdings. The Chicago-based private investment group controls a multi-billion dollar mix of businesses, including real estate investment trusts (REITs), restaurants, and cruise ships. Zell's REITs are #1 in office property (Equity Office Properties Trust), apartments (Equity Residential Properties Trust), and land leased to manufactured home owners (Manufactured Home Communities). Equity Office Properties is one of the largest landlords in San Francisco and Seattle.

A knack for finding and turning around distressed companies earned Zell the nickname "Grave Dancer." Equity Group Investments has rescued many companies floundering in bankruptcy and often buys during downturns. Many acquisitions are made through the Zell/Chilmark Fund.

Zell's Equity Residential Properties continues to build its portfolio through acquisitions and is enjoying the run-up in REIT stocks. Another holding, American Classic Voyages, isn't faring so well. The company took a hit as the Hawaiian cruise industry cooled, and business eroded further after the events of September 11. American Classic Voyages has filed for Chapter 11 reorganization.

Zell has made forays into other investments with mixed success. He bought into sugar mills in Mexico that were nationalized by the government, and he's recently rediscovered a junk-bond investing strategy.

## HISTORY

Sam Zell's first business endeavor was photographing his eighth-grade prom. In 1953 he graduated to reselling 50-cent *Playboy* magazines to schoolmates at a 200% markup.

While at the University of Michigan in the 1960s, Zell teamed with fraternity brother Robert Lurie to manage off-campus student housing. In graduate school, they invested in residential properties and formed Equity Financial and Management Co. after graduation. Their collection of distressed properties grew in the 1970s as Zell made the deals and Lurie made them work. Zell's hands-off management style had its drawbacks, however: In 1976 Zell and three others (including his brother-in-law) were indicted on federal tax-related charges after selling a Reno, Nevada, hotel and apartment complex. The charges were later dropped against Zell and another defendant (only the brother-in-law was convicted).

In the 1980s tax-law changes led the team to begin buying troubled companies. They started in 1983 with Great American Management and Investment, a foundering real estate manager they turned into an investment vehicle. Other targets included Itel (1984, now Anixter International) and oil and gas company Nucorp (1988, now part of insurer CNA Surety). The true attraction in many of these acquisitions, however, lay in tax-loss carryforwards that could be applied against future earnings.

Lurie died in 1990, after which Zell began to consolidate his power and ease out old friends. (Lurie's estate still owns shares of many Zell enterprises.) That year Zell and David Schulte formed the Zell/Chilmark Fund, which soon owned or controlled such companies as Schwinn (sold 1997), Sealy (sold 1997), and Revco (sold 1997). Among the fund's failures was West Coast retailer Broadway Stores, which Zell bought out of bankruptcy in 1992; when California's slumping economy prevented a rapid turnaround, Zell sold it in 1995.

Starting in 1987, Zell formed four real estate funds with Merrill Lynch; six years later, both Equity Residential Properties Trust and Manufactured Home Communities went public. As REITs became popular with investors, more trusts began vying for distressed assets — Zell's traditional lifeblood. In 1997 Zell melded four of his commercial real estate funds into another REIT, Equity Office Properties Trust, and took it public.

In 1998, as investors and financiers looked for fresh opportunities, Zell launched Equity International Properties, a fund targeting acquisitions in Latin America and elsewhere. That year a civil racketeering suit brought against Zell by former executive Richard Perlman shed light on "handshake" loans to top executives and other informal business deals. In 1999 Zell sold Jacor Communications to radio industry consolidator Clear Channel Communications. Equity Group Investments remains diversified, however: In 1999 Equity Office Properties teamed with venture capital firm Kleiner Perkins Caufield & Byers to form Broadband Office offering Internet and phone services to Zell's tenants and those of other property owners.

Equity Office Properties Trust continued its buying into the 21st century, claiming New York-based Cornerstone Properties (2000) and California's Spieker Properties (2001).

**Chairman:** Samuel Zell
**President and CEO:** Sheli Z. Rosenberg, age 59
**COO:** Donald J. Liebentritt
**VP, Treasurer, and Controller:** Greg Stegimen
**VP, Human Resources:** Dan Harris

## LOCATIONS

**HQ:** Equity Group Investments, L.L.C.
2 N. Riverside Plaza, Ste. 600, Chicago, IL 60606
**Phone:** 312-454-1800        **Fax:** 312-454-0610

## PRODUCTS/OPERATIONS

**Selected Affiliates**
American Classic Voyages Co. (36%, cruises)
Anixter International, Inc. (14%, communications
    network equipment)
Capital Trust, Inc. (commercial real estate finance)
Chart House Enterprises, Inc. (38%, restaurants)
Davel Communications, Inc. (14%, pay-telephone
    operator)
Equity International Properties (overseas buyout fund)
Equity Office Properties Trust (4%, office property REIT)
Equity Residential Properties Trust (3%, apartments
    REIT)
Manufactured Home Communities, Inc. (15%, mobile
    home communities REIT)
Transmedia Network (40%, consumer savings programs)
Zell/Chilmark Fund L.P. (investment vulture fund)

## COMPETITORS

Apollo Advisors
Blackstone Group
Carlyle Group
Clayton, Dubilier
Goldman Sachs
JMB Realty
KKR
Thomas Lee
Trump

# ERNST & YOUNG INTERNATIONAL

Accounting may actually be the *second* oldest profession, and Ernst & Young is one of the oldest practitioners. The New York-based concern, one of the Big Five accounting firms, has about 700 offices in about 130 countries.

The firm's audit and accounting business provides internal audit, accounting advisory, and risk management services. It has one of the world's largest tax practices, particularly serving the needs of multinational clients that have to comply with multiple local tax laws.

After spending most of the 1980s and 1990s building their consulting businesses, The Big Five have all moved toward spinning off or otherwise shedding these operations, partly from internal pressures and partly because of the perceived conflict of interest in performing

audits for clients who may also be large consulting customers. Ernst & Young was the first to split off its consultancy, selling it to French consultancy Cap Gemini Group. The Securities and Exchange Commission has since established new rules for disclosure fees paid to auditors, revealing the massive proportion of nonaudit fees and raising further conflict-of-interest concerns.

Ernst & Young is now following the industry trend in adding legal affiliates to provide more comprehensive professional services. The firm has assembled a team of more than 1,850 lawyers in some 60 countries to provide legal services. Ernst & Young also offers a variety of corporate finance, health, and entrepreneurial services.

## HISTORY

When Luca Pacioli's *Summa di Arithmetica* was published in Venice in 1494, it was the first text on double-entry bookkeeping, but it was almost 400 years before accounting became a profession.

In 1849 Frederick Whinney joined the UK firm of Harding & Pullein. Whinney's ledgers were so clear that he was advised to take up accounting, which was a growth field as stock companies proliferated. Whinney became a name partner in 1859 and his sons followed him into the business. The firm became Whinney, Smith & Whinney (WS&W) in 1894.

After WWII, WS&W formed an alliance with Ernst & Ernst (founded in Cleveland in 1903 by brothers Alwin and Theodore Ernst), with each firm operating on the other's behalf across the Atlantic.

Whinney merged with Brown, Fleming & Murray in 1965 to become Whinney Murray. In 1979 Whinney Murray, Turquands Barton Mayhew (also a UK firm), and Ernst & Ernst merged to form Ernst & Whinney.

But Ernst & Whinney wasn't done merging. A decade later, when it was the fourth-largest accounting firm, it merged with #5 Arthur Young, which had been founded by Scotsman Arthur Young in 1895 in Kansas City. Long known as "old reliable," Arthur Young fell on hard times in the 1980s because its audit relationships with failed S&Ls led to expensive litigation (ultimately settled in 1992 for $400 million).

Thus the new firm of Ernst & Young faced a rocky start. In 1990 it fended off rumors of collapse. The next year it slashed payroll, even thinning its partner roster. Exhausted by the

S&L wars, in 1994 the firm replaced its pugnacious general counsel, Carl Riggio, with the more cost-conscious Kathryn Oberly.

In the mid-1990s Ernst & Young concentrated on consulting, particularly in software applications, and grew through acquisitions. In 1997 the firm was sued for a record $4 billion for its alleged failure to effectively handle the 1993 restructuring of the defunct Merry-Go-Round Enterprises retail chain (it settled the suit for $185 million in 1999). On the heels of a merger deal between Coopers & Lybrand and Price Waterhouse, Ernst & Young agreed in 1997 to merge with KPMG International. But Ernst & Young called off the negotiations in 1998, citing the uncertain regulatory process they faced.

In 1999 the firm launched a worldwide media blitz aimed at raising awareness of the firm's full range of services, which that year included the company's new technology incubator.

In 2000 Ernst & Young became the first of the Big Five firms to sell its consultancy, dealing it to France's Cap Gemini Group for about $11 billion. Later that year the company agreed to buy Washington Counsel, a lobbying firm. The company also started a venture to provide online financial advice with E*TRADE and spun off Intellinex, its online corporate training division.

The following year the UK accountancy watchdog group announced it would investigate Ernst & Young for its handling of the accounts of UK-based The Equitable Life Assurance Society. The insurer was forced to close to new business in 2000 because of massive financial difficulties.

**Global Chairman:** James Turley
**CEO:** William L. Kimsey
**Americas CEO:** Richard S. Bobrow
**Vice Chairman Finance, Technology, and Administration:** Hilton Dean
**Vice Chairman Assurance and Advisory Services:** John F. Ferraro
**Vice Chairman Consulting Services:** Antonio Schneider
**Vice Chairman Human Resources:** Lewis A. Ting
**Vice Chairman Intrastructure:** John G. Peetz Jr.
**Vice Chairman Regional Integration and Entrepreneurial Growth Companies:** Jean-Charles Raufast
**Vice Chairman Regional Integration and Planning:** Richard N. Findlater
**Vice Chairman Tax and Legal Services:** Andrew B. Jones
**Executive Partner:** Paul J. Ostling
**General Counsel:** Kathryn A. Oberly

## LOCATIONS

**HQ:** 787 7th Ave., New York, NY 10019
**Phone:** 212-773-3000          **Fax:** 212-773-6350
**Web:** www.eyi.com

## PRODUCTS/OPERATIONS

**Selected Services**

**Assurance and Advisory**
Actuarial services
Audits
Accounting advisory
Employee benefit plan services
Fraud investigation
Information systems security
Internal audit
Enterprise risk management and risk solutions

**Corporate Finance**
Capital markets advisory
Due diligence
IPO services
Litigation advisory
Mergers and acquisitions advisory
Restructuring advisory
Strategic finance
Valuation advisory
Treasury management

**Health**
Audit services
Consulting services
Emerging technologies
Tax services

**Law**
Anti-trust, competition, and regulated marks advisory
Banking and securities advisory
Bankruptcy and insolvency assistance and advisory
Commercial and trade advisory and compliance
Corporate mergers and acquisitions advisory and compliance
E-commerce advisory and compliance
Employment advisory and compliance
Environmental advisory and compliance
Intellectual property advisory, protection, and compliance
Real estate/commercial property advisory and compliance

**Tax**
Consulting on tax consequences of business transactions and decisions
Economics and quantitative analysis
Financial statement effective tax rate management assistance
Global employment solutions
International tax
New tax laws and regulations impact analysis
Online tax advisor
Personal financial counseling
Tax planning
Tax return review and support
Transfer pricing

## COMPETITORS

American Management
Andersen
Bain & Company
BDO International
Deloitte Touche Tohmatsu
Grant Thornton
 International
IBM
KPMG
PricewaterhouseCoopers

## HISTORICAL FINANCIALS & EMPLOYEES

| Partnership FYE: June 30 | Annual Growth | 9/92 | 9/93 | 9/94 | 9/95 | 9/96 | 9/97 | 9/98 | 9/99 | *6/00 | 6/01 |
|---|---|---|---|---|---|---|---|---|---|---|---|
| Sales ($ mil.) | 6.4% | 5,701 | 5,839 | 6,020 | 6,867 | 7,800 | 9,100 | 10,900 | 12,500 | 9,500 | 10,000 |
| Employees | 4.6% | 58,900 | 58,377 | 61,287 | 68,452 | 72,000 | 79,750 | 85,000 | 97,800 | 88,625 | 88,000 |

* Fiscal year change

### SALES HISTORY

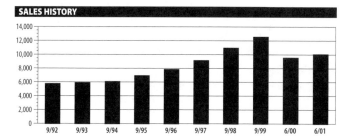

# FARMLAND INDUSTRIES, INC.

## OVERVIEW

Farmland Industries helps its members farm land industriously. The Kansas City, Missouri-based enterprise is the #1 agricultural cooperative in the US. Farmland is owned by about 1,700 local co-ops, comprising 600,000 farmers in the US, Canada, and Mexico. To help farmers grow crops and raise livestock, Farmland provides them with fertilizers, feed, herbicides and pesticides. When the harvest is complete, the co-op provides grain storage, delivery, processing, and marketing services — including

export to more than 60 countries. Higher up the food chain, the co-op is a major meat company. It makes and markets fresh and processed beef, catfish, and pork through its Farmland National Beef (the #4 US beef slaughterer), Southern Farm Fish Processors, and Farmland Foods subsidiaries.

Farmland also has more than 60 joint ventures and alliances, including WILFARM (with Wilbur-Ellis Company, chemical products).

## HISTORY

In 1929 President Herbert Hoover pushed passage of the Agricultural Marketing Act (AMA) to encourage cooperatives as one means to remedy the hard times facing the US agriculture industry in the 1920s. However record grain harvests in 1928 and 1929 foiled its intent: a glut ground down prices, and later the Depression (and drought) dried up markets.

By the time of the AMA, Union Oil Company, Farmland Industries' predecessor, was already in the works. Union Oil was formed in 1929 to provide petroleum supplies to farmers in a period of rapid agricultural mechanization. In the early 1930s, as the government sought to regulate supply by introducing payments for taking land out of production, Union Oil increased the range of its co-op activities. It changed its name to Consumers Cooperative Association in 1935.

Farming did not revive until WWII, though price controls and supports remained an important feature of agricultural policy. Throughout this period the performance of Consumers Cooperative's growing membership of primary producers and local co-ops remained tied to raw commodity prices. In 1959, however, to decrease its reliance on commodity prices, Consumers Cooperative bought a pork processing plant in Denison, Iowa, and began making Farmbest meat products. It was a success, and four years later the co-op opened another plant in Iowa Falls. In 1966 Consumers Cooperative became Farmland Industries, and in the 1970s it expanded into beef production. However, when prices and consumption declined, it exited the field.

Overzealous expansion by American farmers in the 1970s was followed in the 1980s by an industry-wide crisis. When the farm economy went down, it hurt the co-op's sales of inputs such as fertilizers. Cheap fertilizer imports, low crude oil prices, and high natural gas prices also took their toll, and the co-op lost

more than $210 million in 1985 and 1986. James Rainey took over as CEO in 1986 and turned the operation around. Farmland began placing a greater emphasis on food processing and marketing, otherwise known as outputs.

Harry Cleberg succeeded Rainey in 1991. The co-op had stopped handling grains in 1985, after a period of volatile prices, but it profitably re-entered the market in 1992. The next year it bought the Tradigrain unit of British Petroleum (now BP Amoco). The purchase led Farmland into markets outside the US. Also in 1993 the co-op resumed beef processing and expanded its pork processing facilities.

During the late 1990s, the co-op formed joint ventures and partnerships spanning its range of activities — feeds, grain marketing, and energy products — and in 1998 absorbed SF Services, an agricultural cooperative.

In 1999 Farmland and Cenex Harvest States voted to merge their operations; Farmland members approved the deal but Cenex members voted it down. Instead Farmland partnered with Land O'Lakes and Cenex to form Agriliance to supply farm products to members. In 2000 Farmland combined its feed business with Land O' Lakes in a joint venture forming North America's top feed company. In the fall of 2000 company veteran Robert Honse was named CEO as Cleberg retired.

Skyrocketing natural gas prices in 2000 hit the co-op's fertilizer business hard, prompting it to shut down one facility. Laden with debt, in mid-2001 the co-op handed the operation of its 24 grain elevators over to Archer Daniels Midland as part of a new grain-marketing venture with the agribusiness giant. In November 2001 the co-op sold its interest in Country Energy to CHS Cooperatives. Farmland lost $90 million in 2001, but the co-op also reduced its debt that year by $268 million and administrative costs by nearly $40 million.

**Chairman:** Albert J. Shivley, age 58
**Vice Chairman and VP:** Jody Bezner, age 60
**President and CEO:** Robert W. Honse, age 58,
$615,612 pay
**EVP and CFO:** John F. Berardi, age 58, $404,720 pay
**EVP, General Counsel, and Corporate Secretary:**
Robert B. Terry, age 45, $228,766 pay
**EVP; President, Crop Production:** Stan A. Riemann,
age 50, $298,782 pay
**EVP; President, Refrigerated Foods:**
William G. Fielding, age 54, $350,000 pay
**EVP; President, World Grain:** Tim R. Daugherty, age 48
**VP and Controller:** Steve Rhodes
**VP, Human Resources:** Holly D. McCoy
**VP, Strategic Sourcing:** Michael T. Sweat, age 56
**Auditors:** KPMG LLP

## LOCATIONS

**HQ:** 12200 N. Ambassador Dr., Kansas City, MO 64163
**Phone:** 816-713-7000          **Fax:** 816-713-6323
**Web:** www.farmland.com

More than 600,000 farmers and their cooperatives,
located in the US, Canada, and Mexico form Farmland
Industries, which conducts business in nearly 60
countries.

## PRODUCTS/OPERATIONS

**Selected Subsidiaries and Joint Ventures**
Agriliance, LLC (with Land O'Lakes and Cenex Harvest
States to supply fertilizer, pesticides, herbicides, and
seed to farmers)
Farmland Foods (99%, 11 food processing plants)
Farmland Hydro, LP (50%, with Norsk Hydro; phosphate
fertilizer manufacturing)
Farmland MissChem Limited (50%, anhydrous ammonia
manufacturing)
Farmland National Beef Packing Co., LP (71%)
Land O'Lakes Farmland Feed
SF Phosphates, Limited Liability Company (50%,
fertilizer manufacturing)
Southern Farm Fish Processors
Tradigrain SA (international grain trading)
WILFARM, LLC (50%, with Wilbur-Ellis Co.; pesticides)

**Consumer Product Brands**
Black Angus Beef
Carando (bread, specialty meats)
Farmland (processed pork products)
Farmstead
Maple River
OhSe
Regal
Roegelein (processed pork products)
Springwater Farms

## COMPETITORS

| | |
|---|---|
| Ag Processing | GROWMARK |
| Agway | Hormel |
| American Foods | IBP |
| ADM | IMC Global |
| Cargill | JR Simplot |
| Cenex Harvest States | Purina Mills |
| CF Industries | Rose Packing |
| ConAgra | Royal Dutch/Shell |
| ContiGroup | Scoular |
| DeBruce Grain | Smithfield Foods |
| Exxon Mobil | Southern States |
| Gold Kist | Transammonia |

## HISTORICAL FINANCIALS & EMPLOYEES

| Cooperative FYE: August 31 | Annual Growth | 8/92 | 8/93 | 8/94 | 8/95 | 8/96 | 8/97 | 8/98 | 8/99 | 8/00 | 8/01 |
|---|---|---|---|---|---|---|---|---|---|---|---|
| Sales ($ mil.) | 14.7% | 3,429 | 4,723 | 6,678 | 7,257 | 9,789 | 9,148 | 8,775 | 10,709 | 12,239 | 11,763 |
| Net income ($ mil.) | — | 62 | (30) | 74 | 163 | 126 | 135 | 59 | 14 | (29) | (90) |
| Income as % of sales | — | 1.8% | — | 1.1% | 2.2% | 1.3% | 1.5% | 0.7% | 0.1% | — | — |
| Employees | 7.4% | 7,616 | 8,155 | 12,000 | 12,700 | 14,700 | 14,600 | 16,100 | 17,700 | 15,000 | 14,500 |

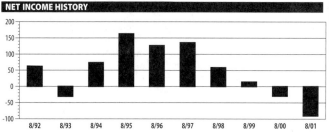

**NET INCOME HISTORY**

**2001 FISCAL YEAR-END**
Debt ratio: 47.3%
Return on equity: —
Cash ($ mil.): 0
Current ratio: 1.21
Long-term debt ($ mil.): 711

# FEDERAL RESERVE SYSTEM

## OVERVIEW

Where do banks go when they need a loan? To the Washington DC-based Federal Reserve System (known as the Fed). The Fed oversees a network of 12 Federal Reserve Banks located in major cities, which in turn provide regulatory oversight for the banks in their districts. The Fed ensures that banks maintain adequate reserves; it provides for their electronic funds transfer and transaction settlements; and by setting the interest rates of loans made to member banks (the prime rate), the Fed sets the pace of lending in the economy. The Fed also maintains active relationships with foreign governments and banks.

The seven-member Board of Governors, chaired by former Ayn Rand compadre Alan Greenspan, oversees its activities. Members are appointed by the US President and confirmed by the Senate for one-time 14-year terms, staggered at two-year intervals to prevent political stacking. As of 2002 two of the seats are currently vacant. The seven governors comprise the majority of the 12-person Federal Open Market Committee, which determines monetary policy. The five remaining members are reserve bank presidents who rotate in one-year terms, with New York always holding a place. Although the Fed enjoys significant political and financial freedom (it even operates at a profit), the chairman is required to testify before Congress twice a year.

National member banks must own stock in their Federal Reserve Bank, though it is optional for state-chartered banks.

## HISTORY

When New York's Knickerbocker Trust Company failed in 1907, it brought on a panic that was stemmed by J. P. Morgan, who strong-armed his fellow bankers into supporting shaky New York banks. The incident demonstrated the need for a central bank.

Morgan's actions sparked fears of his economic power and spurred congressional efforts to establish a central bank. After a six-year struggle between eastern money interests and populist monetary reformers, the 1913 Federal Reserve Act was passed. Twelve Federal Reserve districts were created, but New York's economic might ensured it would be the most powerful.

New York bank head Benjamin Strong dominated the Fed in the 1920s, countering the glut of European gold flooding the US in 1923 by selling securities from the Fed's portfolio. After he died in 1928, the Fed couldn't stabilize prices. Such difficulty, along with low rates encouraging members to use Fed loans for stock speculation, helped set the stage for the 1929 stock market crash.

During the Depression and WWII, the Fed yielded to the demands of the Treasury to buy bonds. But after WWII it sought independence, cultivating Congress to help free it from Treasury demands. This effort was led by chairman William McChesney Martin, with the assistance of New York bank president Alan Sproul (also a rival for the chairmanship). Martin diluted Sproul's influence by governing by consensus with the other bank leaders.

The Fed managed the economy successfully in the postwar boom, but it was stymied by inflation in the late 1960s. In the early 1970s the New York bank also faced the collapse of the fixed currency exchange-rate system and the growth of currency trading. Its role as foreign currency trader became even more crucial as the dollar's value eroded amid rising oil prices and a slowing economy.

The US suffered from double-digit inflation in 1979 as President Jimmy Carter appointed New York Fed president Paul Volcker as chairman. Volcker, believing that raising interest rates a few points would not suffice, allowed the banks to raise their discount rates and increased bank reserve requirements to reduce the money supply. By the time inflation eased, Ronald Reagan was president.

During the 1980s and 1990s, US budget fights limited options for controlling the economy through spending decision, so the Fed's actions became more important. Its higher profile brought calls for more access to its decision-making processes. Alan Greenspan took over as chairman in 1987 (and has since been reappointed chairman by Presidents Bush and Clinton).

While the US economy seemed immune to the Asian currency crisis of 1997 and 1998, the Federal Reserve remained relatively quiescent. But when Russia defaulted on some of its bonds in 1998, leading to the near-collapse of hedge fund Long-Term Capital Management, the New York Federal Reserve Bank brokered a bailout by the fund's lenders and investors.

This led to new guidelines for banks' risk management in 1999. After raising interest rates to stave off inflation during the late go-go 1990s, the Fed cut rates an unprecedented 11 times in 2001 (to a 40-year low of 1.75%) to help spur the flagging post-boom economy.

**Chairman of the Board of Governors:** Alan Greenspan
**Vice Chairman of the Board of Governors:**
  Roger W. Ferguson Jr.
**Member of the Board of Governors:** Laurence H. Meyer
**Member of the Board of Governors:**
  Edward M. Gramlich
**Member of the Board of Governors:** Mark W. Olson
**Member of the Board of Governors:**
  Susan Schmidt Bies, age 53

## LOCATIONS

**HQ:** 20th St. and Constitution Ave., NW,
  Washington, DC 20551
**Phone:** 202-452-3000
**Web:** www.federalreserve.gov

The Federal Reserve System oversees a network of 12
Federal Reserve banks in Atlanta, Boston, Chicago,
Cleveland, Dallas, Kansas City, Minneapolis, New York,
Philadelphia, Richmond, San Francisco, and St. Louis.

## HISTORICAL FINANCIALS & EMPLOYEES

| Government agency<br>FYE: December 31 | Annual<br>Growth | 12/91 | 12/92 | 12/93 | 12/94 | 12/95 | 12/96 | 12/97 | 12/98 | 12/99 | 12/00 |
|---|---|---|---|---|---|---|---|---|---|---|---|
| Assets ($ mil.) | (5.8%) | — | — | — | — | — | — | — | — | 647,460 | 609,877 |
| Net income ($ mil.) | — | — | — | — | — | — | — | — | — | 26,262 | 29,868 |
| Income as % of assets | — | — | — | — | — | — | — | — | — | 4.1% | 4.9% |
| Employees | — | — | — | — | — | — | — | — | — | — | 23,056 |

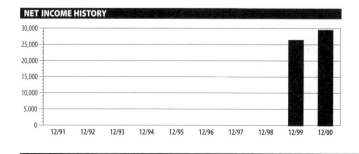

NET INCOME HISTORY

# FELD ENTERTAINMENT, INC.

You might say it's like a three-ring circus around Feld Entertainment. The Vienna, Virginia-based company is one the largest producers of live entertainment shows in the world with productions touring the globe, including its flagship Ringling Bros. and Barnum & Bailey Circus. The company also puts on a number of Disney-themed ice shows, including frozen productions of *Beauty and the Beast* and *Toy Story*, and it owns the Siegfried & Roy Las Vegas stage spectacular.

About 25 million people in 45 countries attend Feld's shows each year.

To keep up with changing times and draw a more affluent audience, Feld created Barnum's Kaleidoscape, a one-ring affair that features more gymnastic artistry than clowning around. Feld Entertainment is owned by chairman and CEO Kenneth Feld (the son of founder Irving Feld), who also personally oversees many of his company's productions.

When five-year-old Irving Feld found a $1 bill in 1923, he told his mother, "I'm going to buy a circus." He started by working the sideshows of traveling circuses before settling in Washington, DC, in 1940. Feld, who was white, opened the Super Cut-Rate Drugstore in a black section of the segregated city with the backing of the NAACP. In 1944 he opened the Super Music City record store and started his own record company, Super Disc. Feld and his brother Israel also began promoting outdoor concerts. When rock and roll became popular in the 1950s, Feld promoted Chubby Checker and Fats Domino, among others.

Feld came a step closer to realizing his dream in 1956 when he began managing the Ringling Bros. and Barnum & Bailey Circus for majority owner John Ringling North. North's circus traced its roots back to 1871 and P. T. Barnum's Grand Traveling Museum, Menagerie, Caravan, and Circus. In 1881 Barnum's circus and James Bailey's circus merged, creating Barnum & Bailey. In 1907 Bailey's widow sold Barnum & Bailey to North's uncles, the Ringling brothers, who had started their circus in 1884.

Among Feld's suggestions to North was moving the circus into air-conditioned arenas, saving $50,000 a week, because 1,800 roustabouts were no longer needed to set up tents. Feld continued to promote music acts, but he suffered a serious blow in 1959 when three of his stars — Buddy Holly, Ritchie Valens, and J. P. Richardson (the Big Bopper) — died in a plane crash.

Feld's dream of owning a circus finally was realized in 1967 when he and investors paid $8 million for Ringling Brothers. He fired most of the circus' performers and opened a Clown College to train new ones. Feld bought a German circus the following year to obtain animal trainer Gunther Gebel-Williams (who spent 30 years with the company). He then split the circus into two units in 1969, so he

could book it in two parts of the country at the same time and double his profits. Feld took the company public that year.

Feld and the other stockholders sold the circus to Mattel in 1971 for $47 million in stock; Feld stayed on as manager and held on to the lucrative concession business, Sells-Floto. He persuaded Mattel to buy the Ice Follies, Holiday on Ice, and the Siegfried & Roy magic show in 1979. Mattel sold the circus back to Feld in 1982 for $22.5 million, along with the ice shows and the magic show. Feld died two years later, and his son Kenneth became head of the company. A chip off the old block, Kenneth fired almost all the circus performers when he took over.

A constant target of animal rights activists, Feld began backing conservation efforts on behalf of the endangered Asian elephant, and established the Center for Elephant Conservation in Florida in 1995. The next year the company changed its name to Feld Entertainment.

Under increasing pressure as creative guru and managerial boss, Feld hired Turner Home Entertainment executive Stuart Snyder as president and COO in 1997, so he could focus on the creative side of the business. That focus produced Barnum's Kaleidoscape in 1999, an upscale version of the original circus, featuring specialty acts, gourmet food, plush seats, and audience interaction. (Plus, for the first time since 1956, a Feld circus was performed under a tent.) Snyder resigned later that year.

In an effort to inject new life into the 130-year-old Ringling Bros. and Barnum & Bailey Circus, Feld Entertainment launched new marketing campaigns in 2001. Also that year, a district court judge dismissed a complaint filed against the company by several animal activist groups, who claimed that Feld Entertainment didn't comply with federal regulations regarding the care of Asian elephants.

## OFFICERS

**Chairman and CEO:** Kenneth Feld, age 53
**CFO:** Mike Ruch
**VP International Sales and Business Development:**
Robert McHugh
**VP Human Resources:** Kirk McCoy

## LOCATIONS

**HQ:** 8607 Westwood Center Dr., Vienna, VA 22182
**Phone:** 703-448-4000 **Fax:** 703-448-4100
**Web:** www.feldentertainment.com

Feld Entertainment produces shows in 45 countries on six continents.

## PRODUCTS/OPERATIONS

**Selected Attractions**
Barnum's Kaleidoscape
Disney On Ice
*Beauty and the Beast*
*Disney Classics Come to Life on Ice!*
*The Jungle Book*
*The Lion King! Live on Ice!*
*Tarzan*
*Toy Story*
Ringling Bros. and Barnum & Bailey Circus
Siegfried & Roy

## COMPETITORS

Cirque du Soleil
Clear Channel Entertainment
Clyde Beatty-Cole Brothers Circus
Great American Circus
Hannaford Family Circus
Corporación Interamericana de Entretenimiento
On Stage Entertainment
Pickle Family Circus
Renaissance Entertainment
Six Flags
TBA
Tom Collins
Walt Disney

## HISTORICAL FINANCIALS & EMPLOYEES

| Private<br>FYE: January 31 | Annual<br>Growth | 1/92 | 1/93 | 1/94 | 1/95 | 1/96 | 1/97 | 1/98 | 1/99 | 1/00 | 1/01 |
|---|---|---|---|---|---|---|---|---|---|---|---|
| Estimated sales ($ mil.) | 5.6% | — | 500 | 570 | 600 | 625 | 550 | 630 | 645 | 675 | 776 |
| Employees | 0.0% | — | 2,500 | 2,500 | 2,500 | 2,500 | 2,500 | 2,500 | 2,500 | 2,500 | 2,500 |

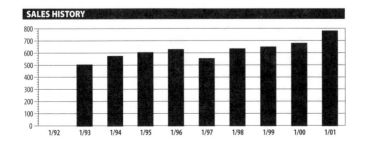

SALES HISTORY

ENTERTAINMENT, INC.

# FMR CORP.

FMR Corp. is *semper fidelis* (ever faithful) to its core business. The Boston-based financial services conglomerate, better known as Fidelity Investments, is the world's #1 mutual fund company. Serving some 17 million customers, FMR manages more than 300 funds and has approximately $1 trillion of assets under management. Its Magellan fund was for many years the US's largest, but it now jockeys with the Vanguard 500 Index Fund for the top spot. The fund's growing bulk raises questions about whether it can retain the agility that historically gave it such impressive growth.

FMR's nonfund products include online brokerage Powerstreet, life insurance, real estate management, securities clearing, and retirement services. FMR has expanded into trust services with its Fidelity Personal Trust Company.

The founding Johnson family controls most of FMR; Abigail Johnson, CEO Ned's daughter and heir apparent, is the largest single shareholder with about 25%.

## HISTORY

Boston money management firm Anderson & Cromwell formed Fidelity Fund in 1930. Edward Johnson became president of the fund in 1943, when it had $3 million invested in Treasury bills. Johnson diversified into stocks, and by 1945 the fund had grown to $10 million. In 1946 he established Fidelity Management and Research to act as its investment adviser.

In the early 1950s Johnson hired Gerry Tsai, a young immigrant from Shanghai, to analyze stocks. He put Tsai in charge of Fidelity Capital Fund in 1957. Tsai's brash, go-go investment strategy in such speculative stocks as Xerox and Polaroid paid off; by the time he left to form his own fund in 1965, he was managing more than $1 billion.

The Magellan Fund started in 1962. The company entered the corporate pension plans market (FMR Investment Management) in 1964, and retirement plans for self-employed individuals (Fidelity Keogh Plan) in 1967. It began serving investors outside the US (Fidelity International) in 1968.

Holding company FMR was formed in 1972, and that year Johnson gave control of Fidelity to his son Ned, who vertically integrated FMR by selling directly to customers rather than through brokers. The next year he formed Fidelity Daily Income Trust, the first money market fund to offer check writing.

Peter Lynch was hired as manager of the Magellan Fund in 1977. During his 13-year tenure, Magellan grew from $20 million to $12 billion in assets and outperformed all other mutual funds. Fidelity started Fidelity Brokerage Services in 1978, becoming the first mutual fund company to offer discount brokerage.

In 1980 the company launched a nationwide branch network and in 1986 entered the credit card business. The Wall Street crash of 1987 forced its Magellan Fund to liquidate almost $1 billion in stock in a single day. That year FMR moved into insurance by offering variable life, single premium, and deferred annuity policies. In 1989 the company introduced the low-expense Spartan Fund, targeted toward large, less-active investors.

Magellan's performance faded in the early 1990s, dropping from #1 performer to #3. Most of Fidelity's best performers were from its 36 select funds, which focus on narrow industry segments. FMR founded London-based COLT Telecom in 1993. In 1994 Ned Johnson gave his daughter and heir apparent, Abigail, a 25% stake in FMR.

Jeffrey Vinik resigned as manager of Magellan in 1996, one of more than a dozen fund managers to leave the firm that year and the next. Robert Stansky took the helm of the $56 billion fund, which FMR decided to close to new investors in 1997. Fidelity had a first that year when it went with an outside fund manager, hiring Bankers Trust (now part of Deutsche Bank) to manage its index funds.

FMR did some housecleaning in the late 1990s selling its Wentworth art galleries (1997) and *Worth* magazine (1998). Despite continued management turnover, it entered Japan and expanded its presence in Canada.

In 1999 the firm formed a joint venture with Charles Schwab; Donaldson, Lufkin & Jenrette, known now as Credit Suisse First Boston (USA); and Spear, Leeds & Kellogg to form an electronic communications network to trade Nasdaq stocks online. That year Fidelity teamed with Internet portal Lycos (now part of Terra Lycos) to develop the company's Powerstreet online brokerage.

FMR opened savings and loan Fidelity Personal Trust Co. in 2000. That year the Magellan Fund for a time lost its longtime title as the US's largest mutual fund to the Vanguard Index 500 Fund. In 2001 the company teamed up with Frank Russell to offer a new fund for wealthy clients.

Chairman and CEO: Edward C. Johnson III
Vice Chairman and COO; President, Fidelity
Investments Institutional Retirement Group:
Robert L. Reynolds
Vice Chairman; President, Fidelity Personal
Investments and Brokerage Group: J. Gary Burkhead
President, Fidelity Management and Research:
Abigail P. Johnson, age 39
EVP and CFO: Stephen P. Jonas
SVP and Chief of Administration and Government
Affairs: David C. Weinstein
VP and General Counsel: Lena G. Goldberg
President, Fidelity Capital: Steven P. Akin
President, Fidelity Corporate Real Estate:
Ronald C. Duff
President, Fidelity Corporate Systems and Services:
Mark A. Peterson
President, Fidelity International Limited:
Barry R.J. Bateman
President, Fidelity Investments Canada:
Jeffrey R. Carney
President, Fidelity Investments European Mutual
Funds: Thomas Balk
President, Fidelity Investments Institutional Brokerage
Group: David F. Denison
President, Fidelity Investments Institutional Services:
Kevin J. Kelly
President, Fidelity Investments Systems:
Donald A. Haile
President, Fidelity Security Services:
George K. Campbell
President, Fidelity Ventures: Timothy T. Hilton
President, Fidelity-Wide Processing: Chuck Griffith
President, Personal Investments: Gail J. McGovern,
age 47
EVP, Fidelity Investments Human Resources:
Ilene B. Jacobs
Auditors: PricewaterhouseCoopers LLP

## LOCATIONS

HQ: 82 Devonshire St., Boston, MA 02109
Phone: 617-563-7000    Fax: 617-476-6150
Web: www.fidelity.com

FMR maintains investor centers in some 30 US states and
Washington, DC. It also has offices in Europe, Asia
and the Pacific Rim, the Middle East, and North America.

## PRODUCTS/OPERATIONS

Selected Subsidiaries
Fidelity Capital
  BostonCoach
  COLT Telecom Group (51%)
  Fidelity Capital Acquisitions Group
  Fidelity Capital Telecommunications & Technology
  Fidelity Technology Solutions
  Fidelity Ventures
  J. Robert Scott
  NetSuite Development
  Pembroke Real Estate
  World Trade Center Boston
Fidelity Financial Intermediary Services
  Fidelity Investments Canada Limited
  Fidelity Investments Institutional Services Company,
    Inc.
Fidelity International Limited (Bermuda)
Fidelity Investments Institutional Retirement Group
  Fidelity Benefits Center
  Fidelity Group Pensions International
  Fidelity Institutional Retirement Services Company
  Fidelity Investments Public Sector Services Company
  Fidelity Investments Tax-Exempt Services Company
  Fidelity Management Trust Company
Fidelity Investments Life Insurance Company
Fidelity Personal Investments and Brokerage Group
  Fidelity Brokerage Technology Group
  Fidelity Capital Markets
  Fidelity Investment Advisor Group
Fidelity Technology & Processing Group
Strategic Advisers, Inc.

## COMPETITORS

| | | |
|---|---|---|
| Alliance Capital | Kaufmann Fund | Putnam |
| Ameritrade | Lehman | Investments |
| AXA Financial | Brothers | Quick & |
| Barclays | Marsh & | Reilly/Fleet |
| Charles Schwab | McLennan | Raymond James |
| Citigroup | MassMutual | Financial |
| Datek Online | Merrill Lynch | T. Rowe Price |
| Dow Jones | MetLife | TD Waterhouse |
| E*TRADE | Morgan Stanley | TIAA-CREF |
| Goldman Sachs | Dean Witter | UBS |
| John Hancock | Northwestern | PaineWebber |
| Financial | Mutual | USAA |
| Services | Prudential | Vanguard Group |

## HISTORICAL FINANCIALS & EMPLOYEES

| Private FYE: December 31 | Annual Growth | 12/91 | 12/92 | 12/93 | 12/94 | 12/95 | 12/96 | 12/97 | 12/98 | 12/99 | 12/00 |
|---|---|---|---|---|---|---|---|---|---|---|---|
| Sales ($ mil.) | 25.3% | — | 1,824 | 2,570 | 3,530 | 4,277 | 5,080 | 5,878 | 6,776 | 8,845 | 11,096 |
| Employees | 17.7% | — | 9,000 | 12,900 | 14,600 | 18,000 | 23,300 | 25,000 | 28,000 | 30,000 | 33,186 |

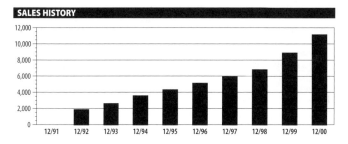

SALES HISTORY

# FOLLETT CORPORATION

## OVERVIEW

Reading is fundamental to Follett's bottom line. River Grove, Illinois-based Follett is the #1 operator of US college bookstores and has about 600 stores serving campuses throughout the US and Canada. In addition to books, campus stores sell items such as clothing, school supplies, and software. Other higher education services include efollett.com (online textbook shopping with a database of 16 million titles).

Follett also brings books to the younger set. The top US wholesaler and distributor of used textbooks to grade schools, Follett also supplies books and audiovisual materials to public and grade school libraries. Other business groups provide library automation and management software, textbook reconditioning, and library management services.

The company has capitalized on the growing trend of universities farming out operations to independent operators. Follett is owned and managed by the Follett family, which has controlled the firm for four generations.

## HISTORY

Follett began in 1873 as a small bookstore opened by the Rev. Charles Barnes in his Wheaton, Illinois, home. By 1893 a recession had rocked the business, and Barnes sought investment from his wife's family, for which he gave up controlling interest. Sales topped $237,000 in 1899.

Initially hired by Barnes in 1901 to help move the store to a new location in Chicago, 18-year-old C. W. Follett stayed on as both salesman and stock clerk. Barnes retired the following year and left the business to his son William and his father-in-law, John Wilcox, who was a major shareholder. In 1917 C. W. bought into the company when William moved to New York (he started what became one of Follett's biggest competitors, Barnes & Noble), and he renamed it J. W. Wilcox & Follett Company. Wilcox died in 1923, and C. W. bought the Wilcox family shares and shortened the name to Wilcox & Follett.

C. W.'s four sons were brought into the business, and each was instrumental in shaping the company's future. Garth created Follett Library Resources, a wholesale service for libraries. Dwight started an elementary textbook publishing division. But Robert would have the most influence: He began wholesaling college textbooks, which led to the creation of Follett College Stores and Follett Campus Resources.

Wilcox & Follett expanded throughout the Depression. During WWII it began publishing kids' books, which were in demand because of a metal toy shortage. C. W. died in 1952 and Dwight took over. Five years later the firm organized into divisions; Follett was created as the parent company. During the 1960s Follett developed the first multiracial textbook series. Dwight built the company to $50 million in annual sales by 1977, when he retired. His son Robert succeeded him and led Follett through tremendous growth in the 1980s.

In 1983 the company sold its publishing division to Esquire Education Group; using funds from this sale, it began acquiring college bookstore chains such as Campus Services. In 1989 Follett developed Tom-Tracks, a computerized textbook system for college bookstores. A year later the company acquired Brennan College Service, adding 57 stores to its chain. Robert's son-in-law Richard Traut, named chairman in 1994, was the first person without the Follett name to hold that position. By 1994 Tom-Tracks had been installed in over 500 bookstores across the country. Also in 1994 Follett introduced Sneak Preview Plus, a CD-ROM product designed to enhance the acquisition process in libraries.

The company acquired used-textbook reseller Western Textbook Exchange (1996), juvenile-book distributor Book Wholesalers (1997), and coursepack printer CAPCO (1998). In early 1998 Follett reorganized its corporate structure by market segments, establishing three divisions: the Elementary/High School Group, the Higher Education Group, and Library Group. Also that year the Follett Campus Resources unit agreed to pay the University of Tennessee $380,000 after the school discovered that the firm had been underpaying students in a book-buyback program for several years. Adding to its bevy of campus bookstores, it signed a contract that year to build a $5 million bookstore at the University of Texas at Arlington. Also in 1998 CFO Kenneth Hull replaced Richard Litzsinger as CEO.

Follett launched efollett.com in early 1999 to sell college textbooks online. That same year Hull also became chairman upon Traut's departure. In November 2000 Christopher Traut became CEO; Hull remained chairman. In April 2001 Hull retired, and Mark Litzsinger succeeded him as chairman.

**Chairman:** R. Mark Litzsinger, age 45
**CEO and President:** Christopher Traut
**VP, Human Resources:** Richard Ellspermann
**Executive VP, Follett Library and School Group:**
Chuck Follett
**VP, Finance and CFO:** Kathryn A. Stanton
**President and CEO, Follett School and Library Group:**
Ross Follett

## LOCATIONS

**HQ:** 2233 West St., River Grove, IL 60171
**Phone:** 708-583-2000          **Fax:** 708-452-9347
**Web:** www.follett.com

Follett has operations in more than 60 countries, including more than 110,000 schools in the US and Canada.

## PRODUCTS/OPERATIONS

**Divisions**

**Elementary/High School Group**
Follett Educational Services (K-12 textbook and workbooks)
Follett Software Company (library automation)
Library Systems & Services (library management)

**Higher Education Group** (college textbook *Blue Book* and distribution, college bookstores, CourseWorks and First*system* software systems, efollett.com, and promotional marketing services)

**Library Group**
Book Wholesalers, Inc. (public libraries)
Follett Audiovisual Resources (comprehensive audiovisual products and services, academic and public libraries)
Follett Library Resources (school libraries)

## COMPETITORS

Baker & Taylor
Barnes & Noble College Bookstores
Barnes & Noble
barnesandnoble.com
Borders
D&H Distributing
Ecampus.com
Educational Development
Indigo Books & Music
Ingram Industries
Kinko's
Nebraska Book
Varsity Group
Wallace's Bookstores
Wal-Mart

## HISTORICAL FINANCIALS & EMPLOYEES

| Private FYE: March 31 | Annual Growth | 3/92 | 3/93 | 3/94 | 3/95 | 3/96 | 3/97 | 3/98 | 3/99 | 3/00 | 3/01 |
|---|---|---|---|---|---|---|---|---|---|---|---|
| Sales ($ mil.) | 12.3% | 549 | 612 | 646 | 713 | 811 | 916 | 1,073 | 1,200 | 1,401 | 1,554 |
| Employees | 2.9% | 6,198 | 6,500 | 6,800 | 7,200 | 7,500 | 8,000 | 7,500 | 8,000 | 8,000 | 8,000 |

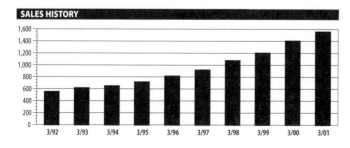

SALES HISTORY

# THE FORD FOUNDATION

As one of the US's largest philanthropic organizations with nearly $15 billion in assets, The Ford Foundation can afford to be generous. The New York City-based not-for-profit foundation offers grants to individuals and institutions in the US and abroad that meet its stated goals of strengthening democratic values, reducing poverty and injustice, promoting international cooperation, and advancing human achievement.

The Ford Foundation gives to a variety of causes in three areas: Asset Building and Community Development (designed to help expand opportunities for the poor and reduce hardship); Peace and Social Justice (promotes peace and the rule of law, human rights, and freedom); and Education, Media, Arts, and Culture (aimed at strengthening education and the arts and at building identity and community). While the foundation normally gives a large number of small grants, in 2000 it launched a 10-year, $330 million initiative to help graduate students in 20 countries.

The foundation is governed by an international board of trustees and no longer has stock in Ford Motor Company or ties to the Ford family. Funds are derived from a diversified investment portfolio that includes publicly traded equity and fixed-income securities.

Henry Ford and his son Edsel gave $25,000 to establish The Ford Foundation in Michigan in 1936, followed the next year by 250,000 shares of nonvoting stock in the Ford Motor Company. The foundation's activities were limited mainly to Michigan until the deaths of Edsel (1943) and Henry (1947) made the foundation the owner of 90% of the automaker's nonvoting stock (catapulting the endowment to $474 million, the US's largest).

In 1951, under a new mandate and president (Paul Hoffman, former head of the Marshall Plan), Ford made broad commitments to the promotion of world peace, the strengthening of democracy, and the improvement of education. Early education program grants overseen by University of Chicago chancellor Robert Maynard Hutchins ($100 million between 1951 and 1953) helped establish major international programs (e.g., Harvard's Center for International Legal Studies) and the National Merit Scholarships.

Under McCarthyite criticism for its experimental education grants, the foundation in 1956 granted $550 million (after selling 22% of its Ford shares) to noncontroversial recipients such as liberal arts colleges and not-for-profit hospitals. The organization's money set up the Radio and Television Workshop (1951); public TV support became a foundation trademark.

International work, begun in Asia and the Middle East (1950) and extended to Africa (1958) and Latin America (1959), focused on education and rural development. The foundation also supported the Population Council and research in high-yield agriculture with The Rockefeller Foundation.

In the early 1960s Ford targeted innovative approaches to employment and race relations.

McGeorge Bundy (former national security adviser to President John F. Kennedy), named president of the foundation in 1966, increased the activist trend with grants for direct voter registration; the NAACP; public-interest law centers serving consumer, environmental, and minority causes; and housing for the poor.

The early 1970s saw support for black colleges and scholarships, child care, and job training for women, but by 1974 inflation, weak stock prices, and overspending had eroded assets. Programs were cut, but continued support for social justice issues led Henry Ford II to quit the board in 1976.

Under lawyer Franklin Thomas (named president in 1979), Ford established the nation's largest community development support organization, Local Initiatives Support. Thomas, the first African-American to lead the foundation, was a catalyst in a series of meetings between white and black South Africans in the mid-1980s.

Thomas stepped down in 1996, and EVP Susan Berresford, the new president, consolidated the foundation's grant programs into three areas: Asset Building and Community Development; Peace and Social Justice; and Education, Media, Arts, and Culture. In the late 1990s Ford was surpassed by various other foundations and had to relinquish its 30-year title as the largest charitable organization in the US.

In 2000 The Ford Foundation announced a $40 million program to provide grants to arts institutions across the US. The foundation later announced its largest grant ever, the 10-year, $330 million International Fellowship Program to support graduate students studying in 20 countries.

**Chairman:** Paul A. Allaire
**President:** Susan V. Berresford
**Controller, Treasurer, and Director Financial Services:** Nicholas M. Gabriel
**EVP, Secretary, and General Counsel:** Barron M. Tenny
**SVP:** Barry D. Gaberman
**VP Asset Building and Community Development:** Melvin L. Oliver
**VP and Chief Investment Officer:** Linda B. Strumpf
**VP Communications:** Alexander Wilde
**VP Education, Media, Arts, and Culture:** Alison R. Bernstein
**VP Peace and Social Justice:** Bradford K. Smith
**Senior Director Office Management Services:** Natalia Kanem
**Director Human Resources:** Bruce D. Stuckey
**Director Economic Development:** Frank F. DeGiovanni
**Director Human Development and Reproductive Health:** Virginia Davis Floyd
**Director Education, Knowledge, and Religion:** Janice Petrovich
**Director Governance and Civil Society:** Michael A. Edwards
**Director Human Rights and International Cooperation:** Alan Jenkins
**Director Community and Resource Development:** Cynthia Duncan
**Assistant Secretary and Associate General Counsel:** Nancy P. Feller
**Auditors:** PricewaterhouseCoopers LLP

## LOCATIONS

**HQ:** 320 E. 43rd St., New York, NY 10017
**Phone:** 212-573-5000       **Fax:** 212-599-4584
**Web:** www.fordfound.org

The Ford Foundation has representatives in New York City, as well as Beijing; Cairo; Hanoi, Vietnam; Jakarta, Indonesia; Johannesburg; Lagos, Nigeria; Makati City, Philippines; Mexico City; Nairobi, Kenya; New Delhi; Rio de Janeiro; Moscow; Santiago, Chile; and Windhoek, Namibia.

## PRODUCTS/OPERATIONS

**Program Area Grants**
Asset Building and Community Development
  Community and Resource Development
  Economic Development
  Human Development and Reproductive Health
Education, Media, Arts, and Culture
  Education, Knowledge, and Religion
  Media, Arts, and Culture
Peace and Social Justice
  Governance and Civil Society
  Human Rights and International Cooperation

## HISTORICAL FINANCIALS & EMPLOYEES

| Foundation FYE: September 30 | Annual Growth | 9/91 | 9/92 | 9/93 | 9/94 | 9/95 | 9/96 | 9/97 | 9/98 | 9/99 | 9/00 |
|---|---|---|---|---|---|---|---|---|---|---|---|
| Sales ($ mil.) | 22.1% | — | 493 | 797 | 489 | 586 | 899 | 1,005 | 1,087 | 1,785 | 2,432 |
| Employees | 0.2% | — | 590 | 590 | 597 | 587 | 570 | 574 | 580 | 576 | 600 |

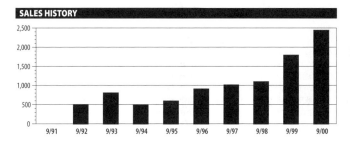

SALES HISTORY

FORD FOUNDATION

# FRY'S ELECTRONICS, INC.

## OVERVIEW

Fry's Electronics keeps its customers angry but entertained. The legendary San Jose, California-based chain — known just as much for its cranky customer service as for its merchandise — has about 20 stores, most of them in the Golden State, yet it ranks among the largest US computer retailers.

Its mammoth stores, some swallowing almost 200,000 sq. ft., cater to the technologically adept shopper. Fry's outlets (a regular stop on bus tours) stock more than 10,000 low-priced electronic items and are known for their whimsical decor and displays. Each follows a theme, from *Alice in Wonderland* to a UFO crash site. The geek-gaws range from silicon chips to potato chips, from *Byte* to *Playboy*, and high-speed PCs (plus software and peripherals) to No-Doz (and other over-the-counter drugs).

But Fry's unfriendly reputation has left it a target of gripe-filled Web postings. Employees are searched at the end of each day as an anti-theft measure. Customers hoping to return items must abide by a process known internally as the "double H," for hoops and hurdles. One manager of an anti-Fry's Web site has likened the experience to a bizarre S&M game that keeps customers coming back for more abuse.

Brothers John (CEO), David (CIO), and Randy Fry (president) own the company, which continues aggressive expansion, including acquiring tech products e-tailer Cyberian Outpost in late 2001. John, a mathematician who collects the writings of Nobel prize winners for fun, is a known cheapskate who hires computer-illiterate sales clerks for a pittance and accepts the resulting high turnover.

## HISTORY

The Fry brothers — David, John, and Randy — wear genes stitched of retailing. Their father, Charles, started Fry's Food Stores in the 1950s in South Bay, California. The 40-store chain was sold for $14 million in 1972 before Charles' progeny heard the retail calling.

Charles gave each of his sons $1 million from the sale of the supermarkets. His eldest son, John, who had gained technical expertise while running the supermarket's computer system, convinced his siblings of the viability of a hard-core computer retail store. The brothers pooled their funds and in 1985 started the first in Sunnyvale, California, along with Kathryn Kolder (EVP). They added a store in Fremont in 1988; the Palo Alto store was completed two years later with an adjacent corporate headquarters.

John mixed his supermarket sales experience with a sharp marketing acumen, selling prime shelf space at smart prices to suppliers. He stocked the stores with everything for a computer user's survival and slashed prices. The first Los Angeles-area store opened in 1992; a second one opened the following year.

Hiring an ex-Lucasfilm designer, John spent $1 million on each location, decorating stores like medieval castles, Mayan temples, and Wild West saloons. In 1994 the Los Angeles computer retail market began to see increased competition from nationwide discount computer superstores. The next year Fry's opened a new store in Woodland Hills with an *Alice in Wonderland* motif. It was the first Southern California Fry's Electronics store to offer appliances and an expanded music department.

The chain continued to gain notoriety for the contempt it seemed to show its customers. Local Better Business Bureaus started ranking Fry's "unsatisfactory" because the stores would not respond to complaints. Visitors were usually met by security guards, scores of hidden surveillance cameras, and employees who were promised bonuses for talking customers out of cash returns.

Still the company thrived, turning over its inventories twice as fast as competitors. One customer who sued Fry's for injuries allegedly received at the hands of store security guards went back for deals soon thereafter. Fry's went on an expansion frenzy in 1996, opening new California stores in Burbank, San Jose, and Anaheim. Moving beyond its Pacific roots, the company in 1997 spent $118 million to buy six of Tandy's failed Incredible Universe retail mega-outlets in Arizona, Oregon, and Texas. The company also won a legal battle with Frenchy Frys, a Seattle vending machine maker, for the right to own and use frys.com URL. The company in 1998 continued to restructure its new stores into Fry's outlets.

Fry's opened a new store in Houston in early 2001 and announced plans that year to open several stores in the Chicago area. In May 2001 Fry's acquired a 10% stake in e-tailer Cyberian Outpost (and acquired the rest in November). Fry's agreed to acquire all of technology products marketer Egghead.com's assets in August; however, in October the deal was called off after Egghead.com said that it did not think Fry's intentions were clearly stated.

**CEO and Director:** John Fry
**President and Director:** William R. Fry
**Chief Information Officer, CFO, and Director:**
 David Fry
**EVP, Business Development; Director:** Kathryn Kolder

## LOCATIONS

**HQ:** 600 East Brokaw Rd., San Jose, CA 95112
**Phone:** 408-487-4500     **Fax:** 408-487-4700
**Web:** www.frys.com

Fry's Electronics has stores in Arizona, California,
Oregon, and Texas.

## PRODUCTS/OPERATIONS

**Selected Computer Products**
Computer chips
Motherboards
PCs
Peripherals
Software

**Other Products**
Audio CDs
Beer
Coffeemakers
Digital mixers
Fax machines
Magazines
Over-the-counter medicines
Potato chips
Razors
Soda
Stereos
Telephones
Telescopes
Televisions
Video systems

## COMPETITORS

| | |
|---|---|
| Best Buy | Insight Enterprises |
| Beyond | Micro Electronics |
| BUY.COM | Micro Warehouse |
| CDW Computer Centers | Office Depot |
| Circuit City | PC Connection |
| CompUSA | PC Mall |
| Cyberian Outpost | RadioShack |
| Dell Computer | Staples |
| Gateway | Systemax |
| Good Guys | Zones |

## HISTORICAL FINANCIALS & EMPLOYEES

| Private<br>FYE: December 31 | Annual<br>Growth | 12/91 | 12/92 | 12/93 | 12/94 | 12/95 | 12/96 | 12/97 | 12/98 | 12/99 | 12/00 |
|---|---|---|---|---|---|---|---|---|---|---|---|
| Estimated sales ($ mil.) | 29.2% | — | — | 250 | 327 | 414 | 535 | 950 | 1,250 | 1,420 | 1,500 |
| Employees | 19.2% | — | — | 1,300 | 1,500 | 1,500 | 2,000 | 4,000 | 4,000 | 4,100 | 4,450 |

**SALES HISTORY**

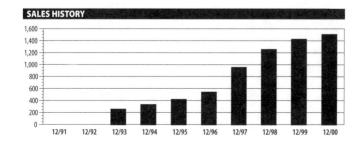

# GIANT EAGLE INC.

## OVERVIEW

Giant Eagle has taken wing to new haunts beyond its hometown of Pittsburgh, Pennsylvania. The supermarket operator has about 145 stores and more than 60 franchised stores in Maryland, western Pennsylvania, Ohio, and West Virginia. It also has a wholesale business. Most of the firm's stores measure about 60,000 sq. ft. As with other birds of the retailing feather, Giant Eagle's stores carry private-label merchandise (Eagle Valley and Giant Eagle) and nonfood items; many have pharmacies and banks, and some offer ready-to-eat meals.

Giant Eagle is the #1 grocer in Pittsburgh, and its 1997 purchase of Riser Foods made it the leader in Cleveland. Now Giant Eagle has expanded again, moving into central Ohio and into Maryland.

The families of Giant Eagle's five founders own the company. CEO David Shapira is the grandson of one of the founders.

## HISTORY

When Joe Porter, Ben Chait, and Joe Goldstein sold their chain of 125 Eagle grocery stores in Pittsburgh to Kroger in 1928, a term in the agreement stated that the men would have to leave the grocery business for three years. In retrospect, Kroger should have made the term last for the length of their lives, because in 1931 the three men joined the owners of OK Grocery — Hyman Moravitz and Morris Weizenbaum — and launched a new chain of grocery stores called Giant Eagle. Eventually, the chain would knock Kroger out of the Pittsburgh market.

Although slowed by the Great Depression, the chain expanded, fighting such large rivals as Acme, A&P, and Kroger for Pittsburgh's food shoppers. The stores were mom-and-pop operations with over-the-counter service until they began converting to self-service during the 1940s. In the 1950s the stores expanded in size to nearly 15,000 sq. ft. Also during that decade, Giant Eagle, with about 30 stores, launched Blue Stamps in answer to Green Stamps and other loyalty programs.

It phased out trading stamps in the 1960s in lieu of everyday low prices. To accommodate its growth, in 1968 Giant Eagle acquired a warehouse in Lawrenceville, Pennsylvania, that more than doubled its storage area. Also that year the firm opened its first 20,000-sq.-ft. Giant Eagle store.

During the inflationary 1970s Giant Eagle introduced generic items and began offering the Food Club line, a private-label brand, in conjunction with wholesaler Topco. It continued its steady expansion, and by 1979 it had become Pittsburgh's leading supermarket chain, as chains such as Kroger, Acme, and A&P were leaving the city.

In 1981 Giant Eagle, with 52 stores, acquired Tamarkin, a wholesale and retail chain in Youngstown, Ohio, part-owned by the Monus family. The purchase moved it into the franchise business, and later that year the first independent Giant Eagle store opened in Monaca (outside Pittsburgh).

The Tamarkin purchase brought together Mickey Monus and Giant Eagle CEO David Shapira, grandson of founder Goldstein. In 1982 they created Phar-Mor, a deep-discount drugstore chain (Wal-Mart's Sam Walton once said it was the only competitor he truly feared). From a single store in Niles, Ohio, Phar-Mor grew rapidly to 310 outlets in 32 states in the early 1990s.

Phar-Mor president Monus helped found the World Basketball League (WBL) in 1987 and became the owner of three teams. In 1992 an auditor discovered two unexplainable Phar-Mor checks to the WBL totaling about $100,000. Investigators soon uncovered three years of overstated inventories and a false set of books; Shapira (who was also CEO of Phar-Mor), Giant Eagle owners (who held a 50% stake in Phar-Mor until 1992), and other investors had been duped of more than $1 billion. Shapira fired Monus and his cronies on July 31, 1992. The next day the WBL folded; about two weeks after that Phar-Mor filed for Chapter 11 bankruptcy. A mistrial in 1994 couldn't save Monus from prison; he was reindicted in 1995 and sentenced to 20 years (later reduced to 12).

Giant Eagle made its largest acquisition in 1997, paying $403 million for Riser Foods, a wholesaler (American Seaway Foods) with 35 company-owned stores under the Rini-Rego Stop-n-Shop banner. The stores were converted to the Giant Eagle banner in 1998 (another 18 independent Stop-n-Shop stores were also converted).

In 2000 Giant Eagle opened several stores in Columbus, Ohio. The grocer moved into Maryland that year when it acquired six Country Market stores in Maryland and Pennsylvania. (It will begin operating the stores in early 2002.) Also in 2001, the grocer founded ECHO Real Estate Services Co. to develop retail, housing, and golf course projects.

**Chairman and CEO:** David S. Shapira
**Vice Chairman:** Anthony Rego
**President and COO:** Raymond Burgo
**SVP and CFO:** Mark Minnaugh
**VP, Personnel:** Raymond A. Huber

## LOCATIONS

**HQ:** 101 Kappa Dr., Pittsburgh, PA 15238
**Phone:** 412-963-6200       **Fax:** 412-968-1561
**Web:** www.gianteagle.com

### 2001 Stores

| | No. |
|---|---:|
| Ohio | |
| Cleveland | 43 |
| Youngstown | 28 |
| Akron/Canton | 20 |
| Columbus | 4 |
| Toledo | 1 |
| Pennsylvania | |
| Pittsburgh | 79 |
| Johnstown/Altoona | 10 |
| Erie | 9 |
| Lake | 5 |
| West Virginia | 6 |
| **Total** | **205** |

## PRODUCTS/OPERATIONS

**Private Labels**
Eagle Valley
Giant Eagle

**Selected Services**
Bakery
Banking services
Childcare
Deli department
Dry cleaning
Fresh seafood
Greeting cards
Pharmacy
Photo developing
Ready-to-eat meals
Ticketmaster outlet
Video rental

## COMPETITORS

Ahold USA
Giant Food
Heinen's
IGA
Kroger
SUPERVALU
Wal-Mart
Wegmans Food Markets
Weis Markets

## HISTORICAL FINANCIALS & EMPLOYEES

| Private<br>FYE: June 30 | Annual<br>Growth | 6/92 | 6/93 | 6/94 | 6/95 | 6/96 | 6/97 | 6/98 | 6/99 | 6/00 | 6/01 |
|---|---|---|---|---|---|---|---|---|---|---|---|
| Estimated sales ($ mil.) | 9.3% | 2,000 | 2,000 | 2,000 | 2,100 | 2,200 | 3,800 | 4,050 | 4,360 | 4,221 | 4,435 |
| Employees | 10.2% | — | 11,800 | 7,200 | 7,200 | 12,000 | 19,200 | 25,000 | 25,600 | 25,600 | 25,600 |

### SALES HISTORY

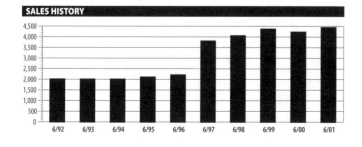

# GOLD KIST INC.

## OVERVIEW

At Gold Kist, high-protein diets aren't just a fad. The Atlanta-based agricultural cooperative is the #2 US chicken producer (behind Tyson Foods) with some 18,000 primarily Southern farmer-members. Poultry operations account for the bulk of its business.

The company divides its operations into co-operative broiler divisions, each with its own chicken flocks, hatcheries, feed mill, and processing plant. It markets whole and cut-up chickens, chicken parts, and other processed products under brands such as Gold Kist Farms and Young 'n Tender to grocery chains, the food service industry, schools, and the military.

Gold Kist has divested its aquaculture and peanut operations to focus more on its chicken business, which has seen an increase in demand owing to concerns about mad cow disease and to a weakened economy that favors chicken over its more expensive rival, beef.

The company's production isn't limited to chicken. The company also processes pork, and it owns 25% of Young Pecan Company, a US pecan processor. The cooperative's other operations include financing for farmers (subsidiary AgraTrade Financing) and metal design and fabrication (subsidiary Luker).

## HISTORY

Georgia native David Brooks, a University of Georgia agronomy professor from the age of 19, left teaching to form Georgia Cooperative Cotton Producers Association in 1933. A Depression-era creation, Brooks saw the Carrollton, Georgia, cotton marketing cooperative as a way to improve the economic well-being of its members through collective price bargaining and the elimination of middlemen. By the end of its first year, Georgia Cotton Producers had grown from 13 members to about 7,000. The co-op expanded into neighboring states during the 1930s and dropped "Georgia" from its name.

The cooperative diversified in the 1940s and 1950s. During WWII the enterprise made ammunition at its fertilizer plants. Cotton Producers moved into pecan and peanut production in 1950s under the Gold Kist label. It also established itself as a major exporter of agricultural products, setting up sales offices in Europe in the late 1940s and Asia and the Middle East in the 1950s. The Gold Kist moniker was slowly adopted as the co-op's name over the next 20 years. When Brooks stepped down from full-time leadership in 1968, Gold Kist was the South's largest farm cooperative.

In the late 1970s the energy crisis, bad harvests, and other factors led to a decline in cooperatives, including Gold Kist, which posted a loss in 1980. The co-op founded Golden Poultry in 1982 to run the Georgia-based broiler complex acquired earlier that year by Agri International, another of its subsidiaries. In 1986 Gold Kist spun off 27% of Golden Poultry, the first farmer-owned cooperative to make such a move. North Carolina-based Carolina Golden Products (a poultry processor partnership between Gold Kist and Golden Poultry) was merged into the company that year.

Gold Kist combined its peanut operations with Archer Daniels Midland's in 1987, forming Golden Peanut Company. Alimenta Processing, the Georgia-based unit of a Swiss firm, became part of Golden Peanut two years later.

The co-op opened its Russellville, Alabama, facility in 1990, increasing its processed-chicken production capacity by half and entering the fast-food market. The co-op moved into pork and pet food processing and catfish farming. Gold Kist merged its pecan operations into Young Pecan Company in 1992. It also beefed up exports (from about $46 million in 1990 to more than $70 million in 1995).

In 1997 Gold Kist bought back the stake in Golden Poultry it did not own. Although low poultry prices and troubled foreign markets hit the company hard in 1998, it continued its plan to focus on food, selling its wholesale and retail farm supply assets — including 100 stores as well as grain buying stations and cotton gins — to the Southern States agricultural cooperative. After reporting a $26 million loss in sales, Gold Kist announced cost-cutting measures in 2000 that included cutbacks in production and a salary freeze.

In 2001 the company recalled more than 420,000 pounds of chicken that may have been contaminated with an insecticide, yet it made a profit that year of more than $33 million thanks in part to more export sales as a result of concerns about mad cow disease. Also that year the company divested its 25% stake in Golden Peanut Company and discontinued its aquaculture operations.

**President and CEO:** John Bekkers, age 56, $612,774 pay
**CFO and Treasurer:** Stephen O. West, age 55
**SVP Planning and Administration:** Michael A. Stimpert, age 57, $351,512 pay
**VP Corporate Relations:** Paul G. Brower, age 62
**VP, General Counsel, and Secretary:** J. David Dyson, age 54
**VP Human Resources:** Harry T. McDonald, age 56
**VP Information Services:** Sandra W. Kearney, age 42
**VP Marketing and Sales:** Jerry L. Stewart, age 61, $313,987 pay
**VP Operations:** Donald W. Mabe, age 47, $266,380 pay
**VP Purchasing:** Marshall Smitherman, age 59
**VP Science and Technology:** Allen C. Merritt, age 55
**Controller:** W. F. Pohl Jr., age 51
**Auditors:** KPMG LLP

## LOCATIONS

**HQ:** 244 Perimeter Center Pkwy. NE, Atlanta, GA 30346
**Phone:** 770-393-5000  **Fax:** 770-393-5262
**Web:** goldkist.com

Gold Kist has operations in Alabama, Florida, Georgia, North Carolina, South Carolina.

## PRODUCTS/OPERATIONS

**Selected Brands**
Big Value
Early Bird
Gold Kist Farms
Medallion
Young 'n Tender

**Selected Subsidiaries and Partnerships**
AgraTrade Financing, Inc. (financing to farmers for poultry and pork facilities)
Luker Inc. (fabricates steel poultry processing equipment)
Young Pecan Company (25%)

## COMPETITORS

Alabama Farmers Cooperatives
Cagle's
ConAgra
ContiGroup
Farmland Industries
Foster Farms
John Sanfilippo & Son
Keystone Foods
Perdue
Pilgrim's Pride
Sanderson Farms
Smithfield Foods
Townsends
Tyson Foods

## HISTORICAL FINANCIALS & EMPLOYEES

| Cooperative<br>FYE: Sunday nearest June 30 | Annual<br>Growth | 6/92 | 6/93 | 6/94 | 6/95 | 6/96 | 6/97 | 6/98 | 6/99 | 6/00 | 6/01 |
|---|---|---|---|---|---|---|---|---|---|---|---|
| Sales ($ mil.) | 3.7% | 1,301 | 1,401 | 1,561 | 1,689 | 1,956 | 2,289 | 1,651 | 1,766 | 1,707 | 1,811 |
| Net income ($ mil.) | — | (2) | 27 | 34 | 12 | 12 | 37 | (103) | 61 | (26) | (33) |
| Income as % of sales | — | — | 1.9% | 2.2% | 0.7% | 1.9% | 0.5% | — | 3.5% | — | — |
| Employees | 3.2% | — | 14,000 | 14,000 | 15,700 | 16,500 | 17,500 | 18,000 | 17,500 | 18,000 | 18,000 |

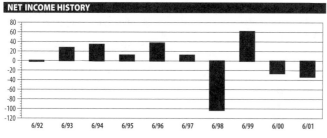

**NET INCOME HISTORY**

**2001 FISCAL YEAR-END**
Debt ratio: 49.4%
Return on equity: —
Cash ($ mil.): 11
Current ratio: 1.44
Long-term debt ($ mil.): 266

# GOLDEN STATE FOODS

Some companies have arch-enemies. Food processor and distributor Golden State Foods has an arch-friend: McDonald's. The fast-food giant with the golden arches is Golden State Foods' only customer. Headquartered in Irvine, California, the company is McDonald's chief supplier of food, providing more than 10,000 individual restaurants worldwide. Its more than 130 products include beef patties, the Big Mac sauce (which the company created), ketchup, mayonnaise, and salad dressing. Golden State Foods operates 12 production plants and distribution centers in Australia, Egypt, Mexico, and the US.

McDonald's and its suppliers have established a symbiotic relationship. Golden State Foods adheres to McDonald's standards and gears its operations toward furthering the restaurant chain's interests. The company serves McDonald's without the benefit of a long-term, written contract, but McDonald's is known for its loyalty to its suppliers.

Investment firm Yucaipa owns a majority of Golden State, and management company Wetterau Associates owns most of the remainder. Both of the firms bought Golden State in 1998 from its management, which kept a small stake in the company.

## HISTORY

In 1947 William Moore founded Golden State Meat, a small meat-supply business that served restaurants and hotels in the Los Angeles area. In 1954 he added several new clients to his business — franchisees of a new chain of hamburger stands called McDonald's that was founded in San Bernardino, California in 1948. In 1961 Ray Kroc, a franchisee from Illinois, bought out the founding McDonald brothers, and the next year he moved to California to oversee a massive expansion in that state.

Moore and Kroc met, were mutually impressed, and became friends. Moore at first tried to get Kroc to buy him out, but Kroc's view of McDonald's did not include micro-managing its supply operations. He wanted to find suppliers the company could trust, and preferred smaller ones that weren't intent on breaking into the retail market. Golden State's relationship with McDonald's was sealed by a handshake between Kroc and Moore.

Moore and a partner bought a McDonald's franchise in 1965; two years later they had five. When Moore's partner died, McDonald's bought the units back for stock, which Moore later sold, using the proceeds to finance a new meat processing plant and warehouse. In 1969 Golden State Meat incorporated as Golden State Foods.

In 1972, after the new facilities were completed, Moore introduced the idea of total distribution. In addition to processing and distributing meat (by now delivered as frozen patties rather than fresh meat, which had limited delivery ranges in the 1950s and 1960s), Moore began supplying most of the needs of the McDonald's stores, making and delivering ketchup, mayonnaise, packaging, and syrup base for soft drinks. This allowed clients to

reduce the number of weekly deliveries they received from as many as 30 to about three. The company went public in 1972, and two years later it dropped all of its other clients to cater exclusively to McDonald's.

Golden State grew in the 1970s, supplying a large share of the millions of McDonald's hamburgers sold every day. Moore died in 1978. Soon thereafter, a group of executives led by newly appointed CEO James Williams began exploring the possibility of taking the company private. In 1980, with backing from Butler Capital, they paid $29 million for the company, which then had sales of $330 million.

During the next decade Golden State expanded its relationship with McDonald's (and with the buying co-ops that supply stores operated by franchisees), opening facilities in other parts of the country. In 1990 the owners of Golden State tried to cash out by putting the company up for sale, but they withdrew it from the market within two years.

Golden State moved its headquarters from Pasadena to Irvine in 1992. In 1996 the company opened a distribution center in Portland, Oregon, and international expansion followed.

Yucaipa and Wetterau Associates, whose management hails from a major midwestern food wholesaler that was sold to SUPERVALU in 1992, bought Golden State in 1998 for about $400 million. The purchase represented Yucaipa's first significant acquisition outside the supermarket arena.

James Williams, who had been with Golden State Foods for 38 years and served as its CEO for more than two decades, resigned in 1999. He was replaced by Mark Wetterau.

**Chairman and CEO:** Mark S. Wetterau
**Vice Chairman and President-International:**
  Richard W. Gochnauer
**President-Liquid Products Group:** Frank Listi
**President-Meat Group:** David Gilbert
**SEVP:** Gene L. Olson
**EVP and CFO:** Mike Waitukaitis

## LOCATIONS

**HQ:** 18301 Von Karman Ave., Ste. 1100,
  Irvine, CA 92612
**Phone:** 949-252-2000    **Fax:** 949-252-2088
**Web:** www.goldenstatefoods.com

Golden State Foods has distribution and processing
facilities in Arizona, California, Georgia, Hawaii, New
York, North Carolina, Oregon, South Carolina, Virginia,
and Washington as well as Australia, Egypt, and Mexico.

## PRODUCTS/OPERATIONS

**Selected Products**
Beef patties
Buns
Ketchup
Jelly
Lettuce
Mayonnaise
Onions
Salad dressing
Sundae toppings

## COMPETITORS

Alliant Exchange
Foodbrands America
International Multifoods
JR Simplot
Keystone Foods
Martin-Brower
MBM
McLane Foodservice
PYA/Monarch
Reyes Holdings
Services Group
Shamrock Foods
SYSCO
U.S. Foodservice

## HISTORICAL FINANCIALS & EMPLOYEES

| Private<br>FYE: December 31 | Annual<br>Growth | 12/91 | 12/92 | 12/93 | 12/94 | 12/95 | 12/96 | 12/97 | 12/98 | 12/99 | 12/00 |
|---|---|---|---|---|---|---|---|---|---|---|---|
| Estimated sales ($ mil.) | 6.9% | — | 1,032 | 1,160 | 1,260 | 1,340 | 1,450 | 1,500 | 1,600 | 1,750 | 1,764 |
| Employees | 2.1% | — | 1,700 | 1,700 | 1,700 | 1,700 | 2,000 | 2,000 | 1,800 | 2,000 | 2,000 |

**SALES HISTORY**

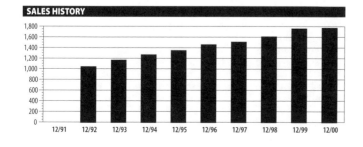

# GOYA FOODS, INC.

## OVERVIEW

Called *frijoles* or *hibicuelas*, beans are beans, and Goya's got 'em. Based in Secaucus, New Jersey, family-owned and -operated Goya Foods produces about 1,000 grocery items commonly found in Hispanic and Caribbean cuisine, including a variety of canned and dried beans, canned meats, olives, rice, seasonings, plantain and yuca chips, and frozen microwaveable entrees. Goya sells more than 20 different rice products and 30 types of beans and peas. Brands include Goya and Kirby. It also sells beverages such as tropical fruit nectars and juices, tropical sodas, a malt drink, and coffee.

Goya has historically served the Hispanic communities in the Northeast and Florida with mostly Cuban, Dominican, and Puerto Rican customers. The company now has products geared toward the tastes of Hispanics in California and the Southwest with roots in Mexico and Central and South America. Additionally, a growing interest in ethnic foods among non-Hispanics is strengthening Goya's sales. Yet it faces competition from food giants such as Kraft Foods, which are releasing lines of Hispanic specialty products. It's also challenged by food manufacturers from Mexico who are turning north to tap the deeper pocketbooks of US consumers.

The company is owned and operated by the Unanue family. President and CEO Joseph Unanue is a son of the founder; six third-generation members of the Unanue family work at the company. Goya is one of the largest Hispanic-owned food companies in the US.

## HISTORY

Immigrants from Spain by way of Puerto Rico, husband and wife Prudencio Unanue and Carolina Casal founded Unanue & Sons in New York City in 1936. The couple imported sardines, olives, and olive oil from Spain, but when the Spanish Civil War (1936-1939) interrupted supply lines, they began importing from Morocco.

In 1949 the company established a cannery in Puerto Rico; the Puerto Rican imports were distributed to a local market of immigrants from the West Indies. Each of the couple's four sons eventually joined the family business, and in 1958 the firm relocated to Brooklyn. The company took its current name, Goya Foods, in 1962 when the family bought the Goya name — originally a brand of sardines — for $1.

The oldest Unanue son, CEO Charles, was fired from Goya in 1969 — and subsequently cut out of Prudencio's will — when he spoke out about an alleged tax evasion scheme. (Legal wrangling between Charles and the rest of the family continued into the late 1990s.) Goya moved to its present New Jersey headquarters in 1974.

Another son, Anthony, died in 1976, as did Prudencio. That year Joseph, another sibling, was named president and CEO. Along with his brother Frank, president of Goya Foods de Puerto Rico, he began a cautious expansion campaign by adding traditional products to the company's existing line of Latin Caribbean and Spanish favorites.

Buoyed by the growing popularity of Mexican food, in 1982 Goya began distributing its products in Texas, targeting the region's sizable Mexican and Central American population. At first, the move proved a disaster. Goya's products were not suited to the Mexican palate, which generally preferred spicier flavors. Likewise, a similar strategy to capture a portion of Florida's huge Cuban market share initially met with only moderate success, but Goya persevered, eventually turning the tables in its favor.

During the 1980s the company also attempted to woo the non-Hispanic market. While Goya's cream of coconut — a key ingredient in pina coladas — found a broader market, its ad campaign featuring obscure actress Zohra Lampert did little to attract a large following of non-Hispanic customers.

Success in that market came in the 1990s. America's interest in the reportedly healthier "Mediterranean diet" boosted sales of Goya's extra virgin olive oil. Recommendations for low-fat, high-fiber diets prompted the company's launch of the "For Better Meals, Turn to Goya" advertising campaign — its first in English — in 1992.

In 1996 Goya sponsored an exhibition of the works of the Spanish master Goya at the New York Metropolitan Museum of Art. Continuing its efforts to reach out to non-Hispanics and English-dominant Hispanics, in 1997 the company began including both English and Spanish on the front of its packaging.

To lure more snackers, the next year Goya added yuca (AKA cassava) chips to its line. In 1999 Goya began packaging its frozen entrees in microwaveable trays. The following year the company announced plans to expand its plants in the Caribbean. In 2001 it bought a new factory in Spain.

**President and CEO:** Joseph A. Unanue
**COO:** Andy Unanue
**VP of Marketing:** Conrad O. Colon
**VP of Computer Information Services:** David Kinkela
**VP of Purchasing:** Joseph Perez
**President, Goya Foods de Puerto Rico:**
  Francisco J. Unanue
**Director of Finance:** Miguel Lugo
**Director of Human Resources:** Ernie Moreno
**Director of Marketing:** Esperanza Carrion
**Director of Public Relations:** Rafael Toro
**Controller:** Tony Diaz
**General Counsel:** Carlos Ortiz
**Assistant Public Relations:** Evanessa Mangual

# LOCATIONS

**HQ:** 100 Seaview Dr., Secaucus, NJ 07096
**Phone:** 201-348-4900    **Fax:** 201-348-6609
**Web:** www.goyafoods.com

Goya Foods has operations in the Dominican Republic, Puerto Rico, Spain, and the US.

# PRODUCTS/OPERATIONS

## Selected Products

**Beverages**
Café Goya
Coconut Water
Malta (malt beverage)
Nectars and juices
Tropical sodas

**Foods and Other Products**
Beans (black-eyed peas, chick peas, lentils, refried)
Bouillon
Cooking sauces
Cooking wine
Cornmeal
Devotional candles
Flour
Frozen foods
Marinades
Meat (chorizo, corned beef, potted, vienna sausage)
Olive oil
Olives
Pasta
Plantain chips
Rice
Seafood
Seasonings
Spices
Yuca chips

# COMPETITORS

| | |
|---|---|
| American Rice | Kraft Foods |
| Authentic Specialty Foods | McCormick |
| Bimbo | Nestlé |
| Chiquita Brands | Pinnacle Foods |
| ConAgra | Corporation |
| Del Monte Foods | Pro-Fac |
| Dole | Riceland Foods |
| Frito-Lay | Riviana Foods |
| Herdez | Seneca Foods |
| Hormel | Unilever |

# HISTORICAL FINANCIALS & EMPLOYEES

| Private FYE: May 31 | Annual Growth | 5/92 | 5/93 | 5/94 | 5/95 | 5/96 | 5/97 | 5/98 | 5/99 | 5/00 | 5/01 |
|---|---|---|---|---|---|---|---|---|---|---|---|
| Sales ($ mil.) | 8.2% | 410 | 453 | 480 | 528 | 560 | 600 | 620 | 653 | 770 | 835 |
| Employees | 5.8% | 1,500 | 1,800 | 2,000 | 2,000 | 2,200 | 3,000 | 3,000 | 2,200 | 2,500 | 2,500 |

## SALES HISTORY

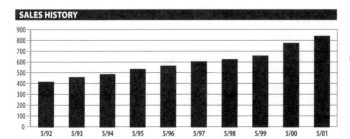

GOYA. FOODS, INC.

# GRANT THORNTON INTERNATIONAL

## OVERVIEW

Grant Thornton International — it's everywhere your business ought to be. The Chicago-based international umbrella organization offers accounting and management consulting through more than 600 offices in 100 countries. Member firms elect representatives to an international policy board that runs the day-to-day operations of the accounting company. The firm is near the top of the so-called "second tier," the companies beneath accounting's Big Five: Andersen (formerly Andersen Worldwide), PricewaterhouseCoopers, KPMG International, Ernst & Young International, and Deloitte Touche Tohmatsu.

Big Five consolidation prompted Grant Thornton International and other second-tier firms to enter such niche areas as information technology and corporate finance. And while the Big Five focus on large corporations, Grant Thornton locks in on midsized companies, helping them with accounting, audit, and tax issues, as well as growth strategies. It is facing new competitors for its target market, with such firms as H&R Block and American Express adding accounting, tax planning, and consulting services.

Despite the difficulties caused by regulatory and cultural differences, accounting firms around the world are attempting to establish global standard practices. On a smaller scale, Grant Thornton's member firms are working to increase cross-border cooperation by pooling resources and cutting costs.

## HISTORY

Cameron, Missouri, accountant Alexander Grant founded Alexander Grant & Co. in 1924 with William O'Brien. They built their firm in Chicago and concentrated on providing services to midwestern clients.

In the 1950s and 1960s, the firm began expanding both domestically and internationally. Alexander Grant & Co. continued to focus on manufacturing and distribution companies.

In 1973 O'Brien died. In 1979 the company began publishing its well-known (and sometimes controversial) index of state business climates. An attempt to merge with fellow second-tier accounting firm Laventhol & Horwath failed that year. The next year Grant Thornton International was formed when Alexander Grant & Co. and its British affiliate, Thornton Baker, combined their offices around the world to form a network. The UK and US branches, however, kept their respective names.

The 1980s brought turmoil and change for the company. Financial scandals led investors and the government to hold accounting firms liable for their audits. Along with the (then) Big Six, Alexander Grant & Co. was hit with several lawsuits alleging fraud and cover-ups. One case marred the firm's squeaky-clean image and caused dozens of clients to jump ship: Just days after Alexander Grant issued it a clean audit, a Florida trading firm was shut down by the SEC. Jilted investors sued to reclaim lost money; Alexander Grant settled for $160 million. Chairman Herbert Dooskin and other leaders also left the company; although they denied it was because of the scandal, their departures left Alexander Grant rudderless during a critical time.

Meanwhile, the company merged with Fox & Co. to create the US's #9 accounting firm. With scandal-scared partners leaving (and taking clients), Fox looked to the merger to shore up its reputation. But Alexander Grant's auditing troubles led some Fox partners and clients to flee from the merged company.

After the fallout from the lawsuits and the merger, the company began rebuilding, taking on new clients, reclaiming lost ones, and refocusing on midsized companies. In 1986 both Alexander Grant & Co. and Thornton Baker took the Grant Thornton name.

The early 1990s recession reduced accounting revenues but increased demand for management consulting. As political and economic barriers fell during the decade, Grant Thornton International grew. The firm entered emerging markets in Africa, Asia, Europe, and Latin America. In 1998 the Big Six became the Big Five; Grant Thornton added refugee firms and partners to its global network. In 1999 the firm's US branch entertained merger offers from H&R Block and PricewaterhouseCoopers, but instead announced plans to reposition itself as a corporate services firm to better compete.

In 2000 the company pulled out of its advisory position to companies involved in controversial diamond mining in war-torn portions of Africa. It also agreed to merge its UK operations with those of HLB Kidsons; the merged firm will retain the Grant Thornton name.

The following year, after disagreements about strategy, US CEO Dom Esposito resigned. UK partner David McDonnell was named the Global CEO.

**Global CEO, Chairman, International Policy Board, and Divisional Director, Europe, Middle East, and Africa:** David C. McDonnell
**Executive Partner; CEO, Grant Thornton LLP:** Edward E. Nusbaum, age 46
**Managing Director:** Robert A. Kleckner
**Treasurer and Director of Administration:** Louis A. Fanchi
**Divisional Director, Latin America and Caribbean:** Shelley Stein
**Divisional Director, Asia Pacific:** Gabriel Azedo
**Divisional Director, North America:** David Hope
**National Director, Human Resources, Grant Thornton LLP:** Debbie Pastor

## LOCATIONS

**HQ:** 1 Prudential Plaza, Ste. 800, 130 E. Randolph Dr., Chicago, IL 60601
**Phone:** 312-856-0001     **Fax:** 312-616-7142
**Web:** www.gti.org

Grant Thornton International has offices in 100 countries in Africa, Asia, Europe, North America, and South America.

## PRODUCTS/OPERATIONS

**Selected Services**
Assurance
Corporate Finance
Family Businesses
International Tax

## COMPETITORS

American Express
American Management
Andersen
Arthur D. Little
Bain & Company
BDO International
Booz-Allen
Boston Consulting
Centerprise Advisors
Deloitte Touche Tohmatsu
Ernst & Young
H&R Block
IBM
KPMG
McGladrey & Pullen
McKinsey & Company
PricewaterhouseCoopers

## HISTORICAL FINANCIALS & EMPLOYEES

| Partnership<br>FYE: December 31 | Annual<br>Growth | 12/91 | 12/92 | 12/93 | 12/94 | 12/95 | 12/96 | 12/97 | 12/98 | 12/99 | 12/00 |
|---|---|---|---|---|---|---|---|---|---|---|---|
| Sales ($ mil.) | 7.1% | — | — | — | — | — | 1,285 | 1,405 | 1,600 | 1,800 | 1,690 |
| Employees | 2.6% | — | — | — | — | — | 18,300 | 18,562 | 20,160 | 20,000 | 20,300 |

### SALES HISTORY

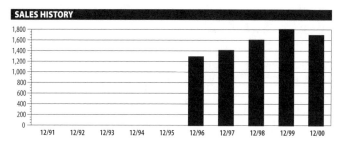

# GRAYBAR ELECTRIC COMPANY, INC.

## OVERVIEW

Graybar Electric Company raises the bar for other distributors. Supplying nearly one million items from thousands of manufacturers, the Clayton, Missouri-based company is a top distributor of electrical and communications products. Graybar Electric also provides equipment leasing and financing through subsidiary Graybar Financial Services.

The construction industry has been the company's traditional market, but rapid changes in telecommunications have prompted it to solidify relationships with major vendors such as Lucent and GE. Customers include electrical contractors, industrial plants, power utilities, and telecommunications providers.

To help bring supply, distribution, and inventory costs down, the company uses electronic data interchange and supplier-assisted inventory management, and urges its suppliers to include bar codes on all products. Graybar Electric has grown by targeting both national and international accounts.

The *FORTUNE* 500 company is owned by its more than 10,000 employees.

## HISTORY

After serving as a telegrapher during the Civil War, Enos Barton borrowed $400 from his widowed mother in 1869 and started an electrical equipment shop in Cleveland with George Shawk. Later that year Elisha Gray, a professor of physics at Oberlin College who had several inventions (including a printing telegraph) to his credit, bought Shawk's interest in the shop. The firm moved to Chicago, where a third partner joined.

The company incorporated as the Western Electric Manufacturing Co. in 1872, with two-thirds of the company's stock held by two Western Union executives. As the telegraph industry took off, the enterprise grew rapidly, providing equipment to towns and railroads in the western US.

Gray and his company missed receiving credit for inventing the telephone in 1875 when Gray's patent application for a "harmonic telegraph" reached the US Patent Office a few hours after Bell's application for his telephone. However, the telephone and the invention of the lightbulb in 1879 opened new doors for Western Electric. The company began to grow into a major corporation, selling and distributing a variety of electrical equipment, including batteries, telegraph keys, and fire-alarm boxes. By 1900 the firm was the world's #1 maker of telephone equipment.

Western Electric formed a new distribution business in 1926, Graybar Electric Co. (from "Gray" and "Barton"), the world's largest electrical supply merchandiser. In 1929 employees bought the company from Western Electric for $3 million in cash and $6 million in preferred stock. During the 1930s it marketed a line of appliances and sewing machines under the Graybar name.

In 1941 the company bought the outstanding shares of stock from Western Electric for $1 million. Graybar Electric was a vital link between manufacturers and US defense needs during WWII. Its men and equipment wired the Panama Canal with telephone cable; it also helped the US military during the Korean and Vietnam Wars.

By 1980 Graybar Electric had reached nearly $1.5 billion in sales. Business was hurt when construction slowed in the late 1980s and the early 1990s, and the company reorganized in 1991, closing regional offices and cutting jobs. Rebounding in 1992 as the US economy improved, Graybar acquired New Jersey-based Square Electric Co.

The company acquired a minority interest in R.E.D. Electronics, a Canadian data communications and computer networking company, and in 1994 realigned its operations into two business segments: electrical products and communications and data products.

The following year Graybar Electric formed the Solutions Providers Alliance with wholesale distributors Kaman Industrial Technologies, VWR Scientific Products, and Vallen Corporation. The national and international network provides products and services to the companies' maintenance, repair, and operations customers. In 1996 AT&T's Global Procurement Group named the company as one of only three suppliers for its electrical products.

Graybar Electric opened a subsidiary in Chile and formed a joint venture, Graybar Financial Services, with Newcourt Financial (formerly AT&T Capital) in 1998. The next year Graybar Electric bought the Connecticut-based electrical wholesaler Frank A. Blesso, and it expanded its distribution partnership with wire and cable manufacturer, Belden Electronics, in 2000.

In 2001 Graybar opened a new distribution location in northeastern Pennsylvania.

**President and CEO:** Robert A. Reynolds
**VP and Treasurer:** John W. Wolf
**VP, Human Resources:** Jack F. Van Pelt

## LOCATIONS

**HQ:** 34 N. Meramec Ave., Clayton, MO 63105
**Phone:** 314-512-9200    **Fax:** 314-512-9453
**Web:** www.graybar.com

Graybar Electric Company has nearly 300 offices and distribution facilities in Canada, Mexico, Puerto Rico, Singapore, and the US.

## PRODUCTS/OPERATIONS

**Selected Products and Services**
Ballasts
Batteries
Cable
Conduit
Connectors
Emergency lighting
Fiber-optic cable
Fittings
Fluorescent lighting
Fuses
Hand tools
Hangers/fasteners
Heating and ventilating equipment
Industrial fans
Lighting
Lubricants
Paints
Smoke detectors
Testing and measuring instruments
Timers
Transfer switches
Transformers
Utility products
Wire

## COMPETITORS

| | |
|---|---|
| Anixter International | Molex |
| Arrow Electronics | Pioneer-Standard |
| Avnet | Electronics |
| Consolidated Electrical | Premier Farnell |
| Cooper Industries | Rexel |
| Eaton | Siemens |
| Emerson | SPX |
| Framatome | Tech Data |
| GE | Tyco International |
| Hagemeyer | WESCO International |
| Matsushita | W.W. Grainger |

## HISTORICAL FINANCIALS & EMPLOYEES

| Private<br>FYE: December 31 | Annual<br>Growth | 12/91 | 12/92 | 12/93 | 12/94 | 12/95 | 12/96 | 12/97 | 12/98 | 12/99 | 12/00 |
|---|---|---|---|---|---|---|---|---|---|---|---|
| Sales ($ mil.) | 13.5% | — | 1,894 | 2,033 | 2,356 | 2,765 | 2,991 | 3,338 | 3,744 | 4,300 | 5,227 |
| Net income ($ mil.) | 26.3% | — | 10 | 15 | 19 | 37 | 45 | 53 | 60 | 65 | 66 |
| Income as % of sales | — | — | 0.5% | 0.7% | 0.8% | 1.3% | 1.5% | 1.6% | 1.6% | 1.5% | 1.3% |
| Employees | 10.6% | — | 4,700 | 5,100 | 5,500 | 6,200 | 6,600 | 7,200 | 7,900 | 8,900 | 10,500 |

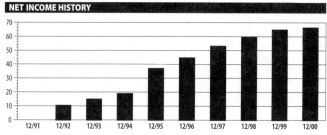

**NET INCOME HISTORY**

**2000 FISCAL YEAR-END**
Debt ratio: 36.8%
Return on equity: 17.2%
Cash ($ mil.): 28
Current ratio: 1.40
Long-term debt ($ mil.): 238

# THE GREEN BAY PACKERS, INC.

## OVERVIEW

Football fans in Green Bay, Wisconsin, bleed green and gold as they chant their mantra, "The Pack is Back." The Green Bay Packers football franchise is among the most storied in the National Football League, winning 12 championship titles, including three Super Bowl victories, since its beginnings in 1919. Icons such as Bart Starr, Ray Nitschke, and legendary coach Vince Lombardi have battled on the frozen tundra at Lambeau Field, where games have been sold out since 1960. (The team's waiting list for season tickets boasts more than 56,000 names.)

In addition to its history, Green Bay is also unique in that it is the only community-owned, not-for-profit franchise in the NFL. It has more than 110,000 shareholders who all have voting rights (a stock split in 1997 gave

1,940 holders most of the voting power), though the stock doesn't increase in value nor pay dividends and can only be sold back to the team. No individual is allowed to own more than 200,000 shares.

After a couple of poor seasons, both athletically and financially, the Packers organization has high hopes for the future. Green Bay voters approved public financing for a $295 million renovation of historic Lambeau Field (which the city owns) in 2000. The project (scheduled to be completed by 2003) will add 10,000 seats to the stadium, which is one of the smallest in the NFL, as well as additional luxury seats. The team is also optimistic about its young head coach Mike Sherman (who was named general manager in 2001) and a group of up-and-coming young players.

## HISTORY

In 1919 Earl "Curly" Lambeau helped organize a professional football team in Green Bay, Wisconsin, with the help of George Calhoun, the sports editor of the *Green Bay Press-Gazette*. At 20 years old, Lambeau was elected team captain and convinced the Indian Packing Company to back the team, giving the squad its original name, the Indians. The local paper, however, nicknamed the team the Packers and the name stuck. Playing on an open field at Hagemeister Park, the team collected fees by passing the hat among the fans. In 1921 the team was admitted into the American Professional Football Association (later called the National Football League), which had been organized the year before.

The Packers went bankrupt after a poor showing its first season in the league, and Lambeau and Calhoun bought the team for $250. With debts continuing to mount, *Press-Gazette* general manager Andrew Turnbull helped reorganize the team as the not-for-profit Green Bay Football Corporation and sold stock at $5 a share. Despite winning three straight championships from 1929-31, the team again teetered on the brink of bankruptcy, forcing another stock sale in 1935. With fortunes dwindling on and off the field, Lambeau retired in 1950. A third stock sale was called for that year, raising $118,000. City Stadium (renamed Lambeau Field in 1965) was opened in 1957. In 1959 the team hired New York Giants assistant Vince Lombardi as head coach.

Under Lombardi, the Packers dominated football in the 1960s, winning five NFL titles.

With players such as Bart Starr and Ray Nitschke, the team defeated the Kansas City Chiefs in the first Super Bowl after the 1966 season. Lombardi resigned after winning Super Bowl II (he passed away in 1970), and the team again fell into mediocrity. Former MVP Starr was called upon to coach in 1974 but couldn't turn the tide before he was released in 1983.

Bob Harlan, who had joined the Packers as assistant general manager in 1971, became president and CEO in 1989. He hired Ron Wolf as general manager in 1991, who in turn hired Mike Holmgren as head coach early the next year. With a roster including Brett Favre, Reggie White, and Robert Brooks, the Packers posted six straight playoff appearances and won its third Super Bowl in 1997. A fourth stock sale (preceded by a 1,000:1 stock split) netted the team more than $24 million.

After Holmgren resigned in 1999 (he left to coach the Seattle Seahawks), former Philadelphia Eagles coach Ray Rhodes tried to lead the team, but lasted only one dismal season. In 2000 Mike Sherman, a former Holmgren assistant, was named the team's 13th head coach. Prompted by falling revenue, the team announced plans to renovate Lambeau Field, and voters in Brown County later approved a sales tax increase to help finance the $295 million project. In 2001 Wolf retired and coach Sherman was tapped as general manager. That year the team signed quarterback Favre to a 10-year, $100 million contract extension.

**President, CEO, and Director:** Robert E. Harlan, age 64
**EVP and COO:** John M. Jones, age 49
**EVP, General Manager, and Head Coach:**
  Michael F. Sherman, age 46
**VP and Director:** John J. Fabry
**VP Football Operations:** Mark Hatley, age 51
**VP Player Finance and General Counsel:**
  Andrew Brandt, age 41
**Secretary:** Peter M. Platten III
**Treasurer and Director:** John R. Underwood
**Executive Committee Member and Director:**
  Donald F. Harden
**Executive Committee Member and Director:**
  Donald J. Schneider
**Executive Committee Member and Director:**
  James A. Temp
**Executive Director of Public Relations:** Lee Remmel,
  age 77
**Director of Administrative Affairs:** Mark Schiefelbein
**Director of Community Relations:** Jeanne McKenna
**Director of Computer Services:** Wayne Wichlacz
**Director of Finance, Compliance, and Benefits:**
  Vicki Vannieuwenhoven
**Director of Marketing:** Jeff Cieply
**Director of Premium Guest Services:** Jennifer Ark
**Director of Pro Personnel:** Reggie McKenzie, age 38
**Director of Tickets:** Mark Wagner
**Auditors:** Wipfli Ullrich Bertelson LLP

## LOCATIONS

**HQ:** 1265 Lombardi Ave., Green Bay, WI 54307
**Phone:** 920-496-5700      **Fax:** 920-496-5712
**Web:** www.packers.com

The Green Bay Packers play at Lambeau Field in Green
Bay, Wisconsin. The team holds its training camp at St.
Norbert College in De Pere, Wisconsin.

## PRODUCTS/OPERATIONS

**2001 Sales**

|  | $ mil. | % of total |
|---|---|---|
| Tickets & media | | |
| TV & radio | 67 | 57 |
| Home game tickets | 17 | 14 |
| Road game tickets | 9 | 9 |
| Marketing & pro shop | 9 | 7 |
| Private box fees | 6 | 5 |
| NFL Properties | 4 | 3 |
| Other | 6 | 5 |
| **Total** | **118** | **100** |

**Championship Titles**
Super Bowl I (1967)
Super Bowl II (1968)
Super Bowl XXXI (1997)
NFC Championships (1996-97)
NFC Central Division (1972, 1995-97)
NFL Championships (1929-31, 1936, 1939, 1944, 1961-
  62, 1965-67)
NFL Western Conference (1936, 1938-39, 1944, 1960-62,
  1965-67)

## COMPETITORS

Chicago Bears
Detroit Lions
Minnesota Vikings
Tampa Bay Buccaneers

## HISTORICAL FINANCIALS & EMPLOYEES

| Not-for-profit<br>FYE: March 31 | Annual<br>Growth | 3/92 | 3/93 | 3/94 | 3/95 | 3/96 | 3/97 | 3/98 | 3/99 | 3/00 | 3/01 |
|---|---|---|---|---|---|---|---|---|---|---|---|
| Sales ($ mil.) | 11.4% | 45 | 54 | 66 | 62 | 70 | 75 | 82 | 103 | 109 | 118 |
| Net income ($ mil.) | (3.6%) | — | — | — | — | — | — | 6 | 6 | 3 | 6 |
| Income as % of sales | — | — | — | — | — | — | — | 7.7% | 6.3% | 2.5% | 4.8% |
| Employees | 9.5% | 62 | 72 | 74 | 80 | 82 | 90 | 92 | 95 | 95 | 140 |

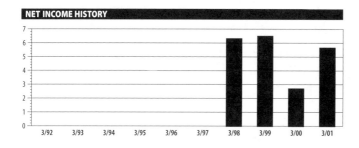

NET INCOME HISTORY

# GUARDIAN INDUSTRIES CORP.

## OVERVIEW

You won't catch Guardian Industries off guard against the fast break — or any other kind of break. Auburn Hills, Michigan-based Guardian is one of the world's leading glassmakers. Guardian primarily manufactures float glass and fabricated glass products for the automotive and construction markets. It also makes architectural glass, fiberglass insulation (Ace, Georgia-Pacific, and True Value brands), and automotive trim parts. Through its Guardian Building Products Group, the company operates Guardian Fiberglass, Builder Marts of America

(BMA, 20%-owned by Ace Hardware), and Cameron Ashley Building Products.

Guardian has been expanding primarily through international acquisitions and by increasing its already significant position in the building materials business. President and CEO William Davidson took Guardian Industries public in 1968 and then bought it back for himself in 1985. A billionaire, Davidson also acts as the managing partner of the Detroit Pistons NBA team.

## HISTORY

Guardian Glass began as a small maker of car windshields in Detroit in 1932 during the Great Depression. The company spent the 1930s and 1940s building its business to gain a foothold in glassmaking, historically one of the world's most monopolized industries. In 1949 PPG Industries and Libbey-Owens-Ford (now owned by the UK's Pilkington) agreed to stop their alleged monopolistic activity. William Davidson took over Guardian Glass from his uncle in 1957. As president, he tried to boost the enterprise's standing in the windshield niche, but PPG and Libbey-Owens-Ford refused to sell him raw glass. That year Guardian Glass filed for bankruptcy to reorganize.

The company emerged from bankruptcy in 1960 (the same year Pilkington developed the float process for glassmaking), and in 1965 it was hit with its first patent-infringement lawsuit. Three years later the company went public, changed its name to Guardian Industries, and was refused a license to use Pilkington's float technology. Guardian began an aggressive acquisition strategy in 1969, and in 1970 it hired Ford's top glass man (who knew the float process) and proceeded to build its first float-glass plant in Michigan. PPG sued Guardian in 1972. Davidson bought the Detroit Pistons in 1974. He applied a do-or-die style that might best be illustrated by the 1979 firing of Piston's coach Dick Vitale, who claims Davidson axed him on his own front doorstep while a curbside limo waited with the motor running.

In 1980 Guardian started making fiberglass and began hiring former workers from insulation maker Manville to duplicate that company's patented technology for fiberglass insulation. Manville successfully sued Guardian in 1981. Guardian opened a Luxembourg plant that year. Pilkington sued Guardian in 1983, but the case was settled out of court three years later. Davidson took Guardian private in 1985,

and in 1988 he bought an Indiana auto trim plant. He also built The Palace of Auburn Hills sports arena in 1988.

The 1990s brought more international expansion for Guardian, which added plants in India, Spain, and Venezuela. It also set up a distribution center in Japan, a country known for its tight control of the glass industry. In 1992 Guardian bought OIS Optical Imaging Systems, a maker of computer display screens. Guardian moved its headquarters to Auburn Hills, Michigan, in 1995. Its purchase of Automotive Moulding the next year boosted its position in the auto plastics and trim market. In 1997 some 30 class-action lawsuits that alleged price-fixing were filed against the top five US glassmakers, including Guardian. The US Justice Department began investigating the matter.

Guardian booted its OIS Optical Imaging Systems unit in 1998, citing ongoing losses. The fiberglass subsidiary bought 50% of Builder Marts of America, ushering Guardian into the market for lumber and roofing products. That year Davidson made a failed attempt to buy the Tampa Bay Lightning hockey team.

In 1999 Guardian bought Siam Guardian Glass Ltd. from Siam Cement Plc, the company's partner in Thailand. The next year Guardian acquired Cameron Ashley Building Products, a distributor with more than 160 branches in the US and Canada. Cameron Ashley distributes pool and patio enclosures, roofing, siding, insulation, industrial metals, and millwork materials to independent building materials dealers, builders, large contractors, and mass retailers.

**President and CEO:** William M. Davidson, age 78
**Group VP, Finance and CFO:** Jeffrey A. Knight
**VP, Human Resources:** Bruce Cummings
**VP and Chief Accounting Officer:** Donald Trofholz
**Treasurer:** Ann Waichunas
**Director of Communications:** Gayle Joseph

## LOCATIONS

**HQ:** 2300 Harmon Rd., Auburn Hills, MI 48326
**Phone:** 248-340-1800     **Fax:** 248-340-9988
**Web:** www.guardian.com

Guardian Industries operates worldwide manufacturing and distribution facilities.

## PRODUCTS/OPERATIONS

**Selected Products and Services**

**Architectural Glass**
Custom fabrication
Float glass
Insulating glass
Laminated glass
Mirrors
Patterned glass
Reflective coated glass
Tempered glass

**Automotive Systems**
Bodyside (mud flaps, wheel covers)
Front and rear end (grilles, rub strips)
Side window (door-frame moldings)
Windshield (window-surround moldings)

**Cameron Ashley**
Aluminum screen doors
Carports
Ceiling tile
Door frames
Doors
Fiberglass insulation
Formica
Metal roofing
Patio covers
Plywood
Rebar
Sheetrock
Storm doors
Windows

**Guardian Fiberglass**
Fiberglass insulation

**Retail Auto Glass**
Auto glass repair
Auto glass replacement
Insurance claim processing

## COMPETITORS

| | |
|---|---|
| Apogee Enterprises | Owens Corning |
| Asahi Glass | Pilkington |
| Corning | PPG |
| CRH | Safelite Glass |
| Donnelly | Saint-Gobain |
| Johns Manville | Vitro |
| Nippon Sheet Glass | |

## HISTORICAL FINANCIALS & EMPLOYEES

| Private<br>FYE: December 31 | Annual<br>Growth | 12/91 | 12/92 | 12/93 | 12/94 | 12/95 | 12/96 | 12/97 | 12/98 | 12/99 | 12/00 |
|---|---|---|---|---|---|---|---|---|---|---|---|
| Estimated sales ($ mil.) | 16.2% | — | 1,200 | 1,200 | 1,500 | 1,700 | 1,900 | 2,000 | 2,200 | 3,650 | 4,000 |
| Employees | 9.1% | — | 10,000 | 9,000 | 10,000 | 12,000 | 13,000 | 14,000 | 15,000 | 15,000 | 20,000 |

### SALES HISTORY

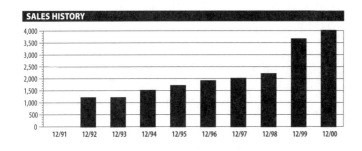

# GUARDIAN LIFE INSURANCE

## OVERVIEW

When your guardian angel fails you, there's Guardian Life Insurance Company of America. The New York City-based mutual company boasts nearly 3 million policy-holding owners.

Guardian offers life insurance, disability income insurance, and — more recently — retirement programs in the US and Puerto Rico. The company has been expanding its traditional employee health indemnity plans to encompass a wider variety of disability, dental, and vision benefits. It is doing this primarily through acquisitions.

In the retirement area, Guardian has long offered the Park Avenue group of mutual funds and annuity products, managed by its Guardian Investor Services. To meet competition in the quickly deregulating financial services area, the company is building its wealth management capabilities to target baby boomers getting ready for retirement. It created broker-dealer Park Avenue Securities and launched Guardian Trust Company to offer trust and investment management services.

As part of these initiatives, Guardian has been on the move to improve customer service and to raise its profile through national advertising. It has also continued acquiring complementary insurers including the acquisition of disability insurance specialist Berkshire Life Insurance.

## HISTORY

Hugo Wesendonck came to the US from Germany in 1850 to escape a death sentence for his part in an abortive 1848 revolution. After working in the silk business in Philadelphia, he moved to New York, which was home to more ethnic Germans than any city outside of Berlin and Vienna.

In 1860 Wesendonck and other expatriates formed an insurance company to serve the German-American community. Germania Life Insurance was chartered as a stock mutual, which paid dividends to shareholders and policy owners. Wesendonck was its first president.

The Civil War blocked the company's growth in the South, but it expanded in the rest of the US; by 1867 it was operating in South America.

After the Civil War, many insurers foundered from high costs. Wesendonck battled this by implementing strict cost controls and limiting commissions, allowing the company to continue issuing dividends and rebates on its policyholders' premiums.

In the 1870s Germania opened offices in Europe, which accounted for much of the company's growth for the next few decades. By 1910, 46% of sales originated in Europe. The company's target clientele in the US decreased between the 1890s and WWI as German immigration slowed, and its market share dropped from ninth in 1880 to 21st in 1910.

During WWI the company lost contact with its German business. Prodded by anti-German sentiment in the US, the company changed its name to The Guardian Life Insurance Company of America in 1917. After WWI the company began winding down its German business (a process that lasted until 1952).

In 1924 Guardian began mutualizing but could not complete the process until 1944 because of probate problems with a shareholder's estate.

After WWII, Guardian offered noncancelable medical insurance (1955) and group insurance (1957). The company formed Guardian Investor Services in 1969 to offer mutual funds; two years later it established Guardian Insurance & Annuity to sell variable contracts. In 1989 it organized Guardian Asset Management to handle pension funds.

In 1993, as indemnity health costs rose, the company moved into managed care via its membership in Private Health Care Systems, a consortium of commercial insurance carriers offering managed health care products and services. This allowed Guardian to offer HMO and PPO products. Guardian entered a joint marketing agreement in 1995 with HMO Physicians Health Services, which contracts with physicians and hospitals in the New York tri-state area. In 1996 the company acquired Managed Dental Care of California and an interest in Physicians Health Services.

Facing deregulation and consolidation in the financial services area, as well as the demutualization of some of its largest competitors, Guardian in the late 1990s decided to add depth to its employee benefits lines and breadth to its wealth management lines.

In 1999 Guardian formed its broker-dealer subsidiary and received a thrift license to facilitate creation of a trust business. Acquisitions included managed dental care companies First Commonwealth and First Choice Dental Network. In 2000 the company moved to boost its disability business with the planned purchase of Berkshire Life Insurance Co.

## OFFICERS

**President, CEO, and Director:** Joseph D. Sargent, age 72
**EVP and COO:** Dennis J. Manning
**EVP and CFO:** Peter L. Hutchings
**EVP and Chief Investment Officer:** Frank J. Jones
**EVP and Director:** Edward K. Kane
**EVP and Chief Actuary:** Armand M. dePalo
**EVP, Equity Products:** Bruce C. Long
**EVP, Group Insurance, Group Pensions, and Corporate Administration:** Gary B. Lenderink
**SVP and Chief Information Officer:** Dennis S. Callahan
**SVP and Corporate Secretary:** Joseph A. Caruso
**SVP, Financial Management and Control:** Stephen A. Scarpati
**SVP, Individual Markets:** Eileen C. McDonnell
**SVP, Human Resources and Administrative Support:** Douglas C. Kramer
**VP and General Counsel:** John Peluso
**Auditors:** PricewaterhouseCoopers LLP

## LOCATIONS

**HQ:** The Guardian Life Insurance Company of America, 7 Hanover Sq., New York, NY 10004
**Phone:** 212-598-8000    **Fax:** 212-919-2170
**Web:** www.glic.com

Guardian Life Insurance Company of America has operations in all 50 states, the District of Columbia, and Puerto Rico.

## PRODUCTS/OPERATIONS

### 2000 Assets

|  | $ mil. | % of total |
|---|---|---|
| Cash & equivalents | 1,261 | 4 |
| Bonds | 11,688 | 36 |
| Stocks | 3,229 | 10 |
| Real estate | 282 | 1 |
| Mortgage loans | 920 | 3 |
| Policy loans | 1,214 | 4 |
| Other investments | 24 | — |
| Assets in separate account | 10,048 | 31 |
| Other assets | 3,693 | 11 |
| **Total** | **32,359** | **100** |

**Selected Services**
Employee benefits
Group pensions and 401(k) products
Individual life and disability income insurance
Investment products (stocks, bonds, mutual funds, and variable annuities & life insurance)

**Subsidiaries**
Berkshire Life Insurance Company of America
First Commonwealth, Inc.
Guardian Asset Management Corporation
Guardian Baillie Gifford, Ltd. (Scotland)
The Guardian Insurance & Annuity Company, Inc.
Guardian Investor Services Corporation
Guardian Reinsurance Services Corporation
The Guardian Trust Company, FSB
Innovative Underwriters, Inc.
Managed Dental Care of California
Managed DentalGuard of Texas
Park Avenue Life Insurance Company
Park Avenue Securities LLC

## COMPETITORS

| | |
|---|---|
| Aetna | MassMutual |
| Allstate | Merrill Lynch |
| American General | MetLife |
| Anthem | New York Life |
| AXA Financial | Northwestern Mutual |
| Charles Schwab | Oxford Health Plans |
| CIGNA | Pacific Mutual |
| Citigroup | Principal Financial |
| CNA Financial | Prudential |
| FMR | UBS PaineWebber |
| GeneralCologne Re | UnitedHealth Group |
| The Hartford | USAA |
| John Hancock Financial Services | WellPoint Health Networks |
| Liberty Mutual | |

## HISTORICAL FINANCIALS & EMPLOYEES

| Mutual company<br>FYE: December 31 | Annual<br>Growth | 12/91 | 12/92 | 12/93 | 12/94 | 12/95 | 12/96 | 12/97 | 12/98 | 12/99 | 12/00 |
|---|---|---|---|---|---|---|---|---|---|---|---|
| Assets ($ mil.) | 15.4% | — | 10,271 | 12,336 | 13,567 | 15,811 | 18,196 | 22,089 | 25,854 | 31,696 | 32,359 |
| Net income ($ mil.) | 19.9% | — | 132 | 249 | 144 | 125 | 173 | 299 | 160 | 325 | 563 |
| Income as % of assets | — | — | 1.3% | 2.0% | 1.1% | 0.8% | 1.0% | 1.4% | 0.6% | 1.0% | 1.7% |
| Employees | (2.8%) | — | 7,502 | 7,126 | 7,602 | 5,322 | 5,155 | 4,800 | — | 5,465 | 6,000 |

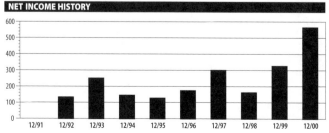

### NET INCOME HISTORY

### 2000 FISCAL YEAR-END

Equity as % of assets: 16.1%
Return on assets: 1.8%
Return on equity: 11.2%
Long-term debt ($ mil.): 0
Sales ($ mil.): 6,569

# HALLMARK CARDS, INC.

Hallmark Cards is the #1 producer of warm fuzzies. The Kansas City, Missouri-based company's greeting cards (sold under brand names such as Hallmark, Shoebox, and Ambassador) are sold in more than 47,000 US retail stores. About 7,500 of these stores bear the Hallmark or Hallmark Gold Crown name (the company owns less than 5% of them, and the rest are franchised). Hallmark markets its products in more than 100 countries.

While Hallmark may be best known for its personal expression products, the company has diversified into a host of other areas. Hallmark owns Binney & Smith, maker of Crayola brand crayons and markers, and mall-based portrait studio chain The Picture People (with nearly 200 studios in the US). The company also produces television movies through Hallmark Entertainment's Crown Media and offers Keepsake brand ornaments. Through its Web site, Hallmark.com, Hallmark offers electronic greeting cards and sells gift items and flowers.

Not resting on well-engraved laurels, Hallmark has announced its intention to triple its revenue by 2010. While it plans to continue expanding its greeting card empire, the company is also intent on stretching its reach in markets such as personal development and family entertainment. Members of the founding Hall family (including chairman Donald Hall) own two-thirds of Hallmark; company employees own the remainder.

Eighteen-year-old Joyce Hall started selling picture postcards from two shoe boxes in his room at the Kansas City, Missouri, YMCA in 1910. His brother Rollie joined him the next year, and the two added greeting cards to their line in 1912. The two opened Hall Brothers, a store that sold postcards, gifts, books, and stationery, but it was destroyed in a 1915 fire. The Halls got a loan, bought an engraving company, and produced their first original cards in time for Christmas.

In 1921 a third brother, William, joined the firm, which started stamping the backs of its cards with the phrase "A Hallmark Card." By 1922 Hall Brothers had salespeople in all 48 states. The firm began selling internationally in 1931.

Hall Brothers patented the "Eye-Vision" display case for greeting cards in 1936 and sold it to retailers across the country. The company aired its first radio ad in 1938. The next year it introduced a friendship card, displaying a cart filled with purple pansies. The card became the company's best-seller. During WWII Joyce Hall persuaded the government not to curtail paper supplies, arguing that his greeting cards were essential to the nation's morale.

The company opened its first retail store in 1950. The following year marked the first production of *Hallmark Hall of Fame,* TV's longest-running dramatic series and winner of more Emmy awards than any other program. Hall Brothers changed its name to Hallmark Cards in 1954 and introduced its Ambassador line of cards five years later.

Hallmark introduced paper party products and started putting *Peanuts* characters on cards in 1960. Donald Hall, Joyce Hall's son, was appointed CEO in 1966. Two years later Hallmark opened Crown Center, which surrounded company headquarters in Kansas City. Disaster struck in 1981 when two walkways collapsed at Crown Center's Hyatt Regency hotel, killing 114 and injuring 225.

Joyce Hall died in 1982, and Donald Hall became both chairman and CEO. Hallmark acquired Crayola crayon maker Binney & Smith in 1984. It introduced Shoebox Greetings, a line of nontraditional cards, in 1986. Irvine Hockaday replaced Donald Hall as CEO the same year (Hall continued as chairman).

The company joined with Information Storage Devices in 1993 to market recordable greeting cards. It unveiled its Web site, Hallmark.com, in 1996 and began offering electronic greeting cards. Hallmark's 1998 acquisition of UK-based Creative Publications boosted the company into the top spot in the British greeting card market. The following year the company acquired portrait studio chain The Picture People and Christian greeting card maker DaySpring Cards. Also in 1999 Hallmark introduced Warm Wishes, a line of 99-cent cards, and it unveiled the Hallmark Home Collection, a line of home furnishings.

The company began testing overnight flower delivery in the US just in time for Valentine's Day 2000. To further its goal of tripling revenues, it reorganized its creative and marketing departments. Hallmark Entertainment subsidiary Crown Media went public in 2000. The company announced that president and CEO Irvine Hockaday would retire at the end of 2001, with vice chairman Donald Hall Jr. taking his place while keeping the VC title. In 2002 Hall took over as CEO.

**Chairman:** Donald J. Hall
**Vice Chairman and CEO:** Donald J. Hall Jr., age 45
**President and CEO, Binney & Smith:** Mark Schwab
**President and CEO, Hallmark Entertainment:**
Robert Halmi Jr., age 44
**SVP Corporate Strategy:** Anil Jagtiani
**SVP Human Resources:** Ralph N. Christensen
**VP Administration and CFO:** Robert J. Druten, age 54
**VP Business Research:** Jay Dittman
**VP Marketing:** John Beeder
**VP Public Affairs and Communications:** Steve Doyal
**VP Marketing:** Greg Field
**Director, Creative Strategy Development:**
Marita Wesely-Clough
**EVP Programming, Crown Media US:** David Kenin,
age 59

## LOCATIONS

**HQ:** 2501 McGee St., Kansas City, MO 64108
**Phone:** 816-274-5111     **Fax:** 816-274-5061
**Web:** www.hallmark.com

Hallmark Cards has operations in Australia, Belgium,
Canada, France, Japan, Mexico, the Netherlands, New
Zealand, Puerto Rico, Spain, the UK, and the US. It
markets its products in more than 100 countries.

## PRODUCTS/OPERATIONS

**Selected Product Lines**
Ambassador (greeting cards)
Hallmark Business Expressions (business greeting cards)
Hallmark en Español (products celebrating Latino
heritage)
Hallmark.com (electronic greeting cards, gifts, flowers)
Keepsake (holiday ornaments and other collectibles)
Mahogany (products celebrating African-American
heritage)
Party Express (party products)
Shoebox (greeting cards)
Tree of Life (products celebrating Jewish heritage)

**Selected Subsidiaries**
Binney & Smith (Crayola brand crayons and markers)
Crown Center Redevelopment (retail complex)
DaySpring (Christian greeting cards)
Hallmark Entertainment (television, movies, and home
video production; majority stake in Crown Media)
Halls Merchandising (department store)
InterArt (Mary Engelbriet and Boyds Bears products)
Irresistible Ink (handwriting service)
Litho-Krome (lithography)
The Picture People (portrait studio chain)
William Arthur (invitations, stationery)

## COMPETITORS

| | |
|---|---|
| 1-800-FLOWERS.COM | Enesco Group |
| American Greetings | Lifetouch |
| Amscan | Olan Mills |
| Andrews McMeel Universal | PCA International |
| AOL Time Warner | SPS Studios |
| Black Dot Group | Syratech |
| Blyth, Inc. | Thomas Nelson |
| CPI Corp. | Viacom |
| CSS Industries | Walt Disney |
| Dixon Ticonderoga | |

## HISTORICAL FINANCIALS & EMPLOYEES

| Private<br>FYE: December 31 | Annual<br>Growth | 12/91 | 12/92 | 12/93 | 12/94 | 12/95 | 12/96 | 12/97 | 12/98 | 12/99 | 12/00 |
|---|---|---|---|---|---|---|---|---|---|---|---|
| Sales ($ mil.) | 3.9% | — | 3,100 | 3,400 | 3,800 | 3,400 | 3,600 | 3,700 | 3,900 | 4,200 | 4,200 |
| Employees | 8.8% | — | 12,487 | 12,600 | 12,800 | 12,100 | 12,600 | 12,554 | 20,945 | 21,000 | 24,500 |

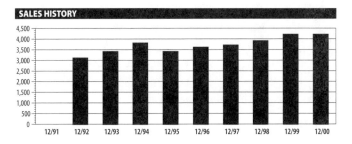

SALES HISTORY

# HARPO, INC.

## OVERVIEW

Everyone knows Oprah Winfrey is an exceptional talk show host, actress, and producer; there's no need to Harpo on it. Winfrey's popular show is just one of the ventures produced by her Chicago-based company, Harpo (Oprah spelled backwards). Her empire is built upon the success of *The Oprah Winfrey Show,* the highest-rated talk show in TV history, which is seen by some 22 million viewers in the US and 112 other countries. Harpo also produces feature films (such as 1998's *Beloved,* which starred Winfrey) and TV movies (*Oprah Winfrey Presents: Tuesdays with Morrie*) and publishes the 2.5 million-circulation *O, The Oprah Magazine* with Hearst.

Worth about $800 million according to *Forbes*, Winfrey's innovative ideas (such as Oprah's Book Club, which can send a little-known title to the top of best seller lists) have earned her show more than 30 Emmys. Oprah refuses to stoop to the level of competitors and continues focusing on topics aimed at improving people's lives.

Oprah's expansive reach is widening through her association with TV producer Marcy Carsey and former Nickelodeon executive Geraldine Laybourne in Oxygen Media, which operates the Oxygen cable TV channel and various Web sites for women (including Oprah.com).

## HISTORY

Oprah Winfrey began her broadcasting career in 1973 at age 19 as a news anchor at Nashville's WTVF-TV. She became an evening news co-anchor in Baltimore in 1976, where she was recruited to co-host WJZ-TV's local talk show *People Are Talking*. At first station management was apprehensive about Winfrey (a black woman in a field dominated by white men), but positive viewer response and healthy ratings put their fears to rest. She moved to Chicago in the early 1980s to host ABC affiliate WLS-TV's *AM Chicago,* which quickly became the city's top morning talk show. It was renamed *The Oprah Winfrey Show* in 1985.

Winfrey's performance in Steven Spielberg's *The Color Purple* in 1985 (her first-ever acting role) won her an Oscar nomination and boosted her ratings when *The Oprah Winfrey Show* debuted nationally in 138 cities the following year thanks to a syndication deal with King World Productions secured by her agent (now Harpo president and COO) Jeffrey Jacobs. Harpo was founded that year.

Winfrey obtained full ownership of her program in 1988. Two years later Harpo Films was created, and Winfrey bought a Chicago studio to produce *Oprah,* becoming only the third woman to own her own production studio (Mary Pickford and Lucille Ball were the others). She introduced the popular Oprah's Book Club in 1996, a show segment in which she selects a book for viewers to read and then discusses on a future show. In 1997 Winfrey launched her Web site, Oprah.com.

A lawsuit brought by Texas cattlemen as the result of a show that year on the UK outbreak of mad cow disease claimed she had caused a drop in beef futures prices (Winfrey didn't emphasize that the disease had not

appeared in the US). However, jurors ruled in her favor in early 1998. Also that year Winfrey renewed her contract until the 2001-02 TV season.

After more than a dozen years at the top, Winfrey saw her program fall to second place in the ratings in 1998 behind Jerry Springer's trash TV talk show (which she called a "vulgarity circus"). Railing against the degeneration of the medium, Winfrey started a new show format called "Change Your Life TV," which aimed to improve viewers' lives by focusing on spirituality and personal empowerment (more poets and pop psychology, fewer prostitutes and porno queens).

Winfrey agreed to produce original programming for Oxygen in 1998, a new cable network for women, in exchange for an equity stake. Oxygen will also acquire the rights to reruns of *The Oprah Winfrey Show* in 2002. CBS bought King World in 1999, and the deal gave King World stockholder Winfrey a $100 million stake in CBS (which is now a stake in Viacom following its buy of CBS). The following year Winfrey launched her own magazine (*O, The Oprah Magazine*) with Hearst that focuses on relationships, health, and fashion.

As part of a strategy of media integration, the magazine, TV show, and Web site began to feature various parts of the same interview in all three formats. Also that year Winfrey renewed her contract with King World to host and produce the Oprah Winfrey Show through the 2003-04 television season. In 2001 Harpo announced that Dr. Phil McGraw (a regular on the Oprah show) would get a spinoff show in 2002.

## OFFICERS

**Chairman:** Oprah Winfrey
**President and COO:** Jeffrey Jacobs
**CFO:** Doug Pattison
**President, Harpo Productions:** Tim Bennett
**President, Harpo Films:** Kate Forte
**Director of Media and Corporate Relations:**
Lisa Halliday
**Director of Human Resources:** Bernice Smith

## LOCATIONS

**HQ:** 110 N. Carpenter St., Chicago, IL 60607
**Phone:** 312-633-0808     **Fax:** 312-633-1976
**Web:** www.oprah.com

## PRODUCTS/OPERATIONS

**Selected Operations**
Harpo Entertainment Group
  Harpo Films
    *Beloved* (1998)
    *Oprah Winfrey Presents: Before Women Had Wings*
    (1997)
    *Oprah Winfrey Presents: The Wedding* (1998)
    *Overexposed* (1992)
    *There Are No Children Here* (1993)
  Harpo Productions
    *Oprah Winfrey Presents: Amy & Isabelle* (2001)
    *Oprah Winfrey Presents: David and Lisa* (1998)
    *Oprah Winfrey Presents: Tuesdays with Morrie*
    (1999)
    *The Oprah Winfrey Show*
    *The Women of Brewster Place* (1989)
  Harpo Video

## COMPETITORS

AOL Time Warner
dick clark productions
Hallmark
Hearst
iVillage
Lifetime
Martha Stewart Living
News Corp.
Sony Pictures Entertainment
Tribune
USA Networks
Viacom

## HISTORICAL FINANCIALS & EMPLOYEES

| Private<br>FYE: December 31 | Annual<br>Growth | 12/91 | 12/92 | 12/93 | 12/94 | 12/95 | 12/96 | 12/97 | 12/98 | 12/99 | 12/00 |
|---|---|---|---|---|---|---|---|---|---|---|---|
| Sales ($ mil.) | 7.0% | — | 105 | 110 | 120 | 130 | 140 | 150 | 162 | 170 | 180 |
| Employees | 5.8% | — | — | 135 | 141 | 166 | 176 | 175 | 190 | 200 | 200 |

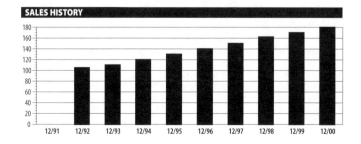

SALES HISTORY

# HARVARD UNIVERSITY

## OVERVIEW

Many parents dream of sending their children to Harvard; some even dream of being able to afford it — $34,350 a year for tuition, fees, and board. Located in Cambridge, Massachusetts, Harvard is the oldest institution of higher learning in the US and one of the world's most prestigious educational institutions. The private, coeducational institution comprises Harvard College (undergraduate) and 10 graduate schools, including the John F. Kennedy School of Government, the Harvard Business School, Harvard Law School, Harvard Medical School, and the Harvard School of Public Health. The Radcliffe Institute for Advanced Study at Harvard was created in

1999 when Radcliffe College and Harvard University merged.

Harvard has more than 18,500 students, roughly two-thirds of whom are enrolled in graduate programs. Among the university's alumni are six US presidents — John Adams, John Quincy Adams, Rutherford B. Hayes, Theodore Roosevelt, Franklin Delano Roosevelt, and John F. Kennedy.

Harvard's reputation for academic excellence is well-founded. More than 30 Harvard faculty members have won Nobel prizes over the years. The university's more than $19 billion makes it the best endowed among US universities.

## HISTORY

In 1636 the General Court of Massachusetts appropriated 400 pounds sterling for the establishment of a college. The first building was completed at Cambridge in 1639 and was named for John Harvard, who had willed his collection of about 400 books and half of his land to the school. The first freshman class had four students.

During its first 150 years, Harvard adhered to the educational standards of European schools, with emphases on classical literature and languages, philosophy, and mathematics. It established its first professorship in 1721 (the Hollis Divinity Professorship) and soon after added professorships in mathematics and natural philosophy. In 1783 the school appointed its first professor of medicine.

Harvard updated its curriculum in the early 1800s, after professor Edward Everett returned from studying abroad with reports of the modern teaching methods in Germany. The university established the Divinity School in 1816, the Law School in 1817, and two schools of science in the 1840s.

In 1869 president Charles Eliot began engineering the development of graduate programs in arts and sciences, engineering, and architecture. He raised standards at the medical and law schools and laid the groundwork for the Graduate School of Business Administration and the School of Public Health. Radcliffe College was founded as "Harvard Annex" in 1879, 15 years after a group of women had begun studying privately with Harvard professors in rented rooms.

Harvard's enrollment, faculty, and endowment grew tremendously throughout the 20th century. The Graduate School of Education opened in 1920, and the first undergraduate

residential house opened in 1930. In the 1930s and 1940s, the school established a scholarship program and a general education curriculum for undergraduates. During WWII Harvard and Radcliffe undergraduates began attending the same classes.

A quota limiting the number of female students was abolished in 1975, and in 1979 Harvard introduced a new core curriculum. Princeton-educated Neil Rudenstine became president in 1991 and vowed to cut costs and to seek additional funding so that no one would be denied a Harvard education for financial reasons.

Harvard made dubious headlines during its 1994-95 academic year, enduring a bank robbery in Harvard Square, three student suicides, and one murder-suicide. The following year Harvard paid a fine of $775,000 after the US Attorney's Office claimed the school's pharmacy had not properly controlled drugs, including antidepressants and codeine cough syrup. The fine was the largest ever paid in the US under the Controlled Substance Act.

In 1998 Harvard's endowment fund acquired insurance services firm White River in one of the largest direct investments ever made by a not-for-profit institution. Also that year the school altered some of its graduation processes and introduced stress-reducing programs in the wake of another student suicide.

In 1999 Radcliffe College merged with Harvard, and the Radcliffe Institute for Advanced Study at Harvard was established. Former Treasury Secretary Lawrence Summers replaced president Neil Rudenstine in 2001.

## OFFICERS

**President:** Lawrence H. Summers
**Provost:** Steven Hyman
**VP Finance:** Elizabeth Huidekoper
**VP Government, Community, and Public Affairs:**
  Alan Stone
**VP Alumni Affairs and Development:**
  Thomas M. Reardon, age 54
**VP and General Counsel:** Anne Taylor
**VP Administration:** Sally H. Zeckhauser
**Treasurer:** D. Ronald Daniel
**Director Human Resources:** Mary Cronin
**Auditors:** PricewaterhouseCoopers LLP

## LOCATIONS

**HQ:** Massachusetts Hall, Cambridge, MA 02138
**Phone:** 617-495-1000        **Fax:** 617-495-0754
**Web:** www.harvard.edu

## PRODUCTS/OPERATIONS

**Selected Programs and Schools**
Undergraduate
  Harvard College
Graduate
  Graduate School of Arts and Sciences
  Graduate School of Design
  Graduate School of Education
  Harvard Business School
  Harvard Divinity School
  Harvard Law School
  Harvard Medical School
  Harvard School of Public Health
  John F. Kennedy School of Government
  School of Dental Medicine

## HISTORICAL FINANCIALS & EMPLOYEES

| School<br>FYE: June 30 | Annual<br>Growth | 6/91 | 6/92 | 6/93 | 6/94 | 6/95 | 6/96 | 6/97 | 6/98 | 6/99 | 6/00 |
|---|---|---|---|---|---|---|---|---|---|---|---|
| Sales ($ mil.) | 6.6% | — | 1,210 | 1,306 | 1,377 | 1,467 | 1,519 | 1,565 | 1,679 | 1,788 | 2,023 |
| Employees | 0.4% | — | 11,000 | 11,000 | 11,000 | 11,100 | 12,150 | 12,782 | 9,701 | 10,500 | 11,360 |

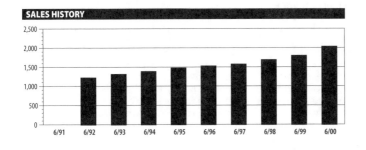

SALES HISTORY

# HAWORTH INC.

## OVERVIEW

Designers at Haworth sit at their cubicles and think about ... more cubicles. Holland, Michigan-based Haworth is a top US maker of office furniture, trailing only #1 Steelcase and neck and neck with Herman Miller. It offers a full range of furniture known for its innovative design, including partitions, desks, chairs, tables, and storage products. The company sells its products in more than 120 countries worldwide through more than 800 dealers.

Haworth, known as an aggressive competitor, has been expanding its presence in Europe, mostly through acquisitions. Operations include Germany's Nestler and Roder, Spain's Kemen, and Canada's SMED International and Groupe Lacasse. The Haworth family, including chairman Richard Haworth, the founder's son, owns the company.

## HISTORY

Gerrard Haworth, an industrial arts high school teacher in Holland, Michigan, started a woodworking business in his garage in 1938. He quit his teaching job 10 years later, took out a mortgage on his house, borrowed $10,000 from his father, and started Modern Products in 1948.

The fledgling company employed only six workers, but that changed two years later when Modern Products received a contract with the United Auto Workers in Detroit. The contract called for an innovative product: a "bank partition" — a partition constructed with wood below but with glass at the top. Believing other companies would want these partitions, Gerrard concentrated on their production. His hunch was correct, and Modern Products boomed throughout the 1950s, gaining a national presence by the decade's end.

Another Haworth, Gerrard's son Richard, went to work for the company in the 1960s, starting by sweeping floors but rising quickly to VP of research and development. When competitor Herman Miller introduced a set of movable panels, shelves, and desktops, it was Richard who developed the counterstroke for Modern Products, creating an insulated movable panel that also reduced noise. The insulated panels started shipping in 1971, helping fuel the company's continued growth.

Four years later, Richard — who would visit competitors' showrooms and take apart their furniture surreptitiously — invented, developed, and patented an even more innovative panel, this one with electrical wiring inside. These panels, called Uni-Group, eliminated the need to call electricians in for rewiring, boosting sales by millions — and ushering in the age of cubicles for office workers everywhere. Also in 1975 Modern Products changed its name to Haworth; the next year Gerrard became chairman and made Richard president.

As president, Richard was at the helm for Haworth's most explosive period of growth;

not only was the office furniture industry booming during the 1980s, but also Haworth was growing at over twice the industry's rate. The company expanded overseas as well, setting up a European division after buying German chair maker Comforto (1988). Seeking to emulate Haworth's success with the pre-wired electrical panel, competitor Steelcase introduced its own version. Haworth, claiming patent infringement, sued Steelcase in 1985, lost in 1988, but then successfully appealed in 1989. Haworth filed a similar patent claim against Herman Miller three years later.

With the office furniture industry tightening in the late 1980s (due in part to a glut of used office supplies), Haworth turned to its international markets. The company purchased two Portuguese furniture makers in 1991 and French and Italian companies (Ordo and Castelli, respectively) the next year. Haworth continued to expand its business line through domestic acquisitions as well, acquiring Globe Business Furniture in 1992 and United Chair and Anderson Hickey three years later.

Haworth's patents on pre-wired partitions entered public domain in 1994. In 1996 and 1997 it had a successful resolution of both its lawsuits against its top two competitors: Herman Miller settled out of court in 1996 for about $44 million, and the next year Steelcase was ordered to pay $211.5 million, one of the largest judgments in patent-litigation history.

In 1999 Haworth expanded its international presence with its purchase of office furniture companies in Germany (dyes, Nestler, Roder, and Art Collection) and Spain (Kemen). The company bought Canada-based SMED International, a designer and manufacturer of office furniture and systems, and a majority stake in Canadian office furniture maker Groupe Lacasse in 2000. For the first time ever, in 2001 Haworth was forced to cut jobs as a result of a slowdown throughout the industry. It also closed a wood-products plant that year.

## HISTORICAL FINANCIALS & EMPLOYEES

| Private<br>FYE: December 31 | Annual<br>Growth | 12/91 | 12/92 | 12/93 | 12/94 | 12/95 | 12/96 | 12/97 | 12/98 | 12/99 | 12/00 |
|---|---|---|---|---|---|---|---|---|---|---|---|
| Sales ($ mil.) | 15.4% | — | 655 | 800 | 1,005 | 1,150 | 1,360 | 1,510 | 1,540 | 1,580 | 2,060 |
| Employees | 11.7% | — | 6,000 | 7,000 | 7,400 | 8,900 | 9,000 | 10,000 | 10,000 | 10,000 | 14,500 |

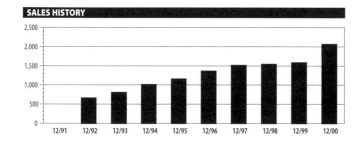

SALES HISTORY

# H. E. BUTT GROCERY COMPANY

H. E. Butt Grocery Company (H-E-B) is the real king of the hill of the Texas Hill Country. The #1 food retailer in Central Texas and its home base of San Antonio, H-E-B is the largest private company in Texas and one of the nation's largest regional supermarket chains. The company runs about 295 supermarkets, mostly in South and Central Texas, although there are 17 in Mexico and one in Louisiana. Most are traditional supermarkets, but there are more than 80 small stores (some flying the Pantry flag) and a handful of Central Market stores (upscale stores offering hard-to-find gourmet and ethnic food items, plus a huge selection of perishables). About 40% of the H-E-B stores have gasoline outlets, and most have pharmacies. H-E-B also operates facilities for processing milk, meat, ice cream, and baked goods, as well as bread and tortillas.

The grocer is familiar with the tastes of Latinos (about half of its market is Hispanic), and H-E-B has moved into Monterrey, Mexico's more affluent neighborhoods, with stores operating under the H-E-B banner and the Economax name (a discount supermarket format). The company plans to have about 40 stores in Mexico by 2004.

The founding Butt family owns the chain.

## HISTORY

Charles C. Butt and his wife, Florence, moved to Kerrville, in the Texas Hill Country, in 1905, hoping the climate would help Charles' tuberculosis. Since Charles was unable to work, Florence began peddling groceries door-to-door for A&P. Later that year she opened a grocery store, C. C. Butt Grocery. However, Florence, a dyed-in-the-wool Baptist, refused to carry such articles of vice as tobacco. The family lived over the store, and all three of the Butt children worked there. The youngest son, Howard, began working there full-time in his teens and took over the business after WWI.

By adopting modern marketing methods such as price tagging (and deciding to sell tobacco), the Butts earned enough to begin expanding. In 1927 Howard opened a second store in Del Rio in West Texas, and over the next few years he opened other stores in the Rio Grande Valley. The company gained patron loyalty by making minimal markups on staples. It moved from Kerrville to Harlingen (1928), then to Corpus Christi (1940) and finally San Antonio (1985).

The company began manufacturing foods in the 1930s, and it invested in farms and orchards. In 1935 Howard (who had adopted the middle name Edward) rechristened the chain the H. E. Butt Grocery Company (H-E-B). He put his three children to work for the company, grooming son Charles for the top spot after Howard Jr. took over the H. E. Butt Foundation from his mother.

While other chains updated their stores during the 1960s, H-E-B plodded. Howard Sr. resigned in 1971 and Charles took over, bringing in fresh management. But this was not enough. Studies showed that the reasons for its lagging market share were its refusal to stock alcohol and its policy of Sunday closing (policies abandoned in 1976). It also drastically undercut competitors, driving many independents out of business. Winning the price wars, H-E-B emerged the dominant player in its major markets.

H-E-B's first superstore, a 56,000-sq.-ft. facility offering general merchandise, photo finishing, and a pharmacy, opened in Austin, Texas, in 1979, and the company concentrated on building more superstores over the next decade. It also installed in-store video rentals and added 35 freestanding Video Central locations (sold to Hollywood Entertainment in 1993).

In 1988 H-E-B launched its H-E-B Pantry division, which remodeled and built smaller supermarkets, mostly in rural Texas towns. Three years later it launched another format, the 93,000-sq.-ft. H-E-B Marketplace in San Antonio, which included restaurants. It also opened the upscale Central Market in Austin with extensive cheese, produce, and wine departments in 1994 (it later opened similar stores in San Antonio and Houston).

Chairman and CEO Charles retired as president in 1996, and James Clingman became the first non-family member to assume the office. That year H-E-B opened its first non-Texas store, in Lake Charles, Louisiana. In 1997 it opened its first Mexican store in an affluent area of Monterrey, followed the next year by a discount supermarket there under the Economax banner. In 1999 the company said it would expand further in Mexico with six to eight new stores per year (it opened seven in 2001). Also in 2001 H-E-B opened its first Dallas/Ft. Worth store — a Central Market.

## LOCATIONS

**HQ:** 646 S. Main Ave., San Antonio, TX 78204
**Phone:** 210-938-8000          **Fax:** 210-938-8169
**Web:** www.heb.com

H. E. Butt Grocery Company operates grocery stores and gas stations in Central, East, and South Texas; Louisiana; and Mexico. The company also operates bakeries; a photo processing lab; and meat, milk, and ice cream plants.

### 2001 Stores

|  | No. |
|---|---|
| Central Texas Region | 63 |
| San Antonio and West Region | 53 |
| Houston East Region | 44 |
| Houston West Region | 42 |
| Border Region | 40 |
| Gulf Coast Region | 31 |
| Houston Region | 6 |
| Mexico | 10 |
| **Total** | **289** |

## COMPETITORS

| | |
|---|---|
| 7-Eleven | IGA |
| Albertson's | Kmart |
| Brookshire Brothers | Kroger |
| Chedraui | Randall's |
| Comerci | Rice Food Markets |
| Grupo Corvi | Soriana |
| Costco Wholesale | Walgreen |
| Eckerd | Wal-Mart |
| Fiesta Mart | Wal-Mart de México |
| Fleming Companies | Whole Foods |
| Gerland's Food Fair | Winn-Dixie |
| Gigante | |

## PRODUCTS/OPERATIONS

**Private Labels**
H-E-B Own Brand
Hill Country Fare

**Store Formats**
Central Market (about 70,000-sq.-ft., upscale supermarkets with expanded organic and gourmet foods; located in major metropolitan markets)
Economax (discount supermarkets, Mexico)
Gas 'N Go (gas stations)
H-E-B (large supermarkets)
H-E-B Marketplace (large supermarkets with specialty departments)
H-E-B Pantry (24,000-30,000 sq. ft., no-frills supermarkets with basic groceries; often located in rural or suburban areas)

## HISTORICAL FINANCIALS & EMPLOYEES

| Private FYE: October 31 | Annual Growth | 10/92 | 10/93 | 10/94 | 10/95 | 10/96 | 10/97 | 10/98 | 10/99 | 10/00 | 10/01 |
|---|---|---|---|---|---|---|---|---|---|---|---|
| Sales ($ mil.) | 12.1% | 3,204 | 4,500 | 4,844 | 5,137 | 5,800 | 6,500 | 7,000 | 7,500 | 8,200 | 8,965 |
| Employees | 19.6% | 12,000 | 19,772 | 25,000 | 25,000 | 42,000 | 45,000 | 45,000 | 45,000 | 50,000 | 60,000 |

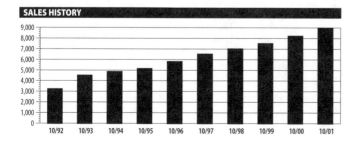

SALES HISTORY

# HEALTH CARE SERVICE

## OVERVIEW

Health Care Service Corporation (HCSC) can't get enough of the Blues.

Chicago-based HCSC owns Blue Cross Blue Shield of Illinois (that state's oldest and largest health insurer) and Blue Cross and Blue Shield of Texas. The Blue Cross and Blue Shield Association licenses its name to the mutually owned HCSC, which offers indemnity insurance, managed care programs, prescription drug plans, Medicare supplement insurance, dental and vision coverage, life and disability insurance, retirement plans, and workers' compensation.

HCSC covers federal employees in Illinois and Texas through the Federal Employee Program, a contract with the US government. It also offers insurance and medical financial services through such subsidiaries as Preferred Financial Group.

To better compete in the health care industry and to benefit from economies of scale, HCSC is working toward an alliance with The Regence Group, which owns the Blues of Idaho, Utah, Oregon, and Washington, that would serve some 10 million members and be the largest not-for-profit health insurance organization in the US. A seventh state could be added to the mix: The company plans to buy Blue Cross Blue Shield of New Mexico.

## HISTORY

The seeds of the Blue Cross organization were sown in 1929, when an official at Baylor University Hospital in Dallas began offering schoolteachers 21 days of hospital care for $6 a year. Fundamental to its coverage was a community rating system, which based premiums on the community's claims experience rather than subscribers' conditions.

In 1935 Elgin Watch Co. owner Taylor Strawn, Charles Schweppe, and other Chicago civic leaders pooled resources to form Hospital Services Corporation to provide the same type of coverage. (The firm adopted the Blue Cross symbol in 1939.) Employees of the Rand McNally cartography company were the first to be covered by the plan.

Soon, four similar plans were launched in other Illinois towns. Between 1947 and 1952, Hospital Services and the other four joined forces, offering coverage nearly statewide. Meanwhile, Blue Shield physician's fee plans in several cities were incorporated as Illinois Medical Service. Illinois Medical Service and Hospital Services operated independently but shared office space and personnel.

A 1975 change in state legislation let the entities merge to become Health Care Service Corp. (HCSC), which offered both Blue Cross and Blue Shield coverage. Following the merger, the company's board of directors (which had been primarily composed of care providers) became dominated by consumers, which helped HCSC become more responsive to its members.

For the next six years, the state denied HCSC any rate increases, leaving it with a frighteningly low $12 million in reserves in 1982.

HCSC achieved statewide market presence in 1982 when it merged with Illinois' last independent Blue Cross plan, Rockford Blue Cross.

In 1986, as managed care swept through the health care industry, only 14% of HCSC's members were enrolled in managed care plans. HCSC created its Managed Care Network Preferred point-of-service plan in 1991; the idea caught on with employers and individuals, and enrollment skyrocketed. By 1994 more than two-thirds of the firm's subscribers participated in some sort of managed care plan. That year it picked up Medicare payment processing for the state of Michigan.

In 1995 HCSC and Blue Cross and Blue Shield of Texas (BCBST) formed an affiliation they hoped would culminate in a merger giving the combined company $6 billion in sales and reserves of more than $1 billion. Texas consumer groups objected to the merger, claiming that Texas residents own BCBST and that Texans should be compensated for the transfer of ownership — especially since BCBST had received state tax breaks for decades in exchange for accepting all applicants. (A Texas judge ruled in favor of the merger in 1998.)

Citing high risks and low margins, HCSC in 1997 dropped its Medicare payment processing contract, which it had held for some 30 years. The next year HCSC agreed to pay $144 million after it pleaded guilty to covering up its poor performance in processing Medicare claims.

In 1999 HCSC agreed to buy Aetna's NylCare of Texas, giving it large, profitable HMOs in Houston and Dallas (completed in 2000). In 2001 it bested Anthem and Wellmark in wooing the troubled Blue Cross Blue Shield of New Mexico; their union is pending.

**President and CEO:** Raymond F. McCaskey
**SVP, Finance and CFO:** Sherman M. Wolff
**SVP, Group Marketing:** Michael M. Seibold
**SVP, Information Technology and Subscriber Services:**
Joanne M. Rounds
**Director, Human Resources:** Robert Ernst
**Auditors:** Arthur Andersen LLP

## LOCATIONS

**HQ:** Health Care Service Corporation
300 E. Randolph, Chicago, IL 60601
**Phone:** 312-653-6000          **Fax:** 312-819-1220
**Web:** www.bcbsil.com

## PRODUCTS/OPERATIONS

**Selected Products and Services**
Dental insurance
Disability insurance
Indemnity insurance
Life insurance
Managed health care plans
Supplemental Medicare coverage
Prescription drug coverage
Retirement plans
Vision insurance
Workers' compensation

**Selected Subsidiaries**
Group Medical and Surgical Service
Preferred Financial Group
    Fort Dearborn Life Insurance Co.
    Medical Life Insurance Company
    Colorado Bankers Life Insurance Company
Rio Grande HMO, Inc.
Texas Gulf Coast HMO, Inc.
Texas Health Plan, Inc.
West Texas Health Plans, L.C.

## COMPETITORS

Aetna
AFLAC
Anthem
CIGNA
Guardian Life
Humana
Kaiser Foundation
Mutual of Omaha
New York Life
Prudential
UnitedHealth Group

## HISTORICAL FINANCIALS & EMPLOYEES

| Mutual company FYE: December 31 | Annual Growth | 12/91 | 12/92 | 12/93 | 12/94 | 12/95 | 12/96 | 12/97 | 12/98 | 12/99 | 12/00 |
|---|---|---|---|---|---|---|---|---|---|---|---|
| Assets ($ mil.) | 14.5% | — | 1,111 | 1,314 | 1,452 | 1,621 | 1,749 | 1,864 | 2,509 | 2,650 | 3,282 |
| Net income ($ mil.) | 12.2% | — | 69 | 98 | 166 | 139 | 89 | 71 | 50 | 111 | 174 |
| Income as % of assets | — | — | 6.2% | 7.5% | 11.4% | 8.6% | 5.1% | 3.8% | 2.0% | 4.2% | 5.3% |
| Employees | 0.9% | — | — | — | — | 5,600 | 5,650 | 5,700 | — | — | — |

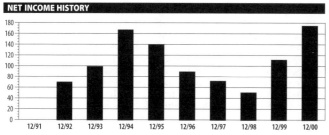

**NET INCOME HISTORY**

**2000 FISCAL YEAR-END**
Equity as % of assets: 39.8%
Return on assets: 5.9%
Return on equity: —
Long-term debt ($ mil.): —
Sales ($ mil.): 10,430

# THE HEARST CORPORATION

OVERVIEW

Like legendary founder William Randolph Hearst's castle, The Hearst Corporation is sprawling. New York City-based Hearst owns 12 daily newspapers (*San Francisco Chronicle, Houston Chronicle*) and 18 weeklies through its Hearst Newspapers unit; 16 US consumer magazines (*Cosmopolitan, Esquire*) through its Hearst Magazine unit; five UK magazines; stakes in cable TV networks (A&E, Lifetime, ESPN); TV and radio stations (through Hearst-Argyle Television); King Features, a features and comic syndicate; and business publishers. Hearst sold the *San Francisco Examiner* to the Fang family in conjunction with its 2000 purchase of the larger *San Francisco Chronicle*.

Although it no longer owns Hearst Castle (deeded to the State of California in 1951), the company has extensive real estate holdings. Online interests include 30% of iVillage, the top Web site for women.

The company is owned by the Hearst family, but managed by a board of trustees. Upon his death, William Randolph Hearst left 99% of the company's common stock to two charitable trusts controlled by a 13-member board that includes five family and eight non-family members. The will includes a clause that allows the trustees to disinherit any heir who contests the will.

## HISTORY

William Randolph Hearst, son of a California mining magnate, started as a reporter — having been expelled from Harvard in 1884 for playing jokes on professors. In 1887 he became editor of the *San Francisco Examiner,* which his father had obtained as payment for a gambling debt. In 1895 he bought the *New York Morning Journal* and competed against Joseph Pulitzer's *New York World.* The "yellow journalism" resulting from that rivalry characterized American-style reporting at the turn of the century.

Hearst branched into magazines (1903), film (1913), and radio (1928). Also during this time it created the Hearst International News Service (it was sold to E.W. Scripps' United Press in 1958 to form United Press International). By 1935 Hearst was at its peak, with newspapers in 19 cities, the largest syndicate (King Features), international news and photo services, 13 magazines, eight radio stations, and two motion picture companies. Two years later Hearst relinquished control of the company to avoid bankruptcy, selling movie companies, radio stations, magazines, and, later, most of his San Simeon estate. (Hearst's rise and fall inspired the 1941 film *Citizen Kane.*)

In 1948 Hearst became the owner of one of the US's first TV stations, WBAL-TV in Baltimore. When Hearst died in 1951, company veteran Richard Berlin became CEO. Berlin sold off failing newspapers, moved into television, and acquired more magazines.

Frank Bennack, CEO since 1979, expanded the company, acquiring newspapers, publishing firms (notably William Morrow, 1981), TV stations, magazines (*Redbook,* 1982; *Esquire,* 1986), and 20% of cable sports network ESPN (1991). Hearst branched into video via a joint

venture with Capital Cities/ABC (1981) and helped launch the Lifetime and Arts & Entertainment cable channels (1984).

In 1991 Hearst launched a New England news network with Continental Cablevision. The following year it brought on board former Federal Communications Commission chairman Alfred Sikes, who quickly moved the company onto the Internet. In 1996 Randolph A. Hearst passed the title of chairman to nephew George Hearst (the last surviving son of the founder, Randolph died in 2000). Broadcaster Argyle Television merged with Hearst's TV holdings in 1997 to form publicly traded Hearst-Argyle Television.

In 1999 Hearst combined its HomeArts Web site with Women.com to create one of the largest online networks for women. It also joined with Walt Disney's Miramax Films to publish entertainment magazine *Talk* and Oprah Winfrey's Harpo Entertainment to publish *O, The Oprah Magazine* (launched in 2000). Also in 1999 the company sold its book publishing operations to News Corp.'s HarperCollins unit, and it agreed to buy the *San Francisco Chronicle* from rival Chronicle Publishing. That deal was called into question over concerns that the *San Francisco Examiner* would not survive and the city would be left with one major paper. To resolve the issue, in 2000 Hearst sold the *Examiner* to ExIn (a group of investors affiliated with the Ted Fang family and other owners of the *San Francisco Independent*). Also in 2000 Hearst bought the UK magazines of Gruner + Jahr, the newspaper and magazine unit of German media juggernaut Bertelsmann.

The following year Hearst gained a 30% stake in iVillage following that company's purchase of rival Women.com Networks.

**Chairman:** George R. Hearst Jr.
**President and CEO:** Frank A. Bennack Jr., age 68
**EVP and COO:** Victor F. Ganzi
**EVP, Hearst Newspapers:** Steven P. Swartz
**SVP; President, Hearst Newspapers:** George B. Irish
**VP and CFO:** Ronald J. Doerfler
**VP; General Manager, Hearst Interactive Sudios:**
Jay Bobowicz
**President and CEO, Hearst-Argyle Television:**
David J. Barrett, age 52
**President and CEO, Hearst Magazines International:**
George Green
**President, Hearst Business Media:** Richard P. Malloch
**President, Hearst Interactive Media:** Alfred C. Sikes,
age 61
**President, Hearst Magazines:** Cathleen P. Black, age 56
**SVP, Human Resources, Hearst Magazines:** Ruth Diem
**SVP, Sales and Marketing, San Francisco Chronicle:**
Margaret Krost

# LOCATIONS

**HQ:** 959 8th Ave., New York, NY 10019
**Phone:** 212-649-2000 **Fax:** 212-765-3528
**Web:** www.hearstcorp.com

Hearst newspapers are published throughout the
US. Hearst magazines are distributed in more than
100 countries.

# PRODUCTS/OPERATIONS

**Selected Operations**

**Broadcasting**
Hearst-Argyle Television (60%)

**Business Publications**
*Diversion*
*First DataBank*
*National Auto Research*

**Entertainment and Syndication**
A&E Television Networks (37.5%, with ABC & NBC)
The History Channel
ESPN (20%)
King Features Syndicate
Lifetime Entertainment Services (50%, with ABC)
Locomotion (with Cisneros Group; all animation TV)
New England Cable News (with AT&T Broadband)

**Interactive Media**
iVillage (30%, Internet site geared towards women)
Also has ownership interest in:
Circles (online loyalty solutions company)
drugstore.com (online pharmacy site)
Hire.com (career job site)
traffic.com (site providing real-time traffic info)

**Magazines**
*Cosmopolitan*
*Country Living*
*Esquire*
*Good Housekeeping*
*Harper's Bazaar*
*House Beautiful*
*Marie Claire* (with Marie Claire Album)
*O, The Oprah Magazine* (with Harpo)
*Popular Mechanics*
*Redbook*
*SmartMoney* (with Dow Jones)
*Talk* (with Disney's Miramax unit)
*Town & Country*

**Major Newspapers**
*Albany Times Union* (New York)
*Houston Chronicle*
*Huron Daily Tribune* (Michigan)
*Laredo Morning Times* (Texas)
*Midland Daily News* (Michigan)
*San Antonio Express-News*
*San Francisco Chronicle*
*Seattle Post-Intelligencer*

**Real Estate**
Hearst Realties
San Francisco Realties
Sunical Land & Livestock Division

# COMPETITORS

| | | |
|---|---|---|
| Advance | E. W. Scripps | Meredith |
| Publications | Freedom | New York Times |
| AOL Time | Communications | News Corp. |
| Warner | Gannett | PRIMEDIA |
| Belo | Hachette | Reader's Digest |
| Bertelsmann | Filipacchi | Reed Elsevier |
| Bloomberg | Médias | Seattle Times |
| Cox Enterprises | IPC Media | Tribune |
| Dennis | Knight Ridder | Viacom |
| Publishing | McGraw-Hill | Walt Disney |
| Emap | MediaNews | Washington Post |

# HISTORICAL FINANCIALS & EMPLOYEES

| Private<br>FYE: December 31 | Annual<br>Growth | 12/91 | 12/92 | 12/93 | 12/94 | 12/95 | 12/96 | 12/97 | 12/98 | 12/99 | 12/00 |
|---|---|---|---|---|---|---|---|---|---|---|---|
| Sales ($ mil.) | 7.0% | — | 1,973 | 2,174 | 2,299 | 2,513 | 2,568 | 2,833 | 2,200 | 2,740 | 3,400 |
| Employees | 4.4% | — | 13,000 | 13,500 | 14,000 | 14,000 | 14,000 | 15,000 | 13,555 | 14,000 | 18,300 |

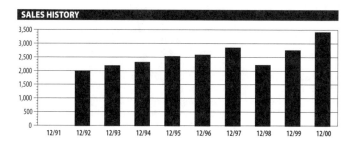

SALES HISTORY

The Hearst Corporation

# HELMSLEY ENTERPRISES, INC.

## OVERVIEW

What word rhyming with "itch" describes Leona Helmsley? Rich! The 1997 death of Harry Helmsley left $5 billion in real estate to the notorious New Yorker. The Helmsley Enterprises portfolio includes millions of square feet of real estate (mostly in New York City) and a lease on the Empire State Building.

Helmsley, who spent the latter part of 1990s out of the limelight, is back in the spotlight once again. After quietly selling off a number of properties, many at a premium in New York's stratospheric real estate market, the "Queen of Mean" is grabbing headlines again: She appears to be winning a public fight with Donald Trump over the terms of the Empire State Building lease, and is being sued for millions for the alleged mistreatment of gay hotel employees.

At its apex, Helmsley's real estate empire included interests in more than 25 million sq. ft. of office space, more than 20,000 apartments, some 7,500 hotel rooms, 50 retail projects, warehouse space, land, garages, restaurants, and real estate companies. To keep the money in the family, the properties were managed by Helmsley-Spear (then 99%-owned by Helmsley, sold in 1997) and Helmsley-Noyes.

Helmsley has sold more than $2 billion worth of property since her husband's death.

## HISTORY

In 1925 Harry Helmsley began his career as a Manhattan rent collector; the work, then done in person, taught him to evaluate buildings and acquainted him with their owners. During the Depression, Helmsley obtained property at bargain prices. He paid $1,000 down for a building with a $100,000 mortgage and later quipped that he did so to provide a job for his father, whom he hired as superintendent. In 1946 he sold the building for $165,000.

In the late 1940s Helmsley teamed up with lawyer Lawrence Wien. Helmsley located properties; Wien financed them through a device of his own invention, the loan syndicate. Prominent properties Helmsley bought into in the 1950s included the Flatiron (1951), Berkeley (1953), and Equitable (1957) buildings. He moved into management in 1955 with the purchase of Leon Spear's property management firm. In 1961 Helmsley bought the Empire State Building for $65 million and sold it to Prudential for $29 million with a 114-year leaseback (which expires in 2075); a public offering for the newly created Empire State Building Co. made up the balance.

In the mid-1960s Helmsley moved into property development, erecting office buildings and shopping centers. He bought the 30-building Furman and Wolfson trust, borrowing $78 million of the $165 million price on the strength of his reputation — the largest signature loan ever.

In 1969 Spear introduced Helmsley to Leona Roberts, a real estate broker who had sold Spear an apartment. Helmsley hired Leona and promoted her to SVP at his Brown, Harris, Stevens real estate brokerage. He divorced his wife and married Leona in 1971. In 1974 he leased a historic building and delegated the renovation to Leona (who built the company's hotel business). The Helmsley Palace opened in 1980 (now the New York Palace, sold 1993).

As Harry's health began to fail, Leona gained control of the empire. Maintenance deteriorated, bookkeeping went lax, and the couple's lavish spending became notorious. In 1988 they were charged with tax evasion. Harry was ruled incompetent to stand trial, but in 1989 Leona was convicted, fined $7.1 million, and sentenced to jail. She spent 21 months incarcerated, the last part of it in a halfway house.

After her 1994 release, Leona was banned from management of the hotels by laws forbidding felon involvement in businesses that serve liquor. She became more involved in the management of Harry's interests and began reshuffling assets, moving management contracts from Helmsley-Spear to Helmsley-Noyes, and selling buildings.

A 1995 suit brought by Harry's partners in Helmsley-Spear accused Leona of looting the company by depriving it of management contracts and loading it with debt to render worthless their right to buy the company under a 1970 option agreement.

In 1997 Harry died, and Leona announced she would sell the 125-property Helmsley portfolio. Leona settled her differences with the Helmsley-Spear partners in 1997, agreeing to sell them the firm for less than $1 million.

Leona sold her favorite, the Helmsley Building on Park Place, in 1998 to the Bass family on condition the building retain the name. She moved closer to a deal in 2000 to buy back the Empire State Building from Donald Trump and partners. The following year Wien's son-in-law Peter Malkin moved to challenge her, forming a plan to buy the skyscraper himself; Leona vowed to block his proposal.

## OFFICERS

**Owner:** Leona Helmsley
**CFO:** Abe Wolf

## LOCATIONS

**HQ:** 230 Park Ave., Room 659, New York, NY 10169
**Phone:** 212-679-3600          **Fax:** 212-953-2810

Helmsley Enterprises operates primarily in New York City.

## PRODUCTS/OPERATIONS

**Selected Owned and/or Managed Properties**
Empire State Building (office building, New York City)
Helmsley Carlton House (hotel, New York City)
Helmsley Middletowne (hotel, New York City)
Helmsley Park Lane (hotel, New York City)
Helmsley Sandcastle (hotel, Sarasota, Florida)
Helmsley Windsor (hotel, New York City)
Lincoln Building (office building, New York City)
New York Helmsley (hotel, New York City)

## COMPETITORS

Alexander's
JMB Realty
Kimco Realty
Lefrak Organization
Lincoln Property
Port Authority of NY & NJ
Tishman Realty
Trammell Crow
TrizecHahn
Trump
Vornado

## HISTORICAL FINANCIALS & EMPLOYEES

| Private<br>FYE: December 31 | Annual<br>Growth | 12/91 | 12/92 | 12/93 | 12/94 | 12/95 | 12/96 | 12/97 | 12/98 | 12/99 | 12/00 |
|---|---|---|---|---|---|---|---|---|---|---|---|
| Estimated sales ($ mil.) | (2.3%) | — | 1,200 | 1,200 | 1,700 | 1,770 | 1,900 | 1,000 | 1,000 | 1,000 | 1,000 |
| Employees | (16.7%) | — | 13,000 | 13,000 | 13,000 | 13,000 | 13,000 | 7,800 | 7,800 | 3,000 | 3,000 |

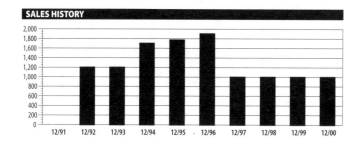

SALES HISTORY

# HICKS, MUSE, TATE & FURST

## OVERVIEW

These Texas Hicks know an investment pool ain't no cement pond. Dallas-based Hicks, Muse, Tate & Furst creates investment pools in the form of limited partnerships. Investors are mostly pension funds but also include financial institutions and wealthy private investors such as Texas' Hunt family. The firm targets under-performing niche companies and builds them up through add-on investments.

As its target industries consolidate — making US acquisitions scarce — Hicks, Muse has increasingly turned to foreign markets. The firm (which sold its AMFM to Clear Channel Communications to create the US's largest radio, television, and outdoor advertising group) exported its media mogul strategy

through investments in Latin America and Europe. Hicks, Muse, along with US-based Liberty Media International, owns CableVision SA, Argentina's largest cable operator.

But all is not well in the world of investments. As the global economy cools, Hicks, Muse has suffered losses and has considered closing funds before they reach their original target amounts. It abandoned plans to buy out manufacturing firm Johns Manville when its stock took a dive, and it and investment partner Kohlberg Kravis Roberts lost a battle with Philip Anschutz for control of Regal Cinemas. The firm, along with UK-based Apax Partners, has agreed to buy British Tele-communication's yellow pages firm Yell.

## HISTORY

The son of a Texas radio station owner, Thomas Hicks became interested in leveraged buyouts as a member of First National Bank's venture capital group. Hicks and Robert Haas formed Hicks & Haas in 1984; the next year that firm bought Hicks Communications, a radio outfit run by Hicks' brother Steven. (This would be the first of many media companies bought or created by the buyout firm, often with Steven Hicks' involvement.)

Hicks & Haas' biggest coup was its mid-1980s buy of several soft drink makers, including Dr Pepper and Seven-Up. The firm took Dr Pepper/Seven-Up public just 18 months after merging the two companies. In all, Hicks & Haas turned $88 million of investor funding into $1.3 billion. The pair split up in 1989; Hicks wanted to raise a large pool to invest, but Haas preferred to work deal by deal.

Hicks raised $250 million in 1989 and teamed with former Prudential Securities banker John Muse. Early investments included Life Partners Group (life insurance, 1990; sold 1996). In 1991 Morgan Stanley's Charles Tate and First Boston's Jack Furst became partners.

As part of its buy-and-build strategy, Hicks, Muse bought DuPont's connector systems unit in 1993, renamed it Berg Electronics, added six more companies to it, and doubled its earnings before selling it in 1998. Not every move was a star in the Hicks, Muse crown. Less-than-successful purchases included bankrupt brewer G. Heileman, bought in 1994 and sold two years later for an almost $100 million loss.

The buyout firm's Chancellor Media radio company went public in 1996. That year Hicks, Muse gained entry into Latin America with its purchases of cash-starved Mexican companies,

including Seguros Commercial America, one of the country's largest insurers. That year also brought International Home Foods (Jiffy Pop, Chef Boyardee) into the Hicks, Muse fold.

In 1997 Chancellor and Evergreen Media merged to form Chancellor Media (renamed AMFM in 1999). The next year Hicks, Muse continued buying US and Latin American media companies. Hicks, Muse and Kohlberg Kravis Roberts' merged their cinema operations to form the US's largest theater chain. The company that year also moved into the depressed energy field (Triton Energy) and formed a $1.5 billion European fund.

Buys in 1999 included UK food group Hillsdown Holdings and one-third of Mexican flour maker Grupo Minsa. The company also agreed to buy Walden (formerly Walden Residential Properties) that year.

Amid assorted media and other buys in 2000, the firm helped put together several joint deals. With investment bank Bear Stearns, it planned to buy construction-materials manufacturer Johns Manville; the deal soured later that year as the economy cooled. After vying with another buyout group for UK food concern United Biscuits, the two competitors teamed up to complete the deal.

Hicks, Muse sold International Home Foods to food giant ConAgra in 2000. The next year it bought bankrupt Vlasic Foods International's North American assets, including Vlasic pickles, Open Pit barbecue sauces, and Swanson frozen dinners. Also in 2001 Hick, Muse, along with US-based Liberty Media International, bought CableVision SA, the largest cable operator in Argentina. It also prepared to sell off its real estate holding, Olympus Real Estate Corp.

**Chairman and CEO:** Thomas O. Hicks, age 55
**President:** Charles W. Tate, age 56
**COO:** John R. Muse, age 50
**CFO:** Darron Ash
**General Counsel:** Michael Salem
**Human Resources Manager:** Lynita Jessen

## LOCATIONS

**HQ:** Hicks, Muse, Tate & Furst Incorporated
200 Crescent Ct., Ste. 1600, Dallas, TX 75201
**Phone:** 214-740-7300      **Fax:** 214-720-7888

Hicks, Muse, Tate & Furst has offices in Dallas and London.

## PRODUCTS/OPERATIONS

**Selected Holdings**
CCI/Triad Systems Corp. (computer systems)
CEI Citicorp Holding (40%, telecommunications and publishing)
Glass Group (automotive information services software)
Grupo Minsa, S.A. de C.V. (32%, corn flour producer, Mexico)
Grupo MVS SA (23%, pay-TV provider and radio station owner, Mexico)
Hedstrom Corp. (playground equipment)
Hillsdown Holdings PLC (food production, office furniture)
Home Interiors & Gifts, Inc. (80%, direct-selling of decorative accessories and gift items)
Ibero-American Media Partners (50%, Latin American media buyout fund)
International Outdoor Advertising (97%; billboards in Argentina, Chile, and Uruguay)
International Wire Holdings Corp. (60%; wire, wire harnesses, and cable)
LIN Holdings (69%, television stations)
Metrocall Inc. (paging systems)
Olympus Real Estate Corp. (real estate equity and mortgage investments)
OmniAmerica Wireless LP (45%, broadcast towers)
Pan-American Sports Network (80%, regional cable sports network)
RCN Corp. (fiber-optic telecommunications networks)
Sunrise Television Corp. (87%, small-market television stations)
Traffic (49%, broadcasting, Brazil)
United Biscuits (Holdings) plc (87%, with Finalrealm; food products; UK)
Viasystems Group (printed circuit boards)
Walden (REIT)

## COMPETITORS

| | | |
|---|---|---|
| Bain Capital | Equity Group | Texas Pacific |
| Berkshire | Investments | Group |
| Hathaway | Haas Wheat | Thomas Lee |
| Boston Ventures | Heico | Vestar Capital |
| Clayton, Dubilier | Maseca | Partners |
| CVC Capital | Investcorp | Vulcan |
| Partners | Jordan Company | Northwest |
| Equitex | KKR | Wingate Partners |
| | Leonard Green | |

# HIGHMARK INC.

## OVERVIEW

Highmark is walking the tightrope between high-minded and high income. The Pittsburgh-based company provides insurance coverage to more than 20 million customers, primarily in Pennsylvania. Highmark offers medical, dental, vision, life, casualty, and other health insurance, as well as such community service programs as the Western Pennsylvania Caring Foundation, which offers free health care coverage to children whose parents earn too much to qualify for public aid but too little to afford private programs.

Highmark continues to operate in western Pennsylvania under the Highmark Blue Cross Blue Shield name and as Pennsylvania Blue Shield statewide. National subsidiaries include United Concordia Companies (dental coverage) and Highmark Life and Casualty Group (disability and life insurance).

## HISTORY

Highmark was created from the merger of Blue Cross of Western Pennsylvania (founded in 1937) and Pennsylvania Blue Shield, created in 1964 when the Medical Service Association of Pennsylvania (MSAP) adopted the Blue Shield name.

The Pennsylvania Medical Society, in conjunction with the state of Pennsylvania, had formed MSAP to provide medical insurance to the poor and indigent. MSAP borrowed $25,000 from the Pennsylvania Medical Society to help set up its operations, and Chauncey Palmer (who had originally proposed the organization) was named president. Individuals paid 35 cents per month, and families paid $1.75 each month to join MSAP, which initially covered mainly obstetrical and surgical procedures.

In 1945 Arthur Daugherty replaced Palmer as president (he served until his death in 1968) and helped MSAP recruit major new accounts, including the United Mine Workers and the Congress of Industrial Organizations. MSAP in 1946 became a chapter of the national Blue Shield association, which was started that year by the medical societies of several states to provide prepaid health insurance plans.

In 1951 MSAP signed up the 150,000 employees of United States Steel, bringing its total enrollment to more than 1.6 million. Growth did not lead to prosperity, though, as the organization had trouble keeping up with payments to its doctors. This shortfall in funds led MSAP to raise its premiums in 1961, at which point the state reminded the association about its social mission and suggested that it concentrate on controlling costs instead of raising rates.

MSAP changed its name to Pennsylvania Blue Shield in 1964. Two years later the association began managing the state's Medicare plan and started the 65-Special plan to supplement Medicare coverage. In the 1970s Pennsylvania Blue Shield again could not keep up with the cost of paying its doctors, which led to more rate increases and closer scrutiny of its expenses. Competition increased in the 1980s as HMOs cropped up around the state. Pennsylvania Blue Shield fought back by creating its own HMO plans — some of which it owned jointly with Blue Cross of Western Pennsylvania — in the 1980s.

After years of slowly collecting noninsurance businesses, Blue Cross of Western Pennsylvania changed its name to Veritus in 1991 to reflect the growing importance of its for-profit operations.

In 1996 Pennsylvania Blue Shield overcame physicians' protests and state regulators' concerns to merge with Veritus. The company adopted the name Highmark to represent its standards for high quality; it took a loss as it failed to meet cost-cutting goals and suffered early-retirement costs related to the merger consolidation. To gain support for the merger, Highmark sold for-profit subsidiary Keystone Health Plan East to Independence Blue Cross in 1997.

In 1999 Highmark teamed with Mountain State Blue Cross Blue Shield to become West Virginia's primary licensee. Rate hikes and investment returns helped propel the company into the black as the decade closed.

In 2001 Highmark announced that it had uncovered almost $5 million in health care insurance fraud over the course of the previous year.

## OFFICERS

**Chairman:** John N. Shaffer
**Vice Chairman:** John A. Carpenter
**President, CEO, and Director:** John S. Brouse
**Group EVP, Health Insurance Operations:**
James Klingensmith
**EVP, Government Business and Corporate Affairs:**
George F. Grode
**EVP, Strategic Business Development:**
Kenneth R. Melani
**SVP, CFO, and Treasurer:** Robert C. Gray
**SVP, Corporate Secretary, and General Counsel:**
Gary R. Truitt
**SVP and General Auditor:** Elizabeth A. Farbacher
**SVP, Human Resources and Administrative Services:**
S. Tyrone Alexander
**Assistant Secretary:** Carrie J. Pecht
**Assistant Treasurer:** Joseph F. Reichard
**Corporate Compliance Officer:** George A. Welsh
**Auditors:** PricewaterhouseCoopers LLP

## COMPETITORS

Aetna
CIGNA
Coventry Health Care
Guardian Life
Humana
New York Life
Prudential
UnitedHealth Group
U.S. Healthcare, Inc.

## LOCATIONS

**HQ:** Fifth Avenue Place, 120 5th Ave.,
Pittsburgh, PA 15222
**Phone:** 412-544-7000     **Fax:** 412-544-8368
**Web:** www.highmark.com

## PRODUCTS/OPERATIONS

**Selected Health Plans and Divisions**
Alliances Ventures
Clarity Vision
Davis Vision
Gateway Health Plan (managed health care delivery
system)
HealthGuard (managed care organization)
HGSAdministrators
Highmark Life & Casualty Group
Insurer Physician Services Organization
Keystone Health Plan Central (HMO; central
Pennsylvania)
Keystone Health Plan West (HMO; western
Pennsylvania)
United Concordia (dental)
Veritus Medicare Services

## HISTORICAL FINANCIALS & EMPLOYEES

| Not-for-profit<br>FYE: December 31 | Annual<br>Growth | 12/91 | 12/92 | 12/93 | 12/94 | 12/95 | 12/96 | 12/97 | 12/98 | 12/99 | 12/00 |
|---|---|---|---|---|---|---|---|---|---|---|---|
| Sales ($ mil.) | 14.3% | — | 3,083 | 3,113 | 3,221 | 3,367 | 6,619 | 7,405 | 7,544 | 8,190 | 9,000 |
| Net income ($ mil.) | 7.0% | — | 141 | 132 | 128 | 43 | (50) | 101 | 62 | 69 | 242 |
| Income as % of sales | — | — | 4.6% | 4.2% | 4.0% | 1.3% | — | 1.4% | 0.8% | 0.8% | 2.7% |
| Employees | 7.3% | — | — | — | 7,200 | 8,000 | 10,500 | 12,000 | 12,000 | 11,000 | 11,000 |

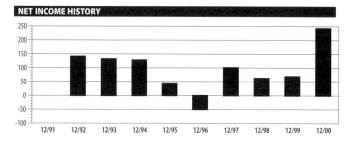

NET INCOME HISTORY

# HOLBERG INDUSTRIES, INC.

## OVERVIEW

Holberg Industries is a parking-space peddler, no longer a fast-food farmer. The Greenwich, Connecticut-based company's 80%-owned subsidiary APCOA/Standard Parking manages about 2,000 parking facilities in more than 200 cities in Canada and the US. The company focuses on urban markets and also operates about 70 airport parking facilities. Its AmeriServe Food Distribution unit, which supplied food, beverages, and equipment to Taco Bell, Pizza Hut, and KFC fast food restaurants in North America, was acquired by McLane Company (the distributing unit of Wal-Mart) after filing for Chapter 11 bankruptcy protection.

Co-founder and CEO John Holten owns a controlling interest in Holberg Industries; Norwegian consumer goods company Orkla owns 34%.

## HISTORY

Norwegian-born John Holten worked at New York City merchant bank DnC Capital in the mid-1980s. There he met Swedish-born managing partner Gunnar Klintberg. In 1986 they formed Holberg Inc. That year, in partnership with Norway's Nora Industrier (now part of Orkla), Holberg bought NEBCO Distribution of Omaha, a Nebraska concession company that had been formed in 1946.

Holberg moved into parking lot management — and formed Holberg Industries — with its 1989 purchase of a controlling stake in the North American operations of APCOA.

APCOA had been founded as Airport Parking Company of America in 1949 by Ted Bonda and future US senator Howard Metzenbaum. At the time, airport parking was unorganized but free. Metzenbaum and Bonda changed all that, garnering a contract in 1951 to manage paid parking facilities at Cleveland Hopkins International Airport. APCOA's guarded, well-lit parking lots were a hit, and the company soon became the preeminent airport parking manager in the US.

Metzenbaum and Bonda sold APCOA to conglomerate International Telephone & Telegraph in 1966. Holding company Delaware North acquired APCOA in 1981 and sold its North American operations to Holberg and APCOA managers in 1989.

In 1990 Holberg Industries created NEBCO EVANS Distribution with its acquisition of Evans Brothers, a Wisconsin-based regional distributor that had begun roasting nuts around 1940. Additional acquisitions in the early 1990s included regional operators L.L. Distribution Systems and Condon Supply, both of Minnesota.

In 1996, when NEBCO EVANS had sales of $400 million, Holberg Industries bought Dallas-based wholesaler AmeriServ Food Co. AmeriServ had been formed by the 1989 combination of distributors Sonneveldt and Interstate Distributors. By the end of 1991, AmeriServ had added four more companies — Alpha Distributors (Wisconsin), First Choice Food Distributors (Texas), Harry H. Post Co. (50%, Colorado), and Food Service Systems (Missouri).

In 1997 Holberg Industries consolidated its $1.4 billion food service operations — including the remaining 50% of Harry H. Post Co. — under the name AmeriServe Food Distribution. Later that year AmeriServe bought PFS, PepsiCo's food service unit, which primarily supplied the KFC, Pizza Hut, and Taco Bell chains. The $830 million deal more than doubled AmeriServe's size.

AmeriServe acquired ProSource in 1998 for $320 million, which added casual dining restaurant chains T.G.I. Friday's and Red Lobster to its customer base; that deal bumped up AmeriServe's sales by about $4 billion.

By 1998 APCOA had 700 parking lots in 30 cities. That year it bought privately held, Chicago-based Standard Parking, which operated 380 garages in 29 cities. Founded in 1929 at a Standard Oil gas station, Standard had made its mark in parking management by playing music in themed garages to help patrons remember where they parked. Myron Warshauer, grandson of Standard's founder, took the wheel of the combined company, APCOA/Standard Parking, which bought several small lot operators in 1998 and 1999.

In 2000 AmeriServe exhibited signs of indigestion when it filed for Chapter 11 bankruptcy protection. The food distributor lost all but one of its customers (TRICON Global Restaurants) and sold off its equipment division that year. Ameriserve was acquired by wholesale distributor McLane Company, a unit of Wal-Mart Stores, and renamed McLane Foodservice Distribution in 2000.

**Chairman and CEO:** John V. Holten, age 44
**Vice Chairman:** Gunnar E. Klintberg
**SVP and CFO:** A. Peter Ostberg
**SVP and Controller:** Susan M. Tessler
**President and CEO, APCOA/Standard Parking:**
  Myron Warshauer, age 60

## LOCATIONS

**HQ:** 545 Steamboat Rd., Greenwich, CT 06830
**Phone:** 203-422-3000      **Fax:** 203-661-5756
**Web:** www.holberg.com

APCOA/Standard Parking manages about 2,000 parking
facilities in 200 cities throughout Canada and the US.

## PRODUCTS/OPERATIONS

**Selected Parking Services**
Lot management services
Value-added services ("Ambiance in Parking")
  Books-To-Go and Film-To-Go (audio and video tape
    lending)
  CarCare service (with Midas International)
  Emergency car services (battery starts, lost car
    assistance)
  Musical-themed floor-reminder systems
  ParkNet (traffic information)
  Standard Parking Exchange (free parking at affiliated
    lots for contract parkers)
  Windshield and headlight cleaning

## COMPETITORS

Ace Parking
Central Parking
Republic Parking

## HISTORICAL FINANCIALS & EMPLOYEES

| Private FYE: December 31 | Annual Growth | 12/91 | 12/92 | 12/93 | 12/94 | 12/95 | 12/96 | 12/97 | 12/98 | 12/99 | 12/00 |
|---|---|---|---|---|---|---|---|---|---|---|---|
| Sales ($ mil.) | (9.8%) | — | — | — | — | — | — | 5,800 | 9,279 | 10,000 | 4,250 |
| Employees | 25.3% | — | — | — | — | — | — | 9,300 | 20,225 | 20,000 | 18,300 |

### SALES HISTORY

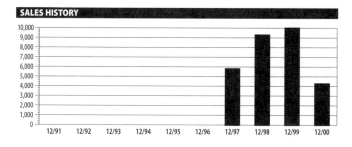

# HUNTSMAN CORPORATION

## OVERVIEW

Chemical production and charitable giving make up the Huntsman Corporation, the world's largest privately held chemical firm. Salt Lake City-based Huntsman makes industrial chemicals, petrochemicals, and specialty chemicals used by companies in the chemical, plastics, detergent, personal care, automotive, high-tech textiles, and packaging industries.

Huntsman makes specialty chemicals for use in foams and coatings; titanium dioxide pigments for use in consumer products (including food and cosmetics); petrochemicals for use in detergents and textiles; and surfactants for use in adhesives and in metalworking and paper processing.

The company doubled in size when it bought the bulk chemical lines of UK-based Imperial Chemical Industries. Peter Huntsman, CEO and son of founder and chairman Jon Huntsman, is reorganizing Huntsman to accommodate new acquisitions and divestitures, which have included the sale of Huntsman Packaging to J. P. Morgan Partners.

Jon Huntsman, a cancer survivor, has given hundreds of millions of dollars to educational and charitable causes and medical research. He has said that the company's divestitures will enable him to give more money to charities, most notably Utah's Huntsman Cancer Institute. Jon Huntsman controls the company.

## HISTORY

First exposed to the use of plastics in the manufacture of egg cartons, Jon Huntsman spent three frustrating years at Dow Chemical. Then, he and his brother Blaine raised $300,000 and received a $1 million loan from Hambrecht & Quist to found Huntsman Container in 1970. When chemical supplies began to run short, Huntsman sold the company to Keyes Fiber in 1976.

After six years, half of which had been spent doing missionary work for the Mormon Church, Huntsman took over polystyrene operations and set his sights on an underused Shell plant in Ohio. With oil and gas titan Atlantic Richfield's backing, Huntsman convinced Shell and a bank to lend him the balance of the purchase price and formed Huntsman Chemical in 1982.

With the acquisition of Hoechst Celanese's polystyrene business in 1986, Huntsman became the #1 producer of styrene in the US. In 1987 it sold 40% of Huntsman Chemical for $52 million and then acquired a New Jersey polypropylene plant from Shell. Huntsman reentered the packaging business in 1989 by acquiring Keyes, the European firm that had once been a part of Huntsman Container.

In 1991 hamburger dynasty McDonald's succumbed to environmentalist pressure and ceased to use the Huntsman-developed polystyrene clamshell containers; as a result, Huntsman lost about 10% of its business. The company acquired packaging assets from Goodyear Tire and Rubber in 1992. The next year Huntsman bought 50% of Chemplex Australia Limited from Consolidated Press Holdings (controlled by Australian tycoon Kerry Packer).

Huntsman and Packer joined forces again in 1994 to buy most of Texaco's unprofitable petrochemical operations (renamed Huntsman Corporation) for $1 billion, which doubled Huntsman's size and added 24 plants in 12 countries. Also that year Huntsman bought Eastman Chemical's worldwide polypropylene business. The next year it formed a joint venture with Texaco to operate Texaco's worldwide lubricant-additives line, and Huntsman reacquired the 17% stake held by Great Lakes Chemical, which had been the only stock in the company held by outsiders.

In 1996 Huntsman placed all of his businesses under a single entity, the Huntsman Corporation. The company bought the last of Texaco's chemicals operations in 1997, moving Huntsman into the propylene oxide market.

Huntsman sold its polystyrene and styrene monomer businesses in the US and Europe to NOVA Chemicals in 1998. In 1999 the company doubled its size with the purchase of Imperial Chemical Industries' polyurethane, aromatics, titanium dioxide, petrochemical, and olefins businesses.

In 2000 Huntsman sold Huntsman Packaging to J. P. Morgan Partners in a deal worth $1 billion. Also, Jon Huntsman stepped down as CEO but remained chairman. He was succeeded by his son, Peter Huntsman. Late that year Huntsman agreed to acquire Rohm and Haas' thermoplastic polyurethane business.

In 2001 the company announced that Bain Capital and Blackstone Capital Partners would acquire a minority interest in Huntsman International Holdings from Imperial Chemical and other private investors for about $550 million.

**Chairman:** Jon M. Huntsman Sr., age 63
**Vice Chairman:** Jon M. Huntsman Jr., age 41
**President, CEO, and Director:** Peter R. Huntsman, age 38
**SVP and CFO:** J. Kimo Esplin, age 38
**SVP and General Counsel; SVP, Chief Legal Officer, and Secretary of Huntsman Polymers:** Robert B. Lence, age 43
**SVP, Environmental, Health, and Safety of Huntsman Corporation, Huntsman Polymers, and Huntsman Petrochemical:** Michael J. Kern, age 50
**SVP, Global Sales and Marketing for Huntsman Corporation, Huntsman Polymers, and Huntsman Petrochemicals:** Donald J. Stanutz, age 50
**SVP, North American Petrochemicals and SVP, Huntsman Polymers:** Thomas J. Keenan, age 48
**SVP, Public Affairs; SVP, Public Affiars, Huntsman Polymers:** Don H. Olsen, age 55
**VP, Administration; VP, Huntsman Polymers:** Sean Douglas, age 36
**VP, Finance:** L. Russell Healy, age 45
**VP, Human Resources:** William Chapman
**VP and Treasurer:** Samuel D. Scruggs, age 41

## LOCATIONS

**HQ:** 500 Huntsman Way, Salt Lake City, UT 84108
**Phone:** 801-584-5700 **Fax:** 801-584-5781
**Web:** www.huntsman.com

Huntsman Corporation has operations worldwide.

## PRODUCTS/OPERATIONS

**Divisions**
Gas Treating Products (like gas-scrubbing agents)
Polymers (including resins)
Polyurethanes (used in products from adhesives to automotive parts)
Surfactants (including oxides and propylene)
Tioxides (titanium dioxides)

**Selected Joint Ventures**
CONDEA-Huntsman GmbH & Co. KG (automobile parts, boat hulls, and marble bath fixtures; Germany)
Huntsman Chemical Company Australia Limited (joint venture with Consolidated Press Holdings)
Polystyrene Australia (joint venture with Dow Chemical (Australia) Ltd.)

## COMPETITORS

| | |
|---|---|
| Akzo Nobel | Hercules |
| American Home Products | ICI |
| BASF AG | Lyondell Chemical |
| Bayer AG | Millennium Chemicals |
| BP | Novartis |
| BP Chemicals | Occidental Petroleum |
| ChevronTexaco | Owens Corning |
| Degussa | Phillips Petroleum |
| Dow Chemical | PPG |
| DuPont | Rohm and Haas |
| Eastman Chemical | Sinopec Shanghai |
| Exxon Mobil | Petrochemical |
| Formosa Plastics | Union Carbide |
| Henkel | |

## HISTORICAL FINANCIALS & EMPLOYEES

| Private<br>FYE: December 31 | Annual<br>Growth | 12/91 | 12/92 | 12/93 | 12/94 | 12/95 | 12/96 | 12/97 | 12/98 | 12/99 | 12/00 |
|---|---|---|---|---|---|---|---|---|---|---|---|
| Sales ($ mil.) | 23.3% | — | — | 1,850 | 3,400 | 4,300 | 4,500 | 4,750 | 5,200 | 7,000 | 8,000 |
| Employees | 19.3% | — | 3,900 | 5,000 | 8,100 | 8,000 | 8,000 | 9,550 | 10,000 | 14,000 | 16,000 |

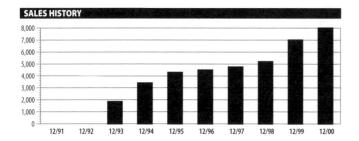

**SALES HISTORY**

**HUNTSMAN**

# HYATT CORPORATION

## OVERVIEW

Chicago is Hyatt's kind of town — as are hundreds of others around the world. Chicago-based Hyatt is one of the largest hotel operators in the nation, with more than 120 full-service luxury hotels and resorts in North America and the Caribbean (Hyatt International, a separate company, operates 60 hotels and 22 resorts in 38 countries). In addition, Hyatt manages casinos at several of its hotels and runs a luxury retirement community called Classic Residence by Hyatt.

Hyatt caters to convention-goers, business travelers, and upscale vacationers. The company offers specially designed Business Plan rooms with fax machines and 24-hour access to copiers, printers, and other business necessities. Camp Hyatt targets family travelers with educational games, activities, and programs for children. The company is experiencing much of its growth outside the US. It has some 17 hotels under construction in countries such as China, India, Poland, Thailand, and the United Arab Emirates.

Led by chairman, president, and CEO Thomas Pritzker, the company is owned by the Pritzker family, one of the wealthiest families in the US.

## HISTORY

Nicholas Pritzker left Kiev for Chicago in 1881, where his family's ascent to the ranks of America's wealthiest families began. His son A. N. left the family law practice in the 1930s and began investing in a variety of businesses. He turned a 1942 investment (Cory Corporation) worth $25,000 into $23 million by 1967. A. N.'s son Jay followed in his father's wheeling-and-dealing footsteps. In 1953, with the help of his father's banking connections, Jay purchased Colson Company and recruited his brother Bob, an industrial engineer, to restructure a company that made tricycles and US Navy rockets. By 1990 Jay and Bob had added 60 industrial companies, with annual sales exceeding $3 billion, to the entity they called the Marmon Group.

The family's connection to Hyatt hotels was established in 1957 when Jay Pritzker bought a hotel called Hyatt House, located near the Los Angeles airport, from Hyatt von Dehn. Jay added five locations by 1961 and hired his gregarious youngest brother, Donald, to manage the hotel company. Hyatt went public in 1967, but the move that opened new vistas for the hotel chain was the purchase that year of an 800-room hotel in Atlanta that both Hilton and Marriott had turned down. John Portman's design, incorporating a 21-story atrium, a large fountain, and a revolving rooftop restaurant, became a Hyatt trademark.

The Pritzkers formed Hyatt International in 1969 to operate hotels overseas, and the company grew rapidly in the US and abroad during the 1970s. Donald Pritzker died in 1972, and Jay assumed control of Hyatt. The family decided to take the company private in 1979. Much of Hyatt's growth in the 1970s came from contracts to manage, under the Hyatt banner, hotels built by other investors. When Hyatt's cut on those contracts shrank in the 1980s, the company launched its own hotel and resort developments under Nick Pritzker, a cousin to Jay and Bob. In 1988, with US and Japanese partners, it built the Hyatt Regency Waikoloa on Hawaii's Big Island for $360 million — a record at the time for a hotel.

The Pritzkers took a side-venture into air travel in 1983 when they bought bedraggled Braniff Airlines through Hyatt subsidiaries as it emerged from bankruptcy. After a failed 1987 attempt to merge the airline with Pan Am, the Pritzkers sold Braniff in 1988.

Hyatt opened Classic Residence by Hyatt, a group of upscale retirement communities, in 1989. The company joined Circus Circus (now Mandalay Resort Group) in 1994 to launch the Grand Victoria, the nation's largest cruising gaming vessel, at Elgin, Illinois. The next year, as part of a new strategy to manage both free-standing golf courses and those near Hyatt hotels, the company opened its first freestanding course: an 18-hole par 71 championship course on Aruba.

President Thomas Pritzker, Jay's son, took over as chairman and CEO of Hyatt following his father's death in early 1999. In 2000 Hyatt announced plans to join rival Marriott International in launching an independent company to provide an online procurement network to serve the hospitality industry. The following year the company announced plans to begin building a new headquarters in 2002. The skyscraper, to be called the Hyatt Center, will be located in Chicago's West Loop.

**Chairman, President, and CEO; Chairman Hyatt International Corporation:** Thomas J. Pritzker
**Vice Chairman; Chairman and President, Hyatt Development Corporation; President, Hyatt Equities:** Nicholas J. Pritzker
**SVP Finance and Administration:** Frank Borg
**Chairman and President, Classic Residence by Hyatt:** Penny S. Pritzker, age 41
**President, Classic Residence by Hyatt:** Ronald J. Richardson
**President, Hyatt Hotels Corporation:** Scott D. Miller
**President, Hyatt International Corporation:** Bernd Chorengel
**EVP and COO, Hyatt Hotels Corporation:** Edward W. Rabin
**SVP, Human Resources, Hyatt Hotels Corporation:** Linda Olson
**SVP Marketing, Hyatt Hotels Corporation:** Tom O'Toole
**SVP Operations, Hyatt Hotels Corporation:** Chuck Floyd
**Divisional VP (Southern), Hyatt Hotels Corporation:** Tim Lindgren
**Divisional VP (Resorts), Hyatt Hotels Corporation:** Victor Lopez, age 51
**Divisional VP (Western), Hyatt Hotels Corporation:** John Orr
**Divisional VP (Central), Hyatt Hotels Corporation:** Steve Sokal

## COMPETITORS

Accor
Cendant
Four Seasons Hotels
Helmsley
Hilton
Host Marriott
Marriott International
Ritz Carlton
Sandals Resorts
Six Continents Hotels
Starwood Hotels & Resorts
Trump

## LOCATIONS

**HQ:** 200 W. Madison St., Chicago, IL 60606
**Phone:** 312-750-1234      **Fax:** 312-750-8550
**Web:** www.hyatt.com

Hyatt Corporation and Hyatt International, a separate entity also controlled by the Pritzker family, own and operate hotels worldwide.

## PRODUCTS/OPERATIONS

**Selected Operations**
Camp Hyatt (activities for children)
Classic Residence by Hyatt (upscale retirement communities)
Hyatt Hotels and Resorts
Regency Casinos

## HISTORICAL FINANCIALS & EMPLOYEES

| Private FYE: January 31 | Annual Growth | 1/91 | 1/92 | 1/93 | 1/94 | 1/95 | 1/96 | 1/97 | 1/98 | 1/99 | 1/00 |
|---|---|---|---|---|---|---|---|---|---|---|---|
| Estimated sales ($ mil.) | 14.4% | — | 1,350 | 1,460 | 950 | 1,240 | 2,500 | 2,900 | 1,378 | 3,400 | 3,950 |
| Employees | 5.7% | — | 51,275 | 52,275 | 47,000 | 54,000 | 65,000 | 80,000 | 80,000 | 80,000 | 80,000 |

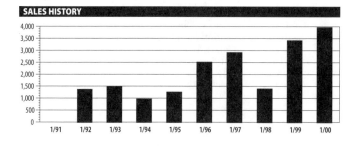

SALES HISTORY

# IGA, INC.

## OVERVIEW

Independent grocers have found they can boost their business by being a little less independent. More than 4,000 stores belong to Chicago-based IGA (which stands for both Independent Grocers Alliance and International Grocers Alliance, according to the company). The alliance is the world's largest voluntary supermarket network, owned by 37 marketing and distribution companies worldwide (including the likes of Fleming Companies and SUPERVALU); it has stores on every inhabited continent — with outlets in nearly all 50 states and about 40 countries. Collectively, its members are one of the largest food operations in terms of sales in North America, and its international operations account for 62% of sales.

In addition to flying the IGA Red Oval banner and having access to IGA Brand private-label products, members receive advertising and marketing services, educational programs, and volume discounts through the food distributors that control it. Some stores in the alliance, which primarily caters to smaller towns, also sell gas.

The association continues its expansion overseas. The first US grocer to go into China and Singapore, IGA is now moving into Europe, particularly focusing on Poland.

## HISTORY

IGA was founded in Chicago in 1926 by a group led by accountant Frank Grimes. During the 1920s chains began to dominate the grocery store industry. Grimes, an accountant for many grocery wholesalers, saw an opportunity to develop a network of independent grocers that could compete with the burgeoning chains. Grimes and five associates — Gene Flack, Louis Groebe, W. K. Hunter, H. V. Swenson, and William Thompson — created IGA.

Their idea was to "level the playing field" for independent grocers and chain stores by taking advantage of volume buying and mass marketing. IGA originally acted as a purchasing agent for its wholesalers but eventually passed that duty to the wholesalers. The group's first members were Poughkeepsie, New York-based grocery distributor W. T. Reynolds Company and the 69 grocery stores it serviced.

IGA focused on adding distributors and retailers, and it soon added wholesaler Fleming-Wilson (now Fleming Companies) and Winston & Newell (now SUPERVALU). In 1930 it hired Babe Ruth as a spokesman; other celebrity endorsers during the period included Jackie Cooper, Jack Dempsey, and Popeye. IGA also sponsored a radio program called the IGA *Home Town Hour*. In 1945 the company introduced the Foodliner format, a design for stores larger than 4,000 sq. ft. The next year IGA introduced the 30-ft.-by-100-ft. Precision Store — designed so customers had to pass all the other merchandise in the store to get to the dairy and bread sections.

Grimes retired as president in 1951. He was succeeded by his son, Don, who continued to expand the company. Don was succeeded in 1968 by Richard Jones, head of IGA member J. M. Jones Co.

Thomas Haggai was named chairman of the company in 1976. A Baptist minister, radio commentator, and former CIA employee, Haggai had come to the attention of Grimes in 1960 when he praised Christian Scientists in one of his radio broadcasts. Grimes, a Christian Scientist, asked Haggai to speak at an IGA convention and eventually asked him to join the IGA board. Haggai, who became CEO in 1986, tightened the restrictions for IGA members, weeding out many of the smaller, low-volume mom-and-pop stores making up much of the group's network.

Haggai also began a push for international expansion. In 1988 the organization signed a deal with Japanese food company C. Itoh (now ITOCHU) to open a distribution outlet in Tokyo.

The 1990s saw expansion into Australia, Papua New Guinea, the Caribbean, China, Singapore, South Africa, and Brazil. IGA also expanded outside the continental US when it entered Hawaii. In 1993 IGA began an international television advertising campaign, a first for the supermarket industry. The next year the company launched its first line of private-label products for an ethnic food market, introducing several Mexican food products. In 1998 the group developed a new format for its stores that included on-site gas pumps

SUPERVALU signed 54 independent grocery stores (primarily in Mississippi and Arkansas and Trinidad in the Caribbean) to the IGA banner in 1999. With more than 60% of sales coming from international operations, IGA realigned its corporate structure in 2001, setting up IGA North America, IGA Southern Hemisphere/Europe/Caribbean, and IGA Asia, each with its own president.

## OFFICERS

**Chairman and CEO:** Thomas S. Haggai
**President, IGA North America:** Duane Martin
**President, IGA Southern Hemisphere, Europe, and Caribbean:** Paulo Goelzer
**President, IGA Asia:** Vincent Kong
**VP, Events:** Barbara G. Wiest
**VP, Information Technology:** Nick Liakopulos
**VP, Retail:** Bill Benzing
**Director of Public Relations:** Shannan Blagg

## LOCATIONS

**HQ:** 8725 W. Higgins Rd., Chicago, IL 60631
**Phone:** 773-693-4520  **Fax:** 773-693-4532
**Web:** www.igainc.com

IGA has operations in 48 states and about 40 other countries, commonwealths, and territories.

### 2000 Sales

|  | $ mil. | % of total |
|---|---|---|
| US & Caribbean | 8,000 | 38 |
| Other regions | 13,000 | 62 |
| **Total** | **21,000** | **100** |

## PRODUCTS/OPERATIONS

### Selected Distributors/Owners
Bozzuto's Inc.
C.I. Foods Systems Co., Ltd. (Japan)
Davids Limited (Australia)
Fleming Companies, Inc.
Foodland Associated Limited (Australia)
Great North Foods
IGA Brasil (includes 16 individual companies)
Martahari Putra Prima Tbk (Indonesia)
McLane Polska (Poland)
Merchants Distributors, Inc.
Metro Cash & Carry (Africa)
Nash Finch Company
NTUC Fairprice (Singapore)
Pearl River Distribution Ltd. (China)
SUPERVALU INC.
Tasmania Independent Wholesalers (Tasmania)
Tripifoods, Inc.
Villa Market JP Co., Ltd. (Thailand)
W. Lee Flowers & Co., Inc.
WALTERMART SUPERMARKETS (Philippines)

### Affiliates
H.Y. Louie (fraternal relationship, Canada)
Sobey's (fraternal relationship, Canada)

### Selected Joint Operations and Services
Advertising
Community service programs
Equipment purchase
IGA Brand (private-label products)
*IGA Grocergram* (in-house magazine)
Internet services
Marketing
Merchandising
Red Oval Family (manufacturer/IGA collaboration on sales, marketing, and other activities)
Volume buying

## COMPETITORS

| | |
|---|---|
| Albertson's | Ito-Yokado |
| AWG | Kroger |
| BJs Wholesale Club | Meijer |
| C&S Wholesale | Metro Cash and Carry |
| Carrefour | Penn Traffic |
| Casino Guichard | Publix |
| Coles Myer | Roundy's |
| Daiei | Royal Ahold |
| Dairy Farm International Holdings | Safeway |
| | Spartan Stores |
| Delhaize | Topco Associates |
| George Weston | Wakefern Food |
| A&P | Wal-Mart |
| Hannaford Bros. | Winn-Dixie |
| H-E-B | |

## HISTORICAL FINANCIALS & EMPLOYEES

| Association<br>FYE: December 31 | Annual<br>Growth | 12/91 | 12/92 | 12/93 | 12/94 | 12/95 | 12/96 | 12/97 | 12/98 | 12/99 | 12/00 |
|---|---|---|---|---|---|---|---|---|---|---|---|
| Estimated sales ($ mil.) | 3.5% | — | 15,900 | 16,500 | 17,000 | 17,100 | 16,800 | 18,000 | 18,000 | 18,000 | 21,000 |
| Employees | (6.7%) | — | — | — | — | 130,000 | 128,000 | 135,000 | 92,000 | 92,000 | 92,000 |

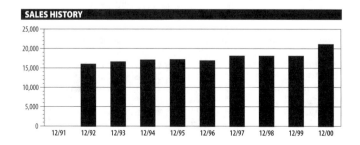

### SALES HISTORY

# INGRAM INDUSTRIES INC.

## OVERVIEW

Book 'em, Martha. Billionaire Martha Ingram heads Nashville Tennessee-based Ingram Industries, whose Ingram Book Group is the US's largest wholesale distributor of trade books and audiobooks to retailers and a leading distributor to libraries. Ingram Book, through its eight fulfillment centers, distributes 175 million titles a year. It serves some 32,000 retail outlets and represents over 13,000 publishers. Its Lightning Source subsidiary offers conversion and distribution services for print-on-demand and e-books.

Although Ingram Book accounts for just over half of Ingram Industries' sales, the company also operates Ingram Marine Group, which ships grain, ore, and other products via its 1,800 barges, and Ingram Insurance Group, which offers high-risk auto insurance in nine states through Permanent General Insurance. Ingram Industries spun off its largest segment, Ingram Micro (the world's largest distributor of microcomputer products), in 1996 and Ingram Entertainment (the US's top distributor of videotapes) in 1997.

Martha Ingram is America's wealthiest active businesswoman, and she and her family own and run Ingram Industries. The family controls about 75% of Ingram Micro's voting stock.

## HISTORY

Orrin Ingram and two partners founded the Dole, Ingram & Kennedy sawmill in 1857 in Eau Claire, Wisconsin, on the Chippewa River, about 50 miles upstream from the Mississippi River. By the 1870s the company, renamed Ingram & Kennedy, was selling lumber as far downstream as Hannibal, Missouri.

Ingram's success was noticed by Frederick Weyerhaeuser, a German immigrant in Rock Island, Illinois, who, like Ingram, had worked in a sawmill before buying one of his own. In 1881 Ingram and Weyerhaeuser negotiated the formation of Chippewa Logging (35%-owned by up-river partners, 65% by down-river interests), which controlled the white pine harvest of the Chippewa Valley. In 1900 Ingram paid $216,000 for 2,160 shares in the newly formed Weyerhaeuser Timber Company. Ingram let his sons and grandsons handle the investment and formed O.H. Ingram Co. to manage the family's interests. He died in 1918.

In 1946 Ingram's descendants founded Ingram Barge, which hauled crude oil to the company's refinery near St. Louis. After buying and then selling other holdings, in 1962 the family formed Ingram Corp., consisting solely of Ingram Barge. Brothers Bronson and Fritz Ingram (the great grandsons of Orrin) bought the company from their father, Hank, before he died in 1963, and the next year they bought half of Tennessee Book, a textbook distributing company founded in 1935. In 1970 they formed Ingram Book Group to sell trade books to bookstores and libraries.

Ingram Barge won a $48 million Chicago sludge-hauling contract in 1971, but later the company was accused of bribing city politicians with $1.2 million in order to land the contract. The brothers stood trial in 1977 for authorizing the bribes; Bronson was acquitted, but the court convicted Fritz on 29 counts. Before Fritz entered prison (he served 16 months of a four-year sentence), he and his brother split their company. Fritz took the energy operations and went bust in the 1980s. Bronson took the barge and book businesses and formed Ingram Industries.

The company formed computer products distributor Ingram Computer in 1982 and between 1985 and 1989 bought all the stock of Micro D, a computer wholesaler. Ingram Computer and Micro D merged to form Ingram Micro. In 1992 it acquired Commtron, the world's #1 wholesaler of prerecorded videocassettes, and merged it into Ingram Entertainment.

When Bronson died in mid-1995, his wife Martha (the PR director) became chairman and began a restructuring. Ingram Industries closed its non-bookstore rack distributor (Ingram Merchandising) in 1995 and sold its oil-and-gas machinery subsidiary (Cactus Co.) in 1996. It spun off Ingram Micro that year, followed in 1997 by Ingram Entertainment. Ingram Industries purchased Christian books distributor Spring Arbor that year and also introduced an on-demand book publishing service (Lightning Print).

The company in late 1998 agreed to sell its book group to Barnes & Noble, but FTC pressure killed the deal in mid-1999. With customers and competitors increasing distribution capacity in the western US, a resulting drop in business led Ingram Industries to cut more than 100 jobs at an Oregon warehouse in 1999.

In 2000 Ingram renamed Lightning Print as Lightning Source. Also that year Ingram announced plans to distribute products other than books for e-tailers (starting with gifts). In March 2001 Ingram took over specialty-book distribution for Borders.

**Chairman:** Martha Ingram
**Vice Chairman; Chairman, Ingram Book Group:**
John Ingram, age 39
**President and CEO; Chairman Ingram Barge Company:**
Orrin H. Ingram II
**VP and Controller:** Mary K. Cavarra
**VP and Treasurer:** Robert W. Mitchell
**VP Human Resources:** Dennis Delaney
**President, Ingram Book Company; COO, Ingram Book
Group:** Jim Chandler
**President and CEO, Ingram Book Group:**
Michael Lovett
**President, Ingram Library Services:** Jim Kelly
**President Spring Arbor Distributors:** Steve Arthur

## LOCATIONS

**HQ:** 1 Belle Meade Place, 4400 Harding Rd.,
Nashville, TN 37205
**Phone:** 615-298-8200          **Fax:** 615-298-8242
**Web:** www.ingram.com

## PRODUCTS/OPERATIONS

**Selected Operations**

**Ingram Book Group**
Ingram Book Company (wholesaler of trade books and
audiobooks)
Ingram Customer Systems (computerized systems and
services)
Ingram International (international distribution of
books and audiobooks)
Ingram Library Services (distributes books, audiobooks,
and videos to libraries)
Ingram Periodicals (direct distributor of specialty
magazines)
Ingram Publisher Services (distribution services for
publishers)
Lightning Source (on-demand printing and electonic
publishing)
Specialty Retail (book distributor to nontraditional book
market)
Spring Arbor Distributors (product and services for
Christian retailers)
White Bridge Communications (consumer marketing
programs for publishers and retailers)

**Ingram Insurance Group**
Permanent General Insurance Co. (automobile
insurance in California, Florida, Georgia, Indiana,
Louisiana, Ohio, South Carolina, Tennessee, and
Wisconsin)

**Ingram Marine Group**
Ingram Barge (grain, ore, and other product shipping)
Ingram Materials Co. (construction materials production)

## COMPETITORS

| | |
|---|---|
| Advanced Marketing | Media Source |
| Allstate | netLibrary, Inc. |
| American Commercial | Progressive Corporation |
| Lines | Publishers Group West |
| American Financial | SAFECO |
| Baker & Taylor | State Farm |
| Chas. Levy | TECO Energy |
| Follett | Thomas Nelson |
| Hudson News | Times Publishing |
| Kirby | |

## HISTORICAL FINANCIALS & EMPLOYEES

| Private<br>FYE: December 31 | Annual<br>Growth | 12/91 | 12/92 | 12/93 | 12/94 | 12/95 | 12/96 | 12/97 | 12/98 | 12/99 | 12/00 |
|---|---|---|---|---|---|---|---|---|---|---|---|
| Sales ($ mil.) | (9.6%) | — | 4,657 | 6,163 | 8,010 | 11,000 | 1,463 | 1,796 | 2,000 | 2,135 | 2,075 |
| Employees | (3.2%) | — | 8,407 | 9,658 | 10,000 | 13,000 | 5,300 | 6,362 | 6,500 | 6,080 | 6,494 |

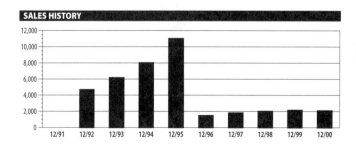

SALES HISTORY

# TEAMSTERS

The International Brotherhood of Teamsters is trying to turn over a new leaf. The largest industrial trade union in the US, and the most (in)famous, the Washington, DC-based Teamsters represents some 1.4 million members, including truckers, UPS workers, airline workers, cab drivers, construction crews, warehouse employees, and other workers in 16 trade groups. The Teamsters (an AFL-CIO affiliate) negotiates with employers for contracts that guarantee its members fair wages and promotion policies, health coverage, job security, and other benefits. It has about 570 local chapters in the US and Canada.

Elected in 1998, Teamsters chief James P. Hoffa (whose father, union leader Jimmy Hoffa, vanished and is assumed dead) is working to usher in a new era for the controversial union. He wants the Teamsters to police themselves so they can end the government's close supervision of the the union. He also is working to re-establish the union as a power in national politics, lobbying against plans to allow trucks from Mexico to traverse US highways.

## HISTORY

Two rival team-driver unions, the Drivers International Union and the Teamsters National Union, merged to form the International Brotherhood of Teamsters in 1903. Led by Cornelius Shea, the Teamsters established headquarters in Indianapolis. Daniel Tobin (president for 45 years, starting in 1907) demanded that union locals obtain executive approval before striking. Membership expanded from the team-driver base, prompting the union to add Chauffeurs, Stablemen, and Helpers to its name (1909).

Following the first transcontinental delivery by motor truck (1912), the Teamster deliverymen traded their horses for trucks. The union then recruited food processing, brewery, and farm workers, among others, to augment Teamster effectiveness during strikes. It joined the American Federation of Labor in 1920.

Until the Depression the Teamsters was still a small union of predominantly urban deliverymen. Then Farrell Dobbs, a Trotskyite Teamster from Minneapolis, organized the famous Minneapolis strikes in 1934 to protest local management's refusal to allow the workers to unionize. Workers clashed with police and National Guard units for 11 days before management acceded to the workers' demands. The strikes demonstrated the potential strength of unions, and Teamsters membership swelled. Although union power ebbed during WWII, the union continued to grow. It moved its headquarters to Washington, DC, in 1953.

The AFL-CIO expelled the Teamsters in 1957 when Teamster ties to the mob became public during a US Senate investigation. New Teamsters boss Jimmy Hoffa eluded indictment and took advantage of America's growing dependence on trucking to negotiate the powerful National Master Freight Agreement (1964). Hoffa also organized industrial workers. He used a union pension fund to make mob-connected loans and was later convicted of jury tampering and sent to prison. In 1975, four years after his release, Hoffa vanished without a trace and is believed to have been the victim of a Mafia hit.

The Teamsters rejoined the AFL-CIO in 1987 and the following year settled a racketeering lawsuit filed by the US Justice Department by allowing government appointees to discipline corrupt union leaders, help run the union, and oversee its elections. The election of self-styled reformer Ronald Carey in 1991 (he received 49% of the vote) seemed to portend real changes for the union; each of his six predecessors had been accused of or imprisoned for criminal activities. However, membership dropped by 40,000 in both 1991 and 1992.

Carey won re-election as union president in 1996 over rival, and son of former boss Jimmy Hoffa, James P. Hoffa (whom Carey accused of having ties to organized crime). A 15-day strike by the Teamsters' UPS employees in 1997 led to the delivery company's agreement to combine part-time jobs into 10,000 new full-time positions. That year Carey's re-election was overturned amid a campaign finance investigation that netted guilty pleas from three Carey associates, and the Teamsters leader was disqualified from running for re-election in 1998. Carey was officially expelled from the Teamsters by the federal government, and Hoffa won the 1998 election over Tom Leedham (who was backed by the union's reform wing).

Promising to fight corruption, Hoffa hired former federal prosecutor Edwin Stier and several former FBI agents to help him operate Project RISE (respect, integrity, strength, and ethics), a new in-house anticorruption program. In 2001 the union began lobbying against plans to allow Mexican trucking companies to transport goods across the US.

## OFFICERS

**General President:** James P. Hoffa, age 60
**General Secretary-Treasurer:** Tom Keegel
**VP At-Large:** Randy Cammack
**VP At-Large:** Fred Gegare
**VP At-Large:** Carl E. Haynes
**VP At-Large:** Ralph J. Taurone
**Central Region VP:** Patrick Flynn
**Central Region VP:** Walter Lytle
**Central Region VP:** Dotty W. Malinsky
**Central Region VP:** Lester A. Singer
**Central Region VP:** Philip E. Young
**Eastern Region VP:** Jack Cipriani
**Eastern Region VP:** John Murphy
**Eastern Region VP:** Dan De Santi
**Eastern Region VP:** Richard Volpe
**Southern Region VP:** Tyson Johnson
**Southern Region VP:** Ken Wood
**Western Region VP:** Chuck Mack
**Western Region VP:** Jon Rabine
**Western Region VP:** Jim Santangelo
**Acting Director of Human Resources Department:**
   Lynda Sist

## PRODUCTS/OPERATIONS

**Trade Divisions**
Airline
Bakery and Laundry
Brewery and Soft Drink
Building Material and Construction
Carhaul
Dairy
Freight
Industrial Trades
Motion Picture and Theatrical Trade
Newspaper, Magazine, and Electronic Media
Parcel and Small Package
Port
Public Services
Tankhaul
Trade Show and Convention Centers
Warehouse

## LOCATIONS

**HQ:** International Brotherhood of Teamsters
   25 Louisiana Ave. NW, Washington, DC 20001
**Phone:** 202-624-6800      **Fax:** 202-624-6918
**Web:** www.teamster.org

### 2000 Membership

|  | % of total |
|---|---|
| United States | |
| Central | 32 |
| East | 28 |
| West | 26 |
| South | 7 |
| Canada | 7 |
| **Total** | **100** |

# INTERNATIONAL DATA GROUP

## OVERVIEW

What better product to peddle in the information age than information. Boston-based International Data Group (IDG) is a publishing and market research giant focused on the high technology sector. It is the world's top tech publisher with some 300 magazines and newspapers in 85 countries, including *Computerworld, CIO,* and *PC World.* Other publishing assets include *CliffsNotes* (study aids) and *Frommer's* (travel guides).

In addition to publishing, the company's International Data Corporation is a leading technology market research and consulting firm, with hundreds of analysts in 43 countries. IDG also produces a number of industry events like MACWORLD Expo and the Internet Commerce Expo and offers career services through JobUniverse.com and ITcareers.com.

Its ExecuTrain unit provides technology training services through more than 250 locations in 40 countries.

While a downturn in the economy in 2000 and 2001 left many of its rivals scrambling for cover, IDG has continued to enjoy growth thanks to its market research and event marketing businesses. However the firm did shed some publishing assets in 2001 including its 75% stake in Hungry Minds (formerly IDG Books Worldwide), publisher of the *For Dummies* series. It also acquired some assets of *Industry Standard* publisher Standard Media (subscriber lists, trademarks, newsletters) following that company's bankruptcy liquidation.

Founder and chairman Patrick McGovern owns a majority stake in IDG; an employee stock plan owns the rest.

## HISTORY

Patrick McGovern began his career in publishing as a paperboy for the *Philadelphia Bulletin.* As a teenager in the 1950s, McGovern was inspired by Edmund Berkeley's book *Giant Brains; or Machines That Think.* He later built a computer and won a scholarship to MIT. There he edited the first computer magazine, *Computers and Automation.* McGovern started market research firm International Data Corporation in 1964 after interviewing the president of computer pioneer UNIVAC. Three years later he launched *Computerworld,* and within a few weeks the eight-page tabloid had 20,000 subscribers. Combined under the name International Data Group, McGovern's company reached $1 million in sales by 1968.

Taking the "International" in its name to heart, IDG began publishing in Japan in 1971 and expanded to Germany in 1975. Following the collapse of Communism in Russia and Eastern Europe the company had 10 publications by 1990. That year two teenage hackers broke into the company's voice mail system and erased orders from customers and messages from writers. The prank cost IDG about $2.4 million. Also in 1990, IDG launched IDG Books Worldwide (renamed Hungry Minds in 2000), which hit it big the next year with *DOS for Dummies.*

With the technology boom of the 1990s, competition in tech publishing heated up. By 1993 several of IDG's magazines, including *InfoWorld, Macworld,* and *PC World,* began losing ad pages to rivals Ziff-Davis and CMP Media. To help stem advertiser attrition, IDG started an incentive program tied to its new online service. In 1995 IDG bought a stake in software companies Architect Software (now Excite@Home) and Netscape (now owned by AOL Time Warner) as part of its move toward Internet-based services.

In 1996 IDG launched *Netscape World: The Web,* a magazine covering the Internet, and introduced more than 30 industry newsletters delivered by e-mail. IDG kicked off its online ad placement service, Global Web Ad Network, in 1997. That year IDG merged *Macworld* with rival Ziff-Davis' *MacUser* in a joint venture called Mac Publishing.

In 1998 IDG pledged $1 billion in venture capital for high-tech startups in China. It also introduced new publications in China, including a Chinese edition of *Cosmopolitan* (with Hearst Magazines) and *China Computer Reseller World.* Later that year the company launched *The Industry Standard* and spun off 25% of IDG Books to the public.

In 1999 it sold a 20% stake in Industry Standard Communications (renamed Standard Media International) to private investors and began laying plans for a possible spinoff in 2000. However, a weakening economy and slowing ad sales in 2000 quieted those plans.

The next year both Standard Media and Hungry Minds announced staff cuts and restructuring. IDG eventually sold its majority interest in Hungry Minds to John Wiley & Sons for about $90 million. Standard Media filed for bankruptcy and liquidated its assets, some of which were bought by IDG. The company also purchased Ziff Davis' 50% stake in their joint-venture Mac Publishing.

**Chairman:** Patrick J. McGovern
**President and CEO:** Kelly P. Conlin
**VP Finance:** Jim Ghirardi
**VP Human Resources:** Karen Budreau
**President and CEO, Bio-IT World Inc.:** Morris R. Levitt
**Auditors:** Deloitte & Touche LLP

## LOCATIONS

**HQ:** 1 Exeter Plaza, 15th Fl., Boston, MA 02116
**Phone:** 617-534-1200    **Fax:** 617-262-2300
**Web:** www.idg.com

International Data Group publishes more than 300 magazines and newspapers in 85 countries.

## PRODUCTS/OPERATIONS

**Selected Operations**
ExecuTrain (majority-owned, technology training)
IDG Communications (periodical publishing)
IDG Research Group (advertising and media research)
IDG.net (online publications hub)
International Data Corporation (IDC, market research)

**Selected Events**
ASPWorld Conference & Expo
CIO Perspectives
ComNet
Internet Commerce Expo
LinuxWorld Conference & Expo
MACWORLD Expo

**Selected Periodicals**
*CIO*
*Computerworld*
*Darwin Magazine*
*GamePro*
*InfoWorld*
*Macworld*
*Network World*
*PC World*
*Publish*

## COMPETITORS

| | |
|---|---|
| CNET Networks | Pearson |
| Forrester Research | Penton Media |
| Freeman Companies | Reed Elsevier |
| Future Network | UMAC |
| Gartner | United Business Media |
| Key3Media | Vivendi Universal |
| Magnamedia Verlag |   Publishing |
| McGraw-Hill | VNU |
| Microsoft | Ziff Davis Media |

## HISTORICAL FINANCIALS & EMPLOYEES

| Private<br>FYE: September 30 | Annual<br>Growth | 9/92 | 9/93 | 9/94 | 9/95 | 9/96 | 9/97 | 9/98 | 9/99 | 9/00 | 9/01 |
|---|---|---|---|---|---|---|---|---|---|---|---|
| Sales ($ mil.) | 15.2% | 840 | 880 | 1,100 | 1,400 | 1,700 | 1,876 | 2,050 | 2,560 | 3,100 | 3,010 |
| Employees | 12.7% | 4,500 | 5,000 | 7,200 | 8,200 | 8,500 | 9,500 | 11,500 | 12,000 | 13,400 | 13,200 |

### SALES HISTORY

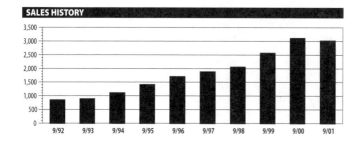

# IMG

Show me the money! The world's largest sports talent and marketing agency, Cleveland-based International Management Group (IMG) is credited with having invented the field of sports management. Along with representing some of the most talented and popular athletes today (Tiger Woods, Venus and Serena Williams), the company serves clients in the arts (Placido Domingo), modeling (Tyra Banks), and broadcasting (Bob Costas).

While representing VIP clients may be how IMG gained its fame, the company is involved in several other aspects of sports promotion as well. Its Trans World International division produces more than 5,000 hours of sports TV programming each year. IMG also gives many

of its clients venues in which to compete by promoting sporting events, and when athletes need training, they can take advantage of IMG's various sports academies.

The company also represents corporate clients (Cisco Systems) and organizations, acts as a literary agent, and is active in real estate, golf course design, and financial consulting through a joint venture with Merrill Lynch (McCormack Advisors International). IMG continues to expand internationally, organizing sporting events such as basketball, baseball, golf, and rugby across Asia, Australia, and Europe. The company is headed by founder and owner Mark McCormack.

## HISTORY

When former amateur golfer Mark McCormack went to Yale Law School in the 1950s, he didn't desert golf entirely. In his free time he set up paid exhibitions for pro golfers he knew from his days on the links, and in 1960 one of these players, Arnold Palmer, asked McCormack to manage his finances so he could concentrate on his game. McCormack went above and beyond the call of duty, signing Palmer to endorsement deals and licensing his name and image. In two years Palmer's annual income skyrocketed from $60,000 to more than $500,000 — a fiscal triumph that would be the bedrock of IMG's business. Throughout the early and mid-1960s, IMG signed up more big-name golfers, as well as stars from other sports such as Jackie Stewart (car racing) and Jean-Claude Killy (skiing).

The addition of foreign stars such as Stewart (Scotland), Killy (France), and Gary Player (South Africa) allowed IMG access to global markets. In the late 1960s as television began to bring sports and its stars into living rooms around the world, IMG used its clients to promote products and services internationally. In 1967 McCormack created a new division of IMG — a TV production company that filmed and distributed sporting events called Trans World International (TWI). The next year IMG signed a contract with Wimbledon's organizers to coordinate video and television licensing.

IMG's entrepreneurial spirit came to the forefront with a vengeance in the 1980s. In addition to managing athletes, sporting events, and sponsors, the company began to skip the middleman and create the sports event itself. IMG debuted the Skins Game in 1983, a golf

invitational featuring four of the sport's top athletes playing for high stakes. IMG also created Saturday afternoon sports staples such as *The Battle of the Network Stars,* shows that featured sports or TV stars competing in a series of events such as the tug-o-war and obstacle courses.

By the 1990s McCormack had situated IMG to take advantage of almost every aspect of televised sports events: Typically, an IMG event involved working with the athletes, the sponsor or sponsors, the event itself, and the television distribution rights. The company continued to expand its clientele beyond sports, adding names such as musician Placido Domingo. By 1997 IMG also counted the Rock and Roll Hall of Fame, the Americas Cup, and the Mayo Clinic as clients.

IMG teamed up with Chase Capital Partners (now J.P. Morgan Partners) in 1998 to form IMG/Chase Sports Capital, a private equity fund with a goal of raising some $200 million to invest in the sports industry. The next year IMG demonstrated a well-honed knack for capitalizing on its clients' appeal by staging a televised golf match between clients Tiger Woods and David Duval, and again in 2000 between Woods and Sergio Garcia. Also that year IMG tried to create a new cable network between TWI and the New York Yankees, but the New York Supreme Court blocked the deal, saying it violated the Yankees' current deal with MSG Network. In 2001 the Yankees broke ties with MSG, paying them $30 million, to form their own network. IMG has expressed interest in joining the new network.

## OFFICERS

**Chairman and CEO:** Mark H. McCormack
**CFO:** Arthur J. LaFave
**Senior Corporate VP:** Stephanie Tolleson, age 45
**VP Human Resources:** Susie Austin

## LOCATIONS

**HQ:** International Management Group
1360 E. 9th St., Ste. 100, Cleveland, OH 44114
**Phone:** 216-522-1200    **Fax:** 216-522-1145
**Web:** www.imgworld.com

IMG has 85 offices in 33 countries.

## PRODUCTS/OPERATIONS

**Selected Clients**
All England Lawn Tennis & Croquet Club (Wimbledon)
America's Cup
Tyra Banks
Mikhail Baryshnikov
Jose Carreras
Vince Carter
Cisco Systems
Bob Costas
Placido Domingo
David Duval
Sergio Garcia
Wayne Gretzky
Stephen Hawking
International Olympic Committee
International Rock and Roll Hall of Fame and Museum
Heidi Klum
Nancy Lopez
John Madden
Major League Baseball
Joe Montana
Colin Montgomerie
Martina Navratilova
Greg Norman
Mark O'Meara
Arnold Palmer
Royal & Ancient Golf Club of St. Andrews
Rugby World Cup
Serena Williams
Venus Williams
Tiger Woods
United States Golf Association

**Selected Sports Academies**
The David Leadbetter Golf Academy
IMG Hockey Academy
International Performance Institute
Nick Bollettieri Tennis Academy
The Soccer and Baseball Academies

**Other Operations**
IMG Golf Course Services (designs, manages, and
   markets golf courses worldwide)
Trans World International (sports television production)

## COMPETITORS

Bull Run
Clear Channel
  Entertainment
Creative Artists
Dentsu
Golden Bear Golf
International Creative
  Management
Interpublic Group
Magnum Sports &
  Entertainment
Sportsworld Media
TBA
United Talent
William Morris
WPP Group

## HISTORICAL FINANCIALS & EMPLOYEES

| Private<br>FYE: December 31 | Annual<br>Growth | 12/91 | 12/92 | 12/93 | 12/94 | 12/95 | 12/96 | 12/97 | 12/98 | 12/99 | 12/00 |
|---|---|---|---|---|---|---|---|---|---|---|---|
| Estimated sales ($ mil.) | 4.7% | — | — | — | — | 1,000 | 1,000 | 1,100 | 1,100 | 1,100 | 1,260 |
| Employees | 12.6% | — | — | — | — | 1,600 | 1,959 | 2,000 | 2,125 | 2,150 | 2,900 |

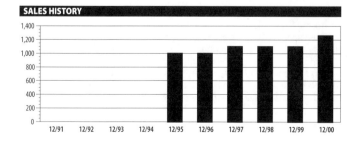

SALES HISTORY

# THE IRVINE COMPANY INC.

At The Irvine Company, everything is going according to plan. *Master* plan, that is.

Newport Beach, California-based Irvine Company creates master-planned communities in well-heeled Orange County, of which the company owns some 50,000 acres (making it California's largest landowner).

The company's land is called Irvine Ranch and includes the US's largest planned community, Irvine, with more than 150,000 residents. The firm's Irvine Spectrum development is one of the nation's largest high-tech research and business centers; the University of California, Irvine, is built on company-donated land. Some 30,000 acres have been set aside for wildlife habitat and open spaces.

The Irvine Company's portfolio also includes two hotels, five marinas, and three golf courses.

The Irvine Company also owns Irvine Apartment Communities, a real estate investment trust (REIT) that owns some 70 apartment complexes in the Irvine Ranch area, as well as in San Diego, San Jose, and Los Angeles.

Chairman Donald Bren, the company's sole owner and one of America's wealthiest men, has continued the Irvine Foundation's 35-year-old master plan, which calls for gradual development of rigorously planned communities. The plan — which has so far helped form the communities of Laguna Beach, Newport Beach, Orange, and Tustin, as well as centerpiece Irvine — is set for completion around 2025, but the company has faced increasing political opposition to its plans from area residents, who tend to become development-weary after they get their piece of the Irvine Ranch.

## HISTORY

A wholesale merchant in San Francisco during the gold rush, James Irvine and two others assembled vast holdings in Southern California in the mid-1800s by buying out the debts of Mexican and Spanish land-grant holders. Irvine bought his partners' shares in 1876 and passed the ranch of 120,000 acres to his son, James II, upon his death in 1886. Eight years later James II incorporated the ranch as The Irvine Company and began turning it into an agribusiness empire, shifting from sheep ranching to cash crop farming.

James II owned the ranch and company until the 1930s, when the death of his son, James III, prompted him to transfer a controlling interest in the company to a not-for-profit foundation. James III's wife, Athalie, and daughter, Joan, inherited 22% of Irvine.

In 1959 company president Myford Irvine, a grandson of James I and uncle to Joan, was found dead from two shotgun wounds. Officials ruled it a suicide, but others weren't so sure.

With Athalie and Joan's encouragement, the company donated land in the early 1960s for the construction of the University of California, Irvine. The company would continue contributing to educational and philanthropic causes as well as donating property for green space to improve Orange County's suburban areas.

The 1960s also saw the Irvine Foundation forming its definitive master plan for pre-arranged communities and marked the company's entry into the real estate development sector. The plan was designed to anticipate and control growth, with provisions for green space and a mix of pricing levels.

Superrich firebrand Joan, who had long accused foundation officers of serving their own interests at the expense of other stockholders, lobbied Congress in the late 1960s to change tax laws pertaining to the foundation. Along with a group of investors led by Donald Bren, Alfred Taubman, and Herbert Allen, Joan trumped a bid by Mobil Oil and in 1977 gained control of the company.

When California's real estate market went sour in 1983, Bren bought a majority interest of the firm. Joan returned to court to protest the price, gaining extra money when the court valued the land at $1.4 billion.

Orange County's record-setting bankruptcy in 1994 (the county lost $1.7 billion in risky investments) threatened the value of The Irvine Company's property portfolio, most of which is located in Orange County. Thanks in part to a frothy economy and settlements from brokerage firms, Orange County and The Irvine Company were spared another 1983-esque bust.

In 1996 Bren bought the company's remaining stock. As part of its expansion into R&D, retail, and office properties in the Silicon Valley area, The Irvine Company opened an office in San Jose the next year, followed by its Eastgate Technology Park in San Diego in 1998.

In 2000 the company laid plans for a retail expansion to its Irvine Spectrum business complex. In 2001 it expanded its Los Angeles-area holdings with the purchase of Century City's Fox Plaza office building.

**Chairman:** Donald L. Bren
**Vice Chairman and COO:** Michael D. McKee
**Vice Chairman:** Raymond L. Watson, age 75
**CFO:** Mark Ley
**President, Irvine Community Development:**
Joseph D. Davis
**President, Investment Properties Group:**
Clarence W. Barker
**Group SVP and Chief Marketing Officer:** W. E. Mitchell
**Group SVP, Corporate Affairs:** Monica Florian
**Group SVP, Entitlement:** Daniel Young
**Group SVP, Urban Planning and Design:**
Robert N. Elliott
**SVP and Corporate Controller:** Mary J. Vietze
**SVP, Human Resources:** Bruce Endsley
**VP, Commercial Land Sales, Investment Property**
**Group:** Larry Williams
**VP, Residential Sales and Marketing:** Don Moe
**Director, Compensation and Benefits:** Pat Neher
**Director, Purchasing:** Heather Colbert
**Director, Training:** Gail Jenson
**President, Apartment Communities, Investment**
**Properties Group:** Max L. Gardner
**President, Retail Properties, Investment Properties**
**Group:** Keith Eyrich
**President, Office Properties, Investment Properties**
**Group:** William Halford

## LOCATIONS

**HQ:** 550 Newport Center Dr., Newport Beach, CA 92658
**Phone:** 949-720-2000      **Fax:** 949-720-2501
**Web:** www.irvineco.com

The Irvine Company owns and develops 54,000 acres of
land in Orange County, California, including the City of
Irvine and parts of Anaheim, Laguna Beach, Newport
Beach, Orange, and Tustin. It also owns properties in
Los Angeles, San Diego, and San Jose.

## PRODUCTS/OPERATIONS

**Selected Divisions**
Investment Properties Group
  Irvine Commercial Land Sales
  Irvine Business Properties (hotels, marinas, and golf
    courses)
  Irvine Industrial (12 million sq. ft. of industrial and
    technology-oriented space)
  Irvine Office Company (7 million sq. ft. of office space)
  Irvine Retail Properties Company (6.1 million sq. ft. of
    shopping and retail space)
Irvine Apartment Communities
Irvine Community Development

## COMPETITORS

Arden Realty
Center Trust
C.J. Segerstrom & Sons
Corky McMillin
Intergroup
KB Home
Kilroy Realty
Majestic Realty
MBK Real Estate
Newhall Land and
  Farming
Pan Pacific

## HISTORICAL FINANCIALS & EMPLOYEES

| Private<br>FYE: June 30 | Annual<br>Growth | 6/91 | 6/92 | 6/93 | 6/94 | 6/95 | 6/96 | 6/97 | 6/98 | 6/99 | 6/00 |
|---|---|---|---|---|---|---|---|---|---|---|---|
| Sales ($ mil.) | 4.6% | — | 700 | 800 | 800 | 700 | 710 | 816 | 1,000 | 1,000 | 1,000 |
| Employees | (2.3%) | — | 300 | 200 | 200 | 200 | 190 | 200 | 236 | 250 | 250 |

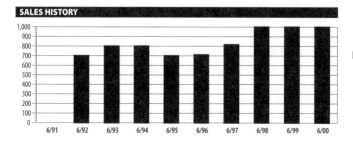

SALES HISTORY

THE IRVINE COMPANY

# J. CREW GROUP, INC.

## OVERVIEW

Getting back to cruising speed has been difficult for the J. Crew Group. With a brand that is sometimes used as an adjective ("That's very J. Crew!"), the New York City-based firm generally focuses on young, college-educated professionals. Timeless casuals, jeans, and other durables account for about 60% of sales. Nearly half of J. Crew's sales come from its 175 or so retail and outlet stores in the US and 70 stores (some within other stores) in Japan (through a partnership with ITOCHU). Another 35% of sales come from about 30 catalog editions that reach about 70 million people each year. Items available from the J. Crew catalog are generally priced between $12 and $100, while the retail stores carry higher-priced apparel. Asian contractors produce about 80% of the company's merchandise.

Hemmed by the stagnant growth of its catalog operations, the company has sold or closed two of its noncore catalog businesses, Popular Club Plan and Clifford & Wills, leaving it with only its namesake operations.

J. Crew has gone through some tough times since the Texas Pacific Group bought a majority stake in the family-run company in 1998. A plan to take the company public was shelved and the company has fallen farther behind rivals such as Abercrombie & Fitch and American Eagle Outfitters.

Emily Cinader Woods, daughter of founder Arthur Cinader, owns nearly 15% of the firm. Investment firm Texas Pacific Group owns more than 60%.

## HISTORY

Although the J. Crew Group started in 1983, the Cinader family's participation in the mail-order catalog business extends back to 1947, when Arthur Cinader's father, Mitchell, along with Saul Charles, founded the Popular Club Plan, a mail-order catalog selling ladies' apparel, furniture, and kitchen supplies.

After inheriting the Popular Club Plan, Arthur observed the remarkable growth in the early 1980s of The Talbots, L.L. Bean, and other clothing catalogs. In 1983 he established his own classic apparel catalog as J. Crew, a name that connoted casual, collegiate clothing. First-year sales were about $3 million.

The following year Arthur offered a job to his eldest daughter, Emily, a recent college graduate. Her first decision was to ban polyester from all J. Crew clothes.

Although early catalogs included clothing from a number of manufacturers, Emily, as the company's chief designer, moved the company to selling its own brand exclusively. J. Crew's early unisex styles were shaped by her desire to wear some of the same clothes she wore while growing up, such as her brother's chinos. Also in 1984 Arthur started the Clifford & Wills catalog operation (low-priced women's clothing). J. Crew catalog sales grew rapidly during the mid-1980s.

In 1989 Emily, then 28, became president of the J. Crew catalog division and launched a risky expansion into retail, with its first store in New York City. Later in 1989 J. Crew unveiled an ambitious store-opening plan (50 stores in five years). However, a weakened economy and sharp competition slowed growth.

The company signed an agreement with ITOCHU to open stores in Japan in 1993.

High executive turnover also stunted growth, possibly attributable to the rough-edged style of Arthur. President and COO Arnold Cohen stepped down in 1993. His replacement, Robert Bernard, resigned in 1996, and Arthur took on his duties.

In an effort to recapitalize the struggling company, the Texas Pacific Group bought its stake in J. Crew in 1997, with an eye toward taking it public when its performance improved. At that time Arthur retired and Emily succeeded her father as J. Crew's chair. In 1998 J. Crew attributed a loss of $27 million to disappointing mail-order sales caused by the USPS strike and a warm fall and winter. The company dismissed 10% of its workforce to reduce overhead costs that year. Also that year J. Crew sold its Popular Club Plan to catalog firm Fingerhut Companies.

Speaking of losing popularity, CEO Howard Socol fell out of favor and left the company in early 1999 after less than a year on the job. Mark Sarvary, former president of Nestlé Frozen Foods, succeeded him. Also in 1999 J. Crew ceased its Clifford & Wills catalog and sold its trademarks and mailing list to Spiegel. In summer 2000 the company launched a bath and body line called So J. Crew, which includes soap, lotion, mouthwash, and candles.

In 2001 J. Crew announced plans to launch a complete line of children's wear for boys and girls ages six to 12. The company laid off about 30 workers at its headquarters after recording disappointing sales.

## HISTORICAL FINANCIALS & EMPLOYEES

| Private<br>FYE: Sat. nearest Jan. 31 | Annual<br>Growth | 1/92 | 1/93 | 1/94 | 1/95 | 1/96 | 1/97 | 1/98 | 1/99 | 1/00 | 1/01 |
|---|---|---|---|---|---|---|---|---|---|---|---|
| Sales ($ mil.) | 6.6% | 466 | 571 | 647 | 738 | 746 | 809 | 834 | 824 | 717 | 826 |
| Net income ($ mil.) | 5.6% | — | 14 | 12 | 15 | 6 | 13 | (27) | (15) | (7) | 22 |
| Income as % of sales | — | — | 2.5% | 1.9% | 2.0% | 0.9% | 1.6% | — | — | — | 2.6% |
| Employees | 15.2% | 2,700 | 3,670 | 4,479 | 5,413 | 5,600 | 6,100 | 6,200 | 8,900 | 8,400 | — |

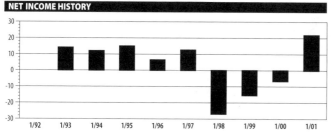

**NET INCOME HISTORY**

**2001 FISCAL YEAR-END**

Debt ratio: 88.6%
Return on equity: —
Cash ($ mil.): 33
Current ratio: 1.34
Long-term debt ($ mil.): 150

# JM FAMILY ENTERPRISES, INC.

## OVERVIEW

The Moran family's car is probably a Lexus. Based in Deerfield Beach, Florida, JM Family Enterprises is a privately owned holding company with about a dozen automotive-related businesses (including JM Lexus, the nation's largest-volume Lexus retailer, in Margate, Florida). It is Florida's second-largest private company, after Publix Super Markets.

Southeast Toyota Distributors, JM's primary subsidiary, operates the world's #1 Toyota distribution franchise, delivering Toyota and Lexus vehicles to more than 160 dealers in Florida, Georgia, Alabama, and the Carolinas. Among its other subsidiaries, JM&A Group provides insurance and warranty services to retailers nationwide. World Omni Financial handles leasing, dealer financing, and other financial services for US auto dealers.

JM is owned by the family of billionaire founder and chairman Jim Moran. Pat Moran, Jim's daughter and company CEO and president, is one of the top female business owners in the US.

## HISTORY

Jim Moran first became visible as "Jim Moran, the Courtesy Man" in Chicago TV advertisements in the 1950s. At that time he ran Courtesy Motors, where he was so successful as the world's #1 Ford dealer that *Time* magazine put his picture on its cover in 1961.

Moran had entered the auto sales business after fixing up and selling a car for more than three times the price he had paid for it. That profit was much better than what he made at the Sinclair gas station he had bought, so he opened a used-car lot. Later, he moved to new-car sales when he bought a Hudson franchise (Ford had rejected him).

Seeing the promise of TV advertising, in 1948 Moran pioneered the forum for Chicago car dealers, not only as an advertiser and program sponsor but also as host of a variety show and a country-and-western barn dance. The increased visibility positioned Moran as Hudson's #1 dealer, but the sales tactics at Courtesy Motors earned an antitrust suit that was settled out of court.

In 1955 Moran started with Ford and, with his TV influence as host of *The Jim Moran Courtesy Hour,* he became the world's #1 Ford dealer in his first month.

He moved to Florida in 1966 after being diagnosed with cancer and given one year to live. Successfully fighting the disease, he bought a Pontiac franchise and later started Southeast Toyota Distributors. In 1969 he formed JM Family Enterprises.

Legal problems cropped up in 1973 when the IRS investigated a Nassau bank serving as a tax haven for wealthy Americans. Moran and three Toyota executives were linked to the bank, and in 1978 Moran was indicted for tax fraud. When an immunity deal fell through, Moran pleaded guilty to seven tax fraud charges in 1984 and was sentenced to two years (suspended), fined more than $12 million, and ordered to perform community service. Moran's legal problems threatened his association with Toyota and were blamed for causing his stroke in 1983.

JM's legal problems continued in the 1980s, partly because of the imposition of auto import restrictions. To get more cars to sell, some Southeast Toyota managers encouraged auto dealers to file false sales reports. Some North Carolina dealers resisted and one sued, settling out of court for $22 million. Other dealers alleged racketeering and fraud on the part of Southeast Toyota, and by the beginning of 1994, JM had paid more than $100 million in fines and settlements for cases stretching back to 1988.

Pat Moran succeeded her father as JM president in 1992. Between 1991 and 1994 three suits were filed against Jim and Southeast Toyota alleging racism against blacks in establishing Toyota dealerships. All three suits were settled.

Jim teamed with Wayne Huizenga in 1996 to launch a national chain of used-car megastores under the name AutoNation USA, which Jim expected would draw buyers to his own auto dealerships. (AutoNation USA's first store was built just two blocks from JM's Coconut Creek Lexus Dealership.) Jim's interest in AutoNation USA was converted into a small percentage (less than 5%) of Republic Industries stock after Huizenga merged AutoNation into waste hauler Republic Industries (now called AutoNation) in 1997.

In late 1998 JM embarked on a national strategy to expand its presence outside the Southeast, establishing an office in St. Louis that handles indirect consumer leasing.

In 2001 *FORTUNE* magazine ranked JM #51 in its list of 100 Best Companies to work for.

**Honorary Chairman:** James M. Moran
**President and CEO:** Patricia Moran
**COO:** Collin Brown
**EVP and CFO:** James R. Foster
**EVP, Human Resources:** Gary L. Thomas

## LOCATIONS

**HQ:** 100 NW 12th Ave., Deerfield Beach, FL 33442
**Phone:** 954-429-2000     **Fax:** 954-429-2244
**Web:** www.jmfamily.com

JM Family Enterprises operates auto retail, distribution, leasing, and financing businesses across the US, mainly in Alabama, Florida, Georgia, and North and South Carolina.

## PRODUCTS/OPERATIONS

**Selected Subsidiaries**

**Finance and Leasing**
World Omni Financial Corp.

**Insurance, Marketing, Consulting, and Related Companies**
Fidelity Insurance Agency
JM&A Group (auto service contracts, insurance)
  Courtesy Insurance Co.
  Fidelity Insurance Agency
  Fidelity Warranty Services
  Jim Moran & Associates
  J.M.I.C. Life Insurance Co.

**Retail Car Sales**
JM Lexus

**Vehicle Processing and Distribution**
Parts Distribution Center
SET Port Processing
Southeast Toyota Distributors

**Selected Affiliate**

Executive Incentives & Travel

## COMPETITORS

| | |
|---|---|
| CarMax | Island Lincoln-Mercury |
| Gulf States Toyota | Morse Operations |
| Hendrick Automotive | United Auto Group |
| Holman Enterprises | |

## HISTORICAL FINANCIALS & EMPLOYEES

| Private<br>FYE: December 31 | Annual<br>Growth | 12/91 | 12/92 | 12/93 | 12/94 | 12/95 | 12/96 | 12/97 | 12/98 | 12/99 | 12/00 |
|---|---|---|---|---|---|---|---|---|---|---|---|
| Sales ($ mil.) | 13.4% | — | 2,600 | 3,500 | 4,200 | 4,500 | 5,100 | 5,400 | 6,200 | 6,600 | 7,100 |
| Employees | 5.0% | — | 2,300 | 2,300 | 2,000 | 2,000 | 3,000 | 2,900 | 3,000 | 3,304 | 3,400 |

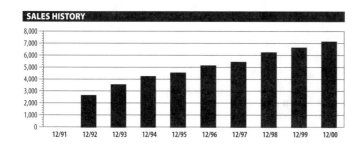

SALES HISTORY

# JOHNSON PUBLISHING COMPANY

## OVERVIEW

Johnson Publishing really caters to the *Jet* set. The Chicago-based company publishes a variety of black-oriented magazines, including flagship *Ebony* and *Jet*. It is one of the largest minority-owned businesses in the US and the nation's largest black-owned publisher. Johnson Publishing also produces a line of hair care products (Supreme Beauty) and cosmetics (Fashion Fair) marketed for African-American women, and each year it hosts the Ebony Fashion Fair, a traveling fashion show that raises money for scholarships and charities in

cities across the US and Canada. The company's book division features titles such as *The New Ebony Cookbook* and the more controversial *Forced Into Glory: Abraham Lincoln's White Dream*.

Johnson Publishing is owned and controlled by founder and CEO John Johnson and his family. Johnson's daughter and heir apparent, Linda Johnson Rice, handles the day-to-day operations as president and COO. His wife, Eunice, produces the Ebony Fashion Fair.

## HISTORY

John H. Johnson launched his publishing business in 1942 while he was still in college in Chicago. The idea for a black-oriented magazine came to him while he was working part-time for Supreme Life Insurance Co. of America, where one of his jobs was to clip magazine and newspaper articles about the black community. Johnson used his mother's furniture as collateral to secure a $500 loan and then mailed $2 charter subscription offers to potential subscribers. He received 3,000 replies and used the $6,000 to print the first issue of *Negro Digest*, patterned after *Reader's Digest*. Circulation was 50,000 within a year.

Johnson started *Ebony* magazine in 1945 (which gained immediate popularity and is still the company's premier publication) and launched *Jet* in 1951, a pocket-sized publication containing news items and features. In the early days Johnson was unable to obtain advertising, so he formed his own Beauty Star mail-order business and advertised its products (dresses, wigs, hair care products, and vitamins) in his magazines. He won his first major account, Zenith Radio, in 1947; Johnson landed Chrysler in 1954, only after sending a salesman to Detroit every week for 10 years. For 20 years, *Ebony* and *Jet* were the only national publications targeting blacks in the US.

By the 1960s Johnson had become one of the most prominent black men in the US. He posed with John F. Kennedy in 1963 to publicize a special issue of *Ebony* celebrating the Emancipation Proclamation. US magazine publishers named him Publisher of the Year in 1972. Johnson launched *Ebony Jr!* (since discontinued) in 1973, a magazine designed to provide "positive black images" for black preteens. His first magazine, *Negro Digest* (renamed *Black World*), became known for its provocative articles, but its circulation

dwindled from 100,000 to 15,000. Johnson retired the magazine in 1975.

Unable to find the proper makeup for his *Ebony* models, Johnson founded his own cosmetics business, Fashion Fair Cosmetics, that year, which carved a niche beside Revlon (which introduced cosmetic lines for blacks) and another black cosmetics company, Johnson Products (unrelated) of Chicago. By 1982 Fashion Fair sales were more than $30 million.

The company got into broadcasting in 1972 when it bought Chicago radio station WGRT (renamed WJPC; that city's first black-owned station). It added WLOU (Louisville, Kentucky) in 1982 and WLNR (Lansing, Illinois; re-launched in 1991 as WJPC-FM) in 1985. By 1995, however, it had sold all of its stations.

Johnson and the company sold their controlling interest in the last minority-owned insurance company in Illinois (and Johnson's first employer), Supreme Life Insurance, to Unitrin (a Chicago-based life, health, and property insurer) in 1991. That year the company and catalog retailer Spiegel announced a joint venture to develop fashions for black women. The two companies launched a mail-order catalog called *E Style* in 1993 and an accompanying credit card the next year.

Johnson Publishing launched its South African edition of *Ebony* in 1995. Johnson was awarded the Presidential Medal of Freedom in 1996. The next year, however, circulation of *Ebony* fell 7% as mainstream magazines began covering black issues more thoroughly and a host of new titles appeared. In response, the company restructured its ventures and closed its *E Style* catalog. Johnson Publishing retired *Ebony Man* (launched in 1985) in 1998 and *Ebony South Africa* in 2000.

**Chairman, Publisher, and CEO:** John H. Johnson, age 83
**President and COO:** Linda Johnson Rice, age 43
**Secretary and Treasurer; Producer and Director, EBONY Fashion Fair:** Eunice W. Johnson
**Editor, EBONY Magazine:** Lerone Bennett Jr.
**VP, Fashion Fair Cosmetics:** J. Lance Clark
**Controller:** Gregory Robertson
**Director Personnel:** LaDoris Foster

## LOCATIONS

**HQ:** Johnson Publishing Company, Inc.
820 S. Michigan Ave., Chicago, IL 60605
**Phone:** 312-322-9200     **Fax:** 312-322-0918
**Web:** www.ebony.com

## PRODUCTS/OPERATIONS

**Selected Operations**

**Fashion and Beauty Aids**
Ebony Fashion Fair (traveling fashion show)
Fashion Fair Cosmetics (color cosmetics, fragrances, skin care)
Supreme Beauty Products (hair care)

**Publishing**
Books
  *Forced Into Glory: Abraham Lincoln's White Dream*
    by Lerone Bennett Jr.
  *The New Ebony Cookbook* by Charlotte Lyons
Magazines
  *Ebony*
  *Jet*

## COMPETITORS

| | |
|---|---|
| Advance Publications | Larry Flynt Publishing |
| Avon | L'Oréal |
| Earl G. Graves | Mary Kay |
| Essence Communications | Revlon |
| Estée Lauder | Time |
| Forbes | Vanguarde Media |
| Hearst | |

## HISTORICAL FINANCIALS & EMPLOYEES

| Private<br>FYE: December 31 | Annual<br>Growth | 12/91 | 12/92 | 12/93 | 12/94 | 12/95 | 12/96 | 12/97 | 12/98 | 12/99 | 12/00 |
|---|---|---|---|---|---|---|---|---|---|---|---|
| Sales ($ mil.) | 4.8% | — | 274 | 294 | 307 | 316 | 326 | 361 | 372 | 387 | 400 |
| Employees | (0.8%) | — | 2,785 | 2,600 | 2,662 | 2,680 | 2,702 | 2,677 | 2,647 | 2,657 | 2,614 |

### SALES HISTORY

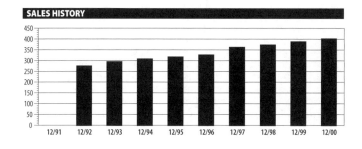

# THE JONES FINANCIAL COMPANIES

"The Wal-Mart of Wall Street" is most at home on Main Street. Des Peres, Missouri-based The Jones Financial Companies is a limited partnership and parent of Edward Jones, one of the largest brokerage networks in the world, with some 7,300 offices in the US, Canada, and the UK. Its brokers cater to individual investors, especially retired persons and small-business owners.

Brokers at Edward Jones sell relatively low-risk investment vehicles (municipal, government, and corporate bonds; established stocks; and high-quality mutual funds) and preach a conservative buy-and-hold approach. The company also sells insurance and engages in investment banking for such clients as Wal-Mart and public agencies. The firm embraces technology, maintaining one of the industry's largest satellite networks (including a dish for each office).

Preferring to build its brokers from the ground up, the firm accepts applicants with no previous experience, trains them extensively, and monitors investment patterns to prevent account churning and investments in risky low-cap stocks. Before they are given such luxuries as office space, assistants, or even a computer, new brokers must make 1,000 cold calls in their chosen community.

John Bachmann, managing partner of Edward Jones, has said the company has no plans to go public.

Jones Financial got its start in 1871 as bond house Whitaker & Co. In 1922 Edward D. Jones (no relation to the Edward D. Jones of Dow Jones fame) opened a brokerage in St. Louis. In 1943 the two firms merged.

Jones' son Edward "Ted" Jones Jr. joined the firm in 1948. Under Ted's leadership (and against his father's wishes), the company focused on rural customers, opening its first branch in the Missouri town of Mexico in 1955 and beginning its march across small-town America. Ted took over as managing partner in 1968, masterminding the company's small-town expansion. (The Wal-Mart comparison is apt; Ted Jones and Sam Walton were good friends.)

Almost from the start, the firm hammered home a conservative investment message focusing on blue-chip stocks and bonds. It expanded steadily throughout the years, adding offices with such addresses as Cedarburg, Wisconsin, and Paris, Illinois.

In the 1970s Edward D. Jones moved into underwriting with clients including Southern Co., Citicorp, and Humana. (It got burned in the mid-1980s on one such deal, when the SEC accused the company of fraud in a bond offering for life insurer D.H. Baldwin Co., which later filed for bankruptcy.)

The company's technological bent was spurred in 1978 after its Teletype network couldn't handle the demand generated by the firm's 220 offices. As a stopgap, the company nixed use of the Teletype for stock quotes, telling its brokers to call Merrill Lynch's toll-free number instead.

Managing partner John Bachmann took over from Ted Jones in 1980. (Bachmann started at the company as a janitor.) A follower of management guru Peter Drucker, Bachmann inculcated the company's brokers with Drucker's customer- and value-oriented principles.

Edward D. Jones began moving into the suburbs and into less-than-posh sections of big cities in the mid-1980s. In 1986 the company started a mortgage program, but the plan was never successful and was ended in 1988. The company weathered the 1987 stock market crash (many brokerages did not), albeit with thinner profit margins.

In 1990 Ted Jones died. The first half of the decade was a time of great expansion for the company as it doubled its number of offices. In 1993 the company opened an office in Canada.

The following year Jones Financial's acquisition of Columbia, Missouri-based thrift Boone National gave it the ability to offer trust and mortgage services to its clients, which helped sales as Jones started facing competition from Merrill Lynch in its small-town niche. The company's rapid expansion and relatively expensive infrastructure (all those one-person offices add up) began to eat at the bottom line, and in 1995 Bachmann stopped expansion so the firm could catch its breath.

In 1997 Edward Jones (which had unofficially dropped its middle "D" to boost name recognition) moved overseas, opening its first offices in the UK, a prime expansion target for the company. The next year the firm teamed up with Mercantile Bank to offer small-business loans. Jones resumed its expansionist push in 1999 and 2000, adding offices in all its markets, but continued to resist online trading. In 2001 the firm began eyeing several European countries as possible expansion targets.

## OFFICERS

**Managing Partner:** John W. Bachmann, age 62, $200,000 pay
**General Partner, Finance and Accounting:** Steven Novik, age 51
**General Partner, Product and Sales Division:** Douglas E. Hill, age 56, $160,000 pay
**General Partner, Human Resources:** Michael R. Holmes, age 42
**General Partner, Information Systems:** Richie L. Malone, age 52, $160,000 pay
**General Partner, Service Division:** Darryl L. Pope, age 61
**Limited Partner, Headquarters Administration:** Robert Virgil Jr., age 66
**Auditors:** Arthur Andersen LLP

## LOCATIONS

**HQ:** The Jones Financial Companies, L.P., LLP
12555 Manchester Rd., Des Peres, MO 63131
**Phone:** 314-515-2000     **Fax:** 314-515-2622
**Web:** www.edwardjones.com

The Jones Financial Companies operates about 7,300 offices in the US, Canada, and the UK.

## PRODUCTS/OPERATIONS

### 2000 Sales

|  | $ mil. | % of total |
|---|---|---|
| Commissions |  |  |
| Mutual funds | 749 | 34 |
| Listed | 272 | 12 |
| Insurance | 222 | 10 |
| OTC | 170 | 8 |
| Principal transactions | 264 | 12 |
| Interest & dividends | 224 | 10 |
| Money market fees | 61 | 3 |
| IRA custodial services fees | 31 | 1 |
| Investment banking | 30 | 1 |
| Other | 189 | 9 |
| **Total** | **2,212** | **100** |

### Selected Subsidiaries

EDJ Holding Co., Inc.
EDJ Leasing Co., LP
Edward D. Jones & Co. Canada Holding Co., Inc.
Edward D. Jones & Co., LP (broker-dealer)
Edward D. Jones Ltd. (UK)
EJ Insurance Agency Holding LLC
EJ Mortgage LLC
  Edward Jones Mortgage (50%)
LHC, Inc.
  Unison Capital Corp., Inc.
Passport Research Ltd. (50%, money market mutual fund adviser)
Unison Investment Trust

## COMPETITORS

A.G. Edwards
Charles Schwab
Citigroup
FleetBoston
Merrill Lynch
Morgan Stanley Dean Witter
Raymond James Financial
TD Waterhouse
UBS PaineWebber
U. S. Bancorp Piper Jaffray
Wells Fargo

## HISTORICAL FINANCIALS & EMPLOYEES

| Private<br>FYE: December 31 | Annual<br>Growth | 12/91 | 12/92 | 12/93 | 12/94 | 12/95 | 12/96 | 12/97 | 12/98 | 12/99 | 12/00 |
|---|---|---|---|---|---|---|---|---|---|---|---|
| Sales ($ mil.) | 18.8% | — | 557 | 642 | 661 | 722 | 952 | 1,135 | 1,450 | 1,787 | 2,212 |
| Net income ($ mil.) | 17.7% | — | 62 | 66 | 54 | 58 | 93 | 114 | 199 | 187 | 230 |
| Income as % of sales | — | — | 11.2% | 10.3% | 8.2% | 8.1% | 9.8% | 10.1% | 13.7% | 10.5% | 10.4% |
| Employees | 15.9% | — | — | 8,330 | 7,418 | 11,717 | 12,148 | 13,691 | 15,795 | 20,541 | 23,432 |

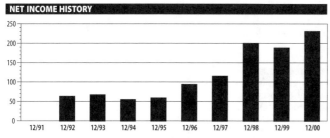

### NET INCOME HISTORY

### 2000 FISCAL YEAR-END

Debt ratio: 4.3%
Return on equity: —
Cash ($ mil.): 176
Current ratio: 0.00
Long-term debt ($ mil.): 30

# JOSTENS, INC.

## OVERVIEW

You can thank Jostens for lovingly documenting your awkward phase. The Minneapolis-based company is the leading US producer of yearbooks and class rings. In addition to yearbooks and class rings, Jostens offers school photography, diplomas, caps and gowns, and other graduation products through a sales force of independent and employee sales representatives.

The company's rings have also commemorated professional sports teams, including more than 20 Super Bowl champions and World Series winners as well as NBA and NHL championship teams and Indianapolis 500 winners. It also has made rings for NCAA champions in football, basketball, baseball, and it has produced medals for the Summer and Winter Olympics.

It also makes recognition products for businesses, which provides organizations with programs to recognize and reward employee service and achievement. Its recognition products include personalized awards, jewelry, and engraved certificates. Jostens also markets recognition products made by other companies, including Lenox, Waterman, and Oneida, and helps manage corporate events. However, the company has announced that it will exit the recognition business.

A private investment group led by Investcorp took Jostens private in May 2000.

## HISTORY

Otto Jostens founded Jostens as a jewelry and watch repair business in Owatonna, Minnesota, in 1897. He began making school awards in 1900 and class rings in 1906. In 1922 Daniel Gainey became Jostens' first ring salesman; the charismatic Gainey recruited more sales representatives and sales followed. Jostens exited the watch repair business in 1930 and built its first ring manufacturing plant; Gainey became chairman and CEO in 1933. Jostens added graduation announcements in 1946 and yearbooks in 1950. In 1952 the company made its first sports championship ring for the NFL's Detroit Lions.

In 1954 Jostens began to expand beyond schools and athletics when it introduced its first line of custom-printed holiday cards for business executives. The company added diplomas to its roster in 1958. In 1959 it further expanded its line of business-related products with the addition of employee recognition awards and achievement certificates. Also that year Jostens bought a jewelry engraved products plant in Princeton, Illinois.

Gainey retired in 1968, and the firm moved to Minneapolis in 1969. Jostens divested some noncore businesses and added sportswear, caps and gowns, and business recognition awards in the 1970s. It bought educational software companies and vocational schools in the mid-1980s but sold the schools in 1987.

In 1990, Jostens acquired recognition products makers Lenox Awards and Gordon B. Miller & Co. Profits slipped in 1992 and 1993. New CEO Robert Buhrmaster, hired in 1992, consolidated operations, cut jobs, centralized management, and sold software and sportswear interests. Paring away slow sellers, Jostens reduced the recognition line by half during 1996 and ring styles from 200 to 75 in 1997.

In 1998 Jostens was hit with a judgment of up to $36 million in an antitrust suit brought by Insilco's Taylor Publishing, a school yearbook rival. A federal judge overturned the verdict in early 1999. Also in 1999 it formed an alliance with Sony to expand its use of digital photography in Canadian schools; related to the deal, Jostens acquired Sony's Canadian school photography business. That same year the company launched jostensalumshop.com which offers collegiate merchandise from more than 300 US colleges and universities.

In late 1999 the company agreed to a $950 million buyout led by Investcorp. Jostens also said it would refocus on its school-based units, eliminating about 100 jobs. The Investcorp-led investment group acquired 94% of Jostens, effectively taking the company private in May 2000. Also in 2000 Jostens acquired a minority stake in Planet Alumni, Inc., operator of planetalumni.com, a Web-based online community that allows users to find former classmates via an online directory, post messages, chat, and post photos.

In December 2001 Jostens announced that it would exit the recognition business.

**Chairman, President, and CEO:** Robert C. Buhrmaster, age 53, $1,347,560 pay
**SVP and General Manager, School Solutions:** Michael L. Bailey, age 45, $884,585 pay
**SVP, Manufacturing and Recognition:** Carl H. Blowers, age 61, $883,430 pay
**VP and General Manager, Business Ventures:** Gregory S. Lea, age 48, $609,757 pay
**VP and Chief Information Officer:** Andrew W. Black, age 38
**VP, Human Resources:** Steven A. Tighe, age 49
**Director of Corporate Development, Treasurer, and Investor Relations:** Jack Larsen
**Manager, Corporate Communications:** Mark Cassutt
**Auditors:** PricewaterhouseCoopers LLP

## LOCATIONS

**HQ:** 5501 Norman Center Dr., Minneapolis, MN 55437
**Phone:** 952-830-3300    **Fax:** 952-830-3293
**Web:** www.jostens.com

Jostens sells its products and services throughout North America through independent and employee sales representatives. It has manufacturing facilities in 10 states and Manitoba, Canada.

## PRODUCTS/OPERATIONS

**Selected Products**
Graduation products
  Announcements
  Caps and gowns
  Diplomas
Jewelry
  Athletic rings
  Class rings
Photography
  Class and individual school pictures
  Prom and special events pictures
  Senior portraits
  Student ID cards
Printing and publishing
  Commercial brochures
  Promotional books and materials
  Yearbooks

## COMPETITORS

CA Short
Commemorative Brands
Herff Jones
Insilco
Lifetouch
Norwood Promotional
 Products
O.C. Tanner

## HISTORICAL FINANCIALS & EMPLOYEES

| Private<br>FYE: Sat. nearest December 31 | Annual<br>Growth | 6/92 | 6/93 | 6/94 | 6/95 | 6/96 | *12/96 | 12/97 | 12/98 | 12/99 | 12/00 |
|---|---|---|---|---|---|---|---|---|---|---|---|
| Sales ($ mil.) | (0.9%) | 876 | 915 | 827 | 665 | 695 | 277 | 743 | 771 | 782 | 805 |
| Net income ($ mil.) | — | 61 | (12) | (16) | 50 | 52 | (1) | 57 | 42 | 43 | (19) |
| Income as % of sales | — | 7.0% | — | — | 7.6% | 7.4% | — | 7.7% | 5.4% | 5.5% | — |
| Employees | (3.6%) | 9,000 | 9,000 | 9,000 | 8,000 | 5,600 | 6,100 | 6,500 | 6,800 | 6,700 | 6,500 |

* Fiscal year change

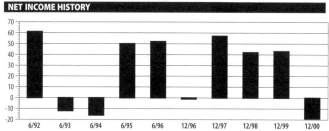

| NET INCOME HISTORY | 2000 FISCAL YEAR-END |
|---|---|

**2000 FISCAL YEAR-END**
Debt ratio: 100.0%
Return on equity: —
Cash ($ mil.): 27
Current ratio: 0.96
Long-term debt ($ mil.): 670

# J.R. SIMPLOT COMPANY

## OVERVIEW

J.R. Simplot is McDonald's primary french fry supplier, and that's no small potatoes. Named after its founder, Boise, Idaho-based agribusiness giant J.R. Simplot is one of the world's largest processors of frozen potatoes. It produces more than 2 billion pounds of fries, hash browns, and nuggets annually. Besides fries, J.R. Simplot's food unit also offers frozen vegetables and fruits. The company offers mostly Simplot-brand and private-label products to food service and retail customers.

The company's spuds sprouted other businesses, including cattle ranches and feedlots (which use feed made from potato peels). Its AgriBusiness Group mines phosphates (for fertilizer and feed) and silica. The company's Turf and Horticulture Group produces grass and turf seed and fertilizer.

Retired since 1994, founder J.R. Simplot is one of the wealthiest Americans. After amassing a mountain of potato money, the spudillionaire moved on to semiconductors and invested heavily in Boise-based Micron Technology.

## HISTORY

J.R. Simplot was born in Dubuque, Iowa, in 1909. His family moved to the frontier town of Declo, Idaho, about a year later. Frustrated with school and an overbearing father, Simplot dropped out at age 14 and moved to a local hotel, where he made money by paying cash for teachers' wage scrip, at 50 cents on the dollar. Simplot then got a bank loan using the scrip as collateral and moved into farming, first by raising hogs and then by growing potatoes. He met Lindsay Maggart, a leading farmer in the area, who taught him the value of planting certified potato seed, rather than potatoes.

Simplot purchased an electric potato sorter in 1928 and eventually dominated the local market by sorting for neighboring farms. By 1940 his company, J.R. Simplot, operated 33 potato warehouses in Oregon and Idaho. The company moved into food processing in the 1940s. In the beginning it produced dried onions and other vegetables for Chicago-based Sokol & Co., and then it moved on to produce dehydrated potatoes. Between 1942 and 1945 J.R. Simplot produced more than 50 million pounds of dehydrated potatoes for the US military. During WW II the company also expanded into fertilizer production, cattle feeding, and lumber. It moved to Boise, Idaho, in 1947.

In the 1950s J.R. Simplot researchers developed a method for freezing french fries. In the mid-1960s Simplot persuaded McDonald's founder, Ray Kroc, to go with his frozen fries, a handshake deal that practically guaranteed Simplot's success in the potato processing industry. By the end of the 1960s, Simplot was the largest landowner, cattleman, potato grower, and employer in the state of Idaho. He also had established fertilizer plants, mining operations, and other businesses in 36 states, as well as in Canada and a handful of other countries.

During the oil crisis of the 1970s, J.R. Simplot began producing ethanol from potatoes.

However, Simplot's empire-building was not without its rough edges. In 1977 he pleaded no contest to federal charges that he failed to report his income, and the next year he was forced to settle charges that he manipulated Maine potato futures.

The company entered the frozen fruit and vegetable business in 1983. Other ventures included using wastewater from potato processing for irrigation and using cattle manure to fuel methane gas plants. Simplot set up a Chinese joint venture in the 1990s to provide processed potatoes to McDonald's and other customers in East Asia.

The company bought the giant ZX cattle ranch near Paisley, Oregon, in 1994. Simplot retired from the board of directors that year and took the title of chairman emeritus; Stephen Beebe was named president and CEO. The 1995 acquisition of Pacific Dunlop led to the creation of Simplot Australia, one of the largest food processors in Australia. Its 1997 stock swap with I. & J. Foods Australia enlarged the subsidiary's frozen food menu.

In 1999 the company sold its Simplot Dairy Products cheese business to France's Besnier Group, and it teamed with Dutch potato processor Farm Frites to enter new markets. The next year it launched agricultural Web site planetAg, bought the turf grass seed assets of AgriBioTech, and added the US potato operations of food giant Nestlé to its pantry. In 2001 the firm said it would build an $80 million potato-processing plant in Manitoba in Canada. Also that year the company said it would not increase the value of its contracts with growers struggling amid low prices in a glutted market.

---

## PRODUCTS/OPERATIONS

**Major Operating Groups**
AgriBusiness Group
  Nitrogen and phosphate fertilizers
  Phosphate and silica ore mining
Corporate Group
  Corporate Development Department
  Corporate Information Systems
  Simplot Aviation (in-company flight services)
  SSI Food Services, Inc. (meat processing and
    packaging)
Food Group (Simplot Foods)
  Avocado products
  Fresh potatoes (Blue Ribbon, Golden Classic)
Frozen fruits and vegetables
  Frozen potato products (fries, nuggets, patties, sticks)
Land and Livestock Group
  Beef production
  Cattle feeding
  Hay, corn, grain production for feedlots

## COMPETITORS

Cargill
ConAgra
ContiGroup
Del Monte Foods
Golden State Foods
Heinz
IBP
IMC Global
McCain Foods
Michael Foods
Potash Corporation
Pro-Fac
Seneca Foods

## HISTORICAL FINANCIALS & EMPLOYEES

| Private<br>FYE: August 31 | Annual<br>Growth | 8/92 | 8/93 | 8/94 | 8/95 | 8/96 | 8/97 | 8/98 | 8/99 | 8/00 | 8/01 |
|---|---|---|---|---|---|---|---|---|---|---|---|
| Sales ($ mil.) | 7.2% | 1,600 | 1,700 | 2,100 | 2,200 | 2,700 | 2,800 | 2,800 | 2,730 | 2,700 | 3,000 |
| Employees | 4.7% | — | 9,000 | 10,000 | 10,000 | 13,000 | 12,000 | 12,000 | 12,000 | 12,000 | 13,000 |

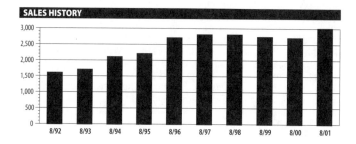

SALES HISTORY

# KAISER FOUNDATION

## OVERVIEW

Kaiser reigns — as a top not-for-profit HMO. Oakland, California-based Kaiser Foundation Health Plan has an integrated care model, offering both hospital and physician care, through a network of hospitals and physician practices operating under the Kaiser Permanente name. Kaiser serves more than 8 million members in nine states and the District of Columbia;

California is its largest market accounting for about 75% of membership.

A string of losses has prompted Kaiser to raise rates and divest underperforming units. Like many competitors, Kaiser also faces the ever-rising costs of health care that threaten the gains it has made to get back in the black.

## HISTORY

Henry Kaiser — shipbuilder, war profiteer, builder of the Hoover and Grand Coulee dams, and founder of Kaiser Aluminum — was a bootstrap capitalist who did well by doing good. A high school dropout from upstate New York, Kaiser moved to Spokane, Washington, in 1906 and went into road construction. During the Depression, he headed the consortium that built the great WPA dams.

It was in building the Grand Coulee Dam that, in 1938, Kaiser teamed with Dr. Sidney Garfield, who earlier had devised a prepayment health plan for workers on California public works projects. As Kaiser moved into steelmaking and shipbuilding during WWII (turning out some 1,400 bare-bones Liberty ships — one per day at peak production), he realized that healthy workers produce more than sick ones. He then called on Garfield to set up on-site clinics funded by the US government as part of operating expenses. Garfield was released from military service by President Roosevelt for the purpose.

After the war, the clinics became war surplus. Kaiser and his wife bought them — at a 99% discount — through the new Kaiser Hospital Foundation. His vision was to provide the public with low-cost, prepaid medical care. He created the health plan — the self-supporting entity that would administer the system — and the group medical organization, Permanente (named after Kaiser's first cement plant site). He then endowed the health plan with $200,000. This plan, the classic HMO model, was criticized by the medical establishment as socialized medicine performed by "employee" doctors.

However, the plan flourished, becoming California's #1 medical system. In 1958 Kaiser retired to Hawaii and introduced his health plan there. But physician resistance limited national growth; HMOs were illegal in some states well into the 1970s.

As health care costs rose, Congress legalized HMOs in all states. Kaiser expanded in the 1980s; as it moved outside its traditional

geographic areas, the company contracted for space in hospitals rather than building them. Growth slowed as competition increased.

Some health care costs in California fell in the early 1990s as more medical procedures were performed on an outpatient basis. Specialists flooded the state, and as price competition among doctors and hospitals heated up, many HMOs landed advantageous contracts. Kaiser, with its own highly paid doctors, was unable to realize the same savings and was no longer the best deal in town. Its membership stalled.

To boost membership and control expenses, Kaiser instituted a controversial program in 1996 in which nurses earned bonuses for cost-cutting. Critics said the program could lead to a decrease in care quality; Kaiser later became the focus of investigations into wrongful death suits linked to cost-cutting in California (where it has since beefed up staffing and programs) and Texas (where it has agreed to pay $1 million in fines).

In 1997 Kaiser tried to boost membership by lowering premiums, but the strategy proved *too* effective: Costs linked to an unwieldy 20% enrollment surge brought a loss in 1997 — Kaiser's first annual loss ever.

A second year in the red in 1998 prompted Kaiser to sell its Texas operations to Sierra Health Services. It also entered the Florida market via an alliance with Miami-based AvMed Health Plan. In 1999 Kaiser announced plans to sell its unprofitable North Carolina operations (it closed the deal the following year).

Kaiser announced plans to charge premiums for its Medicare HMO, Medicare+Choice, to offset the shortfall in federal reimbursements in 2000. In 2001 the company's hospital division bought the technology and assets of defunct Internet grocer Webvan in an effort to increase its distribution activity. Also that year, the son of a deceased anthrax victim sued a Kaiser facility for failing to recognize and treat his father's symptoms.

## OFFICERS

**Chairman and CEO:** David M. Lawrence, age 60
**President:** L. Dale Crandall
**EVP and COO:** William A. Gillespie
**EVP, Health Plan Operations:** Arthur M. Southam, age 43
**EVP; President, California Division:** Richard R. Pettingill
**SVP and Chief Administration Officer:** Robert M. Crane
**SVP, National Contracting Purchasing and Distribution:** Joseph W. Hummel
**SVP, Workforce Development:** Leslie A. Margolin
**SVP, General Counsel, and Secretary:** Kirk E. Miller
**SVP and Director for Care and Services Quality:** Patricia B. Siegel
**SVP and Chief Information Officer:** Timothy E. Sullivan
**VP, Human Resources, Regions Outside of California:** Dresdene Flynn-White

## LOCATIONS

**HQ:** Kaiser Foundation Health Plan, Inc.
1 Kaiser Plaza, Oakland, CA 94612
**Phone:** 510-271-5800     **Fax:** 510-271-6493
**Web:** www.kaiserpermanente.org

Kaiser Foundation Health Plan operates in California, Colorado, Georgia, Hawaii, Maryland, Ohio, Oregon, Virginia, Washington, and the District of Columbia.

### 2000 Membership

| | no. members |
|---|---|
| California | 6,132,515 |
| Mid-Atlantic | 545,064 |
| Northwest | 449,633 |
| Colorado | 371,752 |
| Georgia | 272,633 |
| Hawaii | 220,261 |
| Ohio | 170,830 |
| **Total** | **8,162,688** |

## PRODUCTS/OPERATIONS

**Selected Operations**
Kaiser Foundation Health Plans (health coverage)
Kaiser Foundation Hospitals (community hospitals and outpatient facilities)
Permanente Medical Groups (physician organizations)

## COMPETITORS

Aetna
Blue Cross
Catholic Health East
Catholic Health Initiatives
Catholic Healthcare Network
Catholic Healthcare Partners
Catholic Healthcare West
CIGNA
HCA
Health Net
Humana
Oxford Health Plans
PacifiCare
Sierra Health
UnitedHealth Group
WellPoint Health Networks

## HISTORICAL FINANCIALS & EMPLOYEES

| Not-for-profit FYE: December 31 | Annual Growth | 12/91 | 12/92 | 12/93 | 12/94 | 12/95 | 12/96 | 12/97 | 12/98 | 12/99 | 12/00 |
|---|---|---|---|---|---|---|---|---|---|---|---|
| Sales ($ mil.) | 6.1% | — | 11,032 | 11,930 | 12,268 | 12,290 | 13,241 | 14,500 | 15,500 | 16,841 | 17,700 |
| Employees | 1.0% | — | 82,858 | 84,885 | 84,845 | 85,000 | 90,000 | 100,000 | 100,000 | 90,000 | 90,000 |

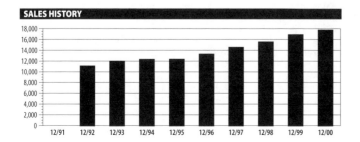

SALES HISTORY

# KEMPER INSURANCE COMPANIES

## OVERVIEW

Kemper fi!

Long Grove, Illinois-based The Kemper Insurance Companies offers personal, risk management, and commercial property/casualty insurance products and services through Lumbermens Mutual Casualty Company and other subsidiaries. Kemper's Business Customer Group provides workers' compensation and property coverage lines, and its Individual and Family Group offers auto and homeowners insurance. The Kemper Casualty Company offers casualty and risk management services to large businesses.

Kemper has completed a realignment of its operations — selling its reinsurance operations, building its specialty casualty business, adding coverage for health care equipment and not-for-profit organizations, acquiring companies involved in workers' compensation and surety bonds, and getting involved in claims management software.

## HISTORY

James Kemper started Lumbermens Mutual in 1912 to provide workers' compensation coverage to Illinois lumberyard owners. The 26-year-old insurance agent perceived a niche when yard owners complained that insurers were overcharging by lumping lumberyards in with the more dangerous logging business. The next year Kemper expanded into fire insurance for lumberyards by founding National Underwriters. Lumbermens began growing, adding offices in Philadelphia, Boston, and Syracuse, New York. By 1921 the company was based in Chicago.

Lumbermens was one of the first auto insurers in the US, and in 1926 it formed American Motorists Insurance Co. specifically for personal and commercial auto insurance. In the early 1930s the firm added boiler and machinery, surety bond, and inland marine coverage. After a receptionist began greeting callers with "Kemper Insurance," Lumbermens subsidiaries all began to be known as the "Kemper companies."

The Kemper family was active in philanthropy, founding a traffic safety institute at Northwestern University in the 1930s and endowing a scholarship fund.

In 1957 Lumbermens began offering marine coverage. The Kemper companies grew to include Federal Kemper Life Assurance in 1961 and American Protection Insurance the next year.

In 1967 Lumbermens, responding to concerns about how a mutual company could own so many subsidiaries, formed public holding company Kemperco (later Kemper Corp.) in which Lumbermens owned controlling interest. In 1981, at age 94, James Kemper died.

Like many other companies, Kemper Corp. set its sights in the 1980s on becoming a financial services powerhouse, buying three brokerages. As cyclic losses inherent in property/casualty insurance dragged down earnings

growth, the company in 1989 began selling those operations back to Lumbermens for stock, decreasing Lumbermens' interest in Kemper Corp. (Property/casualty premiums had dropped from 60% of operating income in 1980 to 49% in 1981 and continued to fall until 1985.)

Additionally, reorganization gave separate management and boards of directors to Kemper Corp. and Kemper National Insurance Cos. (formed by Lumbermens Mutual Casualty Company, American Motorists Insurance Company, and American Manufacturers Mutual Insurance Company). In 1992 the companies' chairmanships were separated as well. Kemper Insurance (originally Kemper National) was formed just in time to be pummeled by the longest and costliest string of natural disasters in the 20th century.

Kemper Corp. became a financial services company with mutual fund offerings. In 1995 it sold its brokerage unit, and in 1996 it was bought by Insurance Partners and Zurich Insurance Group (now Zurich Financial).

Kemper Insurance, meanwhile, was devastated by the 1994 bond crash; earnings sank again in 1996 when the company bolstered environmental and asbestos reserves. Toward the end of the decade, the firm began realigning its insurance offerings, acquiring specialty coverage players and selling Kemper Reinsurance to GE Capital (1998). In 1999 Kemper took advantage of continuing deregulation when it announced plans to open LMC, a thrift serving Illinois.

In 2000 Kemper bolstered its presence in the workers' compensation market when it acquired the policy renewal rights from the Superior National Insurance companies, which were under supervision by the California Insurance Department. The next year Kemper announced the sale of its Canadian subsidiary to UK-based Royal & Sun Alliance Insurance.

**Chairman and CEO:** David B. Mathis, age 62
**President, COO, and Director:** William D. Smith, age 56
**SVP and CFO:** Mural R. Josephson
**SVP and Chief Actuary:** Frederick O. Kist
**SVP, Capital Development:** William A. Hickey
**SVP, Corporate Planning and Administration:**
Mary Ann Eddy
**SVP, Human Resources:** Sue A. Coughlin
**Treasurer:** Michael A. Finelli Jr.
**General Counsel and Corporate Secretary:**
John K. Conway
**General Auditor:** Kent L. Suarez
**President and CEO, GreatLand Insurance Co.:**
W. Taylor
**President and CEO, Kemper Casualty Company; EVP,**
**Lumbermens Mutual Casualty:** Dennis P. Kane
**President and CEO, KEMPES:** Vickie F. Kartchner
**President, American Motorists Insurance Company;**
**EVP, Lumbermens Mutual Casualty:**
Dale S. Hammond
**President, Business Customer Group; EVP,**
**Lumbermens Mutual Casualty:** Douglas A. Batting
**President, Kemper Technology Services; SVP,**
**Lumbermans Mutual Casualty Company:**
Jack E. Scott
**Auditors:** KPMG LLP

## LOCATIONS

**HQ:** The Kemper Insurance Companies
1 Kemper Dr., Long Grove, IL 60049
**Phone:** 847-320-2000       **Fax:** 847-320-2494
**Web:** www.kemperinsurance.com

The Kemper Insurance Companies has operations in
Australia, Belgium, Canada, Germany, Japan, Singapore,
and the US.

## PRODUCTS/OPERATIONS

**Subsidiaries and Affiliates**
Eagle Insurance Group (specialty workers'
compensation)
GreatLand Insurance (commercial insurance products)
Kemper Auto & Home (personal property/casualty)
Kemper Casualty Company
Kemper Environmental (commercial and
environmental insurance and services)
Kemper Risk Management (workers' compensation,
liability, and commercial auto insurance)
Kemper Solutions (risk management programs for
midsized to large customers)
Kemper Cost Management (health care equipment
insurance)
Kemper Professional (individual professional liability)
KEMPES (professional liability, public entity, and
property/casualty)
Lumbermens Mutual Casualty Company

## COMPETITORS

Acordia
Allstate
American Family Insurance
American Financial
AIG
American Safety Insurance
Chubb
CIGNA
CNA Financial
Liberty Mutual
Mutual of Omaha
New York Life
Prudential
Reliance Group Holdings
St. Paul Companies
Travelers

## HISTORICAL FINANCIALS & EMPLOYEES

| Mutual company FYE: December 31 | Annual Growth | 12/91 | 12/92 | 12/93 | 12/94 | 12/95 | 12/96 | 12/97 | 12/98 | 12/99 | 12/00 |
|---|---|---|---|---|---|---|---|---|---|---|---|
| Assets ($ mil.) | 1.3% | — | 8,460 | 9,137 | 8,956 | 9,023 | 8,962 | 9,834 | 9,810 | 9,738 | 9,409 |
| Net income ($ mil.) | 3.7% | — | 86 | 119 | 25 | 169 | 19 | 222 | 227 | 167 | 115 |
| Income as % of assets | — | — | 1.0% | 1.3% | 0.3% | 1.9% | 0.2% | 2.3% | 2.3% | 1.7% | 1.2% |
| Employees | (0.8%) | — | — | 9,000 | 8,295 | 8,837 | 10,068 | 9,500 | 9,000 | — | 8,500 |

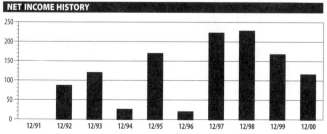

### NET INCOME HISTORY

### 2000 FISCAL YEAR-END
Equity as % of assets: 22.0%
Return on assets: 1.2%
Return on equity: 4.8%
Long-term debt ($ mil.): 0
Sales ($ mil.): 3,014

# KING RANCH, INC.

King Ranch's property is Texas-sized (not really, but it is larger than Rhode Island). The company's 825,000-acre namesake ranch still conducts the farming and ranching that made it famous, but the dwindling demand for beef has made it more dependent on oil and gas royalties, fruit and sugar cane farming in Florida, and tourist dollars (from sightseers, hunters, and birdwatchers). The operations are managed from its Houston corporate headquarters.

Considered the birthplace of the American ranching industry, King Ranch also has introduced the new highly fertile breed of beef cattle: the King Ranch Santa Cruz, which is one-fourth Gelbvieh, one-fourth Red Angus, and one-half Santa Gertrudis. About 60,000 cattle still roam the land, but raising animals isn't the only thing King Ranch cottons to — this sprawl of four noncontiguous ranches is also one of the US's largest cotton producers.

Like a good western movie, some things have ridden into the sunset at King Ranch. The company sold its 670-acre Kentucky Thoroughbred breeding and racing farm, as well as most of its foreign ranches, and its primary oil and gas subsidiary. About 85 descendants of the company's founder, Richard King, own King Ranch.

King Ranch was founded in 1853 by former steamboat captain Richard King and his wife Henrietta, the daughter of a Brownsville, Texas, missionary. On the advice of his friend Robert E. Lee, King used his steamboating profits and occasional strong-arm tactics to buy land — miles of flat, brush-filled, coastal plain and desert south of Corpus Christi, Texas, valued at pennies an acre.

The next year King relocated the residents of an entire drought-ravaged village to the ranch and employed them as ranch hands, known ever after as *kinenos* ("King's men"). The Kings built their homestead in 1858 at a site recommended by Lee.

King Ranch endured attacks from Union guerrillas during the Civil War and Mexican bandits after the war. Times were tough, but King was up to the challenge, always traveling armed and with outriders.

In 1867 the ranch used its famed Running W brand for the first time. After King's death in 1885, Robert Kleberg, who married King's daughter Alice, managed the 1.2 million-acre ranch for his mother-in-law. Henrietta died in 1925 and left three-fourths of the ranch to Alice. Before Robert's death in 1932, control of the ranch passed to sons Richard and Bob. In 1933 Bob negotiated an exclusive oil and gas lease with Houston-based Humble Oil, which later became part of Exxon.

While Richard served in Congress, Bob ran the ranch. He developed the Santa Gertrudis, the first breed of cattle ever created in the US, by crossing British shorthorn cattle with Indian Brahmas. The new breed was better suited to the hot, dry South Texas climate.

Bob made King Ranch a leading breeder of quarter horses, which worked cattle, and Thoroughbreds, which he raced. He bought Kentucky Derby winner Bold Venture in 1936 and a Kentucky breeding farm in 1946; that year a King Ranch horse, Assault, won racing's Triple Crown.

When Bob died in 1974, the family asked James Clement, husband of one of the founders' great-granddaughters, to become CEO and bypassed Robert Shelton, a King relative and orphan whom Bob had raised as his own son. Shelton severed ties with the ranch in 1977 over a lawsuit he filed against Exxon, and partially won, alleging underpayment of royalties.

Under Clement, King Ranch became a multinational corporation. In 1980 it formed King Ranch Oil and Gas (also called King Ranch Energy) to explore for and produce oil and gas in five states and the Gulf of Mexico. In 1988 Clement retired, and Kimberly-Clark executive Darwin Smith became the first CEO not related to the founders. Smith left after one year, and the reins passed to petroleum geologist Roger Jarvis and then to Jack Hunt in 1995.

With the help of scientists, in the early 1990s the company developed a leaner, more fertile breed of the Santa Gertrudis called the Santa Cruz.

In 1998 Stephen "Tio" Kleberg, the only King descendant still actively working the ranch, was pushed from the saddle of daily operations to a seat on the board. King Ranch sold its Kentucky horse farm in 1998 and teamed up with Collier Enterprises that year to purchase citrus grower Turner Foods from utility holding company FPL Group. In 2000 King Ranch sold King Ranch Energy to St. Mary Land and Exploration Co. for $60 million.

**Chairman:** James H. Clement
**President and CEO:** Jack Hunt
**CFO:** Bill Gardiner
**VP Livestock:** Paul Genho
**VP Audit:** Richard Nilles
**Secretary and General Counsel:** Frank Perrone
**Director of Human Resources:** Martha Breit

## LOCATIONS

**HQ:** 3 River Way, Ste. 1600, Houston, TX 77056
**Phone:** 832-681-5700          **Fax:** 832-681-5759
**Web:** www.king-ranch.com

King Ranch operates ranching and farming interests in South Texas and Florida.

**Selected Agricultural Operations**
Florida
  3,100 acres (St. Augustine sod)
  12,000 acres (sugar cane)
  40,000 acres (orange and grapefruit groves)
Texas
  60,000 acres (cotton and grain)

## PRODUCTS/OPERATIONS

**Selected Operations**
Consolidated Citrus Limited
  Partnership (southern Florida citrus groves)
King Ranch Museum
King Ranch Nature Tour Program
King Ranch Saddle Shop (leather products)

## COMPETITORS

Alico
AZTX Cattle
Cactus Feeders
Calcot
Devon Energy
Koch
Southern States
Southwestern Irrigated
  Cotton
Tejon Ranch

## HISTORICAL FINANCIALS & EMPLOYEES

| Private<br>FYE: December 31 | Annual<br>Growth | 12/91 | 12/92 | 12/93 | 12/94 | 12/95 | 12/96 | 12/97 | 12/98 | 12/99 | 12/00 |
|---|---|---|---|---|---|---|---|---|---|---|---|
| Estimated sales ($ mil.) | (1.2%) | — | 330 | 250 | 250 | 250 | 250 | 300 | 300 | 300 | 300 |
| Employees | 0.0% | — | 700 | 700 | 700 | 700 | 700 | 700 | 700 | 700 | 700 |

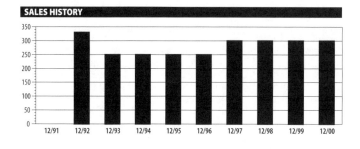

SALES HISTORY

# KINGSTON TECHNOLOGY COMPANY

In the realm of memory, Kingston Technology is a king. The Fountain Valley, California-based company is a leading maker of memory modules — circuit boards that increase the capacity and speed of printers and computers. It also makes flash memory cards used in portable electronic devices such as digital cameras, wireless phones, and personal digital assistants. Kingston has discontinued its offerings of peripheral devices such as processor upgrades, hard drives, and networking equipment (adapters, hubs, routers). Kingston sells worldwide, primarily through resellers and distributors.

In an effort to handle more manufacturing functions for its customers, Kingston has debuted its Payton Technology Project, a specialized factory that tests and packages memory chips before assembling them into customized memory modules. The process is touted as cutting the time required for order fulfillment from weeks to days.

Company co-founders and owners John Tu (president and CEO) and David Sun (COO) promote a casual work atmosphere and treat employees as members of an extended family. (Their work cubicles are identical to their employees'.) Since 1996 they have given more than $100 million in bonuses to workers; in some cases the bonuses have amounted to three times the employees' annual salaries.

Kingston Technology was founded in 1987 by Shanghai-born John Tu and Taiwan-born David Sun, both of whom had moved to California in the 1970s. The pair met in 1982 and started a memory upgrade company called Camminton Technology in Tu's garage. Sales had reached $9 million by 1986, when they sold the business to high-tech firm AST Research for $6 million. The two invested their money in stock market futures but suffered heavy losses when the market crashed in 1987.

That year PC makers were producing computers that lacked the memory needed to run the latest, hottest software, so Tu and Sun sprang into action. With just $4,000 in cash, they started another company that converted inexpensive, outdated chips into memory upgrades. Tu, who was educated in Europe, wanted to call the company Kensington after the gardens in London. A mouse pad company had that name, so Kingston was chosen.

Tu had doubts about the new company and bet Sun a Jaguar that it wouldn't survive the first year of operations. Sun won the car (which he later gave to a veteran employee who dreamed of owning one) and within two years the company had sold nearly $40 million worth of products. In 1989 Kingston began making memory system upgrades; a year later it started producing processor upgrades.

The company was #1 on *Inc.* magazine's list of fastest-growing private US companies in 1992. The next year Kingston began marketing networking and storage products. Its vendor-friendly policy paid off that year, when demand for semiconductors far outstripped supply. Suppliers kept shipping to the company even when orders for other buyers were delayed.

Demand for Kingston's upgrades kicked in when Microsoft launched the Windows 95 operating system, leading many consumers to boost their computers' power so they could run the software.

In 1996 Kingston launched a processor upgrade that gave 486-based computer systems the processing power of a 75 MHz Pentium chip. That year SOFTBANK paid $1.5 billion for 80% of the company but promised to preserve its culture and retain all management — including Tu and Sun — and employees. Sun and Tu set aside $100 million for employee bonuses.

In 1997 Kingston opened a European headquarters in the UK. The next year Kingston opened its first foreign manufacturing facility, in Ireland, and later in 1998 it established one in Taiwan. Also in 1998, in a unique arrangement suggesting that SOFTBANK overpaid when it bought Kingston, Tu and Sun agreed to forgo SOFTBANK's final $333 million payment. The following year Tu and Sun bought back SOFTBANK's stake for about $450 million. Also in 1999 the company opened a manufacturing plant in Malaysia.

In 2000 Kingston debuted its Payton Technology Project, a cutting-edge California plant that combines chip testing and packaging facilities with those for making memory modules. The company claims that Payton's integrated processes reduce product turnaround times from several weeks to several days.

After years of making computer storage devices, Kingston in 2000 formed a separate company, StorCase Technology, which specializes in storage equipment. The following year Kingston discontinued its Peripheral Products Division's offerings.

**President and CEO:** John Tu, age 59
**COO:** David Sun
**CFO:** Koichi Hosokawa
**VP, Administration (HR):** Daniel Hsu

# LOCATIONS

**HQ:** 17600 Newhope St., Fountain Valley, CA 92708
**Phone:** 714-435-2600        **Fax:** 714-435-2699
**Web:** www.kingston.com

Kingston Technology has operations in Australia, China, France, Germany, Ireland, Malaysia, Taiwan, the UK, and the US.

# PRODUCTS/OPERATIONS

**Selected Products**
Flash memory cards (CompactFlash, DataFlash, MultiMediaCard, Solid State Floppy Disc Cards)
Memory modules and add-on boards
Standard memory modules (ValueRAM)

# COMPETITORS

AMD
Amkor
ASE Test Limited
Centon
ChipPAC
Hynix
Intel
Micron Technology
PNY Technologies
Samsung Electronics
SanDisk
Silicon Storage
SimpleTech
Unigen
Viking Components

# HISTORICAL FINANCIALS & EMPLOYEES

| Private<br>FYE: December 31 | Annual<br>Growth | 12/91 | 12/92 | 12/93 | 12/94 | 12/95 | 12/96 | 12/97 | 12/98 | 12/99 | 12/00 |
|---|---|---|---|---|---|---|---|---|---|---|---|
| Sales ($ mil.) | 26.1% | — | 251 | 489 | 800 | 1,300 | 2,100 | 1,000 | 1,000 | 1,400 | 1,600 |
| Employees | 35.6% | — | 175 | 255 | 310 | 450 | 547 | 663 | 670 | 2,000 | 2,000 |

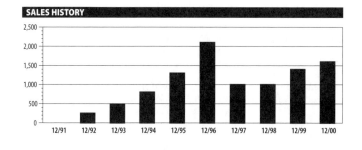

SALES HISTORY

# KINKO'S, INC.

## OVERVIEW

Ask someone what they're doing at Kinko's and they might respond, "Makin' copies." But they might also say they're sending documents around the world electronically, shipping packages, getting business cards printed, checking e-mail, or even accessing the Internet. Ventura, California-based Kinko's began as a one-store, campus-oriented copy shop and has evolved into an entrepreneurial "branch office" for small offices and home businesses. Although the small office/home office market accounts for most of the company's sales, it also provides digital document services to medium and large corporations.

Kinko's operates a global chain of more than 1,100 stores in Australia, Canada, China, Japan, the Netherlands, South Korea, the UK, the United Arab Emirates, and the US. The firm has also launched Kinkos.com, which allows Web users to design products such as business cards and then forward the order to a nearby Kinko's store for printing.

New CEO Gary Kusin, a longtime Dallas businessman, has announced that the company is moving its headquarters to Dallas. He cites the area's central location and low tax rate as reasons for uprooting the company. About 350 staffers will be cut as a result of a restructuring of field support positions.

New York buyout firm Clayton, Dubilier & Rice owns 41% of Kinko's.

## HISTORY

Kinko's is the creation of Paul Orfalea, who suffers from dyslexia and was inappropriately placed for six weeks in a school for the mentally retarded. The red-haired, Afro-sporting Orfalea (nicknamed Kinko) started selling pencils and spiral notebooks on the campus of UC Santa Barbara in 1970. When he saw a 10-cents-a-page photocopy machine in the library, he decided selling copies would be even better. The self-described hippie borrowed $5,000 that year and opened his first Kinko's shop in a former taco stand near the university. He sold school supplies and made copies on a wheeled copy machine that had to be moved outside because the shop was so small.

Orfalea opened a second California store in San Luis Obispo in 1972, and in the mid-1970s he started providing custom publishing materials for colleges. His innovative approach caught on, and by 1980 he had 80 stores in operation, mostly located near colleges.

In 1983 Kinko's opened its first store outside the US, in Canada, and in 1985 it opened its first 24-hour store, in Chicago. The company moved to Ventura, California, in 1988 and shifted its focus to the growing home office market in 1989 following the loss of a $1.9 million copyright-infringement suit for photocopying texts for professors. By 1990 Kinko's had 420 stores.

Kinko's began positioning itself as "Your Branch Office" in 1992. The next year it teamed up with telecommunications company Sprint and introduced videoconferencing services in 100 stores. Kinko's opened an office in South Korea in 1995 and launched Kinkonet, its electronic communications network. The company teamed up with UUNET (now owned by MCI WorldCom) in 1996 to offer Internet access at its stores.

Until that year Orfalea was the sole owner of 110 stores and had partnership arrangements with more than 120 other entrepreneurs, a relationship that allowed Orfalea to control the company's rapidly growing network, while giving plenty of incentive for local expansion. This relaxed style of management also led to some unprofitable operations.

To remedy this, Kinko's went corporate in 1996, selling about 30% of the company to buyout firm Clayton, Dubilier & Rice for $219 million; the funds have been used for new technology and expansion. As part of the deal, Kinko's established a single, unified corporation, rolling into it all of the decentralized joint venture, corporate, and partnership companies operating under the Kinko's name.

In 1997 the company opened its first branch in China and made its first acquisition, document management company Electronic Demand Publishing, which became the core of Kinko's corporate document unit. In 1998 Kinko's opened its first stores in the UK and in the Middle East. The next year it began offering Internet-based custom printing services through an alliance with online print services firm iPrint.com.

In 2000 it launched a new majority-owned Web firm, Kinkos.com. Orfalea resigned as chairman and was replaced by George Tamke that year. Also in 2001 Joseph Hardin Jr. (who had been CEO for more than three years) resigned; Gary Kusin replaced him. The company announced that it would relocate its headquarters to Dallas in 2002, a move that Orfalea had criticized as unnecessary.

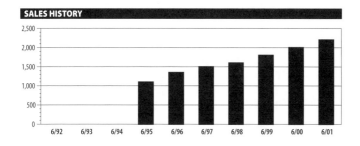

## OFFICERS

**Chairman:** George Tamke Jr.
**President, CEO, and Director:** Gary M. Kusin, age 50
**CFO:** Jeffrey E. Moxie
**SVP and Chief Technology Officer:** Allen Dickason
**SVP Legal:** Jim Cornell
**SVP Human Resources and Administration:**
  Paul Rostron
**SVP Technology and Chief Information Officer:**
  Fred Herczeg
**President, Kinko's International:** Michael Cohn
**Chief Field Operations:** Scott Seay

## LOCATIONS

**HQ:** 255 W. Stanley Ave., Ventura, CA 93002
**Phone:** 805-652-4000     **Fax:** 805-652-4347
**Web:** www.kinkos.com

Kinko's operates more than 1,100 stores in Australia, Canada, China, Japan, the Netherlands, South Korea, the UK, the United Arab Emirates, and the US.

## PRODUCTS/OPERATIONS

**Selected Products and Services**
Binding and finishing services
Business and specialty papers
Computer rentals
Custom printing
Digital printing
E-mail
Fax services
FedEx services
Folding
Instant posters and banners
Internet access
Laminating
Laser printing
Office supplies
Overhead transparencies
Photocopying (black-and-white, color, full-service, self-service, oversize)
Pick up and delivery
Presentation materials
Scanning

## COMPETITORS

Black Dot Group
Champion Industries
EagleDirect.com
Franchise Services
General Binding
IKON
IPI
iPrint
Mail Boxes Etc.
Merrill
Office Depot
OfficeMax
PIP
Pitney Bowes
Staples
TRM
Xerox

## HISTORICAL FINANCIALS & EMPLOYEES

| Private<br>FYE: June 30 | Annual<br>Growth | 6/92 | 6/93 | 6/94 | 6/95 | 6/96 | 6/97 | 6/98 | 6/99 | 6/00 | 6/01 |
|---|---|---|---|---|---|---|---|---|---|---|---|
| Estimated sales ($ mil.) | 12.2% | — | — | — | 1,100 | 1,350 | 1,500 | 1,600 | 1,800 | 2,000 | 2,200 |
| Employees | 4.7% | — | — | — | 19,000 | 23,000 | 24,000 | 24,000 | 25,000 | 26,000 | 25,000 |

### SALES HISTORY

# KNOLL, INC.

## OVERVIEW

If cartoonist Scott Adams worked in a cubicle designed by Knoll, *Dilbert* might never have existed. The East Greenville, Pennsylvania, company makes a variety of distinctively designed, curvilinear office furniture and related accessories, including office systems (cubicles) sold under such names as Equity, Dividends, and Currents.

Other products include rolling chairs, tables, metal and wood desks, file cabinets, lighting, computer and desk accessories, textiles, and leather upholstery. Some products are created by high-profile architects and designers such as Frank Gehry and Vietnam War Memorial architect Maya Lin. Some 30 Knoll products are part of the permanent design

collection of the Museum of Modern Art in New York City.

Knoll markets its products through independent dealers in North America via a network of more than 300 dealerships and 100 showrooms and regional offices. The company also has dealers in South America, Europe, and Asia. It has been increasing its sales force to grow its share of the middle to high-end office furniture market. Knoll has manufacturing sites in East Greenville and Grand Rapids and Muskegon, Michigan. It also has plants in Toronto, Ontario and Foligno and Graffignana, Italy.

Investment firm Warburg Pincus and Knoll management own the company.

## HISTORY

German immigrant Hans Knoll founded Knoll in 1938 (starting in a single room on Manhattan's East Side that he dubbed Factory No. 1) on the premise that modern buildings would require modern furniture. Knoll and his wife, Florence, an architect, sought out noted architects to design the company's products: Eero Saarinen worked for Knoll, and the company later gained the rights to use designs by Ludwig Mies van der Rohe and Marcel Breuer.

Following WWII Hans decided to move manufacturing from New York City. He chose eastern Pennsylvania because of its large population of Pennsylvania-Dutch and German immigrants who came from communities with traditions of painstaking craftsmanship. He found a healthy labor pool among men who had returned from the war and no longer wanted to work on the farm.

Knoll moved into textiles in 1947, but when it was unable to find the quality of upholstery materials it wanted, the company turned to the fashion industry for fabric and ended up using men's suit fabric for most of its first line of upholstered furniture.

Hans died in a car crash in 1955; his widow worked at Knoll for another decade. The company enjoyed the boom years of the 1950s and 1960s, but it ran into trouble when commercial construction dried up in the 1970s. General Felt acquired Knoll in the early 1980s, took it public in 1983, took it private again in 1986, and sold it to Westinghouse in 1990.

Knoll struggled during the early 1990s but eventually got back on track, redesigning its products, consolidating its manufacturing, and restructuring its management contracts.

By the time Westinghouse sold Knoll to its top managers and merchant banker Warburg, Pincus in 1996 for $160 million, the economy had improved and the company was profitable once again.

The company went public in 1997 with John Lynch (who previously worked at Westinghouse) as CEO. Continuing its tradition of hiring high-profile architects, the next year Knoll unveiled a line of furniture created by Vietnam War Memorial designer Maya Lin.

After settling a shareholder lawsuit to block the deal, Knoll returned to private ownership again in 1999 when Warburg, Pincus and a Knoll management group bought the 40% of the company they didn't already own for nearly $500 million.

In 2000 Knoll introduced KnollShop, allowing customers to order furniture online. As part of KnollShop, customers could choose "white glove" service, where company representatives assemble, inspect, and place the furniture for them, so local dealers would not be excluded from the company's move to the Web. Also that year Knoll introduced its Upstart line of office furniture, targeted at dot-com startup companies. In mid-2001 COO Andrew Cogan replaced Lynch as CEO.

**Chairman:** Burton B. Staniar, age 59, $825,004 pay
**CEO and Director:** Andrew B. Cogan, age 38,
  $1,205,000 pay (prior to promotion)
**President and CEO, Knoll North America, and
  Director:** Kathleen G. Bradley, age 51, $2,100,000 pay
  (prior to title change)
**SVP, CFO, Treasurer, and Controller:** Barry L. McCabe,
  age 54
**SVP, Design:** Carl G. Magnusson, age 61
**SVP, General Counsel, and Secretary:**
  Patrick A. Milberger, age 44
**SVP, Operations:** Stephen A. Grover, age 48
**SVP, Sales and Distribution:** Arthur C. Graves, age 54,
  $800,683 pay
**VP, Human Resources:** S. David Wolfe, age 43
**Chief Marketing and Development Officer:**
  Andrew C. McGregor, age 51
**Auditors:** Ernst & Young LLP

## LOCATIONS

**HQ:** 1235 Water St., East Greenville, PA 18041
**Phone:** 215-679-7991   **Fax:** 215-679-1755
**Web:** www.knoll.com

Knoll has three plants in the US, two in Italy, and one in
Canada.

**2000 Sales**

|  | $ mil. | % of total |
|---|---|---|
| US | 1,061 | 91 |
| Europe | 70 | 6 |
| Canada | 32 | 3 |
| **Total** | **1,163** | **100** |

## PRODUCTS/OPERATIONS

**2000 Sales**

|  | % of total |
|---|---|
| Office systems | 71 |
| Other products | 29 |
| **Total** | **100** |

**Selected Products and Brands**
Bookshelves
Credenzas
Desks
KnollExtra (binder bins, bookends, calendars, computer
  accessories, desk pads, file holders, letter trays,
  planters, sorters, wastebaskets)
KnollStudio (lounge seating, side chairs, sofas, tables)
KnollTextiles (panel fabrics, upholstery fabrics, wall
  coverings)
Office seating (Bulldog, Parachute, Sapper, SoHo)
Office systems (Currents, Dividends, Equity, Morrison,
  Reff)
Spinneybeck (leather upholstery)
Storage and filing cabinets (Calibre)
Tables (Interaction, Propeller)

## COMPETITORS

Anderson Hickey
Bush Industries
Global Furniture
Haworth
Herman Miller
HighPoint Furniture
HON INDUSTRIES
Natuzzi
KI
Kimball International
LifeStyle Furnishings International
O'Sullivan Industries
Return Assured
Steelcase
Teknion
Virco Mfg.
Vitra

## HISTORICAL FINANCIALS & EMPLOYEES

| Private<br>FYE: December 31 | Annual<br>Growth | 12/91 | 12/92 | 12/93 | 12/94 | 12/95 | 12/96 | 12/97 | 12/98 | 12/99 | 12/00 |
|---|---|---|---|---|---|---|---|---|---|---|---|
| Sales ($ mil.) | 9.2% | — | 577 | 508 | 563 | 621 | 652 | 811 | 949 | 985 | 1,163 |
| Net income ($ mil.) | — | — | (38) | (40) | (60) | 29 | 25 | 72 | 93 | 78 | 116 |
| Income as % of sales | — | — | — | — | — | 4.7% | 3.9% | 8.8% | 9.8% | 8.0% | 10.0% |
| Employees | 5.7% | — | — | — | — | — | 3,550 | 3,942 | 4,061 | 4,378 | 4,435 |

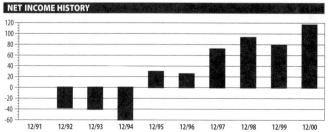

**NET INCOME HISTORY**

**2000 FISCAL YEAR-END**
Debt ratio: 100.0%
Return on equity: —
Cash ($ mil.): 22
Current ratio: 1.14
Long-term debt ($ mil.): 395

# KNOWLEDGE UNIVERSE, INC.

## OVERVIEW

Is knowledge power? Knowledge Universe (KU) thinks so.

Menlo Park, California-based KU's portfolio is divided into two groups: Knowledge Universe Business Group and Knowledge Universe Learning Group. The business group focuses on companies whose products and services aim to improve the productivity of client businesses. The learning group invests in companies that provide education venues such as interactive learning Web sites for children.

The company invests in a variety of firms such as Hoover's (the publisher of this profile); Knowledge Learning Corporation, which operates more than 350 community and corporate-based day care centers; LeapFrog, which makes educational toys and books; and Productivity Point International, which provides comprehensive learning services to business. KU also owns a controlling stake in technology consulting business Nextera Enterprises.

KU is an investment vehicle for Drexel Burnham Lambert vet Michael Milken (chairman of KU); his brother Lowell, who oversees the Milken family philanthropies; and Oracle CEO Larry Ellison. The Milken and Ellison names have attracted a lineup of business luminaries to KU's board. Directors include Rupert Murdoch, former Warner Brothers chairman Terry Semel, and former baseball commissioner Peter Ueberroth.

## HISTORY

After returning from his sojourn "Up North" (as insiders delicately refer to a stretch in prison for SEC rules infractions relating to 1980s-era corporate finance innovations), and after vanquishing cancer, Michael Milken found a new crusade.

In 1996 he and his brother Lowell, along with Larry Ellison, founded Knowledge Universe to invest a seed fund of $500 million in human capital. Cadence Design Systems vet Joe Costello was tapped to lead KU, but he left a few months later, citing strategic differences, and was replaced by former Mattel CEO Thomas Kalinske.

With an aim of providing crib-to-cane educational resources, Knowledge Universe began making acquisitions in 1997 with the purchase of Symmetrix. The management and information technology consulting company, renamed Nextera (from NextERA), acquired other IT and human resources consultancies (including SiGMA Consulting, Planning Technologies, and Sibson & Company) and went public in 1999. When the Milken name failed to wow investors into a meaningful IPO pop, Nextera began repositioning itself as an e-commerce specialist.

KU also bought into Nobel Educational Dynamics (now Nobel Learning Communities, which operates private and specialty schools) and bought up Children's Discovery Centers (now Knowledge Learning Corp., which runs about 300 preschools and day care centers). Also in the educational field, KU announced the formation of Knowledge Universe University, an online university that was designed to offer access to top-notch scholars. But the project languished and eventually morphed into UNext, an online business training venture.

Additional investments reflected Milken's personal interests, including Oncology.com and Tasteforliving.com, a Web site named for a cookbook co-written by Milken, who became a vegetarian during his battle with cancer.

Although KU's aggregate sales exceeded $1 billion by 1999, the company began soft-pedaling its lifetime learning activities in favor of focusing on its incubator and venture capital activities in the area of B2B Internet informational services. In 2000 KU continued to emphasize B2B services with an investment in interactive Webcaster MShow.com.

Knowledge Universe companies made a push into China in 2000. KU's Community of Science, which produces a Web site for university researchers and R&D professionals, launched an Internet portal for Chinese researchers, COS China. Also that year KU's Nobel Learning Communities and South Ocean Development, the largest private school operator in China, signed a deal that includes student and teacher interchange programs, linking of the companies' schools via Web, and the development of preschools in China.

In 2001 KU invested $10 million to launch K12, an Web-based school providing tutoring through complete home school curricula, led by former US Secretary of Education and *Book of Virtues* author William Bennett. Also in 2001 KU's Nibblebox animation company merged with Vivendi Universal's Hypnotic.

## OFFICERS

**Chairman:** Michael Milken
**Vice Chairman:** Steven B. Fink, age 50
**Vice Chairman:** Lowell Milken
**Vice Chairman:** Gregory J. Clark, age 59
**President and Director:** Thomas Kalinske
**CFO and Director; President, Knowledge Universe Business Group and Knowledge Universe Capital:** Randolph C. Read, age 49
**SVP, Corporate Communications:** Geoffrey E. Moore
**Secretary:** Stan Maron

## LOCATIONS

**HQ:** 3551 El Camino Real, Ste. 200, Menlo Park, CA 94027
**Phone:** 650-549-3200      **Fax:** 650-549-3222
**Web:** www.knowledgeu.com

Knowledge Universe has offices in Menlo Park and Los Angeles, California.

## PRODUCTS/OPERATIONS

**Selected Investements**

**Business Group**
AdvanceOnline
eMind.com
EMVentures
Hoover's
KnowledgePlanet.com
MeansBusiness
Nextera Enterprises
Productivity Point International
TEC Worldwide
TeckChek
UNext

**Learning Group**
Community of Science
Charter School USA
K12
Knowledge Learning Corp.
LeapFrog Enterprises, Inc.
Nobel Learning Communities

## COMPETITORS

Bain Capital
BancBoston Capital, Inc.
Fenway Partners
Gores Technology
Internet Capital
Madison Dearborn
Onex
Redbus Group
Veronis Suhler Stevenson
Vulcan Northwest
Warburg Pincus
Welsh Carson

## HISTORICAL FINANCIALS & EMPLOYEES

| Private<br>FYE: December 31 | Annual<br>Growth | 12/91 | 12/92 | 12/93 | 12/94 | 12/95 | 12/96 | 12/97 | 12/98 | 12/99 | 12/00 |
|---|---|---|---|---|---|---|---|---|---|---|---|
| Estimated sales ($ mil.) | 25.7% | — | — | — | — | — | 600 | 1,200 | 1,200 | 1,500 | 1,500 |
| Employees | 11.2% | — | — | — | — | — | — | 8,000 | 8,000 | 11,000 | 11,000 |

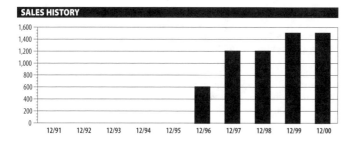

SALES HISTORY

# KOCH INDUSTRIES, INC.

## OVERVIEW

Among really big privately owned businesses, Koch (pronounced "coke") is the real thing. Wichita, Kansas-based Koch Industries, which has extensive operations in oil and gas, agriculture, and chemicals, is the second-largest private company in the US, after grain merchant Cargill.

Koch's petroleum operations include the purchasing, gathering, and trading of crude oil. Its two refineries in Minnesota and Texas process about 600,000 barrels of crude a day, making it a leading producer of gasoline and petrochemicals. Among its fuels are the low-sulfur Blue Planet brand and soybean diesels.

Koch also owns gas gathering systems and about 35,000 miles of pipeline between Texas and Canada, and it purchases, processes, and markets natural gas liquids through a joint venture with Entergy.

Koch's agricultural businesses include cattle ranches (with about 390,000 head of cattle), in Kansas, Montana, and Texas. KoSa, Koch's joint venture with Mexico's Saba family, is a leading polyester producer. Koch also produces paraxylene and high-octane missile fuels.

Brothers Charles and David Koch control the family-run enterprise.

## HISTORY

Fred Koch grew up poor in Texas and worked his way through college at MIT. In 1928 Koch developed a process to refine more gasoline from crude oil, but when he tried to market his invention, the major oil companies sued him for patent infringement. Koch eventually won the lawsuits (after 15 years in court), but the controversy made it tough to attract many US customers. In 1929 Koch took his process to the Soviet Union, but he grew disenchanted with Stalinism and returned home to become a founding member of the anticommunist John Birch Society.

Koch launched Wood River Oil & Refining in Illinois (1940) and bought the Rock Island refinery in Oklahoma (1947). He folded the remaining purchasing and gathering network into Rock Island Oil & Refining (though later sold the refineries). After Koch's death in 1967, his 32-year-old son Charles took the helm and renamed the company Koch Industries. He began a series of acquisitions, adding petrochemical and oil trading service operations.

In the 1980s Koch was thrust into various arenas, legal and political. Charles' brother David, also a Koch Industries executive, ran for US vice president on the Libertarian ticket in 1980. That year the other two Koch brothers, Frederick and William (David's fraternal twin), launched a takeover attempt, but Charles retained control and William was fired from his job as VP.

The brothers traded lawsuits, and in a 1983 settlement Charles and David bought out the dissident family members for just over $1 billion. William and Frederick continued to challenge their brothers in court, claiming they had been shortchanged in the deal (the two estranged brothers eventually lost their case in 1998, and their appeals were rejected in 2000).

In 1987 they even sued their mother over her distribution of trust fund money.

Despite this legal wrangling, Koch Industries continued to expand, purchasing a Corpus Christi, Texas, refinery in 1981. It expanded its pipeline system, buying Bigheart Pipe Line in Oklahoma (1986) and two systems from Santa Fe Southern Pacific (1988).

To strengthen its engineering services presence worldwide, Koch acquired Glitsch International (a maker of separation equipment) from engineering giant Foster Wheeler in 1997. It also acquired USX-Delhi Group, a natural gas processor and transporter.

In 1998 Koch formed the KoSa joint venture with Mexico's Saba family to buy Hoechst's Trevira polyester unit. Lethargic energy and livestock prices in 1998 and 1999, however, led Koch to lay off several hundred employees, sell its feedlots, and divest portions of its natural gas gathering and pipeline systems.

William Koch sued Koch Industries in 1999, claiming the company had defrauded the US government and Native Americans in oil payments on Indian lands. A jury found for William, but he, Charles, and David agreed to settle the case in 2001 — and sat down to dinner together for the first time in 20 years.

In other legal matters, in 2000 Koch agreed to pay a $30 million civil fine and contribute $5 million toward environmental projects to settle complaints over oil spills from its pipelines in the 1990s. The company agreed to pay $20 million in 2001 to settle a separate environmental case concerning a Texas refinery.

Koch combined its pipeline system and trading units with the power marketing businesses of electric utility Entergy in 2001 to form Entergy-Koch, one of the the biggest energy commodity traders in the US.

## OFFICERS

**Chairman and CEO:** Charles G. Koch, age 65
**Vice Chairman:** William W. Hanna, age 65
**President, COO, and Director:** Joseph W. Moeller, age 57
**EVP and Director:** David H. Koch, age 61
**EVP:** Richard H. Fink
**EVP, Operations; Chairman, KoSa:** William R. Caffey
**SVP and CFO:** Sam Soliman
**SVP, Chemicals:** Cy S. Nobles
**SVP, Ventures:** John C. Pittenger
**VP, General Counsel, and Secretary:** Paul Kaleta
**VP, Human Resources:** Paul Wheeler
**VP, Chemical Technology:** John M. Van Gelder
**VP, Mergers and Acquisitions:** M. Brad Hall
**VP and CFO, Ventures:** David Duncan
**VP and Chief Legal Counsel, Ventures:** Joel Telpner
**Chairman, Entergy-Koch and Entergy:** Robert Luft, age 65
**President, Koch Petroleum Group:** David L. Robertson
**President and CEO, Entergy-Koch:** Kyle D. Vann
**President, Ventures:** Ray Gary
**Auditors:** KPMG LLP

## LOCATIONS

**HQ:** 4111 E. 37th St. North, Wichita, KS 67220
**Phone:** 316-828-5500       **Fax:** 316-828-5739
**Web:** www.kochind.com

Koch Industries has operations in the US and 20 other countries.

## PRODUCTS/OPERATIONS

**Selected Operations**
Koch Agriculture Group
Koch Chemical/Environ Technology Group (specialty equipment and services for refining and chemical industry)
    Brown Fintube Company
    The John Zink Company
    Koch-Glitsch, Inc.
    Koch Membrane Systems Inc.
    Koch Modular Process Systems, LLC
    Tru-Tec Services, Inc.
Koch Chemicals Group
    Koch Chemicals (paraxylene)
    KoSa (polyester, 50%)
    Koch Specialty Chemicals (high-octane missile fuel)
Koch Energy Group
    Entergy-Koch L.P. (50%)
    Koch Exploration
Koch Financial Services, Inc.
    Koch Financial Corp.
Koch Gas Liquids Group
Koch Mineral Services (bulk ocean transportation and fuel supply)
    Koch Fertilizer Storage & Terminal Co.
    Koch Pipeline Co. LP
Koch Petroleum Group (crude oil and refined products)
    Koch Materials Co. (asphalt)
Koch Ventures Group (investment in noncore businesses)

## COMPETITORS

| | | |
|---|---|---|
| AEP | Equilon | Phillips |
| ADM | Enterprises | Petroleum |
| Ashland | Exxon Mobil | Reliant Energy |
| Avista | Imperial Oil | Royal |
| BP | Kerr-McGee | Dutch/Shell |
| Cargill | King Ranch | Southern |
| ChevronTexaco | Lyondell | Company |
| Conoco | Chemical | Sunoco |
| ContiGroup | Marathon Oil | Tractebel |
| Duke Energy | Motiva | Ultramar |
| Dynegy | Enterprises | Diamond |
| Enron | Occidental | Shamrock |
| Entergy | Petroleum | UtiliCorp |
| EOTT Energy | Peabody Energy | Williams |
| Partners | PEMEX | Companies |
| | PG&E | |

## HISTORICAL FINANCIALS & EMPLOYEES

| Private FYE: December 31 | Annual Growth | 12/91 | 12/92 | 12/93 | 12/94 | 12/95 | 12/96 | 12/97 | 12/98 | 12/99 | 12/00 |
|---|---|---|---|---|---|---|---|---|---|---|---|
| Sales ($ mil.) | 9.1% | — | 19,914 | 20,000 | 23,725 | 25,200 | 30,000 | 36,200 | 35,000 | 33,050 | 40,000 |
| Employees | (0.5%) | — | 12,000 | 12,000 | 12,000 | 12,500 | 13,000 | 15,600 | 16,000 | 12,500 | 11,500 |

### SALES HISTORY

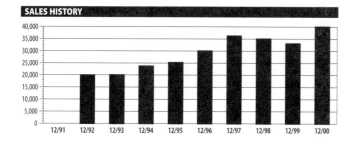

# KOHLBERG KRAVIS ROBERTS & CO.

## OVERVIEW

The master of the 1980s buyout universe, Kohlberg Kravis Roberts (KKR) has shed its hostile takeover image for a kinder, gentler, buy-and-build strategy.

New York City-based KKR assembles funds to buy low and sell high. An active investor, it supervises or installs new management and revamps strategy and corporate structure, selling underperforming units or adding new ones. KKR profits not only from its direct interest in these companies but also from fund and company management fees. It has a joint venture with venture capital firm Accel to provide support for companies integrating online and bricks-and-mortar businesses. KKR's investment

in media company PRIMEDIA (with holdings in such New Economy sob stories as CMGI, Brill Media Ventures, and About.com) has proved costly and KKR is anxious to minimize its losses. Cousins Henry Kravis and George Roberts are the senior partners in KKR.

Since 1976 KKR has invested $100 billion in more than 90 companies, with investors receiving returns of around 23%. As the economy cools, though, the firm is weathering its fair share of tumult. It lost its place as the top fund-raiser to Thomas H. Lee, which closed a record-setting $6.1 billion fund in early 2001.

## HISTORY

In 1976 Jerome Kohlberg left investment bank Bear Stearns to form his own leveraged buyout (LBO) firm; with him he brought protégé Henry Kravis and Kravis's cousin George Roberts. They formed Kohlberg Kravis Roberts & Co. (KKR).

Kohlberg believed LBOs, by giving management ownership stakes in their companies, would yield better results. KKR orchestrated friendly buyouts funded by investor groups and debt. The firm's first buyout was machine-toolmaker Houdaille Industries in 1979.

KKR lost money on its 1981 investment in the American Forest Products division of Bendix. But by 1984 the firm had raised its fourth fund and made its first $1 billion buyout: Wometco Enterprises.

The next year KKR turned mean with a hostile takeover of Beatrice. The deal depended on junk bond financing devised by Drexel Burnham Lambert's Michael Milken and on the sale of pieces of the company. KKR funded the buyouts of Safeway Stores and Owens-Illinois (1986), Jim Walter Homes (1987), and Stop & Shop (1988, sold in 1996).

Unhappy with the firm's image, Kohlberg left in 1987 to form Kohlberg & Co. His suit against KKR over the alleged undervaluing of companies in relation to his departure settlement was resolved for an undisclosed amount.

The Beatrice LBO triggered a rash of similar transactions as the financial industry sought fat fees. The frenzy culminated in 1988 with the $31 billion RJR Nabisco buyout, which brought KKR $75 million in fees. As the US slid into a recession in 1989, LBOs dwindled and KKR turned to managing its acquisitions.

The firm also did some bottom feeding. In 1991 KKR joined with what is now FleetBoston

to buy Bank of New England. The next year it picked up 47% of what is now Advantica Restaurant Group, owner of Denny's (sold 1997).

KKR made its first international foray in 1993 with Russian truck maker Kamaz; it later stalled when Kamaz refused to pay management fees. The next year it freed itself from the RJR morass by swapping its investment in RJR for troubled food company Borden.

In the latter half of the decade, KKR reaped mixed results on its investments, including what is now Spalding Holdings (sporting goods and Evenflo baby products), supermarket chain Bruno's, and KinderCare Learning Centers. The $600 million KKR had sunk into magazine group K-III (now PRIMEDIA) between 1990 and 1994 didn't revive interest in the stock, and it sent Bruno's into bankruptcy in 1998. Disgruntled investors complained about low returns, and in 1996 KKR booted activist megafund CalPERS from its investor ranks.

In 1998 KKR's niche buying continued when it joined with Hicks, Muse, Tate & Furst to buy Regal Cinemas, which it combined with Act III to form the biggest theater chain in the US. In 1999 KKR departed from course and unveiled online mortgage lender Nexstar Financial, its first company built from the ground up.

Still focused on Europe, in 2000 the firm claimed the telecommunications business of Robert Bosch (now Tenovis), UK private equity fund Wassall PLC, and Siemens' banking systems unit. In 2001, KKR joined with Internet VC firm Accel Partners to form Accel-KKR to invest in companies that combine traditional business and Internet assets.

**Founding Partner:** Henry R. Kravis, age 57
**Founding Partner:** George R. Roberts
**General Partner:** Edward A. Gilhuly, age 41
**General Partner:** Perry Golkin
**General Partner:** James H. Greene Jr.
**General Partner:** Robert I. MacDonnell
**General Partner:** Michael W. Michelson, age 50
**General Partner:** Paul E. Raether
**General Partner:** Scott M. Stuart
**General Partner:** Michael T. Tokarz
**Managing Director, Europe:** Johannes Huth
**Chairman, Accel-KKR, Inc.:** Paul M. Hazen, age 59
**Office Manager:** Sandy Cisneros
**Auditors:** Deloitte & Touche LLP

## LOCATIONS

**HQ:** 9 W. 57th St., Ste. 4200, New York, NY 10019
**Phone:** 212-750-8300      **Fax:** 212-750-0003
**Web:** www.kkr.com

Kohlberg Kravis Roberts has offices in London; Menlo Park, California; and New York City.

## PRODUCTS/OPERATIONS

**Selected Investments**

| | |
|---|---|
| Accuride Corporation | MedCath Incorporated |
| Alea Group Holdings AG | NewSouth |
| Alliance Imaging, Inc. | Communications |
| Amphenol Corporation | Nexstar Financial |
| Birch Telecom, Inc. | Corporation |
| Borden, Inc. | Owens-Illinois, Inc. |
| Bristol West Insurance | PRIMEDIA Inc. |
| Group | Regal Cinemas,Inc. |
| CAIS Internet, Inc. | Rockwood Specialties Inc. |
| Centric Software, Inc. | Shoppers Drug Mart Inc. |
| DPL Inc. | Spalding Holdings |
| Evenflo Company, Inc. | Corporation |
| FirstMark | Tenovis Holding GmbH |
| Communications | The Boyds Collection, Ltd. |
| Europe SA | Walter Industries, Inc. |
| IDEX Corporation | Willis Group Limited |
| Intermedia | Wincor Nixdorf Holding |
| Communications Inc. | GmbH & Co. |
| KinderCare Learning | WorldCrest Group |
| Centers, Inc. | Zhone Technologies, Inc. |
| KKF.net AG | Zumtobel AG |
| KSL Recreation | |
| Corporation | |

## COMPETITORS

| | |
|---|---|
| AEA Investors | Heico |
| American Financial | Hicks, Muse |
| Apollo Advisors | Interlaken Investment |
| Bear Stearns | Investcorp |
| Berkshire Hathaway | Jordan Company |
| Blackstone Group | Lehman Brothers |
| Carlyle Group | Leonard Green |
| Clayton, Dubilier | MacAndrews & Forbes |
| CVC Capital Partners | Merrill Lynch |
| Dresdner Kleinwort | Salomon Smith Barney |
| Wasserstein | Holdings |
| Equity Group Investments | Texas Pacific Group |
| Forstmann Little | Thomas Lee |
| GE Capital | Veronis Suhler Stevenson |
| Goldman Sachs | Vestar Capital Partners |
| Haas Wheat | Wingate Partners |

# KOHLER CO.

Kohler sits on the throne of the global bathroom business. Based in Kohler, Wisconsin, the family-owned firm makes bathroom fixtures and is a leader in the US with products sold under the brand names Ann Sacks (ceramic tile, marble, stone products, and antique building materials), Kallista (bathroom and kitchen fixtures), Kohler and Sterling (plumbing products), Robern (mirrored cabinets), and Canac (kitchen and bathroom cabinets). European brands include Jacob Delafon and Neomediam plumbing products, as well as Sanijura bath cabinetry and related products. The company has more than 40 manufacturing facilities in Asia, Europe, the Middle East, and the Americas.

In addition to plumbing products, Kohler makes small engines, generators, and electrical systems, and produces furniture under the Baker and McGuire names. Additional interests include a luxury Wisconsin resort (The American Club), golf courses, a spa, and design showrooms.

Herbert Kohler Jr., the founder's grandson, has reorganized the company. Herbert, who now controls most of the company along with his sister Ruth, has vowed the company will never go public. Kohler is building a new manufacturing facility in Mexico and is expanding some of its US factories.

## HISTORY

In 1873, 29-year-old Austrian immigrant John Kohler and partner Charles Silberzahn founded Kohler & Silberzahn in Sheboygan, Wisconsin. That year they purchased a small iron foundry that made agricultural products for $5,000 from Kohler's father-in-law. In 1880, two years after Silberzahn left the firm, its machine shop was destroyed by fire.

The company introduced enameled plumbing fixtures in the rebuilt factory in 1883. The design caught on, and the business sold thousands of sinks, kettles, pans, and bathtubs. By 1887, when Kohler was incorporated, enameled items accounted for 70% of sales. By 1900 the 250-person company received 98% of its sales from enameled iron products. That year, shortly after John Kohler began building new facilities near Sheboygan (which later became the company village of Kohler), he died at age 56. More trouble followed: Kohler's new plant burned down in 1901, and two of the founder's sons died — Carl at age 24 in 1904 and Robert at age 35 in 1905.

John's eldest surviving son Walter built a boarding hotel to house workers and introduced other employee-benefit programs. He also set up company-paid workers' compensation before the state made it law in 1917.

By the mid-1920s, when Kohler premiered colors in porcelain fixtures and added brass fittings and vitreous china toilets and washbasins to its line, it was the #3 plumbing-product company in the US. As a testament to the design quality of its products, Kohler items were displayed at the New York Museum of Modern Art in 1929. The company also began developing products that would grow in importance in later decades: electric generators and small gasoline engines. In the 1950s Kohler's engines

virtually conquered Southeast Asia, where they were used to power boats, drive air compressors, and pump water for rice paddies in Vietnam and Thailand. While strikes against Kohler in 1897 and 1934 had been resolved quickly, a 1954 strike against the firm lasted six years. The strike gave Kohler the dubious honor of enduring the longest strike in US history.

Small-engine use grew in the US in the 1960s, and Kohler's motors were used in lawn mowers, construction equipment, and garden tractors. The founder's last surviving son, Herbert (a child from John Kohler's second marriage), died in 1968. Under the leadership of Herbert's son, Herbert Jr. (appointed chairman 1972), Kohler expanded its operations, buying Sterling Faucet (1984) and Jacob Delafon (1986). More recent acquisitions include Sanijura (bathroom furniture, France, 1993), Osio (enamel baths, Italy, 1994), Robern (mirrored cabinets, 1995), Holdiam (baths, whirlpools, and sinks; France, 1995), and Canac (cabinets, Canada, 1996).

The company entered a growing plumbing market in China through four joint ventures formed in that country in 1996 and 1997. In 1998 several family and nonfamily shareholders claimed a reorganization plan unfairly forced them out and undervalued their stock. Legal battles over the stock's fair price continued in 1999, and a settlement was reached the following year that granted shareholders a fair price. Herbert and his sister Ruth also gained a firm control of the company. More legal battles continued in 2001 when the company sued Kohler International Ltd., a Canada-based company, for trademark infringement.

**Chairman and President:** Herbert V. Kohler Jr.
**SVP, Finance:** Jeffery P. Cheney
**VP, Human Resources:** Laura Kohler

## LOCATIONS

**HQ:** 444 Highland Dr., Kohler, WI 53044
**Phone:** 920-457-4441    **Fax:** 920-459-1818
**Web:** kohlerco.com

Kohler operates about 45 manufacturing plants and sells its products worldwide.

## PRODUCTS/OPERATIONS

### Selected Operations

### Engines
Commercial turf equipment engines
Consumer lawn and garden equipment engines
Industrial, construction, and commercial equipment engines
Recreational equipment engines

### Furniture
Baker Furniture
McGuire Furniture Company
Milling Road Furniture

### Generators
Kohler rental power
Marine generators
Mobile generators
On-site power systems
  Automatic transfer switches
  Switchgear
Residential generators
Small business generators

### Kitchen and Bath Products
Cabinets and vanities
  Canac (bathroom cabinetry)
  Robern (lighting and mirrored bath cabinetry)
  Sanijura (vanities and other bath furniture)
Plumbing products
  Jacob Delafon (bathtubs, faucets, lavatories, and toilets)
  Kallista (bathroom and kitchen sinks and faucets)
  Kohler (bath and shower faucets, baths, bidet faucets, bidets, body spa systems, glass showers and shower doors, kitchen and bathroom sinks and faucets, master baths, toilets, toilet seats, vanities, whirlpool baths)
  Sterling (bathing fixtures, faucets, sinks, tub/shower enclosures, vitreous china bath fixtures)
Tile and stone products
  Ann Sacks (art tile, glazed tile, knobs and pulls, mosaics, terra cotta)

### Real Estate
The American Club (resort hotel)
Blackwolf Run golf course
Inn on Woodlake
Kohler Stables
Whistling Straits golf course

## COMPETITORS

| | |
|---|---|
| American Standard | Klaussner Furniture |
| Armstrong Holdings | Leggett & Platt |
| Bassett Furniture | Masco |
| Black & Decker | Moen |
| Briggs & Stratton | Mueller Industries |
| Chicago Faucet | Newell Rubbermaid |
| Cooper Industries | NIBCO |
| Crane | Tecumseh Products |
| Dal-Tile | TOTO |
| Dyson-Kissner-Moran | Triangle Pacific |
| Elkay Manufacturing | U.S. Industries |
| Gerber Plumbing Fixtures | Waxman |
| Honda | Yamaha |

## HISTORICAL FINANCIALS & EMPLOYEES

| Private<br>FYE: December 31 | Annual<br>Growth | 12/91 | 12/92 | 12/93 | 12/94 | 12/95 | 12/96 | 12/97 | 12/98 | 12/99 | 12/00 |
|---|---|---|---|---|---|---|---|---|---|---|---|
| Estimated sales ($ mil.) | 9.1% | — | 1,350 | 1,450 | 1,600 | 1,850 | 2,020 | 2,210 | 2,400 | 2,500 | 2,700 |
| Employees | 4.8% | — | 13,778 | 14,257 | 14,500 | 15,000 | 18,000 | 18,000 | 18,000 | 20,000 | 20,000 |

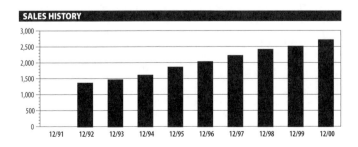

SALES HISTORY

KOHLER.

# KPMG INTERNATIONAL

## OVERVIEW

KPMG is fighting for dominance in the field of accounting, and is willing to not only tie one hand behind its back, but to cut it off entirely. The Amstelveen, Netherlands-based Big Five accounting firm has split its consulting operations from its audit offerings and taken the former public.

Traditionally a confederation of accounting firms, in recent years KPMG has more closely linked its local operations and has organized them into three regional operating units: the Americas, Europe/Middle East/Africa, and Asia/Pacific. With more than 800 offices in nearly 160 countries, KPMG is the most geographically dispersed of the Big Five. In addition to its traditional auditing function, the firm offers tax and financial advisory services; its KLegal International network employs some 1,600 lawyers around the world.

KPMG's consulting operations focus on the Internet. After much regulatory pressure, KPMG Consulting was spun off in an IPO in 2000 that left the firm with a stake of around 20%; Cisco Systems, which had invested $1 billion in the unit, has a 9% stake.

## HISTORY

Peat Marwick was founded in 1911, when William Peat, a London accountant, met James Marwick during an Atlantic crossing. University of Glasgow alumni Marwick and Roger Mitchell had formed Marwick, Mitchell & Company in New York in 1897. Peat and Marwick agreed to ally their firms temporarily, and in 1925 they merged as Peat, Marwick, Mitchell, & Copartners.

In 1947 William Black became senior partner, a position he held until 1965. He guided the firm's 1950 merger with Barrow, Wade, Guthrie, one of the US's oldest firms, and built its consulting practice. Peat Marwick restructured its international practice as PMM&Co. (International) in 1972 (renamed Peat Marwick International in 1978).

The next year several European accounting firms led by Klynveld Kraayenhoff (the Netherlands) and Deutsche Treuhand (Germany) began forming an international accounting federation. Needing an American member, the European firms encouraged the merger of two American firms founded around the turn of the century, Main Lafrentz and Hurdman Cranstoun. Main Hurdman & Cranstoun joined the Europeans to form Klynveld Main Goerdeler (KMG), named after two of the member firms and the chairman of Deutsche Treuhand, Reinhard Goerdeler. Other members were C. Jespersen (Denmark), Thorne Riddel (Canada), Thomson McLintok (UK), and Fides Revision (Switzerland).

Peat Marwick merged with KMG in 1987 to form Klynveld Peat Marwick Goerdeler (KPMG). KPMG lost 10% of its business as competing client companies departed. Professional staff departures followed in 1990 when, as part of a consolidation, the firm trimmed its partnership rolls.

In the 1990s the then-Big Six accounting firms all faced lawsuits arising from an evolving standard holding auditors responsible for the substance, rather than merely the form, of clients' accounts. KPMG was hit by suits stemming from its audits of defunct S&Ls and litigation relating to the bankruptcy of Orange County, California (settled for $75 million in 1998). Nevertheless KPMG kept growing; expand its consulting division with the acquisition of banking consultancy Barefoot, Marrinan & Associates in 1996.

In 1997, after Price Waterhouse and Coopers & Lybrand announced their merger, KPMG and Ernst & Young announced one of their own. But they called it quits the next year, fearing that regulatory approval of the deal would be too onerous.

The creation of PricewaterhouseCoopers (PwC) and increasing competition in the consulting sides of all of the Big Five brought a realignment of loyalties in their national practices. KPMG Consulting's Belgian group moved to PwC, and its French group to Computer Sciences Corporation. Andersen Worldwide nearly wooed away KPMG's Canadian consulting group, but the plan was foiled by the ever-sullen Andersen Consulting group (which is now called Accenture) and by KPMG's promises of more money. Against this background, KPMG sold 20% of its consulting operations to Cisco Systems for $1 billion. In addition to the cash infusion, the deal allowed KPMG to provide installation and system management (neither of which Cisco provides) to Cisco's customers.

In 2000 KPMG announced its IPO plans for the consulting group but continued to rail against the SEC's calls for the severing of relationships between consulting and auditing organizations. That IPO took place in 2001.

**Chairman; KPMG LLP:** Stephen G. Butler
**Acting CEO and COO:** Colin Holland
**CFO:** Joseph E. Heintz
**Regional Executive Partner, Americas:** Lou Miramontes
**Regional Executive Partner, Asia-Pacific:** John Sim
**International Managing Partner, Assurance:**
Hans de Munnik
**International Managing Partner, Consulting:**
Jim McGuire
**International Managing Partner, Financial Advisory
Services:** Gary Colter
**International Managing Partner, Markets:**
Alistair Johnston
**International Managing Partner, Tax and Legal:**
Hartwich Lübmann
**Deputy Chairman, KPMG LLP:** Robert W. Alspaugh
**Chief Marketing Officer, KPMG LLP:**
Timothy R. Pearson
**General Counsel, KPMG LLP:** Claudia L. Taft
**National Industry Director, Banking Practice, KPMG
LLP:** Robert F. Arning
**Partner, Human Resources, KPMG LLP:**
Timothy P. Flynn

## LOCATIONS

**HQ:** Burgemeester Rijnderslaan 20,
1185 MC Amstelveen, The Netherlands
**Phone:** +31-20-656-7890     **Fax:** +31-20-656-77-00
**US HQ:** 345 Park Ave., New York, NY 10154
**US Phone:** 212-758-9700     **US Fax:** 212-758-9819
**Web:** www.kpmg.com

### 2001 Sales

|  | $ mil. | % of total |
|---|---|---|
| Europe/Middle East/Africa | 6,300 | 54 |
| Americas | 4,300 | 37 |
| Asia/Pacific | 1,100 | 9 |
| **Total** | **11,700** | **100** |

## PRODUCTS/OPERATIONS

### 2001 Sales

|  | $ mil. | % of total |
|---|---|---|
| Assurance | 5,800 | 50 |
| Tax & legal | 3,100 | 26 |
| Consulting | 1,500 | 13 |
| Financial advisory | 1,200 | 10 |
| Other | 100 | 1 |
| **Total** | **11,700** | **100** |

### Selected Services

**Assurance**
Advisory services
Financial statement audits
Information risk management
Management assurance services

**Financial Advisory**
Corporate recovery
Corporate finance
Forensic and litigation services
Transaction services

**Tax and Legal**
Business tax services
Global tax services
Indirect tax/customs services
Legal services pertaining to corporate and commercial,
  banking and financial services, competition,
  employment/labor, intellectual property, e-commerce,
  and estates and trusts law
State, local, and property tax services

## COMPETITORS

| | |
|---|---|
| Andersen | H&R Block |
| Aon | Hewitt Associates |
| Arthur D. Little | Marsh & McLennan |
| Bain & Company | McKinsey & Company |
| BDO International | PricewaterhouseCoopers |
| Booz-Allen | Towers Perrin |
| Deloitte Touche Tohmatsu | Watson Wyatt |
| Ernst & Young | |

## HISTORICAL FINANCIALS & EMPLOYEES

| Partnership<br>FYE: September 30 | Annual<br>Growth | 9/92 | 9/93 | 9/94 | 9/95 | 9/96 | 9/97 | 9/98 | 9/99 | 9/00 | 9/01 |
|---|---|---|---|---|---|---|---|---|---|---|---|
| Sales ($ mil.) | 7.4% | 6,150 | 6,000 | 6,600 | 7,500 | 8,100 | 9,200 | 10,600 | 12,200 | 13,500 | 11,700 |
| Employees | 2.6% | 73,488 | 76,200 | 76,200 | 72,000 | 77,000 | 83,500 | 85,300 | 102,000 | 108,000 | 92,800 |

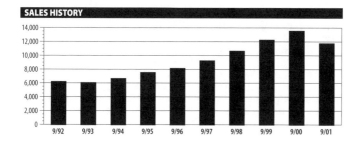

SALES HISTORY

# LAND O'LAKES, INC.

Land O'Lakes makes lakes o' dairy products. Through more than 1,100 community cooperatives, Arden Hills, Minnesota-based Land O'Lakes serves 300,000 farmers and ranchers. The cooperative — the #2 US dairy co-op, behind Dairy Farmers of America — produces packaged milk, margarine, sour cream, and cheeses. The company's oldest product, Land O'Lakes butter, is the leading US butter brand.

The co-op's Agricultural Services division produces animal health products and feed, and it is creating Land O'Lakes Farmland (a joint venture with Farmland Industries) to become the #1 livestock feed producer in the US. It also supplies members with fertilizers and chemical crop protection products. Land O'Lakes Finance provides financing services for beef, dairy, pork, and poultry producers.

In response to a tight consumer packaged goods market, changes in the agriculture business, and the rapidly consolidating dairy market, Land O'Lakes has positioned itself as a national player with member co-ops coast to coast. In 2001 it acquired Purina Mills, a leading US commercial animal feed producer.

## HISTORY

In the old days, grocers sold butter from communal tubs and it often went bad. Widespread distribution of dairy products had to await the invention of fast, reliable transportation. By 1921 the necessary transportation was available. That year about 320 dairy farmers in Minnesota formed the Minnesota Cooperative Creameries Association and launched a membership drive with $1,375, mostly borrowed from the US Farm Bureau.

The co-op arranged joint shipments for members; imposed strict hygiene and quality standards; and aggressively marketed its sweet cream butter nationwide, packaged for the first time in the familiar box of four quarter-pound sticks. A month after the co-op's New York sales office opened, it was ordering 80 shipments a week.

Minnesota Cooperative Creameries, as part of its promotional campaigns, ran a contest in 1924 to name that butter. Two contestants offered the winning name — Land O'Lakes. The distinctive Indian Maiden logo first appeared about the same time, and in 1926 the co-op changed its name to Land O'Lakes Creameries. By 1929, when it began supplying feed, its market share approached 50%.

During WWII, civilian consumption dropped, but the co-op increased production of dried milk to provide food for soldiers and newly liberated concentration camp victims.

In the 1950s and 1960s, Land O'Lakes added ice cream and yogurt producers to its membership and fought margarine makers, yet butter's market share continued to melt. The co-op diversified in 1970 through acquisitions, adding feeds and agricultural chemicals. Two years later Land O'Lakes threw in the towel and came out with its own margarine. Despite the decreasing use of butter nationally, the co-op's market share grew.

Land O'Lakes formed a marketing joint venture, Cenex/Land O'Lakes Agronomy, with fellow co-op Cenex in 1987. As health consciousness bloomed in the 1980s, Land O'Lakes launched reduced-fat dairy products. When margarine consumption declined in the mid-1990s, the co-op scaled down its production and introduced no-fat sour cream dips. Land O'Lakes began ramping up its international projects at the same time: It built a feed mill in Taiwan, introduced feed products in Mexico, and established feed and cheese operations in Poland.

In 1997 the co-op bought low-fat cheese maker Alpine Lace Brands. Land O'Lakes took on the eastern US when it merged with the 3,600-member Atlantic Dairy Cooperative (1997), and it bulked up on the West Coast when California-based Dairyman's Cooperative Creamery Association joined its fold (1998). Cenex/Land O'Lakes Agronomy bought Terra Industries' distribution and seed businesses in 1999.

Land O'Lakes acquired its longtime butter supplier, Madison Dairy Produce, in 2000. Later that year the co-op sold five plants to Dean Foods. The sale included an agreement to continue supplying the plants with raw milk and a joint venture to market specialty fluid milk products under the Land O'Lakes brand. Also in 2000 Land O'Lakes agreed to combine its feed business with those of Farmland Industries to create Land O'Lakes Farmland Feed.

In March 2001 Land O'Lakes bought a Minnesota cheese plant from Kraft Foods, which will be owned and operated by a 50-50 joint venture with Dairy Farmers of America. In October the company acquired Purina Mills, a leading US commercial animal feed producer; Purina Mills will become part of Land O'Lakes Farmland Feed.

**Chairman:** Jim Fife
**President and CEO:** John E. Gherty
**EVP and COO, Agricultural Services:** Duane Halverson
**EVP and COO, Dairy Foods Industrial Group:**
Jack Prince
**EVP and COO, Value Added Group:** Chris Policinski
**SVP and CFO:** Dan Knutson
**VP and General Counsel:** John Rebane
**VP, Human Resources:** Karen Grabow
**VP, Planning and Business Development:**
Jim Wahrenbrock
**VP, Public Affairs:** Don Berg
**VP, Research, Technology, and Engineering:**
David Hettinga
**President, Land O'Lakes Farmland Feed:**
Bob DeGregorio
**Co-President, Agriliance:** Al Giese
**Auditors:** KPMG LLP

**Selected Products**

**Agricultural Supplies and Services**
Animal health products
Animal milk replacers
Crop nutrients
Crop protection products
Feed
Seed

**Dairy Products**
Butter
Cheese (including Alpine Lace)
Eggs
Flavored butter
Light butter
Margarine
Milk
Sour cream

**HQ:** 4001 Lexington Ave. North, Arden Hills, MN 55126
**Phone:** 651-481-2222　　**Fax:** 651-481-2000
**Web:** www.landolakesinc.com

Land O'Lakes operates processing, manufacturing, warehousing, and distribution facilities across the US and internationally.

| | |
|---|---|
| ADM | Parmalat Finanziaria |
| AMPI | Pioneer Hi-Bred |
| California Dairies Inc. | Prairie Farms Dairy |
| Cargill | Saputo |
| Dairy Farmers of America | Schreiber Foods |
| Dean Foods | Suiza Dairy Group |
| Foremost Farms | Unilever |
| Kraft Foods | WestFarm Foods |

| Cooperative<br>FYE: December 31 | Annual<br>Growth | 12/91 | 12/92 | 12/93 | 12/94 | 12/95 | 12/96 | 12/97 | 12/98 | 12/99 | 12/00 |
|---|---|---|---|---|---|---|---|---|---|---|---|
| Sales ($ mil.) | 10.6% | — | 2,562 | 2,733 | 2,859 | 3,014 | 3,486 | 4,195 | 5,174 | 5,613 | 5,756 |
| Net income ($ mil.) | 7.7% | — | 57 | 47 | 75 | 121 | 119 | 95 | 69 | 21 | 103 |
| Income as % of sales | — | — | 2.2% | 1.7% | 2.6% | 4.0% | 3.4% | 2.3% | 1.3% | 0.4% | 1.8% |
| Employees | 3.3% | — | 5,000 | 5,700 | 5,500 | 5,500 | 5,500 | 5,500 | 6,500 | 6,500 | 6,500 |

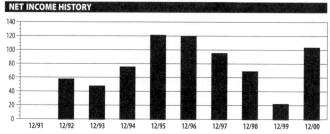

**NET INCOME HISTORY**

**2000 FISCAL YEAR-END**
Debt ratio: 37.0%
Return on equity: —
Cash ($ mil.): 4
Current ratio: 1.36
Long-term debt ($ mil.): 472

# THE LEFRAK ORGANIZATION

## OVERVIEW

There's a whole lotta shaking going on, and it's The Lefrak Organization that's moving the earth. The Rego Park, New York-based building firm is one of the US's largest private landlords, with more than 60,000 apartments in New York City and New Jersey, another 30,000 units under management, and millions of square feet of commercial space. The company is concentrating on its Newport City development, a 600-acre community of apartments, office towers, and stores on the waterfront in Jersey City across the Hudson River from Manhattan. Lefrak has built half a dozen office towers (occupied by CIGNA, U.S. Trust, and UBS PaineWebber, among others) on the site, and plans for further apartment developments and more office buildings are underway.

Lefrak's flagship development, 5,000-unit Lefrak City in Queens, has been home to successive waves of ethnic groups seeking a better life. The company also has holdings in oil exploration (Lefrak Oil & Gas Organization) and entertainment (Lefrak Entertainment operates LMR, the record label that launched Barbara Streisand). It also owns stage and movie theaters and produces television programs, movies, and Broadway shows.

Chairman Samuel LeFrak, famed for his interpretation of the Golden Rule ("he who has the gold makes the rules"), is an active philanthropist, supporting the Guggenheim Museum. He has also contributed to the oceanographic studies of the late sea explorer Jacques Cousteau.

## HISTORY

Harry Lefrak and his father came to the US from Palestine around 1900. They began building tenements to house the flood of immigrants then pouring into New York City. In 1905 they started what is now known as The Lefrak Organization. It diversified into glass and for some time provided raw material for the workshops of Louis Comfort Tiffany. After WWI the glass factory was sold, and the company expanded into Brooklyn, where it developed housing and commercial space in Bedford-Stuyvesant, among other areas.

Samuel, Harry's son, began working in the business early, assisting tradesmen at building sites. He then attended the University of Maryland and returned to the business.

After WWII, business took off, as the company began building low-cost housing. Samuel took over the company in 1948. To keep costs down, Samuel bought clay and gypsum quarries, forests, and lumber mills and cement plants, eventually achieving 70% vertical integration of his operations.

The 1950s building boom was in part spurred by new laws in New York authorizing the issue of state bonds for financing low-interest construction loans, which Lefrak used to build more than 2,000 apartments in previously undeveloped coastal sections of Brooklyn. At its peak, Lefrak turned out an apartment every 16 minutes for rents as low as $21 per room.

In 1960 Lefrak broke ground for Lefrak City, a 5,000-apartment development built on 40 acres in Queens, which featured air-conditioned units and rented for $40 per room.

The next decade brought a real estate slump that endangered the organization's next project,

Battery Park. Lefrak issued public bonds to save it. Samuel also picked up a few more properties during this period, and he capitalized the "F" in his family name but not the company name. (He later said that he did this to distinguish himself from other Lefraks at his club who had been posted for nonpayment of dues.)

Samuel's son Richard became increasingly involved in the business in the 1980s as the organization began an even bigger project: the 600-acre Newport City development, begun in 1989 with plans for almost 10,000 apartments and retail and commercial space.

The company bought 200 oil fields in 1994 to build up its reserves of gas and home-heating oil.

Meanwhile, Lefrak City had "turned," as its original Jewish occupants sought greener fields. As occupancy dropped, the company relaxed its tenant screening, and the development deteriorated (it was subsequently tagged with the sobriquet "Crack City"). In the 1990s, however, it began attracting a mix of African, Jewish, and Central Asian immigrants, whose tightly knit communities improved the development's safety and equilibrium.

Construction of the company's Newport project continued throughout the 1990s with construction of office buildings, apartments, and a hotel (completed in 2000) on the site. As a tight Manhattan office market drove up lease prices, Lefrak's new offices across the Hudson attracted companies in the finance and insurance sectors. Lefrak filled about 3 million sq. ft. in its Newport development during 1999 and 2000.

## OFFICERS

**Chairman:** Samuel J. LeFrak
**President:** Richard S. LeFrak
**COO and CFO:** Judy Watsmann
**SVP Marketing:** Edward Cortese
**VP and General Counsel:** Howard Boris
**VP Commercial:** Marsilia Boyle
**VP Commercial:** Irwin Granville
**VP Construction-Engineering:** Anthony Scavo
**VP Finance and Administration and Treasurer:**
  Mitchell Ingerman
**VP Management:** Charles Mehlman
**VP:** Harrison LeFrak
**Director of Human Resources:** John Farrelly
**Auditors:** Lewis Goldberg

## LOCATIONS

**HQ:** 97-77 Queens Blvd., Rego Park, NY 11374
**Phone:** 718-459-9021   **Fax:** 718-897-0688
**Web:** www.lefrak.com

The Lefrak Organization operates primarily in the New
York metropolitan area.

### Selected Properties

**Commercial Space**
Jersey City, New Jersey
  Newport development
Manhattan
  40 W. 57th St.
  Gateway Plaza at Battery
    Park City
  James Tower

**Residential Apartments**
Jersey City, New Jersey
  Atlantic
  East Hampton
  James Monroe
  Presidential Plaza
  Riverside
  Southampton
  Towers of America
Manhattan
  Gateway Plaza at Battery
    Park City
Queens
  Lefrak City

**Residential Co-op
Properties**
Brooklyn
  Bay Ridge
  Bensonhurst
  Flatbush
  Park Slope
  Sheepshead Bay
Queens
  Elmhurst
  Flushing
  Forest Hills
  Key Gardens
  Rego Park
  Woodside

**Retail**
Jersey City, New Jersey
  Newport Centre Mall

## PRODUCTS/OPERATIONS

**Selected Operations**

**Energy**
Lefrak Oil & Gas Organization

**Entertainment**
Lefrak Entertainment Co.

**Real Estate**
Commercial properties
Residential apartments
Residential co-op properties
Retail properties

## COMPETITORS

Alexander's
Boston Properties
Equity Office Properties
  Trust
Hartz Mountain
Helmsley
Mack-Cali Realty
Port Authority of NY & NJ
Reckson Associates Realty
Starrett Corporation
Tishman Realty
TrizecHahn
Trump
Vornado

## HISTORICAL FINANCIALS & EMPLOYEES

| Private<br>FYE: Last Sunday in November | Annual<br>Growth | 11/91 | 11/92 | 11/93 | 11/94 | 11/95 | 11/96 | 11/97 | 11/98 | 11/99 | 11/00 |
|---|---|---|---|---|---|---|---|---|---|---|---|
| Sales ($ mil.) | 2.2% | — | 3,200 | 3,200 | 3,100 | 3,300 | 3,500 | 3,400 | 2,750 | 3,200 | 3,800 |
| Employees | (1.3%) | — | 18,000 | 18,000 | 17,500 | 17,400 | 17,500 | 18,000 | 16,000 | 16,110 | 16,200 |

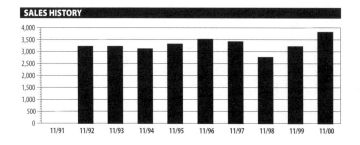

SALES HISTORY

# LEVI STRAUSS & CO.

## OVERVIEW

Levi Strauss & Co. (LS&CO.) has been caught with its pants down in the minds of America's tastemakers: teenagers. The company that invented denim jeans is now trying to reinvent itself. San Francisco-based LS&CO. is the world's largest maker of brand-name clothing. It sells jeans, casual wear, and sportswear under the Levi's, Dockers, and Slates names.

As the jeans market became more competitive, LS&CO. lost its focus. The company got mired in transitioning to contract manufacturers and failed to respond to changing fashions — namely the baggy, wide-leg preferences of the demographically significant US teenage population. Sales and profits have fallen as a result, and the company's US market share, which topped 30% when the 1990s began, has slipped to 12%.

LS&CO. has spent the late 1990s closing factories and cutting jobs in North America and Europe to pare costs. To win back younger shoppers, it has introduced new youth-oriented products, including its unusually cut Engineered Jeans. It is also dumping ads that promote image (which turn off older shoppers) in favor of ads highlighting products.

The family-owned company is controlled by chairman Robert Haas — a great-great-grandnephew of LS&CO.'s founder — and three relatives.

## HISTORY

Levi Strauss arrived in New York City from Bavaria in 1847. In 1853 he moved to San Francisco to sell dry goods to the gold rushers. Shortly after, a prospector told Strauss of miners' problems in finding sturdy pants. Strauss made a pair out of canvas for the prospector; word of the rugged pants spread quickly.

Strauss continued his dry-goods business in the 1860s. During this time he switched the pants' fabric to a durable French cloth called *serge de Nîmes*, soon known as denim. He colored the fabric with indigo dye and adopted the idea from Nevada tailor Jacob Davis of reinforcing the pants with copper rivets. In 1873 Strauss and Davis produced their first pair of waist-high overalls (later known as jeans). The pants soon became *de rigueur* for lumberjacks, cowboys, railroad workers, oil drillers, and farmers.

Strauss continued to build his pants and wholesaling business until he died in 1902. Levi Strauss & Co. (LS&CO.) passed to four nephews who carried on their uncle's jeans business while maintaining the company's philanthropic reputation.

After WWII Walter Haas and Peter Haas (a fourth-generation Strauss family member) assumed leadership of LS&CO. In 1948 they ended the company's wholesaling business to concentrate on Levi's clothing. In the 1950s Levi's jeans ceased to be merely functional garments for workers: They became the uniform of American youth. In the 1960s LS&CO. added women's attire and expanded overseas.

The company went public in 1971. That year it added a women's career line and bought Koret sportswear (sold in 1984). By the mid-1980s profits declined. Robert Haas (Walter's son), a Peace Corps veteran-turned-McKinsey consultant, grabbed the reins at LS&CO. in 1984 and took the company private the next year. He also instilled a touchy-feely corporate culture often at odds with the bottom line.

In 1986 LS&CO. introduced Dockers casual pants. The company's sales began rising in 1991 as consumers forsook designer duds for more practical clothes. However, LS&CO. missed out on the birth of another trend: the split between the fashion sense of US adolescents and their Levi's-loving, baby boomer parents.

In 1996 the company introduced Slates dress slacks. That year LS&CO. bought back nearly one-third of its stock from family and employees for $4.3 billion. Grappling with slipping sales and debt from the buyout, in 1997 LS&CO. closed 11 of its 37 North American plants, laying off 6,400 workers and 1,000 salaried employees (it granted generous severance packages even to those earning minimum wage).

In 1998, citing improved labor conditions in China, LS&CO. announced it would step up its use of Chinese subcontractors. Further restructuring added a third of its European plants to the closures list that year. LS&CO.'s sales fell 13% in fiscal 1998. The next year LS&CO. closed 11 of 22 remaining North American plants. It also unleashed several new jeans brands that eschewed the company's one-style-fits-all approach of old.

In 1999 Haas handed his CEO title to Pepsi executive Philip Marineau. In 2000 the company revealed that its sales fell about 15% in 1999, its third consecutive drop in annual sales. Also that year it launched its ICD+ line in Europe featuring techno jackets wired with mobile phones, MP3 players, headsets, and remote controls.

**Chairman:** Robert D. Haas, age 58, $2,850,000 pay
**President and CEO:** Philip A. Marineau, age 54,
$3,250,000 pay
**SVP and CFO:** William B. Chiasson, age 48,
$1,137,619 pay
**SVP and Chief Information Officer:** David G. Bergen,
age 45
**SVP Worldwide Human Resources:** Fred Paulenich,
age 36
**SVP, General Counsel, and Assistant Secretary:**
Albert F. Moreno, age 57, $781,281 pay
**SVP; President, Levi Strauss Asia Pacific:**
R. John Anderson, age 49
**SVP; President, Levi Strauss Europe, Middle East and
Africa:** Joseph Middleton, age 45
**Auditors:** Arthur Andersen LLP

## LOCATIONS

**HQ:** 1155 Battery St., San Francisco, CA 94111
**Phone:** 415-501-6000     **Fax:** 415-501-3939
**Web:** www.levistrauss.com

Levi Strauss & Co. manufactures and sells its branded
jeans, sportswear, and dress pants through retail
locations and company-owned outlets in more than 80
countries.

**2000 Sales**

|  | % of total |
|---|---|
| US | 68 |
| Europe | 24 |
| Asia/Pacific | 8 |
| **Total** | **100** |

## PRODUCTS/OPERATIONS

**2000 Sales**

|  | % of total |
|---|---|
| Levi's | 75 |
| Dockers | 23 |
| Slates | 2 |
| **Total** | **100** |

**Selected Brand Names**
501
Dockers
Dockers K-1
Dockers Recode
L2
Red Tab Classics
Silvertab
Slates
Sta-Prest

**Operating Divisions**
Asia Pacific Division
Levi Strauss Europe, Middle East, Africa
Levi Strauss, the Americas
    Levi Strauss & Co. (Canada) Inc.
    Levi Strauss Argentina
    Levi Strauss do Brasil
    Levi Strauss Mexico
    Levi Strauss U.S.

## COMPETITORS

| | |
|---|---|
| Calvin Klein | NIKE |
| Fruit of the Loom | OshKosh B'Gosh |
| The Gap | Oxford Industries |
| Guess? | Polo |
| Haggar | Tommy Hilfiger |
| J. Crew | VF |
| J. C. Penney | Warnaco Group |

## HISTORICAL FINANCIALS & EMPLOYEES

| Private<br>FYE: Last Sunday in November | Annual<br>Growth | 11/91 | 11/92 | 11/93 | 11/94 | 11/95 | 11/96 | 11/97 | 11/98 | 11/99 | 11/00 |
|---|---|---|---|---|---|---|---|---|---|---|---|
| Sales ($ mil.) | (2.2%) | — | 5,570 | 5,892 | 6,074 | 6,707 | 7,136 | 6,861 | 5,959 | 5,139 | 4,645 |
| Net income ($ mil.) | (5.9%) | — | 362 | 492 | 558 | 735 | 465 | 138 | 103 | 5 | 223 |
| Income as % of sales | — | — | 6.5% | 8.4% | 9.2% | 11.0% | 6.5% | 2.0% | 1.7% | 0.1% | 4.8% |
| Employees | (8.2%) | — | 34,200 | 36,400 | 36,500 | 37,700 | 37,000 | 37,000 | 30,000 | 30,000 | 17,300 |

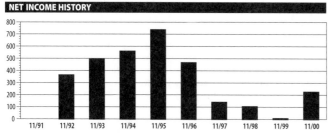

**NET INCOME HISTORY**

**2000 FISCAL YEAR-END**
Debt ratio: 100.0%
Return on equity: —
Cash ($ mil.): 117
Current ratio: 1.43
Long-term debt ($ mil.): 1,895

# LIBERTY MUTUAL INSURANCE

## OVERVIEW

Businesses that want freedom from the tyranny of employees' medical bills have made Boston-based Liberty Mutual Insurance the US's leading workers' compensation insurer. The company, which plans to form a mutual holding company, also offers homeowners and auto insurance, retirement products, and group and individual life insurance. Other services include risk-prevention services, consulting, rehabilitation case management, and physical rehabilitation centers.

After failing to find a buyer, asset manager Liberty Financial is selling itself off little by little. Canadian insurer Sun Life has acquired Keyport Life Insurance and mutual fund distributor Independent Financial Marketing Group. Liberty Financial's investment management segment (including subsidiaries Crabbe Huston, Stein Roe & Farnham, and Liberty Wanger Asset Management) was snapped up by FleetBoston. The company plans to spend the money it receives from the sale of Liberty Financial on new acquisitions. Liberty Mutual has taken what is left of Liberty Financial private and merged it into one of its subsidiaries.

The company's diversification efforts include Liberty International, which provides insurance and occupational health and safety services in such countries as Canada, Japan, Mexico, Singapore, and the UK.

## HISTORY

In the 19th century, Europeans already had a system for providing financial aid to workers injured on the job, but in the US, the first workers' compensation law, for federal employees, wasn't passed until 1908. Massachusetts was one of the first states to enact similar legislation. Liberty Mutual was founded in Boston in 1912 to fill this newly recognized niche.

Liberty Mutual followed the fire insurance practice of taking an active part in loss prevention. It evaluated clients' premises and procedures and recommended ways to prevent accidents. The company rejected the budding industry practice of limiting medical fees, instead studying the most effective ways to reduce the long-term cost of a claim by getting the injured party back to work.

In 1942 the company acquired the United Mutual Fire Insurance Company (founded 1908, renamed Liberty Mutual Fire Insurance Company in 1949). The next year it founded a rehabilitation center in Boston to treat injured workers and to test treatments.

In the 1960s and 1970s Liberty Mutual expanded its line to include life insurance (1963), group pensions (1970), and IRAs (1975).

Seeking to increase its national presence, the company formed Liberty Northwest Insurance Corporation in 1983. It continued expanding its offerings, with new subsidiaries in commercial, personal, and excess lines and, in 1986, by moving into financial services by buying Stein Roe & Farnham (founded 1958).

The expansion/diversification strategy seemed to work. Earnings between 1984 and 1986 more than tripled. Then came the downturn: Recession was followed by a string of natural disasters, and Liberty Mutual's income fell sharply between 1986 and 1988. In 1992 and 1993 the company lost suits to Coors and Outboard Marine for failing to back the companies in environmental litigation cases.

Liberty Mutual restructured in 1994, withdrawing from the group health business and reorganizing claims operations into two units: Personal Markets and Business Markets.

The company expanded its financial services operations in 1995 and 1996, merging its Liberty Financial subsidiary with the already-public Colonial Group; it also acquired American Asset Management and Newport Pacific Management.

In 1997 Liberty Mutual acquired bankrupt workers' compensation provider Golden Eagle Insurance of California; the next year the firm bought Florida's Summit Holding Southeast. Mutual funds were also on the shopping list: Purchases included Société Generale's US mutual funds unit, led by international money dean Jean-Marie Eveillard. The firm also played suitor to high-performance trust fund SIFE; the $450 million proposal was rebuffed as ungenerous. In 1998 the company was slammed by increased claims — many related to a Condé Nast Building construction accident that shut down New York City's Times Square that summer. Liberty Mutual acquired erstwhile competitor Employers Insurance of Wausau that year.

In 1999 the company bought Guardian Royal Exchange's US operations. In a new international initiative that year, Liberty Mutual bought 70% of Singapore-based insurer Citystate Holdings (renamed Liberty Citystate) as its foothold in Asia.

In 2001 Liberty Mutual announced it would form a mutual holding company to raise funds for acquisitions.

**Chairman, President, and CEO:** Edmund F. Kelly
**EVP:** John B. Conners
**EVP:** Gary R. Gregg
**EVP:** Roger L. Jean
**EVP; President, Liberty International:**
Thomas C. Ramey, age 57
**SVP and CFO; VP and CFO, Liberty Mutual Fire Insurance:** J. Paul Condrin III
**SVP and Chief Information Officer:** Terry L. Connor
**SVP and Chief Investment Officer; VP, Liberty Mutual Fire Insurance:** A. Alexander Fontanes
**SVP and General Counsel:** Christopher C. Mansfield
**SVP and Manager of Human Resources and Administration:** Helen E.R. Sayles
**SVP:** Stephen G. Sullivan
**VP and Corporate Actuary:** Douglas M. Hodes
**VP and Secretary:** Dexter R. Legg
**VP and Treasurer:** Elliot J. Williams
**VP and Comptroller:** Dennis Langwell
**Auditors:** Ernst & Young LLP

## LOCATIONS

**HQ:** Liberty Mutual Insurance Companies
175 Berkeley St., Boston, MA 02117
**Phone:** 617-357-9500    **Fax:** 617-350-7648
**Web:** www.libertymutual.com

Liberty Mutual Insurance has about 900 offices in the US and 16 other countries.

## PRODUCTS/OPERATIONS

**2000 Sales**

|  | % of total |
|---|---|
| Commercial marketplace | 37 |
| Personal marketplace | 26 |
| Regional agency markets | 16 |
| International | 11 |
| Financial services | 6 |
| Other | 4 |
| **Total** | **100** |

**Selected Product Lines**
Annuities
Disability insurance
General liability
Individual and group auto and property insurance
Individual and group life
Investment advice and management
Mutual funds
Workers' compensation

**Selected Operating Units**
Liberty Financial Companies
  Colonial Mutual Funds
  Liberty Asset Management Co.
  Newport Pacific Management, Inc.
  Stein Roe & Farnham
Liberty International
  Liberty ART SA (Argentina)
  Liberty Citystate (Singapore)
  Liberty International Canada
  Liberty Japan
  Liberty Mexico Seguros
  Liberty Mutual Insurance Company (Japan)
  Liberty Mutual Insurance Company (UK) Ltd.
  Liberty Paulista de Seguros (Brazil)
  Liberty Seguros SA (Colombia)
  Liberty Venezuela (merger between Seguros Panamerican and Seguros Caracas)
Liberty Mutual Group
  Colorado Casualty
  Golden Eagle Insurance Co.
  Indiana Insurance Company
  Liberty Northwest Insurance Corporation
  Merchants and Businessmen's Insurance Company
  Montgomery Mutual Insurance Company
  Peerless Insurance
  Summit Holding Southeast
  Wausau

## COMPETITORS

| | | |
|---|---|---|
| 21st Century | The Hartford | Prudential |
| Allstate | Lincoln National | SAFECO |
| AIG | MassMutual | St. Paul |
| Charles Schwab | MetLife | Companies |
| CIGNA | New York Life | State Farm |
| Citigroup | Northwestern | T. Rowe Price |
| CNA Financial | Mutual | Washington |
| Fremont General | Progressive | National |
| GenAmerica | Corporation | Corporation |

## HISTORICAL FINANCIALS & EMPLOYEES

| Mutual company FYE: December 31 | Annual Growth | 12/91 | 12/92 | 12/93 | 12/94 | 12/95 | 12/96 | 12/97 | 12/98 | 12/99 | 12/00 |
|---|---|---|---|---|---|---|---|---|---|---|---|
| Assets ($ mil.) | 13.0% | — | 20,216 | 20,544 | 20,644 | 21,791 | 22,690 | 25,230 | 26,254 | 55,259 | 53,826 |
| Employees | 8.7% | — | 19,000 | 22,000 | 22,000 | 23,000 | 23,000 | 23,000 | 24,000 | 37,440 | 37,000 |

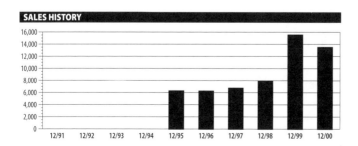

SALES HISTORY

# LIBERTY TRAVEL, INC.

## OVERVIEW

Liberty Travel doesn't mix business and pleasure. The Ramsey, New Jersey-based travel agency is the nation's leading private leisure travel company. It is one of the only large agencies to focus almost entirely on leisure rather than business travel. The company offers trips to more than 200 destinations, including Colorado Rockies ski excursions, Alaskan cruises, and family vacations to Walt Disney World. Liberty specializes in package deals, in which various aspects of a trip (travel and hotel accommodations, meals, rental cars, tours, and activities) are sold in combinations for less than they would cost if purchased individually. The company operates about 200 offices throughout the Northeast and in Florida.

Liberty Travel conducts its business as a true retail operation. A majority of the company's offices are open seven days a week. Its agents rely entirely on commission, and the company stresses salesmanship, providing a comprehensive training program that includes computer training, as well as "vacation class," which covers products and customer service. The agency also has redesigned its offices to entice more clients. Unlike most travel agencies, Liberty does not franchise; it owns all of its offices.

Liberty Travel's GOGO Worldwide Vacations division offers wholesale packages to other travel agencies through some 90 offices in more than 30 states.

## HISTORY

Gilbert Haroche and Fred Kassner began Liberty Travel in 1951 in New York City. From the beginning, the company was unusual. Offices were open from 9 a.m. to 9 p.m. Monday through Friday and from 10 a.m. to 5 p.m. Saturdays and Sundays, unlike most travel agencies, which kept hours somewhat closer to bankers'. At first Haroche and Kassner offered package trips to local resorts, but soon they began encouraging their clients to go to Miami, even in the hottest months. The two men were successful in getting hotel owners to guarantee them rooms in the peak season if they could fill the rooms at other times. They used the term "package trip" to cover not only the rooms but also sightseeing tours and rental cars, combining vacation elements at a lower price than if they had been purchased individually. They also began booking airplane seats in volume, and soon were offering "deluxe economy vacations," vacation packages with upscale accommodations at discount prices that combined airfare and hotel room rates.

GOGO Worldwide Vacations began in 1955 as GOGO Tours, with packages to Florida and Puerto Rico. The company prided itself on offering affordable vacations to the average working family. As disposable income grew, GOGO added the Bahamas and the Caribbean and later included other US, Canadian, and European destinations, as well as trips to South America and parts of Asia.

During the intense competition and fare wars of the 1980s, Liberty joined other travel agencies in charging fees for canceled or revised itineraries. The company also made an early foray into self-ticketing by installing video-display kiosks in New York City shopping centers.

GOGO began upgrading its "Kmart of travel" image in 1995. Since GOGO Tours conjured up images of escorted tours, the company changed its name to GOGO Worldwide Vacations reflecting the more global — and upscale — nature of its packages. The next year it added a hotel rating system and introduced FIRST (Future in Reservation Systems Technology), a real-time booking system available to agents 24 hours a day, seven days a week.

In 1996 Liberty announced plans to open 15 offices a year, a goal it achieved for the next two years. It received more than 1,000 inquiries after announcing it wanted to buy a number of small to midsized travel agencies. In 1997 GOGO began its Intimate Hotels of the Caribbean showcase of some 170 smaller, independent hotels, inns, and guest houses in 28 locations in the Bahamas, Belize, Bermuda, and the Caribbean. Following the trend toward sales over the Internet, both Liberty and GOGO began in 1998 to allow customers to browse and book vacations through their Web site.

Co-founder Fred Kassner died late in 1998. The next year Liberty Travel bought a 10% stake in Global Travel Network, a franchisor of independent travel agents. Global Travel Network was subsequently acquired by Playorena (later renamed ETRAVNET.COM). Also in 1999 Bernie Tessler joined Liberty Travel as COO to help the company focus on its Web site. However, in 2000 he left the company shortly after announcing that the site would undergo an overhaul.

**President and CEO:** Gilbert Haroche
**SVP Finance:** Richard Cowlan
**EVP:** Michelle Kassner
**VP GOGO Worldwide Vacations:** Mike Norton
**VP Information Services:** Bill Hughes
**VP Strategic Planning:** Orest Rusynko
**VP Sales:** Cathy Peleaz
**VP Public Retalions:** Diane Brancella
**Director of Human Resources:** Susan Brennen

## LOCATIONS

**HQ:** 69 Spring St., Ramsey, NJ 07446
**Phone:** 201-934-3500    **Fax:** 201-934-3651
**Web:** www.libertytravel.com

Liberty Travel has about 200 offices, primarily on the
East Coast. GOGO Worldwide Vacations, its sister
company, has about 90 offices in major cities
throughout the US.

**Selected Destinations**

| | |
|---|---|
| Bahamas | Mexico |
| Belize | Acapulco |
| Bermuda | Cancun |
| Canada | Cozumel |
| Alberta | Huatulco |
| British Columbia | Manzanillo |
| Quebec | Puerto Vallarta |
| Caribbean | US |
| Aruba | California |
| Barbados | Colorado |
| Cayman Islands | Florida |
| Dominican Republic | Hawaii |
| Jamaica | Nevada |
| Puerto Rico | New Mexico |
| St. John | New York |
| St. Lucia | Pennsylvania |
| St. Maarten | South Carolina |
| St. Martin | Texas |
| St. Thomas | Utah |
| Costa Rica | Vermont |
| | Virginia |
| | Wyoming |

## COMPETITORS

AAA
Accor
American Express
Carlson Wagonlit
Carnival
Empress Travel
Expedia
Globus/Cosmos
Lowestfare.com
Pleasant Holidays
priceline.com
Rosenbluth International
Royal Caribbean Cruises
TravelFest Superstores, Inc.
WorldTravel

## HISTORICAL FINANCIALS & EMPLOYEES

| Private<br>FYE: December 31 | Annual<br>Growth | 12/91 | 12/92 | 12/93 | 12/94 | 12/95 | 12/96 | 12/97 | 12/98 | 12/99 | 12/00 |
|---|---|---|---|---|---|---|---|---|---|---|---|
| Sales ($ mil.) | 3.2% | — | — | — | — | — | 1,236 | 1,297 | 1,320 | 1,390 | 1,400 |
| Employees | 13.7% | — | — | — | — | — | — | 1,700 | 1,800 | 2,500 | 2,500 |

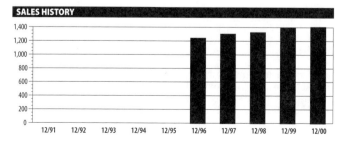

# LIFESTYLE FURNISHINGS

## OVERVIEW

LifeStyle Furnishings International targets the consumers who choose their sofas the same way they choose their clothing: to make a fashion statement. The High Point, North Carolina-based company (formerly one of the "Big Three" home furnishings manufacturers — along with Furniture Brands International and La-Z-Boy) sells principal brands BenchCraft, Beacon Hill, LaBarge, and Lexington. Lifestyle lost its footing in 2001 and slipped out of the furniture industry triad with its sale of Drexel Heritage, Henredon, and Maitland-Smith to Furniture Brands International (in January 2002).

Stressing style, it also sells furniture bearing the names of designers better known for clothing (such as Alexander Julian), celebrities (Arnold Palmer), and institutions (Smithsonian). It sells bedroom, dining room, and living room furniture, plus lamps, mirrors, outdoor furniture, and decorative fabric.

The company sells its products through some 22,000 retailers, 1,500 galleries within stores, department stores, specialty shops, and more than 80 independent stores that sell only LifeStyle products. Its products are also sold through 13 company-owned Beacon Hill designer-exclusive showrooms and through contract distribution channels.

Building supply manufacturer Masco holds a 15% stake in LifeStyle, managers own about 20%, and a Citibank venture capital unit controls the rest.

## HISTORY

LifeStyle Furnishings International was the result of remodeling by its former owner, Michigan-based Masco. The leading US maker of faucets, kitchen cabinets, and other home products, Masco branched into the furniture business in 1986. The company brought brand recognition to the home improvement market (it introduced Delta and Peerless faucets) and saw a similar opportunity in furniture. Masco believed customers would select furniture by name to reflect their individual tastes and styles. The company thought it could quickly make a mark in the fragmented market.

Masco started by buying, rather than building, furniture companies, most in North Carolina. In 1986 it purchased the first member of its furniture family, Henredon, a well-known manufacturer of mid- and high-priced wood and upholstered furniture. Within months Masco scooped up Drexel Heritage. The following year it bought Lexington Furniture. (Masco spent $1 million on computerized routing machines to eliminate a six-month backlog of furniture orders at Lexington.) In 1989 the company took the top spot in the US furniture industry with its $550 million acquisition of Universal Furniture, the #1 supplier of dining room furniture. It also began signing big-name designers (Alexander Julian, artist Bob Timberlake, and others) to create furniture lines. Masco maintained the brands' identities and sought ways to strengthen the group, such as through added buying power.

Trying to create a niche, Masco started its own furniture brand, Lineage, aimed at the middle-income customer in 1991. The line contained eclectic pieces to fit certain lifestyles: "casual living," "gracious living," and "special places."

But Lineage failed, in part because the custom designs turned out to be too expensive and too unusual for the middle market.

On the heels of its divestitures of other non-core interests and disappointed that its furniture division never earned the anticipated profit margin, Masco cleaned house again in 1996. It sold off the furniture unit as LifeStyle Furnishings International for $1.1 billion — a half-billion-dollar loss — to a group of investors led by a venture capital arm of Citibank. But Masco did not cut the apron strings completely. It retained a 15% stake in the company, and Wayne Lyon, who had been Masco's president and COO, left to lead the venture.

The company restructured in 1997 and 1998, closing about 10 manufacturing and distribution plants and laying off 5,000 employees (about 15% of its workforce), mostly from its Universal Furniture operations in Asia.

In 1998 LifeStyle moved its headquarters from Thomasville to High Point, North Carolina. The company filed to go public that year but opted to hold off on an IPO until market conditions become more comfy. In 2000 the company reorganized its upper management to focus on internal efficiency and growth. The company sold its Universal brand to Lacquer Craft, a Chinese furniture maker, in 2001.

In 2002 Lifestyle sold Drexel Heritage, Henredon, and Maitland-Smith to Furniture Brands International — thus relinquishing its solid positioning as one of the "Big Three" in furniture manufacturing. Lifestyle also announced intentions of selling Berkline and BenchCraft units to a management-led buyout team in the future.

## OFFICERS

**Chairman Emeritus:** Tom Cunningham
**Chairman:** Wayne B. Lyon
**President and CEO:** Alan D. Cole
**Group VP; President and CEO, The Berkline Corporation:** Bill Wittenberg
**VP, Corporate Marketing:** Chris Fink
**VP, Human Resources:** William J. Frakes
**VP, Marketing and Business Development:** Robert Stamper
**VP, Treasurer, and CFO:** Ronald J. Hoffman
**President and CEO, BenchCraft:** Greg Henderson

## LOCATIONS

**HQ:** LifeStyle Furnishings International Ltd.
4000 Lifestyle Ct., High Point, NC 27265
**Phone:** 336-878-7000    **Fax:** 336-878-7015
**Web:** www.lifestylefurnishings.com

LifeStyle Furnishings International makes and distributes its products at about 70 facilities in North America, Asia, and Europe.

## PRODUCTS/OPERATIONS

### Selected Products

Accent items
Bedroom sets
Chairs
Dining room sets
Family room sets
Home entertainment centers
Home furnishings fabrics
Home office
Lamps
Living room sets
Mirrors
Outdoor furniture
Recliners
Sleeper sofas
Sofas
Tables

### Selected Brands

Alexander Julian At Home (licensed)
Ametex
BenchCraft
Berkline
Bob Timberlake (licensed)
Jack Nicklaus Collection (licensed)
La Barge
Lexington
Lillian August (licensed)
Nautica Home (licensed)
Palmer Home Collection (licensed)
Pinehurst Collection (licensed)
Robert Allen
Southern Living Collection (licensed)
Sunbury
Tommy Bahama (licensed)
Waverly (licensed)

## COMPETITORS

Ashley Furniture Industries
Bassett Furniture
Bombay Company
Bush Industries
Chromcraft Revington
DMI Furniture
Ethan Allen
F. Schumacher
Flexsteel
Furniture Brands International
Natuzzi
Kimball International
Klaussner Furniture
Knoll
La-Z-Boy
O'Sullivan Industries
P/Kaufman
Rowe Companies
Sauder Woodworking
Stanley Furniture

## HISTORICAL FINANCIALS & EMPLOYEES

| Private<br>FYE: December 31 | Annual<br>Growth | 12/91 | 12/92 | 12/93 | 12/94 | 12/95 | 12/96 | 12/97 | 12/98 | 12/99 | 12/00 |
|---|---|---|---|---|---|---|---|---|---|---|---|
| Sales ($ mil.) | 1.8% | — | — | 1,764 | 1,898 | 1,993 | 1,997 | 1,969 | 2,007 | 2,100 | 2,000 |
| Employees | 0.0% | — | — | — | — | — | — | 30,000 | 30,000 | 30,000 | 30,000 |

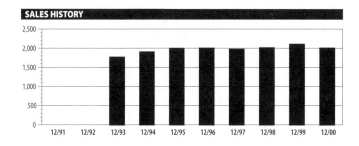

SALES HISTORY

# L.L. BEAN, INC.

## OVERVIEW

Although Leon Leonwood Bean didn't live in a shoe, he did make his living by selling them. Headquartered in Freeport, Maine, L.L. Bean was the first national mail-order house (and now the largest) to specialize in outdoor goods (such as the original Maine Hunting Shoe, which started the company). L.L. Bean publishes catalogs and operates its flagship retail store on Main Street in Freeport (which attracts 3.5 million visitors annually and is open 24 hours a day, 365 days a year). It also sells its wares through about 10 outlet stores in the US, 20-plus stores in Japan, and through its Web site. The company offers more than 16,000 items ranging from outdoor apparel to sporting goods to household furnishings, most of

which carry the L.L. Bean label. It makes more than 300 of its products (such as shoes, tote bags, luggage) in Maine.

L.L. Bean's famous customer service is exemplified by its liberal return policies and perpetual replacement of the rubber soles of its Maine Hunting Shoe. The company also offers seminars and events on such topics as fly fishing, sea kayaking, and outdoor photography. Faced with intense competition from rivals such as Lands' End, L.L. Bean plans to grow by adding to its full-price retail stores. It also has launched Freeport Studio, a more fashion-conscious women's catalog.

The company is controlled by the family of its founder.

## HISTORY

Leon Leonwood Bean started out as a storekeeper in Freeport, Maine. Tired of wet, leaky boots, he experimented with various remedies and in 1911 came up with the Maine Hunting Shoe, a boot with rubber soles and feet and leather uppers. It became his most famous product.

From its outset in 1912, L.L. Bean was a mail-order house. The first batch of boots was a disaster: Almost all of them leaked. But Bean's willingness to correct his product's defects quickly, at his own expense, saved the company.

Maine's hunting licensing system, implemented in 1917, provided the company with a mailing list of affluent recreational hunters in the Northeast, and that year Bean opened a showroom to accommodate the customers stopping by his Freeport workshop.

Bean cultivated the image of the folksy Maine guide, offering durable, comfortable, weather-resistant clothes and reliable camping supplies. In 1920 Bean built a store on Main Street in Freeport. L.L. Bean continued to grow and add products, even during the Depression, and sales reached $1 million in 1937.

During WWII Bean helped design the boots used by the US military, and his company manufactured them, thus remaining afloat as the war years and rationing brought cutbacks in materials and outdoor activities. He began keeping the retail store open 24 hours a day in 1951, noting that he had "thrown away the keys." Bean added a women's department three years later.

Sales rose to $2 million in the early 1960s and were at $4.8 million when Bean died in 1967 at age 94. (He had resisted growing the business bigger, saying, "I'm eating three meals

a day; I can't eat four.") The new president was Bean's grandson Leon Gorman, who had started with L.L. Bean in 1960. His early attempts at updating the mailing operations (mailing labels typed by hand and correspondence kept in cardboard boxes) had been vetoed by his grandfather. Gorman brought in new people and made improvements, including automating the mailing systems, improving the manufacturing systems, and targeting new, nonsporting markets (like women's casual clothes).

L.L. Bean continued its transition by targeting more of its classic customer profile — upper-middle-class college graduates — and sales grew about 20% annually for most of the 1980s. By 1989, however, sales had slowed and growth flattened as the national economy slumped and imitators carried away market share. Unsolicited catalog orders had been coming in from Japan since the late 1980s, so in 1992 L.L. Bean began a joint venture with Seiyu and Matsushita Electric Industrial. Their first store opened that year (the company opened a catalog and service center in Japan in 1995). L.L. Kids began in 1993.

In 1996 the company began an online shopping service. Sparked by the success of its L.L. Kids division, which grew 300% in four years, the company opened a separate children's store in Freeport the next year. In 1999 L.L. Bean introduced Freeport Studio, a more fashion-forward catalog for women. The company opened its second full-line store in 2000 near Washington, DC. L.L. Bean plans to continue opening retail stores in the eastern US.

L.L. Bean veteran Chris McCormick was named president and CEO in May 2001; Gorman remained chairman.

**Chairman:** Leon A. Gorman, age 66
**President and CEO:** Chris McCormick
**SVP and CFO:** Mark Fasold
**SVP, Human Resources:** Bob Peixotto

## LOCATIONS

**HQ:** Casco St., Freeport, ME 04033
**Phone:** 207-865-4761    **Fax:** 207-552-6821
**Web:** www.llbean.com

L.L. Bean sells through direct-mail catalogs, has retail
and outlet stores in the US, and in Japan through a joint
venture with Seiyu and Matsushita Electric Industrial.
It manufactures some of its merchandise in Maine.

## PRODUCTS/OPERATIONS

**Selected Catalogs**
Corporate Sales (custom embroidered clothing and
  luggage)
Fly Fishing (equipment, outer wear, and accessories)
Freeport Studio (fashionable women's apparel and
  accessories)
L.L. Bean
L.L. Bean Hunting
Home (linens, pillows, and decorating)
Outdoor Discovery Schools (classes and symposiums)
Outdoors (seasonal outdoor wear and accessories)
Traveler (clothing, luggage, and accessories)

**Selected Products**
Home and garden accessories
Men's, women's, and children's casual apparel
Outdoor classes
Outer wear
Shoes and boots
Sports gear and apparel
Travel apparel and luggage

## COMPETITORS

| | |
|---|---|
| American Eagle Outfitters | Lands' End |
| American Retail | Levi Strauss |
| Bass Pro Shops | The Limited |
| Brylane | Lost Arrow |
| Cabela's | May |
| Coldwater Creek | Nautica Enterprises |
| Coleman | North Face |
| Columbia Sportswear | Orvis Company |
| Dillard's | OshKosh B'Gosh |
| Fast Retailing | Polo |
| Federated | REI |
| Foot Locker | Sears |
| The Gap | Spiegel |
| Gart Sports | Sports Authority |
| J. Crew | Sportsman's Guide |
| J. Jill Group | Talbots |
| J. C. Penney | Target |
| Johnson Outdoors | Timberland |

## HISTORICAL FINANCIALS & EMPLOYEES

| Private FYE: February 28 | Annual Growth | 2/92 | 2/93 | 2/94 | 2/95 | 2/96 | 2/97 | 2/98 | 2/99 | 2/00 | 2/01 |
|---|---|---|---|---|---|---|---|---|---|---|---|
| Sales ($ mil.) | 7.4% | 632 | 743 | 867 | 976 | 1,078 | 1,040 | 1,068 | 1,070 | 1,100 | 1,200 |
| Employees | 4.0% | 3,300 | 3,500 | 3,500 | 3,800 | 3,800 | 3,500 | 3,600 | 4,000 | 4,000 | 4,700 |

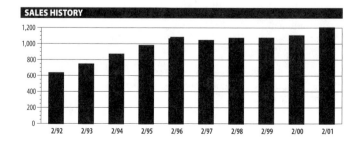

SALES HISTORY

L.L.Bean

# LUCASFILM LTD.

## OVERVIEW

The Force is definitely strong with George Lucas. Based at Skywalker Ranch in Nicasio, California, Lucasfilm (one of five entertainment and technology companies owned by the filmmaker) has produced five of the top 20 grossing films in history, including 1999's *Star Wars: Episode I — The Phantom Menace* (more than $920 million worldwide). Lucasfilm has produced four *Star Wars* films in all, as well as the *Indiana Jones* trilogy and a handful of other films, collecting a total of 17 Academy Awards. The company includes the THX Group, which designs digital sound systems for movie and home theaters. Lucasfilm also manages the business aspects (finances, research services, marketing, and human resources) of the other Lucas companies. The company is building a new headquarters and production center at the Presidio, a former Army base in San Francisco.

## HISTORY

After attending film school at the University of Southern California, George Lucas started his career as a documentary filmmaker, chronicling the production of Francis Ford Coppola's *Finian's Rainbow* in 1968. The two men became fast friends and founded American Zoetrope in 1969, which released Lucas' feature film debut two years later, the science-fiction film *THX 1138* (a full-length version of a student film he made at USC). The film flopped, and Coppola went into production on *The Godfather.* Lucas left American Zoetrope and created his own company, Lucasfilm, in 1971.

Two years later Lucas released *American Graffiti* through Universal Pictures (with some financial help from Coppola). The film was a smash hit; it raked in $115 million in the US and made him a millionaire before the age of 30. It also gave him the clout to try to get his most ambitious project off the ground, a space opera called *Star Wars.* Universal, frustrated with cost overruns on *Graffiti,* wanted no part of Lucas' seemingly ridiculous idea, so he went to 20th Century Fox, which agreed to finance the $10 million film. Lucas gave up his directing fee for a percentage of the box-office take and all merchandising rights. He created Industrial Light & Magic (ILM) and Sprocket Systems (later Skywalker Sound) in 1975 to produce the visual and sound effects needed for the film.

*Star Wars* cost about $12 million, and almost everyone involved was sure it would bomb. Released in 1977, the movie shattered every box-office record, and the merchandising rights Lucas obtained made him a multimillionaire. With his take from *Star Wars,* Lucas was able to finance the film's sequel, *The Empire Strikes Back* (1980), out of his own pocket, meaning he would receive most of the profits (it grossed more than $220 million domestically). Lucasfilm's next production was *Raiders of the Lost Ark* (1981), directed by Lucas' friend Steven Spielberg. It went on to gross more than $380 million worldwide.

The next year Lucas began developing the THX sound system in preparation for the 1983 release of the third *Star Wars* film, *Return of the Jedi* (which hauled in more than $260 million domestically). He also founded LucasArts in 1982 to develop video games. Lucasfilm completed Skywalker Ranch (a facility housing many of its various companies in Marin County, California) in the mid-1980s and filled out the decade with two *Raiders* sequels — *Indiana Jones and the Temple of Doom* (1984, $333 million worldwide) and *Indiana Jones and the Last Crusade* (1989, $495 million worldwide).

Lucasfilm reorganized in 1993 by spinning off LucasArts into a separate company and regrouping ILM and Skywalker Sound into a new company called Lucas Digital. Lucasfilm won local government approval to build an $87 million film studio near Skywalker Ranch in 1996, and the following year it rereleased the *Star Wars Trilogy* to theaters with new special effects in celebration of the 20th anniversary, adding another $250 million to its take. Anticipating the release of the first of three prequels to the *Star Wars Trilogy,* Lucasfilm started signing marketing agreements in 1998 (including deals with Hasbro and Pepsi) that resulted in advance licensing of nearly $3 billion.

*Star Wars: Episode I — The Phantom Menace* opened in May 1999 and has grossed about $920 million worldwide (it finished its initial run second only to *Titanic*). Two more sequels are slated for release in 2002 and 2005. Later in 1999 Lucas announced plans to develop a $250 million digital arts center at the old Presidio army base in San Francisco that will house ILM, LucasArts, Lucas Learning, Lucas Online, THX, and the George Lucas Educational Foundation.

## OFFICERS

**Chairman:** George W. Lucas Jr.
**President:** Gordon Radley
**CFO:** Micheline Chau
**VP Marketing:** Jim Ward
**Director Communications:** Lynne Hale
**Director Human Resources:** Darlene Sattel

## LOCATIONS

**HQ:** 5858 Lucas Valley Rd., Nicasio, CA 94946
**Phone:** 415-662-1800     **Fax:** 415-662-2437
**Web:** www.lucasfilm.com

Lucasfilm operates from Skywalker Ranch in Marin County, Cailfornia, about 30 miles north of San Francisco.

## PRODUCTS/OPERATIONS

**Selected Productions**
*American Graffiti* (1973)
*Howard the Duck* (1986)
*Indiana Jones and the Last Crusade* (1989)
*Indiana Jones and the Temple of Doom* (1984)
*Labyrinth* (1986)
*More American Graffiti* (1979)
*Radioland Murders* (1994)
*Raiders of the Lost Ark* (1981)
*Star Wars: Episode I — The Phantom Menace* (1999)
*Star Wars: Episode II — Attack of the Clones* (2002)
*Star Wars: Episode III* (2005)
*Star Wars: Episode IV — A New Hope* (1977)
*Star Wars: Episode V — The Empire Strikes Back* (1980)
*Star Wars: Episode VI — Return of the Jedi* (1983)
*Tucker: The Man and His Dream* (1988)
*Willow* (1988)
*The Young Indiana Jones Chronicles* (1992-96, TV movies)

## COMPETITORS

Alliance Atlantis Communications
Artisan Entertainment
Dolby
DreamWorks SKG
Fox Entertainment
Lions Gate Entertainment
MGM
Pixar
Sony Pictures Entertainment
Time Warner Entertainment
Universal Studios
USA Networks
Viacom
Walt Disney

## HISTORICAL FINANCIALS & EMPLOYEES

| Private<br>FYE: March 31 | Annual<br>Growth | 3/91 | 3/92 | 3/93 | 3/94 | 3/95 | 3/96 | 3/97 | 3/98 | 3/99 | 3/00 |
|---|---|---|---|---|---|---|---|---|---|---|---|
| Estimated sales ($ mil.) | 37.9% | — | — | — | 160 | 160 | 200 | 250 | 400 | 600 | 1,100 |
| Employees | 118.7% | — | — | — | — | 36 | 100 | 200 | 500 | 1,300 | 1,800 |

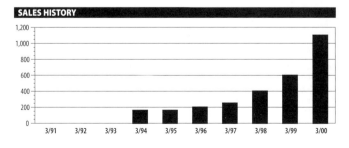

SALES HISTORY

# MACANDREWS & FORBES

Ron Perelman banks on glamour and thrift. The cigar-smoking financier's New York City-based MacAndrews & Forbes Holdings owns 83% of Revlon (cosmetics) and about 28% of the nation's #2 thrift, Golden State Bancorp. The company also has a major stake in M&F Worldwide (licorice extract) and an interest in WeddingChannel.com. Most of Perelman's business strategy involves improving his cash position and paying down debt — hence his IPO of Revlon (1996), the sale of The Coleman Company to Sunbeam (1998), and the sale of two of Revlon's noncore units.

Despite the success of Golden State Bancorp, Perelman's holdings have lost over $2 billion in value since 1999. Revlon is struggling with debt and dwindling market share and Marvel Entertainment went bankrupt under his control. He was the largest single investor in Sunbeam (appliances and Coleman camping equipment) before that company initiated bankruptcy proceedings. He did make a hefty profit when he sold his Mafco Consolidated Group's stake in Consolidated Cigar Holdings to French tobacco manufacturer Seita in 1999.

Perelman is still a media curiosity, largely because of his very public courtship of and wedding to wife #4, actress Ellen Barkin — not to mention a net worth of around $3 billion.

## HISTORY

Ron Perelman grew up working in his father's Philadelphia-based conglomerate, Belmont Industries, but he left at the age of 35 to seek his fortune in New York. In 1978 he bought 40% of jewelry store operator Cohen-Hatfield Industries. The next year Cohen-Hatfield bought a minority stake in MacAndrews & Forbes (licorice flavoring). Cohen-Hatfield acquired MacAndrews & Forbes in 1980.

In 1984 Perelman reshuffled his assets to create MacAndrews & Forbes Holdings, which acquired control of Pantry Pride, a Florida-based supermarket chain, in 1985. Pantry Pride then bought Revlon for $1.8 billion with the help of convicted felon Michael Milken. After Perelman acquired Revlon, he added several other cosmetics vendors, including Max Factor and Yves Saint Laurent's fragrance and cosmetic lines.

In 1988 MacAndrews & Forbes agreed to invest $315 million in five failing Texas savings and loans, which Perelman combined and named First Gibraltar (sold to BankAmerica, now Bank of America, in 1993). The next year MacAndrews & Forbes bought The Coleman Company, a maker of outdoor equipment.

With a growing reputation for buying struggling companies, revamping them, and then selling them at a higher price, Perelman bought Marvel Entertainment Group (Marvel Comics) in 1989 and took it public in 1991. That year he sold Revlon's Max Factor and Betrix units to Procter & Gamble for over $1 billion.

MacAndrews & Forbes acquired 37.5% of TV infomercial producer Guthy-Renker and SCI Television's seven stations and merged them to create New World Television. That company was combined with TV syndicator Genesis Entertainment and TV production house New World Entertainment to create New World Communications Group, which Perelman took public in 1994. That year MacAndrews & Forbes and partner Gerald J. Ford bought Ford Motor's First Nationwide, the US's fifth-largest S&L at that time.

Subsidiaries Mafco Worldwide and Consolidated Cigar Holdings merged with Abex (aircraft parts) to create Mafco Consolidated Group in 1995. Following diminishing comic sales, Perelman placed Marvel in bankruptcy in 1996 and subsequently lost control of the company. In 1997 First Nationwide bought California thrift Cal Fed Bancorp for $1.2 billion. In addition, Perelman sold New World to Rupert Murdoch's News Corp.

In 1998 Perelman orchestrated a $1.8 billion deal in which First Nationwide merged with Golden State Bancorp to form the US's second-largest thrift. Sunbeam bought Perelman's stake in Coleman that year, making Perelman a major Sunbeam shareholder. Also in 1998 MacAndrews & Forbes bought a 72% stake in Panavision (movie camera maker, later increased to 91%) and sold its 64% stake in Consolidated Cigar to French tobacco giant Seita (netting Perelman a smoking $350 million profit).

Perelman's stock in Sunbeam was rendered worthless when the company initiated bankruptcy proceedings in February 2001. He was also sued by angry shareholders after the board of M&F Worldwide, the licorice company he controls, bought Perelman's stock in Panavision at more than five times its market value.

**Chairman, CEO, and CFO:** Ronald O. Perelman, age 58
**Co-Vice Chairman:** Donald G. Drapkin, age 53
**Co-Vice Chairman:** Howard Gittis, age 67
**Director of Human Resources:** Herb Vallier

## LOCATIONS

**HQ:** MacAndrews & Forbes Holdings Inc.
35 E. 62nd St., New York, NY 10021
**Phone:** 212-688-9000 **Fax:** 212-572-8400

MacAndrews & Forbes Holdings' consumer products operations are principally in the US.

## PRODUCTS/OPERATIONS

**Selected Holdings**
e7th (online footwear wholesaler)
Golden State Bancorp (34%, #2 US thrift)
Mafco Consolidated Group
   M&F Worldwide Corp. (32%, licorice extract)
Panavision (91%, movie cameras)
Revlon Inc. (83%, cosmetics and personal care products)
Sunbeam Corporation (about 37%, small appliances and
   Coleman camping gear)
WeddingChannel.com

## COMPETITORS

Alberto-Culver
Alticor
Avon
Bank of America
Body Shop
Brunswick
Chattem
Colgate-Palmolive
Estée Lauder
Golden West Financial
Kellwood
L'Oréal USA
LVMH
Mary Kay
Procter & Gamble
Unilever
Washington Mutual
Wells Fargo

## HISTORICAL FINANCIALS & EMPLOYEES

| Private<br>FYE: December 31 | Annual<br>Growth | 12/91 | 12/92 | 12/93 | 12/94 | 12/95 | 12/96 | 12/97 | 12/98 | 12/99 | 12/00 |
|---|---|---|---|---|---|---|---|---|---|---|---|
| Sales ($ mil.) | 5.8% | — | 3,496 | 2,748 | 3,030 | 4,413 | 6,196 | 6,071 | 4,900 | 5,400 | 5,500 |
| Employees | (3.4%) | — | 25,700 | 23,500 | 22,328 | 22,800 | 30,000 | 29,854 | 19,500 | — | 19,500 |

## SALES HISTORY

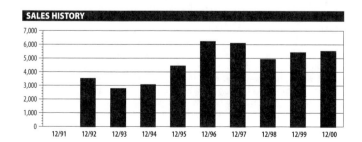

# MAJOR LEAGUE BASEBALL

## OVERVIEW

It may be the national pastime, but Major League Baseball (MLB) is also big business. Based in New York City, MLB oversees 30 baseball franchises in 28 cities, all of which act as separate businesses but adhere to rules and policies laid down by the national organization. It regulates changes in franchise ownership and licenses official league merchandise. It also awards national broadcasting rights, and splits that revenue among the teams. (Each team is free to negotiate its own regional broadcast fees.) Its franchises are divided between the National League (16) and

the American League (14) and play regular-season games between April and October.

MLB's financial future was secured in 2000 when Fox Entertainment agreed to a six-year, $2.5 billion broadcasting contract. But the league and commissioner Bud Selig have made some tough decisions as financial disparity grows between small- and big-market teams. The team owners and the league must negotiate a new labor agreement with players as their contract, forged after a disastrous strike in 1994, expired at the end of the 2001 season.

## HISTORY

The first baseball team to field professional players was the Cincinnati Red Stockings in 1869. Teams in Boston, New York City, and Philadelphia followed suit. In 1876 eight professional teams formed the National League. Competing leagues sprang up and folded, but Ban Johnson's Western League (formed in 1892) seized on territory abandoned by the National League in 1900 and began luring players away from the National League with higher salaries. Renamed the American League, it also began drawing away fans. The two leagues agreed to join forces in 1903 by having their champions meet in the World Series.

The sport flourished until the "black sox" scandal of 1919, in which eight Chicago White Sox players were accused of taking bribes to throw the World Series. The owners hired Judge Kenesaw Mountain Landis as baseball's first commissioner in 1921 to clean up the game's image. A joint committee of owners and players introduced more reforms in 1947, including a player pension fund.

The players formed the Major League Baseball Players' Association (MLBPA) in 1954 and signed the first collective-bargaining agreement with the owners in 1968. The players called their first strike in 1972, a 13-day walkout that won an improved pension plan. They won the right to free agency in 1976; another seven-week strike interrupted the 1981 season.

Salary increases slowed, and the free agent market dried up in the mid-1980s, prompting the MLBPA to sue the owners for collusion. The owners agreed to a settlement of $280 million in 1990. Baseball's eighth commissioner, Fay Vincent, resigned in 1992 after the owners effectively removed all power from the commissioner's office. An executive council of owners led by Milwaukee Brewers owner Bud Selig took control.

Prompted by the owners' decision to unilaterally restrict free agency and withdraw salary arbitration, the players started a 232-day strike in August 1994 that forced the cancellation of the World Series and stretched into the 1995 season. Revenue and income plummeted. Play resumed in 1995 when the owners and the MLBPA approved a new collective-bargaining agreement. Selig stepped down from the Brewers in 1998 to become the game's ninth commissioner.

Having alienated countless fans, baseball was resuscitated in 1998 by Mark McGwire and Sammy Sosa as they pursued Roger Maris' 37-year-old single-season home run record of 61. Fans returned in droves to see McGwire hit 70 homers over the fence that season. (McGwire's record only lasted until the 2001 season when the San Francisco Giants' outfielder Barry Bonds hit 72 homers.)

MLB signed a new six-year, $800 million TV contract with ESPN in 1999.

Sweeping changes took place in 2000 when owners, who had voted the previous year to eliminate the American and National league offices (centralizing power with the commissioner's office), also voted to restore the "best interests of baseball" powers to the commissioner, giving Selig full authority to redistribute wealth, block trades, and fine teams and players. The organization also scored a financial home run when Fox Entertainment agreed to pay $2.5 billion for exclusive rights to televise the All-Star Game and all postseason contests through the 2006 season.

Because of the consistent financial disparity between large- and small-market teams, the league in 2001 voted to eliminate two teams before the start of the 2002 season. But public outcry and lawsuits led the league to delay the move until at least 2003.

**Commissioner:** Allan H. Selig, age 67
**President and COO:** Paul Beeston
**CFO:** Jeffrey White
**EVP Baseball Operations:** Sandy Alderson
**EVP Business:** Timothy J. Brosnan
**SVP Baseball Operations:** Jimmie Lee Solomon
**SVP Security and Facilities Management:**
Kevin M. Hallinan
**VP International Baseball Operations:** Lou Melendez
**VP Marketing:** Kathy Francis
**Executive Director of Public Relations:** Richard Levin
**Executive Director of Human Resources:** Wendy Lewis
**Chairman, MLB Advanced Media:** Bob DuPuy
**President and CEO, MLB Advanced Media:**
Robert A. Bowman, age 45
**Auditors:** Ernst & Young LLP

## LOCATIONS

**HQ:** 245 Park Ave., New York, NY 10167
**Phone:** 212-931-7800    **Fax:** 212-949-8636
**Web:** www.mlb.com

Major League Baseball has 30 franchises in 28 cities in
the US and Canada.

## PRODUCTS/OPERATIONS

**Major League Franchises**

**American League**
Anaheim Angels (1965, California)
Baltimore Orioles (1952)
Boston Red Sox (1901)
Chicago White Sox (1901)
Cleveland Indians (1915)
Detroit Tigers (1900)
Kansas City Royals (1969, Missouri)
Minnesota Twins (1961, Minneapolis)
New York Yankees (1913, New York City)
Oakland Athletics (1968, California)
Seattle Mariners (1977)
Tampa Bay Devil Rays (1998)
Texas Rangers (1972, Arlington)
Toronto Blue Jays (1977)

**National League**
Arizona Diamondbacks (Phoenix, 1998)
Atlanta Braves (1966)
Chicago Cubs (1903)
Cincinnati Reds (1866)
Colorado Rockies (1993, Denver)
Florida Marlins (1993, Miami)
Houston Astros (1964)
Los Angeles Dodgers (1958)
Milwaukee Brewers (1970; switched from American
League, 1998)
Montreal Expos (1969)
New York Mets (1962, New York City)
Philadelphia Phillies (1883)
Pittsburgh Pirates (1887)
St. Louis Cardinals (1900)
San Diego Padres (1969)
San Francisco Giants (1958)

## COMPETITORS

| | |
|---|---|
| FIFA | PGA Tour |
| NASCAR | PGA |
| NBA | World Wrestling |
| NFL | Federation |
| NHL | |

## HISTORICAL FINANCIALS & EMPLOYEES

| Association<br>FYE: October 31 | Annual<br>Growth | 10/91 | 10/92 | 10/93 | 10/94 | 10/95 | 10/96 | 10/97 | 10/98 | 10/99 | 10/00 |
|---|---|---|---|---|---|---|---|---|---|---|---|
| Sales ($ mil.) | 8.4% | — | 1,663 | 1,775 | 1,134 | 1,411 | 1,847 | 2,216 | 3,174 | 2,838 | 3,178 |
| Employees | 7.5% | — | — | 150 | 150 | 170 | 200 | 200 | — | — | — |

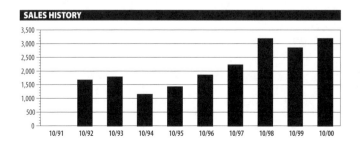

SALES HISTORY

MAJOR LEAGUE BASEBALL

# MARITZ INC.

OVERVIEW

Organizing trips, making employees happy and productive, and collecting data are all in a day's work for Maritz (pronounced "mer-its"). The company, which is headquartered in Fenton, Missouri, has 240 offices in North America and Europe and operates in three areas: travel services, performance improvement, and marketing services. It co-owns (with TUI Business Travel and Internet Travel Group) TQ3 Travel Solutions, the largest travel firm in Europe and a leading global agency with about 1,300 offices in more than 50 countries.

The company's employee motivation and incentive programs help clients improve workforce quality and customer satisfaction. Its

customers include a majority of the *Forbes* 500. Maritz is also one of the largest custom market research providers in the US, specializing in telecommunications and automotive research, and it provides syndicated buyer research services and conducts consumer surveys (Maritz Polls).

Facing heat from online incentive programs, the company launched its own online service, e-Maritz, in 2000. It also started Heybridge, an e-commerce subsidiary that helps small and midsized businesses sell over the Internet. In 2001 it purchased online learning company Librix Learning.

The Maritz family owns the company.

## HISTORY

Edward Maritz, an entrepreneur of Swiss-French descent, founded the E. Maritz Jewelry Manufacturing Company in St. Louis in 1894. By 1900 the wholesaler and manufacturer of men's and women's jewelry was supplying retail jewelers across the South and West. By 1921 Maritz had become a major importer of Swiss watches, which it sold to retail jewelers under the Merit, Cymrex, and Record brands. In the 1920s the company added diamond jewelry and silverware to its product mix. Edward Maritz died in 1929.

To drum up new business during the Depression, Edward's son James began trying to sell watches and jewelry to large corporations for use as sales and service awards, pioneering the incentive market. The first sale for a nationwide employee incentive campaign was to Caradine Hat, a St. Louis hatmaker, in 1930. In 1948 Maritz handled a $2 million incentive program for Chevrolet.

In 1950 the Maritz family split the business into two operations. Brother Lloyd handled the jewelry business (it died in 1955 when Lloyd died); James took over the incentive operations, which flourished. In the 1950s James expanded his company's offerings to include merchandise awards, and in 1958, travel incentive awards (arranged through the newly acquired Holiday House Travel Center of Detroit). The enterprise adopted the corporate name Maritz Inc. in 1961. During the 1960s and early 1970s, Maritz made a series of acquisitions closely allied with its motivation endeavors, including Lee Creative Research, the nucleus of what would become its market research operations (1973). The organization expanded internationally with the opening of Maritz offices in the UK and Mexico in 1974.

In 1980 the company acquired the Wilding division of Bell & Howell (now ProQuest), which it merged with another unit to form Maritz Communications. James died in 1981. Maritz beefed up its travel operations in the 1980s, acquiring corporate travel agency Traveler's Service (St. Louis, 1981), Byfield Travel (Chicago, 1984), Beverly Hills Travel (Los Angeles, 1986), and Travel Counselors International (Virginia, 1986).

After a family boardroom tussle in 1993, William Maritz expanded his control by buying out his sister's 50% stake in the company and putting his two sons on the board. His son Stephen Maritz subsequently took over as president. Maritz acquired The Research Business Group, the UK's largest independently owned marketing research firm (1993), and BLC, the largest performance-improvement company in France (1994). In 1997 the company established an office in Manila, its first in Asia.

In 1998 William Maritz stepped down as CEO and retained the title of chairman; his son Stephen succeeded him. In 1998 and 1999 the company boosted its international presence with acquisitions in Canada (group travel firm Partners in Performance, marketing research firm Thompson Lightstone & Co.) and the Netherlands (Maritz B.V.). Facing competition from online incentive programs, Maritz announced the launch of its own, e-Maritz, in 2000. It also started Heybridge, an e-commerce subsidiary.

In 2001, in an attempt to broaden the scope of its e-learning offerings, the company purchased Librix Learning. Also that year the company joined with Germany's TUI Business Travel and Australia's Internet Travel Group to form global travel firm TQ3 Travel Solutions.

**President and CEO:** W. Stephen Maritz
**SEVP and CFO:** James W. Kienker
**SEVP and Director Corporate Communications:**
Norman L. Schwesig
**SVP:** Jeffrey D. Reinberg
**SVP Human Resources:** Terry L. Goring
**President and COO, eMaritz:** Brian Fitzpatrick
**COO, Heybridge:** Andrew Hodges
**VP, Maritz Europa:** John R. Chalker

## LOCATIONS

**HQ:** 1375 N. Highway Dr., Fenton, MO 63099
**Phone:** 636-827-4000     **Fax:** 636-827-3312
**Web:** www.maritz.com

Maritz operates 240 offices in Canada, France, Germany,
Italy, Mexico, the Netherlands, Spain, the UK, and the US.

## PRODUCTS/OPERATIONS

**Services**
Marketing Research
    Custom marketing research
    Customer satisfaction and customer value analysis
    Data collection (focus groups, telephone interviews)
    Maritz Polls and Maritz Research Reports
    Syndicated buyer research
    Telecommunications research
Performance Improvement
    Communications
    e-Learning
    Fulfillment
    Internet consulting
    Loyalty marketing
    Measurement and feedback
    Rewards and recognition
Travel
    Consulting services
    Corporate travel management
    Group travel services
    Travel award programs

## COMPETITORS

| | |
|---|---|
| ACNielsen | J.D. Power |
| American Express | JTB |
| Carlson | Navigant International |
| Franklin Covey | NFO WorldGroup |
| Gallup | Opinion Research |
| Harris Interactive | Rosenbluth International |
| IMS Health | Thomas Cook AG |
| Information Resources | WorldTravel |

## HISTORICAL FINANCIALS & EMPLOYEES

| Private<br>FYE: March 31 | Annual<br>Growth | 3/92 | 3/93 | 3/94 | 3/95 | 3/96 | 3/97 | 3/98 | 3/99 | 3/00 | 3/01 |
|---|---|---|---|---|---|---|---|---|---|---|---|
| Sales ($ mil.) | 1.3% | 1,173 | 1,260 | 1,442 | 1,078 | 1,795 | 2,010 | 2,170 | 2,200 | 1,325 | 1,318 |
| Employees | 0.4% | — | 6,000 | 6,080 | 6,410 | 7,000 | 7,500 | 6,500 | 6,500 | 6,500 | 6,200 |

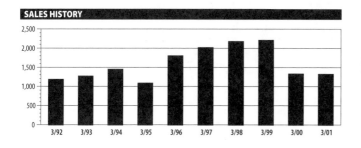

SALES HISTORY

# MARK IV INDUSTRIES, INC.

## OVERVIEW

Mark IV Industries is after the aftermarket. The Amherst, New York-based company makes automotive power-transmission and fluid-handling products for aftermarket customers as well as OEMs. Automotive aftermarket products such as belts and hoses account for about 60% of sales. OEM products include engines, idlers, pulleys, water pumps, and intake manifolds. Mark IV's industrial division makes circulating liquid temperature control systems used to maintain control over the temperature of injection molding machines.

Since unloading its Purolator- and Facet-brand air- and fuel-filtration products, Mark IV has concentrated on divesting other product lines to further focus its product mix. The company has sold its Dayco Industrial Power Transmission (belts) unit to Carlisle Companies, and sold Dayco Industrial's fluid transfer and hydraulic hose unit to Parker Hannifin. European private equity firm BC Partners owns the company.

## HISTORY

Salvatore Alfiero and Clement Arrison founded Mark IV Homes in 1969 as a Pennsylvania-based maker of mobile homes. The two also invested in Glar-Ban International (glass instrument panels), which they used as a vehicle to buy other small manufacturers. Mark IV's mobile-home business prospered until recession caused a 30% sales slump in 1974.

In 1976 Alfiero and Arrison merged Glar-Ban with Mark IV, changed its name to Mark IV Industries, and moved the office to Williamsville, New York (and later to nearby Amherst). By 1981 the company had sold all of its mobile-home operations. Two years later it bought Protective Closures, at the time the US's #1 maker of plastic caps, seals, and plugs for use in manufacturing.

Over the next decade Alfiero's uncanny ability to find and nurture undervalued companies in niche markets led to strong growth. The company bought 40 firms between 1985 and 1991 and catapulted from sales of $39 million in 1985 to more than $1 billion in 1992. Acquisitions in this period included LFE (hydraulic equipment and environmental controls), Conrac (electronic displays), Eagle Signal Controls (traffic signals), and Cetec (audio equipment).

Alfiero used high-yield debt during the 1980s to finance a series of acquisitions, including Mark IV's biggest purchase, the 1988 acquisition of Armtek, an automotive products maker twice its size. Armtek's tire-making business was later sold for $575 million. The company's 1980s shopping spree left it with sizable debt, and Alfiero slowed acquisitions. During the 1990s the company gained from public demands for environmentally safer products, both in fluid-handling (vapor-recovery gasoline hoses) and mass transit operations.

In 1991 Mark IV bought Vapor (then the world's #1 maker of doors for trains and buses). By late 1994 Alfiero had reduced debt and

purchased Purolator Products (automotive and specialized filtration products), Citla (industrial and auto belts and hoses, Mexico), and Hevas (auto tubes and tube assemblies, Sweden). Mark IV added Bjorkmans (tubing, Sweden) and Tubi Speciali Auto (air-conditioning hose assemblies, Italy) in 1995. The following year it bought the Imperial Eastman division (hydraulic and industrial hoses) of Pullman Company.

From 1996 to 1998, the company underwent major restructuring. It sold Vapor, Interstate Highway Signs, its Professional Audio business, the Gulton (satellite data systems) and LFE (computer-based measurement and control systems) units, and Automatic Signal/Eagle Signal (traffic signals). It also closed some facilities, opened new ones, and announced the elimination of some 1,700 jobs. In 1999 Mark IV sold its Purolator automotive filtration business to Arvin Industries, then sold its other filtration businesses to CLARCOR. The company also added Italy-based Lombardini, a maker of diesel engines used in small cars and vans built for Europe's congested urban streets. Partially due to the completion of its restructuring, profits in fiscal 1999 were about half those in 1998.

The company was acquired in 2000 by European private equity firm BC Partners. Later in 2000 Mark IV bought Focon Electronic Systems AS, a Danish maker of railway passenger information systems. The next year Mark IV agreed to sell its Dayco industrial power transmission business (transmission belts and accessories) to Carlisle Companies. In October of 2001 Mark IV sold its Swan garden hose unit to Tekni-Plex, Inc. In December of that year Mark IV sold its Dayco Industrial fluid transfer and hydraulic hose unit to Parker Hannifin.

**President and COO:** William P. Montague
**CFO:** Mark G. Barberio
**SVP; President, Mark IV Automotive:** Kurt J. Johansson
**VP; President, Dayco Industrial Division:**
Richard F. Bing
**President, Transportation Products Group:**
David R. Oliver
**Manager, Human Resources:** Michelle Acquilina

## LOCATIONS

**HQ:** 501 John James Audubon Pkwy.,
Amherst, NY 14226
**Phone:** 716-689-4972      **Fax:** 716-689-6098
**Web:** www.mark-iv.com

Mark IV Industries operates 67 manufacturing plants, 41 distribution and sales facilities, and 13 technical centers in 40 countries.

## PRODUCTS/OPERATIONS

**Selected Automotive Products**

**Aftermarket Products**
Accessory belts
Fuel hoses
Heater hoses
Radiator hoses
Timing belts
Timing belt countershafts
Windshield-washer system hoses

**OEM Products**
Engine division
Air-intake systems (ducts, manifolds)
Belts (poly-rib, raw edge, timing)
Dampers for camshafts
Dampers for crankshafts
Idlers
Pulleys
Surge tanks
Tensioners
Thermostat housings
Water pumps
Platform division
Air-conditioner hose and hose assemblies
Brake-fluid tanks
Canisters, fuel lines, and vapor-recovery systems
Clips and quick connectors
Engine and transmission oil-cooling hose and hose
assemblies
Fuel systems and components
Fuel-filler assemblies
High-technology plastic systems
Noise tuning
Power-steering fluid tanks
Power-steering hoses and hose assemblies
Powertrain division
Continuously variable transmission
Engines (diesel and gasoline)

**Selected Industrial Product**

Circulating liquid temperature control systems

## COMPETITORS

| | |
|---|---|
| Applied Industrial | Robbins & Myers |
| Technologies | SPX |
| BorgWarner | Sun Hydraulics |
| Dana | Tekni-Plex |
| Dover | Tesma |
| Eaton | Tomkins |
| Goodyear | United Technologies |

## HISTORICAL FINANCIALS & EMPLOYEES

| Private<br>FYE: February 28 | Annual<br>Growth | 2/92 | 2/93 | 2/94 | 2/95 | 2/96 | 2/97 | 2/98 | 2/99 | 2/00 | 2/01 |
|---|---|---|---|---|---|---|---|---|---|---|---|
| Sales ($ mil.) | 6.4% | 1,146 | 1,222 | 1,244 | 1,603 | 2,089 | 2,076 | 2,210 | 1,949 | 1,994 | 2,000 |
| Employees | 3.0% | 11,900 | 11,800 | 12,500 | 16,200 | 16,000 | 15,800 | 17,000 | 17,000 | 15,600 | 15,500 |

### SALES HISTORY

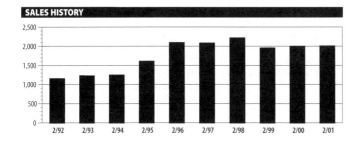

# THE MARMON GROUP, INC.

## OVERVIEW

"The more the merrier" could well be The Marmon Group's motto. A worldwide association of more than 100 manufacturing and service companies, Chicago-based Marmon is one of the largest private conglomerates in the US. Marmon units operate about 550 facilities in 50 countries. Each company works under its own management, and a small corporate office (fewer than 100 employees) oversees and pulls together the conglomerate, acting as combination CFO, tax lawyer, accountant, and broker to member companies.

Marmon companies make medical products, mining equipment, railway equipment, industrial materials and components, industrial and consumer products, transportation equipment, building and commercial products, and water-treatment products. Services include marketing and distribution, contract rail switching, and consumer credit information.

Marmon continues to grow through acquisitions, largely to complement existing businesses in fields such as retail display equipment, fasteners and metal products, and consumer credit information. Marmon is owned by Chicago's Pritzker family, which also owns the Hyatt hotel chain.

## HISTORY

Although the history of The Marmon Group officially begins in 1953, the company's roots are in the Chicago law firm Pritzker and Pritzker, started by Nicholas Pritzker in 1902. Through the firm, the family made connections with First National Bank of Chicago, which A. N. Pritzker, Nicholas' son, used to get a line of credit to buy real estate. By 1940 the firm had stopped accepting outside clients to concentrate on the family's growing investment portfolio.

In 1953 A. N.'s son Jay used his father's connections to get a loan to buy Colson Company, a small, money-losing manufacturer of bicycles, hospital equipment, and other products. Jay's brother, Robert, a graduate of the Illinois Institute of Technology, took charge of Colson and turned it around. Soon Jay began acquiring more companies for his brother to manage.

In 1963 the brothers paid $2.7 million for about 45% of the Marmon-Herrington Company (whose predecessor, Marmon Motor Car, built the car that in 1911 won the first Indianapolis 500). The family now had a name for its industrial holdings — The Marmon Group.

It became a public company in 1966 when it merged with door- and spring-maker Fenestra. However, Jay began to take greater control of the group through a series of stock purchases, and by 1971 The Marmon Group was private once again.

A year earlier the group had acquired a promising industrial pipe supplier, Keystone Tubular Service (which later became Marmon/Keystone). In 1973 Marmon began to acquire stock in Cerro Corp., which had operations in mining, manufacturing, trucking, and real estate; by 1976 the group had bought all of Cerro, thereby tripling its revenues. The brothers sold Cerro's trucking subsidiary, ICX, in 1977 and bought organ maker Hammond Corp., along with Wells Lamont, Hammond's glove-making subsidiary.

Marmon acquired conglomerate Trans Union in 1981. Trans Union brought many operations, including railcar and equipment leasing, credit information services, international trading, and water- and wastewater-treatment systems. Jay acquired Ticketmaster in 1982.

The Pritzkers made a foray into the airline business in 1984 by buying Braniff Airlines. After unsuccessfully bidding for Pan Am in 1987, they sold Braniff in 1988. Disappointments in other Pritzker businesses didn't slow Marmon, which added to its transportation equipment business in 1984 with Altamil, a maker of products for the trucking and aerospace industries.

In 1993 the Pritzkers sold 80% of Ticketmaster to Microsoft co-founder Paul Allen but retained a minority interest. Marmon sold Arzco Medical Systems in 1995.

The Anbuma purchase and Marmon/Keystone's 1997 acquisition of UK tube distributor Wheeler Group exemplify Marmon's practice of building strength through acquisitions in its established markets. In 1998 Marmon purchased more than 30 companies and opened a business development office in Beijing.

Marmon splashed out more than $500 million in 1999 to make 35 acquisitions, including Kerite (power cables), OsteoMed (specialty medical devices), and Bridport (medical and aviation products). Jay Pritzker died that year, and the company announced that his title of chairman will not be filled.

In 2000 Marmon spent another $500 million on more than 20 acquisitions, buying operations engaged in the production of retail display equipment, tank containers, and metal products, among others.

## OFFICERS

**President and CEO:** Robert A. Pritzker
**EVP and Treasurer:** Robert C. Gluth
**SVP, Secretary, and General Counsel:** Robert W. Webb
**SVP:** Henry J. West
**VP:** Mike Hartley
**VP:** David Robert
**President, Comtran:** John DeMarco
**Director Personnel:** Larry Rist
**Auditors:** Ernst & Young LLP

## LOCATIONS

**HQ:** 225 W. Washington St., Chicago, IL 60606
**Phone:** 312-372-9500    **Fax:** 312-845-5305
**Web:** www.marmon.com

The Marmon Group companies operate 550 facilities in 50 countries.

## PRODUCTS/OPERATIONS

### Selected Member Companies

**Automotive Equipment**
Fontaine Modification Co.
Marmon-Herrington Co.
Perfection HY-Test Co.

**Building Products and Fasteners**
Anderson Copper and Brass Co.
Atlas Bolt & Screw Company
Shepherd Products Inc.

**Casters**
Albion Industries, Inc.
Colson Caster Corporation

**Consumer Products, Marketing, and Financial Services**
Beijing Huilian Food Co., Ltd.
Getz Bros. & Co., Inc.
Wells Lamont Corporation

**Credit Data and Information Management**
Trans Union LLC

**Industrial Products**
Amarillo Gear Co.
Koehler-Bright Star, Inc.
Solidstate Controls, Inc.

**Medical Products**
American Medical Instruments, Inc.
B.G. Sulzle, Inc.
Medical Device Technologies, Inc. (MD Tech)
MicroAire Surgical Instruments, Inc.
Surgical Specialties Corporation

**Metal Products and Materials**
Cerro Copper Products Co.
Cerro Metal Products Co.
Penn Aluminum International, Inc.

**Pipe and Tube Distribution**
Marmon/Keystone Corporation
  Future Metals, Inc.
  Huron Steel Company, Inc.

**Railway and Transportation Services**
Exsif Worldwide, Inc.
Penn Machine Co.
Trackmobile, Inc.
Union Tank Car Co.

**Retail and Food-service Equipment**
L.A. Darling Co.
Store Opening Solutions, Inc.
Thorco Industries, Inc.

**Seat Belts and Cargo Restraints**
Am-Safe Inc.
Bridport Aviation

**Water Treatment Systems**
Ecodyne Limited
EcoWater Systems, Inc.
Spectrum Labs, Inc.

**Wire and Cable Products**
Cable USA, Inc.
Hendrix Wire & Cable, Inc.
Rockbestos-Surprenant Cable Corp.

## COMPETITORS

| | | |
|---|---|---|
| Alcatel | Illinois Tool | Superior |
| Balfour Beatty | Works | TeleCom |
| Cable Design | Ingersoll-Rand | Terex |
| Technologies | ITT Industries | TRW |
| Eaton | Masco | USG |
| Equifax | Pirelli S.p.A. | Wolverine Tube |
| GE | | |

## HISTORICAL FINANCIALS & EMPLOYEES

| Private<br>FYE: December 31 | Annual<br>Growth | 12/91 | 12/92 | 12/93 | 12/94 | 12/95 | 12/96 | 12/97 | 12/98 | 12/99 | 12/00 |
|---|---|---|---|---|---|---|---|---|---|---|---|
| Sales ($ mil.) | 6.8% | — | 4,008 | 4,319 | 5,302 | 6,083 | 5,776 | 6,003 | 6,032 | 6,530 | 6,786 |
| Net income ($ mil.) | 9.6% | — | 145 | 207 | 281 | 307 | 305 | 316 | 348 | 351 | 301 |
| Income as % of sales | — | — | 3.6% | 4.8% | 5.3% | 5.0% | 5.3% | 5.3% | 5.8% | 5.4% | 4.4% |
| Employees | 5.0% | — | 27,000 | 27,700 | 28,000 | 30,000 | 35,000 | 33,000 | 35,000 | 40,000 | 40,000 |

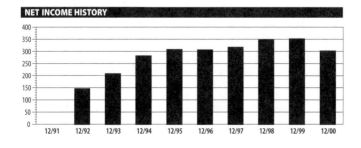

NET INCOME HISTORY

# MARS, INCORPORATED

Mars knows chocolate sales are nothing to snicker at. The McLean, Virginia-based company is the US's #2 candy maker, after Hershey, and one of the nation's largest private companies. Mars' products include M&M's, Snickers, 3 Musketeers, Dove, Milky Way, Skittles, Twix, and Starburst candies. In addition, the company offers ice-cream versions of several of its candy bars, Combos and Kudos snacks, Uncle Ben's rice (the leading branded rice), and pet food under the names Pedigree and Whiskas. It also manufactures drink vending machines,

electronic coin changers, bill acceptors, and other related equipment.

Although the company is surpassed in the US by Hershey, it is ahead of its rival internationally. Mars stays virtually debt-free and uses its profits for international expansion. It now sells its products in more than 100 countries on five continents.

Brothers Forrest Mars Jr. and president and CEO John Mars, along with their sister, VP Jacqueline Badger Mars, own the enterprise. The Mars family is one of the richest in the country.

## HISTORY

Frank Mars invented the Milky Way candy bar in 1923 after his previous three efforts at the candy business left him bankrupt. After his estranged son Forrest graduated from Yale, Mars hired him to work at his candy operation. When Forrest demanded control of one-third of the company and Frank refused, Forrest moved to England with the foreign rights to Milky Way and started his own company (Food Manufacturers) in the 1930s. He made a sweeter version of Milky Way for the UK, calling it a Mars bar. Forrest also ventured into pet food with the 1934 purchase of Chappel Brothers (renamed Pedigree). At one point he controlled 55% of the British pet food market.

During WWII Forrest returned to the US and introduced Uncle Ben's rice (the world's first brand-name raw commodity) and M&M's (a joint venture between Forrest and Bruce Murrie, son of the then-Hershey president). The idea for M&M's was borrowed from British Smarties, for which Forrest obtained rights (from Rowntree Mackintosh) by relinquishing similar rights to the Snickers bar in some foreign markets. The ad slogan "Melts in your mouth, not in your hand" (and the candy's success in non-air-conditioned stores and war zones) made the company an industry leader. Mars introduced M&M's Peanut in 1954. It was one of the first candy companies to sponsor a television show — *Howdy Doody* in the 1950s.

Forrest merged his firm with his deceased father's company in 1964, after buying his dying half-sister's controlling interest in the firm. (He renamed the business Mars at her request.) The merger was the end of an alliance with Hershey, who had supplied Frank with chocolate since his Milky Way inception.

In 1968 Mars bought Kal Kan. (The division now oversees all pet food operations.) In 1973 Forrest, then 69 years old, delegated his company responsibility to sons Forrest Jr. and

John. Five years later the brothers, looking for snacks to offset dwindling candy sales from a more diet-conscious America, bought the Twix chocolate-covered cookie brand. During the late 1980s they bought ice-cream bar maker Dove Bar International and Ethel M Chocolates, producer of liqueur-flavored chocolates, a business their father had begun in his retirement.

Hershey passed Mars as the US's largest candy maker in 1988 when it acquired Cadbury Schweppes' US division (Mounds and Almond Joy). While Hershey chose to stick close to home, Mars ventured abroad. The company entered the huge confectionery market of India in 1989 by building a $10 million factory there. In 1996 the company opened a confectionery processing plant in Brazil. To help improve sales back home, the company expanded on its popular Starburst candy line (1996) and in 1997 launched new ad campaigns, including M&M's spots featuring a trio of animated M&M candies. Mars breathed new life into its moribund market leader with the introduction of Uncle Ben's Rice Bowl frozen meals in the late 1990s.

Forrest Sr. died in July 1999, spurring rumors that Mars would go public or be sold. Instead, the company dismantled most of its sales force, opting to use less-costly food brokers for sales representation. Also in 1999, Forrest Mars Jr. retired from the company, leaving brother John Mars as president and CEO. Still far behind its rival, Mars received a modest boost in US market share when Hershey experienced computer troubles in late 1999.

In 2000 Mars established a subsidiary to manufacture and market Mars' product line in India. Mars announced in 2001 that it was buying French bank BNP Paribas Group's 56.4% stake in French pet food company Royal Canin for about $730 million, with further plans to take full control of Royal Canin by 2003.

---

**Chairman, President, and CEO:** John Franklyn Mars, age 65
**VP:** Jacqueline Badger Mars, age 62
**VP and Secretary:** D. M. Newby
**VP and Treasurer:** R. E. Barnes
**President, Masterfoods USA:** Paul S. Michaels

## LOCATIONS

**HQ:** 6885 Elm St., McLean, VA 22101
**Phone:** 703-821-4900      **Fax:** 703-448-9678
**Web:** www.mars.com

## PRODUCTS/OPERATIONS

**Selected Products**

**Candy**
3 Musketeers
Bounty
Dove
Ethel M Chocolates
Maltesers
M&M's
Mars
Milky Way
Opal Fruit
Revels
Skittles
Snickers
Starburst
Twix

**Ice-Cream Bars**
3 Musketeers
DoveBars
M&M Cookie Ice Cream
  Sandwiches
Milky Way
Snickers
Starburst Ice Bars

**Pet Food**
Bounce
Brekkies

Cesar
Chappie
Dine
Frolic
KiteKat
Loyal
My Dog
Pedigree
Sheba
Trill
Waltham
Whiskas

**Rice and Other Food and Drinks**
Dolmio sauces
Flavia drinks
Masterfoods condiments
  and sauces
Suzi Wan Chinese food
Uncle Ben's Rice

**Snacks**
Combos
Kudos

**Other Products**
Coin changers
Flavia (office beverage systems)
Klix (beverage vending equipment)
Lockets (medicated lozenges)
Smart card payment systems
Tunes (medicated lozenges)

**Selected Divisions**
Information Services International (information and
  systems technology for Mars units)
Masterfoods USA (US business units of M&M/Mars, Kal
  Kan, and Uncle Ben's)
MEI (electronic bill acceptors, coin changers, and card-
  based cashless payment systems)

## COMPETITORS

Cadbury Schweppes
Campbell Soup
Lindt & Sprungli
Colgate-Palmolive
ConAgra
Grupo Corvi
CSM
Doane Pet Care Company
Ezaki Glico
Ferrara Pan Candy
Ferrero
General Mills
Hershey

Heinz
Kraft Foods
Meiji Seika
Nestlé
Quaker Oats
Riceland Foods
Riviana Foods
Russell Stover
Thorntons
Tootsie Roll
Unilever
Wrigley

## HISTORICAL FINANCIALS & EMPLOYEES

| Private<br>FYE: December 31 | Annual<br>Growth | 12/91 | 12/92 | 12/93 | 12/94 | 12/95 | 12/96 | 12/97 | 12/98 | 12/99 | 12/00 |
|---|---|---|---|---|---|---|---|---|---|---|---|
| Estimated sales ($ mil.) | 2.3% | — | 12,500 | 13,000 | 12,500 | 13,000 | 13,000 | 15,000 | 15,000 | 15,000 | 15,000 |
| Employees | 0.9% | — | 28,000 | 27,000 | 28,000 | 28,000 | 28,000 | 28,500 | 30,000 | 28,500 | 30,000 |

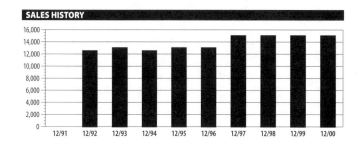

**SALES HISTORY**

# MARY KAY INC.

## OVERVIEW

Mary Kay promoted Girl Power before any of the Spice Girls were even born. The Addison, Texas based company, the US's #2 direct seller of beauty products (after Avon), aims to empower its primarily female employees through careers that allow them ample time for their families. Mary Kay sells more than 200 products in eight product categories: facial skin care, cosmetics, body care, nail care, men's skin care, fragrances, nutritional supplements, and sun protection. Some 800,000 direct-sales consultants demonstrate Mary Kay products in small group settings in the US and about 35 other countries. The US accounts for about 80% of sales.

Founded by a woman — Mary Kay Ash —

for women, Mary Kay has a largely female workforce. Although the company stands by Mary Kay's original goal of providing financial and career opportunities for women, men exert quite a bit of power at the company: Mary Kay's chairman and CEO (Ash's son Richard Rogers) and CFO are both men.

The company gives bonuses each year, ranging from jewelry to the company's trademark pink Cadillacs. During her lifetime, Ash was known for her religious nature as well as her generosity. She suffered a debilitating stroke in 1996 and died on Thanksgiving Day 2001. Her family owns most of the company.

## HISTORY

Before founding her own company in 1963, Mary Kay Ash worked as a Stanley Home Products sales representative. Impressed with the alligator handbag awarded to the top saleswoman at a Stanley convention, Ash was determined to win the next year's prize — and she did. Despite that accomplishment and having worked at Stanley for 11 years, a male assistant she had trained was made her boss after less than a year on the job. Tired of not receiving recognition, Ash and her second husband used their life savings ($5,000) to go into business for themselves. Although her husband died of a heart attack shortly before the business opened, Ash forged ahead with the help of her two grown sons.

She bought a cosmetics formula invented years earlier by a hide tanner. (The mixture was originally used to soften leather, but the tanner noticed how the formula made his hands look younger, and he began applying the mixture to his face, with great results.) Ash kept her first line simple — 10 products — and packaged her wares in pink to contrast with the typical black and red toiletry cases of the day. Ash also enlisted consultants, who held "beauty shows" with five or six women in attendance. Mary Kay grossed $198,000 in its first year.

The company introduced men's skin care products in 1965. Ash bought a pink Cadillac the following year and began awarding the cars as prizes three years later. (By 1981 orders were so large — almost 500 — that GM dubbed the color "Mary Kay Pink.")

Ash became a millionaire when her firm went public in 1968. Mary Kay grew steadily through the 1970s. Foreign operations began in 1971 in Australia, and over the next 25 years

the company entered 24 more countries, including nations in Asia, Europe, Central and South America, and the Pacific Rim.

Sales plunged in the early 1980s, along with the company's stock prices (from $40 to $9 between 1983 and 1985). Ash and her family reacquired Mary Kay in 1985 through a $375 million LBO. Burdened with debt, the firm lost money in the late 1980s. Mary Kay took a number of steps to boost sales and income, doing a makeover on the cosmetics line and advertising in women's magazines again (after a five-year hiatus) to counter its old-fashioned image. The company also introduced recyclable packaging. In 1989 Avon rebuffed a buyout offer by Mary Kay, and both companies halted animal testing.

Mary Kay introduced a bath and body product line in 1991, and its Skin Revival System, launched in 1993, raked in $80 million in its first six months on the market. It began operations in Russia that year; sales there reached $25 million by 1995. Ash suffered a debilitating stroke in 1996.

In 1998 the company began selling through retail outlets in China because of a government ban on direct selling. Changing with the times, Mary Kay added a white sport utility vehicle and new shades of pink to its fleet of 10,000 GM cars that year.

Chairman John Rochon was named CEO in 1999. Also in 1999 Mary Kay launched *Women & Success* (a magazine for consultants) and Atlas (its electronic ordering system).

In June 2001 Richard Rogers, Ash's son and the company chairman, replaced Rochon as CEO. Ash passed away on Thanksgiving Day 2001.

**Chairman and CEO:** Richard Rogers, age 58
**CFO:** David Holl
**EVP, Global Communications and Public Affairs:**
Russell Mack
**EVP, Global Product Technology:** Dennis Greaney
**EVP and Chief Scientific Officer:** Myra O. Barker
**SVP, Global Human Resources and US Branch**
**Operations:** Darrell Overcash
**SVP and Chief Information Officer:** Kregg Jodie
**President, US Sales:** Tom Whatley
**General Counsel:** Brad Glendening

## LOCATIONS

**HQ:** 16251 Dallas Pkwy., Addison, TX 75001
**Phone:** 972-687-6300    **Fax:** 972-687-1609
**Web:** www.marykay.com

Mary Kay employs about 800,000 direct-sales
consultants who sell the company's merchandise in 35
countries in Asia, Australia, Europe, North America, and
South America.

## PRODUCTS/OPERATIONS

**Selected Product Lines**
Body care
Cosmetics
Facial skin care
Fragrances
Men's skin care
Nail care
Nutritional supplements for men
Nutritional supplements for women
Sun protection

## COMPETITORS

Alberto-Culver
Allou
Alticor
Avon
BeautiControl Cosmetics
Body Shop
Clarins
Colgate-Palmolive
Coty
Del Labs
Dial
Estée Lauder
Helen of Troy
Herbalife
Intimate Brands
Johnson & Johnson
L'Oréal
Merle Norman
New Dana Perfumes
Nu Skin
Perrigo
Procter & Gamble
Reliv
Revlon
Schwarzkopf & DEP
Scott's Liquid Gold
Shaklee
Shiseido
Sunrider
Unilever
Wella

## HISTORICAL FINANCIALS & EMPLOYEES

| Private<br>FYE: December 31 | Annual<br>Growth | 12/91 | 12/92 | 12/93 | 12/94 | 12/95 | 12/96 | 12/97 | 12/98 | 12/99 | 12/00 |
|---|---|---|---|---|---|---|---|---|---|---|---|
| Sales ($ mil.) | 8.8% | — | 613 | 737 | 850 | 950 | 1,000 | 1,050 | 1,000 | 1,000 | 1,200 |
| Employees | 7.0% | — | 2,100 | 2,400 | 2,400 | 2,800 | 3,000 | 3,500 | 3,500 | 3,250 | 3,600 |

**SALES HISTORY**

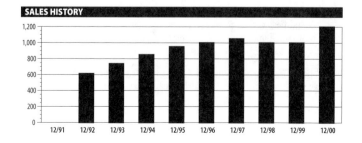

# MASHANTUCKET PEQUOT GAMING

Mashantucket Pequot Gaming Enterprise has taken the Mashantucket Pequot Tribal Nation (with roughly 600 members) from intense poverty to its position as the wealthiest Native American tribe in the US. It owns and operates Mashantucket, Connecticut-based Foxwoods Resort Casino, the largest casino in the world and, many believe, the most profitable. The complex offers more than 5,800 slot machines and 350 gaming tables in five casinos, three hotels (Grand Pequot Tower, Great Cedar Hotel, Two Trees Inn), about 25 restaurants, live entertainment, and a string of retail shops.

The Mashantucket Pequot reservation is a sovereign nation, and the Pequot tribe is not obligated to pay local property or business taxes, or reveal all of its finances. However, estimates of Foxwoods' annual revenues exceed $1 billion. The state of Connecticut receives 25% of the casino's slot machine revenues.

In addition to its gaming operations, the Mashantucket Pequot Tribal Nation owns Fox Navigation (high-speed ferry service) and the Pequot Pharmaceutical Network (mail-order and discount pharmaceuticals). It also owns three Connecticut hotels (Hilton Mystic, Norwich Inn & Spa, Randall's Ordinary Inn) and two golf courses (Foxwoods Golf & Country Club at Boulder Hills and Pequot Golf Club). The Mashantucket Pequot Tribal Nation has even established the Mashantucket Pequot Museum and Research Center dedicated to the tribe's life and history.

Two books released in 2000 and 2001, which questioned the authenticity of the Mashantucket Pequot tribe and claimed that the government was duped into giving them more land for their reservation than they were entitled to, sparked a series of lawsuits from neighboring communities.

## HISTORY

Once a powerful tribe, the Pequots were virtually wiped out in the 17th century by disease and attacks from colonists. More than 350 years later, Richard "Skip" Hayward, a pipefitter making $15,000 a year, led the fight for federal recognition of his nearly extinct Mashantucket Pequot tribe. He was elected tribal chairman in 1975, and the US government officially recognized the tribe in 1983.

The Indian Gaming Regulatory Act of 1988 opened the door for legal gambling on reservations, but tribes still had to negotiate with state governments for authorization. Hayward hired G. Michael "Mickey" Brown as a consultant and lawyer. Brown took the tribe's legal battle to the US Supreme Court, which eventually ruled that the Pequots could build a casino. When some 30 banks turned down the Pequots for a construction loan, Brown introduced Hayward and his tribe to Lim Goh Tong, billionaire developer of the successful Gentings Highlands Casino resort in Malaysia. Tong invested approximately $60 million, and the Foxwoods casino opened in 1992.

Brown brought in Alfred J. Luciani to serve as president and CEO of Foxwoods. Luciani stayed less than a year, however, resigning because of what he called philosophical differences with tribe leadership. Brown took over as CEO in 1993. Although Foxwoods grew rapidly, Brown often wrestled with members of the tribal council over how the business should be run. The next year Brown rehired Luciani to oversee the development of the Grand Pequot Tower hotel.

Brown resigned and Luciani was fired in 1997 after it was revealed that Brown had not fully disclosed his ties with Lim Goh Tong and that, in 1992, Luciani had accepted a $377,000 loan from Gamma International, a vendor that provided keno services to Foxwoods. The Pequots considered these actions to be conflicts of interest. A new management team was brought in, and Floyd "Bud" Celey, a veteran of Hilton Hotels, was appointed CEO.

The Pequots opened the Mashantucket Pequot Museum and Research Center in 1998. When tribal elections were held later that year, Kenneth Reels was elected chairman of the Pequot's tribal governing body, ousting Hayward from the position he had held for more than 20 years. Hayward was elected vice chairman. Mashantucket Pequot Gaming Enterprise concentrated on improving financial accountability in 1999, and the tribe began cutting costs by shuttering unprofitable holdings including Pequot River Shipworks, its shipbuilding business.

Former COO William Sherlock replaced Celey as CEO in 2000. That year the first of two books (the second was published in 2001) questioning the tribe's legitimacy created some controversy for the group. A federal audit in 2000 revealed that the tribe's pharmaceutical firm was giving discount drugs intended for Native Americans to its non-Native American employees.

## LOCATIONS

**HQ:** Mashantucket Pequot Gaming Enterprise Inc.
Rte. 2, Mashantucket, CT 06339
**Phone:** 860-312-3000 **Fax:** 860-312-1599
**Web:** www.foxwoods.com

The Mashantucket Pequot Tribal Nation has holdings in Connecticut and Rhode Island.

## PRODUCTS/OPERATIONS

**Selected Operations**
Foxwoods Resort Casino
 Foxwoods Golf & Country Club at Boulder Hills
 (Richmond, RI)
 Grand Pequot Tower
 Great Cedar Hotel
 Two Trees Inn

**Selected Mashantucket Pequot Tribal Nation Holdings**
Fox Navigation (ferry service)
Hilton Mystic (Mystic, CT)
Mashantucket Pequot Gaming Enterprise (Foxwoods
 Resort Casino; Ledyard, CT)
Mashantucket Pequot Museum and Research Center
 (Mashantucket, CT)
Norwich Inn & Spa (Norwich, CT)
Pequot Golf Club (Stonington, CT)
Pequot Pharmaceutical Network (mail-order and
 discount pharmaceuticals)
Randall's Ordinary Inn (North Stonington, CT)

## COMPETITORS

Aztar
Connecticut Lottery
Harrah's Entertainment
Mohegan Tribal Gaming
New York State Lottery
Park Place Entertainment
Sun International Hotels
Trump Hotels & Casinos

## HISTORICAL FINANCIALS & EMPLOYEES

| Private<br>FYE: September 30 | Annual<br>Growth | 9/91 | 9/92 | 9/93 | 9/94 | 9/95 | 9/96 | 9/97 | 9/98 | 9/99 | 9/00 |
|---|---|---|---|---|---|---|---|---|---|---|---|
| Estimated sales ($ mil.) | 3.8% | — | — | 1,000 | 1,000 | 1,030 | 1,100 | 1,000 | 1,000 | 1,200 | 1,300 |
| Employees | 4.8% | — | — | 9,100 | 10,000 | 11,000 | 12,000 | 11,180 | 11,500 | — | — |

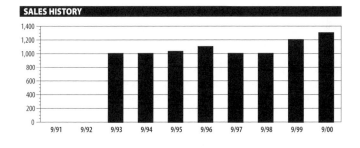

SALES HISTORY

# MASSACHUSETTS MUTUAL

## OVERVIEW

Like so many other large insurance firms, Massachusetts Mutual Life Insurance (Mass Mutual) is determined to transform into a financial services firm. However, you won't catch the Springfield-based firm issuing stock (which it hasn't done since 1866) to get the job done; the management of MassMutual has decided to keep things collective despite pressure from some policyholders.

Through more than 1,300 offices in the US, MassMutual primarily sells pension products and life and disability insurance. Its Financial Services Group offers retirement plans and annuities to individuals and businesses; it also includes The MassMutual Trust Company (private investment and trust services). Other units include OppenheimerFunds (mutual fund management), David L. Babson & Co. (individual and institutional investor services), and Cornerstone Real Estate (real estate equities).

MassMutual International is exporting the company's operations worldwide, with subsidiaries in Argentina, Bermuda, Chile, Hong Kong, Luxembourg, and Taiwan. It focuses on new product development (70% of sales come from products or channels developed within the last two years) and broadened distribution.

## HISTORY

Insurance agent George Rice formed Massachusetts Mutual in 1851 as a stock company based in Springfield. The firm converted to a mutual in 1867. For its first 50 years, MassMutual sold only individual life insurance, but after 1900 it branched out, offering first annuities (1917) and then disability coverage (1918).

The early 20th century was rough on MassMutual, which was forced to raise premiums on new policies during WWI, and then faced the high costs of the 1918 flu epidemic. The firm endured the Great Depression despite policy terminations, expanding its product line to include income insurance. In 1946 MassMutual wrote its first group policy, for Jack Daniel's maker Brown-Forman Distillers. By 1950 the company had diversified into medical insurance.

MassMutual began investing in stocks in the 1950s, switching from fixed-return bonds and mortgages for higher returns. It also decentralized and in 1961 began automating operations. By 1970 the firm had installed a computer network linking it to its independent agents. During this period, whole life insurance remained the core product.

With interest rates increasing during the late 1970s, many insurers diversified by offering high-yield products like guaranteed investment contracts funded by high-risk investments. MassMutual resisted as long as it could, but as interest rates soared to 20%, the company experienced a rash of policy loans, which led to a cash crunch. In 1981, with its policy growth rate trailing the industry norm, MassMutual developed new products, including UPDATE, which offered higher dividends in return for adjustable interest on policy loans.

In the 1980s MassMutual reduced its stock investment (to about 5% of total investments by 1987), allowing it to emerge virtually unscathed from the 1987 stock market crash.

The firm changed course in 1990 and entered financial services. It bought a controlling interest in mutual fund manager Oppenheimer Management. MassMutual announced in 1993 that, with legislation limiting rates, it would stop writing new individual and small-group policies in New York.

The next year the company targeted the neglected family-owned business niche; in 1995 it sponsored the American Alliance of Family-Owned Businesses and rolled out new whole life products aimed at this segment. That year it bought David L. Babson & Company, a Massachusetts-based investment management firm, and opened life insurance companies in Chile and Argentina.

In 1996 MassMutual merged with Connecticut Mutual. Still in the mood to merge, the company entered discussions with Northwestern Mutual in 1998, but culture clashes terminated the talks. Also that year the company helped push through legislation that would allow insurers to issue stock through mutual holding companies, a move which MassMutual itself contemplated in 1999.

MassMutual expanded outside the US at the turn of the century. In 1999 it issued securities in Europe, opened offices in such locales as Bermuda and Luxembourg, and bought the Argentine operations of Jefferson-Pilot. A year later it expanded into Asia when it bought Hong Kong-based CRC Protective Life Insurance (now MassMutual Asia). In 2001 the company entered the Taiwanese market, buying a stake in Mercuries Life Insurance (now MassMutual Mercuries Life Insurance) and acquired Japanese insurer Aetna Heiwa Life (a subsidiary of US health insurer Aetna).

**Chairman, President, and CEO:** Robert J. O'Connell
**EVP and CFO:** Howard E. Gunton
**EVP and Chief Information Officer:** Christine M. Modie
**EVP and Chief Investment Officer:** Stuart H. Reese
**EVP and General Counsel:** Lawrence V. Burkett Jr.
**EVP, Corporate Human Resources:** Susan A. Alfano
**EVP, Individual Life Business:** Matthew E. Winter
**EVP, Life Services/Annuities:** James E. Miller
**EVP, Retirement Services:** Frederick C. Castellani
**SVP, Corporate Communications:** Frances B. Emerson
**SVP, Mergers and Acquisitions:** Paul T. Pasteris
**SVP, Capital Markets & Treasury; President, Financial Products Division:** Toby J. Slodden
**SVP and Chief Compliance Officer:** Margaret Sperry
**SVP, Corporate Services:** Colin C. Collins
**SVP, Disability Income Business:** Richard L. Mucci
**SVP, Retirement Services:** E. Thomas Johnson Jr.
**SVP, Persumma:** J. Spencer Williams
**SVP, Large Corporate Markets:** Anne Melissa Dowling
**SVP, Retail Distribution:** Burvin E. Pugh
**SVP, Life Risk Management:** Theresa H. Forde
**Auditors:** PricewaterhouseCoopers LLP

# LOCATIONS

**HQ:** Massachusetts Mutual Life Insurance Company
1295 State St., Springfield, MA 01111
**Phone:** 413-788-8411    **Fax:** 413-744-6005
**Web:** www.massmutual.com

Massachusetts Mutual Life Insurance operates in
Argentina, Bermuda, Chile, Hong Kong, Luxembourg,
Taiwan, and the US.

# PRODUCTS/OPERATIONS

## 2000 Assets

|  | $ mil. | % of total |
|---|---|---|
| Cash & equivalents | 2,682 | 4 |
| Bonds | 26,152 | 35 |
| Stocks | 487 | 1 |
| Mortgage loans | 7,220 | 10 |
| Real estate | 2,017 | 3 |
| Policy loans | 5,901 | 8 |
| Other investments | 2,550 | 3 |
| Assets in separate account | 25,318 | 34 |
| Other assets | 1,412 | 2 |
| **Total** | **73,739** | **100** |

### Selected Subsidiaries
Antares Capital Corporation (commercial finance)
C.M. Life Insurance Company
Cornerstone Real Estate Advisers, Inc. (real estate equities)
David L. Babson and Company, Inc. (institutional investment services)
MassMutual International, Inc.
  MassLife Seguros de Vida S.A. (Argentina)
  MassMutual Asia (Hong Kong)
  MassMutual Mercuries Life Insurance (Taiwan; 38%)
  Vida Corp. S.A. (Chile)
MassMutual Trust Company, F.S.B.
MML Bay State Life Insurance Company
MML Investors Services, Inc.
OppenheimerFunds, Inc. (mutual funds)

# COMPETITORS

| | | |
|---|---|---|
| Allianz | FMR | Northwestern |
| Allstate | Guardian Life | Mutual |
| American | The Hartford | Principal |
| Financial | Jefferson-Pilot | Financial |
| American | John Hancock | Prudential |
| General | Financial | St. Paul |
| AIG | Services | Companies |
| AXA Financial | Liberty Mutual | State Farm |
| Charles Schwab | Mellon Financial | TIAA-CREF |
| CIGNA | Merrill Lynch | Torchmark |
| Citigroup | MetLife | UBS |
| CNA Financial | Nationwide | PaineWebber |
| Conseco | New York Life | |

# HISTORICAL FINANCIALS & EMPLOYEES

| Mutual company<br>FYE: December 31 | Annual<br>Growth | 12/91 | 12/92 | 12/93 | 12/94 | 12/95 | 12/96 | 12/97 | 12/98 | 12/99 | 12/00 |
|---|---|---|---|---|---|---|---|---|---|---|---|
| Assets ($ mil.) | 11.2% | — | 31,495 | 34,699 | 35,720 | 38,632 | 55,752 | 61,069 | 66,979 | 70,586 | 73,739 |
| Net income ($ mil.) | 26.1% | — | 116 | 139 | 93 | 159 | 239 | 262 | 359 | 441 | 740 |
| Income as % of assets | — | — | 0.4% | 0.4% | 0.3% | 0.4% | 0.4% | 0.4% | 0.5% | 0.6% | 1.0% |
| Employees | 0.7% | — | — | — | — | — | — | — | 7,885 | 7,900 | 8,000 |

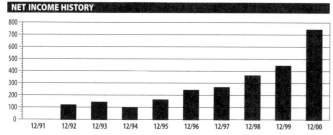

**NET INCOME HISTORY**

**2000 FISCAL YEAR-END**
Equity as % of assets: 5.2%
Return on assets: 1.0%
Return on equity: —
Long-term debt ($ mil.): —
Sales ($ mil.): 15,340

# MASTERCARD INTERNATIONAL

## OVERVIEW

MasterCard International (which plans to merge with European partner Europay) hopes to master the market, but it has a way to go: its approximately 25% share of the payments market is about half that of the leader, Visa. Based appropriately enough in Purchase, New York, MasterCard has cards for shoppers buying on credit (MasterCard) and for debt-shy consumers paying via debit (Maestro).

Under the current arrangement, the company is owned by the 20,000 financial institutions that issue its cards; it markets the brand, provides the transaction authorization network, and collects fees from members. Its cards are accepted at 21 million global locations.

Long considered more downmarket than Visa, MasterCard is working to add affluent users (the World MasterCard offers 24-hour concierge services). The company is working amid growing competition to make its electronic smart card (single-use or refillable chip-based cards used as cash) the industry standard through its 51%-owned subsidiary Mondex International.

MasterCard's quest for market share has led it to announce a merger with Europay, the company's European counterpart, of which it owns 12%. Under the plan, MasterCard will convert from a mutual to a private company with stock issued to member banks. After the merger, European members will own about one-third of the company, while non-Europeans will hold the rest. The new company, to be known as MasterCard Inc., will control the world's largest debit card network but still trail Visa in credit cards.

## HISTORY

A group of bankers formed The Interbank Card Association (ICA) in 1966 to establish authorization, clearing, and settlement procedures for bank credit card transactions. This was particularly important to banks left out of the rapidly growing BankAmericard (later Visa) network sponsored by Bank of America.

By 1969, ICA was issuing the Master Charge card throughout the US and had formed alliances in Europe and Japan. In the mid-1970s ICA modernized its system, replacing telephone transaction authorization with a computerized magnetic strip system. ICA had members in Africa, Australia, and Europe by 1979. That year the organization changed its name (and the card's) to MasterCard.

In 1980 Russell Hogg became president when John Reynolds resigned after disagreeing with the board over company performance and direction. Hogg made major organizational changes and consolidated data processing in St. Louis. MasterCard began offering debit cards in 1980 and traveler's checks in 1981.

MasterCard issued the first credit cards in China in 1987. The next year it bought Cirrus, then the world's largest ATM network. It also secured Eurocard (now Europay) to supervise MasterCard's European operations and help build the brand.

Hogg resigned in 1988 after disagreements with the board and was succeeded by Alex Hart. In 1991 the Maestro debit card was unveiled.

The 1990s were marked by trouble in Europe: The Europay pact hadn't resulted in the boom MasterCard had hoped for, customer service was below par, and competition was keen. Alex Hart retired in 1994 and was succeeded by Eugene Lockhart, who tackled the European woes. Lockhart considered ending the relationship but eventually worked things out with Europay. By the end of the decade, Europay was locked in a vicious battle to undercut Visa's market share through lower fees.

MasterCard in 1995 invested in UK-based Mondex International (now 51% owned by MasterCard International), maker of electronic, set-value, refillable smart cards. But US consumer resistance to cash cards and competition in the more advanced European market delayed growth in this area.

Lockhart resigned in 1997 and was succeeded by former head of overseas operations Robert Selander. The next year the Justice Department sued MasterCard and Visa for prohibiting member banks from issuing competing credit cards, such as American Express' Optima. That year MasterCard and Visa came under scrutiny for attempting to create a debit card industry monopoly.

Yet another management upheaval began in 1999 as the company moved to streamline its organizational structure and shift away from geographical divisions.

In 2000 the Justice Department charged MasterCard and Visa with antitrust practices stemming from the companies' cross-ownership structure and an alleged noncompetitive alliance between them. The next year a federal judge ordered the two companies to allow their member banks to issue rival credit cards, but the card firms are appealing.

**Chairman Emeritus:** Norman J. Tice, age 65
**Chairman:** Donald L. Boudreau
**President and CEO:** Robert W. Selander, age 51,
$2,700,000 pay
**President, Asia/Pacific Region:** André Sekulic
**President, Latin America/Caribbean Region:**
Jean F. Rozwadowski
**President, North American Region:** Ruth Ann Marshall
**President, MasterCard Canada:** Walter M. Macnee
**SEVP, Central Resources:** Christopher D. Thom,
$1,200,000 pay
**SEVP, Customer Group:** Alan J. Heuer, $1,375,000 pay
**SEVP, Global Technology and Operations:**
Jerry McElhatton, $1,300,000 pay
**EVP and CFO:** Denise K. Fletcher, age 52
**EVP and General Manager, Europe and Middle
East/Africa Region:** Donald L. VanStone
**EVP, Customer Group; Chairman and CEO, Cirrus
System:** G. Henry Mundt III
**EVP, Human Resources:** Michael W. Michl,
$755,000 pay
**SVP, Global Payment Solutions:** Steve L. Abrams
**SVP, Global e-Business:** Arthur D. Kranzley
**SVP, Global Sponsorships and Event Marketing:**
John Stuart
**SVP, Deposit Access Systems, North America Region:**
Dan Tuccillo
**Chief Marketing Officer:** Larry Flanagan
**Auditors:** PricewaterhouseCoopers LLP

## LOCATIONS

**HQ:** MasterCard International Incorporated
2000 Purchase St., Purchase, NY 10577
**Phone:** 914-249-2000      **Fax:** 914-249-4206
**Web:** www.mastercard.com

MasterCard International provides services in more than
210 countries.

## PRODUCTS/OPERATIONS

**Products**
Maestro (debit card)
MasterCard (credit card including standard, Gold,
Platinum, and World cards, as well as business,
business debit, corporate, corporate fleet, corporate
purchasing, and executive cards)
MasterCard Global Service (telephone services)
MasterCard Online Exclusives (online promotions for
cardholders)
MasterCard/Cirrus ATM network
Member Protection Program
Mondex (chip-based electronic cash card)

## COMPETITORS

American Express
Morgan Stanley Dean
Witter
Visa

## HISTORICAL FINANCIALS & EMPLOYEES

| Private<br>FYE: December 31 | Annual<br>Growth | 12/91 | 12/92 | 12/93 | 12/94 | 12/95 | 12/96 | 12/97 | 12/98 | 12/99 | 12/00 |
|---|---|---|---|---|---|---|---|---|---|---|---|
| Sales ($ mil.) | 16.9% | — | 451 | 540 | 665 | 816 | 946 | 1,090 | 1,257 | 1,389 | 1,571 |
| Net income ($ mil.) | 46.8% | — | — | — | 12 | 21 | 71 | 40 | 57 | 86 | 118 |
| Income as % of sales | — | — | — | — | 1.8% | 2.6% | 7.6% | 3.6% | 4.6% | 6.2% | 7.5% |
| Employees | 13.2% | — | — | 1,300 | 1,975 | 2,000 | 2,025 | 2,357 | 2,400 | 2,700 | 3,100 |

### NET INCOME HISTORY

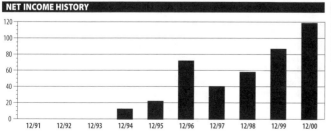

### 2000 FISCAL YEAR-END

Debt ratio: 15.2%
Return on equity: 29.4%
Cash ($ mil.): 193
Current ratio: 1.75
Long-term debt ($ mil.): 83

# MAYO FOUNDATION

OVERVIEW

Mayo can whip up a medical miracle. Rochester, Minnesota-based Mayo Foundation manages the Mayo Clinic, the world-famous private medical facility. Its multidisciplinary approach to care attracts some 500,000 patients a year, including such notables as Ronald and Nancy Reagan and the late King Hussein of Jordan. Affluent patients who can pay — well — for treatment (and who may contribute to the endowment) help subsidize care for those who can't pay.

In addition to the Mayo Clinic, the foundation operates two other Rochester hospitals — Saint Marys and Rochester Methodist. It has clinics in Arizona and Florida and operates 13 hospitals in Iowa, Minnesota, and Wisconsin. At the University of Minnesota, the foundation's education programs include the Mayo Graduate School of Medicine and the Mayo School of Health-Related Sciences.

With managed care limiting patients' ability to use its facilities, Mayo forms referral alliances with hospital groups, HMOs, and other groups. Its charter prevents it from raising prices to compensate for rising health care costs, so the foundation commercializes medical technology, publishes medical literature, and invests in other medical startups to increase income.

HISTORY

In 1845 William Mayo came to the US from England. He was a doctor, veterinarian, river boatman, surveyor, and newspaper editor before settling in Rochester, Minnesota, in 1863.

When a tornado struck Rochester in 1883, Mayo took charge of a makeshift hospital. The Sisters of St. Francis offered to replace the hospital that was lost in the disaster if Mayo would head the staff. He agreed reluctantly. Not only were hospitals then associated with the poor and insane, but his affiliation with the sisters raised eyebrows among Protestants and Catholics.

Saint Marys Hospital opened in 1889. Mayo's sons William and Charles, who were starting their medical careers, helped him. After the elder Mayo retired, the sons ran the hospital. Although the brothers accepted all medical cases, they made the hospital self-sufficient, attracting paying patients by pioneering in specialization at a time when physicians were jacks-of-all-medical-trades.

This specialization attracted other physicians, and by 1907 the practice was known as "the Mayo's clinic." The brothers, in association with the University of Minnesota, established the Mayo Foundation for Medical Research (now the Mayo Graduate School of Medicine), the world's first program to train medical specialists, in 1915.

In 1919 the brothers transferred the clinic properties and miscellaneous financial assets, primarily from patient care profits, into the Mayo Properties Association (renamed the Mayo Foundation in 1964). Under the terms of the endowment, all Mayo Clinic medical staff members became salaried employees. In 1933 the clinic established one of the first blood banks in the US. Both brothers died in 1939.

Part of the association's mission was to fund research. In 1950 two Mayo researchers won a Nobel prize for developing cortisone to treat rheumatoid arthritis. The foundation opened its second medical school, the Mayo Medical School, in 1972.

As insurers in the 1980s pressured to cut hospital admissions and stays, the foundation diversified with for-profit ventures. In 1983 Mayo began publishing the *Mayo Clinic Health Letter,* its first subscription publication for a general audience, and the *Mayo Clinic Family Health Book*. It also began providing specialized lab services to other doctors and hospitals. The addition of Rochester Methodist Hospital (creating the largest not-for-profit medical group in the country) was also a response to financial pressures. Following the money south as affluent folks retired, the foundation opened clinics in Jacksonville (1986); Scottsdale, Arizona (1987); and in nearby Phoenix (1998).

Seeking to expand in its home market, Mayo in 1992 formed the Mayo Health System, a regional network of health care facilities and medical practices. In 1996 former patient Barbara Woodward Lips left $127.9 million to the foundation, the largest bequest in its history.

In the late 1990s the foundation increasingly looked to corporate partnerships to help defray costs and to expand research activities. In 1998 and 1999 Mayo boosted its presence overseas with nonmedical regional offices. Mayo scientists in 2000 announced they had regrown or repaired nerve coverings in mice; this type of damage in humans (caused by such conditions as multiple sclerosis) had been considered irreparable.

**Chairman, Mayo Foundation:** Francis D. Fergusson,
age 56
**President and CEO, Mayo Foundation:** Michael B. Wood
**CFO and Treasurer, Mayo Foundation:** David R. Ebel
**VP and Director for Education:**
Richard M. Weinshilboum
**VP and Chief Administrative Officer:** John H. Herrell,
age 60
**Chief Development Officer:** David W. Lawrence
**Secretary:** Robert K. Smoldt
**General Counsel:** Jill A. Beed
**Chair, Board of Governors, Mayo Clinic Jacksonville:**
Leo F. Black
**Chair, Board of Governors, Mayo Clinic Rochester:**
Robert R. Hattery
**Chair, Board of Governors, Mayo Clinic Scottsdale:**
Michael B. O'Sullivan
**Chair, Human Resources:** Marita Heller

## LOCATIONS

**HQ:** 200 1st St. SW, Rochester, MN 55905
**Phone:** 507-284-2511      **Fax:** 507-284-0161
**Web:** www.mayo.edu

The Mayo Foundation operates facilities in Rochester,
Minnesota; Jacksonville; and Phoenix and Scottsdale,
Arizona, along with a network of community health care
providers in Iowa, Minnesota, and Wisconsin.

## PRODUCTS/OPERATIONS

**2000 Sales**

|  | $ mil. | % of total |
|---|---|---|
| Medical services | 3,054 | 82 |
| Grants & contracts | 141 | 4 |
| Premiums | 134 | 4 |
| Investments | 111 | 3 |
| Other | 270 | 7 |
| **Total** | **3,710** | **100** |

**Principal Divisions**
Charter House, Rochester (Minnesota, retirement
community)
Mayo Clinic Hospital, Phoenix
Mayo Clinic Jacksonville
Mayo Clinic Rochester
Mayo Clinic Scottsdale (Arizona)
Mayo Health System (network of clinics and hospitals in
Iowa, Minnesota, and Wisconsin)
Rochester Methodist Hospital
Saint Marys Hospital, Rochester
St. Luke's Hospital, Jacksonville

**Selected Mayo Publications**

**Publications for Patients**
*Inside Mayo Clinic* (Rochester)
*The Mayo Checkup* (Jacksonville)
*Mayo Clinic Family Health Book*
*Mayo Clinic Guide to Self-Care*
*Mayo Clinic Health Letter*
*Mayo Clinic Heart Book*
*Mayo Clinic on Arthritis*
*Mayo Clinic on High Blood Pressure*
*The Mayo Clinic Williams-Sonoma Cookbook*
*Mayo Clinic Women's HealthSource*

## COMPETITORS

| | |
|---|---|
| Allina Health | Memorial Sloan-Kettering |
| Ascension | Methodist Health Care |
| Catholic Health Initiatives | New York City Health and |
| Catholic Healthcare | Hospitals |
| Partners | Rush System for Health |
| Detroit Medical Center | Scripps |
| HCA | SSM Health Care |
| HMA | Tenet Healthcare |
| HEALTHSOUTH | Trinity Health |
| Henry Ford Health System | Universal Health Services |
| Johns Hopkins Medicine | |

## HISTORICAL FINANCIALS & EMPLOYEES

| Not-for-profit FYE: December 31 | Annual Growth | 12/91 | 12/92 | 12/93 | 12/94 | 12/95 | 12/96 | 12/97 | 12/98 | 12/99 | 12/00 |
|---|---|---|---|---|---|---|---|---|---|---|---|
| Sales ($ mil.) | 12.1% | — | 1,490 | 1,579 | 1,873 | 2,189 | 2,348 | 2,566 | 2,370 | 2,750 | 3,710 |
| Employees | 9.9% | — | 20,615 | 21,770 | 21,856 | 25,433 | 28,671 | 30,497 | 32,531 | 41,265 | 44,000 |

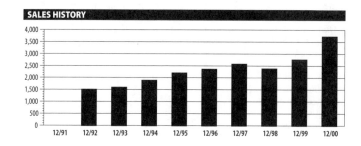

SALES HISTORY

# MCKINSEY & COMPANY

Even the best and the brightest have to hustle at McKinsey & Company. McKinsey, one of the world's leading management consultant firms, is based in New York City and has 84 offices in 43 countries. Distinguished alumni include American Express chairman and CEO Harvey Golub, IBM chairman and CEO Louis Gerstner, and former CBS chairman and CEO Michael Jordan.

The Firm (as it is known to insiders) provides services in strategy, organization, corporate finance, and marketing, among other areas. It also is beefing up its capabilities in information technology, an area on which the consulting industry is increasingly focused. Its customers are mostly private companies, but

McKinsey also serves government organizations, foundations, and associations.

McKinsey's cachet comes from its devotion to the bottom line, meticulous data-gathering, discretion, and a carefully cultivated mystique. Its partners must survive a rigorous up-or-out weeding process in which failure to advance to higher levels means dismissal. The economic downturn has taken its toll on the consulting industry, and McKinsey has found itself competing fiercely with other firms for fewer clients and having more consultants on its hands (employees are staying put instead of leaving for Internet startups and venture capital firms). McKinsey is owned by its partners and led by managing director Rajat Gupta.

## HISTORY

McKinsey & Company was founded in Chicago in 1926 by University of Chicago accounting professor James McKinsey. The company evolved from an auditing practice of McKinsey and his partners, Marvin Bower and A. T. Kearney, who began analyzing business and industry and offering advice. McKinsey died in 1937; two years later, Bower, who headed the New York office, and Kearney, in Chicago, split the firm. Kearney renamed the Chicago office A. T. Kearney & Co., and Bower kept the McKinsey name and built up a practice structured like a law firm.

Bower focused on the big picture instead of on specific operating problems, helping boost billings to $2 million by 1950. He hired staff straight out of prestigious business schools, reinforcing the firm's theoretical bent. Bower implemented a competitive up-or-out policy requiring employees who are not continually promoted to leave the firm. Only 20% of associates become partners.

Before becoming president in 1953, Dwight Eisenhower asked McKinsey to find out exactly what the government did.

By 1959 Bower had opened an office in London, followed by others in Amsterdam; Dusseldorf, Germany; Melbourne; Paris; and Zurich. In 1964 the company founded management journal *The McKinsey Quarterly*. When Bower retired in 1967, sales were $20 million, and McKinsey was the #1 management consulting firm. During the 1970s it faced competition from firms with newer approaches and lost market share. In response, then-managing director Ronald Daniel started specialty practices and expanded foreign operations.

The consulting boom of the 1980s was

spurred by mergers and buyouts. By 1988 the firm had 1,800 consultants, sales were $620 million, and 50% of billings came from overseas.

The recession of the early 1990s hit white-collar workers, including consultants. McKinsey, scrambling to upgrade its technical side, bought Information Consulting Group (ICG), its first acquisition. But the corporate cultures did not meld, and most ICG people left by 1993.

In 1994 the company elected its first managing director of non-European descent, Indian-born Rajat Gupta.

Two years later the traditionally hush-hush firm found itself at the center of that most public 1990s arena, the sexual discrimination lawsuit. A female ex-consultant in Texas sued, claiming McKinsey had sabotaged her career (the case was dismissed).

In 1998 McKinsey partnered with Northwestern University and the University of Pennsylvania to establish a world-class business school in India. The following year graduating seniors surveyed in Europe, the UK, and the US named the company as their ideal employer.

Also in 1999 the company created @McKinsey to help "accelerate" Internet startups. The next year it increased salaries and offered incentives to compete with Internet firms for employees. In 2001 the company expanded its branding business with the acquisition of Envision, a Chicago-based brand consultant.

**Managing Director:** Rajat Gupta
**CFO:** Donna Rosenwasser
**Senior Partner, Global Strategies Group:**
  Lowell L. Bryan
**Director Communications:** Stuart Flack
**Director Personnel:** Jerome Vascellaro

## LOCATIONS

**HQ:** 55 E. 52nd St., New York, NY 10022
**Phone:** 212-446-7000       **Fax:** 212-446-8575
**Web:** www.mckinsey.com

McKinsey & Company has 84 offices in 43 countries.

## PRODUCTS/OPERATIONS

**Selected Areas of Practice**
Automotive
Banking and securities
Chemicals
Consumer industries and packaged goods
Corporate finance
Corporate strategy
High tech
Insurance
Marketing
Operational effectiveness
Payors and providers
Pharmaceuticals and medical products
Pulp and paper
Retail
Telecommunications
Travel and logistics

## COMPETITORS

Accenture
Arthur D. Little
A.T. Kearney
Bain & Company
Booz-Allen
Boston Consulting
Computer Sciences
Deloitte Touche Tohmatsu
Ernst & Young
Grant Thornton International
IBM
KPMG
Marsh & McLennan
Perot Systems
PricewaterhouseCoopers
Towers Perrin

## HISTORICAL FINANCIALS & EMPLOYEES

| Private<br>FYE: December 31 | Annual<br>Growth | 12/91 | 12/92 | 12/93 | 12/94 | 12/95 | 12/96 | 12/97 | 12/98 | 12/99 | 12/00 |
|---|---|---|---|---|---|---|---|---|---|---|---|
| Sales ($ mil.) | 13.6% | — | 1,230 | 1,300 | 1,500 | 1,800 | 2,100 | 2,200 | 2,500 | 2,900 | 3,400 |
| Employees | 11.4% | — | 5,500 | 5,560 | 6,000 | 6,050 | 7,100 | 8,500 | 10,000 | 10,500 | 13,000 |

### SALES HISTORY

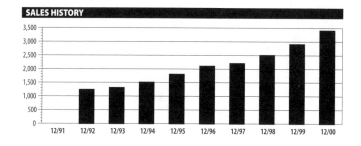

McKinsey&Company, Inc.

# MEIJER, INC.

## OVERVIEW

After "behemoth: something of monstrous size or power," the dictionary might add, "example — a Meijer store." Grand Rapids, Michigan-based Meijer (pronounced "Meyer") has about 150 combination grocery and general merchandise stores averaging 200,000 to 250,000 sq. ft. (about the size of four regular grocery stores), mostly in Michigan but also in Illinois, Indiana, Kentucky, and Ohio.

Although the discount superstore format is most often referred to in conjunction with

Wal-Mart, Meijer is its pioneer. In addition to selling groceries, including private-label products, typical Meijer stores have about 40 departments, such as a bakery, bank, pharmacy, photo lab, and food court; sections selling hardware, electronics, toys, apparel, and shoes; and pet and garden centers. Most stores also sell gasoline and have multiple in-store restaurants, and some have liquor licenses.

The Meijer family owns the company.

## HISTORY

Dutch immigrant and barber Hendrik Meijer owned a vacant space next to his barbershop in Greenville, Michigan. Because of the Depression, he couldn't rent it out. So in 1934 he bought $338.76 in merchandise on credit and started his own grocery store, Thrift Market, with the help of his wife, Gezina; son, Fred; and daughter, Johanna; he made $7 the first day. Meijer had 22 competitors in Greenville alone, but his dedication to low prices (he and Fred often traveled long distances to find bargains) attracted customers. In 1935, to encourage self-service, Meijer placed 12 wicker baskets at the front of the store and posted signs that read, "Take a basket. Help yourself."

A second store was opened in 1942. The company added four more in the 1950s. In 1962 Meijer — then with 14 stores — opened the first one-stop shopping Meijer Thrifty Acres store, similar to a hypermarket another operator had opened in Belgium a year earlier. By 1964, the year that Hendrik died and Fred took over, three of these general merchandise stores were operating. The company entered Ohio in the late 1960s.

Many Meijer stores were equipped with gasoline pumps in the late 1970s. However, a 1978 law prohibiting the sale of gasoline and alcohol at the same site forced the company to separate the two operations.

In the early 1980s Meijer bought 14 Twin Fair stores in Ohio, 10 of which were in Cincinnati, but it sold the stores by 1987 after disappointing results. Meijer had greater success in Columbus, Ohio, where it opened one store that year and immediately captured 20% of the market. In 1988 the company began keeping most stores open 24 hours a day.

Meijer annihilated competitors in Dayton, Ohio, in 1991, when it opened four stores that year. The company entered the Toledo market in 1993 with four stores; after one year it had

taken 11.5% of the market. A foray into the membership warehouse market was abandoned in 1993, just a few months after they had opened, when Meijer said it would close all seven SourceClubs in Michigan and Ohio.

The company entered Indiana in 1994, opening 16 stores in less than two years; it also reached an agreement with McDonald's to open restaurants in several stores. The first labor strike in Meijer's history hit four stores in Toledo that year, leading to pickets at 14 others. Union officials accused the company of using intimidation tactics by its hiring of large, uniformed men in flak jackets and combat boots as security guards. After nine weeks Meijer agreed to recognize the workers' newly attained union affiliation.

In 1995 the company opened 13 stores, including its first in Illinois. It reentered Cincinnati market in 1996, announcing the opening of two new stores there by mailing 80,000 videos to residents. By the end of the year, Meijer had a total of five stores in Cincinnati and had entered Kentucky.

Meijer opened a central kitchen in Indiana to prepare deli salads and some vegetables and process orange juice for its stores in 1997. It opened its first two stores in Louisville, Kentucky, the following year. Meijer broke into the tough Chicago-area market with its first store in 1999.

The next year Meijer opened several "village-style" stores — scaled-down versions (about 155,000 sq. ft.) of its larger stores. Later in 2000 Meijer unveiled what it claims is the largest superstore in North America. The 255,000-sq.-ft. behemoth (compared to a Wal-Mart Supercenter, which averages about 183,106 sq. ft.) features a gourmet coffee shop, a card shop, a bank open seven days a week, and restaurants serving pizza and sushi.

**Chairman Emeritus:** Fred Meijer
**Co-Chairman:** Doug Meijer
**Co-Chairman:** Hendrik G. Meijer, age 48
**President and CEO:** Jim McLean
**SVP, Finance and Administration, and CFO:** Jim Walsh
**SVP, Public & Consumer Affairs:** Brian Breslin
**SVP, Human Resources:** Wendell Ray
**Director of Corporate Relations:** John Zimmerman

## LOCATIONS

**HQ:** 2929 Walker Ave. NW, Grand Rapids, MI 49544
**Phone:** 616-453-6711     **Fax:** 616-791-2572
**Web:** www.meijer.com

### 2001 Stores

|  | No. |
|---|---|
| Michigan | 76 |
| Ohio | 35 |
| Indiana | 25 |
| Kentucky | 8 |
| Ohio | 5 |
| **Total** | **149** |

## PRODUCTS/OPERATIONS

**Selected Meijer Store Departments**

| | |
|---|---|
| Apparel | Jewelry |
| Auto supplies | Lawn and garden |
| Bakery | Music |
| Banking | Nutrition products |
| Books | Paint |
| Bulk foods | Pets and pet supplies |
| Coffee shop | Pharmacy |
| Computer software | Photo lab |
| Dairy | Portrait studio |
| Delicatessen | Produce |
| Electronics | Service meat and seafood |
| Floral | Small appliances |
| Food court | Soup and salad bar |
| Gas station | Sporting goods |
| Hardware | Tobacco |
| Health and beauty | Toys |
| products | Wall coverings |
| Home fashions | Wine |

## COMPETITORS

| | |
|---|---|
| Albertson's | Kroger |
| ALDI | Marsh Supermarkets |
| Ames | Penn Traffic |
| CVS | Phar-Mor |
| D&W Food Centers | Roundy's |
| Dollar General | Schnuck Markets |
| Dominick's | Schottenstein Stores |
| Eagle Food | Spartan Stores |
| Family Dollar Stores | SUPERVALU |
| Fleming Companies | Target |
| A&P | Value City |
| Home Depot | Walgreen |
| IGA | Wal-Mart |
| Kmart | Winn-Dixie |

## HISTORICAL FINANCIALS & EMPLOYEES

| Private<br>FYE: January 31 | Annual<br>Growth | 1/92 | 1/93 | 1/94 | 1/95 | 1/96 | 1/97 | 1/98 | 1/99 | 1/00 | 1/01 |
|---|---|---|---|---|---|---|---|---|---|---|---|
| Sales ($ mil.) | 7.2% | 5,370 | 5,390 | 4,250 | 5,160 | 5,640 | 6,000 | 6,900 | 8,300 | 9,500 | 10,000 |
| Employees | 5.4% | 50,000 | 60,000 | 65,000 | 70,000 | 65,000 | 73,000 | 77,000 | 80,000 | 80,000 | 80,000 |

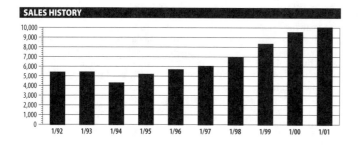

SALES HISTORY

# MENARD, INC.

If sticks and stones break bones, what can two-by-fours and 2-in. nails do? That is what Eau Claire, Wisconsin-based Menard is wondering now that its biggest rivals (#1 home improvement giant The Home Depot and #2 Lowe's) are hammering away at its home turf. The third-largest home improvement chain in the US, Menard has more than 150 stores in nine midwestern states.

Although its outlets are typically smaller than those of Home Depot, the stores offer a similar selection of products by building large warehouses adjacent to stores and then quickly restocking merchandise when it's sold. Products include lumber, building materials, tools, and hardware, all laid out on easy-to-reach, supermarket-styled shelves. That shopper-friendly approach has helped it find a niche with consumers scared away by large warehouse retailers. To help keep expenses low and prices cheap, Menard makes some of its merchandise, including picnic tables and doors.

Billionaire founder John Menard owns and runs the chain; other family members are engaged in its everyday operations. John Menard also owns an Indy car-racing team.

## HISTORY

John Menard was the oldest of eight children on a Wisconsin dairy farm. To pay for attending the University of Wisconsin at Eau Claire, he and some fellow college students built pole barns in the late 1950s. Learning that other builders had trouble finding lumber outlets open on the weekends, Menard began buying wood in bulk and selling it to them. He added other supplies in 1960 and sold his construction business in 1970 as building supply revenues became his chief source of income.

He founded Menard in 1972 as the do-it-yourself craze was beginning, but he wanted an operation run more like mass merchandiser Target, with easy-to-reach shelves, wide aisles, and tile floors rather than the cold, cumbersome layout used by lumberyards. To realize that concept, Menard built warehouses and stockrooms behind the stores so he could restock merchandise quickly.

Menard's vision worked, and he began building his midwestern empire, often acquiring abandoned retail sites that were inexpensive and in good locations. By 1986 Menard was in Iowa, Minnesota, North and South Dakota, and Wisconsin, and by 1990 it had 46 stores. In the early 1990s Menard began enlarging its operations to serve the ever-growing number of stores, opening a huge warehouse and distribution center and a manufacturing facility that made doors, Formica countertops, and other products. It entered Nebraska in 1990 and opened its first store in Chicago the next year. By 1992 there were more than 60 stores.

That year Menard made *The National Enquirer* with a story about the firing of a store manager who had built a wheelchair-accessible home for his 11-year-old daughter who had spina bifida, violating a company theft-prevention policy forbidding store managers to build their own homes. The company insisted that the man was fired in part because of poor work performance.

Menard continued to expand to new areas, operating stores in Indiana and Michigan by 1992. As it continued expanding in the Chicago area, it offered varying store formats, ranging from a full line of building materials to smaller Menards Hardware Plus stores. By 1994 Menard had 85 stores, many bigger than 100,000 sq. ft.

In 1995 and 1996 the company was plagued with lawsuits filed by customers charging false arrest and imprisonment for shoplifting. An on-duty police officer apprehending a shoplifting suspect at a store was even stopped and searched.

Competition also heated up then. The Home Depot's push into the Midwest — including opening several stores directly across the street from Menard — spurred Menard to fight back by lowering prices and opening nearly 40 stores. The fight forced smaller chains like Handy Andy out of business.

In 1997 Menard and his company were fined $1.7 million after dumping bags of toxic ash from its manufacturing facility at residential trash pick-up sites rather than at properly regulated outlets (it had been fined for similar violations in 1989 and 1994). In response to a price war initiated by Home Depot, in 1998 Menard dropped sales prices by 10%.

The following year competitor Lowe's began moving into Menard's biggest market, Chicago. Menard began opening larger stores in 2000 (about 162,000 sq. ft., or some 74,000 sq. ft. bigger than the older stores). In 2001 it began beefing up its lines of home appliances, adding more washers, dryers, dishwashers, refrigerators, and ranges.

## OFFICERS

**President and CEO:** John R. Menard
**CFO and Treasurer:** Earl R. Rasmussen
**Operations Manager:** Larry Menard
**Director of Human Resources:** Terri Jain
**Senior Merchandiser:** Ed Archibald
**General Counsel:** Dawn M. Sands

## LOCATIONS

**HQ:** 4777 Menard Dr., Eau Claire, WI 54703
**Phone:** 715-876-5911  **Fax:** 715-876-2868

Menard owns home improvement stores in Illinois,
Indiana, Iowa, Michigan, Minnesota, Nebraska, North
Dakota, South Dakota, and Wisconsin.

## PRODUCTS/OPERATIONS

**Operations**
Menards (home improvement stores)
Midwest Manufacturing and Distributing (product
  manufacturing and distribution)

**Selected Menards Departments**
Appliances
Building materials
Electrical (wiring, lighting)
Floor coverings
Hardware
Lumberyard
Millwork (doors, cabinetry, molding)
Plumbing
Seasonal (Christmas, lawn and garden)
Tools
Wall coverings (wallpaper, paint)

## COMPETITORS

84 Lumber
Ace Hardware
Carolina Holdings
Carter Lumber
Do it Best
Fastenal
Home Depot
Lanoga
Lowe's
Payless Cashways
Primus
Sears
Seigle's Home and Building Centers
Sherwin-Williams
Sutherland Lumber
TruServ
Wal-Mart
Wickes
Wolohan Lumber

## HISTORICAL FINANCIALS & EMPLOYEES

| Private<br>FYE: January 31 | Annual<br>Growth | 1/92 | 1/93 | 1/94 | 1/95 | 1/96 | 1/97 | 1/98 | 1/99 | 1/00 | 1/01 |
|---|---|---|---|---|---|---|---|---|---|---|---|
| Estimated sales ($ mil.) | 17.2% | — | 1,400 | 1,750 | 2,300 | 2,700 | 3,200 | 3,700 | 4,000 | 4,500 | 5,000 |
| Employees | 6.2% | — | — | 5,000 | 5,800 | 6,534 | 7,000 | 7,000 | 7,000 | 7,000 | 7,600 |

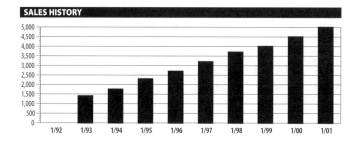

SALES HISTORY

# METROMEDIA COMPANY

## OVERVIEW

Metromedia has a large stake in steak with a variety of trimmings: restaurants, telecommunications, and energy firms. Billionaire investors John Kluge and Stuart Subotnick run the East Rutherford, New Jersey-based company through a partnership.

Metromedia is the franchisor for three of the nation's best-known steak houses: Bonanza, Ponderosa Steakhouse, and Steak and Ale, as well as the Bennigan's pub-style restaurant chain. Under the Metromedia Restaurant Group

banner, the company has some 1,000 restaurants in the US and overseas.

One of the nation's largest private companies, Metromedia also owns controlling interests in telecom firms Metromedia International Group, which has holdings in eastern Europe and former Soviet republics, Metromedia Fiber Network, and energy broker Metromedia Energy (formerly CPM Energy).

## HISTORY

German immigrant John Kluge, born in 1914, came to Detroit at age eight with his mother and stepfather. He later worked at the Ford assembly line. At Columbia University he studied economics and (to the chagrin of college administrators) poker, building a tidy sum with his winnings by graduation. Kluge worked in Army intelligence during WWII. After the war he bought WGAY radio in Silver Spring, Maryland, and went on to buy and sell other small radio stations.

Kluge began to diversify, entering the wholesale food business in the mid-1950s. In 1959 he purchased control of Metropolitan Broadcasting, including TV stations in New York and Washington, and took it public. He renamed the company Metromedia in 1960.

Metromedia added independent stations — to the then-legal limit of seven — in other major markets, paying relatively little compared to network affiliate prices. The stations struggled through years of infomercials but thrived in the late 1970s and early 1980s. Metromedia's stock price rose from $4.50 in 1974 to more than $500 in 1983. The company also acquired radio stations, the Harlem Globetrotters, and the Ice Capades.

In 1983 Kluge bought paging and cellular telephone licenses across the US. He later acquired long-distance carriers in Texas and Florida. In 1984 Metromedia went private in a $1.6 billion buyout and began to sell off its assets in 1985. It sold its Boston TV station to Hearst and its six other TV stations to Rupert Murdoch for a total of $2 billion. In 1986 it sold its outdoor advertising firm, nine of its 11 radio stations, and the Globetrotters and Ice Capades. Kluge then sold most of the company's cellular properties to SBC Communications. In 1990 it sold its New York cellular operations to LIN Broadcasting and its Philadelphia cellular operations to Comcast.

Building what Kluge envisioned as his steak

house empire, the firm bought the Ponderosa steak house chain (founded in the late 1960s) in 1988 from Asher Edelman and later added Dallas-based USA Cafes (Bonanza steak houses, founded 1964) and S&A Restaurant Corp. (Steak and Ale, founded 1966; Bennigan's, founded 1976). Also in 1988 Kluge rescued friend Arthur Krim, whose Orion Pictures was threatened by Viacom, by buying control of the filmmaker.

Kluge's grand steak house vision did not come to fruition. Increased competition squeezed profits at Ponderosa and Bonanza. The restaurant group also was plagued by management shakeups, aging facilities, food-quality issues, and even bad press. (Bennigan's was ranked the worst casual dining chain in the US in a 1992 Consumer Reports poll.)

In 1989 Kluge merged Metromedia Long Distance with the long-distance operations of ITT. Renamed Metromedia Communications in 1991, the company merged with other long-distance providers to become MCI WorldCom. (Kluge sold his 16% of MCI WorldCom to the public in 1995.)

Kluge created Metromedia International Group in 1995 by merging Orion Pictures, Metromedia International Telecommunications, MCEG Sterling (film and television production), and Actava Group (maker of Snapper lawn mowers and sporting goods). Metromedia Restaurant Group announced a $190 million refinancing agreement for S&A Restaurant Corp. in 1998 to expand and refurbish its restaurants; it closed 28 unprofitable restaurants that year and launched a franchise program to grow its Bennigan's and Steak and Ale chains.

Metromedia expanded its Bennigan's units in Korea in 1999 and the next year announced it would build 65 new restaurants in the US and expand to more than 200 units internationally.

**Chairman and President:** John W. Kluge, age 87
**EVP; President and CEO, Metromedia International Group:** Stuart Subotnick, age 59
**SVP Finance and Treasurer:** Robert A. Maresca
**SVP, Secretary, and General Counsel:** David A. Persing, age 43
**SVP; President, Kluge and Company:** Silvia Kessel, age 50
**VP and Controller:** David Gassler
**Director of Human Resources:** Jamie Smith-Wagner

## LOCATIONS

**HQ:** 1 Meadowlands Plaza, East Rutherford, NJ 07073
**Phone:** 201-531-8000     **Fax:** 201-531-2804
**Web:** www.metromediarestaurants.com

## PRODUCTS/OPERATIONS

**Selected Subsidiaries and Affiliates**
Metromedia Energy (energy and long-distance telephone service)
Metromedia Fiber Network, Inc. (competitive local-exchange carrier)
   AboveNet Communications, Inc. (data center operations)
   SiteSmith, Inc. (Internet infrastructure management services)
Metromedia International Group, Inc. (telecommunications)
   Snapper (power lawnmowers, lawn tractors, power tillers, snow throwers)
Metromedia Restaurant Group (Bennigan's, Bonanza, Ponderosa, Steak and Ale)

## COMPETITORS

Applebee's
AT&T
Brinker
BT
Buffets
Carlson Restaurants Worldwide
Darden Restaurants
Deutsche Telekom
Global TeleSystems
Hellenic Telecommunications
Level 3 Communications
Lone Star Steakhouse
O'Charley's
Outback Steakhouse
The Restaurant Company
Rostelecom
Ryan's Family Steak Houses
Sprint FON
Verizon
WorldCom
Worldwide Restaurant Concepts

## HISTORICAL FINANCIALS & EMPLOYEES

| Private<br>FYE: December 31 | Annual<br>Growth | 12/91 | 12/92 | 12/93 | 12/94 | 12/95 | 12/96 | 12/97 | 12/98 | 12/99 | 12/00 |
|---|---|---|---|---|---|---|---|---|---|---|---|
| Estimated sales ($ mil.) | (2.3%) | — | 1,804 | 1,900 | 2,000 | 1,900 | 1,900 | 1,950 | 1,500 | 1,610 | 1,500 |
| Employees | (22.3%) | — | — | — | — | — | — | 63,000 | 62,700 | 32,000 | 29,500 |

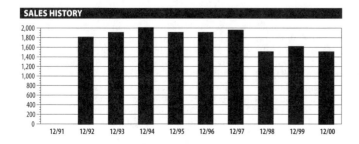

SALES HISTORY

# MTA

Getting around New York City is the goal of natives and tourists alike. Getting them around is the goal of the Metropolitan Transportation Authority (MTA), the largest provider of public transportation in the US.

Serving nearly 8 million people a day, New York City's MTA operates buses in all five boroughs (the Bronx, Brooklyn, Manhattan, Queens, and Staten Island), provides subway service to all but Staten Island, and operates the Staten Island Railway. The authority also provides bus and railway service to Connecticut and Long Island and maintains tunnels and toll bridges.

The MTA, a public-benefit corporation

chartered by the New York Legislature, is working to become more self-sufficient. It has cut expenses through more efficient administration and maintenance. The MTA has also automated electronic fare with its MetroCard and toll collection with E-Z Pass.

Meanwhile, the MTA continues improvements that give its growing ridership a rush. It has plans to establish a direct subway line to LaGuardia Airport as well as extend subway and rail lines into Manhattan's East Side. The MTA's free subway-to-bus transfers, volume discounts, and monthly passes have resulted in a lowering of the average fare for the first time in the subway's history.

## HISTORY

Mass transit began in New York City in the 1820s with the introduction of horse-drawn stagecoaches run by small private firms. By 1832 a horse-drawn railcar operating on Fourth Avenue offered a smoother and faster ride than its street-bound rivals.

By 1864 residents were complaining that horsecars and buses were overcrowded and that drivers were rude. (Horsecars were transporting 45 million passengers annually.) In 1870 a short subway under Broadway was opened, but it remained a mere amusement. Elevated steam railways were built, but people avoided them because of the smoke, noise, and danger from explosions. Cable cars arrived in the 1880s, and by the 1890s electric streetcars became important.

Construction of the first commercial subway line was completed in 1904. The line was operated by Interborough Rapid Transit (IRT), which leased the primary elevated rail line in 1903 and had effective control of rail transit in Manhattan and the Bronx. In 1905 IRT merged with the Metropolitan Street Railway, which ran most of the surface railways in Manhattan, giving the firm almost complete control of the city's rapid transit. Public protests led the city to grant licenses to Brooklyn Rapid Transit (later BMT), creating the Dual System.

By the 1920s the transit system was again in crisis, largely because the two lines were not allowed to raise their five-cent fares. With the IRT and BMT in receivership in 1932, the city decided to own and operate part of the rail system and organized the Independent (IND) rail line. Pressure for public ownership and operation of the transit system resulted in the city's purchase of all of IRT's and BMT's assets in 1940 for $326 million.

In 1953 the legislature created the New York City Transit Authority, the first unified system. In 1968, two years after striking transit workers left the city in a virtual gridlock, the Metropolitan Transit Authority began to coordinate the city's transit activities with other commuter services.

The 1970s and 1980s saw the city's transit infrastructure and service deteriorate as crime, accidents, and fares rose. But by the early 1990s a modernization program had begun to make improvements: Subway stations were repaired, graffiti was removed from trains, and service was extended. By 1994 the agency said subway crime was down 50% from 1990, and ridership had increased.

The MTA set up a five-year plan in 1995 to cut expenses by $3 billion. Only 18 months later and already two-thirds of the way to reaching the goal, the authority said it would cut another $230 million and return the savings to customers as fare discounts. The agency agreed in 1996 to sell Long Island Rail Road's freight operations.

In 1998 the MTA capital program completed the $200 million restoration of the Grand Central Terminal. The next year the MTA ordered 500 new clean-fuel buses. But the agency suffered a setback when New York State's $3.8 billion Transportation Infrastructure Bond Act, which included $1.6 billion for MTA improvements, was rejected by voters in 2000.

MTA subway lines in lower Manhattan suffered extensive damage from the September 11, 2001 terrorist attacks that destroyed the World Trade Center's twin towers. The attacks left the MTA (which was already seeking billions of dollars for improvements) with $530 million worth of damage.

## OFFICERS

**Chairman:** Peter S. Kalikow
**Vice Chairman:** David S. Mack
**Executive Director and Board Member:** Marc V. Shaw
**Deputy Executive Director Corporate Affairs and Communications:** Christopher P. Boylan
**Deputy Executive Director Operations and Chief of Staff:** Forrest R. Taylor
**President, MTA Bridges and Tunnels:** Michael C. Ascher
**President, MTA Long Island Bus:** Neil S. Yellin
**President, MTA Long Island Rail Road:** Kenneth J. Bauer
**President, MTA Metro-North Railroad:** Peter A. Cannito
**President, MTA New York City Transit:** Lawrence G. Reuter
**Director Budgets and Financial Management:** Gary G. Caplan
**Director Human Resources:** Dave Knapp
**Auditor General:** Nicholas DiMola
**Chief of Police:** James D. O'Donnell
**Auditors:** PricewaterhouseCoopers LLP

## LOCATIONS

**HQ:** Metropolitan Transportation Authority
347 Madison Ave., New York, NY 10017
**Phone:** 212-878-7000      **Fax:** 212-878-0186
**Web:** www.mta.nyc.ny.us

MTA New York City Transit operates buses in all five New York City boroughs and provides subway service to all but Staten Island. It also maintains seven bridges and two tunnels in New York City. The MTA Staten Island Railway extends from the Staten Island Ferry landing 14 miles south to Tottenville. MTA Metro-North Railroad has rail lines to outlying counties in New York and Connecticut. MTA Long Island Bus operates buses in Nassau, Queens, and Suffolk counties. MTA Long Island Rail Road has rail lines to Nassau and Suffolk counties.

## PRODUCTS/OPERATIONS

### 2000 Sales

|  | % of total |
|---|---|
| Operating revenues | 45 |
| State/regional taxes | 19 |
| Tolls | 14 |
| Local subsidies | 4 |
| State subsidies | 3 |
| Other | 15 |
| **Total** | **100** |

### Selected Operating Units

The Long Island Rail Road Company (MTA Long Island Rail Road)
Metro-North Commuter Railroad Company (MTA Metro-North Railroad)
Metropolitan Suburban Bus Authority (MTA Long Island Bus)
New York City Transit Authority (MTA New York City Transit)
Staten Island Rapid Transit Operating Authority (MTA Staten Island Railway)
Triborough Bridge and Tunnel Authority (MTA Bridges and Tunnels)

## COMPETITORS

Coach USA
Laidlaw
Amtrak
Port Authority of NY & NJ

## HISTORICAL FINANCIALS & EMPLOYEES

| Government-owned FYE: December 31 | Annual Growth | 12/91 | 12/92 | 12/93 | 12/94 | 12/95 | 12/96 | 12/97 | 12/98 | 12/99 | 12/00 |
|---|---|---|---|---|---|---|---|---|---|---|---|
| Sales ($ mil.) | (2.3%) | — | 4,845 | 5,036 | 5,189 | 5,005 | 5,381 | 5,511 | 5,707 | 5,590 | 4,033 |
| Net income ($ mil.) | — | — | (173) | (136) | (156) | (154) | 440 | (93) | (7) | (489) | (386) |
| Income as % of sales | — | — | — | — | — | — | 8.2% | — | — | — | — |
| Employees | (0.2%) | — | 63,868 | 64,838 | 65,465 | 58,201 | 56,551 | 57,563 | 57,551 | 58,000 | 62,800 |

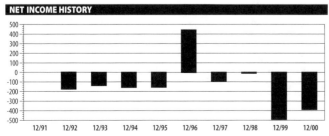

**NET INCOME HISTORY**

**2000 FISCAL YEAR-END**
Debt ratio: 46.9%
Return on equity: —
Cash ($ mil.): 66
Current ratio: 1.50
Long-term debt ($ mil.): 13,995

# MICRO ELECTRONICS, INC.

## OVERVIEW

"We're not greedy," says Micro Electronics co-founder and president John Baker. "We don't need it all" — just a healthy chunk of the computer, software, and peripheral sales market.

Hilliard, Ohio-based Micro Electronics, which operates nearly 20 Micro Center chain stores, has declared itself a leader by means of its "technical retailing" concept. Micro Center is the largest of Micro Electronics' divisions. Its stores (average 45,000 sq. ft.) carry about 36,000 products in 700 different categories. Store departments include books, education, Macintosh products, mobile computing, name brand systems, private-label computers (under the WinBook and PowerSpec brands), peripherals, and software. The company typically locates its stores in major cities with high-tech centers, office complexes, and universities.

Micro Center's technical retailing strategy includes intensive training for salespeople.

Customer surveys helped the company create its version of a computer department store (featuring a dozen departments divided by business and home, education, and entertainment interests), which consistently wins industry accolades.

Other Micro Electronics divisions include MEI-Micro Center (the company's mail-order operation) and Micro Center Computer Education (which has taught hundreds of thousands of students everything from general computing to programming and support). The company is selling its corporate sales unit.

Baker, who owns the company with other private investors, has been approached to sell Micro Electronics or take it public, but he has refused because of his belief in his long-term business plan.

## HISTORY

John Baker had studied agricultural economics, taken pharmacy classes, and worked in the insurance business before becoming interested in computers in 1976, when he read an article about microcomputing. Determined to learn more, he took a job at a Radio Shack store in Columbus, Ohio. By 1980 Baker was a store manager, but he was given a choice of quitting or being fired after a disagreement with the company over how to market computer equipment. That year he and another Radio Shack refugee, Bill Bayne, pooled their resources ($35,000) and opened the first Micro Center, in the same mall. The store was a success and within a few years had grown from 1,200 to 44,000 sq. ft. The resulting company, Micro Electronics, soon added mail-order and manufacturing operations.

The company established its Corporate Sales Micro Center subsidiary in 1983 to provide hardware, software, and services to large purchasers such as corporations and institutions.

Early on Micro Electronics began making private-label computers, but it left the business in 1985 after having trouble with the FCC (which the company has not elaborated on). In 1986 Micro Center stores added a computer education department, which evolved into the company's Micro Center Computer Education unit. The company returned to the private-label market in 1987, making Laser brand computers.

By 1988 there were only two Micro Center stores, both in Ohio. Initially, Baker expanded the company slowly, insisting that the business

finance its growth internally, without significant debt. "What grows fast, dies fast," he has said. "We won't die fast."

Growth of Micro Electronics' retail operations picked up speed in the 1990s. In 1991 the company started conducting in-store customer surveys to help maximize sales through well-designed store layouts.

Micro Electronics opened a direct marketing unit in 1993 for its WinBook computers. The company's Laser Computer brand was replaced by the PowerSpec brand in 1994. Micro Center opened a store in Houston that year and one in Dallas the next.

Micro Electronics' sales topped $1 billion for the first time in 1996. That year the company moved to its new 200,000-sq.-ft. headquarters near Columbus, Ohio, and added its first store in the Chicago area. In 2000 the company agreed to sell its corporate sales business to SARCOM, a computer services company. That year Micro Electronics added digital imaging departments to all its stores.

**CEO:** Dale Brown
**President:** John Baker
**CFO:** James Koehler
**Director of Human Resources:** Deanna Lyon

## LOCATIONS

**HQ:** 4119 Leap Rd., Hilliard, OH 43026
**Phone:** 614-850-3000      **Fax:** 614-850-3001
**Web:** www.microelectronics.com

Micro Electronics operates 18 Micro Center stores in 12 states.

## PRODUCTS/OPERATIONS

**Selected Operations**
MEI-Micro Center
Micro Center
Micro Center Education
PowerSpec PC
Redemtech
WinBook Computer
  Corporation
WinBook Corporation

**Selected Products**
Accessories
Add-in boards and
  upgrades
Audio/speakers/music
Books
Computers
  Desktops
  Handhelds
  Notebooks
Consumer electronics
Digital image/scanners
Drives/data storage
Input devices
Media
Memory
Modems

Monitors
Networking
Paper supplies
Power protection
Print supplies
Printers
Software

**Micro Center Computer
Education Courses**
Accounting and finance
Databases
Desktop publishing and
  graphics
Integration
Internet
Macintosh computers
Microsoft certification
Novell networking
Operating systems and
  environments
PCs
Programming and support
Project management
Spreadsheets
Word processing

## COMPETITORS

Best Buy
BUY.COM
CDW Computer Centers
Circuit City
CompUSA
Cyberian Outpost
Dell Computer
Fry's Electronics
Gateway
Insight Enterprises

Micro Warehouse
Office Depot
OfficeMax
PC Connection
PC Mall
RadioShack
Staples
Systemax
Zones

## HISTORICAL FINANCIALS & EMPLOYEES

| Private<br>FYE: September 30 | Annual<br>Growth | 9/92 | 9/93 | 9/94 | 9/95 | 9/96 | 9/97 | 9/98 | 9/99 | 9/00 | 9/01 |
|---|---|---|---|---|---|---|---|---|---|---|---|
| Estimated sales ($ mil.) | 9.6% | 400 | 515 | 780 | 930 | 1,000 | 1,110 | 1,000 | 1,000 | 750 | 916 |
| Employees | 11.0% | 900 | 980 | 980 | 1,800 | 2,600 | 1,800 | 1,950 | 2,000 | 2,000 | 2,300 |

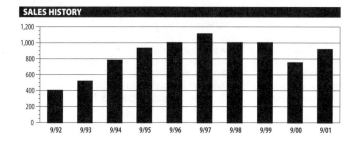

**SALES HISTORY**

míCRO CENTER

# MICRO WAREHOUSE, INC.

## OVERVIEW

You can walk through the aisles of Micro Warehouse without leaving home. The Norwalk, Connecticut-based firm sells more than 30,000 computer products mainly through its core catalogs (MacWAREHOUSE, MicroWAREHOUSE, DataCommWAREHOUSE, and Inmac), but also through specialty catalogs, its Web sites, and telemarketers. Each year Micro Warehouse distributes more than 120 million catalogs worldwide (the US represents nearly 75% of sales). Products include computers, hardware, software, networking equipment, accessories, and peripherals; customers include business, education, and government clients, as well as individuals (about 15% of sales).

Increased competition from manufacturers that market their products directly (such as Compaq, Dell, and Gateway) forced Micro Warehouse to restructure across the board. The company dumped unprofitable operations outside the US (including its European headquarters) and trimmed its workforce.

A group of investors including CEO Jerome York, Gary Wilson, and Freeman Spogli & Co. bought Micro Warehouse in early 2000.

## HISTORY

Peter Godfrey joined Robert Bartner in 1974 to run Fiona Press, an adult magazine publisher (sold to Paragon Publishing in 1992). In 1985 the two, with independent publisher Felix Dennis, founded *MacUser* magazine, which they sold to Ziff-Davis in 1986. The next year they founded Micro Warehouse and launched *MacWAREHOUSE* to sell Macintosh computer products.

The company expanded its mailing list by getting subscriber names from technical magazines and registered user names from its suppliers. In 1989 it added the *MicroWAREHOUSE* catalog for PC users. International expansion was key to growth in the early 1990s. Micro Warehouse established operations in the UK in 1991. The next year it went public and set up operations in France and Germany.

Micro Warehouse was distributing 30 million catalogs to almost 2 million customers by 1993. That year it introduced four specialty catalogs (DataCommWAREHOUSE, Micro SuppliesWAREHOUSE, Paper design-WAREHOUSE, and CD-ROM WAREHOUSE) and invested nearly $5 million in telemarketing and computer centers around the globe.

Bartner retired as chairman in 1994, and was replaced by CEO Godfrey. Micro Warehouse spent 1994 and the next year focused on balancing its Mac- and PC-related sales and expanding internationally. By 1994 the company had entered Canada, Japan, and Mexico. That year it added two more catalogs, *Micro SystemsWAREHOUSE* and *Home Computer-WAREHOUSE*. In 1995 it acquired Technomatic (UK), Mac Direct and Castle Computing (both in Australia), and Canada's Mac Store.

That year Micro Warehouse placed its catalog on the Web. The company also combined *CD-ROM WAREHOUSE, MacWAREHOUSE,* and *MicroWAREHOUSE* and launched *Mac SystemsWAREHOUSE.* It discontinued some specialty catalogs (including *Paper designWAREHOUSE*). Sales for 1995 increased almost 60% from 1994.

Micro Warehouse's 1996 acquisitions included computer networking retailer Inmac Corporation, Helsinki-based Business Forum, and Wintel (PC products based on Intel chips and Windows software) direct marketer USA Flex. That year the SEC began investigating alleged accounting irregularities, and CFO Steve Purcell and chief accounting officer Eric Furman resigned. The Inmac acquisition contributed to a dip in profits for 1996.

Godfrey had turned over the CEO reins to former Ingram Micro head Chip Lacy that year, but took over again in 1997 when Lacy resigned after clashing with board members over strategy. Also in 1997 the company bought software reseller Online Interactive and created a Web auction site. Late that year the company began a major restructuring that included closing some overseas facilities, selling some Mac-dependent operations, and closing its European headquarters in the UK. It took a $68 million charge and was left in the red for 1997.

In 1998 Micro Warehouse paid nearly $30 million to settle shareholder suits over the accounting irregularities from 1996. The company also cut its workforce by 14%. In 1999 the company shut down Webauction.com (online auctions) and Computersbynet.com (discount computers). The SEC also settled its case against Micro Warehouse, the company neither admitting nor denying allegations.

In early 2000 Godfrey resigned and a group of investors including Gary Wilson, Jerome York, and Freeman Spogli & Co. bought Micro Warehouse. York, formerly of International Business Machines and Chrysler, was appointed chairman, president, and CEO.

**Chairman, President, and CEO:** Jerome B. York, age 63
**CFO:** Laurie Schmalkuche
**EVP Operations:** Jeffrey Gentile
**VP Human Resources:** Michelle Visosky

## LOCATIONS

**HQ:** 535 Connecticut Ave., Norwalk, CT 06854
**Phone:** 203-899-4000    **Fax:** 203-899-4203
**Web:** www.warehouse.com

Micro Warehouse has operations in Canada, France, Germany, the Netherlands, Sweden, the UK, and the US.

## COMPETITORS

Apple Computer
ASI Corp.
Excite@Home
Best Buy
Beyond
Black Box
BUY.COM
CDW Computer Centers
Circuit City
Comark
Compaq
CompuCom
CompUSA
Computacenter
Cyberian Outpost
Dell Computer
Fry's Electronics
GameStop
Gateway
GTSI
Insight Enterprises
MCSi
Micro Electronics
Office Depot
OfficeMax
PC Connection
PC Mall
PC Warehouse
Provell
SARCOM
Software Spectrum
Systemax
Tech Data
Zones

## HISTORICAL FINANCIALS & EMPLOYEES

| Private<br>FYE: December 31 | Annual<br>Growth | 12/91 | 12/92 | 12/93 | 12/94 | 12/95 | 12/96 | 12/97 | 12/98 | 12/99 | 12/00 |
|---|---|---|---|---|---|---|---|---|---|---|---|
| Sales ($ mil.) | 32.7% | — | 270 | 450 | 776 | 1,308 | 1,916 | 2,126 | 2,220 | 2,400 | 2,600 |
| Employees | 19.5% | — | 721 | 1,496 | 2,300 | 3,100 | 3,481 | 4,133 | 3,595 | 3,200 | 3,000 |

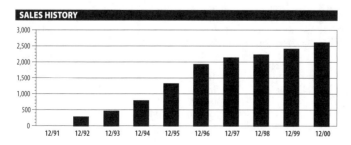

SALES HISTORY

MicroWAREHOUSE

# MIDAMERICAN ENERGY HOLDINGS

## OVERVIEW

MidAmerican Energy Holdings keeps roaming farther and farther from its California roots. The Des Moines, Iowa-based diversified energy company, which once focused on building and operating geothermal, hydroelectric, and natural gas power plants worldwide, now gets most of its revenues from its energy distribution operations.

Subsidiary MidAmerican Energy Company generates 4,500 MW of electricity (primarily from coal) and transmits and distributes it to about 670,000 customers in the midwestern US; it distributes natural gas to about 650,000 in the same region. It also sells wholesale energy to other utilities and marketers. Northern Electric, a UK regional electricity company, serves about 1.5 million electricity customers and about 470,000 gas customers; it also generates and markets electricity.

MidAmerican Energy Holdings' majority-owned residential real estate brokerage, HomeServices.Com, operates in 12 states. Subsidiary CalEnergy has 1,400 MW of capacity in independent power projects (mostly geothermal), as well as gas exploration and production operations, in Australia, Poland, the Philippines, the UK, and the US.

MidAmerican Energy Holdings was purchased by Warren Buffett's Berkshire Hathaway and other investors in 2000. Because of regulatory restrictions on utility ownership, Berkshire owns the majority of MidAmerican Energy Holdings' stock but has less than 10% of its voting control. Buffett business partner and Berkshire director Walter Scott controls a majority of MidAmerican Energy Holdings' voting rights.

## HISTORY

Amid oil shortages, polluted air, and concerns about the safety of nuclear power plants, Charles Condy formed California Energy in 1971 to sell oil and gas partnerships and to consult on the development of geothermal power plants.

In 1978 Congress passed the Public Utility Regulatory Policies Act (PURPA) to wean the US from foreign oil by encouraging efficient use of fossil fuels and development of renewable and alternative energy sources. Grasping the potential of the changing energy environment, CalEnergy signed a 30-year deal with the US government in 1979 to develop the geothermal Coso Project, northeast of Los Angeles. In the 1980s CalEnergy focused entirely on geothermal development and started producing power at the Coso Project in 1987, the year the company went public.

Omaha, Nebraska-based construction firm Peter Kiewit Sons' injected some much-needed capital when it began buying a stake in the company in 1990. CalEnergy restructured in 1991, moving its headquarters from San Francisco to Omaha. It also acquired Desert Peak and Roosevelt Hot Springs geothermal areas in the US and made plans to enter markets in Asia. In 1993 the Philippine government contracted CalEnergy to develop geothermal projects. CalEnergy also obtained the rights to exploit geothermal fields in Indonesia. In 1994 the company opened a geothermal plant in Yuma, Arizona.

In 1996 CalEnergy doubled its size by acquiring rival Magma Power, and it began geothermal projects in the Salton Sea and the Imperial Valley in California. It also took advantage of the growing deregulation trend in the UK by acquiring a controlling stake in Northern Electric, a major British regional electricity company with about 1.5 million customers in northeast England and Wales.

Completing its transformation into a global power player, CalEnergy acquired gas plants in Poland and Australia in 1997. It also attracted 300,000 new gas customers in the UK. The company bought back Kiewit's stake that year. In 1998 CalEnergy subsidiary CalEnergy International Ltd. was part of a consortium (the PowerBridge Group) that won a contract to develop, synchronize, and transmit up to 1,000 MW of electricity from Lithuania to Poland, at an estimated cost of $400 million.

The next year CalEnergy bought MidAmerican Energy Holdings, an electric utility, for about $2.4 billion. CalEnergy then took the MidAmerican name and moved its headquarters to Des Moines, Iowa. Subsidiary MidAmerican Realty Services went public as HomeServices.Com; MidAmerican Energy Holdings retained a majority stake. In 2000 Warren Buffett's Berkshire Hathaway led an investor group, which included MidAmerican Energy Holdings CEO David Sokol, in purchasing MidAmerican Energy Holdings for about $2 billion and $7 billion in assumed debt.

In 2001 MidAmerican Energy Holdings announced plans to buy out minority shareholders in HomeServices.Com.

Chairman and CEO: David L. Sokol, age 44
President and COO; CEO, Northern Electric and MidAmerican Energy: Gregory E. Abel, age 38
SVP and CFO: Patrick J. Goodman, age 34
SVP and Chief Administrative Officer: Keith D. Hartje, age 51
SVP Mergers and Acquisitions, General Counsel, and Secretary: Steven A. McArthur, age 43
VP Human Resources: Maureen Sammon
President and COO, MidAmerican Energy: Ronald W. Stepien, age 54
President and COO, Northern Electric: P. Eric Connor, age 52
Managing Director, CalEnergy Gas: Peter Youngs
Auditors: Deloitte & Touche LLP

## LOCATIONS

HQ: MidAmerican Energy Holdings Company
666 Grand Ave., Des Moines, IA 50309
Phone: 515-242-4300          Fax: 515-281-2389
Web: www.midamerican.com

MidAmerican Energy Holdings has energy operations in Illinois, Iowa, Nebraska, and South Dakota, and in Australia, the Philippines, Poland, and the UK.

## PRODUCTS/OPERATIONS

### 2000 Sales

|  | $ mil. | % of total |
|---|---|---|
| MidAmerican Energy Co. | 2,378 | 47 |
| Northern Electric | 2,017 | 39 |
| HomeServices.Com | 473 | 9 |
| CalEnergy | 244 | 5 |
| Adjustments | (9) | — |
| **Total** | **5,103** | **100** |

### Selected Subsidiaries

CalEnergy Company (power production facility development)
HomeServices.Com Inc. (83%, real estate brokerage)
MidAmerican Energy Company (electricity and natural gas distribution)
Northern Electric plc (electricity and natural gas distribution, UK)

## COMPETITORS

AES
Alliant Energy
Calpine
Dynegy
Edison International
El Paso
Enron
Entergy
International Power
Peoples Energy
Scottish and Southern Energy
Scottish Power
Trigen Energy
TXU Europe
UtiliCorp

## HISTORICAL FINANCIALS & EMPLOYEES

| Private<br>FYE: December 31 | Annual<br>Growth | 12/91 | 12/92 | 12/93 | 12/94 | 12/95 | 12/96 | 12/97 | 12/98 | 12/99 | 12/00 |
|---|---|---|---|---|---|---|---|---|---|---|---|
| Sales ($ mil.) | 60.3% | — | 117 | 132 | 155 | 355 | 519 | 2,166 | 2,555 | 4,399 | 5,103 |
| Net income ($ mil.) | 18.6% | — | 34 | 47 | 37 | 63 | 93 | (84) | 127 | 167 | 133 |
| Income as % of sales | — | — | 28.8% | 35.7% | 23.8% | 17.9% | 17.8% | — | 5.0% | 3.8% | 2.6% |
| Employees | 59.8% | — | 225 | 249 | 278 | 593 | 4,400 | 4,300 | 3,703 | 9,700 | 9,550 |

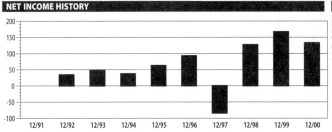

### NET INCOME HISTORY

### 2000 FISCAL YEAR-END

Debt ratio: 66.7%
Return on equity: 10.8
Cash ($ mil.): 38
Current ratio: 0.63
Long-term debt ($ mil.): 5,229

# MILLIKEN & COMPANY INC.

## OVERVIEW

From outer space to tennis courts, Milliken & Company is part of the fabric of society. The Spartanburg, South Carolina-based company is one of the world's largest textile manufacturers. Its more than 48,000 textile and chemical products include finished fabrics for space suits, rugs, and carpets, as well as woven and knitted fabrics used in automobiles, sails, tennis balls, and computer ribbons. Milliken's dyes infuse products such as Crayola crayons with color, its clarifying agents make plastics clear, and its chemicals help produce more durable car dashboards. The company has

about 1,300 patents and operates 65 facilities worldwide, including an extensive textile research center.

Milliken has introduced a new line of carpets (its largest product line ever). It is also expanding operations, in part with the addition of a manufacturing facility to produce plastic-clarifying agents.

Milliken has about 200 shareholders (mostly from the Milliken family), but brothers Roger and Gerrish Milliken control the company. Roger, a billionaire who supporters conservative causes, has led the company since 1947.

## HISTORY

Seth Milliken and William Deering formed a company in 1865 to become selling agents for textile mills in New England and the South. Deering left the partnership, and in 1869 he founded Deering Harvester (now Navistar).

Milliken set up operations in New York before the turn of the century, began buying the accounts receivables of cash-short textile mill operators, and invested in some of the companies.

In his position as agent and financier, Milliken was able to spot failing mills. He bought out the distressed owners at a discount and soon became a major mill owner himself. In 1905 Milliken and his allies waged a bitter proxy fight and court case to win control of two mills, earning Milliken a fearsome reputation.

H. B. Claflin, a New York dry-goods wholesaler that also operated department stores, owed money to Milliken. When Claflin went bankrupt in 1914, Milliken got some of the stores, which became Mercantile Stores. The Milliken family retained about 40% of the chain (sold to Dillard's in 1998).

Roger Milliken, grandson of the founder, became the president of the company in 1947 and has ruled with a firm hand. He fired his brother-in-law W. B. Dixon Stroud in 1955, and none of Roger's children, nephews, or nieces has ever been allowed to work for the company. The workers at Milliken's Darlington, South Carolina, mill voted to unionize in 1956. The next day Milliken closed the plant, beginning 24 years of litigation that ended at the US Supreme Court. Milliken settled with its workers for $5 million.

In the 1960s the company introduced Visa, a finish for easy-care fabrics. Milliken launched its Pursuit of Excellence program in 1981; the program stressed self-managed teams of employees and eliminated 700 management positions. Roger also emphasized research, training, and

new technology, including automation. Tom Peters dedicated his 1987 bestseller, *Thriving on Chaos,* to Roger.

Away from that limelight, Milliken is (and has always been) a secretive, closely held business. In 1989 that secrecy and family control were threatened when members of the Stroud branch of the family sued the company in the Delaware courts and then sold a small number of shares to Erwin Maddrey and Bettis Rainsford, executives of Milliken competitor Delta Woodside. The courts ruled in favor of Milliken in 1992; Maddrey and Rainsford were required to sign confidentiality agreements before receiving Milliken information.

In 1991 the company introduced Fashion Effects, a process that allowed it to customize drapery designs. Roger financially backed opponents of NAFTA in 1993.

The company's largest factory, in La Grange, Georgia, was destroyed by fire in 1995, but was rebuilt the next year.

Milliken is known by competitors for its unofficial motto: "Steal ideas shamelessly." Woven-filament maker NRB sued Milliken in 1997 for corporate spying, and the following year industrial textile maker Johnston Industries filed a similar lawsuit. Milliken settled both cases out of court.

In 1999 Milliken began using its Millitron dye technology to produce residential carpets and rugs. It also introduced new lines of patterned rugs (Royal Dynasty, Prestige, American Heritage) — its largest line to date. In 2000 the company built a manufacturing facility in South Carolina to expand its production of Millard-brand clarifying agents.

**Chairman and CEO:** Roger Milliken
**President and COO:** Thomas J. Malone
**CFO:** John Lewis
**VP, Human Resources:** Tommy Hodge
**Director, Public Affairs:** Richard Dillard

## LOCATIONS

**HQ:** 920 Milliken Rd., Spartanburg, SC 29304
**Phone:** 864-503-2020    **Fax:** 864-503-2100
**Web:** www.milliken.com

Milliken & Company has more than 60 manufacturing
facilities and operations worldwide.

## PRODUCTS/OPERATIONS

**Selected Products**

**Fabrics, Carpet, and Rugs**
Area rugs
Automotive upholstery
Carpet and carpet tiles
Commercial table linen fabrics (Ambassador, Embassy,
  and Visa)
Entrance and logo mats (KEX)
Fabrics for computer printer ribbons
Knit and woven apparel fabrics
Lining fabrics (Bemburg)
Nylon fabric for sails
Shop towels
Tennis ball felt
Uniform fabrics

**Chemicals**
Carpet cleaner (Capture)
Clarifying agents for plastics (Millad)
Colorants and tints (ClearTint, Liquitint, Reactint)
Metal working chemical additives
Resin intermediates
Specialty chemicals
Textile chemicals
Turf maintenance chemicals

## COMPETITORS

Asahi Kasei
Avondale Incorporated
Beaulieu Of America
Burlington Industries
Coats
Collins & Aikman
Crompton
Dixie Group
Dow Chemical
DuPont
Galey & Lord
Interface
Johnston Industries
JPS Industries
Mohawk Industries
R. B. Pamplin
Reliance Industries
Samsung
Shaw Industries
Springs Industries
Texfi Industries
Thomaston Mills
Unifi
WestPoint Stevens

## HISTORICAL FINANCIALS & EMPLOYEES

| Private<br>FYE: November 30 | Annual<br>Growth | 11/91 | 11/92 | 11/93 | 11/94 | 11/95 | 11/96 | 11/97 | 11/98 | 11/99 | 11/00 |
|---|---|---|---|---|---|---|---|---|---|---|---|
| Estimated sales ($ mil.) | 5.3% | — | 2,640 | 2,707 | 2,706 | 2,800 | 3,000 | 3,200 | 3,100 | 3,500 | 4,000 |
| Employees | 4.6% | — | 14,000 | 14,000 | 13,500 | 13,500 | 15,000 | 16,000 | 16,000 | 18,000 | 20,000 |

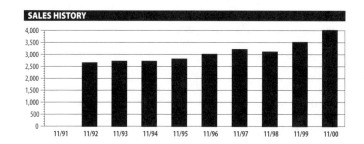

SALES HISTORY

# MOTIVA ENTERPRISES LLC

## OVERVIEW

Volatile oil prices and stiff competition provided the motivation to create Motiva Enterprises. The Houston-based company was created to combine the East Coast and Gulf Coast refining and marketing operations of Texaco, Shell Oil, and Saudi Aramco. Motiva and Equilon, a sister joint venture formed by Shell and Texaco that operates in the West and Midwest, together form the largest gasoline retailer in the US.

With a long-term agreement with Saudi Aramco for crude oil supply, Motiva has holdings in almost 50 product terminals and operates three refineries on the Gulf Coast and one in Delaware with a total capacity of 825,000 barrels a day. It operates about 13,000 Shell and Texaco gas stations.

ChevronTexaco and Saudi Aramco each own 35% of Motiva, and Shell owns 30%. In 2001 Texaco agreed to sell its stakes in Motiva (to Shell and Saudi Aramco) and Equilon (to Shell) to gain regulatory clearance to be acquired by Chevron. When the deals are completed, Shell and Saudi Aramco will each own 50% of Motiva, and Shell will take full ownership of Equilon.

## HISTORY

Although Motiva was not created until 1998, two of its key players, Texaco and Saudi Aramco, had been doing business together in various ventures since 1936. But they had never tried anything on the scale of the Star Enterprise joint venture approved by Texaco CEO James Kinnear and Saudi Oil Minister Hisham Nazer in late 1988. The deal, valued at nearly $2 billion, was the largest joint venture of its kind in the US.

The agreement to create Star Enterprise sprang, in part, from Texaco's tumultuous ride following its purchase of Getty Oil in 1983. Texaco was sued by Pennzoil for preempting Pennzoil's bid for Getty, and Pennzoil won a $10.5 billion judgment in 1985. Texaco filed for bankruptcy in 1987 and eventually settled with Pennzoil for $3 billion.

In 1988 Texaco emerged from bankruptcy after announcing a deal with Saudi Aramco at a stockholder meeting. Texaco got a much-needed injection of cash, and Saudi Aramco gained a steady US outlet for its supply of crude. The Saudis had been at odds with their OPEC partners for several years, and in late 1985 then-Saudi Oil Minister Sheikh Yamani and Saudi Aramco began increasing production, leading to an oil price crash in 1986. Nazer replaced Yamani and changed Saudi Aramco's strategy. To secure market share, the Saudis started signing long-term supply contracts.

The deal with Texaco gave Saudi Aramco a 50% interest in Texaco's refining and marketing operations in the East and on the Gulf Coast — about two-thirds of Texaco's US downstream operations — including three refineries and its Texaco-brand stations. In return, the Saudis paid $812 million cash and provided three-fourths of Star's initial inventory, about 30 million barrels of oil. They also agreed to a 20-year, 600,000-barrel-a-day commitment of crude. Each company named three representatives to Star's management.

The new company soon initiated a modernization and expansion program: It acquired 65 stations, built 30 new outlets, and remodeled another 172 during 1989. In 1994 the company began franchising its Texaco-brand Star Mart convenience stores. By mid-1995 it had sold 30 franchises.

Facing a more competitive oil marketing environment in the US, Shell Oil approached Texaco in 1996 with the possibility of merging some of their operations. In 1998 Shell and Texaco formed Equilon Enterprises, a joint venture that combined their western and midwestern refining and marketing activities.

Later that year Shell and Texaco/Saudi Aramco (Star Enterprises) formed Motiva to merge the companies' refining and marketing businesses on the East Coast and Gulf Coast. Shell and Texaco also formed two more Houston companies as satellite firms for Motiva and Equilon: Equiva Trading Company, a general partnership that provide supplies and trading services, and Equiva Services, which provides support services. L. Wilson Berry, the former president of Texaco Refining and Marketing, took over as CEO of Motiva.

In 1999 Motiva and Equilon together bought 15 product terminals from Premcor. To boost profits, the Motiva board appointed Texaco downstream veteran Roger Ebert as its new CEO in 2000, replacing Berry, who announced his resignation after a Motiva board meeting.

US government regulators in 2001 required that Texaco sell its Motiva and Equilon stakes in order to be acquired by Chevron. Shell and Saudi Aramco agreed to buy Texaco's stake in Motiva, and Shell agreed to buy Texaco's stake in Equilon.

**President and CEO:** Roger L. Ebert
**CFO:** William M. Kaparich
**VP Commercial Marketing and Distribution:**
  Ralph Grimmer
**VP Human Resources and Corporate Services, Motiva**
  **Enterprises and Equilon Enterprises:**
  Bruce Culpepper
**VP Refining, Motiva Enterprises and Equilon**
  **Enterprises:** Carmine Falcone
**VP Sales and Marketing:** Larry Burch
**VP Sales and Marketing:** Hugh Cooley
**Chief Diversity Officer, Motiva Enterprises and Equilon**
  **Enterprises:** John Jefferson
**General Counsel:** Rick Frazier

## LOCATIONS

**HQ:** 1100 Louisiana St., Houston, TX 77002
**Phone:** 713-277-8000      **Fax:** 713-277-7856
**Web:** www.equilonmotivaequiva.com

Motiva operates Shell and Texaco gas stations in 20
northeastern and southeastern states. It has refineries in
Convent and Norco, Louisiana; Delaware City, Delaware;
and Port Arthur, Texas.

## COMPETITORS

7-Eleven
BP
CITGO
Cumberland Farms
Dairy Mart
Exxon Mobil
Gulf Oil
Marathon Ashland
 Petroleum
Phillips Petroleum
Racetrac Petroleum
Sunoco
Ultramar Diamond
 Shamrock
Valero
Wawa

## HISTORICAL FINANCIALS & EMPLOYEES

| Joint venture<br>FYE: December 31 | Annual<br>Growth | 12/91 | 12/92 | 12/93 | 12/94 | 12/95 | 12/96 | 12/97 | 12/98 | 12/99 | 12/00 |
|---|---|---|---|---|---|---|---|---|---|---|---|
| Sales ($ mil.) | 90.3% | — | — | — | — | — | — | — | 5,371 | 12,196 | 19,446 |
| Net income ($ mil.) | 143.1% | — | — | — | — | — | — | — | 78 | (69) | 461 |
| Income as % of sales | — | — | — | — | — | — | — | — | 1.5% | — | 2.4% |
| Employees | 46.1% | — | — | — | — | — | — | — | 3,750 | — | 8,000 |

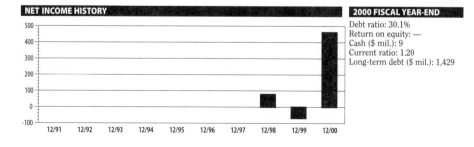

**NET INCOME HISTORY**

**2000 FISCAL YEAR-END**
Debt ratio: 30.1%
Return on equity: —
Cash ($ mil.): 9
Current ratio: 1.20
Long-term debt ($ mil.): 1,429

# MTS, INCORPORATED

## OVERVIEW

Whether pop music rocks your world or Broadway tunes set your feet a-tappin', MTS offers a Tower of choices. West Sacramento, California-based MTS — owner of Tower Records — is the second-largest specialty retailer of music in the US (after Musicland), with more than 170 company-owned music, book, and video stores in eight countries; its franchise agreements encompass 10 additional countries. The company also publishes free music magazines such as *Pulse!* and runs several WOW! stores with The Good Guys, an electronics retailer.

Pioneers of specialty retailing's superstore concept, MTS has fewer stores than other major music chains, it is known for broad selection and high volume. Unlike other specialty retailers, managers at each store are granted discretion in maintaining the level and mix of their inventories.

The chain has faced increasing competition from discounters such as Wal-Mart, from industry consolidation, and from online retailers. Big losses have prompted the company to adopt a restructuring plan and it has indefinitely postponed the idea of going public.

MTS was founded by self-described "aging hippie" Russell Solomon (who scorns corporate stuffiness and confiscates neckties from visiting executives and displays them outside his office). Russell and son Michael T. Solomon (for whom the company is named) own all but 1% of MTS.

## HISTORY

Russell Solomon began selling used jukebox records in 1941 in his father's Tower Cut Rate Drug Store at age 16. He joined the Army after dropping out of high school and went back to work in his father's store after his 1946 discharge. In 1952 he took over the record inventory from his father's store and began wholesaling, setting up record departments in drugstores and department stores.

Solomon's record wholesaling business went broke and creditors forced him to liquidate in 1960. Days later, with $5,000 from his father, Solomon incorporated MTS (named after Solomon's son Michael T.) and soon opened the first Tower Records in Sacramento, California. A month later a second Sacramento store was born. The first Tower Books opened in 1963, adjacent to one of the record stores.

By the 1967 "Summer of Love," Solomon was noticing the diverse musical tastes of the flower children who hung out in his stores. With the music business exploding, he figured serving the market would require stocking stores with a huge selection. In 1968 the first store outside Sacramento was opened, Tower Records' landmark Columbus Street store in San Francisco. At the time it was the largest record store in the US.

In 1970 Tower Records opened in Los Angeles on the Sunset Strip. The company started expanding outside California in 1976 (mainly in the West) and overseas in 1979 (Japan). The first Tower Video opened in Sacramento in 1981; three more opened the next year. The East Coast got its first Tower Records in 1983 (New York City); at the time the 35,000-sq.-ft. store was the world's largest.

That year the company debuted *Pulse!* magazine, an in-store freebie with record reviews and artist interviews. The company's real expansion began in 1989; by 1994 Tower Records, with 127 outlets, had more than doubled its stores. That year it opened its first multimedia store, offering books, videos, records, and CD-ROMs under one roof.

MTS opened the largest record shop in the world (an eight-floor megastore in Tokyo) and the first WOW! store (a joint venture with electronics retailer The Good Guys) in Las Vegas in 1995. That year it started selling CDs on the Internet via America Online; it added its own online store in 1996. In 1998 MTS sold $110 million in bonds to raise money for expansion. Also that year president and CEO Russell Solomon passed his Tower-guarding duties and his titles to son Michael.

To counteract growing losses, MTS began several experiments in 2000, including the creation of kiosks that allow customers to download songs digitally and burn their own CDs. A similar project allows customers to pay for music from Tower's Web site and then immediately download it.

In 2001 MTS adopted a restructuring plan that included closing and liquidating most stand-alone and combination bookstores and selling the company's operations in Argentina, Hong Kong, Taiwan, and Singapore and converting them to franchises. It also decided to shut down its operations in Canada. The company's large losses in fiscal 2001 were attributed mostly to the restructuring and the closure of some of its international operations.

**Chairman:** Russell M. Solomon, age 76, $932,780 pay
**President and CEO:** Michael T. Solomon, age 53,
$460,400 pay
**EVP and COO:** Stanley L. Goman, age 53, $322,349 pay
**EVP, CFO, Secretary, and Treasurer:**
DeVaughn D. Searson, age 57, $322,378 pay
**EVP and Chief Advertising Officer:** Ronald Nugent,
age 52, $254,629 pay
**SVP, European Operations:** Andy D. Lown, age 36
**SVP, Far East Operations:** Keith Cahoon, age 45,
$165,120 pay
**Director of Human Resources:** Shauna Pompei
**Auditors:** Arthur Andersen LLP

## LOCATIONS

**HQ:** 2500 Del Monte St., West Sacramento, CA 95691
**Phone:** 916-373-2500   **Fax:** 916-373-2535
**Web:** www.towerrecords.com

**2001 Sales**

|  | % of total |
|---|---|
| US | 58 |
| Japan | 34 |
| UK & Ireland | 5 |
| Other countries | 3 |
| **Total** | **100** |

## PRODUCTS/OPERATIONS

**2001 Sales**

|  | % of total |
|---|---|
| Recorded music | 86 |
| Video products | 10 |
| Complementary products | 4 |
| **Total** | **100** |

**Selected Operations**
Internet
  TowerRecords.com
Music magazines
  *Bounce* (Japan)
  *Pass* (Taiwan)
  *Pulse!* (US)
  *Pulse Latino* (Latin America)
  *Top* (UK)
Stores
  Tower
  WOW! (jointly operated with The Good Guys)

## COMPETITORS

| | |
|---|---|
| Amazon.com | Hollywood Entertainment |
| Barnes & Noble | Kmart |
| Bertelsmann | Movie Gallery |
| Best Buy | MP3.com |
| Blockbuster | Musicland |
| BMG Entertainment | Napster |
| Books-A-Million | National Record Mart |
| Borders | Target |
| CDnow | Trans World |
| Circuit City | Entertainment |
| Columbia House | Virgin Group |
| Costco Wholesale | Wal-Mart |
| EMI Group | WHSmith |
| Hastings Entertainment | Wherehouse |
| HMV | Entertainment |

## HISTORICAL FINANCIALS & EMPLOYEES

| Private FYE: July 31 | Annual Growth | 7/92 | 7/93 | 7/94 | 7/95 | 7/96 | 7/97 | 7/98 | 7/99 | 7/00 | 7/01 |
|---|---|---|---|---|---|---|---|---|---|---|---|
| Sales ($ mil.) | 5.6% | — | 699 | 809 | 951 | 1,001 | 992 | 1,008 | 1,026 | 1,100 | 1,080 |
| Net income ($ mil.) | — | — | 15 | 17 | 15 | 10 | 4 | 10 | (8) | (10) | (90) |
| Income as % of sales | — | — | 2.1% | 2.1% | 1.6% | 1.0% | 0.4% | 1.0% | — | — | — |
| Employees | (0.0%) | — | — | — | — | — | 6,800 | 7,200 | 7,500 | 7,158 | 6,795 |

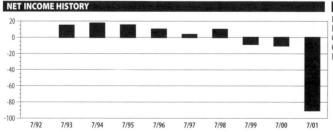

**NET INCOME HISTORY**

**2001 FISCAL YEAR-END**
Debt ratio: 84.7%
Return on equity: —
Cash ($ mil.): 32
Current ratio: 0.83
Long-term debt ($ mil.): 118

# MUTUAL OF OMAHA

## OVERVIEW

In the wild kingdom that is today's insurance industry, The Mutual of Omaha Companies wants to distinguish itself from the pack. But the venerable insurer is not immune to the health industry's upheaval.

Increased cost-mindedness among clout-wielding managed care organizations has put traditional indemnity insurers — who have less power to bargain for lower-cost services — at a disadvantage, as have state laws mandating coverage for persons regardless of underwriting policy. Mutual of Omaha is exiting the health business in some areas and is adding managed care services. It is focused on growing its health care networks internally, rather than by acquisition, to ensure its standards are met. These networks are largely in underserved rural areas, where the firm has kept a strong presence. Other services include disability coverage, employee health, mutual funds, pension plans, homeowner and auto coverage, and brokerage.

Mutual of Omaha is involved in wildlife conservation and protection. Starting with sponsorship of the long-running *Mutual of Omaha's Wild Kingdom,* this interest has evolved into a grant and scholarship program run by the company's Wildlife Heritage Center.

## HISTORY

Charter Mutual Benefit Health & Accident Association got its start in Omaha, Nebraska, in 1909. A year later, half of its founders quit, leaving a group headed by pharmaceuticals businessman H. S. Weller in charge. He tapped C. C. Criss as principal operating officer, general manager, and treasurer. Criss brought in his wife, Mabel, and brother Neil to help run the business.

Formed to offer accident and disability protection at a time when there were many fraudulent benefit societies, Charter Mutual Benefit Health faced consumer resistance that slowed growth in its first 10 years. By 1920 it was licensed in only nine states. Experience helped it refine its products and improve its policies' comprehensibility. By 1924 the firm had more than doubled its penetration, gaining licensing in 24 states.

The US was nearing the depths of the Depression when Weller died in 1932. Criss succeeded him as president. The stock crash had brought a steep decline in the value of the firm's asset base, and premium income dropped (accompanied by an increase in claims). Even so, Mutual Benefit Health expanded its agency force, the scope of its benefits, and its operations. It went into Canada in 1935 and began a campaign to obtain licensing throughout the US.

By 1939 the company was licensed in all 48 states. During WWII it wrote coverage for civilians killed or injured in acts of war in the US (including Hawaii) and Canada. With paranoia running high and consumer goods in short supply, the insurance industry boomed during the war (and payouts on stateside act-of-war claims were low to nonexistent). Criss retired in 1949.

Gearing up its post-war sales efforts, in 1950 the company changed its name to Mutual of Omaha and adopted its distinctive chieftain logo. During the 1950s it added specialty accident and group medical coverage. In 1963 it made an advertising coup when it launched *Mutual of Omaha's Wild Kingdom.* Hosted by zoo director Marlin Perkins and, later, naturalist sidekick Jim Fowler, the show was one of the most popular nature programs of all time. Later that decade the company added investment management to its services.

Changes in the health care industry during the 1990s led Mutual of Omaha to de-emphasize its traditional indemnity products in favor of building managed care alternatives. In 1993 the company joined with Alegent Health System to form managed care company Preferred HealthAlliance. Mutual of Omaha also stopped writing new major medical coverage in such states as California, Florida, New Jersey, and New York, where state laws made providing health care onerous. This led the company to cut its workforce by about 10% in 1996.

In 1997 the firm launched a medical savings account program and a new, bundled 401(k) plan. It sold its Canadian insurance operations in 1998 and discontinued its Tele-Trip flight-accident insurance line. In 1999 it bought out Alegent's interest in their joint venture and entered the credit card business (offering First USA Visa cards). The company also began offering critical illness insurance by which patients diagnosed with certain serious illnesses receive one lump-sum payment of up to $750,000.

In 2000 the firm lifted its $25,000 limit for coverage of AIDS-related illnesses (its standard limit is $1 million); the company had been sued over the policy.

## OFFICERS

**Chairman and CEO:** John W. Weekly
**President and COO:** John A. Sturgeon
**EVP and Chief Investment Officer:** Rick Witt
**EVP and Comptroller:** Tommie D. Thompson
**EVP and Chief Actuary:** Cecil D. Bykerk
**EVP and Executive Counsel:** Lawrence F. Harr
**EVP and General Counsel:** Thomas J. McCusker
**EVP, Corporate Services and Corporate Secretary:**
M. Jane Huerter
**EVP, Customer Service Operation:** Kimberly S. Harm
**EVP, Government Affairs:** William C. Mattox
**EVP, Group Benefit Services:** Randall C. Horn
**EVP, Health Care Management:** Stephen R. Booma
**EVP, Information Services:** James L. Hanson
**EVP, Human Resources:** Rick Frederick
**Public Relations Officer:** Joe Clauson
**Auditors:** Deloitte & Touche LLP

## LOCATIONS

**HQ:** The Mutual of Omaha Companies
Mutual of Omaha Plaza, Omaha, NE 68175
**Phone:** 402-342-7600      **Fax:** 402-351-2775
**Web:** www.mutualofomaha.com

The Mutual of Omaha Companies operate throughout
the US.

## PRODUCTS/OPERATIONS

**Selected Services and Products**
Annuities
Dental insurance
Disability insurance
Individual life and health insurance
Long-term-care insurance
Major medical
Mutual funds
Property/casualty coverage

**Selected Subsidiaries and Affiliates**
Companion Life Insurance Company
innowave (water purification products)
Kirkpatrick Pettis (brokerage)
Mutual of Omaha Insurance Company
Mutual of Omaha Investor Services (mutual funds)
Omaha Property and Casualty Insurance Company
United of Omaha Life Insurance Company
United World Life Insurance Company

## COMPETITORS

| | |
|---|---|
| Aetna | Liberty Mutual |
| Allstate | MassMutual |
| American National | MetLife |
| Insurance | MONY |
| Assurant Group | Morgan Stanley Dean |
| AXA Financial | Witter |
| Blue Cross | New York Life |
| CIGNA | Northwestern Mutual |
| CNA Financial | Prudential |
| Guardian Life | State Farm |
| John Hancock Financial | USAA |
| Services | |

## HISTORICAL FINANCIALS & EMPLOYEES

| Mutual company<br>FYE: December 31 | Annual<br>Growth | 12/91 | 12/92 | 12/93 | 12/94 | 12/95 | 12/96 | 12/97 | 12/98 | 12/99 | 12/00 |
|---|---|---|---|---|---|---|---|---|---|---|---|
| Assets ($ mil.) | 8.2% | — | 7,714 | 8,600 | 9,551 | 10,659 | 11,726 | 12,639 | 13,231 | 13,959 | 14,465 |
| Net income ($ mil.) | 11.5% | — | 65 | 94 | 82 | 122 | 105 | 181 | 117 | 90 | 156 |
| Income as % of assets | — | — | 0.8% | 1.1% | 0.9% | 1.1% | 0.9% | 1.4% | 0.9% | 0.6% | 1.1% |
| Employees | (1.5%) | — | — | 7,665 | 8,330 | 8,163 | 7,047 | 7,309 | 7,111 | — | — |

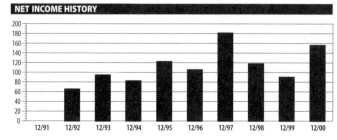

**NET INCOME HISTORY**

**2000 FISCAL YEAR-END**
Equity as % of assets: 17.2%
Return on assets: 1.1%
Return on equity: —
Long-term debt ($ mil.): —
Sales ($ mil.): 4,240

# MUZAK LLC

## OVERVIEW

Having trouble stopping *The Pink Panther Theme* from playing inside your head? Do you constantly hear *Crocodile Rock* in the background? No need to see a mental health professional, you're merely one of the 100 million people who hear Muzak's tunes each day. The king of canned music, Fort Mill, South Carolina-based Muzak offers 60 music channels delivered via satellite (72% of business), local broadcast transmission, tapes, and CDs. Among its 325,000 customers are retailers, grocery stores, hotels, office buildings, and factories. Not limited to Mantovani, the company's

offerings cover genres such as classical, country, Latin, oldies, and contemporary. Muzak serves customers in 15 countries from its network of offices. In addition to providing music, Muzak also sells, installs, and maintains equipment such as sound systems and intercoms.

The company made numerous acquisitions in the late 1990s and is hoping to restore profitability by renewing its focus on its core services. Investment firm ABRY Partners owns about 62% of the company; radio station giant Clear Channel, about 21%.

## HISTORY

George Squier patented a system for transmitting phonograph music over electrical lines in 1922. He sold the rights to utility North American Company, and together they formed a subsidiary to begin testing the system in Cleveland. In 1934 Squier coined the term Muzak ("muz" from music and "ak" from Kodak, his favorite company) before he died that year. The company moved to New York in 1936.

In the 1930s Muzak was used in then-newfangled elevators to calm riders (hence the term "elevator music"). In 1938 Warner Bros. bought the company but sold it the next year to US Senator William Benton (who was also the publisher of *Encyclopaedia Britannica*). Experiments showed that music could increase productivity, and during WWII Muzak systems were installed in factories.

After the war the company continued to work on Stimulus Progression — the idea of regulating worker productivity through music. During the 1950s the company began using audio tapes to deliver its music to customers. The company was sold to Wrather Corp. in 1957.

In 1972 Teleprompter bought the company and began distributing its music via satellite. Westinghouse bought Teleprompter in 1981 and sold it to Marshall Field V in 1986. Field bought Seattle-based Yesco, a producer of "foreground" music for retailers, and merged the two the next year. Muzak moved its headquarters from New York to Seattle.

Led by Yesco's management, Muzak greatly expanded the number of channels it offered, from one to 12, and it began updating its sound to appeal to baby boomers. The new channels did not offer the traditonal symphonic re-recordings of soft favorites; instead they featured original recordings, including jazz, contemporary pop, and country music. The

company also introduced music video feeds for retailers, nightclubs, restaurants, and bars. Field sold Muzak to its management and New York investment firm Centre Capital in 1992.

In 1996 the company called off plans to go public. Saddled with debt from the buyout and mounting losses, it ousted CEO John Jester in 1997 and replaced him with William Boyd, who refocused the company on its core music business.

In 1998 the company began buying competitors and its own independent affiliates.

In 1999 Muzak merged with Audio Communications Network, a Muzak franchiser owned by media investment firm ABRY Partners, and the Muzak affiliates owned by Capstar (Capstar later became part of AMFM, which was subsequently acquired by radio station owner Clear Channel). Later that year Muzak made a string of acquisitions, including Data Broadcasting's InStore Satellite Network, a music and ad business.

In 2000 Muzak moved its headquarters to Fort Mill, South Carolina. Extending its acquisitive streak, the company acquired Telephone Audio Productions (audio marketing and messaging) and Muzak franchisee Vortex Sound Communications.

To pay for all those acquisitions, Muzak sold $85 million worth of preferred stock to Bank of America, New York Life, L.P., and Northwestern Investment in late 2000.

**Chairman:** R. Steven Hicks, age 50
**CEO:** William A. Boyd, age 59
**COO, CFO, and Treasurer:** Stephen P. Villa, age 37
**SVP Owned Operations:** Steven M. Tracy, age 50, $118,750 pay
**VP:** Royce G. Yudkuff, age 44
**VP and Secretary:** Peni Garber, age 37
**VP, General Counsel and Assisntant Secretary:** Michael F. Zendan II, age 37
**VP Marketing:** Kenny Kahn
**VP Team Member Services (HR):** Frank Messana
**Chief Technology Officer:** David Moore
**Auditors:** PricewaterhouseCoopers LLP

## LOCATIONS

**HQ:** 3318 Lakemont Boulevard, Fort Mill, SC 29708
**Phone:** 803-396-3000          **Fax:** 803-396-3077
**Web:** www.muzak.com

Muzak offers its services in 15 countries.

## PRODUCTS/OPERATIONS

### 2000 Sales

|  | $ mil. | % of total |
|---|---|---|
| Music & related services | 138 | 72 |
| Equipment & related services | 54 | 28 |
| **Total** | **192** | **100** |

### Selected Products

Audio Architecture (music programming)
Audio Marketing (music and messages for phone systems)
Video System Design (video programming)

### Selected Music Genres

Classical
County
Jazz
Latin
Mature adult
Oldies
Popular contemporary
Popular contemporary instrumentals
Specialty
Urban

## COMPETITORS

DMX/AEI MUSIC
MP3.com
PlayNetwork
TM Century

## HISTORICAL FINANCIALS & EMPLOYEES

| Private<br>FYE: December 31 | Annual<br>Growth | 12/91 | 12/92 | 12/93 | 12/94 | 12/95 | 12/96 | 12/97 | 12/98 | 12/99 | 12/00 |
|---|---|---|---|---|---|---|---|---|---|---|---|
| Sales ($ mil.) | 17.1% | — | 55 | 59 | 83 | 87 | 87 | 91 | 100 | 130 | 192 |
| Net income ($ mil.) | — | — | (6) | (4) | (7) | (6) | (11) | (13) | (12) | (22) | (44) |
| Income as % of sales | — | — | — | — | — | — | — | — | — | — | — |
| Employees | 14.3% | — | — | — | — | 715 | 751 | 667 | 1,041 | 1,324 | 1,395 |

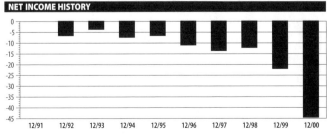

**NET INCOME HISTORY**

**2000 FISCAL YEAR-END**
Debt ratio: 64.0%
Return on equity: —
Cash ($ mil.): 3
Current ratio: 1.13
Long-term debt ($ mil.): 284

# NASD

Bull market or bear, NASD will be there.

The National Association of Securities Dealers (NASD) controls the NASD Automated Quotations (Nasdaq) stock market, the US's #2 securities market, and #3 American Stock Exchange (AMEX), giving listed companies and investors a choice between auction (AMEX) or electronic trading (Nasdaq). Nasdaq and AMEX may lack the clout and market capitalization of the New York Stock Exchange, but, with some 4,800 and 600 listed companies, respectively, the two surpass the NYSE's approximately 3,000.

Per SEC orders, NASD Regulation watches over more than 5,500 securities firms and some 650,000 securities professionals; it is kept separate from NASD's market operations.

Despite the tech bust and economic slowdown, NASD has proceeded with its foreign expansion plans, kicking off Nasdaq Japan and Nasdaq Canada and acquiring a controlling interest in Nasdaq Europe (formerly Easdaq). To stay competitive with electronic communications networks (ECNs), Nasdaq is creating one of its own (SuperMontage). It is also spinning off all but about 20% Nasdaq, which is set to become a publicly traded exchange.

## HISTORY

The National Association of Securities Dealers (NASD) was founded in 1939 as a self-regulating entity for over-the-counter (OTC) securities traders who traded directly with companies or with market makers authorized to trade their stock. Traders shopped by phone to get the best price from the market makers, and up-to-date OTC quotes were unobtainable. NASD set trading qualifications, administered licensing tests, set standards for underwriting compensation, and disciplined wayward traders.

In 1963 the SEC asked the NASD to develop an automated OTC quotations system. Work began in 1968 on facilities in Trumbull, Connecticut, and Rockville, Maryland. The system went online in 1971 and soon turned into an electronic trading medium because it made dealer quotes more competitive and instantly visible. By 1972 volume exceeded 2 billion shares, and two years later the Nasdaq claimed a share volume nearly one-third of NYSE's. By 1980 it reported having almost 60% of the NYSE's volume, although Nasdaq counted both sides of many trades.

In 1975 Congress gave NASD responsibility for regulating the municipal securities market and asked the SEC to develop a national market system for share trading. The SEC handed the task to NASD. The market started trading in 1982 with 40 stocks, establishing a two-tier system: one for the crème de la crème, such as MCI (now WorldCom) and Microsoft, and one for smaller or newer issues. The system is continually updated; new technology made it a model for other exchanges.

To improve responsiveness to small investors, NASD instituted the SOES (small order entry system) after the 1987 stock crash, when many traders bailed themselves out before executing customer sell orders. So-called SOES bandits (dealers who used the system to make frequent small trades) increased the market's volatility and made Nasdaq vulnerable to NYSE's contention that auction exchanges were fairer to investors. An SEC investigation resulted in a requirement that dealers execute small customer orders along with their own and at the best prices. In 1997 the new rules were phased in and spreads dropped by an average of 35% without affecting volume.

A 1997 proposal to cap investor arbitration awards at $750,000, regardless of actual damages, met with criticism, since arbitration had been instituted in 1987 because the parties could receive remedies comparable to those available in court. Reform-minded Wall Streeter Frank Zarb took over in 1997. Nasdaq and the American Stock Exchange (AMEX) merged the next year. NASD reluctantly complied when the SEC asked it to join the NYSE in real-time trade price reporting.

With for-profit, around-the-clock competitors like The Island ECN and Archipelago in mind, NASD prepared in 1999 to spin off Nasdaq as a for-profit exchange (overwhelmingly approved in 2000). Nasdaq also extended official pricing to 6:30 p.m. (eastern time).

In 2000 Nasdaq converted stock prices from fractions to decimals, mandated by regulators. That year it joined with SOFTBANK to build Nasdaq Japan, an Internet-based market of primarily Japanese tech companies. In 2001 the flaccid economy led Nasdaq to trim about 10% of its staff — its first job cuts since just after the 1987 crash. Zarb also retired that year.

In the wake of the terrorism attacks that shook Wall Street and the nation in 2001, Nasdaq and the New York Stock Exchange began discussing a disaster plan under which the two would cooperate should a future incident cripple either market.

## OFFICERS

**Chairman, President, and CEO:** Robert R. Glauber, age 62
**Vice Chairman; Chairman and CEO, The American Stock Exchange:** Salvatore F. Sodano
**EVP and Chief Administrative Officer:** Michael D. Jones
**EVP, Corporate Development, Strategy and Technology:** Douglas Shulman
**SVP, Human Resources:** Diane E. Carter
**Vice Chairman, The Nasdaq Stock Market:** Alfred R. Berkeley III
**Director; CEO, The Nasdaq Stock Market:** Hardwick Simmons
**President, The Nasdaq Stock Market:** Richard G. Ketchum
**Chairman and CEO, Nasdaq International; EVP, Strategic Development, The Nasdaq Stock Market:** John L. Hilley
**CEO, Nasdaq Europe:** Michael O. Sanderson
**President, Nasdaq US Markets, The Nasdaq Stock Market:** J. Patrick Campbell
**President, Nasdaq International:** John T. Wall
**President and CEO, Nasdaq-Japan Planning Company:** Tatsuyuki Saeki
**President, The American Stock Exchange:** Peter Quick
**President, NASD Regulation:** Mary L. Schapiro, age 46
**CFO, The Nasdaq Stock Market:** David P. Warren
**EVP of Operations & Technology and CIO, The Nasdaq Stock Market:** Steve Randich
**EVP and Chief Legal Officer, The Nasdaq Stock Market:** Edward S. Knight
**EVP, The Nasdaq Stock Market:** John N. Tognino
**Auditors:** Ernst & Young LLP

## LOCATIONS

**HQ:** National Association of Securities Dealers
1735 K St. NW, Washington, DC 20006
**Phone:** 202-728-8000   **Fax:** 202-293-6260
**Web:** www.nasd.com

National Association of Securities Dealers has 15 regulation and dispute resolution offices throughout the US. The company's stock exchange operations have offices in London; Menlo Park, California; New York; Trumbull, Connecticut; and Washington, DC.

## PRODUCTS/OPERATIONS

**Selected Subsidiaries**
The American Stock Exchange, Inc.
NASD Dispute Resolution, Inc.
NASD Regulation, Inc.
Nasdaq International Ltd.
The Nasdaq Stock Market, Inc.
Securities Dealers Insurance Co., Inc.
Securities Dealers Risk Purchasing Group

## COMPETITORS

Archipelago
Bloomberg
E*TRADE
Goldman Sachs
Instinet
Island ECN
MarketXT
NYSE

## HISTORICAL FINANCIALS & EMPLOYEES

| Not-for-profit FYE: December 31 | Annual Growth | 12/91 | 12/92 | 12/93 | 12/94 | 12/95 | 12/96 | 12/97 | 12/98 | 12/99 | 12/00 |
|---|---|---|---|---|---|---|---|---|---|---|---|
| Sales ($ mil.) | 24.8% | — | 264 | 332 | 372 | 438 | 556 | 634 | 740 | 1,177 | 1,555 |
| Net income ($ mil.) | 15.9% | — | 35 | 39 | 21 | 17 | 55 | 36 | 47 | 154 | 114 |
| Income as % of sales | — | — | 13.2% | 11.7% | 5.6% | 3.9% | 9.9% | 5.7% | 6.4% | 13.1% | 7.3% |
| Employees | 6.1% | — | 1,991 | 2,145 | 2,328 | 2,000 | 2,218 | 2,200 | 2,900 | 3,000 | 3,200 |

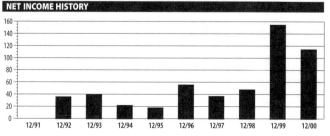

**NET INCOME HISTORY**

**2000 FISCAL YEAR-END**
Debt ratio: 2.8%
Return on equity: 15.4%
Cash ($ mil.): 604
Current ratio: 1.66
Long-term debt ($ mil.): 25

# NBA

## OVERVIEW

The NBA may have drawn one too many technical fouls over the past few seasons, but that's all about to change thanks to a little magic from the Washington Wizards. After a less than stellar 1998-99 season that saw a contentious lockout and the retirement of its most popular player, Michael Jordan, the New York City-based National Basketball Association has seen its attendance and TV ratings decline dramatically. Add to that a host of on-and-off court image problems, and 17-year commissioner David Stern has his work cut out for him to return the league to its glory days of the 1980s. But now that Jordan has made his second return

as a player to the NBA with the Wizards, the 2001-02 ratings will likely skyrocket.

The NBA has 29 teams, including one Canadian club, playing in the Eastern and Western Conferences. It also operates the Women's NBA, which features sister teams in 16 NBA cities. Although attendance and TV ratings are dropping, the league still manages to bring in the dough through lucrative merchandising deals and TV contracts. However, matters aren't helped any by the fact that the average ticket price for an NBA game has passed the $50 mark, the most expensive in professional sports.

## HISTORY

Dr. James Naismith, a physical education teacher at the International YMCA Training School in Springfield, Massachusetts, invented basketball in 1891. Naismith nailed peach baskets at both ends of the school's gym, gave his students a soccer ball, and one of the world's most popular sports was born.

In the beginning many YMCAs deemed the game too rough and banned it, so basketball was limited to armories, gymnasiums, barns, and dance halls. To pay the rent for the use of the hall, teams began charging spectators fees for admission, and leftover cash was divided among the players. The first pro basketball game was played in 1896 in Trenton, New Jersey. A group of arena owners looking to fill their halls when their hockey teams were on the road formed the Basketball Association of America in 1946. It merged with the midwestern National Basketball League in 1949 to form the 17-team National Basketball Association (NBA).

Six teams dropped out in 1950. The league got an unexpected boost the next year when a point-shaving scandal rocked college basketball. The bad publicity for the college game made the pros look relatively clean, and it helped attract more fans. Another boost came through innovation when the league introduced the 24-second shot clock in 1954, which sped up the game and increased scoring.

Basketball came into its own in the late 1950s and 1960s, thanks to the popularity of such stars as Wilt Chamberlain, Bill Russell, and Bob Cousy. A rival league, the American Basketball Association (ABA), appeared on the scene in 1967 with its red, white, and blue basketball. Salaries escalated as the two leagues competed for players. The leagues merged in 1976.

By the early 1980s the NBA was suffering major image problems (drugs, fighting, racial issues) and began to wane in popularity. The league was resuscitated by exciting new players such as Magic Johnson, Larry Bird, and Michael Jordan, and, in 1984, a new commissioner, David Stern. Although increased commercialism drove some purists crazy, big-name players and big-time rivalries helped sell the NBA's most important commodity — sport as entertainment.

Stern went to work cleaning up the league's image and financial problems, pushing through a strict antidrug policy and a salary cap (the first such cap in major US sports). He also signed big marketing deals with such sponsors as Coca-Cola and McDonald's. The NBA added its first two non-US teams in 1995, the Toronto Raptors and Vancouver Grizzlies. (The Grizzlies moved to Memphis, Tennessee in 2001.) The league also launched the Women's NBA (WNBA) in 1997.

On July 1, 1998, the NBA owners voted to lock out players, leading to the first work stoppage in the NBA's 52-year history. The dispute lasted six months, and the NBA's 1998-99 season was pared down to 50 games from the standard 82.

Concerned with the rash of players either leaving college early or skipping it entirely for the NBA, the league announced the formation of a developmental league (akin to baseball's minor leagues) in 2000. Also in 2001 the NBA got a much-needed shot in the arm when Michael Jordan announced that he would come out of retirement for a second time to play for the Washington Wizards.

## OFFICERS

**Commissioner:** David J. Stern, age 58
**Deputy Commissioner and COO:** Russell T. Granik
**SVP Basketball Operations:** Stu Jackson
**SVP Business Affairs:** Harvey E. Benjamin
**SVP Consumer Products:** Christopher Heyn
**SVP Finance:** Robert Criqui
**SVP International:** Andrew Messick, age 36
**SVP Marketing and Team Business Operations:**
Bernie Mullin
**SVP New League Development:** Rob Levine
**VP Internet Services:** Brenda Spoonemore
**VP Marketing Partnerships:** Jonathan Press
**VP Team Marketing Services:** Bill Sutton
**Chief of Staff, President and COO, NBA
Entertainment:** Adam Silver
**President, NBA Television and New Media Ventures:**
Ed Desser
**President, Women's National Basketball Association:**
Val Ackerman
**EVP Global Media Properties and Marketing
Partnerships, NBA Entertainment:** Heidi Ueberroth
**EVP Programming and Executive Producer, NBA
Entertainment:** Gregg Winik
**SVP and COO, WNBA:** Paula Hanson
**SVP Operations and Technology, NBA Entertainment:**
Steve Hellmuth
**Human Resources:** Patrica E. Swedin

## LOCATIONS

**HQ:** National Basketball Association
Olympic Tower, 645 5th Ave., New York, NY 10022
**Phone:** 212-407-8000        **Fax:** 212-754-6414
**Web:** www.nba.com

## PRODUCTS/OPERATIONS

### NBA Teams

| Eastern Conference | Western Conference |
|---|---|
| Atlantic Division | Midwest Division |
| Boston Celtics | Dallas Mavericks |
| Miami Heat | Denver Nuggets |
| New Jersey Nets | Houston Rockets |
| New York Knicks | Memphis Grizzlies |
| Orlando Magic | Minnesota Timberwolves |
| Philadelphia 76ers | San Antonio Spurs |
| Washington Wizards | Utah Jazz |
| Central Division | Pacific Division |
| Atlanta Hawks | Golden State Warriors |
| Charlotte Hornets | Los Angeles Clippers |
| Chicago Bulls | Los Angeles Lakers |
| Cleveland Cavaliers | Phoenix Suns |
| Detroit Pistons | Portland Trail Blazers |
| Indiana Pacers | Sacramento Kings |
| Milwaukee Bucks | Seattle SuperSonics |
| Toronto Raptors | |

### WNBA Teams

| Eastern Conference | Western Conference |
|---|---|
| Charlotte Sting | Houston Comets |
| Cleveland Rockers | Los Angeles Sparks |
| Detroit Shock | Minnesota Lynx |
| Indiana Fever | Phoenix Mercury |
| Miami Sol | Portland Fire |
| New York Liberty | Sacramento Monarchs |
| Orlando Miracle | Seattle Storm |
| Washington Mystics | Utah Starzz |

## COMPETITORS

Major League Baseball
NASCAR
NFL
NHL
PGA Tour
World Wrestling
Federation

## HISTORICAL FINANCIALS & EMPLOYEES

| Association<br>FYE: August 31 | Annual<br>Growth | 8/91 | 8/92 | 8/93 | 8/94 | 8/95 | 8/96 | 8/97 | 8/98 | 8/99 | 8/00 |
|---|---|---|---|---|---|---|---|---|---|---|---|
| Sales ($ mil.) | 12.5% | — | 843 | 999 | 1,030 | 1,259 | 1,403 | 1,664 | 1,874 | 956 | 2,164 |
| Employees | 12.2% | — | — | — | 450 | 550 | 650 | 850 | 1,000 | 800 | — |

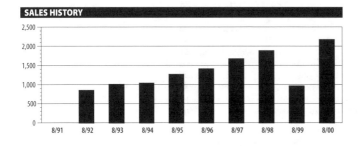

SALES HISTORY

# NATIONAL FOOTBALL LEAGUE

## OVERVIEW

In the world of professional sports, the National Football League (NFL) is blitzing the competition. The New York City-based organization oversees America's most popular spectator sport, acting as a trade association for 31 franchise owners to promote the sport, license team names and logos, collect dues and royalties, and develop new programs. Its NFL Properties division generates billions through merchandising and licensing, while NFL Enterprises negotiates national broadcasting rights for the teams, including its current eight-year, $17.6 billion TV deal struck in 1998. The franchises operate as separate businesses but share the revenue generated through broadcasting.

While the NFL has called many of the right plays the past few years, the league sees big challenges as well as opportunities on the horizon. In 2002 the NFL will welcome the Houston Texans as its 32nd franchise, but a reorganization of its two conferences could upset some fans. Meanwhile, the league is capitalizing on the Internet as a revenue source it signed a four-year $300 million deal with SportsLine.com, AOL, and CBS in 2001 to promote and maintain the league's NLF.com site.

## HISTORY

Descended from the English game of rugby, American football was developed in the late 1800s by Walter Camp, a player from Yale University who is generally credited with introducing new rules for downs and scoring. Professional teams sprang up in the 1890s, but football remained relatively unorganized until 1920, when George Halas and college star Jim Thorpe helped organize the American Professional Football Association. The new league featured 14 teams from the Midwest and East, including Halas' Staleys (now the Chicago Bears) and the Racine Cardinals (now the Arizona Cardinals). In 1922 the association changed its name to the National Football League.

The new league suffered many growing pains over the next decade, but by the 1930s the NFL had settled on 10 teams including the Green Bay Packers (joined in 1921), the New York Giants (1925), and the Philadelphia Eagles (1933). Interest in the game remained somewhat regional, however, until the late 1940s and 1950s. In 1946 the Cleveland Rams moved to Los Angeles, and in 1950 the NFL expanded with three teams joining from the defunct All-American Football Conference. Television showed its potential in 1958 when that year's championship game, the first to be televised nationally, kept audiences riveted with an overtime victory by the Baltimore Colts over the Giants. In 1962 the NFL signed its first league-wide television contract with CBS for $4.65 million.

The 1960s brought a new challenge in the form of the upstart American Football League (AFL). Concerned that the AFL would steal players with higher salaries and draw away fans, NFL commissioner Pete Rozelle negotiated a deal in 1966 to combine the leagues.

That season concluded with the first AFL-NFL World Championship Game, which was renamed the Super Bowl in 1969. When the merger was completed in 1970, the new NFL sported 26 teams.

Football's popularity exploded during the 1970s, helped by the rise of franchise dynasties such as the Pittsburgh Steelers (four Super Bowl wins) and the Dallas Cowboys (five NFC titles). In 1982 the Oakland Raiders moved to Los Angeles after a jury ruled against the NFL's attempts to keep the team in Oakland. The decision prompted other teams to relocate in search of better facilities and more revenue. (The Raiders returned to Oakland in 1995.) Rozelle stepped down in 1989 and was replaced by Paul Tagliabue.

During the 1990s the league expanded to 30 teams, adding the Carolina Panthers and Jacksonville Jaguars in 1995. The next year Art Modell moved his Cleveland Browns franchise to Baltimore to become the Ravens (the city of Cleveland held onto the rights to the Browns name and history and the franchise was revived in 1999), and in 1997 the Houston Oilers defected to Tennessee and were renamed the Titans. The next year brought new television deals worth $17.6 billion over eight years.

The NFL made plans for new expansion in 1999, awarding a franchise to Robert McNair of Houston, who paid a record $700 million franchise fee and $310 million for a new stadium. Named the Houston Texans, the team is set to start play in 2002. (The NFL plans to realign the NFC and AFC that year, shifting to eight divisions with four teams each.) In 2001 the NFL struck a four-year $300 million deal with SportsLine.com, CBS, and AOL to operate and promote the league's NFL.com Web site.

**Commissioner:** Paul J. Tagliabue
**CFO:** Barbara A. Kaczynski
**EVP and League Counsel:** Jeff Pash
**EVP Business, Properties, and Club Services:**
Roger Goodell
**EVP Labor Relations; Chairman, NFLMC:**
Harold R. Henderson
**EVP New Media and Enterprises:** Thomas E. Spock
**SVP Broadcast Planning:** Dennis Lewin
**SVP Communications and Government Affairs:**
Joe Browne
**SVP Events:** Jim Steeg
**SVP Football Operations:** George Young
**SVP New Media:** Christopher J. Russo
**VP Player and Employee Development:** Lem Burnham
**Executive Director, NFLPA:** Gene Upshaw
**President and CEO, NFL Europe:** Oliver Luck
**Managing Director, NFL Europe:** Jim Connelly
**SVP and Managing Director, NFL International:**
Douglas Quinn
**Senior Director Human Resources and Administration:**
John Buzzeo
**Auditors:** Arthur Andersen LLP

## LOCATIONS

**HQ:** 280 Park Ave., New York, NY 10017
**Phone:** 212-450-2000          **Fax:** 212-681-7573
**Web:** www.nfl.com

The National Football League oversees 31 franchises in
30 cities. It also has six franchises in Europe.

## PRODUCTS/OPERATIONS

**National Football League Franchises**

**American Football Conference**
Baltimore Ravens
Buffalo Bills
Cincinnati Bengals
Cleveland Browns
Denver Broncos
Indianapolis Colts
Jacksonville Jaguars
Kansas City Chiefs
Miami Dolphins
New England Patriots
New York Jets
Oakland Raiders
Pittsburgh Steelers
San Diego Chargers
Seattle Seahawks
Tennessee Titans

**National Football Conference**
Arizona Cardinals
Atlanta Falcons
Carolina Panthers
Chicago Bears
Dallas Cowboys
Detroit Lions
Green Bay Packers
Minnesota Vikings
New Orleans Saints
New York Giants
Philadelphia Eagles
San Francisco 49ers
St. Louis Rams
Tampa Bay Buccaneers
Washington Redskins

## COMPETITORS

| | |
|---|---|
| CART | NHL |
| FIFA | PGA |
| Major League Baseball | World Wrestling |
| NASCAR | Federation |
| NBA | |

## HISTORICAL FINANCIALS & EMPLOYEES

| Not-for-profit FYE: March 31 | Annual Growth | 3/92 | 3/93 | 3/94 | 3/95 | 3/96 | 3/97 | 3/98 | 3/99 | 3/00 | 3/01 |
|---|---|---|---|---|---|---|---|---|---|---|---|
| Sales ($ mil.) | 12.5% | — | — | 1,753 | 1,730 | 2,059 | 2,331 | 2,448 | 3,271 | 3,602 | 4,000 |
| Employees | 4.0% | — | — | — | — | — | — | 400 | 400 | 450 | 450 |

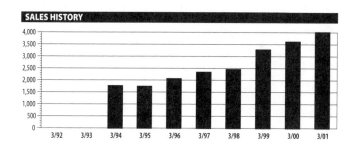

SALES HISTORY

# NATIONAL GEOGRAPHIC SOCIETY

## OVERVIEW

If your only brush with the National Geographic Society involves maneuvering around the stacks of yellow magazines wedged into every corner of Grandma's attic, you might be surprised to learn what the organization's been up to lately. Still publishing its flagship *National Geographic* magazine (with 10 million member/subscribers), the Washington, DC-based, not-for-profit organization has branched across the media spectrum to enhance our familiarity with all things geographic.

For-profit subsidiary National Geographic Ventures has expanded the organization's presence on TV and the Web, as well as in map-making and retail. The company operates the National Geographic Channel with NBC and FOX. The National Geographic Society hasn't abandoned its roots, though: it continues to fund geographic expeditions (it has financed more than 7,000 treks) and sponsor exhibits, lectures, and education programs.

As competition from relative newcomers such as Discovery Communications intensifies, the commercialization of the National Geographic Society has been accelerating.

## HISTORY

In 1888 a group of scientists and explorers gathered in Washington, DC, to form the National Geographic Society. Gardiner Hubbard was its first president. The organization mailed the first edition of its magazine, dated October 1888, to 165 members. The magazine was clothed in a brown cover and contained a few esoteric articles, such as "The Classification of Geographic Forms by Genesis." The organization's tradition of funding expeditions began in 1890 when it sent geologist Israel Russell to explore Alaska. It began issuing regular monthly editions of *National Geographic* in 1896.

Following Hubbard's death in 1897, his son-in-law, inventor Alexander Graham Bell, became president. Aiming to boost the magazine's popularity, he hired Gilbert Grosvenor (who later married Bell's daughter) as editor. Grosvenor turned the magazine from a dry, technical publication to one of more general interest.

Under Grosvenor the magazine pioneered the use of photography, including rare photographs of remote Tibet (1904), the first hand-tinted colored photos (1910), the first underwater color photos (1920s), and the first color aerial photographs (1930).

The organization sponsored Robert Peary's trek to the North Pole in 1909 and Hiram Bingham's 1912 exploration of Machu Picchu in Peru. National Geographic expanded into cartography with the creation of a maps division in 1915. Grosvenor became president in 1920.

By 1930 circulation was 1.2 million (up from 2,200 in 1900). Grosvenor's policy of printing only "what is of a kindly nature ... about any country or people" resulted in two articles that were criticized for their kindly portrayal of pre-war Nazi Germany. (However, National Geographic maps and photographs were used by the US government for WWII intelligence.) That policy eased over the years, and in 1961 a *National Geographic* article described the growing US involvement in Vietnam.

Grosvenor retired in 1954. His son Melville Bell Grosvenor, who became president and editor in 1957, accelerated book publishing and created a film unit that aired its first TV documentary in 1965. Melville retired in 1967.

Melville's son Gilbert Melville Grosvenor took over as president in 1970. The organization debuted its *National Geographic Explorer* television series in 1985. National Geographic branched into commercial ventures in 1995 when it created for-profit subsidiary National Geographic Ventures to expand its presence on television and the Internet, as well as with maps and retail.

Grosvenor became chairman in 1996, and Reg Murphy took over as president. Murphy shook up the organization by laying off nearly a quarter of its staff and stepping up its profit-making activities. National Geographic branched into cable television in 1996 when it partnered with NBC to launch a documentary channel (FOX bought into the partnership three years later).

John Fahey replaced Murphy as president in 1998. The following year National Geographic unveiled its *Adventure* magazine. To fight a circulation decline, the organization began offering *National Geographic* on newsstands for the first time in 1999. In 2000 National Geographic Ventures acquired recreational topographic map company Wildflower Productions. As part of an agreement to buy 30% of travel portal iExplore, National Geographic also agreed to license the use of its name for the first time in the organization's history.

## HISTORICAL FINANCIALS & EMPLOYEES

| Not-for-profit<br>FYE: December 31 | Annual<br>Growth | 12/91 | 12/92 | 12/93 | 12/94 | 12/95 | 12/96 | 12/97 | 12/98 | 12/99 | 12/00 |
|---|---|---|---|---|---|---|---|---|---|---|---|
| Sales ($ mil.) | 1.2% | — | 453 | 423 | 419 | 423 | 401 | 489 | 537 | 600 | 500 |
| Employees | (3.6%) | — | 2,005 | 1,700 | 1,493 | 1,551 | 1,300 | 1,214 | 1,410 | — | 1,500 |

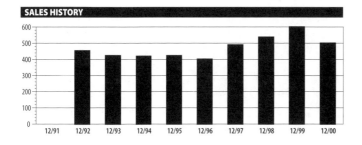

SALES HISTORY

NATIONAL
GEOGRAPHIC
SOCIETY

# NATIONAL HOCKEY LEAGUE

## OVERVIEW

Contrary to popular humor, you don't have to go to a fight to see a hockey match break out in the NHL. Nevertheless, for the New York City-based National Hockey League's 30 US and Canadian teams, there's plenty of opportunity for fisticuffs in each game. The clubs are organized into two conferences with three divisions each. Seven minor and semi-pro hockey leagues also play under the NHL banner.

League revenue has increased markedly over the past few seasons, more so with the five-year TV contract with ABC and ESPN that began with the 2000-01 season.

But the NHL still has a long way to go to catch up to the other professional sports leagues in popularity. Commissioner Gary Bettman's top priorities include changing the slow, low-scoring image of the game (rule changes the past two seasons have helped improve the pace).

League play has been marred by violence, including a near epidemic of concussions. Equipment used by players — including the size and construction of elbow and shoulder pads, which increasingly have been used as weapons — is under scrutiny. The lack of marquee players of Wayne Gretzky's stature is also seen as a detriment to the league's success.

## HISTORY

The National Hockey League traces its heritage to 1893, when the Stanley Cup (donated by Lord Stanley, Governor General of Canada) was first awarded to the Montreal Amateur Athletic Association hockey club of the Amateur Hockey Association of Canada. The National Hockey Association (NHA) was the first professional league to award the Cup (a large silver chalice with a new layer added each year, passed to the winning team and engraved with the names of that team's players) in 1910.

The NHA folded in 1917 when feuding brought the need for a new image. That year Frank Calder, a British scholar and former sports journalist who came to Canada to be a soccer player, decided to keep the NHA's teams intact, rename the organization the National Hockey League (NHL), and appoint himself president. The league consisted of four teams that played a 22-game schedule.

The original Ottawa Senators (the team went under in 1934 and reemerged as an expansion team in 1992) were the league's first dynasty, winning four Cups from 1920-27. The NHL added its first US team in 1925 when the Boston Bruins joined the league, and the 1920s saw continued expansion, but the NHL remained amorphous as many teams joined up and dropped out during the decade. Hordes of players went to WWII, forcing the NHL to field teams whose players were too young, too old, or barely able to skate. The league almost shut down, but the Canadian government encouraged play to continue, claiming it boosted national morale.

The Montreal Canadiens (winners of 24 Stanley Cups, more than any other franchise by far) dominated the NHL for most of the next three decades. The NHL, after representing a small number of teams for many years, launched its largest expansion in league history in 1967 when six US-based franchises joined up. The league expanded to 21 teams in 1979 by absorbing its rival professional league, the World Hockey Association. US interest in the sport stagnated for many years, however, as it was largely considered a Canadian sport, and its reputation for brutal violence turned off many fans. The NHL tried to put an end to its slugfest image by implementing new rules in 1992, reducing violent play, and emphasizing a quicker game based on skill and style.

Several expansion teams (Anaheim, Florida, Tampa Bay, Ottawa, San Jose) were added to the NHL throughout the 1990s, a decade marred by the only major labor dispute in the league's history. Team owners instituted a player lockout in 1994 and delayed the season but ultimately failed in their goal of implementing a salary cap (the current contract between the players' union and owners runs through 2004). In 1997 the NHL added four new expansion teams (Atlanta; Columbus, Ohio; Minnesota; and Nashville, Tennessee), introducing them over a four-year period.

The league's plan to boost popularity by using pro players in the 1998 Winter Olympics games in Nagano, Japan, was thwarted by limited, late-night coverage. Later that year NHL team owners agreed to a $600 million, five-year television contract with Walt Disney's ABC and ESPN starting with the 2000-01 season.

In 2000, as part of a plan to bring its entire Internet business under the NHL roof, the league bought IBM's interest in NHL Interactive CyberEnterprises for $10 million. Also that year the Minnesota Wild and the Columbus Blue Jackets expansion teams took to the ice.

## OFFICERS

**Commissioner:** Gary B. Bettman, age 49
**EVP and COO:** Jon Litner
**EVP and Chief Legal Officer:** William Daly
**SVP:** Richie Woodworth
**SVP New Business Development; President, NHL Interactive and CyberEnterprises:** Keith Ritter
**SVP Television and Media Ventures:** Doug Perlman
**VP and CFO:** Craig Harnett
**VP Broadcasting and Programming:** Adam Acone
**VP Club Marketing:** Scott Carmichael
**VP Corporate Marketing:** Andrew Judelson
**VP Human Resources:** Janet A. Meyers
**Group VP Consumer Products Marketing:** Brian Jennings
**Group VP and Managing Director, NHL International:** Ken Yaffe
**President, NHL Enterprises:** Ed Horne
**Director of Officiating:** Andy van Hellemond
**Auditors:** PricewaterhouseCoopers LLP

## LOCATIONS

**HQ:** 1251 Avenue of the Americas, 47th Fl., New York, NY 10020
**Phone:** 212-789-2000     **Fax:** 212-789-2020
**Web:** www.nhl.com

The National Hockey League has 24 teams in the US and six in Canada.

## PRODUCTS/OPERATIONS

**NHL Teams**

| Eastern Conference | Western Conference |
|---|---|
| Atlantic Division | Central Division |
| New Jersey Devils | Chicago Blackhawks |
| New York Islanders | Columbus Blue Jackets |
| New York Rangers | Detroit Red Wings |
| Philadelphia Flyers | Nashville Predators |
| Pittsburgh Penguins | St. Louis Blues |
| Northeast Division | Northwest Division |
| Boston Bruins | Calgary Flames |
| Buffalo Sabres | Colorado Avalanche |
| Montreal Canadiens | Edmonton Oilers |
| Ottawa Senators | Minnesota Wild |
| Toronto Maple Leafs | Vancouver Canucks |
| Southeast Division | Pacific Division |
| Atlanta Thrashers | Mighty Ducks of |
| Carolina Hurricanes | Anaheim |
| Florida Panthers | Dallas Stars |
| Tampa Bay Lightning | Los Angeles Kings |
| Washington Capitals | Phoenix Coyotes |
|  | San Jose Sharks |

**Minor and Semi-Pro Leagues**
American Hockey League
Central Hockey League
East Coast Hockey League
International Hockey League
United Hockey League
West Coast Hockey League
Western Professional Hockey League

## COMPETITORS

CART
Indy Racing League
Major League Baseball
NASCAR
NBA
NFL
PGA

## HISTORICAL FINANCIALS & EMPLOYEES

| Association FYE: June 30 | Annual Growth | 6/91 | 6/92 | 6/93 | 6/94 | 6/95 | 6/96 | 6/97 | 6/98 | 6/99 | 6/00 |
|---|---|---|---|---|---|---|---|---|---|---|---|
| Sales ($ mil.) | 18.8% | — | — | — | 604 | 763 | 728 | 1,099 | 1,336 | 1,476 | 1,697 |
| Employees | 27.3% | — | — | — | 110 | 150 | 200 | 257 | 289 | — | — |

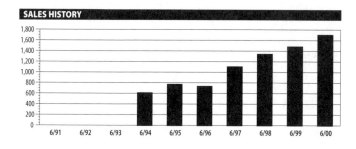

SALES HISTORY

# AMTRAK

Is Amtrak the big engine that couldn't? The Washington, DC-based National Railroad Passenger Corporation, better known as Amtrak, is a private, for-profit company — that can't seem to make a profit.

Amtrak, which has a monopoly on US intercity passenger rail service and serves 500 communities in 45 states, carries 22.5 million passengers each year. The company is governed by a seven-member Reform Board (which until 1997 was a nine-member board of directors) established by Congress. The board consists of the Secretary of Transportation and six other members appointed by the President of the US and approved by the Senate.

Almost wholly owned by the US Department of Transportation, Amtrak hasn't once turned a profit in its nearly 30-year history. To change that, Congress approved a one-time $2.3 billion capital expenditure that Amtrak is using to

establish a new, high-speed commuter rail service between Boston and Washington, DC (with more routes planned outside the Northeast) and to improve infrastructure, equipment, and customer service. Amtrak is also adding revenues by carrying mail and time-sensitive cargo to help free itself from government handouts by 2003, and it moved to cut costs in 2001 by offering voluntary separation and early retirement packages to 2,900 management employees.

The September 11, 2001, terrorist attacks on the US presented a new challenge for Amtrak: Flight cancellations and travelers' reluctance to return to the skies boosted demand for passenger rail services by more than 30% in the first two weeks after the attacks. To accelerate improvements to its system in order to keep some of those new passengers on the trains, Amtrak has asked for a fresh infusion of government help.

## HISTORY

US passenger train travel peaked in 1929, with 20,000 trains in operation. But the spread of automobiles, bus service, and air travel cut into business, and by the late 1960s only about 500 passenger trains remained running in the US. In 1970 the combined losses of all private train operations exceeded $1.8 billion in today's dollars. That year Congress passed the Rail Passenger Service Act, which created Amtrak to preserve America's passenger rail system. Although railroads were offered stock in the corporation for their passenger equipment, most just wrote off the loss.

Amtrak began operating in 1971 with 1,200 cars, most built in the 1950s. Although the company lost money from the outset ($153 million in 1972), it continued to be bankrolled by Uncle Sam, despite much criticism. Amtrak ordered its first new equipment in 1973, the year it also began taking over stations, yards, and service staff. The company didn't own any track until 1976, when it purchased hundreds of miles of right-of-way track from Boston to Washington, DC.

After a 1979 study showed Amtrak passengers to be by far the most heavily subsidized travelers in the US, Congress ordered the company to better utilize its resources. The 1980s saw Amtrak leasing its rights-of-way along its tracks in the Northeast corridor to telecommunications companies, which installed fiber-optic cables, and beginning mail and freight services for extra revenue.

In the early 1990s Amtrak faced a number of

challenges: Midwest flooding, falling airfares, and safety concerns over a number of rail accidents, particularly the 1993 wreck of the Sunset Limited near Mobile, Alabama, in which 47 people were killed (the worst accident in Amtrak's history). In 1994 Amtrak's Board of Directors (at Congress' behest) adopted a plan to be free of federal support by 2002 (later adjusted to 2003). In 1995 the company began planning high-speed trains for its heavily traveled East Coast routes.

In 1997 Amtrak began increasing its freight hauling and had its first profitable product line: the Metroliner route between New York and Washington, DC. Amtrak's board of directors was replaced by Congress that year with a seven-member Reform Board. Chairman and president Thomas Downs resigned that year, and Tommy Thompson, then governor of Wisconsin, took over as chairman. Former Massachusetts governor Michael Dukakis was named vice chairman, and George Warrington stepped in as Amtrak's president and CEO.

Technical problems in 1999 delayed Amtrak's introduction of the Acela high-speed train in the Northeast until late 2000, when service began in the Boston-Washington, DC, corridor. In 2001 Amtrak pitched a 20-year plan, involving an annual outlay of $1.5 billion in federal funds, for expanding and modernizing its passenger service to help alleviate highway and airport congestion nationwide. Thompson left the Amtrak board in 2001 after he was named US secretary of health and human services.

Vice Chairman: Michael S. Dukakis
President, CEO, and Director: George D. Warrington
CFO: Arlene R. Friner
EVP Marketing and Sales: Barbara J. Richardson
EVP Operations: E. S. Bagley Jr.
SVP and General Counsel: James T. Lloyd
VP and Counsel, Business Diversity and Strategic
  Initiatives: Wanda Morris Hightower
VP Freight Railroad Affairs: Lee W. Bullock
VP Government Affairs: Sandy J. Brown
VP High-Speed Rail Development: David J. Carol
VP Human Resources: Lorraine A. Green
VP Labor Relations: Joseph M. Bress
VP Procurement: Michael Rienzi
VP Service Operations: Anne W. Hoey
President, Amtrak Intercity: Edward V. Walker
President, Amtrak Mail & Express: Lee H. Sargrad
President, Amtrak West: Gilbert O. Mallery
Corporate Secretary: Stewart G. Simonson
Auditors: KPMG LLP

## LOCATIONS

HQ: National Railroad Passenger Corporation
  60 Massachusetts Ave. NE, Washington, DC 20002
Phone: 202-906-3000      Fax: 202-906-3306
Web: www.amtrak.com

The National Railroad Passenger corporation (or
Amtrak) is the only intercity passenger rail service in
the US with routes across the entire country. The
company serves 45 states.

## PRODUCTS/OPERATIONS

**2000 Sales**

|  | % of total |
|---|---|
| Passenger tickets | 52 |
| Other | 48 |
| **Total** | **100** |

## COMPETITORS

America West
AMR
Burlington Northern
  Santa Fe
Coach USA
Continental Airlines
Delta
FedEx
Greyhound
Metra
Northwest Airlines
Port Authority of NY & NJ
Roadway
Schneider National
Southwest Airlines
TWA
UAL
Union Pacific
UPS
U.S. Postal Service
US Airways
Yellow

## HISTORICAL FINANCIALS & EMPLOYEES

| Government-owned FYE: September 30 | Annual Growth | 9/91 | 9/92 | 9/93 | 9/94 | 9/95 | 9/96 | 9/97 | 9/98 | 9/99 | 9/00 |
|---|---|---|---|---|---|---|---|---|---|---|---|
| Sales ($ mil.) | 5.0% | 1,359 | 1,325 | 1,403 | 1,413 | 1,497 | 1,555 | 1,674 | 2,285 | 2,042 | 2,111 |
| Net income ($ mil.) | — | (722) | (712) | (731) | (986) | (808) | (764) | (762) | (353) | (702) | (768) |
| Income as % of sales | — | — | — | — | — | — | — | — | — | — | — |
| Employees | 0.6% | 23,741 | 24,000 | 24,000 | 24,000 | 24,100 | 23,000 | 23,000 | 24,000 | 25,000 | 25,000 |

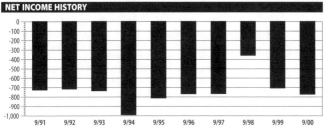

**NET INCOME HISTORY**

**2000 FISCAL YEAR-END**
Debt ratio: 36.6%
Return on equity: —
Cash ($ mil.): 99
Current ratio: 0.45
Long-term debt ($ mil.): 2,798

# NATIONWIDE

## OVERVIEW

Call it truth in advertising — Nationwide has offices throughout the US.

The Columbus, Ohio-based company is a leading US property/casualty insurer that, while still a mutual firm, operates in part through Nationwide Financial, a publicly held insurance company of which it owns 80%.

In addition to personal and commercial property/casualty coverage, life insurance, and financial services, Nationwide offers surplus lines, professional liability, workers' compensation, managed health care, and other coverage. The company sells its products through such affiliates as Farmland Insurance, GatesMcDonald, and Scottsdale Insurance.

Although its name reflects the scope of its domestic operations, Nationwide is turning its attention to foreign soil. As competition in the deregulating insurance and financial services industry heats up globally, the company is building its international operations (it's already in some 35 countries) through purchases, focusing particularly on asset management and other financial services. Domestically, Nationwide is focusing on wealth management and retirement products.

## HISTORY

In 1919 members of the Ohio Farm Bureau Federation, a farmers' consumer group, established their own automobile insurance company. (As rural drivers, they didn't want to pay city rates.) To get a license from the state, the company, called Farm Bureau Mutual, needed 100 policyholders. It gathered more than 1,000. Founder Murray Lincoln headed the company until 1964.

The insurer expanded into Delaware, Maryland, North Carolina, and Vermont in 1928, and in 1931 it began selling auto insurance to city folks. It expanded into fire insurance in 1934 and life insurance the next year.

During WWII growth slowed, although the company had operations in 12 states and Washington, DC, by 1943. It diversified in 1946 when it bought a Columbus, Ohio, radio station. By 1952 the firm had resumed expansion and changed its name to Nationwide.

The company was one of the first auto insurance companies to use its agents to sell other financial products, adding life insurance and mutual funds in the mid-1950s. Nationwide General, the country's first merit-rated auto insurance firm, was formed in 1956.

Nationwide established Neckura in Germany in 1965 to sell auto and fire insurance. Four years later it bought GatesMcDonald, a provider of risk, tax, benefit, and health care management services. It organized its property/casualty operations into Nationwide Property & Casualty in 1979.

The company experienced solid growth throughout the 1980s by establishing or purchasing insurance firms, among them Colonial Insurance of California (1980), Financial Horizons Life (1981), Scottsdale (1982), and, the largest, Employers Insurance of Wausau (1985). Wausau wrote the country's first workers' compensation policy in 1911.

Earnings were up and down in the 1990s as the company invested in Wausau and in consolidating office operations. Nationwide set up an ethics office in 1995, a time of increased scrutiny of insurance industry sales practices, and made an effort to hire more women as agents. In 1996 the Florida Insurance Commission claimed the company discriminated against customers on the basis of age, gender, health, income, marital status, and location. Nationwide countered that the allegations originated from displeased agents.

In 1997 the company settled a lawsuit by agreeing to stop its redlining practices (it avoided selling homeowners' insurance to urban customers with homes valued at less than $50,000 or more than 30 years old, which allegedly discriminated against minorities).

As the century came to a close, Nationwide began to narrow its focus on its core businesses. It spun off Nationwide Financial Services so the unit could have better access to capital, and it expanded both at home and abroad through such purchases as ALLIED Group (multiline insurance), CalFarm (agricultural insurance in California), and AXA subsidiary PanEuroLife (asset management in Europe). It jettisoned such operations as West Coast Life Insurance, its Wausau subsidiary, and its ALLIED Life operations. The company's discrimination woes came back to haunt it in 1999, and it created a $750,000 fund to help residents of poor Cincinnati neighborhoods buy homes.

At the end of 2000 Nationwide Health Plans asked regulators for permission to exit the profit-poor HMO business. The division plans to maintain its more popular PPO operations. In 2001 Nationwide's expansion in Europe continued with the purchase of UK fund manager Gartmore Investment Management.

## OFFICERS

**Chairman and CEO:** William G. Jurgensen
**EVP and CFO:** Robert A. Oakley
**EVP and Chief Administrative Officer:** Donna A. James
**EVP and Chief Investment Officer:**
Robert J. Woodward Jr.
**EVP, Corporate Strategy:** Michael S. Helfer
**SVP and Chief Communications Officer:**
John R. Cook Jr.
**SVP and General Counsel:** Patricia R. Hatler
**SVP, Corporate Relations, Nationwide and Nationwide Financial Services:** Gregory Lashutka, age 57
**SVP, Fixed Income Securities:** Edwin P. McCausland
**SVP, Corporate Strategy:** David A. Diamond
**President and CEO, Villanova Capital:** Paul J. Hondros
**President and Managing Director, Nationwide Global Holdings:** Richard D. Headley
**President and COO, Nationwide Financial, Nationwide Life Insurance, and Nationwide Life & Annuity Insurance:** Joseph J. Gasper
**President, Nationwide Agencies:** Thomas L. Crumrine
**President and COO, Nationwide Insurance:**
Galen R. Barnes
**President and COO, Scottsdale Insurance Companies:**
R. Max Williamson
**President, NFS Distributors:** Richard A. Karas
**President and COO, Allied Insurance:**
Steve S. Rasmusser
**SVP, Business Development and Sponsor Relations, Nationwide Insurance:** David K. Hollingsworth
**SVP and Chief Actuary, Nationwide Financial:**
Phillip C. Gath
**Auditors:** KPMG LLP

## LOCATIONS

**HQ:** One Nationwide Plaza, Columbus, OH 43215
**Phone:** 614-249-7111    **Fax:** 614-249-7705
**Web:** www.nationwide.com

Nationwide operates in more than 35 countries around the world.

## PRODUCTS/OPERATIONS

**2000 Assets**

|  | $ mil. | % of total |
|---|---|---|
| Cash & equivalents | 1,271 | 1 |
| Bonds | 27,742 | 24 |
| Stocks | 4,071 | 4 |
| Mortgage loans & real estate | 7,570 | 6 |
| Assets in separate account | 67,759 | 58 |
| Other assets | 8,626 | 7 |
| **Total** | **117,039** | **100** |

**Selected Subsidiaries and Affiliates**
GatesMcDonald
Nationwide Agribusiness
  Farmland Insurance
Nationwide Federal Credit Union
Nationwide Financial (81.5%)
  The 401k Company
  National Deferred Compensation
  Nationwide Advisory Services
  Nationwide Home Mortgage Company
  Nationwide Retirement Plan Services, Inc.
  Nationwide Retirement Solutions
  PEBSCO Nationwide Retirement Solutions
  Pension Associates, Inc.
Nationwide Global
  PanEuroLife
Nationwide Insurance
  Allied Insurance
  CalFarm Insurance
  Nationwide Health Plans
Nationwide Realty Investors
Scottsdale Insurance

## COMPETITORS

| | | |
|---|---|---|
| Allstate | The Hartford | Pacific Mutual |
| American Financial | John Hancock Financial Services | Principal Financial |
| AXA | Liberty Mutual | Prudential |
| AXA Financial | MassMutual | St. Paul Companies |
| Blue Cross | MetLife | State Farm |
| CIGNA | New York Life | UnitedHealth Group |
| Citigroup | Northwestern Mutual | USAA |
| CNA Financial | | |
| Guardian Life | | |

## HISTORICAL FINANCIALS & EMPLOYEES

| Mutual company FYE: December 31 | Annual Growth | 12/91 | 12/92 | 12/93 | 12/94 | 12/95 | 12/96 | 12/97 | 12/98 | 12/99 | 12/00 |
|---|---|---|---|---|---|---|---|---|---|---|---|
| Assets ($ mil.) | 15.3% | — | 37,582 | 42,213 | 47,696 | 57,420 | 67,624 | 83,214 | 98,280 | 115,760 | 117,039 |
| Net income ($ mil.) | 21.6% | — | 69 | 501 | 445 | 183 | 250 | 1,031 | 963 | 526 | 331 |
| Income as % of assets | — | — | 0.2% | 1.2% | 0.9% | 0.3% | 0.4% | 1.2% | 1.0% | 0.5% | 0.3% |
| Employees | 0.9% | — | 32,500 | 32,583 | 32,600 | 32,949 | 33,184 | 29,051 | 32,815 | 35,000 | 35,000 |

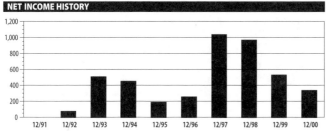

**NET INCOME HISTORY**

**2000 FISCAL YEAR-END**
Equity as % of assets: 7.2%
Return on assets: 0.3%
Return on equity: —
Long-term debt ($ mil.): 558
Sales ($ mil.): 32,834

# NUMMI

## OVERVIEW

Like a Samurai assembly worker with American roots, Fremont, California-based New United Motor Manufacturing, Inc. (NUMMI) has the capacity to make 240,000 cars and 150,000 pickups a year. The 50-50 joint venture between General Motors (GM) and Toyota makes Tacoma light pickups and Corolla sedans for Toyota, and Chevrolet Prizm sedans (formerly called Geos; the Prizm model may soon be discontinued and replaced with a next-generation model) made for GM. NUMMI is the exclusive manufacturer of Tacoma light pickup trucks for the North American market.

NUMMI began as an experiment to see if Japanese management techniques emphasizing team decision-making would work in the US. The experiment has been a success story. Toyota's strategy to build more vehicles in the markets it serves (rather than transport them) helps the company reduce costs. NUMMI's production methods are considered to be among the world's most efficient.

Although GM may discontinue its only model produced at the Fremont facility (Chevrolet Prizm), the US automaker has hinted about building a replacement new "life-style vehicle" (built in both right- and left-hand drive models for sales in Japan, as well as in the US). GM and Toyota have agreed to a five-year research deal to explore development of alternative-fuel vehicles.

## HISTORY

Rivals General Motors (GM) and Toyota applied the old adage, "If you can't beat 'em, join 'em," in forming their 50-50 joint venture New United Motor Manufacturing (NUMMI). In the early 1980s GM was losing ground in the small-car market, and Japan's Toyota wanted to build cars in the US to ease trade tension. GM head Roger Smith and Toyota chairman Eiji Toyoda met in 1982 to discuss ways to achieve their goals.

After a year of negotiations, the two companies announced their partnership at GM's plant (which GM had closed in 1982) in Fremont, California. Toyota put up $100 million, and GM provided the plant (valued at $89 million) and $11 million cash. The companies also raised $350 million to build a stamping plant.

To gain FTC approval, the companies agreed to limit the venture to 12 years (extended later), make no more than 250,000 cars a year for GM, and refrain from sharing strategic information. In 1984 the FTC approved the deal and NUMMI was born.

The Fremont plant had a reputation for poor labor relations, and Toyota originally refused to rehire any of the workers from the plant; after prolonged negotiations with the UAW, it agreed to hire 50% plus one of the former workers. From the outset NUMMI was different, with fewer management layers and a blurred distinction between blue- and white-collar workers.

NUMMI's first car, a Chevy Nova, rolled off the assembly line in late 1984. The company began producing the Corolla FX, a two-door version of the four-door Nova, in 1986. NUMMI earned kudos for high worker morale and productivity and was selected that year as a case study on positive labor-management

relations for the International Labor Organization Conference.

Despite its success on some fronts, NUMMI's sales slid during the late 1980s. It had earned a reputation for high-quality cars, but it struggled with high overhead and weak Nova sales. In 1988 NUMMI halted Nova and Corolla FX production to build Geo Prizm and Corolla sedans.

By late 1989 NUMMI's production numbers had begun to rebound. In 1990 NUMMI began a major expansion as it geared up to build Toyota's half-ton pickup. Its first Toyota 4X2 pickup (the Toyota Hi-Lux pickup truck) rolled off the assembly line in 1991, followed by the Toyota 4X4 pickup the next year.

In 1993 the FTC approved an indefinite extension of the original 12-year GM-Toyota agreement. Also that year NUMMI began building the Toyota Xtracab, and it began constructing a plastics plant to build bumper coverings for Prizms and Corollas. It also expanded the paint, body welding, and assembly plant facilities. Although Toyota had produced half of its North America-bound pickups in Japan and half in the US for years, it shifted all compact truck production to the NUMMI plant with the 1995 launch of the Tacoma. NUMMI built its 3 millionth vehicle in 1997 and marked the event by donating three vehicles to charitable agencies in the Fremont area.

In 1998 GM changed the name of the Geo Prizm to the Chevrolet Prizm. The companies agreed in 1999 to a five-year partnership to develop and possibly produce alternative fuel vehicles. GM alluded to discontinuing the Prizm in 2000, possibly to be replaced by a next-generation model.

**President and CEO:** Kanji Ishii
**VP, Human Resources:** Patricia Pineda
**Treasurer and General Manager Finance:** Y. Toyoda

## LOCATIONS

**HQ:** New United Motor Manufacturing, Inc.
45500 Fremont Blvd., Fremont, CA 94538
**Phone:** 510-498-5500       **Fax:** 510-770-4160
**Web:** www.nummi.com

New United Motor Manufacturing has a manufacturing plant in Fremont, California.

## PRODUCTS/OPERATIONS

**Selected Models**
Chevrolet Prizm (sedan)
Toyota Corolla (sedan)
Toyota Tacoma (pickup)

## COMPETITORS

DaimlerChrysler
Fiat
Ford
Fuji Heavy Industries
Honda
Hyundai
Isuzu
Kia Motors
Mack Trucks
Mazda
Nissan
Peugeot Motors of America, Inc.
Saab Automobile
Suzuki Motor
Volkswagen

# NYC HEALTH AND HOSPITALS

New York City Health and Hospitals Corp-oration (HHC) runs one of the largest munici-pal health service systems in the US.

The company has facilities in all five bor-oughs. It operates 11 acute care hospitals (in-cluding Bellevue, the nation's oldest public hospital), as well as community clinics, diag-nostic and treatment centers, long-term care facilities, and the city's correctional medical services. MetroPlus is the system's HMO.

In recent years HHC has lost paying patients to newer, better-equipped facilities, and is left caring for a deluge of medically indigent and Medicaid patients, who tend to be sicker than the general population since they wait longer to seek care.

To streamline, HHC has slashed jobs, worked to reduce the average length of stay of patients, and cut back on unnecessary facilities.

## HISTORY

The City of New York in 1929 created a de-partment to manage its hospitals for the poor. During the Depression, more than half of the city's residents were eligible for subsidized care, and its public hospitals operated at full capacity.

Four new hospitals opened in the 1950s, but the city was already having trouble maintain-ing existing facilities and attracting staff (young doctors preferred private, insurance-supported hospitals catering to the middle class.) Meanwhile, technological advances and increased demand for skilled nurses made hos-pitals more expensive to operate. The advent of Medicaid in 1965 was a boon for the system be-cause it brought in federal money.

In 1969 the city created the New York City Health and Hospitals Corporation (HHC) to manage its public health care system — and, it was hoped, to distance it from the political arena. But HHC was still dependent on the city for funds, arousing criticism from those who had hoped for more autonomy. A 1973 state re-port claimed that the people of New York City were not "materially better served by the Health and Hospitals Corporation than by its predecessor agencies."

City budget shortfalls in the mid-1970s led to cutbacks at HHC, including nearly 20% of staff. Later in the decade, several hospitals closed and some services were discontinued. Ed Koch became mayor in 1978 and gained more control over HHC's operations. Struggles between his administration and the system led three HHC presidents to resign by 1981. That year Koch crony Stanley Brezenoff assumed the post and helped transform HHC into a city pseudo-department.

The early 1980s brought greater prosperity to the system. Reimbursement rates and col-lections procedures improved, allowing HHC to upgrade its record-keeping and its ambula-tory and psychiatric care programs. In the late 1980s, sharp increases in AIDS and crack addiction cases strained the system, and a sluggish economy decreased city funding. Criticism mounted in the early 1990s, with al-legations of wrongful deaths, dangerous facili-ties, and lack of Medicaid payment controls. HHC lost patients to managed care providers, and revenues plummeted. In 1995 a city panel recommended radically revamping the system.

Faced with declining revenues and criticism from Mayor Rudolph Giuliani that HHC was "a jobs program," the company began cutting jobs and consolidating facilities in 1996. Under Giuliani's direction, HHC made plans to sell its Coney Island, Elmhurst, and Queens hospital centers. In 1997 the New York State Supreme Court struck down Giuliani's privatization ef-forts, saying the city council had a right to re-view and approve each sale. In 1998 Giuliani continued to seek to restructure HHC, and the agency itself contended it was making progress toward its restructuring goals, which were aimed at giving HHC more autonomy as well as more fiscal responsibility. In anticipation of a budget shortfall that year, the system laid off some 900 support staff employees. In 1999 the state court of appeals ruled HHC could not legally lease or sell its hospitals.

In 2000 HHC launched its effort to improve its physical infrastructure, by beginning the rebuilding and renovation of facilities in Brooklyn, Manhattan, and Queens. The organi-zation also began converting to an electronic (and thus more efficient) clinical information system. In 2001 HHC forged ahead with fur-ther restructuring initiatives. It introduced the Open Access plan, a cost-cutting measure de-signed to expedite the processes involved in outpatient visits.

## OFFICERS

**Chairman:** Richard T. Roberts
**VC:** Edward J. Rappa
**President and CEO:** Luis R. Marcos
**SVP Communications and Marketing:**
Jane D. Zimmerman
**SVP Corporate Planning, Community Health, and Intergovernmental Relations:** LaRay Brown
**SVP Finance and Capital and CFO:** Rick Langfelder
**SVP Medical and Professional Affairs:** Van Dunn
**SVP Operations:** Frank J. Cirillo
**SVP, Brooklyn Staten Island Family Health Network; Executive Director, Kings County Hospital Center:**
Jean Leon
**SVP, Generations Plus Northern Manhattan Health Network; Executive Director, Lincoln Medical and Mental Health Center, and Metropolitan Hospital Center:** Jose Sanchez
**SVP, North Bronx HealthCare Network; Executive Director, Jacobi Medical Center, and North Central Bronx Hospital:** Joseph S. Orlando
**SVP, Queens Health Network; Executive Director, Elmhurst Hospital Center:** Pete Velez
**SVP, South Manhattan Network; Executive Director, Bellevue Hospital Center:** Carlos Perez
**VP Human Resources and Workforce Development:**
Pamela S. Silverblatt
**General Counsel:** Alan D. Aviles
**Auditors:** KPMG LLP

## LOCATIONS

**HQ:** New York City Health and Hospitals Corporation
125 Worth St., Ste. 510, New York, NY 10013
**Phone:** 212-788-3321    **Fax:** 212-788-0040
**Web:** www.ci.nyc.ny.us/html/hhc

### HHC Networks

**Brooklyn Staten Island Family Health Network**
Coney Island Hospital
Dr. Susan Smith McKinney Nursing and Rehabilitation Center
East New York Diagnostic & Treatment Center
Kings County Hospital Center
Sea View Hospital Rehabilitation Center and Home

**Generations Plus Northern Manhattan Health Network**
Harlem Hospital Center
Lincoln Medical and Mental Health Center
Metropolitan Hospital Center
Morrisania Diagnostic & Treatment Center
Renaissance Diagnostic & Treatment Center
Segundo Ruiz Belvis Diagnostic & Treatment Center

**North Bronx Network**
Jacobi Medical Center
North Central Bronx Hospital

**North Brooklyn Health Network**
Cumberland Diagnostic & Treatment Center
Woodhull Medical and Mental Health Center

**Queens Health Network**
Elmhurst Hospital Center
Queens Hospital Center

**South Manhattan Healthcare Network**
Bellevue Hospital Center
Coler/Goldwater Memorial Hospital
Gouverneur Nursing Facility and Diagnostic & Treatment Center

## COMPETITORS

Carondelet Health
Catholic Healthcare Network
Columbia University
Cornell University
Memorial Sloan-Kettering
Montefiore Medical
Mount Sinai
NYU
North Shore-Long Island Jewish Health System
Saint Vincent Catholic Medical Centers

## HISTORICAL FINANCIALS & EMPLOYEES

| Government-owned FYE: June 30 | Annual Growth | 6/91 | 6/92 | 6/93 | 6/94 | 6/95 | 6/96 | 6/97 | 6/98 | 6/99 | 6/00 |
|---|---|---|---|---|---|---|---|---|---|---|---|
| Sales ($ mil.) | 2.4% | — | — | 3,468 | 3,949 | 4,134 | 4,460 | 4,069 | 3,835 | 4,131 | 4,100 |
| Employees | (4.8%) | — | — | — | 45,000 | 41,711 | 35,000 | 33,000 | 31,600 | 33,403 | 33,500 |

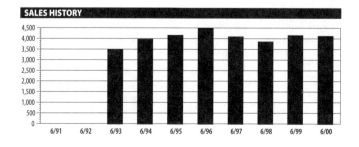

SALES HISTORY

# NEW YORK LIFE INSURANCE

## OVERVIEW

New York Life Insurance has been in the Big Apple since it was just a tiny seed.

The New York City-based insurer is adding products but retaining its core business: Life insurance and annuities. Its New York Life International is reaching out geographically, especially to areas where the life insurance market is not yet mature, such as Asia. The company has operations in Argentina, China, Hong Kong, India, Indonesia, Mexico, the Philippines, South Korea, Taiwan, Thailand, the US, and Vietnam.

As customer focus shifts from death benefits to retirement, New York Life has added such products and services as mutual funds and securities brokerage for individuals. It put its asset management businesses under one umbrella (New York Life Asset Management); it also offers its asset management services to institutional investors. Other lines of business include special group policies sold through AARP and to federal government contractors.

After state legislators failed to approve a mutual holding company structure, New York Life announced it would not follow its rivals in demutualizing for fear of being gobbled up in a merger. The insurer will instead use its considerable war chest to further build international and asset management operations.

## HISTORY

In 1841 actuary Pliny Freeman and 56 New York businessmen founded Nautilus Insurance Co., the third US policyholder-owned company. It began operating in 1845 and became New York Life in 1849.

By 1846 the company had the first life insurance agent west of the Mississippi River. Although the Civil War disrupted southern business, New York Life honored all its obligations and renewed lapsed policies when the war ended. By 1887 the company had developed its branch office system. By the turn of the century, the company had established an agent compensation plan that featured a lifetime income after 20 years of service (discontinued in 1991). New York Life moved into Europe in the late 1800s but withdrew after WWI.

In the early 1950s the company simplified insurance forms, slashed premiums, and updated mortality tables from the 1860s. In 1956 it became the first life insurer to use data-processing equipment on a large scale.

In the 1960s New York Life helped develop variable life insurance, which featured variable benefits and level premiums; it added variable annuities in 1968. Steady growth continued to the late 1970s, when high interest rates led to heavy policyholder borrowing. The outflow of money convinced New York Life to make its products more competitive as investments.

The company formed New York Life and Health Insurance Co. in 1982. It acquired MacKay-Shields Financial, which oversees its MainStay mutual funds, in 1984. The company's first pure investment product, a real estate limited partnership, debuted that year. When limited partnerships proved riskier than most insurance customers bargained for, investors sued New York Life; in 1996 the company negotiated a plan to liquidate the partnerships and reimburse investors.

Expansion continued in 1987 when it bought a controlling interest in a third-party insurance plan administrator and group insurance programs. The company also acquired Sanus Corp. Health Systems.

New York Life formed an insurance joint venture in Indonesia in 1992 and entered South Korea and Taiwan. The next year it bought Aetna UK's life insurance operations.

In 1994 New York Life grew its health care holdings, adding utilization review and physician practice management units. Allegations of churning (agents inducing customers to buy more expensive policies) led New York Life to overhaul its sales practices in 1994; it settled the resulting lawsuit for $300 million in 1995. Soon came claims that agents hadn't properly informed customers that some policies were vulnerable to interest-rate changes and that customers might be entitled to share in the settlement. Some agents lashed out, saying New York Life fired them so it wouldn't have to pay them retirement benefits.

As health care margins decreased and the insurance industry consolidated, New York Life in 1998 sold its health insurance operations and said it would demutualize — a plan ultimately foiled by the state legislature.

In 2000 the company bought two Mexican insurance firms, including the nation's #2 life insurer, Seguros Monterrey. It received Office of Thrift Supervision permission to open a bank, New York Life Trust Company. Also that year, the company created a subsidiary to house its asset management businesses and entered the Indian market through its joint venture with Max India.

## OFFICERS

**Chairman, President, and CEO:** Seymour Sternberg, age 57
**Vice Chairman; Chairman and CEO, New York Life International:** Gary G. Benanav
**Vice Chairman:** Frederick J. Sievert
**EVP:** Phillip J. Hildebrand
**EVP, Chief Investment Officer and Director:** Richard M. Kernan Jr.
**EVP and Secretary:** George J. Trapp
**EVP; Chairman and CEO, New York Life Investment Management LLC:** Gary E. Wendlandt
**SVP and General Counsel:** Shelia K. Davidson
**SVP and Treasurer:** Jay S. Calhoun
**SVP and Chief Information Officer:** Judith E. Campbell
**SVP and Controller:** Richard D. Levy
**SVP and Chief Actuary:** Stephen N. Steinig
**SVP and General Auditor:** Thomas J. Warga
**SVP:** Frank M. Boccio
**SVP:** Jessie M. Colgate
**SVP:** Solomon Goldfinger
**SVP:** Robert J. Hebron
**SVP, Human Resources:** Richard A. Hansen
**SVP:** Carolyn M. Buscarino
**SVP:** Eric B. Campbell
**Auditors:** PricewaterhouseCoopers LLP

## LOCATIONS

**HQ:** New York Life Insurance Company
51 Madison Ave., New York, NY 10010
**Phone:** 212-576-7000    **Fax:** 212-576-8145
**Web:** www.newyorklife.com

New York Life Insurance Company operates in Argentina, China, Hong Kong, India, Indonesia, Mexico, the Philippines, South Korea, Taiwan, Thailand, the US, and Vietnam.

## PRODUCTS/OPERATIONS

**2000 Assets**

|  | $ mil. | % of total |
|---|---|---|
| Cash | 802 | 1 |
| Bonds | 56,751 | 58 |
| Stocks | 3,846 | 4 |
| Mortgage loans | 9,409 | 10 |
| Real estate | 523 | 1 |
| Policy loans | 5,954 | 6 |
| Assets in separate account | 11,922 | 12 |
| Other assets | 7,894 | 8 |
| **Total** | **97,101** | **100** |

**Selected Operations**
New York Life Asset Managment LLC
  MacKay Shields LLC
  Madison Square Advisors LLC
  MainStay Management LLC,
  Monitor Capital Advisors LLC
  New York Life Benefit Services LLC
New York Life Insurance and Annuity Corporation
  (individual life insurance and annuities)
New York Life International, Inc.
NYLIFE Administration Corp. (long-term care and other specialty programs)
New York Life Benefit Services, Inc. (retirement benefits administration)

## COMPETITORS

| | | |
|---|---|---|
| AEGON | CNA Financial | Morgan Stanley |
| Allianz | Fortis | Dean Witter |
| Allstate | Guardian Life | Mutual of |
| American | The Hartford | Omaha |
| General | Jefferson-Pilot | Northwestern |
| AIG | John Hancock | Mutual |
| American | Financial | Principal |
| National | Services | Financial |
| Insurance | Kemper | Prudential |
| AXA | Insurance | State Farm |
| AXA Financial | MassMutual | T. Rowe Price |
| Charles Schwab | Merrill Lynch | TIAA-CREF |
| CIGNA | MetLife | UBS |
| Citigroup | MONY | PaineWebber |

## HISTORICAL FINANCIALS & EMPLOYEES

| Mutual company FYE: December 31 | Annual Growth | 12/91 | 12/92 | 12/93 | 12/94 | 12/95 | 12/96 | 12/97 | 12/98 | 12/99 | 12/00 |
|---|---|---|---|---|---|---|---|---|---|---|---|
| Assets ($ mil.) | 6.4% | — | 59,169 | 66,791 | 68,926 | 74,281 | 78,809 | 84,067 | 90,367 | 94,979 | 97,101 |
| Net income ($ mil.) | 20.5% | — | 271 | 368 | 404 | 625 | 579 | 650 | 753 | 555 | 1,205 |
| Income as % of assets | — | — | 0.5% | 0.6% | 0.6% | 0.8% | 0.7% | 0.8% | 0.8% | 0.6% | 1.2% |
| Employees | 6.4% | — | — | — | 8,130 | 8,442 | 12,190 | 12,570 | 13,000 | 7,349 | 11,800 |

### NET INCOME HISTORY

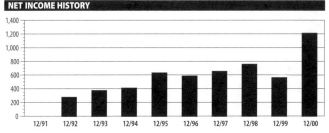

### 2000 FISCAL YEAR-END

Equity as % of assets: 9.0%
Return on assets: 1.3%
Return on equity: —
Long-term debt ($ mil.): 0
Sales ($ mil.): 21,996

# NEW YORK STATE LOTTERY

## OVERVIEW

Winning the New York State Lottery could make you king of the hill, the top of the heap. Based in Schenectady, New York, the lottery is one of the largest in the US, and is the nation's second-oldest (after New Hampshire). It has raised some $20 billion for state educational programs (which get nearly 40% of sales) since it was started in 1967. It offers both numbers games (such as Lotto and Take Five) and instant-win contests. The lottery sells its tickets through more than 17,000 retailers and some 14,000 online terminals (maintained by Rhode Island-based GTECH Holdings). In addition to education, proceeds from the lottery have helped pay for the construction of New York City Hall, as well as bridges and roads for the state. The lottery returns about half the money it takes in as prizes; 3% of sales are used to cover administrative costs, while retailers get 6%.

Sales rose in 2001 after falling off the year before. The New York State lottery has faced competition from the multistate Powerball and The Big Game lotteries available in neighboring states. New York's legislature resisted approving a multistate game, but finally caved in late in 2001 and authorized a bill allowing New Yorkers to buy Powerball tickets. The news comes as a relief to Greenwich, Connecticut, residents, who saw thousands of out-of-staters overrun its town in hopes of cashing in on a summer jackpot that grew to $300 million.

## HISTORY

In the mid-1960s the New York state legislature succeeded in sending a lottery amendment to voters, and 60% of New Yorkers voted in favor of the amendment in 1966. Lottery sales began in 1967 with a raffle-style drawing game. In its first year of operation, the lottery contributed more than $26 million to the state's education fund.

New York introduced its first instant game in 1976, with sales topping $18 million the first week. The state debuted its six-of-six lotto game two years later. Sales were slow until 1981, when Louie "the Light Bulb" Eisenberg — the state's first lottery celebrity — won $5 million, the largest single-winner prize at that time.

GTECH Holdings won the contract to operate New York's lottery terminal sales in 1987. The Quick Pick option — through which a terminal chooses a player's numbers — was introduced in 1989, as was a new lotto game and the state's first online computer terminal game. Autoworker Antonio Bueti set a record for the largest individual prize, winning $35 million in 1990. A jackpot of $90 million was split among nine players in 1991.

Through the mid-1990s, however, lackluster lottery sales were blamed on the Persian Gulf War, the recession, and poor publicity. During 1993 and 1994, lottery management revamped the state's lottery infrastructure and redesigned some games. The investment paid off in October 1994 when lotto fever pushed a jackpot to $72.5 million. During the height of the frenzy, sales reached $46,000 a minute.

Quick Draw, which lets players choose numbers every five minutes, was added in 1995. Sales of the game topped $1 million on the second day and soon it was grossing nearly $12 million a week. Real estate mogul Donald Trump unsuccessfully sued to stop Quick Draw, claiming that it was more addictive than (his) casinos and would encourage organized crime. That year the New York State Lottery became the first to reach $3 billion in sales in a single year.

In 1996 the state pulled its Quick Draw advertising after critics complained it encouraged compulsive gambling. Lottery officials replaced enticing ads with advertising stressing the lottery's benefits to state education. The lottery was the subject of a sting operation that year led by Governor George Pataki to crack down on lottery vendors selling tickets to minors. In 1997 the lottery spawned its own game show with the debut of *NY Wired,* a half-hour weekly program pitting vendor representatives against each other for cash prizes given to audience members and schools.

With sales slipping, the state left longtime ad partner DDB Needham Worldwide (now DDB Worldwide) in 1998 and signed a $28 million contract with Grey Advertising. Lottery director Jeff Perlee resigned the next year. He was replaced by Margaret DeFrancisco, who helped drum up sales with Millennium Millions, which paid out a record $100 million prize to Johnnie Ely, a cook from the South Bronx, on the eve of 2000. Two players shared a record $130 million jackpot later in the year.

After holding out for years, the New York legislature in 2001 authorized a bill that would allow state residents to participate in the multistate Powerball lottery.

## OFFICERS

**Director:** Margaret R. DeFrancisco
**Director of Administration:** Jerry Woitkoski
**Director Marketing and Sales:** Connie H. Laverty
**Director of Operations:** Daniel J. Codden
**Regional Director, Long Island:** James Benoit
**Regional Director, Western New York:**
  Joanne Thompson
**Regional Director, Central New York:** William Lonczak
**Regional Director, New York City:** Charles O'Donnell
**Director Human Resources:** Charlie Titus
**Auditors:** KPMG LLP

## LOCATIONS

**HQ:** One Broadway Center, Schenectady, NY 12301
**Phone:** 518-388-3300      **Fax:** 518-388-3368
**Web:** www.nylottery.org

## PRODUCTS/OPERATIONS

**Selected Games**
Numbers games
  New York Lotto
  Numbers
  Pick 10
  Quick Draw
  Take Five
  Win 4
Instant-win games
  Blackjack
  Cash Flurries
  Fortune Cookie
  Go for the Green
  Ho Ho Doubler
  Hot Shots
  Loose Change
  Lucky 7s
  Pot o' Gold
  Red Hot Hearts
  Take 5
  Top 10
  Win 4

## COMPETITORS

Connecticut Lottery
Massachusetts State Lottery
Multi-State Lottery
New Hampshire Lottery
New Jersey Lottery
Pennsylvania Lottery
Vermont Lottery

## HISTORICAL FINANCIALS & EMPLOYEES

| Government-owned FYE: March 31 | Annual Growth | 3/92 | 3/93 | 3/94 | 3/95 | 3/96 | 3/97 | 3/98 | 3/99 | 3/00 | 3/01 |
|---|---|---|---|---|---|---|---|---|---|---|---|
| Sales ($ mil.) | 8.2% | 2,063 | 2,360 | 2,369 | 3,028 | 3,752 | 4,136 | 4,185 | 3,831 | 3,674 | 4,185 |
| Net income ($ mil.) | 5.9% | 867 | 1,001 | 1,011 | 1,244 | 1,400 | 1,543 | 1,529 | 1,413 | 1,365 | 1,447 |
| Income as % of sales | — | 42.0% | 42.4% | 42.7% | 41.1% | 37.3% | 37.3% | 36.5% | 36.9% | 37.2% | 34.6% |
| Employees | 4.7% | 231 | 233 | 241 | 239 | 310 | 340 | 350 | 345 | 350 | 350 |

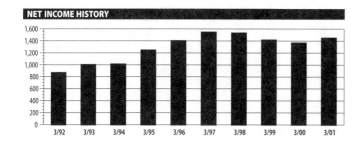

**NET INCOME HISTORY**

# NEW YORK STOCK EXCHANGE, INC.

Bulls and bears and boards, oh my! The New York Stock Exchange (NYSE), aka the Big Board, is the US's oldest and the world's largest stock market. Its more than 3,000 listings include most large US companies. The member-owned, not-for-profit corporation also attracts foreign companies seeking the liquidity available only in US markets.

NYSE is touting its people-driven auction exchange — where stock prices are set largely by a throng of traders in an area the size of a football field — against the electronic exchange run by archrival Nasdaq. (The NYSE is scurrying to find ways to trade Nasdaq stocks on the NYSE board, and vice versa.) The Big Board also faces competition from foreign exchanges and such electronic communications networks (ECNs) as The Island and Instinet. Even though NYSE argues that such trades hamper investors' ability to see the big picture, the exchange accommodates brokers making large-block trades off the floor.

To better compete, the NYSE is planning to go public as a for-profit company. IPO proceeds might be used to buy any of the several systems vying to become new exchanges. For-profit status would let NYSE's management move more decisively without interference from major members (many of whom also happen to hold stakes in competing ECNs).

The urge to merge among other exchanges has not been lost on the staid firm. NYSE has announced plans to join forces with nine other exchanges to form a 24-hour platform.

To prevent a monopoly on stock sales by securities auctioneers, 24 New York stockbrokers and businessmen agreed in 1792 to avoid "public auctions," to charge a commission on sales of stock, and to "give preference to each other" in their transactions. The Buttonwood Agreement, named after a tree on Wall Street under which they met, established the first organized stock market in New York. The Bank of New York was the first corporate stock traded under the Buttonwood tree.

Excluded traders continued dealing on the streets of New York until 1921 and later formed the American Stock Exchange.

In 1817 the brokers created the New York Stock & Exchange Board, a stock market with set meeting times. The NYS&EB began to require companies to qualify for trading (listing) by furnishing financial statements in 1853. The board became the New York Stock Exchange 10 years later.

Stock tickers began recording trades in 1867, and two years later the NYSE consolidated with competitors the Open Board of Brokers and the Government Bond Department. Despite repeated panics and recessions in the late 1800s, the stock market remained unregulated until well into the 20th century.

In the 1920s the NYSE installed a centralized stock quote service. Post-war euphoria brought a stock mania that fizzled in the crash of October 1929. The subsequent Depression brought investigation and federal regulation to the securities industry.

The NYSE registered as an exchange in 1934. In 1938 it reorganized, with a board of directors representing member firms, nonmember brokers, and the public; it also hired its first full-time president, member William McChesney Martin. As a self-regulating body, the NYSE policed the activities of its members.

The NYSE began electronic trading in the 1960s; in 1968 it broke 1929's one-day record for trading volume (16 million shares). It became a not-for-profit corporation in 1971.

Despite upgrades, technology was at least partly to blame for the 1987 crash: A cascade of large sales triggered by computer programs fueled the market's fall. NYSE's income suffered, leading to a $3 million loss in 1990.

In 1995 Richard Grasso became the first NYSE staff employee named chairman. The exchange followed the other US stock markets in 1997 by switching trade increments from one-eighth point to one-sixteenth point (known as a "teenie" by arbitrageurs). The NYSE used a veiled threat to move to New Jersey to win itself the promise of some growing space. In 1999 the exchange named Karen Nelson Hackett as its first female governor.

The Big Board in 2000 announced plans to go public, but the move has frequently been stalled. It also extended its official pricing until 6:30 p.m. (eastern time). In 2001 the NYSE said it would team with exchanges in Amsterdam, Australia, Brussels, Hong Kong, Mexico, Paris, Sao Paulo, Tokyo, and Toronto to create a 24-hour global equity market. In the wake of the terrorism attacks that shook Wall Street and the nation that year, the NYSE and Nasdaq began discussing a disaster plan that would see the two cooperating should a future incident cripple either market.

**Chairman and CEO:** Richard A. Grasso, age 54
**Vice Chairman:** Charles J. Bocklet Jr.
**Vice Chairman:** David H. Komansky, age 61
**President, COO, and Director:** William R. Johnston
**Group EVP:** Robert G. Britz
**EVP:** Catherine R. Kinney, age 49
**Group EVP:** Edward A. Kwalwasser
**Group EVP:** Georges Ugeux
**EVP and General Counsel:** Richard P. Bernard
**EVP, Human Resources:** Frank Z. Ashen
**EVP, Market Operations:** Richard A. Edgar
**SVP, Floor Operations:** Anne E. Allen
**SVP and Corporate Secretary:** James E. Buck
**SVP, International Corporate:** Dorothy A. Carey
**SVP, Strategic Planning and Chief Economist:**
James L. Cochrane
**SVP, New Listings and Client Service:**
Noreen M. Culhane
**SVP, Enforcement:** David P. Doherty
**SVP, Regulatory Systems and Corporate Network:**
Donald G. Dueweke
**SVP and Associate General Counsel:** James F. Duffy
**SVP and CFO:** Keith R. Helsby
**Auditors:** PricewaterhouseCoopers LLP

## LOCATIONS

**HQ:** 11 Wall St., New York, NY 10005
**Phone:** 212-656-3000      **Fax:** 212-656-2126
**Web:** www.nyse.com

## PRODUCTS/OPERATIONS

**2000 Sales**

|  | $ mil. | % of total |
|---|---|---|
| Listing fees | 278 | 34 |
| Trading fees | 142 | 18 |
| Market data fees | 140 | 17 |
| Regulatory fees | 130 | 16 |
| Facility & equipment fees | 46 | 6 |
| Membership fees | 10 | 1 |
| Other | 69 | 8 |
| **Total** | **815** | **100** |

**Services**
Market regulation
Member regulation
Securities clearing
Securities depository
Securities information

## COMPETITORS

Archipelago
Bloomberg TRADEBOOK
CBOE
Chicago Mercantile
  Exchange
E*TRADE
Instinet
Investment Technology
Island ECN
Knight Trading
London Stock Exchange
NASD
NYFIX

## HISTORICAL FINANCIALS & EMPLOYEES

| Not-for-profit<br>FYE: December 31 | Annual<br>Growth | 12/91 | 12/92 | 12/93 | 12/94 | 12/95 | 12/96 | 12/97 | 12/98 | 12/99 | 12/00 |
|---|---|---|---|---|---|---|---|---|---|---|---|
| Sales ($ mil.) | 8.7% | — | 418 | 445 | 452 | 501 | 562 | 639 | 729 | 735 | 815 |
| Net income ($ mil.) | 7.5% | — | 41 | 54 | 44 | 57 | 74 | 86 | 101 | 75 | 73 |
| Income as % of sales | — | — | 9.8% | 12.1% | 9.7% | 11.3% | 13.3% | 13.5% | 13.9% | 10.2% | 8.9% |
| Employees | 0.0% | — | — | 1,500 | 1,450 | 1,450 | 1,475 | 1,475 | 1,500 | — | — |

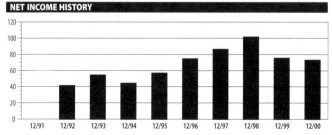

**NET INCOME HISTORY**

**2000 FISCAL YEAR-END**
Debt ratio: 0.0%
Return on equity: —
Cash ($ mil.): 17
Current ratio: 2.99
Long-term debt ($ mil.): 0

# NORTHWESTERN MUTUAL

Northwestern Mutual would "enter the 21st Century as we left the 19th," according to its former chairman and CEO, John Ericson (who retired in mid-2001). Well not exactly.

Although the Milwaukee-based company has resisted the industry trend of demutualizing and remains committed to ownership by its about 3 million policyholders, The Quiet Company has begun blowing its own horn — in a diffident upper Midwest way. Reorganized to highlight its wealth management products, the company is raising its profile through aggressive advertising.

Northwestern Mutual's 7,500 agents (meticulously recruited and trained) sell a lineup of life and health insurance and retirement products, including fixed and variable annuities and mutual funds to a clientele of small businesses and prosperous individuals.

Other operations, which are increasing in importance, are investment bank Robert W. Baird & Co. and asset manager Frank Russell Company (of Russell 2000 stock index fame). Targeting wealthy individuals over 55, the company has opened its own personal trust services company, Northwestern Mutual Trust.

## HISTORY

In 1854, at age 72, John Johnston, a successful New York insurance agent, moved to Wisconsin to become a farmer. Three years later Johnston returned to the insurance business when he and 36 others formed Mutual Life Insurance (changed to Northwestern Mutual Life Insurance in 1865). From the beginning the company's goal was to become better, not just bigger.

The company continued to offer level-premium life insurance in the 1920s, while competitors offered new types of products. This failure to rise to new demands brought a decline in market share that lasted into the 1940s.

Northwestern automated in the late 1950s. In 1962 it introduced the Insurance Service Account, whereby all policies owned by a family or business could be consolidated into one monthly premium and paid with pre-authorized checks. In 1968 Northwestern inaugurated Extra Ordinary Life, which combined whole and term life insurance, using dividends to convert term to paid-up whole life each year. EOL soon became the company's most popular product.

Suffering from a low profile, in 1972 the insurer kicked off its "The Quiet Company" ad campaign during the summer Olympics. Public awareness of Northwestern jumped. But even in advertising, the company was staid; a revamped Quiet Company campaign made a return Olympic appearance 24 years later in another effort to raise the public's consciousness.

In the 1980s Northwestern began financing leveraged buyouts, gaining direct ownership of companies. Investments included two-thirds of flooring maker Congoleum (with other investors); it also bought majority interests in Milwaukee securities firm Robert W. Baird (1982; now 64%) and mortgage guarantee insurer MGIC Investment (1985; now 11%).

The firm stayed out of the 1980s mania for fast money and high-risk diversification. Instead, it devoted itself almost religiously to its core business, despite indications that it was a shrinking market.

In the early 1990s new life policy purchases slowed and the agency force declined — ominous signs, since insurers make their premium income on retained policies, and continued sales are crucial to growth. Northwestern reversed the trend, adding administrative support for its agents, using database marketing to target new customers, and increasing the cross-selling of products among existing customers. The result was a record-setting 1996.

With the financial services industry consolidating, Northwestern in 1997 moved into the mutual fund business by setting up its nine Mason Street Funds.

In the 1990s many large mutuals sought to demutualize, and in 1998 Northwestern, politically influential in Wisconsin, successfully lobbied for legislation to permit demutualization, citing the need to be able to move quickly in shifting markets.

In 1999 the company acquired Frank Russell, a pension management firm. The acquisition gave Northwestern a foothold in global investment management and analytical services (the Russell 2000 index).

The company followed up with an all-out reorganization, separating the office of president from the duties of chairman and CEO, and naming, for the first time, an EVP of marketing. In 2001 the firm opened Northwestern Mutual Trust, a wholly owned personal trust services subsidiary.

**CEO and President:** Edward J. Zore, age 55
**COO:** John M. Bremer, age 53
**SEVP, Insurance:** Peter W. Bruce, age 55
**EVP and Chief Investment Officer:** Mason G. Ross
**EVP, Agencies:** William H. Beckley, age 52
**EVP, Planning and Technology:** Deborah A. Beck, age 52
**EVP, Marketing:** Bruce L. Miller
**SVP and Chief Actuary:** William C. Koenig
**SVP, Corporate and Government Relations:**
Frederic H. Sweet
**SVP, Life Insurance:** Richard L. Hall
**SVP, Public Markets:** Mark G. Doll
**SVP, Field System Administration:** Donald L. Mellish
**SVP, Securities and Real Estate:** John E. Schlifske
**SVP, Information Systems:** Walt J. Wojcik
**SVP, Annuity and Accumulation Products:**
Leonard F. Stecklein
**VP and Controller:** Gary E. Long
**VP, Annuity and Accumulation Products:**
Meridee J. Maynard
**VP, Communications:** W. Ward White
**VP, General Counsel:** Robert J. Berden
**VP, Technology Research and Web Resources:**
Martha M. Valerio
**VP, Human Resources:** Susan A. Lueger
**Auditors:** PricewaterhouseCoopers LLP

**HQ:** Northwestern Mutual Life Insurance
720 E. Wisconsin Ave., Milwaukee, WI 53202
**Phone:** 414-271-1444    **Fax:** 414-299-7022
**Web:** www.northwesternmutual.com

Northwestern Mutual Life Insurance has agents and offices throughout the US.

**2000 Assets**

|  | $ mil. | % of total |
|---|---|---|
| Cash & temporary investments | 1,217 | 1 |
| Bonds | 40,607 | 44 |
| Stocks | 6,216 | 7 |
| Mortgage loans | 14,431 | 16 |
| Real estate | 1,627 | 2 |
| Policy loans | 8,504 | 9 |
| Other investments | 4,508 | 5 |
| Assets in separate account | 12,497 | 13 |
| Other assets | 2,518 | 3 |
| **Total** | **92,125** | **100** |

**Selected Subsidiaries**
Frank Russell Company (investment management and securities brokerage)
Mason Street Funds (mutual funds)
Robert W. Baird & Co. Incorporated (asset management)

| | |
|---|---|
| Alliance Capital | MassMutual |
| American General | Merrill Lynch |
| AXA Financial | MetLife |
| CIGNA | MONY |
| Citigroup | Morgan Stanley Dean |
| CNA Financial | Witter |
| Conseco | Mutual of Omaha |
| FMR | Nationwide |
| Fortis | New York Life |
| GenAmerica | Pacific Mutual |
| Guardian Life | Principal Financial |
| The Hartford | Prudential |
| John Hancock Financial | T. Rowe Price |
| Services | TIAA-CREF |
| Liberty Mutual | |

| Mutual company FYE: December 31 | Annual Growth | 12/91 | 12/92 | 12/93 | 12/94 | 12/95 | 12/96 | 12/97 | 12/98 | 12/99 | 12/00 |
|---|---|---|---|---|---|---|---|---|---|---|---|
| Assets ($ mil.) | 11.1% | — | 39,679 | 44,061 | 48,112 | 54,876 | 62,680 | 71,081 | 77,995 | 85,985 | 92,125 |
| Net income ($ mil.) | 28.6% | — | 244 | 330 | 279 | 459 | 620 | 689 | 809 | 1,337 | 1,829 |
| Income as % of assets | — | — | 0.6% | 0.7% | 0.6% | 0.8% | 1.0% | 1.0% | 1.0% | 1.6% | 2.0% |
| Employees | 2.1% | — | 3,298 | 3,500 | 3,300 | 3,344 | 3,513 | 3,818 | 4,117 | 3,700 | 3,900 |

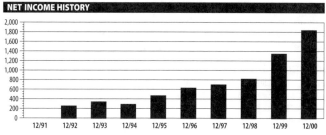

Equity as % of assets: 6.4%
Return on assets: 2.1%
Return on equity: —
Long-term debt ($ mil.): —
Sales ($ mil.): 15,382

# NORTHWESTERN UNIVERSITY

## OVERVIEW

Near the city of big shoulders is a place that shapes broad minds. Located in the Chicago suburb of Evanston, Northwestern University is widely recognized as one of the country's top learning institutions, serving more than 17,500 full- and part-time students through two campuses. Its 240-acre main campus is home to most of Northwestern's 12 schools and colleges, while some 2,300 students take graduate courses at its 20-acre Chicago campus. The downtown location is home to Northwestern's School of Law, Medical School, and McGaw Medical Center. With tuition and expenses running more than $30,000 a year, about 60% of undergraduates receive some form of financial aid from the school.

Among Northwestern's top-ranked programs are its law school, medical school, and its engineering program. Its J. L. Kellogg Graduate School of Management is ranked second in the nation by *Business Week*. Its journalism and drama programs produced such alumni as Charlton Heston, Gary Marshall, and Julia Louis-Dreyfus. US Supreme Court Justice John Paul Stevens is also a former Wildcat.

Northwestern is home to several research centers, continuing education services, and community outreach programs. The university also supports 19 intercollegiate athletic programs. It is the only private institution in the Big 10 conference.

The school's endowment has also swelled to more than $2.8 billion, and it has exceeded its goal to raise $1 billion, Campaign Northwestern, by more than $15 million. The money will be used to increase endowment for student scholarships and fellowships, to help repair and build facilities, and fund more faculty positions.

## HISTORY

Northwestern University's Methodist founders met in 1850 to create an institution of higher learning serving the original Northwest Territory. The university was chartered in 1851, and two years later it acquired 379 acres of property north of Chicago on Lake Michigan. The town of Evanston was later named after John Evans, one of the school's founders.

Classes began in the fall of 1855 with two professors and 10 students. By 1869 Northwestern had more than 100 students and began to admit women. In 1870 Northwestern signed an affiliation agreement with the Chicago Medical College (founded 1859), and three years later it joined with the original University of Chicago (no relation to the current institution) to create the Union College of Law. When the University of Chicago closed in 1886 due to financial difficulties, Northwestern took control of the law school. The university reorganized in 1891, consolidating its affiliated professional schools (dentistry, law, medicine, and pharmacy) into the university.

By 1900 Northwestern had become the third-largest university in the US (after Harvard and Michigan), with an enrollment of 2,700. In the 1920s the university created the Medill School of Journalism, named for Joseph Medill, the founder of the *Chicago Tribune*. In 1924 the school's athletic teams adopted the nickname Wildcats, and two years later the university completed the primary buildings that form its Chicago campus. Northwestern suffered a drop in enrollment during the Depression, but after WWII it saw student numbers swell as veterans took advantage of the GI Bill. Expansion continued throughout the 1960s and 1970s.

In 1985 the school and the City of Evanston began developing a research center to attract more high-tech industries to the area. The university's graduate school of business achieved national prominence in 1988 after it was ranked #1 in the US by *Business Week*. In 1995 Henry Bienen, a dean at Princeton, became the school's 15th president. That year Northwestern's football team, forever the doormat of the Big 10, achieved national fame when it won the conference championship.

In 1998 faculty member Professor John Pople won the Nobel prize in Chemistry, the first Nobel prize awarded to a faculty member while teaching at the university. Northwestern won a significant legal battle in 1998 when a judge ruled that the university was not obligated to pay a faculty member simply because he had been granted tenure. To help pay for needed expansion, Bienen launched Campaign Northwestern that year with the goal of raising $1 billion. Encouraged by their successful efforts, the college in 2000 raised its fundraising goal to $1.4 billion from $1 billion.

The university's dental school closed its doors in 2001, citing the financial difficulties confronting private schools in providing a competitive dental education.

## LOCATIONS

**HQ:** 633 Clark St., Evanston, IL 60208
**Phone:** 847-491-3741    **Fax:** 847-491-8406
**Web:** www.nwu.edu

Northwestern University has one campus in Chicago and one in Evanston, Illinois.

## PRODUCTS/OPERATIONS

**Selected Undergraduate Colleges and Schools**
Medill School of Journalism
Robert McCormick School of Engineering and Applied Sciences
School of Education and Social Policy
School of Music
School of Speech
Weinberg College of Arts and Sciences

**Selected Graduate Schools**
The Graduate School
J. L. Kellogg Graduate School of Management
Medill School of Journalism
Medical School
Robert McCormick School of Engineering and Applied Sciences
School of Education and Social Policy
School of Law
School of Music
School of Speech

**Selected Research Centers and Institutes**
Banking Research Center
Center for Biotechnology
Center for Catalysis and Surface Science
Center for Sleep and Circadian Biology
Center for Mathematical Studies in Economics and Management Science
Center for Reproductive Science
Center for the Study of Ethical Issues in Business
Center for Quantum Devices
Center for Quality Engineering and Failure Prevention
Heizer Center for Entrepreneurial Studies
Institute for Environmental Catalysis
Institute for Health Services Research and Policy Studies
Institute for Neuroscience
Institute for Policy Research
Kellogg Environmental Research Center
Materials Research Center
Program of African Studies
Traffic Institute
Transportation Center

## HISTORICAL FINANCIALS & EMPLOYEES

| School<br>FYE: August 31 | Annual<br>Growth | 8/91 | 8/92 | 8/93 | 8/94 | 8/95 | 8/96 | 8/97 | 8/98 | 8/99 | 8/00 |
|---|---|---|---|---|---|---|---|---|---|---|---|
| Sales ($ mil.) | 5.1% | — | 587 | 628 | 676 | 708 | 779 | 721 | 816 | 782 | 875 |
| Employees | 0.1% | — | — | 5,650 | 5,650 | 5,800 | 5,800 | 5,978 | 5,985 | — | 5,700 |

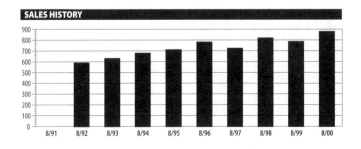

**SALES HISTORY**

# OCEAN SPRAY CRANBERRIES, INC.

## OVERVIEW

It's not just sour grapes: Ocean Spray Cranberries knows that cranberries can spoil, too. Based in Lakeville-Middleboro, Massachusetts, the company — a marketing cooperative owned by more than 900 cranberry and grapefruit growers in the US and Canada — controls about 50% of the US cranberry juice market. Surplus harvests of cranberries and competition from store brands have cut into its market share and forced layoffs. Competition from industry giants like Coca-Cola and Pepsi, both of which are trying to increase market share in the non-carbonated drinks sector, also hurts Ocean-Spray.

The company made its name through a quest for quality and successful marketing that elevated the fruit's status. To expand beyond the berry's traditional role, Ocean Spray has turned the fruit into a chewy snack (Craisins), and cranberries now show up in co-branded cookies and cereal. Promotion efforts have been aided by research showing that cranberry juice can reduce urinary tract infections.

Ocean Spray's Washington State-based subsidiary, Milne Fruit Products, processes fruit into juice ingredients.

## HISTORY

Ocean Spray Cranberries traces its roots to Marcus Urann, president of the Cape Cod Cranberry Company. In 1912 Urann, who became known as the "Cranberry King," began marketing a cranberry sauce that was packaged in tins and could be served year-round. Inspired by the sea spray that drifted off the Atlantic and over his cranberry bogs, Urann dubbed his concoction Ocean Spray Cape Cod Cranberry Sauce.

It didn't take long for other cranberry growers to make their own sauces, and rather than compete, the Cranberry King consolidated. In 1930 Urann merged his company with A.D. Makepeace Company and with Cranberry Products, forming a national cooperative called Cranberry Canners. During the 1940s it added growers in Wisconsin, Oregon, and Washington and, to reflect its new scope, changed its name to National Cranberry Association.

Canadian growers were added to the fold in 1950. Urann retired in 1955, and two years later the co-op introduced its first frozen products. To take advantage of the popular Ocean Spray brand name, in 1959 the company changed its name to Ocean Spray Cranberries.

Two weeks before Thanksgiving that year, the US Department of Health mistakenly announced that aminotriazole, a herbicide used by some cranberry growers, was linked to cancer in laboratory rats. Sales of what consumers called "cancer berries" plummeted, and Ocean Spray nearly folded. However, the US government came to the rescue with subsidies in 1960, and the company stayed afloat.

The scare convinced Ocean Spray it needed to cut its dependence on seasonal demand, and it began to diversify more aggressively into the juice business, introducing a heavily promoted new line of juices blending cranberries with apples, grapes, and other fruits.

Ocean Spray allowed Florida's Indian River Ruby Red grapefruit growers to join the co-op in 1976. The company acquired Milne Food Products, a manufacturer of fruit concentrates and purees, in 1985, and three years later it signed a Japanese distribution deal.

To maintain its edge in a growing but increasingly competitive market, Ocean Spray automated plants and allied with food giants to create cranberry-flavored treats such as cookies (Nabisco, 1993) and cereal (Kraft Foods, 1996). In 1998 it unsuccessfully sued to block PepsiCo's purchase of juice maker Tropicana on grounds that it would interfere with PepsiCo's distribution of Ocean Spray's drinks. Ocean Spray also introduced a line of 100% juice blends to compete with rivals such as former co-op member Northland Cranberries, and it bought a stake in Nantucket Allserve, maker of Nantucket Nectars.

Bumper harvests from 1997 through 1999 led to lower cranberry prices. As a result, in 1999 the company announced its third round of layoffs since 1997 (bringing the total to 500). It also suspended its practice of buying back the stock of its growers, who must buy shares to join the co-op.

Amid criticism that it has been unable to compete effectively with for-profit rivals, Ocean Spray hired former Pillsbury executive Robert Hawthorne as CEO in 2000. Grower-owners voted not to explore a sale of the company at its 2001 annual meeting, a vote of confidence for the new management. The company supported a 32% crop reduction to help eliminate the crop surpluses that cause depressed prices.

## OFFICERS

**Chairman:** Sherwood Johnson
**CEO:** H. Robert Hawthorne, age 56
**President and COO:** Randy Papadellis
**CFO:** Timothy Chan
**VP Human Resources:** John Soi
**VP New Product Development:** Karl R. Johnson
**Manager Corporate Communications and Public Affairs:** Chris Phillips

## LOCATIONS

**HQ:** 1 Ocean Spray Dr., Lakeville-Middleboro, MA 02349
**Phone:** 508-946-1000   **Fax:** 508-946-7704
**Web:** www.oceanspray.com

Ocean Spray Cranberries has seven receiving stations and eight processing and bottling plants in Florida, Massachusetts, Nevada, New Jersey, Oregon, Texas, Washington, Wisconsin, and British Columbia, Canada.

## PRODUCTS/OPERATIONS

**Selected Juice Products and Labels**
Apple Juice
Black Cherry Blast
Cranapple
Cranberry Juice Cocktail
Cran*Blueberry
Cran*Cherry
Cran*Currant
Cran*Grape
Cranicot
Cran*Mango
Cran*Raspberry
Cran*Strawberry
Cran*Tangerine
Fruit Punch
Grapefruit Juice
Kiwi Strawberry
Lightstyle (Cranberry, Cran*Grape, Cran*Mango, Cran*Raspberry)
Mandarin Magic
¡Mango Mango!
Mauna La'i (Island Guava, ParadisePassion)
Orange Juice
Pink Grapefruit
Premium 100% Juice
Reduced (Cranapple, Cranberry Juice Cocktail, Cran-Raspberry)
Ruby Red & Mango
Ruby Red & Tangerine Grapefruit
Ruby Red Grapefruit

**Other Products**
Craisins (sweetened dried cranberries)
Cran Raspberry sauce
Cranberry sauce (jellied, whole)
Fresh cranberries

## COMPETITORS

| | | |
|---|---|---|
| Cadbury | Florida's Natural | Pepsi-Cola |
| Schweppes | Hansen Natural | Philip Morris |
| Campbell Soup | J. M. Smucker | Quaker Oats |
| Chiquita Brands | National Grape | Sunkist |
| Clement Pappas | Cooperative | Triarc |
| Cliffstar | Northland | Tropicana |
| Coca-Cola | Cranberries | Products |
| Dole | Odwalla | |

## HISTORICAL FINANCIALS & EMPLOYEES

| Cooperative FYE: August 31 | Annual Growth | 8/91 | 8/92 | 8/93 | 8/94 | 8/95 | 8/96 | 8/97 | 8/98 | 8/99 | 8/00 |
|---|---|---|---|---|---|---|---|---|---|---|---|
| Sales ($ mil.) | 2.2% | — | 1,091 | 1,168 | 1,221 | 1,361 | 1,433 | 1,438 | 1,480 | 1,360 | 1,300 |
| Employees | (1.2%) | — | 2,200 | 2,300 | 2,300 | 2,300 | 2,300 | 2,300 | 2,350 | 2,000 | 2,000 |

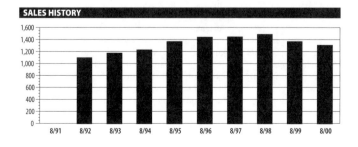

SALES HISTORY

# THE OHIO STATE UNIVERSITY

## OVERVIEW

The first class at Ohio State University (OSU) comprised 24 students. Today the university is Ohio's largest institution of higher learning and has the nation's second-largest single-campus enrollment (about 48,000 students at its Columbus campus), behind The University of Texas at Austin. OSU also has four regional campuses and two agricultural institutes. The university has a 4,600-member faculty offering instruction in more than 175 undergraduate programs, 120 master's degree programs, and more than 90 doctoral programs.

Among OSU's colleges and schools are the Austin E. Knowlton School of Architecture, the College of Medicine and Public Health, and the Fisher College of Business. Noteworthy university alumni include astronaut Nancy Sherlock Currie, golfer Jack Nicklaus, author John Jakes, and Olympian Jesse Owens.

Near the close of 2000, OSU unveiled an academic plan under which the university will spend $750 million to advance its national academic standing.

## HISTORY

In 1870 the Ohio legislature, prompted by Governor Rutherford B. Hayes, agreed to establish the Ohio Agricultural and Mechanical College in Columbus on property provided by the Morrill Act of 1862 (the land-grant institution act, which gave land to states and territories for the establishment of colleges).

After a heated battle over whether the college should teach only agricultural and mechanical arts or foster a broad-based liberal arts curriculum, the college opened in 1873 offering agriculture, ancient languages, chemistry, geology, mathematics, modern languages, and physics courses. Two years later the school appointed its first female faculty member. The Ohio State University became the school's name in 1878; that year it graduated its first class. OSU graduated its first female student the next year.

OSU grew dramatically, adding schools of veterinary medicine (1885), pharmacy (1885), law (1891), and dairy sciences (1895). It awarded its first Masters of Arts degree in 1886. The university continued to expand in the early 20th century, with enrollment surpassing 3,000 in 1908; by 1923 it had reached 10,000. New schools were added in education (1907), medicine and dentistry (1913), and commerce and journalism (1923). During WWI Ohio State designated part of its campus as training grounds and established the only college schools in the nation for airplane and balloon squadrons. Ohio Stadium was dedicated in 1922.

During the Great Depression Ohio State cut back salaries and course offerings. In the 1940s the school geared for war once again by establishing radiation and war research labs, as well as programs and services for students who were drafted. OSU captured its first national football championship in 1942.

The 1950s ushered in the era of legendary

OSU football coach Woody Hayes. Hayes led his beloved Buckeyes to three national championships and nine Rose Bowl appearances before he was discharged for striking a Clemson player in 1978. The 1950s also saw the addition of four regional campuses at Lima, Mansfield, Marion, and Newark.

In the early 1960s the university was engaged in internal free-speech battles. By the end of that decade, enrollment had surpassed 50,000. OSU opened its School of Social Work in 1976.

In 1986 OSU and rival Michigan shared the Big 10 football conference title. Enrollment at OSU topped 54,000 in 1990 but then began declining. In response, the university tried to cut costs and beef up revenues. One way was through alliances: In 1992 it teamed with research group Battelle to develop a testing system for new drugs for the Food and Drug Administration. But when more savings were needed in 1995 and 1996, the university began streamlining operations, merging journalism and communications, and consolidating several veterinary departments. However, it also approved the creation of a new school of public health to provide education in environmental health, epidemiology, and health care management and financing.

But sports were not forgotten, and in 1996 OSU broke ground on the $84 million Schottenstein Center, a multipurpose facility for the university's basketball and ice hockey teams. In 1997 president Gordon Gee announced that he was leaving OSU for Brown University. The next year William Kirwan from the University of Maryland came on board as president.

In 2000 the university's "Affirm Thy Friendship" contribution campaign came to a close. The campaign increased OSU's endowment from $493 million in 1993 to $1.3 billion in 2000.

## OFFICERS

**President:** William E. Kirwan, age 63
**EVP and Provost:** Edward J. Ray
**SVP Business & Finance and CFO:** William Shkurti
**VP Agricultural Administration and Executive Dean:**
Bobby D. Moser
**VP University Development:** Jerry A. May
**Vice Provost Graduate Studies and Dean of the
Graduate School:** Susan L. Huntington
**VP Health Sciences:** Manuel Tzagournis
**Interim VP Student and Urban/Community Affairs:**
William Hall II
**VP Research:** C. Bradley Moore
**Associate VP Human Resources:** Larry M. Lewellen
**Secretary of the Board of Trustees, Special Assistant to
the President for Government Relations:**
William Napier
**VP and General Counsel:** Virginia Trethewey
**Auditors:** Deloitte & Touche LLP

## LOCATIONS

**HQ:** 1800 Cannon Dr., Columbus, OH 43210
**Phone:** 614-292-6446      **Fax:** 614-292-2387
**Web:** www.osu.edu

The Ohio State University has campuses in Columbus,
Lima, Mansfield, Marion, and Newark. It has two
agricultural centers in Wooster, Ohio.

## PRODUCTS/OPERATIONS

**Selected Colleges and Schools**
Austin E. Knowlton School of Architecture
College of Biological Sciences
College of Dentistry
College of Education
College of Engineering
College of Food, Agricultural, and Environmental
Sciences
College of Human Ecology
College of Humanities
College of Law
College of Mathematical and Physical Sciences
College of Medicine and Public Health
College of Nursing
College of Optometry
College of Social and Behavioral Sciences
College of Social Work
College of the Arts
College of Veterinary Medicine
Graduate School
Max M. Fisher College of Business
School of Natural Resources
University College

## HISTORICAL FINANCIALS & EMPLOYEES

| School<br>FYE: June 30 | Annual<br>Growth | 6/92 | 6/93 | 6/94 | 6/95 | 6/96 | 6/97 | 6/98 | 6/99 | 6/00 | 6/01 |
|---|---|---|---|---|---|---|---|---|---|---|---|
| Sales ($ mil.) | 0.0% | 1,656 | 1,409 | 1,506 | 1,575 | 1,531 | 1,630 | 1,749 | 1,923 | 1,554 | 1,661 |
| Employees | 0.9% | 29,565 | 29,576 | 29,658 | 29,500 | 29,266 | 29,000 | 31,268 | 29,502 | 31,302 | 32,000 |

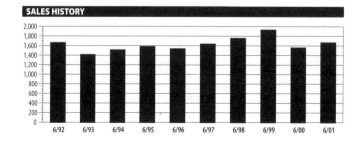

SALES HISTORY

# PACIFIC MUTUAL HOLDING

## OVERVIEW

Pacific Mutual Holding is into cross-breeding. The Newport Beach, California-based insurer is a mutual holding company that owns stock holding company Pacific LifeCorp, which is the parent of Pacific Life Insurance, the Golden State's largest life insurer. Pacific Mutual's conversion from a pure mutual to a mutual holding company gives it more flexibility and the option of an IPO; meanwhile, policyholders retain ownership of the company, but hold no stock.

Targeting individuals and small businesses, Pacific Life sells individual insurance, pension products, and annuities. Its subsidiaries focus on such activities as employee health and life insurance, brokerage services (Pacific Select Distributors), portfolio management, and reinsurance (World-Wide Reassurance). Affiliate PIMCO Advisors, of which Pacific Life owns 31%, is an investment management partnership majority-owned by German insurer Allianz.

The company plans to grow by introducing new products and adding new investment options to its variable product line.

## HISTORY

Pacific Mutual began business in 1868 in Sacramento, California, as a stock company. Its board was dominated by California business and political leaders, including three of the "Big Four" who created the Central Pacific Railroad (Charles Crocker, Mark Hopkins, and Leland Stanford) and three former governors (Stanford, Newton Booth, and Henry Huntley Haight). Stanford (founder of Stanford University) was the company's first president and policyholder.

By 1870 Pacific Mutual was selling life insurance throughout most of the western US. Expansion continued in the early 1870s into Colorado, Kentucky, Nebraska, New York, Ohio, and Texas. The company ventured into Mexico in 1873 but sold few policies. It had more luck in China, accepting its first risk there in 1875, and in Hawaii, where it started business in 1877. In 1881 Pacific Mutual moved to San Francisco.

Leland Stanford died in 1893. His widow and eponymous university, though rich in assets, found themselves struggling through a US economic depression. The benefit from Stanford's policy kept the university open until the estate was settled.

In 1905 Conservative Life bought the firm. The Pacific Mutual name survived the acquisition just as its records survived the fire that ravaged San Francisco after the 1906 earthquake. Pacific Mutual then relocated to Los Angeles.

The company squeaked through the Depression after a flood of claims on its noncancellable disability income policies forced Pacific Mutual into a reorganization plan initiated by the California insurance commissioner (1936). After WWII, Pacific Mutual entered the group insurance and pension markets.

After 83 years as a stock company and an eight-year stock purchasing program, Pacific Mutual became a true mutual in 1959.

Pacific Mutual relocated to Newport Beach in 1972. During the 1980s it built up its financial services operations, including its Pacific Investment Management Co. (PIMCO, founded 1971). The company was in trouble even before the stock crash of 1987 because of health care costs and over-investment in real estate. That year it brought in CEO Thomas Sutton, who sold off real estate and emphasized HMOs and fee-based financial services.

In the 1990s the company cut costs and increased its fee income. PIMCO Advisors, L.P., was formed in 1994 when PIMCO merged with Thomson Advisory Group. The merger gave Pacific Mutual a retail market for its fixed-income products, a stake in the resulting public company, and sales that offset interest rate variations and changes in the health care system.

The company assumed failed Confederation Life Insurance Co.'s corporate-owned life insurance business and merged insolvent First Capital Life into Pacific Life as Pacific Corinthian Life in 1997. That year Pacific Mutual became the first top-10 US mutual to convert to a mutual holding company, thus allowing it the option of issuing stock to fund acquisitions. Because the firm remained partially mutual, however, policyholders retained ownership but got no shares of Pacific LifeCorp, its new stock company.

In an attempt to compete with one-stop financial service behemoths like Citigroup, Pacific Mutual began selling annuities through a Compass Bank subsidiary in 1998. The next year the firm made plans to acquire controlling interests in broker-dealer M.L. Stern and investment adviser Tower Asset Management. In 2000 the world's #2 insurer, Allianz, bought all of PIMCO Advisors other than the interest retained by Pacific Mutual when it spun off the investment manager.

Chairman and CEO, Pacific Mutual Holding Company,
  Pacific LifeCorp, and Pacific Life Insurance:
  Thomas C. Sutton, age 58
**President, Pacific Life:** Glenn S. Schafer, age 51
**EVP and CFO, Pacific Life:** Khanh T. Tran, age 44
**EVP, Pacific Life, Annuities Division:** Bill Robinson
**EVP, Group Insurance Division:** David W. Gartley
**EVP, Pacific Life, Institutional Products Division; EVP
  and Chief Credit Officer, Pacific Financial Products:**
  Mark W. Holmlund
**EVP, Pacific Life, Life Insurance Division:**
  Lynn C. Miller
**EVP, Pacific Life, Real Estate Division:** Michael S. Robb
**EVP, Pacific Life, Securities Division; EVP and Chief
  Credit Officer, Pacific Financial Products:**
  Larry J. Card
**SVP and General Counsel, Pacific Life:**
  David R. Carmichael
**SVP, Administration, Pacific Life, Annuities Division:**
  Robert C. Hsu
**SVP, Finance and Administration, Pacific Life, Life
  Insurance Division:** S. Gene Schofield
**SVP, Guaranteed Products and Operations, Pacific Life,
  Institutional Products Division:** John E. Milberg
**SVP, Human Resources, Pacific Life:** Anthony J. Bonno
**SVP, Marketing Operations, Pacific Life, Life Insurance
  Division:** James T. Morris
**SVP, Public Affairs, Pacific Life:** Robert G. Haskell
**SVP, Risk and Financial Management, Pacific Life,
  Institutional Products Division:** Henry M. McMillan
**SVP, Sales Office Marketing, Pacific Life, Life
  Insurance Division:** Michael A. Bell
**SVP, Sales, Pacific Life, Annuities Division:**
  Dewey P. Bushaw
**SVP, Strategic Planning and Development, Pacific Life:**
  Marc S. Franklin

**HQ:** Pacific Mutual Holding Company
  700 Newport Center Dr., Newport Beach, CA 92660
**Phone:** 949-219-3011    **Fax:** 949-219-7614
**Web:** www.pacificlife.com

Pacific Mutual Holding has insurance operations
throughout the US (except in New York) and in the UK.

**2000 Assets**

|  | $ mil. | % of total |
|---|---|---|
| Cash & equivalents | 211 | — |
| Bonds | 15,136 | 28 |
| Stocks | 179 | — |
| Mortgage loans | 3,026 | 6 |
| Policy loans | 4,680 | 9 |
| Other investments | 2,968 | 5 |
| Assets in separate account | 25,918 | 47 |
| Other assets | 2,655 | 5 |
| **Total** | **54,773** | **100** |

**Selected Subsidiaries and Affiliates**
Associated Securities Corp.
Aviation Capital Group
M.L. Stern & Co., LLC
Mutual Service Corporation
Pacific Financial Products, Inc.
Pacific Life & Annuity Company
Pacific Life Insurance Company
Pacific LifeCorp.
Pacific Select Distributors, Inc. (formerly Pacific Mutual
  Distributors)
PIMCO Advisors L.P. (31%)
PMRealty Advisors, Inc.
World-Wide Reassurance Company Limited (UK)

| | |
|---|---|
| Acordia | MetLife |
| Aetna | MONY |
| AXA Financial | Nationwide |
| Blue Cross | New York Life |
| Charles Schwab | Northwestern Mutual |
| CIGNA | PacifiCare |
| Citigroup | Principal Financial |
| GenAmerica | Provident Mutual |
| Guardian Life | Prudential |
| Hartford | St. Paul Companies |
| Health Net | StanCorp Financial Group |
| John Hancock Financial | State Farm |
| Services | USAA |
| Liberty Mutual | WellPoint Health |
| Lincoln National | Networks |
| MassMutual | |

| Mutual company FYE: December 31 | Annual Growth | 12/91 | 12/92 | 12/93 | 12/94 | 12/95 | 12/96 | 12/97 | 12/98 | 12/99 | 12/00 |
|---|---|---|---|---|---|---|---|---|---|---|---|
| Assets ($ mil.) | 21.5% | — | 11,547 | 13,346 | 14,728 | 17,589 | 27,065 | 34,009 | 39,884 | 50,123 | 54,773 |
| Net income ($ mil.) | 37.3% | — | 79 | 119 | 81 | 85 | 167 | 176 | 242 | 371 | 995 |
| Income as % of assets | — | — | 0.7% | 0.9% | 0.5% | 0.5% | 0.6% | 0.5% | 0.6% | 0.7% | 1.8% |
| Employees | 6.0% | — | 2,265 | 2,400 | 2,400 | 2,700 | 2,750 | 3,422 | 2,700 | 3,799 | 3,600 |

Equity as % of assets: 5.9%
Return on assets: 1.8%
Return on equity: 30.8
Long-term debt ($ mil.): 359
Sales ($ mil.): 4,417

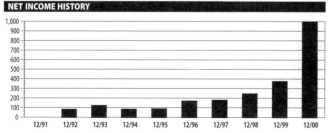

# PARSONS CORPORATION

## OVERVIEW

No village vicar, this Parsons shepherds a flock of construction projects from Abu Dhabi to Zaire. One of the world's largest engineering, procurement, and construction firms, the Pasadena, California-based company operates through five main groups: advanced technologies, communications, transportation, energy and chemicals, and infrastructure and technology.

Parsons provides construction, program, and project management services, as well as engineering, planning, and design services. The company's projects have included rail systems, bridges, and highways. Parsons has also designed power plants, overseen the cleanup of hazardous nuclear waste, and built airports, dams, resorts, and shopping centers. The firm's clients include local, state, and federal government agencies and private industries.

The company, which is owned by its employees, has diversified in order to compete in every major region of the world.

## HISTORY

Ralph Parsons, the son of a Long Island fisherman, was born in 1896. At age 13 he started his first business venture, a garage and machine shop, which he operated with his brother. After a stint in the US Navy, Parsons joined Bechtel as an aeronautical engineer. The company changed its name to Bechtel-McCone-Parsons Corporation in 1938. However, Parsons later sold his shares in that company and left in 1944 to start his own design and engineering firm, the Ralph M. Parsons Co., after splitting with partner John McCone (who later headed the CIA).

Parsons Co. expanded into the chemical and petroleum industries in the early 1950s. During that decade it oversaw the building of several natural gas and petroleum refineries overseas, including the world's largest, in Lacq, France.

In the early 1960s the company began working in Kuwait, which later proved to be one of its biggest markets. By 1969 Parsons had built oil refineries for all of the major oil companies, designed launch sites for US missiles, and constructed some of the largest mines in the world. In 1969 the company went public. With annual sales of about $300 million, it ranked second only to Bechtel in the design and engineering field. Ralph Parsons died in 1974.

The company built oil and gas treatment and production plants in Alaska in the 1970s and reorganized itself into The Parsons Corporation and RMP International in 1978. It went private in 1984 as The Parsons Corporation, taking advantage of a new tax law that favored corporations with employee stock ownership plans (ESOPs). Not all employees were happy, though. Several groups sued, maintaining that the plan disproportionately benefited executives, and that the buyout left the ESOP with all of the debt but no decision-making power. A Labor Department investigation later exonerated Parsons executives.

Parsons had just finished work on a power plant in Kuwait when Iraq invaded in 1990. Several employees were detained by the Iraqis but were released shortly before the Persian Gulf War. Two years later the company returned to Kuwait to rebuild some of the country's demolished infrastructure.

In 1995 Parsons acquired Gilbert/Commonwealth, an engineering company that specializes in designing nuclear power plants as part of an effort to bolster Parsons' ability to compete for power plant projects in industrializing countries. That year Parsons was awarded a contract to help build the Seoul International Airport, one of the largest airport projects in the world.

James McNulty, who had led the company's infrastructure and technology group, replaced Leonard Pieroni as CEO in 1996 after Pieroni died in the Bosnia plane crash that also claimed the life of US Secretary of Commerce Ronald Brown. Later that year a Parsons-led consortium won a $164.5 million contract for infrastructure projects in Bosnia.

Parsons restructured in 1997 to focus on energy, transportation, and infrastructure projects. A Parsons/Inelectra joint venture won a $150 million construction contract in 1998 to develop Cerro Negro's heavy oil production facilities in Venezuela, and the next year Parsons was chosen to manage construction of a $5 billion refinery in Bahrain, a $1.4 billion gas plant in Saudi Arabia, and a $1 billion polyethylene project in Abu Dhabi.

Parsons partnered with TRW in 2000 to create TRW Parsons Management & Operations to bid on the DOE's Yucca Mountain site in Nevada, a potential repository for the US's high-level radioactive waste and spent nuclear fuel. It also was awarded a three-year contract to help rebuild the war-torn Serbian province of Kosovo and the next year was awarded a similar contract for Bosnia-Herzegovina.

**Chairman and CEO:** James F. McNulty
**President and COO:** Frank A. DeMartino
**EVP and CFO:** Curtis A. Bower
**SVP and General Counsel:** Gary L. Stone
**SVP, Government Relations:** James E. Thrash
**VP, Human Resources:** David R. Goodrich
**VP and General Manager, Asset Management:**
Ronald L. Freeland
**President, Parsons Advanced Technologies:**
Clifford E. Eby
**President, Parsons Energy and Chemicals Group:**
William E. Hall
**President, Parsons Infrastructure and Technology
Group:** Richard G. Miller
**President, Parsons Transportation Group:**
James R. Shappell
**SVP, Parsons Infrastructure and Technology Group:**
Milton Hunter

## LOCATIONS

**HQ:** 100 W. Walnut St., Pasadena, CA 91124
**Phone:** 626-440-2000          **Fax:** 626-440-2630
**Web:** www.parsons.com

Parsons Corporation provides heavy construction
services in all 50 states and 80 other countries.

## PRODUCTS/OPERATIONS

### Selected Markets and Services

**Parsons Advanced Technologies Group**
Call centers
Criminal justice
Energy market data
Environmental data management
Revenue collection and management systems
Transportation data management
Vehicle inspection and compliance

**Parsons Communications Group**
Cable and component assembly
Equipment testing and system commissioning
Network planning and installation
Physical plants
Procurement, planning, and logistics
Project management
Wireless and wireline network management systems

**Parsons Energy and Chemicals Group**
Gas processing
Oil and gas production and gas treatment
Petrochemical and chemical plants
Power
Refining
Sulfur management

**Parsons Infrastructure and Technology Group**
Commercial and institutional facilities
Entertainment
Infrastructure
Mobile source air quality
Water resources

**Parsons Transportation Group**
Aviation
Bridges
Highways
Railroads
Systems Engineering
Tunneling
Urban transport

## COMPETITORS

| | |
|---|---|
| ABB | IT Group |
| AECOM | Jacobs Engineering |
| BE&K | Lend Lease |
| Bechtel | Louis Berger Group |
| Black & Veatch | MA Mortenson |
| Bouygues | Michael Baker |
| Day & Zimmermann | Peter Kiewit Sons' |
| Fluor | Raytheon |
| Foster Wheeler | Turner Corporation |
| Gilbane | Tutor-Saliba |
| Granite Construction | URS |
| Halliburton | Washington Group |
| Hyundai Engineering and | Waste Management |
| Construction | |

## HISTORICAL FINANCIALS & EMPLOYEES

| Private<br>FYE: December 31 | Annual<br>Growth | 12/91 | 12/92 | 12/93 | 12/94 | 12/95 | 12/96 | 12/97 | 12/98 | 12/99 | 12/00 |
|---|---|---|---|---|---|---|---|---|---|---|---|
| Sales ($ mil.) | 5.6% | — | 1,556 | 1,547 | 1,597 | 1,467 | 1,600 | 1,263 | 1,600 | 1,800 | 2,400 |
| Employees | 3.8% | — | 10,000 | 10,000 | 9,500 | 10,600 | 10,000 | 10,400 | 11,000 | 11,000 | 13,500 |

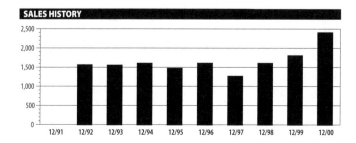

### SALES HISTORY

# PENSION BENEFIT GUARANTY

## OVERVIEW

Even in these days of the 401(k), some retired Americans still rely on their pensions. The Pension Benefit Guaranty Corporation (PBGC) makes sure they can. Washington, DC-based PBGC is a government corporation that insures nearly 40,000 single-company pension funds and 1,800 multi-employer plans (collective-bargaining agreements involving two or more employers); all together, these plans cover about 43 million workers. Governed by a board that includes the secretaries of labor, commerce, and the treasury, PBGC audits pension plans to spot those that are at risk. It is funded by employer-paid insurance premiums (about $19 per employee), as well as investment income, assets from administered plans, and recoveries from companies with terminated plans.

PBGC terminates pension plans when it determines that a company can no longer pay benefits; it can take a portion of a company's assets to ensure that pension obligations are met. When PBGC takes over a failed plan, it pays each individual pensioner covered by the plan up to $40,000 annually.

Many companies are moving from traditional defined benefit pension plans to so-called defined contribution plans, usually reducing the benefits of long-time workers in the process. Workers and their advocates criticize the switched plans, but they don't come under PBGC's jurisdiction unless they fail.

## HISTORY

The Employment Retirement Income Security Act (ERISA) of 1974 established the Pension Benefit Guaranty Corporation (PBGC) to protect workers' pension benefits. The poor economy of the day guaranteed PBGC plenty of business. By 1975 more than 1,000 companies were unable to meet pension obligations. Other companies tried to avoid entering the system by terminating their plans before a 1996 deadline; the Supreme Court in 1980 upheld PBGC's contention that these companies were obligated to pay benefits to vested workers.

ERISA's provisions initially let companies voluntarily terminate their plans by paying PBGC a portion of their assets; many companies took this route until Congress limited the provision. Pensions faced a new threat in the late 1980s, as many buyout deals were structured to use company pension plans as part of their funding; Congress put a stop to that practice in 1990.

Companies found themselves caught between conflicting requirements of the PBGC (ever watchful for underfunded pension plans) and the IRS (which penalized overfunded plans). PBGC's deficit grew as it took on more and more pension payment liabilities; companies continued to jeopardize plans by using funds for other purposes. On behalf of 40,000 workers, PBGC in 1988 sued companies that allegedly terminated their plans illegally between 1976 and 1981 (the suit was settled in 1995 for $100 million.)

In 1989 new director James Lockhart began airing PBGC's plight, claiming that the pension system would follow the savings and loan industry into collapse. In the early 1990s his predictions seemed reasonable; PBGC's deficit was driven sky-high by such bankruptcies as Pan Am (1991), TWA, and Munsingwear (1992). Under Lockhart's guidance, the PBGC began publishing the "iffy fifty" — the 50 most underfunded pensions in the country.

Martin Slate succeeded Lockhart in 1993 and toned down the Chicken Little rhetoric, although that year PBGC announced that underfunding had nearly doubled between 1987 and 1992. Help arrived in the form of 1994's Retirement Protection Act, which put some teeth into pension laws. Under the reforms, PBGC required some employers to notify workers and retirees about the funding of their plans; it also changed the rules for annual reporting to the PBGC. The next year President Clinton vetoed the budget bill, which would have allowed companies to take money from their pension plans.

Slate died in 1997 and David Strauss took over. After two decades in the red, PBGC in 1998 marked its third consecutive year in the black. The organization was sued by several former Pan Am workers who claimed PBGC had shorted their benefits. That year PBGC announced that LTV, the giant steel company that went bankrupt in 1993, could resume monthly pension payments to retired workers.

In 1999 PBGC defended itself against critics who claimed it took too long to determine benefits from bankrupt companies, and often required pensioners to repay thousands of dollars that had been paid in estimated benefits.

In 2000 with a $10 billion surplus under PBGC's belt, Strauss said that Congress should permit well-funded pensions a holiday from paying premiums.

**Chairman:** Alexis M. Herman
**Executive Director:** David M. Strauss
**Deputy Executive Director and COO:** Joseph Grant
**Deputy Executive Director and CFO:**
  N. Anthony Calhoun
**Chief Negotiator:** Andrea E. Schneider
**General Counsel:** James J. Keightley
**Director Budget:** Henry R. Thompson
**Director Communications and Public Affairs:**
  Judith Welles
**Director Contracts and Controls Review:** Marty Boehm
**Director Corporate Policy and Research:**
  Stuart A. Sirkin
**Director Facilities and Services:** Janet Smith
**Director Financial Operations:** Hazel Broadnax
**Director Human Resources:** Sharon Barbee-Fletcher
**Director Information Resources Management:**
  Cristin M. Birch
**Director Insurance Operations:** Bennie Hagans
**Director Participant and Employer Appeals:**
  Harriet D. Verburg
**Director Procurement:** Robert Herting
**Assistant Executive Director Legislative Affairs:**
  Judy Schub
**Auditors:** PricewaterhouseCoopers LLP

## LOCATIONS

**HQ:** Pension Benefit Guaranty Corporation
  1200 K St. NW, Washington, DC 20005
**Phone:** 202-326-4040      **Fax:** 202-326-4042
**Web:** www.pbgc.gov

## PRODUCTS/OPERATIONS

**2000 Assets**

|  | $ mil. | % of total |
|---|---|---|
| Cash & equivalents | 349 | 2 |
| Fixed maturity securities | 12,390 | 58 |
| Equities | 8,189 | 38 |
| Other investments | 48 | — |
| Receivables | 431 | 2 |
| Other | 2 | — |
| **Total** | **21,409** | **100** |

**2000 Sales**

|  | $ mil. | % of total |
|---|---|---|
| Underwriting | 836 | 25 |
| Investing | 2,462 | 75 |
| **Total** | **3,298** | **100** |

## COMPETITORS

CIGNA
Putnam Investments
Vanguard Group

## HISTORICAL FINANCIALS & EMPLOYEES

| Government agency FYE: September 30 | Annual Growth | 9/91 | 9/92 | 9/93 | 9/94 | 9/95 | 9/96 | 9/97 | 9/98 | 9/99 | 9/00 |
|---|---|---|---|---|---|---|---|---|---|---|---|
| Assets ($ mil.) | 16.3% | — | — | — | 8,659 | 10,848 | 12,548 | 15,910 | 18,376 | 19,123 | 21,409 |
| Employees | 2.2% | — | — | — | 687 | 660 | 764 | 750 | 750 | — | — |

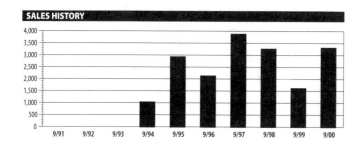

SALES HISTORY

# PENSKE CORPORATION

With eyes on the finish line — and the bottom line, Roger Penske, known to be a lead-footed and hard-driving executive, heads the closely held Detroit-based Penske Corporation, which operates nearly 10 automotive and transportation businesses.

The company's Penske Truck Leasing Company (79%-owned by GE Capital) is the US's #2 truck-rental operation, after Ryder. Penske Automotive operates five upscale car dealerships in southern California, and it has a nearly 60% stake in publicly traded United Auto Group (UAG), which has more than 120 franchise dealerships in 19 states, Puerto Rico, and Brazil. Penske also owns a 15% stake in electronic fuel-injection systems maker Diesel

Technology. (Robert Bosch owns the rest.) It also operates Penske Auto Centers through more than 630 Kmart locations nationwide.

Penske just can't seem to resist that new car smell. The company has sold its racetrack interests and upped its stake in the struggling UAG. Roger Penske personally visited most of UAG's dealerships to help return the chain to profitablity. He now heads UAG and holds a 57% stake in Penske Corporation. Penske has sold its 49% stake in heavy-duty truck engine maker Detroit Diesel to DaimlerChrysler. The company has souped up its Penske Truck Leasing unit with the purchase of Rollins Truck Leasing, the US's third-largest truck rental and leasing player.

As a teen Roger Penske earned money by repairing and reselling cars. At 21 he entered his first auto race; he was running second when his car overheated. His winning ways, however, were soon apparent, and in 1961 *Sports Illustrated* named him race car driver of the year.

Nonetheless, in 1965 Penske went looking for a day job. With a $150,000 loan from his father, he bought a Chevrolet dealership in Philadelphia and retired from racing to avoid loading his balance sheet with steep life-insurance premiums for the CEO. Penske teamed with driver Mark Donohue in 1966 to form the Penske Racing Team. Donohue died in a crash in 1975, but team Penske continued.

In 1969 Penske started a regional truck-leasing business, incorporated under the name Penske. The company established auto dealerships in Pennsylvania and Ohio in the early 1970s. In 1975 the company bought the Michigan International Speedway. Penske and fellow racing team owner Pat Patrick started the race-sponsoring organization Championship Auto Racing Teams (CART) in 1978.

In 1982 Penske's truck-leasing business formed a joint venture with rental company Hertz to form Hertz Penske Truck Leasing. Penske expanded its auto dealerships in the 1980s by acquiring dealerships in California, including Longo Toyota in 1985.

Racing legend Al Unser Sr. surprised Indy 500 watchers in 1987 by driving a car borrowed from an exhibition in a hotel lobby to a first place finish for the Penske Racing Team.

In 1988 Penske bought 80% of GM's Detroit Diesel engine-making unit, which had a market share of only 3% and had lost some

$600 million over the previous five years. Penske trimmed $70 million from the unit's budget by firing 440 salaried employees, streamlining manufacturing processes, and cutting administration expenses. Detroit Diesel's market share doubled in its first two years as a Penske unit. Also in 1988 Penske purchased Hertz's stake in Hertz Penske Truck Leasing, which it later combined with the truck-rental division of appliance maker General Electric to create Penske Truck Leasing.

By 1993 Detroit Diesel's market share had grown to more than 25%. That year the engine maker went public. Penske bought 860 Kmart auto centers for $112 million in 1995. The company's racing business, Penske Motorsports, went public in 1996, but Penske retained a 55% stake in the company. Also that year Penske bought Truck-Lite, Quaker State's automotive lighting unit. Penske Truck Leasing formed Penske Logistics Europe in 1997 to offer information systems and other integrated logistics services on that continent.

Penske sold its Penske Motorsports operations, which included racetracks in California, Michigan, North Carolina, and Pennsylvania, to International Speedway in 1999. Also that year Penske invested about $83 million for a 38% stake in car retailer UnitedAuto Group (UAG) and Roger Penske became CEO of Penske. In 2000 the company sold its 48.6% stake in Detroit Diesel to DaimlerChrysler.

The following year Penske increased its stake in UAG to 57%, and added three additional dealerships. Later in 2001 Penske Truck Leasing acquired Rollins Truck Leasing (the US's third-largest player behind Ryder and Penske) for $754 million.

**Chairman and CEO:** Roger S. Penske, age 64
**EVP, Administration:** Paul F. Walters
**SVP, Corporate Finance:** J. Patrick Conroy
**VP, Human Resources:** Randall W. Johnson

## LOCATIONS

**HQ:** 13400 Outer Dr. West, Detroit, MI 48239
**Phone:** 313-592-5000 **Fax:** 313-592-5256
**Web:** www.penske.com

Penske operations include Penske Automotive, with five
dealerships in southern California; Penske Auto Centers,
with about 630 repair shops located in Kmart stores;
Penske Truck Leasing, with about 750 worldwide rental
locations; and UnitedAuto Group, with more than 123
franchise dealerships in 19 states, Brazil, and Puerto Rico.

## PRODUCTS/OPERATIONS

**Selected Subsidiaries and Affiliates**
Davco, Inc. (fuel filters and engine accessories)
Diesel Technology (15%, fuel-injection system
  manufacturing)
Penske Auto Centers, Inc. (retail auto-service outlets)
Penske Automotive (retail auto sales)
Penske Truck Leasing Co. LP (21%, truck rental and
  leasing)
Truck-Lite (automotive lighting)
UnitedAuto Group (57%, retail auto sales)

## COMPETITORS

AMERCO
AutoNation
DaimlerChrysler
Discount Tire
Fiat
General Motors
Goodrich
Isuzu
Mack Trucks
Navistar
PACCAR
Prospect Motors
Ryder
Tasha Inc.
Volvo

## HISTORICAL FINANCIALS & EMPLOYEES

| Private<br>FYE: December 31 | Annual<br>Growth | 12/91 | 12/92 | 12/93 | 12/94 | 12/95 | 12/96 | 12/97 | 12/98 | 12/99 | 12/00 |
|---|---|---|---|---|---|---|---|---|---|---|---|
| Sales ($ mil.) | 17.2% | — | 2,800 | 3,250 | 3,287 | 3,900 | 5,200 | 5,800 | 6,000 | 6,400 | 10,000 |
| Employees | 15.3% | — | 10,906 | 11,500 | 16,000 | 16,700 | 25,000 | 28,000 | 28,000 | 34,000 | 34,000 |

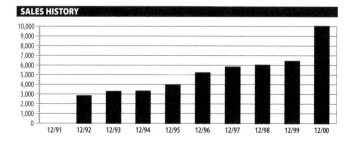

SALES HISTORY

# PERDUE FARMS INCORPORATED

Bird is the word at Perdue Farms, the leading chicken producer in the Northeast and near the top of the pecking order of all US poultry companies. Each week the Salisbury, Maryland-based company supplies supermarkets, restaurants, and other customers with some 46 million pounds of chicken products and nearly 4 million pounds of turkey products. It sells its products primarily in the East, Midwest, and South, and it exports to more than 50 countries.

Perdue is vertically integrated: It hatches the eggs, grows the birds, and then processes and ships the meat. The company processes grain to make its own feeds and vegetable oils.

Perdue also turns poultry by-products into pet food ingredients. And in a joint venture with AgriRecycle it makes fertilizer from used chicken litter. In recent years the company has doubled the size of its food service division and has placed greater emphasis on value-added chicken products.

The family-owned company is headed by James Perdue, who appears Perdue ads, just like his famous father, Frank, did before him. Perdue produces its own breed of chicken, the skin of which is a distinct yellow color resulting from a diet that includes marigold petals.

If asked which came first, the chickens or the eggs, the Perdue family will tell you the eggs did. Arthur Perdue, a railroad express worker, bought 23 layer hens in 1920 and started supplying the New York City market with eggs from a henhouse in his family's backyard in Salisbury, Maryland. His son Frank joined the business in 1939.

The Perdues sold broiling chickens to major processors such as Swift and Armour in the 1940s and pioneered chicken crossbreeding to develop new breeds. The family started contracting with farmers in the Salisbury area in 1950 to grow broilers for them. Frank became president of the company in 1952. The next year it began mixing its own feed.

Frank persuaded his father to borrow money to build a soybean mill in 1961. (Arthur had not willingly gone into debt in his more than 40 years in the poultry industry.) The soybean mill was part of Frank's plan to vertically integrate the company — with grain storage facilities, feed milling operations, soybean processing plants, mulch plants, hatcheries, and 600 contract chicken farmers — to counter the threat of processors buying chickens directly from farmers rather than through middlemen like the Perdues. To differentiate their products, the company applied the Perdue name to packages on retail meat counters in 1968.

Two years later the company began a breeding and genetic research program. Over the following years Frank transformed himself from country chicken salesman to media poultry pitchman when the company decided to use him as spokesperson in its print, radio, and TV ads. Catchy slogans ("It takes a tough man to make a tender chicken") combined with Frank's whiny voice and sincere face helped

sales. As Perdue Farms expanded geographically into new eastern markets such as Philadelphia, Boston, and Baltimore, it acquired the broiler facilities of other processors.

In 1983 James Perdue, Frank's only son, joined the company as a management trainee. The following year Perdue added processors in Virginia and Indiana and introduced turkey products. In 1986 it acquired Intertrade, a feed broker, and FoodCraft, a food equipment maker. However, after enjoying a rising demand for poultry by an increasingly health-conscious society in the 1970s and early 1980s, the company found its sales leveling off in the late 1980s. When North Carolina fined Perdue for unsafe working conditions in 1989, the company increased its emphasis on safety.

James, who had become chairman of the board in 1991, replaced his folksy father in 1994 as the company's spokesman in TV ads. In the early 1990s Perdue's management determined that future sales growth lay in food service, international sales, and prepared foods; therefore, the poultry company quietly began laying the groundwork to support these new markets.

Perdue launched its Cafe Perdue entree meal kits in 1997. The following year it purchased Italian entree maker De Luca. Also in 1998, through a joint venture, Perdue opened a poultry processing plant in Shanghai, China.

Early in 1999 the company purchased Advantage Foods, a poultry processor that specializes in deboning chicken for portion-control chicken breasts. At the end of 2000, faced with depressed market prices, Perdue announced it would be cutting jobs. Employees who worked as chicken catchers for Perdue won $2.4 million in a 2001 settlement over claims filed in 1998 for unpaid overtime.

**Chairman and CEO:** James A. Perdue
**President and COO:** Robert Turley
**CFO:** Michael Cooper
**SVP of Retail, Sales, and Marketing:** Steve Evans
**SVP of Supply Chain Management:** Larry Winslow
**VP of Human Resources:** Rob Heflin
**President and General Manager, Specialty Foods:**
Randy Day
**President and General Manager, Grain and Oilseed
Division:** Dick Willey
**Director of Corporate Affairs:** Tita Sherrier
**Director of Environmental Service:** John Chlada

# LOCATIONS

**HQ:** 31149 Old Ocean City Rd., Salisbury, MD 21804
**Phone:** 410-543-3000      **Fax:** 410-543-3292
**Web:** www.perdue.com

Perdue Farms has operations in Alabama, Connecticut, Delaware, Florida, Indiana, Kentucky, Maryland, New Jersey, North Carolina, Pennsylvania, South Carolina, Tennessee, Virginia, and West Virginia.

# PRODUCTS/OPERATIONS

### Selected Poultry Products and Brands

**Fresh Poultry**
Chicken parts (Prime Parts)
Ground chicken
Roasters, turkeys, and Cornish hens
Seasoned chicken
Skinless, boneless poultry cuts
Turkey burgers
Turkey sausage

**Fully Cooked Poultry**
Cutlets
Nuggets
Rotisserie-style chicken (Tender Ready, food service)
Tenders

**Other Brands**
Chef's Choice
Cookin' Good
Ed & Joan DeLuca
Fit 'N Easy
Gol-pak
Shenandoah
Short Cuts

**Other Products**

Pet food ingredients
Vegetable oils

# COMPETITORS

| | |
|---|---|
| AJC International | Hormel |
| Cagle's | Keystone Foods |
| Cargill | Pilgrim's Pride |
| ConAgra | Sanderson Farms |
| ContiGroup | Smithfield Foods |
| Foster Farms | Townsends |
| Gold Kist | Tyson Foods |

# HISTORICAL FINANCIALS & EMPLOYEES

| Private<br>FYE: March 31 | Annual<br>Growth | 3/92 | 3/93 | 3/94 | 3/95 | 3/96 | 3/97 | 3/98 | 3/99 | 3/00 | 3/01 |
|---|---|---|---|---|---|---|---|---|---|---|---|
| Sales ($ mil.) | 9.0% | 1,239 | 1,300 | 1,600 | 1,700 | 2,100 | 2,200 | 2,200 | 2,515 | 2,501 | 2,700 |
| Employees | 5.1% | 12,500 | 13,300 | 18,600 | 18,600 | 19,000 | 18,000 | 18,000 | 20,500 | 19,500 | 19,500 |

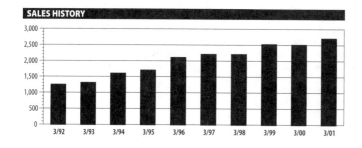

SALES HISTORY

# PETCO ANIMAL SUPPLIES, INC.

## OVERVIEW

Petco Animal Supplies is hot on the tail of the #1 US pet supply specialty retailer, PETsMART. San Diego-based Petco is the #2 pet supply chain, with more than 530 stores in some 40 states and Washington, DC. Its 15,000-sq.-ft. superstores offer about 10,000 different items, including premium pet foods (Iams, Nutro, Science Diet), toys, animal habitats, grooming and veterinary supplies, collars, and leashes. Critter-wise, it sells reptiles, birds, fish, and small mammals, and it sponsors pet adoption for cats and dogs with local animal welfare organizations.

Like its chief competitor, Petco has grown through rapid yet costly acquisitions. Now with its purchases fully integrated, the firm is focusing on growing through internal expansion, with plans to open 50 stores per year, especially in the Southeast. Petco has also leapt paws first into online retailing through Petco.com and Petopia.com, which the company bought in December 2000 (it already owned 26%) and folded into Petco.com.

In late 2000 buyout specialists led by Leonard Green acquired Petco for almost $600 million. The company filed to go public in December 2001.

## HISTORY

Petco evolved from Upco, a suburban San Diego veterinary supply store opened in 1965. In 1979 it moved into mainstream pet supplies and changed its name to Petco Animal Supplies. It had 40 stores by 1988, when it was bought by the Spectrum Group and the Thomas H. Lee Co. That year Petco bought two pet supply chains, more than tripling its store count. Management then began a strategy of having periodic, heavily promoted sales. However, this raised advertising costs and made customer traffic irregular. By 1990 Petco was in trouble.

The chain installed a new management team headed by CEO Brian Devine, a former Toys "R" Us executive. It launched an everyday-low-pricing strategy for its popular premium pet food lines and it worked to open stores near supermarkets to draw shoppers to Petco. Those moves helped to increase traffic and resulted in more impulse purchases of toys and grooming supplies.

Sales stabilized, and by the time Petco went public in 1994, it had 198 stores. Over the next five years, the firm made 19 acquisitions, adding 208 stores in 28 states, including Pet USA, Super Pets, PAWS, and Pet Food Savemart. It added eight stores in the New York area when it bought Pet Nosh for $17 million in 1996. The company also greatly expanded its presence in the upper Midwest in 1996, when it paid approximately $55 million for Minnesota-based Pet Food Warehouse, a 28-store chain serving Minnesota, Wisconsin, North Dakota, South Dakota, and Iowa.

Sales grew rapidly, increasing 50% per year between 1994 and 1997. Yet integration of new stores proved costly and competition had heated up. Major discounters such as Wal-Mart as well as supermarket chains began to add more premium pet foods to their shelves, drawing away many Petco customers.

The company continued its streak of acquisitions in 1997, buying Chicago-based PetCare Plus, an 80-store chain in Alabama, Arkansas, Illinois, Indiana, Kansas, Kentucky, Michigan, Missouri, and Tennessee. Merger and acquisition costs contributed to losses in 1997 and 1998.

In 1998 Petco curtailed the pace of its acquisitions, adding only four stores. Also that year the company launched a major national advertising campaign designed to draw consumers back from the supermarket and into the pet store. Petco also established its "PETCO Animal Lovers Save" (P.A.L.S.) customer loyalty program, rewarding frequent customers with discounts on store merchandise.

Still, 1999 profits were again affected by merger costs relating to purchases made in 1997. In July 1999 Petco took a 26% interest in e-commerce firm Petopia.com, looking to mark its territory in the already dog-eat-dog online pet supply market.

A poor stock showing led the company to accept a May 2000 buyout offer from Leonard Green & Partners and Texas Pacific Group. The acquisition was completed five months later for nearly $600 million.

In December 2000 the company bought the remaining shares in Petopia.com, with plans to merge it with existing Petco online operations. Also in 2000 the company expanded its P.A.L.S. program to offer customers free pet food. Petco filed to go public in December 2001.

**Chairman, President, and CEO:** Brian K. Devine
**EVP Operations:** Bruce C. Hall
**SVP and CFO:** James M. Myers
**SVP Business Development:** William M. Woodard
**SVP Human Resources and Administration:**
  Janet D. Mitchell

## LOCATIONS

**HQ:** 9125 Rehco Rd., San Diego, CA 92121
**Phone:** 858-453-7845    **Fax:** 858-677-3095
**Web:** www.petco.com

Petco Animal Supplies has more than 500 stores in 40
states and central distribution centers in California,
Illinois, and New Jersey.

## PRODUCTS/OPERATIONS

**Selected Merchandise**
Aquariums
Bird cages
Carriers
Collars
Dog houses
Grooming supplies
Leashes
Pet apparel
Pet food
Terrariums
Treats
Toys
Veterinary products
Vitamins

**Selected Services**
Obedience training
Professional grooming
Veterinary care

## COMPETITORS

| | |
|---|---|
| Ahold USA | Pet Valu |
| Albertson's | PETsMART |
| Costco Wholesale | Safeway |
| Kmart | Target |
| Kroger | Wal-Mart |

## HISTORICAL FINANCIALS & EMPLOYEES

| Private<br>FYE: Sat. nearest January 31 | Annual<br>Growth | 1/92 | 1/93 | 1/94 | 1/95 | 1/96 | 1/97 | 1/98 | 1/99 | 1/00 | 1/01 |
|---|---|---|---|---|---|---|---|---|---|---|---|
| Sales ($ mil.) | 30.2% | 107 | 117 | 148 | 189 | 271 | 500 | 750 | 840 | 990 | 1,151 |
| Net income ($ mil.) | — | 2 | 1 | (1) | 5 | 8 | (12) | (13) | (2) | 22 | (29) |
| Income as % of sales | — | 1.8% | 0.4% | — | 2.4% | 3.1% | — | — | — | 2.2% | — |
| Employees | 30.1% | 1,200 | 1,636 | 2,200 | 2,016 | 3,115 | 5,700 | 9,400 | 9,300 | 10,200 | 12,800 |

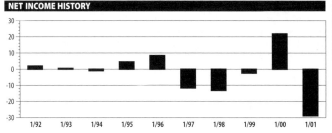

**NET INCOME HISTORY**

**2001 FISCAL YEAR-END**
Debt ratio: 100.0%
Return on equity: —
Cash ($ mil.): 18
Current ratio: 1.30
Long-term debt ($ mil.): 380

# PETER KIEWIT SONS', INC.

## OVERVIEW

By building everything from tunnels to high-rises, Peter Kiewit Sons' has become a heavyweight in the heavy construction industry. The Omaha, Nebraska-based company is one of the largest general contractors in the US. Roughly 50% of its projects are transportation-related, including airports, bridges, highways, mass transit systems, and railroads. Another 20% falls under the power, heat, and cooling umbrella, and commercial buildings, water treatment and sewage facilities, and mining and petroleum infrastructure make up the balance. The firm specializes in design-build projects and often works through joint ventures. More than 75% of its business comes from government contracts.

The construction business has the undivided attention of Kiewit these days. It has spun off its asphalt and ready-mix concrete business as Kiewit Materials and has created a unit to focus on construction for the offshore drilling industry. The company also provides construction for Level 3 Communications (a telecommunications and computer services business it divested in 1998), which accounts for about 40% of sales.

Kiewit has no trouble answering to both its shareholders and its employees — they are one and the same. The company is owned by current and former employees and Kiewit family members.

## HISTORY

Born to Dutch immigrants, Peter Kiewit and brother Andrew founded Kiewit Brothers, a brickyard, in 1884 in Omaha, Nebraska. By 1912 two of his sons worked at the yard, which was named Peter Kiewit & Sons. When Peter Kiewit died in 1914, his son Ralph took over, and the firm took the name Peter Kiewit Sons'. Another son, Peter, joined Ralph at the helm in 1924 after dropping out of Dartmouth and later took over.

During the Depression, Kiewit managed huge federal public works projects, and in the 1940s it focused on war-related emergency construction projects.

One of the firm's most difficult projects was top-secret Thule Air Force Base in Greenland, above the Arctic Circle. For more than two years 5,000 men worked around the clock, beginning in 1951; the site was in development for 15 years. In 1952 the company won a contract to build a $1.2 billion gas diffusion plant in Portsmouth, Ohio. It also became a contractor for the US interstate highway system (begun in 1956).

Peter Kiewit died in 1979, after stipulating that the largely employee-owned company should remain under employee control and that no one employee could own more than 10%. His 40% stake, when returned to the company, transformed many employees into millionaires. Walter Scott Jr., whose father had been the first graduate engineer to work for Kiewit, took charge. Scott made his mark by parlaying money from construction into successful investments.

When the construction industry slumped, Kiewit began looking for other investment opportunities, and in 1984 it acquired packaging company Continental Can Co. (selling off noncore insurance, energy, and timber assets). Continental was saddled with a 1983 class action lawsuit alleging that it had plotted to close plants and lay off workers before they were qualified for pensions. In 1991 Kiewit agreed to pay $415 million to settle the lawsuit.

In 1986 Kiewit loaned money to a business group to build a fiber-optic loop in Chicago; by 1987 it had launched MFS Communications to build local fiber loops in downtown districts. In 1992 Kiewit split its business into two pieces: the construction group, which was strictly employee-owned, and a diversified group, to which it added a controlling stake in phone and cable TV company C-TEC in 1993. That year Kiewit took MFS public; by 1995 it had sold all its shares, and the next year MFS was bought by telecom giant WorldCom.

In 1996 Kiewit assisted CalEnergy (now MidAmerican Energy) in a hostile $1.3 billion takeover of the UK's Northern Electric. Kiewit got stock in CalEnergy and a 30% stake in the UK electric company, all of which it sold to CalEnergy in 1998.

That year Kiewit spun off its telecom and computer services holdings into Level 3 Communications. Scott, who had been hospitalized the year before for a blood clot in his lung, stepped down as CEO, and Ken Stinson, CEO of Kiewit Construction Group, took over Peter Kiewit Sons'.

In 1999 Kiewit acquired a majority interest in Pacific Rock Products, a construction materials firm in Canada. Kiewit spun off its asphalt, concrete, and aggregates operations in 2000 as Kiewit Materials. Also that year the company created Kiewit Offshore Services to focus on construction for the offshore drilling industry.

**Chairman Emeritus:** Walter Scott Jr., age 69
**Chairman and CEO, Peter Kiewit Sons' and Kiewit Construction:** Kenneth E. Stinson, age 58, $3,686,556 pay
**President, COO, and Director; President, Kiewit Western:** Bruce E. Grewcock, age 47, $816,600 pay
**EVP and Director; EVP, Kiewit Pacific:** Richard W. Colf, age 57, $818,700 pay
**EVP and Director; EVP, Kiewit Pacific:** Allan K. Kirkwood, age 57, $918,700 pay
**EVP and Director:** Roy L. Cline, age 63, $608,604 pay
**VP and Treasurer:** Michael J. Piechoski, age 47
**VP, General Counsel, and Secretary:** Tobin A. Schropp, age 38
**VP, Human Resources and Administration:** John B. Chapman, age 55
**VP:** Ben E. Muraskin, age 37
**VP:** Gerald S. Pfeffer, age 55
**VP:** Stephen A. Sharpe, age 49
**Controller:** Gregory D. Brokke, age 38
**Auditors:** PricewaterhouseCoopers LLP

## LOCATIONS

**HQ:** Kiewit Plaza, Omaha, NE 68131
**Phone:** 402-342-2052　　**Fax:** 402-271-2939
**Web:** www.kiewit.com

Peter Kiewit Sons' has projects in 43 states and Washington, DC, Puerto Rico, and seven Canadian provinces.

**2000 Sales**

|  | $ mil. | % of total |
|---|---|---|
| US | 4,269 | 96 |
| Canada | 194 | 4 |
| **Total** | **4,463** | **100** |

## PRODUCTS/OPERATIONS

**2000 New Contracts**

|  | % of total |
|---|---|
| Transportation (highways, bridges, airports, railroads & mass transit) | 48 |
| Power, heat & cooling | 19 |
| Commercial buildings | 15 |
| Water supply | 10 |
| Mining | 3 |
| Other | 5 |
| **Total** | **100** |

## COMPETITORS

| | |
|---|---|
| ABB | Jacobs Engineering |
| Bechtel | Parsons |
| Black & Veatch | Perini |
| Bovis Lend Lease | Raytheon |
| EMCOR | Skanska |
| Fluor | Turner Corporation |
| Foster Wheeler | Tutor-Saliba |
| GE Power Systems | Washington Group |
| Granite Construction | Whiting-Turner |
| Halliburton | Williams Companies |
| ITOCHU | |

## HISTORICAL FINANCIALS & EMPLOYEES

| Private<br>FYE: Last Saturday in December | Annual<br>Growth | 12/91 | 12/92 | 12/93 | 12/94 | 12/95 | 12/96 | 12/97 | 12/98 | 12/99 | 12/00 |
|---|---|---|---|---|---|---|---|---|---|---|---|
| Sales ($ mil.) | 10.4% | — | 2,020 | 2,179 | 2,991 | 2,902 | 2,904 | 2,764 | 3,403 | 4,013 | 4,463 |
| Net income ($ mil.) | (0.1%) | — | 181 | 261 | 110 | 244 | 221 | 155 | 288 | 165 | 179 |
| Income as % of sales | — | — | 9.0% | 12.0% | 3.7% | 8.4% | 7.6% | 5.6% | 8.5% | 4.1% | 4.0% |
| Employees | 4.9% | — | 7,600 | 10,620 | 14,000 | 14,300 | 14,000 | 16,200 | 16,200 | 20,300 | 11,146 |

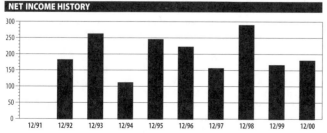

**NET INCOME HISTORY**

**2000 FISCAL YEAR-END**
Debt ratio: 1.7%
Return on equity: —
Cash ($ mil.): 302
Current ratio: 1.82
Long-term debt ($ mil.): 12

# THE PORT AUTHORITY OF NY & NJ

## OVERVIEW

The Port Authority of New York and New Jersey bridges the often-troubled waters between the two states — and helps with other transportation needs of more than 400 million customers who rely on the Port Authority's services. The bi-state agency operates and maintains tunnels, bridges, airports, a commuter rail system, shipping terminals, and other facilities within the Port District, an area surrounding the Statue of Liberty. The Port Authority, whose main New York City office was destroyed on September 11, 2001, is being run from temporary headquarters in Jersey City, New Jersey.

A self-supporting public agency, the Port Authority receives no state or local tax money but relies on tolls, fees, and rents. The governors of the two states each appoint six of the 12 members of the board of commissioners and review the board's decisions.

The Port Authority's facilities include such international symbols of transportation and commerce as the George Washington Bridge, the Holland and Lincoln tunnels, LaGuardia and John F. Kennedy airports, and the New York-New Jersey Port. The World Trade Center was counted among those before its twin towers and much of the rest of the complex were destroyed in a terrorist attack on September 11, 2001. Executive Director Neil Levin was killed in the attack, and 73 other Port Authority employees were listed as dead or missing.

The Port Authority Trans-Hudson (PATH) rapid-transit system carries nearly 75 million passengers per year.

## HISTORY

New York and New Jersey spent much of their early history fighting over their common waterways. In 1921 a treaty creating a single, bistate agency, the Port of New York Authority, was ratified by the New York and New Jersey state legislatures.

The agency struggled at first, although its early projects, such as the Goethals Bridge (1928, linking Staten Island to New Jersey), were far from timid. It merged with the Holland Tunnel Commission in 1930, which brought a steady source of revenue. In 1931 the George Washington Bridge (spanning the Hudson River from Manhattan to New Jersey) was completed. The Lincoln Tunnel (also linking Manhattan to New Jersey) opened in 1937.

After WWII the Port Authority broadened its focus to include commercial aviation. In 1947 the agency took over LaGuardia Airport, and the next year it dedicated the New York International Airport (renamed John F. Kennedy International Airport in 1963).

As trucking supplanted railroads in the late 1950s, The Port Authority experimented with more-efficient ways of transferring cargo. In 1962 it built the first containerport in the world. That year the agency acquired a commuter rail line connecting Newark to Manhattan, which became the Port Authority Trans-Hudson (PATH).

In the early 1970s the Port Authority completed the World Trade Center. The agency changed its name to the Port Authority of New York and New Jersey in 1972 to reflect its role in mass transit between the two states. Critics, however, frequently assailed the agency for inefficiency and pork-barrel politics. In 1993 terrorists detonated a truck bomb in one of the World Trade Center towers, but within a year the building had largely recovered.

George Marlin became executive director in 1995. He cut operating expenses for the first time since 1943 and through budget cuts and layoffs, saved $100 million in 1996. He stepped down in 1997, and Robert Boyle took the post. That year the agency broke ground on Terminal 4 at JFK International Airport.

New York City mayor Rudolph Giuliani proposed legislation in 1999 to place the Port Authority's LaGuardia and JFK airports under City Hall jurisdiction. An 18-month standoff between the governors of New York and New Jersey regarding disputes over leases and agency spending was settled in 2000, which allowed the Port Authority to move forward with projects that had been blocked. Also in 2000 Boyle announced plans to resign. Neil Levin, New York's state insurance superintendent and a former Goldman Sachs vice president, replaced him the next year.

After the Port Authority and Vornado Realty Trust in 2001 failed to finalize an agreement for Vornado to lease the World Trade Center, the Port Authority that year signed a 99-year, $3.2 billion deal to lease portions of the World Trade Center's office space to a group led by Silverstein Properties while leasing the retail space to Westfield America.

Less than two months later, the World Trade Center's twin towers were destroyed when terrorists hijacked passenger jets and flew them into the buildings.

## OFFICERS

**Chairman:** Lewis M. Eisenberg
**Vice Chairman:** Charles A. Gargano
**Acting Executive Director:** Ronald Shiftan, age 56
**COO; VP and General Manager, PATH:**
Ernesto L. Butcher
**CFO:** Charles F. McClafferty
**Chief Engineer:** Francis J. Lombardi
**Treasurer:** Bruce Bohlen
**Comptroller:** Margaret R. Zoch
**Director Audit:** John D. Brill
**Director Aviation:** William R. DeCota
**Director Human Resources:** Paul Segalini
**Director Media Relations:** Kayla Bergeron
**Director Priority Capital Programs:** Anthony Cracchiolo
**Director Real Estate; VP and Secretary, Newark Legal Center:** Cherrie Nanninga
**Director Tunnels, Bridges and Terminals:** Ken Philmus
**General Counsel; VP and Secretary, New York & New Jersey Railroad:** Jeffrey S. Green
**Auditors:** Deloitte & Touche LLP

## LOCATIONS

**HQ:** The Port Authority of New York and New Jersey
241 Erie St., Jersey City, NJ 07310
**Phone:** 201-216-2924
**Web:** www.panynj.gov

The Port Authority of New York and New Jersey has operations in the five city boroughs and 12 counties in New Jersey and New York. The agency has overseas offices in Belgium, China, Hong Kong, Japan, Singapore, South Korea, and the UK.

## PRODUCTS/OPERATIONS

**2000 Sales**

| | $ mil. | % of total |
|---|---|---|
| Air terminals | 1,437 | 55 |
| Interstate transportation | 664 | 25 |
| World Trade Center | 348 | 13 |
| Port commerce | 114 | 4 |
| Economic development | 85 | 3 |
| **Total** | **2,648** | **100** |

### Selected Locations

**Aviation**
Downtown Manhattan Heliport (New York)
John F. Kennedy International Airport (New York)
LaGuardia Airport (New York)
Newark International Airport (New Jersey)
Teterboro Airport (New Jersey)

**Commercial Real Estate**
Bathgate Industrial Park (Bronx, New York)
Industrial Park at Elizabeth (New Jersey)
Queens West (mixed-use waterfront development; Queens, New York)
The Teleport (communications center; Staten Island, New York)

**Port Commerce**
Auto Marine Terminal (Bayonne, New Jersey)
Brooklyn-Port Authority Marine Terminal (New York)
Howland Hook Marine Terminal (New York)
Port Newark/Elizabeth Marine Terminal (New Jersey)
Red Hook Container Terminal (New York)

**Tunnels, Bridges, and Terminals**
Bayonne Bridge (Staten Island to Bayonne, New Jersey)
George Washington Bridge (Manhattan to Ft. Lee, New Jersey)
George Washington Bridge Bus Terminal
Goethals Bridge (Staten Island to Elizabeth, New Jersey)
Holland Tunnel (Manhattan to Jersey City, New Jersey)
Lincoln Tunnel (Manhattan to Union City, New Jersey)
Outerbridge Crossing (Staten Island to Perth Amboy, New Jersey)
Port Authority Bus Terminal (Manhattan)

**Other**
The Port Authority Trans-Hudson System (rail transportation between New York and New Jersey)
World Trade Center (office complex, Manhattan, prior to its destruction by terrorists in 2001)

## COMPETITORS

| | |
|---|---|
| Coach USA | Amtrak |
| Covanta | Reckson Associates Realty |
| Helmsley | Tishman Realty |
| Lefrak Organization | Trump |
| MTA | |

## HISTORICAL FINANCIALS & EMPLOYEES

| Government-owned FYE: December 31 | Annual Growth | 12/91 | 12/92 | 12/93 | 12/94 | 12/95 | 12/96 | 12/97 | 12/98 | 12/99 | 12/00 |
|---|---|---|---|---|---|---|---|---|---|---|---|
| Sales ($ mil.) | 4.0% | — | 1,934 | 1,921 | 1,980 | 2,083 | 2,154 | 2,206 | 2,361 | 2,548 | 2,648 |
| Net income ($ mil.) | 12.6% | — | 144 | 108 | 153 | 177 | 199 | 282 | 299 | 314 | 372 |
| Income as % of sales | — | — | 7.4% | 5.6% | 7.7% | 8.5% | 9.2% | 12.8% | 12.7% | 12.3% | 14.1% |
| Employees | (3.7%) | — | 9,500 | 9,350 | 9,200 | 9,250 | 8,100 | 7,500 | 7,200 | 7,200 | 7,000 |

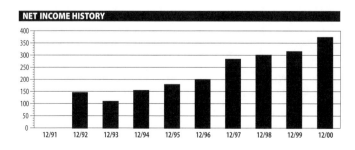

**NET INCOME HISTORY**

# PRICEWATERHOUSECOOPERS

## OVERVIEW

After putting it all together, they almost had to take it apart. New York City-based PricewaterhouseCoopers (PwC) was formed in the 1998 merger of the fourth- and sixth-largest accounting firms. It is now the world's largest professional services company. PwC nearly sought a buyer for its consulting arm in light of SEC concerns about conflicts of interest for firms auditing and consulting for the same clients. Such concerns have been heightened by shareholders of failed companies who suspect accounting firms of cooking their clients' books in order to keep up revenue from non-auditing services. Instead of splitting PwC and its Big Four brethren, the SEC imposed strict

disclosure rules for accounting firms, which may still lead to industry reforms.

In addition to its auditing business, PwC provides tax compliance, procurement, human resources, technology, and real estate services on an outsourcing basis. It also offers financial advice and insurance management services.

PricewaterhouseCoopers also has extensive online offerings, including GlobalVatOnLine, which compiles rules, regulations, and rates on value added taxes. Unfortunately, the economy at home can't sustain PwC at its full size; the company has released about 15% of its US staff and has announced cuts in other areas.

## HISTORY

In 1850 Samuel Price founded an accounting firm in London and in 1865 took on partner Edwin Waterhouse. The firm and the industry grew rapidly, thanks to the growth of stock exchanges that required uniform financial statements from listees. By the late 1800s Price Waterhouse (PW) had become the world's best-known accounting firm.

US offices were opened in the 1890s, and in 1902 United States Steel chose the firm as its auditor. PW benefited from tough audit requirements instituted after the 1929 stock market crash. In 1935 the firm was given the prestigious job of handling Academy Awards balloting. It started a management consulting service in 1946. But PW's dominance slipped in the 1960s, as it gained a reputation as the most traditional and formal of the major firms.

Coopers & Lybrand, the product of a 1957 transatlantic merger, wrote the book on auditing. Lybrand, Ross Bros. & Montgomery was formed in 1898 by William Lybrand, Edward Ross, Adam Ross, and Robert Montgomery. In 1912 Montgomery wrote *Montgomery's Auditing,* which became the bible of accounting.

Cooper Brothers was founded in 1854 in London by William Cooper, eldest son of a Quaker banker. In 1957 Lybrand joined up to form Coopers & Lybrand. During the 1960s the firm expanded into employee benefits and internal control consulting, building its technology capabilities in the 1970s as it studied ways to automate the audit process.

Coopers & Lybrand lost market share as mergers reduced the Big Eight accounting firms to the Big Six. After the savings and loan debacle of the 1980s, investors and the government wanted accounting firms held liable not only for the form of audited financial statements

but for their veracity. In 1992 the firm paid $95 million to settle claims of defrauded investors in MiniScribe, a failed disk-drive maker. Other hefty payments followed, including a $108 million settlement relating to the late Robert Maxwell's defunct media empire.

In 1998 Price Waterhouse and Coopers & Lybrand combined PW's strength in the media, entertainment, and utility industries, and Coopers & Lybrand's focus on telecommunications and mining. But the merger brought some expensive legal baggage involving Coopers & Lybrand's performance of audits related to a bid-rigging scheme involving former Arizona governor Fife Symington.

Feeling the pinch of competition and the aftereffects of its megamerger, PwC announced it would cut 1,000 jobs and replace obsolete positions with e-business consultants to cut costs. The year 2000 began on a sour note: An SEC conflict-of-interest probe turned up more than 8,000 alleged violations, most involving PwC partners owning stock in their firm's audit clients.

As the SEC grew ever more shrill in its denunciation of the potential conflicts of interest arising from auditing companies that the firm hoped to recruit or retain as consulting clients, PwC saw the writing on the wall and in 2000 began making plans to split the two operations. That year the company announced it would start an Internet security software subsidiary called BeTrusted. In 2001 PwC paid $55 million to shareholders of MicroStrategy Inc., who charged that the audit firm defrauded them by approving MicroStrategy's inflated earnings and revenues figures.

Global Chairman: Andrew Ratcliffe
Global CEO: Samuel A. DiPiazza
Global COO: Thomas O'Neill
Global CFO: Geoffrey E. Johnson
Global Chief Administrative Officer: Amyas CE Morse
Global General Counsel: Lawrence Keeshan
Global Human Capital Leader: Amy DiGeso, age 49
Global Risk Management Leader: Ian Brindle
Global Consumer and Industrial Products Leader:
  Thomas W. Cross
Global Industries, Markets and Strategic Planning
  Leader: Rocco J. Maggiotto
Global Technology, Information, Communications, and
  Entertainment Leader: Francis A. Doyle
Global Services Leader: Bruce W. Hucklesby
Global Assurance and Business Advisory Services
  Leader: J. Frank Brown
Global Business Process Outsourcing Leader:
  John C. Barnsley
Global Financial Services Leader: Jeremy Scott
Global Management Consulting Services Leader:
  Scott C. Hartz
Global Geography Leader: Rolf Windmöller
Global Tax and Legal Services Leader:
  Paul J.M. van Leent
Global Chief Development, Independence and Risk
  Officer: John J. Roberts
Global Energy and Mining Leader: Geoffrey C. Green

HQ: 1301 Avenue of the Americas, New York, NY 10019
Phone: 646-471-4000       Fax: 646-394-1301
Web: www.pwcglobal.com

Selected Industries Served

Consumer and Industrial Products
Consumer packaged goods
Forestry
Industrial products
Pharmaceuticals
Retail

Energy and Mining
Energy
Mining
Utilities

Financial Services
Banking
Capital markets
Insurance
Investment management
Real estate

Services Industry
Education/Not-for-profit
Engineering and construction
Government
Health care
Hospitality and leisure
Posts
Transport

Technology Info-Com and Entertainment
Entertainment and media
Technology
Telecommunications

| | |
|---|---|
| American Management | Getronics |
| Andersen | H&R Block |
| A.T. Kearney | Hewitt Associates |
| Atos Origin | IBM |
| Bain & Company | ICL |
| BDO International | KPMG |
| Booz-Allen | Marsh & McLennan |
| Boston Consulting | McKinsey & Company |
| Deloitte Touche Tohmatsu | Perot Systems |
| EDS | Towers Perrin |
| Ernst & Young | Watson Wyatt |

| Partnership FYE: June 30 | Annual Growth | 6/92 | 6/93 | 6/94 | 6/95 | 6/96 | 6/97 | 6/98 | 6/99 | 6/00 | 6/01 |
|---|---|---|---|---|---|---|---|---|---|---|---|
| Sales ($ mil.) | 22.8% | 3,781 | 3,890 | 3,980 | 4,460 | 5,020 | 5,630 | 15,000 | 15,300 | 21,500 | 24,000 |
| Employees | 14.2% | 48,600 | 48,781 | 50,122 | 53,000 | 56,000 | 60,000 | 140,000 | 155,000 | 150,000 | 160,000 |

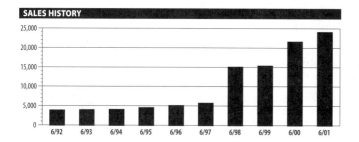

SALES HISTORY

PRICEWATERHOUSECOOPERS

# PUBLIX SUPER MARKETS, INC.

## OVERVIEW

What's eating at Winn-Dixie Stores and other supermarket chains located in Florida? Publix Super Markets. The Lakeland, Florida-based company is one of the nation's largest grocers, with more than 650 stores (about 80% are located in Florida; the rest are in Alabama, Georgia, and South Carolina). By emphasizing service and a family-friendly image rather than price, Publix has grown faster and been more profitable than Winn-Dixie and other rivals. The company, the nation's largest employee-owned supermarket chain, is controlled — and run — by members of the founding Jenkins family.

Although it has Florida's shoppers, Publix has lost a few legal battles brought by its employees. It has settled three suits (over gender and race discrimination) but currently is embroiled in another suit alleging it discriminated against Hispanics. Despite the lawsuits, Publix was featured in *FORTUNE* magazine's "Most Admired Companies" list.

The company plans to test an online grocery and delivery service, PublixDirect, in 2001. Publix also says it will add more than 300 stores in the next five years.

## HISTORY

George Jenkins, age 22, resigned as manager of the Piggly Wiggly grocery in Winter Haven, Florida, in 1930. With money he had saved to buy a car, he opened his own grocery store, Publix, next door to his old employer. The small store (named after a chain of movie theaters) prospered despite the Depression, and in 1935 Jenkins opened another Publix in the same town.

Five years later, after the supermarket format had become popular, Jenkins closed his two smaller locations and opened a new, more modern Publix Market. With pastel colors and electric-eye doors, it was also the first US store to feature air conditioning.

Publix Super Markets bought the All-American chain of Lakeland, Florida (19 stores), in 1944 and moved its corporate headquarters to that city. The company began offering S&H Green Stamps in 1953, and in 1956 it replaced its original supermarket with a mall featuring an enlarged Publix and a Green Stamp redemption center. Publix expanded into South Florida in the late 1950s and began selling stock to employees.

As Florida's population grew, Publix continued to expand, opening its 100th store in 1964. Publix was the first grocery chain in the state to use bar code scanners — all its stores had the technology by 1981. The company beat Florida banks in providing ATMs and in the 1980s it opened debit card stations.

Publix continued to grow in the 1980s, safe from takeover attempts because of its employee ownership. In 1988 the company installed the first automated checkout systems in South Florida, giving patrons an always-open checkout lane.

The chain stopped offering Green Stamps in 1989, and most of the $19 million decrease in Publix advertising expenditures was attributed to the end of the 36-year promotion. That year, after almost six decades, "Mr. George" — as founder Jenkins was known — stepped down as chairman in favor of his son Howard. (George died in 1996.)

In 1991 Publix opened its first store outside Florida, in Georgia, as part of its plan to become a major player in the Southeast. Publix entered South Carolina in 1993 with one supermarket; it also tripled its presence in Georgia to 15 stores.

The United Food and Commercial Workers Union began a campaign in 1994 against alleged gender and racial discrimination in Publix's hiring, promotion, and compensation policies. The next year the union claimed the company was rewrapping and redating meats not sold by their "sell by" dates.

Publix opened its first store in Alabama in 1996. That year a federal judge allowed about 150,000 women to join a class-action suit filed in 1995 by 12 women who had sued Publix charging that the company consistently channeled female employees into low-paying jobs with little chance for good promotions. The case, said to be the biggest sex discrimination lawsuit ever, was set to go to trial, but in 1997 the company paid $82.5 million to settle that suit and another $3.5 million to settle a complaint of discrimination against black applicants and employees.

Publix promised to change its promotion policies and to work with employees on their careers; however, two more lawsuits alleging discrimination against women and blacks were filed later in 1997 and 1998. The suit filed in behalf of women was denied class-action status in 2000. Later that year the company settled the racial discrimination lawsuit for $10.5 million. Howard Jenkins stepped down as CEO in mid-2001; his cousin Charlie Jenkins took the helm.

**Chairman:** Howard M. Jenkins, age 50, $456,170 pay
**Vice Chairman:** Hoyt R. Barnett, age 57, $341,288 pay
**CEO and COO:** Charles H. Jenkins Jr., age 58,
$435,482 pay (prior to title change)
**President:** W. Edwin Crenshaw, age 50, $412,414 pay
**CFO and Treasurer:** David P. Phillips, age 41
**SVP:** Tina P. Johnson, age 41
**SVP and Chief Information Officer:** Daniel M. Risener,
age 60, $283,161 pay
**SVP:** James J. Lobinsky, age 61
**SVP:** Thomas M. O'Connor, age 53
**VP Human Resources:** James H. Rhodes II, age 56
**Auditors:** KPMG LLP

## LOCATIONS

**HQ:** 1936 George Jenkins Blvd., Lakeland, FL 33815
**Phone:** 863-688-1188    **Fax:** 863-284-5532
**Web:** www.publix.com

Publix Super Markets operates more than 650 grocery
stores in Alabama, Florida, Georgia, and South Carolina.
The company also has three dairy processing plants
(Deerfield Beach and Lakeland, Florida, and
Lawrenceville, Georgia) and a deli plant and a bakery in
Lakeland. Publix operates eight distribution centers in
Florida (Boynton Beach, Deerfield Beach, Jacksonville,
Lakeland, Miami, Orlando, and Sarasota) and Georgia
(Lawrenceville).

**2000 Stores**

|  | No. |
|---|---|
| Florida | 509 |
| Georgia | 111 |
| South Carolina | 23 |
| Alabama | 4 |
| **Total** | **647** |

## PRODUCTS/OPERATIONS

**Selected Supermarket Departments**
Bakery
Banking
Dairy
Deli
Ethnic foods
Floral
Groceries
Health and beauty care
Housewares
Meat
Pharmacy
Photo processing
Produce
Seafood

**Foods Processed**
Baked goods
Dairy products
Deli items

## COMPETITORS

| | |
|---|---|
| Albertson's | Nash Finch |
| ALDI | The Pantry |
| Bruno's Supermarkets | Rite Aid |
| Costco Wholesale | Royal Ahold |
| CVS | Ruddick |
| Delhaize America | Sedano's Management |
| Fleming Companies | Smart & Final |
| Hurry | Walgreen |
| IGA | Wal-Mart |
| Ingles Markets | Whole Foods |
| Kmart | Winn-Dixie |
| Kroger | |

## HISTORICAL FINANCIALS & EMPLOYEES

| Private<br>FYE: Last Sat. in December | Annual<br>Growth | 12/91 | 12/92 | 12/93 | 12/94 | 12/95 | 12/96 | 12/97 | 12/98 | 12/99 | 12/00 |
|---|---|---|---|---|---|---|---|---|---|---|---|
| Sales ($ mil.) | 10.4% | — | 6,664 | 7,473 | 8,665 | 9,393 | 10,431 | 11,224 | 12,067 | 13,069 | 14,724 |
| Net income ($ mil.) | 15.6% | — | 166 | 184 | 239 | 242 | 265 | 355 | 378 | 462 | 530 |
| Income as % of sales | — | — | 2.5% | 2.5% | 2.8% | 2.6% | 2.5% | 3.2% | 3.1% | 3.5% | 3.6% |
| Employees | 7.1% | — | 73,000 | 82,000 | 90,000 | 95,000 | 103,000 | 111,000 | 117,000 | 120,000 | 126,000 |

### NET INCOME HISTORY

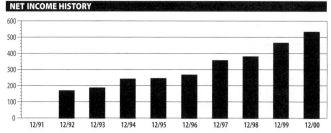

### 2000 FISCAL YEAR-END

Debt ratio: 0.0%
Return on equity: —
Cash ($ mil.): 397
Current ratio: 1.15
Long-term debt ($ mil.): 0

# QUAD/GRAPHICS, INC.

When you think of Quad/Graphics, think ink. The Pewaukee, Wisconsin-based company is the nation's #1 privately owned printer of catalogs, magazines, books, inserts, and other commercial products. Its 22 printing facilities provide comprehensive pre-press, press, and post-press services for clients such as *People, Newsweek,* Bloomingdale's, and Victoria's Secret. The company, which offers 100% digital imaging capabilities, operates internationally through joint ventures in Argentina, Brazil, and Poland.

Quad is one of the most employee- and community-oriented companies in the industry. The firm has been recognized for its fun work atmosphere and provides on-site day care centers, health clubs, and medical clinics. In addition, it sponsors sports leagues (softball, bowling), awards college scholarships to employees' children, and provides interest-free auto loans. Quad/Graphic's Windhover Fund manages the philanthropic distribution of 5% of the company's pretax profit for social, cultural, and educational projects.

Founder and president Harry Quadracci and company employees own Quad/Graphics.

## HISTORY

Ink runs in Harry V. Quadracci's family. His father, Harry R., founded a printing business — Standard Printing — in Racine, Wisconsin, in 1930, when he was 16. Four years later Quadracci sold out to William A. Krueger. Though he worked to build Krueger into a major regional printer, the elder Quadracci had little equity in the company.

In the 1960s son Harry V. joined Krueger as a company lawyer. Within a few years he had worked his way up to plant manager. Krueger was a union shop, and in those days unions dictated the work rules and often salary levels. In 1970 there was a three-and-a-half-month strike. At odds with new management and reportedly dissatisfied with the way Krueger caved in to union demands and the adversarial relationship between company and union, the younger Quadracci left.

After 18 months of unemployment, in 1971 Quadracci formed a limited partnership with 12 others to get a loan to buy a press, which was installed in a building in Pewaukee, Wisconsin. The next year his father joined the company as chairman. Within two years the partners had recouped their initial investment, but the business' future remained in question until about 1976. One of its most innovative moves was to make its delivery fleet drivers into entrepreneurs by requiring them to find cargo to haul on their return trips.

Working on a shoestring, Quadracci hired inexperienced workers and trained them, moving them up as the company grew. The need to improvise fostered a flexibility that Quadracci institutionalized by keeping management layers flat and remaining accessible to his employees. Beginning in 1974, Quadracci rewarded his workers with equity in the company.

In the 1980s Quad/Graphics' commitment to technology enabled it to offer better service than many of its competitors. It was also immune to the merger-and-acquisition fever of the time. Free of acquisition debt, the company had excellent credit and was able to finance equipment upgrades with bank loans. Quad expanded by opening a plant in Saratoga Springs, New York (1985), and buying a plant in Thomaston, Georgia (1989).

But there were missteps, such as its 1985 attempt to break into the newspaper coupon insert business dominated by Treasure Chest Advertising. Quad/Graphics sold that operation three years later. The company was not immune to the national economic downturn that began about that time, which forced it to lay off employees in the late 1980s and early 1990s and prompted it to reduce weekend overtime pay (from double time to time-and-a-half). The firm was also hit when a major customer consolidated its printing outside the Midwest. In response, Quad/Graphics increased its capacity in other regions of the US during the 1990s.

In 1996 the company bought 40% of Argentine printer Anselmo L. Morvillo. Benefiting from the UPS strike and changes in the postal regulations, in 1997 Quad/Graphics expanded its shipping services with Parcel/Direct, targeting parcels for large shippers such as catalog merchants, in cooperation with the US Postal Service. Also that year it created a joint venture color printing firm with Brazil's Folha Group.

In 1998 Quad/Graphics expanded its international reach, agreeing to a joint venture in Poland. The next year it was awarded the prepress business of Condé Nast magazines. In 2000 it launched a business-to-business portal called Smart Tools. The following year Quad/Graphics announced plans to begin construction of a new printing plant in Oklahoma; the plant is slated to begin production in 2003.

## OFFICERS

**President:** Harry V. Quadracci
**EVP:** Thomas A. Quadracci
**SVP Sales and Administration:** Carl L. Bennett
**VP Finance and CFO:** John C. Fowler
**VP and Controller:** Linda Larson
**VP Employee Services:** Emmy M. LaBode

## LOCATIONS

**HQ:** W224 N3322 Duplainville Rd., Pewaukee, WI 53072
**Phone:** 414-566-6000
**Web:** www.qg.com

Quad/Graphics has production plants in Georgia, New York, West Virginia, and Wisconsin. It also operates joint ventures in Argentina, Brazil, and Poland.

## PRODUCTS/OPERATIONS

**Selected Services**
Binding and finishing
Color correction
Design
Desktop production
Direct mailing
Imaging and photography
Ink jetting
Integrated circulation
Mailing and distribution
Mailing list management
Parcel fulfillment
Printing
Scanning

## COMPETITORS

Applied Graphics
Arandell
Banta
Black Dot Group
Consolidated Graphics
Dai Nippon Printing
Merrill
Quebecor World
Queens Group, Inc.
R. R. Donnelley
Taylor Corporation
Toppan Printing
Vertis

## HISTORICAL FINANCIALS & EMPLOYEES

| Private<br>FYE: December 31 | Annual<br>Growth | 12/91 | 12/92 | 12/93 | 12/94 | 12/95 | 12/96 | 12/97 | 12/98 | 12/99 | 12/00 |
|---|---|---|---|---|---|---|---|---|---|---|---|
| Sales ($ mil.) | 15.2% | — | 582 | 703 | 801 | 1,002 | 1,042 | 1,200 | 1,400 | 1,500 | 1,800 |
| Employees | 10.3% | — | 6,400 | 6,800 | 7,500 | 8,444 | 9,500 | 11,000 | 11,000 | 13,000 | 14,000 |

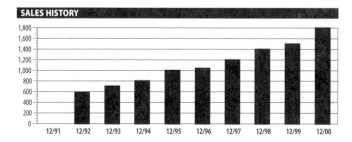

SALES HISTORY

# QUALITY STORES, INC.

## OVERVIEW

It might seem as if there are no more categories for retailers to kill, but Muskegon, Michigan-based Quality Stores (formerly Central Tractor Farm & Country) is cultivating yet another in America's farmlands: tractor parts. The agricultural supply retailer offers just about anything a farmer, gardener, or do-it-yourselfer would want, from tools and fencing to pet supplies and tractor parts (but not tractors). Quality Stores operates more than 300 stores under six different banners, although all are being converted to the Quality Farm & Country name; most are located in rural towns in 31 states.

The company also sells products through its FarmandCountry.com Web site (which offers twice the number of products as its bricks-and-mortar counterparts and an "Ask the Expert" forum for farmers and ranchers), and also through an annual catalog distributed to about 500,000 homes in rural and agricultural communities. Liquidity problems prompted the company to file for Chapter 11 bankruptcy protection in November 2001 and announce the closure of about 90 stores.

QSI is a wholly owned subsidiary of QSI Holdings, which is an affiliate of investment firm J.W. Childs Associates. Chairman Jerry Horn, who is also a partner with J.W. Childs Associates, owns about 10% of QSI.

## HISTORY

Jack Brody and his wife, Rae, founded a tractor salvage company in 1935 in Boone, Iowa, and started a mail-order parts business the next year. The Brodys moved to Des Moines in 1944 and opened their first retail store, the Central Tractor Farm & Family Center, in the 1950s. The firm added stores mainly in the Northeast because of that region's large number of small farms (and the prevalence of old farm equipment). By the 1980s it was adding one or two stores a year.

In 1988 New York investment firm Butler Capital bought the retailer from the Brody family for about $45 million. James McKitrick was hired from retailer Builders Emporium and named president and CEO in 1992. The new management team added only six stores between 1989 and 1993.

By 1994 the company had nearly 60 stores. That year it went public (Butler Capital retained 65% of the company's stock). Also that year the company changed its stores' names to CT Farm & Country and changed its corporate name to Central Tractor Farm & Country.

In 1996 Central Tractor added another 31 stores when it acquired Big Bear Farm Stores. Also in 1996 the company opened 14 new stores. Central Tractor doubled in size later in 1996 when it paid $139 million for ConAgra's Country General Store chain which had 114 locations, primarily in the Midwest. The next year Boston investment firm J.W. Childs Equity Partners bought the company for $156 million.

Country General was founded in 1959 in Grand Island, Nebraska, as Wheelers. The Wheeler family quickly expanded the chain to nine stores in Nebraska. In the mid 1980s the Wheeler family sold Country General to ConAgra. ConAgra also acquired family-run stores throughout the Midwest and Southeast, including S&S Stores, Town & Country Supply, Anfinson's, Sandvig's, and Security Feed and Seed. The farm giant gathered all these stores together under the Country General name. In 1999 it bought the US's #3 farming goods retailer, Quality Stores, a chain of more than 100 Quality Farm and Fleet and County Post stores in Michigan and Ohio.

Founded in 1962 by brothers George and Jack Hilt, Quality Farm and Fleet Wholesale Supply opened its first store in Hudsonville, Michigan. By 1971, the company had 12 stores in Michigan, Ohio, and Indiana. Quality Farm and Fleet expanded its product line to include home improvement products for do-it-yourselfers. In 1980, Quality Farm and Fleet changed its name to Quality Stores, Inc.

The merger of Central Tractor and Quality Stores created the largest specialty farming goods retailer in the US. The new entity adopted the name Quality Stores, Inc. and made its headquarters in Michigan.

The company launched an online retail site, FarmandCountry.com, in June 2000. That year it closed 28 underperforming stores, in part because of liquidity problems caused by management. As a result, 10 executives were terminated, including CEO James McKitrick. Jerry Horn, former chairman of General Nutrition Cos., was named chairman, president, and CEO of the company in November. In mid-2001 the company named turnaround specialist Peter Fitzsimmons as CEO, but kept Horn as chairman. Despite these efforts, QSI filed for Chapter 11 bankruptcy protection and announced the closing of about 90 stores in November 2001.

Chairman: Jerry Horn, age 63
CEO: Peter D. Fitzsimmons, age 44
SVP and COO: William A. Waack, age 37, $155,048 pay
SVP of Finance, CFO, and Secretary:
Thomas J. Reinebach, age 51, $149,039 pay
VP: Steven G. Segal, age 40
VP: Adam L. Suttin, age 33
VP of Merchandising: John J. Keenan Jr., $86,731 pay
VP of Human Resources and Administration:
Ted G. Britton, $108,954 pay

## LOCATIONS

HQ: 455 E. Ellis Rd., Muskegon, MI 49443
Phone: 231-798-8787    Fax: 231-798-8414

### 2001 Stores

| | No. |
|---|---|
| Nebraska | 46 |
| Ohio | 42 |
| Michigan | 40 |
| New York | 26 |
| Pennsylvania | 25 |
| Indiana | 18 |
| Colorado | 17 |
| California | 16 |
| Iowa | 15 |
| South Dakota | 11 |
| Virginia | 11 |
| Georgia | 10 |
| West Virginia | 9 |
| Kansas | 7 |
| Kentucky | 7 |
| North Carolina | 6 |
| South Carolina | 6 |
| Minnesota | 5 |
| North Dakota | 5 |
| Maryland | 4 |
| Wyoming | 4 |
| New Jersey | 3 |
| Delaware | 2 |
| Florida | 2 |
| Oklahoma | 2 |
| Tennessee | 2 |
| Other states | 6 |
| **TOTAL** | **347** |

## PRODUCTS/OPERATIONS

### 2001 Sales

| | % of total |
|---|---|
| Lawn & garden supplies & seasonal | 23 |
| Agricultural (tractor parts, accessories) | 21 |
| Specialty hardware | 16 |
| Rural automotive | 13 |
| Work wear | 11 |
| Pet supplies | 9 |
| General consumer goods | 7 |
| **Total** | **100** |

### Selected Products

**Agricultural**
Animal health supplies
Fencing materials
Tillage and harvesting parts
Tractor parts

**General Consumer Products**
Camping supplies
Charcoal grills
Collectible toys
Coolers
Guns and ammunition
Hunting accessories

**Lawn and Garden Supplies and Seasonal**
Fans
Fertilizers
Lawn fencing
Lawn tractors and mowers
Plants, trees, and shrubs
Space heaters and stoves
Weed killers

**Pet Supplies**
Animal feed
Pet supplies

**Rural Automotive**
Accessories
Automotive parts
Batteries
General automotive items

**Specialty Hardware**
Air compressors
Generators
Hand tools
Lighting
Motors
Paint
Plumbing supplies
Power tools

**Work Wear**
Flannel shirts
Hunting clothing
Outerwear
Overalls
Work jeans

## COMPETITORS

Ace Hardware
Agway
Home Depot
Kmart
Lowe's
Sears
Southern States
Tractor Supply
TruServ
Wal-Mart

## HISTORICAL FINANCIALS & EMPLOYEES

| Private FYE: January 31 | Annual Growth | 10/91 | 10/92 | 10/93 | 10/94 | 10/95 | 10/96 | 10/97 | 10/98 | *1/00 | 1/01 |
|---|---|---|---|---|---|---|---|---|---|---|---|
| Sales ($ mil.) | 25.8% | — | — | 226 | 254 | 252 | 293 | 411 | 587 | 1,092 | 1,126 |
| Net income ($ mil.) | — | — | — | 2 | 4 | 6 | 9 | 0 | 10 | 3 | (51) |
| Income as % of sales | — | — | — | 0.9% | 1.7% | 2.2% | 3.0% | 0.0% | 1.7% | 0.3% | — |
| Employees | 31.5% | — | — | 870 | 1,940 | 1,970 | 2,492 | 4,500 | 4,500 | 9,343 | 5,900 |

* Fiscal year change

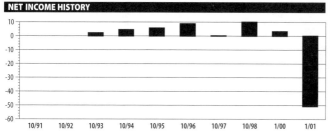

**NET INCOME HISTORY**

**2001 FISCAL YEAR-END**
Debt ratio: 67.4%
Return on equity: —
Cash ($ mil.): 3
Current ratio: 1.77
Long-term debt ($ mil.): 397

# RAND MCNALLY & COMPANY

## OVERVIEW

Rand McNally lets you know where you stand. The largest commercial mapmaker in the world, the Skokie, Illinois-based company is best known for its flagship Rand McNally Road Atlas — the best-selling product in the history of mapmaking. In addition to maps and atlases, Rand McNally produces travel and reference software (TripMaker, StreetFinder), educational products for classrooms, and mileage and routing software for the transportation industry. The company also makes maps for the Canadian market through its Rand McNally Canada unit. It sells its products online and through some 50,000 retail outlets across the US, including nearly 30 Rand McNally stores.

Rand McNally sold a number of subsidiaries in 1997 and renewed its focus on geographic information. Controlling interest in the formerly family-owned company was sold to the secretive AEA Investors group later that year, a move that paved the way for growth in mapmaking. Rand McNally has been buying smaller, regional mapmakers in keeping with that strategy.

Although it created a Web site in 1996, Rand McNally didn't begin focusing on the Internet in earnest until 1999, years later than online rivals such as MapQuest.com and Maps.com. In 2000 it relaunched its Web site in hopes of catching up with its online competitors.

## HISTORY

Rand McNally was founded by William Rand and Andrew McNally in 1856. In 1864 the pair bought the job-printing department of the *Chicago Tribune,* and they expanded into the printing of railroad tickets and schedules. They published their first book, a Chicago business directory, in 1870.

In 1872 the company printed its first map for the *Railway Guide.* Rand McNally later expanded into publishing paperback novels (popular among train travelers), and by 1891 annual sales topped $1 million.

During the 1890s McNally bought Rand's share of the business, and the company branched into printing school textbooks. Rand McNally's first photo auto guide was issued in 1907, and the company introduced its first complete US road atlas in 1924.

When Hitler invaded Poland in 1939, Rand McNally's New York stock of European maps sold out in one day. WWII necessitated the revision of a number of maps — a challenge that the company continued to face throughout the 20th century.

Although the company had abandoned adult fiction and nonfiction in 1914, it reentered the field in 1948 when a company official persuaded explorer Thor Heyerdahl to write a book for the company about his adventures. First published in 1950, Heyerdahl's *Kon-Tiki* sold more than a million copies in its first six years.

Rand McNally produced its first four-color road atlas in 1960, and during the 1970s it began publishing travel guides for Mobil Oil. The next decade the company published several new road atlases to fill the void created when gas stations discontinued their practice of giving away free road maps. Rand McNally sold its textbook publishing business to Houghton

Mifflin in 1980, and five years later it began computerizing its cartography operation.

In 1993 the company acquired Allmaps Canada Limited (now Rand McNally Canada). It introduced *TripMaker,* a CD-ROM vacation-planning program, the next year. Also in 1994 Rand McNally won a contract to create maps for a *Reader's Digest* atlas. The company debuted its StreetFinder street-level software in 1995 and created its Cartographic and Information Services division in 1996. It also established a Web site that year.

In 1997, as part of a plan to focus on mapmaking and providing geographic information, Rand McNally sold a number of its subsidiaries. AEA Investors bought a controlling interest in the company later in 1997, bringing an end to more than 140 years of McNally family control (though it did retain a minority stake). While Rand McNally was still profitable, the sale to AEA underscored the challenges facing the company: Growth in earnings had slowed, and technological changes (Internet maps and software) had altered the mapmaking industry.

Rand McNally expanded in 1999 with acquisitions of mapmakers Thomas Bros. Maps and King of the Road Map Service. Later that year Henry Feinberg resigned as chairman and CEO. Richard Davis was appointed CEO, and John Macomber became chairman.

In 2000 the company relaunched its Web site with additional trip planning capabilities. Also that year it became the primary North American distributor of *National Geographic* maps and COO Norman Wells replaced Davis as CEO.

In 2001 Michael Hehir was named CEO, Wells replaced Macomber as chairman, and Macomber remained as a director on the board.

**Chairman:** Norman E. Wells Jr., age 52
**President, CEO, and Director:** Michael Hehir
**SVP and General Manager, Consumer Travel Solutions:** Victoria Donnowitz
**SVP, Global Business Solutions:** Robert P. Denaro
**VP and General Counsel:** Deborah Lipoff
**VP, Human Resources:** Mary Lynn Smedinghoff
**VP, Information Services:** Ken Levin
**Group Controller:** David Jones
**President, randmcnally.com:** Chris Heivly
**Auditors:** Arthur Andersen LLP

## LOCATIONS

**HQ:** 8255 N. Central Park Ave., Skokie, IL 60076
**Phone:** 847-329-8100    **Fax:** 847-329-6361
**Web:** www.randmcnally.com

Rand McNally operates in the US and Canada. It has retail stores in 14 US states.

## PRODUCTS/OPERATIONS

**Selected Print Products**
*Business Travelers' Briefcase Atlas*
*Motor Carriers' Road Atlas*
*Rand McNally Pocket City Atlas*
*Rand McNally Road Atlas*
*The Thomas Guides*

**Selected Sales Channels**
Rand McNally (retail stores)
randmcnally.com (e-commerce)

**Selected Software**
New Millennium World Atlas Deluxe Edition
Rand McNally StreetFinder Deluxe
Rand McNally TripMaker Deluxe

## COMPETITORS

AAA
Analytical Surveys
Barnes & Noble
Borders
DeLorme
Educational Insights
Encyclopædia Britannica
ESRI
Expedia
Globe Pequot
Langenscheidt
Lonely Planet
MapInfo
MapQuest.com
Michelin
National Geographic
Piersen Graphics
TravRoute
Vicinity

## HISTORICAL FINANCIALS & EMPLOYEES

| Private<br>FYE: December 31 | Annual<br>Growth | 12/91 | 12/92 | 12/93 | 12/94 | 12/95 | 12/96 | 12/97 | 12/98 | 12/99 | 12/00 |
|---|---|---|---|---|---|---|---|---|---|---|---|
| Sales ($ mil.) | (6.5%) | — | 342 | 395 | 438 | 469 | 163 | 175 | 175 | 179 | 200 |
| Employees | (15.9%) | — | 4,000 | 4,000 | 4,200 | 4,650 | 1,000 | 1,000 | 1,000 | 920 | 1,000 |

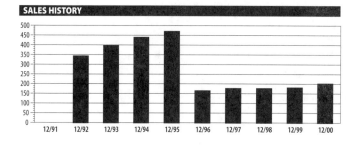

**SALES HISTORY**

RAND McNALLY

# RECREATIONAL EQUIPMENT, INC.

## OVERVIEW

For serious climbers and casual outdoor lovers alike, Recreational Equipment, Inc. (REI) is a breath of fresh, mountain air. The Kent, Washington-based company is one of the nation's largest consumer cooperatives, with more than 1.8 million member-owners. Through about 60 outlets in 24 states (and one store in Tokyo, a market REI plans to exit), REI sells high-end gear, clothing, and footwear (including private-label goods) for adventurous outdoor activities like climbing, kayaking, and skiing, as well as for hiking, bicycling, and camping. The company also repairs gear, and it sells merchandise online and through occasional catalogs.

REI donates to conservation and recreation groups and operates an adventure travel service. Its stores offer product demonstrations, educational seminars, and a gift registry. The company's MSR (Mountain Safety Research) subsidiary makes mountaineering equipment, outdoor clothing, and camping products.

Customers can become co-op members by paying a $15 onetime fee; its privileges include getting about 10% of their annual purchases refunded in the form of patronage dividends. Listed by *FORTUNE* as one of the "100 Best Companies to Work For" in the US, the co-op offers profit sharing and deep discounts to its employees.

## HISTORY

After being disappointed by the price and quality of an ice axe he had ordered, avid mountaineer Lloyd Anderson decided he could do better. He searched through catalogs and eventually found an axe to his liking, at half the price. Impressed with his nose for good deals, Anderson's mountain climbing friends began asking him to make purchases for them. Anderson founded Recreational Equipment, Inc. (REI) in his Seattle garage in 1938 with his wife, Mary, and 21 other outdoorsmen and women looking for high-quality mountaineering equipment at low prices. Uncomfortable about making money off of his friends, Anderson formed a co-op, returning a portion of profits to its members. Each of the co-op's original members put a dollar in to join.

REI's first retail location, opened in 1944, consisted of three shelves in the back of a Seattle gas station and sold mostly Army surplus. The company didn't hire its first full-time employee until 1953.

Growth was slow yet steady. In 1971 the company operated one store; by 1983 REI had seven stores and had added several product lines and a catalog business. That year Wally Smith became the company's CEO.

REI benefited from the growing interest in outdoor activities, expanding to 17 stores in 13 states in 1987. By 1991, when it built its first distribution center, it had 27 stores in 16 states. The co-op reached for a new frontier in 1996 when it began selling on the Internet. Also in 1996 the company opened its flagship store in Seattle with features including a 30-foot waterfall, a seven-story climbing wall, a landscaped bike trail, and a "rain room"

where customers could test the their rain gear under showers.

It launched its REI-Outlet.com Web site in 1998 to sell discounted merchandise. Also that year, for the first time in its history, REI shut down two of its stores, in Mission Viejo, California, and Orem, Utah, because of low sales volumes.

The co-op began a Japanese retail Web site in 1999; it had made catalog sales in Japan for nearly a decade. Also in 1999 REI decided to scale back on its catalog mailings, instead focusing its direct-selling efforts on e-commerce.

Smith, who grew the company from nine to 54 stores during his 17-year reign, retired in early 2000 and was replaced by COO Dennis Madsen, a 34-year company veteran. Sally Jewell, a former executive with Washington Mutual Bank, was named to succeed Madsen as COO.

Trekking overseas, the company opened its first international location in Tokyo in April 2000. The co-op rankled its rank and file in May 2000 when it announced it would move manufacturing to Mexico and close subsidiary THAW by year's end. In June 2001 REI announced plans to exit the Japanese market, closing its store in Japan and shutting down its Japanese Web site.

## OFFICERS

**Chairman:** Tom Harville
**Vice Chairman:** Frances M. Conley, age 58
**President and CEO:** Dennis Madsen
**EVP and COO:** Sally Jewell
**SVP and CFO:** Brad Johnson
**SVP Merchandising and Logistics:** Matt Hyde
**SVP Retail:** Bob Stadshaug
**VP Finance and Corporate Treasurer:** Atsuko Tamura
**VP Human Resources:** Glen Simmons
**VP Online and Direct Sales:** Joan Broughton
**VP REI Brand Products:** Mike Boshart
**VP Retail Operations:** Dave Towe
**VP Retail Sales:** Brian Unmacht
**VP Retail Store Development:** Jerry Chevassus

## LOCATIONS

**HQ:** 6750 S. 228th St., Kent, WA 98032
**Phone:** 253-395-3780     **Fax:** 253-395-4352
**Web:** www.rei.com

## PRODUCTS/OPERATIONS

**Selected Products and Services**
Bicycles and accessories
Books and maps
Camping gear
Canoes, kayaks, and related gear
Climbing gear
Clothing (children's, men's, and women's)
Fitness gear
Footwear
Gift registry
Racks (bike, boat, and ski mounts)
REI photo service (with PhotoWorks)
REI repair service
Sleeping bags
Snow sports gear
Tents
Travel accessories

## COMPETITORS

| | |
|---|---|
| Academy | Kellwood |
| Bass Pro Shops | Lands' End |
| Big 5 | L.L. Bean |
| Cabela's | Lost Arrow |
| Coleman | North Face |
| Dick's Sporting Goods | Orvis Company |
| Eastern Mountain Sports | Spiegel |
| Galyans Trading | Sport Chalet |
| Gart Sports | Sports Authority |
| Hibbett Sporting Goods | Sportsman's Guide |
| Johnson Outdoors | Track 'n Trail |

## HISTORICAL FINANCIALS & EMPLOYEES

| Cooperative FYE: December 31 | Annual Growth | 12/91 | 12/92 | 12/93 | 12/94 | 12/95 | 12/96 | 12/97 | 12/98 | 12/99 | 12/00 |
|---|---|---|---|---|---|---|---|---|---|---|---|
| Sales ($ mil.) | 8.3% | — | — | — | 432 | 448 | 484 | 536 | 587 | 621 | 698 |
| Net income ($ mil.) | — | — | — | — | 14 | 13 | 15 | 15 | 14 | 10 | (11) |
| Income as % of sales | — | — | — | — | 3.2% | 2.8% | 3.2% | 2.8% | 2.4% | 1.7% | — |
| Employees | 9.9% | — | — | — | — | — | 4,800 | 5,100 | 6,000 | 6,000 | 7,000 |

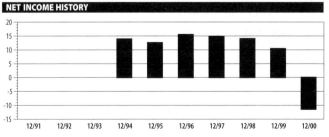

**NET INCOME HISTORY**

**2000 FISCAL YEAR-END**
Debt ratio: 33.3%
Return on equity: —
Cash ($ mil.): 44
Current ratio: 1.03
Long-term debt ($ mil.): 94

# REGAL CINEMAS, INC.

## OVERVIEW

Regal Cinemas reigns supreme in the land of movie theaters. The Knoxville, Tennessee-based company is the world's largest movie exhibitor with more than 4,000 screens at about 350 theaters in 32 states (most of which are in mid-sized urban and large suburban markets). Regal also features IMAX 3-D at a few theaters and runs several FunScapes centers that offer family entertainment (such as food courts, miniature golf, and video games) in addition to movie theaters.

Faced with mounting debt from the rapid construction of its many, pricey new multiplexes — which include amenities like stadium seating and coffee bars — as well as an industry with a glut of theatres, Regal has started to scale back its expansion plans.

Investment firms Hicks, Muse, Tate & Furst and Kohlberg Kravis Roberts own the company. However, Qwest Communications chairman Philip Anschutz has bought about $425 million of Regal's debt, which is likely to leave him in control of the company after a restructuring. (Anschutz also gained control of United Artists Theatre Circuit movie chain in 2001, leaving some to speculate he may combine the two entities.)

## HISTORY

Former grocer Mike Campbell got into the cinema business in 1981 when the New Tazewell, Tennessee, movie theater closed down. He and Neal Melton, also a grocery store manager, bought the theater, refurbished it, and reopened it in 1982 with the blockbuster *E.T. The Extra-Terrestrial*. With the profits from their successful venture, they soon began to expand. Their company, Premiere Cinemas, had 26 theaters by 1989 — the year Cinemark bought them out for $21 million.

With the proceeds from that deal, they immediately founded Regal Cinemas and opened a 10-screen theater in Florida in 1990. Also in 1990 the company made its first acquisition, buying the Searstown Twin Theatre in Titusville, Florida. During the 1990s the movie theater business began a period of consolidation, and Regal was soon swept up in the movement. By the time Regal went public three years later, it had acquired 95 theaters with 630 screens, built 30 new theaters, and added 35 new screens to existing theaters.

In 1993 the company opened its first theater cafe, in a Regal Cinema in Hundington Valley, Pennsylvania. In 1994 Regal acquired Litchfield Luxury Theatres, and in 1995 the company bought the Neighborhood Entertainment theater chain. Also in 1995 Regal opened the first FunScapes family centers.

In 1996 the company bought the 56-screen Georgia State Theatre chain, and it entered the West Coast market for the first time with the acquisition of 69 screens from George Krikorian. In 1997 Regal paid $200 million for Birmingham, Alabama-based Cobb Theatres which operated about 67 theatres with 650 screens in the southeastern US. Also that year it acquired Magic Cinemas, and it signed a deal with IMAX to build up to 10 of IMAX's 3-D movie theatres at Regal locations.

In the feel-good movie deal of 1998 (at least for Campbell), investment firms Kohlberg Kravis Roberts and Hicks, Muse, Tate & Furst bought Regal Cinemas, for $1.2 billion and the assumption of $300 million in debt. The two investment firms combined Regal with Act III Cinemas, which KKR had acquired in 1997 for $600 million in cash and debt. The two had originally planned to include United Artist Theatre Group in the deal as well, but Hicks, Muse's attempt to purchase that theater chain fell though. Campbell remained chief of the new multiplex megacompany as chairman, president, and CEO.

Regal continued to expand in 1999 with more than 90 new theaters and more than 1,500 new screens either built or in planning stages. However, this rapid expansion led to huge losses in 2000, opening the door for Denver billionaire Philip Anschutz to bail the company out.

In 2001 Anschutz and Los Angeles-based investment company Oaktree Capital Management announced that it had acquired about $350 million of Regal's $1 billion in bank debt, paying about 75 cents on the dollar. The deal gave the Anschutz group a controlling interest in the company, which will undergo a reorganization. Anschutz also holds a controlling interest in United Artists Theatre Group.

**Chairman, President, and CEO:** Michael L. Campbell
**SVP, CFO, and Treasurer:** Amy Miles, age 34
**SVP and Head Film Buyer:** Denise K. Gurin, age 49
**SVP and Chief Information Officer:** J.E. Henry, age 52
**SVP Constructions:** Ron Reid, age 59
**SVP, General Counsel, and Secretary:** Peter B. Brandow, age 40
**SVP Operations:** Mike Levesque, age 41
**SVP and Chief Purchasing Officer:** Robert J. Del Moro, age 41
**SVP and Human Resources Counsel:** Raymond L. Smith, age 37
**SVP Real Estate:** Jon Rober
**SVP Sales and Marketing:** Dick Westerling, age 49
**EVP and COO:** Gregory W. Dunn, age 41
**VP and Controller:** Macon Fields
**VP Operations, West:** Curtis Ewing
**VP Operations, South:** Bill Koontz
**VP Security and Quality Control:** F. Leon Hurst
**VP Technical Services:** Roger Frazee
**VP Theatre Equipment:** Ray Dunlap
**VP Advertising:** Rich Rachgiven
**Auditors:** Deloitte & Touche LLP

## LOCATIONS

**HQ:** 7132 Mike Campbell Dr., Knoxville, TN 37918
**Phone:** 865-922-1123          **Fax:** 865-922-6739
**Web:** www.regalcinemas.com

Regal Cinemas has about 350 theaters in 32 states.

## PRODUCTS/OPERATIONS

**2000 Sales**

|  | $ mil. | % of total |
|---|---|---|
| Admissions | 767 | 68 |
| Concessions | 310 | 27 |
| Other | 54 | 5 |
| **Total** | **1,131** | **100** |

## COMPETITORS

AMC Entertainment
Carmike Cinemas
Century Theatres
Cinemark USA
Edwards Theatres
GC Companies
Loews Cineplex
 Entertainment
National Amusements
Pacific Theatres
United Artists Theatre

## HISTORICAL FINANCIALS & EMPLOYEES

| Private<br>FYE: December 31 | Annual<br>Growth | 12/91 | 12/92 | 12/93 | 12/94 | 12/95 | 12/96 | 12/97 | 12/98 | 12/99 | 12/00 |
|---|---|---|---|---|---|---|---|---|---|---|---|
| Sales ($ mil.) | 52.2% | — | 39 | 57 | 136 | 190 | 270 | 479 | 707 | 1,037 | 1,131 |
| Net income ($ mil.) | — | — | 2 | 5 | 7 | 17 | 30 | 25 | (74) | (89) | (367) |
| Income as % of sales | — | — | 5.1% | 8.0% | 5.1% | 9.1% | 11.0% | 5.3% | — | — | — |
| Employees | 45.1% | — | — | 1,120 | 2,716 | 3,816 | 4,227 | 7,605 | 12,000 | 17,249 | 15,159 |

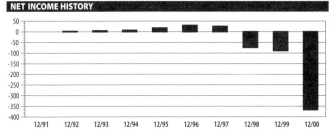

**NET INCOME HISTORY**

**2000 FISCAL YEAR-END**
Debt ratio: 0.0%
Return on equity: —
Cash ($ mil.): 119
Current ratio: 0.08
Long-term debt ($ mil.): 4

# THE ROCKEFELLER FOUNDATION

## OVERVIEW

The Rockefeller Foundation is one of the nation's oldest private charitable organizations. Based in New York City, it supports grants, fellowships, and conferences for programs it hopes will lead to a better world. These programs (or themes) include initiatives to foster fair implementation of health care, job opportunities for America's urban poor, creative expression through the humanities and arts, and agricultural policies that ensure food distribution to people in developing countries. Its cross theme of global inclusion binds its programs to a global focus, ensuring that globalization gets doled out democratically and helps populations typically alienated from the global economy.

The foundation maintains no ties to the Rockefeller family or its other philanthropies. An independent board of trustees sets program guidelines and approves all expenditures.

President Gordon Conway has introduced a reorganization focusing on the role of globalization in aiding the poor. The foundation's former divisions — such as Agricultural Sciences, Equal Opportunity, and Health Sciences — now come under the themes of Food Security, Working Communities, and Health Equity. Its non-New York City offices (Bangkok; Mexico City; Nairobi, Kenya; Harare, Zimbabwe; and San Francisco) are taking on increasing responsibility in carrying out the group's global mission.

## HISTORY

Oil baron John D. Rockefeller, one of America's most criticized capitalists, was also one of its pioneer philanthropists. Before founding The Rockefeller Foundation in 1913, he funded the creation of The University of Chicago (with $36 million over a 25-year period) and formed organizations for medical research (1901), the education of southern African-Americans (1903), and hookworm eradication in the southern US.

Rockefeller turned the control of the foundation over to his son John D. Rockefeller Jr. in 1916. The younger Rockefeller separated the foundation from the family's interests and established an independent board. (The board later rejected a proposal from John Sr. to replace school textbooks that he claimed promoted Bolshevism.)

In the mid-1920s the foundation started conducting basic medical research. In 1928 it absorbed several other Rockefeller philanthropies, adding programs in the natural and social sciences and the arts and humanities. During the 1930s the foundation developed the first effective yellow fever vaccine (1935), continued its worldwide battles against disease, and supported pioneering research in the field of biology. Other grants supported the performing arts in the US and social science research. During WWII it supplied major funding for nuclear science research tools (spectroscopy, X-ray diffraction).

After the war, with an increasing number of large public ventures modeled after the foundation (e.g., the UN's World Health Organization) taking over its traditional physical and natural sciences territory, the organization dissolved its famed biology division in 1951. The following year emphasis swung to agricultural studies under chairman John D. Rockefeller III. The organization took wheat seeds developed at its Mexican food project to Colombia (1950), Chile (1955), and India (1956); a rice institute in the Philippines followed (1960). The Green Revolution sprouted 12 more developing-world institutes.

In the 1960s the foundation began dispatching experts to African and Latin American universities in an effort to raise the level of training at those institutions. The long bear market of the 1970s caused the foundation's assets to drop to a low of $732 million (1977).

In 1990 the organization set up the Energy Foundation, a joint effort with the Pew Charitable Trusts and the MacArthur Foundation, to explore alternate energy sources.

In the mid-1990s the Republican-led Congress launched three probes into the foundation and several other not-for-profits over allegations of political activities that could jeopardize their tax status.

In 1998 Gordon Conway, a British agricultural ecologist, became the foundation's 12th (and first foreign) president. He implemented a retooling of the organization's programs in 1999. He also led an effective campaign against bioengineering giant Monsanto's (now part of Pharmacia Corp.) plan to market "sterile seeds" that do not regenerate. In 2000 James Orr III, a Rockefeller board member and CEO of Boston's United Asset Management Corporation, succeeded Alice Ilchman as chairman of the board of trustees.

## LOCATIONS

**HQ:** 420 5th Ave., New York, NY 10018
**Phone:** 212-869-8500     **Fax:** 212-764-3468
**Web:** www.rockfound.org

The Rockefeller Foundation has field offices in Kenya, Mexico, Thailand, Zimbabwe, and the US, and maintains the Bellagio Study and Conference Center in northern Italy.

## PRODUCTS/OPERATIONS

**2000 Grants**

|  | % of total |
|---|---|
| Working communities | 20 |
| Global inclusion | 20 |
| Food security | 19 |
| Health equity | 15 |
| Creativity & culture | 12 |
| Special programs | 10 |
| Regional programs | 4 |
| **Total** | **100** |

**Themes**

Creativity & Culture (renews and preserves the cultural heritage of people excluded from the globalizing economy; promotes public exchanges of ideas; supports diversity and creativity in humanities and arts)

Food Security (generates agricultural institutions, policies, and innovations to help rural poor in developing countries)

Global Inclusion (seeks to ensure that globalization processes are carried out fairly and democratically, benefiting those most in need)

Health Equity (seeks to improve the implementation of health care in developing countries)

Working Communities (seeks to increase employment, improve schools, and encourage democratic participation in poor urban neighborhoods in the US)

## HISTORICAL FINANCIALS & EMPLOYEES

| Foundation FYE: December 31 | Annual Growth | 12/91 | 12/92 | 12/93 | 12/94 | 12/95 | 12/96 | 12/97 | 12/98 | 12/99 | 12/00 |
|---|---|---|---|---|---|---|---|---|---|---|---|
| Sales ($ mil.) | (5.4%) | — | 198 | 208 | 21 | 319 | 413 | 510 | 388 | 680 | 127 |
| Employees | 6.2% | — | 142 | 147 | 137 | 130 | 152 | 149 | 150 | 220 | 230 |

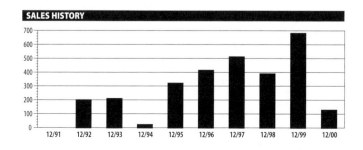

SALES HISTORY

# ROLL INTERNATIONAL

Frankly, Scarlett, you deserve a commemorative plate. So thought husband-and-wife team Stewart and Lynda Rae Resnick, owners of the world's top collectibles company, The Franklin Mint. That frippery firm is part of the couple's Los Angeles-based Roll International, which also owns Paramount Farms (processes pistachios), Paramount Citrus (California-based citrus products), and Teleflora (floral wire service). Roll also operates The Franklin Mint Museum, which has displayed such pop culture items as Jacqueline Kennedy Onassis' triple-strand faux pearl necklace.

Based near Philadelphia and with operations in about 15 countries, The Franklin Mint is the centerpiece of the Resnicks' empire. (It has no connection to the US Mint.) The company develops up to 1,200 products each year and has sold everything from *Gone With the Wind* figurines and *Star Trek* chess sets to limited-edition Monopoly games and even the Elvis Presley commemorative .45 automatic. The Franklin Mint produces many of its wares under licensing agreements with the likes of the Vatican, The Coca-Cola Company, and Harley-Davidson, among others. Products are sold by mail order, through its Web site, and in 50 company-owned and independent retail outlets.

Stewart Resnick, a UCLA Law School graduate, is recognized as the financial and organizational brains of Roll International. Lynda Rae, an art lover and marketing guru, started her own advertising agency when she was 19 years old. Each had established careers when they married in the early 1970s. Together they have built their company through a series of acquisitions.

Among the Resnicks' first purchases was Teleflora, which they bought in 1979. Originally called Telegraph Delivery Service, Teleflora had been founded in 1934 by Edwin Douglas. The Resnicks also bought alarm company American Protection Industries (API), which they set up as their holding company.

In 1985 the Resnicks acquired The Franklin Mint from Warner Communications (now AOL Time Warner) for around $167 million. Founded in 1964 by Joseph Segal (who in 1986 started the QVC television shopping network) as General Numismatics, the company originally focused on coins and other metal objects. It went public in 1965 and changed its name to The Franklin Mint in 1968. The Franklin Mint was purchased by Warner in 1981, but it failed to prosper. The Resnicks, who had been eyeing the company for some time, saw a greater opportunity in the collectibles market rather than in coins and greatly expanded that part of the business. In 1991 The Franklin Mint turned its first profit since 1987.

The Resnicks bought Mobil's Apex Orchards, an almond and pistachio grower in the San Joaquin Valley, in 1986. The next year they added the California agribusinesses of Texaco (now ChevronTexaco) to their holdings. (Texaco had become owner of the Central California operations when it acquired Getty Oil in 1984.) The Resnicks formed their agribusiness unit, Paramount Farms, in 1989.

That year they sold API; however, they retained the name until 1993, when they renamed their holding company Roll International, after another agricultural company they had acquired.

The couple had planned to take The Franklin Mint public in 1992, but its poor earnings prior to 1991 and a cool IPO market changed their minds. Instead they focused on expanding the mint's line of collectibles through licensing agreements and added commemorative plates to their line. In the early 1990s the company began opening The Franklin Mint retail stores. In 1993 Paramount Farms and the Pistachio Producers of California teamed up to form the CAL-PURE marketing co-op, offering pistachios under the Sunkist name.

The Franklin Mint had 50 gallery shops in US shopping centers and more than $600 million in US sales by 1996. The following year Teleflora bought Redbook Florist Services, giving it more subscribers (though still lower sales) than rival floral company FTD.

Also in 1997 Lynda Resnick bought the high-collared "Elvis dress" worn by the late Diana, Princess of Wales, for over $150,000 for display in The Franklin Mint Museum. A memorial fund for Diana sued The Franklin Mint in 1998, charging it with unauthorized use of the princess' image on various items. (The suit was subsequently dismissed.) That year the Resnicks looked into selling the company, reportedly because its legal problems had tarnished Lynda's standing among American socialites. In 1999 Lynda was named a trustee for the Aspen Institute, a high-brow intellectual group for societal leaders. Paramount Citrus became the US's largest fresh citrus marketer after it purchased 4,000 acres from Dole Food for $55 million in 2000.

## HISTORICAL FINANCIALS & EMPLOYEES

| Private<br>FYE: December 31 | Annual<br>Growth | 12/91 | 12/92 | 12/93 | 12/94 | 12/95 | 12/96 | 12/97 | 12/98 | 12/99 | 12/00 |
|---|---|---|---|---|---|---|---|---|---|---|---|
| Sales ($ mil.) | (1.9%) | — | 960 | 1,180 | 1,300 | 1,360 | 1,280 | 1,511 | 725 | 700 | 825 |
| Employees | (4.7%) | — | 7,500 | 7,500 | 7,500 | 7,700 | 7,500 | 7,500 | 7,500 | 5,000 | 5,100 |

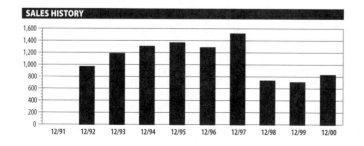

SALES HISTORY

Teleflora

# ROSENBLUTH INTERNATIONAL

Rosenbluth International makes billions by keeping its customers second. Philadelphia-based Rosenbluth, whose corporate philosophy was revealed in chairman and CEO Hal Rosenbluth's 1992 book *The Customer Comes Second* (after employees), is a leader in travel management services. The company's mascot is a salmon, because of its ability to successfully swim upstream against the tide.

Placing emphasis on corporate travel, Rosenbluth has more than 1,300 locations worldwide and serves the travel needs of clients, including DuPont, ChevronTexaco, NIKE, and J.P. Morgan Chase. Known for keeping pace with evolving travel technology, the company offers its services with the aid of travel systems such as its @Rosenbluth (a business travel management system), Discount Analysis Containing Optimal Decision Algorithms (DACODA, maximizes savings on airlines tickets), and Custom-Res (a global reservation system). Through Rosenbluth Interactive, Rosenbluth operates biztravel.com, a travel Web site dedicated to business travelers.

In addition to providing traditional travel services (airline, hotel, and car rental reservations), Rosebluth has branched into virtual travel management, offering its clients services such as Web conferencing. Founded in 1892 by Marcus Rosenbluth, the company still is owned and operated by his family, including his great-grandson, chairman and CEO Hal Rosenbluth.

## HISTORY

In 1892 Marcus Rosenbluth began selling immigration packages from his storefront shop to neighbors in Philadelphia's Brewerytown. After collecting $50 in various currencies, he would arrange passage for an immigrant family's European relative to Ellis Island, often greeting the American-to-be personally and helping complete forms in the new language.

Rosenbluth's travel company rode out the ups and downs of two world wars and the emerging commercial airline industry. By the time Rosenbluth's great-grandson Hal Rosenbluth came aboard in 1974, the mostly consumer leisure travel agency was making more than $20 million a year. In the year of airline deregulation (1978), a lightbulb went on as Hal Rosenbluth observed reservation agents working on the company's corporate accounts. He soon demoted himself from vice president to reservations agent and began steering the company toward corporate accounts.

Before deregulation, airlines focused on service; fares were regulated by law and rarely changed. Businesses were interested mostly in who could deliver their tickets the fastest. With deregulation, fares changed with dizzying frequency. Yield management replaced service. Travelers needed help sorting through the confusion, and Rosenbluth saw the opportunity to meet their needs.

In the early 1980s accounts with Bethlehem Steel and DuPont helped Rosenbluth gain a national presence. A less than ecstatic reception in Atlanta in 1985 motivated the company to upgrade its high-tech pricing and reservations system and lure corporate accounts with promises of savings and good service.

Hal Rosenbluth became CEO in 1987, and the next year Rosenbluth sought to grow overseas by forming Rosenbluth International Alliance (RIA), a network of independent business travel agencies.

Hal Rosenbluth's book, *The Customer Comes Second,* was published in 1992. Rosenbluth abandoned RIA in 1993 (buying some of the businesses and setting up new ones) when it found it could not control the quality of service it offered to multinationals. Crunched by low air fares, the company began reorganizing operations in 1994 along the lines of a family farm, breaking up the company into 100-plus branches serving specific clients and regions. It also laid off about 10% of its workforce.

In 1997 the company geared itself for global growth by forming a strategic alliance with The SABRE Group to integrate SABRE's technology into its travel reservations systems. One year later Rosenbluth bought Swedish travel firm Business Express.

Rosenbluth acquired travel services firm Aquarius Travel in 1999. Later that year the company expanded into Web-based travel services when it bought a majority of Internet travel services company biztravel.com. In 2000 Rosenbluth unveiled Rosenbluth Everywhere, a custom online and wireless travel service. The company also expanded into non-travel call center services and made headlines when biztravel.com offered travelers refunds for flights that arrived late. In 2001 the company entered a partnership with large Chinese travel agency China Comfort.

**Chairman and CEO:** Hal F. Rosenbluth, age 49
**President and COO:** Alex Wasilov
**CFO:** Thomas Sukay
**SVP North America:** Ron DiLeo
**VP Business Development, Central U.S. Region:**
Yma Sherry
**VP Business Development, Western U.S. Region:**
R. Timothy Small
**VP Strategic Markets:** Pieter Reider
**VP Sales and Marketing, North America:**
Wendy Gonzalez
**VP Business Development, Asia Pacific:** Peter Lau
**VP Corporate Communications and Government**
**Relations:** Mary Trupo
**VP Human Resources Development:** Cecily Carel
**VP Global Supplier Relations:** Michael Boult
**VP:** Joe Terrion
**SVP and Chief Information Officer:** John Dabek

**HQ:** 2401 Walnut St., Philadelphia, PA 19103
**Phone:** 215-977-4000      **Fax:** 215-977-4028
**Web:** www.rosenbluth.com

Rosenbluth International has operations in 24 countries worldwide.

**Selected Products and Services**
@Rosenbluth (business travel management system)
biztravel.com (Web site dedicated to business travelers)
Custom-Res (global reservation system)
Discount Analysis Containing Optimal Decision (system
for maximizing savings on airline tickets)
E-Ticket Tracking Solution (electronic ticket tracking
System)
Global Distribution Network (electronic reservation
system)
Res-Monitor® (low-fare search system)
Rosenbluth's Electronic Messaging Services (e-mail
based travel management system)
Travelution (discount airline tickets Web site)

Airtours
American Express
Carlson Wagonlit
Expedia
JTB
Kuoni Travel
Maritz
Pleasant Holidays
Preussag
priceline.com
Travelocity
WorldTravel

| Private<br>FYE: December 31 | Annual<br>Growth | 12/91 | 12/92 | 12/93 | 12/94 | 12/95 | 12/96 | 12/97 | 12/98 | 12/99 | 12/00 |
|---|---|---|---|---|---|---|---|---|---|---|---|
| Sales ($ mil.) | 11.4% | — | — | — | — | 3,200 | 3,500 | 4,000 | 3,500 | 4,500 | 5,500 |
| Employees | 5.1% | — | — | — | — | — | 4,500 | 4,500 | 4,500 | 4,500 | 5,500 |

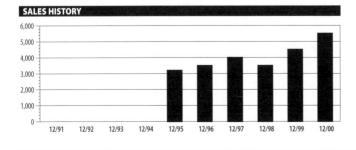

# ROTARY INTERNATIONAL

## OVERVIEW

The rotary phone may be gone, but Rotary International is still going strong. The Evanston, Illinois-based service organization has a membership of nearly 1.2 million in about 30,000 clubs across 163 countries. With the motto "Service Above Self" as its banner, Rotary International is active in addressing a variety of issues including AIDS, hunger, and polio. Through the not-for-profit Rotary Foundation, the organization invests $90 million each year in international education and humanitarian programs (funds are raised through voluntary contributions). Rotary International also sponsors Interact clubs for secondary school students, as well as a network of about 6,500 Rotaract clubs for members ages 18-30.

Membership in Rotary clubs is by invitation only. Each club strives to include representatives from major businesses, professions, and institutions in its community. Governed by a 19-member board, the organization maintains offices worldwide.

Along with other service organizations, Rotary International has been confronted with a new issue — social and attitudinal trends that have made it more difficult to attract new members. While Rotary International has fared better than some counterparts, a decline in civic-mindedness and the fact that contemporary corporations tend not to stress membership in service organizations present new challenges for the organization.

## HISTORY

On February 23, 1905, lawyer Paul Harris met with three friends in an office in Chicago's Unity Building. Inspired by the fellowship and tolerance of his boyhood home in Wallingford, Vermont, Harris proposed organizing a men's club to meet periodically for the purpose of camaraderie and making business contacts. The new endeavor was organized as the Rotary Club of Chicago (the name arose from the club's custom of rotating its meeting place) and had 30 members by the end of the year.

As additional clubs followed, the organization assumed its role as a civic and service organization (the installation of public comfort stations in Chicago's City Hall was one of its first projects). At the first convention of the National Association of Rotary Clubs in 1910, Harris was elected president. International clubs soon followed, and by 1921 there were Rotary clubs on each continent.

In 1932, while struggling to revive a company with financial difficulties, Rotarian Herbert Taylor devised a statement of business ethics that later became the Rotarian mantra. Taylor's "4-Way Test" consisted of the following questions: "Is it the truth? Is it fair to all concerned? Will it build goodwill and better friendships? Will it be beneficial to all concerned?"

During WWI Rotary clubs promoted war relief and peace fund efforts. Following WWII the clubs assisted in efforts to aid refugees and prisoners of war. The extent of Rotarian involvement in international issues became clear when 49 members assisted in drafting the United Nations Charter in 1945.

The first significant contributions to The Rotary Foundation followed Harris' death in 1947. These funds formed the bedrock for the foundation's programs, and in 1965 the foundation created its Matching Grants and Group Study Exchange programs. Rotary International also welcomed younger members in the 1960s by creating its Interact and Rotaract clubs in 1962 and 1968, respectively.

The largest meeting of Rotarians occurred in 1978 when almost 40,000 members attended the organization's Tokyo convention. But controversy was fast approaching the male-only organization. In 1978 a California Rotary club defied the male-only requirement and admitted two women. Claiming that the club had violated the organization's constitution, Rotary International revoked the club's charter. A lengthy court battle ensued, and a series of appeals landed the issue on the docket of the US Supreme Court. In 1987 the court ruled that the all-male requirement was discriminatory. Two years later Rotary International officially did away with its all-male status.

In the 1990s membership in Rotary clubs grew, but at a slower pace than in the organization's past. Mary Wolfenberger was appointed the organization's first female CFO in 1993 (resigned 1997). In 1998 Rotary International joined with the United Nations to launch a series of humanitarian service projects in developing areas.

In 1999 the organization spearheaded events to help flood victims in North Carolina and refugees in the Balkans. In 2000 the group created a program specializing in peace and conflict resolution.

**President:** Frank J. Devlyn
**VP:** Louis Piconi
**CFO:** Ladd Waldo
**Chairman, The Rotary Foundation:** Herbert G. Brown
**Vice Chairman:** Luis Vicente Giay
**Treasurer:** Noel Friar
**Director Corporate Services:** Mark A. Garazaglia
**Director Human Resources:** C. Engblom
**President-Elect:** Richard D. King

## LOCATIONS

**HQ:** 1 Rotary Center, 1560 Sherman Ave.,
Evanston, IL 60201
**Phone:** 847-866-3000     **Fax:** 847-866-9732
**Web:** www.rotary.org

Rotary International has clubs in 163 countries.

## PRODUCTS/OPERATIONS

**Selected Issues Addressed**
AIDS
Drug-abuse prevention
Environment
Family
Hunger
Literacy
Polio
Urban violence prevention
Youth

**Selected Programs**
Educational programs
    Ambassadorial Scholarships
    Grants for University Teachers
    Group Study Exchange (GSE)
    Rotary Friendship Exchange
Humanitarian grants
    Discovery Grants
    Grants for Rotary Volunteers
    Matching Grants
    New Opportunities Grants
    Peace Program Grants
    PolioPlus Program

## HISTORICAL FINANCIALS & EMPLOYEES

| Not-for-profit FYE: June 30 | Annual Growth | 6/91 | 6/92 | 6/93 | 6/94 | 6/95 | 6/96 | 6/97 | 6/98 | 6/99 | 6/00 |
|---|---|---|---|---|---|---|---|---|---|---|---|
| Sales ($ mil.) | 2.5% | — | 51 | 52 | 59 | 60 | 62 | 72 | 73 | 62 | 62 |
| Employees | (4.0%) | — | 554 | 617 | 450 | 350 | 400 | 400 | 400 | 400 | 400 |

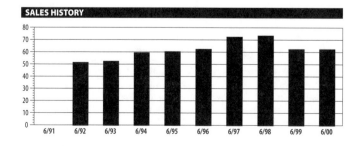

SALES HISTORY

# ROUNDY'S, INC.

## OVERVIEW

Roundy's has plenty of square deals for independent grocers, supplying them with name-brand and private-label food and general merchandise. The Pewaukee, Wisconsin-based wholesaler is a cooperative of nearly 60 members, which operate about 100 supermarkets primarily in Wisconsin, but also in Illinois. (These operations account for about 30% of sales.) Roundy's also distributes to about 700 other independent grocery stores in 14 states, primarily throughout the Midwest and South (nearly 45% of sales). Roundy's offers its members and customer stores a host of support services, including accounting and inventory control, advertising, and store financing. Co-op members own all of the voting shares (about 65% of the total company); employees and other investors control the rest.

Roundy's also owns about 50 supermarkets, the majority of which are Park & Save or Pick 'n Save warehouse stores offering complete food and general merchandise lines at discounted prices. The rest are conventional retail stores operating under the Park & Shop and Orchard Foods banners.

## HISTORY

Migration from the eastern US and overseas was boosting Milwaukee's ranks when William Smith, Judson Roundy, and Sidney Hauxhurst formed grocery wholesaler Smith, Roundy & Co. in 1872. Smith left the firm in 1878 for his first of two terms as Wisconsin's governor, and William Peckham joined the enterprise, which was then renamed Roundy, Peckham & Co. Two years later Charles Dexter joined the company, by then operating in five midwestern states and running a manufacturing business.

The wholesaler became Roundy, Peckham & Dexter Co. in 1902, following the death of Hauxhurst (Roundy died in 1907). The company introduced its first private-label product — salt — in 1922. In 1929 Dexter (then 84) came up with a plan to publicize the Roundy's name by handing out cookbooks that called for the company's goods.

Roy Johnson, who joined the company in 1912, was named president near the end of the Depression. In the 1940s the wholesaler acquired smaller companies in the region. The company became Roundy's in 1952 when Roundy, Peckham & Dexter was bought by a group comprising hundreds of Wisconsin grocery retailers. Johnson remained head of the new company until his death in 1962. James Aldrich led the company for the next 11 years.

In 1970 Roundy's started Insurance Planners, which offered insurance to retailers. Vincent Little became president of the company in 1973. Two years later Roundy's began a real estate subsidiary (Ronco Realty) and opened its first Pick 'n Save Warehouse Foods store.

The company expanded in the 1980s through the purchase of distributors in Indiana, Michigan, Ohio, and Wisconsin. The acquisitions included Cardinal Food Group in 1984 and Viking Foods in 1985. Expansion hurt profits, and dividends were suspended in 1984 and 1985. In the late 1980s several Pick 'n Save stores opened throughout Wisconsin and other midwestern states. Owners grew suspicious of Little's accounting practices and the special treatment given a Roundy's-owned store run by his son, and in 1986 they forced him out of his president and CEO positions. John Dickson replaced him.

By 1994 Pick 'n Save had vastly upgraded its image — one store sold $1,000 cognac and featured an $18,000 cappuccino machine. However, sales dropped off for the third straight year. Roundy's and rival wholesaler Spartan Stores announced merger plans in late 1994 but called off the deal seven weeks later. COO Gerald Lestina was named CEO in 1995, replacing Dickson, who continued as chairman. Dickson died later that year.

Roundy's did not pay its members a dividend in 1995 as it made an effort to offset losses in Michigan and Ohio. To ease those losses, in 1997 the company closed 12 poorly performing stores in those states. A year later a fire destroyed its Evansville, Indiana, warehouse; the company rebuilt the facility that year. Also in 1999 Roundy's purchased three supermarkets in Indiana from Kroger and The John C. Groub Company.

The Mega Marts and Ultra Mart chains, which together operate 24 Pick 'n Save stores, primarily in Wisconsin, were acquired by Roundy's in 2000. The following year Roundy's launched an online grocery shopping service, called Pick 'n Save Online Shopping, in two test stores in Wisconsin (with plans for more locations). Also in 2001 the company purchased its competitor, The Copps Corporation, acquiring 21 stores in north and central Wisconsin and a wholesale business that distributes to retailers in Wisconsin and northern Michigan.

## OFFICERS

**President and CEO:** Gerald F. Lestina, age 58,
$641,250 pay
**VP and CFO:** Robert D. Ranus, age 60, $324,000 pay
**VP of Administration:** David C. Busch, age 52
**VP of Advertising:** Londell J. Behm, age 50
**VP of Corporate Relief:** Gary L. Fryda, age 48
**VP of Distribution:** John E. Paterson, age 53
**VP of Human Resources:** Debra A. Lawson, age 45
**VP of Marketing:** Marion H. Sullivan, age 54,
$256,500 pay
**VP of Planning and Information Services:**
Charles H. Kosmaler Jr., age 58
**VP of Sales and Development:** Michael J. Schmitt,
age 52, $256,500 pay
**VP, Secretary, and Treasurer:** Edward G. Kitz, age 47
**VP of Wholesale:** Ralph D. Beketic, age 54, $283,500 pay
**Auditors:** Deloitte & Touche LLP

## LOCATIONS

**HQ:** 23000 Roundy Dr., Pewaukee, WI 53072
**Phone:** 262-953-7999    **Fax:** 262-953-6580
**Web:** www.roundys.com

Roundy's distributes products to more than 800 stores
(including about 20 company-owned stores) in Arkansas,
Illinois, Indiana, Kentucky, Michigan, Minnesota,
Missouri, New York, Ohio, Oklahoma, Pennsylvania,
Tennessee, West Virginia, and Wisconsin.

## PRODUCTS/OPERATIONS

**2000 Sales**

|  | % of total |
|---|---|
| Independent retailers | 43 |
| Company-owned stores | 30 |
| Co-op members | 27 |
| **Total** | **100** |

### Selected Products and Services

**Selected Private and Controlled Labels**
Buyers' Choice
Old Time
Roundy's
Shurfine

**Product Lines**
Bakery goods
Dairy products
Dry groceries
Fresh produce
Frozen foods
General merchandise
Meats

**Selected Services**
Centralized bakery purchasing
Financing
Group advertising
Insurance
Inventory control
Merchandising
Ordering assistance
Point-of-sale support
Pricing services
Purchasing reports
Real estate services
Retail accounting
Retail training
Store development
Store engineering

## COMPETITORS

Albertson's
ALDI
AWG
Central Grocers
  Cooperative
Certified Grocers Midwest
Costco Wholesale
Dominick's
Eagle Food
Fleming Companies
A&P
GSC Enterprises

Hy-Vee
IGA
Kmart
Kroger
Meijer
Nash Finch
S. Abraham & Sons
Spartan Stores
SUPERVALU
Topco Associates
Wal-Mart

## HISTORICAL FINANCIALS & EMPLOYEES

| Cooperative<br>FYE: Sat. nearest Dec. 31 | Annual<br>Growth | 12/91 | 12/92 | 12/93 | 12/94 | 12/95 | 12/96 | 12/97 | 12/98 | 12/99 | 12/00 |
|---|---|---|---|---|---|---|---|---|---|---|---|
| Sales ($ mil.) | 2.3% | — | 2,491 | 2,480 | 2,462 | 2,488 | 2,579 | 2,611 | 2,579 | 2,727 | 2,991 |
| Net income ($ mil.) | 14.1% | — | 7 | 8 | 7 | 9 | 10 | 11 | 12 | 18 | 21 |
| Income as % of sales | — | — | 0.3% | 0.3% | 0.3% | 0.4% | 0.4% | 0.4% | 0.5% | 0.6% | 0.7% |
| Employees | 7.5% | — | 5,088 | 4,884 | 4,775 | 4,839 | 5,481 | 5,071 | 5,193 | 5,617 | 9,071 |

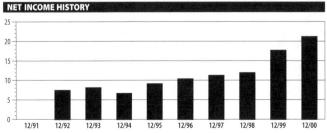

**NET INCOME HISTORY**

**2000 FISCAL YEAR-END**
Debt ratio: 52.5%
Return on equity: —
Cash ($ mil.): 40
Current ratio: 1.13
Long-term debt ($ mil.): 167

# RUSSELL STOVER CANDIES INC.

## OVERVIEW

Whether grabbed as a last-minute anniversary offering or tucked into an Easter basket, Russell Stover Candies knows that chocolate is always welcome. As the largest maker of boxed chocolates in the US, the Kansas City, Missouri-based company is the #3 confectioner in the US, after Hershey and Mars. Faced with the reputation of being your grandmother's favorite chocolates, Russell Stover is hoping to attract younger customers with licensed characters (Elvis, Looney Tunes, Peanuts). It also is putting more focus on new products such as individually wrapped candy-bar aisle treats — a market area it previously ignored — and

more sugar-free items for diabetics and others. Its Whitman's affiliate makes the famous Whitman's Sampler. (Most of the company's sales come from various samplers.) And Russell Stover makes Pangburn's candy, including the Millionaires brand (also in a sugarless version).

Russell Stover's candies are sold in supermarkets, card and gift shops, drugstores, mass merchandisers, and about 50 Russell Stover Candies retail stores. Brothers Tom and Scott Ward are co-presidents; the Ward family owns the company.

## HISTORY

Russell William Stover began selling Mrs. Stover's Bungalow Candies with his wife, Clara, in 1923. Russell had more than 10 years of experience in the candy industry, including a 1921-23 partnership with Christian Nelson, who created the I-Scream bar (chocolate-coated ice cream). Russell changed the name to Eskimo Pie, and the two did well selling the patented item until look-alikes started popping up; the patent was eventually declared invalid, and Russell sold his interest and moved to Denver.

There the Stovers' homemade candies were an instant hit, and by 1925 they were selling their candies in seven local stores. That year they opened candy factories in Denver and in Kansas City, Missouri, to keep up with demand. With Russell as president and Clara as VP, Mrs. Stover's flourished through the rest of the decade and even managed to turn a profit during the lean times of the Depression. A third factory opened in Lincoln, Nebraska, in 1942, and the company's name was changed to Russell Stover Candies a year later.

By the time Russell died in 1954, the company was selling about 11 million pounds of candy a year through about 2,000 department stores and 40 Russell Stover Candies shops. The Stover family and partners carried on until 1960, when they sold the business to Louis Ward, then president of the Ward Paper Box Co., for about $7 million.

Evidently Ward enjoyed boxing chocolates more than making boxes, because he took the company national, expanding sales on the East Coast and building a factory in Clarksville, Virginia, in 1969. Ward maintained the use of higher-cost small-batch production processes and continued, in many cases, using recipes unchanged since the 1940s. The firm used marketing to sweeten its sales in the 1970s and

1980s, introducing heart-shaped boxes, cherry cordials, and miniature chocolates. By the mid-1980s Russell Stover was the king of boxed chocolates. The company soon diversified into a wide range of Easter basket items and gift packs. In the late 1980s Russell Stover began roasting its own nuts and established a candy school.

In 1993 the senior Ward retired after suffering a stroke, and his sons stepped in. That year the company acquired Whitman's Candies. Candy-bar sales had flattened in the early 1990s, and big players such as Mars and Hershey began going after Russell Stover's market by introducing boxed chocolate products.

The Ward brothers fought back. They began licensing the rights to use artwork and cartoon characters in 1994 and opened new plants in Abilene (1995) and Iola, Kansas (1997). The firm introduced bagged candy the following year. In 1999, the company jumped into the candy bar market with a version of the s'more — a sticky sandwich of graham cracker, marshmallow, and chocolate traditionally made around campfires.

Russell Stover acquired the trademarks of bankrupt Pangburn Candy, makers of Millionaires-brand boxed chocolates, for $4.5 million in 1999. It also completed a 462,000-sq.-ft. candy plant and kitchen in Corsicana, Texas, the company's fourth new plant in three years. In 2000 Russell Stover closed its plant in Marion, South Carolina. In response to news reports of children working as slaves on Ivory Coast cocoa bean farms, Russell Stover co-president Thomas Ward said in 2001 that the company's supplier contracts forbid the use of child labor.

Co-President and COO: Thomas S. Ward
Co-President: Scott H. Ward
CFO: Dick Masinton
VP Human Resources: Robinn S. Weber
VP Logistical Operations and Product Scheduling:
  Robert G. Maack
VP Marketing: John O'Hara
VP Sales: Mark Frame

## LOCATIONS

HQ: 4900 Oaks St., Kansas City, MO 64112
Phone: 816-842-9240   Fax: 816-842-5593
Web: www.russellstover.com

Russell Stover Candies has factories in Colorado, Kansas
Tennessee, Texas, and Virginia. Products are sold in
Australia, Canada, New Zealand, Puerto Rico, and the US.

## PRODUCTS/OPERATIONS

Selected Products
Assorted chocolates
Cherry Cordials
Chocolate Covered Nuts
French Chocolate Mints
Fruit Flavored Jellies
Millionaires (regular and sugar free)
Miniature Chocolates
Mint Patties
PB & Grape Jelly Cup
PB & Red Raspberry Cup
Pecan Delights
Traditional S'mores Candy Bar

## COMPETITORS

| | |
|---|---|
| Archibald Candy | Jelly Belly Candy |
| Brach's | Just Born |
| Cadbury Schweppes | Mars |
| Campbell Soup | Nestlé |
| Chase General | Rocky Mountain Chocolate |
| Lindt & Sprungli | See's Candies |
| DFG Confectionery | Sherwood Brands |
| Ferrero | Tootsie Roll |
| Hershey | World's Finest Chocolate |

## HISTORICAL FINANCIALS & EMPLOYEES

| Private<br>FYE: February 28 | Annual<br>Growth | 2/92 | 2/93 | 2/94 | 2/95 | 2/96 | 2/97 | 2/98 | 2/99 | 2/00 | 2/01 |
|---|---|---|---|---|---|---|---|---|---|---|---|
| Sales ($ mil.) | 1.6% | — | — | — | — | — | 442 | 510 | 500 | 500 | 471 |
| Employees | (3.1%) | — | — | — | — | — | 5,900 | 6,000 | 6,300 | 6,200 | 5,200 |

## SALES HISTORY

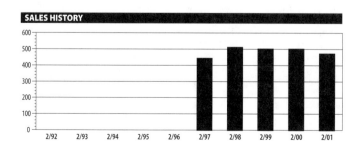

# SALVATION ARMY USA

## OVERVIEW

The name Salvation Army may only ring a bell with you around Christmas, but Salvation Army USA is always working. Active as a church and a charity, the organization serves nearly 37 million people a year. The Alexandria, Virginia-based organization's many programs help alcoholics, drug addicts, the elderly, the homeless, the handicapped, the suicidal, prison inmates, students, and the unemployed. It also provides disaster relief in the US and abroad. The Salvation Army usually tops the list of US not-for-profits in terms of donations received: In 2000 contributions reached about $523 million.

Along with promoting charity, the Salvation Army seeks to save souls. As an evangelical church, it preaches the message of salvation through Jesus Christ. Before joining the organization and becoming a soldier (a lay member),

one must sign an agreement known as the "Articles of War," a commitment to the avoidance of gambling, debt, and profanity and to abstention from alcohol, tobacco, and other recreational drugs. The US organization includes some 125,000 soldiers, more than 3 million volunteers, and nearly 5,400 officers, who are also ordained ministers.

Officers are expected to wear their uniforms at all times and to work full-time for the Salvation Army. They receive no salary; instead, they are provided with room and board and given a limited stipend.

The Salvation Army USA is only one of scores of national Salvation Army organizations around the world, which report to the group's global leader, General John Gowans, at its international headquarters in the UK.

## HISTORY

William Booth (1829-1912) started preaching the gospel as a Wesleyan Methodist in the UK, but the church expelled him because he insisted on preaching outside and to everyone, including the poor. In 1865 he moved to the slums of London's East End and attracted large crowds with his volatile sermons. Opposition to his message of universal salvation for drunks, thieves, prostitutes, and gamblers often caused riots. In fact, the first women in the organization wore bonnets designed with a dual purpose in mind — warmth and protection from flying objects.

At a meeting in 1878, a sign was used referring to the "Salvation Army." Booth adopted the reference as both the name and the style of his organization. Members became soldiers, evangelists were officers, and Booth was referred to as "General." Prayers became knee drills, and contributions were called cartridges.

The Salvation Army marched across the Atlantic to the US in 1880, led by seven women and one man. Women have always played an active role in the Salvation Army, both as officers and soldiers. Booth's wife, Catherine Mumford, was a leading suffragette, and Booth advocated equal rights for women.

In 1891 a crab pot was placed on a San Francisco street to collect donations, with a sign reading "Keep the Pot Boiling." The idea led to the Salvation Army's annual Christmas kettle program.

During WWI the organization became famous for the doughnuts that it served the doughboys fighting on the front lines. After

some internal dissension, the Salvation Army took its only public political stance in 1928 with the endorsement of Herbert Hoover for his support of Prohibition during his presidential campaign. The charity opened its first home for alcoholics in 1939, in Detroit. After WWII the Salvation Army began using such radio and TV programs as *Heartbeat Theater* and *Army of Stars* to spread its message.

Over the years the Salvation Army has provided assistance to victims of hurricanes, floods, and earthquakes. Volunteers rendered almost 70,000 service hours in the aftermath of the Oklahoma City bombing in 1995, counseling more than 1,600 victims and family members, helping with funeral arrangements, and providing food, clothing, and travel assistance. Indicative of the organization's readiness and extensive reach, its volunteers were helping victims in Guam within minutes of the 1997 Korean Air plane crash. It was quickly on the scene after a Jonesboro, Arkansas, shooting incident in 1998 when four students and one teacher were killed by fellow students. Late that year the organization received the largest donation in its history — $80 million from Joan Kroc, wife of McDonald's co-founder Ray Kroc.

In 2000 General Paul Rader retired, and with incoming General John Gowans the organization initiated its first reform in more than 100 years by allowing officers to marry outside the ranks. Following the September 11 attacks in 2001, the Salvation Army provided assistance to rescue workers and families affected by the tragedy through its Disaster Relief Fund.

## OFFICERS

**General (International Director):** John Gowans
**Chairman National Advisory Board:** Donald V. Fites
**Commissioner (National Commander):** John Busby
**Colonel (National Chief Secretary):** Thomas C. Lewis
**Colonel (National Secretary for Personnel):**
  Myrtle V. Ryder
**Lieutenant Colonel (National Treasurer and Secretary
  Business Administration):** Don McDougald
**Commissioner (Southern Territorial Commander):**
  Raymond S. Cooper
**Commissioner (Western Territorial Commander):**
  David Edwards
**Commissioner (Central Territorial Commander):**
  Lawrence Moretz
**Commissioner (Eastern Territorial Commander):**
  Joseph J. Noland
**Commissioner (National President Women's
  Organizations):** Elsie Busby
**Auditors:** PricewaterhouseCoopers LLP

## LOCATIONS

**HQ:** 615 Slaters Ln., Alexandria, VA 22313
**Phone:** 703-684-5500       **Fax:** 703-684-3478
**Web:** www.salvationarmyusa.org

Salvation Army USA operates service centers, local
churches, and social service programs and facilities
throughout the US and provides disaster relief
worldwide.

## PRODUCTS/OPERATIONS

**Selected Services**
Alcohol and drug treatment centers
Clinics and hospitals
Convalescent homes
Counseling
Crisis counseling
Food distribution centers
Handicapped housing
Homeless shelters
Institutes for the blind
Leprosy clinics
Military canteens and hostels
Nurseries and day care centers
Occupational centers
Prison ministry
Probation housing
Refugee centers
Science and trade schools
Student housing
Welfare aid

## HISTORICAL FINANCIALS & EMPLOYEES

| Not-for-profit<br>FYE: September 30 | Annual<br>Growth | 9/91 | 9/92 | 9/93 | 9/94 | 9/95 | 9/96 | 9/97 | 9/98 | 9/99 | 9/00 |
|---|---|---|---|---|---|---|---|---|---|---|---|
| Sales ($ mil.) | 4.3% | — | 1,287 | 1,398 | 1,355 | 1,421 | 2,070 | 2,525 | 2,078 | 1,707 | 1,803 |
| Employees | 2.2% | — | — | — | 39,591 | 38,999 | 44,626 | 40,770 | 39,883 | 43,318 | 45,096 |

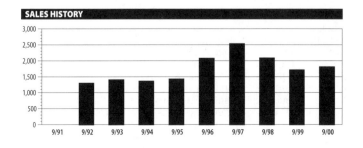

SALES HISTORY

# S&P COMPANY

## OVERVIEW

For those who consider Coors Light or Miller Genuine Draft too froufrou, consider the brands of S&P. Based in Mill Valley, California, S&P (no, not the financial service) owns a stable of nonpremium beer brands through its Pabst Brewing Company. Its brands include Pabst, Pearl, and Lone Star. The company added Old Milwaukee, Schlitz, and Colt 45 to its ice chest with its 1999 purchase of most of Stroh Brewery's brands. Once the #4 brewer in the US, Pabst has been battered by the stiff competition from Anheuser-Busch, Miller Brewing, and Adolph Coors.

The company shutdown its 115-year-old brewery in San Antonio, Texas, and its Pennsylvania plant and transferred the brewing of its brands to Miller. Pabst will continue to own the brands and market the products.

S&P's founder, Paul Kalmanovitz, traditionally bought past-their-prime breweries and rode the brands down, allocating few resources to advertising, brewery upgrades, or new products. Instead, S&P bought California real estate. S&P is owned by the Kalmanovitz Charitable Trust. Federal law requires the trust give up control of the company before June 2005.

## HISTORY

Born in Poland in 1905, Paul Kalmanovitz went to sea and jumped ship in Philadelphia in 1926. After moving to California, he worked as a handyman and driver for film magnate Louis B. Mayer and then bought an auto shop and a bar. During WWII, he and partner Nathan Sherry (the "S" in S&P) bought bars around Union Station in Los Angeles (a major transit point for troops). Kalmanovitz bought out Sherry and bought restaurants and nightclubs before buying his first brewery, bankrupt Maier Brewing Co., in 1958. In 1971 he bought (and then dismantled) General Brewing.

Falstaff Brewing caught his eye in 1975. Falstaff began in 1917 when Joseph Griesedieck bought Forest Park Brewing Company. Falstaff later acquired other breweries, including Fred Krug Brewery (1935), Narragansett (1966), and Ballantine (1972). Once S&P took control, it cut Falstaff's annual advertising budget from $2.6 million to $23,000 and later closed its breweries.

S&P bought the Pearl brewery in 1978. Pearl was founded in 1885 when several San Antonio businessmen bought City Brewery and began producing Pearl beer. The name was changed to Pearl Brewing Company in 1952, and in 1961 it acquired Goetz Brewing and its Country Club Malt Liquor and Goetz Pale Near Beer brands.

In a 1985 takeover, Kalmanovitz acquired Pabst, which had begun in 1844 when Jacob Best and his sons began making beer in Milwaukee as Best & Company. Pabst was the US's #1 beer through the turn of the century, with sales throughout the US, across Europe, and as far afield as China. By the 1970s Pabst was the US's #3 brewer. Its decline was attributed to its failure to introduce new brands. In 1983 Pabst acquired Olympia Brewing Co. (founded 1896).

Kalmanovitz plowed the profits of his eroding beer interests into real estate until he died in 1987. His wife, Lydia, died seven years later. After her death, relatives attempted to gain larger shares of the estate, charging, among other things, trustees of the Kalmanovitz's had influenced her to change her will and had kept her isolated.

Financial information obtained from court filings revealed that Pabst was losing money. S&P closed the antiquated Milwaukee plant in 1996 and farmed all Pabst production out to rival brewer Stroh, throwing about 400 Pabst workers out of their jobs. That year the company also stopped paying retirement benefits for more than 700 retirees. (After a class action suit, S&P agreed in 1998 to pay $66 million to a pension fund over the next 15 years.)

Meanwhile, members of the Kalmanovitz family appealed the dismissal of their challenge to Lydia's will. In 1999 S&P bought several beverage brands and a Pennsylvania brewery from Stroh in a $500 million deal that also involved Miller's purchase of Hamm's, Henry Weinhard's, Mickeys, and Olde English 800 from Pabst.

In 2000 plans were announced to close the landmark Pearl Brewery in San Antonio (operating since 1886). That year the Kalmanovitz Charitable Trust was awarded ownership of S&P, ending the battles with disgruntled relatives. However, federal law prohibits charitable foundations from owning active investments and the trust must sell the company before June 2005.

In March 2001 the company agreed to move production of the Pabst-owned brands to Miller Brewing's plants. Pabst's San Antonio brewery shut down in May 2001 and the Pennsylvania plant closed the following September.

## HISTORICAL FINANCIALS & EMPLOYEES

| Private<br>FYE: June 30 | Annual<br>Growth | 6/92 | 6/93 | 6/94 | 6/95 | 6/96 | 6/97 | 6/98 | 6/99 | 6/00 | 6/01 |
|---|---|---|---|---|---|---|---|---|---|---|---|
| Estimated sales ($ mil.) | 3.6% | 566 | 628 | 595 | 600 | 550 | 550 | 500 | 1,200 | 1,000 | 775 |
| Employees | (24.4%) | — | 2,800 | 2,400 | 1,300 | 1,604 | 1,600 | 1,500 | 700 | 750 | 300 |

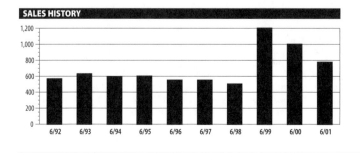

SALES HISTORY

# SAS INSTITUTE INC.

## OVERVIEW

SAS Institute answers SOS cries from companies drowning in data. The Cary, North Carolina-based company is the world's largest privately held software specialist, with 17,000 customers in 110 countries. SAS (pronounced "sass") leads the market in data warehousing and data mining software used by large corporations and government agencies to gather, manage, and analyze voluminous amounts of information stored on mainframes and databases. Clients such as Boeing, IBM, Merrill Lynch, and Pfizer use its software to find patterns in customer purchases, create mailing lists for repeat buyers, and target new business.

SAS also offers integrated software and support packages for specific industries with applications for financial reporting and consolidation, exploratory oil and gas analysis, and information technology systems management. Nearly half of its sales come from outside of North America.

Co-founder and CEO James Goodnight, one of the few billionaires who still spends most mornings churning software code, is looking to the Web for new growth in the data warehousing market. SAS is the industry leader in research and development, reinvesting 30% of its sales — more than double the average.

To help attract new employees, SAS is at long last contemplating a public offering. Instead of throwing money into marketing and recruiting, Goodnight's mission is to invest in the care and comfort of his workers. With perks including an on-site school, medical center (health care is complimentary), swimming pool, unlimited sick days, meditation room, putting green, and baseball field, SAS maintains an employee turnover rate of below 4% (the industry average is 20%).

Goodnight owns two-thirds of the company, and co-founder and EVP John Sall owns the remaining third.

## HISTORY

SAS Institute was started in 1976 by North Carolina State University professors James Goodnight and John Sall. The two had developed a mainframe statistical analysis system (SAS) for the US Department of Agriculture to analyze data around the state. Its popularity grew at other southern campuses, enabling the two professors to go out on their own.

The company began rewriting SAS System software in 1984 to make it independent of hardware systems. While rewriting the package in C language, it ran into a problem — none of the commercial C compilers supported the IBM 370 mainframe architecture. SAS Institute then began developing MultiVendor Architecture in C to enable the package to be hardware- and platform-independent.

SAS acquired Lattice Inc., a prominent maker of C language code translators, in 1986 to assist in the adaptation of SAS software to the PC environment. The next year the complete version of SAS System for the PC was released, and in 1988 the company unveiled systems for UNIX platforms.

In 1989 SAS released JMP software for the Apple Macintosh, developed a cooperative software program with IBM, and began offering consulting services. By 1990 the company had redesigned its SAS System software so it would be completely hardware-independent in the mainframe and minicomputer domains. SAS also introduced a new menu-driven, task-oriented interface to the SAS System that enabled access to those with limited computer experience.

The company released its first vertical market product for the pharmaceuticals and biotechnology industries in 1992, and the next year it introduced software for building customized executive information systems. By 1994 almost all the top 100 companies in the *FORTUNE* 500 had site license agreements for SAS software.

In 1997 SAS acquired Abacus Concepts' StatView software, a statistical analysis program for the life sciences market. It also teamed up with Hewlett-Packard to create the Data Insight and Discovery Center, a data mining lab for financial services firms seeking information about their customers.

In 1998 SAS formed an alliance with business and information technology consulting firm American Management Systems to offer customized data warehousing and decision support systems to their clients. In 2000 the company spun off its first subsidiary, iBiomatics, to help life sciences professionals share information about drug compounds over the Internet. As part of a push to go public, the company hired Andre Boisvert, its first president and COO.

A year later, however, Boisvert abruptly resigned; Goodnight reassumed his duties, raising questions about SAS's plans to go public. Also in 2001 the company re-absorbed iBiomatics.

**Chairman, President, and CEO:** James H. Goodnight
**EVP and Chief Administrative Officer:**
W. Greyson Quarles Jr.
**EVP:** John Sall
**SVP and Chief Technology Officer:** Keith V. Collins
**SVP, Business Development and Channel Operations:**
Graeme Woodley
**SVP, Chief Marketing Officer:** Jim Davis
**VP, Alliance Development:** Zul Abbany
**VP, Marketing, Europe:** Phil Winters
**VP, Professional Services:** Jay Finnigan
**VP, Public Sector Sales, SAS North America:**
Jeffrey C. Babcock
**VP, SAS Business Solutions Division:** Richard G. Roach
**VP, US Commercial Sales:** Kelly Ross
**President, SAS International:** Art Cooke
**Counsel to the President, Government Relations and**
**Public Policy:** Mary U. Musacchia
**Director, Clinical Software Research and Development:**
Andrew Fagan
**Director, Corporate Communications:** Betty Fried
**Director, Genomic and Discovery Software Research**
**and Development:** Russ Wolfinger
**Director, Human Resources:** Jeff Chambers
**Director, Market Intelligence:** John H. McIntyre
**Director, Pharmaceutical Practice, SAS North America:**
Angela Lightfoot

## LOCATIONS

**HQ:** SAS Campus Dr., Cary, NC 27513
**Phone:** 919-677-8000      **Fax:** 919-677-4444
**Web:** www.sas.com

SAS Institute has offices worldwide and customers in
110 countries.

**2000 Sales**

|  | % of total |
|---|---|
| The Americas | 52 |
| Europe, Middle East & Africa | 37 |
| Asia/Pacific & Latin America | 11 |
| **Total** | **100** |

## PRODUCTS/OPERATIONS

**2000 Sales**

|  | % of total |
|---|---|
| Finance & insurance | 25 |
| Government | 14 |
| Manufacturing | 14 |
| Sales & service | 13 |
| Telecommunications | 12 |
| Health care | 9 |
| Information technology services | 9 |
| Education | 4 |
| **Total** | **100** |

**Selected Applications**

| | |
|---|---|
| Application software development | Geographic reporting |
| Credit analysis | Human resources management |
| Customer relationship management | Information technology systems management |
| Data analysis | Management science |
| Database marketing | Market research |
| E-commerce | Portfolio analysis |
| Enterprise performance management | Process management |
| Enterprise resource planning system optimization | Project management |
| | Public sector |
| | Quality improvement |
| Experimental design | Resource optimization |
| Financial consolidation, reporting, and analysis | Risk management |
| Financial management | Statistical analysis |
| Forecasting | Supplier relationship management |

## COMPETITORS

| | | |
|---|---|---|
| Accrue Software | Hummingbird | PeopleSoft |
| Ascential Software | Hyperion Information | Progress Software |
| Brio Software | Builders | Sagent |
| Business Objects | IBM | Technology |
| Cognos | Microsoft | SAP |
| Computer Associates | MicroStrategy NetGenesis | Siebel Systems SPSS |
| E.piphany | Oracle | Sybase |

## HISTORICAL FINANCIALS & EMPLOYEES

| Private FYE: December 31 | Annual Growth | 12/91 | 12/92 | 12/93 | 12/94 | 12/95 | 12/96 | 12/97 | 12/98 | 12/99 | 12/00 |
|---|---|---|---|---|---|---|---|---|---|---|---|
| Sales ($ mil.) | 15.0% | — | 366 | 420 | 482 | 562 | 653 | 750 | 871 | 1,020 | 1,120 |
| Employees | 16.0% | — | 2,600 | 2,897 | 3,260 | 4,138 | 4,500 | 5,108 | 5,400 | 6,400 | 8,500 |

**SALES HISTORY**

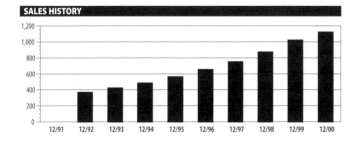

# S.C. JOHNSON & SON, INC.

OVERVIEW

The Karate Kid might use S.C. Johnson & Son's Pledge to wax on, wax off. The Racine, Wisconsin-based maker of household cleaning, insect control, personal care, and storage products has not stopped trying to polish off the competition. S.C. Johnson is one of the world's largest makers of consumer chemical specialty products: Glade air freshener, Pledge furniture polish, Windex cleaner, Shout stain remover, Ziploc baggies, Raid insecticide, and OFF! insect repellent are #1 in their market categories.

The company has operations in more than 65 countries.

S.C. Johnson's commercial products division (Johnson Wax Professional and Johnson Polymer) has been spun off as a private company owned by the Johnson family. Great-grandson of the company's founder and one of the richest people in the US, chairman emeritus Samuel Johnson and his immediate family own 60% of S.C. Johnson; descendants of the founder's daughter own almost 40%.

HISTORY

Samuel C. Johnson, a carpenter whose customers were as interested in his floor wax as in his parquet floors, founded S.C. Johnson in Racine, Wisconsin, in 1886. Forsaking carpentry, Johnson began to manufacture floor care products. The company, named S.C. Johnson & Son in 1906, began establishing subsidiaries worldwide in 1914. By the time Johnson's son and successor, Herbert Johnson, died in 1928, annual sales were $5 million. Herbert Jr. and his sister, Henrietta Lewis, received 60% and 40% of the firm, respectively. The original section of S.C. Johnson's headquarters, designed by Frank Lloyd Wright and called "the greatest piece of 20th-century architecture" in the US, was finished in 1939.

In 1954, with $45 million in annual sales, Herbert Jr.'s son Samuel Curtis Johnson joined the company as new products director. Two years later it introduced Raid, the first water-based insecticide, and soon thereafter, OFF! insect repellent. Each became a market leader. The company unsuccessfully attempted to diversify into paint, chemicals, and lawn care during the 1950s and 1960s. The home care products segment prospered, however, with the introduction of Pledge aerosol furniture polish and Glade aerosol air freshener.

After Herbert Jr. suffered a stroke in 1965, Samuel became president. In 1975 the firm banned the use of the chlorofluorocarbons (CFCs) in its products, three years before the US government banned CFCs. Samuel started a recreational products division that was bought by the Johnson family in 1986. That company went public in 1987 as Johnson Worldwide Associates, with the family retaining control.

The company launched Edge shaving gel and Agree hair products in the 1970s but had few products as successful in the 1980s. It moved into real estate with Johnson Wax Development (JWD) in the 1970s, but sold JWD's assets in the late 1980s.

S. Curtis Johnson, Samuel's son, joined the company in 1983. In 1986 S.C. Johnson bought Bugs Burger Bug Killers, moving into commercial pest control; in 1990 it entered into an agreement with Mycogen to develop biological pesticides for household use.

In 1993 it bought Drackett, bringing Drano and Windex to its product roster along with increased competition from heavyweights such as Procter & Gamble and Clorox. That year S.C. Johnson sold the Agree and Halsa lines to DEP. In 1996 it launched a line of water-soluble pouches for cleaning products that allow work to be done without touching hazardous chemicals. President William Perez became CEO the next year.

S.C. Johnson bought Dow Chemical's DowBrands unit, maker of bathroom cleaner (Dow), plastic bags (Ziploc), and plastic wrap (Saran Wrap), for $1.2 billion in 1998. It then sold off other Dow brands (cleaners Spray 'N Wash, Glass Plus, Yes, and Vivid) to the UK's Reckitt & Colman to settle antitrust issues.

A year later S.C. Johnson sold its skin care line, including Aveeno, to health care products maker Johnson & Johnson, and spun off its commercial products unit as a private firm owned by the Johnson family. Boosting its home cleaning line, in 1999 it introduced two new products: AllerCare (for dust mite control) and Pledge Grab-It (electrostatically charged cleaning sheets).

In 2000 S.C. Johnson pulled its AllerCare carpet powder and allergen spray from store shelves after some consumers had negative reactions to the fragrance additive in the products. That year H. Fisk Johnson succeeded his father (who became chairman emeritus) as chairman.

In 2001 the company was fined $950,000 for selling banned Raid Max Roach Bait traps in New York after agreeing to pull them from store shelves.

**Chairman Emeritus:** Samuel C. Johnson, age 73
**Chairman:** Herbert F. Johnson, age 43
**President and CEO:** William D. Perez, age 53
**President Asia Pacific:** Joseph T. Mallof, age 50
**President North America:** David L. May
**President Europe, Africa, and Near East:**
Steven P. Stanbrook
**EVP Americas:** Pedro Cleza
**SVP General Counsel and Secretary:** David Hecker
**SVP Worldwide Corporate Affairs:** Jane M. Hutterly
**SVP Worldwide Human Resources:** Gayle P. Kosterman
**SVP and CFO:** W. Lee McCollum, age 52
**SVP Worldwide Manufacturing and Procurement:**
Nico J. Meiland
**VP Human Resources, North America:**
Wesley A. Coleman
**VP Enterprise Resource Planning:** David C. Henry
**VP and Chief Information Officer:** Daniel E. Horton
**VP Corporate Treasurer:** William H. Van Lopik
**VP Corporate Controller:** Jeffrey M. Waller

# LOCATIONS

**HQ:** 1525 Howe St., Racine, WI 53403
**Phone:** 262-260-2000     **Fax:** 262-260-6004
**Web:** www.scjohnson.com

S.C. Johnson & Son has operations in 65 countries
worldwide.

# PRODUCTS/OPERATIONS

**Selected Products and Brands**

**Air Care**
Air freshener (Glade)
Pillow and mattress covers (AllerCare)

**Home Cleaning**
Bathroom/drain (Drano, Scrubbing Bubbles, Vanish,
Dow)
Cleaners (Fantastik, Windex)
Floor care (Pledge, Pledge Grab-It, Johnson)
Furniture care (Pledge)
Laundry/carpet care (Shout)

**Home Storage**
Plastic bags (Ziploc)
Plastic wrap (Handi-Wrap, Saran Wrap)

**Insect Control**
Insecticides (Raid, Raid Max)
Repellents (Deep Woods OFF!, OFF!, OFF! Skintastic)

**Personal Care**
Men's grooming (Edge)
Women's shaving (Skintimate)

# COMPETITORS

| | |
|---|---|
| Alticor | Lilly Industries |
| Blyth, Inc. | 3M |
| Church & Dwight | Pactiv |
| Clorox | Procter & Gamble |
| Colgate-Palmolive | Reckitt Benckiser |
| Dial | Shaklee |
| DuPont | Unilever |
| Gillette | United Industries |
| IWP International | Yankee Candle |

# HISTORICAL FINANCIALS & EMPLOYEES

| Private<br>FYE: Friday nearest June 30 | Annual<br>Growth | 6/92 | 6/93 | 6/94 | 6/95 | 6/96 | 6/97 | 6/98 | 6/99 | 6/00 | 6/01 |
|---|---|---|---|---|---|---|---|---|---|---|---|
| Estimated sales ($ mil.) | 3.5% | 3,300 | 3,550 | 3,800 | 4,000 | 4,000 | 4,300 | 5,000 | 4,200 | 4,200 | 4,500 |
| Employees | (3.7%) | 13,400 | 13,100 | 13,100 | 13,400 | 12,100 | 12,500 | 13,200 | 9,500 | 9,500 | 9,500 |

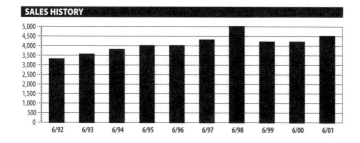

SALES HISTORY

# SCHNEIDER NATIONAL, INC.

OVERVIEW

Big trucks are wheeling hefty sales for Schneider National, the US's largest truckload carrier. Hauling out of Green Bay, Wisconsin, Schneider National transports customers' cargo from the Shaky Side (trucker slang for the West Coast) to the Dirty Side (the East Coast). The Schneider Van division is the most recognizable of the groups, with 14,000 bright-orange trucks and more than 40,000 trailers providing one-way, long-haul, single-load trucking throughout Canada, parts of Mexico, and the US.

The Schneider Dedicated Operations unit supplies customers with their own personal Schneider fleets, including trucks, trailers, and drivers. Other divisions include Schneider Bulk (liquid chemical transport), Schneider Specialized (trailers and hauling services for unique shipments), and Schneider TruckRail (containers and trailers designed for use on rail or over

the road). The company also acts as a middle-man through Schneider Brokerage, which finds carriers for shippers, and Schneider Finance, which sells and leases truck equipment.

Schneider National also rides the information superhighway. Its Logistics subsidiary cuts shipping costs of large US and European customers by finding efficient ways to use their supply chains, shipping routes, and carriers. The unit, which works with carriers in all modes of transportation, offers a real-time cargo tracking system with customer access over the Internet.

Schneider National has set the industry standard with satellite-tracking systems on board trucks and is adding tracking systems to its trailer fleet as well. Hard-driving owner and CEO Donald Schneider, son of the company founder, has kept the largely nonunionized Schneider National in the hammer lane.

HISTORY

A. J. "Al" Schneider bought a truck in 1935 with money earned from selling the family car. He drove the truck for three years, got another, and then leased them both to another firm. Becoming general manager of Bins Transfer & Storage in 1938, Schneider bought the company that year and changed the name to Schneider Transport & Storage. In 1944 Schneider stopped storing household goods and continued as an intrastate carrier in Wisconsin through the 1950s, transporting food and household goods. The Interstate Commerce Commission granted its first interstate license to Schneider in 1958.

Al's son Donald joined the company as general manager in 1961, and in 1962 the company dropped "Storage" from its name to become Schneider Transport. The 1960s also saw the first of many acquisitions. Donald became CEO in 1973, overseeing more acquisitions and the creation of Schneider National as a holding company for the organization. Donald also saw to the installation of computerized control systems, the first of many technical innovations Schneider would use in its trucks.

With the Motor Carrier Act's passage in 1980, restrictions eased and interstate shipping opened up. Schneider (and its competitors) saw the sky as the limit and founded Schneider Communications, a long-distance provider, in 1982. Eager to escape the Teamsters' thrall but choosing not to go head-to-head with the powerful union, Schneider formed Schneider National Carriers as a

nonunion company out of three 1985 acquisitions, which signed on new recruits, while Schneider Transport remained unionized. The company focused on guaranteeing on-time delivery in the deregulated market: In 1988 Schneider became the first trucking company to install a satellite-tracking system in its trucks, setting the industry standard.

Schneider further expanded its services in the 1990s, starting with Schneider Specialized Services for carrying difficult items. It moved into Canada and Mexico in 1991. In 1993 the company formed Schneider Logistics to help companies streamline their shipping operations. It sold Schneider Communications to Frontier Communications in 1995. The company moved into Europe in 1997.

It continued buying other US trucking firms, including Landstar Poole and Builder's Transport (both in 1998), mainly to acquire their drivers for its expanding fleet. In 1999 Schneider acquired the glass-transportation business of A. J. Metler & Rigging.

In 2000 Schneider acquired the freight payment services of Tranzact Systems and further boosted its e-commerce offerings through alliances with ContractorHub.com and Paperloop.com. The company also made plans to spin off Schneider Logistics and sell part of it to the public, but unfavorable market conditions put the IPO on hold. Schneider added expedited services to its portfolio in 2001 to provide time-definite delivery in Canada, Mexico, and the US.

**President and CEO:** Donald J. Schneider
**COO:** Christopher B. Lofgren
**CFO:** Tom Gannon
**VP Human Resources:** Tim Fliss

## LOCATIONS

**HQ:** 3101 S. Packerland Dr., Green Bay, WI 54306
**Phone:** 920-592-2000          **Fax:** 920-592-3063
**Web:** www.schneider.com

Schneider National has operations throughout Canada, parts of Mexico, and the US. Its Schneider Logistics subsidiary has operations throughout North America and Europe. The company's major operating centers in North America are located in Akron, Ohio; Charlotte, North Carolina; Chicago; Dallas; Des Moines, Iowa; Evergreen, Alabama; Green Bay, Wisconsin; Harrisburg, Pennsylvania; Indianapolis; Los Angeles; Memphis; Portland, Oregon; and Toronto.

## PRODUCTS/OPERATIONS

**Selected Transportation Units**
Schneider Brokerage (dry van/refrigerated and flatbed/open equipment brokerage)
Schneider Bulk (liquid chemical transport services)
Schneider Dedicated Operations (carrier management and coordination)
Schneider Optimodal (rail-based containers and trailers)
Schneider Specialized (open equipment service)
Schneider TruckRail (intermodal container service)
Schneider Van (one-way truckload service)

## COMPETITORS

Burlington Northern Santa Fe
Cannon Express
Celadon
CHR
CSX
J. B. Hunt
Landstar System
Norfolk Southern
Roadway
Ryder
Swift Transportation
Union Pacific
Werner

## HISTORICAL FINANCIALS & EMPLOYEES

| Private<br>FYE: December 31 | Annual<br>Growth | 12/91 | 12/92 | 12/93 | 12/94 | 12/95 | 12/96 | 12/97 | 12/98 | 12/99 | 12/00 |
|---|---|---|---|---|---|---|---|---|---|---|---|
| Sales ($ mil.) | 14.2% | — | 1,066 | 1,175 | 1,325 | 1,700 | 2,156 | 2,510 | 2,711 | 3,000 | 3,089 |
| Employees | 5.8% | — | 12,000 | 13,950 | 15,300 | 15,500 | 17,550 | 16,500 | 17,000 | 19,000 | 18,775 |

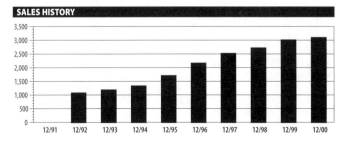

SALES HISTORY

# SCHWAN'S SALES ENTERPRISES

## OVERVIEW

With a fleet of unintentionally retro-hip freezer trucks, Schwan's Sales Enterprises is definitely cool. The Marshall, Minnesota-based company maintains a home delivery system that brings more than 300 frozen food products directly to customers in 48 mainland states. Orders can include bagels, casseroles, enchiladas, stir fry, or wraps, but it's Schwan's ice cream that has a devoted following.

Schwan's is also the #2 US frozen pizza maker behind Kraft Foods. It sells the Tony's, Red Baron, and Freschetta frozen pizza brands in grocery stores. The company sells Chicago Town pizza in western Europe and supplies schools and other institutional cafeterias with frozen pizza and sandwiches.

The secretive family of late founder Marvin Schwan (who gave no interviews after 1982) owns Schwan's. Marvin's children settled a 1995 lawsuit filed against their uncle, Alfred Schwan, and a friend of their father's for mismanagement of the estate in 1997. Details of the settlement were not made public.

## HISTORY

Paul Schwan bought out his partner in their dairy in 1948 and began manufacturing ice cream using his own recipes. His son, Marvin Schwan, made deliveries for the dairy for a few years. After attending a two-year college, Marvin came back in 1950 to work at the dairy full-time. Two years later he began using his delivery experience to take advantage of the increase in homes with freezers. He bought an old truck for $100 and began a rural route selling ice cream to farmers. He quickly developed a loyal customer base and expanded to two routes the following year.

In the 1960s the company diversified with two acquisitions: a prepared sandwich company and a condensed fruit juice company. A new holding company, Schwan's Sales Enterprises, was established in 1964. Schwan's began delivering pizza the next year. Paul died in 1969.

Deciding that frozen pizza was not a fad, Marvin bought Kansas-based Tony's Pizza in 1970 and quickly rose to the top of the new industry. In the late 1970s Schwan's entered the commercial leasing business, and it later added more leasing companies under the Lyon Financial Services umbrella.

The company entered the institutional pizza market in the mid-1980s and edged out competitors Sabatasso Foods and Better Baked Pizza. Schools liked Schwan's use of their government surplus cheese to make pizzas, which the company then sold to the schools at a discount.

In 1992 the company bought two Minnesota-based food companies: Panzerotti, a stuffed pastry business, and Monthly Market, a specialty retailer that sells groceries to fund-raising groups. It also began selling its pizzas in the UK. The next year Schwan's bought Chicago Brothers Frozen Pizza, a San Diego-based company specializing in deep-dish pizza.

Marvin died of a heart attack in 1993 at age 64, with his worth estimated at more than $1 billion. The previous year he had willed two-thirds of the company's stock to a charitable Lutheran trust, which was to be bought out by Schwan's after his death. In 1994 his brother, Arthur, and Marvin's friend Lawrence Burgdorf made arrangements to have the company repurchase the foundation's shares for a total of $1.8 billion. But Marvin's four children filed a lawsuit in 1995 against their uncle and Burgdorf over the action. They claimed the men did not have the financial health of the company at heart and were divided in their loyalty. The children, on the other hand, were called money-hungry and callous to their father's last wishes. (The case was settled in 1997 but no information was released.)

A rash of salmonella poisoning was linked to the company's ice-cream products in 1994. (An investigation revealed the contamination came from leased trucks.) Two years later the company introduced Freschetta, its version of a rising-crust style of pizza, to compete with Kraft Food's fast-selling DiGiorno pizza.

Lenny Pippin became the company's fourth CEO in 1999, replacing Alfred, who remained on as chairman. Schwan's exited the Canadian market at the end of 1999 due to perennial losses. In 2000 Schwan's introduced irradiated frozen ground beef patties and struck an agreement with another company to electronically pasteurize some of its products. Also that year it sold its Lyon Financial Services subsidiary, which leases equipment and provides financial management. Schwan's also sold the assets and trademarks of its Chicago Brothers food operations in 2000.

In mid-2001 Schwan's expanded its offerings by acquiring frozen dessert maker Edwards Fine Foods from private equity firm Ripplewood Holdings.

**Chairman:** Alfred Schwan
**President and CEO:** M. Lenny Pippin, age 53
**VP Finance:** Don Miller
**VP Human Resources:** Dave Paskach

## LOCATIONS

**HQ:** Schwan's Sales Enterprises, Inc.
115 W. College Dr., Marshall, MN 56258
**Phone:** 507-532-3274        **Fax:** 507-537-8226
**Web:** www.schwans.com

Schwan's Sales Enterprises has manufacturing facilities in the US and in Europe; its products are sold in the 48 contiguous states and western Europe.

## PRODUCTS/OPERATIONS

**Selected Products**
Casseroles
Desserts
Entrees
Ice cream
Pizza (Chicago Town, Freschetta, Red Baron, Tony's)
Sandwiches
Stir Fry
Wraps

**Selected Subsidiaries and Operations**
Orion Food Systems
Schwan's Food Service
SSE Manufacturing

## COMPETITORS

| | |
|---|---|
| Aurora Foods | Little Caesar |
| Celentano Brothers | Nation Pizza Products |
| ConAgra | Nestlé |
| Domino's Pizza | Papa John's |
| Dreyer's | SYSCO |
| Kraft Foods | TRICON |

## HISTORICAL FINANCIALS & EMPLOYEES

| Private<br>FYE: December 31 | Annual<br>Growth | 12/91 | 12/92 | 12/93 | 12/94 | 12/95 | 12/96 | 12/97 | 12/98 | 12/99 | 12/00 |
|---|---|---|---|---|---|---|---|---|---|---|---|
| Estimated sales ($ mil.) | 7.2% | — | 1,780 | 2,100 | 2,200 | 2,350 | 2,500 | 2,900 | 2,875 | 3,350 | 3,100 |
| Employees | 0.0% | — | — | 6,000 | 6,000 | 6,000 | 6,000 | 6,000 | 6,000 | 6,000 | 6,000 |

### SALES HISTORY

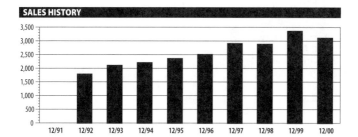

# SCIENCE APPLICATIONS

Good things happen when you apply yourself. San Diego-based Science Applications International Corporation (SAIC) is a leading provider of systems integration, engineering, and R&D services to the US government (which accounts for about 55% of sales), including the Defense Department and NASA. A growing percentage of sales, however, comes from services including software installation and plant automation services for telecommunications, health care, and oil and gas companies. SAIC also has its hands in undersea data collection, space systems engineering, and national security projects. Its billion-dollar Telcordia Technologies subsidiary, formerly the Bellcore research unit of the Baby Bells, supplies networking and operations software to telecoms such as Sprint.

SAIC has transformed itself from a defense contractor with few peers into a highly respected engineering firm and the largest employee-owned tech company in the US. Employees own about 80% of SAIC. Founder, chairman, and CEO Robert Beyster (who has guided the company to record revenues for each of the last 32 years) asserts that employee ownership has been key to the company's success, and has shown little interest (or need) in pursuing in IPO; the company last received outside funding in 1970, when it received $200,000 from private investors.

## HISTORY

Physicist Robert Beyster, who worked at Los Alamos National Laboratory in the 1950s, was hired by General Atomic in 1957 to establish and manage its traveling wave linear accelerator. When the company was sold to Gulf Oil in 1968, research priorities changed and Beyster left. He founded Science Applications Inc. (SAI) the following year and built his business from consulting contracts with Los Alamos and Brookhaven National Laboratories.

During the first year Beyster instituted an employee ownership plan that rewarded workers that brought onboard new business with stock in SAI. Beyster's idea was to share the success of SAI and to raise capital.

In 1970 the company established an office in Washington, DC, to court government contracts. Despite a recession, SAI continued to grow during the 1970s, and by 1979 sales topped $100 million. The following year SAI restructured, becoming a subsidiary of Science Applications International Corporation (SAIC), a new holding company.

During the 1980s defense buildup, an emphasis on high-tech weaponry and SAI's high-level Pentagon connections (directors have included former defense secretaries William Perry and Melvin Laird and former CIA director John Deutch) brought in contracts for submarine warfare systems and technical development for the Strategic Defense Initiative ("Star Wars").

As defense spending slowed with the end of the Cold War, SAIC began casting a wider net. By 1991 computer systems integration and consulting accounted for 25% of sales, which surpassed the $1 billion mark.

SAIC made several purchases during the mid-1990s, including transportation communications firm Syntonic, Internet domain name registrar Network Solutions, Inc. (NSI), and government think tank Aerospace Corp. In 1997 SAIC acquired Bellcore (the research lab of the regional Bells, now Telcordia Technologies), and reduced its stake in NSI through a public offering. SAIC formed several alliances in 1998, including a joint venture with Rolls-Royce to service the aerospace, energy, and defense industries.

The next year SAIC expanded its information technology (IT) expertise with the acquisition of Boeing's Information Services unit. It also acquired the call center software operations of Elite Information Group. SAIC in 2000 realized a significant gain on its $5 million purchase of NSI when e-commerce software maker VeriSign bought the minority-owned (23%) subsidiary for $17 billion.

In 2001 SAIC signed a variety of large contracts, including an outsourcing agreement with BP to manage that company's North American application and hosting services, as well as a $3 billion deal to provide support (in conjunction with Bechtel Group) for the Department of Energy's civilian radioactive waste management program.

## OFFICERS

**Chairman, President, and CEO:** J. Robert Beyster, age 76
**EVP and CFO:** Thomas E. Darcy, age 50
**EVP and Secretary:** J. Dennis Heipt, age 57
**EVP, Federal Business and Director:** Duane P. Andrews, age 56
**EVP, Strategic Initiatives and Director:** J. P. Walkush, age 48
**EVP, Systems Integration and Director:** John H. Warner Jr., age 60
**EVP and Director:** John E. Glancy, age 54
**EVP and Director:** S. D. Rockwood, age 57
**EVP:** D. H. Foley, age 56
**EVP:** R. A. Rosenberg, age 66
**EVP:** William A. Roper Jr., age 55
**EVP:** A. L. Slotkin, age 54
**SVP and Controller:** P. N. Pavlics, age 40
**SVP and General Counsel:** D. E. Scott, age 44
**SVP, Health Solutions Group:** Michael A. Mark
**SVP, Human Resources:** Bernard Theull
**VP and Treasurer:** Steven P. Fisher, age 40
**CEO, Telcordia Technologies and Director:** Richard C. Smith, age 59
**Deputy Director, Aerospace Center:** Phillip S. Meilinger
**Auditors:** Deloitte & Touche LLP

## LOCATIONS

**HQ:** Science Applications International Corporation
10260 Campus Point Dr., San Diego, CA 92121
**Phone:** 858-546-6000 **Fax:** 858-546-6800
**Web:** www.saic.com

Science Applications International has offices in more than 150 cities worldwide.

### 2001 Sales

|  | $ mil. | % of total |
|---|---|---|
| US | 5,456 | 93 |
| Venezuela | 302 | 5 |
| UK | 125 | 2 |
| Other countries | 13 | — |
| **Total** | **5,896** | **100** |

## PRODUCTS/OPERATIONS

**Selected Services**

**Energy**
Information systems
Plant monitoring systems
Project management
Quality assurance
Reliability engineering evaluations
Safety evaluations
Security
Technical reviews

**Environmental**
Feasibility studies
Monitoring
Regulatory compliance support and training
Remedial actions and investigations
Sampling
Site assessments
Technology evaluations

**Health**
Medical information systems
Research support
Technology development

**Information Technology**
Information protection and e-business security

Intranet consulting and network design
Outsourcing

**National Security**
Advanced research
Management support
Operational support
Systems engineering and integration
Technical support
Technology development

**Telecommunications**
Consulting and engineering
Network design and implementation
Software development and enhancements

**Other Services**
Automated toll collection
Computer and information security
Material control
NASA engineering support
Undersea data collection, transmission, and analysis

## COMPETITORS

Accenture
American Management
CACI International
Cap Gemini
Computer Sciences
DynCorp
EDS
GRC International
IBM
Keane
PRC
QinetiQ
SRI International
Titan
Unisys

## HISTORICAL FINANCIALS & EMPLOYEES

| Private<br>FYE: January 31 | Annual<br>Growth | 1/92 | 1/93 | 1/94 | 1/95 | 1/96 | 1/97 | 1/98 | 1/99 | 1/00 | 1/01 |
|---|---|---|---|---|---|---|---|---|---|---|---|
| Sales ($ mil.) | 18.4% | 1,285 | 1,504 | 1,671 | 1,922 | 2,156 | 2,402 | 3,089 | 4,740 | 5,530 | 5,896 |
| Net income ($ mil.) | 58.0% | 34 | 38 | 42 | 49 | 57 | 64 | 85 | 151 | 620 | 2,059 |
| Income as % of sales | — | 2.6% | 2.5% | 2.5% | 2.6% | 2.7% | 2.7% | 2.7% | 3.2% | 11.2% | 34.9% |
| Employees | 13.3% | 13,510 | 15,839 | 17,800 | 20,500 | 21,100 | 22,600 | 30,300 | 35,200 | 39,078 | 41,500 |

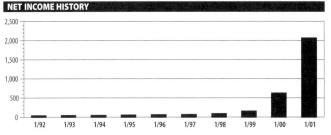

### NET INCOME HISTORY

### 2001 FISCAL YEAR-END
Debt ratio: 3.4%
Return on equity: —
Cash ($ mil.): 644
Current ratio: 1.63
Long-term debt ($ mil.): 119

# SEAGATE TECHNOLOGY, INC.

OVERVIEW

Seagate Technology markets the drives and drives the market. The Scotts Valley, California-based company is a leading independent maker of storage drives for computers. It makes disk drives and tape drives for everything from PCs to large-scale computer networks. Seagate sells its products mainly to manufacturers. Its Crystal Decisions subsidiary (formerly Seagate Software) offers business intelligence software.

In an industry niche that has been hurt by falling prices in the PC market, Seagate has managed to stay at the front of the disk drive provider line by significantly undercutting competitors' disk drive prices, instituting global lay-off initiatives, and consolidating facilities to cut costs. The company continues to position itself as a provider of all technologies that store, retrieve, and manage information. Its acquisition of XIOtech gave the company a foothold in the storage area networking market.

## HISTORY

Seagate Technology was founded in 1979 by Alan Shugart, an 18-year veteran of IBM who had made floppy disks standard on microcomputers; manufacturing expert and longtime technology industry veteran Tom Mitchell; design engineer Douglas Mahon; and Finis Conner. Seagate pioneered the miniaturizing of larger mainframe hard disk drives for PCs.

Seagate's first product, a 5.25-in. hard disk, sold briskly. With IBM as a customer, the company had grabbed half of the market for small disk drives by 1982; sales reached $344 million by 1984. But Seagate's heavy dependence on IBM showed its double edge as dwindling PC demand prompted IBM to cut orders. Sales in 1985 dropped to $215 million and profits to $1 million (from $42 million). Seagate transferred its manufacturing to Singapore and cut its California workforce in half. That year Conner, after a quarrel with Shugart, left Seagate to start his own disk drive company, Conner Peripherals (Mitchell later joined him).

Using acquisitions to grow, the company purchased Grenex (thin-film magnetic media, 1984), Aeon (aluminum substrates, 1987), and Integrated Power Systems (custom semiconductors, 1987). Seagate also lured back IBM, which had turned to an alternate supplier in the interim.

With sales more than doubling in 1986 and again in 1987, Seagate continued to invest in 5.25-in. production, ignoring signs of a coming 3.5-in. drive standard. The strong market in 1988 for the smaller drives prompted the company's quick shift to 3.5-in. production. Seagate's purchase of Imprimis in 1989 made it the world's premier independent drive maker and a leader in high-capacity drives.

In 1993 the company acquired a stake in flash memory storage specialist SunDisk. That year, when Sun Microsystems accounted for 11% of sales, Seagate was the only profitable independent disk drive company. In 1994 it began pursuing its software initiative, acquiring companies including Palindrome and Crystal Computer Services.

Shugart, an iconoclast who once ran his dog for Congress, had a small comeuppance in 1996 when Seagate paid just over $1 billion for Conner Peripherals, which had banked on 3.5-in. disk drives from the start and had gone public in 1988. By the time of the acquisition, Conner was a leading maker of disk and tape drives, storage systems, and software.

Seagate merged Conner's software subsidiary with its own holdings to form Seagate Storage Management Group, and continued to expand by buying management software companies.

An industry slump, production problems, and lowered PC demand prompted Seagate to cut 20% of its workforce, streamline development, fire Shugart, and replace him with president and COO — and former investment banker — Stephen Luczo. The downturn took its toll when the company suffered a $530 million loss for fiscal 1998. The next year Seagate gained a stake of about 33% in VERITAS Software when it sold its network and storage management software operations to that company for $3.1 billion. Seagate also announced that it would lay off another 10% of its workforce of nearly 80,000.

In early 2000 the company acquired XIOtech, which makes virtual storage and storage area network systems. Later that year Seagate entered into an intricate deal with VERITAS, whereby the software maker bought back the stake owned by Seagate. As part of the deal, Seagate was taken private in a buyout led by Silver Lake Partners and Texas Pacific Group.

Also in 2000, COO William Watkins, who joined Seagate when it bought Conner Peripherals, replaced Luczo as president; Luczo remained CEO. The following year the company renamed its Seagate Software division Crystal Decisions.

CEO: Stephen J. Luczo
President and COO: William D. Watkins
EVP and Chief Administrative Officer: Donald L. Waite
EVP and Chief Technology Officer:
Townsend H. Porter Jr.
EVP, Business and Corporate Development:
Jeremy Tennenbaum
EVP, Finance and CFO: Charles C. Pope
EVP, Global Disc Storage Operations:
David Wickersham, age 44
EVP, Global Sales, Marketing, Product Line
Management, and Customer Service Operations:
Brian S. Dexheimer
Research Director: Mark Kryder
Auditors: Ernst & Young LLP

## LOCATIONS

HQ: 920 Disc Dr., Scotts Valley, CA 95067
Phone: 831-438-6550       Fax: 831-438-7205
Web: www.seagate.com

Seagate Technology has sales offices in Australia, France, Germany, Hong Kong, Ireland, Japan, the Netherlands, Singapore, Sweden, Taiwan, the UK, and the US.

## PRODUCTS/OPERATIONS

Selected Products
Disk drives
   Desktop (Barracuda)
   Server/multiuser and workstation systems
      (Barracuda, Cheetah)
Network storage systems
   Network attached storage devices (NASRaQ)
   Storage area network systems (XIOtech)
Query and report writing and analysis software (Crystal
   Decisions)
Tape drives
   DAT (Scorpion)
   Linear Tape Open (Viper)
   Travan (Hornet)

## COMPETITORS

| | |
|---|---|
| Compaq | Maxtor |
| EMC | NEC |
| Exabyte | Network Appliance |
| Fujitsu | Overland Data |
| Hewlett-Packard | Samsung |
| Hitachi | StorageTek |
| Imation | Toshiba |
| IBM | Western Digital |
| Iomega | |

## HISTORICAL FINANCIALS & EMPLOYEES

| Private<br>FYE: Friday nearest June 30 | Annual<br>Growth | 6/91 | 6/92 | 6/93 | 6/94 | 6/95 | 6/96 | 6/97 | 6/98 | 6/99 | 6/00 |
|---|---|---|---|---|---|---|---|---|---|---|---|
| Sales ($ mil.) | 10.6% | — | 2,875 | 3,044 | 3,500 | 4,540 | 8,588 | 8,940 | 6,819 | 6,802 | 6,448 |
| Net income ($ mil.) | 22.0% | — | 63 | 195 | 225 | 260 | 213 | 658 | (530) | 1,176 | 310 |
| Income as % of sales | — | — | 2.2% | 6.4% | 6.4% | 5.7% | 2.5% | 7.4% | — | 17.3% | 4.8% |
| Employees | 4.6% | — | 42,000 | 43,000 | 43,000 | 53,000 | 65,000 | 111,000 | 87,000 | 82,000 | 60,000 |

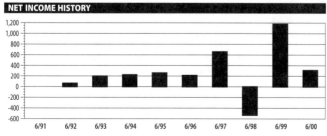

NET INCOME HISTORY

2000 FISCAL YEAR-END
Debt ratio: 15.5%
Return on equity: 8.4%
Cash ($ mil.): 875
Current ratio: 2.37
Long-term debt ($ mil.): 703

# SEALY CORPORATION

## OVERVIEW

Sealy is a slumbering giant. The Trinity, North Carolina-based company is North America's #1 maker of bedding products. Its mattresses and box springs are sold under such leading brand names as Sealy, Stearns & Foster, and Barrett. These are sold through more than 7,000 retail outlets, including sleep shops, furniture stores, mass merchandisers, and department stores, as well as to the hospitality industry. It also licenses the Sealy name to makers of other bedding products (pads, pillows) and home furnishings (sofas, futons).

Most of Sealy's sales come from the US, but its products also are sold abroad. The company is making acquisitions and building plants to expand its business in Latin America. Like rivals Serta and Simmons, Sealy is privately owned. Boston-based investment firm Bain Capital, which controls bedding retailers Mattress Discounters and Sleep Country Canada, and Sealy management own the company.

## HISTORY

Daniel Haynes, a cotton gin builder, first made a new, more resilient type of cotton-filled mattress in 1881 in Sealy, Texas. In 1889 he patented a machine to mass-produce his increasingly popular product. Haynes sold manufacturing rights to firms in other cities, and in 1906 he sold his patents to a Texas firm that renamed itself Sealy.

Sealy expanded by advertising in national magazines and finding licensees to open mattress factories. By 1920 the company had 28 licensed plants. When doctors in the 1940s advised that people with back problems sleep on firm mattresses, Sealy designed the Orthopedic Firm-O-Rest; it was renamed the Posturepedic in 1950 after the FTC banned the use of the medical term "orthopedic" in brand names.

In the 1950s Sealy sprung out geographically (it added Canadian licensees in 1954) and financially (sales quintupled to $48 million during the decade). During the 1960s it became the first mattress firm to advertise on prime-time TV.

The princess had her uncomfortable pea; Sealy had The Ohio Mattress Company, one of its independent licensees. In the 1950s Ohio Mattress began entering other licensees' territories (despite exclusive territory agreements) and lowering its prices to force its new rivals to sell out. In 1963 Ernest Wuliger succeeded his father as president of Ohio Mattress and began an aggressive expansion campaign. He acquired a Sealy licensee in Texas and Oklahoma in 1967, but Sealy bought some of the licensees that Wuliger wanted. The Supreme Court found Sealy guilty that year of antitrust violations regarding price-fixing and exclusive territories. Still, by the end of the 1960s, Sealy had sales of $113 million and additional international licensees.

Wuliger took Ohio Mattress public in 1970. The next year Wuliger began a series of

antitrust lawsuits against Sealy that lasted fifteen years. Ohio Mattress acquired bedding maker Stearns & Foster (1983) and Woodstuff Manufacturing (1985). In 1986 the legal bedding battle ended, and Ohio Mattress was awarded $77 million. Instead, in 1987 Ohio Mattress opted to buy Sealy and all but one of Sealy's nine US licensees. It acquired the holdout licensee's Sealy license later in 1987 and became the leading mattress manufacturer.

Investment firm Gibbons Goodwin van Amerongen led a $965 million, junk-bond-financed LBO of Ohio Mattress in 1989; it renamed the company Sealy in 1990. Amid a downturn in the junk-bond market, from 1991 to 1993 Sealy changed owners twice, ending up with investment fund Zell/Chilmark. It also found itself in bed with a variety of new CEOs. Right after the LBO, Wuliger — and many of Wuliger's top managers — resigned due to conflicts with the new owners. COO Malcolm Candlish was promoted to CEO. Candlish resigned in 1992, citing disagreements with new directors, and was replaced by Lyman Beggs, who lasted until 1995, when he was replaced by Ronald Jones, former head of Masco Home Furnishings.

In 1997 investment firm Bain Capital bought a majority stake in Sealy. The company relocated from Ohio to North Carolina the next year. Sealy lost $34 million in fiscal 1998 in part due to early debt repayment related to the Bain Capital buyout.

In 2000 Sealy acquired the Bassett bedding license and Carrington-Chase brand from Premier Bedding. Sealy also bought control of Argentina-based bedding maker Rosen and built a factory in Brazil. The following year Sealy announced it would close its Tennessee bedding plant because it wasn't profitable. Marking its entrance into Europe, Sealy agreed to acquire Paris-based Sapsa Bedding in March 2001.

**Chairman and CEO:** Ronald L. Jones, age 58,
$1,641,569 pay

**President and COO:** David J. McIlquham, age 46,
$428,816 pay (prior to promotion)

**Corporate VP and General Manager Domestic Bedding:**
Douglas E. Fellmy, age 51, $395,056 pay

**Corporate VP and General Manager International:**
Lawrence J. Rogers, age 52, $398,385 pay

**Corporate VP Administration and CFO:** E. Lee Wyatt,
age 48

**Corporate VP, General Counsel, and Secretary:**
Kenneth L. Walker, age 52

**Corporate VP Human Resources:** Jeffrey C. Claypool,
age 53

**Corporate VP Marketing:** Mark Hobson

**Corporate VP National Accounts:** Chuck Dawson

**Corporate VP Research and Development:**
Bruce G. Barman, age 55

**Corporate VP Sales:** Al Boulden

**Corporate VP Technology, Quality and Maufacturing
Engineering:** James F. Goughenour

**VP Operations, East Region:** Dan Hige

**VP Operations, West Region:** Kevin Hogan

## LOCATIONS

**HQ:** Sealy Drive 1 Office Pkwy., Trinity, NC 27370
**Phone:** 336-861-3500      **Fax:** 336-861-3501
**Web:** www.sealy.com

Sealy has more than 30 manufacturing facilities in
Argentina, Brazil, Canada, Mexico, Puerto Rico, and the
US. It has licensees in Australia, Israel, Jamaica, Japan,
New Zealand, South Africa, Thailand, and the UK.

## PRODUCTS/OPERATIONS

**Brand Names**
Bassett
Bed Time
Carrington-Chase
Meyer
Sealy
Sealy Back Saver
Sealy Correct Comfort
Sealy Kids
Sealy OrthoZone
Sealy Posture Premier
Sealy Posturematic
Sealy Posturepedic
Sealy Posturepedic Crown Jewel
Stearns & Foster

## COMPETITORS

Premier Bedding Group
Select Comfort
Serta
Simmons
Spring Air

## HISTORICAL FINANCIALS & EMPLOYEES

| Private<br>FYE: Sun. nearest Nov. 30 | Annual<br>Growth | 11/91 | 11/92 | 11/93 | 11/94 | 11/95 | 11/96 | 11/97 | 11/98 | 11/99 | 11/00 |
|---|---|---|---|---|---|---|---|---|---|---|---|
| Sales ($ mil.) | 7.1% | — | — | 683 | 698 | 654 | 698 | 805 | 891 | 986 | 1,102 |
| Net income ($ mil.) | 2.3% | — | — | 26 | 29 | 20 | (1) | 7 | (34) | 16 | 30 |
| Income as % of sales | — | — | — | 3.8% | 4.2% | 3.0% | — | 0.9% | — | 1.6% | 2.7% |
| Employees | 3.3% | — | — | 4,844 | 4,345 | 4,520 | 4,875 | 5,456 | 5,193 | 5,460 | 6,077 |

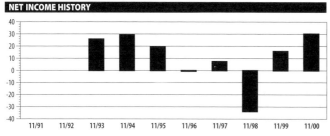

**NET INCOME HISTORY**

**2000 FISCAL YEAR-END**
Debt ratio: 100.0%
Return on equity: —
Cash ($ mil.): 18
Current ratio: 1.15
Long-term debt ($ mil.): 652

# SEMATECH, INC.

## OVERVIEW

SEMATECH's work has been seminal to maintaining Moore's Law — the dictum that semiconductor power doubles every 18 months. The Austin, Texas-based industry consortium — whose name stands for "semiconductor manufacturing technology" — funds research in areas such as design, front-end processes, lithography, and interconnect systems to improve semiconductor manufacturing techniques. The organization is credited with updating the equipment used in American factories and helping US chip makers recover their global dominance. Its members include US chip makers Agere, Advanced Micro Devices, Conexant, Hewlett-Packard, IBM, Intel, Motorola, and Texas Instruments; European firms Infineon, Philips, and STMicroelectronics; and Hynix and Taiwan Semiconductor

in Asia. Members, whose dues support the consortium, send employees to Texas for group projects.

SEMATECH has lost members — in part because of the US chip industry's return to dominance, in part because of its inclusion of non-US firms — but continues to tackle difficult technological issues related to the shrinking size of chips and use of new materials. When government funding came to an end in 1996, SEMATECH knew it had to evolve or become extinct. It has widened its focus to issues facing chip companies worldwide. However, some members have objected to expansion that detracts from individual member goals. SEMATECH is also teaming up with other international research organizations, including Selete, its Japanese counterpart.

## HISTORY

In 1986 Japan surpassed the US to become the leading maker of semiconductors. The Semiconductor Industry Association (SIA), a US chip industry trade group formed SEMATECH in 1987 with funding for five years from the US Defense Department's Defense Advanced Research Projects Agency, and another $100 million per year from 14 member companies.

Former Xerox research executive Bill Spencer became CEO of SEMATECH in 1990. Despite its technological advances, critics complained that the organization benefited its largest members. In the early 1990s Micron Technology and LSI Logic (its smallest members) and Harris Corp. dropped out.

SEMATECH's government funding was extended (although lowered) in 1992. When the US regained its world manufacturing chip title that year, many credited SEMATECH for the turnaround.

In 1994 SEMATECH began phasing out federal backing. Citing the main challenge to US chip makers as technology limits, not foreign competition, the organization in 1996 invited European and Asian manufacturers to join an initiative to make larger semiconductor wafers. When government funding came to an end in 1996, SEMATECH formed an international branch and increased its dues (from $10 million to $15 million) to cover lost funding.

In 1997 Mark Melliar-Smith was named CEO; Spencer remains chairman. In 1998 five companies from Asia and Europe formed the new International SEMATECH. That year

National Semiconductor left SEMATECH, citing financial difficulties.

In 1999 Motorola, concerned about the organization's international push, gave the required two years notice that it would withdraw. Compaq — which became a member when it acquired Digital Equipment (but not that company's chip operations) in 1997 — also made plans to leave. SEMATECH was instrumental in two major chip industry developments implemented in 1999: migration to 300 millimeter (12-in.) silicon wafers and adoption of copper interconnect technology.

By 2000 SEMATECH and International SEMATECH became a single entity. Also that year the research organization accelerated its international involvement through pacts with Selete, the organization's Japanese counterpart, and Belgian research agency IMEC.

Also in 2000 International SEMATECH began licensing its TP2 tool performance tracking software, which automatically collects performance data on operations and equipment in semiconductor manufacturing facilities.

In 2001 Bob Helms, a Texas Instruments engineer and Stanford University emeritus professor, succeeded Melliar-Smith as the consortium's president and CEO.

**Chairman:** O. B. Bilous
**Vice Chairman:** William J. Spencer
**President and CEO:** Bob Helms
**COO:** Rinn Cleavelin
**Chief Administrative Officer:** David Saathoff
**General Counsel:** Robert Falstad
**Financial Planner:** Stuart Clark
**Director, Account Management:** Tom Bowers
**Director, Advanced Technology Development Facility:**
  Juergen Woehl
**Director, Environment, Safety, and Health:**
  Coleen Miller
**Director, Front End Processes:** Mike Jackson
**Director, Interconnect:** Paul Winebarger
**Director, Lithography:** Gerhard Gross
**Director, Manufacturing Methods and Productivity:**
  Scott Kramer
**Director, Supplier Relations:** David Anderson
**Associate Director, Advanced Technology Development
  Facility:** Dan Holladay
**Associate Director, Interconnect:** Ken Monnig
**Associate Director, Manufacturing Methods and
  Productivity:** Randy Goodall
**Technical Manager, Metrology/Yield Management Tools:**
  Alain Diebold
**Program Manager, 157nm:** Rich Harbison
**Human Resources:** Linda Cline
**Auditors:** PricewaterhouseCoopers LLP

## LOCATIONS

**HQ:** 2706 Montopolis Dr., Austin, TX 78741
**Phone:** 512-356-3500       **Fax:** 512-356-3086
**Web:** www.sematech.org

SEMATECH includes members from France, Germany,
the Netherlands, South Korea, Taiwan, and the US.

## PRODUCTS/OPERATIONS

**Research and Development Programs**
Advanced tool development facilities and facilities design
Environment, safety, and health
Front-end processes
Interconnect
Lithography
Manufacturing methods and productivity

**SEMATECH Members**
Advanced Micro Devices
Agere
Conexant
Hewlett-Packard
Hynix
IBM
Infineon
Intel
Motorola
Philips
STMicroelectronics
Taiwan Semiconductor Manufacturing Corp.
Texas Instruments

## COMPETITORS

Intel
IBM
MIT
MCC
Research Triangle Institute
SAIC
Southwest Research
  Institute
SRI International
University of California

# SKADDEN, ARPS

## OVERVIEW

Attorneys at Skadden, Arps, Slate, Meagher & Flom have probably heard every lawyer joke in circulation, and they are laughing all the way to the bank. The New York City-based law firm is one of the largest in the world and #1 in the US. It has more than 1,600 attorneys operating from 22 offices in Asia, Australia, Europe, and North America. Skadden, Arps' provides legal counsel to government, industrial, financial, and corporate clients.

Widely known for its mergers and acquisitions practice, Skadden, Arps is a giant in the field; in 2000 alone it handled more than 65 deals valued at $1 billion or more. For example, the firm represented Germany's Mannesmann in the largest merger in history when it was acquired by Vodafone Group for about $180 billion. The firm also has first-rate bankruptcy, litigation, and securities practices.

## HISTORY

Marshall Skadden, Leslie Arps, and John Slate hung out their shingle in New York City on April Fool's Day, 1948. Skadden and Arps came from a Wall Street law firm, and Slate had been counsel to Pan American World Airways. Without the reputation and connections of the established New York law firms, the firm found work one case at a time from referrals, handling mainly commercial, corporate, and litigations work. Marshall Skadden died in 1958.

Denied the luxury of steady clients, the firm was forced to be innovative and, at times, unorthodox. Joe Flom, who had joined as the firm's first associate, specialized in corporate law and proxy fights. During the 1960s, when tender offers and hostile takeovers increased, many of the more venerable firms referred clients engaged in the undignified corporate raids to Flom to preserve their gentlemanly reputations. With "white shoe" lawyers on Wall Street hesitant to tread into the uncivilized region of corporate takeovers, Skadden, Arps went for it, and the firm virtually pioneered the business of mergers and acquisitions (M&A) under Flom.

When Congress passed the Williams Act in 1968, which "legitimized" tender offers by providing regulation, other law firms started to get in on the act. Skadden, Arps was way ahead of the game, however, and as corporations and lawyers realized that aggressive legal tactics helped win corporate takeover battles, it also became apparent that Joe Flom was the expert. As takeover fights became more frequent in the early 1970s, the firm earned more than just respect. Earnings came not just from some of the highest hourly rates in the industry, but from hefty retainers (now a common practice at many firms) on the theory that association with Flom would scare raiders off. The only other name that could strike such fear in people's hearts was Marty Lipton of rival takeover specialists Wachtell, Lipton, Rosen & Katz. From the late 1970s through the 1980s, Skadden, Arps was involved in almost every important M&A case in the US.

The firm used its success in mergers and acquisitions to build its practice in other areas. In the early 1980s it branched into bankruptcy, product liability, and real estate law. By then it had opened offices in Boston; Chicago; Los Angeles; Washington, DC; and Wilmington, Delaware. Les Arps died in 1987.

With the boom in M&A activity and bankruptcies in the late 1980s, the firm grew to almost 2,000 lawyers by 1989. Then came the recession, and M&A work virtually dried up. Skadden, Arps responded by shedding more than 500 lawyers between 1989 and 1990. It also scrambled to diversify and expand internationally. As takeover activity rebounded in the mid-1990s, the diversification strategy actually began to work against Skadden, Arps because profits didn't skyrocket like those of M&A specialist firms.

The firm opened an office in Singapore in 1995 to coordinate its Asian business, signaling that city's growing importance as a financial center. Two years later two-thirds of the firm's Beijing team defected to a rival firm. Headquarters shrugged it off and flew in replacements. Skadden, Arps won one of its highest profile cases in 1998 when the sexual harassment suit brought against President Clinton by Paula Jones was thrown out.

With its M&A practice in full swing again, Skadden, Arps was involved in 70 announced M&A deals in 1999, including the $75 billion merger of oil companies Exxon and Mobil. It also became the first US law firm to reach $1 billion in revenue in 2000. (In 2001 it passed the $1 billion mark again.) The company announced an alliance with Italian law firm Studio Chiomenti in mid-2001.

**Executive Partner:** Robert C. Sheehan
**Finance Director:** Karl Duchek
**Director of Associate Development:** Jodie R. Garfinkel
**Director of Human Resources:** Laurel Henschel
**Director of Legal Hiring:** Carol Lee H. Sprague
**Director of Marketing & Communications:**
Sally Feldman, age 43
**Director of Technology:** Harris Z. Tilevitz
**Senior Partner:** Joseph H. Flom
**Senior Partner, Corporate Practice:** Roger S. Aaron
**Senior Partner Litigation:** William P. Frank
**Managing Partner, Chicago:** Wayne W. Whalen
**Managing Partner, New York:** Irene A. Sullivan
**Managing Partner, Reston:** Ronald Barusch

## LOCATIONS

**HQ:** Skadden, Arps, Slate, Meagher & Flom LLP
4 Times Square, New York, NY 10036
**Phone:** 212-735-3000     **Fax:** 212-735-2000
**Web:** www.skadden.com

**US Offices**
Boston
Chicago
Houston
Los Angeles
New York City
Newark, NJ
Palo Alto, CA
San Francisco
Washington, DC
Wilmington, DE

**International Offices**
Beijing
Brussels
Frankfurt
Hong Kong
London
Moscow
Paris
Singapore
Sydney
Tokyo
Toronto

## PRODUCTS/OPERATIONS

**Selected Practice Areas**
Antitrust
Banking and institutional investing
Corporate finance
Government affairs
Health care
Insurance
Intellectual property
International trade
Internet and e-commerce
Labor and employment law
Litigation
Mass torts and insurance litigation
Mergers and acquisitions
Real estate
Tax
Trusts and estates
White-collar crime

## COMPETITORS

| | |
|---|---|
| Baker & McKenzie | Paul, Weiss, Rifkind |
| Cleary, Gottlieb | Shearman & Sterling |
| Clifford Chance | Sidley Austin Brown & |
| Cravath, Swaine | Wood |
| Davis Polk | Simpson Thacher |
| Debevoise & Plimpton | Sullivan & Cromwell |
| Jones, Day | Wachtell, Lipton |
| Latham & Watkins | Weil, Gotshal |
| Mayer, Brown & Platt | White & Case |

## HISTORICAL FINANCIALS & EMPLOYEES

| Partnership FYE: December 31 | Annual Growth | 12/91 | 12/92 | 12/93 | 12/94 | 12/95 | 12/96 | 12/97 | 12/98 | 12/99 | 12/00 |
|---|---|---|---|---|---|---|---|---|---|---|---|
| Sales ($ mil.) | 12.8% | — | 440 | 478 | 582 | 635 | 710 | 826 | 890 | 1,025 | 1,154 |
| Employees | 4.4% | — | 3,000 | 3,200 | 3,100 | 3,000 | 3,150 | 3,000 | 3,200 | 3,600 | 4,235 |

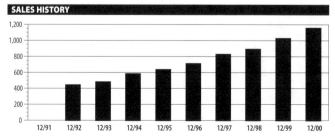

SALES HISTORY

SKADDEN
ARPS
SLATE
MEAGHER &
FLOM

# SKIDMORE OWINGS & MERRILL, LLP

## OVERVIEW

Reaching for the sky, Skidmore Owings & Merrill (SOM) is responsible for the look of some of the world's tallest buildings. One of the largest architecture and engineering firms in the world, the New York City-based partnership also provides graphics, interior design, and urban design and planning. Although it earned its reputation with its signature highrises, including the Sears Tower and John Hancock Center, the company also takes on institutional projects such as airports, convention centers, office buildings, and schools. It also performs interior design work and renovation projects for older buildings.

The company has offices in five US cities, London, and Hong Kong, and has completed projects in more than 50 countries. However, its plans to build the world's tallest structure, a 112-story high-rise in Chicago near the Sears Tower, ran awry in 2000 when financing for the project failed to materialize.

One of the stalwarts of modernist design, SOM has used its reputation for innovation to put its stamp on cities throughout Asia (though some critics sniff that it has lost its creative distinction and become the IBM of architectural firms).

## HISTORY

While studying and working in Paris in 1929, Louis Skidmore met two architects involved in planning the 1933-1934 Century of Progress Exposition in Chicago. He arranged to be appointed chief designer for the exposition and asked Nathaniel Owings, his brother-in-law, to assist him, thus beginning their professional association.

After the exposition, the two pursued separate paths, only to come together again in 1936 to found a small design firm in Chicago bearing their names. Trading on corporate relationships developed at the exposition, the two men soon had enough work for three draftsmen.

The next year the firm opened a New York office and worked on the 1939 New York World's Fair. Gordon Bunshaft came on in 1937 and spent the next 42 years with the firm, becoming one of its most famous and influential architects. By 1939, when architectural engineer John Merrill joined the firm, it had developed a reputation for clean, functional design.

In 1940 Skidmore & Owings won the contract that brought it to national prominence — designing the defense community of Oak Ridge, Tennessee, part of the Manhattan (atomic bomb) Project.

After WWII, the firm, now Skidmore Owings & Merril (SOM), grew rapidly, opening a San Francisco office in 1946. The company's modernist style was so distinctive by 1950 that SOM became the first architectural firm to be granted an exhibition at New York's Museum of Modern Art. Two years later it had 14 partners and four offices.

The 1960s saw more noteworthy commissions, and in 1961 SOM received the first architectural excellence award for firms given by the American Institute of Architects (it would win the recognition again in 1996, the only firm to win twice). It opened its Washington, DC, office in 1967 and was commissioned to develop the master plan for the Washington Mall. In the 1970s the firm's presence was keenly felt in Chicago, where, under the modernist influence of architect Bruce Graham, its designs included the John Hancock building and the Sears Tower.

SOM opened its first foreign office in London in 1986. That decade the firm's old-fashioned commitment to modernism in the face of postmodernism hurt its bottom line. By the time it had adapted, the building boom of the 1980s had gone bust. Several offices closed and half of SOM's staff was laid off in 1990. To keep the company alive, SOM's first chairman, David Childs (appointed in 1991), cut costs and perks. He also steered the firm toward institutional work and integrating design services for clients, instead of separating work by specialties. Meanwhile, as some second-generation stars retired, their retirement draws were a drain on company finances. SOM renegotiated with some retired partners, but others (including John Merrill's son) sued in 1996.

The Asian financial crisis halted some projects in 1997, and SOM began focusing more on work in the US. In an ironic turn of events, award-winning designer Joseph Gonzalez resigned after 20 years with the firm when it was learned that he was not licensed.

In 1999 China opened the SOM-designed 88-story Jin Mao Building in Shanghai, China's tallest and the world's third-tallest structure after the Petronas Twin Towers in Malaysia and SOM's Sears Tower. SOM's plans to design the world's tallest building, a 112-story Chicago skyscraper, received a major setback in 2000 when financing for the project fell through.

## OFFICERS

**Chairman:** Marilyn J. Taylor
**President and CEO:** H. Guy Leibler
**CFO:** Joseph Dailey
**Chief Information Officer:** Yangwei Yee
**General Counsel:** Richard E. Viktora
**Manager Human Resources:** Barbara Schiola
**Auditors:** Arthur Andersen LLP

## LOCATIONS

**HQ:** 14 Wall St., New York, NY 10005
**Phone:** 212-298-9300    **Fax:** 212-298-9500
**Web:** www.som.com

## PRODUCTS/OPERATIONS

### Selected Services

**Architecture**
Conceptual and architectural design
Construction administration
Site and building evaluations

**Graphics**
Corporate and institutional print communications
Design of signage and wayfinding systems
Environmental design

**Interiors**
Building systems analysis
Relocation strategies
Space planning and strategic facilities analysis

**Mechanical/Electrical/Plumbing Engineering Design**
Building telecommunications systems
Fire and life safety engineering
Heating, ventilation, and air-conditioning
Lighting systems and daylighting studies

**Planning and Urban Design**
Environmental analysis and planning
Master planning and design
Site selection studies

**Structural and Civil Engineering**
Fire engineering
Foundation design
High-rise and long-span structural systems design
Structural aspects of renovating and modernizing
  historic structures
Structural seismic analysis and engineering design

### Selected Projects

100 East Pratt/IBM (Baltimore, 1993)
AT&T Corporate Center (Chicago, 1989)
Bank of America (San Francisco, 1971)
Banque Lambert (Brussels, 1965)
Broadgate Development (London, 1992)
Brunswick Building (Chicago, 1965)
Chase Manhattan Bank (New York, 1961)
Exchange House (London, 1990)
Haj Terminal at International Airport (Jeddah, Saudi
  Arabia; 1982)
Hirshhorn Museum and Sculpture Garden (Washington,
  DC; 1974)
Hong Kong Convention and Exhibition Center (1997)
Inland Steel (Chicago, 1956)
Jin Mao Building (Shanghai, 1999)
John Hancock Center (Chicago, 1970)
LBJ Library (University of Texas, Austin; 1971)
Lever House (New York, 1952)
Library at Northwestern University (Evanston, IL; 1971)
Lincoln Center for the Performing Arts, Library-
  Museum (New York, 1965)
Lisbon University (1997)
Ludgate Office Complex (London, 1992)
Manufacturers Hanover Trust Company Bank and Office
  Building (New York, 1954)
New York City Building (1939 World's Fair)
Oak Ridge defense community (Tennessee, 1942-1946)
Regenstein Library (University of Chicago, 1970)
Rowes Wharf (Boston, 1987)
San Francisco International Airport Terminal (1998)
Sears Tower (Chicago, 1974)
University of Illinois at Chicago (1965)
US Air Force Academy (Colorado Springs, CO; 1962)
Vila Olimpica (Barcelona, Spain; 1992)
Weyerhaeuser Headquarters (Tacoma, WA; 1971)
Worldwide Plaza (New York, 1991)

## COMPETITORS

| | |
|---|---|
| A. Epstein & Sons | Jacobs Engineering |
| AECOM | Loebl Schlossman & Hackl |
| Einhorn Yaffee Prescott | Louis Berger Group |
| Architecture | Murphy/Jahn |
| Ellerbe Beckett | Parsons Brinckerhoff |
| FFNS | Perkins & Will |
| Hellmuth, Obata + | STV |
| Kassabaum | Takenaka |
| Holabird and Root | URS |

## HISTORICAL FINANCIALS & EMPLOYEES

| Partnership<br>FYE: September 30 | Annual<br>Growth | 9/91 | 9/92 | 9/93 | 9/94 | 9/95 | 9/96 | 9/97 | 9/98 | 9/99 | 9/00 |
|---|---|---|---|---|---|---|---|---|---|---|---|
| Sales ($ mil.) | 5.9% | — | 63 | 68 | 79 | 87 | 82 | 88 | 90 | 100 | 100 |
| Employees | 3.4% | — | 687 | 746 | 733 | 800 | 800 | 850 | 850 | 900 | 900 |

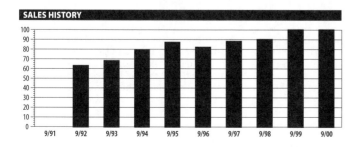

SALES HISTORY

# SMITHSONIAN INSTITUTION

The Smithsonian Institution wears many hats, from the one worn by Harrison Ford in the *Indiana Jones* trilogy to the one worn by Abraham Lincoln the night he was assassinated. The Smithsonian is the world's largest museum, home to more than 140 million objects (only a small portion of which are on display at any one time) in 16 museums and galleries, most of which are located on the National Mall in Washington, DC (two museums are in New York City). More than 40 million visitors each year peruse exhibits on art, film and television, history, music, science, and many other subjects, featuring such disparate items as the desk on which Thomas Jefferson wrote the Declaration of Independence,

the ruby slippers worn by Judy Garland in *The Wizard of Oz,* and the Wright Brothers' first airplane.

The Smithsonian Institution also operates the National Zoo, as well as several research facilities. Admission is free at most of its museums and the zoo. The Smithsonian receives almost 50% of its operating revenue from the federal government and is also active in soliciting contributions from individuals, corporations, and foundations. A board of regents that includes former Vice President Al Gore, Chief Justice William Rehnquist, six members of Congress, and eight private citizens leads the institution.

## HISTORY

English chemist James Smithson wrote a proviso to his will in 1826 that would lead to the creation of the Smithsonian Institution. When he died in 1829, he left his estate to his nephew, Henry James Hungerford, with the stipulation that if Hungerford died without heirs, the estate would go to the US to create "an Establishment for the increase and diffusion of knowledge among men." Hungerford died in 1835 without any heirs, and the US government inherited more than $500,000 in gold.

Congress squandered the money after it was received in 1838, but perhaps feeling pangs of guilt, covered the loss. The Smithsonian was finally created in 1846, and Princeton physicist Joseph Henry was named as its first secretary. That year it established the Museum of Natural History, the Museum of History and Technology, and the National Gallery of Art. The Smithsonian's National Museum was developed around the collection of the US Patent Office in 1858. The Smithsonian continued to expand, adding the National Zoological Park in 1889 and the Smithsonian Astrophysical Observatory in 1890.

The Freer Gallery, a gift of industrialist Charles Freer, opened in 1923. The National Gallery was renamed the National Collection of Fine Arts in 1937, and a new National Gallery, created with Andrew Mellon's gift of his art collection and a building, opened in 1941. The Air and Space Museum was established in 1946.

More museums were added in the 1960s, including the National Portrait Gallery in 1962 and the Anacostia Museum (exhibits and materials on African-American history) in 1967. The Kennedy Center for the Performing Arts was opened in 1971. The Collection of Fine Arts was renamed the National Museum of

American Art and the Museum of History and Technology was renamed the National Museum of American History in 1980.

The Smithsonian placed its first-ever contribution boxes in four of its museums in 1993. A planned exhibit featuring the Enola Gay — the plane that dropped the atomic bomb on Hiroshima — created a firestorm in 1994 with critics charging that the exhibit downplayed Japanese aggression and US casualties in WWII. The original exhibit was canceled in 1995, the director of the Air and Space Museum resigned, and a scaled-down version of the exhibit premiered.

Large contributions from private donors continued in the 1990s; the Mashantucket Pequot tribe gave $10 million from its casino operations in 1994 for a planned American Indian museum, and prolific electronics inventor Jerome Lemelson donated $10.4 million in 1995. The museum celebrated its sesquicentennial in 1996 amid news that $500 million in repairs were needed over the next 10 years.

In 1997 California real estate developer Kenneth Behring gave the largest cash donation ever to the museum — $20 million for the National Museum of Natural History. Short of funds, the Smithsonian had to cut back on its 150th anniversary traveling exhibit that year. The Smithsonian announced a $26 million renovation for the National Museum of Natural History in 1998. Two years later Kenneth Behring quadrupled his record breaking 1997 donation of $20 million by giving $80 million to the National Museum of American History in 2000.

## LOCATIONS

**HQ:** 1000 Jefferson Dr. SW, Washington, DC 20560
**Phone:** 202-357-2700  **Fax:** 202-786-2377
**Web:** www.si.edu

The Smithsonian Institution has museums and galleries located in New York City and Washington, DC; its research centers are located in the US and Panama.

## PRODUCTS/OPERATIONS

**1999 Sales**

|  | $ mil. | % of total |
|---|---|---|
| Federal appropriations | 402.6 | 46 |
| General trust | 242.7 | 28 |
| Donors & sponsors | 157.4 | 18 |
| Government grants & contracts | 66.9 | 8 |
| **Total** | **869.6** | **100** |

**Museums and Research Centers**
Anacostia Museum and Center for African American History & Culture
Archives of American Art
Arthur M. Sackler Gallery
Arts and Industries Building
Center for Folklife Programs and Cultural Heritage
Conservation and Research Center
Cooper-Hewitt, National Design Museum (New York City)
Freer Gallery of Art
Hirshhorn Museum and Sculpture Garden
National Air and Space Museum
National Museum of African Art
National Museum of American History
National Museum of Natural History
National Museum of the American Indian (New York City)
National Portrait Gallery
National Postal Museum
National Zoological Park
Smithsonian American Art Museum
Renwick Gallery
Smithsonian Astrophysical Observatory
Smithsonian Center for Latino Initiatives
Smithsonian Center for Materials Research and Education
Smithsonian Environmental Research Center
Smithsonian Institution Building (The Castle)
Smithsonian Marine Station at Fort Pierce
Smithsonian Tropical Research Institute

## HISTORICAL FINANCIALS & EMPLOYEES

| Not-for-profit<br>FYE: September 30 | Annual<br>Growth | 9/90 | 9/91 | 9/92 | 9/93 | 9/94 | 9/95 | 9/96 | 9/97 | 9/98 | 9/99 |
|---|---|---|---|---|---|---|---|---|---|---|---|
| Sales ($ mil.) | 3.0% | — | — | 706 | 730 | 605 | 750 | 703 | 729 | 774 | 870 |
| Employees | (0.9%) | — | — | 6,800 | 6,800 | 6,671 | 6,600 | 6,487 | 6,469 | — | 6,400 |

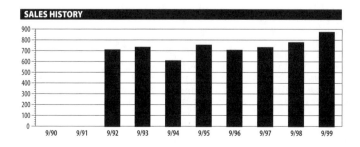

SALES HISTORY

SMITHSONIAN INSTITUTION

# SPRINGS INDUSTRIES, INC.

## OVERVIEW

If coordinated home furnishings put a spring in your step, you'll love Springs Industries, one of the largest makers of home furnishings in the US. The Fort Mill, South Carolina-based company is best known for its bed and bath products — sheets, comforters, pillows, rugs, shower curtains, and towels — sold under the Springmaid and Wamsutta brands, among others. Springs also makes baby bedding, infant apparel, window blinds, and a line of fabrics for the home-sewing market. Springs makes licensed brands (Disney, John Deere) and private-label items (for Wal-Mart, Target).

Springs sells its home furnishings to catalog retailers, department stores, and mass merchandisers (Wal-Mart represents 27% of sales) and through about 60 company-owned outlet stores. Historically an apparel textile maker, Springs has spent the past decade refocusing on home fashions through sales and acquisitions.

The Close family, descendants of co-founder Leroy Springs, owns 55% of the company. Springs formed a partnership with private equity firm Heartland Industrial Partners and took Springs private in September 2001; Heartland owns the remaining 45%. Chairwoman Crandall Close Bowles is the great-great-granddaughter of Leroy Springs.

## HISTORY

Springs Industries began in 1887 as Fort Mill Manufacturing Co., a cotton miller organized by Samuel Elliott White and a group of investors, including Leroy Springs, White's future son-in-law. Springs later founded his own cotton mill, Lancaster Cotton Mills, in 1895 and gained control of Fort Mill Manufacturing in 1914, three years after White died.

Leroy's only son, Elliott Springs, became president in 1931 when his father died. Left with massive debt and six aging cotton mills, Elliott rejuvenated the company by modernizing mill equipment and consolidating the plants into the Springs Cotton Mills (1933). During WWII the company's seven mills made fabric for military use.

In 1945 Springs started the Springmaid line of bedding and fabrics. Elliott's satiric, risque, but effective ads (beginning in 1948) helped the company become a leading producer of sheets.

Elliott died in 1959 and his son-in-law, William Close, became president. With profits sharply declining, the company went public as Springs Mills in 1966.

The first nonfamily member to be president, Peter Scotese from Federated Department Stores, was hired in 1969. The next year Springs began working with designer Bill Blass. It diversified into synthetic fabrics in 1971 by buying a minority interest in a Japanese textile plant producing Ultrasuede for apparel and cars.

Springs acquired Graber Industries (window-decorating products) in 1979 and three years later changed its name to Springs Industries. In 1985 it acquired M. Lowenstein, which made Wamsutta home furnishings; the deal also gave it Clark-Schwebel Fiber Glass (industrial fabrics). Springs added Carey-McFall (Bali blinds) in 1989.

Declining economic conditions throughout the textile industry in the late 1980s and early 1990s forced Springs to close plants and trim its weakened finished-fabrics segment (the downsizing continued into 1993). A $70 million charge in 1990 led to a $7 million loss, its first in 25 years as a public company.

Historically a maker of apparel fabrics, Springs had grown vulnerable to imports and launched a long-term plan to focus on home furnishings through sales and acquisitions. In 1991 the company set up a bath group with the purchase of C. S. Brooks. Springs became a leading seller of home textiles in Canada the next year by buying the marketing and sales units of C. S. Brooks Canada and Springmaid distributor Griffiths-Kerr.

Expanding in 1995, Springs acquired Dundee Mills (baby and health care products, towels) and Nanik Window Coverings (blinds, shutters). Crandall Close Bowles became the eighth president of Springs in 1997. The next year she took over the chairman and CEO posts from Walter Elisha.

To further focus on its home furnishings business, in 1998 the company sold its Ultra-Suede business (but kept its UltraLeather business) and its industrial products division. In 1999 Springs finally exited the apparel fabrics business when it sold its Springfield division to a management group.

In April 2001 the Close family agreed to partner with private equity firm Heartland Industrial Partners to take Springs private. In September that year the deal was completed, increasing the family's stake to 55%; Heartland owns the remaining 45%.

## OFFICERS

**Chairwoman, President, and CEO:**
Crandall Close Bowles, age 53, $637,504 pay
**EVP and CFO:** Kenneth E. Kutcher, age 48
**EVP; President, Home Furnishings Operating Group:**
Stephen P. Kelbley, age 58, $389,773 pay
**EVP; President, Sales and Marketing Group:**
Thomas P. O'Connor, age 54, $396,672 pay
**SVP and Chief Information Officer:** Ray E. Greer,
age 46
**SVP and Chief Purchasing Officer:** John R. Cowart,
age 50
**SVP, General Counsel, and Secretary:**
C. Powers Dorsett, age 56, $285,013 pay
**SVP, Global Sourcing and International Marketing:**
Dale Williams
**SVP, Human Resources:** Gracie P. Coleman, age 49
**SVP; President, Textile Manufacturing:**
William K. Easley, age 57
**VP and Controller:** Charles M. Metzler, age 48
**VP and Treasurer:** Samuel J. Ilardo, age 45
**VP, Corporate Communications:** Ted Matthews
**Auditors:** Deloitte & Touche LLP

## LOCATIONS

**HQ:** 205 N. White St., Fort Mill, SC 29715
**Phone:** 803-547-1500      **Fax:** 803-547-1636
**Web:** www.springs.com

Springs Industries operates 40 manufacturing plants in
13 states.

### 2000 Sales

|                 | % of total |
| --------------- | ---------: |
| US              | 94         |
| Other countries | 6          |
| **Total**       | **100**    |

## PRODUCTS/OPERATIONS

**Selected Products and Brand Names**

**Home Furnishings** (sheets, comforters, infant bedding,
towels, shower curtains, bath rugs, ceramic bath
accessories, fabric)
Daisy Kingdom
Dundee
Performance
Regal
Springmaid
Texmade (in Canada)
Wabasso (in Canada)
Wamsutta

**Window Furnishings and Related Hardware**
Bali
CrystalPleat
FashionPleat
Graber
Maestro
Nanik

## COMPETITORS

| | |
| --- | --- |
| Avondale Incorporated | Milliken |
| Burlington Industries | Mohawk Industries |
| Coats | National Textiles |
| Croscill | Newell Rubbermaid |
| Crown Crafts | Pillowtex |
| Dan River | R. B. Pamplin |
| Galey & Lord | Thomaston Mills |
| Gerber Childrenswear | WestPoint Stevens |
| Guilford Mills | William Carter |
| Hunter Douglas | |

## HISTORICAL FINANCIALS & EMPLOYEES

| Private<br>FYE: Sat. nearest December 31 | Annual<br>Growth | 12/91 | 12/92 | 12/93 | 12/94 | 12/95 | 12/96 | 12/97 | 12/98 | 12/99 | 12/00 |
| --- | --- | --- | --- | --- | --- | --- | --- | --- | --- | --- | --- |
| Sales ($ mil.) | 1.8% | — | 1,976 | 2,023 | 2,069 | 2,233 | 2,243 | 2,226 | 2,181 | 2,220 | 2,275 |
| Net income ($ mil.) | 5.3% | — | 45 | (25) | 62 | 72 | 85 | 69 | 37 | 69 | 67 |
| Income as % of sales | — | — | 2.3% | — | 3.0% | 3.2% | 3.8% | 3.1% | 1.7% | 3.1% | 2.9% |
| Employees | (1.7%) | — | 20,900 | 20,300 | 20,500 | 23,700 | 20,700 | 19,500 | 17,500 | 18,500 | 18,200 |

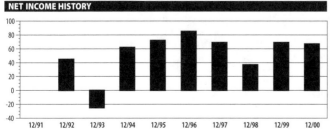

**NET INCOME HISTORY**

**2000 FISCAL YEAR-END**

Debt ratio: 25.7%
Return on equity: 8.4%
Cash ($ mil.): 3
Current ratio: 3.09
Long-term debt ($ mil.): 283

# SRI INTERNATIONAL

*Business Week* magazine called SRI International "Silicon Valley's soul." The Menlo Park, California-based not-for-profit research organization conceived such innovations as the computer mouse, magnetic encoding for checks, the videodisc, and high-definition television, not to mention some of the foundations of personal computing, the Internet, and stealth technology. SRI focuses on technology research and development, business strategies, and issues analysis. It has about 600 patents and patent applications around the globe. The organization's 1,400 scientists, researchers, policy experts, and support staff work at research centers worldwide. Its commercial clients include Ingersoll-Rand, Samsung, and Visa.

Government agencies that have used SRI's services include the US Department of Defense, the Department of Energy, NASA, and the National Cancer Institute.

SRI has two subsidiaries: Sarnoff Corporation (formerly a unit of General Electric) specializes in creating and commercializing electronic, biomedical, and information technologies, and SRI Consulting focuses on such issues as organizational management, marketing technologies, and the commercialization of processes. SRI has spun off more than 20 companies, and Sarnoff has spun off more than a dozen (*Business Week* also called SRI "Spin-Off City").

In the 1920s Stanford University professor Robert Swain envisioned a research center devoted to chemistry, physics, and biology. Swain received support from university president Ray Lyman and alumnus Herbert Hoover, but the Great Depression and WWII postponed the venture.

Finally, in 1946, the Stanford Research Institute was formed in conjunction with the university. That year the David Sarnoff Research Center invented the color TV tube under the wing of RCA Laboratories.

During Stanford Research's early years, it worked on such projects as logistics for Disneyland, magnetic ink for character recognition, and strategies for combating air pollution. The think tank was the focus of student protests in the 1960s because of its defense work. In 1969 Stanford Research Institute was one of four nodes on the first computer network, the ARPANET. It became fully independent in 1970 as SRI International.

In the 1960s and 1970s, SRI won large contracts from the US Department of Defense for research in such areas as radar, speech recognition, and noise cancellation technologies. It got a tremendous boost in 1987 when longtime client General Electric gave SRI the Sarnoff Research Center (as a tax write-off) plus $250 million in business, along with $65.2 million in cash.

In 1993 SRI founded Pangene to commercialize gene cloning and analysis technology. The next year it founded GeneTrace to develop genetics-related products for biomedical research and Nuance Communications to commercialize speech recognition products. In

1995 it created Intuitive Surgical, which develops minimally invasive surgical technologies.

SRI developed two key components for use in an improved mail sorting program, which the US Postal Service announced in 1997 it would use to save millions in processing costs. The David Sarnoff Research Center changed its name to Sarnoff Corporation that year. SRI joined Motorola in 1997 to make semiconductors for digital TVs.

In 1998 SRI and the National Science Foundation teamed to develop innovative science and math teaching programs. The following year SRI began working with network equipment leader Cisco Systems and the US Army to develop a voice and multimedia communications system for the military.

In 2000 SRI spun off AtomicTangerine, an e-business venture consulting firm. That same year SRI and Palm, Inc. teamed together to launch the Palm Education Pioneers Program. The program will give Palm handheld computers to about 100 K-12 teachers. SRI will develop and conduct a research program to evaluate effectiveness of Palm technology in the classroom. The research group also announced in 2000 that it would team with Mattel to develop toys using the institute's research in robotics, embedded systems, speech recognition, and wireless systems.

In 2001 SRI partnered with SPEEDCOM Wireless to codevelop wireless technology.

## OFFICERS

**Chairman:** Samuel H. Armacost, age 61
**President, CEO, and Director:** Curtis R. Carlson
**EVP, Asian Programs and International Development:**
Paul J. Jorgensen
**SVP and CFO:** Thomas Furst
**SVP, Commercial Business Development:**
Harold E. Kruth
**VP, Engineering and Systems:** John W. Prausa
**VP, Information and Computing Sciences Division:**
William Mark
**VP, Information, Telecommunications, and
Automation:** Michael S. Frankel
**VP, Intellectual Property:** Steven Weiner
**VP, Legal and Business Affairs and General Counsel:**
Richard Abramson
**VP, Pharmaceutical Discovery:** Michael Tracy
**VP, Physical Sciences:** Lawrence H. Dubois
**VP, Policy Division:** Dennis Beatrice
**VP, Ventures and Strategic Business Development:**
Norman Winarsky
**Director; President and CEO, Sarnoff Corporation:**
James E. Carnes
**Senior Director, Corporate Communications:**
Alice R. Resnick
**Senior Director, Human Resources:** Jeanie Tooker
**Program Director, Instrumentation and Simulation
Systems:** Chris Terndrup
**Educational Psychologist and Director, Center for
Technology in Learning:** Barbara Means
**Senior Research Scientist, Center for Technology in
Learning:** William Penuel

## LOCATIONS

**HQ:** 333 Ravenswood Ave., Menlo Park, CA 94025
**Phone:** 650-859-2000      **Fax:** 650-326-5512
**Web:** www.sri.com

SRI International has offices in Greenland, Japan, South
Korea, the UK, and the US.

## PRODUCTS/OPERATIONS

**Business Areas**
Automation and Robotics
Automotive and Commercial Equipment Technologies
Biopharmaceutical Development
Chemistry, Materials, and Applied Physics
Communications Technologies
Defense and Intelligence
Information Science and Software Development
(human-computer interaction)
Medical Devices
Pharmaceutical Discovery
Policy (analysis of social, technological, and economic
changes)
Product Engineering
Sensors and Measurement Systems
Systems and Services

**Subsidiaries**
Sarnoff Corporation (commercialization of innovative
electronics, biomedical, and information technologies)
SRI Consulting (management consulting)

**Selected SRI Spinoffs**
AlterEgo Networks (wireless networking device services)
AtomicTangerine (information security consulting)
Intuitive Surgical, Inc. (technologies and techniques for
minimally invasive surgery)
Nuance Communications, Inc. (speech recognition
technology)
Pangene Corp. (genetic engineering technology)
Songbird Hearing, Inc. (development of a disposable
hearing aid)

## COMPETITORS

| | |
|---|---|
| Akzo Nobel | LECG |
| Andersen | Lucent |
| Arthur D. Little | McKinsey & Company |
| Battelle Memorial | MCC |
| Bayer | PAREXEL |
| Booz-Allen | Quintiles Transnational |
| CACI International | Rand |
| Educational Testing | SAIC |
| Service | Southwest Research |
| DuPont | Institute |
| Kendle | |

## HISTORICAL FINANCIALS & EMPLOYEES

| Not-for-profit<br>FYE: December 31 | Annual<br>Growth | 12/91 | 12/92 | 12/93 | 12/94 | 12/95 | 12/96 | 12/97 | 12/98 | 12/99 | 12/00 |
|---|---|---|---|---|---|---|---|---|---|---|---|
| Sales ($ mil.) | (7.5%) | — | 305 | 312 | 312 | 320 | 326 | 363 | 174 | 160 | 164 |
| Employees | (6.1%) | — | 2,321 | 2,170 | 1,973 | 1,900 | 2,700 | 2,783 | 1,500 | 1,400 | 1,400 |

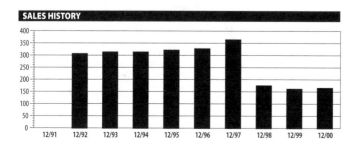

SALES HISTORY

# STANFORD UNIVERSITY

## OVERVIEW

One of the premier universities in the US, Stanford University is the West Coast's answer to the Ivy League. The Stanford, California-based private university regularly scores high national rankings for both its undergraduate and graduate programs, especially in business, education, engineering, and law. It boasts more than 14,000 students at its seven schools; its 1,600 faculty members include 12 Nobel prize winners and 18 National Medal of Science winners. Stanford is also widely recognized as one of the top US research universities and sports a host of laboratories and research centers, including the Stanford Institute for Economic Policy Research and the Stanford

Linear Accelerator Center. Its nearly $9 billion endowment is one of the largest in the US.

In 2000 the school welcomed its 10th president, former provost John Hennessey, who launched a campaign to raise $1 billion, the largest drive ever undertaken by a university. It quickly reached half that goal thanks to donations from alumni like Jerry Yang (cofounder of Yahoo!), Charles Schwab, and Texas billionaire and trustee chairman Robert Bass. However, its alumni ranks lost a prominent member in 2001 when William Hewlett passed away.

## HISTORY

In 1885 Leland Stanford Sr. and his wife, Jane, established Leland Stanford Junior University in memory of their son Leland Jr., who had died of typhoid at age 15. Stanford made his fortune selling provisions to California gold miners and as a railroad magnate whose Central Pacific Railroad built tracks eastward and eventually completed the transcontinental railway. Stanford also served as California's governor and as a US senator.

The Stanfords donated more than 8,000 acres of land from their own estate to establish an unconventional university, one that was both coeducational and nondenominational. Stanford opened its doors in 1891 to a freshman class of 559 students. It awarded its first degrees four years later, and among the graduates was future US president Herbert Hoover.

Leland Stanford Sr. died in 1893, and in 1903 Jane Stanford turned the university over to the board of trustees. After weathering significant damage in 1906 from the Great San Francisco Earthquake, the university established a law school in 1908 and its medical school five years later.

During WWI the university mobilized half of its students into the Students' Army Training Corps. The School of Education was established in 1917, followed by the School of Engineering and Graduate School of Business eight years later. In 1933 a rule limiting the number of women admitted to Stanford was abolished.

Wallace Sterling, who became president of the university after WWII, initiated the transformation of Stanford into a world-class institution with a reputation for teaching and research. Under Sterling the university initiated development on the Stanford Research Park.

In 1958 Stanford opened its first overseas

campus (near Stuttgart, Germany), and the Stanford Medical Center was completed the following year. The university created a computer science department in 1965 and two years later opened the Stanford Linear Accelerator Center dedicated to physics research.

Donald Kennedy became president in 1980. During his tenure, it was revealed that Stanford had overcharged the Office of Naval Research for indirect costs associated with research. The scandal led to Kennedy's resignation in 1992, and in 1994 the Office of Naval Research and the university settled a related lawsuit for $1.2 million and a stipulation that Stanford had not committed any wrongdoing. Gerhard Casper succeeded Kennedy as president.

In 1997 Stanford and the University of California at San Francisco combined their teaching hospitals in a public/private merger. Two years later, after the controversial experiment had harmed both hospitals' financial picture, the merger was terminated, and the two hospitals agreed to go their separate ways.

In 1999 Casper announced his intention to resign as president. The school tapped provost John Hennessy as his replacement. Soon after his appointment in 2000, Hennessy launched a campaign to raise $1 billion. Former Stanford professor and Netscape co-founder Jim Clark donated $150 million later that year to support Stanford's biomedical engineering and sciences program. (The donation was the university's largest since its founding grant.) The school also launched a new company called e-Skolar, which is developing an online search engine for the medical industry.

## LOCATIONS

**HQ:** 857 Serra St., Stanford, CA 94305
**Phone:** 650-723-2300      **Fax:** 650-725-0247
**Web:** www.stanford.edu

Stanford University's campus is located in Stanford, California. The university also offers study programs in Argentina, Chile, France, Germany, Italy, Japan, Mexico, Russia, and the UK.

## PRODUCTS/OPERATIONS

**2000 Revenues**

|  | $ mil | % of total |
|---|---|---|
| Sponsored research | 674 | 34 |
| Investment income | 490 | 25 |
| Tuition and fees | 280 | 14 |
| Health care services | 157 | 8 |
| Gifts | 113 | 6 |
| Other | 243 | 13 |
| **Total** | **1,957** | **100** |

**Selected Schools**
Undergraduate
  School of Earth Sciences
  School of Engineering
  School of Humanities and Sciences
Graduate
  School of Business
  School of Earth Sciences
  School of Engineering
  School of Education
  School of Humanities and Sciences
  School of Law
  School of Medicine

**Selected Interdisciplinary Research Centers**
Center for Computer Research in Music and Acoustics
Center for Integrated Facility Engineering
Center for Integrated Systems
Stanford Integrated Manufacturing Association

**Selected Laboratories, Centers, and Institutes**
Center for Research on Information Storage Materials
Center for the Study of Language and Information
Edward L. Ginzton Laboratory
Institute for International Studies
Institute for Research on Women and Gender
Stanford Center for Buddhist Studies
Stanford Humanities Center
Stanford Institute for Economic Policy Research
W.W. Hansen Experimental Physics Laboratory

**Selected Medical Research Facilities**
Center for Biomedical Ethics
Center for Research in Disease Prevention
Human Genome Center
Richard M. Lucas Center for Magnetic Resonance
  Spectroscopy & Imaging
Sleep Disorders Center

**Other Selected Research Facilities**
Hoover Institution on War, Revolution and Peace
Hopkins Marine Station
Martin Luther King, Jr. Papers Project
Stanford Linear Accelerator Center

## HISTORICAL FINANCIALS & EMPLOYEES

| School FYE: August 31 | Annual Growth | 8/91 | 8/92 | 8/93 | 8/94 | 8/95 | 8/96 | 8/97 | 8/98 | 8/99 | 8/00 |
|---|---|---|---|---|---|---|---|---|---|---|---|
| Sales ($ mil.) | 6.5% | — | — | 1,262 | 1,243 | 1,171 | 1,416 | 1,474 | 1,558 | 1,749 | 1,957 |
| Employees | 4.7% | — | — | — | — | — | 8,702 | 8,677 | 9,535 | — | — |

### SALES HISTORY

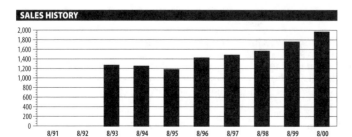

Stanford University

# STATE FARM INSURANCE

## OVERVIEW

State Farm wants to protect customers from harm. Bloomington, Illinois-based property/casualty insurer State Farm provides accident, health, and life insurance and annuities to customers in the US and Canada through more than 16,000 independent agents. State Farm insures about 20% of the automobiles on US roads and is also a major provider of homeowners insurance. Since its founding, the company has been run by two families, the Mecherles (1922-1954) and the Rusts (1954-present).

State Farm's not-so-secret weapon against increased competition is a federal savings bank charter that offers deposit accounts, CDs, mortgages, and auto and home equity loans in Illinois and Missouri. The company is expanding its financial services and has started offering mutual funds. Cashing in on the currently lucrative insurance climate, State Farm has formed Bermuda-based reinsurer Da Vinci Re together with RenaissanceRe.

## HISTORY

Retired farmer George Mecherle formed State Farm Mutual Automobile Insurance in Bloomington, Illinois, in 1922. State Farm served only members of farm bureaus and farm mutual insurance companies, charging a one-time membership fee and a premium to protect an automobile against loss or damage.

Unlike most competitors, State Farm offered six-month premium payments. The insurer billed and collected renewal premiums from its home office, relieving the agent of the task. In addition, State Farm determined auto rates by a simple seven-class system, while competitors varied rates for each model.

State Farm in 1926 started City and Village Mutual Automobile Insurance to insure non-farmers' autos; it became part of the company in 1927. Between 1927 and 1931 it introduced coverage for borrowed cars, wind damage, and vehicles used to transport schoolchildren.

State Farm expanded to California in 1928 and formed State Farm Life Insurance the next year. In 1935 it established State Farm Fire Insurance. George Mecherle became chairman in 1937, and his son Ramond became president.

During the 1940s State Farm focused on urban areas after most of the farm bureaus formed their own insurance companies. In the late 1940s and 1950s, it moved to a full-time agency force. Homeowners coverage was added to the insurer's offerings under the leadership of Adlai Rust, who led State Farm from 1954 until 1958, when Edward Rust took over. He died in 1985 and his son, Edward Jr., currently holds the top spot.

Between 1974 and 1987 the insurer was hit by several gender-discrimination suits (a 1992 settlement awarded $157 million to 814 women). State Farm has since tried to hire more women and minorities.

In the early 1990s serial disasters, including Hurricane Andrew and the Los Angeles riots, proved costly. The 1994 Northridge

earthquake alone generated more than $2.5 billion in claims and contributed to a 72% decline in earnings.

State Farm — the top US home insurer since the mid-1960s — canceled 62,500 residential policies in South Florida in 1996 to cut potential hurricane loss an estimated 11%. In response, Florida's insurance regulators rescinded a previously approved rate hike. That year the company agreed to open more urban neighborhood offices to settle a discrimination suit brought by the Department of Housing and Urban Development, which accused State Farm of discriminating against potential customers in minority-populated areas.

Legal trouble continued. In 1997 State Farm settled with a California couple who alleged the company forged policyholders' signatures on forms declining coverage and concealed evidence to avoid paying earthquake damage claims. That year a policyholder sued to keep State Farm from "wasting company assets" on President Clinton's legal defense against Paula Jones' sexual harassment charges (Clinton held a State Farm personal liability policy).

Relations with its sales force already rocky, State Farm in 1998 proposed to reduce up-front commissions and cut base pay in favor of incentives for customer retention and cross-selling. Reduced auto premiums and increased catastrophe claims from across the US eroded State Farm's bottom line that year. A federal thrift charter obtained in 1998 let the company launch banking operations the next year.

State Farm is appealing a 1999 Illinois state court judgment that it pay $1.2 billion to policyholders for using aftermarket parts in auto repairs. In 2000 the company was hit with a class-action lawsuit about its denial of personal-injury claims; previous suits had been individual cases.

## OFFICERS

**Chairman and CEO:** Edward B. Rust Jr., age 51
**EVP, Chief Agency Officer, Chief Marketing Officer, and Director:** Charles R. Wright
**SVP and General Counsel:** Kim M. Brunner
**SVP, Investments:** Paul Eckley
**SVP, Investments:** Kurt G. Moser
**VP, Corporate Secretary, and Counsel:** Laura P. Sullivan
**VP, Human Resources:** Arlene Hogan
**Vice Chairman, CFO, and Treasurer, State Farm Mutual Automobile Insurance and Director:** Roger S. Joslin, age 65
**Vice Chairman, President, and COO, State Farm Mutual Automobile Insurance and Director:** Vincent J. Trosino
**President and CEO, State Farm Federal Savings Bank:** Stanley R. Ommen
**EVP and Chief Administrative Officer, State Farm Fire and Casualty:** W. Donald Sullivan
**EVP and Chief Administrative Officer, State Farm Life Insurance:** Roger B. Tompkins
**EVP and Chief Administrative Officer, State Farm Mutual Automobile Insurance:** James E. Rutrough
**SVP, State Farm Mutual Automobile Insurance:** John P. Coffey
**SVP, State Farm Mutual Automobile Insurance:** Barbara Cowden
**SVP, State Farm Mutual Automobile Insurance:** Jack W. North
**Auditors:** PricewaterhouseCoopers LLP

## LOCATIONS

**HQ:** 1 State Farm Plaza, Bloomington, IL 61710
**Phone:** 309-766-2311      **Fax:** 309-766-3621
**Web:** www.statefarm.com

State Farm Insurance Companies has operations in Canada and throughout the US.

## PRODUCTS/OPERATIONS

**Group Companies**
State Farm County Mutual Insurance Company of Texas (high-risk auto insurance)
State Farm Federal Savings Bank
State Farm Fire and Casualty Company (homeowners, boat owners, and commercial insurance)
State Farm Florida Insurance Company (homeowners and renters insurance)
State Farm General Insurance Company (property insurance)
State Farm Indemnity Company (auto insurance in New Jersey)
State Farm Life Insurance Company
State Farm Mutual Automobile Insurance Company (auto and health insurance)

## COMPETITORS

| | |
|---|---|
| Allstate | MetLife |
| American Family Insurance | Nationwide |
| | Progressive Corporation |
| AIG | Prudential |
| Berkshire Hathaway | SAFECO |
| GEICO | Travelers |
| The Hartford | USAA |
| Liberty Mutual | Zurich Financial Services |

## HISTORICAL FINANCIALS & EMPLOYEES

| Mutual company<br>FYE: December 31 | Annual<br>Growth | 12/91 | 12/92 | 12/93 | 12/94 | 12/95 | 12/96 | 12/97 | 12/98 | 12/99 | 12/00 |
|---|---|---|---|---|---|---|---|---|---|---|---|
| Assets ($ mil.) | 13.3% | — | — | — | — | — | — | 82,296 | 88,366 | 80,114 | 119,602 |
| Net income ($ mil.) | (51.5%) | — | — | — | — | — | — | 3,581 | 996 | 1,033 | 408 |
| Income as % of assets | — | — | — | — | — | — | — | 4.4% | 1.1% | 1.3% | 0.3% |
| Employees | 2.0% | — | — | — | — | — | — | — | 76,257 | 79,300 | 79,300 |

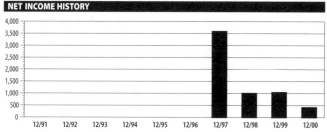

**NET INCOME HISTORY**

**2000 FISCAL YEAR-END**
Equity as % of assets: 36.6%
Return on assets: 0.4%
Return on equity: —
Long-term debt ($ mil.): —
Sales ($ mil.): 47,863

# STATE UNIVERSITY OF NEW YORK

Higher education gives some New Yorkers a SUNY disposition. The State University of New York (SUNY), based in Albany, New York, maintains 64 institutions across the state, including 13 university colleges and four university centers, 30 community colleges, five technical colleges, and two health centers. With an enrollment of 373,000, SUNY is essentially tied with California State University for the title of largest university system in the US. In all, SUNY's institutions offer more than 5,000 programs of study ranging from the health sciences to ceramics; it hands out some 70,000 diplomas each year, including nearly 9,000 postgraduate degrees. Most students are residents of New York State. SUNY is also top-notch in

research, boasting nearly $800 million in federal, state, and local grants and contracts. Its laboratories have helped pioneer magnetic resonance imaging, implantable heart pacemakers, and supermarket bar code scanners.

To support the institution, the state of New York provides $1.7 billion in funding, a third of its total revenue, while tuition and fees account for only 15% (less than $800 million). University services, including residence halls, food services, and university hospitals, bring in an additional $1.3 billion. New chancellor Robert King is challenging SUNY administrators and the state to increase those levels of funding to help keep the university competitive against other top-flight institutions.

The State University of New York was organized in 1948, but it traces its roots back to several institutions founded in the 19th century. In 1844 the New York state legislature authorized the creation of the Albany Normal School, which was charged with educating the state's secondary school teachers. Two years later, the University of Buffalo was chartered to provide academic, theological, legal, and medical studies. More normal schools later were founded between 1861 and 1889 in Brockport, Buffalo, Cortland, Fredonia, Geneseo, New Paltz, Oneonta, Oswego, Plattsburgh, and Potsdam.

In the early 1900s the state established several agricultural colleges, including schools in Canton (1907), Alfred (1908), Morrisville (1910), Farmingdale (1912), and Cobleskill (1916). New York also set up several schools as units of Cornell University, including colleges of veterinary medicine (1894), agriculture (1909), home economics (1925), and industrial and labor relations (1945).

After WWII, veterans began to fill US colleges and universities, taking advantage of the GI Bill to secure a college education. The legislature set up SUNY in 1948 to consolidate 29 institutions under a single board of trustees charged with meeting the growing demand. The board coordinated the state colleges into a single body and established four-year liberal arts colleges, professional and graduate schools, and research centers. During the 1950s and 1960s, new campuses were created at Binghamton, Stony Brook, Old Westbury, Purchase, and Utica/Rome, and enrollment began to take off, jumping from 30,000 in 1955 to 63,000 in 1959.

By the early 1970s SUNY had more than

320,000 students at 72 institutions. But budget constraints later that decade led to higher tuition, reduced enrollment goals, and employment cutbacks. In 1975 eight community colleges in New York City were transferred to City University. SUNY's enrollment began growing again during the 1980s, reaching more than 400,000 by 1990. Early in the decade, the institution began implementing SUNY 2000, a plan that called for increasing access to education and diversifying undergraduate studies. Following his election in 1994, Governor George Pataki proposed more than $550 million in cuts to the SUNY system.

In 1997 John Ryan replaced Thomas Bartlett as chancellor. The following year SUNY became the exclusive sponsor of The College Channel, a guide to colleges and college life aimed at high school juniors and seniors and broadcast by PRIMEDIA's Channel One. In 1999 the governor's budget director, Robert King, was named chancellor to replace the retiring Bartlett. In 2000 SUNY faced rising budget shortfalls at its teaching hospitals, in part because money was being siphoned off to other areas. That year King announced a set of initiatives to raise an additional $1.5 billion in federal research grants and $1 billion in private donations over five years. He also wants to increase revenues from university services and is asking the state to chip in $2 billion more than current funding levels for capital improvements.

## LOCATIONS

**HQ:** State University Plaza, Albany, NY 12246
**Phone:** 518-443-5555          **Fax:** 518-443-5321
**Web:** www.suny.edu

## PRODUCTS/OPERATIONS

### 2000 Revenue

|  | $ mil. | % of total |
|---|---|---|
| State appropriations |  |  |
| University operations | 1,634 | 32 |
| Hospitals & clinics | 210 | 4 |
| Sales & services |  |  |
| University hospitals & clinics | 821 | 16 |
| Residence halls | 205 | 4 |
| Food service | 131 | 3 |
| Educational activities | 31 | 1 |
| Other | 123 | 3 |
| Grants, gifts & contracts |  |  |
| Federal | 631 | 12 |
| Private | 248 | 5 |
| State | 160 | 3 |
| Local | 4 | — |
| Other | 11 | — |
| Tuition & fees | 774 | 15 |
| Federal appropriations | 18 | 1 |
| Endowment income | 3 | — |
| Other sources | 72 | 1 |
| **Total** | **5,076** | **100** |

### Selected Institutions

Colleges of Technology
  Alfred
  Canton
  Cobleskill
  Delhi
  Morrisville
  University Colleges of Technology
Health Science Centers
  Brooklyn
  Syracuse
Statutory Colleges
  College of Agriculture and Life Sciences at Cornell
    University
  College of Ceramics at Alfred University
  College of Human Ecology at Cornell University
  College of Veterinary Medicine at Cornell University
  School of Industrial and Labor Relations at Cornell
    University
University Centers
  Albany
  Binghamton
  Buffalo
  Stony Brook
University Colleges
  Brockport
  Buffalo State
  Cortland
  Empire State
  Fredonia
  Geneseo
  New Paltz
  Old Westbury
  Oneonta
  Oswego
  Plattsburgh
  Potsdam
  Purchase

## HISTORICAL FINANCIALS & EMPLOYEES

| School<br>FYE: June 30 | Annual<br>Growth | 6/91 | 6/92 | 6/93 | 6/94 | 6/95 | 6/96 | 6/97 | 6/98 | 6/99 | 6/00 |
|---|---|---|---|---|---|---|---|---|---|---|---|
| Sales ($ mil.) | 5.1% | — | 3,407 | 3,692 | 4,018 | 4,167 | 4,136 | 4,244 | 4,564 | 4,628 | 5,076 |
| Employees | 4.6% | — | 47,514 | 47,574 | 48,194 | 52,000 | 55,000 | 56,135 | 65,000 | 65,000 | — |

## SALES HISTORY

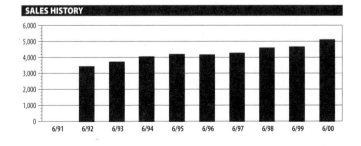

# STATER BROS. HOLDINGS INC.

## OVERVIEW

David felled one Goliath, but could he have toppled three? That's the task ahead of Colton, California-based Stater Bros. Holdings. With 155 supermarkets in six heavily populated Southern California counties, the company is not exactly tiny. (In 1999 it added nearly 45 stores that it bought from Albertson's.) But its foes — highly profitable Albertson's, burgeoning Fred Meyer (with the Ralph's and Food 4 Less chains; now part of Kroger), and Safeway (Vons) — are the biggest names in the US supermarket industry.

Competition from the grocery giants, and the purchase of those additional stores from Albertson's, has put a strain on the company's profits. To distinguish itself from rivals, the chain refuses to offer promotional games and frequent shopper cards, boasting everyday low prices instead. Stater Bros. also owns 50% of milk and juice processor Santee Dairies (Kroger owns the other 50%); Santee serves Stater Bros. Markets and Ralph's, as well as independent grocers.

Stater Bros. is owned by La Cadena Investments, a general partnership consisting of Stater Bros. chairman, president, and CEO Jack Brown and other top company executives.

## HISTORY

In 1936, at age 23, Cleo Stater and his twin brother, Leo, mortgaged a Chevrolet to make a down payment on a modest grocery store where Cleo had been working for five years in their hometown of Yucaipa, California. Later that year the brothers bought their second grocery in the nearby community of Redlands. Their younger brother, Lavoy, soon joined them to help build the company. In 1938 the brothers opened the first Stater Bros. market in Colton; by 1939 they had a chain of four stores.

The small, family-owned grocery chain continued to grow. In 1948 Stater Bros. opened its first supermarket (which was several times larger than its other stores and had its own parking lot) in Riverside. By 1950 the company had 12 stores.

Stater Bros. consolidated its offices and warehouse in Colton in the early 1960s and continued its expansion into nearby communities. By 1964 it operated 27 supermarkets in 18 cities in Los Angeles, Orange, Riverside, and San Bernardino counties. In 1968 the brothers sold the company's 35 stores to Long Beach, California-based petroleum services provider Petrolane for $33 million. Lavoy succeeded Cleo as president.

As a division of Petrolane, Stater Bros. kept growing. In the 1970s the company introduced a new store design that expanded sales area but required less land and a smaller building. The number of stores more than doubled (to over 80) between 1968 and 1979, when Lavoy retired.

Ron Burkle, VP of Administration for Petrolane, and his father, Joe, president of Stater Bros., attempted to buy the chain for $100 million in 1981. Infuriated by the low bid, Petrolane fired Ron and demoted his father, who left that year. Jack Brown was named president in his place. Petrolane sold the chain in 1983 to La Cadena Investments, a private company that included Brown and other top Stater Bros. executives.

Leo died in 1985. That year the company went public to reduce debt from the 1983 LBO and to provide funds for an extensive expansion plan. It also incorporated as Stater Bros. Inc. In 1986 a proxy fight for control of the company erupted between Brown's La Cadena group and chairman Bernard Garrett, who owned about 41% of Stater Bros. Brown had been suspended as president and CEO (Joe Burkle returned in his place), but Los Angeles-based investment firm Craig Corp. bought Garrett's stake and Brown returned; he was later made chairman. That year Stater Bros. also became a co-owner in Santee Dairies with Hughes Markets.

In 1987 Craig and Stater Bros. executives took the grocery chain private again. Also that year Craig reduced its stake in Stater Bros., transferring some stock to La Cadena. Stater Bros. Holdings was created as a parent company for the grocery chain.

Stater Bros. expressed an interest in buying rival Alpha Beta stores when they were put up for sale, but Yucaipa Companies bought them in 1991. Craig considered selling its stake in Stater Bros. the following year; it finally sold its half of the company to La Cadena in 1996.

In 1999 Stater Bros. acquired 33 Albertson's and 10 Lucky stores, as well as one store site. (The FTC required Albertson's to sell the stores in order to acquire American Stores, Lucky's parent.) The acquisition and the early retirement of debt resulted in its 1999 losses. In September 2001 company co-founder Cleo passed away.

**Chairman, President, and CEO:** Jack H. Brown, age 61, $3,044,000 pay
**Vice Chairman:** Thomas W. Field Jr., age 67
**EVP and COO:** Donald I. Baker, age 59, $360,000 pay
**SVP and CFO:** Phillip J. Smith, age 53, $150,000 pay
**SVP Administration:** George Frahm
**Group SVP Administration:** A. Gayle Paden, age 64, $316,000 pay
**Group SVP Development:** H. Harrison Lightfoot, age 62, $323,000 pay
**VP Human Resources:** Kathy Finazzo
**VP Insurance Administration:** Dean Jackson
**Secretary:** Bruce D. Varner, age 64
**Auditors:** Ernst & Young LLP

## LOCATIONS

**HQ:** 21700 Barton Rd., Colton, CA 92324
**Phone:** 909-783-5000    **Fax:** 909-783-3930
**Web:** www.staterbrosmarkets.org

Stater Bros. Holdings operates one distribution center and about 155 supermarkets in Southern California.

### 2001 Stores

|  | No. |
|---|---|
| San Bernardino County | 46 |
| Riverside County | 40 |
| Orange County | 30 |
| Los Angeles County | 27 |
| San Diego County | 10 |
| Kern County | 2 |
| **Total** | **155** |

## PRODUCTS/OPERATIONS

**Selected Departments and Products**
Bakery
Convenience foods
Dairy products
Delicatessen
Fresh produce
Frozen foods
General merchandise
Meats
Seafood

## COMPETITORS

Albertson's
Arden Group
Costco Wholesale
Fred Meyer
Longs
Safeway
Smart & Final
Trader Joe's Co
Walgreen
Wal-Mart
Whole Foods

## HISTORICAL FINANCIALS & EMPLOYEES

| Private<br>FYE: Last Sunday in September | Annual<br>Growth | 9/92 | 9/93 | 9/94 | 9/95 | 9/96 | 9/97 | 9/98 | 9/99 | 9/00 | 9/01 |
|---|---|---|---|---|---|---|---|---|---|---|---|
| Sales ($ mil.) | 5.9% | 1,538 | 1,526 | 1,540 | 1,580 | 1,705 | 1,718 | 1,726 | 1,830 | 2,418 | 2,574 |
| Net income ($ mil.) | 0.1% | 8 | 6 | 9 | 7 | 16 | 13 | 3 | (9) | (6) | 8 |
| Income as % of sales | — | 0.5% | 0.4% | 0.6% | 0.4% | 0.9% | 0.8% | 0.1% | — | — | 0.3% |
| Employees | 4.5% | 8,500 | 9,800 | 10,000 | 9,800 | 8,900 | 8,900 | 8,700 | 12,700 | 12,100 | 12,600 |

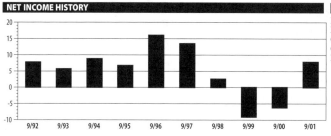

**NET INCOME HISTORY**

**2001 FISCAL YEAR-END**
Debt ratio: 100.0%
Return on equity: —
Cash ($ mil.): 102
Current ratio: 1.64
Long-term debt ($ mil.): 467

# SUNKIST GROWERS, INC.

## OVERVIEW

Sunkist is ripe in the minds of shoppers. One of the most recognized brands in the US, the Sunkist name on fruit-bowl staples commands higher prices in supermarkets. Sherman Oaks, California-based citrus cooperative Sunkist Growers counts more than 6,500 California and Arizona farmers as its members/owners. The co-op markets fresh oranges, lemons, grapefruit, and tangerines, as well as citrus juice and peel products.

The co-op turns the fruit that doesn't meet fresh market standards into juices and oils used in food products. Sunkist has licensing agreements with companies in more than 55 countries. Through those agreements, the Sunkist name and logo appear on scores of beverages and other products, such as vitamins and snacks. The co-op's fruits are exported around the world; Japan, South Korea, and Hong Kong are its largest export customers.

## HISTORY

Sunkist Growers was founded in the early 1890s as the Pachappa Orange Growers, a group of California citrus farmers determined to control the sale of their fruit. Success attracted new members, and in 1893 the Southern California Fruit Exchange was born. The name "Sunkissed" was coined by an ad copywriter in 1908, and it was soon reworked into "Sunkist" and registered as a trademark, becoming the first brand name for a fresh produce item. Eventually the co-op renamed itself after its popular brand: It became Sunkist Growers in 1952. Sunkist began licensing its trademark to other companies in the early 1950s.

As early as 1916, efforts to increase citrus consumption included designing and marketing glass citrus juicers and encouraging homemakers to "Drink an Orange." The co-op also promoted the practice of putting lemon slices in tea or water and funded early research on the health benefits of vitamins (vitamin C in particular). In 1925 tissue wrappers gave way to stamping the Sunkist name directly on each piece of fruit.

Although Sunkist pioneered bottled orange juice in 1933, its juice marketing efforts were never as successful as those of its Florida competitors. Florida oranges are drippy and dowdy and thus better suited for juicing. Capitalizing on this aspect, Florida growers dominated the market for fresh and frozen juice.

In 1937 Congress created a system of citrus shipment quotas and limits (known as "marketing orders") that ultimately proved most beneficial to large citrus cooperatives. By the early 1990s the marketing order system was under political attack, and in 1992 the Justice Department filed civil prosecution against Sunkist, alleging that the co-op had reaped unfair extra profits by surpassing its lemon shipment limits. In 1994, after much legal wrangling, the quotas were abolished and the Justice Department dropped its case against Sunkist.

Inconveniently warm weather and increasing competition from imported citrus marked the harvests of 1996. That year the co-op had trouble maintaining discipline among its members; some undercut Sunkist price levels, while others flooded the market to sell their fruit at the higher early market prices, creating a supply surplus. Also that year the co-op relinquished the marketing of all Sunkist juices in North America to Florida-based Lykes Bros. in a licensing agreement.

The co-op agreed in 1998 to distribute grapefruit from Florida's Tuxedo Fruit, providing Sunkist with winter grapefruit supply and increasing its year-round consumer appeal. Also in 1998 Russell Hanlin, Sunkist president and CEO since 1978, was succeeded by Vince Lupinacci, who had held positions with Pepsi and Six Flags, became the first person from outside the citrus business to hold Sunkist's top post.

In 1998 the company sold 90 million cartons of fresh citrus — the greatest volume in its history — despite increased competition from imported Latin American, South African, and Spanish crops, a damaging California freeze, and the ill effects of El Niño. The next year production was almost halved because of adverse weather.

Lupinacci resigned in 2000, citing personal and family reasons. Chairman Emeritus James Mast then took the helm as acting president. Although the company grew its market through exports to China in 2000, its profits were squeezed that year by increasing foreign competition, a citrus glut, and lessened demand. In mid-2001 Jeff Gargiulo replaced Mast as Sunkist's president and CEO.

**Chairman:** Al Williams
**President and CEO:** Jeffrey D. Gargiulo
**VP of Corporate Relations:** Michael Wooton
**VP of Finance and Administration:** H. B. Flach
**Corporate Secretary:** Linda D. Shepler
**Director of Human Resources:** John R. McGovern

Alico
Chiquita Brands
Dole
Fresh Del Monte Produce
UniMark Group

**HQ:** 14130 Riverside Dr., Sherman Oaks, CA 91423
**Phone:** 818-986-4800      **Fax:** 818-379-7405
**Web:** www.sunkist.com

### 2000 Sales

|  | % mil. | % of total |
|---|---|---|
| Fresh fruit |  |  |
|  Domestic | 518 | 61 |
|  Export | 218 | 25 |
| Fruit products | 69 | 8 |
| Other | 42 | 6 |
| **Total** | **847** | **100** |

| Cooperative<br>FYE: October 31 | Annual<br>Growth | 10/91 | 10/92 | 10/93 | 10/94 | 10/95 | 10/96 | 10/97 | 10/98 | 10/99 | 10/00 |
|---|---|---|---|---|---|---|---|---|---|---|---|
| Sales ($ mil.) | (2.4%) | — | 1,029 | 1,093 | 1,005 | 1,096 | 1,025 | 1,075 | 1,069 | 862 | 847 |
| Net income ($ mil.) | — | — | — | — | — | — | — | — | 6 | 6 | (4) |
| Income as % of sales | — | — | — | — | — | — | — | — | 0.5% | 0.7% | — |
| Employees | (0.5%) | — | 900 | 1,200 | 1,138 | 1,150 | 878 | 813 | 875 | — | — |

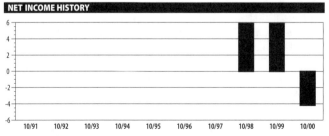

Debt ratio: 17.7%
Return on equity: —
Cash ($ mil.): 0
Current ratio: 1.27
Long-term debt ($ mil.): 11

# TIAA-CREF

If you were one of the US's largest private pension systems, you'd throw your weight around boardrooms too. The Teachers Insurance and Annuity Association-College Retirement Equities Fund (TIAA-CREF) is known for active and choosy investing.

The New York City-based not-for-profit organization provides benefits for more than 2 million members of the academic community and for investors outside academia's ivied confines. TIAA-CREF continues its historical core business of offering members financial advice, investment information, pensions, and annuities. TIAA-CREF Enterprises targets the general public with such offerings as mutual funds, tuition financing, and education IRAs; this unit includes TIAA-CREF Trust (trusts, estate planning, investment management).

TIAA-CREF is not afraid to use its clout to sway portfolio companies' management. The organization is a vocal critic of extravagant executive compensation packages. With an increasing share of its investment assets overseas, TIAA-CREF is also leading the crusade for global corporate governance standards.

## HISTORY

With $15 million, the Carnegie Foundation for the Advancement of Teaching in 1905 founded the Teachers Insurance and Annuity Association (TIAA) in New York City to provide retirement benefits and other forms of financial security to educators. When Carnegie's original endowment was found to be insufficient, another $1 million reorganized the fund into a defined-contribution plan in 1918. TIAA was the first portable pension plan, letting participants change employers without losing benefits and offering a fixed annuity. The fund required infusions of Carnegie cash until 1947.

In 1952 TIAA CEO William Greenough pioneered the variable annuity, based on common stock investments, and created the College Retirement Equities Fund (CREF) to offer it. Designed to supplement TIAA's fixed annuity, CREF invested participants' premiums in stocks. CREF and TIAA were subject to New York insurance (but not SEC) regulation.

During the 1950s, TIAA led the fight for Social Security benefits for university employees and began offering group total disability coverage (1957) and group life insurance (1958).

In 1971 TIAA-CREF began helping colleges boost investment returns from endowments, then moved into endowment management. It helped found a research center to provide objective investment information in 1972.

For 70 years retirement was the only way members could exit TIAA-CREF. Their only investment choices were stocks through CREF or a one-way transfer into TIAA's annuity accounts based on long-term bond, real estate, and mortgage investments. In the 1980s CREF indexed its funds to the S&P average.

By 1987's stock crash, TIAA-CREF had a million members, many of whom wanted more protection from stock market fluctuations.

After the crash, Clifton Wharton (the first African-American to head a major US financial organization) became CEO; the next year CREF added a money market fund, for which the SEC required complete transferability, even outside TIAA-CREF. Now open to competition, TIAA-CREF became more flexible, adding investment options and long-term-care plans.

John Biggs became CEO in 1993. After the 1994 bond crash, TIAA-CREF began educating members on the ABCs of retirement investing, hoping to persuade them not to switch to flashy short-term investments and not to panic during such cyclical events as the crash.

In 1996 it went international, buying interests in UK commercial and mixed-use property. TIAA-CREF filed for SEC approval of more mutual funds in 1997. Although Federal tax legislation took away TIAA-CREF's tax-exempt status in 1997, the change was made without decreasing annuity incomes for the year.

The status change let TIAA-CREF offer no-load mutual funds to the public in 1998. A trust company and financial planning services were added; all new products were sold at cost, with TIAA-CREF waiving fees. TIAA-CREF in 1998 became the first pension fund to force out an entire board of directors (that of sputtering cafeteria firm Furr's/Bishop's). Also that year TIAA-CREF's crusade to curb "dead hand" poison pills (an antitakeover defense measure) found favor with the shareholders of Bergen Brunswig (now AmerisourceBergen), Lubrizol, and Mylan Laboratories. Late in 1999, the organization sold half of its stake in the Mall of America to Simon Property Group, keeping 27%. The next year it made a grab for more market share when it launched five new mutual funds.

**Chairman, President, and CEO:** John H. Biggs
**Vice Chairman and Chief Investment Officer:**
 Martin L. Leibowitz
**EVP and General Counsel:** Charles H. Stamm
**EVP and Chief Actuary:** Harry I. Klaristenfeld
**EVP, Finance and Planning:** Richard L. Gibbs
**EVP, Human Resources:** Matina S. Horner, age 62
**EVP, Consulting Services:** David A. Shunk
**EVP, Retirement Services:** James A. Wolf
**EVP, External Affairs:** Don Harrell
**EVP, Shared Services:** Mary Ann Werner
**EVP, CREF Investments:** Scott C. Evans
**EVP, TIAA Investments:** John A. Somers
**EVP, Information Technology:** C. Victoria Apter
**EVP, Shared Services:** Ira J. Hoch
**EVP, Retirement Services:** Frances Nolan
**EVP, Marketing:** Deanne J. Shallcross
**VP and Corporate Secretary:** E. Laverne Jones
**President, Investment Products:** Martin E. Galt III
**President, TIAA-CREF Trust:** Joseph J. Gazzoli
**President, TIAA-CREF Enterprises:** John J. McCormack
**Auditors:** Deloitte & Touche LLP

## LOCATIONS

**HQ:** Teachers Insurance and Annuity Association-
 College Retirement Equities Fund
 730 3rd Ave., New York, NY 10017
**Phone:** 212-490-9000        **Fax:** 212-916-4840
**Web:** www.tiaa-cref.org

The Teachers Insurance and Annuity Association-College
Retirement Equities Fund (TIAA-CREF) operates across
the US.

## PRODUCTS/OPERATIONS

**2000 Assets**

|  | $ mil. | % of total |
|---|---|---|
| Cash & equivalents | 361 | — |
| Bonds | 95,288 | 34 |
| Stocks | 149,414 | 53 |
| Mortgage loans | 21,953 | 8 |
| Real estate | 5,296 | 2 |
| Other investments | 4,844 | 2 |
| Assets in separate account | 3,409 | 1 |
| Other assets | 818 | — |
| **Total** | **281,383** | **100** |

**Selected Subsidiaries and Units**
Teachers Advisors, Inc. (mutual fund management
 services)
TIAA-CREF Enterprises (for the general public)
TIAA-CREF Institute (think tank)
TIAA-CREF Life Insurance Company (insurance and
 personal annuities)
TIAA-CREF Trust Company, FSB (trust services)
TIAA-CREF Tuition Financing, Inc. (state tuition savings
 program management)

## COMPETITORS

| | |
|---|---|
| Aetna | MassMutual |
| American Express | Merrill Lynch |
| American General | MetLife |
| AXA Financial | New York Life |
| Berkshire Hathaway | Northwestern Mutual |
| Charles Schwab | Principal Financial |
| CIGNA | Prudential |
| Citigroup | T. Rowe Price |
| FleetBoston | U.S. Global Investors |
| FMR | USAA |
| John Hancock Financial | Vanguard Group |
| Services | |

## HISTORICAL FINANCIALS & EMPLOYEES

| Not-for-profit<br>FYE: December 31 | Annual<br>Growth | 12/91 | 12/92 | 12/93 | 12/94 | 12/95 | 12/96 | 12/97 | 12/98 | 12/99 | 12/00 |
|---|---|---|---|---|---|---|---|---|---|---|---|
| Sales ($ mil.) | 4.7% | — | — | — | — | — | 31,024 | 41,437 | 35,054 | 38,665 | 37,273 |
| Employees | 2.7% | — | — | — | — | — | 4,490 | 4,920 | 5,000 | 5,000 | 5,000 |

### SALES HISTORY

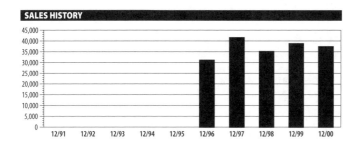

# TENNESSEE VALLEY AUTHORITY

## OVERVIEW

Although the Tennessee Valley Authority (TVA) may not be an expert on Tennessee attractions like Dollywood and the Grand Ole Opry, it is an authority on power generation. The Knoxville-based federal corporation is the US's largest government-owned electricity generator (nearly 30,400 MW of capacity) and the sole power wholesaler, by law, in an 80,000-sq.-mi. territory that includes most of Tennessee and portions of six neighboring states.

TVA transmits power to 158 locally owned distribution utilities (about 84% of sales), which supply electricity to 8.3 million consumers. It also provides power for industrial facilities and government agencies, and it manages the Tennessee River system for power production and flood control. Established by Congress during the Depression as part of the New Deal, TVA began as an effort to spur economic development in its area.

TVA's rates are among the nation's lowest, which would-be competitors attribute to its exemption from federal and state income and property taxes. To prepare for deregulation, the authority is trying to reduce its $25 billion debt.

## HISTORY

In 1924 the Army Corps of Engineers finished building the Wilson Dam on the Tennessee River in Alabama to provide power for two WWI-era nitrate plants. With the war over, the question of what to do with the plants became a political football.

An act of Congress created the Tennessee Valley Authority (TVA) in 1933 to manage the plants and Tennessee Valley waterways. New Dealers saw TVA as a way to revitalize the local economy through improved navigation and power generation. Power companies claimed the agency was unconstitutional, but by 1939, when a federal court ruled against them, TVA had five operating hydroelectric plants and five under construction.

During the 1940s TVA supplied power for the war effort, including the Manhattan Project in Tennessee. During the postwar boom between 1945 and 1950, power usage in the Tennessee Valley nearly doubled. Despite adding dams, TVA couldn't keep up with demand, so in 1949 it began building a coal-fired unit. Because coal-fired plants weren't part of TVA's original mission, in 1955 a Congressional panel recommended the authority be dissolved.

TVA survived, but its funding was cut. In 1959 it was allowed to sell bonds, but no longer received direct government appropriations for power operations. In addition, it had to pay back the government for past appropriations.

TVA began to build the first unit of an ambitious 17-plant nuclear power program in Alabama in 1967. However, skyrocketing costs forced it to raise rates and cut maintenance on its coal-fired plants, which led to breakdowns. In 1985 five reactors had to be shut down because of safety concerns.

In 1988 former auto industry executive Marvin Runyon was appointed chairman of the agency. "Carvin' Marvin" cut management, sold three airplanes, and got rid of peripheral businesses, saving $400 million a year. In 1992 Runyon left to go to the postal service and was replaced by Craven Crowell, who began preparing TVA for competition in the retail power market.

TVA ended its nuclear construction program in 1996 after bringing two nuclear units on line within three months, a first for a US utility. The next year it raised rates for the first time in 10 years, planning to reduce its debt. In response to a lawsuit filed by neighboring utilities, it agreed to stop "laundering" power by using third parties to sell outside the agency's legally authorized area.

In 1999 the authority finished installing almost $2 billion in scrubbers and other equipment at its coal-fired plants so that it could buy Kentucky coal along with cleaner Wyoming coal. That year, however, the EPA charged TVA with violating the Clean Air Act by making major overhauls on some of its older coal-fired plants without getting permits or installing updated pollution-control equipment. It ordered TVA to bring most of its coal-fired plants into compliance with more current pollution standards. The next year TVA contested the order in court, stating compliance would jack up electricity rates.

Also in 2000 TVA agreed to produce tritium, a radioactive gas that boosts the power of nuclear weapons, for the US Department of Energy (a first for a civilian nuclear power generator). TVA was also fined by the US Nuclear Regulatory Commission for laying off a nuclear plant whistleblower. Crowell resigned in 2001, and Glenn McCullough Jr. was named chairman.

**Chairman:** Glenn L. McCullough Jr.
**President and COO:** Oswald Zeringue
**EVP Business Services and Chief Administrative Officer:** Norm Zigrossi
**EVP Customer Service and Marketing:** Mark O. Medford
**EVP Financial Services and CFO:** David N. Smith
**EVP Fossil Power Group:** Joseph R. Bynum
**EVP Human Resources:** John E. Long Jr.
**EVP River System Operations and Environment:** Kathryn J. Jackson
**EVP Transmission and Power Supply:** Terry Boston
**EVP TVA Nuclear and Chief Nuclear Officer:** John A. Scalice
**SVP and General Counsel:** Edward S. Christenbury
**SVP Power Resources and Operations Planning:** Gregory M. Vincent
**SVP Strategic Initiatives:** Peyton T. Hairston Jr.
**Acting VP Communications:** Carolyn Bradley
**Auditors:** PricewaterhouseCoopers LLP

# LOCATIONS

**HQ:** 400 W. Summit Hill Dr., Knoxville, TN 37902
**Phone:** 865-632-2101
**Web:** www.tva.gov

The Tennessee Valley Authority's service area covers most of Tennessee and parts of Alabama, Georgia, Kentucky, Mississippi, North Carolina, and Virginia.

# PRODUCTS/OPERATIONS

**2001 Sales**

|  | $ mil. | % of total |
|---|---|---|
| Electricity |  |  |
|   Municipalities & cooperatives | 5,908 | 84 |
|   Industries | 659 | 9 |
|   Federal agencies & other | 330 | 5 |
| Other | 102 | 2 |
| **Total** | **6,999** | **100** |

# HISTORICAL FINANCIALS & EMPLOYEES

| Government-owned<br>FYE: September 30 | Annual<br>Growth | 9/92 | 9/93 | 9/94 | 9/95 | 9/96 | 9/97 | 9/98 | 9/99 | 9/00 | 9/01 |
|---|---|---|---|---|---|---|---|---|---|---|---|
| Sales ($ mil.) | 3.7% | 5,065 | 5,276 | 5,401 | 5,375 | 5,693 | 5,552 | 6,729 | 6,595 | 6,762 | 6,999 |
| Net income ($ mil.) | — | 120 | 311 | 151 | 10 | 61 | 8 | 233 | 119 | 24 | (3,311) |
| Income as % of sales | — | 2.4% | 5.9% | 2.8% | 0.2% | 1.1% | 0.1% | 3.5% | 1.8% | 0.4% | — |
| Employees | (4.4%) | 19,493 | 18,974 | 19,027 | 16,559 | 16,021 | 14,500 | 13,818 | 13,322 | 13,400 | 13,000 |

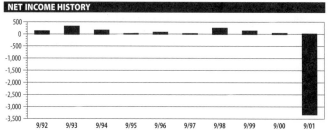

**NET INCOME HISTORY**

**2001 FISCAL YEAR-END**

Debt ratio: 93.2%
Return on equity: —
Cash ($ mil.): 343
Current ratio: 0.24
Long-term debt ($ mil.): 19,851

# THE TEXAS A&M UNIVERSITY

## OVERVIEW

Don't even think about trying to douse the Aggie school spirit. Renowned for their enthusiasm and school traditions, students at the namesake school of The Texas A&M University System don't mind standing for an entire football game or saluting the school mascot (a pooch named Reveille). But behind the fervor is solid education: College Station, Texas-based Texas A&M University System teaches more than 90,000 students at nine universities. Texas A&M in College Station is the largest campus, with an enrollment exceeding 44,000.

A&M's schools are well regarded for engineering and agricultural studies, as well as business administration and veterinary medicine. The system also operates eight state

agricultural and engineering extension agencies and a health sciences center (including Baylor College of Dentistry in Dallas). The system (along with the University of Texas) is endowed by the state's Permanent University Fund, valued at about $7.7 billion.

In the wake of a bonfire collapse which took the lives of 12 students in 1999, A&M has been charged by outsiders with trying to conceal the university's involvement in the accident. Still others have called on A&M to loosen some of its traditions. However, the school, students, and alumni have all stood fast against the tide. A&M has also embarked on a mission to renovate its facilities, announcing a $2 billion capital spending campaign in 2000.

## HISTORY

The Texas Constitution of 1876 created an agricultural and mechanical college and stated that "separate schools shall be provided for the white and colored children, and impartial provisions shall be made for both." The white school, the Agricultural and Mechanical College of Texas (later Texas A&M), began instruction that year. Texas A&M was a men's school at first, and membership in its Corps of Cadets was mandatory. The Agricultural and Mechanical College of Texas for Colored Youth (later Prairie View A&M) opened in 1878.

To help fund the agricultural colleges and The University of Texas, the Legislature established the Permanent University Fund in 1876 to hold more than one million acres of land in West Texas as an endowment. An additional million was added in 1883. The Santa Rita well on the university land struck oil in 1923 and money flowed into the Permanent University Fund's coffers. Under the provisions of the constitution, The University of Texas got two-thirds of the income, and A&M got the rest.

In 1948 The Texas A&M College System was established to oversee Texas A&M, Prairie View A&M, Tarleton State, and Arlington State (which left the system in 1965 and is now The University of Texas at Arlington). By 1963 enrollment system-wide had reached 8,000. That year the system changed its name to The Texas A&M University System, the same year that Texas A&M went coed.

By the mid-1980s enrollment had surpassed 35,000 students. The system grew quickly in 1989 when it added Texas A&I University (now Texas A&M University-Kingsville), Corpus Christi State (now Texas A&M University-Corpus Christi), and Laredo State University

(now Texas A&M International). West Texas State College in Canyon joined the system in 1990 and became West Texas A&M University in 1993.

The 91-year-old Baylor College of Dentistry (in Dallas) and East Texas State University, well-known for training future teachers, joined the A&M system in 1996 (East Texas State was divided into Texas A&M University-Commerce and Texas A&M-Texarkana). In 1997 the system opened the first portion of the $82 million George Bush Presidential Library and Museum.

In early 1998 the system signed an alliance with the private South Texas College of Law in Houston, which was opposed by the Texas Higher Education Coordinating Board. (In 1999 a judge ruled that the two schools had to discontinue their affiliation.) That year Texas Instruments donated $5.1 million to the system (one of the largest donations in the institution's history) for the creation of an analog technology program. Chancellor Barry Thompson announced he would retire in 1999. The system appointed former Army general Howard Graves as the new chancellor.

Tragedy struck the College Station campus later in 1999 when logs being stacked for the annual bonfire celebrating The University of Texas/Texas A&M football game collapsed and killed 12 people. Clinging to the 90-year tradition, many Aggies past and present insisted the bonfire go on in future years. In 2000 Graves announced a $2 billion, five-year capital improvement plan.

**Chairman, Board of Regents:** Erle Nye, age 63
**Vice Chairman:** Dionel E. Avilés
**Chancellor:** Howard D. Graves
**Vice Chancellor of Academic and Student Affairs:**
Leo Sayavedra
**Vice Chancellor of Agriculture and Life Sciences:**
Edward A. Hiler
**Vice Chancellor of Business Services (CFO):**
Tom D. Kale
**Vice Chancellor of Engineering:** C. Roland Haden
**Vice Chancellor of Governmental Affairs:**
Stanton C. Calvert
**Vice Chancellor of Health Affairs; President, The Texas
A&M University System Health Science Center:**
Nancy W. Dickey
**Deputy Chancellor:** Jerry Gatson
**Associate Vice Chancelllor of Human Resources:**
Patti Couger
**Associate Vice Chancellor of Budgets and Accounting:**
B. J. Crain
**Associate Vice Chancellor and Treasurer:**
Greg Anderson
**Associate Vice Chancellor of Planning and Institutional
Research:** Glenn Dowling
**Associate Vice Chancellor of Distance Learning and
Information Technology:** LeAnn McKinzie
**President, Prairie View A&M University:**
Charles A. Hines
**President, Tarleton State University:** Dennis P. McCabe
**President, Texas A&M International University:**
Ray Keck III
**President, Texas A&M University:** Ray M. Bowen
**President, Texas A&M University-Commerce:**
Keith McFarland
**Auditors:** Texas State Auditor

# LOCATIONS

**HQ:** The Texas A&M University System
John B. Connally Bldg., 301 Tarrow, 3rd Fl.,
College Station, TX 77840
**Phone:** 979-458-6000       **Fax:** 979-845-2490
**Web:** tamusystem.tamu.edu

# PRODUCTS/OPERATIONS

**2000 Revenues**

|  | % of total |
|---|---|
| Federal & state appropriations | 38 |
| Grants & contracts |  |
| Federal | 15 |
| State | 4 |
| Other | 3 |
| Tuition & fees | 17 |
| Sales & services | 11 |
| Investment & endowment income | 6 |
| Gifts | 3 |
| Other income & fees | 3 |
| **Total** | **100** |

**Selected Texas A&M University System Components**
Health Science Center
  Baylor College of Dentistry
  College of Medicine
  Graduate School of Biomedical Sciences
  Institute of Biosciences and Technology
  School of Rural Public Health
State agencies
  Texas Agricultural Experiment Station
  Texas Agricultural Extension Service
  Texas Engineering Experiment Station
  Texas Engineering Extension Service
  Texas Forest Service
  Texas Transportation Institute
  Texas Veterinary Medical Diagnostic Laboratory
  Texas Wildlife Damage Management Service
Universities
  Prairie View A&M University
  Tarleton State University
  Texas A&M International University
  Texas A&M University
  Texas A&M University-Commerce
  Texas A&M University-Corpus Christi
  Texas A&M University-Kingsville
  Texas A&M University-Texarkana
  West Texas A&M University

# HISTORICAL FINANCIALS & EMPLOYEES

| School<br>FYE: August 31 | Annual<br>Growth | 8/91 | 8/92 | 8/93 | 8/94 | 8/95 | 8/96 | 8/97 | 8/98 | 8/99 | 8/00 |
|---|---|---|---|---|---|---|---|---|---|---|---|
| Sales ($ mil.) | 10.6% | — | 1,172 | 1,212 | 1,287 | 1,299 | 1,425 | 1,550 | 1,695 | 1,792 | 2,620 |
| Employees | 4.9% | — | 15,670 | 15,966 | 16,367 | 20,000 | 22,600 | 22,800 | 23,300 | 23,000 | 23,000 |

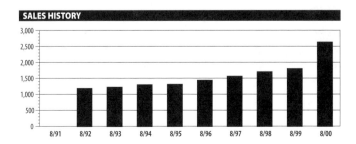

SALES HISTORY

# TEXAS LOTTERY COMMISSION

## OVERVIEW

Everything is big in Texas, including the size of its lottery payoffs and the odds against becoming a Texas-sized millionaire. The Austin-based Texas Lottery Commission oversees one of the largest state-run lotteries in the US. Created in 1991, it has generated more than $7 billion for the state's coffers. The lottery offers four numbers games, including Lotto Texas, Pick 3, Cash 5, and Texas Two Step, as well as an ever-changing variety of "scratchers," the instant-win tickets sold through retailers and vending machines leased from Cincinnati-based Interlott Technologies. More than 55% of ticket sales are paid out in prizes, while the state's Foundation School Fund gets about 30%. The remaining money goes to cover administration costs and to pay commissions to retailers.

The Lone Star lottery seems to be rebounding, with rising sales after three years of losses. The company is discontinuing its slumping Texas Million lottery game. It also changed its Texas Lotto game so that customers must match six numbers out of 54 numbers instead of 50. The extra four numbers changed the odds of winning from about one in 16 million to one in 26 million.

## HISTORY

A state lottery had been an issue in Texas for years before it was discussed in earnest in the mid-1980s. Falling oil and gas revenue had plunged the state into a recession, raising the specter of tax increases. In 1985 the state budget had a shortfall of $1 billion; that figure tripled by 1987. Adding fuel to the fire, the Texas Supreme Court ruled in 1989 that Texas had to change the way it funded public schools to avoid penalizing poor school districts. The ruling forced the state to seek new sources of revenue. In 1991 Governor Ann Richards called a special session of the legislature to deal with the fiscal crisis, and House Bill 54 was passed, creating the state lottery. The measure was approved by 64% of voters.

In May of 1992, Richards bought the symbolic first ticket at an Austin feed store (it was not a winner). Fourteen hours later Texans had spent nearly $23 million on tickets — breaking the California Lottery's first-day sales record — and had won $10 million in prizes. More than 102 million tickets were sold the first week. GTECH Holdings was awarded a five-year contract that year for lotto operations. Lotto Texas started in November with a winner taking nearly $22 million. By the end of fiscal 1992, lotto sales in Texas had topped $1 billion. In its first 15 months, it contributed $812 million to the state's coffers.

In March 1994 five winners split a record $77 million jackpot. By that autumn sales had surpassed $5 billion. In November a Mansfield, Texas, gas station owner picked up the largest single-winner jackpot, $54 million. By the end of 1994, Texas had the largest state lottery in the US. Cumulative sales topped $8 billion in mid-1995. In its first 37 months of operation, the Texas Lottery contributed $2.5 billion to the state's general fund. Cash 5 debuted that year, and instant ticket vending machines were installed at some sites.

In 1996 lottery director Nora Linares was dismissed following allegations that one of her friends received $30,000 from GTECH as a "hunting consultant." When a GTECH official was convicted in New Jersey of taking kickbacks from a lobbyist, questions were raised concerning payments to GTECH's Texas lobbyist, former Texas Lieutenant Governor Ben Barnes. In 1997 Texas canceled its contract with GTECH to operate the lottery through 2002 and reopened bidding; GTECH filed suit to enforce the contract. Executive director Lawrence Littwin later was dismissed by the commission. Littwin sued GTECH, claiming the company had gotten him fired (the case was settled in 1999). Linda Cloud, his replacement, reinstated GTECH's contract. That year the Texas legislature voted to increase the amount going to the state and to reduce prize payouts.

Lottery sales fell sharply in 1998, due in part to the reduced prize money. To combat suffering sales, the legislature reversed itself the next year and restored the level of prize payouts. The commission proposed lengthening the odds of winning to create larger jackpots, but public outcry scuttled the plan. In 2000 the commission agreed to change the wording on its scratch tickets after a San Antonio College professor and his students argued that breaking even is not winning. The following year it introduced its first new lottery game in about three years, Texas Two Step, and discontinued Texas Million following slumping sales.

**Chairman:** C. Thomas Clowe
**Executive Director:** Linda Cloud
**Deputy Executive Director:** Patsy Henry
**Director Communications:** Keith Elkins
**Director Financial Administration:** Bart Sanchez
**Director Human Resources:** Jim Richardson
**Director Lottery Operations:** Gary Grief
**Director Marketing:** Toni Smith
**Director Security:** Mike Pitcock
**General Counsel:** Kimberly Kiplin

## LOCATIONS

**HQ:** 611 E. 6th St., Austin, TX 78701
**Phone:** 512-344-5000  **Fax:** 512-344-5490
**Web:** www.txlottery.org

## PRODUCTS/OPERATIONS

**2000 Sales**

|  | % of Total |
| --- | --- |
| Prize money | 57 |
| Schools | 31 |
| Administrative costs | 7 |
| Retailers | 5 |
| **Total** | **100** |

**Selected Games**

**Lottery games**
  Cash 5
  Lotto Texas
  Pick 3
  Texas Two Step

**Scratch-off games**
  $25,000 Diamonds
  9's In A Line
  Break the Bank
  Cupid Cash
  Fast Cash
  High 5
  Jingle Bucks
  Masquerade Match Up
  Pot O' Gold
  Rake in the Cash
  Texas Gold Gusher
  Triple 3
  Triple Blackjack
  Weekly Grand

## COMPETITORS

Multi-State Lottery
New Mexico Lottery

## HISTORICAL FINANCIALS & EMPLOYEES

| Government-owned<br>FYE: August 31 | Annual<br>Growth | 8/91 | 8/92 | 8/93 | 8/94 | 8/95 | 8/96 | 8/97 | 8/98 | 8/99 | 8/00 |
| --- | --- | --- | --- | --- | --- | --- | --- | --- | --- | --- | --- |
| Sales ($ mil.) | 26.7% | — | 594 | 1,863 | 2,772 | 3,052 | 3,449 | 3,761 | 3,106 | 3,156 | 3,940 |
| Net income ($ mil.) | — | — | 250 | 660 | 932 | 1,014 | 1,101 | 1,421 | 1,213 | (118) | (116) |
| Income as % of sales | — | — | 42.1% | 35.4% | 33.6% | 33.2% | 31.9% | 37.8% | 39.0% | — | — |
| Employees | 0.4% | — | 325 | 325 | 325 | 325 | 325 | 304 | 335 | 300 | 335 |

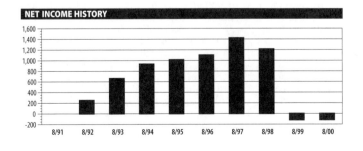

NET INCOME HISTORY

# TEXAS PACIFIC GROUP

## OVERVIEW

He may not be the Oracle of Omaha, but David Bonderman is certainly no Trickster from Texas. Like investor Warren Buffett, Bonderman's Texas Pacific Group (TPG) invests in brands, buying and resuscitating consumer and *luxe* labels, as well as less recognizable technology and telecommunication companies. When the markets get rough, TPG is happy to wait for some calm, but it prefers firms with lower valuations. TPG usually holds onto a company for at least five years, although consistent moneymakers are likely to be kept indefinitely. The Fort Worth, Texas-based firm's holdings include health care (Oxford Health Plans, Magellan Health Services), food (Del Monte), clothing (J. Crew), motorcycles (Ducati), and technology (ZiLOG, Motorola spinoff ON Semiconductor). Its venture capital affiliate TPG Ventures invests in telecommunications and technology companies.

Affiliated funds include the Newbridge partnerships (overseas investments) and Colony Capital (real estate). TPG is an active investor, often taking control of the firms in which it invests. It profits not only from the rise in value of its holdings but also from fund management.

With buying opportunities drying up in the US, the firm is leading the way overseas. The recession in Europe has caused acquisition prices to drop. TPG has stepped in to buy MEMC Electronic Materials from German industrial group E.ON AG and the directories business of Norwegian telecom Telenor Media.

## HISTORY

The story of Texas Pacific Group is largely the story of David "Bondo" Bonderman. The magna cum laude Harvard law grad — an ardent Democrat and former law professor — built a reputation as an adviser who helped Texas billionaire Robert Bass rack up triple-digit returns.

After a decade with Bass, Bonderman struck out on his own in 1992. James Coulter, recruited to the Bass organization out of Stanford University's business school, went with him. William Price, a former Bain & Company consultant who advised Bonderman on some of his Bass deals, joined them, as did Richard Schifter (airlines background) and David Stanton (technology expertise).

Bonderman raised eyebrows in 1993 when TPG affiliate Air Partners recapitalized Continental Airlines, then in its second bankruptcy. At the time the airline industry was losing billions, and Bonderman was a little-known quantity. After an extensive restructuring and management shakeup, Bonderman turned Continental into the US's #5 airline, logging record profits for four consecutive quarters.

This type of deal would become Bonderman's modus operandi: Jumping into troubled waters shunned by others, turning the company around, then (often) selling his interest for a profit. Of the head-rolling that frequently occurs after buyouts, Bonderman once said, "Generally speaking, you like to dance with the girl that brung you, and if you can't, sometimes you have to shoot her." In 1994 Bonderman worked his magic with America West Airlines. As with Continental, TPG sold shares in a second offering that made millions.

Taking a cue from Robert Mondavi, TPG in 1996 bought Nestlé's debt-ridden Wine World Estates (with help from investment group Silverado Partners), renamed it Beringer Wine Estates Holdings, and took it public in 1997 in an IPO twice as big as Mondavi's.

In 1997 TPG bought clothier J. Crew Group. In an era of falling petroleum prices, the firm gambled on Appalachian energy company Belden & Blake and teamed with Genesis Health Ventures and Cypress Group to buy a stake in ailing elder care operator Multicare. It also bought Del Monte Foods, the world's #1 maker of canned fruits and vegetables (taking it public in 1999).

Bonderman and Air Partners in 1998 sold their interest in Continental to Northwest Airlines. Following its strategy of buying turnarounds, TPG threw lifelines to HMO Oxford Health Plans (1998) and Magellan Health Services (1999). It also built its technology holdings, investing in integrated circuits maker ZiLOG (1998) and leading a management buyout of a Motorola unit that is now ON Semiconductors.

The group jumped into a European investment hotbed, taking a majority stake in Punch Taverns Group, which bought 3,600 pubs from Allied Domecq. In 1999 TPG bought the Bally fashion house and a stake in Italian scooter maker Piaggio. It failed, however, to turn around Favorite Brands, selling the marshmallow and candy maker to Nabisco. In 2000 TPG said it would buy a stake in French "smart card" maker Gemplus. It also agreed to sell Beringer to Foster's Brewing Group.

**CEO and Managing Partner:** David Bonderman
**CFO:** Jim O'Brien
**Treasurer:** Michelle Reese
**Human Resources Manager:** Jennifer Dixon
**General Partner, TPG Ventures for European Investment:** Badri Nathan

## LOCATIONS

**HQ:** 301 Commerce St., Ste. 3300,
Fort Worth, TX 76102
**Phone:** 817-871-4000     **Fax:** 817-871-4010
**Web:** www.texpac.com

Texas Pacific Group has offices in Fort Worth, Texas; San Francisco; Washington, DC; and London.

## PRODUCTS/OPERATIONS

**Selected Holdings**
America West Airlines
Bally Management (shoes and accessories)
Belden & Blake Corp. (oil and gas)
Del Monte Foods Company
Denbury Resources Inc. (oil and gas)
Ducati Motor SpA
Genesis Health Ventures Inc.
GlobeSpan (semiconductors)
J. Crew Group Inc.
Magellan Health Services Inc.
MEMC Electronic Materials (silicon wafers for
   semiconductors)
ON Semiconductor
Oxford Health Plans, Inc.
Paradyne Networks, Inc. (broadband accessory devices)
Piaggio
Punch Taverns Ltd.
Ryanair Holdings (airlines)
Zhone Technologies (data networking equipment)
ZiLOG Inc. (semiconductors)

## COMPETITORS

AEA Investors
Berkshire Hathaway
Blackstone Group
Clayton, Dubilier
Goldman Sachs
Haas Wheat
Heico
Hicks, Muse
Jordan Company
Keystone
KKR
Sevin Rosen Funds
Thomas Lee
Wingate Partners

# TISHMAN REALTY & CONSTRUCTION

The Tishman name has been a constant in New York for the last century. Tishman Realty & Construction, descendant of a company founded in 1898 to build tenements, offers a full range of real estate services such as project design, construction, leasing, and financing.

Tishman Realty & Construction built such landmarks as Madison Square Garden in New York, Disney's EPCOT Center in Orlando, Florida, and the John Hancock Center in Chicago. The company also erected the World Trade Center complex, including its landmark twin towers, which dominated the New York skyline until both were destroyed in a terrorist attack in 2001.

Tishman's E Walk entertainment and retail development is under construction in New York's Times Square district; the project will include the Westin New York hotel, specialty retail shops, and entertainment venues.

Affiliates of Tishman Realty & Construction include Tishman Construction, which carries out development and construction; Tishman Technologies, which equips buildings with data and communications infrastructure; Tishman Real Estate Services, which provides leasing, landlord and tenant representation, and other commercial real estate services; and Tishman Realty, which finances the firm's activities.

Chairman and CEO John Tishman has expanded the company beyond its Big Apple origins, most notably through a partnership with the Walt Disney Company to build hotels and theme parks in Florida. Tishman Realty & Construction is owned by the Tishman family.

Julius Tishman escaped the Russian pogroms of the late 19th century by emigrating to the US in 1885. Five years later he opened a store in Newburgh, New York. In 1898, as eastern European immigrants inundated New York City, Tishman began building tenements on the Lower East Side. He named his business Julius Tishman & Sons. By the 1920s the firm had moved uptown and upscale, building luxury apartment buildings. The firm went public in 1928 as Tishman Realty & Construction, with the family retaining an ownership stake. Julius was chairman; son David was CEO.

The pitfalls of going public were soon obvious. The offering raised less than $2 million, not enough to finance projects, and because the stock market favored profit generation over asset appreciation, the company was undervalued. When the Depression hit, David's involvement as a director of the Bank of the United States and the family's participation in bad loans made by the bank forced the firm to sell assets. Tishman's lenders, including insurer Metropolitan Life, took over some of its buildings, leaving the firm to manage them. In the 1930s and 1940s, the company focused mainly on managing its properties. It continued its construction operations on a contract basis for the Federal Housing Authority.

After WWII, Tishman moved away from residential development and into office construction. Meanwhile, David's younger brothers Paul and Norman began jockeying for position to replace him as CEO; in 1948 David chose Norman to succeed him (Paul resigned to form his own construction company). A nephew, John, became head of the firm's construction arm.

By the early 1950s, Tishman had moved into management and leasing services and expanded nationally, opening offices in Chicago and Los Angeles. In 1962 David relinquished his chairmanship to Norman, who was in turn replaced as CEO by his brother Bob. Under Bob's leadership, Tishman divested residential properties to focus on office space, mostly company-owned.

In 1972 the company completed the World Trade Center complex, including twin 110-story towers that were then the tallest buildings in the world. The iconic structures stood more than 1,300 feet above Manhattan until they collapsed as a result of a terrorist attack in 2001.

Tishman was hit hard by recession in the 1970s. In 1976 Bob took the company private again, selling off New York assets and splitting the company into Tishman Speyer Properties (headed by Bob and son-in-law Jerry Speyer), Tishman Management and Leasing (now part of Grubb & Ellis), and Tishman Realty & Construction (headed by John and promptly bought by the Rockefeller Center Corporation).

John Tishman bought back Tishman Realty & Construction in 1980 and steered it into high-profile partnerships with the likes of the Walt Disney Company. He also added project management and real estate financial services to his company's repertoire and continued to take part in highly visible construction projects.

## OFFICERS

**Chairman and CEO:** John L. Tishman
**President:** Daniel R. Tishman
**CFO:** Larry Schwarzwalder
**SVP:** Richard M. Kielar
**Chairman and CEO, Tishman Hotel and Tishman Realty Corp.:** John A. Vickers
**President and COO, Tishman Urban Development:** John T. Livingston
**President, Tishman Realty Corp.:** William J. Sales
**President, Tishman Real Estate Services:** Joseph J. Simone
**Director Human Resources:** Christine Smith

## LOCATIONS

**HQ:** Tishman Realty & Construction Co. Inc.
666 5th Ave., New York, NY 10103
**Phone:** 212-399-3600    **Fax:** 212-397-1316
**Web:** www.tishman.com

Tishman Realty & Construction Company has offices in Atlantic City and Newark, New Jersey; Boston; Chicago; Los Angeles; New York City; Orlando, Florida; San Francisco; and Washington, DC.

## PRODUCTS/OPERATIONS

**Selected Subsidiaries**
Tishman Construction Corp. (construction operations)
Tishman Hotel Corp. (hotel development and management)
Tishman Interiors Corp. (interior build-out and renovation)
Tishman Real Estate Management Co. (property management for third-party clients)
Tishman Real Estate Services Co. (real estate consulting and management)
Tishman Research Corp. (building materials research and consulting)
Tishman Technologies Corp. (communication and data systems development)

## COMPETITORS

| | |
|---|---|
| CB Richard Ellis | Lefrak Organization |
| Cushman & Wakefield | Lincoln Property |
| Gilbane | Reckson Associates Realty |
| Grubb & Ellis | Starrett Corporation |
| Insignia Financial Group | Trammell Crow |
| JMB Realty | Trump |
| Jones Lang LaSalle | Witkoff Group |

## HISTORICAL FINANCIALS & EMPLOYEES

| Private<br>FYE: June 30 | Annual<br>Growth | 6/92 | 6/93 | 6/94 | 6/95 | 6/96 | 6/97 | 6/98 | 6/99 | 6/00 | 6/01 |
|---|---|---|---|---|---|---|---|---|---|---|---|
| Sales ($ mil.) | 14.1% | 500 | 527 | 540 | 572 | 580 | 650 | 937 | 1,005 | 1,109 | 1,640 |
| Employees | 7.7% | — | 510 | 575 | 575 | 600 | 620 | 650 | 800 | 890 | 920 |

### SALES HISTORY

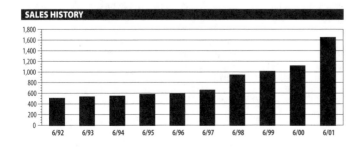

# TOPCO ASSOCIATES, INC.

## OVERVIEW

Armed with aluminum foil rather than a fencing foil, it's still "all for one and one for all" for food wholesaler Topco Associates. Based in Skokie, Illinois, the wholesale grocery cooperative is the second largest in the US, trailing only Wakefern Food.

The co-op distributes more than 7,000 private-label items to its members, who sell them under Topco brands such as Kingston, Food Club, Top Care, and Top Crest. Topco also helps members market their own brands. Products offered by Topco include frozen food, regional dairy and bakery items, cheese, groceries, health and beauty products, general merchandise, and pharmaceutical items. It also offers perishables such as processed and

fresh meat, seafood, poultry, deli items, produce, and floral items.

Topco is owned by 28 supermarkets, representing about 3,000 stores, and two food services companies, and a hardware co-op. Its size enables it to purchase large volumes at lower prices than its member-owners could get if they bought the goods on their own. The co-op's combined buying power also cuts costs for its member store and warehouse equipment purchases; a financial services program creates savings for utilities, auditing, coupon processing, telecommunications, and utilities. Most of Topco's members are in the US market; Topco also has members in Israel and Japan.

## HISTORY

Food Cooperatives was founded in Wisconsin in 1944 to procure dairy bags and paper products during wartime shortages. A few years later it merged with Top Frost Foods, with which it had some common members. In 1948 the name Topco Associates was adopted (created by combining the word "Top" from Top Frost with the "Co" in Cooperatives). The member companies involved in the merger included Alpha Beta, Big Bear Stores, Brockton Public Market, Fred Meyer, Furr's, Hinky Dinky, Penn Fruit Company, and Star Markets.

Topco initially sold basic commodities to private-label retailers. It added fresh produce in 1958 and expanded its product line further in 1960, moving into general merchandise, health and beauty care items, and store equipment. In 1961, when the company moved its headquarters to Skokie, Illinois, revenues topped the $100 million mark. In the 1960s other leading supermarkets, including Giant Eagle, King Soopers, McCarty-Holman, and Tom Thumb, joined Topco.

Also that decade it came under attack from the Justice Department when it was accused of antitrust activity in granting its members exclusive distribution rights for Topco-branded products. In 1972 the Supreme Court ruled against Topco. It then agreed to sell products under the private labels of its members.

In the late 1970s the company introduced Valu Time, the first nationally marketed line of branded generic products. This concept was then adopted by many US supermarkets. By 1979 Topco surpassed $1 billion in revenues.

By the end of the 1980s, Topco's membership had expanded to include Randall's, Riser Foods, Pueblo International, Schnuck Markets,

and Smith's Food & Drug Centers. In 1988 it introduced World Classics, a premium line of high-volume, high-margin products promoted as national brands.

During the early 1990s Topco ran through a number of CEOs. In 1990 Robert Seelert replaced 10-year CEO Marcel Lussier. In 1992 John Beggs took over, and the next year Steven Rubow was handed the reins.

The early 1990s also saw rapid growth, with 20 new members bringing the company's total to 46 by 1995 (its membership later declined in number through acquisition and consolidation). Topco also expanded internationally, with the membership of Oshawa Group in Canada and the associate membership of Seiyu in Japan in 1995. Also that year the company lured upscale Kings Super Markets away from distributor White Rose.

Topco began offering members utility accounting and natural gas services through Illinova Energy Partners in 1998. In 1999 the company expanded its Top Care line of personal care products, using a variety of packaging designed to resemble several name brands within a single category. CEO Steve Rubow retired in late 1999 and was replaced by Steve Lauer. Topco took aim at consumers who prefer natural foods in 2000, launching the Full Circle line of 60 organically grown items in 15 different categories. In October 2001 Topco announced that it would combine its operations with Shurfine International's operations to form a new company, Topco Associates LLC, that will be jointly owned by Topco Associates, Inc. (85.7%) and Shurfine (14.3%).

**Chairman:** Charles D'Amour
**President and CEO:** Steven K. Lauer
**SVP Corporate Brands:** Daniel F. Mazur
**SVP Cost Containment Programs/Support Services:**
Ian Grossman
**SVP Member Development:** Kenneth H. Guy
**SVP Perishables:** Russel Wolfe
**SVP World Brands:** Michael Ricciardi
**VP Dairy:** Laird Snelgrove
**VP Meat Operations:** Rick Findlay
**VP Non-Foods:** Curt Maki
**VP Produce and Floral Operations:** Bert Boyd
**Controller:** Debbie Byers
**Manager Human Resources:** Dennis Pieper
**Auditors:** KPMG LLP

## LOCATIONS

**HQ:** 7711 Gross Point Rd., Skokie, IL 60077
**Phone:** 847-676-3030        **Fax:** 847-676-4949
**Web:** www.topcoess.com

Topco Associates purchases products on behalf of its
members in Israel, Japan, Puerto Rico, and the US.

## PRODUCTS/OPERATIONS

**Selected Private-Label Brands**
Food Club
Full Circle
GreenMark
Kingston
Pet Club
Top Care
Top Crest
Top Frost
Valu Time

**Selected Member Companies**

| | |
|---|---|
| Ace Hardware | K-VA-T Food Stores |
| Ahold USA | Meijer |
| Alex Lee | Penn Traffic |
| Big Y Foods | Piggly Wiggly Carolina |
| Blue Square-Israel | Premier Foodservice |
| Dillon Companies | Distributors of America |
| Eagle Food Centers | Pueblo International |
| F.A.B. | Quality Food Centers |
| Fred W. Albrecht Grocery | Raley's Supermarkets |
| Co. | Schnuck Markets |
| Furr's Supermarkets | Fresh Brands (Piggly |
| Genuardi's Family Markets | Wiggly) |
| Giant Eagle | Shaw's Supermarkets |
| Gooding's Supermarkets | Smith's Food |
| Haggen | The Seiyu |
| Jitney-Jungle Stores of | Ukrop's Super Markets |
| America | Weis Markets |
| Kings Super Markets | |

## COMPETITORS

Shurfine International

## HISTORICAL FINANCIALS & EMPLOYEES

| Cooperative FYE: March 31 | Annual Growth | 3/92 | 3/93 | 3/94 | 3/95 | 3/96 | 3/97 | 3/98 | 3/99 | 3/00 | 3/01 |
|---|---|---|---|---|---|---|---|---|---|---|---|
| Sales ($ mil.) | 0.9% | 2,900 | 3,000 | 3,500 | 3,700 | 3,900 | 3,700 | 3,900 | 4,000 | 3,400 | 3,150 |
| Employees | (4.2%) | 400 | 375 | 400 | 375 | 390 | 400 | 365 | 359 | 275 | 271 |

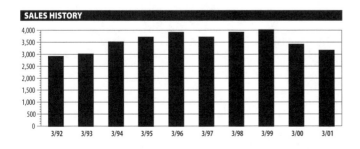

SALES HISTORY

# TOWERS PERRIN

This tower of consulting power plays a horn lots of companies want to hear. Towers Perrin, one of the leading management consulting firms in the world, serves an extensive list of corporate clients in 23 countries, including more than 700 of the *FORTUNE* 1000 companies. Headquartered in New York City, the firm's core focus is on human resources and management consulting, employee benefits, and health industry consulting. Its Tillinghast-Towers Perrin unit focuses on risk management and actuarial services to financial companies, while Towers Perrin Reinsurance serves clients primarily as a reinsurance intermediary. In

addition to consulting, the company produces several publications and surveys investigating business trends and challenges.

While guiding its clients through the downsizing and consolidating that characterized the 1990s, Towers Perrin also has been working to streamline its own operations. The company has pared down its client roster, mainly keeping its biggest customers. At the same time it has been creating new business by expanding into new practice areas, such as public relations and corporate communications. The firm is owned by more than 630 partners.

In 1934 Towers, Perrin, Forster & Crosby (TPF&C) was formed in Philadelphia by John Towers, Charles Perrin, H. Walter Forster, Arthur Crosby, H. Pratt Weaver, and Walter Chase (all former partners in predecessor firm Henry W. Brown and Company, which was founded in 1871). TPF&C specialized in reinsurance, pensions, and other employee benefits consulting. Among its initial clients were General Foods and International Harvester. Business prospered in the 1930s as companies wrestled with newly enacted Social Security and minimum wage laws. TPF&C's reinsurance division was particularly busy in London with brokers active among Lloyd's syndicates. In 1938 Walter Forster, considered "the father of pension planning," was named president.

TPF&C expanded its consulting business with a move into Chicago in 1946 and expanded beyond US borders into Montreal 10 years later. In the 1960s the firm bought companies, added offices, and expanded services to include compensation and organization consulting in response to proliferation of federal employment laws. Revenues grew from $4 million in 1960 to $14 million in 1969. Quentin Smith was named CEO in 1972 and intensified the company's growth through acquisitions. TPF&C moved from Philadelphia to New York City in 1975.

In 1983 TPF&C entered general management consulting with the purchase of Cresap, McCormick & Paget (founded in 1946) and garnered notice for the number of consultants it graduated into the CEO and chairmanship ranks at major corporations. Continuing to bulk up in an effort to keep up with first-tier competitors, TPF&C bought insurance actuarial consultancy Tillinghast, Nelson & Warren in 1986. The next year the company changed

its name to Towers Perrin. Smith retired in 1988 and James Kielly took over as CEO.

A consulting industry slump in the early 1990s, in part resulting from a lack of new federal legislation, prompted a 10% staff cut at Towers Perrin in 1991. That year John Lynch rose to the position of CEO. (He added the title of chairman the next year.) The company expanded into workplace diversity consulting in 1992. An internal restructuring produced unprofitable projects and led to staff resignations, a surprising move for a firm traditionally noted for low turnover.

In 1994 Towers Perrin rejected a takeover bid from benefit and actuarial consulting specialist Buck Consultants, a company one-quarter the size of its acquisition target. One Towers Perrin executive called the move "the goofiest thing we've ever seen." Reports later surfaced that some Towers Perrin customers who paid high fees between 1994 and 1996 for workplace diversity recommendations received 100-page reports containing identical, generic suggestions and plans. Most clients accepted the proposals.

The company continued to expand through acquisitions, particularly outside the US and in healthcare services. It bought health care adviser Partners Consulting Group in 1997, Canadian consulting firm Tandem International and Atlanta-based Miller/Howard Consulting Group in 1998. The following year Towers Perrin was appointed investment consultant to The Monetary Authority of Singapore, which plans to place $10 billion with fund managers over the next three years.

In 2001 the company created Towers Perrin Technology Solutions to help companies use the Internet to manage their human resources.

---

**Chairman and CEO:** Mark Mactas
**CFO:** Mark L. Wilson
**Managing Director E-commerce and Strategic Planning:** Patricia Milligan
**Managing Director Executive Compensation and People Performance Solutions:** Donald L. Lowman
**Managing Director Global Retirement Services, Health & Welfare, and Administration Services:** Robert G. Hogan
**Managing Director Human Resources:** Anne Donovan Bodnar
**Managing Director International Operations (Europe, Latin America, Asia, Australia):** Michael Ponicall
**Managing Director North America:** Garrett L. Dietz

## LOCATIONS

**HQ:** 335 Madison Ave., New York, NY 10017
**Phone:** 212-309-3400      **Fax:** 212-309-0975
**Web:** www.towers.com

Towers Perrin has 78 offices in 23 countries.

## PRODUCTS/OPERATIONS

**Selected Operations**

**Tillinghast-Towers Perrin**
Customer Value Management
Distribution Strategy and Effectiveness
Health Sector Consulting
Market Analysis and Positioning
Mergers, Acquisitions and Restructuring
Organizational Effectiveness
Reinsurance Intermediary and Consulting Services
RiskValueInsights

**Towers Perrin**
Change Management
Human Resource Administration
Human Resource Strategy and Management
Mergers, Acquisitions and Restructuring
Organization and Process Redesign
Total Rewards
  Benefits
  Compensation
  Learning and Development
  Work Environment
Workforce and Organization Research

**Selected Publications**

*2000 HR Service Center Survey*
*AlfaBeta* (investment issues and pension funds, Canada)
*Custody World* (custody information)
*Pensions & Benefits Today* (pension and benefits, Canada)
*Perspectives on Reward Management* (executive compensation)
*Perspectives on Total Rewards* (business improvement)
*SuperNews* (superannuation plans, Australia)
*Towers Perrin Monitor* (client newsletter)
*Worldwide Pay and Benefits Headlines* (compensation trends)

## COMPETITORS

Accenture
Aon
A.T. Kearney
Bain & Company
Booz-Allen
Boston Consulting
Buck Consultants
Deloitte Touche Tohmatsu
Ernst & Young
Gallup
Hewitt Associates
KPMG
Marsh & McLennan
Marsh
McKinsey & Company
PricewaterhouseCoopers
Watson Wyatt

## HISTORICAL FINANCIALS & EMPLOYEES

| Private FYE: December 31 | Annual Growth | 12/91 | 12/92 | 12/93 | 12/94 | 12/95 | 12/96 | 12/97 | 12/98 | 12/99 | 12/00 |
|---|---|---|---|---|---|---|---|---|---|---|---|
| Sales ($ mil.) | 9.4% | — | 705 | 709 | 767 | 822 | 855 | 1,000 | 1,125 | 1,338 | 1,448 |
| Employees | 8.3% | — | 4,730 | 5,000 | 5,000 | 5,050 | 6,361 | 6,350 | 6,314 | 8,600 | 8,919 |

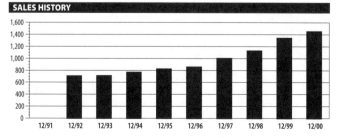

**SALES HISTORY**

*Towers Perrin*

# THE TRUMP ORGANIZATION

When it comes to betting on big business, The Donald always pulls out a Trump card. Through his New York City-based Trump Organization, Donald J. Trump owns and develops several pieces of prime NYC real estate, including Trump International Hotel and Tower, 40 Wall Street, and half-ownership of the Empire State Building (the land on which it stands). He is also 50% owner, with Conseco, of the General Motors Building at Trump International Plaza. The company has raised the world's tallest residential building, the 72-story Trump World Tower in New York.

Meanwhile, Trump continues to retain interests in the projects that made him famous, such as Trump Tower (he owns the lower 26 floors, plus his three-floor apartment), and Trump Palace.

Beyond Manhattan, Trump owns the Mar-A-Lago resort and the Trump Plaza condominium complex in Palm Beach, Florida. He also has a 42% stake in, and is chairman of, the publicly traded Trump Hotels & Casino Resorts, which operates three Atlantic City casinos — Trump Taj Mahal, Trump Plaza, and Trump Marina — as well as the Trump Indiana riverboat casino.

The Donald continues to excel on the strength of his deal-making prowess; the flamboyant tycoon is renowned for setting up real estate partnerships in which other firms put up most of the cash while he retains most of the control. In the Trump World Tower, for example, he invested $6.5 million, while Korean firm Daewoo pumped in more than $58 million. Trump also has profited from his famous moniker — which he has trademarked — and his public image.

The third of four children, Donald Trump was the son of a successful builder in Queens and Brooklyn. After graduating from the Wharton School of Finance in 1968, his first job was to turn around a 1,200-unit foreclosed apartment complex in Cincinnati that his father had bought for $6 million with no money down. Managing the Cincinnati job gave Trump a distaste for the nonaffluent; he wanted to get to Manhattan to meet all the right people.

Operating as the Trump Organization, he took options on two Hudson River sites in 1975 for no money down and began lobbying the city to finance his construction of a convention center. The center was built, but not by Trump, who nevertheless got about $800,000 and priceless publicity. He and hotelier Jay Pritzker turned the Commodore Hotel near Grand Central Station into the Grand Hyatt Hotel in 1975. Trump married fashion model Ivana Zelnicek two years later.

In 1981 he built the posh Trump Tower on Fifth Avenue and proceeded to wheel and deal himself into 1980s folklore. In 1983 he joined with Holiday Inn to build the Trump Casino Hotel (now Trump Plaza) in Atlantic City using public-issue bonds (he bought out Holiday Inn's interest in 1986), and he acquired the Trump Castle from Hilton in 1985. In 1987 he ended up with the unfinished Taj Mahal in Atlantic City, then the world's largest casino, after a battle with Merv Griffin for Resorts International (Griffin won). He bought the Plaza Hotel in Manhattan in 1988, and the Eastern air shuttle (renamed the Trump Shuttle) the next year.

As the 1990s dawned, though, Trump's balance sheet was loaded with about $3 billion in debt. At the same time, his marriage to Ivana broke up in a splash of publicity. Trump's 70 creditor banks consolidated and restructured his debt in 1990. He married Marla Maples in 1993. (They divorced in 1998.)

In 1995 Trump formed Trump Hotels & Casino Resorts and took it public. He also paid a token $10 for 40 Wall St. (now home to American Express). The next year he unloaded more than $1.1 billion of his debt by selling the Taj Mahal and Trump's Castle to Trump Hotels. That year Trump bought the Miss Universe, Miss USA, and Miss Teen USA beauty pageants.

In 1997 he published *The Art of the Comeback,* a follow-up to *The Art of the Deal* (1987), and started work on Trump Place, a residential development on New York's Upper West Side. In 1999 he began building the Trump World Tower — a 90-story residential building near the United Nations complex.

In 2000 Trump and publisher Hollinger International announced plans to transform the former riverfront headquarters of the *Chicago Sun-Times* into a residential and commercial development. Originally planned to be the world's tallest skyscraper, the development would have returned to Chicago the lofty title it lost to the Petronas Towers (Kuala Lumpur, Malaysia). Trump decided to scale back the project in the wake of the 2001 terrorist attacks on the World Trade Center towers in New York.

## OFFICERS

**Chairman, President, and CEO:** Donald J. Trump, age 54
**CFO:** Allen Weisselberg
**EVP Acquisitions and Finance:** Abraham Wallach
**VP Finance:** John P. Burke, age 53
**VP Human Resources:** Norma Foerderer
**Corporate Secretary:** Rhona Graff-Riccio
**General Counsel:** Bernard Diamond

## LOCATIONS

**HQ:** 725 5th Ave., New York, NY 10022
**Phone:** 212-832-2000     **Fax:** 212-935-0141
**Web:** www.trumponline.com

## PRODUCTS/OPERATIONS

**Trump Hotels & Casino Resorts, Inc.**
Trump Indiana (mooring for a 37,000-sq.-ft. yacht casino; Buffington Harbor, IN)
Trump Marina (casino resort; Atlantic City, NJ)
Trump Plaza ( hotel/casino; Atlantic City, NJ)
Trump Taj Mahal (hotel/casino; Atlantic City, NJ)

**Other Holdings**
40 Wall Street
Briar Hall Country Club (Westchester County, NY)
Empire State Building (50%)
General Motors Building at Trump International Plaza (50%)
Mar-A-Lago (private club; Palm Beach, FL)
Miss Teen USA pageant
Miss Universe pageant
Miss USA pageant
Trump International Golf Club (West Palm Beach, FL)
Trump International Hotel and Tower
Trump Palace
Trump Parc
Trump Place
Trump Tower
Trump World Tower

## COMPETITORS

| | |
|---|---|
| Alexander's | MGM Mirage |
| Aztar | Park Place Entertainment |
| Harrah's Entertainment | Port Authority of NY & NJ |
| Helmsley | Ritz Carlton |
| Hyatt | Rouse |
| Lefrak Organization | Tishman Realty |
| Marriott International | Vornado |
| Mashantucket Pequot Gaming | |

## HISTORICAL FINANCIALS & EMPLOYEES

| Private<br>FYE: December 31 | Annual<br>Growth | 12/91 | 12/92 | 12/93 | 12/94 | 12/95 | 12/96 | 12/97 | 12/98 | 12/99 | 12/00 |
|---|---|---|---|---|---|---|---|---|---|---|---|
| Estimated sales ($ mil.) | 24.3% | — | 1,400 | 2,000 | 2,750 | 4,000 | 6,000 | 6,500 | 6,800 | 7,000 | 8,000 |
| Employees | 3.3% | — | 17,000 | 15,000 | 15,000 | 19,000 | 19,000 | 22,000 | 22,000 | 22,000 | 22,000 |

**SALES HISTORY**

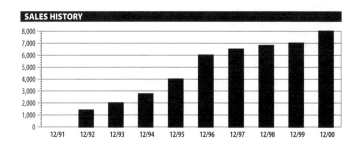

# TRUSERV CORPORATION

## OVERVIEW

To compete against home improvement giants such as The Home Depot and Lowe's, Chicago-based TruServ is relying on pure service. The troubled company is the #1 hardware cooperative in the US, serving about 7,700 independent retailers there and in Canada. Its True Value, Coast to Coast, and ServiStar chains sell lumber and building materials, home and garden supplies, and hardware. (Most Coast to Coast and ServiStar stores converted to the True Value banner.) The firm also operates the Taylor Rental and Grand Rental Station chains and serves the C&S Choices and Home & Garden Showplace chains. In addition, TruServ makes paint and accessories.

TruServ was formed with the marriage of Cotter & Company (wholesaler to the True Value chain) and ServiStar Coast to Coast (operator of Coast to Coast hardware stores and several other chains). The merger has given members — many of them mom-and-pop outlets — more buying clout to compete against the do-it-yourself mega-retailers, plus retail advice and advertising support. The company is fending off growing competitors such as Ace Hardware and Do it Best, which are aggressively wooing TruServ dealers.

## HISTORY

Noting that hardware retailers had begun to form wholesale cooperatives to lower costs, John Cotter, a traveling hardware salesman, and associate Ed Lanctot started pitching the wholesale co-op idea in 1947 to small-town and suburban hardware retailers, and by early 1948 they had enrolled 25 merchants for $1,500 each. Cotter became chairman of the new firm, Cotter & Company.

The co-op created the Value & Service (V&S) store trademark in 1951 to emphasize the advantages of an independent hardware store. Acquisitions included the 1963 purchase of Chicago-based wholesaler Hibbard, Spencer, Bartlett, giving Cotter 400 new members and the well-known True Value trademark, which soon replaced V&S signs. Four years later Cotter broadened its focus by buying the General Paint & Chemical Company (Tru-Test paint). The V&S name was revived in 1972 for a five-and-dime store co-op, V&S Variety Stores.

Cotter died in 1989. By that time there were almost 7,000 True Value Stores. Cotter moved into Canada in 1992 by acquiring hardware distributor and store operator Macleod-Stedman (275 outlets).

Juggling variety-store and hardware merchandise and delivering very small amounts of merchandise to a lukewarm co-op membership did not allow for economies of scale, so in 1995 the company quit its manufacturing operations and its US variety stores (though it still serves variety stores in Canada, operating as C&S Choices), tightened membership requirements, and introduced new services.

Two years later Cotter formed TruServ by merging with hardware wholesaler Servistar Coast to Coast. ServiStar had its origins in the nation's first hardware co-op, American Hardware Supply, which was founded in Pittsburgh in 1910 by M. R. Porter, John Howe, and E. S. Corlett. By 1988, the year it changed its name to Servistar, the co-op topped $1 billion in sales.

Servistar expanded in the upper Midwest and on the West Coast in 1990 when it acquired the assets of the Coast to Coast chain (founded in 1928 as a franchise hardware store in Minneapolis); Servistar brought Coast to Coast out of bankruptcy two years later, making it a co-op. Merging its 1992 acquisition of Taylor Rental Center with its Grand Rental Station stores in 1993 made Servistar the #1 general rental chain. In 1996 it consolidated Coast to Coast's operations into its own and changed its name to Servistar Coast to Coast.

President Don Hoye became CEO of the company in 1999. That year TruServ slashed 1,000 jobs and declared it would convert all its hardware store chains to the True Value banner. But TruServ lost $131 million in 1999 over bookkeeping gaffs, and co-op members received no dividends. Of 2,800 ServiStar dealers, only 1,900 raised the True Value flag. Others either declined to switch or were never offered the change because other True Value stores already shared their market area. In addition, stores began deserting the co-op because of inventory and other problems.

As competition continued to increase in 2001, the company was facing falling sales and a $200 million loan default. It also faced lawsuits from shareholders and retailers alleging unfair practices intended to pressure them into adopting the cooperative's flagship True Value banner. It streamlined its executive structure and announced plans to cut up to 10% of its workforce and divest its Canadian interests. In 2001 Hoye resigned. CFO and COO Pamela Forbes Lieberman was named the new CEO.

## OFFICERS

**Chairman:** Joe W. Blagg
**Vice Chairman:** James D. Howenstine
**CEO and Acting CFO:** Pamela Lieberman, age 46
**SVP and Chief Information Officer:** Neil A. Hastie
**SVP, Human Resources, Chief Administrative Officer, and General Counsel:** Robert Ostrov
**SVP, Logistics:** Michael Rosen
**SVP Sales, Marketing, Advertising, and Merchandising:** Robert Liebgott, age 50
**SVP, Supply Chain and Business Segments:** William Godwin
**Auditors:** PricewaterhouseCoopers LLP

## LOCATIONS

**HQ:** 8600 W. Bryn Mawr Ave., Chicago, IL 60631
**Phone:** 773-695-5000    **Fax:** 773-695-6516
**Web:** www.truserv.com

TruServ is a hardware store cooperative serving some 7,700 stores in the US and Canada.

## PRODUCTS/OPERATIONS

**Selected Operations**
C&S Choices
Coast to Coast
Grand Rental Station
Home & Garden Showplace
Induserve Supply
ServiStar
Taylor Rental
True Value

## COMPETITORS

84 Lumber
Ace Hardware
Akzo Nobel
Benjamin Moore
Carolina Holdings
Do it Best
Fastenal
Hertz
Home Depot
House2Home
Kmart
Lanoga
Lowe's
McCoy
Menard
Payless Cashways
Reno-Depot
Sears
Sherwin-Williams
Sutherland Lumber
United Rentals
Valspar
Wal-Mart
Wickes
Wolohan Lumber

## HISTORICAL FINANCIALS & EMPLOYEES

| Cooperative<br>FYE: Sat. nearest Dec. 31 | Annual<br>Growth | 12/91 | 12/92 | 12/93 | 12/94 | 12/95 | 12/96 | 12/97 | 12/98 | 12/99 | 12/00 |
|---|---|---|---|---|---|---|---|---|---|---|---|
| Sales ($ mil.) | 6.8% | — | 2,356 | 2,421 | 2,574 | 2,437 | 2,442 | 3,332 | 4,328 | 4,502 | 3,994 |
| Net income ($ mil.) | (6.9%) | — | 61 | 57 | 60 | 59 | 52 | 43 | 20 | (131) | 34 |
| Income as % of sales | — | — | 2.6% | 2.4% | 2.3% | 2.4% | 2.1% | 1.3% | 0.5% | — | 0.9% |
| Employees | (0.3%) | — | 4,400 | 4,400 | 4,200 | 4,186 | 3,825 | 5,800 | 6,500 | 5,500 | 4,300 |

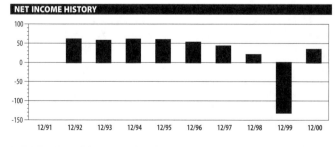

**NET INCOME HISTORY**

**2000 FISCAL YEAR-END**
Debt ratio: 5.7%
Return on equity: —
Cash ($ mil.): 19
Current ratio: 0.82
Long-term debt ($ mil.): 9

# TY INC.

## OVERVIEW

Ty's Beanies aren't so weeny. The Westmont, Illinois-based company makes Beanie Babies, the plush collectibles that are small in size but big in stature. The plastic-pellet-filled creatures, with colorful names such as Cheezer the mouse and Jester the clownfish, have a cult-like following among kids and adults alike. In addition to the more than 325 varieties of Beanie Babies (but only 40 or 50 in circulation at any one time), Ty's products include Baby Ty Pillow Pals, Attic Treasures, and Ty Classics (stuffed animals); Beanie Buddies (bigger versions of traditional Beanies); and Beanie Kids (humanoid Beanies).

Beanies are recognizable by their heart-shaped tags, but if the company itself had a tag, it might well be shaped like a brain. Ty's marketing smarts have kept Beanies popular for years rather than for a single holiday season, à la Furby or Tickle Me Elmo. Rather than flood the market with Beanies through the likes of Toys "R" Us and Wal-Mart, Ty sells them only through specialty toy and gift retailers. It also limits production so that supply never outstrips demand.

The firm doesn't advertise, relying instead on the word of mouth that is rampant in Beanie culture. Books, magazines, newsletters, and Web sites stoke collectors' enthusiasm. Ty's "retirement" of a Beanie can cause its price among collectors to skyrocket from its $5-$7 retail debut to hundreds or even thousands of dollars. This collectors' market — which Ty frowns upon (officially, anyway) — shows signs of fading, however.

Mysterious, gimmicky founder Ty Warner owns Ty, whose success has enabled him to buy two Four Seasons luxury hotels (in New York City and Montecito, California).

## HISTORY

Ty Warner, the son of a plush-toy salesman, started his toy career selling stuffed animals to specialty shops for stuffed bear manufacturer Dakin. Warner left Dakin in 1980, moved to Europe for a few years, and in the mid-1980s returned to the US and founded Ty. It first designed a line of $20, understuffed Himalayan cats.

Beanie Babies first debuted at a 1993 trade show. In January 1994 the first nine Beanies went up for sale — at prices low enough for kids to afford — in Chicago specialty stores. As Warner had learned at Dakin, selling stuffed animals through specialty retailers rather than through mass merchandisers meant bigger profits for suppliers and longer-term popularity. By 1995 there were about 30 different Beanie Babies, and Ty's estimated sales were $26 million.

The popularity of Beanies exploded in 1996, first in the Midwest, then along the East Coast, and then across the US. By midyear, Beanies — and the public's mania for getting them before they sold out — were receiving widespread media coverage. Ty heightened the frenzy among collectors when it started announcing Beanie retirements on its Web site in 1997.

McDonald's got on the bandwagon in 1997: The fast-food giant issued some 100 million "teenie" Beanie Babies in a Happy Meal promotion. McDonald's ran out of the toys and had to end the promotion early, causing a public relations mess. McDonald's doubled its toy order in 1998 and teamed up with Ty again in 1999 and 2000.

In 1998 Warner paid $10 million for a 7% stake in marketing company Cyrk. In return, Cyrk (now Simon Worldwide) developed the Beanie Babies Official Club, which turned stores that sell Beanies into "official headquarters" offering club membership kits. Ty introduced its Attic Treasures and Beanie Buddies lines that year.

By spring 1998 Beanies had become a customs issue at the US-Canadian border, where limits of one imported Beanie per person resulted in tears and fisticuffs. (Ty raise the personal limit to 30.) That summer the crowds at Major League Baseball games featuring Beanie giveaways were 26% bigger than average.

Warner bought the Four Seasons hotel in New York City in 1999, paying the equivalent of the retail price of roughly 46 million Beanies. He also provided auditing documents and correspondence to *The New York Post* indicating that Ty had 1998 profits of more than $700 million — more than Hasbro and Mattel combined.

After an August 1999 announcement that it would retire the Beanies at the end of the year, the company held a New Year's vote to determine their fate. In the most shocking outcome since *Rocky IV*, the public voted overwhelmingly in favor of continuing the Beanies. Ty introduced its humanoid Beanie Kids line in early 2000. Later that year he bought the Four Seasons Biltmore Hotel in Montecito, California.

## HISTORICAL FINANCIALS & EMPLOYEES

| Private<br>FYE: December 31 | Annual<br>Growth | 12/91 | 12/92 | 12/93 | 12/94 | 12/95 | 12/96 | 12/97 | 12/98 | 12/99 | 12/00 |
|---|---|---|---|---|---|---|---|---|---|---|---|
| Estimated sales ($ mil.) | 100.0% | — | — | — | — | 25 | 250 | 400 | 1,000 | 1,250 | 800 |
| Employees | 82.1% | — | — | — | — | 50 | 200 | 500 | 1,000 | 1,000 | 1,000 |

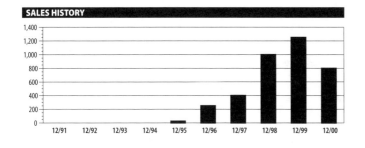

**SALES HISTORY**

# UNIFIED WESTERN GROCERS, INC.

## OVERVIEW

What do you name a company resulting from the unification of two wholesale grocery distributors on the West Coast unite? Unified Western Grocers, of course. Formed when Certified Grocers of California merged with United Grocers of Oregon in 1999, the Commerce, California-based cooperative supplies food and general merchandise to about 3,700 stores, mostly independents located in Arizona, California, Colorado, Hawaii, Nevada, Oregon, Utah, and Washington. The co-op is owned by some 670 retail members who receive dividends each year based on the amount they purchase.

Unified distributes name-brand deli items, dry groceries, frozen foods, meat, and baked and dairy goods. The co-op also provides a full line of food and nonfood items under such private labels as Springfield, Gingham, Special Value, Western Family, and Valley Fare. In addition to distribution, the company provides its members support services, including financing, insurance, real estate, and store development.

Consolidation and the trend toward self-distribution among food retailers has hurt wholesale grocery distributors. To match the buying power afforded to large supermarket chains and wholesalers, the two co-ops merged to become Unified. Unified has begun its own store format, Apple Markets, to replace older stores. Unified also owns nine SavMax, three Apple Market, and two Thriftway stores on the West Coast.

## HISTORY

Certified Grocers of California evolved from a group of 15 independent Southern California grocers that formed a purchasing cooperative in 1922 to compete against large grocery chains. Certified Grocers of California incorporated in 1925 and issued stock to 50 members.

The co-op merged with a small retailer-owned wholesale company called Co-operative Grocers in 1928. In 1929 it acquired Walker Brothers Grocery and nearly tripled the previous year's sales. By 1938 the co-op had grown to 310 members and 380 stores, and sales passed $10 million.

Certified launched a line of private-label products under the Springfield name in 1947. In the early 1950s it added nonfood items and began processing its own private-label coffee and bean products. The co-op added delicatessen items in 1956. During the 1960s and 1970s, Certified added a meat center, a frozen food and deli warehouse, a produce distribution center, a creamery, a central bakery, and a specialty foods warehouse.

In 1989 the co-op opened several membership warehouse stores called Convenience Clubs. The Save Mart and Boys Markets chains left the fold in 1991. The co-op lost about 30% of its business during the next two years, including the Bel Air and Williams Bros. chains. After disappointing returns, in 1992 Certified sold its warehouse stores, cut staff, and consolidated warehouses.

CFO (and former Atlantic Richfield executive) Al Plamann was appointed CEO in 1994, succeeding Everett Dingwell. In 1996 the co-op began to convert its customers' older retail stores to Apple Markets in Southern California. That year revenues dipped as the result of reduced purchases from some supermarkets and the sale in 1996 of one of its subsidiaries, Hawaiian Grocery Stores. Member chain Stumps converted to the Apple Markets banner in 1998. Faced with a declining customer base, in 1999 Certified merged with United Grocers of Oregon to form Unified Western Grocers.

Dr. R. Norton, F. L. Freeburg, and A. C. Brinckerhoff founded United Grocers of Oregon in 1915 as a way for grocers in Portland to cooperate in the purchase of merchandise. The next year the co-op had 35 members. In the 1950s United formed a trucking department and established a general merchandise division. The company also grew rapidly in the 1950s through acquisitions, buying Northwest Grocery Company and the Fridegar Grocery Company. In 1963 United formed its frozen food department when it purchased Raven Creamery.

By 1975 the company's Northwest Grocery Company subsidiary had 14 Cash and Carry warehouses that sold goods to small grocers and restaurants. In 1995 the company bought California food distributor Market Wholesale. Three years later United sold its Cash and Carry warehouse-style stores to Smart & Final.

Upon completion of United's merger with Certified in 1999, Certified's Plamann was named to head the new organization.

The next year it bought the specialty foods business of J. Sosnick and Son, another California company. The company attributed net losses during 2001 to delays in moving the source for northern California specialty merchandise from southern to northern California and to the costs of entering the Washington marketplace, among other factors.

**President and CEO:** Alfred A. Plamann, age 58, $500,000 pay
**EVP, Finance and Administration and CFO:** Richard J. Martin, age 53, $266,154 pay
**EVP, General Counsel, and Secretary:** Robert M. Ling Jr., age 41, $237,115 pay
**EVP Sales and Marketing:** Charles J. Pilliter, age 52, $234,231 pay
**SVP Retail Development; President, SavMax Foods:** Harley J. Delano, age 63
**SVP Non Foods and Specialty Products:** George D. Gardner, age 47, $175,000 pay
**SVP Procurement:** Philip S. Smith, age 50
**VP and Controller:** William O. Cote, age 43
**VP and Treasurer:** David A. Woodward, age 58
**VP Human Resources:** Don Giltin
**Auditors:** Deloitte & Touche LLP

## LOCATIONS

**HQ:** 5200 Sheila St., Commerce, CA 90040
**Phone:** 323-264-5200       **Fax:** 323-265-4006
**Web:** www.certifiedgrocers.com

Unified Western Grocers distributes to about 3,700 member stores in Arizona, California, Colorado, Hawaii, Nevada, Oregon, Utah, and Washington.

## PRODUCTS/OPERATIONS

**Selected Co-op Members**
Alamo Market
Andronico's Markets
Bales For Food
Berberian Enterprises, Inc.
Bristol Farms Markets, Inc.
Estacada Foods, Inc.
Evergreen Markets, Inc.
Gelson's Markets
Goodwin & Sons, Inc.
Howard's On Scholls
Joe Notrica, Inc.
K. V. Mart Co.
Mar-Val Food Stores, Inc.
Mollie Stone's Markets
Pioneer Super Save, Inc.
Pokerville Select Market
Pro & Son's, Inc.
Sentry Market
Stump's Market, Inc.
Super A Foods, Inc.
Super Center Concepts, Inc.
Sweet Home Thriftway
Tresierras Bros. Corp.
Wright's Foodliner

**Selected Support Services**
Financing
Information technology
Insurance
Private labels
Real estate development
Security
Store design

## COMPETITORS

| | |
|---|---|
| Albertson's | Safeway |
| Associated Food | Shurfine International |
| Associated Grocers | SUPERVALU |
| Core-Mark | Topco Associates |
| Fleming Companies | Wal-Mart |
| Kroger | WinCo Foods |
| Nash Finch | |

## HISTORICAL FINANCIALS & EMPLOYEES

| Cooperative FYE: Sat. nearest Sept. 30 | Annual Growth | 9/92 | 9/93 | 9/94 | 9/95 | 9/96 | 9/97 | 9/98 | 9/99 | 9/00 | 9/01 |
|---|---|---|---|---|---|---|---|---|---|---|---|
| Sales ($ mil.) | 2.3% | 2,378 | 2,007 | 1,874 | 1,823 | 1,949 | 1,927 | 1,832 | 1,894 | 3,067 | 2,929 |
| Net income ($ mil.) | — | (4) | 0 | (2) | 1 | 2 | 2 | 3 | 3 | (11) | (13) |
| Income as % of sales | — | — | — | — | 0.0% | 0.1% | 0.1% | 0.2% | 0.1% | — | — |
| Employees | 3.8% | 3,000 | 2,500 | 2,600 | 2,470 | 2,400 | 2,400 | 2,200 | 3,945 | 4,000 | 4,200 |

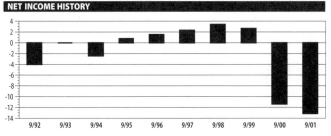

### NET INCOME HISTORY

### 2001 FISCAL YEAR-END
Debt ratio: 76.5%
Return on equity: —
Cash ($ mil.): 15
Current ratio: 0.15
Long-term debt ($ mil.): 288

# UNITED STATES POSTAL SERVICE

## OVERVIEW

Through snow, rain, heat, and gloom of night, the United States Postal Service (USPS) delivers about 40% of the world's mail, more than 200 billion pieces a year. The independent government agency, which is based in Washington, DC, relies on postage and fees to fund operations.

USPS has a monopoly on the delivery of nonurgent letters but faces stiff competition from UPS and FedEx in services such as package delivery. Another challenge for the agency is the growing use of the Internet, which the USPS expects will cause the volume of "snail mail" to decline.

To keep pace, the USPS is launching e-commerce initiatives such as computerized postage. The agency has also tapped into online shopping with its priority mail, merchandise return, and delivery confirmation services. It has formed limited alliances with express delivery companies, including a deal in which FedEx provides air transportation for express mail, priority, and first-class mail shipments (but doesn't deliver the mail).

At the same time, the agency has been hit hard by rising fuel costs. With an eye on its bottom line, the USPS has scaled down its construction program, and in 2001 it moved to impose a rare midyear rate hike.

The US president appoints nine of the 11 members of the board that oversees the USPS. The presidential appointees select the postmaster general, who, along with the deputy postmaster general, is a board member.

## HISTORY

The second-oldest agency of the US government (after Indian Affairs), the Post Office was created by the Continental Congress in 1775 with Benjamin Franklin as postmaster general. The postal system came to play a vital role in the development of transportation in the US.

At that time, postal workers were riders on muddy paths delivering letters without stamps or envelopes. Letters were delivered only between post offices. Congress approved the first official postal policy in 1792: Rates ranged from six cents for less than 30 miles to 25 cents for more than 450. Letter carriers began delivering mail in cities in 1794.

First based in Philadelphia, in 1800 the Post Office moved to Washington, DC. In 1829 Andrew Jackson elevated the position of postmaster general to cabinet rank — it became a means of rewarding political cronies. Mail contracts subsidized the early development of US railroads. The first adhesive postage stamp appeared in the US in 1847.

Uniform postal rates (not varying with distance) were instituted in 1863, the year free city delivery began. The start of free rural delivery in 1896 spurred road construction in isolated US areas. Parcel post was launched in 1913, and new mail-order houses such as Montgomery Ward and Sears, Roebuck flourished.

The famous pledge beginning "Neither snow nor rain ..." — not an official motto — was first inscribed at the main New York City post office in 1914. Scheduled airmail service between Washington, DC, and New York City began in 1918, stimulating the development of commercial air service. The ZIP code was introduced in 1963.

As mail volume grew, postal workers became increasingly militant under work stress. (Franklin's pigeonhole sorting method had barely changed.) A work stoppage in the New York City post office in 1970 spread within nine days to 670 post offices, and the US Army was deployed to handle the mail. Later that year the Postal Reorganization Act was passed. The law established a board of governors to handle postal affairs and choose the postmaster general, who became CEO of an independent agency, the United States Postal Service (USPS). The next year USPS negotiated the first US government collective bargaining labor contract.

In 1996 USPS overhauled rates, cutting prices for larger mailers who prepared their mail for automation and raising prices for small mailers who didn't.

Postmaster General Marvin Runyon — whose six-year tenure took the agency from the red into the black — retired in 1998 and was succeeded by USPS veteran William Henderson. Nodding to the Internet, USPS in 1999 contracted with outside vendors to enable customers to buy and print stamps online.

In 2001 USPS formed a strategic alliance with rival FedEx through which FedEx agreed to provide air transportation for USPS mail, in return for the placement of FedEx drop boxes in post offices. Later that year the company halted construction projects as part of a cost-cutting effort and announced further rate increases. Henderson stepped down in 2001, and EVP Jack Potter was named to replace him. That same year several postal workers in a Washington, DC, branch office were exposed to anthrax-tainted letters.

## OFFICERS

**Chairman:** Robert F. Rider, age 72
**Vice Chairman:** S. David Fineman
**Postmaster General and CEO:** John E. Potter, age 45
**Deputy Postmaster General and Chief Marketing Officer:** John Nolan
**EVP and CFO:** Richard J. Strasser Jr.
**SVP and Chief Technology Officer:** Norman E. Lorentz
**SVP Future Business Design:** Allen R. Kane
**SVP Government Relations:** Debrorah K. Willhite
**SVP HR:** Suzanne Medvidovich
**SVP Operations:** Patrick R. Donahoe
**VP and General Counsel:** Mary S. Eleano
**VP Area Operations, Great Lakes Area:** J.T. Weeker
**VP Area Operations, Mid-Atlantic Area:**
Henry A. Pankey
**VP Area Operations, Midwest Area:** William H. McComb
**VP Area Operations, New York Metro Area:**
David Solomon
**VP Area Operations, Northeast Area:** Jon Steele
**VP Area Operations, Pacific Area:** Jesse Durazo
**VP Area Operations, Southeast Area:** Robert T. Davis
**Acting VP Area Operations, Southwest Area:**
George Lopez
**VP Area Operations, Western Area:** Craig G. Wade
**Auditors:** Ernst & Young LLP

## LOCATIONS

**HQ:** 475 L'Enfant Plaza SW, Washington, DC 20260
**Phone:** 202-268-2500    **Fax:** 202-268-4860
**Web:** www.usps.gov

## PRODUCTS/OPERATIONS

**2001 Sales**

|  | $ mil. | % of total |
|---|---|---|
| First-class mail | 35,876 | 54 |
| Standard mail | 15,705 | 24 |
| Priority mail | 4,916 | 7 |
| Periodicals | 2,205 | 3 |
| Packages | 1,994 | 3 |
| International | 1,732 | 3 |
| Express mail | 996 | 2 |
| Other services | 2,495 | 4 |
| Adjustments | (85) | — |
| **Total** | **65,834** | **100** |

**Selected Services**

Certified mail
Collection-on-delivery (COD)
Delivery confirmation (via the Web)
Digital Certificate (proof of identification for electronic transactions)
Express mail
First-class mail
Free mail for the blind and disabled
International mail
Mail forwarding
Merchandise return (downloadable return-mail labels)
Money orders
Passport applications
PC Postage
Periodicals
Post office boxes
Postage meters
Priority mail
Registered mail
Return receipt
Special delivery
Standard mail

## COMPETITORS

| | |
|---|---|
| Airborne | FedEx |
| BAX Global | Mail Boxes Etc. |
| CNF | Roadway |
| DHL | UPS |

## HISTORICAL FINANCIALS & EMPLOYEES

| Government-owned<br>FYE: September 30 | Annual<br>Growth | 9/92 | 9/93 | 9/94 | 9/95 | 9/96 | 9/97 | 9/98 | 9/99 | 9/00 | 9/01 |
|---|---|---|---|---|---|---|---|---|---|---|---|
| Sales ($ mil.) | 4.0% | 46,151 | 47,418 | 49,252 | 54,294 | 56,402 | 58,216 | 60,072 | 62,726 | 64,540 | 65,834 |
| Net income ($ mil.) | — | (536) | (1,765) | (914) | 1,770 | 1,567 | 1,264 | 550 | 363 | (199) | (1,680) |
| Income as % of sales | — | — | — | — | 3.3% | 2.8% | 2.2% | 0.9% | 0.6% | — | — |
| Employees | 1.1% | 725,290 | 691,723 | 728,944 | 753,384 | 760,966 | 765,174 | 792,041 | 800,000 | 787,538 | 797,795 |

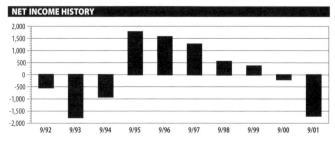

**NET INCOME HISTORY**

**2001 FISCAL YEAR-END**
Debt ratio: 100.0%
Return on equity: —
Cash ($ mil.): 1,005
Current ratio: 0.11
Long-term debt ($ mil.): 5,751

# UNITED WAY OF AMERICA

United Way of America (UWA) has been described as a mutual fund for charitable causes, and with about 45,000 agencies receiving financial support from UWA's 1,400 local organizations, the epithet seems fitting. Headquartered in Alexandria, Virginia, the not-for-profit organization focuses on health and human services causes. Its local organizations help to fund a multitude of endeavors, including the American Cancer Society, Big Brothers/Big Sisters, Catholic Charities, Girl Scouts and Boy Scouts, and the Salvation Army. During a fund-raising campaign that began in 1999, UWA raised

nearly $3.8 billion (about 50% from employee contributions and more than 20% from corporations). Its administrative expenses average 10% of funds raised.

Each of the local organizations is an independent entity governed by local volunteers, and UWA acts as a national services and training center, supporting the local organizations with services such as national advertising and research. To advance the understanding of its role, UWA has launched an initiative to raise awareness of how it serves local communities.

The first modern Community Chest was created in 1913, laying the foundation for the practice of allocating funds among multiple causes. Five years later, representatives from 12 fund-raising organizations met in Chicago and established the American Association for Community Organizations, the predecessor of the present-day United Way. Contributing to the community became more widespread in the 1920s, and by 1929 more than 350 Community Chests had been established.

Payroll deductions for charitable contributions debuted in 1943. In 1946 the United Way's predecessor organization initiated a cooperative relationship with the American Federation of Labor and the Congress of Industrial Organizations (which merged to become the AFL-CIO in 1955) to provide services to members of organized labor. (The relationship continues today, with the organizations collaborating on projects such as recruiting members of organized labor to lead health and human services organizations.)

The Uniform Federal Fund-Raising Program was created by order of President Dwight Eisenhower in 1957, enabling federal employees to contribute to charities of their choice. (The program later evolved into the Combined Federal Campaign.) Six years later, Los Angeles became the first city to adopt the United Way name when more than 30 local Community Chests and United Fund organizations merged. The national organization, which had been operating under the United Community Funds and Councils (UCFCA) name, adopted the United Way of America (UWA) name in 1970. It established its headquarters in Alexandria, Virginia, the next year.

Congress made its first emergency food and shelter grant to the private sector in 1983, and UWA was selected as its fiscal agent.

UWA created its Emergency Food and Shelter National Board Program the same year. In 1984 UWA created the Alexis de Tocqueville Society to solicit larger donations from individuals (it attracted such members as Bill Gates and Walter Annenberg).

In 1992 William Aramony, UWA's president for more than two decades, resigned after coming under fire for his lavish expenditures. Former Peace Corps head Elaine Chao was tapped to replace him, and in 1995 Aramony was sentenced to seven years in prison for defrauding the organization of about $600,000. Former UWA CFO Thomas Merlo and Stephen Paulachak (former president of a UWA spinoff) were convicted on related charges. After four years spent burnishing UWA's tarnished image, Chao resigned in 1996, and was succeeded the following year by Betty Beene, who had headed UWA operations in Houston and New York.

In an effort to stress the manner in which its local organizations benefit their communities, UWA launched a brand initiative campaign in 1998. The following year UWA's local organization in Santa Clara, California, found itself in serious financial straits when donations began slipping despite its location in the wealthy Silicon Valley. Infoseek (now Walt Disney Internet Group's GO.com) founder Steve Kirsch and Microsoft founder Bill Gates chipped in $1 million and $5 million, respectively, to help keep the organization afloat.

Beene, who drew the ire of some chapters for suggesting a national pledge-processing center and national standards, announced in 2000 that she would step down in January 2001. Later that year, the United Way named Brian Gallagher as its new president and CEO. Also that year UWA began funneling more funds into smaller community projects instead of national charities.

## OFFICERS

**Chairman:** Ellie Ferdon
**President and CEO:** Brian A. Gallagher
**Human Resources:** Paul Springer
**Auditors:** Arthur Andersen LLP

## LOCATIONS

**HQ:** 701 N. Fairfax St., Alexandria, VA 22314
**Phone:** 703-836-7100       **Fax:** 703-683-7840
**Web:** national.unitedway.org

United Way of America has 1,400 local organizations
across the US.

## PRODUCTS/OPERATIONS

**Selected Recipients of United Way Funds**
American Cancer Society
American Red Cross
Big Brothers/Big Sisters of America
Boy Scouts of America
Catholic Charities USA
Girl Scouts of the United States of America
The Salvation Army
The Urban League

## HISTORICAL FINANCIALS & EMPLOYEES

| Not-for-profit<br>FYE: December 31 | Annual<br>Growth | 12/91 | 12/92 | 12/93 | 12/94 | 12/95 | 12/96 | 12/97 | 12/98 | 12/99 | 12/00 |
|---|---|---|---|---|---|---|---|---|---|---|---|
| Sales ($ mil.) | 3.2% | — | 3,040 | 3,050 | 3,078 | 3,148 | 3,250 | 3,400 | 3,580 | 3,770 | 3,910 |
| Employees | 0.0% | — | — | — | — | — | 10,000 | 10,000 | 10,000 | 10,000 | 10,000 |

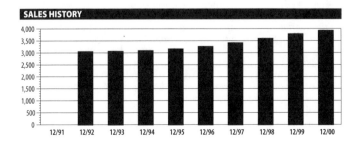

SALES HISTORY

# UNIVERSITY OF CALIFORNIA

## OVERVIEW

UC is striving not to become known as the "University for Caucasians." Struggling with minority recruitment in an era without affirmative action, the Oakland-based University of California (UC) maintains nine primary campuses: Berkeley, Davis, Irvine, Los Angeles, Riverside, San Diego, San Francisco, Santa Barbara, and Santa Cruz. It also plans to open a campus in Merced in 2004. Nearly 174,000 graduate and undergraduate students attend UC schools.

UC students can study in more than 150 disciplines. The university has three law schools, five medical schools, and one of the nation's leading continuing education programs. In addition, it manages three national laboratories for the federal government and produces more research leading to patented inventions than any other US university.

In the wake of California's Proposition 209, which eliminated state affirmative action programs, enrollment of minorities has dropped, as well as the hiring of female faculty. To help raise minority admissions, UC guarantees admission to the top 4% of students at each California high school or the top 12.5% statewide. A new proposal by president Richard Atkinson would accept the top 12.5% of students at each school who first complete a transfer program at a California community college.

## HISTORY

The founders of California's government provided for a state university via a clause in the state's constitution in 1849. The origins of the College of California, opened in Oakland in 1869, date back to the Contra Costa Academy, a small school established by Yale alumnus Henry Durant in 1853. (Durant ran Contra Costa, and then the college, until 1872.) Women were allowed to enter the school in 1870. The college moved to Berkeley and graduated its first class (12 men) in 1873.

As California's economy and population grew, so did its university system. Renamed University of California (UC) in 1879, it had 1,000 students by 1895. Agriculture, mining, geology, and engineering were among its first fields. A second campus was established at Davis in 1905, followed by campuses in San Diego (1912) and Los Angeles (1919).

The Depression brought cutbacks in funding for UC, but the system rebounded in the 1940s. It opened its fifth campus (Santa Barbara) in 1944, and during WWII it also began gaining recognition for research. Between 1945 and 1965 enrollment quadrupled, spurred by war veterans taking advantage of The GI Bill, and a population shift to the West. The state legislature formulated the Master Plan for Higher Education in 1960, which reorganized university administration and established admission requirements. Campuses were established at Irvine and Santa Cruz in 1965.

The first of several important demonstrations in the 1960s at UC Berkeley came in 1964 over the university's attempts to ban political activity on a strip of UC-owned land. The People's Park riot of 1969, touched off when UC tried to close a parcel of land in Berkeley that students had turned into a kind of playground for the counterculture, left one dead and more than 50 wounded.

Aware of the changing demographics of its student body, especially its growing Asian enrollment (28% in 1990), UC Berkeley gave the chancellor's job to Chang-Lin Tien in 1990 — the first person of Asian descent to hold that position at a major US university (Tien served as chancellor until 1997). A California recession in the early 1990s resulted in budget cuts for UC. Strapped for cash, the university launched a for-profit entity in 1992 to tap its extensive library of patents.

UC San Diego chancellor Richard Atkinson succeeded Jack Peltason as UC president in 1995, the same year the UC Board of Regents approved a new campus — the university's 10th — in the San Joaquin Valley. That year it voted to phase out race- and sex-based affirmative action. The board, in an effort to be competitive with other top universities in recruiting faculty, voted to offer health benefits to the partners of gay employees in 1997. Also that year UC created the California Digital Library and began putting its library collection online.

Entrepreneur Alfred Mann donated $100 million to UCLA in 1998 for biomedical research. Admissions of non-Asian-American minorities to the fall freshman classes of UCLA and UC Berkeley fell sharply that year. The following year the UC system began guaranteeing admission to the top 4% of students in each of the state's high schools. UC took some heat in 1999 and 2000 for two separate instances of security breaches at the Los Alamos National Laboratory in New Mexico.

**Chairman:** S. Sue Johnson
**President:** Richard C. Atkinson
**SVP Business and Finance:** Joseph P. Mullinix
**SVP Academic Affairs and Provost:** C. Judson King
**VP Agriculture and Natural Resources:** W. R. Gomes
**VP Budget:** Lawrence C. Hershman
**VP Clinical Services Development:** William H. Gurtner
**VP Financial Management:** Anne C. Broome
**VP Health Affairs:** Michael V. Drake
**VP Legal Affairs and General Counsel:** James E. Holst
**VP University and External Relations:** Bruce B. Darling
**VP Educational Outreach:** Alex M. Saragoza
**Assistant VP Human Resources:** Lubbe Levin
**Auditors:** Pricewaterhouse Coopers LLP

## LOCATIONS

**HQ:** 1111 Franklin St., Oakland, CA 94607
**Phone:** 510-987-0700    **Fax:** 510-987-0894
**Web:** www.ucop.edu

**Campuses**
UC Berkeley (31,011 students)
UC Davis (25,092)
UC Irvine (18,166)
UC Los Angeles (35,796)
UC Merced (to open in 2004)
UC Riverside (10,602)
UC San Diego (19,347)
UC San Francisco (3,511)
UC Santa Barbara (19,363)
UC Santa Cruz (10,981)

## PRODUCTS/OPERATIONS

**2001 Sales**

|  | $ mil. | % of total |
| --- | --- | --- |
| Sales & services | 4,313 | 27 |
| State appropriations | 3,368 | 21 |
| Department of Energy Laboratories | 3,101 | 20 |
| Federal appropriations | 1,851 | 12 |
| Tuition & fees | 1,190 | 7 |
| Private gifts | 1,034 | 6 |
| Investment income | 628 | 4 |
| Local government grants & contracts | 121 | 1 |
| Other | 281 | 2 |
| **Total** | **15,887** | **100** |

**Department of Energy Laboratories**
Ernest Orlando Lawrence Berkeley National Laboratory (Berkeley, CA)
Lawrence Livermore National Laboratory (Livermore, CA)
Los Alamos National Laboratory (New Mexico)

## HISTORICAL FINANCIALS & EMPLOYEES

| School FYE: June 30 | Annual Growth | 6/92 | 6/93 | 6/94 | 6/95 | 6/96 | 6/97 | 6/98 | 6/99 | 6/00 | 6/01 |
| --- | --- | --- | --- | --- | --- | --- | --- | --- | --- | --- | --- |
| Sales ($ mil.) | 8.9% | 7,394 | 7,548 | 7,895 | 7,958 | 8,363 | 9,022 | 9,375 | 13,074 | 14,048 | 15,887 |
| Employees | (2.1%) | 132,279 | 131,661 | 132,964 | 131,660 | 137,874 | 130,000 | 130,000 | 99,890 | 103,767 | 108,827 |

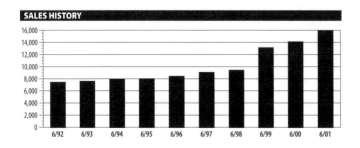

SALES HISTORY

# THE UNIVERSITY OF CHICAGO

Few institutions of higher education can match the scholarship of The University of Chicago (U of C). Located in the Hyde Park area of the Windy City, the university is a bastion of liberal education. While its list of those who graduated is impressive, the list of those who did not is equally prominent, including Oracle's Larry Ellison and author Kurt Vonnegut. The U of C has been home to more than 70 Nobel prize recipients, including physicist Enrico Fermi and economist Paul Samuelson, and it has an extraordinary predilection for producing Nobelists in Economics, including Milton Friedman, George Stigler, and Gary Becker.

The university's undergraduate college offers more than 40 areas of specialization, including fields of study ranging from history to physics to visual arts. Among the university's four graduate divisions and six graduate

professional schools are the renowned University of Chicago Law School and Graduate School of Business, both of which are ranked in the top 10 by *U.S. News & World Report*.

The more than 12,000 students attending the U of C study primarily at its 200-acre main campus on the South Side of Chicago, but the university's Graduate School of Business also maintains campuses in downtown Chicago; Barcelona, Spain; and Singapore. Among the many institutions affiliated with the U of C are the University of Chicago Medical Center, the Enrico Fermi Institute, the Argonne National Laboratory, and the Yerkes Observatory. The University of Chicago Press publishes 250 to 300 new titles each year, as well as more than 50 journals and is the largest university press in the US.

The University of Chicago took its name from the first U of C, a small Baptist school that operated from 1858-1886. In 1891 William Rainey Harper, the man who was to become the University's first president, convinced Standard Oil's John D. Rockefeller to provide a founding gift of $600,000. Members of the American Baptist Education Society chipped in another $400,000, and department store owner Marshall Field donated the land for the campus.

The university opened in 1892 with a faculty of 103 and 594 students. As it grew, the university took over property that had been used in the Columbian Exposition of 1892-93, eventually surrounding the fair's former midway. (The school's football team later earned the nickname "Monsters of the Midway" while being coached by the legendary Amos Alonzo Stagg before withdrawing from intercollegiate play in 1939.) Legend has it that the University retains the right to rejoin the Big Ten.

Only four years after its founding, the university's enrollment of 1,815 exceeded Harvard's. By 1907, 43% of its 5,000 students were women. Robert Maynard Hutchins, president from 1929-1951, revolutionized the university and American higher education by insisting on the study of original sources (the Great Books) and competency testing through comprehensive exams. He organized the college and graduate divisions into their present structure, reaffirming the role of the university as a place for intellectual exploration rather than vocational training. In 1942 the U of C ushered in the nuclear age when Enrico Fermi created the first

controlled nuclear chain reaction in the school's abandoned football stadium.

From the 1950s through the 1970s, the university purchased and restored Frank Lloyd Wright's famed Robie House and built the Joseph Regenstein Library (1970). In 1978 Hanna Holborn Gray was named president of U of C, becoming the first woman to be named president of a major university. Gray abolished the decade old Lacivious Costume Ball, a major social event (some would say the only social event) at the university. Hugo Sonnenschein succeeded Gray in 1993. The beginning of his tenure coincided with a period of financial difficulty for the school, as increases in costs outpaced revenue growth. In 1996 Sonnenschein announced plans to boost enrollment by as much as 30% in order to invigorate the school's finances.

U of C graduate and former professor Myron Scholes shared the Nobel Prize in Economics in 1997. The following year the university signed a controversial (within the U of C community) agreement to supply content to Internet distance-learning startup UNext.com, founded by trustee Andrew Rosenfield. Cardean University, UNext.com's online university, began operating in 2000.

Sonnenschein resigned that year and was replaced by Don Randel, former provost of Cornell University. Also in 2000 the University of Chicago Graduate School of Business opened a campus in Singapore, and U of C economist James Heckman was awarded a Nobel prize for his work in microeconomics.

## LOCATIONS

**HQ:** 5801 S. Ellis Ave., Chicago, IL 60637
**Phone:** 773-702-1234   **Fax:** 773-702-0809
**Web:** www.uchicago.edu

The University of Chicago has campuses in the Hyde
Park area of Chicago; downtown Chicago; Barcelona,
Spain; and Singapore.

## PRODUCTS/OPERATIONS

**Selected Affiliated Institutions**
Argonne National Laboratory
Argonne National Laboratory/University of Chicago
Development Corporation (ARCH)
Chapin Hall Center for Children and the Laboratory
Schools
Enrico Fermi Institute
James Franck Institute
National Opinion Research Center
Oriental Institute
University of Chicago Medical Center
Yerkes Observatory

**Selected Graduate Schools and Programs**
Divinity School
Graduate School of Business
Graham School of General Studies
Harris Graduate School of Public Policy Studies
Law School
Pritzker School of Medicine
School of Social Service Administration

**Selected Libraries**
D'Angelo Law Library
Eckhart Library (mathematics, mathematical statistics,
and computer science)
Harper Memorial Library for the College
John Crerar Library (natural sciences, medicine, and
technology)
Jones Library (chemistry)
Joseph Regenstein Library (humanities and social
sciences)
School of Social Service Administration Library
Yerkes Observatory Library (astronomy and
astrophysics)

## HISTORICAL FINANCIALS & EMPLOYEES

| School<br>FYE: June 30 | Annual<br>Growth | 6/91 | 6/92 | 6/93 | 6/94 | 6/95 | 6/96 | 6/97 | 6/98 | 6/99 | 6/00 |
|---|---|---|---|---|---|---|---|---|---|---|---|
| Sales ($ mil.) | 5.0% | — | 1,113 | 1,150 | 1,217 | 1,313 | 1,395 | 1,377 | 892 | 848 | 1,639 |
| Employees | 0.1% | — | — | 11,800 | 11,400 | 10,954 | 12,000 | 12,000 | 12,869 | 11,900 | 11,900 |

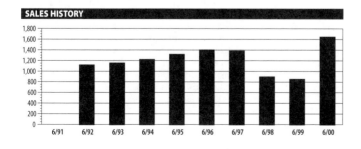

SALES HISTORY

# THE UNIVERSITY OF TEXAS SYSTEM

## OVERVIEW

Students at The University of Texas System are looking to lock horns with higher education. Based in Austin, the UT System is one of the largest university systems in the US, with more than 153,000 students at its nine campuses throughout the state. (Its flagship university in Austin, with more than 50,000 students, is the largest single campus in the US.) Many of UT's graduate programs rank near the top tiers, including business, education, engineering, and law. It also attracts more than $1 billion in research grants and contracts (mostly from the federal government), making it one of the nation's top research institutes. In addition, the UT System runs six health institutions and four medical schools. Its $10 billion endowment fund, managed by the University of Texas Investment Management Co., is the third-largest in the country (behind Harvard and Yale).

With the bulging ranks of Generation Y looming on the horizon, the UT System expects its enrollment to swell to 250,000 by the end of the decade. To accommodate the increase, the system has laid out plans for nearly $3 billion in capital spending for new and improved facilities. It also hopes the improvements will put it on par with research institutions like California State.

## HISTORY

The Texas Declaration of Independence (1836) admonished Mexico for having failed to establish a public education system in the territory, but attempts to start a state-sponsored university were stymied until after Texas achieved US statehood and fought in the Civil War. A new constitution in 1876 provided for the establishment of "a university of the first class," and in 1883 The University of Texas (UT) opened in Austin. Eight professors taught 218 students in two curricula: academics and law.

The school's first building opened in 1884, and in 1891 the university's medical school opened in Galveston. By 1894 UT-Austin had 534 students and a football team. UT opened a Graduate School in 1910 and various other colleges over the years. The university added its first academic branch campus when the Texas State School of Mines and Metallurgy (opened in 1914 in El Paso) became part of the system in 1919.

UT's financial future was secured in 1923 when oil was found on West Texas land that had been set aside by the legislature as an education endowment. The income from oil production, as well as the proceeds of surface-use leases, became the Permanent University Fund (PUF), from which only interest and earnings on the revenues can be used: two-thirds by UT and one-third by Texas A&M University. UT continued to grow, thanks to the PUF, which topped $100 million by 1940.

UT sported the stigma of racial prejudice (as did many other institutions at the time) when it refused to admit Heman Sweatt, a black student, to its law school in 1946. The Supreme Court ordered UT to admit him in 1950, the same year the UT System was officially organized.

In 1962, in one of the nation's most highly publicized crimes, Charles Whitman killed 14 people and wounded 31 others with a high-powered rifle fired from atop the UT-Austin administration tower. The observation deck wasn't closed until 1975, however, after a series of suicides. (It was reopened in 1999.)

In the meantime, UT added a medical center in Dallas and several graduate schools in Austin. The 1960s through the 1980s were a time of geographic expansion for the system as it absorbed other institutions, started several new campuses, and expanded its network of medical centers. In 1996 the UT System became the first public university to establish a private investment management company (University of Texas Investment Management Co.) to invest PUF money (by that time over $9 billion) and other funds.

The race issue reared its head again in 1996 when a Federal court ruled in the Hopwood decision (named for the plaintiff) that the UT System could no longer use race to determine scholarships and admissions. Minority enrollments declined the following year, prompting the Texas Legislature to enact a law granting admission to the top 10% of graduates from any Texas high school to the state university of their choice. Chancellor William Cunningham announced plans in 2000 to expand the UT System by 100,000 students over the decade. After he resigned that year, R. D. Burck took over as his successor. In 2001 UT received a $50 million donation from Texan and Minnesota Vikings owner Red McCombs, the largest gift in the school's history. Later that year, Burck announced his intention to step down by 2003.

## OFFICERS

**Chairman, Board of Regents:** Tom Loeffler
**Vice Chairman, Board of Regents:**
Rita Crocker Clements
**Executive Secretary, Board of Regents:**
Francie A. Fredrick
**Chancellor:** R. D. Burck
**Executive Vice Chancellor Academic Affairs:**
Edwin R. Sharpe
**Executive Vice Chancellor Business Affairs:**
Kerry L. Kennedy
**Executive Vice Chancellor Health Affairs:**
Charles B. Mullins
**Vice Chancellor and General Counsel:**
Cullen M. Godfrey
**Vice Chancellor Development and External Relations:**
Shirley Bird Perry
**Vice Chancellor Federal Relations:** Mark Franz
**Vice Chancellor Governmental Relations:** Tom Scott
**President, University of Texas at Arlington:**
Robert E. Witt
**President, University of Texas at Austin:**
Larry R. Faulkner
**President, University of Texas at Dallas:**
Franklyn G. Jenifer, age 61
**President, University of Texas at El Paso:**
Diana S. Natalicio, age 61
**President, University of Texas Pan American:**
Miguel A. Nevarez
**President, University of Texas of the Permian Basin:**
Charles A. Sorber
**President, University of Texas at San Antonio:**
Ricardo Romo
**President, University of Texas at Tyler:**
Rodney H. Mabry
**Director Human Resources:** Gerald Schroeder
**Auditors:** Texas State Auditor

## LOCATIONS

**HQ:** 601 Colorado St., Austin, TX 78701
**Phone:** 512-499-4200     **Fax:** 512-499-4218
**Web:** www.utsystem.edu

The University of Texas System has component
institutions in Arlington, Austin, Brownsville, Dallas,
Edinburg, El Paso, Galveston, Houston, Odessa, San
Antonio, and Tyler, Texas.

## PRODUCTS/OPERATIONS

**University of Texas System Component Institutions**

**Academic Institutions**
The University of Texas at Arlington (est. 1895; 19,148
students)
The University of Texas at Austin (est. 1883; 50,010
students)
The University of Texas at Brownsville (est. 1991; 9,094
students)
The University of Texas at Dallas (est. 1961; 10,137
students)
The University of Texas at El Paso (est. 1914; 14,695
students)
The University of Texas - Pan American (Edinburg; est.
1927; 12,520 students)
The University of Texas of the Permian Basin (Odessa;
est. 1969; 2,222 students)
The University of Texas at San Antonio (est. 1969; 18,607
students)
The University of Texas at Tyler (est. 1971; 3,392
students)

**Health Institutions**
The University of Texas Health Science Center at
Houston (est. 1972; 3,170 students)
The University of Texas Health Science Center at San
Antonio (est. 1959; 2,557 students)
The University of Texas Health Center at Tyler (est.
1947)
The University of Texas M.D. Anderson Cancer Center
(Houston; est. 1941)
The University of Texas Medical Branch at Galveston
(est. 1891; 1,952 students)
The University of Texas Southwestern Medical Center at
Dallas (est. 1943; 1,554 students)

## HISTORICAL FINANCIALS & EMPLOYEES

| School<br>FYE: August 31 | Annual<br>Growth | 8/91 | 8/92 | 8/93 | 8/94 | 8/95 | 8/96 | 8/97 | 8/98 | 8/99 | 8/00 |
|---|---|---|---|---|---|---|---|---|---|---|---|
| Sales ($ mil.) | 7.1% | — | 3,433 | 3,744 | 4,030 | 4,300 | 4,624 | 4,803 | 5,244 | 4,131 | 5,943 |
| Employees | 2.1% | — | 67,210 | 67,985 | 70,000 | 72,395 | 74,364 | 75,517 | 77,112 | — | 79,430 |

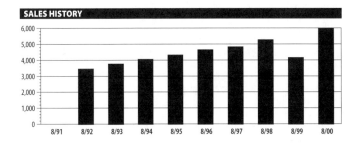

**SALES HISTORY**

# THE UNIVERSITY OF WISCONSIN

## OVERVIEW

There is no School of Cheese in the University of Wisconsin System, but there are 13 four-year universities, 13 two-year campuses, and a statewide extension program. Based in Madison, the University of Wisconsin System is one of the largest public university systems in the US, with more than 150,000 students.

The University of Wisconsin at Madison is the system's flagship school and has more than 40,000 students. It is ranked in the top 10 of US public schools by *U.S. News & World Report*

and offers undergraduate, graduate, and doctoral studies to its students. The school's graduate program in sociology is considered one of the best in the nation. The system's other major campus is the University of Wisconsin at Milwaukee, with nearly 23,000 students.

One-third of the UW System's annual budget comes from state funds. Student fees, federal grants, fund raising, and other sources account for the remainder.

## HISTORY

When Wisconsin became a state in 1848, its constitution called for the establishment of a state university. A board of regents was named, and it first established a preparatory school because regents felt Wisconsin's secondary schools were not advanced enough to prepare students for university studies. The school began classes in 1849 with 20 students in the Madison Female Academy Building. The University of Wisconsin's first official freshman class began studies in the fall of 1850. A campus was established a mile west of the state capitol in Madison. By 1854, when it held its first commencement (with two graduates), the school had 41 students.

Enrollment dipped during the Civil War (all but one of the school's senior class joined the army) but soon rebounded, and by 1870 the university had almost 500 students. Meanwhile, it established a school of agriculture (in 1866) and a school of law (1868). The state established normal schools (teachers' colleges) in Platteville (1866), Whitewater (1868), Oshkosh (1871), and River Falls (1874).

There was also a teachers' course for women at the university in Madison. However, when John Bascom became president in 1874, he transformed the university into a truly coeducational institution, putting women "in all respects on precisely the same footing" with the men.

While the university at Madison remained Wisconsin's primary seat of learning, the state continued to establish normal schools. It opened institutions in Milwaukee (1885), Superior (1893), Stevens Point (1894), La Crosse (1909), and Eau Claire (1916). The nine normal schools eventually became a system of state colleges called Wisconsin State Universities.

The university at Madison also continued to grow, and by the late 1920s it had almost 9,000 students. WWII brought a drop in enrollment, but afterward it took off, jumping from about 7,000 in 1945 to over 22,000 by the late 1950s.

The University of Wisconsin-Milwaukee branch was founded in 1956. Other branch campuses were established in Green Bay (1965) and Kenosha (1968).

The Madison campus became a focal point for student protests during the Vietnam War. Events came to a head in 1970 when President Fred Harrington resigned during a four-day standoff between students and the National Guard. War protesters also placed a bomb outside Sterling Hall, which housed the Army Math Research Center; the explosion killed one student and injured three others.

The state legislature merged the University of Wisconsin and the Wisconsin State Universities in 1971 to create The University of Wisconsin System. By the early 1980s it had an enrollment of nearly 160,000. Later that decade, however, it tightened admission standards and enrollment began to fall.

A property tax reform bill passed by the state legislature in 1994 cut into The University of Wisconsin System's funding the next year. The system announced it would cut 500 jobs in 1997, use more part-time instructors, and increase class sizes to deal with the $43 million it lost in the budget cuts.

UW-Madison broke ground on the $22 million Fluno Center for Executive Education in 1998, a 100-room dorm, classroom building, and dining hall rolled into one. The next year enrollment at The University of Wisconsin System's two-year colleges broke 10,000 for the first time in five years. The licensing of technologies invented at the UW-Madison campus was expanded to include all four-year universities in the UW System in 2000. The University of Wisconsin System's mandatory student fee system was ruled unconstitutional later that year.

## OFFICERS

**President:** Katharine C. Lyall, age 59
**SVP Administration:** David W. Olien
**VP University Relations:** Linda Weimer
**VP Finance:** Deborah A. Durken
**VP Budget Planning:** Kathleen R. Sell
**Associate VP Academic Affairs:** Sharon L. James
**Assistant VP Administrative Services:** Ellen James
**Assistant VP Acadamec Affairs, Senior Advisor of President, Multicultural Affairs:** Andrea-Teresa Arenas
**Assistant VP Capital Planning and Budget:** Nancy J. Ives
**Associate VP Learning and Information Technology:** Edward Meachen
**Associate VP Human Resources:** George H. Brooks
**Associate VP Policy Analysis and Research:** Frank Goldberg
**Director Budget Planning:** Melissa Kepner
**Director Information Services:** Nancy Crabb
**Director Internal Audit:** Ronald L. Yates
**Controller:** Mike Kraus
**General Counsel:** Elizabeth Rindskopf Parker
**Auditors:** State of Wisconsin Legislative Audit Bureau

## LOCATIONS

**HQ:** The University of Wisconsin System
Van Hise Hall, 1220 Linden Dr., Madison, WI 53706
**Phone:** 608-262-2321     **Fax:** 608-262-3985
**Web:** www.uwsa.edu

**University Campuses**
UW-Baraboo/Sauk County (two-year college, 676 students)
UW-Barron County (two-year college, 534)
UW-Eau Claire (four-year university, 10,402)
UW-Fond Du Lac (two-year college, 558)
UW-Fox Valley (two-year college, 1,510)
UW-Green Bay (four-year university, 5,442)
UW-La Crosse (four-year university, 9,295)
UW-Madison (four-year university, 40,045)
UW-Manitowoc (two-year college, 505)
UW-Marathon County (two-year college, 1,167)
UW-Marinette (two-year college, 546)
UW-Marshfield/Wood County (two-year college, 595)
UW-Milwaukee (four-year university, 22,964)
UW-Oshkosh (four-year university, 10,783)
UW-Parkside (four-year university, 4,951)
UW-Platteville (four-year university, 5,340)
UW-Richland (two-year college, 434)
UW-River Falls (four-year university, 5,711)
UW-Rock County (two-year college, 823)
UW-Sheboygan (two-year college, 749)
UW-Stevens Point (four-year university, 8,544)
UW-Stout (four-year university, 7,517)
UW-Superior (four-year university, 2,741)
UW-Washington County (two-year college, 857)
UW-Waukesha (two-year college, 1,956)
UW-Whitewater (four-year university, 10,653)

## PRODUCTS/OPERATIONS

### 2000 Sales

|  | $ mil. | % of total |
|---|---|---|
| State appropriations | 961 | 33 |
| Federal grants | 501 | 17 |
| Student fees | 494 | 17 |
| Enterprises | 473 | 16 |
| Gifts & trusts | 298 | 10 |
| Operations | 80 | 3 |
| Cost reimbursement | 67 | 2 |
| Hospital | 31 | 1 |
| Federal appropriations | 17 | 1 |
| **Total** | **2,922** | **100** |

## HISTORICAL FINANCIALS & EMPLOYEES

| School<br>FYE: June 30 | Annual<br>Growth | 6/91 | 6/92 | 6/93 | 6/94 | 6/95 | 6/96 | 6/97 | 6/98 | 6/99 | 6/00 |
|---|---|---|---|---|---|---|---|---|---|---|---|
| Sales ($ mil.) | 3.5% | — | 2,226 | 2,309 | 2,442 | 2,556 | 2,612 | 2,399 | 2,543 | 2,558 | 2,922 |
| Employees | (2.8%) | — | 30,090 | 30,269 | 30,341 | 30,410 | 28,626 | 25,399 | 25,500 | 25,889 | 23,981 |

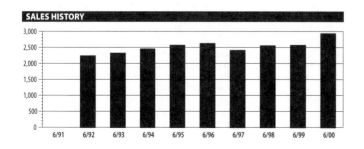

SALES HISTORY

The University of Wisconsin

System

# USAA

Whether the country is at war or at peace, USAA's relationship with the US military stands firm.

With more than 4 million customers, the San Antonio-based mutual company primarily serves military personnel and their families. In addition to property/casualty (available only to military personnel) and life insurance, USAA offers several financial services through more than 85 subsidiaries and affiliates. These services include discount brokerage, investment management, and banking. It uses direct marketing via the telephone and Internet to distribute its products. The company also sells

merchandise (jewelry, major appliances, electronic and consumer goods) in seasonal catalogs and offers long-distance telephone services.

After dropping in the early 1990s, USAA's claims continue to rise, outpacing premium income. Technology costs have also cut into its bottom line. However, the company is expecting its membership to continue growing, projecting it to nearly double by 2010. Cutting costs, USAA has streamlined operations by reducing staff and closing down divisions, including mailing, printing, and information technology offices.

In 1922 a group of 26 US Army officers gathered in a San Antonio hotel and formed their own automobile insurance association. The reason? As military officers who often moved, they had a hard time getting insurance because they were considered transient. So the officers decided to insure each other. Led by Major William Garrison, who became the company's first president, they formed the United States Army Automobile Insurance Association.

In 1924, when US Navy and Marine Corps officers were allowed to join, the company changed its name to United Services Automobile Association. By the mid-1950s the company had some 200,000 members.

In the 1960s USAA Life Insurance Company (1963) and USAA Casualty Insurance Company (1968) were formed. In 1969 Robert McDermott, a retired US Air Force brigadier general, became president. He cut employment through attrition, established education and training seminars for employees, and invested in computers and telecommunications (drastically cutting claims-processing time).

McDermott added new products and services, such as mutual funds, real estate investments, and banking. Under McDermott, USAA's membership grew from 653,000 in 1969 to over 3 million in 1993.

In the 1970s, in an effort to go paperless, USAA became one of the insurance industry's first companies to switch from mail to toll-free (800) numbers. Early the next decade the company introduced its discount purchasing program, USAA Buying Services. In 1985 it opened the USAA Federal Savings Bank. In the late 1980s USAA began installing an optical storage system to automate some customer service operations.

McDermott retired in 1993 and was

succeeded by Robert Herres. The following year USAA Federal Savings Bank began developing a home banking system, offering members information and services over advanced screen telephones provided by IBM.

In the early 1990s USAA's real estate activities increased dramatically. In 1995 USAA restructured its interest in the Fiesta Texas theme park in San Antonio in order to focus on previously developed properties in geographically diverse areas. That year Six Flags Theme Parks (now Six Flags, Inc.) assumed operation and management of Fiesta Texas (it purchased it from USAA in 1998).

USAA began including enlisted military personnel as members in 1997. It also started to experiment with a "plain English" mutual fund prospectus. In 1998 USAA began offering Choice Ride in Orlando, Florida. For about $1,100 per quarter and a promise not to drive except in emergencies, the pilot program provided 36 round trips and a 90% discount on car insurance, in hopes of keeping older drivers from unnecessarily getting behind the wheel.

That year, as part of its new Financial Planning Network, USAA began offering retirement and estate planning assistance aimed at 25- to 55-year-olds for a yearly $250 fee. In 1999 claims doubled largely due to the impact of Hurricane Floyd and spring hail storms hitting military communities in North Carolina and Virginia.

That year USAA also moved to consolidate its customers' separate accounts (such as mutual fund holdings, stocks and bonds, and life insurance products) into one main account to strengthen customer relationships and reduce operational costs. In 2000, after completing a number of technology projects, the association laid off workers for the first time in its history.

## OFFICERS

**Chairman:** Robert T. Herres
**President and CEO:** Robert G. Davis
**SVP, CFO, and Corporate Treasurer:** Joe Robles Jr.
**SVP and Chief Communications Officer:**
Wendi E. Strong
**SVP, Secretary, and General Counsel:** Bradford W. Rich
**SVP, Human Resources:** Elizabeth Conklyn
**Auditors:** KPMG LLP

## LOCATIONS

**HQ:** 9800 Fredericksburg Rd., USAA Building,
San Antonio, TX 78288
**Phone:** 210-498-2211        **Fax:** 210-498-9940
**Web:** www.usaa.com

USAA has major regional offices in California, Colorado,
Florida, Virginia, and Washington. It maintains
international offices in London and Frankfurt.

## PRODUCTS/OPERATIONS

**Selected Operations**
USAA Alliance Services Company (merchandising and
member services)
USAA Federal Savings Bank
USAA Investment Management Company (mutual funds,
investment and brokerage services)
USAA Property & Casualty (including automobile, home,
boat, and flood insurance)
USAA Real Estate Company

## COMPETITORS

| | |
|---|---|
| 21st Century | Kemper Insurance |
| Allstate | Liberty Mutual |
| American Express | MassMutual |
| American Financial | MetLife |
| American General | Morgan Stanley Dean |
| AXA Financial | Witter |
| Berkshire Hathaway | Mutual of Omaha |
| Charles Schwab | Nationwide |
| Chubb | New York Life |
| CIGNA | Northwestern Mutual |
| Citigroup | Pacific Mutual |
| CNA Financial | Prudential |
| FMR | St. Paul Companies |
| Guardian Life | State Farm |
| The Hartford | T. Rowe Price |
| John Hancock Financial | UBS PaineWebber |
| Services | |

## HISTORICAL FINANCIALS & EMPLOYEES

| Mutual company<br>FYE: December 31 | Annual<br>Growth | 12/91 | 12/92 | 12/93 | 12/94 | 12/95 | 12/96 | 12/97 | 12/98 | 12/99 | 12/00 |
|---|---|---|---|---|---|---|---|---|---|---|---|
| Assets ($ mil.) | 9.2% | — | 16,235 | 18,494 | 19,548 | 22,244 | 23,622 | 25,007 | 28,831 | 30,323 | 32,794 |
| Net income ($ mil.) | 21.6% | — | 140 | 676 | 564 | 730 | 855 | 1,189 | 980 | 765 | 669 |
| Income as % of assets | — | — | 0.9% | 3.7% | 2.9% | 3.3% | 3.6% | 4.8% | 3.4% | 2.5% | 2.0% |
| Employees | 5.2% | — | 14,667 | 15,905 | 15,233 | 15,677 | 16,571 | 17,967 | 20,120 | 21,795 | 22,000 |

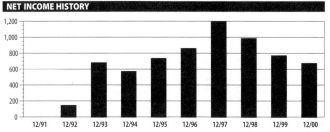

**NET INCOME HISTORY**

**2000 FISCAL YEAR-END**
Equity as % of assets: 21.5%
Return on assets: 2.1%
Return on equity: —
Long-term debt ($ mil.): —
Sales ($ mil.): 8,551

# THE VANGUARD GROUP, INC.

## OVERVIEW

If you buy low and sell high, invest for the long term, don't panic, and generally disapprove of those whippersnappers at Fidelity, then you may end up in the Vanguard of the financial market.

Based in Malvern, Pennsylvania, The Vanguard Group offers a line of highly sought-after mutual funds and brokerage services; it is the #2 fund manager after FMR (aka Fidelity). Vanguard's fund options include stock, bond, mixed, and international offerings; its Vanguard 500 Index Fund now competes with longtime king, Fidelity's Magellan, as the largest US fund. The company is known as much for its puritanical thriftiness and conservative investing (it actively discourages short-term investing with redemption fees, defining "short-term" as three years) as it is for its line of index funds, which track the performance of such groups of stock as the S&P 500.

Unlike other funds, Vanguard is set up like a mutual insurance company. The funds (and by extension, their investors) own the company, so fees are low to nonexistent; funds are operated on a tight budget so as not to eat into results. The company spends next to nothing on advertising, relying instead on strong returns and word-of-mouth. As part of the low-cost culture, managers at Vanguard may be switched at a moment's notice to answering telephones when market conditions prompt a flood of calls from concerned investors.

Largely in response to the popularity of Web-based discount brokerages, Vanguard has been quietly touting its previously low-profile brokerage division. The company is also expanding in Europe. In addition, Vanguard is developing cheap ways to dole out advice, especially through the use of toll-free numbers and the Internet. It has also inked an agreement with Hamilton Lane Advisors, a small Pennsylvania private equity firm that will afford Vanguard's wealthiest clients access to such products as venture, mezzanine, and buyout funds.

## HISTORY

A distant cousin of Daniel Boone, Walter Morgan knew a few things about pioneering. He was the first to offer a fund with a balance of stocks and bonds, serendipitously introduced early in 1929, months before the stock market collapsed. Morgan's balanced Wellington fund (named after Napoleon's vanquisher) emerged effectively unscathed.

John Bogle's senior thesis on mutual funds impressed fellow Princeton alum Morgan, who hired Bogle in 1951. Morgan retired in 1967 and picked Bogle to replace him. That year Bogle engineered a merger with old-school investment firm Thorndike, Doran, Paine and Lewis. After culture clashes and four years of shrinking assets, the Thorndike-dominated board fired Bogle, who appealed to the mutual funds and their separate board of directors. The fund directors decided to split up the funds and the advisory business.

Bogle named the fund company The Vanguard Group, after the flagship of Lord Nelson, another Napoleon foe. Vanguard worked like a cooperative; mutual fund shareholders owned the company, so all services were provided at cost. The Wellington Management Company remained Vanguard's distributor until 1977, when Bogle convinced Vanguard's board to drop the affiliation. Without Wellington as the intermediary, Vanguard sold its funds directly to consumers as no-load funds (without service charges). In 1976 the company launched the Vanguard Index 500, the first index fund. These measures attracted new investors in droves.

Vanguard rode the 1980s boom. Its Windsor fund grew so large the company closed it, launching Windsor II in 1985. Vanguard weathered the 1987 crash and began the 1990s as the US's #4 mutual fund company. FMR's actively managed funds, most notably its Magellan fund, led the market then. The retirement of legendary Magellan manager Peter Lynch and the fund's consequential underperformance spurred a rush to index funds. Vanguard moved up to #2.

Vanguard played against type in 1995 when it introduced the Vanguard Horizon Capital Growth stock fund, an aggressively managed fund designed to vie directly with Fidelity's funds. In 1997 Vanguard added brokerage services and began selling its own and other companies' funds on the Internet to allow clients to consolidate their financial activities. In 1998 Bogle passed the chairmanship to CEO John Brennan, a soft-spoken technology wonk. Walter Morgan died that year at age 100.

Investors were ruffled when 70-year-old Bogle announced that corporate age limits would force him to leave the board of directors at the end of 1999. The Vanguard 500 Index Fund briefly passed Fidelity's Magellan as the US's largest mutual fund in 2000.

**Chairman, President, and CEO:** John J. Brennan
**SVP and CFO:** Ralph K. Packard
**Managing Director:** Ian A. MacKinnon
**Managing Director:** James H. Gately
**Managing Director:** F. William McNabb III
**Managing Director and Secretary:**
Raymond J. Klapinsky
**Managing Director, Human Resources:**
Kathleen C. Gubanich

## LOCATIONS

**HQ:** 100 Vanguard Blvd., Malvern, PA 19355
**Phone:** 610-648-6000      **Fax:** 610-669-6605
**Web:** www.vanguard.com

The Vanguard Group has offices in Malvern,
Pennsylvania; Charlotte, North Carolina; Philadelphia;
and Phoenix, as well as in Australia and Europe.

## PRODUCTS/OPERATIONS

**Selected Vanguard Funds**
Vanguard 500
Vanguard Admiral Treasury Money Market Fund
Vanguard Balanced Index Fund
Vanguard Calvert Social Index Fund
Vanguard Capital Opportunity Fund
Vanguard Emerging Markets Stock Index Fund
Vanguard Energy Fund
Vanguard Equity Income Fund
Vanguard European Stock Index Fund
Vanguard Global Asset Allocation Fund
Vanguard Global Equity Fund
Vanguard GNMA Fund
Vanguard Gold and Precious Metals Fund
Vanguard Growth and Income Fund
Vanguard Growth Index Fund
Vanguard Health Care Fund
Vanguard High-Yield Corporate Fund
Vanguard Inflation-Protected Securities Fund
Vanguard International Growth Fund
Vanguard International Value Fund
Vanguard LifeStrategy Growth Fund
Vanguard LifeStrategy Income Fund
Vanguard Mid-Cap Index Fund
Vanguard Pacific Stock Index Fund
Vanguard Preferred Stock Fund
Vanguard Prime Money Market Fund
Vanguard Small-Cap Growth Index Fund
Vanguard Small-Cap Value Index Fund
Vanguard STAR Fund
Vanguard Tax-Managed Growth and Income Fund
Vanguard Tax-Managed International Fund
Vanguard Total Bond Market Index Fund
Vanguard Total Stock Market Index Fund
Vanguard U.S. Growth Fund
Vanguard U.S. Value Fund
Vanguard Utilities Income Fund
Vanguard Wellesley Income Fund
Vanguard Wellington Fund
Vanguard Windsor Fund

## COMPETITORS

| | |
|---|---|
| Alliance Capital | Mellon Financial |
| Barclays | Merrill Lynch |
| Charles Schwab | Prudential |
| FMR | T. Rowe Price |
| Franklin Resources | USAA |

## HISTORICAL FINANCIALS & EMPLOYEES

| Private<br>FYE: December 31 | Annual<br>Growth | 12/91 | 12/92 | 12/93 | 12/94 | 12/95 | 12/96 | 12/97 | 12/98 | 12/99 | 12/00 |
|---|---|---|---|---|---|---|---|---|---|---|---|
| Estimated sales ($ mil.) | 21.1% | — | — | — | — | — | — | 900 | 1,200 | 1,500 | 1,600 |
| Employees | 30.1% | — | — | — | — | — | — | 5,000 | 10,000 | 11,000 | 11,000 |

### SALES HISTORY

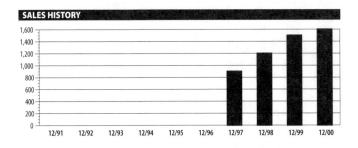

THE**Vanguard**GROUP.

# VERTIS INC.

## OVERVIEW

Although it has changed its name, Vertis hopes its advertising business will blossom. The Baltimore-based company (formerly Big Flower Holdings) is among the leading providers of targeted marketing and advertising services in the US. It operates through three primary units — TC Advertising, LTC Group, and Webcraft. TC Advertising serves more than 300 newspapers and some 700 retailers by producing advertising inserts and circulars, printing newspaper TV listing guides, and offering circulation-building services. Vertis also is involved in digital services, online marketing, and strategic consulting (through LTC Group), as well as direct mailing, response

management, Internet integration, and database management (through Webcraft).

Vertis has undergone significant restructuring in recent years. It began relying less and less on its traditional commercial printing business in the late 1990s as it expanded into other areas of marketing and advertising. Later it consolidated its three primary divisions (all the better to create cross-selling opportunities), took itself private, moved its headquarters from New York City to TC Advertising's home base of Baltimore, and changed its name from Big Flower Holdings to Vertis. An investor group including Evercore Partners and Thomas H. Lee Company owns the company.

## HISTORY

Brothers Robert and Paul Milhous founded Treasure Chest Advertising (later changed to TC Advertising) in 1967 to publish the Treasure Chest of Values, a weekly shopping newspaper. Within five years the company was printing advertising circulars from six plants across the US. In 1982 Treasure Chest began printing color comics and TV program listings. By the early 1990s the Milhouses were ready to sell out. Investment banker Theodore Ammon, who gave up a partnership in Kohlberg Kravis Roberts to strike out on his own, founded BFP Holdings in 1993 and paid $235 million for the company.

In 1994 BFP Holdings acquired two additional operations — Retail Graphic Holding and KTB Associates — which expanded its capacity and customer base in both the advertising insert and newspaper TV magazine segments. It raised about $100 million through an IPO in November 1995. Almost immediately afterward, the newly public company — renamed Big Flower Press Holdings — purchased LaserTech Color (now LTC Group, outsourced digital pre-media and content management services). A disastrous Christmas for retailers and high paper prices in 1995 lowered its earnings and sent stock prices to the basement.

In 1996 Big Flower bought direct mail and specialty printer Webcraft Technologies, which focused on fragrance samplers, rub-off promotional games, and lottery tickets. (The lottery unit was sold later that year.) The company also purchased a full-service direct mail company, Scanforms, which increased its customer base among financial services and publishing companies. In addition, it added Internet production services to its repertoire with the acquisition of Pacific Color Connection. Big

Flower reached $1 billion in sales in 1996, just three years after its formation.

The following year Big Flower continued its rapid expansion strategy with the purchase of UK-based Olwen Direct Mail Limited, which marked the company's first international acquisition. It also bought two companies, Columbine JDS Systems and Broadcast Systems Software, which diversified Big Flower into broadcast media services. In 1997 the company underwent a legal restructuring; afterward Big Flower Holdings emerged as the parent of Big Flower Press Holdings.

The company's European presence was further expanded in 1998 with the purchase of two prepublication service providers — Production Response Systems and Lifeboat Matey, which operate as the Fusion Group. Also that year the company invested in the Internet advertiser 24/7 Media (now 24/7 Real Media) and acquired a software development and database marketing company (Reach America), a digital prepublication company (Enterton Group), and a marketing services company (ColorStream). In 1999 a group led by leveraged-buyout firm Thomas H. Lee Co. purchased Big Flower for about $800 million.

In 2000 Big Flower consolidated its major operating units, took itself private, moved its headquarters to Baltimore, and changed its name to Vertis as part of an ongoing restructuring. In connection with the restructuring, CEO Ed Reilly resigned and was replaced by Don Roland, who joined TC Advertising in 1983 and became its CEO in 1995.

**Chairman, President, and CEO:** Donald E. Roland
**COO:** Herbert W. Moloney III
**CFO:** Dean D. Durbin
**SVP Human Resources:** Catherine S. Leggett
**VP, Secretary and General Counsel:** John V. Howard Jr.
**Auditors:** Deloitte & Touche LLP

## LOCATIONS

**HQ:** 250 W. Pratt St., Baltimore, MD 21201
**Phone:** 410-528-9800    **Fax:** 410-528-9288
**Web:** www.vertisinc.com

## PRODUCTS/OPERATIONS

**Selected Products and Services**
Advertising inserts and circulars
Consumer and media research
Database management
Digital media production
Digital workflow management
Direct mail printing
Electronic prepress services
eMarketing
Fragrance marketing
Internet integration
Media placement
Newspaper circulation-building products
Newspaper TV listing guides
Personalization
Promotional campaign planning
Strategic consulting

## COMPETITORS

| | |
|---|---|
| ACG Holdings | Mail-Well |
| Acxiom | Quad/Graphics |
| ADVO | Quebecor World |
| Applied Graphics | R. R. Donnelley |
| Avanti/Case-Hoyt | Schawk |
| Experian | Seven Worldwide |
| Harte-Hanks | Valassis |

## HISTORICAL FINANCIALS & EMPLOYEES

| Private<br>FYE: December 31 | Annual<br>Growth | 12/91 | 12/92 | 12/93 | 12/94 | 12/95 | 12/96 | 12/97 | 12/98 | 12/99 | 12/00 |
|---|---|---|---|---|---|---|---|---|---|---|---|
| Sales ($ mil.) | 17.9% | — | 536 | 555 | 565 | 532 | 1,202 | 1,377 | 1,740 | 1,800 | 2,000 |
| Employees | 20.9% | — | — | — | 3,200 | 4,000 | 6,410 | 8,500 | 10,000 | 10,000 | 10,000 |

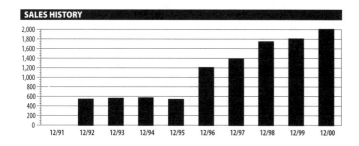

SALES HISTORY

# VISA INTERNATIONAL

## OVERVIEW

Visa International, the reigning emperor of e-money, is putting its plastic where its mouth is. With a Visa card of any stripe (or microchip), the company's 1 billion customers can get service at more than 21 million merchant locations worldwide. Foster City, California-based Visa operates the world's #1 payment system, with more than half of the market, followed by MasterCard and American Express. The classic credit card has been joined by smart cards, debit cards, and disposable cash cards.

Visa International operates through six autonomous regional groups and is owned by its 21,000 member financial institutions.

Visa is accelerating its push to introduce chip cards over magnetic stripe technology, and it is maneuvering its Open Platform technology into position against the MasterCard-supported Mondex platform and Microsoft's Smart Card for Windows. Winner takes all in this contest, with losers having to adapt to new systems or face a shrinking market share.

## HISTORY

Although the first charge card was issued by Western Union in 1914, it wasn't until 1958 that Bank of America (BofA) issued its Bank-Americard, which combined the convenience of a charge account with credit privileges. When BofA extended its customer base outside California, the interchange system controlling payments began to falter because of design problems and fraud.

In 1968 Dee Hock, manager of the Bank-Americard operations of the National Bank of Commerce in Seattle, convinced member banks that a more reliable system was needed. Two years later National BankAmericard Inc. (NBI) was created as an independent corporation (owned by 243 banks) to buy the BankAmericard system from BofA.

With its initial ad slogan, "Think of it as Money," the Hock-led NBI developed Bank-Americard into a widely used form of payment in the US. A multinational corporation, IBANCO, was formed in 1974 to carry the operations into other countries. People outside the US resisted BankAmericard's nominal association with BofA, and in 1977 Hock changed the card's name to Visa. NBI became Visa USA, and IBANCO became Visa International.

By 1980 Visa had debuted debit cards, begun issuing traveler's checks, and created an electromagnetic point-of-sale authorization system. Visa developed a global network of ATMs in 1983; it was expanded in 1987 by the purchase of a 33% stake in the Plus System of ATMs, then the US's second-largest system. Hock retired in 1984 with the company well on its way to realizing his vision of a universal payment system.

The company built the Visa brand image with aggressive advertising, such as sponsorship of the 1988 and 1992 Olympics, and by co-branding (issuing cards through other organizations with strong brand names, such as Blockbuster and Ford).

In 1994 Visa teamed with Microsoft and others to develop home banking services and software. Visa Cash was introduced during the 1996 Olympics. Visa pushed its debit cards in 1996 and 1997 with humorous ads featuring presidential also-ran Bob Dole and showbiz success story Daffy Duck. The company expanded its smart card infrastructure in 1997. It published, with MasterCard, encryption and security software for online transactions. The gloves came off the next year as the companies vied to convince the world to rally around their respective e-purse technology standards.

During the 1990s Visa fought American Express' attempts to introduce a bank credit card of its own by forbidding Visa members in the US from issuing the product; the Justice Department responded with an antitrust suit against Visa and MasterCard. The case went to trial in 2000 with the government claiming that Visa and MasterCard stifle competition and enjoy an exclusive cross-ownership structure.

Also that year, the company made a deal with Gemplus, a French smart card company, to enable payments over wireless networks; Visa also inked a billing deal with wireless technology company Aether Systems.

The company continued its technology push in 2000 with a deal with Financial Services Technology Consortium to test biometrics (the use of fingerprints, irises, and voice recognition to identify cardholders). The company also prepared to launch a pre-paid card, Visa Buxx, targeted at teenagers. Also that year the European Union launched an investigation into the firm's transaction fees, alleging that the fees could restrict competition. The following year Visa International agreed to drop its fee to 0.7% of the transaction value over five years.

In 2001 a federal judge ordered Visa and MasterCard to allow their member banks to issue rival credit cards, but the card firms are appealing the ruling.

**President and CEO:** Malcolm Williamson
**CFO:** Ken Sommer
**EVP, Human Resources:** Elizabeth Rounds
**EVP and General Counsel:** Guy Rounsaville
**SVP, Public Policy:** Mark MacCarthy
**President, Visa, Asia Pacific Region:** Rupert Keeley
**President, Visa USA:** Carl Pascarella, age 58
**President, Visa Canada:** Derek A. Fry
**President, Visa Central and Eastern Europe, Middle East, and Africa Region:** Anne L. Cobb
**President, Visa European Union (EU):**
Johannes I. van der Velde
**President, Visa Latin America and Caribbean:**
Jonathan Sanchez-Jaimes
**EVP, Global Marketing Partnerships and Sponsorships:**
Tom Shepard
**EVP, Emerging Markets and Technology and COO, Visa, Asia Pacific:** Paul Vessey
**VP, Visa, U.S.A:** Kelly Presta
**Head of Sales and Intergrated Solutions Group, Visa, Asia U.S.A.:** Paul Gardner

**HQ:** 900 Metro Center Blvd., Foster City, CA 94404
**Phone:** 650-432-3200    **Fax:** 650-432-3087
**Web:** www.visa.com

Visa International provides consumer payment services at more than 21 million locations worldwide.

**Products and Services**
ATMs (almost 650,000 locations)
Electron (debit card outside of US)
Interlink (debit card)
smartVisa card (computer-chip-embedded card that is accepted worldwide)
Visa Business card (for small businesses and professionals)
Visa Cash (smart cards)
Visa Classic card (credit/debit card issued by Visa's 21,000 member banks)
Visa Corporate card (for travel and entertainment expenses)
Visa Debit card (accesses bank account for immediate settlement of payments)
Visa Gold card (higher spending limits)
VisaNet (electronic transaction processing network)
Visa Purchasing card (for corporate purchases)
Visa Travelers Cheques
Visa TravelMoney (prepaid card in any currency)

| | |
|---|---|
| American Express | Morgan Stanley Dean |
| Citigroup | Witter |
| MasterCard | |

| Private FYE: September 30 | Annual Growth | 9/91 | 9/92 | 9/93 | 9/94 | 9/95 | 9/96 | 9/97 | 9/98 | 9/99 | 9/00 |
|---|---|---|---|---|---|---|---|---|---|---|---|
| Estimated sales ($ mil.) | 15.9% | — | 920 | 1,040 | 1,260 | 1,330 | 1,650 | 2,050 | 2,550 | 2,800 | 3,000 |
| Employees | 9.1% | — | 2,500 | 3,000 | 3,500 | 4,000 | 4,800 | 5,000 | 5,000 | 5,000 | 5,000 |

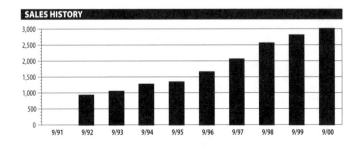

SALES HISTORY

# VULCAN NORTHWEST INC.

## OVERVIEW

Paul Allen is making sci-fi fantasies reality. One of the US's richest men (in such rarefied company as Gates, Buffett, and Ellison), Allen invests in companies that promote a "wired world."

Based in Bellevue, Washington, Vulcan Northwest is the umbrella organization for Allen's ventures, including his interest in Microsoft (5%, which he uses to fund his acquisitions) and charities supporting the arts, medical research, land conservation, and other causes. Allen has stakes in dozens of companies offering computer, multimedia, or communications products and services. His Vulcan

Ventures finds investment opportunities; think tank Interval Research develops new technology and business opportunities promoting Allen's vision. His sister Jody Patton oversees both his business and charitable ventures.

Many of Allen's investments in the "wired world" took a beating with the stock market downturn. He even saw his own personal wealth take a dip, but that hasn't stopped him. Among his latest projects is the Final Encyclopedia. Straight out of a sci-fi novel, the project is looking to put together the ultimate reference source in a form accessible to everyone.

## HISTORY

Paul Allen and Bill Gates first worked together on computer projects as schoolmates in Seattle. They developed a program to determine traffic patterns and launched Traf-O-Data, an operation that failed because the state provided the information for free. When Allen saw an article on the MITS Altair 8800 minicomputer in 1975, he and Gates realized it needed a simplified programming language to make it useful. They offered MITS a modified version of BASIC they had written for Traf-O-Data. The company set them up in an office in Albuquerque, New Mexico. They then began their biggest collaboration of all: Microsoft. While Gates concentrated on business, Allen focused on technical issues.

They moved to Bellevue, a Seattle suburb, in 1979. The next year IBM asked them to create a programming language for a PC project. Allen bought Q-DOS (quick and dirty operating system) from Seattle Computer; the pair tweaked it and renamed it MS-DOS. Allen and Gates made a key decision to structure their contract with IBM to allow clones. They also helped design many aspects of the original IBM PC.

Allen developed Hodgkin's disease in 1982. Facing his own mortality, he ended his daily involvement in Microsoft (keeping a chunk of the company and a board seat) and began to play more (traveling and playing the electric guitar).

With his cancer in remission in 1985, Allen founded multimedia software company Asymetrix. The next year he set up Vulcan Northwest to hold his diversified interests and Vulcan Ventures. He also began helping startups, indulging his interests (buying the NBA's Portland Trail Blazers in 1988 and donating some $60 million to build a museum honoring his musical idol, Jimi Hendrix, and other

Pacific Northwest artists), and funding Seattle-area civic improvements.

In 1990 Allen hired William Savoy to help organize his finances; Savoy later became president of Vulcan Ventures. Seeing a need for more R&D in the US, Allen in 1992 started Interval Research. He also invested in America Online (sold 1994). In 1993 Allen bought 80% of Ticketmaster (sold 1997), and in 1995 invested in DreamWorks SKG, the multimedia company of Steven Spielberg, Jeffrey Katzenberg, and David Geffen.

Allen made a rare buy outside the entertainment and high-tech worlds with a 1996 investment in power turbine maker Capstone Turbine. To prevent the Seattle Seahawks from moving to California, Allen bought the team in 1997 and made plans for a new stadium. He consolidated his management operations under Vulcan Northwest and dissolved Paul Allen Group (founded 1994), keeping Vulcan Ventures.

Allen moved into cable in 1998 and 1999; his Charter Communications eventually became the #4 US cable firm. In 1999 several Allen investments (Charter Communications, Vulcan Ventures, RCN, High Speed Access, and Go2Net) joined to form wired world venture Broadband Partners.

In 2000 it was nearly impossible to ignore Allen's influence on Seattle as several major projects took shape or were completed, including the new Seahawks' arena, the rock 'n' roll museum, and the renovation of a 90-year-old train station as part of a complex that will include Vulcan's new headquarters. That year he provided a $100 million infusion to struggling Oxygen Media. In 2001 Vulcan Ventures bought sports games Web site operator Small World Media to boost its sports holdings.

**Chairman:** Paul G. Allen
**CEO:** Jody Patton
**Senior Executive; President and CEO, Asymetrix:** Jim Billmaier
**Senior Executive; Chairman, Asymetrix Learning Systems; Vice Chairman, Portland Trailblazers and Seattle Seahawks:** Bert Kolde
**Senior Executive; President, Vulcan Ventures:** William D. Savoy, age 36
**CFO:** Joseph Franzi
**Director, Human Resources:** Pam Faber
**Director, Public Relations:** Susan Pierson

**HQ:** 110 110th Ave. NE, Ste. 550, Bellevue, WA 98004
**Phone:** 425-453-1940      **Fax:** 425-453-1985
**Web:** www.paulallen.com

**Selected Holdings**
800.com (online consumer electronics retailer)
Charter Communications (cable-TV system)
Command Audio (audio-on-demand service)
CyberSource (ecommerce transaction services)
Digeo Broadband Inc. (broadband services)
DreamWorks SKG (entertainment company)
Drugstore.com (online retailer)
e-steel (Internet marketplace)
IFILM (film industry online content provider)
imandi.com (online marketplace)
Instantiations, Inc. (Java-based software developer)
inviso (display developer)
iVAST (broadband content provider)
Kestrel Solutions (optical fiber networking)
Metricom, Inc. (wireless data-transmission products)
myplay, inc. (digital music services)
Oxygen Media (Internet and television content provider)
Portland Trail Blazers (professional basketball team)
RCN Corporation (broadband fiber-optic networks)
Replay TV, Inc. (television programming technology provider)
ScienceMedia (science and health online products)
Seattle Seahawks (professional football team)
The Sporting News (print and online sports magazine)
Stamps.com (online postage retailer)
Telescan, Inc. (online investor information)
TiVo (television programming technology provider)
Transmeta (microprocessors)
USA Networks (broadcasting and other media, retail, and Internet services)
Vulcan Ventures, Inc. (investments)
Wavtrace (wireless technology)
Wink Communications (television advertising technology)

| | | |
|---|---|---|
| Accel Partners | Hummer | SOFTBANK |
| Austin Ventures | Winblad | Sutter Hill |
| Benchmark | Institutional | Trinity Ventures |
| Capital | Venture | US Venture |
| Boston Ventures | Partners | Partners |
| Draper Fisher | Kleiner Perkins | Venrock |
| Jurvetson | Matrix Partners | Associates |
| Flatiron Partners | Mayfield Fund | Veronis Suhler |
| Harris & Harris | Menlo Ventures | Stevenson |
| | Microsoft | |

# WAFFLE HOUSE INC.

There might be 50 ways to leave your lover, but the Waffle House claims it knows 844,739 ways to cook a hamburger. Based in Norcross, Georgia, the company owns or franchises some 1,300 restaurants in more than 20 states, mainly in the Southeast. Each unit is a mecca of starchy goodness with a menu that offers waffles (pecan and regular) and a host of other breakfast foods, including hash browns, omelets, eggs, and grits. The restaurants — which are open 24 hours a day, every day of the year — also serve non-breakfast fare such as burgers, chili, soup, melts, sandwiches, and desserts. The restaurants are casual with a greasy spoon feel and a jukebox that features

such pro-waffle ditties as "Waffle Do Wop" and "Waffle House Family, Part 1," performed by the wife of chairman and CEO Joe W. Rogers Jr. (son of founder Joe Rogers Sr.).

The employee-owned company has been fighting the perception of race and gender discrimination after several lawsuits. Waffle House is notoriously media-wary, does little advertising, and releases few details to the public. Although it hasn't romanced the media, the company has developed close relationships with food suppliers to serve exclusively Coca-Cola soft drinks, Minute Maid orange juice, and Heinz condiments.

Joe Rogers Sr. and Tom Fortner opened the first Waffle House restaurant on Labor Day, 1955, in Avondale Estates, Georgia. Rogers and Fortner based their restaurant's strategy on simple Southern cooking and low overhead. Little has changed at the Waffle House — the same black-on-yellow signs hang over each restaurant, and the menu could serve as a time capsule from 1955 (prices aside).

Joe Rogers Jr. became CEO in 1973. He built a reputation for management skills, establishing a rigorous training program for store managers and instituted incentive-based compensation in an effort to retain employees.

In 1981 the US Department of Labor took exception to the company's practice of paying inordinately low wages to restaurant managers who also served as cooks. The company won the case in 1983 and has since become tight-lipped about its operations.

In 1997 the Waffle House had another scrape with the law. A US district judge found the company guilty of sexual harassment and "egregious conduct" against a former human resources employee. The judge ordered the company to pay $8.1 million in damages. The following year Waffle House showed signs of rethinking its tight-lipped stance when it hired a public relations firm.

Waffle House's largest franchisee, Northlake Foods, was hit by a racial discrimination suit in 1999. Five African-American men alleged that they were denied service by a white cook at an Atlanta-area restaurant. Also that year a Mobile, Alabama, Waffle House waitress won $10 million from a lottery ticket left by a customer as a tip. Four of her co-workers won a share in the winnings after demonstrating in

court that the employees had a "share the wealth" agreement.

In 2000 the company found itself the subject of another race-related lawsuit when a manager said he was ordered to fire black employees in order to have the restaurant's staff reflect the racial makeup of its mostly white town. The following year a federal judge ordered Waffle House franchisee Treetop Enterprises to pay nearly $3 million to 125 employees who worked more than 80 hours a week despite allegedly being hired to work 53-hour weeks.

Waffle House's legal troubles continued to stack up in early 2002. Four people filed a federal lawsuit accusing employees at a Gastonia, North Carolina, franchise of racial discrimination and mistreatment, including spraying water and spilling coffee on them, using a racial slur, serving white customers before black customers, and not allowing black customers in the restaurant even though there were seats available.

The same day that suit was filed, the Supreme Court voted to allow the Equal Employment Opportunity Commission the right to sue Waffle House on behalf of an employee who had been fired after he had suffered a seizure while on the job. The employee had previously signed an arbitration agreement waiving his right to sue.

**Chairman and CEO:** Joe W. Rogers Jr.
**VP Finance:** T.J. Turner
**Area VP:** Roger Turner
**VP Human Resources:** Ann Parker

## LOCATIONS

**HQ:** 5986 Financial Dr., Norcross, GA 30071
**Phone:** 770-729-5700     **Fax:** 770-729-5999
**Web:** www.wafflehouse.com

Waffle House owns and franchises restaurants in 21 states.

## COMPETITORS

Advantica Restaurant Group
Bob Evans
CBRL Group
Furr's
IHOP
Luby's
Shoney's

## HISTORICAL FINANCIALS & EMPLOYEES

| Private<br>FYE: June 30 | Annual<br>Growth | 6/92 | 6/93 | 6/94 | 6/95 | 6/96 | 6/97 | 6/98 | 6/99 | 6/00 | 6/01 |
|---|---|---|---|---|---|---|---|---|---|---|---|
| Estimated sales ($ mil.) | 3.8% | — | — | — | 500 | 525 | 525 | 600 | 540 | 580 | 625 |
| Employees | 0.0% | — | — | — | 6,000 | 6,000 | 6,000 | 6,000 | 6,000 | 6,000 | 6,000 |

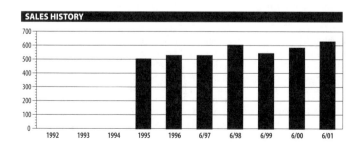

SALES HISTORY

# WAKEFERN FOOD CORPORATION

## OVERVIEW

At Wakefern Food the little guys are Goliath. The largest supermarket co-op in the US, Elizabeth, New Jersey-based Wakefern is owned by more than 40 independent grocers who operate some 200 ShopRite supermarkets in five northeastern states. The company provides members and other customers more than 20,000 name-brand items, including groceries, dairy and meat products, produce, frozen foods, and general merchandise. It also sells more than 3,000 items under the ShopRite label, and it offers members support services, including advertising, insurance, merchandising, and store design.

More than half of the ShopRite stores offer full-service pharmacies, and others offer specialty services such as banking, coffee shops, and photo labs that are quickly becoming the norm in food retailing. Members range from single-store owners to Big V Supermarkets, Wakefern's largest customer, with some 30 ShopRite stores. All members are given one vote in the co-op, regardless of size.

## HISTORY

Wakefern Food was founded in 1946 by seven New York- and New Jersey-based grocers: Louis Weiss, Sam and Al Aidekman, Abe Kesselman, Dave Fern, Sam Garb, and Albert Goldberg (the company's name is made up of the letters of the first five of those founders). Like many cooperatives, the association sought to lower costs by increasing its buying power as a group.

They each put in $1,000 and began operating a 5,000-sq.-ft. warehouse, often putting in double time to keep both their stores and the warehouse running. The shopkeepers' collective buying power proved valuable, enabling the grocers to stock many items at the same prices as their larger competitors.

In 1951 Wakefern members began pooling their resources to buy advertising space. A common store name — ShopRite — was chosen, and each week co-op members met to decide which items would be sale priced. Within a year, membership had grown to over 50. Expansion became a priority, and in the mid-1950s co-op members united in small groups to take over failed supermarkets. One such group, called the Supermarkets Operating Co. (SOC), was formed in 1956. Within 10 years it had acquired a number of failed stores, remodeled them, and given them the ShopRite name.

In the late 1950s sales at ShopRite stores slumped after Wakefern decided to buck the supermarket trend of offering trading stamps (which could then be exchanged for gifts), figuring that offering the stamps would ultimately lead to higher food prices. The move initially drove away customers, but Wakefern cut grocery prices across the board and sales returned. The company also embraced another supermarket trend: stocking stores with nonfood items.

The co-op was severely shaken in 1966 when SOC merged with General Supermarkets, a similar small group within Wakefern, becoming Supermarkets General Corp. (SGC). SGC was a powerful entity, with 71 supermarkets, 10 drugstores, six gas stations, a wholesale bakery, and a discount department store. Many Wakefern members opposed the merger and attempted to block the action with a court order. By 1968 SGC had beefed up its operations to include department store chains as well as its grocery stores. In a move that threatened to break Wakefern, SGC broke away from the co-op, and its stores were renamed Pathmark.

Wakefern not only weathered the storm, it grew under the direction of chairman and CEO Thomas Infusino, elected shortly after the split. The co-op focused on asserting its position as a seller of low-priced products. Wakefern developed private-label brands, including the ShopRite brand. In the 1980s members began operating larger stores and adding more nonfood items to the ShopRite product mix. With its number of superstores on the rise and facing increased competition from club stores in 1992, Wakefern opened a centralized, nonfood distribution center in New Jersey.

In 1995, 30-year Wakefern veteran Dean Janeway was elected president of the co-op. In 1997 the co-op purchased two of its customer's stores in Pennsylvania, then threatened to close them when contract talks with the local union deteriorated. The following year Wakefern settled the dispute, then sold the stores.

The company partnered with Internet bidding site priceline.com in 1999, offering customers an opportunity to bid on groceries and then pick them up at ShopRite stores. Big V, Wakefern's biggest customer, filed for Chapter 11 bankruptcy protection in 2000 and said it was ending its distribution agreement with the co-op. In 2001, however, Wakefern entered into an agreement to purchase most of Big V's assets, pending approval by bankruptcy court.

**Chairman and CEO:** Thomas Infusino
**President:** Dean Janeway
**CFO:** Ken Jasinkiewicz
**EVP:** Joseph Sheridan
**VP Corporate and Consumer Affairs:** Mary Ellen Gowin
**VP Human Resources:** Ernie Bell
**Chief Information Officer:** Natan Tabak

## LOCATIONS

**HQ:** 600 York St., Elizabeth, NJ 07207
**Phone:** 908-527-3300     **Fax:** 908-527-3397
**Web:** www.shoprite.com

Wakefern Food's 40-plus members operate about 200 ShopRite supermarkets in Connecticut, Delaware, New Jersey, New York, and Pennsylvania.

## PRODUCTS/OPERATIONS

**Major Members**
Big V Supermarkets
Foodarama Supermarkets
Inserra Supermarkets
Village Super Market

**Selected Private Labels**
Black Bear (deli items)
Chef's Express
Reddington Farms (poultry)
ShopRite

## COMPETITORS

| | |
|---|---|
| C&S Wholesale | Pathmark |
| Di Giorgio | Royal Ahold |
| Fleming Companies | Shurfine International |
| A&P | Stop & Shop |
| IGA | SUPERVALU |
| King Kullen Grocery | Wal-Mart |
| Krasdale Foods | |

## HISTORICAL FINANCIALS & EMPLOYEES

| Cooperative FYE: September 30 | Annual Growth | 9/91 | 9/92 | 9/93 | 9/94 | 9/95 | 9/96 | 9/97 | 9/98 | 9/99 | 9/00 |
|---|---|---|---|---|---|---|---|---|---|---|---|
| Sales ($ mil.) | 7.6% | — | — | — | 3,740 | 3,700 | 4,304 | 4,613 | 5,000 | 5,500 | 5,800 |
| Employees | 8.9% | — | — | — | 3,000 | 3,700 | 3,000 | 3,200 | 3,000 | 4,000 | 5,000 |

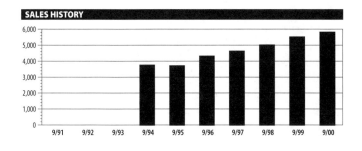

**SALES HISTORY**

# WHITE CASTLE SYSTEM, INC.

## OVERVIEW

White Castle System opts for square burgers instead of round tables. The Columbus, Ohio-based company was the country's first fast-food hamburger chain and still owns all 350 of its restaurants, located primarily in 12 eastern and midwestern states. White Castle steam-cooks its square, palm-sized burgers (also known as Slyders) on a bed of onions, the same way it did when the company was founded in 1921. Subsidiary PSB makes stainless-steel fixtures and equipment (including kitchen equipment used in White Castle restaurants), as well as lawn spreaders under the PrizeLAWN brand.

Little has changed at White Castle over its 80-year history, from its Slyders to its castle-shaped buildings. That has helped the chain establish strong loyalty among both customers and employees. Its turnover rate for salaried employees is far below the industry average. But White Castle's reluctance to franchise and its lack of TV advertising, among other things, have allowed McDonald's and Burger King to dominate the market. Chairman, president, and CEO E. W. Ingram III (grandson of co-founder E. W. Ingram) and his family own the company.

## HISTORY

Walter Anderson, a cook in Wichita, Kansas, invented a new way to cook hamburger patties by steam-grilling the meat over a bed of onions. In 1916 he opened his first hamburger stand. Looking to build his string of three stands, Anderson joined real estate broker E. W. "Billy" Ingram in 1921 and opened the first White Castle restaurant in Wichita. At the time, many Americans were skeptical about the sanitary quality of hamburger meat, so Anderson and Ingram chose a name that stood for purity (White) and for strength and permanence (Castle). Whether it was the appellation or the Slyders, White Castle restaurants were a success, and about 100 restaurants opened between 1923 and 1931.

In 1933 Anderson sold his share in the company to Ingram, who moved the company head-quarters to Columbus, Ohio, the next year. For the next several decades, White Castle distinguished itself with innovative products and ideas. To prove the nutritional value of its food, White Castle once paid a university student to eat nothing but White Castle hamburgers for an entire summer. The student, who ate about 20-24 burgers daily, survived, but on the advice of a chemist, the company added more flour to its bun to make the meal more nutritious.

The first company in the food industry to use paper cartons, White Castle created its Porcelain Steel Building subsidiary to build its restaurants (some of which were movable) and much of its kitchen equipment. Marketing innovations included the creation of Julia Joyce, a fictional character played by a local housewife. Joyce would give other housewives a tour of White Castle kitchens, showcasing the sanitary conditions while handing out free coupons.

Beef shortages during WWII led to the closure of about a third of the company's restaurants. Those lean times were not helped by

Ingram's refusal to hire women or black workers. White Castle yielded on the former by the end of the 1940s but did not hire sizable numbers of black employees until two decades after the war. During the 1950s and 1960s, the franchise-oriented operations of Burger King and McDonald's eclipsed White Castle, in part because the company refused to exploit suburban expansion and TV advertising.

After Billy Ingram died in 1966, his son E. W. Ingram Jr. took control of the company. While the fast-food market exploded during the 1970s, White Castle continued its steady but slow growth. In 1977 E. W. Ingram Jr. handed the reins of the company over to his son, E. W. Ingram III. Two years later White Castle opened its first drive-through restaurant.

In 1981 the company started a toll-free number through which US customers could order frozen burgers and have them delivered within 24 hours. The program was so successful that it spawned White Castle Distributing, which debuted in 1986 to market the company's burgers in grocery stores; distribution spread to convenience stores and vending machines by 1995.

The next year the company formed an agreement with Church's Chicken to open co-branded restaurants nationwide. After introducing its first breakfast sandwich in 1998, White Castle launched a Web site the following year, whatyoucrave.com, featuring tasty tidbits on everything trivial about White Castle. Also in 1999, 31 new members were inducted into its 25-Year Club and received the royal treatment, including limousines, a banquet, and a gold watch.

## HISTORICAL FINANCIALS & EMPLOYEES

| Private<br>FYE: December 31 | Annual<br>Growth | 12/91 | 12/92 | 12/93 | 12/94 | 12/95 | 12/96 | 12/97 | 12/98 | 12/99 | 12/00 |
|---|---|---|---|---|---|---|---|---|---|---|---|
| Sales ($ mil.) | 3.5% | — | — | — | 325 | 350 | 360 | 384 | 400 | 400 | 400 |
| Employees | (3.1%) | — | — | — | — | — | — | 11,000 | 10,000 | 10,000 | 10,000 |

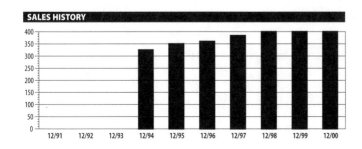

SALES HISTORY

# WINGATE PARTNERS

## OVERVIEW

It's a win-win situation for Wingate Partners. The Dallas-based equity investment firm buys controlling interests in manufacturing, distribution, and service businesses and transforms them into moneymakers, which it may operate or sell. Forgoing opportunities in such businesses as banking, media, technology, and real estate, Wingate generally targets companies that are underperforming or in industries in transition; these companies usually have sales between $100 million and $500 million and may or may not be profitable when purchased. It typically invests between $10 million and

$20 million in a holding. Wingate often makes more expensive purchases in conjunction with other investors.

An active investor, Wingate usually takes seats on the boards of companies it holds, and sometimes manages them. The company's holdings include building products maker Kevco. Wingate has launched three investment funds with a combined capitalization of $290 million. Investors include Yale University, The Ford Foundation, BankAmerica Capital, and the Hall family (of Hallmark cards fame).

## HISTORY

In 1987 experienced investors Frederick Hegi and James Callier teamed up with Tom Sturgess, a former senior executive with the distribution arm of meatpacker Swift Independent, to form Wingate. Hegi, who began his career as an investment manager at First National Bank of Chicago, was part of an investment group that had acquired Swift. Callier had been a McKinsey & Company management consultant and an investor in his own right.

The trio found 11 prominent individual and institutional investors — including Carl Lindner, Henry Hillman, Hughes Aircraft Pension Fund, the University of Texas endowment fund, and several insurance companies — to establish the $67 million Wingate Partners L.P. fund to support Wingate's acquisition strategy.

The investment fund's initial purchase was manufactured home builder Redman Industries and its aluminum window manufacturing unit, Redman Building Products, in 1988. To bring the underperforming Redman operations into profitability, Wingate began cutting costs and paring noncore businesses. Wingate also bought children's car seat and crib maker Century Products (an unprofitable subsidiary of Gerber Products) that year.

In 1991 the company bought Loomis Armored; it took three years for Wingate to return the armored-car company to profitability (Loomis Armored had recorded three years of losses prior to its purchase by Wingate.) In 1992 Wingate bought Associated Stationers, a network of stationery distribution centers.

By the time Wingate took Redman Industries public in 1993 (earning about $69 million), it had turned the company around. Wingate held on to Redman Building Products

(the window unit) until 1997, when it was sold to Robert Bass' Keystone Inc.

When Wingate launched its second investment fund in 1994, it raised $130 million. Investors included BankAmerica Capital Corp., Common Fund, Duke University, The Ford Foundation, the Hall family, Hughes Aircraft Pension Fund, the Kauffman Foundation, The University of Texas, Yale University, and several wealthy families in Dallas, Denver, and Kansas City.

With Wingate Partners II, the firm jumped on the health care bandwagon. Teaming with the former CEO of a hospital chain, Wingate formed rollup company AmeriStat Mobile Medical Services in 1994 to acquire ambulance companies. After making 10 such buys, the business was sold to ambulance operator Laidlaw in 1995.

Wingate bought Associated Stationers' rival United Stationers in 1995 and merged the former competitors under the United name. Wingate co-founder Sturgess served as United Stationers' chairman, CEO, and president until his resignation in 1996 (he still serves on Wingate's advisory board.) In 1997 Wingate merged its Loomis Armored unit with Borg-Warner Security's Wells Fargo Armored Service subsidiary to form Loomis, Fargo & Co.

In 1998 the firm separately sold Century Products' stroller and car seat operations and its crib-making division, Okla Homer Smith. That year Wingate sold ITCO to Heafner Tire Group, a nationwide tire distributor and retailer. In 1999 the company bought 46% of manufactured-housing building products distributor Kevco and acquired three automotive parts distributors to form Pro Parts Xpress.

Wingate in 2000 launched its third fund and sold its United Stationers stake. The next year it sold its half of Loomis.

## OFFICERS

**Founding Partner and Principal:** Frederick B. Hegi Jr.
**Principal:** Jay I. Applebaum, age 38
**Principal:** Michael B. Decker, age 52
**Principal:** V. Edward Easterling Jr., age 41
**Principal:** James A. Johnson, age 47
**VP:** Jason H. Reed, age 33
**Controller:** Alna Evans

## LOCATIONS

**HQ:** 750 N. St. Paul St., Ste. 1200, Dallas, TX 75201
**Phone:** 214-720-1313          **Fax:** 214-871-8799
**Web:** www.wingatepartners.com

## PRODUCTS/OPERATIONS

**Selected Holdings**
ENSR International (environmental consulting)
Kevco, Inc. (building products)
National Spirit Group (student sports and spirits
   products and services)
Pro Parts Xpress (auto parts distributor)

## COMPETITORS

AEA Investors
Apollo Advisors
Berkshire Hathaway
Blackstone Group
Clayton, Dubilier
Forstmann Little
Haas Wheat
Heico
Hicks, Muse
Interlaken Investment
KKR
Texas Pacific Group
Thomas Lee

# W.K. KELLOGG FOUNDATION

## OVERVIEW

You might say the W.K. Kellogg Foundation is a cereal philanthropist. Founded by corn flake pioneer Will Keith Kellogg, the Battle Creek, Michigan-based Kellogg Foundation gives more than $200 million in grants each year to programs promoting health, education, and agriculture. More than 20% of its funding goes to youth and education programs, while other initiatives fund projects aimed at rural development and fostering volunteerism. It also contributes millions to local projects in Battle

Creek. It makes grants primarily in the US, but also in Latin America and Southern Africa.

The foundation is guided by its founder's desire "to help people help themselves" and prefers funding programs that offer long-term solutions rather than quick handouts. Its $4.5 billion trust ranks the Kellogg Foundation as one of the largest in the world. It owns about one-third of the Kellogg Company and is governed by an independent board of trustees.

## HISTORY

Born in 1860, Will Keith Kellogg's early jobs included those of stock boy and traveling broom salesman. He later went to work as a clerk (and later bookkeeper and manager) at the Battle Creek Sanitarium, a renowned homeopathic hospital where his older brother, John Harvey Kellogg, was physician in chief. The brothers' experiments to improve vegetarian diets led to a happy accident in 1894 that resulted in the first wheat flakes. In 1906 W.K. Kellogg started the Battle Creek Toasted Corn Flake Company. Through marketing genius and innovative products, Kellogg's company became a leader in the industry.

A philanthropist by inclination, Kellogg established the Fellowship Corporation in 1925 to build an agricultural school and a bird sanctuary, as well as to set up an experimental farm and a reforestation project. He also gave $3 million to hometown causes, such as the Ann J. Kellogg School for disabled children, and for the construction of an auditorium, a junior high school, and a youth recreation center.

After attending a White House Conference on Child Health and Protection, Kellogg established the W.K. Kellogg Child Welfare Foundation in 1930. A few months later he broadened the focus of the charter and renamed the institution the W.K. Kellogg Foundation. That year the foundation began its landmark Michigan Community Health Project (MCHP), which opened public health departments in counties once thought too small and poor to sustain them. In 1934 Kellogg placed more than $66 million in Kellogg Company stock and other investments in a trust to fund his foundation.

During WWII the foundation expanded its programming to Latin America, funding advanced schooling for dentists, physicians, and other health professionals. After the war it broadened its programming to include agriculture to help war-torn Europe. It funded projects

in Germany, Iceland, Ireland, Norway, and the UK. Following Kellogg's death in 1951, the organization began providing support for graduate programs in health and hospital administration, as well as for rural leadership and community colleges.

During the 1970s the foundation lent its support to the growing volunteerism movement and to aiding the disadvantaged, with a special emphasis on programs for minorities. A review of operations in the late 1970s led the Kellogg Foundation to reassert its emphasis on health, education, agriculture, and leadership. The foundation also expanded its programs to Southern Africa.

In 1986 The Kellogg Foundation began funding the Rural America Initiative — a series of 28 projects meant to develop leadership, train local government officials, and revitalize rural areas. William Richardson became president and CEO of the foundation in 1995, leaving his post as president of The Johns Hopkins University. Also during the 1990s, the foundation supported the Community-Based Public Health Initiative, which assisted universities in educating public health professionals by presenting community-based approaches to students and faculty.

In 1998 the organization announced a five-year, $55 million plan to bring health care to the nation's poor and homeless. Also that year it gave Portland State University a $600,000 grant to develop its Institute for Nonprofit Management. In 1999 the Kellogg Foundation started its first geographically based program, pledging $15 million in grants for development of Mississippi River Delta communities in Arkansas, Louisiana, and Mississippi. In 2001 the foundation announced it would invest $10 million in new education projects.

**President and CEO:** William C. Richardson, age 60
**SVP and Corporate Secretary:** Gregory A. Lyman
**SVP Programs:** Anne C. Petersen
**VP and Chief Investment Officer:** Paul J. Lawler
**VP Programs:** Richard M. Foster
**VP Programs:** Gail D. McClure
**VP Programs:** Dan E. Moore
**VP Programs:** Gloria R. Smith
**Director Marketing and Communications:**
  Karen E. Lake
**Assistant VP:** James E. McHale
**VP Finance and Treasurer:** La June Montgomery-Tally
**Auditors:** PricewaterhouseCoopers LLP

## LOCATIONS

**HQ:** 1 Michigan Ave. East, Battle Creek, MI 49017
**Phone:** 616-968-1611      **Fax:** 616-968-0413
**Web:** www.wkkf.org

### 2000 Grants

|  | $ mil. | % of total |
|---|---|---|
| US | 167 | 81 |
| Latin America & the Caribbean | 22 | 10 |
| Africa | 15 | 7 |
| Other regions | 4 | 2 |
| **Total** | **208** | **100** |

## PRODUCTS/OPERATIONS

### 2000 Grants

|  | % of total |
|---|---|
| Youth & education | 22 |
| Health | 16 |
| Cross-cutting themes | 10 |
| Food systems & rural development | 10 |
| Programs operated | 10 |
| Cross-goal initiatives | 10 |
| Philanthropy & volunteerism | 8 |
| Special opportunities | 4 |
| Greater Battle Creek | 4 |
| Recurring grants | 4 |
| Other | 2 |
| **Total** | **100** |

## HISTORICAL FINANCIALS & EMPLOYEES

| Foundation FYE: August 31 | Annual Growth | 8/91 | 8/92 | 8/93 | 8/94 | 8/95 | 8/96 | 8/97 | 8/98 | 8/99 | 8/00 |
|---|---|---|---|---|---|---|---|---|---|---|---|
| Sales ($ mil.) | 2.6% | — | 226 | 256 | 235 | 271 | 298 | 374 | 330 | 327 | 277 |
| Employees | (1.1%) | — | — | — | — | 264 | 276 | 280 | 286 | 290 | 250 |

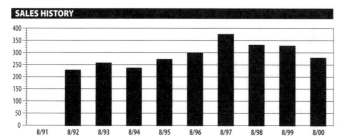

SALES HISTORY

W.K. KELLOGG FOUNDATION

# W. L. GORE & ASSOCIATES, INC.

## OVERVIEW

While Al Gore didn't invent the Internet, Newark, Delaware-based W. L. Gore and Associates did invent GORE-TEX, a lightweight, waterproof, and windproof fabric used in products that range from dental floss to space suits. The fabric is popular for hats, jackets, and hiking boots, since it allows perspiration to escape and blocks rain and wind. The company also produces synthetic blood vessels (the inert material is resistant to infection), electronic cables, filters, and guitar strings.

Gore is known for its unusual style of management — the lattice system. There is no fixed authority, as the company has "sponsors," not bosses, and all employees are considered associates. Company goals and tasks are determined by consensus. To foster this type of reliance and cooperation, each company facility has no more than 200 employees.

In order to compete with similar products produced in the Far East, the company continuously expands the number of uses for its GORE-TEX material. New products include n-LIGHTEN, a multi-channel optical transmitter and receiver developed in connection with Flextronics.

The company, which is headed by Robert Gore, the founder's son, is 75% owned by the Gore family. Gore associates own the rest.

## HISTORY

In 1941 Bill Gore, a DuPont scientist, started researching and developing plastics, polymers, and resins. One project at DuPont that Gore worked on was the development of a synthetic substance commonly known as teflon.

Seeing an untapped market for teflon-type products, Gore quit DuPont and in 1958 started his own business. He worked with his wife and his son Bob, a chemical engineering student. Bob helped him develop the company's first major product line — teflon-insulated electronic wires and cables.

With the success of its cables, the company was able to move out of the family basement and into a facility in Newark, Delaware. By 1965 Gore employed 200 people and soon implemented the lattice structure of management, eschewing demands for personal commitments and emphasizing cooperation and teamwork as paramount tenets of the business. A second plant was opened in Flagstaff, Arizona, in 1967.

Bob Gore, who had earned a doctorate in chemistry, hit the synthetic plastic motherlode in 1969. While experimenting with teflon, he discovered a way to stretch the material at microscopic levels, creating a fabric with holes large enough for body heat and moisture to escape, but small enough to deflect raindrops. Gore applied for a patent on its GORE-TEX fabric in 1970 and received it six years later. The company experienced an explosive period of growth as GORE-TEX found its way into space suits, sporting apparel, filters, and artificial arteries. Bob Gore became the company's president during this time.

By the 1980s GORE-TEX-related products generated the majority of sales. Globally, Gore operated about 30 plants, locating most in smaller cities since the Gores believed that small towns offered a better quality of life. Bill Gore died in 1986. The business continued and developed new uses for GORE-TEX. Various patent lawsuits emerged at the time, and when the company lost a case in 1990, Gore's exclusive patent on GORE-TEX ended, although it retained patents on certain products and processes.

The door was open for competition by 1993, but Gore still had the advantages of experience and a perception of higher quality and durability. It continued to introduce new uses for GORE-TEX, spooling out dental floss in 1993. The company also moved into the computer market that year by acquiring Supercomputer Systems.

Gore expanded its US medical product line in 1996 by marketing a membrane made from GORE-TEX-related material for use as a replacement for dura mater (the membrane that protects the brain and spinal cord) and in 1997 with the purchase of Prograft Medical.

In 1999 Gore introduced its REMEDIA catalytic filter system, which destroys carcinogenic dioxins and furans produced during industrial combustion by converting them into water and harmless chemicals.

The company exited the circuit packaging business in 2000 when it sold its Eau Claire, Wisconsin, plants to 3M. That year it introduced ReviveX Water and Stain Repellent, a product that restores water repellency in outerwear. The following year Gore entered into a strategic agreement with Singapore-based photonic component manufacturer Flextronics Photonics to manufacture optical transmitter and receiver modules.

**President and CEO:** Robert W. Gore
**CFO:** Charles Carroll
**Director, Human Resources:** Sally Gore

## LOCATIONS

**HQ:** 555 Paper Mill Rd., Newark, DE 19711
**Phone:** 302-738-4880     **Fax:** 302-738-7710
**Web:** www.gore.com

W. L. Gore and Associates operates manufacturing
facilities in China, Germany, Japan, the UK, and the US,
with sales and customer service offices in those
countries as well as in Argentina, Austria, Chile,
Finland, France, Greece, Hong Kong, India, Italy,
Malaysia, the Netherlands, Singapore, South Korea,
Spain, Sweden, Switzerland, and Taiwan.

## PRODUCTS/OPERATIONS

### Selected Divisions, Products, and Brands

**Consumer Products**
CleanStream vacuum cleaner filters
ELIXER guitar strings
GLIDE dental floss
ReviveX water and stain repellent

**Electronics**
Cable and assembly products
  Fiber-optic cables
  Flat cables
  High data rate cables
  Hook-up wire
  Microwave products
  Round cables
Electronic packaging and materials
  Conductive adhesives
  EMI/RFI shielding - GORE-SHIELD
  PWB materials
  Thermal interfaces

**Fabrics**
ACTIVENT fabrics
CROSSTECH fabrics
DRYLOFT fabrics
GORE WINDSTOPPER fabrics
GORE-TEX BEST DEFENSE outerwear
GORE-TEX fabrics
GORE-TEX OCEAN TECHNOLOGY outerwear

**Medical and Health Care**
GLIDE floss
GORE cast liner
GORE surgical-barrier fabrics
Implantable medical devices
  GORE RESOLUT XT regenerative material
  GORE subcutaneous augmentation material
  GORE-TEX DualMesh biomaterial
  GORE-TEX MycroMesh biomaterial
  GORE-TEX regenerative material
  GORE-TEX stretch vascular graft
  GORE-TEX suture
  GORE-TEX vascular grafts
  PRECLUDE dura substitute
  PRECLUDE peritoneal membrane
  SEAMGUARD staple line-reinforcement material

**Membrane Filtration and Separations**
Cleanroom garments
CleanStream vacuum cleaner filters
Disk drive filters
Filter bags and cartridges
GORE-SORBER exploration survey
GORE-SORBER screening survey
Liquid filtration tubular filter socks
Microfiltration filter media
Particulate and fluid filters for nonimpact printing
  components
PRIMEA power assemblies
PRISTYNE UX filter media
RASTEX sewing thread and weaving fiber
REMEDIA catalytic filter system

**Sealants and Fibers Technologies**
GFO fiber packing
GORE-TEX gasket tape
GORE-TEX joint sealant
ONE-UP pump diaphragms
RASTEX fiber
SEQUEL fiber packing
TENARA fiber
TENARA sewing thread

## COMPETITORS

| | |
|---|---|
| Belden | Malden Mills |
| Burlington Industries | Milliken |
| CardioTech | Superior TeleCom |
| Donaldson | Thoratec Corp |
| Kellwood | Timberland |
| L.L. Bean | |

## HISTORICAL FINANCIALS & EMPLOYEES

| Private<br>FYE: March 31 | Annual<br>Growth | 3/92 | 3/93 | 3/94 | 3/95 | 3/96 | 3/97 | 3/98 | 3/99 | 3/00 | 3/01 |
|---|---|---|---|---|---|---|---|---|---|---|---|
| Sales ($ mil.) | 8.1% | — | 750 | 804 | 825 | 958 | 1,064 | 1,150 | 1,280 | 1,350 | 1,400 |
| Employees | 3.6% | — | — | 5,170 | 5,700 | 5,860 | 6,100 | 6,600 | 7,000 | 5,888 | 6,600 |

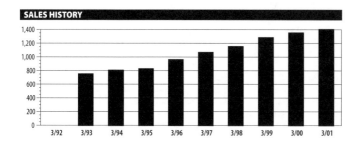

SALES HISTORY

# THE YUCAIPA COMPANIES LLC

The Yucaipa Companies has a hungry eye for bargains. The Los Angeles-based investment company (controlled by billionaire businessman Ron Burkle) forged its reputation as the ultimate grocery shopper, executing a series of grocery chain mergers and acquisitions that put the company on the supermarket map. It owned a minority interest in the Fred Meyer grocery chain until Kroger bought Fred Meyer in 1999. Yucaipa now owns 2% of Kroger. The company also maintains a link to the food industry through a 70% stake in Golden State Foods, one of McDonald's largest suppliers, and 9% of major food distributor Fleming. In addition, Yucaipa's portfolio includes Alliance Entertainment (a distributor of music, videos,

and games); a stake in Simon Worldwide (formerly Cyrk), a promotional marketing company whose largest customer is McDonald's; and 6% of retail behemoth Kmart Corporation.

In 1999 Burkle and former Walt Disney president Michael Ovitz launched CheckOut Entertainment Network, the operator of CheckOut.com, an entertainment Web site at which Web surfers could buy books, music, and video games. Yucaipa also invested in other Internet ventures, including GameSpy (online games) and OneNetNow (online communities). However, as the Internet economy faltered, Yucaipa began exiting the industry; it sold CheckOut.com in 2001.

Ronald Burkle launched his career in the grocery industry as a box boy at his dad's Stater Bros. grocery store. By age 28 Burkle had moved up to SVP of administration, but he was fired after botching a buyout of the company in 1981.

Burkle and former Stater Bros. colleagues Mark Resnik and Douglas McKenzie founded Yucaipa (named after Burkle's hometown in California) in 1986 when they bought Los Angeles gourmet grocery chain Jurgensen's. The next year Yucaipa bought the Kansas-based Falley's, which had 20 Food 4 Less stores in California.

In 1989 Yucaipa merged with Breco Holding, operator of 70 grocery stores. It also bought Northern California's Bell Markets. Yucaipa acquired ABC Markets in Southern California in 1990. The next year the company bought the 142-store chain Alpha Beta. In the 1992 Los Angeles riots 36 Yucaipa stores were damaged, but Yucaipa rebuilt, working with unions to keep workers employed until the stores were operational.

The company acquired the 28-store Smitty's Super Valu chain (now Fred Meyer Marketplace) in 1994. The following year Yucaipa bought the 70-year-old family-owned chain Dominick's Finer Foods. Later in 1995 Yucaipa's Food 4 Less chain merged with Los Angeles competitor Ralphs Grocery (founded in 1873 by George Ralphs), making Yucaipa #1 in Southern California.

Yucaipa sold Smitty's to Utah-based Smith's in 1996, acquiring a minority stake in Smith's (Burkle became Smith's CEO). Dominick's went public in 1996, and Yucaipa retained a minority stake. The next year Fred Meyer

bought Smith's for $1.9 billion. Burkle became the acquiring company's chairman, and Yucaipa gained a 9% interest in Fred Meyer.

In 1998 Fred Meyer bought Ralphs and 155-store Quality Food Centers (QFC). Yucaipa and Wetterau Associates, a management firm, also bought Golden State Foods, giving Yucaipa a 70% stake in the McDonald's food supplier. Yucaipa sold Dominick's to Safeway.

After Kroger bought Fred Meyer in 1999, Yucaipa turned away from the consolidating grocery industry and moved into cyberspace. Burkle teamed with Mike Ovitz (former Walt Disney president) to create the CheckOut.com e-commerce Web site (launched mid-1999). Yucaipa hired Richard Wolpert, former president of Disney Online, to oversee its Internet and technology activities.

Yucaipa added to its portfolio in 1999 by taking stakes in GameSpy (online games), OneNetNow (online communities), ClubMom (Web site for mothers), and Cyrk (now Simon Worldwide, promotional marketing). It also bought music, video, and games distributor Alliance Entertainment. Music and video retailer Wherehouse Entertainment became a 50%-owner of CheckOut.com after it merged its online retailing operations with CheckOut.com in 1999.

In 2000 the company digressed from its focus on the Web to invest in Kole Imports, an importer of merchandise sold in discount stores. The next year it returned to its roots, buying 9% of food distributor Fleming. Also in 2001 the struggling CheckOut.com was sold to digital music supplier Amplified Inc., and Yucaipa bought a 6% stake in retail chain Kmart Corporation.

**Managing Partner Yucaipa, Chairman-Alliance:**
Ronald W. Burkle, age 48
**Legal:** Robert P. Bermingham
**Human Resources:** Marla Hunter

## LOCATIONS

**HQ:** 9130 W. Sunset Blvd., Los Angeles, CA 90069
**Phone:** 310-789-7200        **Fax:** 310-884-2600

## PRODUCTS/OPERATIONS

**Selected Investments**
Alliance Entertainment (music, videos, and game
  distribution)
Fleming Companies (9%, wholesale food distributor)
Golden State Foods (70%, McDonald's supplier)
Kmart Corporation (6%, discount retailer)
Kole Imports (minority stake, discount merchandise
  importer)
The Kroger Co. (2%, grocery stores)
Simon Worldwide (20%, promotional marketing)

## COMPETITORS

Baker & Taylor
Equity Marketing
HA-LO Industries
Handleman
Ingram Entertainment
Keystone Foods
Martin-Brower
Norwood Promotional
  Products
Wal-Mart

# Hoover's Handbook of Private Companies

## KEY PRIVATE COMPANIES

## 24 HOUR FITNESS WORLDWIDE INC.

8 Columbus Ave.
San Francisco, CA 94111
Phone: 415-249-6800
Fax: 800-535-3799
Web: www.24hourfitness.com

CEO: Mark S. Mastrov
CFO: Colin Heggie
HR: Sandi Stevens
Type: Private

2000 Sales: $911.0 million
1-Yr. Sales Change: 23.8%
Employees: 26,794
FYE: December 31

If you're holding too much weight, 24 Hour Fitness Worldwide has the solution. It owns and operates some 437 fitness centers (under the 24 Hour Fitness, Q Clubs, and Hart's Athletic Clubs names) that offer aerobic, cardiovascular, and weight lifting activities. Some facilities also feature squash, racquetball, and basketball courts; swimming pools; steam and sauna rooms; tanning rooms; and whirlpools. The centers (the majority of which are open 24 hours a day) are located in 15 states in the US, as well as in countries throughout Europe and Asia. 24 Hour Fitness intends to continue to expand. Investment partnership McCown De Leeuw & Co. is the leading investor in the firm.

**KEY COMPETITORS**
Bally Total Fitness
The Sports Club
YMCA

## 84 LUMBER COMPANY

Route 519
Eighty Four, PA 15330
Phone: 724-228-8820
Fax: 724-228-4145
Web: www.84lumber.com

CEO: Joseph A. Hardy Sr.
CFO: Dan Wallach
HR: —
Type: Private

2000 Sales: $1,775.0 million
1-Yr. Sales Change: (1.4%)
Employees: 5,000
FYE: December 31

With its no-frills stores (most don't have — or need — air conditioning or heating), 84 Lumber Company has built itself to be a low-cost provider of lumber and building materials. Through about 415 stores, the company sells lumber, siding, drywall, windows, and other supplies, as well as kits to make barns, playsets, decks, and even homes. Professional builders and remodelers account for 75% of sales; other customers include do-it-yourselfers and commercial builders. Its stores are in more than 30 states, mainly in the East, Southeast, and Midwest; 84 Lumber also sells products internationally. CEO Joseph Hardy Sr. founded 84 Lumber in 1956; his daughter, president Maggie Hardy Magerko, owns about 80% of the firm.

**KEY COMPETITORS**
Carolina Holdings
Payless Cashways
Sutherland Lumber

 See pages 26–27 for a full profile of this company.

## AAA

1000 AAA Dr.
Heathrow, FL 32746
Phone: 407-444-7000
Fax: 407-444-7380
Web: www.aaa.com

CEO: Robert L. Darbelnet
CFO: John Schaffer
HR: Carol Droessler
Type: Not-for-profit

2000 Sales: —
1-Yr. Sales Change: —
Employees: —
FYE: December 31

This isn't your father's AAA. The not-for-profit organization (formerly the American Automobile Association) still offers its trademark emergency roadside assistance to members, but it has expanded its offerings to include various financial services as well. AAA Financial Services offers credit cards, personal loans, online banking, and vehicle financing and leasing. AAA also sells insurance, operates more than 1,000 travel agencies, and publishes TourBook guides and maps. Members can take advantage of AAA's travel benefits in 110 countries. Founded in Chicago in 1902 by nine auto clubs, AAA has about 100 clubs and about 1,000 US and Canadian offices. The organization has more than 42 million members.

**KEY COMPETITORS**
GE Capital
Shell
State Farm

## AARP

601 E St. NW
Washington, DC 20049
Phone: 202-434-2277
Fax: 202-434-2525
Web: www.aarp.org

CEO: William D. Novelli
CFO: Jocelyn Davis
HR: J. Robert Carr
Type: Association

2000 Sales: $502.1 million
1-Yr. Sales Change: 3.5%
Employees: 2,000
FYE: December 31

AARP is gearing up for the geezer boom. Open to anyone age 50 or older (dues are $10 per year), the not-for-profit organization is changing its image to lure baby boomers reaching the age of eligibility. It is the largest organization of older adults in the US with about 34 million members and is also the largest lobbyist for the elderly (it spends more than $50 million on lobbying and related activities). On a mission to enhance the quality of life for older Americans, AARP is active in four areas: information and education, community service, advocacy, and member services. It also publishes the monthly *AARP Bulletin* and the bimonthly *Modern Maturity* magazine.

 **See pages 28–29 for a full profile of this company.**


## ABBEY CARPET COMPANY, INC.

3471 Bonita Bay Blvd.
Bonita Springs, FL 34134
Phone: 941-948-0900
Fax: 941-948-0999
Web: www.abbeycarpet.com

CEO: Phil Gutierrez
CFO: Herb Gray
HR: Patti Peterson
Type: Private

2000 Sales: $1,280.0 million
1-Yr. Sales Change: 28.0%
Employees: —
FYE: December 31

Beating out even McDonald's as the first registered franchise in California, Abbey Carpet Company has become one of the nation's top franchise operations. The company runs a network of more than 750 independently owned and operated stores across the US, the Bahamas, and Puerto Rico. It sells brand-name carpet at mill-direct prices, as well as area rugs; hardwood, laminate, and vinyl floorings; ceramic tile; and window coverings. It also offers its own line of carpet and home fashion products. Founded in 1958 by Milton Levinson, Abbey Carpet began as a single floor-covering store in Sacramento, California. Chairman and CEO Phil Gutierrez has owned Abbey Carpet since 1983.

**KEY COMPETITORS**
Carpet One
Home Depot
Lowe's


## ACE HARDWARE CORPORATION

2200 Kensington Ct.
Oak Brook, IL 60523
Phone: 630-990-6600
Fax: 630-990-6838
Web: www.acehardware.com

CEO: David F. Hodnik
CFO: Rita D. Kahle
HR: Fred J. Neer
Type: Cooperative

2000 Sales: $2,945.2 million
1-Yr. Sales Change: (7.4%)
Employees: 5,513
FYE: December 31

Ace is the place for thousands of hardware retailers. The nations' #2 hardware cooperative (behind TruServ), Ace Hardware operates about 5,000 hardware stores in the US and about 65 other countries. The co-op distributes to its retailers from more than 20 wholesale warehouses and backs dealers with national advertising, insurance, and training. Dealers receive dividends from Ace's profits. Ace also manufactures paint and offers hardware and household items under the Ace brand. Formed in the 1920s, Ace has responded to strong competition from warehouse-style rivals The Home Depot and Lowe's by remodeling its stores and updating its image.

**KEY COMPETITORS**
Home Depot
Lowe's
TruServ

 **See pages 30–31 for a full profile of this company.**

## ADVANCE PUBLICATIONS, INC.

950 Fingerboard Rd.
Staten Island, NY 10305
Phone: 718-981-1234
Fax: 718-981-1456
Web: www.advance.net

CEO: Samuel I. "Si" Newhouse Jr.
CFO: Arthur Silverstein
HR: Arthur Silverstein
Type: Private

2000 Sales: $4,542.0 million
1-Yr. Sales Change: 7.4%
Employees: 23,000
FYE: December 31

Advance Publications gets its marching orders from the printed page. One of the top US periodical publishers, Advance owns 26 daily newspapers around the country, including *The Star-Ledger* (New Jersey) and *The Cleveland Plain Dealer*. It also owns American City Business Journals (40 weekly papers) and Parade Publications (*Parade Magazine* Sunday insert). Advance is the #2 magazine publisher in the US (behind Time, Inc.) through units Condé Nast Publications, with its 16 popular titles such as *Allure, Glamour,* and *Vanity Fair,* and trade journal publisher Fairchild Publications. Advance also has stakes in cable TV systems and Discovery Communications. Samuel "Si" Newhouse Jr. and his brother Donald own the company.

**KEY COMPETITORS**
Gannett
Hearst
Time

 **See pages 32–33 for a full profile of this company.**


## ADVANTAGE/ESM FEROLIE

2 Van Riper Rd.
Montvale, NJ 07645
Phone: 201-307-9100
Fax: 201-782-0878
Web: www.feroliegroup.com

CEO: Lawrence J. Ferolie
CFO: Cathy Ross
HR: Julie Shasteen
Type: Private

2000 Sales: $1,100.0 million
1-Yr. Sales Change: 0.0%
Employees: 615
FYE: December 31

A food broker serving the northeastern United States, Advantage/ESM Ferolie broke into the business in 1948. The company provides sales and marketing services for packaged food and packaged goods companies. Through exclusive area and regional contracts, the group arranges distribution to warehouse stores, drugstores, supermarkets, and mass merchandisers. Some of Advantage/ESM Ferolie's biggest clients are Gillette's Duracell, Fort James, Kraft Foods, Unilever's Lipton, and McCormick & Company. The company is affiliated with Advantage Sales & Marketing, a partnership of food brokerages operating across the US. Founded by A. Joseph Ferolie, the company remains family-owned.

**KEY COMPETITORS**
Atlantic Mktg
Crossmark
Marketing Specialists


## ADVENTIST HEALTH

2100 Douglas Blvd.
Roseville, CA 95661
Phone: 916-781-2000
Fax: 916-783-9909
Web: www.adventisthealth.org

CEO: Donald R. Ammon
CFO: Douglas E. Rebok
HR: Roger Ashley
Type: Not-for-profit

2000 Sales: $2,510.4 million
1-Yr. Sales Change: 22.8%
Employees: 16,500
FYE: December 31

They even stay open on Saturdays. Adventist Health is a not-for-profit health care system with strong ties (financially, organizationally, and spiritually) to the Seventh-Day Adventist Church. The West Coast wing of an international organization operating more than 160 Adventist health care operations, Adventist Health runs about 20 hospitals (with some 3,200 beds), almost 20 home health services facilities, and various other outpatient facilities and hospices in California, Hawaii, Oregon, and Washington. The organization also works with its own churches and those of other denominations to offer such preventative health services as medical screenings, immunizations, and health education.

**KEY COMPETITORS**
Catholic Healthcare West
Los Angeles County
  Department of Health
Tenet Healthcare

## ADVOCATE HEALTH CARE

2025 Windsor Dr.
Oak Brook, IL 60523
Phone: 630-572-9393
Fax: 630-572-9139
Web: www.advocatehealth.com

CEO: Richard R. Risk
CFO: Lawrence J. Majka
HR: Ben Grigaliunas
Type: Not-for-profit

2000 Sales: $1,675.2 million
1-Yr. Sales Change: 4.7%
Employees: 24,500
FYE: December 31

Advocating wellness in Chicagoland from Palos Heights to Palatine, Advocate Health Care is an integrated health care network with more than 200 sites serving the Chicago area. Advocate's operations include eight acute-care hospitals (including Christ Medical Center and Lutheran General Hospital) with more than 3,000 beds, as well as home health care and ambulatory care services. Advocate also has teaching affiliations with area medical schools such as the University of Illinois at Chicago. In addition, Advocate manages a medical ethics center that helps its staff and clients address such issues as cloning and physician-assisted suicide.

**KEY COMPETITORS**
HCA
Provena Health
Rush System for Health

## AECOM TECHNOLOGY CORPORATION

555 S. Flower
Los Angeles, CA 90071
Phone: 213-593-8000
Fax: 213-593-8729
Web: www.aecom.com

CEO: Raymond W. Holdsworth
CFO: Joseph A. Incaudo
HR: —
Type: Private

2001 Est. Sales: $1,575.0 mil.
1-Yr. Sales Change: 15.4%
Employees: 12,800
FYE: September 30

AECOM Technology means never having to say Architecture, Engineering, Construction management, Operation, and Maintenance. The holding company develops, designs, builds, and maintains facilities for public and private entities around the world through its eight firms. AECOM is a top design engineering firm in Asia and the Middle East and a global leader in the water, transportation, and wastewater sectors. The employee-owned company has expanded in Europe by acquiring UK-based companies such as transportation infrastructure group Maunsell and water and wastewater construction group Metcalf & Eddy. AECOM is also buying UK-based building engineering and transportation planning specialist Oscar Faber.

**KEY COMPETITORS**
ABB
Bechtel
Louis Berger Group

## AEI RESOURCES, INC.

2000 Ashland Dr.
Ashland, KY 41101
Phone: 606-928-3433
Fax: 606-928-0450
Web: www.aeiresources.com

CEO: Donald Brown
CFO: Rick Fasold
HR: Robert Schmidt
Type: Private

2000 Est. Sales: $1,500.0 mil.
1-Yr. Sales Change: 12.7%
Employees: —
FYE: December 31

You can't buy a vowel from AEI Resources, but you can get some coal from the company, one of the nation's largest producers of steam coal. Most of AEI's sales are generated through long-term contracts to supply electric utilities. The company operates mines in Colorado, Illinois, Indiana, Kentucky, Tennessee, and West Virginia. Through its Mining Machinery subsidiary, AEI also provides trucking services, major equipment rebuilds, and mining equipment. The company also manufactures Addcar-brand highwall mining equipment. The Addington family — including AEI chairman Larry and his brothers, Robert and Bruce — control the company.

**KEY COMPETITORS**
CONSOL Energy
Joy Global
Peabody Energy

# AFL-CIO

| | | |
|---|---|---|
| 815 16th St. NW | CEO: John J. Sweeney | Sales: — |
| Washington, DC 20006 | CFO: Richard L. Trumka | 1-Yr. Sales Change: — |
| Phone: 202-637-5000 | HR: Carl Garland | Employees: — |
| Fax: 202-637-5058 | Type: Labor union | FYE: June 30 |
| Web: www.aflcio.org | | |

The AFL-CIO (American Federation of Labor and Congress of Industrial Organizations) is an umbrella organization representing more than 13 million workers. An alliance of 66 autonomous national and international unions, the AFL-CIO negotiates with employers and works to improve working and living standards for union members. Its membership includes actors and airline pilots, farmworkers and firefighters, and police and postal employees. The organization is aggressively focusing on recruitment as membership declines because of the decreasing number of workers in manufacturing, construction, and other traditionally unionized industries.

 See pages 34–35 for a full profile of this company.


# AG PROCESSING INC

| | | |
|---|---|---|
| 12700 W. Dodge Rd. | CEO: Martin P. Reagan | 2000 Sales: $1,961.7 million |
| Omaha, NE 68103 | CFO: Kenneth S. Grubbe | 1-Yr. Sales Change: (6.3%) |
| Phone: 402-496-7809 | HR: Judy Ford | Employees: 2,500 |
| Fax: 402-498-5548 | Type: Cooperative | FYE: August 31 |
| Web: www.agp.com | | |

Soy far, soy good for Ag Processing (AGP), one of the largest soybean processors in the US. AGP's chief soybean products include vegetable oil and commercial animal feeds. The cooperative is also promoting its corn-based ethanol and soybean oil-based bio-fuels, fuel additives, and solvents. AGP processes some 15,000 acres of soybeans a day from its members' farms. Its grain division has the capacity to store more than 50 million bushels. The co-op's owners include 300,000 members from 16 states and Canada. The members, most of whom are in the Midwest, are represented through nearly 300 local co-ops and 10 regional co-ops. AGP and Archer Daniels Midland co-own Consolidated Nutrition, a leading US feed manufacturer.

**KEY COMPETITORS**
ADM
Cargill
ConAgra

 See pages 36–37 for a full profile of this company.


# A. G. SPANOS COMPANIES

| | | |
|---|---|---|
| 1341 W. Robinhood Dr. | CEO: Dean A. Spanos | 2001 Est. Sales: $1,560.0 mil. |
| Stockton, CA 95207 | CFO: Jeremiah T. Murphy | 1-Yr. Sales Change: (1.9%) |
| Phone: 209-478-7954 | HR: Charlene Flynn | Employees: 600 |
| Fax: 209-478-3309 | Type: Private | FYE: September 30 |
| Web: www.agspanos.com | | |

From California to Florida, A.G. Spanos Companies spans many operations: building, managing, and selling multifamily housing units, constructing master-planned communities, and developing land. The firm has built more than 80,000 apartments in 32 states since its founding in 1960. Major projects include Spanos Park, a $1 billion master-planned community in founder and chairman Alex G. Spanos' hometown of Stockton, California, and luxury apartment construction in 18 states. Spanos stills owns the firm, operated by sons Dean and Michael Spanos. Alex Spanos also owns the NFL's San Diego Chargers.

**KEY COMPETITORS**
Centex
Del Webb
Irvine Company

## AGAMERICA, FCB

3636 American River Dr.
Sacramento, CA 95864
Phone: 916-485-6000
Fax: 916-485-6171
Web: www.agamwestfcb.com

CEO: James D. Kirk
CFO: David B. Newlin
HR: John Lovstad
Type: Cooperative

2000 Sales: $833.9 million
1-Yr. Sales Change: 13.0%
Employees: —
FYE: December 31

AgAmerica aggrandizes farm credit in the western US. The cooperative is one of six regional banks in the federal Farm Credit System, providing loans and banking services to local Farm Credit offices. The bank has a joint management agreement with its sister Western Farm Credit Bank; their combined resources serve more than 80,000 borrowers, including aquatic producers, farmers, ranchers, rural homeowners, timber harvesters, and rural utility providers in more than a dozen states. AgAmerica offers operating and land loans, rural home mortgages, crop insurance, and such financial services as farm record-keeping and financial planning. The bank raises its funds through the sale of securities.

**KEY COMPETITORS**
AgFirst
AgriBank
National Rural Utilities Cooperative Finance

## AGFIRST FARM CREDIT BANK

1401 Hampton St.
Columbia, SC 29201
Phone: 803-799-5000
Fax: 803-254-1776
Web: www.agfirst.com

CEO: F. A. "Andy" Lowrey
CFO: Larry R. Doyle
HR: Pat N. Roche
Type: Cooperative

2000 Sales: $1,108.4 million
1-Yr. Sales Change: 10.8%
Employees: —
FYE: December 31

AgFirst puts farms first. AgFirst Farm Credit Bank is a large agricultural lender for the southeastern US and Puerto Rico, offering more than $9 billion in loans to some 79,000 farmers, ranchers, and rural homeowners. It is one of six regional farm credit banks that make up the Farm Credit System (FCS) cooperative. AgFirst originates real estate, operating, and rural home mortgage loans. The company also offers crop, life, and other insurance, equipment leasing, and tax services. Clients also include rural utility businesses, agricultural cooperatives, and agribusinesses. The bank does not accept deposits; it raises money by selling bonds and notes on the capital markets.

**KEY COMPETITORS**
AgAmerica
AgriBank
National Rural Utilities Cooperative Finance

## AGRIBANK, FCB

375 Jackson
St. Paul, MN 55164
Phone: 651-282-8800
Fax: 651-282-8666
Web: www.agribank.com

CEO: William J. Collins
CFO: Diane M. Cole
HR: Sandra L. Schmiesing
Type: Cooperative

2000 Sales: $1,774.3 million
1-Yr. Sales Change: 9.3%
Employees: —
FYE: December 31

AgriBank sees green in green acres. AgriBank is one of six intermediary banks in the Farm Credit System, a nationwide network of cooperatives that provide loans and financial services for farmers and rural homeowners. Farm Credit Services co-ops write loans for land, equipment, and other farm operating costs; they in turn own Agribank, which provides loans and wholesale banking services to the co-ops. Agribank's district includes some 40 FCS offices representing more than 200,000 member-owners in about a dozen midwestern and southern states. Land loans comprise about 60% of Agribank's loan portfolio; operating loans account for about 30%. It also provides credit to rural electric, water, and telephone systems.

**KEY COMPETITORS**
Ag Services
AgAmerica
AgFirst

## AGWAY INC.

333 Butternut Dr.
DeWitt, NY 13214
Phone: 315-449-7061
Fax: 315-449-6008
Web: www.agway.com

CEO: Donald P. Cardarelli
CFO: Peter J. O'Neill
HR: Richard Opdyke
Type: Cooperative

2001 Sales: $1,548.3 million
1-Yr. Sales Change: 8.5%
Employees: 4,700
FYE: June 30

It's either Agway or the highway for many farmers. The agricultural co-op boasts 69,000 members, primarily in the Northeast. The co-op's Agricultural Group sells feeds, seeds, fertilizers, and other farm supplies to members and other growers. Agway's Country Products Group processes and markets fresh produce (mostly under the Country Best label), sunflower seeds, and beans, and invests in new agricultural technology. Agway Energy Products sells fuel and HVAC systems and markets electricity and gas in deregulated states. Agway also offers leasing and insurance services. The co-op has sold its stores, which retain the Agway name, and dealer supply network. It is selling its bean and soybean operations.

**KEY COMPETITORS**
ADM
Farmland Industries
Purina Mills

 See pages 38–39 for a full profile of this company.

## AID ASSOCIATION FOR LUTHERANS/LUTHERAN BROTHERHOOD

625 4th Ave. South
Minneapolis, MN 55415
Phone: 612-340-7000
Fax: 612-340-4070
Web: www.aal.org

CEO: Bruce J. Nicholson
CFO: Laurence W. Stranghoener
HR: Jennifer H. Martin
Type: Not-for-profit

2000 Sales: $2,322.0 million
1-Yr. Sales Change: 6.0%
Employees: 2,086
FYE: December 31

The Spirit has moved Aid Association for Lutherans (AAL) to merge with Lutheran Brotherhood. Until a new name for the 3 million member-strong fraternal organization is chosen later in 2002, the resulting entity is simply known as Aid Association for Lutherans/Lutheran Brotherhood (AAL/LB). The merger brings under one steepled roof some $55 billion in assets under management in mutual funds, bank and trust services (AAL Bank and Trust and LB Community Bank & Trust will eventually merge), and other financial services. AAL/LB also has about $145 billion in life insurance in force.

**KEY COMPETITORS**
Citigroup
FMR
State Farm

## AIR WISCONSIN AIRLINES CORPORATION

W6390 Challenger Dr., Ste. 203
Appleton, WI 54914
Phone: 920-739-5123
Fax: 920-739-1325
Web: www.airwis.com

CEO: Geoffrey T. Crowley
CFO: Rose M. Lussier
HR: Lisa Conover
Type: Private

2000 Sales: $2,051.7 million
1-Yr. Sales Change: —
Employees: 2,861
FYE: December 31

Not limited to the state that shares its name, Air Wisconsin Airlines flies some 4 million passengers to more than 40 cities in 21 states in the US. The regional carrier operates as United Express, providing connecting service to and from United Airlines' hubs in Denver and Chicago. Air Wisconsin's fleet consists mostly of regional jets. The smaller, more fuel-efficient aircraft make flying to less populated destinations more cost effective than using larger jets. The airline plans to expand its regional jet fleet and has firm orders to acquire 51 Canadair jets. Like many airlines in the wake of the September 11 US terrorist attacks, Air Wisconsin cut its flight schedule and trimmed its staff.

**KEY COMPETITORS**
Frontier Airlines
Mesa Air
Midwest Express

## ALCOA FUJIKURA LTD.

800 Crescent Centre Dr., Ste. 600
Franklin, TN 37067
Phone: 615-778-6000
Fax: 615-778-5927
Web: www.alcoa-fujikura.com

CEO: Robert S. Hughes II
CFO: Barbara Smith
HR: Brett Blair
Type: Joint venture

2000 Sales: $2,200.0 million
1-Yr. Sales Change: 69.2%
Employees: 36,000
FYE: December 31

Alcoa Fujikura's customers use its products for wheeled and wired stuff. A joint venture between US-based aluminum producer Alcoa and Japanese wire and cable maker Fujikura, Alcoa Fujikura makes fiber-optic products for electric utilities and telecommunications and broadcasting, as well as electrical distribution systems for the automotive industry. Its fiber-optic products range from cable and connectors to couplers and fusion splicing systems. The automotive division makes electronic controllers, plastic components, printed circuit boards, and wiring. Alcoa Fujikura also offers engineering, installation, and testing services. The company's clients include BellSouth, Ford, Harley-Davidson, and Verizon.

**KEY COMPETITORS**
Corning
Furukawa Electric
Stoneridge

## ALEX LEE, INC.

120 4th St. SW
Hickory, NC 28602
Phone: 828-323-4424
Fax: 828-323-4435
Web: www.alexlee.com

CEO: Boyd George
CFO: Ronald W. Knedlik
HR: Glenn DeBiasi
Type: Private

2001 Sales: $1,890.0 million
1-Yr. Sales Change: 11.8%
Employees: 8,500
FYE: September 30

The George family mixed food wholesaling and retail well before it became a trend among consolidators. Founded by Alex and Lee George, Alex Lee has been distributing food to retailers through Merchants Distributors, Inc. (MDI) since 1931. MDI serves about 600 retailers in the Mid-Atlantic and Southeast, including IGA stores and Galaxy Food Centers. The company became a food service supplier in the 1960s through Institution Food House, and in 1984 it bought the Lowe's Food chain, which has more than 100 stores in North Carolina and Virginia. In 1998 Alex Lee started Consolidation Services to provide logistic services to vendors, distributors, and manufacturers. The George family controls Alex Lee.

**KEY COMPETITORS**
Fleming Companies
Kroger
SUPERVALU

## ALLIED WORLDWIDE, INC.

5001 US Hwy. 30 West
Ft. Wayne, IN 46818
Phone: 219-429-2511
Fax: 219-429-1853

CEO: Jim Rogers
CFO: —
HR: Todd Schorr
Type: Private

2000 Sales: $2,372.0 million
1-Yr. Sales Change: 7.2%
Employees: 7,000
FYE: December 31

Whether you're moving across the street, across town, or across the country, Allied Worldwide will get your belongings where they need to be. Formed in 1999 through a merger of North American Van Lines and Allied Van Lines, the group is one of the largest relocation companies in the world. In addition, Allied Worldwide operates the Allied Pickfords and Pickfords companies, providing household moving services in 36 countries in Asia, Australia, Europe, and North America. The group maintains a fleet of nearly 4,000 tractors and 6,000 trailers, and more than 1,000 straight trucks. Allied Worldwide is controlled by investment firm Clayton, Dubilier & Rice.

**KEY COMPETITORS**
AMERCO
Atlas World
UniGroup

## ALLINA HEALTH SYSTEM

| | | |
|---|---|---|
| 5601 Smetana Dr. | CEO: Gordon M. Sprenger | 2000 Sales: $2,600.0 million |
| Minnetonka, MN 55343 | CFO: David Jones | 1-Yr. Sales Change: 0.0% |
| Phone: 952-992-2000 | HR: Mike Howe | Employees: 21,500 |
| Fax: 952-992-2126 | Type: Not-for-profit | FYE: December 31 |
| Web: www.allina.com | | |

Oh Allina, oh don't you cry for me. For I come from Minnesota with a health care plan for me. Allina Health System is a not-for-profit health care system that focuses on prevention and community programs as an alternative means of keeping its members healthy. Allina's health plans, doctors, and hospitals cover Minnesota, North and South Dakota, and Wisconsin. The system's Medica Health Plans offers a variety of plans and serves more than a million members. The Allina Medical Group operates about 20 hospitals and nearly 50 clinics offering inpatient and ambulatory care. Allina also operates nursing homes and provides home health care. The company has faced government allegations of improper billing and spending.

**KEY COMPETITORS**
HCA
Mayo Foundation
SSM Health Care


## ALTICOR INC.

| | | |
|---|---|---|
| 7575 Fulton St. East | CEO: Dick DeVos | 2001 Sales: $3,500.0 million |
| Ada, MI 49355 | CFO: Lynn Lyall | 1-Yr. Sales Change: 0.0% |
| Phone: 616-787-1000 | HR: Robin Horder-Koop | Employees: 10,500 |
| Fax: 616-682-4000 | Type: Private | FYE: August 31 |
| Web: www.alticor.com | | |

At the core of Alticor, there is Amway. Alticor was formed in 2000 as a holding company for four businesses: direct-selling giant Amway, Web-based sales firm Quixtar, Pyxis Innovations (corporate development for Alticor and affiliates), and Access Business Network (manufacturing, logistics services). Access Business' biggest customers are Amway and Quixtar, but Access also serves outsiders. Amway, which accounts for the bulk of Alticor's revenues, sells more than 450 products through 3 million independent distributors. Quixtar sells Amway and other products online. Alticor is owned by Amway founders, the DeVos and Van Andel families.

**KEY COMPETITORS**
Avon
CCL Industries
PFSweb


## A-MARK FINANCIAL CORPORATION

| | | |
|---|---|---|
| 100 Wilshire Blvd., 3rd Fl. | CEO: Steven C. Markoff | 2001 Sales: $2,600.0 million |
| Santa Monica, CA 90401 | CFO: Joseph Ozaki | 1-Yr. Sales Change: 43.5% |
| Phone: 310-319-0200 | HR: Cary Wehrli | Employees: 102 |
| Fax: 310-319-0346 | Type: Private | FYE: July 31 |
| Web: www.amark.com | | |

Calling all gold bugs: A-Mark Financial trades, markets, and finances rare coins, precious metals, and collectibles. A-Mark Precious Metals trades in gold, silver, platinum, and palladium coins, bars, ingots, and medallions for central banks, corporations, and individuals worldwide. A-Mark distributes coins for government mints, including those of Australia, Canada, South Africa, and the US. Subsidiary A-M Handling provides melting and assay services. Affiliates include collectibles auctioneer Superior Stamps & Collectibles, which offers rare coins and bullion. Chairman, president, and owner Steven Markoff, a supporter of the medical marijuana movement, founded the company in 1965.

**KEY COMPETITORS**
Anglo American
Degussa
DGSE Companies

## AMERICAN BUILDERS & CONTRACTORS SUPPLY CO., INC.

1 ABC Pkwy.
Beloit, WI 53511
Phone: 608-362-7777
Fax: 608-362-6215
Web: www.abc-supply.com

CEO: Kenneth A. Hendricks
CFO: Kendra Story
HR: Lisa Indgjer
Type: Private

2000 Sales: $1,238.9 million
1-Yr. Sales Change: 3.5%
Employees: 3,121
FYE: December 31

American Builders & Contractors Supply Co. (which operates as ABC Supply) has put roofs over millions of heads. A leading supplier of roofing, siding, windows, and related builder's supplies, ABC Supply has about 200 outlets in more than 40 states. It carries its own brand of products (Amcraft, Mule-Hide), and it offers doors, windows, tools, and such from about 100 vendors. ABC Supply distributes its products via a fleet of some 2,700 vehicles. It also operates a building supply catalog. ABC Supply, which markets its products mostly to small- and medium-sized contractors, was founded in 1982 by CEO Kenneth Hendricks. Hendricks and his wife, EVP Diane, own the company.

**KEY COMPETITORS**
Cameron Ashley
Georgia-Pacific Group
North Pacific Group

## AMERICAN CANCER SOCIETY, INC.

1599 Clifton Rd. NE
Atlanta, GA 30329
Phone: 404-320-3333
Fax: 404-329-5787
Web: www.cancer.org

CEO: John R. Seffrin
CFO: Peter Tartikoss
HR: Aurelia C. Stanley
Type: Not-for-profit

2000 Sales: $812.0 million
1-Yr. Sales Change: 20.8%
Employees: 5,000
FYE: August 31

The American Cancer Society (ACS) works as a firefighter for your lungs. Dedicated to the elimination of cancer, the not-for-profit organization is staffed by professionals and more than 2 million volunteers at some 3,400 local units across the country. ACS is the largest source of private cancer research funds in the US. In addition to research, the ACS supports detection, treatment, and education programs. The organization encourages prevention efforts with programs such as the Great American Smokeout. Patient services include moral support, transportation to and from treatment, and camps for children who have cancer. Programs account for about 71% of expenses; 29% goes to administration and fund-raising.

 **See pages 40–41 for a full profile of this company.**

## AMERICAN CENTURY COMPANIES, INC.

4500 Main St., Ste. 1500
Kansas City, MO 64111
Phone: 816-531-5575
Fax: 816-340-7962
Web: www.americancentury.com

CEO: William M. Lyons
CFO: Robert T. Jackson
HR: Jerry Bartlett
Type: Private

2000 Est. Sales: $1,110.0 mil.
1-Yr. Sales Change: 23.3%
Employees: 3,000
FYE: December 31

American Century Companies, through subsidiary American Century Investment Management, oversees a family of more than 60 mutual funds. The firm employs direct marketing to sell its four distinct groups of funds: capital preservation, income, growth and income, and growth. The company's brokerage services afford investors access to stocks, fixed income, and precious metal investments, as well as approximately 9,000 mutual funds managed by other firms. American Century caters to individuals, investment professionals, businesses, not-for-profits, and retirement plans. J.P. Morgan Chase & Co. owns a 45% stake in American Century Investments, which is controlled by founder James Stowers Jr. and his family.

**KEY COMPETITORS**
FMR
T. Rowe Price
Vanguard Group

## AMERICAN CRYSTAL SUGAR COMPANY

101 N. Third St.
Moorhead, MN 56560
Phone: 218-236-4400
Fax: 218-236-4422
Web: www.crystalsugar.com

CEO: James J. Horvath
CFO: Joseph J. Talley
HR: Randy Johnson
Type: Cooperative

2001 Sales: $866.4 million
1-Yr. Sales Change: 18.4%
Employees: 1,250
FYE: August 31

Call it saccharine, but for American Crystal Sugar, business is all about sharing. The sugar beet cooperative is owned by more than 3,000 growers in the Red River Valley of North Dakota and Minnesota. American Crystal, formed in 1899 and converted into a co-op in 1973, divides the 35-mile-wide valley into five districts, each served by a processing plant. During an annual eight-month "campaign," the plants operate continuously, producing sugar, molasses, and beet pulp. Its products (under the Crystal name, the licensed Pillsbury brand, and private labels) are sold through marketing co-ops United Sugars and Midwest Agri-Commodities. American Crystal also owns 46% of corn sweeteners joint venture ProGold.

**KEY COMPETITORS**
Florida Crystals
Imperial Sugar
U.S. Sugar

## AMERICAN FAMILY INSURANCE GROUP

6000 American Pkwy.
Madison, WI 53783
Phone: 608-249-2111
Fax: 608-243-4921
Web: www.amfam.com

CEO: Harvey R. Pierce
CFO: J. Brent Johnson
HR: Vicki L. Chvala
Type: Mutual company

2000 Sales: $4,388.4 million
1-Yr. Sales Change: 6.3%
Employees: 7,300
FYE: December 31

Even singles can get insured through American Family Insurance Group. The company specializes in property/casualty insurance, but it also offers life, health, and homeowners coverage, as well as investment and retirement-planning products. It is among the largest US mutual companies that concentrates on auto insurance (State Farm is the biggest). American Family also provides coverage for apartment owners, restaurants, contractors, and other businesses. Through the company's consumer finance division, agents can also offer their customers home equity and personal lines of credit. American Family operates primarily in the Midwest.

**KEY COMPETITORS**
Allstate
Nationwide
State Farm

📖 See pages 42–43 for a full profile of this company.

## THE AMERICAN RED CROSS

430 17th St. NW
Washington, DC 20006
Phone: 202-737-8300
Fax: 703-248-4256
Web: www.redcross.org

CEO: Harold Decker
CFO: John D. Campbell
HR: Nancy Breseke
Type: Not-for-profit

2000 Sales: $2,528.6 million
1-Yr. Sales Change: 4.4%
Employees: 35,000
FYE: June 30

The American Red Cross is a member of the International Red Cross and Red Crescent Movement, a not-for-profit organization that helps victims, especially after disasters. Chartered by Congress in 1905, the American Red Cross isn't a government agency. Its staff is largely volunteer — more than 1.3 million of them. Aside from helping victims of more than 60,000 disasters each year, the Red Cross teaches CPR, first aid and AIDS awareness courses; provides counseling and emergency message transmission for US military personnel; and maintains the nation's largest blood, plasma, and tissue banks. The American Red Cross' mission was highlighted after the 2001 terrorist attacks on New York City and Washington, DC.

 See pages 44–45 for a full profile of this company.

## AMERICAN RETAIL GROUP INC.

| | | |
|---|---|---|
| 6251 Crooked Creek Rd. | CEO: Hans Brenninkmeyer | 2001 Est. Sales: $1,300.0 mil. |
| Norcross, GA 30092 | CFO: Michele Toth | 1-Yr. Sales Change: 8.3% |
| Phone: 770-662-2500 | HR: Elaine Gregg | Employees: 11,000 |
| Fax: 770-448-9831 | Type: Private | FYE: January 31 |

It's all in the family with retail clothing giant American Retail Group (ARG). ARG is the US piece of the Brenninkmeyer family's $7 billion global retail puzzle. The company sells mid-priced apparel and outdoor clothing through nearly 1,000 stores in the US. Its chains include Miller's Outpost, Eastern Mountain Sports, Maurice's, Anchor Blue Clothing, Levi's Outlet by M.O.S.T., Dockers Outlet by M.O.S.T., and Juxtapose; it shuttered its Uptons chain in 1999. The Brenninkmeyers, who entered US retailing in 1948, are a secretive bunch, sometimes sending their children to college under assumed names. The brood runs its empire from a secluded compound in the Netherlands and employs more than 200 family members.

**KEY COMPETITORS**
J. C. Penney
Kmart
Sears

## AMERICAN STOCK EXCHANGE, INC.

| | | |
|---|---|---|
| 86 Trinity Place | CEO: Salvatore F. Sodano | 2000 Sales: $270.4 million |
| New York, NY 10006 | CFO: Raqui Selwanes | 1-Yr. Sales Change: 16.9% |
| Phone: 212-306-1000 | HR: Katie Casey | Employees: — |
| Fax: 212-306-1218 | Type: Subsidiary | FYE: December 31 |
| Web: www.amex.com | | |

Don't confuse AMEX (The American Stock Exchange) with that credit card in your wallet. The exchange is a subsidiary of the National Association of Securities Dealers (NASD). It provides a floor-based auction market that complements the NASD's Automated Quotations system (Nasdaq) market. (Both are units of NASD.) AMEX lists more than 600 smaller, newer issues and specializes in trading derivatives, foreign issues, and American depositary shares; index fund trading now makes up a significant chunk of its daily volume. The market is the second-largest options exchange (behind the Chicago Board Options Exchange).

**KEY COMPETITORS**
CBOE
Instinet
NYSE

See pages 46–47 for a full profile of this company.

## AMERICAN UNITED LIFE INSURANCE COMPANY

| | | |
|---|---|---|
| 1 American Sq. | CEO: Jerry D. Semler | 2000 Sales: $1,907.1 million |
| Indianapolis, IN 46206 | CFO: Constance E. Lund | 1-Yr. Sales Change: 78.3% |
| Phone: 317-285-1877 | HR: Mark Roller | Employees: 1,634 |
| Fax: — | Type: Mutual company | FYE: December 31 |
| Web: www.aul.com | | |

American United Life Insurance Company is licensed in 49 states and the District of Columbia; it also does business in Latin America. The insurer specializes in pensions and annuities, and it offers individual and group life insurance and disability coverage. The company touts its reinsurance unit (which dates from 1904) as the oldest in the US. American United Life Insurance was formed from the 1936 merger of United Mutual Life Insurance (founded in 1877) and American Central Life Insurance (1899). The company has restructured into a mutual holding company, which gives it a more favorable tax status as well as allowing it to form publicly traded subsidiaries.

**KEY COMPETITORS**
CNA Financial
Lincoln National
Principal Financial

## AMICA MUTUAL INSURANCE COMPANY

| | | |
|---|---|---|
| 10 Lincoln Center Blvd. | CEO: Thomas A. Taylor | 2000 Sales: $1,075.1 million |
| Lincoln, RI 02865 | CFO: Robert A. DiMuccio | 1-Yr. Sales Change: (0.6%) |
| Phone: 401-334-6000 | HR: Richard S. Glover | Employees: — |
| Fax: 401-333-4610 | Type: Mutual company | FYE: December 31 |
| Web: www.amica.com | | |

Amica is an amicable source for your insurance needs. Amica Mutual Insurance Company provides a variety of personal insurance products, including auto, home, marine, personal liability, and life policies. The company is a mutual insurance company, which means it is owned by its policyholders. Amica sells its policies directly to customers in all states except Hawaii through about 40 offices. With its roots as an auto insurer going back to 1907 (when fire coverage was a car owner's most important need, because of exploding gas tanks) Amica was formed in 1973 through the consolidation of Automobile Mutual Insurance Company of America and Factory Mutual Liability Insurance Company of America.

**KEY COMPETITORS**
Allstate
CNA Financial
State Farm

## AMSTED INDUSTRIES INCORPORATED

| | | |
|---|---|---|
| 205 N. Michigan Ave., 44th Fl. | CEO: W. Robert Reum | 2001 Sales: $1,650.0 million |
| Chicago, IL 60601 | CFO: Robert Chiapetta | 1-Yr. Sales Change: (7.0%) |
| Phone: 312-645-1700 | HR: Shirley Whitesell | Employees: 10,300 |
| Fax: 312-819-8523 | Type: Private | FYE: September 30 |
| Web: www.amsted.com | | |

Wilbur and Orville Wright's first flight might never have succeeded without an assist from Amsted's Diamond Chain subsidiary. A maker of roller chains for a variety of equipment and machinery, Diamond Chain also produced the propeller chain for the Wright brothers' aircraft. AMSTED's other subsidiaries include American Steel Foundries (cast steel freight car components), Griffin Pipe Products (ductile iron pressure and sewer pipe), and Means Industries (automotive steering and transmission components). Customers include industrial distributors, locomotive and railcar manufacturers, and automotive OEMs. Employee-owned, AMSTED has more than 55 plants worldwide.

**KEY COMPETITORS**
ABC-NACO
ALSTOM
Bethlehem Steel

## ANDERSEN

| | | |
|---|---|---|
| 33 W. Monroe St. | CEO: Joseph Berardino | 2001 Sales: $9,340.0 million |
| Chicago, IL 60603 | CFO: Barbara J. Duganier | 1-Yr. Sales Change: 11.2% |
| Phone: 312-580-0033 | HR: Kay G. Priestly | Employees: 85,000 |
| Fax: 312-507-6748 | Type: Partnership | FYE: August 31 |
| Web: www.andersen.com | | |

Andersen (formerly Andersen Worldwide) is facing an identity crisis. After a long stint as the largest of the Big Five accounting/consulting firms, it has fallen victim both to industry consolidation (the formation of PricewaterhouseCoopers dislodged it from the top spot) and to its own success in building Andersen Consulting (now called Accenture), which finally seceded from the partnership. Andersen, ranking a big fifth out of the Big Five, does its accounting business under the Andersen name (formerly Arthur Andersen); the company has been growing a new consulting arm specializing in human resources and risk management consulting, legal services business, and outsourced business support services.

**KEY COMPETITORS**
Ernst & Young
KPMG
PricewaterhouseCoopers

 See pages 48–49 for a full profile of this company.

## ANDERSEN CORPORATION

| | | |
|---|---|---|
| 100 4th Ave. North | CEO: Donald Garofalo | 2000 Sales: $1,700.0 million |
| Bayport, MN 55003 | CFO: Michael O. Johnson | 1-Yr. Sales Change: 13.3% |
| Phone: 651-264-5150 | HR: Jan Grose | Employees: 6,000 |
| Fax: 651-264-5107 | Type: Private | FYE: December 31 |
| Web: www.andersencorp.com | | |

Windows of opportunity open and shut daily for Andersen, one of the US's leading makers of wood-clad windows and patio doors. The Andersen brand is one of the most-recognized brands in the industry, and the company sells its products globally to architects, contractors, and building owners. Andersen offers a wide array of window designs (including hinged, bay, and double-hung), hinged patio doors (sold under the Frenchwood brand), and skylights. The company has expanded its ownership of distribution centers by purchasing Morgan Products, the largest US distributor of Andersen products. The Andersen family owns the majority of the company.

**KEY COMPETITORS**
JELD-WEN
Pella
Sierra Pacific Industries

 **See pages 50–51 for a full profile of this company.**


## ANDERSON NEWS COMPANY

| | | |
|---|---|---|
| 6016 Brookvale Ln., Ste. 151 | CEO: Charles Anderson | 2001 Est. Sales: $1,100.0 mil. |
| Knoxville, TN 37919 | CFO: John Campbell | 1-Yr. Sales Change: (8.3%) |
| Phone: 865-584-9765 | HR: Donna Norris | Employees: 6,600 |
| Fax: 865-584-3498 | Type: Private | FYE: December 31 |
| Web: www.andersonnews.com | | |

Anderson News is the covergirl of the magazine wholesale industry. The company (which bought Aramark's magazine distribution operations in 1998) leads the merger-happy industry with about a 40% US market share. Anderson News distributes thousands of magazine titles to about 40,000 outlets, including bookstores, mass merchants, grocery and convenience stores, discount retailers, and just about any other place that sells something to read. The company also distributes newspapers, books, videos, and music. Anderson News was founded in 1917 by CEO Charles Anderson's grandfather; it is still family-owned. The founding Anderson family also runs the #3 US bookstore chain, Books-A-Million.

**KEY COMPETITORS**
Chas. Levy
Hudson News
Jim Pattison Group


## THE ANDREW W. MELLON FOUNDATION

| | | |
|---|---|---|
| 140 E. 62nd St. | CEO: William G. Bowen | 2000 Sales: $438.8 million |
| New York, NY 10021 | CFO: T. Dennis Sullivan | 1-Yr. Sales Change: (67.6%) |
| Phone: 212-838-8400 | HR: Gretchen Wagner | Employees: 42 |
| Fax: 212-223-2778 | Type: Foundation | FYE: December 31 |
| Web: www.mellon.org | | |

Recipients of funds from The Andrew W. Mellon Foundation don't take the organization for granted. Ranking among the 10 largest charitable foundations in the US, the organization's more than $210 million in grants include awards for higher education (about 60%), performing arts, conservation, and public affairs. Grant recipients have included the American Council of Learned Societies, the Museum of Modern Art, and the University of Virginia. The foundation was created in 1969 when Paul Mellon and Ailsa Mellon Bruce, the son and daughter of banking titan Andrew W. Mellon, merged their charitable foundations (Old Dominion Foundation and Avalon Foundation).

## APEX OIL COMPANY, INC.

8182 Maryland Ave.
St. Louis, MO 63105
Phone: 314-889-9600
Fax: 314-854-8539
Web: www.apexoil.com

CEO: P. A. "Tony" Novelly
CFO: John L. Hank Jr.
HR: Gale Brasswell
Type: Private

2001 Sales: $2,000.0 million
1-Yr. Sales Change: 17.6%
Employees: 175
FYE: September 30

At the top of its game, Apex Oil is engaged in the wholesale sales, storage, and distribution of petroleum products. Its range of refined products includes asphalt, kerosene, fuel oil, diesel fuel, heavy oil, gasoline, and bunker fuels. The company's terminals are located on the East Coast, Gulf Coast, in California, and in the Midwest. Internationally, Apex Oil has a terminal in Caracas, Venezuela, and has additional activities in Bermuda, Monaco, and the Netherlands. The company is also engaged in a tug boats and barge business and has a storage and truck rack operation. Founded in 1932 by Samuel Goldstein, Apex Oil is controlled by CEO Tony Novelly.

**KEY COMPETITORS**
Chemoil
Crown Central Petroleum
Getty Petroleum Marketing

## APPLERA CORPORATION

301 Merritt 7
Norwalk, CT 06851
Phone: 203-840-2000
Fax: 203-840-2312
Web: www.applera.com

CEO: Tony L. White
CFO: Dennis L. Winger
HR: Barbara J. Kerr
Type: Holding company

2001 Sales: $1,644.1 million
1-Yr. Sales Change: 19.9%
Employees: 5,544
FYE: June 30

If you are exploring the latest frontiers, Applera has some of the tools you may need. Its Applied Biosystems unit makes data-managing life science systems used in the drug, food, agriculture, and chemical manufacturing industries; it accounts for most of Applera's sales. The company's Celera Genomics unit sequenced the human genome and licenses its genetic databases to biotech and drug companies for medical discoveries. The three companies are combining their expertise to identify gene markers for diseases, then develop and commercialize drugs based on their findings.

**KEY COMPETITORS**
Affymetrix
Amersham Biosciences
Human Genome Sciences

## ARCTIC SLOPE REGIONAL CORPORATION

301 Arctic Slope Ave., Ste. 300
Anchorage, AK 99518
Phone: 907-852-8633
Fax: 907-852-5733
Web: www.asrc.com

CEO: Jacob Adams
CFO: Frank Zirnkilton
HR: Karen Burnell
Type: Private

2000 Sales: $1,038.0 million
1-Yr. Sales Change: 16.9%
Employees: 5,973
FYE: December 31

The Inupiat people have survived the Arctic for centuries, and now they're surviving in the business world. The Inupiat-owned Arctic Slope Regional Corporation (ASRC) was set up to manage 5 million acres on Alaska's North Slope after the Alaska Native Claims Settlement Act in 1971 cleared the way for oil development in the area. ASRC gets about two-thirds of sales from its energy services subsidiaries (Natchiq) and its petroleum refining and marketing units (Petro Star). Other operations include construction, engineering, technical services, and manufacturing. With other native corporations ASRC has formed Alaska Native Wireless, a partnership with AT&T Wireless that has won more than 40 mobile licenses in the US.

**KEY COMPETITORS**
Alaska Communications
Systems Group
Baker Hughes
Tesoro Petroleum

## ARMY AND AIR FORCE EXCHANGE SERVICE

| | | |
|---|---|---|
| 3911 S. Walton Walker Blvd. | CEO: Maj. Gen. Charles J. Wax, USAF | 2001 Sales: $7,368.8 million |
| Dallas, TX 75236 | CFO: Terry B. Corley | 1-Yr. Sales Change: 5.4% |
| Phone: 214-312-2011 | HR: James K. Winters | Employees: 52,400 |
| Fax: 214-312-3000 | Type: Government agency | FYE: January 31 |
| Web: www.aafes.com | | |

Be all that you can be and buy all that you can buy at the PX (Post Exchange). The Army and Air Force Exchange Service (AAFES) runs more than 12,000 facilities — including PXs and BXs (Base Exchanges) — at US Army and Air Force bases worldwide. Its outlets range from tents to shopping centers that have retail stores, fast-food outlets, movie theaters, beauty shops, and gas stations. AAFES serves active-duty military personnel, reservists, retirees, and their family members. A government agency under the Department of Defense (DoD), it receives no funding from the DoD. More than 70% of profits are used to fund amenities such as libraries and youth programs. Other profits are used to build or refurbish stores.

**KEY COMPETITORS**
Kmart
Target
Wal-Mart

See pages 52–53 for a full profile of this company.

## ARTHUR D. LITTLE, INC.

| | | |
|---|---|---|
| 25 Acorn Park | CEO: — | 2000 Est. Sales: $650.0 mil. |
| Cambridge, MA 02140 | CFO: — | 1-Yr. Sales Change: 3.3% |
| Phone: 617-498-5000 | HR: Michael Eisenbud | Employees: 3,000 |
| Fax: 617-498-7200 | Type: Private | FYE: December 31 |
| Web: www.arthurdlittle.com | | |

Being the world's first consulting firm is no small feat for Arthur D. Little. Founded by a chemist of the same name in 1886, Arthur D. Little (ADL) specializes in environment and risk consulting, management consulting, and technology and product development, and also invests in new commercial ventures. It operates from about 50 offices and laboratories in more than 30 countries. Other operations include the Arthur D. Little School of Management (a graduate program in management) and Arthur D. Little Enterprises, which commercializes products developed by the firm's staff. ADL's staff of about 3,000 owns the company. ADL has filed for Chapter 11 bankruptcy as part of a plan to be acquired by Cerberus Capital Management.

**KEY COMPETITORS**
Accenture
Booz-Allen
McKinsey & Company

See pages 54–55 for a full profile of this company.

## ASBURY AUTOMOTIVE GROUP, INC.

| | | |
|---|---|---|
| 3 Landmark Sq., Ste. 500 | CEO: Thomas R. Gibson | 1999 Sales: $4,000.0 million |
| Stamford, CT 06901 | CFO: Thomas F. Gilman | 1-Yr. Sales Change: 29.0% |
| Phone: 203-356-4400 | HR: Phillip R. Johnson | Employees: 5,400 |
| Fax: 203-356-4450 | Type: Private | FYE: December 31 |
| Web: www.asburyauto.com | | |

Asbury Automotive Group is the largest privately owned dealership group in the US. The company, which has grown through acquisitions, sells about 30 auto brands through nine major dealership groups (about 90 locations) in Arkansas, Florida, Georgia, Mississippi, Missouri, North Carolina, Oregon, Texas, and Virginia. Asbury Automotive sells more than 150,000 new and used cars annually. The company's strategy is to buy majority interests in multi-location dealerships with at least $150 million in annual sales, transforming each into a joint venture. Investment firms Ripplewood Holdings and Freeman Spogli & Co. own Asbury Automotive. In July 2001 the company announced plans to go public.

**KEY COMPETITORS**
AutoNation
Hendrick Automotive
VT

## ASCENSION HEALTH

4600 Edmundson Rd.
St. Louis, MO 63134
Phone: 314-253-6700
Fax: 314-253-6807
Web: www.ascensionhealth.org

CEO: Douglas D. French
CFO: Anthony J. Filer
HR: David A. Smith
Type: Not-for-profit

2000 Sales: $6,400.0 million
1-Yr. Sales Change: 0.0%
Employees: 67,000
FYE: June 30

Things are looking up for Ascension Health. Formed in the 1999 merger of the Daughters of Charity National Health System and the Sisters of St. Joseph Health System, the network consists of some 60 Roman Catholic hospitals, as well as nursing homes, psychiatric wards, long-term care centers, and other health care facilities in about 15 states and the District of Columbia. Its facilities are primarily located in the southern, midwestern, and northeastern areas of the US. Ascension Health is a leading Catholic hospital system and the largest not-for-profit health care system in the US. Although several clergy members sit on its governing board, the organization is led by a non-clergy CEO.

**KEY COMPETITORS**
Catholic Health Initiatives
HCA
Tenet Healthcare

 **See pages 56–57 for a full profile of this company.**


## THE ASCII GROUP, INC.

7101 Wisconsin Ave., Ste. 1000
Bethesda, MD 20814
Phone: 301-718-2600
Fax: 301-718-0435
Web: www.ascii.com

CEO: Alan D. Weinberger
CFO: Steve Reynolds
HR: —
Type: Consortium

Sales: —
1-Yr. Sales Change: —
Employees: —
FYE: December 31

ASCII has got the skinny on high-tech bargaining power. The ASCII Group is one of the world's largest buying consortiums for independent, full-service computer resellers, representing more than 2,000 US and Canadian members. Paying a monthly fee entitles members to buy volume products and negotiate better deals with hardware and software distributors. ASCII also offers discounts on credit card processing and leasing rates, online pricing, financing, health and business insurance, and other business service program offerings from companies such as Hertz and Airborne Freight. Chairman and CEO Alan Weinberger founded the group in 1984.

**KEY COMPETITORS**
Arrow Electronics
Avnet
Pioneer-Standard Electronics


## ASHLEY FURNITURE INDUSTRIES, INC.

1 Ashley Way
Arcadia, WI 54612
Phone: 608-323-3377
Fax: 800-678-4492
Web: www.ashleyfurniture.com

CEO: Ron Wanek
CFO: Richard Barclay
HR: Jim Dotta
Type: Private

2000 Sales: $952.0 million
1-Yr. Sales Change: 16.7%
Employees: 5,000
FYE: December 31

Furniture buyers took a shine to Ashley Furniture Industries when it added a tough, high-gloss polyester finish to its furniture in 1986. The company is one of the nation's largest furniture manufacturers. Ashley Furniture makes and imports upholstered, leather, and hardwood furniture, as well as bedding. It has manufacturing plants and distribution centers in California, Florida, New Jersey, Washington, Wisconsin, and overseas. It has tapped into retail through more than 100 Ashley Furniture HomeStores — independently owned shops that sell only Ashley Furniture products. Founded by Carlyle Weinberger in 1945, Ashley Furniture is owned by father-and-son duos Ron and Todd Wanek and Chuck and Ben Vogel.

**KEY COMPETITORS**
Furniture Brands International
La-Z-Boy
LifeStyle Furnishings International

## ASI CORP.

| | | |
|---|---|---|
| 48289 Fremont Blvd. | CEO: Marcel Liang | 2000 Sales: $818.0 million |
| Fremont, CA 94538 | CFO: Dean Madsen | 1-Yr. Sales Change: 12.1% |
| Phone: 510-226-8000 | HR: Crystal Yuan | Employees: 500 |
| Fax: 510-226-8858 | Type: Private | FYE: December 31 |
| Web: www.asi2000.com | | |

ASI has a whole lotta sales going on. The company, a wholesale distributor of computer software and hardware, sells more than 3,000 products, including CD-ROM drives, modems, monitors, PCs, networking equipment, and storage devices. ASI also assembles microcomputers, which it sells under the NSpire name, and offers standard and custom configurations. The company sells to systems integrators and resellers throughout North America. Vendor partners include 3Com, Microsoft, Samsung, and Toshiba. President Christine Liang, who founded ASI in 1987, owns 51% of the company.

**KEY COMPETITORS**
Arrow Electronics
Ingram Micro
Tech Data


## ASPLUNDH TREE EXPERT CO.

| | | |
|---|---|---|
| 708 Blair Mill Rd. | CEO: Scott Asplundh | 2000 Sales: $1,473.0 million |
| Willow Grove, PA 19090 | CFO: Joseph P. Dwyer | 1-Yr. Sales Change: 17.7% |
| Phone: 215-784-4200 | HR: Jean Nichols | Employees: 25,500 |
| Fax: 215-784-4493 | Type: Private | FYE: December 31 |
| Web: www.asplundh.com | | |

How much wood would a woodchuck chuck, if a woodchuck would chuck wood? A lot, if the woodchuck were named Asplundh. The company is the world's largest tree-trimming business, clearing tree limbs from power lines for utilities and municipalities in Australia, Canada, New Zealand, and the US. The company also offers utility-related services such as meter reading, pipeline maintenance, storm emergency services, street light maintenance and construction, underground pipeline location, and utility pole maintenance. The Asplundh family owns and manages the company, which was founded in 1928.

**KEY COMPETITORS**
Davey Tree
Monroe and Lewis Tree Service
Wright Tree Service


## ASSOCIATED FOOD STORES, INC.

| | | |
|---|---|---|
| 1850 W. 2100 South | CEO: Richard A. Parkinson | 2001 Sales: $1,200.0 million |
| Salt Lake City, UT 84119 | CFO: S. Neal Berube | 1-Yr. Sales Change: 26.1% |
| Phone: 801-973-4400 | HR: Fred Ferguson | Employees: 1,400 |
| Fax: 801-978-8551 | Type: Cooperative | FYE: March 31 |
| Web: www.afstores.com | | |

Associated Food Stores, a regional cooperative wholesale distributor, goes to extremes — mountain cold and desert heat — in supplying about 600 independent supermarkets. Member stores (who own the cooperative) are spread throughout Arizona, Colorado, Idaho, Montana, Nevada, Oregon, Utah, and Wyoming. The co-op owns about 25% of Western Family, a grocery wholesalers' partnership that produces Western Family private-label merchandise. It acquired three of its four largest customers (Macey's, Dan's, and Lin) in 1999 to avoid losing them to acquisition-hungry supermarket chains. The co-op was formed in 1940 by Donald Lloyd, president of the Utah Retail Grocers Association, and 34 other retailers.

**KEY COMPETITORS**
Fleming Companies
SUPERVALU
Unified Western Grocers

## ASSOCIATED GROCERS, INC.

3301 S. Norfolk
Seattle, WA 98118
Phone: 206-762-2100
Fax: 206-764-7731
Web: www.agseattle.com

CEO: Robert E. Hoyt
CFO: Jeffrey R. Kessler
HR: Harold "Buzz" Ravenscraft
Type: Private

2000 Sales: $1,100.0 million
1-Yr. Sales Change: 0.0%
Employees: 1,500
FYE: September 30

Associated Grocers (AG) feeds the ability of its member/owners to remain competitive. The cooperative distributes food and nonfood goods and provides support services to about 400 independent grocery retailers in Alaska, Hawaii, Oregon, and Washington as well as Guam and the Pacific Rim. It distributes more than 12,000 items, including products under the Western Family, Ovenworks, and Javaworks names. AG (not to be confused with Associated Grocers in other regions) was formed in 1934 to support 11 Seattle-based neighborhood grocers. The co-op's AG/Fleming Northwest joint venture with Fleming Cos. provides food marketing and distribution to about 75 Washington and Oregon supermarkets.

**KEY COMPETITORS**
Kroger
Unified Western Grocers

## ASSOCIATED MILK PRODUCERS INCORPORATED

315 N. Broadway
New Ulm, MN 56073
Phone: 507-354-8295
Fax: 507-359-8651
Web: www.ampi.com

CEO: Mark Furth
CFO: Steve Sorenson
HR: Leigh Heilman
Type: Cooperative

2000 Sales: $1,000.0 million
1-Yr. Sales Change: (9.1%)
Employees: 1,600
FYE: December 31

Associated Milk Producers Incorporated's dairy business is solid. Shying away from the liquid stuff, it transforms milk into more than five billion pounds of butter, cheese, and other solid milk products each year. A regional cooperative of 4,800 dairy farms from Iowa, Minnesota, Missouri, Nebraska, North and South Dakota, and Wisconsin, AMPI operates 14 manufacturing plants. The co-op produces 60% of all the instant milk sold in the US and is a large cheddar producer. Aside from its own State brand of cheese and butter, AMPI primarily makes private-label products and is seeking stability in value-added products such as shelf-stable cheese sauces.

**KEY COMPETITORS**
Dairy Farmers of America
Foremost Farms
Land O'Lakes

 See pages 58–59 for a full profile of this company.

## THE ASSOCIATED PRESS

50 Rockefeller Plaza
New York, NY 10020
Phone: 212-621-1500
Fax: 212-621-5447
Web: www.ap.org

CEO: Louis D. Boccardi
CFO: Patrick T. O'Brien
HR: James M. Donna
Type: Cooperative

2000 Sales: $574.0 million
1-Yr. Sales Change: 0.3%
Employees: 3,700
FYE: December 31

For more than 150 years, The Associated Press (AP) has been associated with news reports from around the globe. AP is the world's largest newsgathering organization, with about 240 news bureaus serving more than 120 countries. It provides news, photos, graphics, and audiovisual services that reach more than 1 billion people daily through print, radio, and television. In addition to its traditional news services, the not-for-profit cooperative, which is owned by its 1,550 member newspapers, runs an international television division (APTN), a digital ad delivery service (AP AdSEND), an ad processing and billing service, photo archives, and a continuous online news service (The WIRE).

**KEY COMPETITORS**
Dow Jones
Reuters
UPI

See pages 60–61 for a full profile of this company.

## ASSOCIATED WHOLESALE GROCERS, INC.

5000 Kansas Ave.
Kansas City, KS 66106
Phone: 913-288-1000
Fax: 913-288-1508
Web: www.awginc.com

CEO: Gary Phillips
CFO: Robert C. Walker
HR: Frank Tricamo
Type: Cooperative

2000 Sales: $3,200.0 million
1-Yr. Sales Change: (5.0%)
Employees: 3,300
FYE: December 31

Associated Wholesale Grocers (AWG) knows its customers can't live by bread and milk alone. The AWG cooperative supports 850 memberstores with wholesale grocery sales, advertising and market support, store decorating and design, and selecting appropriate technology. The co-op's territory covers primarily Arkansas, Kansas, Missouri, and Oklahoma, but also six other midwestern and southern states. The co-op offers its members the use of such banners as Country Mart, Thriftway, Price Chopper, and Sun Fresh. AWG also operates more than 30 of its own Falley's and Food 4 Less stores in Kansas and Missouri, and it distributes brand-name and private-label goods through four distribution centers in the Midwest.

**KEY COMPETITORS**
Fleming Companies
IGA
Nash Finch

 **See pages 62–63 for a full profile of this company.**

## ASSOCIATED WHOLESALERS, INC.

Route 422
Robesonia, PA 19551
Phone: 610-693-3161
Fax: 610-693-3171
Web: www.awiweb.com

CEO: J. Christopher Michael
CFO: Thomas C. Teeter
HR: Audrey Hausmann
Type: Cooperative

2001 Sales: $923.0 million
1-Yr. Sales Change: 5.0%
Employees: 1,500
FYE: July 31

Being associated with Associated Wholesalers, Inc. (AWI) means having a supplier of food and nonfood items. The retailer-owned cooperative supplies health and beauty care items, meat, dairy products, produce, bakery products, and canned goods to independent grocers. AWI primarily serves the eastern US, from Maine to West Virginia. In addition to merchandise, the co-op also provides training and technical services to members, and it operates a handful of its own Shurfine Markets. AWI operates two distribution centers in Pennsylvania — one in Robesonia that supplies food and one in York that handles general merchandise.

**KEY COMPETITORS**
Di Giorgio
Fleming Companies
SUPERVALU

## AUSTIN INDUSTRIES INC.

3535 Travis St., Ste. 300
Dallas, TX 75229
Phone: 214-443-5500
Fax: 214-443-5581
Web: www.austin-ind.com

CEO: William T. Solomon
CFO: Paul W. Hill
HR: Linda Bayless
Type: Private

2000 Sales: $1,216.6 million
1-Yr. Sales Change: 45.6%
Employees: 6,000
FYE: December 31

Paving the way for progress, Austin Industries provides civil, commercial, and industrial construction services. Its oldest subsidiary, Austin Bridge & Road, provides road, bridge, and parking lot construction across Texas. Subsidiary Austin Commercial, known for its high-rises, builds corporate headquarters, technology sites, and hospitals throughout the central and southwestern US. Austin Commercial is tackling its first major sports arena, American Airlines Center, in Dallas. Austin Industrial focuses on construction, instrumentation, and electrical services for the chemical, refining, power, and manufacturing industries, mostly in the US South and Southeast. The employee-owned firm was founded in 1918.

**KEY COMPETITORS**
Beck Group
Granite Construction
Turner Industries

## BAIN & COMPANY

2 Copley Place
Boston, MA 02116
Phone: 617-572-2000
Fax: 617-572-2427
Web: www.bain.com

CEO: Orit Gadiesh
CFO: Len Banos
HR: Elizabeth Corcoran
Type: Partnership

2000 Est. Sales: $810.0 mil.
1-Yr. Sales Change: 15.7%
Employees: 2,700
FYE: December 31

"Bainies" are always ready when corporate titans need a little direction. A leader in strategic consulting, Bain & Company (whose consultants are called Bainies) offers services such as business unit, organizational, and corporate strategy; distribution and logistics advice; mergers and acquisitions consulting; and marketing strategy. It works for clients in a variety of industries, including consumer products, financial services, technology, and telecommunications. The firm also offers services for startups through its bainlab unit. Bain has 26 offices in nearly 20 countries. Although founded by the same individuals, Bain & Company and investment firm Bain Capital are separate concerns.

**KEY COMPETITORS**
Booz-Allen
Boston Consulting
McKinsey & Company

See pages 64–65 for a full profile of this company.

## BAKER & MCKENZIE

1 Prudential Plaza, 130 E. Randolph Dr., Ste. 2500
Chicago, IL 60601
Phone: 312-861-8800
Fax: 312-861-2899
Web: www.bakerinfo.com

CEO: Christine Lagarde
CFO: Robert S. Spencer
HR: Wilbert Williams
Type: Partnership

2001 Sales: $1,000.0 million
1-Yr. Sales Change: 6.4%
Employees: 8,000
FYE: June 30

Baker & McKenzie knows that size has its advantages (and disadvantages). Baker is the world's second-largest law firm — behind the UK's Clifford Chance — with more than 3,000 lawyers and another 1,000 fee earners serving in more than 60 offices across some 35 countries. It offers expertise in such areas as international trade and tax. Although Baker's size helps attract attorneys as well as clients, the firm also has had to fight the image that it is focused more on franchising (some refer to it as McFirm) than quality legal work. Russell Baker and John McKenzie founded the firm in 1949 with a focus on building an international practice; in 1999 Baker became one of the first major practices to appoint a woman as its top partner.

**KEY COMPETITORS**
Clifford Chance
Jones, Day
Sidley Austin Brown & Wood

See pages 66–67 for a full profile of this company.

## BAKER & TAYLOR CORPORATION

2709 Water Ridge Pkwy.
Charlotte, NC 28217
Phone: 704-357-3500
Fax: 704-329-8989
Web: www.btol.com

CEO: Gary M. Rautenstrauch
CFO: Edward H. Gross
HR: Claudette Hampton
Type: Private

2001 Sales: $1,000.0 million
1-Yr. Sales Change: (11.5%)
Employees: 2,500
FYE: June 30

If you've strolled through a library recently, you probably saw a lot of books from Baker & Taylor (B&T). The #1 book supplier to libraries, B&T has three operating units. Its institutional segment distributes books, tapes, calendars, CDs, DVDs, and videos to some 8,000 schools and libraries around the world. It retail unit supplies storefront and Internet retailers, including Amazon.com, and independent booksellers with nearly 4 million book titles and more than 135,000 video, DVD, and CD titles. Informata.com is B&T's business-to-business e-commerce arm. Investment firm The Carlyle Group and its affiliates own nearly 85% of B&T. Management, employees, and other private investors own the rest.

**KEY COMPETITORS**
Ingram Entertainment
Ingram Industries
Valley Media

See pages 68–69 for a full profile of this company.

## BANNER HEALTH SYSTEM

| | | |
|---|---|---|
| 4310 17th Ave. SW | CEO: Peter S. Fine | 2000 Sales: $1,734.6 million |
| Fargo, ND 58103 | CFO: Ron Bunnell | 1-Yr. Sales Change: 11.1% |
| Phone: 701-277-7500 | HR: Gerri Toomey | Employees: 24,500 |
| Fax: 701-277-7636 | Type: Not-for-profit | FYE: December 31 |
| Web: www.bannerhealth.com | | |

Formed from the merger of Lutheran Health Systems and Samaritan Health System, Banner Health System is one of the largest non-church-affiliated, not-for-profit health systems in the country. The organization operates hospitals and nursing homes in 14 western states. Its Banner Health Arizona division focuses on home care, heart care, cancer care, women's health, and outpatient services, along with behavioral health and rehabilitation. The Banner Health Colorado division consists of a network of community hospitals; it also supplies home medical equipment in Colorado.

**KEY COMPETITORS**
Catholic Healthcare West
HCA
Triad Hospitals

## BARNES & NOBLE COLLEGE BOOKSTORES, INC.

| | | |
|---|---|---|
| 33 E. 17th St. | CEO: Max J. Roberts | 2001 Sales: $1,200.0 million |
| New York, NY 10003 | CFO: Barry Brover | 1-Yr. Sales Change: 30.4% |
| Phone: 212-539-2000 | HR: Gail Gittleson | Employees: 9,000 |
| Fax: 212-780-1866 | Type: Private | FYE: April 30 |
| Web: www.bkstore.com | | |

Barnes & Noble College Bookstores is the scholastic sister company of Barnes & Noble (B&N), the US's largest bookseller. Started in 1873, the company operates more than 400 campus bookstores nationwide, selling textbooks, trade books, school supplies, collegiate clothing, and emblematic merchandise. Universities, medical and law schools, and community colleges hire Barnes & Noble College Bookstores to replace traditional campus cooperatives. (The schools get a cut of the sales.) The company also runs online retailer textbooks.com. B&N's chairman and CEO Leonard Riggio owns a controlling interest in Barnes & Noble College Bookstores.

**KEY COMPETITORS**
Follett
Nebraska Book
Wallace's Bookstores

## BARTLETT AND COMPANY

| | | |
|---|---|---|
| 4800 Main St., Ste. 600 | CEO: James B. Heberstreit | 2000 Est. Sales: $810.0 mil. |
| Kansas City, MO 64112 | CFO: Arnie Wheeler | 1-Yr. Sales Change: 14.9% |
| Phone: 816-753-6300 | HR: Bill Webster | Employees: 575 |
| Fax: 816-753-0062 | Type: Private | FYE: December 31 |

When the cows come home, Bartlett and Company will be ready. The company's primary business is grain merchandising, but it also runs cattle feedlots and mills flour. Bartlett operates grain storage facilities in Kansas City, Kansas; St. Joseph and Waverly, Missouri; and Nebraska City, Nebraska. It has terminal elevators in Iowa, Kansas, and Missouri, as well as more than 10 country elevators. Bartlett's cattle operations are based in Texas; its flour mills are in Kansas, North Carolina, and South Carolina. The Bartlett and Company Grain Charitable Foundation makes financial gifts to local causes. Founded in 1907 as Bartlett Agri Enterprises, the company is still owned by the founding Bartlett family.

**KEY COMPETITORS**
ADM
Cargill
DeBruce Grain

## BARTON MALOW COMPANY

27777 Franklin Rd., Ste. 800
Southfield, MI 48034
Phone: 248-351-4500
Fax: 248-351-5795
Web: www.bmco.com

CEO: Ben C. Maibach III
CFO: Mark A. Bahr
HR: Judith Willard
Type: Private

2001 Sales: $1,160.0 million
1-Yr. Sales Change: 13.1%
Employees: 1,640
FYE: March 31

Barton Malow scores by building end zones and home plates. The construction management and general contracting firm also ranks highly for its schools, hospitals, offices, and plants. Barton Malow's services range from planning to completion on projects in 38 states and the District of Columbia, including Atlanta's Phillips Arena, Boston's Shriners Hospital, and General Motors' Truck Product Center. Barton Malow Design provides architecture and engineering services, and the company's Barton Malow Rigging unit installs process equipment and machinery. Chairman Ben Maibach Jr. and his family own a majority stake in the firm, which was founded in 1924 by C. O. Barton.

**KEY COMPETITORS**
Gilbane
Hunt Construction
Walbridge Aldinger

## BASHAS' INC.

22402 S. Basha Rd.
Chandler, AZ 85248
Phone: 480-895-9350
Fax: 480-895-1206
Web: www.bashas.com

CEO: Edward N. Basha Jr.
CFO: Darl J. Andersen
HR: Michael Gantt
Type: Private

2000 Est. Sales: $1,200.0 mil.
1-Yr. Sales Change: (0.8%)
Employees: 8,800
FYE: December 31

Bashas' has blossomed in the Arizona desert. Founded in 1932 and owned by the Basha family, the food retailer has grown to about 95 stores, primarily throughout Arizona, but with one store each in California and New Mexico. Its holdings include Bashas' traditional supermarkets, AJ's Fine Foods (gourmet-style supermarkets), and Bashas' Mercado and Food City supermarkets, which cater to Hispanics in southern Arizona. Bashas' also operates a handful of supermarkets (including its New Mexico store) in the Navajo Nation. The company offers online grocery shopping through its Groceries On The Go service.

**KEY COMPETITORS**
Albertson's
Kroger
Safeway

## BASS PRO SHOPS, INC.

2500 E. Kearney
Springfield, MO 65898
Phone: 417-873-5000
Fax: 417-831-2802
Web: www.basspro.com

CEO: John L. Morris
CFO: Toni Miller
HR: Mike Roland
Type: Private

2000 Est. Sales: $990.0 mil.
1-Yr. Sales Change: 4.2%
Employees: 8,200
FYE: December 31

Bass Pro Shops (BPS) knows how to reel in the shoppers. Each of its 14 Outdoor World stores (in 10 states) covers about 280,000 sq. ft. The cavernous outlets sell boats, campers, equipment, and apparel for most outdoor activities and offer features such as archery ranges, giant fish tanks, snack bars, and video arcades. The first Outdoor World store, in Missouri, has been that state's #1 tourist attraction since it opened in 1981. BPS catches shoppers at home with its seasonal and specialty catalogs and through its TV and radio programs. It owns Tracker Marine (boat manufacturing), American Rod & Gun (sporting goods wholesale), and runs a resort in the Ozark Mountains. Founder and CEO John Morris owns BPS.

**KEY COMPETITORS**
Academy
MarineMax
Wal-Mart

## BATTELLE MEMORIAL INSTITUTE

505 King Ave.
Columbus, OH 43201
Phone: 614-424-6424
Fax: 614-424-5263
Web: www.battelle.org

CEO: Carl F. Kohrt
CFO: Mark W. Kontos
HR: Bob Lincoln
Type: Not-for-profit

2001 Est. Sales: $1,029.0 mil.
1-Yr. Sales Change: 8.3%
Employees: 7,607
FYE: September 30

When you use a photocopier, hit a golf ball, or listen to a CD, you're using technologies developed by Battelle Memorial Institute. This nonprofit trust, founded in Gordon Battelle's 1923 will, operates one of the world's largest research enterprises. Originally formed to promote metallurgy and related industries, the institute has diversified into research and development for agriculture, automobiles, chemicals, energy, software, and medicine. It works with corporations and governments in about 30 countries. Primarily a contract research provider, the institute continues to explore next-generation technologies including advanced medical products, alternative fuels, and recycling processes.

**KEY COMPETITORS**
MITRE
SAIC
SRI International

 See pages 70–71 for a full profile of this company.


## BAYLOR HEALTH CARE SYSTEM

3500 Gaston Ave.
Dallas, TX 75246
Phone: 214-820-0111
Fax: 214-820-7499
Web: www.baylordallas.edu

CEO: Joel T. Allison
CFO: John L. Hess
HR: Venita McCellon-Allen
Type: Not-for-profit

2000 Sales: $875.0 million
1-Yr. Sales Change: (4.0%)
Employees: —
FYE: June 30

The Baylor Health Care System (BHCS) offers a bundle of services. Founded in 1981, it was governed by Baylor University until establishing autonomy in 1997. The not-for-profit medical network, which serves seven counties in the Dallas-Ft. Worth metroplex, includes the Baylor University Medical Center complex, one of the state's major teaching and referral facilities. Other system members include rehabilitation facilities, primary care centers, senior health centers, family health centers, community hospitals, and medical centers. The system also provides home health care and specialty pediatric services.

**KEY COMPETITORS**
CHRISTUS Health
HCA
Texas Health Resources


## BCOM3 GROUP, INC.

35 W. Wacker Dr.
Chicago, IL 60601
Phone: 312-220-1000
Fax: 312-220-3299
Web: www.bcom3group.com

CEO: Roger A. Haupt
CFO: —
HR: Beth Reeves
Type: Private

2000 Sales: $1,833.7 million
1-Yr. Sales Change: (5.1%)
Employees: 17,000
FYE: December 31

Three's not a crowd for advertising conglomerate Bcom3. Formerly BDM, the company was formed from the 2000 merger of The Leo Group and The MacManus Group. The combined unit, which brings such agencies as Leo Burnett, D'Arcy, and N.W. Ayer under one roof, is now among the world's top ad firms. In addition to advertising, Bcom3 provides a variety of business services, including marketing, media buying, and public relations through units such as Manning, Selvage & Lee and Starcom MediaVest. It operates through more than 520 companies in nearly 90 countries. Bcom3's clients include Kellogg's and Procter & Gamble. Top executives control almost 80% of the company; top Japanese ad conglomerate Dentsu has a 20% stake.

**KEY COMPETITORS**
Interpublic Group
Omnicom
WPP Group

See pages 72–73 for a full profile of this company.

## BE&K INC.

2000 International Park Dr.
Birmingham, AL 35243
Phone: 205-972-6000
Fax: 205-972-6651
Web: www.bek.com

CEO: T. Michael Goodrich
CFO: Clyde M. Smith
HR: Kimberly S. Patterson
Type: Private

2001 Sales: $1,776.0 million
1-Yr. Sales Change: 29.6%
Employees: 10,799
FYE: March 31

Like a busy bee building hives for the queen, BE&K keeps up its reputation as a top US engineering and construction contractor. The company provides design, build, and maintenance services for industrial process facilities, including the cement, chemical, petrochemical, pharmaceutical, and pulp and paper industries. BE&K also serves the telecommunications, manufacturing, environmental, energy, and commercial sectors. The company was founded in 1972 by partners Peter Bolvig, William Edmonds, and Chairman Ted Kennedy (who retain ownership). Overseas operations began in Poland in 1984 through a strategic relationship with International Paper; BE&K now operates on five continents.

**KEY COMPETITORS**
CH2M Hill
Parsons
URS

## BEAULIEU OF AMERICA, LLC

1502 Coronet Dr.
Dalton, GA 30720
Phone: 706-695-4624
Fax: 706-695-6237
Web: www.beaulieu-usa.com

CEO: Carl M. Bouckaert
CFO: Jim WIlliams
HR: Angela Davis
Type: Private

2000 Est. Sales: $1,800.0 mil.
1-Yr. Sales Change: 5.9%
Employees: 11,000
FYE: December 31

Beaulieu Of America (BOA) knows beautiful places from wall to wall. The company is the largest privately held carpet company in the world and the third largest overall, after Shaw and Mohawk. Its products include area rugs, berber carpet, artificial turf, mats, and wall coverings. A vertically integrated company, BOA produces polypropylene fibers for its own carpets as well as for other carpet companies. In 1998 BOA pled guilty to making illegal contributions to a GOP presidential candidate in 1995. BOA was fined and its officers performed 500 hours of community service. Chairman and CEO Carl Bouckaert and his wife, Mieke, whose family made carpets in Europe, founded Beaulieu in 1978; the Bouckaerts control BOA.

**KEY COMPETITORS**
Interface
Mohawk Industries
Shaw Industries

## BECHTEL GROUP, INC.

50 Beale St.
San Francisco, CA 94105
Phone: 415-768-1234
Fax: 415-768-9038
Web: www.bechtel.com

CEO: Riley P. Bechtel
CFO: Georganne Proctor
HR: Jim Illich
Type: Private

2000 Sales: $15,108.0 million
1-Yr. Sales Change: 19.9%
Employees: 40,000
FYE: December 31

If only the pharaohs could have hired the Bechtel Group. Bechtel, which has made a name for itself on projects as big as the Pyramids, designs and builds facilities for industries ranging from aerospace to waste management. The engineering, construction, and project management firm operates in 66 countries, completing more than 1,000 projects a year. Notable projects include the construction of the Hoover Dam and cleanup of the Chernobyl nuclear plant. Subsidiary Bechtel Enterprises invests in infrastructure projects and arranges financing for its clients. Chairman and CEO Riley Bechtel is the fourth generation of Bechtels to head the company. The billionaire Bechtel family owns a controlling stake in the firm.

**KEY COMPETITORS**
Fluor
Foster Wheeler
Skanska

See pages 74–75 for a full profile of this company.

## THE BECK GROUP

| | | |
|---|---|---|
| 1700 Pacific Ave., Ste. 3800 | CEO: Lawrence A. Wilson | 2000 Sales: $990.0 million |
| Dallas, TX 75201 | CFO: Patricia Priest | 1-Yr. Sales Change: 69.5% |
| Phone: 214-965-1100 | HR: Jerry Cooper | Employees: 710 |
| Fax: 214-965-1300 | Type: Private | FYE: December 31 |
| Web: www.beckgroup.com | | |

At the beck and call of commercial developers, The Beck Group has built everything from racetracks to runways, hotels, and hospitals. The firm provides design/build, general contracting, and construction management services in the US and Mexico. It offers facility development, construction financing, and such construction services as scheduling, contract administration, and procurement support. The Beck Group also provides real estate development services. Its projects include Dallas' Cotton Bowl, the Texas Motor Speedway outside Fort Worth, the Museum of Contemporary Art in Los Angeles, and California's Beverly Hills Hotel. Members of the Beck family own the company, which was founded in 1912 by Henry Beck.

**KEY COMPETITORS**
Austin Industries
Bechtel
Turner Corporation


## BELK, INC.

| | | |
|---|---|---|
| 2801 W. Tyvola Rd. | CEO: John M. Belk | 2001 Sales: $2,269.7 million |
| Charlotte, NC 28217 | CFO: John R. Belk | 1-Yr. Sales Change: 5.8% |
| Phone: 704-357-1000 | HR: Carolyn McGinnis | Employees: 21,000 |
| Fax: 704-357-1876 | Type: Private | FYE: January 31 |
| Web: www.belk.com | | |

Department store operator Belk has shed a lot of bulk. Now a relatively svelte 207-store retailer operating in 13 states, the chain was a confederation of 112 separate companies before its 1998 reorganization. Belk stores, located in the Southeast and Mid-Atlantic (primarily in the Carolinas and Georgia), offer mid-priced brand-name and private-label apparel, shoes, cosmetics, and home furnishings. Its stores usually anchor malls or shopping centers in small to medium-sized markets. The Belk family runs the show and owns most of the company, which is the biggest privately held department store chain in the US. Belk grew from a single store (called New York Racket) opened in Monroe, North Carolina, in 1888.

**KEY COMPETITORS**
Dillard's
Federated
Saks Inc.

 See pages 76–77 for a full profile of this company.


## BEN E. KEITH COMPANY

| | | |
|---|---|---|
| 601 E. 7th St. | CEO: Robert Hallam | 2001 Sales: $1,068.0 million |
| Fort Worth, TX 76102 | CFO: Mel Cockrell | 1-Yr. Sales Change: 11.4% |
| Phone: 817-877-5700 | HR: Sam Reeves | Employees: 2,347 |
| Fax: 817-338-1701 | Type: Private | FYE: June 30 |
| Web: www.benekeith.com/main.html | | |

Ben E. Keith is your bud if you like eating out and drinking Bud. The company delivers a full line of foods (produce, dry groceries, frozen food, meat), paper goods, equipment, and supplies to more than 12,000 customers in Arkansas, Kansas, Louisiana, New Mexico, Oklahoma, and Texas. It is one of the world's largest Anheuser-Busch distributors, delivering beer in 49 Texas counties. Ben E. Keith's customers include restaurants, hospitals, schools, and other institutional businesses. Founded in 1906 as Harkrider-Morrison, the company assumed its current name in 1931 in honor of Ben E. Keith, who served as the company's president until 1959. Its owners include Robert and Howard Hallam.

**KEY COMPETITORS**
Alliant Exchange
SYSCO
U.S. Foodservice

## BERWIND GROUP

3000 Centre Square West, 1500 Market St.
Philadelphia, PA 19102
Phone: 215-563-2800
Fax: 215-563-8347
Web: www.berwind.com

CEO: Hellene Runtagh
CFO: James Cook
HR: Catherine Warrin
Type: Private

2000 Est. Sales: $850.0 mil.
1-Yr. Sales Change: (15.0%)
Employees: 4,150
FYE: December 31

Berwind Group's multi-industry operations range from manufacturing to real estate and financial services. Founded in 1874 to mine Appalachian coal, the firm began leasing its mining operations in 1962 to fund investments in new ventures. Berwind's Interlogix subsidiary makes items such as intrusion and fire detection sensors, facility integration control systems, and surveillance equipment. Berwind Property Group owns commercial, retail, and residential real estate nationwide, and Berwind Financial Group provides investment banking services. Berwind Natural Resources and Berwind Pharmaceutical Services round out the group's operations. The Berwind family owns the company.

**KEY COMPETITORS**
DuPont
FMC
W.W. Grainger


## BIG V SUPERMARKETS, INC.

176 N. Main St.
Florida, NY 10921
Phone: 845-651-4411
Fax: 845-651-7048

CEO: James A. Toopes Jr.
CFO: Anthony J. Moccio
HR: Kay Hastings
Type: Private

2000 Sales: $980.0 million
1-Yr. Sales Change: 14.4%
Employees: 5,700
FYE: December 31

Big V Supermarkets is keeping its fingers crossed rather than flashing victory signs as it struggles amid reorganization proceedings. The company runs some 30 grocery stores, mostly in New York's Hudson Valley and in New Jersey. Battered by competition, Big V filed for Chapter 11 bankruptcy protection in late 2000 and said it was ending its distribution agreement with Wakefern Food, the #1 retailer-owned supermarket cooperative. In 2001, however, Big V agreed to sell most of its assets to Wakefern, pending court approval. The company began as a single Victory Supermarket in 1942 and was publicly held until a management-led LBO in 1987. Thomas H. Lee Company bought the Big V chain in 1990.

**KEY COMPETITORS**
A&P
Pathmark
Stop & Shop


## BIG Y FOODS, INC.

2145 Roosevelt Ave.
Springfield, MA 01102
Phone: 413-784-0600
Fax: 413-732-7350
Web: www.bigy.com

CEO: Donald H. D'Amour
CFO: Herb Dotterer
HR: Jack Henry
Type: Private

2001 Sales: $1,150.0 million
1-Yr. Sales Change: 6.2%
Employees: 7,800
FYE: June 30

Why call it Big Y? Big Y Foods began as a 900-sq.-ft. grocery at a Y intersection in Chicopee, Massachusetts. It now operates about 45 supermarkets in Massachusetts and Connecticut. More than half of its stores are Big Y World Class Markets, offering specialty areas such as bakeries and floral shops, as well as banking. The rest consist of Big Y Supermarkets and one Table & Wine store, which sells gourmet food, wine, and liquor. Some Big Y stores provide babysitting, dry cleaning, photo processing, and even propane sales, and their delis and Food Courts offer prepared foods. Big Y is owned and run by the D'Amour family; Paul D'Amour bought the original store in 1936 and was quickly joined by teenage brother Gerald.

**KEY COMPETITORS**
Shaw's
Stop & Shop
SUPERVALU

## BILL & MELINDA GATES FOUNDATION

1551 Eastlake Ave. East
Seattle, WA 98102
Phone: 206-709-3100
Fax: 206-709-3180
Web: www.gatesfoundation.org

CEO: William H. Gates Sr.
CFO: Allan C. Golston
HR: Julie Olson
Type: Foundation

2000 Sales: $303.5 million
1-Yr. Sales Change: 9.8%
Employees: 6
FYE: December 31

You don't have to be one of the richest men in the world to attract attention to your charitable foundation, but it doesn't hurt. Established in 1994, The William H. Gates Foundation was thrust into the spotlight in 1999 after receiving more than $2 billion from Microsoft chairman and foundation namesake Bill Gates. Later that year it combined with affiliate Gates Learning Foundation to form the Bill & Melinda Gates Foundation. Its contributions fund work in the areas of world health (vaccine research) and education; it also supports community service initiatives in the Pacific Northwest. William Gates Sr. runs the foundation, which is the largest in the US, with an endowment of about $21 billion.

 See pages 78–79 for a full profile of this company.


## BILL HEARD ENTERPRISES

200 Brookstone Center Pkwy., Ste. 205
Columbus, GA 31904
Phone: 706-323-1111
Fax: 706-321-9488
Web: www.billheard.com

CEO: William T. Heard
CFO: Ronald A. Feldner
HR: Jim Matthews
Type: Private

2000 Sales: $1,796.0 million
1-Yr. Sales Change: 25.3%
Employees: 3,100
FYE: December 31

The South is alive with the sound of Chevys — music to the ears of Bill Heard Enterprises. The largest Chevrolet dealer in the world (according to Chevrolet Motor Division), Bill Heard has about 15 dealerships in Alabama, Arizona, Florida, Georgia, Tennessee, and Texas. The dealer sells both new and used vehicles and auto supplies and offers repair services; it also owns Oldsmobile and Cadillac franchises in Atlanta and Columbus, Georgia. William Heard Sr. opened his first dealership in 1919. He switched to selling Chevrolets exclusively in 1932, and his son and grandsons, who now run the family-owned business, continue to focus on Chevy sales.

**KEY COMPETITORS**
AutoNation
CarMax
United Auto Group


## BJC HEALTH SYSTEM

4444 Forest Park Ave.
St. Louis, MO 63108
Phone: 314-286-2000
Fax: 314-286-2060
Web: www.bjc.org

CEO: Steven H. Lipstein
CFO: Edward Stiften
HR: Robert Cannon
Type: Not-for-profit

2000 Sales: $2,100.0 million
1-Yr. Sales Change: 30.6%
Employees: 26,038
FYE: December 31

BJC brings Jews and Christians together for the good of its patients. BJC Health System is the product of the 1993 merger of Barnes-Jewish, Inc., and Christian Health System. The not-for-profit system operates 12 hospitals and about 100 primary care and home health facilities in and around St. Louis — both in Missouri and Illinois. Specialized services include hospice care, rehabilitation services, and occupational health and workers' compensation. BJC also offers a dental plan with HMO, PPO, and fee-for-service options. BJC Health System is affiliated with Washington University Medical Center.

**KEY COMPETITORS**
Ascension
Sisters of Mercy
SSM Health Care

## BLACK & VEATCH

8400 Ward Pkwy.
Kansas City, MO 64114
Phone: 913-458-2000
Fax: 913-458-2934
Web: www.bv.com

CEO: Leonard C. Rodman
CFO: Karen L. Daniel
HR: Jim Farr
Type: Private

2000 Sales: $2,358.0 million
1-Yr. Sales Change: (0.7%)
Employees: 8,500
FYE: December 31

From Argentina to Zimbabwe, Black & Veatch provides the ABCs of construction and engineering. The firm engages in all phases of building projects, including design and engineering, financing and procurement, and construction. Since 1915 Black & Veatch has handled jobs ranging from the elegant (reconstructing a Renaissance building in the Czech Republic) to the industrial (building a coal-fired power plant in Guatemala). Having more than 90 offices worldwide, Black & Veatch targets the infrastructure, process, and power markets. Other markets include high-tech, information technology, management consulting, telecommunications, and water/wastewater. The employee-owned firm is one of the US's largest private companies.

**KEY COMPETITORS**
AMEC
Foster Wheeler
MWH Global

## BLOOMBERG L.P.

499 Park Ave.
New York, NY 10022
Phone: 212-318-2000
Fax: 212-893-5999
Web: www.bloomberg.com

CEO: Lex Fenwick
CFO: —
HR: Linda Norris
Type: Private

2000 Est. Sales: $2,800.0 mil.
1-Yr. Sales Change: 21.7%
Employees: 7,200
FYE: December 31

What do you do when you've conquered Wall Street? You become mayor of the city the famous financial district calls home. Founder Michael Bloomberg left his corporate empire in 2001 after winning the top spot in the nation's largest city. Bloomberg's mainstay is its eponymous proprietary terminals, which provide real-time, around-the-clock financial news, market data, and analysis. With more than 156,000 terminals installed, Bloomberg, along with rival Reuters, ranks among the world's largest providers of such devices. The company also has a syndicated news service; publishes books and magazines; and disseminates business information via TV, radio, and the Web. Michael Bloomberg controls the company; Merrill Lynch owns a 20% stake.

**KEY COMPETITORS**
Dow Jones
Reuters
Thomson Corporation

 See pages 80–81 for a full profile of this company.

## BLUE CROSS AND BLUE SHIELD ASSOCIATION

225 N. Michigan Ave.
Chicago, IL 60601
Phone: 312-297-6000
Fax: 312-297-6609
Web: www.bcbs.com

CEO: Scott P. Serota
CFO: Ralph Rambach
HR: Bill Colbourne
Type: Association

2000 Sales: $126,000.0 million
1-Yr. Sales Change: 34.5%
Employees: 150,000
FYE: December 31

The Blue Cross and Blue Shield Association coordinates about 45 chapters that provide health insurance to at least 80 million Americans through HMOs, preferred provider organizations, point-of-service plans, and fee-for-service plans. The chapters also administer Medicare plans for the federal government. To compete with managed care companies that can reject poor insurance risks, Blues are merging within the national alliance, creating for-profit units, forming joint ventures with for-profit providers, or dropping their not-for-profit status and going public. Accordingly, the national association is increasingly acting as a brand manager and marketing organization for licensees.

**KEY COMPETITORS**
Aetna
Health Net
Kaiser Foundation

 See pages 82–83 for a full profile of this company.

## BLUE CROSS AND BLUE SHIELD OF MASSACHUSETTS, INC.

LandMark Center
Boston, MA 02215
Phone: 617-246-5000
Fax: 617-246-4347
Web: www.bcbsma.com

CEO: William C. Van Faasen
CFO: Allen P. Maltz
HR: Robert Martin
Type: Not-for-profit

2000 Sales: $2,700.0 million
1-Yr. Sales Change: 27.4%
Employees: 2,601
FYE: December 31

Hobbled by its past, Blue Cross and Blue Shield of Massachusetts is working its way back into the race. Serving more than 1.8 million members, it offers indemnity insurance, HMOs, preferred provider organizations, and Medicare extension programs. The not-for-profit organization runs HMO Blue, HMO Blue New England, and Blue Choice New England, as well as Access Blue, in which HMO members may see specialists without referrals. Things are turning around for Blue Cross and Blue Shield of Massachusetts: To refocus on health insurance, it sold 10 health centers and plans to sell its dental insurance. It is also entering the risky business of reinsurance.

**KEY COMPETITORS**
Anthem
Harvard Pilgrim
Tufts Health Plan

 See pages 84–85 for a full profile of this company.


## BLUE CROSS BLUE SHIELD OF MICHIGAN

600 E. Lafayette Blvd.
Detroit, MI 48226
Phone: 313-225-8000
Fax: 313-225-5629
Web: www.bcbsm.com

CEO: Richard E. Whitmer
CFO: Mark R. Bartlett
HR: George F. Francis III
Type: Not-for-profit

2000 Sales: $10,507.0 million
1-Yr. Sales Change: 12.5%
Employees: —
FYE: December 31

Blue Cross Blue Shield of Michigan is one of the nation's top Blue Cross Blue Shield health insurance associations, serving more than 4.7 million members, including autoworkers for GM and Ford. The company's insurance plans include traditional indemnity, Blue Preferred (PPO), and Blue Care Network (HMO). Blue Cross Blue Shield of Michigan also offers dental, vision, and Medicare supplement coverage, as well as workers' compensation insurance, health assessment, and health care management services. For-profit subsidiary Preferred Provider Organization of Michigan offers private health care management services.

**KEY COMPETITORS**
Henry Ford Health System
United American Healthcare
UnitedHealth Group

 See pages 86–87 for a full profile of this company.


## BON SECOURS HEALTH SYSTEM, INC.

1505 Marriottsville Rd.
Marriottsville, MD 21104
Phone: 410-442-5511
Fax: 410-442-1082
Web: www.bshsi.com

CEO: Christopher M. Carney
CFO: Michael W. Cottrell
HR: David D. Jones
Type: Not-for-profit

2000 Est. Sales: $1,700.0 mil.
1-Yr. Sales Change: 54.5%
Employees: 27,000
FYE: August 31

Bon Secours Health System succors the poor and sick. A not-for-profit organization dedicated to providing health care to all, the company was created in 1983 by the Sisters of Bon Secours, an international Roman Catholic order established in 1824 in Paris. Bon Secours Health System is composed of 24 acute-care hospitals, nine long-term-care facilities, and a psychiatric hospital. The system also operates ambulatory sites, nursing care centers, assisted-living facilities, hospices, and home health care services. Acquisitive Bon Secours has operations in nine states, primarily on the East Coast.

**KEY COMPETITORS**
Catholic Health East
Johns Hopkins Medicine
MedStar

## BONNEVILLE POWER ADMINISTRATION

905 NE 11th Ave.
Portland, OR 97232
Phone: 503-230-3000
Fax: 503-230-3816
Web: www.bpa.gov

CEO: Steve Wright
CFO: James H. Curtis
HR: Roy P. Smithey
Type: Government-owned

2000 Sales: $3,041.0 million
1-Yr. Sales Change: 16.1%
Employees: 2,732
FYE: September 30

Bonneville Power Administration (BPA) keeps the lights on in the Pacific Northwest. The US Department of Energy power marketing agency operates a 15,000-mile high-voltage transmission grid that delivers 46% of the electrical power consumed in eight states. The electricity that BPA wholesales is generated primarily by 29 federal hydroelectric plants and one private nuclear facility. BPA has added hydroelectric power from British Columbia, gas-fired peak generators, and wind energy to its power mix since low supplies and high demand brought the region to the brink of brownout in 2000. Founded in 1937, the utility sells primarily to public utilities; most of its big industrial customers, aluminum smelters, have shut down.

**KEY COMPETITORS**

AES
Dynegy
Reliant Energy

## BOOZ-ALLEN & HAMILTON INC.

8283 Greensboro Dr.
McLean, VA 22102
Phone: 703-902-5000
Fax: 703-902-3333
Web: www.bah.com

CEO: Ralph W. Shrader
CFO: Doug Swenson
HR: DeeAnne Aguirre
Type: Private

2001 Sales: $2,000.0 million
1-Yr. Sales Change: 11.1%
Employees: 11,000
FYE: March 31

Booz-Allen & Hamilton has been on a big consulting bender for more than 80 years. Founded in 1914, the management and technology consulting firm has a staff of more than 11,000 across the US and more than 30 other countries. Its commercial unit provides a variety of productivity, management, and strategy consultation services to companies in such industries as communications, energy, engineering, and financial services. The technology business unit works primarily with the defense departments and other areas of the US government, as well as other national governments, providing engineering and technology and managing consulting services.

**KEY COMPETITORS**

Accenture
McKinsey & Company
PricewaterhouseCoopers

 **See pages 88–89 for a full profile of this company.**

## BORDEN, INC.

180 E. Broad St.
Columbus, OH 43215
Phone: 614-225-4000
Fax: —
Web: www.bordenfamily.com

CEO: C. Robert Kidder
CFO: William H. Carter
HR: Nancy A. Reardon
Type: Private

2000 Sales: $1,524.0 million
1-Yr. Sales Change: 12.0%
Employees: 4,000
FYE: December 31

*Barbarians at the Gate* or *The Wheeler Dealers*? First traded for a portion of RJR Nabisco, Borden, Inc., is no longer in the dairy business, having traded Elsie the cow for a barn full of test tubes. Borden's decentralized units include Borden Chemical (formaldehyde, melamine, resins) and Elmer's Products, a leading producer of household and school glues (Elmer's and Krazy Glue). Borden sold its Borden Foods and Wise Foods operations to BW Holdings, an affiliate of Kohlberg Kravis Roberts & Co., Borden's parent company. (BW Holdings has since sold Wise.) However, Borden still manages Borden Foods (pastas, bouillons) as well as housewares maker World Kitchen (Pyrex, Corelle, and Corning; formerly Corning Consumer Products).

**KEY COMPETITORS**

Ashland
Georgia-Pacific Corporation
Kraft Foods

**See pages 90–91 for a full profile of this company.**

## BOSCOV'S DEPARTMENT STORES

| | | |
|---|---|---|
| 4500 Perkiomen Ave. | CEO: Edwin A. Lakin | 2001 Sales: $1,000.0 million |
| Reading, PA 19606 | CFO: Russell C. Diehm | 1-Yr. Sales Change: 4.4% |
| Phone: 610-779-2000 | HR: Ed Elko | Employees: 10,000 |
| Fax: 610-370-3495 | Type: Private | FYE: January 31 |
| Web: www.boscovs.com | | |

Outlet mall capital Reading, Pennsylvania, has conceived more than bargain shopping. It's given us Boscov's Department Stores, which operates about 35 general department stores that anchor malls mainly in Pennsylvania, but also in Delaware, Maryland, New Jersey, and New York. The stores sell men's, women's, and children's apparel, shoes, and accessories, as well as jewelry, cosmetics, housewares, appliances, toys, and sporting goods. Some stores also feature travel agencies, vision centers, hair salons, and restaurants. The firm's charge card services are handled by its Boscov's Receivable Finance subsidiary. Boscov's was founded by Solomon Boscov in 1911 in Reading and is still owned by the Boscov family.

**KEY COMPETITORS**
Federated
J. C. Penney
Sears


## BOSE CORPORATION

| | | |
|---|---|---|
| The Mountain | CEO: Amar G. Bose | 2001 Sales: $1,250.0 million |
| Framingham, MA 01701 | CFO: Daniel A. Grady | 1-Yr. Sales Change: 13.6% |
| Phone: 508-879-7330 | HR: John Ferrie | Employees: 7,000 |
| Fax: 508-766-7543 | Type: Private | FYE: March 31 |
| Web: www.bose.com | | |

Bose doesn't subscribe to the theory that bigger is better. One of the world's leading speaker makers, the company has been concentrating on making its speakers smaller to better blend into home and office decors. Bose makes a variety of audio products, including auto sound systems and speakers, home stereo speakers, music systems, PC sound systems, aviation headsets, and professional loudspeakers. Its critically acclaimed Wave radio (compact in size but not in sound) has been a success despite its $350 price tag. Bose makes its products in North America and Ireland and has 90 stores worldwide. Founder Amar Bose, a MIT professor, is the company's largest shareholder.

**KEY COMPETITORS**
Bang & Olufsen
Harman International
Matsushita

 See pages 92–93 for a full profile of this company.


## THE BOSTON CONSULTING GROUP

| | | |
|---|---|---|
| Exchange Place, 31st Fl. | CEO: Carl Stern | 2000 Sales: $1,100.0 million |
| Boston, MA 02109 | CFO: Hugh Simon | 1-Yr. Sales Change: 16.0% |
| Phone: 617-973-1200 | HR: — | Employees: 4,300 |
| Fax: 617-973-1399 | Type: Private | FYE: December 31 |
| Web: www.bcg.com | | |

Global corporations are willing to give much more than a penny for the thoughts of Boston Consulting Group (BCG). Founded in 1963 by consulting pioneer Bruce Henderson, BCG serves global leaders in such industries as consumer goods, finance, and telecommunications. The firm is noted for its work in developing several of its own innovative ideas such as "time-based competition" (rapid response to change) and "deconstruction" (an end to vertical integration). It also is recognized as a leader in e-commerce consulting, and about 20% of its North American revenue comes from this type of consulting. The employee-owned company has about 2,000 consultants working in about 50 offices worldwide.

**KEY COMPETITORS**
Accenture
Booz-Allen
McKinsey & Company

 See pages 94–95 for a full profile of this company.

## BOSTON UNIVERSITY

| | | |
|---|---|---|
| 147 Bay State Rd. | CEO: Jon Westling | 2000 Sales: $971.5 million |
| Boston, MA 02215 | CFO: Kenneth G. Condon | 1-Yr. Sales Change: (0.4%) |
| Phone: 617-353-2000 | HR: Manuel Monteiro | Employees: 8,500 |
| Fax: 617-353-0088 | Type: School | FYE: June 30 |
| Web: web.bu.edu | | |

You'll probably amount to a lot more than a hill of beans after graduating from Boston University. Founded as a Methodist seminary in 1839, BU has almost 30,000 students at its campus on the banks of the Charles River. The private university has 15 graduate and undergraduate schools and colleges, including schools of education, law, management, medicine, social work, and theology. It also supports a number of research programs, such as the Center for Space Physics, the Einstein Papers Project (which aims to publish 25 volumes of the physicist's writings), and the Center for Human Genetics. Four Nobel laureates — Elie Wiesel, Derek Walcott, Saul Bellow, and Sheldon Glashow — are among more than 3,000 faculty members.

## BOZZUTO'S INC.

| | | |
|---|---|---|
| 275 School House Rd. | CEO: Michael A. Bozzuto | 2001 Sales: $830.0 million |
| Cheshire, CT 06410 | CFO: Robert Wood | 1-Yr. Sales Change: 6.8% |
| Phone: 203-272-3511 | HR: Pat Grossi | Employees: 1,025 |
| Fax: 203-250-2953 | Type: Private | FYE: September 30 |
| Web: www.bozzutos.com | | |

If you shop at an IGA supermarket within 250 miles of Cheshire, Connecticut, then Bozzuto's will keep you grinning. The company distributes food and other items to independent supermarkets belonging to the IGA network. The wholesaler supplies more than 100 stores with food, tobacco products, and household items under national brands as well as the IGA and Bestway labels. It also provides store design, administrative, marketing, and inventory management services. Bozzuto's owns Adams Super Food Stores, a Cheshire-based supermarket chain. Founded in 1945 as John Bozzuto & Sons, Bozzuto's serves stores in New England, New York, and New Jersey.

**KEY COMPETITORS**
C&S Wholesale
Di Giorgio
SUPERVALU

## BRASFIELD & GORRIE, LLC

| | | |
|---|---|---|
| 729 S. 30th St. | CEO: M. Miller Gorrie | 2000 Sales: $849.0 million |
| Birmingham, AL 35233 | CFO: Randall J. Freeman | 1-Yr. Sales Change: 31.4% |
| Phone: 205-328-4000 | HR: Kelly Crane | Employees: 2,000 |
| Fax: 205-251-1304 | Type: Private | FYE: December 31 |
| Web: www.brasfieldgorrie.com | | |

Brasfield & Gorrie makes a big splash in the southeastern US. Among its construction projects are the VisionLand amusement and water park in Alabama and hotels, health care facilities, industrial plants, retail complexes, and water-treatment plants. Commercial and industrial construction together account for two-thirds of its revenues. It provides general contracting, design-build, and construction management services through offices in Alabama, Florida, Georgia, North Carolina, and Tennessee, and it has completed projects in 16 states. Founded in 1922 by Thomas C. Brasfield, the company was sold to owner and CEO Miller Gorrie in 1964.

**KEY COMPETITORS**
Austin Industries
BE&K
Beck Group

## BREED TECHNOLOGIES, INC.

5300 Allen K. Breed Hwy.
Lakeland, FL 33811
Phone: 863-668-6000
Fax: 863-668-6007
Web: www.breedtech.com

CEO: John Riess
CFO: Douglas D. Watts
HR: Brenda Stanley
Type: Private

1998 Sales: $1,385.3 million
1-Yr. Sales Change: 74.3%
Employees: 16,300
FYE: June 30

BREED Technologies is a leading manufacturer of air bags and air bag components. The company also makes steering wheels and seat belts. BREED's line of air bag products includes sensors, inflators, driver-side and steering-wheel air bag combinations, and side-impact air bag systems. The company supplies air bag systems to most of the world's carmakers. BREED was taken private in late 2000 after emerging from bankruptcy protection; earlier, the company pulled out of a merger agreement with Harvard Industries. BREED's bank lenders control the company.

**KEY COMPETITORS**
Autoliv
Robert Bosch
TRW


## BROOKSHIRE GROCERY COMPANY

1600 W. South West Loop 323
Tyler, TX 75701
Phone: 903-534-3000
Fax: 903-534-2206
Web: www.brookshires.com

CEO: Tim Brookshire
CFO: Marvin Massey
HR: Tim Brookshire
Type: Private

2001 Est. Sales: $1,700.0 mil.
1-Yr. Sales Change: 6.3%
Employees: 10,750
FYE: September 30

By selling staples, specialties, and Southern hospitality, Brookshire Grocery Company has grown into a chain of about 135 Brookshire's and Super 1 Food supermarkets in Texas, Arkansas, and Louisiana. The company also owns two distribution centers, a dairy plant, a fleet of nearly 350 trucks, and bakery, ice cream, drink, and ice manufacturing facilities. Brookshire's stores average about 40,000 sq. ft., while its warehouse-style Super 1 Foods stores average 80,000 sq. ft. More than 40 of Brookshire Grocery's stores sell gasoline. Originally part of the Brookshire Brothers grocery chain (dating back to 1921), the company split from it in 1939. The Brookshire family is still among the company's owners.

**KEY COMPETITORS**
Albertson's
Kroger
Wal-Mart


## BROWN AUTOMOTIVE GROUP LTD.

10287 Lee Hwy.
Fairfax, VA 22030
Phone: 703-352-5555
Fax: 703-352-5591
Web: www.brownscar.com

CEO: Charles S. Stringfellow Jr.
CFO: Charles S. Stringfellow Jr.
HR: —
Type: Private

2000 Sales: $2,500.0 million
1-Yr. Sales Change: 4.2%
Employees: 3,000
FYE: December 31

Color them diverse. Brown Automotive Group, the largest auto dealer in the mid-Atlantic region, sells about a dozen makes of automobiles from about 40 dealerships in the Washington, DC, and Baltimore areas, as well as in Charlottesville and Richmond, Virginia. The company's new-car makes include DaimlerChrysler, General Motors, Honda, Jaguar, Mazda, Mercedes, Nissan, Saab, Subaru, Toyota, and Volkswagen. It also sells used cars and operates five collision centers. Although the company was formed by William Schuiling in 1983, it traces its origins to Schuiling's purchase of one of Brown Automotive's Pontiac dealerships in Arlington, Virginia, in the early 1970s. The company also develops real estate in Maryland.

**KEY COMPETITORS**
Jim Koons Automotive
Ourisman Automotive
Rosenthal Automotive

## BUFFETS, INC.

| | | |
|---|---|---|
| 1460 Buffet Way | CEO: Kerry A. Kramp | 2000 Sales: $1,021.0 million |
| Eagan, MN 55121 | CFO: Clark C. Grant | 1-Yr. Sales Change: 9.0% |
| Phone: 651-994-8608 | HR: K. Michael Shrader | Employees: 25,200 |
| Fax: 651-365-2356 | Type: Private | FYE: December 31 |
| Web: www.buffet.com | | |

You don't have to worry about getting seconds at Buffets. The company operates one of the country's largest chains of buffet restaurants, with more than 400 locations in more than 35 states (it also franchises 24 restaurants). Operating mostly under the Old Country Buffet and HomeTown Buffet brands, the company's locations are self-service buffets featuring entrees, sides, and desserts for an all-inclusive price. Buffets' other brands include Original Roadhouse Grill, Granny's Buffet, Country Roadhouse Buffet & Grill, Tahoe Joe's Famous Steakhouse, and Soup 'N Salad Unlimited. In 2000 private equity firm Caxton-Iseman Capital bought Buffets for $643 million.

**KEY COMPETITORS**

Investor's Management
Ryan's Family Steak Houses
Shoney's


## BUILDER MARTS OF AMERICA, INC.

| | | |
|---|---|---|
| 1 Independence Pointe | CEO: Duane Faulkner | 2000 Est. Sales: $1,000.0 mil. |
| Greenville, SC 29615 | CFO: R. Steven Robins | 1-Yr. Sales Change: 19.4% |
| Phone: 864-297-6101 | HR: Kay Gould | Employees: 200 |
| Fax: 864-281-3381 | Type: Private | FYE: December 31 |
| Web: www.buildermarts.com | | |

Business is building at Builder Marts of America (BMA). BMA supplies products and services to about 4,500 building supply retailers nationwide. Its offerings include lumber and other forest products; building materials; hardlines, including paint, power tools, and plumbing; millwork, such as steel doors and wood windows; and other products. In 2000 glassmaker Guardian Industries' Building Products Group, which owns more than 50% of BMA, bought the lumber and building materials division of TruServ and folded it into BMA, making it the US's largest buying group for such products. The same year BMA purchased Cameron Ashley Building Products. Ace Hardware has a minority stake in BMA, which was formed in 1966.

**KEY COMPETITORS**

Home Depot
Lowe's
Lumbermens Merchandising


## BUILDERS FIRSTSOURCE, INC.

| | | |
|---|---|---|
| 2200 Ross Ave., Ste. 4900 West | CEO: Floyd F. Sherman | 2000 Sales: $1,710.0 million |
| Dallas, TX 75201 | CFO: Charles L. Horn | 1-Yr. Sales Change: (10.0%) |
| Phone: 214-880-3500 | HR: — | Employees: 6,800 |
| Fax: 214-880-3599 | Type: Private | FYE: December 31 |
| Web: www.buildersfirstsource.com | | |

Builders FirstSource, like an ambitious weight lifter, is bulking up an already well-built form. It aims to be a leading supplier to professional builders — it sells doors, hardware, windows, lumber, and other building products. It also provides engineering services. Since its founding in 1997 as Stonegate Resources, the company has grown, primarily through acquisitions, to include more than 80 distribution centers and about 60 manufacturing plants in 13 states. It is growing in the eastern and southern areas of the US through acquisitions and internal development. The company was founded by a management team headed by former CEO John Roach and private investment firm Littlejohn & Levy.

**KEY COMPETITORS**

84 Lumber
CertainTeed
U.S. Industries

## BURT AUTOMOTIVE NETWORK

5200 S. Broadway
Englewood, CO 80110
Phone: 800-535-2878
Fax: 303-789-6706
Web: www.burt.com

CEO: Lloyd G. Chavez
CFO: John Held
HR: Todd van Maldeghem
Type: Private

2000 Sales: $1,129.6 million
1-Yr. Sales Change: 12.6%
Employees: 1,200
FYE: December 31

John Elway may have retired, but don't think that Burt Automotive Network has stopped trying to sack him. In Denver, Burt goes head-to-head with the John Elway AutoNation USA dealerships once owned (and still named for) the former Broncos star. Burt operates eight dealerships in Colorado that sell new passenger vehicles from DaimlerChrysler, GM, Toyota, Subaru, Nissan, and Ford. It also sells commercial trucks and used cars and offers parts and repair services. Burt, owned by CEO Lloyd G. Chavez, is one of the largest Hispanic-owned businesses in America. A salesman with Burt since 1950, Chavez became the majority owner in 1982 and bought the rest of the company in 1987.

**KEY COMPETITORS**
AutoNation
MNL, Inc.
Phil Long Dealerships

## CALIFORNIA DAIRIES INC.

11709 E. Artesia Blvd.
Artesia, CA 90701
Phone: 562-865-1291
Fax: 562-860-8633

CEO: Gary Korsmeier
CFO: Joe Heffington
HR: Holly Misenhimer
Type: Cooperative

2000 Sales: $1,900.0 million
1-Yr. Sales Change: 18.8%
Employees: —
FYE: April 30

Herding dairies to give them greater "ag"-gregate strength has made California Dairies one of the largest dairy cooperatives in the US. Formed from the 2000 merger of three California dairy cooperatives (California Milk Producers, Danish Creamery Association, and San Joaquin Valley Dairymen), California Dairies' 700 members account for almost half of its home state's milk production. The co-op's five plants process milk, cheese, and other dairy products, including powdered milk. California Dairies, the nation's second-largest agricultural cooperative after Farmland Industries, also markets the milk its members produce.

**KEY COMPETITORS**
Dairy Farmers of America
Dean Foods
Land O'Lakes

## CALIFORNIA PUBLIC EMPLOYEES' RETIREMENT SYSTEM

Lincoln Plaza, 400 P St.
Sacramento, CA 95814
Phone: 916-326-3000
Fax: 916-558-4001
Web: www.calpers.ca.gov

CEO: James E. Burton
CFO: Vincent P. Brown
HR: Tom Pettey
Type: Government-owned

2000 Sales: $18,845.2 million
1-Yr. Sales Change: (9.8%)
Employees: 1,594
FYE: June 30

You don't need calipers to measure CalPERS, the California Public Employees' Retirement System. It's one of the largest public pension systems in the US, with more than $140 billion in assets. Serving nearly 2,500 government agencies, CalPERS manages retirement and health plans for more than a million California employees and retirees and their dependants. An active investor, CalPERS has become a voice to reckon with in the world of corporate governance, focusing on company performance, executive compensation and, occasionally, social issues. CalPERS is a recognized trendsetter in negotiating for such services as insurance; rates established by CalPERS often serve as benchmarks for other employers.

**KEY COMPETITORS**
AXA Financial
FMR
TIAA-CREF

 See pages 96–97 for a full profile of this company.

## CALIFORNIA STATE LOTTERY COMMISSION

| | | |
|---|---|---|
| 600 N. 10th St. | CEO: Joan Wilson | 2000 Sales: $2,598.4 million |
| Sacramento, CA 95814 | CFO: — | 1-Yr. Sales Change: 3.9% |
| Phone: 916-324-9639 | HR: Loretta Stillwell | Employees: 650 |
| Fax: 916-327-0489 | Type: Government-owned | FYE: June 30 |
| Web: www.calottery.com | | |

There's still a gold rush going on in the Golden State, but you won't need a pick or a shovel to get in on the action. The California State Lottery Commission offers a string of scratch-off games (Wild 7's, Double Doubler) and numbers games (Fantasy 5, SuperLotto Plus) for Californians' wagering pleasure. Scratch-off and Fantasy 5 players also can win chances to spin a wheel for prizes on the *Big Spin* TV show. State law requires that at least 34% of lottery proceeds go to public education in California; since its 1985 inception, the lottery has provided more than $13 billion to that cause. Most of those funds are used to attract and retain teachers.

**KEY COMPETITORS**
Multi-State Lottery
Oregon State Lottery
Washington State Lottery

## TRUSTEES OF THE CALIFORNIA STATE UNIVERSITY

| | | |
|---|---|---|
| 401 Golden Shore | CEO: Charles B. Reed | 2001 Sales: $4,050.0 million |
| Long Beach, CA 90802 | CFO: Richard P. West | 1-Yr. Sales Change: 6.5% |
| Phone: 562-951-4000 | HR: Jackie McClain | Employees: 40,000 |
| Fax: — | Type: School | FYE: June 30 |
| Web: www.calstate.edu | | |

California State University (CSU) is neck and neck with the State University of New York (SUNY) as the nation's largest university system. With the baby boomers' children reaching college age and college participation increasing, CSU's student body has grown to around 390,000. The system has campuses in 23 cities, including Bakersfield, Los Angeles, San Francisco, and San Jose. CSU emphasizes teacher training and is responsible for some 60% of the state's educators. To prepare for a student population expected to grow about 40% by 2010, CSU is focusing on distance education (via teleconferencing and the Internet) and experimenting with year-round schooling.

 See pages 98–99 for a full profile of this company.

## CALVIN KLEIN, INC.

| | | |
|---|---|---|
| 205 W. 39th St., 4th Fl. | CEO: Barry Schwartz | 2000 Est. Sales: $170.0 mil. |
| New York, NY 10018 | CFO: Len LaSalandra | 1-Yr. Sales Change: (2.9%) |
| Phone: 212-719-2600 | HR: — | Employees: — |
| Fax: 212-730-4818 | Type: Private | FYE: December 31 |

Spanning the style spectrum — from streetwise to sophisticated — Calvin Klein is known for its simple (but not cheap) clothes, fragrances, and accessories. The company makes its flagship ready-to-wear collection of women's clothing, but gets most of its revenue from licensing its name to makers of jeans, underwear, and fragrances. Altogether, Calvin Klein-licensed products rake in more than $5 billion a year in retail sales. The company also licenses more than 40 retail stores worldwide. Looking to keep a trim bottom line, Calvin Klein has cut jobs and is shutting down its self-manufactured sportswear division in the US. The firm was founded in 1968 by CEO Barry Schwartz and Calvin Klein, who are its sole owners.

**KEY COMPETITORS**
Donna Karan
Polo
Tommy Hilfiger

See pages 100–101 for a full profile of this company.

## C&S WHOLESALE GROCERS, INC.

Old Ferry Rd.
Brattleboro, VT 05301
Phone: 802-257-4371
Fax: 802-257-6727
Web: www.cswg.com

CEO: Richard B. Cohen
CFO: Mark Gross
HR: Charlotte Edwards
Type: Private

2001 Sales: $8,500.0 million
1-Yr. Sales Change: 21.4%
Employees: 7,000
FYE: September 30

C&S Wholesale Grocers is at the bottom of the food chain — and likes it that way. The company is one of the US's largest food wholesalers, delivering groceries to some 4,000 independent supermarkets, major supermarket chains, mass marketers (including Wal-Mart), and wholesale clubs from Maine to Maryland. The company sells more than 53,000 items, including general groceries, produce, and nonfood items. It runs facilities in Connecticut, Maryland, Massachusetts, New Jersey, New York, Pennsylvania, and Vermont. An affiliate of C&S Wholesale bought bankrupt supermarket chain (and a top C&S customer) The Grand Union Company in 2001. Chairman and CEO Richard Cohen owns the company, which his grandfather started in 1918.

**KEY COMPETITORS**
Di Giorgio
Fleming Companies
SUPERVALU

 See pages 102–103 for a full profile of this company.

## CANTOR FITZGERALD, L.P.

Data Center Address: 120 W. Passaic St.
Rochelle Park, NJ 07662
Phone: 201-556-1500
Fax: —
Web: www.cantor.com

CEO: Howard W. Lutnick
CFO: —
HR: —
Type: Private

2000 Est. Sales: $990.0 mil.
1-Yr. Sales Change: —
Employees: 1,100
FYE:

Broker Cantor Fitzgerald specializes in fixed-income securities, institutional equities, derivatives, and foreign stocks. The largest trader of US Treasuries, the firm operates such marketplaces as the Cantor Exchange, a full-time electronic exchange for US Treasury futures. Cantor offers electronic trading of municipal and US government bonds and sovereign debt. It helped pioneer the trading of air pollution credits as a commodity and controls eSpeed, an electronic trading platform it spun off in 1999. Once known as the "broker to the stars" (clients included Zsa Zsa Gabor and Clint Eastwood), the firm was founded in 1945. Still suffering from its losses in the World Trade Center attack, the firm has ceased voice-broking activities.

**KEY COMPETITORS**
CBOT
Instinet
Lehman Brothers

## CARDONE INDUSTRIES INC.

5501 Whitaker Ave.
Philadelphia, PA 19124
Phone: 215-912-3000
Fax: 215-912-3700
Web: www.cardone.com

CEO: Michael Cardone Jr.
CFO: —
HR: —
Type: Private

2000 Sales: $4,900.0 million
1-Yr. Sales Change: —
Employees: 3,500
FYE: December 31

Old car parts get a new lease on life thanks to Cardone Industries. The company is a leading remanufacturer of automotive parts for the aftermarket. Cardone focuses on six basic product lines: brakes (master cylinders, calipers), drivetrain parts (constant-velocity drive axles), electronics (climate and spark controls, fuel-display modules), motors (window-lift and wiper), pumps (water and vacuum), and steering (rack and pinion units, power-steering filters). The company remanufactures its products in Pennsylvania and has warehouse facilities in California, as well as Belgium and Canada. The Cardone family controls the business.

**KEY COMPETITORS**
Champion Parts
Delco Remy
Motorcar Parts

## CAREGROUP, INC.

375 Longwood Ave., 3rd Fl.
Boston, MA 02215
Phone: 617-975-5000
Fax: 617-975-6065
Web: www.caregroup.org

CEO: James L. Reinertsen
CFO: Eugene C. Wallace
HR: William Behrendt
Type: Private

2000 Sales: $1,290.0 million
1-Yr. Sales Change: 1.6%
Employees: 13,000
FYE: September 30

Thanks to CareGroup, there's well-being in Beantown. Formed in the 1997 union of several Boston-area health care organizations, CareGroup serves Massachusetts through its flagship, the Beth Israel Deaconess, and five other hospitals. With more than 1,000 beds, the system provides comprehensive acute care as well as specialty clinics and research facilities. CareGroup is affiliated with Harvard University, the Joslin Diabetes Center, and the Mind/Body Medical Institute. CareGroup's not-for-profit Provider Service Network (an alliance with Lahey Clinic) serves more than 400,000 managed-care patients. CareGroup is selling parts of the Beth Israel Deaconess hospital to pay debt and boost operating capital.

**KEY COMPETITORS**
Baystate Health Systems
HCA
Partners HealthCare

## CARGILL, INCORPORATED

15407 McGinty Rd. West
Wayzata, MN 55391
Phone: 952-742-7575
Fax: 952-742-7393
Web: www.cargill.com

CEO: Warren R. Staley
CFO: Robert L. Lumpkins
HR: Nancy P. Siska
Type: Private

2001 Sales: $49,400.0 million
1-Yr. Sales Change: 3.8%
Employees: 90,000
FYE: May 31

Cargill may be private, but all of its parts are highly visible. The US's largest private corporation, Cargill's diversified operations include grain, cotton, sugar, and petroleum trading; financial trading; food processing; futures brokering; feed and fertilizer production; and steelmaking. The company is the leading grain exporter in the US, and its Excel unit is the #3 meat packer (behind ConAgra and IBP). Cargill's brands include Diamond Crystal (salt), Gerkens (cocoa), Honeysuckle White (poultry), and Sterling Silver (fresh meats). Created with one grain elevator in 1865, the company operates from more than 1,000 locations in over 70 countries. Descendants of the founders own about 85% of Cargill.

**KEY COMPETITORS**
ADM
Bunge Limited
Corn Products International

 See pages 104–105 for a full profile of this company.

## CARILION HEALTH SYSTEM

1212 3rd St.
Roanoke, VA 24016
Phone: 540-981-8080
Fax: 540-344-5716
Web: www.carilion.com

CEO: Edward Murphy
CFO: Donald E. Lorton
HR: Brucie Boggs
Type: Not-for-profit

2000 Sales: $1,079.7 million
1-Yr. Sales Change: 10.6%
Employees: 10,000
FYE: September 30

Carilion Health System rings true for residents of western Virginia. Founded in 1899 as the Roanoke Hospital Association, the system today includes about 10 hospitals, a nursing home, and a cancer center, with a total of about 1,300 beds. Its Medical Center for Children in Roanoke serves as a regional pediatric referral site, and its Carilion Behavioral Health has become one of the most comprehensive psychiatric service networks in its area. Through its 60%-owned, for-profit Carilion Health Plans subsidiary, the system markets its own HMO and point-of-service health care plans. Carilion has also formed a biomedical research institute together with Virginia Tech and the University of Virginia.

**KEY COMPETITORS**
HCA
Mid Atlantic Medical
Sentara Healthcare

## CARLSON COMPANIES, INC.

| | | |
|---|---|---|
| PO Box 59159 | CEO: Marilyn Carlson Nelson | 2000 Sales: $9,800.0 million |
| Minneapolis, MN 55459 | CFO: Martyn R. Redgrave | 1-Yr. Sales Change: 0.0% |
| Phone: 763-212-5000 | HR: Rosalyn Mallet | Employees: 192,000 |
| Fax: 763-212-2219 | Type: Private | FYE: December 31 |
| Web: www.carlson.com | | |

Carlson Companies began in 1938 as the Gold Bond Stamp Company but has evolved into a leisure services juggernaut. The company owns 50% of travel giant Carlson Wagonlit (French hotelier Accor owns the rest). It also owns more than 745 hotels under brands such as Radisson and Country Inns & Suites By Carlson. Carlson's restaurant empire includes the 670-unit T.G.I. Friday's chain. A specialist in relationship marketing, Carlson Marketing Group offers services such as sales promotion and customer loyalty programs. CEO Marilyn Carlson Nelson and director Barbara Carlson Gage, the daughters of late founder Curtis Carlson, each own half of the company.

**KEY COMPETITORS**
American Express
Darden Restaurants
Marriott International

 See pages 106–107 for a full profile of this company.


## CARLSON WAGONLIT TRAVEL

| | | |
|---|---|---|
| 1405 Xenium Ln. | CEO: Hervé Gourio | 2000 Sales: $12,000.0 million |
| Plymouth, MN 55441 | CFO: Tim Hennessy | 1-Yr. Sales Change: 9.1% |
| Phone: 763-212-4000 | HR: Cindy Rodahl | Employees: 20,100 |
| Fax: — | Type: Joint venture | FYE: December 31 |
| Web: www.carlsonwagonlit.com | | |

Carlson Wagonlit Travel did not get its middle name from Indians trying to explain to pioneers that their covered wagons were on fire. The company is descended from both the creator of the Orient Express (Wagons-Lits) and the oldest US travel agency chain (Ask Mr. Foster). It manages business travel from more than 3,000 travel offices worldwide. The company is the #2 travel firm in the world, behind American Express. It is co-owned by the US firm Carlson Companies (whose US leisure and franchise operations also fall under the Carlson Wagonlit brand) and France's Accor Group. Carlson Wagonlit has locations in more than 140 countries.

**KEY COMPETITORS**
American Express
Preussag
WorldTravel

 See pages 108–109 for a full profile of this company.


## THE CARLYLE GROUP

| | | |
|---|---|---|
| 1001 Pennsylvania Ave. NW, Ste. 220 South | CEO: Frank C. Carlucci | Sales: — |
| Washington, DC 20004 | CFO: John F. Harris | 1-Yr. Sales Change: — |
| Phone: 202-347-2626 | HR: Mori Sabet | Employees: — |
| Fax: 202-347-1818 | Type: Private | FYE: December 31 |
| Web: www.thecarlyegroup.com | | |

With former US Defense Secretary Frank Carlucci as its chairman, it's no surprise that The Carlyle Group is drawn to defense. Defense and aerospace firms such as United Defense Industries make up a significant share of the world's largest private equity firm's portfolio. Also represented are information technology, health care, real estate, and bottling companies. Since Carlucci joined in 1989, a host of staffers from the Reagan and first Bush administrations have stinted at the company, including ex-Secretary of State James Baker and ex-budget chief Richard Darman. Former President Bush and former UK Prime Minister John Major have also made appearances.

**KEY COMPETITORS**
Goldman Sachs
Hicks, Muse
KKR

 See pages 110–111 for a full profile of this company.

## CARONDELET HEALTH SYSTEM

13801 Riverport Dr., Ste. 300
St. Louis, MO 63043
Phone: 314-770-0333
Fax: 314-770-0444
Web: www.chs-stl.com

CEO: Andrew W. Allen
CFO: Paul Briggs
HR: Nancy Heet
Type: Not-for-profit

2000 Sales: $995.0 million
1-Yr. Sales Change: (0.5%)
Employees: 16,000
FYE: June 30

Through a network of about 20 facilities, Carondelet Health System carries on its healing mission in eight widely scattered states from New York to California. Besides hospitals, the system operates behavioral treatment centers, hospice centers, and rehabilitation facilities. The not-for-profit is sponsored by the Sisters of St. Joseph Carondelet, a Roman Catholic order founded in 17th century France. Some members of the order emigrated to the US in 1836 and founded a school for the deaf in St. Louis, and their mission spread across the country. Carondelet's efforts to care for underinsured or uninsured patients have caused it financial hardship; the system sold two hospitals to Tenet Healthcare.

**KEY COMPETITORS**
Ascension
Catholic Health Initiatives
Tenet Healthcare

## CARPENTER CO.

5016 Monument Ave.
Richmond, VA 23220
Phone: 804-359-0800
Fax: 804-353-0694
Web: www.carpenter.com

CEO: Stanley F. Pauley
CFO: Dave Morman
HR: Tom Newport
Type: Private

2000 Sales: $1,075.0 million
1-Yr. Sales Change: 10.0%
Employees: 6,200
FYE: December 31

It's a cushy job for Carpenter Co., making polyurethane foam and chemicals and polyester fiber used as cushioning by the automotive, bedding, floor covering, and furniture industries, among others. The company started out making foam rubber; it now manufactures air filter media, expanded polystyrene building materials, and a tire fill product as a replacement for air in off-road construction vehicles. Carpenter has facilities throughout the US, as well as in Canada, Denmark, France, Germany, Spain, Sweden, and the UK. The company also sells consumer products — which include craft fiber products, mattress pads, and pillows — through retailers.

**KEY COMPETITORS**
Acordis
Foamex
Owens Corning

## CARPET CO-OP ASSOCIATION OF AMERICA

1765 The Exchange, Ste. 400
Atlanta, GA 30339
Phone: 770-984-9791
Fax: 770-984-9771
Web: www.carpetone.com

CEO: Howard Brodsky
CFO: Ed Muchnick
HR: Lisa Miles
Type: Cooperative

2000 Sales: $3,140.0 million
1-Yr. Sales Change: 12.1%
Employees: 350
FYE: September 30

You might say Carpet Co-op Association of America's business is "floor"ishing. Its more than 1,400 member-owner stores (most operate under the Carpet One name) sell name-brand carpets and floor coverings such as ceramic tile, laminates, and hardwoods. The co-op also includes Stone Mountain Carpet Mill Outlets (closeout prices), ProSource Wholesale Floorcoverings, and International Design Guild (high-end showrooms in Australia and North America). Carpet One is one of the world's largest floor covering retailers (with stores in the US, Canada, Australia, New Zealand, and Guam) and the exclusive US marketer of Bigelow and Lees carpet brands. Executives Howard Brodsky and Alan Greenberg started the co-op in 1985.

**KEY COMPETITORS**
Abbey Carpet
Home Depot
Lowe's

## CARQUEST CORPORATION

2635 Millbrook Rd.
Raleigh, NC 27604
Phone: 919-573-2500
Fax: 919-573-2501
Web: www.carquest.com

CEO: A.E. Lottes III
CFO: —
HR: Louise Veasman
Type: Private

2000 Est. Sales: $2,000.0 mil.
1-Yr. Sales Change: 0.0%
Employees: 36,000
FYE: December 31

CARQUEST is driven by its mission to get its parts into your car. The replacement auto parts distribution group is owned by its seven member warehouse distributors (the largest is North Carolina-based General Parts). The CARQUEST group includes a network of more than 60 distribution centers serving more than 4,000 retail outlets in the US and Canada. Focusing on professional installers, the company sells its own line of auto parts (made by Moog Automotive, Dana, Gabriel, and others). Auto repair shops can join CARQUEST's Tech-Net Professional Service program, which provides members with a marketing plan and other services, as well as a diagnostic telephone hotline.

**KEY COMPETITORS**
AutoZone
Genuine Parts
Pep Boys

See pages 112–113 for a full profile of this company.


## CATHOLIC HEALTH EAST

14 Campus Blvd., Ste. 300
Newtown Square, PA 19073
Phone: 610-355-2000
Fax: 610-355-2050
Web: www.che.org

CEO: Daniel F. Russell
CFO: C. Kent Russell
HR: George F. Longshore
Type: Not-for-profit

2000 Sales: $4,300.0 million
1-Yr. Sales Change: 0.0%
Employees: 44,000
FYE: December 31

Catholic Health East serves believers and nonbelievers alike as one of the leading religious health care systems in the US, along with Ascension Health and Catholic Health Initiatives. The system offers health care through more than 30 hospitals, about 30 nursing homes, and some 20 independent- and assisted-living facilities, primarily on the East Coast. The network also offers adult day care, home health services, and hospice care. Catholic Health East continues to struggle to preserve its charitable mission in the face of industry consolidation, rising health care costs, and declining membership in religious orders.

**KEY COMPETITORS**
Ascension
Bon Secours Health
Catholic Health Initiatives

See pages 114–115 for a full profile of this company.


## CATHOLIC HEALTH INITIATIVES

1999 Broadway, Ste. 2605
Denver, CO 80202
Phone: 303-298-9100
Fax: 303-298-9690
Web: www.catholichealthinit.org

CEO: Patricia A. Cahill
CFO: Sister Geraldine Hoyler
HR: Michael Fordyce
Type: Not-for-profit

2001 Sales: $5,742.0 million
1-Yr. Sales Change: 3.4%
Employees: 66,000
FYE: June 30

Giant not-for-profit Catholic Health Initiatives is an amalgamation of four Roman Catholic health care systems (Catholic Health Corporation of Omaha, Nebraska; Franciscan Health System of Aston, Pennsylvania; Sisters of Charity Health Care Systems of Cincinnati; and Sisters of Charity of Nazareth Health Care System of Bardstown, Kentucky). A leading Roman Catholic health care system, Catholic Health Initiatives operates more than 60 hospitals and more than 40 long-term care, assisted-living, and residential facilities. The organization is sponsored by 12 different congregations and serves communities in some 20 states.

**KEY COMPETITORS**
Ascension
Beverly Enterprises
HCA

See pages 116–117 for a full profile of this company.

## CATHOLIC HEALTHCARE NETWORK

155 E. 56th St., 2nd Fl.
New York, NY 10022
Phone: 212-752-7300
Fax: 212-752-7547
Web: www.chcn.org

CEO: Mary Healey-Sedutto
CFO: Gerard Vilucci
HR: —
Type: Not-for-profit

1998 Sales: $4,523.3 million
1-Yr. Sales Change: (22.7%)
Employees: —
FYE: December 31

While it may not have the high profile of the late Mother Teresa, New York's Catholic Healthcare Network is nonetheless dedicated to providing health care (rooted in the values of the Catholic Church) to people who need it, regardless of their income or status. The network includes about a dozen hospitals and nursing homes, as well as affiliated health care providers such as rehabilitation facilities and medical centers (including non-Catholic institutions). Catholic Healthcare Network is sponsored by the Archdiocese of New York.

**KEY COMPETITORS**
New York City Health and Hospitals
North Shore-Long Island Jewish Health System
Saint Vincent Catholic Medical Centers


## CATHOLIC HEALTHCARE PARTNERS

615 Elsinore Place
Cincinnati, OH 45202
Phone: 513-639-2800
Fax: 513-639-2700
Web: www.health-partners.org

CEO: Michael D. Connelly
CFO: Rick Annis
HR: Rick Frederick
Type: Not-for-profit

2000 Sales: $2,372.7 million
1-Yr. Sales Change: 19.6%
Employees: 27,941
FYE: December 31

Catholic Healthcare Partners offers health care services, primarily in Ohio but also in Indiana, Kentucky, Pennsylvania, and Tennessee through the more than 100 corporations that make up its system. Facilities include about 30 hospitals, some 30 long-term-care facilities, housing sites for the elderly, and wellness centers. The system also offers physician practices, hospice and home health care, and outreach services. Catholic Healthcare Partners is co-sponsored by the Sisters of Mercy in Cincinnati and in Dallas, Pennsylvania; The Sisters of the Humility of Mary in Villa Maria, Pennsylvania; The Franciscan Sisters of the Poor; and Covenant Health Systems.

**KEY COMPETITORS**
Catholic Health Initiatives
HCA
OhioHealth


## CATHOLIC HEALTHCARE WEST

1700 Montgomery St., Ste. 300
San Francisco, CA 94111
Phone: 415-438-5500
Fax: 415-438-5724
Web: www.chw.edu

CEO: Lloyd H. Dean
CFO: Michael Blaszyk
HR: Ernie Urquhart
Type: Not-for-profit

2000 Sales: $4,800.0 million
1-Yr. Sales Change: 14.3%
Employees: 40,000
FYE: June 30

Catholic Healthcare West has found it takes a lot of *nunsense* to become one of the largest private, nonprofit providers in California. Catholic Healthcare West's system stretches from Redding to San Diego in the Golden State, as well as into Arizona and Nevada. It includes more than 45 acute care hospitals, skilled nursing facilities, and medical centers. Catholic Healthcare West also has an alliance with Scripps, a major San Diego-based health care provider. The organization formed when the hospital operations of several Roman Catholic women's religious orders consolidated, along with some non-Catholic community hospitals.

**KEY COMPETITORS**
HCA
Sutter Health
Tenet Healthcare

📖 See pages 118–119 for a full profile of this company.

## CB RICHARD ELLIS SERVICES, INC.

200 N. Sepulveda Blvd., Ste. 300
El Segundo, CA 90245
Phone: 310-563-8600
Fax: 310-563-8670
Web: www.cbrichardellis.com

CEO: Raymond E. Wirta
CFO: James H. Leonetti
HR: Pam Perry
Type: Private

2000 Sales: $1,323.6 million
1-Yr. Sales Change: 9.1%
Employees: 9,600
FYE: December 31

CB Richard Ellis Services is the largest commercial real estate services company in the US. It provides a complete array of commercial real estate services, including real estate brokerage, commercial mortgage origination and servicing (through its L.J. Melody subsidiary), and facility management services to businesses around the world. The company manages hundreds of millions of square feet of commercial space and has about 250 offices in more than 40 countries in Africa, Asia, Europe, and North and South America. A product of the merger of the commercial portion of Coldwell Banker and the non-UK-based operations of Richard Ellis, the company has been taken private by CEO Ray Wirta and others.

**KEY COMPETITORS**
Cushman & Wakefield
Jones Lang LaSalle
Trammell Crow

 See pages 120–121 for a full profile of this company.


## CENEX HARVEST STATES COOPERATIVES

5500 Cenex Dr.
Inver Grove Heights, MN 55077
Phone: 651-451-5151
Fax: 651-451-5073
Web: www.cenexharveststates.com

CEO: John D. Johnson
CFO: John Schmitz
HR: Dick Baldwin
Type: Cooperative

2000 Sales: $8,571.4 million
1-Yr. Sales Change: 33.2%
Employees: 5,308
FYE: August 31

Cenex Harvest States Cooperatives goes with the grain. The #2 agricultural co-op (behind Farmland Industries), CHS represents some 325,000 farmers, primarily in the Midwest and Northwest. CHS trades grain and sells supplies to members through more than 330 stores. It also processes soybeans for use in salad dressings, margarines, and animal feeds, and it markets petroleum. In addition, CHS grinds wheat into flour used in pastas and bread; subsidiary Sparta Foods makes tortillas. The co-op's joint ventures include Agriliance (with Farmland Industries and Land O'Lakes), which sells crop nutrient and protection products, and United Harvest (with Mitsui), which markets grain.

**KEY COMPETITORS**
ADM
Cargill
ConAgra

See pages 122–123 for a full profile of this company.


## CENTRAL NATIONAL-GOTTESMAN INC.

3 Manhattanville Rd.
Purchase, NY 10577
Phone: 914-696-9000
Fax: 914-696-1066

CEO: Kenneth L. Wallach
CFO: Joshua J. Eisenstein
HR: Louise Caputo
Type: Private

2000 Sales: $1,825.0 million
1-Yr. Sales Change: 9.9%
Employees: 900
FYE: December 31

Got pulp? Central National-Gottesman does. Founded in 1886, the family-owned company distributes pulp, paper, paperboard, and newsprint in about 75 countries worldwide. In addition to its North America operations, the company operates about 25 overseas offices in 22 countries located in Asia, Europe, and Latin America. The Central National-Gottesman network includes the Lindenmeyr family of companies, which specialize in the distribution of fine paper as well as papers for books and magazines. The company's extensive list of suppliers includes paper industry leaders International Paper (#1) and Weyerhaeuser.

**KEY COMPETITORS**
Perry Koplik
Unisource
WWF Paper

## CERULEAN COMPANIES, INC.

3350 Peachtree Rd. NE
Atlanta, GA 30326
Phone: 404-842-8000
Fax: 404-842-8801
Web: www.cerulean-companies.com

CEO: Richard D. Shirk
CFO: Gregg Chandler
HR: Eula Austin
Type: Private

2000 Sales: $2,033.8 million
1-Yr. Sales Change: 22.9%
Employees: 2,900
FYE: December 31

Cerulean Companies has the Blues in Georgia — Blue Cross and Blue Shield. Cerulean, which has been acquired by WellPoint Health Networks, was formed as the holding company for Blue Cross and Blue Shield of Georgia (Georgia Blue) when it became a for-profit company. Through its subsidiaries, Cerulean offers a variety of insurance plans, including HMO, PPO, indemnity, and point-of-service products; this business serves some 1.8 million members. Cerulean also provides supplemental products such as dental and vision coverage, as well as 65PLUS, a Medicare supplement. Subsidiary Greater Georgia Life Insurance writes group life, accident, and disability insurance.

**KEY COMPETITORS**
Aetna
Humana
UnitedHealth Group

## CF INDUSTRIES, INC.

1 Salem Lake Dr.
Long Grove, IL 60047
Phone: 847-438-9500
Fax: 847-438-0211
Web: www.cfindustries.com

CEO: R. C. Liuzzi
CFO: Stephen R. Wilson
HR: Francie Lucente
Type: Cooperative

2000 Sales: $1,100.9 million
1-Yr. Sales Change: 0.6%
Employees: 1,474
FYE: December 31

The grass is always greener at CF Industries. Organized in 1946 as Central Farmers Fertilizer Company, CF Industries is an interregional agricultural cooperative that manufactures and markets fertilizers, including nitrogen products (ammonia, granular urea, and UAN solutions), phosphates, and potash (potassium) products to its members in 45 states and two Canadian provinces. The co-op is owned by nine regional agricultural co-ops, including GROWMARK, Land O'Lakes, and CENEX Harvest States Cooperative. CF Industries operates nitrogen and phosphate plants, a phosphate mine, and a network of distribution terminals and storage facilities by which it offers products worldwide.

**KEY COMPETITORS**
IMC Global
Potash Corporation
Terra Industries

## CFM INTERNATIONAL, INC.

1 Neumann Way
Cincinnati, OH 45215
Phone: 513-563-4180
Fax: 513-552-3306
Web: www.cfm56.com

CEO: Pierre Fabre
CFO: —
HR: —
Type: Joint venture

2000 Sales: $6,700.0 million
1-Yr. Sales Change: —
Employees: —
FYE: December 31

CFM International makes sure that hundreds of aircraft don't have to just wing it. The company, a joint venture of US-based General Electric (GE) and France's Snecma, manufactures aircraft engines for more than 300 commercial and military customers worldwide. The company's name stems from a combination of CF6 and M56, designations for commercial aircraft engines made, respectively, by GE and Snecma. GE makes CFM's engine cores and assembles roughly half of its engines; Snecma manufactures the fans and rotors and assembles the rest of the engines. CFM's engines can be found in Boeing 737s, the DC8, Airbus A320s, and the AWACS.

**KEY COMPETITORS**
Honeywell International
Pratt & Whitney
Rolls-Royce

## CH2M HILL COMPANIES, LTD.

| | | |
|---|---|---|
| 6060 S. Willow Dr. | CEO: Ralph R. Peterson | 2000 Sales: $1,706.7 million |
| Greenwood Village, CO 80111 | CFO: Samuel H. Iapalucci | 1-Yr. Sales Change: 44.1% |
| Phone: 303-771-0900 | HR: Fred Berry | Employees: 10,600 |
| Fax: 303-846-2231 | Type: Private | FYE: December 31 |
| Web: www.ch2m.com | | |

CH2M's name is a company (not a chemical) compound derived from the initials of its founders — Cornell, Howland and Hayes (2 H's), and Merryfield — plus Hill, from its first merger. CH2M Hill Companies offers its clients engineering consulting services related to industrial facility design, transportation, water treatment, and environmental remediation. Specialties include sewer and waste-treatment design, hazardous-waste cleanup, and transportation projects such as highways and bridges. The firm operates from more than 140 offices worldwide. US government contracts account for more than 30% of annual revenues. Employees own CH2M Hill, which was founded in 1946 in Corvallis, Oregon.

**KEY COMPETITORS**
Bechtel
Foster Wheeler
MWH Global

## CHARLES PANKOW BUILDERS, LTD.

| | | |
|---|---|---|
| 2476 N. Lake Ave. | CEO: Rik Kunnath | 2000 Est. Sales: $1,000.0 mil. |
| Altadena, CA 91001 | CFO: Tim Murphy | 1-Yr. Sales Change: 122.2% |
| Phone: 626-791-1125 | HR: Patty Bevans | Employees: 135 |
| Fax: 626-794-1539 | Type: Private | FYE: December 31 |
| Web: www.pankow.com | | |

Charles Pankow Builders has some concrete ideas on how to construct high-rises. The design/build general contractor specializes in quake-resistant concrete frames, putting up department stores, hotels, condominiums, medical facilities, and office buildings, primarily in California and Hawaii. The company also has operations in other US states. Affiliate Pankow Special Projects focuses on small-scale projects such as renovations and seismic upgrades. Pankow's new framing system, developed with researchers at the University of Washington and the National Institute of Standards and Technology, has been used for San Francisco's tallest precast concrete building. Chairman Charles Pankow founded the company in 1963.

**KEY COMPETITORS**
Hathaway Dinwiddie Construction
Swinerton
Webcor Builders

## CHEMCENTRAL CORPORATION

| | | |
|---|---|---|
| 7050 W. 71st St. | CEO: John R. Yanney | 2000 Sales: $917.0 million |
| Bedford Park, IL 60499 | CFO: John G. LaBahn | 1-Yr. Sales Change: 4.1% |
| Phone: 708-594-7000 | HR: — | Employees: 1,050 |
| Fax: 708-594-6382 | Type: Private | FYE: December 31 |
| Web: www.chemcentral.com | | |

CHEMCENTRAL is in the center of a chemically dependent world. The company is one of the top chemical distributors in North America. It carries products made by BASF, Dow Chemical, DuPont, and others. Key customers for CHEMCENTRAL's more than 8,000 chemical products include companies that manufacture adhesives, caulks, and sealants; cleaning agents; cosmetics and personal care products; inks and paint coatings; and plastic and rubber compounds. Established in 1926 as the William J Hough Company of Chicago, CHEMCENTRAL now has more than 100 warehouse, distribution, and sales units worldwide.

**KEY COMPETITORS**
Aceto
Ashland
Stinnes

## CHEMOIL CORPORATION

| | | |
|---|---|---|
| 4 Embarcadero Center, Ste. 1800 | CEO: Robert V. Chandran | 2000 Sales: $1,100.0 million |
| San Francisco, CA 94111 | CFO: Manolete Gonzalez | 1-Yr. Sales Change: 120.0% |
| Phone: 415-268-2700 | HR: Lucius C. Conrad | Employees: 70 |
| Fax: 415-268-2701 | Type: Private | FYE: December 31 |
| Web: www.chemoil.com | | |

Chemoil is hunkered down in the bunker fuel distribution business. Founded in 1981, the company supplies marine bunker fuels to about 330 shipping companies worldwide. Chemoil operates refineries and terminals and distributes fuel from ports in six US ports (including New York and Los Angeles), the Netherlands, and Singapore. The company supplies more than 4,000 vessels a year. Fuel is delivered mostly by tankers, barges, and tugboats owned and operated by Chemoil or its affiliates, which include KC Marine (New York), King Shipping (Houston), Unilloyd (Rotterdam), and Westoil Marine (Los Angeles). Chemoil is 50%-owned by Japanese trading company ITOCHU, which is helping to fund its expansion to new ports.

**KEY COMPETITORS**
BP
Statia Terminals
Tesoro Petroleum


## CHEVRON PHILLIPS CHEMICAL COMPANY LP

| | | |
|---|---|---|
| 1301 McKinney | CEO: Jim Gallogly | 2000 Sales: $7,470.0 million |
| Houston, TX 77010 | CFO: Kent Potter | 1-Yr. Sales Change: — |
| Phone: 713-754-2000 | HR: Sherry Richard | Employees: — |
| Fax: — | Type: Joint venture | FYE: December 31 |
| Web: www.cpchem.com | | |

A coin toss determined which company's name would go first when Chevron (now ChevronTexaco) and Phillips Petroleum formed a new joint venture, Chevron Phillips Chemical Company (CPChem). A leading maker of olefins and polyolefins (synthetic fibers), CPC also produces aromatics, alpha olefins, and styrenics. CPChem derives plastics, resins, additives, specialty chemicals, and lubricants from petroleum and natural gas. CPChem is North America's largest producer of high-density polyethylene (HDPE) used in blow/injection molding, plastic bags and pipes, and films, and is near the top in ethylene and aromatics production. Most of the company's operations are located in the US.

**KEY COMPETITORS**
BP
Equistar Chemicals
Shell


## CHEVY CHASE BANK, F.S.B.

| | | |
|---|---|---|
| 8401 Connecticut Ave. | CEO: B. Francis Saul II | 2000 Sales: $903.4 million |
| Chevy Chase, MD 20815 | CFO: Stephen R. Halpin | 1-Yr. Sales Change: 70.1% |
| Phone: 301-986-7000 | HR: Russ McNish | Employees: 3,487 |
| Fax: 301-986-4733 | Type: Private | FYE: September 30 |
| Web: www.chevychasebank.com | | |

Chevy Chase Bank is one of the largest banks serving the Washington, DC, area (including parts of Maryland and northern Virginia) with such traditional retail services as checking and savings accounts, CDs, and IRAs. The savings bank serves customers through more than 160 branches, as well as through the Internet and through "video banking" (videoconferencing kiosks in stores and malls that give customers a warmer and fuzzier way to bank electronically). The bank's loan portfolio includes commercial, construction, consumer, and mortgage loans. Chairman and CEO B. Francis Saul II controls the bank through various companies.

**KEY COMPETITORS**
Allfirst Financial
First Virginia
Riggs National

## CHICK-FIL-A INC.

5200 Buffington Rd.
Atlanta, GA 30349
Phone: 404-765-8000
Fax: 404-765-8971
Web: www.chick-fil-a.com

CEO: S. Truett Cathy
CFO: James B. "Buck" McCabe
HR: Renea Boozer
Type: Private

2000 Sales: $1,086.0 million
1-Yr. Sales Change: 16.1%
Employees: 40,000
FYE: December 31

Beloved by bovines, Chick-fil-A is the nation's #2 fast-food chicken restaurant chain (behind TRICON's KFC and ahead of AFC's Popeyes/Church's). It serves chicken entrees, sandwiches, and salads at some 980 stores in about 35 US states and in South Africa. Although nearly 45% its restaurants are located in shopping malls, the company is focusing most of its expansion efforts on free-standing outlets. Chick-fil-A also licenses units inside hospitals, schools, airports, and other nontraditional locations. Founder and owner S. Truett Cathy, a devout Baptist, closes his stores on Sundays and boasts of a high management retention rate.

**KEY COMPETITORS**
AFC Enterprises
KFC
McDonald's

 See pages 124–125 for a full profile of this company.


## CHRISTUS HEALTH

6363 N. Hwy. 161, Ste. 450
Irving, TX 75038
Phone: 214-492-8500
Fax: 214-492-8540
Web: www.christushealth.org

CEO: Thomas C. Royer
CFO: Jay Herron
HR: Mary Lynch
Type: Not-for-profit

2001 Sales: $2,200.0 million
1-Yr. Sales Change: 5.8%
Employees: 8,000
FYE: June 30

CHRISTUS has plenty to be merry about. The not-for-profit system was formed in 1999 by a merger of Incarnate Word Health System and Sisters of Charity Health System. CHRISTUS Health operates more than 30 hospitals and other health care facilities in some 70 communities in four states, as well as in Mexico. Facilities range from acute-care hospitals to outpatient centers and also include hospice centers, medical education centers, and long-term acute-care facilities. CHRISTUS' predecessor organizations have their roots in the religious order Sisters of Charity of the Incarnate Word, founded when three French nuns arrived in Texas in 1866 to care for the poor and sick.

**KEY COMPETITORS**
Memorial Hermann Healthcare
Sisters of Mercy
Triad Hospitals


## CINEMARK USA, INC.

3900 Dallas Pkwy., Ste. 500
Plano, TX 75093
Phone: 972-665-1000
Fax: 972-665-1004
Web: www.cinemark.com

CEO: Lee Roy Mitchell
CFO: Robert D. Copple
HR: Brad Smith
Type: Private

2000 Sales: $786.3 million
1-Yr. Sales Change: 10.3%
Employees: 8,000
FYE: December 31

Cinemark USA has left its mark on the cinema landscape. The movie exhibitor has more than 2,900 screens in more than 270 theaters in the US and 12 other countries (mostly in Latin America). Cinemark operates multiplex theaters (89% with a minimum of eight screens) in midsized cities and in suburban areas of major metropolitan markets. Some larger theaters operate under the Tinseltown name. About 15% of the company's theaters are discount operations. Cinemark also has online ticketing available at nearly 20% of its theaters. Chairman and CEO Lee Roy Mitchell owns about 24% of the company and controls 100% of the voting shares; Cypress Merchant Banking Partners owns 42%.

**KEY COMPETITORS**
AMC Entertainment
Loews Cineplex Entertainment
Regal Cinemas

 See pages 126–127 for a full profile of this company.

## CINGULAR WIRELESS

Glenridge Highlands Two
Atlanta, GA 30342
Phone: 404-236-6000
Fax: 404-236-6005
Web: www.cingular.com

CEO: Stephen M. Carter
CFO: Richard G. Lindner
HR: Rickford D. Bradley
Type: Joint venture

2000 Sales: $12,647.0 million
1-Yr. Sales Change: 39.9%
Employees: —
FYE: December 31

BellSouth *plus* SBC *times* wireless assets *equals* Cingular Wireless. With a name chosen to emphasize unity and the individual customer, the two regional Bell companies have combined assets to create the second-largest wireless carrier in the US, behind Verizon Wireless. Cingular Wireless has more than 21 million mobile phone and wireless data customers in 38 states, the District of Columbia, and two US territories. The joint venture is 60%-owned by SBC and 40% by BellSouth, according to the contributions made by the two companies, which share control of Cingular Wireless. Eleven brand names used by the SBC and BellSouth wireless units have been replaced by the Cingular Wireless brand.

**KEY COMPETITORS**
AT&T Wireless
Sprint PCS
Verizon Wireless

---

## THE CITY UNIVERSITY OF NEW YORK

535 E. 80th St.
New York, NY 10021
Phone: 212-794-5555
Fax: 212-794-5590
Web: www.cuny.edu

CEO: Matthew Goldstein
CFO: Sherry F. Brabham
HR: —
Type: School

2001 Sales: $1,927.4 million
1-Yr. Sales Change: 1.4%
Employees: —
FYE: June 30

Do students at City University of New York (CUNY) give their teachers bigger apples? The college has 20 campuses in the five boroughs of New York City and is the US's largest urban university system. About 200,000 undergraduate and graduate students are enrolled at CUNY. The university also teaches some 150,000 students in adult and continuing education programs. CUNY has 10 colleges, six community colleges, a doctoral-granting graduate school, a four-year technical school, and medical and law schools. Its 900-plus programs range from specialized, career-oriented courses to traditional liberal arts curricula. CUNY's student body is an ethnically diverse one, including students from 145 countries.

 See pages 128–129 for a full profile of this company.

---

## CLARK ENTERPRISES, INC.

7500 Old Georgetown Rd.
Bethesda, MD 20814
Phone: 301-272-8100
Fax: 301-272-1928
Web: www.clarkus.com

CEO: A. James Clark
CFO: Lawrence C. Nussdorf
HR: Ann Timmons
Type: Private

2000 Est. Sales: $2,400.0 mil.
1-Yr. Sales Change: 33.3%
Employees: 4,500
FYE: December 31

Convention does not bind Clark Enterprises. Besides constructing convention centers, Clark Enterprises' Clark Construction unit builds hotels, office buildings, stadiums, and transportation facilities. Clark Enterprise has built several Maryland projects, including Oriole Park at Camden Yards (home to baseball's Baltimore Orioles), and many other recognizable structures around the country, such as the Los Angeles Convention Center, the US Federal Courthouse in Boston, and the 30th Street Station in Philadelphia. Other subsidiaries provide general contracting and design/build construction, including international projects. CEO James Clark owns Clark Enterprises.

**KEY COMPETITORS**
Bechtel
Fluor
Turner Corporation

## CLARK RETAIL GROUP, INC.

3003 Butterfield Rd.
Oak Brook, IL 60523
Phone: 630-366-3000
Fax: 630-366-3440
Web: www.clarkretail.com

CEO: Brandon K. Barnholt
CFO: Jeff Jones
HR: Lou Kartsimas
Type: Private

2000 Sales: $2,600.0 million
1-Yr. Sales Change: 79.3%
Employees: 6,000
FYE: December 31

Clark Retail Group hopes to reach out to those on the go. It operates or franchises more than 1,300 gas stations and convenience stores, many operated by subsidiary Clark Retail Enterprises. Store names include Clark, Light House, Oh! Zone, On The Go, Minit Mart, and White Hen Pantry. Clark Retail Enterprises was formed when an affiliate of investment firm Apollo Management bought the retail assets of oil refiner Clark USA in 1999. As part of the deal, Clark Retail Enterprises began life with a two-year petroleum supply agreement with its former owner. Clark Retail Group's holdings span much of the Central US and Massachusetts, with about 400 locations in the Chicago area alone.

**KEY COMPETITORS**
BP
CITGO
Exxon Mobil

## CLUBCORP, INC.

3030 LBJ Fwy., Ste. 700
Dallas, TX 75234
Phone: 972-243-6191
Fax: 972-888-7338
Web: www.clubcorp.com

CEO: Robert H. Dedman Jr.
CFO: Jeffrey P. Mayer
HR: Albert E. Chew III
Type: Private

2000 Sales: $1,068.8 million
1-Yr. Sales Change: 4.0%
Employees: 24,000
FYE: December 31

ClubCorp makes its green from the green — the golf green, that is. The world's largest operator of golf courses, country clubs, private business clubs, and resorts, the company owns and operates more than 220 properties in nearly a dozen countries. Its holdings include Mission Hills Country Club near Palm Springs, California, and North Carolina's Pinehurst Resort and Country Club (site of the 1999 US Open). The company also owns 25% of ClubLink, a leading Canadian developer and operator of golf courses, and 30% of PGA European Tour Courses, an operator of tournament golf courses across Europe. Founder and chairman Robert Dedman and his family own 75% of ClubCorp.

**KEY COMPETITORS**
American Golf
Golf Trust of America
National Golf Properties

 See pages 130–131 for a full profile of this company.

## COCA-COLA BOTTLING COMPANY OF CHICAGO

7400 N. Oak Park Ave.
Niles, IL 60714
Phone: 847-647-0200
Fax: 847-647-9306

CEO: Marvin J. Herb
CFO: Thomas T. Martin
HR: Robert T. Palo
Type: Private

2000 Est. Sales: $1,015.0 mil.
1-Yr. Sales Change: 8.0%
Employees: 4,000
FYE: December 31

Quenching big thirsts in "the City of the Big Shoulders" and beyond, the Coca-Cola Bottling Company of Chicago bottles and distributes soft drinks for The Coca-Cola Company. Its major brands include Coca-Cola classic, diet Coke, Sprite, and Barq's. It also bottles Sunkist, Tab, and Welch's and rolls out bottled water and sports drinks. The Coca-Cola Bottling Company of Chicago serves Illinois, Wisconsin, and Indiana, as well as parts of Pennsylvania and New York. Bought by Marvin Herb in 1981, the firm is part of one of the top bottling groups in the US (Herb Coca-Cola). The world's top bottler, Coca-Cola Enterprises, has acquired the company along with others in the Herb Coca-Cola franchise group.

**KEY COMPETITORS**
Dr Pepper/Seven Up Bottling
Pepsi Bottling
PepsiAmericas

## COLFAX CORPORATION

9211 Forest Hill Ave., Ste. 109
Richmond, VA 23235
Phone: 804-560-4070
Fax: 804-560-4076
Web: www.colfaxcorp.com

CEO: John Young
CFO: Scott Faison
HR: —
Type: Private

2000 Est. Sales: $900.0 mil.
1-Yr. Sales Change: (10.0%)
Employees: 3,500
FYE: December 31

Colfax Corporation's businesses consist of a Power Transmission Group (Warner Electric, Boston Gear, Ameridrives), and a Pump Group (ALLWEILLER and Imo Pump). Warner Electric makes industrial clutches and brakes for applications ranging from lawn tractors to tractor-trailer rigs. Boston Gear offers 30,000 motion control products and components, while Ameridrives makes such power transmission products as gear couplings, spindles, and universal joints. Colfax's German subsidiary ALLWEILLER offers an array of industrial pumps designed to move everything from soft drinks to sewage. Imo Pumps makes two- and three-screw pumps used in machinery lubrication, fuel oil transport, and burner service.

**KEY COMPETITORS**
Flowserve
Parker Hannifin
Robbins & Myers

## COLLIERS INTERNATIONAL PROPERTY CONSULTANTS INC.

84 State St., 3rd Fl.
Boston, MA 02019
Phone: 617-722-0221
Fax: 617-722-0224
Web: www.colliers.com

CEO: Margaret Wigglesworth
CFO: Margaret Carlson
HR: Margaret Carlson
Type: Private

2000 Sales: $1,000.1 million
1-Yr. Sales Change: 11.1%
Employees: 9,000
FYE:

Colliers International is one of the largest commercial real estate dealers in the world. With some 250 offices in more than 50 countries, the company is a partnership of more than 40 independently owned firms. Colliers International agencies provide brokerage, corporate, construction consulting, investment sales, and property development and management services to tenants, owners, and investors. Colliers Macauley Nicolls (dba Colliers International) is the group's largest member, with offices in nearly 90 cities worldwide. Originally founded in 1832, Colliers Jardine represents the Asia/Pacific region. All told, Colliers International firms manage about 400 million sq. ft. of property on six continents.

**KEY COMPETITORS**
CB Richard Ellis
Grubb & Ellis
Jones Lang LaSalle

## COLT'S MANUFACTURING COMPANY, INC.

545 New Park Ave.
West Hartford, CT 06110
Phone: 860-236-6311
Fax: 860-244-1442
Web: www.colt.com

CEO: William M. Keys
CFO: Tom Siegel
HR: Mike Magouirk
Type: Private

1999 Est. Sales: $100.0 mil.
1-Yr. Sales Change: 4.2%
Employees: 700
FYE: December 31

Colt's Manufacturing is in the gunfight of its life. Through its subsidiaries, Colt's Manufacturing makes handguns (Cowboy, Defender) and semiautomatic rifles for civilian use, and military weapons (M-16, M-4 Carbine) for the US and other governments. Founded in 1836 by Samuel Colt, the company is about 83%-owned by investment firm Zilkha & Co., which has been reviving the company since 1994. Colt's, which has struggled recently, sold military weapons manufacturer Saco Defense to General Dynamics. Wounded by lawsuits, Colt's is discontinuing a number of handguns and is focusing research on "smart gun" technology (in which weapons can only be fired by the weapon's owner).

**KEY COMPETITORS**
Beretta
Saf-T-Hammer
Sturm, Ruger

📖 See pages 132–133 for a full profile of this company.

## COLUMBIA FOREST PRODUCTS INC.

222 SW Columbia, Ste. 1575
Portland, OR 97201
Phone: 503-224-5300
Fax: 503-224-5294
Web: www.columbiaforestproducts.com

CEO: Harry L. Demorest
CFO: Cliff Barry
HR: —
Type: Private

2000 Sales: $800.0 million
1-Yr. Sales Change: 10.3%
Employees: 3,500
FYE: December 31

Columbia Forest Products is a clear-cut leader as North America's largest manufacturer of hardwood plywood, veneer, and laminated products. The employee-owned company makes products used in flooring, cabinets, architectural millwork, and commercial fixtures. Specializing in Northern Appalachian hardwoods, Columbia Forest Products' rotary veneer is used by the cabinetry, door, furniture, and decorative plywood industries. The company sells its products to OEMs, wholesale distributors, and mass merchandisers. Columbia Forest Products operates 25 plants in the US and Canada.

**KEY COMPETITORS**
Armstrong Holdings
Roseburg Forest Products
Weyerhaeuser

## COLUMBIA HOUSE COMPANY

Columbia House, 1221 Avenue of the Americas
New York, NY 10020
Phone: 212-596-2001
Fax: 212-596-2213
Web: www.columbiahouse.com

CEO: Scott Flanders
CFO: —
HR: Bob Consiglio
Type: Joint venture

2000 Sales: $1,200.0 million
1-Yr. Sales Change: 20.0%
Employees: —
FYE: December 31

If the house is a-rockin', it's probably Columbia House. A 50-50 joint venture between entertainment giants Sony and AOL Time Warner, Columbia House is the top club-based direct marketer of music and videos in North America. The company sells more than 16,000 music selections and 7,000 video titles via mail-order and its namesake Web site. Started in 1955, Columbia House boasts more than 14 million members in the US, Canada, and Mexico. The company agreed to merge with online music retailer CDnow in 1999; the deal was called off in March 2000, however, not long after parent Time Warner announced its intent to merge with America Online. (The merger was completed in January 2001.)

**KEY COMPETITORS**
Amazon.com
Bertelsmann
Musicland

## COLUMBIA UNIVERSITY

2690 Broadway
New York, NY 10027
Phone: 212-854-1754
Fax: 212-749-0397
Web: www.columbia.edu

CEO: George Rupp
CFO: John Masten
HR: Colleen M. Crooker
Type: School

2001 Est. Sales: $1,700.0 mil.
1-Yr. Sales Change: (5.0%)
Employees: 7,072
FYE: June 30

Predating the American Revolution, Columbia University (founded as King's College in 1754) is the fifth-oldest institution of higher learning in the US. With a student population of almost 23,000 students and a campus spread across 36 acres in Manhattan, Columbia's 16 schools and colleges grant undergraduate and graduate degrees in about 70 disciplines, including its well-known programs in journalism, law, and medicine. Columbia also has a strong reputation for research and ranks #1 among universities earning funds through patents and royalties. The Ivy League university added former vice president Al Gore as one of its 7,000 faculty members in 2001.

 See pages 134–135 for a full profile of this company.

## COMARK, INC.

444 Scott Dr.
Bloomingdale, IL 60108
Phone: 800-888-5390
Fax: 630-351-7497
Web: www.comark.com

CEO: Chuck Wolande
CFO: Gary D. Kovanda
HR: Larry Fazzini
Type: Private

2001 Sales: $1,560.0 million
1-Yr. Sales Change: 0.6%
Employees: 1,364
FYE: March 31

Comark serves up a computer feast, soup to nuts. Founded in 1977 by fraternity brothers Philip Corcoran and Chuck Wolande, Comark is a leading private reseller of computers, peripherals, and computer supplies in the US. The company sells to large global companies, government agencies, and schools. It has developed partnerships with industry leaders such as IBM, Hewlett-Packard, and Compaq to sell and provide service for their products. Comark's services include asset management and network, system, and Internet consulting and implementation. The company's offices are located primarily in the midwestern and eastern US. Corcoran and Wolande own the company.

**KEY COMPETITORS**

CompuCom
Ingram Micro
Tech Data

 See pages 136–137 for a full profile of this company.

## CONAIR CORPORATION

1 Cummings Point Rd.
Stamford, CT 06904
Phone: 203-351-9000
Fax: 203-351-9180
Web: www.conair.com

CEO: Barry Haber
CFO: Pat Yannotta
HR: John Mayorek
Type: Private

2000 Sales: $1,082.0 million
1-Yr. Sales Change: 16.6%
Employees: 4,461
FYE: December 31

Counterintelligence has shown that Conair has a place in many bathrooms and kitchens. Conair makes personal products and small appliances. Its home and professional beauty lines include curling irons, hair dryers, shavers, mirrors, and salon products (Jheri Redding, Rusk). Its Cuisinart unit produces blenders, food processors, and other kitchen appliances. Conair also sells the Interplak electric toothbrush, telephones, answering machines, and private-label appliances and personal products for retailers. Leandro Rizzuto, who founded Conair in 1959 with his parents, owns the company.

**KEY COMPETITORS**

Applica
Helen of Troy
SEB

## CONCERT COMMUNICATIONS COMPANY

11921 Freedom Dr.
Reston, VA 20190
Phone: 703-707-4000
Fax: 703-707-4018
Web: www.concert.com

CEO: Gerald R. Weis
CFO: R. Wayne Jackson
HR: Christine Brennan
Type: Joint venture

2000 Sales: $7,000.0 million
1-Yr. Sales Change: 133.3%
Employees: 2,000
FYE: March 31

The fat lady is clearing her throat for the end of Concert Communications, the global joint venture between BT Group (formerly British Telecommunications) and AT&T (each owns 50%). Operating since 1998, Concert provides voice and data telecom services to multinational corporations and handles international traffic for telecom carriers and ISPs, as a carrier's carrier. It also serves customers through a network of distributors. But the venture has racked up huge losses, and the two parent companies have agreed the show must not go on. BT Group and AT&T have agreed to unwind Concert and divide the assets. Services will be continued while the venture is being dissolved. Concert's final chorus is expected in 2002.

**KEY COMPETITORS**

Cable and Wireless
Equant
WorldCom

## CONNECTICUT LOTTERY CORPORATION

270 John Downey Dr.
New Britain, CT 06051
Phone: 860-348-4001
Fax: 860-348-4015
Web: www.ctlottery.org

CEO: James Vance
CFO: —
HR: Karen Mehigen
Type: Government-owned

2000 Sales: $837.5 million
1-Yr. Sales Change: (3.8%)
Employees: —
FYE: June 30

The Connecticut Lottery gives residents of the Constitution State a chance to amend their incomes. The organization operates a variety of scratch-off instant games and daily numbers games (Cash 5, Nightly Numbers, Play 4). It also offers Classic Lotto twice-a-week jackpot games and the multistate Powerball Lottery. Players who buy Instant Powerball TV Game scratch-off tickets also are eligible to win a chance to get their 15 minutes of fame by competing on *Powerball - The Game Show,* a weekly lottery game show hosted by none other than Bob Eubanks. The Connecticut Lottery pays out about 60% of lottery revenue in prizes and about 30% to Connecticut's general fund.

**KEY COMPETITORS**
Massachusetts State Lottery
New York State Lottery
Pennsylvania Lottery

## THE CONNELL COMPANY

One Connell Dr.
Berkeley Heights, NJ 07922
Phone: 908-233-0700
Fax: 908-233-1070
Web: www.connellco.com

CEO: Grover Connell
CFO: Terry Connell
HR: Maureen Waldron
Type: Private

2000 Sales: $2,425.0 million
1-Yr. Sales Change: 5.4%
Employees: 240
FYE: December 31

The Connell Company, a leading international distributor of sugar and rice, is ready to sweeten the pot. Connell's core business is rice distribution, conducted through subsidiary Connell Rice & Sugar. The company's support operations have grown into full subsidiaries including brokerage of flour and sugar sales, commercial real estate development, equipment leasing (including forklift trucks), exporting, and financial services (such as underwriting airlines' purchases of aircraft). The company has offices in Malaysia, Taiwan, Thailand, and the US. Connell has remained a family-owned business since it was founded in 1926. President and CEO Grover Connell has been a generous supporter of Democratic politicians.

**KEY COMPETITORS**
Cargill
GE Capital
Riceland Foods

## CONNELL LIMITED PARTNERSHIP

1 International Place
Boston, MA 02110
Phone: 617-737-2700
Fax: 617-737-1617
Web: www.connell-lp.com

CEO: William F. Connell
CFO: —
HR: Maurice "Bud" Heller
Type: Private

2000 Sales: $1,185.0 million
1-Yr. Sales Change: 2.2%
Employees: 2,000
FYE: December 31

The die was cast in 1987 when several subsidiaries organized to create Connell Limited Partnership, a maker of aluminum and industrial equipment. The company's Danly Die Set makes die sets and supplies for die makers. Its Wabash Alloys unit recycles scrap aluminum for steelmakers and the die- and sand-casting industries. Its IEM unit offers bushings and wear plate products. Yuba Heat Transfer provides heat-transfer equipment and feedwater heaters to the petroleum, chemical, and pulp and paper industries. Connell sold its Mayville Metal products to APW Limited. Chairman and CEO William Connell owns the company.

**KEY COMPETITORS**
Actuant
IMCO Recycling
TAT Technologies

## CONRAIL INC.

| | | |
|---|---|---|
| 2001 Market St. | CEO: Gregory R. Weber | 2000 Sales: $985.0 million |
| Philadelphia, PA 19103 | CFO: Joseph Rogers | 1-Yr. Sales Change: (55.2%) |
| Phone: 215-209-2000 | HR: Anthony Carlini | Employees: — |
| Fax: 215-209-4068 | Type: Private | FYE: December 31 |
| Web: www.conrail.com | | |

Conrail is the holding company for Consolidated Rail, a freight railroad in the heavily industrialized Northeast. Most of its lines and facilities have been divided between its joint owners, rail operators CSX (42%) and Norfolk Southern (58%), following an agreement that took effect in 1999. Conrail, however, continues to manage and operate some lines and facilities in the Philadelphia and Detroit metropolitan areas and in much of New Jersey. To serve customers along those lines, both CSX and Norfolk Southern pay a fee to Conrail for line access; Conrail acts as the local switching and terminal management agent.

**KEY COMPETITORS**
A-P-A Transport
Emons Transportation
Guilford Transportation

## CONSOLIDATED ELECTRICAL DISTRIBUTORS INC.

| | | |
|---|---|---|
| 31356 Via Colinas, Suite 107 | CEO: Keith W. Colburn | 2000 Est. Sales: $2,500.0 mil. |
| Westlake Village, CA 91362 | CFO: — | 1-Yr. Sales Change: (7.4%) |
| Phone: 818-991-9000 | HR: Marie Lipp | Employees: 5,500 |
| Fax: 818-991-6842 | Type: Private | FYE: December 31 |
| Web: www.cedcareers.com | | |

With more than 440 locations nationwide, electrical equipment wholesaler Consolidated Electrical Distributors (CED) has its US distribution wired. The family-owned business is the third-largest electrical distributor in the US. It supplies load centers, panel boards, transformers, switches, and similar products to construction contractors and industrial users. Founded in 1957 as The Electric Corporation of San Francisco, the company buys electrical distributors, usually keeping the acquired company's name and local management team. The Colburn family owns CED, and Keith Colburn runs the firm.

**KEY COMPETITORS**
Anixter International
Graybar Electric
WESCO International

## CONSUMERS UNION OF UNITED STATES, INC.

| | | |
|---|---|---|
| 101 Truman Ave. | CEO: James Guest | 2000 Sales: $140.4 million |
| Yonkers, NY 10703 | CFO: Conrad Harris | 1-Yr. Sales Change: 0.3% |
| Phone: 914-378-2000 | HR: Rick Lustig | Employees: 450 |
| Fax: 914-378-2900 | Type: Not-for-profit | FYE: May 31 |
| Web: www.consumersunion.org | | |

Consumers Union of United States (CU) inspires both trust and fear. Best known for publishing *Consumer Reports* magazine (4.1 million subscribers), the not-for-profit organization also serves as a consumer watchdog through newsletters, books, TV and radio programming, the Internet, and *Zillions* children's magazine. CU derives revenue from sales of its publications, from car and insurance pricing services, and from contributions, fees, and grants. It tests and rates thousands of products annually. CU also testifies on consumer issues and files lawsuits on behalf of consumers. Its Consumer Policy Institute focuses on research and education in issues such as air pollution.

**KEY COMPETITORS**
Consumers' Research
Hearst
Underwriters Labs

 See pages 138–139 for a full profile of this company.

## CONTIGROUP COMPANIES, INC.

277 Park Ave.
New York, NY 10172
Phone: 212-207-5100
Fax: 212-207-2910
Web: www.contigroup.com

CEO: Paul J. Fribourg
CFO: Michael J. Zimmerman
HR: Teresa E. McCaslin
Type: Private

2001 Sales: $4,000.0 million
1-Yr. Sales Change: (60.0%)
Employees: 14,500
FYE: March 31

It's farther up the food chain now, but ContiGroup Companies (CGC, formerly Continental Grain) is still a big name in agribusiness. CGC has exited the grain export business and now operates through ContiBeef (a national leader in cattle feeding), Premium Standard Farms (#2 US pork producer, after Smithfield Foods), and Wayne Farms, a major poultry processor. Overseas the company has interests in feed milling and aquaculture. CGC also owns 78% of bankrupt ContiFinancial (consumer/commercial loans). CGC's investment arm, ContiInvestments, manages diverse holdings. Chairman Paul Fribourg (the founder's great-great-great-grandson) and his family own CGC.

**KEY COMPETITORS**
Cactus Feeders
Smithfield Foods
Tyson Foods

 See pages 140–141 for a full profile of this company.


## CONTRAN CORPORATION

5430 LBJ Fwy., Ste. 1700
Dallas, TX 75240
Phone: 972-233-1700
Fax: 972-448-1444

CEO: Harold C. Simmons
CFO: Bob D. O'Brien
HR: Keith A. Johnson
Type: Private

2000 Sales: $1,200.0 million
1-Yr. Sales Change: 3.4%
Employees: 9,000
FYE: December 31

Founded by Texas billionaire Harold Simmons, Contran is a holding company that controls more than 90% of Valhi, Inc., a publicly traded company. Through subsidiaries and affiliations, Valhi conducts diversified operations involved in chemicals (NL Industries), titanium metals (Titanium Metals Corporation), waste management services (Waste Control Specialties), computer support systems, and precision ball bearing slides and locking systems (CompX International). Contran also has a controlling interest in Keystone Consolidated Industries, a maker of fencing and wire products. Trusts benefiting Simmons' daughters and his grandchildren (with Simmons as the sole trustee) own almost all of Contran.

**KEY COMPETITORS**
RTI International Metals
Steelcase
Waste Management


## CONVERSE INC.

One Fordham Rd.
North Reading, MA 01864
Phone: 978-664-1100
Fax: 978-664-7472
Web: www.converse.com

CEO: Jack Boys
CFO: Lisa Kempa
HR: Susan Rogato
Type: Private

2000 Sales: $209.1 million
1-Yr. Sales Change: (9.8%)
Employees: 1,510
FYE: December 31

Once-popular basketball shoe maker Converse is trying to rebound. Converse has sold nearly 575 million pairs of that American classic, the Chuck Taylor All Star canvas basketball shoe, which has appealed to everyone from computer programmers to clothing designers to rock stars, nevermind gym rats and neighborhood kids. It also licenses sports apparel from head to toe. Its products are sold in 110 countries through about 5,500 sporting goods, department, and shoe stores, as well as about 25 company-operated retail outlets. Following years of declining sales, the company filed for Chapter 11 bankruptcy protection in 2001. Footwear Acquisition has purchased the company, which intends to continue operations.

**KEY COMPETITORS**
adidas-Salomon
NIKE
Reebok

 See pages 142–143 for a full profile of this company.

## CORE-MARK INTERNATIONAL, INC.

395 Oyster Point Blvd., Ste. 415
South San Francisco, CA 94080
Phone: 650-589-9445
Fax: 650-952-4284
Web: www.coremark.com

CEO: Robert A. Allen
CFO: Leo F. Korman
HR: Henry J. Hautau
Type: Private

2000 Sales: $3,035.4 million
1-Yr. Sales Change: 7.0%
Employees: 2,582
FYE: December 31

Got a late-night craving for sweets or a smoke? Core-Mark International distributes cigarettes and candy — plus health and beauty aids, fast food, snacks,
groceries, beverages, batteries, and film — to retailers in the western US and
Canada. Cigarettes (including its Best Buy brand) bring in more than 70% of
sales. Core-Mark also offers store services, including help with displays, promotions, and marketing. It operates 15 distribution centers in the western US
and four in Canada. Core-Mark's customers range from drugstores and convenience, liquor, and grocery stores to movie theaters and prisons. Investment
firm Jupiter Partners owns 75% of Core-Mark; the company's senior management owns 22%.

**KEY COMPETITORS**
Fleming Companies
McLane
SUPERVALU


## CORNELL UNIVERSITY

Cornell University Campus, 305 Day Hall
Ithaca, NY 14853
Phone: 607-255-2000
Fax: 607-255-5396
Web: www.cornell.edu

CEO: Hunter R. Rawlings III
CFO: Harold D. Craft Jr.
HR: Mary George Opperman
Type: School

2001 Sales: $1,459.1 million
1-Yr. Sales Change: (38.0%)
Employees: 12,866
FYE: June 30

To excel at Cornell you'll need every one of your brain cells. The Ivy League
university has been educating young minds since its founding in 1865. Its
more than 20,000 students can select from seven undergraduate and four
graduate and professional colleges and schools. In addition to its Ithaca, New
York, campus, the university also offers two medical graduate and professional
colleges and schools in New York City and has set up education-outreach centers in every county and borough of New York. Cornell's faculty includes a
handful of Nobel laureates, and the university has a robust research component studying everything from animal health to space to waste management.


## CORPORATE SOFTWARE & TECHNOLOGY, INC.

2 Edgewater Dr.
Norwood, MA 02062
Phone: 781-440-1000
Fax: 781-440-7070
Web: www.corpsoft.com

CEO: Marc Chatel
CFO: Michael Clarke
HR: Jim Boger
Type: Private

2000 Sales: $1,000.0 million
1-Yr. Sales Change: 0.0%
Employees: 750
FYE: December 31

Corporate Software & Technology (CS&T) gets the most out of its name. The
software reseller specializes in software asset management services, which
help organizations manage, control, and evaluate their network and desktop
applications in order to get the most out of their software investments.
Targeting large enterprises, schools, and government agencies, CS&T sells
software from such industry leaders as Computer Associates, Microsoft, and
Symantec. Spun off from Stream International in 1997, CS&T is a subsidiary
of investment firm REBAR (formerly Magellan Holdings). REBAR was created
in 1999 by CS&T chairman Howard Diamond and 19 other execs to buy back
CS&T shares owned by printer R. R. Donnelley & Sons.

**KEY COMPETITORS**
CompuCom
EDS
Merisel

## CORPORATION FOR PUBLIC BROADCASTING

| | | |
|---|---|---|
| 901 E St. NW | CEO: Robert T. Coonrod | 2000 Sales: $384.0 million |
| Washington, DC 20004 | CFO: Elizabeth A. Griffith | 1-Yr. Sales Change: 35.7% |
| Phone: 202-879-9600 | HR: Alicia Schoshinski | Employees: 90 |
| Fax: 202-879-9768 | Type: Not-for-profit | FYE: September 30 |
| Web: www.cpb.org | | |

The Corporation for Public Broadcasting (CPB) is often on the *Frontline* of political controversy. The not-for-profit organization has come under fire from political factions opposed to government cultural spending. Appropriations from Congress help CPB fund cultural, educational, and informational programming for more than 1,000 public television and radio stations, mostly Public Broadcasting Service, National Public Radio, and Public Radio International stations. Funding has been approved through 2003, despite a 1999 investigation that revealed some PBS stations had given their mailing lists to the Democratic party for fundraising purposes.

**KEY COMPETITORS**
A&E Networks
BBC
Discovery Communications

 See pages 144–145 for a full profile of this company.

## COX ENTERPRISES, INC.

| | | |
|---|---|---|
| 1400 Lake Hearn Dr. | CEO: James C. Kennedy | 2000 Sales: $7,823.6 million |
| Atlanta, GA 30319 | CFO: Robert C. O'Leary | 1-Yr. Sales Change: 28.3% |
| Phone: 404-843-5000 | HR: Marybeth H. Leamer | Employees: 74,000 |
| Fax: 404-843-5109 | Type: Private | FYE: December 31 |
| Web: www.coxenterprises.com | | |

The Cox family has been working at this enterprise for more than 100 years. One of the largest media conglomerates in the US, family-owned Cox Enterprises publishes 18 daily newspapers (including *The Atlanta Journal-Constitution*) and about 30 weeklies and shoppers and owns 15 TV stations through Cox Television. It also owns about 63% of Cox Radio (more than 80 radio stations) and 68% of Cox Communications, one of the US's largest cable systems with more than 6 million subscribers. Cox's Manheim Auctions runs more than 100 automobile auctions worldwide and owns a majority-stake in AutoTrader.com, and Cox Interactive Media operates more than 20 city-specific Web sites.

**KEY COMPETITORS**
AT&T Broadband
Gannett
Tribune

 See pages 146–147 for a full profile of this company.

## CROWLEY MARITIME CORPORATION

| | | |
|---|---|---|
| 155 Grand Ave. | CEO: Thomas B. Crowley Jr. | 2000 Est. Sales: $800.0 mil. |
| Oakland, CA 94612 | CFO: John Calvin | 1-Yr. Sales Change: 3.2% |
| Phone: 510-251-7500 | HR: Susan Rogers | Employees: 5,000 |
| Fax: 510-251-7788 | Type: Private | FYE: December 31 |
| Web: www.crowley.com | | |

Crowley Maritime has pushed and pulled its way into prominence as one of the largest tug and barge operators in the world. The company transports freight, petroleum products, and breakbulk (entire refineries and other structures that cannot be broken down) by ship. It provides trucking services, ship assists, towing, logistics, and marine salvage. The company has some 60,000 containers and trailers, and its fleet includes tugboats, tankers, barges, and specialized cargo vessels. Crowley Maritime has more than 100 offices worldwide; it has expanded with the acquisition of Marine Transport. CEO Thomas Crowley (grandson of the founder), his family, and employees own about 85% of the company, which was founded in 1892.

**KEY COMPETITORS**
APL
CSX
Hamburg Süd

## CROWN CENTRAL PETROLEUM CORPORATION

One North Charles Street
Baltimore, MD 21201
Phone: 410-539-7400
Fax: 410-659-4778

CEO: Frank B. Rosenberg
CFO: John E. Wheeler Jr.
HR: J. Michael Mims
Type: Private

2000 Sales: $1,961.4 million
1-Yr. Sales Change: 54.4%
Employees: 2,636
FYE: December 31

Independent oil refiner and marketer Crown Central Petroleum's family jewels include two refineries in Texas with a total capacity of 152,000 barrels per day, more than 330 retail service stations in the mid-Atlantic and southeastern US, and 13 product terminals. Crown Central also offers fleet fueling services. The company has come under attack for a four-year labor lockout at its Houston-area refinery, civil rights violations, and excessive toxic releases. It is considering selling its refineries and its terminals. Chairman Henry Rosenberg and his family, through their Rosemore, Inc., took full ownership of Crown Central in 2001 after overcoming a competing bid from rival shareholder Apex Oil.

**KEY COMPETITORS**
Motiva Enterprises
Phillips Petroleum
Valero

## CROWN EQUIPMENT CORPORATION

40 S. Washington St.
New Bremen, OH 45869
Phone: 419-629-2311
Fax: 419-629-9241
Web: www.crownlift.com

CEO: James F. Dicke II
CFO: Kent Spille
HR: Randy Niekamp
Type: Private

2001 Sales: $1,127.0 million
1-Yr. Sales Change: 11.6%
Employees: 7,290
FYE: March 31

Crown Equipment Corporation is a leading maker of electric heavy-duty lift trucks for maneuvering goods in warehouses and distribution centers. The company's products include narrow-aisle stacking equipment, powered pallet trucks, order-picking equipment, and forklift trucks. Its equipment can move four-ton loads and stack pallets nearly 45 feet high. Crown Equipment sells its products globally through retailers. The company, founded in 1945 by brothers Carl and Allen Dicke, originally made temperature controls for coal furnaces. It began making material-handling equipment in the 1950s. The Dicke family still controls Crown Equipment.

**KEY COMPETITORS**
Caterpillar
Ingersoll-Rand
Komatsu

## CUMBERLAND FARMS, INC.

777 Dedham St.
Canton, MA 02021
Phone: 781-828-4900
Fax: 781-828-9012
Web: www.cumberlandfarms.com

CEO: Lily H. Bentas
CFO: Donald Holt
HR: Foster G. Macrides
Type: Private

2001 Sales: $1,500.0 million
1-Yr. Sales Change: 57.9%
Employees: 6,545
FYE: September 30

Tracing its roots to a one-cow dairy, Cumberland Farms owns and operates about 1,000 convenience stores (three-fourths of which sell gasoline) in 11 eastern seaboard states from Maine to Florida. The company has its own grocery distribution and bakery operations to supply its stores. In addition, Cumberland Farms' majority stake in Gulf Oil, a petroleum wholesaler, gives it the right to use and license Gulf trademarks in Delaware, New Jersey, New York, most of Ohio, Pennsylvania, and the New England states. The company, the first operator of convenience stores in New England, was founded in 1938 by Vasilios and Aphrodite Haseotes. The Haseotes' children, including CEO Lily Bentas, own the company.

**KEY COMPETITORS**
7-Eleven
BP
Exxon Mobil

## CUSHMAN & WAKEFIELD INC.

| | | |
|---|---|---|
| 51 W. 52nd St. | CEO: Arthur Mirante II | 2000 Sales: $820.0 million |
| New York, NY 10019 | CFO: Thomas Dowd | 1-Yr. Sales Change: 17.1% |
| Phone: 212-841-7500 | HR: Carolyn F. Sessa | Employees: 11,500 |
| Fax: 212-841-7867 | Type: Private | FYE: December 31 |
| Web: www.cushwake.com | | |

Cushman & Wakefield serves the real estate needs of corporations and financial institutions around the globe. The commercial real estate brokerage and services company, founded in 1917 by Bernard Wakefield and J. Clydesdale Cushman, has more than 170 offices in about 50 countries. Cushman & Wakefield operates in Africa, Asia, Europe, the Middle East, and North and South America. Landmark projects include the American Express Tower in Manhattan and the Sears Tower in Chicago. The company has begun an Internet venture with Business Integration Group to offer online real estate management services. The Rockefeller Group, a Mitsubishi Estate subsidiary, owns about 80% of Cushman & Wakefield.

**KEY COMPETITORS**
CB Richard Ellis
Grubb & Ellis
Trammell Crow


## DADE BEHRING INC.

| | | |
|---|---|---|
| 1717 Deerfield Rd. | CEO: James Reid-Anderson | 2000 Sales: $1,184.0 million |
| Deerfield, IL 60015 | CFO: John Duffey | 1-Yr. Sales Change: (9.6%) |
| Phone: 847-267-5300 | HR: Robert Luse | Employees: 7,500 |
| Fax: 847-267-5408 | Type: Private | FYE: December 31 |
| Web: www.dadebehring.com | | |

Dade Behring just wants to make *sure* that blood is thicker than water. Among the company's products are diagnostic instruments that test how well blood coagulates. Other products test for infectious diseases; measure levels of cholesterol, glucose, iron, or sodium in the body; diagnose cardiac disease; monitor therapeutic drugs; and test for illicit drug use. With sales offices worldwide, the company has almost 25,000 customers, mainly clinical laboratories and hospitals. Dade Behring has a staff of more than 1,000 providing support services to its product's users.

**KEY COMPETITORS**
Beckman Coulter
Johnson & Johnson
Roche


## DAIRY FARMERS OF AMERICA

| | | |
|---|---|---|
| 10220 N. Executive Hills Blvd. | CEO: Gary E. Hanman | 2000 Sales: $6,700.0 million |
| Kansas City, MO 64153 | CFO: Jerry Bos | 1-Yr. Sales Change: (11.8%) |
| Phone: 816-801-6455 | HR: Harold Papen | Employees: — |
| Fax: 816-801-6456 | Type: Cooperative | FYE: December 31 |
| Web: www.dfamilk.com | | |

Dairy Farmers of America (DFA) are partners in cream and ready to curdle their competitors. Formed by the merger of four separate dairy cooperatives, DFA is now the world's largest dairy cooperative, with 27,000 members in 45 states. The co-op produces more than a quarter of the US milk supply. It also produces cheese, butter, and other products for wholesale and retail customers worldwide. To better compete with larger food manufacturers, DFA is seeking strength in value-added products and joint ventures to distribute its milk and milk-based food ingredients to wider regions.

**KEY COMPETITORS**
Danone
Dean Foods
Land O'Lakes

 See pages 148–149 for a full profile of this company.

## DAIRYLEA COOPERATIVE INC.

| | | |
|---|---|---|
| 5001 Brittonfield Pkwy. | CEO: Richard P. Smith | 2000 Sales: $811.5 million |
| East Syracuse, NY 13057 | CFO: Edward Bangel | 1-Yr. Sales Change: (7.9%) |
| Phone: 315-433-0100 | HR: Edward Bangel | Employees: 205 |
| Fax: 315-433-2345 | Type: Cooperative | FYE: March 31 |
| Web: www.dairylea.com | | |

Yes, the farmer takes a wife, then hi-ho, the derry-o, the farmer takes membership in milk marketing organizations such as Dairylea Cooperative. Owned by more than 2,800 dairy farmers in the northeastern US, Dairylea markets 5 billion pounds of milk for its farmers annually to customers such as Kraft Foods and Great Lakes Cheese Company. The cooperative invests in dairy companies and provides members with financial and farm management services, as well as insurance. Dairylea, the largest milk marketer in the Northeast, has a joint marketing venture with Dairy Farmers of America and other cooperatives. Dairylea's Empire Livestock subsidiary markets livestock.

**KEY COMPETITORS**
Agri-Mark
AMPI
Foremost Farms


## DART CONTAINER CORPORATION

| | | |
|---|---|---|
| 500 Hogsback Rd. | CEO: Kenneth B. Dart | 2000 Est. Sales: $1,200.0 mil. |
| Mason, MI 48854 | CFO: William Myer | 1-Yr. Sales Change: 9.1% |
| Phone: 517-676-3800 | HR: Mark Franks | Employees: 5,000 |
| Fax: 517-676-3883 | Type: Private | FYE: December 31 |
| Web: www.dartcontainer.com | | |

Dart Container is a world cup winner — maybe not in soccer, but it is the world's top maker of foam cups and containers, with about half of the global market in cups. The company uses a secret method of molding expandable polystyrene to make its products, which include cups, lids, dinnerware, and cutlery. To cut costs, Dart Container makes its own feedstocks, builds its own molding machinery, and operates its own distribution trucks. The company runs four polystyrene-recycling plants and operates in the US and through subsidiaries in Argentina, Australia, Canada, Mexico, and the UK. Although often embroiled in litigation, the Dart family continues to own the company.

**KEY COMPETITORS**
sf holdings
Smurfit-Stone Container
Temple-Inland

 See pages 150–151 for a full profile of this company.


## DAVID WEEKLEY HOMES

| | | |
|---|---|---|
| 1111 N. Post Oak Rd. | CEO: David Weekley | 2000 Sales: $828.0 million |
| Houston, TX 77055 | CFO: Jim Alexander | 1-Yr. Sales Change: 16.5% |
| Phone: 713-963-0500 | HR: Mike Gentry | Employees: 1,010 |
| Fax: 713-963-8822 | Type: Private | FYE: December 31 |
| Web: www.davidweekleyhomes.com | | |

A development home developed to your taste? Founded in 1976, David Weekley Homes builds houses offering hundreds of floor plans and custom upgrades for its customers. Priced from $120,000 to about $650,000, the builder's homes range in size from about 1,500 sq. ft. to more than 4,000 sq. ft. Weekley constructs on home buyers' lots, but it primarily works in its own planned communities in the southeastern US and in Colorado, Oklahoma, and Texas. The company built a home in Tampa in conjunction with the *Today* show, allowing viewers to vote on and determine every aspect of the home's construction, from the floor plan to the bathroom's color scheme. Founder and chairman David Weekley owns the firm.

**KEY COMPETITORS**
D.R. Horton
Engle Homes
Town and Country Homes

## DAVID WILSON'S AUTOMOTIVE GROUP

| | | |
|---|---|---|
| 1400 N. Tustin | CEO: David Wilson | 2000 Sales: $1,033.0 million |
| Orange, CA 92867 | CFO: Ted Tomasek | 1-Yr. Sales Change: 161.5% |
| Phone: 714-639-6750 | HR: Vicki Murphy | Employees: 450 |
| Fax: 714-771-0363 | Type: Private | FYE: December 31 |

First Orange County, then the world — or at least Arizona. David Wilson's Automotive Group has its roots in Orange County, California. Owner David Wilson bought the first of his eight dealerships, Toyota of Orange, in 1985; his Ford of Orange is the county's largest Ford dealership. The company has two other Toyota dealerships and two Lexus dealerships in California. In 1998 the company expanded east, opening a Honda dealership in Scottsdale, Arizona. The company added a Toyota location in Arizona in 1999. The company's dealerships also sell used cars and offer parts and service departments; some offer fleet services.

**KEY COMPETITORS**
AutoNation
Marty Franich
Tuttle-Click


## THE DAY & ZIMMERMANN GROUP, INC.

| | | |
|---|---|---|
| 1818 Market St. | CEO: Harold L. "Hal" Yoh III | 2000 Sales: $1,554.0 million |
| Philadelphia, PA 19103 | CFO: Joe Ritzel | 1-Yr. Sales Change: (5.8%) |
| Phone: 215-299-8000 | HR: Judith Jones Blanks | Employees: 26,000 |
| Fax: 215-299-8355 | Type: Private | FYE: December 31 |
| Web: www.dayzim.com | | |

The Day & Zimmermann Group offers services as distinct as day and night. The company provides engineering and construction management, security, munitions assembly and disposal, and technical and administrative staffing services worldwide. Its clients are US and foreign defense and energy agencies, utilities, and educational, financial, and health organizations. The company also operates dedicated offices for individual clients, such as giants DuPont and Lucent. The company has boosted its munitions business by buying Mason & Hanger Engineering, which subsequently lost a $1.5 billion, five-year contract at the Pantex nuclear bomb plant in Texas. Founded in 1901, the company is owned by the family of CEO Harold Yoh III.

**KEY COMPETITORS**
Alliant Techsystems
Fluor
Manpower


## DEBRUCE GRAIN, INC.

| | | |
|---|---|---|
| 4100 N. Mulberry Dr. | CEO: Paul DeBruce | 2001 Sales: $1,200.9 million |
| Kansas City, MO 64116 | CFO: Curt Heinz | 1-Yr. Sales Change: 36.6% |
| Phone: 816-421-8182 | HR: Joni Hawn | Employees: 330 |
| Fax: 816-584-2350 | Type: Private | FYE: March 31 |
| Web: www.debruce.com | | |

Got a few tons of wheat and no place to keep it? DeBruce Grain stores, handles, and sells grain and fertilizer for the agribusiness industry. The company runs 13 grain elevators in Iowa, Kansas, Nebraska, and Texas with a combined capacity of 47 million bushels of grain. DeBruce Grain's office in Mexico merchandises grain grown in both countries. The company also markets fertilizer (by the bag, truck, or barge-load), and it brokers truck freight through subsidiary DeBruce Transportation. DeBruce has paid a $685,000 fine in relation to the 1998 explosion, which killed seven workers, of its Haysville, Kansas, facility — the largest grain elevator in the world. Owner and CEO Paul DeBruce founded the company in 1978.

**KEY COMPETITORS**
Ag Processing
Cargill
Scoular

## DELAWARE NORTH COMPANIES INC.

40 Fountain Plaza
Buffalo, NY 14202
Phone: 716-858-5000
Fax: 716-858-5266
Web: www.delawarenorth.com

CEO: Jeremy M. Jacobs
CFO: —
HR: Karen Kemp
Type: Private

2000 Sales: $1,500.0 million
1-Yr. Sales Change: 7.1%
Employees: 25,000
FYE: December 31

When it comes to corn dogs and nachos, Delaware North is ready to make a lot of concessions. A giant in the food concession industry, the company has a string of subsidiaries ready to make hungry folks happy. Among the company's holdings are Sportservice (food service at sports stadiums), CA One Services (airport food service), and Delaware North Parks Services (visitor services for national parks and tourist attractions). It also operates Boston's FleetCenter and owns a handful of pari-mutuel facilities across the US. Delaware North was founded in 1915 by brothers Charles, Louis, and Marvin Jacobs. The Jacobs family (including CEO Jeremy Jacobs, owner of the NHL's Boston Bruins) still owns the company.

**KEY COMPETITORS**
ARAMARK
HMSHost
Sodexho Alliance

## DELCO REMY INTERNATIONAL, INC.

2902 Enterprise Dr.
Anderson, IN 46013
Phone: 765-778-6499
Fax: 765-778-6404
Web: www.delcoremy.com

CEO: Thomas J. Snyder
CFO: David E. Stoll
HR: Roderick English
Type: Private

2000 Sales: $1,090.9 million
1-Yr. Sales Change: 14.4%
Employees: 7,707
FYE: July 31

Carmakers get cranked up with the help of Delco Remy International, which manufactures and distributes starters and alternators for carmakers and light- and heavy-duty truck makers. The company, which is owned by Citicorp Venture Capital, also remanufactures engines, fuel systems, starters, transmissions, alternators, and torque converters for the automotive aftermarket. Delco's OEM customers include companies such as General Motors, Ford, Navistar, Freightliner, and Caterpillar; retail customers include Pep Boys, AutoZone, and other parts chains. The company was 53%-owned by Citicorp Venture Capital until 2001, at which point Citicorp took advantage of Delco Remy's low stock price and took the company private.

**KEY COMPETITORS**
Genuine Parts
Motorcar Parts
Robert Bosch

 See pages 152–153 for a full profile of this company.

## DELOITTE TOUCHE TOHMATSU

1633 Broadway
New York, NY 10019
Phone: 212-492-4000
Fax: 212-492-4111
Web: www.deloitte.com

CEO: James E. Copeland Jr.
CFO: William A. Fowler
HR: James H. Wall
Type: Partnership

2001 Sales: $12,400.0 million
1-Yr. Sales Change: 10.7%
Employees: 95,000
FYE: May 31

Once, the smallest of the largest accounting/consulting companies, Deloitte Touche Tohmatsu (DTT) is now firmly in the middle of the pack. DTT offers a variety of traditional audit and fiscal oversight services to a multinational clientele through some 700 offices in about 130 countries. Its Deloitte Consulting unit, the firm's fastest growing business line, offers strategic and management consulting in addition to information technology and human resources consulting services. The regulatory pressure Deloitte (and other Big Five firms) had faced to split their consulting and audit operations may be reapplied by new SEC disclosure requirements that reveal the ratio of auditing/ consulting revenues.

**KEY COMPETITORS**
Andersen
Ernst & Young
KPMG

 See pages 154–155 for a full profile of this company.

## DELTA DENTAL PLAN OF CALIFORNIA

| | | |
|---|---|---|
| 100 1st St. | CEO: Gary D. Radine | 2000 Sales: $2,800.0 million |
| San Francisco, CA 94105 | CFO: Elizabeth Russell | 1-Yr. Sales Change: 3.7% |
| Phone: 415-972-8300 | HR: Teri Forestieri | Employees: 2,400 |
| Fax: 415-972-8366 | Type: Not-for-profit | FYE: December 31 |
| Web: www.deltadentalca.org | | |

Delta Dental Plan of California doesn't just help keep the mouths of movie stars clean. A not-for-profit organization, the company is a member of the Delta Dental Plans Association and has affiliates nationwide. Delta Dental provides dental coverage through HMOs, preferred provider plans (PPOs), and such government programs as California's Denti-Cal. The company serves more than 13 million enrollees; its programs cover more than one-third of California residents. Together with Delta Dental of Pennsylvania, Delta Dental of California formed Dentegra Group, a holding company that serves some 16 million members throughout the US.

**KEY COMPETITORS**
PacifiCare
SafeGuard Health Enterprises
WellPoint Health Networks


## DEMOULAS SUPER MARKETS INC.

| | | |
|---|---|---|
| 875 East St. | CEO: — | 2000 Est. Sales: $1,800.0 mil. |
| Tewksbury, MA 01876 | CFO: Donald Mulligan | 1-Yr. Sales Change: 0.0% |
| Phone: 978-851-8000 | HR: Lucille Lopez | Employees: 11,000 |
| Fax: 978-640-8390 | Type: Private | FYE: December 31 |

Supermarket or soap opera? Demoulas Super Markets operates almost 60 grocery stores under the Market Basket and Demoulas Super Market names in Massachusetts and New Hampshire. The firm also has real estate interests. The company was founded in 1954 when brothers George and Mike Demoulas bought their parents' mom-and-pop grocery store. The men agreed that, upon one brother's death, the other would care for the deceased's family and maintain the firm's 50-50 ownership. In 1990 George's family alleged that Mike had defrauded them of all but 8% of the company's stock; the 10-year court battle was decided in favor of George's family, giving it 51% of the company. By then Mike had resigned as CEO; the post remains vacant.

**KEY COMPETITORS**
Hannaford Bros.
Shaw's
Stop & Shop


## DETROIT MEDICAL CENTER

| | | |
|---|---|---|
| 3663 Woodward Ave., Ste. 200 | CEO: Arthur T. Porter | 2000 Sales: $1,600.0 million |
| Detroit, MI 48201 | CFO: Nickolas Vitale | 1-Yr. Sales Change: 10.2% |
| Phone: 313-578-2000 | HR: Ruthann Voelker | Employees: 16,500 |
| Fax: 313-578-3225 | Type: Not-for-profit | FYE: December 31 |
| Web: www.dmc.org | | |

The seeds for the Detroit Medical Center were planted in 1955, when four Detroit hospitals joined to provide coordination between the hospitals and Wayne State University's medical school. Today the medical center (which became a not-for-profit corporation in 1985) serves patients in southeastern Michigan with more than 2,000 beds and some 3,000 physicians. The center is made up of seven hospitals, more than 100 outpatient facilities, and two nursing centers. The Detroit Medical Center is the teaching and clinical research site for Wayne State, now one of the US's largest medical schools; it is also allied with the Barbara Ann Karmanos Cancer Institute and the Kresge Eye Institute.

**KEY COMPETITORS**
Henry Ford Health System
Trinity Health
William Beaumont Hospital

## DEVCON CONSTRUCTION INCORPORATED

690 Gibraltar Dr.
Milpitas, CA 95035
Phone: 408-942-8200
Fax: 408-262-2342
Web: www.devcon-const.com

CEO: Gary Filizetti
CFO: Bret Sisney
HR: Jennifer Cooke
Type: Private

2001 Sales: $1,351.0 million
1-Yr. Sales Change: 3.9%
Employees: 550
FYE: March 31

The dot-com deathwatch hasn't hurt Devcon Construction — it's still riding the coattails of Silicon Valley's business boom. The area's top commercial contractor, Devcon has built more than 35 million sq. ft. of office, industrial, and commercial space in Northern California. Founded in 1976, Devcon specializes in high-tech projects, including industrial research and development facilities for clients such as Cisco Systems and Silicon Graphics. Devcon also provides engineering, design/build, and interior design services. In addition to company facilities, other projects include hotels, restaurants, retail stores, and schools.

**KEY COMPETITORS**
DPR Construction
Rudolph & Sletten
Webcor Builders

## DFS GROUP LIMITED

First Market Tower
San Francisco, CA 94105
Phone: 415-977-2700
Fax: 415-977-4289
Web: www.dfsgroup.com

CEO: Edward J. Brennan
CFO: Caden Wang
HR: Peggy Tate
Type: Private

2000 Est. Sales: $1,800.0 mil.
1-Yr. Sales Change: 38.5%
Employees: 9,000
FYE: December 31

Some travelers prefer seeing the sights, but as DFS Group knows, some prefer seeing a good sale. The world's largest travel retailer, DFS (Duty Free Shoppers) runs 150 stores, located primarily in the Asia/Pacific region and on the US West Coast. The stores offer upscale brands of perfume, jewelry, liquor, tobacco, clothing, and other high-end goods. DFS is famous for its airport stores, but it also runs about 15 Galleria stores in downtown and resort locations, which feature in-store luxury boutiques and entertainment attractions. The company operates onboard cruise line retailers through its Miami Cruiselines Services unit. French conglomerate LVMH owns 61% of the company. Co-founder Robert Miller owns 38%.

**KEY COMPETITORS**
BAA
King Power
Richemont

 See pages 156–157 for a full profile of this company.

## DI GIORGIO CORPORATION

380 Middlesex Ave.
Carteret, NJ 07008
Phone: 732-541-5555
Fax: 732-541-3590
Web: www.whiterose.com

CEO: Richard B. Neff
CFO: Lawrence S. Grossman
HR: Jackie Simmons
Type: Private

2000 Sales: $1,488.1 million
1-Yr. Sales Change: 5.3%
Employees: 1,373
FYE: December 31

Di Giorgio delivers little apples (and other foods) to the Big Apple. Founded in 1920, the firm is a food wholesaler and distributor primarily in New York City, Long Island, and New Jersey. It offers more than 17,000 products to more than 1,800 stores ranging from independents and members of cooperatives to regional chains. (A&P accounts for about 25% of sales.) Although Di Giorgio distributes national brands, it also supplies frozen and refrigerated products under its White Rose brand, a name known in New York for well over a century. Di Giorgio co-chairman and CEO Richard Neff owns more than 99%, primarily through his sole general partnership in Rose Partners; co-chairman and president Stephen Bokser owns about 1%.

**KEY COMPETITORS**
C&S Wholesale
Krasdale Foods
Wakefern Food

## DICK CORPORATION

P.O. Box 10896
Pittsburgh, PA 15236
Phone: 412-384-1000
Fax: 412-384-1150
Web: www.dickcorp.com

CEO: David E. Dick
CFO: Jeffrey L. Konn
HR: Janet Love
Type: Private

2000 Sales: $1,050.0 million
1-Yr. Sales Change: 52.4%
Employees: 3,000
FYE: December 31

Without any help from Tom or Harry, Dick Corp., a general contracting, construction, and management firm, builds commercial, institutional, power, industrial, bridge, and highway projects nationwide. Dick International is expanding the company's foreign operations beyond the Caribbean into Europe, Latin America, and the Middle East. Major projects include PNC Park, the new home of the Pittsburgh Pirates, and a terminal at Ronald Reagan Washington National Airport. CEO David Dick and President Douglas Dick, part owners of the Pittsburgh Pirates, run the family-owned firm founded by their grandfather, Noble Dick, in 1922.

**KEY COMPETITORS**
Jacobs Engineering
Peter Kiewit Sons'
Turner Corporation


## DICK'S SPORTING GOODS, INC.

200 Industry Dr.
Pittsburgh, PA 15275
Phone: 412-809-0100
Fax: 412-809-0724
Web: www.dickssportinggoods.com

CEO: Ed Stack
CFO: Michael Hines
HR: Lynn Uram
Type: Private

2001 Est. Sales: $900.0 mil.
1-Yr. Sales Change: 0.0%
Employees: 9,100
FYE: February 28

See Dick's shoppers run, putt, dunk, dribble — and buy. Fast-growing Dick's Sporting Goods operates more than 100 stores in 20 states in the eastern US. Dick's stores average about 50,000 sq. ft. and contain smaller shops featuring sporting goods, apparel, and footwear for leisure pursuits ranging from football and golf to hunting and camping. The company also sells online. Dick Stack opened his first store in 1948 with $300 from his grandmother's cookie jar; the chain is now headed by his son, Ed. Dick's is owned by the Stack family and private investors, including French retailer Carrefour and the Vulcan Northwest venture capital firm.

**KEY COMPETITORS**
Foot Locker
Sports Authority
Wal-Mart


## DILLINGHAM CONSTRUCTION CORPORATION

5960 Inglewood Dr.
Pleasanton, CA 94588
Phone: 925-463-3300
Fax: 925-847-7029
Web: www.dillinghamconstruction.com

CEO: D. E. Sundgren
CFO: Larry L. Magelitz
HR: Bob Schwab
Type: Private

2001 Est. Sales: $1,258.0 mil.
1-Yr. Sales Change: 1.5%
Employees: 6,500
FYE: October 31

Dillingham Construction doesn't dillydally around when it comes to civil, commercial, industrial, and marine construction. Founded in the 1880s by Benjamin Dillingham to build a railroad through the swamps of Hawaii, the firm now completes projects internationally. It offers design/build, construction management, maintenance, and emergency response services for such projects as dams, highways, industrial plants, offices, housing, and rapid transit systems. It also makes hot mix asphalt, recycles pavement, and performs seismic retrofits. Subsidiaries include contractor Nielsen Dillingham and Dillingham Dredging. Japan's Shimizu Corporation owns a 45% stake in the firm; employees own the remaining 55%.

**KEY COMPETITORS**
Bechtel
DPR Construction
Peter Kiewit Sons'

## DISCOUNT TIRE CO.

14631 N. Scottsdale Rd.
Scottsdale, AZ 85254
Phone: 480-951-1938
Fax: 480-951-0206
Web: www.discounttire.com

CEO: Gary Van Brunt
CFO: Christian Roe
HR: Staci Adams
Type: Private

2000 Sales: $1,192.0 million
1-Yr. Sales Change: 15.6%
Employees: 8,987
FYE: December 31

Concerned about that upcoming "re-tire-ment"? Discount Tire Co., one of the largest independent tire dealers in the US, can provide several options. With about 420 stores in more than 15 states, the company sells leading brands (Michelin, Goodyear, Uniroyal) and private-label tires, as well as wheels and suspension products. Discount Tire operates mostly in the Midwest and Southwest and fixes flat tires for free, regardless of where they were bought. Some of the company's West Coast stores operate as America's Tire Co. because of a name conflict. Discount Tire also sells tires online through Discount Tire Direct. Owner Bruce Halle founded the company in 1960 with six tires — four of them recaps.

**KEY COMPETITORS**
Sears
TBC
Wal-Mart

## DISCOVERY COMMUNICATIONS, INC.

7700 Wisconsin Ave.
Bethesda, MD 20814
Phone: 301-986-0444
Fax: 301-771-4064
Web: www.discovery.com

CEO: John S. Hendricks
CFO: Gregory B. Durig
HR: Pandit Wright
Type: Joint venture

2000 Sales: $1,730.0 million
1-Yr. Sales Change: 23.6%
Employees: 4,000
FYE: December 31

Discover science and nature in the comfort of your living room with Discovery Communications (DCI). Shows such as *Walking With Dinosaurs* and *Raising the Mammoth* make the Discovery Channel one of the top-rated cable networks in the US. DCI owns other cable networks as well, including The Learning Channel, Travel Channel, and Animal Planet. Its programs reach more than 500 million subscribers in about 150 countries. DCI also has 170 Discovery Channel retail stores, and its Internet unit, Discovery.com (which it may take public), houses various nature and science Web sites. Liberty Media Corp. (49%), Cox Communications (25%), and Advance/Newhouse Communications (25%) own DCI.

**KEY COMPETITORS**
AOL Time Warner
Viacom
Walt Disney

 See pages 158–159 for a full profile of this company.

## DO IT BEST CORP.

6502 Nelson Rd.
Fort Wayne, IN 46801
Phone: 219-748-5300
Fax: 219-748-5620
Web: www.doitbest.com

CEO: Michael J. McClelland
CFO: Dave Dietz
HR: Nancy Harris
Type: Cooperative

2000 Sales: $2,440.0 million
1-Yr. Sales Change: 10.2%
Employees: 1,307
FYE: June 30

If you're building a house or fixing one up, you might as well Do it Best — at least, that's the hope of the hardware industry's third-largest cooperative. Trailing TruServ and Ace Hardware, Do it Best has about 4,400 member-owned stores in the US and 40 other countries. The stores stock some 70,000 hardware and building products, which are also sold online. (Its Web site offers tips for do-it-yourselfers and project advice as well.) The co-op, whose buying power enables members to get retail products at competitive prices, also offers unifying branding programs using the Do it Center and Do it Best names. Do it Best (formerly Hardware Wholesalers) began in 1945; it bought the Our Own Hardware co-op in 1998.

**KEY COMPETITORS**
Ace Hardware
Home Depot
TruServ

## DOANE PET CARE COMPANY

| | | |
|---|---|---|
| 210 Westwood Place South, Ste. 400 | CEO: Douglas J. Cahill | 2000 Sales: $891.9 million |
| Brentwood, TN 37027 | CFO: Philip K. Woodlief | 1-Yr. Sales Change: 15.7% |
| Phone: 615-373-7774 | HR: Debra J. Shecterle | Employees: 3,585 |
| Fax: 615-309-1187 | Type: Private | FYE: December 31 |

Doane Pet Care has no quibble with kibble. A leading maker of private-label dog and cat food both in North America and in Europe, the company makes dry and semi-moist foods, as well as soft treats and dog biscuits. Wal-Mart accounts for more than 40% of its sales; other customers include about 400 mass merchandisers, grocery and pet store chains, and farm and feed stores. Doane also makes products for other pet food companies. The highly leveraged company has expanded into Asia, Europe, and Latin America through several domestic and overseas acquisitions. Doane is owned by a number of investors and investment firms, including affiliates of J.P. Morgan Chase & Co. and Credit Suisse First Boston (USA).

**KEY COMPETITORS**
Heinz
Mars
Nestlé Purina PetCare

## DOCTOR'S ASSOCIATES INC.

| | | |
|---|---|---|
| 325 Bic Dr. | CEO: Frederick A. DeLuca | 2000 Sales: $4,720.0 million |
| Milford, CT 06460 | CFO: Carmela DeLuca | 1-Yr. Sales Change: 47.5% |
| Phone: 203-877-4281 | HR: Wendy Kopazna | Employees: 730 |
| Fax: 203-876-6695 | Type: Private | FYE: December 31 |
| Web: www.subway.com | | |

You don't have to go underground to catch this Subway. The sandwich chain, owned by Doctor's Associates, has more than 15,000 restaurants in 75 countries — second only to McDonald's in number of units. Virtually all Subway restaurants are franchises and offer such fare as hot and cold sandwiches, turkey wraps, and salads. Subways are located in freestanding buildings, as well as in airports, convenience stores, sports facilities, and other locations. Subway's heavy reliance on franchising hasn't been without controversy, and the company has weathered a number of legal skirmishes with disgruntled franchisees. President and CEO Fred DeLuca and chairman Peter Buck own the company they founded in 1965.

**KEY COMPETITORS**
Blimpie
McDonald's
TRICON

📖 See pages 160–161 for a full profile of this company.

## DOMINO'S INC.

| | | |
|---|---|---|
| 30 Frank Lloyd Wright Dr. | CEO: David A. Brandon | 2000 Sales: $1,166.1 million |
| Ann Arbor, MI 48106 | CFO: Harry J. Silverman | 1-Yr. Sales Change: 0.8% |
| Phone: 734-930-3030 | HR: Patricia A. Wilmot | Employees: 14,600 |
| Fax: 734-668-1946 | Type: Private | FYE: December 31 |
| Web: www.dominos.com | | |

No pawn in the pizza wars, Domino's is scrabbling away to ensure that success is in the cards. The world's #1 pizza delivery company and the #2 pizza chain overall (behind TRICON's Pizza Hut), Domino's Pizza has more than 7,100 stores (most are franchised) in about 65 countries. While the company built its reputation with speedy delivery, it also has begun to emphasize quality with its new Italian Originals line of Italian-spiced pizzas. Domino's founder Thomas Monaghan retired in 1998, selling his 93% stake to Boston-based investment firm Bain Capital. CEO David Brandon has initiated a restructuring involving closing or selling 142 stores and ousting about 100 managers.

**KEY COMPETITORS**
Little Caesar
Papa John's
Pizza Hut

📖 See pages 162–163 for a full profile of this company.

## DON MASSEY CADILLAC, INC.

| | | |
|---|---|---|
| 40475 Ann Arbor Rd. | CEO: Donald Massey | 2000 Sales: $922.0 million |
| Plymouth, MI 48170 | CFO: Mike Carusello | 1-Yr. Sales Change: (7.8%) |
| Phone: 734-453-7500 | HR: Lowell Peterson | Employees: — |
| Fax: 734-453-6680 | Type: Private | FYE: December 31 |
| Web: www.donmasseycadillac.com | | |

High rollers seeking a high-dollar ride can find one at Don Massey Cadillac. One of the nation's leaders in auto retail sales, Don Massey Cadillac has about 20 dealerships located throughout California, Colorado, Florida, Kentucky, Michigan, North Carolina, Tennessee, and Texas. The company sells new and used cars, primarily General Motors automobiles (Buicks, Cadillacs, Chevrolets, Oldsmobiles), but it also sells Hondas at its Nashville dealership. In addition, its Arapahoe, Colorado, location deals exclusively in used automobiles. Each location offers parts and service departments. Founded in 1961, Don Massey Cadillac is owned by president and CEO Don Massey.

**KEY COMPETITORS**
AutoNation
Hendrick Automotive
Phil Long Dealerships

## DOT FOODS, INC.

| | | |
|---|---|---|
| Route 99 South | CEO: Patrick F. Tracy | 2000 Sales: $1,107.0 million |
| Mount Sterling, IL 62353 | CFO: William Metzinger | 1-Yr. Sales Change: 0.0% |
| Phone: 217-773-4411 | HR: Mike Hulsen | Employees: 1,607 |
| Fax: 217-773-3321 | Type: Private | FYE: December 31 |
| Web: www.dotfoods.com | | |

Dot Foods, the largest food service redistributor in the US, was born in a station wagon that hauled dairy goods around as Associated Dairy Products. The company now runs more than 400 trucks (under the name Dot Transportation), which roll cross-country to receive groceries, flatware, serving ware, utensils, and janitorial supplies from food and equipment manufacturers and redistribute them to food processors and food service distributors. The company owns facilities in California, Georgia, Illinois, Maryland, and Missouri, and it serves customers in all 50 states. Dot has formed a subsidiary, edotfoods, to handle its e-commerce ventures. Robert and Dorothy Tracy founded the family-owned company in 1960.

**KEY COMPETITORS**
Alliant Exchange
Purity Wholesale Grocers
SYSCO

## DOW CORNING CORPORATION

| | | |
|---|---|---|
| 2200 W. Salzburg Rd. | CEO: Gary E. Anderson | 2000 Sales: $2,750.9 million |
| Midland, MI 48686 | CFO: Gifford E. Brown | 1-Yr. Sales Change: 5.7% |
| Phone: 989-496-4000 | HR: Burnett S. Kelly | Employees: 9,000 |
| Fax: 989-496-4393 | Type: Joint venture | FYE: December 31 |
| Web: www.dowcorning.com | | |

Cosmetic surgery has caused major health problems at Dow Corning. A 50-50 joint venture of chemical titan Dow Chemical and glass giant Corning, Dow Corning is operating under bankruptcy protection as a result of thousands of claims by women alleging the company's silicone-gel breast implants harmed them. Dow Corning produces more than 7,000 silicone-based products such as adhesives, insulating materials, and lubricants for aerospace, automotive, and electrical uses. Because silicone does not conduct electricity, it is also used in its hard polycrystalline form (silicon) as the material on which semiconductors are built. With manufacturing plants worldwide, the company sells about 60% of its products outside the US.

**KEY COMPETITORS**
BASF AG
ICI
3M

📖 See pages 164–165 for a full profile of this company.

## DPR CONSTRUCTION, INC.

| | | |
|---|---|---|
| 1450 Veterans Blvd. | CEO: Peter Nosler | 2000 Sales: $1,958.0 million |
| Redwood City, CA 94063 | CFO: Michael Hanf | 1-Yr. Sales Change: 63.2% |
| Phone: 650-474-1450 | HR: Jorinne Liberatore | Employees: 3,100 |
| Fax: 650-474-1451 | Type: Private | FYE: December 31 |
| Web: www.dprinc.com | | |

Building on its success, DPR Construction caters to microelectronics, biotechnology, pharmaceuticals, and health care companies. It operates primarily in the western US, and is one of Silicon Valley's biggest contractors. DPR also specializes in corporate office construction and entertainment projects (such as theme parks and studios); clients include Apple Computer, Disney, Kaiser Permanente, Pixar Animation, and WorldCom. The company was founded in 1990 when Douglas Woods, Peter Nosler, and Ronald Davidowski (the D, P, and R) left rival Rudolph & Sletten.

**KEY COMPETITORS**
Devcon Construction
Turner Corporation
Webcor Builders

## DR PEPPER/SEVEN UP BOTTLING GROUP, INC.

| | | |
|---|---|---|
| Sherry Ln. Ste. 500 | CEO: Jim L. Turner | 2000 Sales: $1,900.0 million |
| Dallas, TX 75225 | CFO: Holly Loworn | 1-Yr. Sales Change: 0.0% |
| Phone: 214-530-5000 | HR: Kellie Defratus | Employees: 8,000 |
| Fax: 214-530-5036 | Type: Private | FYE: December 31 |

Dr Pepper/Seven Up Bottling Group (DPSUBG) rings up sweet results for Cadbury Schweppes, the world's #3 soft drink firm. It is a leading bottler of soft drinks in the US, distributing in much of California, Texas, and a number of western states from 14 distribution centers. Besides the Dr Pepper and 7 UP brands (owned by Cadbury Schweppes), it also bottles other brands, including A&W Root Beer, Canada Dry, Hawaiian Punch, and RC Cola. DPSUBG was formed in 1999 when Dr Pepper Bottling Company of Texas and American Bottling merged. Cadbury Schweppes and The Carlyle Group own 40% and 53% of the company, respectively. CEO Jim Turner joined Dr Pepper Bottling Company of Texas in 1982 and built it by acquiring franchises.

**KEY COMPETITORS**
Coca-Cola Enterprises
Cott
Pepsi Bottling

## DREAMWORKS SKG

| | | |
|---|---|---|
| 1000 Flower St. | CEO: Steven Spielberg | 2000 Sales: $1,873.0 million |
| Glendale, CA 91201 | CFO: Ronald L. Nelson | 1-Yr. Sales Change: 50.8% |
| Phone: 818-733-7000 | HR: Heidi Gonggryp | Employees: 1,500 |
| Fax: 818-733-9918 | Type: Private | FYE: December 31 |
| Web: www.dreamworks.com | | |

DreamWorks SKG has moguls times three. Created in 1994 by principal partners Steven Spielberg (famed film director/producer), Jeffrey Katzenberg (former Disney film executive and animation guru), and David Geffen (recording industry maven), DreamWorks has established itself in the entertainment industry after a rocky start. The company produces films (Best Picture winner *Gladiator, Shrek*), TV shows (*Spin City, The Job, Undeclared*), and music, including the soundtracks to DreamWorks films and record deals with artists such as Henry Rollins. DreamWorks has pulled out of the GameWorks video arcade business it started with SEGA and Universal Studios. Microsoft co-founder Paul Allen is also a major investor in DreamWorks.

**KEY COMPETITORS**
Fox Entertainment
Viacom
Walt Disney

 See pages 166–167 for a full profile of this company.

## DUCHOSSOIS INDUSTRIES, INC.

845 Larch Ave.
Elmhurst, IL 60126
Phone: 630-279-3600
Fax: 630-530-6091
Web: www.duchossoisindustries.com

CEO: Craig J. Duchossois
CFO: Robert L. Fealy
HR: Melody Ditori
Type: Private

2000 Est. Sales: $1,200.0 mil.
1-Yr. Sales Change: (20.0%)
Employees: 7,000
FYE: December 31

Business is no longer a horse race for Duchossois Industries. The former owner of Chicago's famed Arlington International Racecourse, Duchossois Industries sold its interests in the track to Churchill Downs Incorporated. Through its subsidiaries, the company makes garage door openers and keyless entry systems (Chamberlain Group). The family of chairman Richard Duchossois owns Duchossois Industries. As a result of the sale of Arlington International Racecourse, Richard Duchossois now holds a 30% interest in Churchill Downs. The company sold its railroad car unit (Thrall) to Trinity Industries.

**KEY COMPETITORS**
GATX
Johnstown America
Stanley Works

## DUKE ENERGY FIELD SERVICES CORPORATION

370 17th St., Ste. 900
Denver, CO 80202
Phone: 303-595-3331
Fax: 303-595-0480
Web: www.defieldservices.com

CEO: Jim W. Mogg
CFO: John Jackson
HR: David Goode
Type: Private

2000 Sales: $9,093.4 million
1-Yr. Sales Change: 162.9%
Employees: 3,400
FYE: December 31

Duke Energy Field Services (DEFS) is a midstream maven. Formed when Duke Energy and Phillips Petroleum combined their gas gathering, processing, and marketing operations, the company is one of the largest midstream natural gas operators in the US, with 57,000 miles of gathering pipeline and 71 processing plants. DEFS also owns several NGL (natural gas liquids) processing facilities and is the US's largest NGL producer at 400,000 barrels per day. The company sells about 40% of its NGL production to Phillips under a long-term contract. Duke Energy owns about 70% of DEFS; Phillips owns 30%. DEFS is the general partner of TEPPCO Partners, L.P., which owns a network of refined products and crude oil pipelines.

**KEY COMPETITORS**
Dynegy
Enterprise
Koch

## DUKE UNIVERSITY

Allen Bldg, Ste. 211
Durham, NC 27708
Phone: 919-684-8111
Fax: 919-684-3200
Web: www.duke.edu

CEO: Nannerl O. "Nan" Keohane
CFO: Tallman Trask III
HR: H. Clint Davidson Jr.
Type: School

2000 Sales: $2,200.0 million
1-Yr. Sales Change: 5.8%
Employees: 20,020
FYE: June 30

The devils at Duke University shouldn't feel blue: *U.S. News & World Report* ranks the school among the top 10 US universities. Venerable Duke is home to almost 12,000 Blue Devils attending classes in its nine schools and colleges, including the Trinity School of Art and Sciences, the Fuqua School of Business, and the Edmund T. Pratt Jr. School of Engineering. Both its law school and medical school are highly regarded nationally. The private institution has an endowment of more than $1.3 billion. Founded in 1838 as Trinity College, Duke adopted its present name in 1924 after American Tobacco Co. magnate James Duke established the Duke Endowment.

## DUNAVANT ENTERPRISES, INC.

3797 New Getwell Rd.
Memphis, TN 38118
Phone: 901-369-1500
Fax: 901-369-1608
Web: www.dunavant.com

CEO: William B. Dunavant Jr.
CFO: —
HR: Cheryl Cooley
Type: Private

2001 Sales: $1,030.0 million
1-Yr. Sales Change: 0.8%
Employees: 2,400
FYE: June 30

King Cotton is alive and well in Memphis. Homegrown Dunavant Enterprises is one of the largest cotton traders in the world. The company was founded in 1960 by William Dunavant, his son Billy (who is allergic to cotton), and Samuel T. Reeves. (The elder Dunavant died shortly after the founding, and Reeves left in 1995 to form Pinnacle Trading.) The company, which grew by selling aggressively to China and the Soviet Union, maintains offices in Asia, Australia, Europe, Mexico, South America, the former Soviet Union, and the southern US. The company's other business interests include cotton trucking, warehousing, and real estate. Dunavant Enterprises is owned by the Dunavant family and company employees.

**KEY COMPETITORS**
Calcot
Cargill
Plains Cotton


## DUNN INDUSTRIES, INC.

929 Holmes
Kansas City, MO 64106
Phone: 816-474-8600
Fax: 816-391-2510

CEO: Terrence P. Dunn
CFO: Gordon Lansford
HR: —
Type: Private

2000 Sales: $1,311.0 million
1-Yr. Sales Change: 23.3%
Employees: 3,000
FYE: December 31

Although its beginnings date back to 1924, this company is far from done. Family-owned Dunn Industries owns construction companies, including flagship J. E. Dunn Construction, Witcher Construction, and Dunn Industrial Group. Dunn provides construction and program management, as well as designs and builds institutional, commercial, and industrial projects. Long focusing on projects in western and midwestern states, the company has expanded into the Southeast through its acquisition of Atlanta-based general contractor R.J. Griffin. J.E. Dunn is construction manager for Kansas City-based Sprint's world headquarters; at 4 million sq. ft. of office space it's the largest construction project ever in the Midwest.

**KEY COMPETITORS**
Bechtel
Foster Wheeler
Turner Corporation


## DYNCORP

11710 Plaza America Dr.
Reston, VA 20190
Phone: 703-261-5000
Fax: 703-261-4800
Web: www.dyncorp.com

CEO: Paul V. Lombardi
CFO: Patrick C. FitzPatrick
HR: James Campbell
Type: Private

2000 Sales: $1,809.1 million
1-Yr. Sales Change: 34.5%
Employees: 20,842
FYE: December 31

DynCorp is more than good enough for government work. One of the largest employee-owned high-tech companies in the US, DynCorp offers a variety of technical and professional services, including enterprise management, consulting, information technology, outsourcing, training, and engineering services. The US government accounts for 98% of sales. Founded in 1946, DynCorp was taken private in a 1987 buyout led by company management. Employees own about 70% of the company; an additional 10% is held in an employee retirement trust. DynCorp has sold its Management Resources unit to consultant TekInsight.com (which has changed its name to DynTek) in exchange for a 40% stake in that company.

**KEY COMPETITORS**
EDS
SAIC

## THE DYSON-KISSNER-MORAN CORPORATION

| | | |
|---|---|---|
| 565 5th Ave., 4th Fl. | CEO: Robert R. Dyson | 2001 Est. Sales: $850.0 mil. |
| New York, NY 10017 | CFO: M. J. Zilinskas | 1-Yr. Sales Change: 6.3% |
| Phone: 212-661-4600 | HR: — | Employees: 4,600 |
| Fax: 212-986-7169 | Type: Private | FYE: January 31 |

Privately held investment firm Dyson-Kissner-Moran, through takeovers and strategic acquisitions, has diversified its holdings to include businesses from manufacturing to arts and crafts. The firm typically uses its own capital to fund acquisitions and usually leaves them intact after the purchase. Founded in the mid-1950s, its purchases have included Household Finance and electronic-parts maker Kearney-National. Dyson-Kissner-Moran is controlled by the family of co-founder Charles Dyson (prominent philanthropist, LBO pioneer, and #5 on Richard Nixon's political enemies list), who died in 1997. His son Robert is the firm's chairman and CEO.

**KEY COMPETITORS**
Haas Wheat
Hicks, Muse
KKR


## EAGLE-PICHER INDUSTRIES, INC.

| | | |
|---|---|---|
| 250 E. 5th St., Ste. 500 | CEO: — | 2000 Sales: $837.6 million |
| Cincinnati, OH 45201 | CFO: Bert Iedema | 1-Yr. Sales Change: (8.3%) |
| Phone: 513-721-7010 | HR: David E. Wilson | Employees: 5,400 |
| Fax: 513-721-2341 | Type: Private | FYE: November 30 |
| Web: www.epcorp.com | | |

From filters to forklifts, Eagle-Picher Industries (EPI) makes products for the automotive, aerospace, construction, telecommunications, pharmaceutical, and food and beverage industries. EPI's automotive group leads in sales (58%) with products that include precision-machined components, rubber-coated parts, and fluid systems. The company's Technologies Segment makes batteries for satellites, launch vehicles, and missiles, as well as boron for nuclear applications. Its Machinery Segment makes forklifts and elevating wheel tractor scrapers (exclusively for Caterpillar), and its Materials Segment produces diatomaceous earth and perlite filter aids. Dutch investment firm Granaria Holdings owns EPI.

**KEY COMPETITORS**
Federal-Mogul
Linamar
Newcor


## E. & J. GALLO WINERY

| | | |
|---|---|---|
| 600 Yosemite Blvd. | CEO: James E. Coleman | 2000 Est. Sales: $1,650.0 mil. |
| Modesto, CA 95354 | CFO: Tony Youga | 1-Yr. Sales Change: 8.9% |
| Phone: 209-341-3111 | HR: Mike Chase | Employees: 3,600 |
| Fax: 209-341-3569 | Type: Private | FYE: December 31 |
| Web: www.gallo.com | | |

Let them drink wine! E. & J. Gallo Winery brings merlot to the masses. The world's largest wine maker makes about 25% of the wine sold in the US, thanks in part to its inexpensive jug brands Carlo Rossi and Gallo as well as the fortified Thunderbird brand. The vintner cultivates 3,000-plus acres in Sonoma County, California; makes its own labels and bottles; and is the leading US wine exporter. It imports and sells Italian wine Ecco Domani and is a leading brandy producer. Gallo once only sold wine in the low-to-moderate price range, but has successfully expanded into premium wines such as Turning Leaf and Gossamer Bay, which don't have the Gallo name on the label. The Gallo family owns the vintner.

**KEY COMPETITORS**
Beringer Blass
Constellation Brands
Robert Mondavi

 See pages 168–169 for a full profile of this company.

## EARLE M. JORGENSEN COMPANY

3050 E. Birch St.
Brea, CA 92821
Phone: 714-579-8823
Fax: 714-577-3784
Web: www.emjmetals.com

CEO: Maurice S. Nelson Jr.
CFO: William Johnson
HR: Inger Dickinson
Type: Private

2001 Sales: $1,059.7 million
1-Yr. Sales Change: 12.9%
Employees: 2,010
FYE: March 31

Earle M. Jorgensen Company (EMJ) is one of the US's largest independent steel distributors. The company sells tubing, pipes, and bar, as well as structural, plate, and sheet metal products. EMJ makes its products from carbon steel, alloy steel, stainless steel, and aluminum. It markets to the automotive, agriculture, chemical, medical, oil, defense, food, petrochemical, and machinery-manufacturing industries. The company operates more than 32 service centers, a cutting center, and a tube-honing facility. Employees own about 30% of EMJ; investment firm Kelso & Company owns most of the rest.

**KEY COMPETITORS**
Co-Steel
LTV
United States Steel

## EBSCO INDUSTRIES INC.

5724 Hwy. 280 East
Birmingham, AL 35242
Phone: 205-991-6600
Fax: 205-995-1636
Web: www.ebscoind.com

CEO: James T. Stephens
CFO: Richard L. Bozzelli
HR: Pat R. Sisbarro
Type: Private

2001 Sales: $1,375.0 million
1-Yr. Sales Change: 0.0%
Employees: 4,500
FYE: June 30

Is there anything EBSCO doesn't do? EBSCO Industries (short for Elton B. Stephens Company) provides fulfillment, sales, telemarketing, and promotional services to magazine publishers. The company is also a commercial printer and academic and educational publisher, and it serves the library market with online information resource operations. In addition, EBSCO makes retail point-of-purchase displays, promotional products, fishing lures, rifles, and specialty office and computer furniture. It has 80 subsidiaries in more than 20 countries. The company was founded by Elton Stephens (chairman) and his wife, Alys, in 1944; the Stephens family owns EBSCO.

**KEY COMPETITORS**
Quebecor
Reed Elsevier
RoweCom

 See pages 170–171 for a full profile of this company.

## EBY-BROWN COMPANY

280 W. Shuman Blvd., Ste. 280
Naperville, IL 60566
Phone: 630-778-2800
Fax: 630-778-2830
Web: www.eby-brown.com

CEO: Thomas G. Wake
CFO: Mark Smetana
HR: Steve Bundy
Type: Private

2000 Sales: $3,400.0 million
1-Yr. Sales Change: 22.6%
Employees: 2,011
FYE: December 31

Eby-Brown makes its money on vices such as munchies and nicotine. The company is a leading supplier of more than 11,000 name-brand products, including tobacco, candy, snacks, health and beauty aids, and general merchandise, to convenience stores. The company's nine distribution centers serve 28 midwestern and southeastern states and more than 25,000 stores, including the Speedway and SuperAmerica chains owned by Marathon Ashland Petroleum. Eby-Brown also has a marketing division that offers its customers advertising and promotion services. Co-CEOs Tom and Dick Wake, the sons of William Wake (who started the company more than 100 years ago), own and operate Eby-Brown.

**KEY COMPETITORS**
GSC Enterprises
McLane
Spartan Stores

## THE EDWARD J. DEBARTOLO CORPORATION

7620 Market St.
Youngstown, OH 44512
Phone: 330-965-2000
Fax: 330-965-2077

CEO: Marie Denise DeBartolo York
CFO: Lynn E. Davenport
HR: Linda Pearce
Type: Private

2000 Est. Sales: $250.0 mil.
1-Yr. Sales Change: (1.6%)
Employees: 4,000
FYE: June 30

Survey says . . . lawsuit! *Family Feud* is the name of the game at The Edward J. DeBartolo Corporation. The siblings who owned the parent company of the San Francisco 49ers, a racetrack, real estate interests, and an 11% stake in Simon Property Group have been fighting over the business for some time. After former CEO Eddie DeBartolo Jr. pleaded guilty in 1998 to a felony charge for failing to report wrongdoing, his sister, chairman Denise DeBartolo York, took over the firm and sued her brother (for debt owed to the company). He countersued, and they eventually reached a settlement to divide the firm's assets (she got the company name, the 49ers, and the racetrack; he got real estate and the Simon Property Group stock).

**KEY COMPETITORS**
Fair Grounds
Harrah's Entertainment
St. Louis Rams

 See pages 172–173 for a full profile of this company.


## EMORY UNIVERSITY

1380 S. Oxford Rd. SE
Atlanta, GA 30322
Phone: 404-727-6123
Fax: 404-727-0646
Web: www.emory.edu

CEO: William M. Chace
CFO: John L. Temple
HR: Alice R. Miller
Type: School

2001 Sales: $1,800.0 million
1-Yr. Sales Change: 2.3%
Employees: 19,000
FYE: August 31

"Have a Coke and a smile" means a little more to Emory University than it does to the rest of the world. The school, which boasts more than 11,400 students and 2,500 faculty members, was transformed from Emory College to Emory University in 1915 by a $1 million donation from Coca-Cola Company owner Asa Candler. Today, about 40% of Emory's endowment consists of Coca-Cola stock. The university offers undergraduate, graduate, and professional degrees in a wide range of fields, including medicine, theology, law, nursing, and business. Founded in 1836, the private university also maintains several research centers and operates a joint venture with HCA to offer managed health care.


## EMPIRE HEALTHCHOICE, INC.

11 W. 42nd St.
New York, NY 10036
Phone: 212-476-1000
Fax: 212-476-1281
Web: www.empirehealthcare.com

CEO: Michael A. Stocker
CFO: John W. Remshard
HR: Ronald Mason
Type: Not-for-profit

2000 Sales: $4,240.0 million
1-Yr. Sales Change: 25.9%
Employees: 6,500
FYE: December 31

Empire HealthChoice, better known by its popular name Empire Blue Cross and Blue Shield, serves more than 4 million customers in eastern New York, making it a leading health care provider in its market. It offers indemnity coverage and managed care products, including HMO, PPO, and EPO (exclusive provider organization offering no out-of-network benefits) plans. Empire also operates for-profit subsidiaries, including accident and health insurance provider Empire HealthChoice Assurance and Empire HealthChoice HMO. Empire has announced plans to convert to for-profit status, but says it will form a charitable foundation to help care for New York's poor and uninsured.

**KEY COMPETITORS**
Aetna
Health Insurance of New York
Oxford Health Plans

 See pages 174–175 for a full profile of this company.

## ENCYCLOPAEDIA BRITANNICA, INC.

| | | |
|---|---|---|
| 310 S. Michigan Ave. | CEO: Ilan Yeshua | 2000 Est. Sales: $275.0 mil. |
| Chicago, IL 60604 | CFO: Richard Anderson | 1-Yr. Sales Change: (1.4%) |
| Phone: 312-347-7000 | HR: William J. Bowe | Employees: 300 |
| Fax: 312-347-7399 | Type: Private | FYE: September 30 |
| Web: corporate.britannica.com | | |

Encyclopaedia Britannica thinks it knows everything, and it probably does. The company publishes reference works including its flagship 32-volume *Encyclopaedia Britannica* (first published in 1768), *The Annals of America,* and *Great Books of the Western World.* It also publishes a variety of dictionaries through its Merriam-Webster subsidiary (*Merriam Webster's Collegiate Dictionary, Merriam Webster's Biographical Dictionary*), which the firm wants to sell to raise capital. Most of the company's products are available online, as well as on CD-ROM and DVD. Swiss financier Jacob Safra owns the company.

**KEY COMPETITORS**
Berkshire Hathaway
Grolier
Microsoft

 See pages 176–177 for a full profile of this company.

## ENTERPRISE RENT-A-CAR

| | | |
|---|---|---|
| 600 Corporate Park Dr. | CEO: Andrew C. Taylor | 2001 Sales: $6,300.0 million |
| St. Louis, MO 63105 | CFO: John T. O'Connell | 1-Yr. Sales Change: 12.5% |
| Phone: 314-512-5000 | HR: Ed Adams | Employees: 50,000 |
| Fax: 314-512-4706 | Type: Private | FYE: July 31 |
| Web: www.enterprise.com | | |

Enterprise Rent-A-Car has a pickup line that gets noticed. The company, which offers to ferry customers to the rental office, is the largest car rental firm in the US. With about 500,000 cars in its rental fleet, Enterprise operates in the US, Canada, Germany, Ireland, and the UK. The company targets customers whose own cars are in the shop or who need a rental for short trips; it has also begun serving the airport market. Enterprise subsidiaries lease vehicles, manage fleets for other companies, and sell cars and trucks. Controlled by founder Jack Taylor and his family, Enterprise has spun off its non-automotive operations (prison supplies, hotel amenities, balloons, footwear, a golf course) as Centric Group.

**KEY COMPETITORS**
AutoNation
Budget Group
Hertz

 See pages 178–179 for a full profile of this company.

## EPIX HOLDINGS CORPORATION

| | | |
|---|---|---|
| 3710 Corporex Park Dr | CEO: Steve Rosenthal | 2000 Sales: $1,300.0 million |
| Tampa, FL 33619 | CFO: Thomas S. Taylor | 1-Yr. Sales Change: 30.0% |
| Phone: 813-664-0404 | HR: Melanie Maskel | Employees: 450 |
| Fax: 813-621-6816 | Type: Private | FYE: December 31 |
| Web: www.pti-info.com | | |

When it comes to epic human resources concerns, more and more employers are using EPIX solutions. EPIX Holdings (formerly Payroll Transfers) is a leading professional employer organization (PEO) that provides human resources management for its clients' permanent full-time workers. The company's services include insurance, tax administration, employee benefits programs, regulatory compliance, and payroll processing. The company provides administrative services for some 48,000 employees from more than 3,000 small and midsized businesses throughout the US. EPIX, which was founded in 1989, is backed by Texas financier Robert Bass' Keystone group, among other investment firms.

**KEY COMPETITORS**
Administaff
Gevity HR
TeamStaff

## EQUILON ENTERPRISES LLC

| | | |
|---|---|---|
| 1100 Louisiana Dr. | CEO: Rob J. Routs | 2000 Sales: $50,010.0 million |
| Houston, TX 77210 | CFO: Ronald B. Blakely | 1-Yr. Sales Change: 70.1% |
| Phone: 713-277-7000 | HR: Bruce Culpepper | Employees: 13,000 |
| Fax: 713-277-7856 | Type: Joint venture | FYE: December 31 |
| Web: www.equilonmotivaequiva.com | | |

For oil refiner and marketer Equilon Enterprises and its sister company, Motiva, East is East and West is West, and never the twain shall meet. Equilon, which was formed in 1998, operates four refineries in the western US with a total capacity of 480,000 barrels a day, and it markets petroleum products at 9,000 Shell and Texaco outlets in the West and Midwest. Motiva does the same in the eastern US. Together Motiva and Equilon form the #1 US gasoline retailing business. Shell Oil owns 56% of Equilon, and ChevronTexaco owns 44%. In order to gain regulatory clearance to be acquired by Chevron, Texaco agreed in 2001 to sell its stakes in Equilon (to Shell) and Motiva (to Shell and Saudi Aramco).

**KEY COMPETITORS**
7-Eleven
BP
Exxon Mobil

## EQUISTAR CHEMICALS, LP

| | | |
|---|---|---|
| 1221 McKinney St., Ste. 700 | CEO: Dan F. Smith | 2000 Sales: $7,495.0 million |
| Houston, TX 77010 | CFO: Kelvin R. Collard | 1-Yr. Sales Change: 37.9% |
| Phone: 713-652-7300 | HR: John A. Hollinshead | Employees: 3,700 |
| Fax: 713-652-4151 | Type: Partnership | FYE: December 31 |
| Web: www.equistarchem.com | | |

Credit good chemistry, but Equistar Chemical — a partnership of Lyondell (about 40%), Millennium Chemicals, and Occidental Petroleum (about 30% each) — is one of the world's largest producers of ethylene and its derivatives, olefins, and polymers. Equistar's two segments, petrochemicals (75% of sales) and polymers (25%), make products for use in the manufacture of items ranging from food and beverage packaging to carpet facing, paints, wire insulation, and cleaners. Through a joint venture with DuPont, the company also produces ethylene glycol (antifreeze, polyester fibers, resins, and films). Millennium was trying to sell its share of Equistar but stopped when it received no offers.

**KEY COMPETITORS**
Dow Chemical
ExxonMobil Chemical
Huntsman

## EQUITY GROUP INVESTMENTS, L.L.C.

| | | |
|---|---|---|
| 2 N. Riverside Plaza, Ste. 600 | CEO: Sheli Z. Rosenberg | Sales: — |
| Chicago, IL 60606 | CFO: Greg Stegimen | 1-Yr. Sales Change: — |
| Phone: 312-454-1800 | HR: Dan Harris | Employees: — |
| Fax: 312-454-0610 | Type: Private | FYE: December 31 |

Billionaire Sam Zell's Equity Group Investments is the parent of affiliates involved in real estate, restaurants, cruise ships, and other ventures. Zell has made his niche — and a lot of money — by purchasing distressed properties and turning them into profitable investments (for which he earned the nickname "Grave Dancer"). Zell's REIT portfolio makes him the US's largest owner of property leased by manufactured homeowners (Manufactured Home Communities), office buildings (Equity Office Properties Trust), and apartments (Equity Residential Properties Trust). As bargains dry up in the US, Zell is heading overseas to buy real estate and companies with his Equity International Properties fund.

**KEY COMPETITORS**
Blackstone Group
Goldman Sachs
Thomas Lee

 See pages 180–181 for a full profile of this company.

## ERGON, INC.

| | | |
|---|---|---|
| 2829 Lakeland Dr. | CEO: Leslie Lampton Sr. | 2000 Est. Sales: $1,900.0 mil. |
| Jackson, MS 39208 | CFO: Kathy Stone | 1-Yr. Sales Change: 35.7% |
| Phone: 601-933-3000 | HR: Lance Maserov | Employees: 2,000 |
| Fax: 601-933-3355 | Type: Private | FYE: December 31 |
| Web: www.ergon.com | | |

That'll work! Ergon (named after the Greek word for work) operates in six major business segments: asphalt and emulsions; information technology; oil and gas; real estate; refining and marketing; and transportation and terminaling. In addition to providing a range of petroleum products and services, the company also manufactures and markets computer technology services and sells road maintenance systems, including emulsions and special coatings.

**KEY COMPETITORS**
Ferrellgas Partners
Koch
Marathon Oil

## ERNST & YOUNG INTERNATIONAL

| | | |
|---|---|---|
| 787 7th Ave. | CEO: William L. Kimsey | 2001 Sales: $10,000.0 million |
| New York, NY 10019 | CFO: Hilton Dean | 1-Yr. Sales Change: 5.3% |
| Phone: 212-773-3000 | HR: Lewis A. Ting | Employees: 88,000 |
| Fax: 212-773-6350 | Type: Partnership | FYE: June 30 |
| Web: www.eyi.com | | |

Ernst & Young International, one of the Big Five accounting firms, offers accounting services from roughly 700 offices in more than 130 countries. In addition to corporate audit services, Ernst & Young provides internal audit, accounting advisory, online security, and risk management services. Its tax practice, one of the world's largest, helps its international clients cope with the tax laws of many countries. The firm also offers a number of corporate finance, health, and legal services. Pressure from regulators to divorce accountancy from consultancy resulted in Ernst & Young's sale of its consultancy business, the first of the Big Five to do so; French company Cap Gemini bought it.

**KEY COMPETITORS**
Deloitte Touche Tohmatsu
KPMG
PricewaterhouseCoopers

 **See pages 182–183 for a full profile of this company.**

## ESPN, INC.

| | | |
|---|---|---|
| 935 Middle St. | CEO: George W. Bodenheimer | 2000 Sales: $2,600.0 million |
| Bristol, CT 06010 | CFO: Christine Driessen | 1-Yr. Sales Change: — |
| Phone: 860-766-2000 | HR: — | Employees: 2,500 |
| Fax: 860-766-2213 | Type: Joint venture | FYE: September 30 |
| Web: espn.go.com | | |

ESPN is a superstar of the sports broadcasting world. The company is the leading cable sports broadcaster with six domestic networks — including its flagship ESPN, ESPN2 (sporting events and news), ESPN Classic (historical sports footage), and ESPNEWS (24-hour news and information) — that reach more than 85 million US homes. It also reaches another 110 million homes worldwide with its ESPN International unit. In addition, ESPN creates content for radio and operates one of the most popular sports sites on the Internet. ESPN also has lent its name to a magazine and a chain of eight sports-themed restaurants. Founded in 1979, ESPN is 80% owned by Walt Disney (through ABC); Hearst has a 20% stake.

**KEY COMPETITORS**
CBS
Fox Entertainment
Turner Broadcasting

## EXPRESS PERSONNEL SERVICES

| | | |
|---|---|---|
| 6300 NW Expwy. | CEO: Robert A. Funk | 2000 Sales: $916.0 million |
| Oklahoma City, OK 73132 | CFO: Thomas Richards | 1-Yr. Sales Change: — |
| Phone: 405-840-5000 | HR: Larry Ferree | Employees: 262,000 |
| Fax: 405-773-6401 | Type: Private | FYE: December 31 |
| Web: www.expresspersonnel.com | | |

When you need a worker fast, Express Personnel Services delivers. The professional staffing company provides work for some 260,000 employees from more than 400 offices in the US and six other countries (Belarus, Canada, Russia, South Africa, the UK, and the Ukraine). As well as temporary staffing, its divisions provide professional placement and contract staffing through Express Professional Staffing and Robert William James & Associates. Management and labor relations services are offered through Express Consulting Services. The company is owned by founder and CEO Robert Funk, who also owns the Oklahoma City Blazers hockey team and Express Ranches, one of the nation's largest cattle breeders.

**KEY COMPETITORS**
Adecco
Kelly Services
Manpower

## FARMLAND INDUSTRIES, INC.

| | | |
|---|---|---|
| 12200 N. Ambassador Dr. | CEO: Robert W. Honse | 2001 Sales: $11,763.4 million |
| Kansas City, MO 64163 | CFO: John F. Berardi | 1-Yr. Sales Change: (3.9%) |
| Phone: 816-713-7000 | HR: Holly D. McCoy | Employees: 14,500 |
| Fax: 816-713-6323 | Type: Cooperative | FYE: August 31 |
| Web: www.farmland.com | | |

Farmland Industries provides its members with nearly everything they need — except for rain. Farmland is the #1 agricultural cooperative in the US and is a competitor in agribusiness worldwide, exporting products (mainly grain) to about 60 countries. It is a major beef packer in the US and also a top producer of pork products. Farmland Industries is owned by about 1,700 local co-ops that are made up of about 600,000 farmers in the US, Canada, and Mexico. The co-op provides farmers with feed, fertilizer, and pesticides; it also processes, stores, and markets their crops and livestock.

**KEY COMPETITORS**
Cargill
Cenex Harvest States
IBP

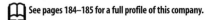 See pages 184–185 for a full profile of this company.

## THE FAULKNER ORGANIZATION

| | | |
|---|---|---|
| 4437 Street Rd. | CEO: Hank Faulkner | 2000 Sales: $821.0 million |
| Trevose, PA 19053 | CFO: Bill Febold | 1-Yr. Sales Change: 1.8% |
| Phone: 215-364-3980 | HR: Walt Huber | Employees: — |
| Fax: 215-364-0706 | Type: Private | FYE: December 31 |
| Web: www.faulknerfamily.com | | |

The sound and the fury of Buicks moving off the lot is coming from The Faulkner Organization, one of the Delaware Valley's largest-volume automotive dealers. The company operates about 20 automobile dealerships in Pennsylvania and Delaware. Its domestic car franchises include Pontiac, Buick, GMC, Cadillac, Ford, Oldsmobile, Chevrolet, Mercury, and Saturn; its import franchises sell Toyotas, Hondas, Mitsubishis, and Mazdas. In addition to new and used cars, the company sells auto parts and offers automotive repairs, car financing, fleet services, and credit life insurance. Founded in 1932 by Henry Faulkner, the company is still owned and operated by the Faulkner family.

**KEY COMPETITORS**
Brown Automotive
Pacifico
Planet Automotive Group

## FEDERAL RESERVE BANK OF NEW YORK

33 Liberty St.
New York, NY 10045
Phone: 212-720-5000
Fax: 212-720-7459
Web: www.newyorkfed.org

CEO: William J. McDonough
CFO: Jamie B. Stewart Jr.
HR: Robert C. Scrivani
Type: Member-owned banking authority

2000 Sales: $13,456.0 million
1-Yr. Sales Change: 16.2%
Employees: 3,400
FYE: December 31

The Federal Reserve Bank of New York is the largest in the Federal Reserve System, which oversees US banks. One of 12 regional banks, it issues currency, clears money transfers, and lends to banks in its district. In addition to the duties which it shares with other Reserve Banks, the New York Fed trades US government securities to regulate the money supply, intervenes on foreign exchange markets, and stores monetary gold for foreign central banks, governments, and agencies. The New York Fed's district is relatively small (made up of New York, Puerto Rico, the US Virgin Islands, and parts of New Jersey and Connecticut), but the bank is the largest in the Federal Reserve System in assets and volume of transactions.

## FEDERAL RESERVE SYSTEM

20th St. and Constitution Ave., NW
Washington, DC 20551
Phone: 202-452-3000
Fax: —
Web: www.federalreserve.gov

CEO: Alan Greenspan
CFO: —
HR: —
Type: Government agency

2000 Sales: $197.7 million
1-Yr. Sales Change: (11.1%)
Employees: 23,056
FYE: December 31

The Federal Reserve System, made famous by the bullish stock market of the 1990s, sets discount interest rates (the rate at which its member banks may borrow), which in turn influences the pace of lending and — many believe — the pace of the economy itself. The Fed, as it is known, through a nationwide network of 12 banks representing 12 regions, also regulates and examines US banks, clears money transfers, issues currency, and buys or sells government securities to regulate the money supply. Through its powerful New York bank, the Fed conducts the US's foreign currency transactions, buys or sells on the world market to support the dollar's value, and stores gold for foreign governments and international agencies.

 **See pages 186–187 for a full profile of this company.**

## FEDERATED INSURANCE COMPANIES

121 E. Park Sq.
Owatonna, MN 55060
Phone: 507-455-5200
Fax: 507-455-5452
Web: www.federatedinsurance.com

CEO: Al Annexstad
CFO: Raymond R. Stawarz
HR: Bryan Brose
Type: Mutual company

2000 Sales: $1,153.2 million
1-Yr. Sales Change: 8.6%
Employees: 3,100
FYE: December 31

Federated Insurance is a mutual company with a specific focus. Consistent with its century-old roots as an insurer for Minnesota farm implement dealers, Federated offers group life and health coverage, as well as workers' compensation, automobile, property/casualty, retirement planning, and individual life insurance to a narrow niche of businesses — auto and tire dealers, service stations, building contractors, equipment dealers, machine shops, and printers. Operating nationwide, Federated Insurance markets its policies directly and through an independent sales force.

**KEY COMPETITORS**
Blue Cross
CNA Financial
State Farm

## FELD ENTERTAINMENT, INC.

| | | |
|---|---|---|
| 8607 Westwood Center Dr. | CEO: Kenneth Feld | 2001 Est. Sales: $776.0 mil. |
| Vienna, VA 22182 | CFO: Mike Ruch | 1-Yr. Sales Change: 15.0% |
| Phone: 703-448-4000 | HR: Kirk McCoy | Employees: 2,500 |
| Fax: 703-448-4100 | Type: Private | FYE: January 31 |
| Web: www.feldentertainment.com | | |

A lot of clowning around has helped Feld Entertainment become one of the largest live entertainment producers in the world. The company entertains some 10 million people each year through its centerpiece, Ringling Bros. and Barnum & Bailey Circus, which visits about 90 locations. It also produces the upscale Barnum's Kaleidoscape, which features acrobats and aerialists instead of elephants and clowns. In addition, Feld produces several touring ice shows, including Disney On Ice shows such as *Beauty and the Beast* and *Toy Story*, and it owns the Siegfried & Roy show in Las Vegas. Chairman and CEO Kenneth Feld, whose father Irving began managing the circus in 1956, owns the company.

**KEY COMPETITORS**
Cirque du Soleil
Clear Channel Entertainment
Six Flags

 See pages 188–189 for a full profile of this company.

## FISHER DEVELOPMENT, INC.

| | | |
|---|---|---|
| 1485 Bayshore Blvd., Ste. 152 | CEO: Robert S. Fisher | 2000 Sales: $1,229.0 million |
| San Francisco, CA 94124 | CFO: Dennis Kreuser | 1-Yr. Sales Change: 113.0% |
| Phone: 415-468-1717 | HR: Barry Langford | Employees: 1,229 |
| Fax: 415-468-6241 | Type: Private | FYE: December 31 |
| Web: www.fisherinc.com | | |

Retail contractor Fisher Development leaves Gaps wherever it goes. Founded in 1971, the company serves as general contractor for The Gap clothing chain on as many as 500 jobs a year. Keeping it all in the family, Fisher Development founder and owner Robert Fisher is the brother of Gap retail stores founder Donald Fisher; an audit committee at The Gap reviews the deals annually. The company also builds and renovates for Gap-owned Banana Republic and Old Navy, as well as Harry and David, Crate & Barrel, among others. The #1 retail interior contractor in the US, Fisher Development has expanded its work into Europe.

**KEY COMPETITORS**
Abrams Industries
Capitol Construction
Whiting-Turner

## FLINT INK CORPORATION

| | | |
|---|---|---|
| 4600 Arrowhead Dr. | CEO: H. Howard Flint II | 2000 Sales: $1,080.0 million |
| Ann Arbor, MI 48105 | CFO: Michael J. Gannon | 1-Yr. Sales Change: (10.0%) |
| Phone: 734-622-6000 | HR: Glenn T. Autry | Employees: 3,700 |
| Fax: 734-622-6060 | Type: Private | FYE: December 31 |
| Web: www.flintink.com | | |

The world's #2 ink maker (behind Sun Chemical), Flint Ink sells its products across several continents and has drawn a bull's-eye on becoming #1. The company hopes to accomplish this goal through its acquisition strategy. Flint Ink has plants throughout the Americas, Australasia, and Europe. The company's customers include printing facilities that produce magazines, newspapers, catalogs, and packaging materials. Flint Ink also makes specialty inks (for example, for printing lottery tickets) and environment-friendly vegetable oil-based inks. The Flint family owns the company and Howard Flint II represents the third generation of the family to head the firm, which was founded in 1920.

**KEY COMPETITORS**
Akzo Nobel
Borden
Dainippon Ink and Chemicals

## FLYING J INC.

| | | |
|---|---|---|
| 1104 Country Hills Dr. | CEO: J. Phillip Adams | 2001 Sales: $4,349.0 million |
| Ogden, UT 84403 | CFO: Paul F. Brown | 1-Yr. Sales Change: 108.2% |
| Phone: 801-624-1000 | HR: Jerry Beckman | Employees: 11,000 |
| Fax: 801-624-1587 | Type: Private | FYE: January 31 |
| Web: www.flyingj.com | | |

Flying J puts out a welcome mat for truck drivers throughout North America. From its humble beginnings in 1968 with four locations, the company is now one of the largest US truck-stop operators — running about 130 amenity-loaded Flying J Travel Plazas in 39 states and Canada. Flying J and its subsidiaries go beyond the usual truck-stop fare (food, fuel, showers) by offering truckers extra services, including fuel cost analysis, bulk-fuel programs, truck fleet sales, advertising, banking, financing, and insurance. The company also owns oil and gas reserves as well as a 25,000-barrel-a-day oil refinery. Founder and chairman Jay Call owns a majority stake in Flying J, which plans to add about 35 plazas by 2002.

**KEY COMPETITORS**
Petro Stopping Centers
Pilot
TravelCenters of America


## FMR CORP.

| | | |
|---|---|---|
| 82 Devonshire St. | CEO: Edward C. "Ned" Johnson III | 2000 Sales: $11,096.0 million |
| Boston, MA 02109 | CFO: Stephen P. Jonas | 1-Yr. Sales Change: 25.4% |
| Phone: 617-563-7000 | HR: Ilene B. Jacobs | Employees: 33,186 |
| Fax: 617-476-6150 | Type: Private | FYE: December 31 |
| Web: www.fidelity.com | | |

FMR, aka Fidelity Investments, is a financial services conglomerate offering mutual funds, life insurance, discount brokerage, and retirement services. Fidelity, the #1 mutual fund company worldwide, manages more than 300 funds for some 17 million customers. FMR also has major holdings in telecommunications (COLT Telecom Group), real estate (Boston World Trade Center), and transportation (BostonCoach). Edward Johnson formed Fidelity Management and Research in 1946 as the investment adviser to the Fidelity Fund. FMR is still controlled by the Johnson family, including CEO Ned, the founder's son, and granddaughter Abigail, who owns about 25% of the firm. It has operations in the US, the UK, and the Pacific Rim.

**KEY COMPETITORS**
Charles Schwab
T. Rowe Price
Vanguard Group

 See pages 190–191 for a full profile of this company.


## FOLLETT CORPORATION

| | | |
|---|---|---|
| 2233 West St. | CEO: Christopher Traut | 2001 Sales: $1,554.0 million |
| River Grove, IL 60171 | CFO: Kathryn A. Stanton | 1-Yr. Sales Change: 10.9% |
| Phone: 708-583-2000 | HR: Richard Ellspermann | Employees: 8,000 |
| Fax: 708-452-9347 | Type: Private | FYE: March 31 |
| Web: www.follett.com | | |

Not all kids like to read, but (fortunately for Follett) by the time they reach college, they don't have a choice. Follett is the #1 operator of US college bookstores and has about 600 campus bookstores throughout the US and Canada. Its campus stores sell other items, including clothing and school supplies. The company's business groups, which operate in about 60 countries, also provide books and audiovisual materials to grade school and public libraries, library automation and management software, textbook reconditioning, and other services. Its efollett.com Web site sells new and used college textbooks (its database has about 16 million titles). The Follett family has owned the company for four generations.

**KEY COMPETITORS**
Baker & Taylor
Barnes & Noble College
 Bookstores
Ingram Industries

 See pages 192–193 for a full profile of this company.

## THE FORD FOUNDATION

320 E. 43rd St.
New York, NY 10017
Phone: 212-573-5000
Fax: 212-599-4584
Web: www.fordfound.org

CEO: Susan V. Berresford
CFO: Nicholas M. Gabriel
HR: Bruce D. Stuckey
Type: Foundation

2000 Sales: $2,432.0 million
1-Yr. Sales Change: 36.2%
Employees: 600
FYE: September 30

The Ford Foundation's charitable giving covers a wide spectrum, from A (Association for Asian Studies) to Z (Zanzibar International Film Festival). It relies on a nearly $15 billion diversified investment portfolio to fund grants and loans for individuals and institutions that meet its stated goals of strengthening democratic values, reducing poverty and injustice, promoting international cooperation, and advancing human achievement. The foundation's three main program areas are Asset Building and Community Development; Peace and Social Justice; and Education, Media, Arts, and Culture.

 See pages 194–195 for a full profile of this company.

## FOREMOST FARMS USA, COOPERATIVE

E10889A Penny Lane
Baraboo, WI 53913
Phone: 608-355-8700
Fax: 608-355-8699
Web: www.foremostfarms.com

CEO: Donald Storhoff
CFO: Duaine Kamenick
HR: Jim Kasten
Type: Cooperative

2000 Sales: $1,093.1 million
1-Yr. Sales Change: (16.0%)
Employees: 1,646
FYE: December 31

No jokes about "herd mentality," please. Foremost Farms USA — owned by more than 5,100 dairy farmers in seven midwestern states, mainly Wisconsin — is one of the largest dairy cooperatives in the US. From about 25 plants the cooperative churns out solid and fluid dairy products for retail and food service customers under brands including Foremost, Golden Guernsey Dairy, and Morning Glory Dairy, as well as private labels. To reduce dependence on commodity products the coop is developing new products (flavored milks, natural fruit juices), and expanding its mozzarella capacity to meet consumer demand. Cheese makes up nearly 50% of its sales.

**KEY COMPETITORS**
AMPI
Dairy Farmers of America
Land O'Lakes

## FOSTER FARMS

1000 Davis St.
Livingston, CA 95334
Phone: 209-394-7901
Fax: 209-394-6342
Web: www.fosterfarms.com

CEO: Paul Carter
CFO: Larry Keillor
HR: Tim Walsh
Type: Private

2000 Sales: $1,127.0 million
1-Yr. Sales Change: 2.5%
Employees: 9,500
FYE: December 31

As the West Coast's top poultry company, Foster Farms has a secure place in the pecking order. The company's vertically integrated operations see chickens and turkeys from the incubator to grocers' meat cases (under the Foster Farms brand). In addition to hatching, raising, slaughtering, and processing chickens and turkeys into fresh and value-added products for the grocery and food service industries, the company grinds its own feeds. Already strong in western states, Foster Farms has cast its gaze eastward hoping to compete nationally and has bought the chicken operations of local rival Zacky Farms. Max and Verda Foster founded the company in 1939; it is still owned by the Foster family.

**KEY COMPETITORS**
Perdue
Tyson Foods
Zacky Farms

## FRANK CONSOLIDATED ENTERPRISES

| | | |
|---|---|---|
| 666 Garland Place | CEO: Jim Frank | 2000 Sales: $1,431.0 million |
| Des Plaines, IL 60016 | CFO: Mary Ann O'Dwyer | 1-Yr. Sales Change: 4.9% |
| Phone: 847-699-7000 | HR: Joan Richards | Employees: 591 |
| Fax: 847-699-4047 | Type: Private | FYE: August 31 |
| Web: www.wheels.com | | |

Frank Consolidated Enterprises has an old lease on life. Its Wheels subsidiary, which claims to have pioneered the auto leasing concept, provides administrative, management, and financing services to help corporations manage their vehicle fleets. The company manages more than 240,000 vehicles. It operates in the US as Wheels and in other countries through Interleasing, an alliance of international fleet management and leasing companies. Wheels was founded in 1939 by Zollie Frank. Frank's family still owns the parent company; his widow serves as its chair and son Jim is its president and CEO. Frank Consolidated Enterprises also owns Z Frank Chevrolet, a Chicago-based auto dealership, which another son runs.

**KEY COMPETITORS**
Enterprise Rent-A-Car
GE Capital
PHH Arval


## FREEDOM COMMUNICATIONS, INC.

| | | |
|---|---|---|
| 17666 Fitch Ave. | CEO: Samuel Wolgemuth | 2000 Est. Sales: $850.0 mil. |
| Irvine, CA 92614 | CFO: David Kuykendall | 1-Yr. Sales Change: 13.3% |
| Phone: 949-253-2300 | HR: Barbara Adams | Employees: 8,000 |
| Fax: 949-474-7675 | Type: Private | FYE: December 31 |
| Web: www.freedom.com | | |

Southern California is the real cradle of Freedom. Media conglomerate Freedom Communications owns more than two dozen daily newspapers, including its flagship, California's *Orange County Register,* with a circulation of about 360,000. In addition, the company owns 37 weekly papers, eight television stations, and 18 niche magazines (including *Latin Trade, Home HealthCare Consultant,* and *MODE*). Freedom Communications also operates more than 50 Web sites, which range from online versions of its printed properties to regional information guides. The company is owned by the family of founder R. C. Hoiles.

**KEY COMPETITORS**
Advance Publications
E. W. Scripps
Gannett


## THE FREEMAN COMPANIES

| | | |
|---|---|---|
| 1421 W. Mockingbird Ln. | CEO: Donald S. Freeman Jr. | 2001 Sales: $878.0 million |
| Dallas, TX 75247 | CFO: Bob Liles | 1-Yr. Sales Change: 17.1% |
| Phone: 214-670-9000 | HR: Suzanne Cragg | Employees: 34,000 |
| Fax: 214-670-9100 | Type: Private | FYE: June 30 |
| Web: www.freemanco.com | | |

The Freeman Companies knows there no business like the trade show business. The firm stages thousands of conventions, corporate meetings, expositions, and trade shows every year and prepares exhibits for its clients. Freeman's operations include Freeman Decorating (event design and production), Freeman Exhibit (exhibit rental and production), Sullivan Transfer (heavy hauling), and Stage Rigging (theatrical rigging). The company's AVW Audio Visual (presentation technologies) unit has merged with Berkshire Partners' TELAV to form AVW/TELAV. Freeman Companies was founded by D.S. "Buck" Freeman in 1927; the company is owned by the Freeman family (including chairman and CEO Donald Freeman) and company employees.

**KEY COMPETITORS**
Key3Media
Viad
VNU

## FRY'S ELECTRONICS, INC.

| | | |
|---|---|---|
| 600 East Brokaw Rd. | CEO: John Fry | 2000 Est. Sales: $1,500.0 mil. |
| San Jose, CA 95112 | CFO: David Fry | 1-Yr. Sales Change: 5.6% |
| Phone: 408-487-4500 | HR: Kathryn Kolder | Employees: 4,450 |
| Fax: 408-487-4700 | Type: Private | FYE: December 31 |
| Web: www.frys.com | | |

Service may be heavy-handed, but where else can you buy appliances, build a computer, grab some Ho-Ho's or Maalox, and find the latest *Playboy* or *Byte*? The 19-store Fry's Electronics chain offers all that plus low prices, extensive inventory (including Crock-Pots, vacuums, stereos, TVs, and computer software and hardware), and whimsically themed displays (such as Wild West or UFO motifs). The technogeek's superstore — whose notoriously bad service is chronicled on unaffiliated Web pages — began in 1985 as the brainchild of CEO John Fry (with brothers Randy and David) and EVP Kathryn Kolder. The Fry brothers, who got their start at Fry's Food Stores, still own the company.

**KEY COMPETITORS**
Best Buy
CompUSA
Good Guys

 See pages 196–197 for a full profile of this company.

## FURRS SUPERMARKETS, INC.

| | | |
|---|---|---|
| 4411 The 25 Way NE, Suite 100 | CEO: Steven L. Mortensen | 2000 Est. Sales: $1,000.0 mil. |
| Albuquerque, NM 87109 | CFO: Steven Stork | 1-Yr. Sales Change: 0.0% |
| Phone: 505-998-3877 | HR: Delwyn James | Employees: 5,000 |
| Fax: 505-944-2671 | Type: Private | FYE: December 31 |
| Web: www.furrs.com | | |

Out in the West Texas town of El Paso, folks buy their fajita fixin's at Furrs Supermarkets — or at least they did until the troubled chain (no longer related to Furr's Cafeterias) sold half of its stores to wholesaler Fleming and closed the rest. Prior to the sale, Furrs operated 71 grocery stores in New Mexico and West Texas. Founded as Furr's Inc. in 1904, the company became Furrs Supermarkets in 1991. Windward Capital Partners owned about 60% of the company, which filed for Chapter 11 bankruptcy protection in February 2001. Furrs auctioned off its assets in June 2001; Fleming won the bid and sold 36 stores to independent grocers and several major chains. Furrs closed the 35 stores that Fleming didn't want.

**KEY COMPETITORS**
Albertson's
Smith's Food & Drug
United Supermarkets

## G-I HOLDINGS, INC.

| | | |
|---|---|---|
| 1361 Alps Rd. | CEO: Richard A. Weinberg | 2000 Est. Sales: $1,200.0 mil. |
| Wayne, NJ 07470 | CFO: John Rebele | 1-Yr. Sales Change: 5.3% |
| Phone: 973-628-3000 | HR: John Schneid | Employees: 5,500 |
| Fax: 973-628-3326 | Type: Private | FYE: December 31 |

Working hard to keep a roof over your head? G-I Holdings (formerly GAF Corporation) is one of the US's oldest sources for commercial and residential roofing materials, with more than 25 plants in the US. Through its Building Materials Corporation of America subsidiary, the company makes flashing, vents, and complete roofing systems. Other products include the Timberline and Sovereign brands of residential shingles and GAF CompositeRoof for commercial asphalt roofing. Customers include contractors, distributors, and national retail outlets, including Home Depot. Citing increased exposure to asbestos liability claims, G-I Holdings has filed for bankruptcy protection. Chairman Samuel Heyman owns 99% of the company.

**KEY COMPETITORS**
Bridgestone/Firestone
Elcor
Owens Corning

## GALE & WENTWORTH, L.L.C.

Park Avenue at Morris County
Florham Park, NJ
Phone: 973-301-9500
Fax: 973-301-9501
Web: www.galewent.com

CEO: Stanley C. Gale
CFO: Kathleen Wielkopolski
HR: Johanna Thacker
Type: Private

2000 Sales: $892.0 million
1-Yr. Sales Change: —
Employees: 430
FYE: December 31

Real estate is a breeze for Gale & Wentworth, which offers US and UK investors and businesses real estate services, including consulting, property management, and construction. The company manages maintenance, security, and other concerns for property owners; represents businesses in lease and sale transactions; provides outsourcing for clients' office support needs; and oversees construction projects. Gale & Wentworth, which manages some 50 million sq. ft., also invests in property through joint ventures with such financiers as Morgan Stanley Dean Witter. Workstage, Gale & Wentworth's joint venture with office furniture maker Steelcase, develops customized office buildings. CEO Stanley Gale controls the firm.

**KEY COMPETITORS**
CB Richard Ellis
Colliers International
Shorenstein

## GENERAL PARTS, INC.

2635 Millbrook Rd.
Raleigh, NC 27604
Phone: 919-573-3000
Fax: 919-573-3553

CEO: O. Temple Sloan Jr.
CFO: Bill Kuykendall
HR: Deborah Tyson
Type: Private

2000 Sales: $1,459.0 million
1-Yr. Sales Change: (0.2%)
Employees: 12,000
FYE: December 31

Feel free to salute General Parts, distributor of replacement automotive parts, supplies, and tools for every make and model of foreign and domestic car, truck, bus, and farm or industrial vehicle. The largest member of the CARQUEST network, employee-owned General Parts, with about 1,200 company-owned stores, distributes its products to more than 4,000 CARQUEST and other auto parts stores across North America through 35 distribution centers. The company, which has been growing through acquisitions, sells its parts to do-it-yourself mechanics, professional installers, body shops, farmers, and fleet owners (commercial customers account for about 80% of CARQUEST's sales). The company owns CARQUEST Canada.

**KEY COMPETITORS**
Advance Auto Parts
AutoZone
Genuine Parts

## GENLYTE THOMAS GROUP LLC

4360 Brownsboro Rd., Ste. 300
Louisville, KY 40207
Phone: 502-893-4690
Fax: 502-895-6618
Web: www.genlytethomas.com

CEO: Larry K. Powers
CFO: William G. Ferko
HR: Manny Cadima
Type: Joint venture

2000 Sales: $1,007.7 million
1-Yr. Sales Change: 3.0%
Employees: 3,317
FYE: December 31

At the marriage of The Genlyte Group and Thomas Industries, which formed Genlyte Thomas Group, they must have played "You Light Up My Life." The joint venture — in which Genlyte owns 68%, Thomas 32% — plays a leading role in the North American lighting market. Genlyte Thomas' lighting fixtures and controls are used both indoors and outdoors, for decoration, landscaping, and tracking. Brand names include Bronzelite, Capri, Lightolier, and ZED. The company markets to distributors, who resell the products for use in the construction and remodeling of residential, commercial, and industrial facilities. Genlyte Thomas' flagship Lightolier division is teaming up with Steelcase to develop workplace lighting.

**KEY COMPETITORS**
Catalina Lighting
Cooper Industries
GE

## GENMAR HOLDINGS, INC.

| | | |
|---|---|---|
| 80 S. 8th Street | CEO: Grant E. Oppegaard | 2000 Sales: $858.0 million |
| Minneapolis, MN 55402 | CFO: Roger R. Cloutier II | 1-Yr. Sales Change: 21.8% |
| Phone: 612-339-7600 | HR: David Vigdal | Employees: 6,500 |
| Fax: 612-337-1930 | Type: Private | FYE: June 30 |
| Web: www.genmar.com | | |

Genmar Holdings trolls for sales by cruising the pleasure boat market with a line of luxury yachts, recreational powerboats, and fishing boats. The company builds more than 300 different boat models ranging in size from 53-foot yachts (servants not included) to fishing skiffs. Its brands include Glastron, Ranger, and Wellcraft. Genmar markets its boat through about 1,300 independent dealers in the US and 30 other countries. The company — which is a combination of 12 different boat manufacturers acquired over 24 years — is controlled by chairman Irwin Jacobs (investor and former corporate raider). In 2001, through JTC Acquisitions, Genmar acquired bankrupt Outboard Marine's US boating and trailer assets.

**KEY COMPETITORS**
Brunswick
Fountain Powerboat
Yamaha Motor


## GEOLOGISTICS CORPORATION

| | | |
|---|---|---|
| 1251 E. Dyer Rd. | CEO: Robert Arovas | 2000 Sales: $1,500.0 million |
| Santa Ana, CA 92705 | CFO: Michael Bible | 1-Yr. Sales Change: (3.7%) |
| Phone: 714-513-3000 | HR: Bob Westman | Employees: — |
| Fax: 714-513-3120 | Type: Private | FYE: December 31 |
| Web: www.geo-logistics.com | | |

GeoLogistics gets goods going, globally. With operations in 140 countries, the company provides multi-modal freight-forwarding, customs brokerage, warehousing, and distribution services, as well as logistics and supply chain management, and trade-show logistics. Shipments can be tracked through GeoLogistics's Internet-based GeoVista system. Almost half of the company's sales come from Europe, with the remainder split between Asia and the US. To focus on core logistics operations, GeoLogistics has sold its moving van unit, The Bekins Company, to Bekins agents. Investment firms Questor Management, William E. Simon & Sons, and Oaktree Capital Management control GeoLogistics, which was founded in 1996.

**KEY COMPETITORS**
EGL
Fritz
Panalpina


## GEORGE E. WARREN CORPORATION

| | | |
|---|---|---|
| 605 17th St. | CEO: Thomas L. Corr | 2000 Est. Sales: $1,300.0 mil. |
| Vero Beach, FL 32960 | CFO: Jonathan W. Taylor | 1-Yr. Sales Change: 1.5% |
| Phone: 561-778-7100 | HR: Martin Paris | Employees: 25 |
| Fax: 561-778-7171 | Type: Private | FYE: December 31 |

By barge, by pipeline, by tank truck by George, George E. Warren is a major private wholesale distributor of petroleum in the eastern US. Founded in Boston by George E. Warren in 1907 as a coal and oil distributor, it moved to Florida in the early 1990s. The company distributes its product mostly by barge and pipeline, though it uses some tank trucks as well. The company has distribution facilities in the southeastern and southwestern US. Its products include propane, propylene, ethylene, gasoline, and heating oil and are sold to multiple industries. President Thomas Corr owns the company.

**KEY COMPETITORS**
Martin Resource Management
Penn Octane
Sun Coast Resources

## GEORGIA LOTTERY CORPORATION

| | | |
|---|---|---|
| 250 Williams St., Ste. 3000 | CEO: Rebecca Paul | 2000 Sales: $2,310.0 million |
| Atlanta, GA 30303 | CFO: Andy Davis | 1-Yr. Sales Change: 13.8% |
| Phone: 404-215-5000 | HR: Margaret Bode | Employees: 250 |
| Fax: 404-215-8886 | Type: Government-owned | FYE: June 30 |
| Web: www.galottery.com | | |

Lottery fans with an eye toward education may have Georgia on their minds. Established in 1993, the Georgia Lottery has contributed more than $4 billion to the state's education coffers. In addition to the HOPE program, which has helped nearly 600,000 students attend college with lottery-funded scholarships, the lottery helps finance a prekindergarten program and public school capital improvements. More than 7,000 retailers throughout Georgia sell tickets for lottery games, including instant-ticket games, online games, keno-style games, and a Powerball-like game aptly named Big Game. In its first year the Georgia Lottery reached $1.1 billion in sales, and it has been growing ever since.

**KEY COMPETITORS**
Multi-State Lottery
Florida Lottery
Virginia Lottery

## GIANT EAGLE INC.

| | | |
|---|---|---|
| 101 Kappa Dr. | CEO: David S. Shapira | 2001 Sales: $4,435.0 million |
| Pittsburgh, PA 15238 | CFO: Mark Minnaugh | 1-Yr. Sales Change: 5.1% |
| Phone: 412-963-6200 | HR: Raymond A. Huber | Employees: 25,600 |
| Fax: 412-968-1561 | Type: Private | FYE: June 30 |
| Web: www.gianteagle.com | | |

With its talons firmly wrapped around western Pennsylvania, Giant Eagle is eyeing new territory. The #1 food retailer in Pittsburgh, it operates some 145 supermarkets (about 60,000 sq. ft. in size) and has more than 60 franchisees in Maryland, western Pennsylvania, Ohio, and northern West Virginia. In addition to food, many Giant Eagle stores feature video rental, banking, photo processing, and ready-to-eat meals. The company became the #1 food seller in eastern Ohio through a 1997 acquisition, and Giant Eagle has expanded to Cleveland, Toledo and Columbus. Chairman and CEO David Shapira is the grandson of one of the five men who founded the company in 1931. The founders' families own Giant Eagle.

**KEY COMPETITORS**
Ahold USA
Kroger
SUPERVALU

 See pages 198–199 for a full profile of this company.

## GILBANE, INC.

| | | |
|---|---|---|
| 7 Jackson Walkway | CEO: Paul J. Choquette Jr. | 2000 Sales: $2,388.0 million |
| Providence, RI 02903 | CFO: Ken Alderman | 1-Yr. Sales Change: 9.6% |
| Phone: 401-456-5800 | HR: Dan M. Kelly | Employees: 1,510 |
| Fax: 401-456-5936 | Type: Private | FYE: December 31 |
| Web: www.gilbaneco.com | | |

Family-owned Gilbane has been the bane of its rivals for four generations. Subsidiary Gilbane Building provides construction management, contracting, and design and build services to construct office buildings, manufacturing plants, schools, prisons, and more for the firm's governmental, commercial, and industrial clients. Projects include the National Air and Space Museum, Lake Placid's 1980 Winter Olympics facilities, and the proposed WWII memorial in Washington, DC. The other subsidiary, Gilbane Properties, develops and finances public and private projects and acts as a property manager. CEO Paul Choquette is a descendant of William and Thomas Gilbane, who founded the firm in 1873.

**KEY COMPETITORS**
Bechtel
Bovis Lend Lease
Parsons

## GLAZER'S WHOLESALE DRUG COMPANY INC.

| | | |
|---|---|---|
| 14860 Landmark Blvd. | CEO: Bennett Glazer | 2000 Sales: $1,480.0 million |
| Dallas, TX 75240 | CFO: Cary Rossel | 1-Yr. Sales Change: 33.3% |
| Phone: 972-702-0900 | HR: Rusty Harmount | Employees: 3,200 |
| Fax: 972-702-8508 | Type: Private | FYE: December 31 |
| Web: www.glazers.com | | |

Glazer's Wholesale Drug, named during Prohibition when only drugstores and drug wholesalers could deal in liquor, is a wholesale distributor of alcoholic beverages. It is the largest distributor of malts, spirits, and wines in Texas and one of the largest US wine and spirits distributors. It also operates in Arizona (Alliance Beverage), Arkansas, Indiana (Olinger Distributing), Iowa, Louisiana, Missouri, and Ohio. The company distributes Robert Mondavi wines and Brown-Forman and Bacardi spirits, among others. Glazer's has been acquiring wholesalers and distributors in the Midwest, including Mid-Continent Distributor (Missouri). CEO Bennett Glazer and family own Glazer's.

**KEY COMPETITORS**
Gallo
National Wine & Spirits
Southern Wine & Spirits


## GLOBAL COMPANIES LLC

| | | |
|---|---|---|
| 800 South St. | CEO: Alfred A. Slifka | Sales: — |
| Waltham, MA 02454 | CFO: Thomas McManmon | 1-Yr. Sales Change: — |
| Phone: 781-894-8800 | HR: Barbara Rosenblum | Employees: — |
| Fax: 781-398-4160 | Type: Private | FYE: December 31 |
| Web: www.globalp.com | | |

Global Companies imports petroleum products from global sources, but its marketing is mainly regional. Formerly Global Petroleum, the company wholesales heating oil, residual fuel oil, diesel oil, kerosene, and gasoline to customers in the northeastern US. It also sells gasoline and diesel directly to more than 85 branded service stations and makes financing available for upgrades or new construction. The company makes proprietary diesel oil and home heating oil. Its alliance with National Grid USA offers oil, natural gas, and electricity to commercial and industrial customers. Founded in 1933 by CEO Alfred Slifka's father, Global Companies is controlled by Spanish oil company Repsol-YPF.

**KEY COMPETITORS**
Crown Central Petroleum
Getty Petroleum Marketing
Gulf Oil


## GOLD KIST INC.

| | | |
|---|---|---|
| 244 Perimeter Center Pkwy. NE | CEO: John Bekkers | 2001 Sales: $1,810.8 million |
| Atlanta, GA 30346 | CFO: Stephen O. West | 1-Yr. Sales Change: 6.1% |
| Phone: 770-393-5000 | HR: Harry T. McDonald | Employees: 18,000 |
| Fax: 770-393-5262 | Type: Cooperative | FYE: June 30 |
| Web: goldkist.com | | |

At Gold Kist, the chickens don't even get to see the road, much less cross it. An agricultural cooperative of 18,000 farmers (mainly in the South), Gold Kist is the #2 US chicken producer (behind Tyson Foods), selling fresh and frozen whole chickens, parts, and processed chicken products (patties, nuggets) to the food service industry, school and military food programs, and grocery chains. It also processes pork and is involved in metal fabrication as well as financing for farmers. Gold Kist produces nuts through its 25% stake in US pecan processor Young Pecan Company. The company has divested its aquaculture and peanut operations to focus more on its chicken business.

**KEY COMPETITORS**
Perdue
Pilgrim's Pride
Tyson Foods

📖 See pages 200–201 for a full profile of this company.

## GOLDEN RULE INSURANCE COMPANY

712 11th St.
Lawrenceville, IL 62439
Phone: 618-943-8000
Fax: 618-943-9151
Web: www.goldenrule.com

CEO: John Whelan
CFO: —
HR: —
Type: Private

2000 Sales: $829.0 million
1-Yr. Sales Change: 13.7%
Employees: 1,084
FYE: December 31

Follow the golden rule and you will find insurance. Golden Rule Insurance provides health insurance, life insurance, and annuities. The company focuses on group and individual health plans, which include employer-sponsored health plans and medical savings account plans. Other products include Asset-Care (a long-term care insurance policy that combines life insurance and asset management), ValuTerm (term life insurance), and WealthBuilder (fixed rate annuities). Golden Rule operates in all US states except New York. Throughout the 1980s and 1990s the company was accused of hardball tactics aimed at denying policyholder claims and "cherry picking" (denying sick and therefore high-risk individuals) customers.

**KEY COMPETITORS**
Aetna
UnitedHealth Group
WellPoint Health Networks

## GOLDEN STATE FOODS

18301 Von Karman Ave., Ste. 1100
Irvine, CA 92612
Phone: 949-252-2000
Fax: 949-252-2088
Web: www.goldenstatefoods.com

CEO: Mark S. Wetterau
CFO: Mike Waitukaitis
HR: —
Type: Private

2000 Sales: $1,764.0 million
1-Yr. Sales Change: 0.8%
Employees: 2,000
FYE: December 31

Did somebody say McDonald's? Food processor and distributor Golden State Foods is listening. The company is one of the fast-food giant's major suppliers, providing its restaurants with more than 130 products. These include beef patties, the Big Mac sauce (which it formulated), buns, ketchup, mayonnaise, and salad dressing. McDonald's is the company's sole customer. Golden State Foods has 12 plants and distribution centers in Australia, Egypt, Mexico, and the US. The company was founded in 1947 by the late William Moore. Investment firm Yucaipa owns a majority of Golden State, while management company Wetterau Associates owns most of the rest.

**KEY COMPETITORS**
JR Simplot
Keystone Foods
Martin-Brower

 See pages 202–203 for a full profile of this company.

## THE GOLUB CORPORATION

501 Duanesburg Rd.
Schenectady, NY 12306
Phone: 518-355-5000
Fax: 518-356-9597
Web: www.pricechopper.com

CEO: Neil M. Golub
CFO: John Endres
HR: Margaret Davenport
Type: Private

2001 Sales: $2,000.0 million
1-Yr. Sales Change: 14.3%
Employees: 19,500
FYE: April 30

Supermarket operator The Golub Corporation offers tasty come-ons such as table-ready meals, gift certificates, automatic discount cards, and a hotline where cooks answer food-related queries. Golub operates about 100 Price Chopper supermarkets in Connecticut, Massachusetts, New Hampshire, upstate New York, northeastern Pennsylvania, and Vermont. It also runs Mini Chopper service stations and convenience stores. Golub has discontinued its HouseCalls home delivery service. Brothers Bill and Ben Golub founded the company in 1932. The Golub family owns 56% of Golub and has turned down offers to sell the company. Employees own the other 44% of Golub.

**KEY COMPETITORS**
Ahold USA
Big Y Foods
Hannaford Bros.

## GOODMAN MANUFACTURING COMPANY, L.P.

1501 Seamist Dr.
Houston, TX 77008
Phone: 713-861-2500
Fax: 713-861-2176
Web: www.goodmanmfg.com

CEO: John B. Goodman
CFO: Tanya Klepser
HR: Cliff Reilly
Type: Private

2000 Est. Sales: $1,100.0 mil.
1-Yr. Sales Change: (49.1%)
Employees: 3,750
FYE: December 31

Goodman knows how to cool off a hot situation. Goodman Manufacturing Company, through its Amana Heating and Air Conditioning, Goodman Manufacturing, and Quietflex divisions, makes air-conditioning, ventilation, and heating equipment for residential and commercial use. Goodman, which sells its products through independent installers and distributors worldwide, is among the top US makers of air conditioners. Its brands include Amana, Caloric, Goodman, GmC, Modern Maid, and Janitrol. In July 2001 the company sold its Amana Appliance division (washers, dryers, microwaves, and refrigerators) to Maytag for $325 million. Goodman is owned by the family of Harold Goodman, who founded the company in 1977.

**KEY COMPETITORS**
Carrier
Fedders
GE Appliances

## GOODWILL INDUSTRIES INTERNATIONAL, INC.

9200 Rockville Pike
Bethesda, MD 20814
Phone: 301-530-6500
Fax: 301-530-1516
Web: www.goodwill.org

CEO: George W. Kessinger
CFO: Samuel W. Cox
HR: Patricia Williams
Type: Not-for-profit

2000 Sales: $1,850.0 million
1-Yr. Sales Change: 12.1%
Employees: 77,895
FYE: December 31

Founded to give those in need "a hand up, not a handout," Goodwill Industries International supports the operations of about 215 independent Goodwill chapters worldwide. Though known mainly for its more than 1,700 thrift stores, Goodwill focuses on providing rehabilitation, training, placement, and employment services for those with disabilities and other barriers to employment. Goodwill is one of the world's largest providers of such services, as well as one of the world's largest employers of the disabled. Funding comes primarily from the retail stores, contract services provided to local employers, and grants. Nearly 84% of revenues go to job training and rehabilitation programs.

## GORDON FOOD SERVICE

333 50th St. SW
Grand Rapids, MI 49548
Phone: 616-530-7000
Fax: 616-261-7600
Web: www.gfs.com

CEO: Dan Gordon
CFO: Steve Plakmeyer
HR: David Vickery
Type: Private

2001 Est. Sales: $2,600.0 mil.
1-Yr. Sales Change: 20.9%
Employees: 4,550
FYE: October 31

Gordon Food Service (GFS) helps satisfy the appetites of Midwesterners and Canadians. A food distributor serving schools, restaurants, and other institutions, GFS boasts more than 12,000 items ranging from fresh produce to sanitation systems. The company also makes its own line of foods under names such as Triumph Packaging and Ready, Set, Serve. Not merely a food distributor, GFS also sells food in bulk through its more than 75 GFS Marketplace retail stores across four states (think Sam's Club without the membership fee). The late Isaac VanWestenbrugge (great-grandfather of president Dan Gordon) founded the company as a butter and egg distributor in 1897. GFS is still owned by the Gordon family.

**KEY COMPETITORS**
McLane Foodservice
SYSCO
U.S. Foodservice

## GORES TECHNOLOGY GROUP

| | | |
|---|---|---|
| 10877 Wilshire Blvd., Ste. 1805 | CEO: Alec Gores | 2000 Sales: $1,200.0 million |
| Los Angeles, CA 90024 | CFO: Cathy Scanlon | 1-Yr. Sales Change: 50.0% |
| Phone: 310-209-3010 | HR: David Strain | Employees: 3,000 |
| Fax: 310-209-3310 | Type: Private | FYE: December 31 |
| Web: www.gores.com | | |

In the gory aftermath of the Tech Wreck, Gores Technology Group can probably find a bargain. The company buys and manages technology firms, particularly software, hardware, services, and telecommunications concerns. Targets typically have revenues between $10 million and $1 billion and are often spin-offs of noncore operations from Global 2000 companies. Gores Technology usually takes full ownership. Since its founding by chairman Alec Gores in 1992, it has bought some 35 companies around the world worth about $2 billion, including the personal computer operations of Micron Electronics (now Interland) and software maker The Learning Company, which then sold its education business to Ireland's Riverdeep software firm.

**KEY COMPETITORS**
Carlyle Group
KKR
Platinum Equity

## GOULD PAPER CORPORATION

| | | |
|---|---|---|
| 11 Madison Ave. | CEO: Harry E. Gould Jr. | 2000 Sales: $810.0 million |
| New York, NY 10010 | CFO: Dan J. Lala | 1-Yr. Sales Change: 0.6% |
| Phone: 212-301-0000 | HR: Barbara O'Grady | Employees: 455 |
| Fax: 212-320-4333 | Type: Private | FYE: December 31 |
| Web: www.gouldpaper.com | | |

Paper is as good as gold for Gould Paper, one of the largest privately owned distributors of printing and fine writing paper in the US. The company sells papers for multiple markets, including fine arts papers, commercial printing and lithography, book and magazine publishing, direct mail and catalogs, envelopes, and specialty converting papers. Gould Paper also makes agricultural equipment for harvesting and mowing. Harry Gould Sr. (father of chairman, president, and company owner Harry Gould Jr.) formed the company in 1924 as a printing paper merchant primarily for the greeting card industry. The company has expanded over the years by acquiring other paper companies.

**KEY COMPETITORS**
Clifford Paper
International Paper
Midland Paper

## GOYA FOODS, INC.

| | | |
|---|---|---|
| 100 Seaview Dr. | CEO: Joseph A. Unanue | 2001 Est. Sales: $835.0 mil. |
| Secaucus, NJ 07096 | CFO: Miguel Lugo | 1-Yr. Sales Change: 8.4% |
| Phone: 201-348-4900 | HR: Ernie Moreno | Employees: 2,500 |
| Fax: 201-348-6609 | Type: Private | FYE: May 31 |
| Web: www.goyafoods.com | | |

Goya Foods wants its palette of products to please more than Hispanic palates. One of the biggest Hispanic-owned companies in the US, Goya produces about 1,000 grocery products, including a variety of canned and dried beans, rice, olives, olive oils, frozen foods, fruit juices and nectars, sauces, and seasonings. In addition to Goya, it uses the Kirby brand name. A growing taste for ethnic foods across the US is fueling Goya's growth beyond its Hispanic roots. However, the company faces increased competition from food giants such as Kraft Foods, as well as imports from Mexico. Goya is owned by one of the richest Hispanic *familias* in the US, the Unanues, who founded the company in 1936.

**KEY COMPETITORS**
Del Monte Foods
Kraft Foods
Nestlé

 See pages 204–205 for a full profile of this company.

## GRAHAM PACKAGING COMPANY, L. P.

2401 Pleasant Valley Rd.
York, PA 17402
Phone: 717-849-8500
Fax: 717-848-4836
Web: www.grahampackaging.com

CEO: Philip R. Yates
CFO: John E. Hamilton
HR: George Lane
Type: Private

2000 Sales: $824.6 million
1-Yr. Sales Change: 15.2%
Employees: 4,000
FYE: December 31

Grocery aisle stockers and mechanics handle Graham Packaging's products everyday. The company makes customized blow molded plastic containers for the food and beverage, household and personal care, and automotive markets. Typical products include containers for frozen juices, pasta sauce, teas, fabric and dish detergents, and motor oil. Graham Packaging operates 57 plants in North America (80% of sales), Europe, and Latin America. One-third of the company's manufacturing plants are located on the grounds of its customer's production facilities. Its customers include Minute Maid, Hershey Foods, Procter & Gamble, and Pennzoil-Quaker State. The company, controlled by Blackstone Group, has suspended its IPO plans.

**KEY COMPETITORS**
Amcor
Consolidated Container
Crown Cork & Seal


## GRANT THORNTON INTERNATIONAL

1 Prudential Plaza, Ste. 800
Chicago, IL 60601
Phone: 312-856-0001
Fax: 312-616-7142
Web: www.gti.org

CEO: David C. McDonnell
CFO: Louis A. Fanchi
HR: Debbie Pastor
Type: Partnership

2000 Sales: $1,690.0 million
1-Yr. Sales Change: (6.1%)
Employees: 20,300
FYE: December 31

Grant Thornton International is a kid brother to the Big Five. The international umbrella organization of accounting and management consulting firms operates from more than 600 offices in 100 countries, placing it among the top second-tier companies that trail around behind the biggest of the big guys (Andersen, PricewaterhouseCoopers, Ernst & Young International, KPMG International, and Deloitte Touche Tohmatsu). With the lowering of trade barriers in Latin America and Europe, Grant Thornton has moved to help smaller firms develop business in these emerging markets.

**KEY COMPETITORS**
Andersen
Ernst & Young
PricewaterhouseCoopers

 See pages 206–207 for a full profile of this company.


## GRAYBAR ELECTRIC COMPANY, INC.

34 N. Meramec Ave.
Clayton, MO 63105
Phone: 314-512-9200
Fax: 314-512-9453
Web: www.graybar.com

CEO: Robert A. Reynolds
CFO: John W. Wolf
HR: Jack F. Van Pelt
Type: Private

2000 Sales: $5,227.4 million
1-Yr. Sales Change: 21.6%
Employees: 10,500
FYE: December 31

Keeping connected is no problem for Graybar Electric, one of the largest distributors of electrical products in the US. Purchasing from thousands of manufacturers, the company distributes nearly 1 million electrical and communications components, including wire, cable, and lighting products. Its customers include electrical contractors, industrial plants, power utilities, and telecommunications providers. Subsidiary Graybar Financial Services offers equipment leasing and financing. Employee-owned Graybar Electric has nearly 300 offices and distribution facilities in Canada, Mexico, Puerto Rico, Singapore, and the US.

**KEY COMPETITORS**
Arrow Electronics
WESCO International
W.W. Grainger

 See pages 208–209 for a full profile of this company.

## GREAT DANE LIMITED PARTNERSHIP

| | | |
|---|---|---|
| 602 E. Lathrop Ave. | CEO: C. F. "Kit" Hammond III | 2000 Est. Sales: $1,310.0 mil. |
| Savannah, GA 31402 | CFO: Tom Horan | 1-Yr. Sales Change: (6.4%) |
| Phone: 912-644-2100 | HR: Thor Egede-Nissen | Employees: 5,000 |
| Fax: 912-644-2166 | Type: Private | FYE: December 31 |
| Web: www.greatdanetrailers.com | | |

Great Dane is really going places — the company is one of the largest manufacturers of truck trailers in North America. Great Dane makes refrigerated (reefer) and freight vans and platform trailers. The company has nine manufacturing plants in the US and sales, parts, and service centers across the US, Canada, Mexico, and South America. It also sells used trailers. Great Dane is a unit of Chicago-based investment group CC Industries, which is controlled by the Henry Crown family. The company started in 1900 as a maker of steel products and switched to trailer making in 1931.

**KEY COMPETITORS**
Lufkin Industries
Utility Trailer
Wabash National


## GREEN BAY PACKAGING INC.

| | | |
|---|---|---|
| 1700 N. Webster Ct. | CEO: William F. Kress | 2000 Sales: $826.0 million |
| Green Bay, WI 54307 | CFO: Walter J. Dauska | 1-Yr. Sales Change: 11.9% |
| Phone: 920-433-5111 | HR: Ron Chase | Employees: 3,025 |
| Fax: 920-433-5337 | Type: Private | FYE: December 31 |
| Web: www.gbp.com | | |

Green Bay Packaging is always packed and ready to go. The company is an integrated and diversified paperboard packaging manufacturer. In addition to corrugated containers, the company also makes pressure-sensitive label stock, folding cartons, linerboard, and lumber products. Its Fiber Resources division in Arkansas manages 195,000 acres of company-owned forests and, through contractors, produces lumber, wood chips, recycled paper, and wood fuel. Green Bay Packaging also offers fiber procurement, wastepaper brokerage, and paper-slitting services. Founded by corrugated paper pioneer George Kress in 1933, the company operates 29 divisions in 14 states. The Kress family controls Green Bay Packaging.

**KEY COMPETITORS**
Georgia-Pacific Group
International Paper
Mead


## THE GREEN BAY PACKERS, INC.

| | | |
|---|---|---|
| 1265 Lombardi Ave. | CEO: Robert E. Harlan | 2001 Sales: $118.0 million |
| Green Bay, WI 54307 | CFO: John M. Jones | 1-Yr. Sales Change: 8.4% |
| Phone: 920-496-5700 | HR: Mark Schiefelbein | Employees: 140 |
| Fax: 920-496-5712 | Type: Not-for-profit | FYE: March 31 |
| Web: www.packers.com | | |

On the frozen tundra of Lambeau Field, the legendary Green Bay Packers battle for pride in the National Football League. The team, founded in 1919 by Earl "Curly" Lambeau, has been home to such football icons as Bart Starr, Ray Nitschke, and legendary coach Vince Lombardi and boasts a record 12 championship titles, including three Super Bowl victories. The team is also the NFL's only community-owned franchise, being a not-for-profit corporation with more than 110,000 shareholders. (The shares do not increase in value nor pay dividends, and can only be sold back to the team.) While fans have kept home games sold out since 1960, the team is counting on a $295 million stadium renovation to boost revenue.

**KEY COMPETITORS**
Chicago Bears
Detroit Lions
Minnesota Vikings

 See pages 210–211 for a full profile of this company.

## GROCERS SUPPLY CO., INC.

| | | |
|---|---|---|
| 3131 E. Holcombe Blvd. | CEO: Max Levit | 2000 Est. Sales: $1,550.0 mil. |
| Houston, TX 77021 | CFO: Michael Castleberry | 1-Yr. Sales Change: 10.7% |
| Phone: 713-747-5000 | HR: Curtis Hopkins | Employees: 2,000 |
| Fax: 713-746-5611 | Type: Private | FYE: May 31 |
| Web: www.grocerssupply.com | | |

Need crackers in Caracas or vanilla in Manila? Grocers Supply Co. distributes groceries near and far. The company (not to be confused with fellow Texas distributor GSC Enterprises) distributes food, health and beauty items, household products, and school and office supplies to convenience stores and supermarkets. Grocers Supply mainly serves customers throughout Texas and Louisiana. Its Grocers Supply International (GSI) division ships supplies to oil company operations, other commercial customers, and US embassies around the world. GSI boasts that it will buy anything to ship anywhere for anyone, including macaroons in Rangoon, or even oleo in Tokyo. Grocers Supply is owned by the Levit family.

**KEY COMPETITORS**
C.D. Hartnett
GSC Enterprises
McLane

## GROUP HEALTH COOPERATIVE OF PUGET SOUND

| | | |
|---|---|---|
| 521 Wall St. | CEO: Cheryl M. Scott | 2000 Sales: $1,400.0 million |
| Seattle, WA 98121 | CFO: Jim Truess | 1-Yr. Sales Change: 0.0% |
| Phone: 206-326-3000 | HR: John Nagelmann | Employees: 9,873 |
| Fax: 206-448-5963 | Type: Not-for-profit | FYE: December 31 |
| Web: www.ghc.org | | |

Group Health Cooperative of Puget Sound is a not-for-profit managed health care group serving counties in Washington and northern Idaho. Members may participate in HMO, PPO, or point-of-service health plans. The co-op is governed by an 11-person board elected by the organization's members. Specialized services include mental health and substance abuse treatment, hospice services, and HIV/AIDS case management. Group Health Cooperative of Puget Sound has an alliance with Virginia Mason Medical Center (to share medical centers and hospitals), as well as with Kaiser Permanente, one of the nation's largest nonprofit health care systems. The organization is owned by its nearly 600,000 members.

**KEY COMPETITORS**
Adventist Health
Health Net
PacifiCare

## GROWMARK, INC.

| | | |
|---|---|---|
| 1701 Towanda Ave. | CEO: Bill Davisson | 2000 Sales: $1,392.1 million |
| Bloomington, IL 61701 | CFO: Jeff Solberg | 1-Yr. Sales Change: 20.4% |
| Phone: 309-557-6000 | HR: Wes Ehler | Employees: 1,000 |
| Fax: 309-829-8532 | Type: Cooperative | FYE: August 31 |
| Web: www.growmark.com | | |

Retail farm-supply and grain-marketing cooperative GROWMARK can mark its growth by the grain. Through its member-owner co-ops — about 100 in retail and 250-plus in grain marketing — GROWMARK serves farmers in the midwestern US and Ontario, Canada. Under the Fast Stop name, the co-op runs fuel stations and convenience stores. Its FS- and NK-brand grains include alfalfa, corn, wheat, and soybeans. GROWMARK also offers fertilizer, seeds, and buildings such as grain bins. GROWMARK partners with Archer Daniels Midland, fertilizer maker and distributor CF Industries, pet food producer PRO-PET, and has an energy alliance with Countrymark Cooperative and Land O'Lakes.

**KEY COMPETITORS**
Agway
Cenex Harvest States
Farmland Industries

## GSC ENTERPRISES, INC.

130 Hillcrest Dr.
Sulphur Springs, TX 75482
Phone: 903-885-0829
Fax: 903-885-6928
Web: www.grocerysupply.com

CEO: Michael K. McKenzie
CFO: Kerry Law
HR: Theresa Patterson
Type: Private

2000 Sales: $1,082.0 million
1-Yr. Sales Change: (2.6%)
Employees: 1,100
FYE: December 31

GSC Enterprises brings the groceries to the grocery store. The wholesale distributor (whose name stands for "Grocery Supply Company," not to be confused with Grocers Supply Co.) supplies independently owned convenience stores, grocers, discounters, and other retailers and wholesalers. It serves a total of some 15,000 stores in about 15 states in the Southwest, Southeast, and Midwest. GSC stocks and distributes tobacco, candy, grocery items, prepared foods (Chicago Style Pizza, Chester Fried Chicken, Deli-Fast Foods), and other items. The firm also owns Fidelity Express, which sells money orders in stores. GSC is owned by the McKenzie family, descendants of two of the men who founded it in 1947.

**KEY COMPETITORS**
Eby-Brown
Fleming Companies
SUPERVALU

## GUARDIAN INDUSTRIES CORP.

2300 Harmon Rd.
Auburn Hills, MI 48326
Phone: 248-340-1800
Fax: 248-340-9988
Web: www.guardian.com

CEO: William M. Davidson
CFO: Jeffrey A. Knight
HR: Bruce Cummings
Type: Private

2000 Est. Sales: $4,000.0 mil.
1-Yr. Sales Change: 9.6%
Employees: 20,000
FYE: December 31

Giving its customers a break would never occur to Guardian Industries, one of the world's largest glassmakers. With plants in 17 countries on five continents, Guardian primarily produces float glass and fabricated glass products for the automobile and construction markets. It also makes architectural glass, fiberglass, and automotive trim parts. Through its Guardian Building Products Group, the company operates Guardian Fiberglass, Builder Marts of America (BMA) — 20% owned by Ace Hardware, and Cameron Ashley Building Products. President and CEO William Davidson took Guardian Industries public in 1968 and bought it back for himself in 1985. Davidson is the managing partner of the Detroit Pistons NBA team.

**KEY COMPETITORS**
Asahi Glass
Owens Corning
PPG

 See pages 212–213 for a full profile of this company.

## THE GUARDIAN LIFE INSURANCE COMPANY OF AMERICA

7 Hanover Sq.
New York, NY 10004
Phone: 212-598-8000
Fax: 212-919-2170
Web: www.glic.com

CEO: Joseph D. Sargent
CFO: Peter L. Hutchings
HR: Douglas C. Kramer
Type: Mutual company

2000 Sales: $6,568.6 million
1-Yr. Sales Change: 4.5%
Employees: 6,000
FYE: December 31

Guardian Life Insurance Company of America has chosen to remain part of the old guard — a mutual — while many of its competitors are going public. The company provides individual and group insurance and investment products. Facing deregulation and industry consolidation, the company is increasing its traditional indemnity group health insurance to encompass a comprehensive line of employee benefits, including HMO, PPO, and dental and vision plans, as well as disability plans. It is growing its retirement and wealth management offerings with the addition of brokerage and trust services. Guardian Life Insurance has operations in all 50 states, the District of Columbia, and Puerto Rico.

**KEY COMPETITORS**
Aetna
MetLife
Prudential

 See pages 214–215 for a full profile of this company.

## GULF OIL, L.P.

90 Everett Ave.
Chelsea, MA 02150
Phone: 617-889-9000
Fax: 617-884-0637
Web: www.gulfoil.com

CEO: John Kaneb
CFO: Alice Kuhne
HR: Karen Channel
Type: Partnership

2001 Sales: $1,970.0 million
1-Yr. Sales Change: 9.4%
Employees: 200
FYE: September 30

Gulf Oil bridges the gap between petroleum producers and retail sales outlets. The petroleum wholesaler distributes gasoline and diesel fuel to 1,800 Gulf-branded stations in 11 northeastern states. Gulf Oil, which owns and operates 12 storage terminals, also distributes motor oils, lubricants, and heating oil to commercial, industrial, and utility customers. The company has alliances with terminal operators in areas in the Northeast where it does not have a proprietary terminal. Noteworthy for providing the world's first drive-in service station, Gulf Oil was established in 1901 with an oil strike in Spindletop, Texas. The oil company restructured into seven operating companies in the 1970s.

**KEY COMPETITORS**
Amerada Hess
Getty Petroleum Marketing
Motiva Enterprises

## GULF STATES TOYOTA, INC.

7701 Wilshire Place Dr.
Houston, TX 77040
Phone: 713-580-3300
Fax: 713-744-3332

CEO: Toby Hynes
CFO: Frank Gruen
HR: Dominic Gallo
Type: Private

2000 Est. Sales: $3,250.0 mil.
1-Yr. Sales Change: 2.9%
Employees: 1,650
FYE: December 31

Even good ol' boys buy foreign cars from Gulf States Toyota. One of only two US Toyota distributors not owned by Toyota Motor Sales (the other is JM Family Enterprises' Southeast Toyota Distributors), the company distributes Toyota and Lexus cars, trucks, and sport utility vehicles in Arkansas, Louisiana, Mississippi, Oklahoma, and Texas. Founded in 1969 by Thomas Friedkin and still owned by The Friedkin Companies, Gulf States distributes new Toyotas, parts, and accessories to around 140 dealers in its region. Because Toyota has had success converting Internet leads into actual sales, Gulf States offers customizable Web site packages to its entire dealership network.

**KEY COMPETITORS**
Ford
General Motors
Nissan

## HALE-HALSELL CO.

9111 E. Pine St.
Tulsa, OK 74115
Phone: 918-835-4484
Fax: 918-641-5471

CEO: Robert D. Hawk
CFO: Michael Owens
HR: Ron Stacey
Type: Private

2000 Sales: $837.0 million
1-Yr. Sales Change: 0.0%
Employees: 4,638
FYE: December 31

Hale-Halsell Co. doesn't make cattle drives, but the food retailer and wholesaler does round up and move out grocery goods throughout Arkansas, Kansas, Missouri, Oklahoma, and Texas. On the retail side, the company operates about 120 Git-N-Go convenience stores and 12 SUPER H supermarkets, primarily in small Oklahoma towns. Hale-Halsell also runs a restaurant supply business. Tom Hale and Hugh Halsell started the company in 1901 to supply settlers in the newly opened Native American lands in Oklahoma. Hale-Halsell is majority-owned by Hale's descendant, Elmer Hale Jr.

**KEY COMPETITORS**
Fleming Companies
Kroger
Wal-Mart

## HALLMARK CARDS, INC.

2501 McGee St.
Kansas City, MO 64108
Phone: 816-274-5111
Fax: 816-274-5061
Web: www.hallmark.com

CEO: Donald J. Hall Jr.
CFO: Robert J. Druten
HR: Ralph N. Christensen
Type: Private

2000 Sales: $4,200.0 million
1-Yr. Sales Change: 0.0%
Employees: 24,500
FYE: December 31

As the #1 maker of meaningful missives, Hallmark Cards is the Goliath of greeting cards. The company's cards are sold under brand names such as Hallmark, Shoebox, and Ambassador and can be found in more than 47,000 US retail stores (about 7,500 of these stores bear the Hallmark name; the company owns less than 5% of these stores, and the rest are franchised). Hallmark also owns Binney & Smith (maker of Crayola brand crayons) and portrait studio chain The Picture People. It offers electronic greeting cards through its Web site, Hallmark.com, and produces television movies through Hallmark Entertainment's Crown Media. Members of the founding Hall family own two-thirds of Hallmark; company employees own the remainder.

**KEY COMPETITORS**
American Greetings
CSS Industries
Viacom

 See pages 216–217 for a full profile of this company.

## HARBOUR GROUP INDUSTRIES, INC.

7701 Forsyth Blvd., Ste. 600
St. Louis, MO 63105
Phone: 314-727-5550
Fax: 314-727-9912
Web: www.harbourgroup.com

CEO: Sam Fox
CFO: Mike Santoni
HR: Harriet Lovins
Type: Private

Sales: —
1-Yr. Sales Change: —
Employees: —
FYE: December 31

Troubled manufacturers can seek refuge with Harbour Group Industries, a conglomerate that acquires companies whose products include auto accessories, fluid handling equipment, plastics-processing equipment, heat exchangers, and textile machinery. Since its founding in 1976, Harbour Group has acquired about 125 companies in 23 different industries; most companies have been combined with similar acquisitions. Harbour Group takes a long-term approach with its acquisitions by assisting them with management and investments. Chairman and CEO Sam Fox controls the company.

**KEY COMPETITORS**
AptarGroup
Swagelok
United States Surgical

## HARPO, INC.

110 N. Carpenter St.
Chicago, IL 60607
Phone: 312-633-0808
Fax: 312-633-1976
Web: www.oprah.com

CEO: Oprah Winfrey
CFO: Doug Pattison
HR: Bernice Smith
Type: Private

2000 Sales: $180.0 million
1-Yr. Sales Change: 5.9%
Employees: 200
FYE: December 31

Harpo toots Oprah's horn. Unrelated to the silent Marx brother, Harpo (Oprah spelled backward) controls the entertainment interests of talk show host/actress/producer extraordinaire Oprah Winfrey, ranked by *Forbes* as one of the top 400 wealthiest Americans. *The Oprah Winfrey Show* is the highest-rated TV talk show in history (22 million viewers each week, about three-fourths of whom are women), seen in almost every US market and in more than 110 countries. Harpo also produces feature films (*Beloved,* which also starred Winfrey) and made-for-TV movies (*Oprah Winfrey Presents: Tuesdays with Morrie*) and launched *O, The Oprah Magazine* in 2000 with Hearst at a circulation of about 2.5 million. Winfrey founded Harpo in 1986.

**KEY COMPETITORS**
AOL Time Warner
Lifetime
USA Networks

 See pages 218–219 for a full profile of this company.

## THE HARTZ MOUNTAIN CORPORATION

400 Plaza Dr.
Secaucus, NJ 07094
Phone: 201-271-4800
Fax: 201-271-0164
Web: www.hartz.com

CEO: Robert Devine
CFO: Bill Salomon
HR: Kelly Shevlin
Type: Private

2000 Est. Sales: $977.0 mil.
1-Yr. Sales Change: 225.7%
Employees: 2,100
FYE: December 31

Hartz Mountain Corporation has something for pets of all sizes. The company markets about 1,500 pet care products including nutritional products for small pets, birds, and aquariums; over-the-counter animal health products (including flea and tick treatments); and toys and accessories for dogs, cats, and birds. Max Stern founded the company in 1926 after emigrating from Germany. The Stern family operated the company for more than 75 years under the Hartz Group umbrella along with the family's real estate operations. The company is buying the Alley Cat and Meow Mix brands from Nestlé Purina PetCare. An investment group, including members of Hartz management, bought the Hartz Mountain pet products business in 2001.

**KEY COMPETITORS**
Iams
Mars
Nestlé Purina PetCare

## HARVARD PILGRIM HEALTH CARE, INC.

93 Worcester St.
Wellesley, MA 02481
Phone: 617-745-1000
Fax: 617-509-7590
Web: www.harvardpilgrim.org

CEO: Charles D. Baker Jr.
CFO: Sujata S. Sanghvi
HR: Deborah Hicks
Type: Not-for-profit

2000 Sales: $2,100.0 million
1-Yr. Sales Change: (18.1%)
Employees: 1,500
FYE: December 31

This Harvard bleeds green rather than crimson. Harvard Pilgrim Health Care provides managed health care for Massachusetts and New England. The company offers its nearly 800,000 members HMO, preferred provider organization (PPO), point-of-service, and Medicaid/Medicare plans through more than 120 affiliated hospitals in New England. Harvard Pilgrim Health Care also offers HPHConnect, for online benefits administration. Harvard Pilgrim is recovering after being placed into receivership by the state of Massachusetts in 1999. Restructuring and raising premiums brought a healthier bottom line but also a significant reduction in membership.

**KEY COMPETITORS**
Blue Cross (MA)
CIGNA
Tufts Health Plan

## HARVARD UNIVERSITY

Massachusetts Hall
Cambridge, MA 02138
Phone: 617-495-1000
Fax: 617-495-0754
Web: www.harvard.edu

CEO: Lawrence H. Summers
CFO: Elizabeth Huidekoper
HR: Mary Cronin
Type: School

2000 Sales: $2,022.6 million
1-Yr. Sales Change: 13.2%
Employees: 11,360
FYE: June 30

Harvard — maybe you've heard of it? With an alumni roster that includes six US presidents, the university is one of the world's most prestigious. The oldest institution of higher learning in the US, Harvard is home to Harvard College (undergraduate studies) and 10 graduate schools (John F. Kennedy School of Government, the Harvard Business School, Harvard Law School, Harvard Medical School). The Radcliffe Institute for Advanced Study at Harvard was created when Radcliffe College and Harvard University merged in 1999. At more than $19 billion, Harvard's endowment is the largest of any US university (Yale ranks #2). President Neil Rudenstine stepped down in June 2001 and was replaced by former Treasury Secretary Lawrence Summers.

 See pages 220–221 for a full profile of this company.

## HAWORTH INC.

| | | |
|---|---|---|
| 1 Haworth Center | CEO: Gerald B. Johanneson | 2000 Sales: $2,060.0 million |
| Holland, MI 49423 | CFO: Calvin W. Kreuze | 1-Yr. Sales Change: 30.4% |
| Phone: 616-393-3000 | HR: Nancy Teutsch | Employees: 14,500 |
| Fax: 616-393-1570 | Type: Private | FYE: December 31 |
| Web: www.haworth.com | | |

Haworth isn't as square thinking as you might think it would be. The company is one of the top office furniture manufacturers in the US (behind #1 Steelcase and neck and neck with Herman Miller). Haworth grows through acquisitions and operates in more than 120 countries, offering typical office furniture, including desks, storage products, panel systems, tables, and chairs. The company — whose invention of pre-wired partitions made today's cubicled workplace possible — has a reputation for being efficient and aggressive and for regularly underpricing competitors. Haworth is owned by the family of Gerrard Haworth, who founded the company in 1948.

**KEY COMPETITORS**
Herman Miller
HON INDUSTRIES
Steelcase

 See pages 222–223 for a full profile of this company.

## H. B. ZACHRY COMPANY

| | | |
|---|---|---|
| 527 Logwood | CEO: Henry Bartell Zachry Jr. | 2000 Sales: $1,400.0 million |
| San Antonio, TX 78221 | CFO: Joe J. Lozano | 1-Yr. Sales Change: 17.2% |
| Phone: 210-475-8000 | HR: Barry Lacey | Employees: 14,000 |
| Fax: 210-475-8060 | Type: Private | FYE: December 31 |
| Web: www.zachry.com | | |

H. B. Zachry began building roads and bridges in 1924, and now his son and grandsons are running the show. The construction and industrial service firm's business today includes building and maintaining power and chemical plants, steel and paper mills, refineries, roadways, dams, airfields, and pipelines. Operating mostly in the southern US, H. B. Zachry has built facilities for companies such as Phillips, DuPont, Samsung, Alcoa, and Shell. It also works internationally and reconstructed the US Embassy in Moscow. Zachry also holds interests in ranches, oil exploration, cement, hospitality, realty, and entertainment companies, as well as the San Antonio Spurs basketball team.

**KEY COMPETITORS**
Bechtel
Fluor
Peter Kiewit Sons'

## H. E. BUTT GROCERY COMPANY

| | | |
|---|---|---|
| 646 S. Main Ave. | CEO: Charles C. Butt | 2001 Est. Sales: $8,965.0 mil. |
| San Antonio, TX 78204 | CFO: Jack C. Brouillard | 1-Yr. Sales Change: 9.3% |
| Phone: 210-938-8000 | HR: Susan Allford | Employees: 60,000 |
| Fax: 210-938-8169 | Type: Private | FYE: October 31 |
| Web: www.heb.com | | |

The Muzak bounces between Tejano and country, and the tortillas and ribs are big sellers at H. E. Butt Grocery (H-E-B). Texas' largest private company and the #1 food retailer in South and Central Texas, H-E-B owns some 295 supermarkets, including a growing number of large (70,000 sq. ft.) gourmet Central Markets in major metropolitan areas and more than 80 smaller (24,000-30,000 sq. ft.) Pantry Foods stores, often in more rural areas. H-E-B also has one store in Louisiana and 17 upscale and discount stores in Mexico. Most of the H-E-B stores have pharmacies and about 40% sell gasoline. H-E-B processes some of its own meat, dairy products, and bread. The company is owned by the Butt family, which founded H-E-B in 1905.

**KEY COMPETITORS**
Albertson's
Randall's
Wal-Mart

See pages 224–225 for a full profile of this company.

## HEAFNER TIRE GROUP, INC.

12200 Herbert Wayne Ct., Ste. 150
Huntersville, NC 28078
Phone: 704-992-2000
Fax: 704-992-1384
Web: www.heafnertiregroup.com

CEO: Richard P. "Dick" Johnson
CFO: William E. Berry
HR: J. David Phillips
Type: Private

2000 Sales: $1,087.3 million
1-Yr. Sales Change: 19.7%
Employees: 2,600
FYE: December 31

Heafner Tire Group's business starts where the rubber meets the road. The company is the largest independent distributor of tires and related products in the US. Tire brands include industry leaders Michelin and Bridgestone/Firestone as well as Goodyear, which also makes Heafner's Regal house brand through its Kelly-Springfield subsidiary. Heafner Tire's distribution business is split into three divisions serving 35 states. The company is selling its retail stores to focus on national distribution; it has sold 130 Winston Tire Centers on the West Coast and is selling about 30 T.O. Haas Tire Co. outlets as well. Heafner Tire plans to acquire other distributors. Charlesbank Equity Fund IV owns 94% of the company.

**KEY COMPETITORS**
Discount Tire
Goodyear
TBC

## HEALTH CARE SERVICE CORPORATION

300 E. Randolph
Chicago, IL 60601
Phone: 312-653-6000
Fax: 312-819-1220
Web: www.bcbsil.com

CEO: Raymond F. McCaskey
CFO: Sherman M. Wolff
HR: Robert Ernst
Type: Mutual company

2000 Sales: $10,429.7 million
1-Yr. Sales Change: 16.1%
Employees: —
FYE: December 31

Health Care Service Corporation (HCSC) has the Blues. HCSC is made up of Blue Cross Blue Shield of Illinois (that state's oldest and largest health insurer) and Blue Cross and Blue Shield of Texas. A licensee of the Blue Cross and Blue Shield Association, the mutual company provides a range of group and individual insurance and medical plans, including indemnity insurance and managed care programs. HCSC also offers life insurance, retirement services, and medical financial services through subsidiaries. The firm is set to align with The Regence Group, which operates the Blues of Oregon, Idaho, Washington, and Idaho, as well as buy the Blues of New Mexico.

**KEY COMPETITORS**
Humana
Prudential
UnitedHealth Group

 <section>See pages 226–227 for a full profile of this company.</section>

## HEALTH INSURANCE PLAN OF GREATER NEW YORK

7 W. 34th St.
New York, NY 10001
Phone: 212-630-5000
Fax: 212-630-8747
Web: www.hipusa.com

CEO: Anthony L. Watson
CFO: Michael Fullwood
HR: Fred Blickman
Type: Not-for-profit

2000 Sales: $2,409.7 million
1-Yr. Sales Change: 8.4%
Employees: —
FYE: December 31

This firm says it's HIP to be healthy. Health Insurance Plan of Greater New York (HIP) is a not-for-profit HMO founded in the 1940s to provide low-cost health care to New York City employees; HIP now boasts nearly 800,000 members. The organization provides medical, lab, and pharmacy services through some 14,000 physicians and about 100 facilities around New York City. Efforts in the 1990s to expand out-of-state proved disastrous; its New Jersey effort was closed by regulators, and HIP sold its Florida affiliate after accumulating huge losses. Back home, HIP has faced allegations from regulators of lavish executive lifestyles and too-cozy relationships with contractors.

**KEY COMPETITORS**
Aetna
Empire Blue Cross
Oxford Health Plans

## HEALTH MIDWEST

| | | |
|---|---|---|
| 2304 E. Meyer Blvd. | CEO: Richard Brown | 2000 Sales: $863.8 million |
| Kansas City, MO 64132 | CFO: Thomas Langenberg | 1-Yr. Sales Change: (2.3%) |
| Phone: 816-276-9297 | HR: Dennis Johnson | Employees: 12,000 |
| Fax: 816-276-9222 | Type: Not-for-profit | FYE: December 31 |
| Web: www.healthmidwest.org | | |

Health Midwest takes care of Kansas. It operates about 15 hospitals in the metropolitan Kansas City area. With about 3,000 physicians, Health Midwest is not only a huge health care provider, but also a major employer. Services include primary care, rehabilitation, and home health care. Specialized programs include childbirth classes, health screenings, hospice services, and behavioral health services. Joining forces with St. Luke's Shawnee Mission Health System, Health Midwest plans to open a comprehensive cancer care program in the region. Health care giant HCA, Inc., exited the Kansas City area after confronting intense competition from Health Midwest.

**KEY COMPETITORS**
Catholic Health Initiatives
Sisters of Charity of
  Leavenworth
Triad Hospitals

## THE HEARST CORPORATION

| | | |
|---|---|---|
| 959 8th Ave. | CEO: Frank A. Bennack Jr. | 2000 Est. Sales: $3,400.0 mil. |
| New York, NY 10019 | CFO: Ronald J. Doerfler | 1-Yr. Sales Change: 24.1% |
| Phone: 212-649-2000 | HR: Ruth Diem | Employees: 18,300 |
| Fax: 212-765-3528 | Type: Private | FYE: December 31 |
| Web: www.hearstcorp.com | | |

Family-owned Hearst Corporation is a media giant with interests in newspapers (Hearst Newspapers), magazines (Hearst Magazines), and business publishing; TV and radio (Hearst Argyle TV); a cartoon and features service (King Features); cable network programming; and online services. The company owns 12 daily newspapers, including the *San Francisco Chronicle* (which Hearst acquired after a lengthy antitrust inquiry that also resulted in the sale of rival paper *San Francisco Examiner*) and the *Houston Chronicle;* 18 weeklies; 16 US consumer magazines, including *Cosmopolitan;* stakes in cable TV networks, including A&E, Lifetime, and ESPN; and business publishers. Hearst also owns about 30% of iVillage, the Web network aimed at women.

**KEY COMPETITORS**
Advance Publications
Gannett
Viacom

 See pages 228–229 for a full profile of this company.

## HELMSLEY ENTERPRISES, INC.

| | | |
|---|---|---|
| 230 Park Ave., Room 659 | CEO: Leona Helmsley | 2000 Est. Sales: $1,000.0 mil. |
| New York, NY 10169 | CFO: Abe Wolf | 1-Yr. Sales Change: 0.0% |
| Phone: 212-679-3600 | HR: — | Employees: 3,000 |
| Fax: 212-953-2810 | Type: Private | FYE: December 31 |

Helmsley Enterprises is the repository of the real estate empire amassed by the late Harry Helmsley over a period of 50 years. Helmsley's widow and heir, Leona, has interests in such high-profile properties as the Helmsley Park Lane, Carlton House, and the Helmsley Windsor. Other holdings include apartment buildings and millions of square feet of primarily New York real estate, not to mention a lease held on the Empire State Building (which is owned by Donald Trump and others) until 2075. The portfolio was valued at $5 billion before Leona Helmsley began to sell properties from it after her husband's death; the company still controls real estate valued at about half that amount.

**KEY COMPETITORS**
Lefrak Organization
Tishman Realty
Vornado

 See pages 230–231 for a full profile of this company.

## HENDRICK AUTOMOTIVE GROUP

6000 Monroe Rd., Ste. 100
Charlotte, NC 28212
Phone: 704-568-5550
Fax: 704-566-3295
Web: www.hendrickauto.com

CEO: Jim C. Perkins
CFO: James F. Huzl
HR: Tim Taylor
Type: Private

2000 Sales: $2,482.7 million
1-Yr. Sales Change: (1.6%)
Employees: —
FYE: December 31

For megadealer Hendrick Automotive Group, variety is the spice of life. The company sells new and used cars and light trucks from about 20 automakers, including General Motors, Honda, and Porsche. Hendrick has a network of about 50 dealerships in nine states ranging from the Carolinas to California. The company also offers financing, leasing, and insurance, as well as automobile parts, accessories, service, and body repair. Founder Rick Hendrick pleaded guilty in 1997 to mail fraud relating to alleged bribes of American Honda executives; he was later pardoned by President Bill Clinton. Hendrick owns the company.

**KEY COMPETITORS**
AutoNation
Sonic Automotive
United Auto Group


## HENRY FORD HEALTH SYSTEM

1 Ford Place
Detroit, MI 48202
Phone: 313-876-8700
Fax: 313-876-9243
Web: www.henryfordhealth.org

CEO: Gail L. Warden
CFO: David Mazurkiewicz
HR: Robert Rieny
Type: Not-for-profit

2000 Sales: $1,900.0 million
1-Yr. Sales Change: 54.7%
Employees: 16,000
FYE: December 31

In 1915 automaker Henry Ford founded the hospital that would be the starting point for southeastern Michigan's not-for-profit Henry Ford Health System, a hospital network that is also involved in medical research and education. The system includes six hospitals with about 2,000 beds, more than 30 other health care facilities, and over 2,000 physicians representing a wide range of specialties. The system's Health Alliance Plan provides managed care and health insurance to more than 500,000 members. The Henry Ford Health Sciences Center Research Institute, the Josephine Ford Cancer Center, and other research centers and affiliated hospitals are also part of the health care system.

**KEY COMPETITORS**
Detroit Medical Center
Trinity Health
William Beaumont Hospital


## HENSEL PHELPS CONSTRUCTION CO.

420 6th Ave.
Greeley, CO 80632
Phone: 970-352-6565
Fax: 970-352-9311
Web: www.henselphelps.com

CEO: Jerry L. Morgensen
CFO: Stephen J. Carrico
HR: —
Type: Private

2001 Sales: $1,368.0 million
1-Yr. Sales Change: 0.8%
Employees: 2,200
FYE: May 31

Hensel Phelps Construction builds it all, from the courthouse to the Big House. Launched as a homebuilding firm by Hensel Phelps in 1937, the employee-owned company now focuses on such nonresidential projects as prisons, airport facilities, hotels, government and corporate complexes, convention centers, sport arenas, and department stores. Hensel Phelps offers design/build, construction management, and turnkey services to clients, as well as financing and cost estimates. Through offices in six states, Hensel Phelps operates nationwide. Major clients include ChevronTexaco, IBM, the Pentagon, United Airlines, and Neiman Marcus.

**KEY COMPETITORS**
Clark Enterprises
PCL Construction
Turner Corporation

## THE HERB CHAMBERS COMPANIES

259 McGrath Hwy.
Somerville, MA 02145
Phone: 617-666-8333
Fax: 617-666-8448
Web: www.chamberscars.com

CEO: Herbert G. Chambers
CFO: Bruce Spatz
HR: —
Type: Private

2000 Sales: $974.2 million
1-Yr. Sales Change: 21.7%
Employees: 1,000
FYE: December 31

Step into the chambers of The Herb Chambers Companies and you'll find a wide range of cars. The company runs about 20 dealerships in New England that sell just about everthing from pricey new cars from BMW, Cadillac, Lexus, Mercedes-Benz, and Porsche to more affordable offerings from Honda, Hyundai, Kia, Mazda, Saturn, and Toyota; dealerships also offer used cars. All of its cars are available online, and customers can buy a car, sight unseen, via fax, phone, or e-mail, and have the dealer deliver it. Herb Chambers also offers parts and service and online credit applications. Owner and CEO Herb Chambers started his automotive empire with a Cadillac/Oldsmobile dealership in New London, Connecticut, in 1985.

**KEY COMPETITORS**
AutoNation
Group 1 Automotive
United Auto Group

## HEWITT ASSOCIATES LLC

100 Half Day Rd.
Lincolnshire, IL 60069
Phone: 847-295-5000
Fax: 847-295-7634
Web: www.hewitt.com

CEO: Dale L. Gifford
CFO: Dan DeCanniere
HR: David Wille
Type: Private

2001 Sales: $1,500.0 million
1-Yr. Sales Change: 17.6%
Employees: 12,933
FYE: September 30

If any of a company's resources are human, chances are it'll need the assistance of Hewitt Associates. Hewitt Associates' consulting services cover human resources, employee benefits, compensation, financial management, and administrative issues for more than 2,300 clients (which together have more than 12 million employees). The Hewitt 401(k) Index tracks 401(k) activity by tracing the movements of 1.5 million 401(k) participants, and the company also offers investment consulting services. Hewitt Associates, which has about 80 offices in 37 countries, was founded by Ted Hewitt in 1940.

**KEY COMPETITORS**
Buck Consultants
Towers Perrin
Watson Wyatt

## HICKS, MUSE, TATE & FURST INCORPORATED

200 Crescent Ct., Ste. 1600
Dallas, TX 75201
Phone: 214-740-7300
Fax: 214-720-7888

CEO: Thomas O. Hicks
CFO: Darron Ash
HR: Lynita Jessen
Type: Private

Sales: —
1-Yr. Sales Change: —
Employees: —
FYE: December 31

Hicks, Muse, Tate & Furst likes to buy, buy, buy & buy. (It sells sometimes, too.) The leveraged buyout firm assembles limited partnership investment pools and targets companies in specific niches that can be used to form a nucleus for other investments. Hicks, Muse (which sold its AMFM broadcast group to rival Clear Channel Communications to form the US's largest radio/TV/outdoor advertising firm) was moving abroad with media and food-company acquisitions in Latin America and Europe but the global downturn put the kibosh on those worldly aspirations. Hicks, Muse also has holdings in manufacturing, real estate, and other sectors.

**KEY COMPETITORS**
Clayton, Dubilier
Investcorp
KKR

See pages 232–233 for a full profile of this company.

## HIGHMARK INC.

| | | |
|---|---|---|
| 5th Ave. Place, 120 5th Ave. | CEO: John S. Brouse | 2000 Sales: $9,000.0 million |
| Pittsburgh, PA 15222 | CFO: Robert C. Gray | 1-Yr. Sales Change: 9.9% |
| Phone: 412-544-7000 | HR: S. Tyrone Alexander | Employees: 11,000 |
| Fax: 412-544-8368 | Type: Not-for-profit | FYE: December 31 |
| Web: www.highmark.com | | |

Highmark aims to be at the acme of HMOs. Operating under the Highmark Blue Cross Blue Shield name in western Pennsylvania and as Pennsylvania Blue Shield in the rest of the state, Highmark provides health-related coverage to more than 20 million customers. It also processes Medicare claims (Veritus Medicare and HGSAdministrators Medicare Services), offers administrative and information services (Alliance Ventures), and sells group life, disability, and employer stop loss insurance through its Highmark Life and Casualty Group subsidiary. The company also provides community service programs, such as the Western Pennsylvania Caring Foundation.

**KEY COMPETITORS**
Aetna
CIGNA
UnitedHealth Group

 See pages 234–235 for a full profile of this company.

## HOBBY LOBBY STORES, INC.

| | | |
|---|---|---|
| 7707 SW 44th St. | CEO: David Green | 2000 Sales: $905.0 million |
| Oklahoma City, OK 73179 | CFO: Patrick Jones | 1-Yr. Sales Change: 13.4% |
| Phone: 405-745-1100 | HR: — | Employees: 13,500 |
| Fax: 405-745-1636 | Type: Private | FYE: December 31 |
| Web: www.hobbylobby.com | | |

If something wicker this way comes, Hobby Lobby Stores might be the source. The company operates about 250 stores in 24 states, selling arts and craft supplies, candles, baskets, silk flowers, home decorating accessories, and frames. Hobby Lobby is the #3 craft retailer (after Michaels Stores and Jo-Ann Stores), and it prefers to set up shop in second-generation retail sites (such as vacated supermarkets and Wal-Mart stores). Sister companies supply Hobby Lobby with merchandise. Distribution is controlled through one center in Oklahoma City. CEO David Green, who owns the company with his wife, Barbara, founded the company in 1972 and operates it according to biblical principles, including closing stores on Sunday.

**KEY COMPETITORS**
Garden Ridge
Jo-Ann Stores
Michaels Stores

## HOFFMAN CORPORATION

| | | |
|---|---|---|
| 805 SW Broadway, Ste. 2100 | CEO: Cecil W. Drinkward | 2000 Sales: $954.0 million |
| Portland, OR 97205 | CFO: Scott Fredricks | 1-Yr. Sales Change: 138.5% |
| Phone: 503-221-8811 | HR: Dick Burnham | Employees: 1,460 |
| Fax: 503-221-8934 | Type: Private | FYE: December 31 |
| Web: www.hoffmancorp.com | | |

Hoffman cherishes a challenge — such as building the nation's deepest subway station in Portland, Oregon, or the snakelike, metal-clad Experience Music Project in Seattle. The company's main subsidiary, Hoffman Construction, builds civic, commercial, and industrial facilities, primarily in the western and midwestern US. One of the top builders of manufacturing facilities, Hoffman also serves such sectors as education, health care, and power generation. Its in-house abilities include plumbing and high-tech cleanroom process systems (Hoffman Mechanical), substructures and superstructures (Hoffman Structures), and specialty electrical wiring (HT Electric). Employees own the company, which was founded in 1922.

**KEY COMPETITORS**
Bovis Lend Lease
Skanska
Turner Corporation

## HOLBERG INDUSTRIES, INC.

545 Steamboat Rd.
Greenwich, CT 06830
Phone: 203-422-3000
Fax: 203-661-5756
Web: www.holberg.com

CEO: John V. Holten
CFO: A. Peter Ostberg
HR: —
Type: Private

2000 Sales: $4,250.0 million
1-Yr. Sales Change: (57.5%)
Employees: 18,300
FYE: December 31

Holberg Industries' customers used to be able to drive through, now they just park it. The company owns about 80% of APCOA/Standard Parking, which runs about 2,000 parking lots, mainly at airports and in urban areas, throughout the US. Holberg Industries once ran Ameriserve Food Distribution, which provided food, beverages, and supplies to Pizza Hut, Taco Bell, and KFC; it sold that unit to distributor McLane Company (a unit of Wal-Mart Stores) in November 2000. John Holten owns a controlling interest in Holberg Industries, which he co-founded in 1986; Norwegian consumer products company Orkla owns 34%.

**KEY COMPETITORS**
Ace Parking
Central Parking
Republic Parking

 **See pages 236–237 for a full profile of this company.**


## HOLIDAY COMPANIES

4567 W. 80th St.
Bloomington, MN 55437
Phone: 952-830-8700
Fax: 952-830-8864
Web: www.holidaystationstores.com

CEO: Ronald A. Erickson
CFO: Dennis Lindahl
HR: Bob Nye
Type: Private

2000 Sales: $1,200.0 million
1-Yr. Sales Change: 9.1%
Employees: 5,500
FYE: December 31

Wholesaling has taken a vacation at Holiday Companies. It sold its Fairway Foods distributions buiness to Fleming Companies in 2000 and now owns convenience stores and sporting good stores in the upper Midwest and Northwest. Holiday Companies owns more than 250 Holiday Stationstores in 11 states and also has 37 franchised stores. These sell gas supplied by the company's Erickson Petroleum subsidiary. It also owns 35 sporting goods stores (mostly Gander Mountain stores). The company was founded in 1928 as a general store in a small Wisconsin town by two Erickson brothers, whose descendents own and operate the company.

**KEY COMPETITORS**
7-Eleven
Casey's General Stores
Exxon Mobil


## HOLMAN ENTERPRISES

7411 Maple Ave.
Pennsauken, NJ 08109
Phone: 856-663-5200
Fax: 856-665-3444
Web: www.holmanauto.com

CEO: Joseph S. Holman
CFO: Robert Campbell
HR: Paul Toepel
Type: Private

2000 Sales: $2,200.0 million
1-Yr. Sales Change: 2.5%
Employees: 2,800
FYE: December 31

Holman sells a whole lot of cars. Family-owned Holman Enterprises owns more than 20 car and truck dealerships in southern New Jersey and southern Florida. Founded in 1924, Holman sells Ford, Lincoln, Mercury, Saturn, BMW, Infiniti, Jaguar, and Rolls-Royce cars and Ford, Kenworth, and Sterling trucks. The company also offers collision repair services. Holman's RMP engine and parts distributor sells small parts and powertrains authorized by Ford. Its Automotive Resources International unit, one of the largest independently owned vehicle fleet leasing management groups in the world, also operates a truck parts and accessories company.

**KEY COMPETITORS**
AutoNation
Penske
United Auto Group

## HONICKMAN AFFILIATES

| | | |
|---|---|---|
| 8275 Rte. 130 | CEO: Jeffrey Honickman | 2000 Est. Sales: $980.0 mil. |
| Pennsauken, NJ 08110 | CFO: Walt Wilkinson | 1-Yr. Sales Change: (2.5%) |
| Phone: 856-665-6200 | HR: June Raufer | Employees: 5,000 |
| Fax: 856-661-4684 | Type: Private | FYE: December 31 |

Honickman Affiliates doesn't mind bottling its creative juices. The firm is one of the nation's largest private bottlers — bottling and distributing soft drinks primarily in Maryland, New Jersey, New York, Ohio, and Virginia through more than 10 plants. A major bottler of Pepsi-Cola brands and Cadbury Schweppes brands including 7 UP, it also sells Canada Dry, Mott's, Snapple, and South Beach Beverage Company's SoBe beverages. It distributes Coors beers in New York and brews up private label soft drinks. Honickman is buying smaller bottlers and is a PepsiCo anchor bottler candidate. Chairman and owner Harold Honickman started the company in 1957 when his father-in-law built a bottling plant for him.

**KEY COMPETITORS**
Coca-Cola Enterprises
Cott
Philadelphia Coca-Cola

## HORSESHOE GAMING HOLDING CORP.

| | | |
|---|---|---|
| 2300 Empress Drive | CEO: Jack Binion | 2000 Sales: $1,012.8 million |
| Joliet, IL 60434 | CFO: Kirk C. Saylor | 1-Yr. Sales Change: 92.7% |
| Phone: 815-773-0700 | HR: David Carroll | Employees: 9,699 |
| Fax: 815-744-9455 | Type: Private | FYE: December 31 |
| Web: www.horseshoegaming.com | | |

Bring your lucky charms to casinos owned by Horseshoe Gaming Holding Corp. The company owns a Horseshoe Casino and Hotel in Bossier City, Louisiana, as well as one in Tunica, Mississippi. In 2001 Horseshoe Gaming sold its Empress Casino riverboat and hotel in Joliet, Illinois, but it retains an Empress location in Hammond, Indiana. Illinois officials denied the company a license to operate the Empress riverboat in Joliet, alleging that owner and CEO Jack Binion failed to comply with state regulations after buying the casino. The company appealed the decision but later struck a deal that forced it to sell the location to Argosy Gaming.

**KEY COMPETITORS**
Casino Magic
Park Place Entertainment
Pinnacle Entertainment

## HOUCHENS INDUSTRIES INC.

| | | |
|---|---|---|
| 900 Church St. | CEO: Jim Gipson | 2001 Sales: $820.0 million |
| Bowling Green, KY 42101 | CFO: Mark Iverson | 1-Yr. Sales Change: 11.6% |
| Phone: 270-843-3252 | HR: Sharon Grooms | Employees: 5,200 |
| Fax: 270-781-6377 | Type: Private | FYE: September 30 |

Houchens Industries operates stores for shoppers more interested in supper than super. Eschewing the industry trend toward massive superstores, the company's 36 Houchens Markets in Kentucky average less than 20,000 sq. ft. Its more than 160 Save-A-Lot stores (licensed from SUPERVALU) offer limited selections and cover 15,000 sq. ft. or less. The Save-A-Lot stores are in 11 states from Georgia to New York. Houchens also owns more than 40 Jr. Foods convenience stores and 20 Tobacco Shoppe discount cigarette outlets, mostly in Kentucky and Tennessee. It bought cigarette maker Commonwealth Brands in 2001. Founded as BG Wholesale in 1918 by Ervin Houchens, the company is entirely owned by its employees.

**KEY COMPETITORS**
Kroger
K-VA-T Food Stores
Winn-Dixie

## H.T. HACKNEY CO.

| | | |
|---|---|---|
| 502 S. Gay St. | CEO: William B. Sansom | 2000 Sales: $2,000.0 million |
| Knoxville, TN 37902 | CFO: Mike Morton | 1-Yr. Sales Change: 0.0% |
| Phone: 865-546-1291 | HR: — | Employees: 3,000 |
| Fax: 865-546-1501 | Type: Private | FYE: December 31 |

The H.T. Hackney Company began delivering goods to small grocers by horse and buggy in 1891; it now supplies 30,000 independent grocers and convenience stores in more than 20 states east of the Mississippi. H.T. Hackney distributes more than 10,000 name-brand items, including frozen food, tobacco products, health and beauty items, and deli products. In addition, it owns convenience store wholesaler Eli Witt, has furniture-making operations (Volunteer Fabricators), and distributes petroleum through its Hackney Petroleum division. Looking to expand its convenience store business, in September 2000 the company acquired six gas stations from Aztex Enterprises. Chairman and CEO Bill Sansom owns H.T. Hackney.

**KEY COMPETITORS**
Eby-Brown
GSC Enterprises
McLane

## HUNT CONSOLIDATED INC.

| | | |
|---|---|---|
| Fountain Place | CEO: Ray L. Hunt | 2000 Est. Sales: $2,000.0 mil. |
| Dallas, TX 75202 | CFO: Donald Robillard | 1-Yr. Sales Change: 66.7% |
| Phone: 214-978-8000 | HR: Charles Mills | Employees: 2,500 |
| Fax: 214-978-8888 | Type: Private | FYE: December 31 |

Hunt Consolidated is a holding company for the oil and real estate businesses of Ray Hunt, son of legendary Texas wildcatter and company founder H.L. Hunt. Founded in 1934 (reportedly with H. L.'s poker winnings), Hunt Oil is an oil and gas production and exploration company with primary interests in North and South America. Hoping to repeat huge discoveries in Yemen, Hunt is exploring in Ghana, Newfoundland, and Madagascar. It has also teamed up with Repsol YPF and S.K. Corp. on an exploration project in Peru and has expanded its Canadian operations through the acquisition of Chieftain International. Hunt Realty handles commercial and residential real estate development and investment management activities.

**KEY COMPETITORS**
BP
Exxon Mobil
Lincoln Property

## HUNT CONSTRUCTION GROUP

| | | |
|---|---|---|
| 2450 S. Tibbs Ave. | CEO: Robert G. Hunt | 2000 Sales: $1,352.0 million |
| Indianapolis, IN 46241 | CFO: Steve Atkins | 1-Yr. Sales Change: 4.0% |
| Phone: 317-227-7800 | HR: Debbie Molina | Employees: 710 |
| Fax: 317-227-7810 | Type: Private | FYE: December 31 |
| Web: www.huntconstructiongroup.com | | |

Hunt Construction Group knows that if they build it, you will come. A private company held by the Hunt Corporation based in Scottsdale, Arizona (not to be confused with office and art supply vendor Hunt Corporation), the construction firm is a leading builder of sports complexes, from the old Three Rivers Stadium to Heinz Field, new home of the Pittsburgh Steelers. The company's portfolio also includes aviation facilities, convention centers, corporate office buildings, government buildings, hospitals, hotels, industrial operations, research development centers, and universities. The group, formerly Huber, Hunt & Nichols, changed its name to more accurately reflect the ownership of the corporation.

**KEY COMPETITORS**
Barton Malow
Gilbane
Turner Corporation

## HUNTSMAN CORPORATION

500 Huntsman Way
Salt Lake City, UT 84108
Phone: 801-584-5700
Fax: 801-584-5781
Web: www.huntsman.com

CEO: Peter R. Huntsman
CFO: J. Kimo Esplin
HR: William Chapman
Type: Private

2000 Sales: $8,000.0 million
1-Yr. Sales Change: 14.3%
Employees: 16,000
FYE: December 31

Huntsman Corporation would like to sell you some chemicals — for a good cause. The company is the largest privately held chemical business in the world and was founded by Jon Huntsman, a philanthropist who devotes a large portion of earnings to charities. The company makes petrochemicals (used in detergents and textiles); surfactants (used in adhesives and paper processing); polyurethanes (used in foams and coatings); and titanium dioxide pigments (used in consumer products). Huntsman sells its chemicals to companies in the plastics, automotive, construction, high-tech, health care, personal care, and textiles industries. Huntsman controls the company.

**KEY COMPETITORS**
BASF AG
Dow Chemical
DuPont

 **See pages 238–239 for a full profile of this company.**


## HYATT CORPORATION

200 W. Madison St.
Chicago, IL 60606
Phone: 312-750-1234
Fax: 312-750-8550
Web: www.hyatt.com

CEO: Thomas J. Pritzker
CFO: Frank Borg
HR: Linda Olson
Type: Private

2000 Sales: $3,950.0 million
1-Yr. Sales Change: 16.2%
Employees: 80,000
FYE: January 31

Hyatt is at your service. One of the nation's largest hotel operators, the company has more than 120 full-service luxury hotels and resorts in North America and the Caribbean (Hyatt International, a separate entity, operates more than 80 hotels and resorts in 38 other countries). Many of Hyatt's hotels and resorts feature professionally designed golf courses and supervised activities for children (Camp Hyatt). The company also operates casinos and luxury retirement communities (Classic Residence by Hyatt). The Pritzker family owns both the US and foreign Hyatt operations.

**KEY COMPETITORS**
Hilton
Marriott International
Starwood Hotels & Resorts

**See pages 240–241 for a full profile of this company.**


## HY-VEE, INC.

5820 Westown Pkwy.
West Des Moines, IA 50266
Phone: 515-267-2800
Fax: 515-267-2817
Web: www.hy-vee.com

CEO: Ronald D. Pearson
CFO: John Briggs
HR: Jane Knaack-Esbeck
Type: Private

2001 Est. Sales: $4,000.0 mil.
1-Yr. Sales Change: 11.1%
Employees: 46,000
FYE: September 30

Give Hy-Vee a high five for being one of the largest privately owned US supermarket chains — despite serving some modestly sized midwestern towns. The company runs more than 210 Hy-Vee supermarkets in Illinois, Iowa, Kansas, Minnesota, Missouri, Nebraska, and South Dakota. About half of its supermarkets are in Iowa, as are most of its 25-plus Drug Town drugstores. It distributes products to its stores through several subsidiaries, including Lomar Distributing (specialty foods), Perishable Distributors of Iowa (fresh foods), and Florist Distributing (flowers). Charles Hyde and David Vredenburg founded the employee-owned firm in 1930. The company's moniker is a combination of the founders' names.

**KEY COMPETITORS**
Albertson's
Eagle Food
Fareway Stores

## IASIS HEALTHCARE CORPORATION

| | | |
|---|---|---|
| 113 Seaboard Ln., Ste. A200 | CEO: David R. White | 2001 Sales: $889.5 million |
| Franklin, TN 37067 | CFO: W. Carl Whitmer | 1-Yr. Sales Change: 9.1% |
| Phone: 615-844-2747 | HR: Russ Follis | Employees: 8,100 |
| Fax: 615-846-3006 | Type: Private | FYE: September 30 |
| Web: www.iasishealthcare.com | | |

If you're sick in the suburbs, IASIS Healthcare provides a medical oasis. Formed largely from castoffs of hospital operators Tenet Healthcare and Paracelsus Healthcare (now Clarent Hospital Corporation) and a series of management buyouts in 1999, the company owns and operates 14 hospitals in Arizona, Florida, Texas, and Utah. Its operations in Arizona include outpatient surgical centers and Health Choice, a Medicaid-managed health plan that serves some 43,000 individuals. IASIS focuses on building networks of mid-sized hospitals in growing urban and suburban regions. Private equity firm Joseph Littlejohn & Levy owns more than 85% of the company.

**KEY COMPETITORS**
HCA
Tenet Healthcare
Triad Hospitals

## ICC INDUSTRIES INC.

| | | |
|---|---|---|
| 460 Park Ave. | CEO: John Oram | 2000 Est. Sales: $1,300.0 mil. |
| New York, NY 10022 | CFO: Susan Abinder | 1-Yr. Sales Change: 8.3% |
| Phone: 212-521-1700 | HR: Frances Foti | Employees: 1,900 |
| Fax: 212-521-1794 | Type: Private | FYE: December 31 |
| Web: www.iccchem.com | | |

ICC Industries keeps pharmaceutical companies supplied with the raw materials used in manufacturing drugs. An international maker and marketer of chemicals, plastics, and pharmaceutical products, ICC also trades and distributes nutritional supplements and food ingredients. Its main subsidiary, ICC Chemical Corporation, maintains trading and marketing offices in Asia, Europe, South America, and the US. The company's Prior Energy Corporation has natural gas distribution interests in several southern states. ICC Industries also owns about 65% of Pharmaceutical Formulations, a manufacturer and distributor of generic over-the-counter drugs. The Farber family, including chairman John Farber, owns ICC.

**KEY COMPETITORS**
Formosa Plastics
IFF
IVAX

## ICON HEALTH & FITNESS, INC.

| | | |
|---|---|---|
| 1500 S. 1000 West | CEO: Scott R. Watterson | 2001 Est. Sales: $850.0 mil. |
| Logan, UT 84321 | CFO: S. Fred Beck | 1-Yr. Sales Change: 16.0% |
| Phone: 435-750-5000 | HR: Doug Younker | Employees: 5,000 |
| Fax: 435-752-6290 | Type: Private | FYE: May 31 |
| Web: www.iconfitness.com | | |

ICON Health & Fitness has muscle as the leading US maker of home fitness equipment. ICON's products include treadmills, elliptical trainers, and weight benches. Brands include Weider, HealthRider, IMAGE, NordicTrack, ProForm, JumpKing, Weslo, and the licensed Reebok name. ICON also offers fitness accessories, spas, and commercial fitness equipment. It makes most of its products in Utah and sells them through retailers, infomercials, online, and its catalog, Workout Warehouse. Sears has an exclusive license to sell NordicTrack-brand apparel. Bain Capital, Credit Suisse, and founders Scott Watterson and Gary Stevenson own more than 90% of ICON. The company intends to license its brand names to other manufacturers.

**KEY COMPETITORS**
Brunswick
Cybex International
Guthy-Renker

## IGA, INC.

8725 W. Higgins Rd.
Chicago, IL 60631
Phone: 773-693-4520
Fax: 773-693-4532
Web: www.igainc.com

CEO: Thomas S. Haggai
CFO: —
HR: —
Type: Association

2000 Sales: $21,000.0 million
1-Yr. Sales Change: 16.7%
Employees: 92,000
FYE: December 31

IGA grocers are independent, but not that independent. The world's largest voluntary supermarket network, IGA has more than 4,000 stores, including members in nearly all 50 states in the US and in about 40 other countries. Collectively, its members are among North America's leaders in terms of supermarket sales. IGA (for either International or Independent Grocers Alliance, the company says) is owned by 37 worldwide marketing and distribution companies, including Fleming Companies and SUPERVALU. Members can sell IGA Brand private-label products and take advantage of joint operations and services such as advertising and volume buying. The first US grocer in China, IGA has moved into Europe with its operations in Poland.

**KEY COMPETITORS**
Kroger
Safeway
Wakefern Food

 See pages 242–243 for a full profile of this company.

## ILLINOIS DEPARTMENT OF THE LOTTERY

201 E. Madison
Springfield, IL 62702
Phone: 217-524-5157
Fax: 217-524-5154
Web: www.illinoislottery.com

CEO: Lori Montana
CFO: Dave Mizeur
HR: Thomas Frefcura
Type: Government-owned

2000 Sales: $1,503.0 million
1-Yr. Sales Change: (1.1%)
Employees: —
FYE: June 30

Just because the Cubs can't win in Illinois doesn't mean you can't. Created in 1974, the Illinois Department of the Lottery runs numbers games, including Pick 3 and Pick 4, and participates in the seven-state Big Game in which players can win jackpots starting at $5 million (odds of winning: 1 in 76 million). It also offers instant-win scratch-off games. Of the money collected from ticket sales, 55% is paid in prizes and 34% goes to the state's Common School Fund, which helps finance K-12 public education. The rest covers retailer commissions and expenses. The Illinois Lottery operates through more than 8,000 retail businesses.

**KEY COMPETITORS**
Kentucky Lottery
Multi-State Lottery
Hoosier Lottery

## INDIANA UNIVERSITY

107 S. Indiana Ave.
Bloomington, IN 47405
Phone: 812-855-4848
Fax: 812-855-7002
Web: www.indiana.edu

CEO: Myles Brand
CFO: Judith G. Palmer
HR: Linda Rasmussen
Type: School

2001 Sales: $1,782.5 million
1-Yr. Sales Change: 7.5%
Employees: —
FYE: June 30

Indiana University has been educating residents of the Hoosier state since its founding in 1820. With a total student population exceeding 92,000, the university has eight campuses including flagship institution IU-Bloomington and seven commuter campuses in Fort Wayne, Gary, Indianapolis, Kokomo, New Albany, Richmond, and South Bend. IU-Bloomington offers students more than 100 academic programs in more than a dozen schools. Its graduate schools offer advanced degrees in a variety of areas ranging from business to music to law. IU-Bloomington also is home to a string of centers and institutes, including the Advanced Research & Technology Institute and the Center for International Business Education and Research.

## INGRAM ENTERTAINMENT HOLDINGS INC.

2 Ingram Blvd.
La Vergne, TN 37089
Phone: 615-287-4000
Fax: 615-287-4982
Web: www.ingramentertainment.com

CEO: David B. Ingram
CFO: William D. "Donnie" Daniel
HR: Andy Grossberg
Type: Private

2000 Sales: $1,057.0 million
1-Yr. Sales Change: (8.5%)
Employees: 1,200
FYE: December 31

Companies selling books and CDs might get the star treatment, but Ingram Entertainment Holdings doesn't mind its supporting role. Ingram is the #1 independent video, DVD, and computer game distributor in the US. It also distributes software, audio books, electronics, and used videos and games. From 17 US locations, Ingram serves more than 17,000 video stores, mass retailers, e-tailers, drugstores, and supermarkets (including Blockbuster, Tower Records, and Walgreens). Ingram offers direct-to-consumer fulfillment services for e-commerce sites and has a majority stake in ad agency Frank, Best & Ingram. David Ingram owns 95% of Ingram Entertainment, which was spun off from family-owned Ingram Industries in 1997.

**KEY COMPETITORS**
Alliance Entertainment
Baker & Taylor
Handleman

## INGRAM INDUSTRIES INC.

1 Belle Meade Place, 4400 Harding Rd.
Nashville, TN 37205
Phone: 615-298-8200
Fax: 615-298-8242
Web: www.ingram.com

CEO: Orrin H. Ingram II
CFO: Robert W. Mitchell
HR: Dennis Delaney
Type: Private

2000 Sales: $2,075.0 million
1-Yr. Sales Change: (2.8%)
Employees: 6,494
FYE: December 31

Ingram Industries is into books, boats, and bad drivers. Ingram Book Group is the #1 wholesale book distributor in the US; it ships more than 175 million books and audiotapes annually, serving some 32,000 retail outlets and 13,000 publishers. Ingram Marine Group operates Ingram Materials and 1,800 barges through Ingram Barge. Ingram's Permanent General Insurance covers high-risk drivers in nine states. The Ingram family, led by chairman Martha Ingram, owns and runs Ingram Industries and controls about 75% of the voting shares of top computer products wholesaler Ingram Micro. Martha's son David owns top video distributor Ingram Entertainment.

**KEY COMPETITORS**
American Commercial Lines
Baker & Taylor
State Farm

 See pages 244–245 for a full profile of this company.

## INOVA HEALTH SYSTEM

2990 Telestar Ct.
Falls Church, VA 22042
Phone: 703-289-2000
Fax: 703-205-2161
Web: www.inova.org

CEO: Knox Singleton
CFO: Richard Magenheimer
HR: Ellen Menard
Type: Not-for-profit

2000 Sales: $1,009.4 million
1-Yr. Sales Change: 4.8%
Employees: 13,000
FYE: December 31

Inova keeps No. Va. healthy. Founded in 1956 as a country hospital in Fairfax, Virginia, Inova Health System is a not-for-profit health care provider, offering acute and subacute care, long-term care, home health care, mental health, and satellite emergency care services in the Virginia suburbs of Washington, DC. Inova's network includes five hospitals (including a children's hospital) with about 1,400 beds, as well as assisted living centers for seniors and several family practice locations. Through the Inova Health System Foundation, the company coordinates philanthropy programs for the community.

**KEY COMPETITORS**
HCA
Johns Hopkins Medicine
MedStar

## INSERRA SUPERMARKETS, INC.

| | | |
|---|---|---|
| 20 Ridge Rd. | CEO: Lawrence R. Inserra | 2000 Sales: $834.0 million |
| Mahwah, NJ 07430 | CFO: Theresa Inserra | 1-Yr. Sales Change: 6.2% |
| Phone: 201-529-5900 | HR: Marie Larson | Employees: 3,900 |
| Fax: 201-529-1189 | Type: Private | FYE: December 31 |

The Big Apple need never be short of apples (or oranges, for that matter) thanks to Inserra Supermarkets. Inserra owns and operates about 20 ShopRite supermarkets and superstores in northern New Jersey and southeastern New York State (most are in the Rockland county area). Inserra's superstores feature bagel bakeries, cafes, and pharmacies. The company also offers banking services in selected stores through agreements with Poughkeepsie Savings Bank, Statewide Savings Bank, and others. Owned by the Inserra family, the retailer is one of 40-plus members that make up cooperative Wakefern Food, the owner of the ShopRite name.

**KEY COMPETITORS**
A&P
Royal Ahold

## INTELSAT, LTD.

| | | |
|---|---|---|
| 3400 International Dr. NW | CEO: Conny Kullman | 2000 Sales: $1,097.3 million |
| Washington, DC 20008 | CFO: Joseph Corbett | 1-Yr. Sales Change: 12.3% |
| Phone: 202-944-6800 | HR: Benjamin Katcoff | Employees: — |
| Fax: 202-944-7890 | Type: Private | FYE: December 31 |
| Web: www.intelsat.int | | |

The bird's-eye view of earth enjoyed by Intelsat's 20 geostationary satellites has become a private eye's view. The former International Telecommunications Satellite Organization, set up by governments around the world in 1964, reorganized as a private company, Intelsat, Ltd., in 2001. The new Intelsat is owned by telecom companies in more than 145 countries. Its owners are Intelsat's major customers, accounting for more than 75% of sales. The satellite system provides Internet, broadcast, telephony, and corporate network services in more than 200 countries and territories worldwide. Intelsat is upgrading its satellite fleet, which it plans to expand to 24 by 2003.

**KEY COMPETITORS**
Eutelsat
Hughes Electronics
SES Global

## INTERMOUNTAIN HEALTH CARE

| | | |
|---|---|---|
| 36 S. State St. | CEO: William H. Nelson | 2000 Sales: $2,552.1 million |
| Salt Lake City, UT 84111 | CFO: Everett Goodwin | 1-Yr. Sales Change: 6.8% |
| Phone: 801-442-2000 | HR: Phyllis Domm | Employees: 23,000 |
| Fax: 801-442-3327 | Type: Not-for-profit | FYE: December 31 |
| Web: www.ihc.com | | |

Intermountain Health Care (IHC) is a not-for-profit health care organization operating more than 20 hospitals, 16 home health care agencies, an air ambulance service, and some 75 physician and urgent care clinics in Utah and Idaho. IHC has affiliations with more than 2,000 physicians, including about 400 in its IHC Physician Group. IHC Health Plans offers health insurance programs to large and small employers. The company was formed in 1975 when the Church of Jesus Christ of Latter Day Saints (the Mormons) decided to donate 15 of their hospitals to the communities they served.

**KEY COMPETITORS**
HCA
Iasis Healthcare
Trinity Health

## INTERNATIONAL BROTHERHOOD OF TEAMSTERS

| | | |
|---|---|---|
| 25 Louisiana Ave. NW | CEO: James P. Hoffa | Sales: — |
| Washington, DC 20001 | CFO: Tom Keegel | 1-Yr. Sales Change: — |
| Phone: 202-624-6800 | HR: Lynda Sist | Employees: — |
| Fax: 202-624-6918 | Type: Labor union | FYE: December 31 |
| Web: www.teamster.org | | |

The International Brotherhood of Teamsters is the largest and arguably most (in)famous labor union in the US. With about 1.4 million members, the Teamsters represents 16 trade groups, including truckers, UPS workers, warehouse employees, cab drivers, airline workers, and construction crews. The union negotiates with employers for contracts that guarantee members fair wages and raises, health coverage, job security, paid time off, promotions, and other benefits. The Teamsters union has about 570 local chapters in the US and Canada. Working to shed its notorious image, Teamsters president James Hoffa has proposed ethics policies aimed at rooting out internal corruption and ties to organized crime.

 See pages 246–247 for a full profile of this company.


## INTERNATIONAL DATA GROUP

| | | |
|---|---|---|
| 1 Exeter Plaza, 15th Fl. | CEO: Kelly P. Conlin | 2001 Sales: $3,010.0 million |
| Boston, MA 02116 | CFO: Jim Ghirardi | 1-Yr. Sales Change: (2.9%) |
| Phone: 617-534-1200 | HR: Karen Budreau | Employees: 13,200 |
| Fax: 617-262-2300 | Type: Private | FYE: September 30 |
| Web: www.idg.com | | |

International Data Group (IDG) is a publishing giant with digital appeal. The world's top technology publisher, IDG produces some 300 magazines and newspapers in 85 countries, including *PC World* and *CIO*. In addition to publishing, IDG provides technology market research through its International Data Corporation and produces a number of industry events. In 2001 the firm sold its 75% stake in of Hungry Minds (formerly IDG Books Worldwide), the oracle for the tech-unsavvy with its *For Dummies* series of books. Chairman Patrick McGovern, who founded IDG in 1964, holds a majority stake in the company; an employee stock plan owns the rest.

**KEY COMPETITORS**
Pearson
United Business Media
Ziff Davis Media

 See pages 248–249 for a full profile of this company.


## INTERNATIONAL MANAGEMENT GROUP

| | | |
|---|---|---|
| 1360 E. 9th St., Ste. 100 | CEO: Mark H. McCormack | 2000 Est. Sales: $1,260.0 mil. |
| Cleveland, OH 44114 | CFO: Arthur J. LaFave | 1-Yr. Sales Change: 14.5% |
| Phone: 216-522-1200 | HR: Susie Austin | Employees: 2,900 |
| Fax: 216-522-1145 | Type: Private | FYE: December 31 |
| Web: www.imgworld.com | | |

Led by founder and owner Mark McCormack, International Management Group (IMG) is the world's largest sports talent and marketing agency. In addition to representing sports idols (Tiger Woods), IMG also counts artists (Placido Domingo), models (Tyra Banks), and broadcasters (Bob Costas) among its clients. Its Trans World International division produces more than 5,000 hours of sports TV programming each year. IMG also promotes sports events, which are often expressly designed to feature some of its clients. In addition, IMG represents corporate clients and organizations, acts as a literary agent, and is active in sports academies, golf course design, and financial consulting.

**KEY COMPETITORS**
Clear Channel Entertainment
Creative Artists
William Morris

 See pages 250–251 for a full profile of this company.

## INVESTORS MANAGEMENT CORP.

5151 Glenwood Ave.
Raleigh, NC 27612
Phone: 919-781-9310
Fax: 919-881-4686
Web: www.goldencorral.net

CEO: Ted Fowler
CFO: Richard Urquhart
HR: Paul Weber
Type: Private

2000 Sales: $968.0 million
1-Yr. Sales Change: 7.7%
Employees: 16,000
FYE: December 31

Investors Management Corporation hopes you'll join them in an eat-out at the Golden Corral. The holding company has more than 460 Golden Corral family-style restaurants (about 70% are franchised, the rest company-owned) in 40 states. The restaurants offer hot meats, pasta, pizza, and fresh vegetables on the trademark 140-item Golden Choice Buffet, which averages about $6 a plate. Golden Corral restaurants also feature a steak menu, as well as a Brass Bell Bakery, which serves fresh pastries and baked goods every fifteen minutes. Founded in 1973 by chairman James Maynard, Golden Corral is one of the nation's largest family-style restaurant chains.

**KEY COMPETITORS**
Advantica Restaurant Group
Buffets
Ryan's Family Steak Houses

## THE IRVINE COMPANY INC.

550 Newport Center Dr.
Newport Beach, CA 92658
Phone: 949-720-2000
Fax: 949-720-2501
Web: www.irvineco.com

CEO: Donald L. Bren
CFO: Mark Ley
HR: Bruce Endsley
Type: Private

2000 Est. Sales: $1,000.0 mil.
1-Yr. Sales Change: 0.0%
Employees: 250
FYE: June 30

The Irvine Company develops residential and commercial real estate in Southern California. Owning more than 50,000 acres, the firm is famous for its master-planned communities stretching for miles in southern Orange County. The firm also develops hotels, office buildings, and retail properties, and it has been expanding into Los Angeles, San Diego, and the Silicon Valley. Its core holdings are derived from the 120,000-acre Irvine Ranch, formed in the mid-1800s when James Irvine bought out the debts of Mexican land-grant holders. Chairman Donald Bren, one of America's wealthiest men, owns the company. The Irvine Company reacquired its former spinoff, real estate investment trust (REIT) Irvine Apartment Communities.

**KEY COMPETITORS**
Corky McMillin
KB Home

 See pages 252–253 for a full profile of this company.

## J. CREW GROUP, INC.

770 Broadway
New York, NY 10003
Phone: 212-209-2500
Fax: 212-209-2666
Web: www.jcrew.com

CEO: Mark A. Sarvary
CFO: Scott M. Rosen
HR: David F. Kozel
Type: Private

2001 Sales: $826.0 million
1-Yr. Sales Change: 15.3%
Employees: —
FYE: January 31

The crews depicted in the flashy catalogs of the J. Crew Group are far from motley. J. Crew sells classic-styled jeans, khakis, and other basic (but pricey) items to young professionals through its catalogs, Web site, and in about 175 retail and factory outlets in the US. It also has about 70 outlets in Japan through a joint venture with ITOCHU. The company has sold off its two non-J.Crew brand catalogs and now its sales come entirely from J. Crew brand items. Texas Pacific Group owns more than 60% of J. Crew; Emily Cinader Woods, daughter of founder Arthur Cinader, owns nearly 15%.

**KEY COMPETITORS**
The Gap
Lands' End
L.L. Bean

See pages 254–255 for a full profile of this company.

## JEA

| | | |
|---|---|---|
| 21 W. Church St. | CEO: Walter P. Bussells | 2000 Sales: $933.6 million |
| Jacksonville, FL 32202 | CFO: Ronald M. Baker | 1-Yr. Sales Change: 2.1% |
| Phone: 904-665-6000 | HR: Joan Clark | Employees: 2,361 |
| Fax: 904-665-7008 | Type: Government-owned | FYE: September 30 |
| Web: www.jea.com | | |

As long as sparks are flying in Jacksonville, everything is A-OK with JEA. The municipal utility provides electricity to more than 360,000 customers in Jacksonville and parts of three adjacent counties in Florida. Established in 1895, JEA has a generating capacity of 2,825 MW (about 53% of its power is derived from coal-fired plants). The company also resells electricity to other utilities, including FPL, which accounts for 15% of electricity sales. JEA also provides water and wastewater services; it serves 198,000 water customers from 100 wells and 32 treatment plants, and 147,000 wastewater customers with six regional treatment plants.

**KEY COMPETITORS**
Florida Public Utilities
FPL
United Water Resources


## JELD-WEN, INC.

| | | |
|---|---|---|
| 401 Harbor Isles Blvd. | CEO: Roderick C. Wendt | 2000 Est. Sales: $2,000.0 mil. |
| Klamath Falls, OR 97601 | CFO: Karen Hoggarth | 1-Yr. Sales Change: 0.0% |
| Phone: 541-882-3451 | HR: Eileen Harris | Employees: 20,000 |
| Fax: 541-885-7454 | Type: Private | FYE: December 31 |
| Web: www.jeld-wen.com | | |

JELD-WEN can improve your outlook — whether it's by providing new windows for your home, or by offering accommodations at a scenic resort. A leading maker of windows and doors, JELD-WEN owns more than 150 companies in the US, Canada, and Europe. These companies manufacture such products as interior and exterior doors, garage doors, door frames, moldings, windows, and patio doors. JELD-WEN also sells time-shares at resorts such as Oregon's Eagle Crest and Running Y Ranch. The company's other interests include specialty wood products (including wood pellets used in fireplaces), real estate, and marketing communications. Chairman Richard Wendt and his siblings founded JELD-WEN in 1960.

**KEY COMPETITORS**
Andersen Corporation
Nortek
Pella


## J. F. SHEA CO., INC.

| | | |
|---|---|---|
| 655 Brea Canyon Rd. | CEO: John F. Shea | 2000 Sales: $1,863.0 million |
| Walnut, CA 91789 | CFO: James G. Shontere | 1-Yr. Sales Change: 3.8% |
| Phone: 909-594-9500 | HR: Howard Hulme | Employees: 2,200 |
| Fax: 909-594-0935 | Type: Private | FYE: December 31 |
| Web: www.jfshea.com | | |

J. F. Shea helped construct the Washington, DC, subway system, the Golden Gate Bridge, and the Hoover Dam, and now it wants to build your house. The company's Shea Homes division builds single-family houses and planned communities, mainly for move-up buyers. J. F. Shea also manages apartments and commercial buildings. The company's Heavy Construction division specializes in underground projects, including dams, pipelines, and tunnels, and its Redding division produces gravel, asphalt, and concrete products. J. F. Shea's proposed buyout of Sun City developer Del Webb in 2000 was rebuffed (rival Pulte bought Del Webb the next year). Founded as a plumbing company in 1876, J. F. Shea is still owned by the Shea family.

**KEY COMPETITORS**
KB Home
Pulte Homes
Tutor-Saliba

## JIM KOONS AUTOMOTIVE

2000 Chain Bridge Rd.
Vienna, VA 22182
Phone: 703-356-0400
Fax: 703-442-5777
Web: www.koons.com

CEO: James E. Koons
CFO: Tim O'Connell
HR: Ed Wauth
Type: Private

2000 Sales: $940.7 million
1-Yr. Sales Change: 71.0%
Employees: —
FYE: December 31

Wheelin' and dealin' on the Web, Jim Koons Automotive sells new and used cars the old-fashioned way and through the Internet. Its 15 locations in the Washington, DC, area (Virginia and Maryland) offer cars made by DaimlerChrysler, Ford, GM, Mazda, Toyota, and Volvo. Three locations specialize in used cars. Internet customers can select new car options, obtain quotes, make appointments for parts and service, and access online coupons for oil changes and other services. President Jim Koons' father, John Koons Sr., the first auto dealer to enter the Automotive Hall of Fame, founded the company in 1964. The Koons family owns the company.

**KEY COMPETITORS**
Brown Automotive
Ourisman Automotive
Rosenthal Automotive

## JITNEY-JUNGLE STORES OF AMERICA, INC.

1770 Ellis Ave., Ste. 200
Jackson, MS 39204
Phone: 601-965-8600
Fax: 601-965-7247
Web: www.jitney.com

CEO: Ronald E. Johnson
CFO: Greg Presley
HR: Jerry L. Jones
Type: Private

1998 Sales: $2,054.1 million
1-Yr. Sales Change: 79.4%
Employees: 17,000
FYE: December 31

How easy was it to steer a Jitney through the fierce grocery jungle? Not very. Jitney-Jungle Stores of America (JJSA) was slammed by larger rivals, such as Wal-Mart, forcing it to seek Chapter 11 bankruptcy protection and then sell its assets in 2001. JJSA ran about 140 stores in four southern states, including conventional stores (Jitney-Jungle, Delchamps), food-and-drug-combination stores (Jitney Premier, Delchamps Premier), discount stores (Sack & Save), 10 liquor stores, and nearly 45 gas stations. Investment firm Bruckmann, Rosser, Sherill & Co. owned 84% of JJSA. In early 2001 JJSA sold some 125 stores to grocers Winn-Dixie Stores and Bruno's Supermarkets. Winn-Dixie is operating stores under the Jitney-Jungle banner.

**KEY COMPETITORS**
Kroger
Wal-Mart
Winn-Dixie

## JM FAMILY ENTERPRISES, INC.

100 NW 12th Ave.
Deerfield Beach, FL 33442
Phone: 954-429-2000
Fax: 954-429-2244
Web: www.jmfamily.com

CEO: Patricia Moran
CFO: James R. Foster
HR: Gary L. Thomas
Type: Private

2000 Sales: $7,100.0 million
1-Yr. Sales Change: 7.6%
Employees: 3,400
FYE: December 31

Founder and chairman Jim Moran and president and CEO Pat Moran (Jim's daughter) make JM Family Enterprises a family affair. JM, owned by the Moran family, is a holding company with about a dozen automotive-related businesses (including the nation's largest-volume Lexus retailer). JM's major subsidiary, Southeast Toyota Distributors, is the world's largest Toyota distribution franchise, delivering Toyota cars, trucks, and vans to more than 160 dealers in Alabama, Florida, Georgia, and North and South Carolina. Other JM divisions include JM&A Group and World Omni Financial, which provide consumer auto leasing, warranty services, insurance, dealer financing, and other related financial services to US auto dealers.

**KEY COMPETITORS**
Gulf States Toyota
Morse Operations
United Auto Group

 See pages 256–257 for a full profile of this company.

## J. M. HUBER CORPORATION

| | | |
|---|---|---|
| 333 Thornall St. | CEO: Peter T. Francis | 2000 Sales: $1,022.0 million |
| Edison, NJ 08837 | CFO: Philip Betsch | 1-Yr. Sales Change: 19.5% |
| Phone: 732-549-8600 | HR: Gary Crowell | Employees: 2,880 |
| Fax: 732-549-2239 | Type: Private | FYE: December 31 |
| Web: www.huber.com | | |

Toothpaste, paint, and tires — J. M. Huber claims to make them even better. Founded in 1883 by Joseph Maria Huber, the company makes specialty additives and minerals used to thicken and improve the cleaning properties of toothpaste, the brightness and gloss of paper, the strength and durability of rubber, and flame retardant properties of wire and cable. The international firm also makes oriented strand board (a plywood substitute) and sells wood to the furniture, construction, and paper industries. Huber manages a half-million acres of timberland in Maine and the southeastern US, and owns about 100 million tons of coal reserves. The company also is an oil and gas producer. Heirs of the founder own J. M. Huber.

**KEY COMPETITORS**
Baker Hughes
Georgia-Pacific Group
Minerals Technologies

## JMB REALTY CORPORATION

| | | |
|---|---|---|
| 900 N. Michigan Ave., Ste. 1100 | CEO: Rigel Barber | 2000 Est. Sales: $1,000.0 mil. |
| Chicago, IL 60611 | CFO: Steve Lovelett | 1-Yr. Sales Change: 0.0% |
| Phone: 312-440-4800 | HR: Gail Silver | Employees: — |
| Fax: 312-915-1768 | Type: Private | FYE: December 31 |

JMB wants to make State Street a great street again and bring glitter back to the Steel City's Golden Triangle. A major US commercial real estate investment firm, JMB Realty owns, develops, and manages real estate projects throughout North America, including regional malls, hotels, planned communities, and office complexes. JMB is heavily involved in ambitious retail developments in Chicago's Loop and downtown Pittsburgh. JMB was founded in 1968 by Robert Judelson, Judd Malkin, and Neil Bluhm; Judelson (the "J" of JMB) is no longer involved with JMB, but Malkin remains as chairman and Bluhm is president.

**KEY COMPETITORS**
Edward J. DeBartolo
Lincoln Property
Trammell Crow

## JOHNS HOPKINS MEDICINE

| | | |
|---|---|---|
| 720 Rutland Ave. | CEO: Edward D. Miller | 2000 Sales: $2,121.2 million |
| Baltimore, MD 21205 | CFO: Richard A. Grossi | 1-Yr. Sales Change: 6.9% |
| Phone: 410-955-5000 | HR: Pamela D. Paulk | Employees: 23,550 |
| Fax: — | Type: Not-for-profit | FYE: June 30 |
| Web: www.hopkinsmedicine.org | | |

Hopping John is a recipe for black-eyed peas; Johns Hopkins Medicine is a recipe for Baltimore's health care. The not-for-profit system includes Johns Hopkins University School of Medicine and the Johns Hopkins Hospital & Health System. Staffed by medical school faculty, the system boasts three acute-care hospitals, as well as facilities that offer long-term care, home care, managed care, and outpatient services. Johns Hopkins Medicine's international division oversees telemedicine programs (that allow remote access to Johns Hopkins physicians) in Europe, the Far East, the Middle East, and South America. The system also performs clinical research trials and is a leading recipient of federal research funding.

**KEY COMPETITORS**
Bon Secours Health
Mayo Foundation
MedStar

## THE JOHNS HOPKINS UNIVERSITY

3400 N. Charles St.
Baltimore, MD 21218
Phone: 410-516-8000
Fax: —
Web: www.jhu.edu

CEO: William R. Brody
CFO: James T. McGill
HR: Audrey Smith
Type: School

2001 Sales: $2,100.0 million
1-Yr. Sales Change: 18.7%
Employees: 28,000
FYE: June 30

Founded in 1876 with a $7 million bequest from its namesake, The Johns Hopkins University established its reputation from the beginning by molding itself in the image of a European research institution. While renowned for its School of Medicine, the private university offers eight academic divisions spanning fields of study including business, engineering, and music. Its nearly 18,000 students and 2,600 full-time faculty members are scattered across campuses in the Baltimore and Washington, DC areas, as well as at international programs in Nanjing, China; Bologna, Italy; and Florence, Italy.

## JOHNSON PUBLISHING COMPANY, INC.

820 S. Michigan Ave.
Chicago, IL 60605
Phone: 312-322-9200
Fax: 312-322-0918
Web: www.ebony.com

CEO: John H. Johnson
CFO: Eunice W. Johnson
HR: LaDoris Foster
Type: Private

2000 Sales: $400.4 million
1-Yr. Sales Change: 3.5%
Employees: 2,614
FYE: December 31

Snubbed by advertisers when he founded his company 60 years ago, John Johnson has pushed his magazine company to the front of the pack. Led by its flagship publication, *Ebony,* family-owned Johnson Publishing Company is the largest black-owned publishing firm in the country. It also publishes *Jet* and operates a book division. Off the printed page, Johnson Publishing markets the Fashion Fair cosmetics line and hosts the Ebony Fashion Fair, a benefit fashion show that visits cities in the US and Canada each year. Chairman and CEO John Johnson, who founded the firm in 1942, has turned over most of the day-to-day operations to daughter Linda Johnson Rice (president and COO).

**KEY COMPETITORS**
Essence Communications
L'Oréal

 **See pages 258–259 for a full profile of this company.**

## THE JONES FINANCIAL COMPANIES, L.P., LLP

12555 Manchester Rd.
Des Peres, MO 63131
Phone: 314-515-2000
Fax: 314-515-2622
Web: www.edwardjones.com

CEO: John W. Bachmann
CFO: Steven Novik
HR: Michael R. Holmes
Type: Private

2000 Sales: $2,212.0 million
1-Yr. Sales Change: 23.8%
Employees: 23,432
FYE: December 31

This is not your father's broker — or, well, maybe it is. The Jones Financial Companies is the parent of Edward Jones (formerly called Edward D. Jones & Co.), an investment brokerage network catering to individual investors. Most of its clients are retired people and small-business owners in rural communities and suburbs. The firm has some 7,300 satellite-linked offices in the US, Canada, and the UK. Brokers offer relatively low-risk investment vehicles such as government bonds, blue-chip stocks, and high-quality mutual funds. Edward Jones also provides investment banking for such clients as Wal-Mart. The firm accepts brokers with no experience, provides extensive training, and closely monitors their activities.

**KEY COMPETITORS**
A.G. Edwards
Merrill Lynch
Raymond James Financial

 **See pages 260–261 for a full profile of this company.**

## JORDAN AUTOMOTIVE GROUP

| | | |
|---|---|---|
| 609 E. Jefferson Blvd. | CEO: Craig Kapson | 2000 Est. Sales: $2,000.0 mil. |
| Mishawaka, IN 46545 | CFO: George Merryman | 1-Yr. Sales Change: 0.0% |
| Phone: 219-259-1981 | HR: Sheryl Scialpi | Employees: 200 |
| Fax: 219-255-0984 | Type: Private | FYE: December 31 |
| Web: www.jordanauto.com | | |

Jordan Automotive scores points for being one of the nation's largest Ford dealers and one of the largest fleet dealers. The family-owned company runs six franchises in Indiana that sell new and used vehicles, including Ford, Toyota, Volvo, Mitsubishi, Lincoln-Mercury, and Kia models. It also has parts and service departments. Jordan Automotive's fleet business, Jordan Commercial & Fleet Sales, provides flat beds, dump trucks, construction trucks, and other heavy-duty vehicles. Chairman Jordan Kapson founded the company as a single Dodge dealership in 1949 after working at his father-in-law's dealership; his son Craig is the company's president.

**KEY COMPETITORS**
Bob Rohrman Auto
Kelley Automotive
United Auto Group

## JORDAN INDUSTRIES, INC.

| | | |
|---|---|---|
| Arborlake Center, Ste. 550, 1751 Lake Cook Rd. | CEO: John W. "Jay" Jordan II | 2000 Sales: $807.0 million |
| Deerfield, IL 60015 | CFO: Thomas C. Spielburger | 1-Yr. Sales Change: 3.9% |
| Phone: 847-945-5591 | HR: — | Employees: 6,967 |
| Fax: 847-945-5698 | Type: Private | FYE: December 31 |
| Web: www.jordanindustries.com | | |

Although not related to Michael, with a name like Jordan Industries, it's no wonder this company does it all. The private holding company is involved in markets as diverse as automotive products, bicycle reflector kits, software application development, Bibles, electric motors, and specialty advertising products. It owns more than 20 companies, which are divided into five separate business units: Motors and Gears (Merkle-Korff), Jordan Auto Aftermarket (Dacco), Consumer and Industrial Products, Specialty Printing and Labeling (JII Promotions, Inc.), and Jordan Specialty Plastics. Chairman and CEO John W. Jordan II owns more than 40% of the company.

**KEY COMPETITORS**
Aftermarket Technology
Baldor Electric
BorgWarner

## JOSTENS, INC.

| | | |
|---|---|---|
| 5501 Norman Center Dr. | CEO: Robert C. Buhrmaster | 2000 Sales: $805.0 million |
| Minneapolis, MN 55437 | CFO: — | 1-Yr. Sales Change: 2.9% |
| Phone: 952-830-3300 | HR: Steven A. Tighe | Employees: 6,500 |
| Fax: 952-830-3293 | Type: Private | FYE: December 31 |
| Web: www.jostens.com | | |

No one photographs bad hair days like Jostens. The company is the leading US producer of yearbooks and class rings, and it sells other graduation products such as diplomas, announcements, caps, and gowns. Its rings are also used to commemorate professional sports champions. Jostens takes and sells class and individual pictures for schools in the US and Canada. It also makes products for businesses, such as personalized awards and engraved certificates, as well as markets recognition products made by other companies (but it is exiting the recognition business). Jostens also provides corporate recognition services, including event planning. A private investment group led by Investcorp took Jostens private in May 2000.

**KEY COMPETITORS**
Commemorative Brands
Herff Jones
Lifetouch

 See pages 262–263 for a full profile of this company.

## JOURNAL COMMUNICATIONS INC.

| | | |
|---|---|---|
| 333 W. State St. | CEO: Steven J. Smith | 2000 Sales: $810.3 million |
| Milwaukee, WI 53203 | CFO: Paul M. Bonaiuto | 1-Yr. Sales Change: 7.2% |
| Phone: 414-224-2000 | HR: Daniel L. Harmsen | Employees: 7,300 |
| Fax: 414-224-2469 | Type: Private | FYE: December 31 |
| Web: www.jc.com | | |

Journal Communications can easily chronicle its operations. The diversified media company generates most of its sales from newspaper publishing, including its flagship *Milwaukee Journal Sentinel,* nearly 50 weekly newspapers and community shoppers, and about a dozen business and specialty publications. It also owns 36 radio stations serving eight markets and four TV stations. In addition, Journal Communications has commercial printing operations, offers direct marketing services, and owns Norlight Telecommunications. The *Journal Sentinel* resulted from a merger between *The Milwaukee Journal* (1882) and *The Milwaukee Sentinal* (1837) in 1995. An employee stock trust owns 90% of the company.

**KEY COMPETITORS**
Gannett
Lee Enterprises
Tribune

## JPI

| | | |
|---|---|---|
| 600 E. Las Colinas Blvd., Ste. 1800 | CEO: Frank Miller III | 2000 Est. Sales: $1,000.0 mil. |
| Irving, TX 75039 | CFO: Frank B. Schubert | 1-Yr. Sales Change: 66.7% |
| Phone: 972-556-1700 | HR: John O'Connor | Employees: 1,500 |
| Fax: 972-556-3784 | Type: Private | FYE: December 31 |
| Web: www.jpi.com | | |

JPI can walk your dog or rent you a bike but what it does best is build and manage apartments. One of the largest luxury multifamily apartment developers in the US, JPI also manages more than 24,000 units in about a dozen states. The company typically buys underperforming properties in desirable areas and upgrades them with such features as parking garages, fitness centers, and 24-hour concierge services. JPI's student complexes include amenities like game rooms and fitness centers. Founded in 1976 as Jefferson Properties, Inc., JPI was a subsidiary of Southland Financial until the early 1990s when Hunt Realty Corp invested in it.

**KEY COMPETITORS**
Castle & Cooke
Gables Residential Trust
Trammell Crow Residential

## J.R. SIMPLOT COMPANY

| | | |
|---|---|---|
| 1 Capital Center, 999 Main St., Ste. 1300 | CEO: Stephen A. Beebe | 2001 Sales: $3,000.0 million |
| Boise, ID 83702 | CFO: Dennis Mogensen | 1-Yr. Sales Change: 11.1% |
| Phone: 208-336-2110 | HR: Ted Roper | Employees: 13,000 |
| Fax: 208-389-7515 | Type: Private | FYE: August 31 |
| Web: www.simplot.com | | |

J.R. Simplot hopes you'll have fries with that. Potato potentate J. R. "Jack" Simplot simply shook hands with McDonald's pioneer Ray Kroc in the mid-1960s, and his company's french fry sales have sizzled ever since. J.R. Simplot produces more than 2 billion pounds of French fries annually, making it one of the largest processors of frozen potatoes. Other operations include cattle ranches and feedlots (with feed from potato peels), phosphate mining (for fertilizer), and frozen fruit and vegetable processing. It offers products mainly to food service and retail customers under its Simplot brand and private labels. Although officially retired, Simplot, founder of the family-owned firm, is one of the richest Americans.

**KEY COMPETITORS**
Cargill
IMC Global
McCain Foods

 See pages 264–265 for a full profile of this company.

## J.S. ALBERICI CONSTRUCTION CO., INC.

2150 Kienlen Ave.
St. Louis, MO 63121
Phone: 314-261-2611
Fax: 314-261-4225
Web: www.alberici.com

CEO: Robert F. McCoole
CFO: Greg Hesser
HR: Carolyn Eskew
Type: Private

2000 Sales: $836.9 million
1-Yr. Sales Change: (3.3%)
Employees: 430
FYE: December 31

When it comes to heavy construction, J.S. Alberici may not have written the book, but it has certainly earned a footnote or two. Founded in 1918, J.S. Alberici Construction Co. has built numerous projects across the US and has operated in Argentina, Austria, Brazil, Canada, Israel, and Mexico. Markets it serves include aerospace, automotive, energy, health care, industrial process, and manufacturing. Alberici offers general contracting, construction management, design-build services, heavy demolition, and steel fabrication and erection. The company also provides environmental services. The employee-owned firm has worked on such projects as a DaimlerChrysler plant and a Boeing rocket factory.

**KEY COMPETITORS**
Fluor
Raytheon
Washington Group

## KAISER FOUNDATION HEALTH PLAN, INC.

1 Kaiser Plaza
Oakland, CA 94612
Phone: 510-271-5800
Fax: 510-271-6493
Web: www.kaiserpermanente.org

CEO: David M. Lawrence
CFO: —
HR: Dresdene Flynn-White
Type: Not-for-profit

2000 Sales: $17,700.0 million
1-Yr. Sales Change: 5.1%
Employees: 90,000
FYE: December 31

Kaiser Foundation Health Plan aims to be the emperor of the HMO universe. With more than 8 million members in 9 states and the District of Columbia, it is one of the largest not-for-profit managed health care companies in the US. Kaiser sponsors the Permanente Medical Groups, associations consisting of more than 11,000 doctors that provide medical care to Kaiser health plan subscribers under the Kaiser Permanente name. The company also runs a network of Kaiser Foundation hospitals. Faced with skyrocketing costs and stiff competition from commercial providers of managed care, Kaiser sold its unprofitable operations in North Carolina and plans to do the same in Kansas.

**KEY COMPETITORS**
Aetna
PacifiCare
WellPoint Health Networks

See pages 266–267 for a full profile of this company.

## K-B TOYS

100 West St.
Pittsfield, MA 01201
Phone: 413-496-3000
Fax: 413-496-3616
Web: www3.kbkids.com/kbhome

CEO: Michael L. Glazer
CFO: Robert J. Feldman
HR: Gerry Murray
Type: Private

2001 Est. Sales: $2,000.0 mil.
1-Yr. Sales Change: 13.2%
Employees: 13,000
FYE: January 31

K-B Toys hopes toy buyers will take their haul from the mall. The toy retailer — one of the largest toy companies in the US — operates 1,350 stores under four different formats: K-B Stores in malls, K-B Works in strip centers, K-B Toy Outlets in outlet malls, and K-B Toy Express in malls selling closeout toys during the Christmas season. It also sells toys online through Kbkids.com and eToys.com (K-B Toys bought the inventory and rights to the defunct eToys business in 2001). While many shoppers have begun buying toys from big box retailers such as Toys "R" Us, K-B Toys believes it can succeed as the dominant mall-based toy retailer. The company is owned by private equity firm Bain Capital.

**KEY COMPETITORS**
Target
Toys "R" Us
Wal-Mart

## KEMPER INSURANCE COMPANIES

1 Kemper Dr.
Long Grove, IL 60049
Phone: 847-320-2000
Fax: 847-320-2494
Web: www.kemperinsurance.com

CEO: David B. Mathis
CFO: Mural R. Josephson
HR: Sue A. Coughlin
Type: Mutual company

2000 Sales: $3,014.1 million
1-Yr. Sales Change: 3.5%
Employees: 8,500
FYE: December 31

Customers of all types keep company with The Kemper Insurance Companies. Kemper offers an array of personal, risk management, and commercial property/casualty products. Its Lumbermens Life Agency offers personal term life and disability income insurance, wealth accumulation programs, and other services. Kemper Insurance also provides automobile, homeowners, and general liability coverage. The company has realigned its operations to focus on property/casualty coverage and risk management services. Kemper Insurance operates throughout the US, as well as overseas.

**KEY COMPETITORS**
Liberty Mutual
St. Paul Companies
Travelers

 See pages 268–269 for a full profile of this company.


## KEYSTONE FOODS LLC

401 City Ave., Ste. 800
Bala Cynwyd, PA 19004
Phone: 610-667-6700
Fax: 610-667-1460
Web: www.keystonefoods.com

CEO: Herbert Lotman
CFO: Michael Mardy
HR: Jerry Gotro
Type: Private

2000 Sales: $2,650.0 million
1-Yr. Sales Change: 2.2%
Employees: 6,700
FYE: December 31

Keystone Foods hopes you won't just have the salad. The company is one of the largest makers of hamburger patties and processed poultry. It's a major supplier to McDonald's restaurants; in the 1970s Keystone persuaded the fast-food giant to switch to frozen beef to reduce the health risks associated with fresh beef. Overseas its operations include McKey Food Services and MacFood Services (some are joint ventures). In addition to its worldwide meat processing facilities, which crank out millions of burgers daily, Keystone also operates M&M Restaurant Supply, and has begun to supply fresh beef to a U.S. grocery retailer. Chairman and CEO Herbert Lotman owns the company, which started in the early 1960s.

**KEY COMPETITORS**
Golden State Foods
IBP
Tyson Foods


## KING RANCH, INC.

3 River Way, Ste. 1600
Houston, TX 77056
Phone: 832-681-5700
Fax: 832-681-5759
Web: www.king-ranch.com

CEO: Jack Hunt
CFO: Bill Gardiner
HR: Martha Breit
Type: Private

2000 Est. Sales: $300.0 mil.
1-Yr. Sales Change: 0.0%
Employees: 700
FYE: December 31

Meanwhile, back at the ranch ... the sprawling King Ranch, that is. King Ranch, founded in 1853, extends beyond the legendary 825,000 acres that are home to about 60,000 cattle and a wide variety of animal species. The business oversees ranching and farming interests in Texas and Florida, but these days it also benefits from oil and gas royalties, farming (cotton, citrus, and sugar), and retail operations (designer saddles, leather goods). In addition, King Ranch also beefs up revenues with tourist dollars from hunters and sightseers. It sold its Kentucky horse farm, once a producer of champion thoroughbreds, and its primary oil and gas subsidiary. About 85 descendants of founder Richard King own King Ranch.

**KEY COMPETITORS**
AZTX Cattle
Cactus Feeders
Koch

See pages 270–271 for a full profile of this company.

## KINGSTON TECHNOLOGY COMPANY

| | | |
|---|---|---|
| 17600 Newhope St. | CEO: John Tu | 2000 Sales: $1,600.0 million |
| Fountain Valley, CA 92708 | CFO: Koichi Hosokawa | 1-Yr. Sales Change: 14.3% |
| Phone: 714-435-2600 | HR: Daniel Hsu | Employees: 2,000 |
| Fax: 714-435-2699 | Type: Private | FYE: December 31 |
| Web: www.kingston.com | | |

Kingston Technology is a kingpin of the memory game. The company is a top maker of memory boards that boost the capacity and speed of computers and printers, and also makes flash memory cards for portable devices such as cellular phones and personal digital assistants. (It has discontinued its offerings of other peripheral devices.) The company is known for its friendliness both to employees (casual clothing and generous bonuses are the norm) and to business partners. (It is sometimes the first to receive scarce components, thanks to its good relations with suppliers.) Founders John Tu (president and CEO) and David Sun (COO), who do business from cubicles identical to their employees', own the company.

**KEY COMPETITORS**
Micron Technology
SanDisk
Unigen

 See pages 272–273 for a full profile of this company.

## KINKO'S, INC.

| | | |
|---|---|---|
| 255 W. Stanley Ave. | CEO: Gary M. Kusin | 2001 Est. Sales: $2,200.0 mil. |
| Ventura, CA 93002 | CFO: Jeffrey E. Moxie | 1-Yr. Sales Change: 10.0% |
| Phone: 805-652-4000 | HR: Paul Rostron | Employees: 25,000 |
| Fax: 805-652-4347 | Type: Private | FYE: June 30 |
| Web: www.kinkos.com | | |

Kinko's has come a long way since its founding as a college town copy shop. It operates more than 1,100 business service centers 24 hours a day in Asia, Australia, Europe, and North America. Originally providing self-service copying, Kinko's now offers a full range of services, including binding and finishing services, color printing, document management, and Internet access. Most of the company's sales come from small office/home office customers, but it also provides digital document services to large companies. Kinko's also allows customers to design products and place orders through its Kinkos.com Web site. Buyout firm Clayton, Dubilier & Rice owns 41% of Kinko's.

**KEY COMPETITORS**
Mail Boxes Etc.
Office Depot
Xerox

 See pages 274–275 for a full profile of this company.

## KINRAY, INC.

| | | |
|---|---|---|
| 152-35 10th Ave. | CEO: Stewart Rahr | 2000 Sales: $1,710.0 million |
| Whitestone, NY 11357 | CFO: Bill Bodinger | 1-Yr. Sales Change: 13.2% |
| Phone: 718-767-1234 | HR: Howard Hershberg | Employees: 400 |
| Fax: 718-767-4388 | Type: Private | FYE: December 30 |
| Web: www.kinray.com | | |

Kinray, one of the US's largest privately held wholesale drug distributors, is nothing if not independent. It provides generic, branded, and repackaged drugs, health and beauty products, medical equipment, vitamins and herbals, and diabetes-care products; it also has a 600-item private label program. The company serves nearly 2,000 pharmacies in the northeastern US. Kinray spearheaded the creation of the Wholesale Alliance Cooperative, a group of about 20 independent regional drug distributors that aims to help preserve the viability of small pharmacies (who are customers to the wholesalers). The company was founded in 1936 by Joseph Rahr. His son, CEO and president Stewart Rahr, owns the company.

**KEY COMPETITORS**
Cardinal Health
McKesson
Quality King

## KLAUSSNER FURNITURE INDUSTRIES, INC.

405 Lewallen St.
Asheboro, NC 27203
Phone: 336-625-6174
Fax: 336-626-0905
Web: www.klaussner.com

CEO: J. B. Davis
CFO: Dave Bryant
HR: Mark Walker
Type: Private

2000 Est. Sales: $950.0 mil.
1-Yr. Sales Change: 16.6%
Employees: 7,000
FYE: December 31

Klaussner Furniture Industries makes furniture for the couch potato in all of us. It is one of the US's largest makers of upholstered furniture. Klaussner sells fabric- and leather-upholstered sofas and recliners, dining furniture, and office furniture under the JDI, Realistic, Revolution Motion, Paoli, Tellus, and Klaussner brand names. It also offers sofas and chairs under the licensed Sealy name. Its 20 plants produce items exported to more than 40 countries. Klaussner also owns about 20% of furniture retailer Jennifer Convertibles. Chairman Hans Klaussner has owned the company since 1979; it was founded in 1964 as Stuart Furniture Industries.

**KEY COMPETITORS**
Furniture Brands International
LifeStyle Furnishings
 International
Steelcase

## KNOLL, INC.

1235 Water St.
East Greenville, PA 18041
Phone: 215-679-7991
Fax: 215-679-1755
Web: www.knoll.com

CEO: Andrew B. Cogan
CFO: Barry L. McCabe
HR: S. David Wolfe
Type: Private

2000 Sales: $1,163.5 million
1-Yr. Sales Change: 18.2%
Employees: 4,435
FYE: December 31

Designer cubicles make for happier workers, or so goes the gospel at Knoll. Knoll makes office furniture and accessories, such as rolling chairs, tables, metal and wood desks, file cabinets, lighting, and computer and desk accessories. Its cubicles — or office systems — are distinctively designed and sold under the names Reff, Morrison, Equity, Dividends, and Currents. Many of its products are created by high-profile designers such as Vietnam War Memorial architect Maya Lin. Knoll also sells textiles and leather upholstery. It sells through independent dealers in North and South America, Europe, and Asia; the US represents 91% of sales. Knoll management and investment firm Warburg Pincus own the company.

**KEY COMPETITORS**
Haworth
Herman Miller
Steelcase

 See pages 276–277 for a full profile of this company.

## KNOWLEDGE UNIVERSE, INC.

3551 El Camino Real, Ste. 200
Menlo Park, CA 94027
Phone: 650-549-3200
Fax: 650-549-3222
Web: www.knowledgeu.com

CEO: Thomas Kalinske
CFO: Randolph C. Read
HR: —
Type: Private

2000 Est. Sales: $1,500.0 mil.
1-Yr. Sales Change: 0.0%
Employees: 11,000
FYE: December 31

There's a world of information out there, and Knowledge Universe (KU) wants to capitalize on it. Founded in 1996, the company is owned by Michael Milken (known for his innovative use of high-yield bonds and cancer-research philanthropy, or his term in jail for securities violations, depending on your perspective), his brother Lowell, and Oracle CEO Lawrence Ellison. KU invests in Internet-oriented companies (Hoover's, Inc.), daycare and childhood learning companies (Nobel Learning Communities), and B2B companies, principally in business and human resources consulting and online training. KU owns a controlling stake in Nextera Enterprises, an information technology consulting company.

**KEY COMPETITORS**
Bain Capital
Gores Technology
Internet Capital

 See pages 278–279 for a full profile of this company.

## KOCH INDUSTRIES, INC.

| | | |
|---|---|---|
| 4111 E. 37th St. North | CEO: Charles G. Koch | 2000 Est. Sales: $40,000.0 mil. |
| Wichita, KS 67220 | CFO: Sam Soliman | 1-Yr. Sales Change: 21.0% |
| Phone: 316-828-5500 | HR: Paul Wheeler | Employees: 11,500 |
| Fax: 316-828-5739 | Type: Private | FYE: December 31 |
| Web: www.kochind.com | | |

Koch Industries is the real thing when there's money to be made. Koch (pronounced "coke") is the second-largest private US company (after Cargill), with extensive holdings in petroleum, agriculture, and chemicals. Its two refineries process about 600,000 barrels of crude oil a day. Koch also processes natural gas liquids and operates gas gathering systems and a 35,000-mile pipeline system between Texas and Canada. KoSa, its venture with Mexico's Saba family, is a leading polyester producer. Other operations include minerals trading and transport, asphalt marketing, manufacturing equipment for processing industries, and ranching. Brothers Charles and David Koch control the company.

**KEY COMPETITORS**
Cargill
Enron
Marathon Oil

 See pages 280–281 for a full profile of this company.


## KOHLBERG KRAVIS ROBERTS & CO.

| | | |
|---|---|---|
| 9 W. 57th St., Ste. 4200 | CEO: Henry R. Kravis | Sales: — |
| New York, NY 10019 | CFO: — | 1-Yr. Sales Change: — |
| Phone: 212-750-8300 | HR: Sandy Cisneros | Employees: — |
| Fax: 212-750-0003 | Type: Partnership | FYE: December 31 |
| Web: www.kkr.com | | |

The barbarians at the gate are now knocking politely. Kohlberg Kravis Roberts (popularly known as KKR) assembles multibillion-dollar funds to invest in individual companies via leveraged buyouts (mostly friendly, these days). KKR collects fees for its management activities and takes an active role in increasing the value of companies. Holdings include stakes in debt-ridden publishing company PRIMEDIA (*Seventeen*, Channel One), diversified manufacturer Borden, and online mortgage lender Nexstar Financial. KKR is shopping in Europe, where bloated corporations are shedding non-core operations to streamline. KKR's senior partners are cousins Henry Kravis and George Roberts.

**KEY COMPETITORS**
Clayton, Dubilier
Forstmann Little
Hicks, Muse

 See pages 282–283 for a full profile of this company.


## KOHLER CO.

| | | |
|---|---|---|
| 444 Highland Dr. | CEO: Herbert V. Kohler Jr. | 2000 Sales: $2,700.0 million |
| Kohler, WI 53044 | CFO: Jeffery P. Cheney | 1-Yr. Sales Change: 8.0% |
| Phone: 920-457-4441 | HR: Laura Kohler | Employees: 20,000 |
| Fax: 920-459-1818 | Type: Private | FYE: December 31 |
| Web: kohlerco.com | | |

When plumbing powerhouse Kohler says profits are in the toilet, it's not complaining. Kohler makes bathroom products under the names Ann Sacks (ceramic tile, marble, stone products); Kallista (bathroom fixtures and accessories); and Hytec, Kohler, and Sterling (plumbing products). European brands include Jacob Delafon and Neomediam plumbing products and Sanijura bath cabinetry and related products. Kohler also makes small engines, generators, electrical switchgear, and high-end furniture. In addition, the company owns The American Club resort, golf courses, and other real estate. Chairman Herbert Kohler Jr. and his sister Ruth Kohler, grandchildren of the firm's founder, control most of the company.

**KEY COMPETITORS**
American Standard
Masco
Moen

 See pages 284–285 for a full profile of this company.

## KPMG INTERNATIONAL

| | | |
|---|---|---|
| 345 Park Ave. | CEO: Colin Holland | 2001 Sales: $11,700.0 million |
| New York, NY 10154 | CFO: Joseph E. Heintz | 1-Yr. Sales Change: (13.3%) |
| Phone: 212-758-9700 | HR: Timothy P. Flynn | Employees: 92,800 |
| Fax: 212-758-9819 | Type: Partnership | FYE: September 30 |
| Web: www.kpmg.com | | |

KPMG is changing PDQ, along with the rest of its peers. The company's effort to globalize its accounting and consulting services, which are provided from more than 830 offices in almost 160 nations, has led to a reorganization of its operations into three regional units: the Americas, Europe/Middle East/Africa, and Asia/Pacific. The firm offers assurance, tax, legal, and financial advisory services; its consulting business focuses on Internet applications and integration. KPMG separated its accounting and consulting operations, sold about 20% of the consulting business to networking equipment maker Cisco Systems and then took it public; the firm now owns about 20% of KPMG Consulting, while Cisco owns about 10%.

**KEY COMPETITORS**
Andersen
Ernst & Young
PricewaterhouseCoopers

 See pages 286–287 for a full profile of this company.


## K-VA-T FOOD STORES, INC.

| | | |
|---|---|---|
| 201 Trigg St. | CEO: Steven Smith | 2000 Sales: $963.0 million |
| Abingdon, VA 24210 | CFO: Robert L. Neeley | 1-Yr. Sales Change: 9.4% |
| Phone: 276-628-5503 | HR: Donnie Meadows | Employees: 8,690 |
| Fax: 276-628-1592 | Type: Private | FYE: December 31 |
| Web: www.foodcity.com | | |

What do you call a chain of supermarkets in Kentucky, Virginia, and Tennessee? How about K-VA-T Food Stores? K-VA-T is one of the largest grocery chains in the region, with about 85 supermarkets primarily under the Food City banner (and a handful of Super Dollar Supermarkets). Originally a Piggly Wiggly franchise with three stores, K-VA-T was founded in 1955. It has expanded by acquiring stores from other regional food retailers, opening new stores, and adding services such as more than 30 pharmacies, about 20 Gas'N Go gasoline outlets, and banking. Its Mid-Mountain Foods provides warehousing and distribution services. The founding Smith family owns a majority of K-VA-T; employees own the rest of the company.

**KEY COMPETITORS**
Delhaize America
Kroger
Wal-Mart


## LAND O'LAKES, INC.

| | | |
|---|---|---|
| 4001 Lexington Ave. North | CEO: John E. Gherty | 2000 Sales: $5,756.3 million |
| Arden Hills, MN 55126 | CFO: Dan Knutson | 1-Yr. Sales Change: 2.6% |
| Phone: 651-481-2222 | HR: Karen Grabow | Employees: 6,500 |
| Fax: 651-481-2000 | Type: Cooperative | FYE: December 31 |
| Web: www.landolakesinc.com | | |

Land O'Lakes butters up its customers. Its network of more than 1,100 community cooperatives serves 300,000 farmers and ranchers. The dairy co-op (#2 in the US, behind Dairy Farmers of America) provides its members with wholesale fertilizer and crop protection products, seed, and animal feed. Its oldest product, Land O'Lakes butter, is the #1 butter brand in the US. Land O'Lakes also produces packaged milk, margarine, sour cream, and cheese. The dairy industry and its markets have been consolidating, and the co-op has responded with acquisitions and joint ventures: It's forming a joint venture with Farmland Industries called Land O'Lakes Farmland; the venture will be the largest feed company in North America.

**KEY COMPETITORS**
Dairy Farmers of America
Kraft Foods
Unilever

 See pages 288–289 for a full profile of this company.

## LANDMARK COMMUNICATIONS, INC.

| | | |
|---|---|---|
| 150 W. Brambleton Ave. | CEO: John O. "Dubby" Wynne | 2000 Sales: $805.0 million |
| Norfolk, VA 23510 | CFO: Lemuel E. Lewis | 1-Yr. Sales Change: 10.3% |
| Phone: 757-446-2000 | HR: Charlie W. Hill | Employees: 5,000 |
| Fax: 757-446-2983 | Type: Private | FYE: December 31 |
| Web: www.landmarkcom.com | | |

Landmark Communications' media properties are all over the map. Its core newspaper business includes three metropolitan dailies and some 50 community papers. Landmark puts many of those papers on the Internet through its InfiNet access and site-hosting unit (equally owned with partners Knight Ridder and Gannett). Founded in 1905 by Samuel Slover, Landmark also owns an outdoor advertising company. In addition to publishing, the company owns the Weather Channel and two CBS-affiliated TV stations in Las Vegas, as well as Nashville, Tennessee. Chairman Frank Batten Jr. (Slover's great-nephew) and his family own the company.

**KEY COMPETITORS**
Community Newspaper
 Holdings
Knight Ridder
Media General


## LANE INDUSTRIES, INC.

| | | |
|---|---|---|
| 1 Lane Center | CEO: Forrest M. Schneider | 2000 Sales: $1,000.0 million |
| Northbrook, IL 60062 | CFO: — | 1-Yr. Sales Change: 0.0% |
| Phone: 847-498-6789 | HR: Linda Datz | Employees: 7,000 |
| Fax: 847-498-2104 | Type: Private | FYE: December 31 |

From the seeds of a humble office machine and supplies manufacturer grew the mighty oak of Lane Industries. The diversified holding company's oldest investment is its nearly two-thirds stake in General Binding, a maker of binding and laminating equipment, marker boards, and paper shredders, founded by William Lane II in 1947. Lane Industries is also active in the lodging industry through Lane Hospitality, which owns or operates more than 30 hotels, resorts, and time-share properties. Through Lane Security, the company owns Protection Service Industries, a security alarm firm in California, Arizona, and New Mexico. Lane Industries also has farming and ranching interests. The Lane family owns the company.

**KEY COMPETITORS**
Fellowes
Starwood Hotels & Resorts
Tyco International


## LANOGA CORPORATION

| | | |
|---|---|---|
| 17946 NE 65th St. | CEO: Paul Hylbert | 2000 Sales: $1,300.0 million |
| Redmond, WA 98052 | CFO: William Brakken | 1-Yr. Sales Change: 3.9% |
| Phone: 425-883-4125 | HR: — | Employees: 5,360 |
| Fax: 425-882-2959 | Type: Private | FYE: December 31 |
| Web: www.lanogacorp.com | | |

Lanoga is a lumbering giant. The company is one of the top US retailers of lumber and building materials, catering to professional contractors as well as consumers. Operating more than 190 stores in about 18 states, Lanoga has grown through dozens of small acquisitions. Its divisions include United Building Centers (about 130 stores in the Midwest and Rocky Mountain states), Lumbermen's Building Centers (about 50 stores in the Northwest and Arizona), Spenard Builders Supply (a dozen or so stores in Alaska), and the Home Lumber Company (five stores in Colorado). The firm was founded in 1855 by cousins William Laird and Matthew Norton. Descendants of the company's founders own Lanoga.

**KEY COMPETITORS**
84 Lumber
Home Depot
Lowe's

## LARRY H. MILLER GROUP

5650 S. State St.
Murray, UT 84107
Phone: 801-264-3100
Fax: 801-264-3198
Web: www.lhm.com

CEO: Larry H. Miller
CFO: Clark Whitworth
HR: Carolyn Ashburn
Type: Private

2000 Sales: $1,367.1 million
1-Yr. Sales Change: 0.5%
Employees: —
FYE: December 31

You wouldn't hire the Larry H. Miller Group for your late night bebop, but the firm does know a little something about all that jazz. Its interests include automobiles, television, and basketball. The company operates about 40 auto dealerships in Arizona, Colorado, Idaho, New Mexico, Oregon, and Utah; most are in Utah. Its dealerships sell Toyota, Cadillac, Chevrolet, Honda, Lexus, and other makes of cars. The company also owns the Utah Jazz professional basketball team, its home (the Delta Center arena), the WNBA's Utah Starzz, and Salt Lake City TV station KJZZ. In addition, the group, owned by its CEO with the same name, operates Larry Miller Advertising and publishes *Spirit* magazine.

**KEY COMPETITORS**
AutoNation
Burt Automotive
Earnhardt's Auto Centers

## LDI, LTD.

54 Monument Circle, Ste. 800
Indianapolis, IN 46204
Phone: 317-237-2251
Fax: 317-237-2280
Web: www.ldiltd.com

CEO: Andre B. Lacy
CFO: Michael P. Hutson
HR: Joyce Schooley
Type: Private

2000 Est. Sales: $900.0 mil.
1-Yr. Sales Change: 5.3%
Employees: —
FYE: December 31

The "D" is definitely for "diversified" at LDI. The holding company, whose initials stand for "Lacy Diversified Industries," deals in clothing, motorcycle parts, bicycle frames, and auto products. It owns Tucker Rocky Distributing, a distributor of apparel and aftermarket equipment for the watercraft, motorcycle, and snowmobile markets. LDI's Answer Products Inc. manufactures and distributes the Manitou brand of bicycle frames and suspension forks, as well as parts and apparel. LDI has a 74% stake in FinishMaster, the #1 automotive paints and coating distributor in the US. LDI sold its Major Video Concepts video distribution business. Founded in 1912 as U.S. Corrugated-Fiber Box Co., LDI is owned by CEO Andre Lacy.

**KEY COMPETITORS**
Cannondale
Genuine Parts
Global Motorsport Group

## THE LEFRAK ORGANIZATION

97-77 Queens Blvd.
Rego Park, NY 11374
Phone: 718-459-9021
Fax: 718-897-0688
Web: www.lefrak.com

CEO: Samuel J. LeFrak
CFO: Judy Watsmann
HR: John Farrelly
Type: Private

2000 Sales: $3,800.0 million
1-Yr. Sales Change: 18.8%
Employees: 16,200
FYE: November 30

"If you build it, they will come" could be The Lefrak Organization's motto. The private firm is one of the largest residential development and management companies in the New York metropolitan area. In addition to a variety of smaller properties, its major developments include Lefrak City (5,000 units) and Battery Park (2,200 units), both in New York City, and Newport City (about 10,000 units), which is still under construction in Jersey City, New Jersey. Owned by the LeFrak family, the company also owns and manages a variety of commercial and retail properties throughout the city. Subsidiaries include Lefrak Oil & Gas Organization and Lefrak Entertainment (a production company).

**KEY COMPETITORS**
Hartz Mountain
Mack-Cali Realty
Vornado

📖 See pages 290–291 for a full profile of this company.

## LEPRINO FOODS COMPANY

1830 W. 38th Ave.
Denver, CO 80211
Phone: 303-480-2600
Fax: 303-480-2605
Web: www.leprinofoods.com

CEO: Wes Allen
CFO: Ron Klump
HR: Dave Swan
Type: Private

2001 Est. Sales: $1,700.0 mil.
1-Yr. Sales Change: 3.0%
Employees: 2,500
FYE: October 31

To pizza chains such as Domino's, Pizza Hut, and Little Caesar, Leprino Foods really is the big cheese. The company is the world's largest maker of mozzarella cheese, which it sells to pizza chains and food manufacturers. Leprino's other dairy products include premium block mozzarella and provolone, as well as sweet whey, whey protein concentrate, and lactose for use in animal feeds, baby formula, and baked goods. The firm gets its milk supply from the nation's large dairy co-ops. Subsidiary Leprino Transportation Company operates refrigerated tractor trailers that transport the company's products nationwide. Italian immigrant Michael Leprino Sr. founded the company in 1950. It is still owned by the Leprino family.

**KEY COMPETITORS**
Saputo
Schreiber Foods

## LES SCHWAB TIRE CENTERS

646 NW Madras Hwy.
Prineville, OR 97754
Phone: 541-447-4136
Fax: 541-416-5208
Web: www.lesschwab.com

CEO: Philip Wick
CFO: Tom Freedman
HR: Larry Smith
Type: Private

2000 Est. Sales: $800.0 mil.
1-Yr. Sales Change: 0.0%
Employees: 6,000
FYE: December 31

If you're seeking tires, Les Schwab Tire Centers aims to help. Of course, it doesn't hurt that the owner wrote the bible of tire retailing: *Pride in Performance — Keep It Going*. Les Schwab Tire Centers prides itself on continued customer service; it sells tires and batteries and does alignment, brake, and shock work at more than 300 stores in Alaska, California, Idaho, Montana, Nevada, Oregon, and Washington. With a story that rivals Moses', founder and chairman Les Schwab was reared in a logging camp and went to school in a converted boxcar. In 1952 he bought a tire shop that eventually became Les Schwab Tire Centers. The firm, owned by Schwab and his family, plans to open 15 to 20 new stores a year.

**KEY COMPETITORS**
Discount Tire
Sears
Wal-Mart

## LEVI STRAUSS & CO.

1155 Battery St.
San Francisco, CA 94111
Phone: 415-501-6000
Fax: 415-501-3939
Web: www.levistrauss.com

CEO: Philip A. Marineau
CFO: William B. Chiasson
HR: Fred Paulenich
Type: Private

2000 Sales: $4,645.1 million
1-Yr. Sales Change: (9.6%)
Employees: 17,300
FYE: November 30

Good ol' trusty Levi's are one thing. Hip, funky, stylish Levi's are another. Blue-jeans maker Levi Strauss & Co. (LS&CO.) wants to be known for both. LS&CO., the world's #1 maker of brand-name clothing, sells jeans and sportswear under the Levi's, Dockers, and Slates names in over 80 countries. Levi's jeans — department store staples — were once the uniform of American youth, but LS&CO. lost touch with the trends in recent years, and slow sales have led the company to slash its US workforce. To re-tap the youth market, LS&CO. is adding hip styles like its unusually cut Engineered Jeans; it also is licensing its brands for youth-oriented products. The Haas family (relatives of founder Levi Strauss) owns LS&CO.

**KEY COMPETITORS**
The Gap
Tommy Hilfiger
VF

 See pages 292–293 for a full profile of this company.

## LIBERTY MUTUAL INSURANCE COMPANIES

175 Berkeley St.
Boston, MA 02117
Phone: 617-357-9500
Fax: 617-350-7648
Web: www.libertymutual.com

CEO: Edmund F. "Ted" Kelly
CFO: J. Paul Condrin III
HR: Helen E.R. Sayles
Type: Mutual company

2000 Sales: $13,470.0 million
1-Yr. Sales Change: (13.1%)
Employees: 37,000
FYE: December 31

Liberty Mutual wants more liberty. The US's #1 workers' compensation insurer hopes to gain more flexibility in dealing with rapidly changing markets by reorganizing as a mutual holding company. The company stresses loss prevention (analyzing work sites and practices for safety) and rehabilitation services and has alliances with health care providers to manage disability care. Noncommercial lines include homeowners, auto, and group life. Liberty Mutual has taken asset management subsidiary Liberty Financial private and merged it into a subsidiary. The company has more than 900 offices in some 15 countries, including Canada, Japan, Mexico, Singapore, and the UK.

**KEY COMPETITORS**
Allstate
Prudential
State Farm

 See pages 294–295 for a full profile of this company.


## LIBERTY TRAVEL, INC.

69 Spring St.
Ramsey, NJ 07446
Phone: 201-934-3500
Fax: 201-934-3651
Web: www.libertytravel.com

CEO: Gilbert Haroche
CFO: Richard Cowlan
HR: Susan Brennen
Type: Private

2000 Sales: $1,400.0 million
1-Yr. Sales Change: 0.7%
Employees: 2,500
FYE: December 31

Give me liberty, or give me travel? Liberty Travel gives you both. The company is one of the US leaders in leisure vacations and owns 200 offices in the Northeast and in Florida; it sells directly to the holiday traveler. Liberty's sister company GOGO Worldwide Vacations serves the travel agent community with customized land-only and air-inclusive travel packages from almost 90 offices in more than 30 states. It also operates Air France Holidays. Gilbert Haroche and the late Fred Kassner founded the privately held Liberty Travel in 1951; Haroche still owns the company.

**KEY COMPETITORS**
American Express
Carlson Wagonlit
WorldTravel

 See pages 296–297 for a full profile of this company.


## LIFE CARE CENTERS OF AMERICA

3570 Keith St. NW
Cleveland, TN 37312
Phone: 423-472-9585
Fax: 423-339-8337
Web: www.lcca.com

CEO: Lane Bowen
CFO: Steve Ziegler
HR: Mark Gibson
Type: Private

2000 Est. Sales: $1,265.0 mil.
1-Yr. Sales Change: 4.5%
Employees: 29,350
FYE: December 31

Life Care Centers of America is a privately owned operator of retirement and health care centers in the US. The company manages more than 200 facilities in 28 states — including retirement communities, assisted living facilities, and nursing homes — and provides such specialized services as home health care. Founder Forrest Preston opened his first center in 1970, and the company continues to tout a "corporate culture grounded in the Judeo-Christian ethic." However Life Care has faced complaints of poor-quality care, typical of complaints that plague the industry overall.

**KEY COMPETITORS**
Beverly Enterprises
Mariner Post-Acute Network
Sun Healthcare

## LIFESTYLE FURNISHINGS INTERNATIONAL LTD.

4000 Lifestyle Ct.
High Point, NC 27265
Phone: 336-878-7000
Fax: 336-878-7015
Web: www.lifestylefurnishings.com

CEO: Alan D. Cole
CFO: Ronald J. Hoffman
HR: William J. Frakes
Type: Private

2000 Sales: $2,000.0 million
1-Yr. Sales Change: (4.8%)
Employees: 30,000
FYE: December 31

LifeStyle Furnishings International is rearranging the house. The company (formerly one of the "Big Three" home furnishings makers — along with Furniture Brands International and La-Z-Boy), sells bedroom, dining room, living room, outdoor, and upholstered furniture and fabrics under Ametex, BenchCraft, Berkline, Lexington, and Robert Allen brands. Its sale of Henredon, Drexel Heritage, and Maitland-Smith (in early 2002) knocked Lifestyle out of the furniture industry triad. Made mostly in North America and Asia, the company sells its products through specialty and department stores, as well as independent shops that carry only LifeStyle products. A venture capital unit of Citibank controls the company.

**KEY COMPETITORS**
Furniture Brands International
Klaussner Furniture
La-Z-Boy

See pages 298–299 for a full profile of this company.


## LINCOLN PROPERTY COMPANY

Lincoln Plaza
Dallas, TX 75201
Phone: 214-740-3300
Fax: 214-740-3313
Web: www.lincolnproperty.com

CEO: Mack Pogue
CFO: Nancy Davis
HR: Luanne Hudson
Type: Private

2000 Sales: $1,251.0 million
1-Yr. Sales Change: (14.4%)
Employees: 4,900
FYE: June 30

Lincoln Property is one of the US's largest diversified real estate companies — honest! Lincoln began by building apartments in the Dallas area, then expanded into commercial and retail projects. It now has residential properties comprising more than 140,000 units and has developed about 140 million sq. ft. of commercial properties nationwide (still managing 90 million). The firm is divided into commercial and residential divisions, and offers management and investment services. It has a joint venture with Lend Lease to develop commercial property and with Sam Zell's Equity Residential Properties to build apartments. Mack Pogue cofounded Lincoln in 1965 with Trammell Crow, whose stake Pogue bought out in 1977.

**KEY COMPETITORS**
JMB Realty
Tishman Realty
Trammell Crow Residential


## LINSCO/PRIVATE LEDGER CORP.

9785 Town Center Dr.
San Diego, CA 92121
Phone: 858-450-9606
Fax: 858-546-8324
Web: www.lpl.com

CEO: Todd A. Robinson
CFO: David Collett
HR: Gina Cannella
Type: Private

2000 Sales: $806.0 million
1-Yr. Sales Change: 130.3%
Employees: 800
FYE: December 31

Linsco/Private Ledger, one of the largest independent brokerage firms in the US, advises its clients on stocks and bonds, mutual funds, commodities, options, annuities, real estate investment trusts (REITs), and other investment vehicles. Clients are charged a flat fee rather than a commission percentage. As an independent, Linsco/Private Ledger doesn't sell a portfolio of its own but provides access to others across the nation. The company has more than 3,800 representatives (independent contractors) in some 1,800 locally owned and operated branch offices in all 50 states and the District of Columbia. Linsco/Private Ledger's offices are in Boston and San Diego.

**KEY COMPETITORS**
Charles Schwab
Merrill Lynch
Morgan Keegan

## L.L. BEAN, INC.

Casco St.
Freeport, ME 04033
Phone: 207-865-4761
Fax: 207-552-6821
Web: www.llbean.com

CEO: Chris McCormick
CFO: Mark Fasold
HR: Bob Peixotto
Type: Private

2001 Est. Sales: $1,200.0 mil.
1-Yr. Sales Change: 9.1%
Employees: 4,700
FYE: February 28

Enjoy the outdoors or just want to look like you do? Outdoor specialty cata-
loger L.L. Bean also operates a flagship retail store and a children's clothing
store in Freeport, Maine (both are open 24 hours a day, year-round). It is
opening more retail stores throughout the US. L.L. Bean also has 10 US factory outlets and more than 20 retail stores in Japan, and it sells its merchandise online. Known for customer service (including unlimited returns), it
offers more than 16,000 items ranging from outdoor wear to household furnishings. L.L. Bean also conducts classes on topics such as bicycle maintenance, camping, and sea kayaking. The firm was founded in 1912 by Leon
Leonwood Bean and is controlled by his descendants.

**KEY COMPETITORS**
Bass Pro Shops
Lands' End
Spiegel

 **See pages 300–301 for a full profile of this company.**

## THE LONGABERGER COMPANY

1500 E. Main St.
Newark, OH 43055
Phone: 740-322-5000
Fax: 740-322-5240
Web: www.longaberger.com

CEO: Tami Longaberger
CFO: Stephanie Imhoff
HR: Ann Dunlap
Type: Private

2000 Sales: $1,000.0 million
1-Yr. Sales Change: 22.1%
Employees: 8,000
FYE: December 31

A tisket, a tasket, a Longaberger basket. The Longaberger Company is the #1
maker of handmade baskets in the US, selling nearly 10 million a year. The
baskets are sold in the US through in-home shows conducted by
Longaberger's 70,000 independent sales associates. Baskets account for half of
sales, but the company also sells pottery, fabrics, window treatments, and
wrought-iron home accessories. Longaberger's home office is a seven-story
rendition of a basket with two 75-ton handles on top. The company also owns
a golf course, a hotel, and Longaberger Homestead (an events area with shops
and restaurants). The family-owned firm is run by the daughters of the late
Dave Longaberger, who founded the company in 1973.

**KEY COMPETITORS**
Euromarket Designs
Pier 1 Imports
Williams-Sonoma

## LOS ANGELES DEPARTMENT OF WATER AND POWER

111 N. Hope St.
Los Angeles, CA 90012
Phone: 213-367-1338
Fax: 213-367-1455
Web: www.ladwp.com

CEO: David A. Wiggs Jr.
CFO: —
HR: —
Type: Government-owned

2001 Sales: $3,628.0 million
1-Yr. Sales Change: 24.8%
Employees: 7,000
FYE: June 30

The Los Angeles Department of Water and Power (LADWP) keeps the movie
cameras running and the swimming pools full. The largest municipally owned
utility in the US, LADWP provides electricity to 1.4 million residential and
business customers and water to 3.8 million consumers. The company owns
interests in generating facilities that give it about 1,000 MW of capacity; it also
buys and sells wholesale power. Most of the city's water supply is transported
through two aqueduct systems from the eastern Sierra Nevada Mountains;
other water sources include wells in the San Fernando Valley and local
groundwater basins. As a city-owned utility, LADWP's monopoly status was
unaffected by deregulation in California.

## LOUISIANA STATE UNIVERSITY SYSTEM

| | | |
|---|---|---|
| 3810 W. Lakeshore Dr. | CEO: William Jenkins | 2000 Sales: $1,366.7 million |
| Baton Rouge, LA 70808 | CFO: Jerry J. Baudin | 1-Yr. Sales Change: (31.5%) |
| Phone: 225-388-6935 | HR: Forest C. Benedict | Employees: 26,000 |
| Fax: 225-388-5524 | Type: School | FYE: June 30 |
| Web: www.lsu.edu | | |

The Louisiana State University (LSU) System oversees a string of higher education institutions across the Bayou State. Flagship institution LSU Agricultural and Mechanical College in Baton Rouge was founded in 1853 and boasts more than 31,000 students (about 15% are graduate students) and a faculty of 1,300. The Baton Rouge campus is home to the Paul M. Hebert Law Center; the LSU Agricultural Center; the LSU Medical Center; the LSU School of Veterinary Medicine; the Center for Coastal, Energy, and Environmental Resources; and the Pennington Biomedical Research Center (nutritional research). Notable LSU alumni include political strategist James Carville, basketball great Shaquille O'Neal, and actress Joanne Woodward.

## LOYOLA UNIVERSITY OF CHICAGO

| | | |
|---|---|---|
| 6525 N. Sheridan Rd. | CEO: Michael R. Quinlan | 2000 Sales: $822.3 million |
| Chicago, IL 60626 | CFO: David Meagher | 1-Yr. Sales Change: (10.3%) |
| Phone: 773-274-3000 | HR: Thomas M. Kelly | Employees: 7,200 |
| Fax: 312-915-6455 | Type: School | FYE: June 30 |
| Web: www.luc.edu | | |

Loyola University of Chicago is a Jesuit university with a reach that extends beyond the Windy City. In addition to its four Chicago-area campuses, the university also maintains an undergraduate campus in Rome. Loyola University's 12,600 students can choose from 46 undergraduate, 59 graduate, 36 doctoral, and three professional programs. Established in 1870, the university has struggled financially after spinning off its medical center (and the center's surplus revenue) as a subsidiary in 1995. It also is fighting declining enrollment and an eroding endowment (worth about $300 million). After surviving calls for his ouster by students and staff, president Rev. John Piderit resigned in 2001.

## LUCASFILM LTD.

| | | |
|---|---|---|
| 5858 Lucas Valley Rd. | CEO: Gordon Radley | 2000 Est. Sales: $1,100.0 mil. |
| Nicasio, CA 94946 | CFO: Micheline Chau | 1-Yr. Sales Change: 83.3% |
| Phone: 415-662-1800 | HR: Darlene Sattel | Employees: 1,800 |
| Fax: 415-662-2437 | Type: Private | FYE: March 31 |
| Web: www.lucasfilm.com | | |

Emperor Lucas knows what the people want. With five of the top 20 grossing films of all time, Lucasfilm is one of the most successful independent production companies in the history of cinema. One of five companies owned by filmmaker George Lucas (the brain behind the *Star Wars* films and the *Indiana Jones Trilogy*), Lucasfilm's productions have garnered a total of 17 Academy Awards. Its latest film, *Star Wars: Episode I — The Phantom Menace* (released in May 1999), has grossed about $920 million worldwide and finished in the #2 spot behind *Titanic*. Created in 1971, Lucasfilm handles the business affairs of each company in the Lucas empire and includes the THX Group (theater and home theater sound systems).

**KEY COMPETITORS**
DreamWorks SKG
Universal Studios
Walt Disney

 See pages 302–303 for a full profile of this company.

## LUMBERMENS MERCHANDISING CORPORATION

| | | |
|---|---|---|
| 137 W. Wayne Ave. | CEO: Anthony J. DeCarlo | 2000 Est. Sales: $2,100.0 mil. |
| Wayne, PA 19087 | CFO: David J. Gonze | 1-Yr. Sales Change: 10.5% |
| Phone: 610-293-7000 | HR: Patricia Moynihan | Employees: — |
| Fax: 610-293-7098 | Type: Cooperative | FYE: September 30 |
| Web: www.cyberyard.com/cybyrdnational/pages | | |

Membership has its privileges. Through Lumbermens Merchandising Corporation (LMC), lumber retailers in the eastern half of the US pool their buying resources to leverage volume discounts from vendors and increase their own efficiency. LMC's network of members includes more than 1,000 building material locations. LMC is the largest dealer-owned lumber building materials buying group in the US. The cooperative holds members to strict confidentiality, in part to safeguard vendor contracts. In addition to lumber and panel products, LMC also supplies its members with non-wood products, millwork, and hardware. LMC is planning to expand into the western portion of the US.

**KEY COMPETITORS**
BMA
Cameron Ashley
Do it Best

## M. FABRIKANT & SONS

| | | |
|---|---|---|
| 1 Rockefeller Plaza, 28th Fl. | CEO: Matthew Fortgang | 2001 Sales: $930.0 million |
| New York, NY 10020 | CFO: Michael Shaffet | 1-Yr. Sales Change: (7.0%) |
| Phone: 212-757-0790 | HR: Susan Fortgang | Employees: 800 |
| Fax: 212-262-9757 | Type: Private | FYE: July 31 |

A major US diamond wholesaler, family-owned M. Fabrikant & Sons claims to be one of the oldest diamond and jewelry companies in the world. With holdings that include about 20 companies in 10 countries, the company purchases, manufactures, and sells to retailers a full range of loose and polished diamonds; diamond, gold, and silver jewelry; and colored stones, such as rubies, emeralds, sapphires, opals, and pearls. Leer Tokyo Pearl, Fabrikant's joint venture with a Japanese firm, supplies the US market with Japanese, Tahitian, and Australian pearls. Fabrikant began as a loose diamond wholesaler in New York City in 1895.

**KEY COMPETITORS**
Lazare Kaplan
Michael Anthony Jewelers

## MA LABORATORIES, INC.

| | | |
|---|---|---|
| 2075 N. Capitol Ave. | CEO: Abraham Ma | 2000 Sales: $855.0 million |
| San Jose, CA 95132 | CFO: Ricky Chow | 1-Yr. Sales Change: 6.9% |
| Phone: 408-941-0808 | HR: Shareen Wu | Employees: 300 |
| Fax: 408-941-0909 | Type: Private | FYE: December 31 |
| Web: www.malabs.com | | |

If you need a computer part, just ask your MA. Distributor MA Laboratories, one of the largest privately held companies in the Silicon Valley, provides computer resellers and systems integrators with more than 1,800 high-tech gadgets and computer items. MA Labs sells just about everything commonly found in or near a computer, including hard drives, motherboards, CD-ROMs, video cards, and memory modules. Other products include monitors, software, fax modems, network cards, digital cameras, notebook computers, and accessories. Among MA's suppliers are 3Com, Advanced Micro Devices, Hewlett-Packard, IBM, Intel, Microsoft, Sony, and Toshiba. MA Labs was founded in 1983 by owner and CEO Abraham Ma.

**KEY COMPETITORS**
Bell Microproducts
Ingram Micro
Tech Data

## M. A. MORTENSON COMPANY

| | | |
|---|---|---|
| 700 Meadow Ln. North | CEO: M. A. Mortenson Jr. | 2000 Sales: $1,080.0 million |
| Minneapolis, MN 55422 | CFO: Peter A. Conzemius | 1-Yr. Sales Change: 11.6% |
| Phone: 763-522-2100 | HR: Daniel R. Haag | Employees: — |
| Fax: 763-520-3430 | Type: Private | FYE: December 31 |
| Web: www.mortenson.com | | |

It's all bricks and mortar for M. A. Mortenson Companies, one of the largest US contractors. The company can offer several levels of services to clients, from site selection and design to financing and construction. The company builds aviation, education, health care, and sports facilities as well as power plants and dams. Mortenson works primarily in the US, where it has built the arena for the Minnesota Wild hockey team, University of Minnesota hospital projects, Denver International Airport, Coors Field in Denver, and Iowa's tallest building, the 44-story 801 Grand in Des Moines. The family-owned company was founded in 1954 by M. A. Mortenson Sr., whose son M. A. Mortenson Jr. runs the company today.

**KEY COMPETITORS**
Bechtel
Parsons
Turner Corporation

## MACANDREWS & FORBES HOLDINGS INC.

| | | |
|---|---|---|
| 35 E. 62nd St. | CEO: Ronald O. Perelman | 2000 Est. Sales: $5,500.0 mil. |
| New York, NY 10021 | CFO: Ronald O. Perelman | 1-Yr. Sales Change: 1.9% |
| Phone: 212-688-9000 | HR: Herb Vallier | Employees: 19,500 |
| Fax: 212-572-8400 | Type: Private | FYE: December 31 |

Through MacAndrews & Forbes Holdings, financier Ron Perelman is focused on makeup and money. The holding company has investments in an array of public and private companies, most notably Revlon (the #2 cosmetics company in the US), Golden State Bancorp (the nation's #2 thrift), M&F Worldwide (licorice flavors), and WeddingChannel.com. Perelman is intent on reversing the fortunes of Revlon, which has been hobbled by debt and dwindling market share; his stake in Sunbeam (small appliances and Coleman camping equipment) became worthless when that company declared bankruptcy in 2001. He did make a hefty profit when Consolidated Cigar Holdings (the #1 US cigar maker) was sold to French tobacco maker Seita in early 1999.

**KEY COMPETITORS**
Estée Lauder
L'Oréal USA
Procter & Gamble

 See pages 304–305 for a full profile of this company.

## MAJOR LEAGUE BASEBALL

| | | |
|---|---|---|
| 245 Park Ave. | CEO: Allan H. "Bud" Selig | 2000 Sales: $3,177.6 million |
| New York, NY 10167 | CFO: Jeffrey White | 1-Yr. Sales Change: 12.0% |
| Phone: 212-931-7800 | HR: Wendy Lewis | Employees: — |
| Fax: 212-949-8636 | Type: Association | FYE: October 31 |
| Web: www.mlb.com | | |

This organization succeeds when you catch a fever — baseball fever, that is. Major League Baseball (MLB) runs the game of professional baseball and oversees 30 franchises in 28 cities. Each team operates as a separate business but is regulated and governed by MLB. The organization sets official rules, regulates team ownership, and collects licensing fees for merchandise. It also sells national broadcasting rights and distributes fees to the teams. MLB was formed when the rival National and American Leagues joined together in 1903. The game's resurgent popularity is being threatened by financial disparity among teams and renewed labor tensions. As a result, the league is eliminating two teams, which are yet to be determined, before the 2002 season.

**KEY COMPETITORS**
NBA
NFL
NHL

 See pages 306–307 for a full profile of this company.

## MARATHON ASHLAND PETROLEUM LLC

539 S. Main St.
Findlay, OH 45840
Phone: 419-422-2121
Fax: 419-425-7040
Web: www.mapllc.com

CEO: Gary R. Heminger
CFO: Garry L. Peiffer
HR: Rodney P. Nichols
Type: Joint venture

2000 Sales: $28,885.0 million
1-Yr. Sales Change: 42.3%
Employees: 28,000
FYE: December 31

It's not hard to find Marathon Ashland Petroleum (MAP) on the map — the company has operations in 23 states in the US and is charting a course to sustain its position as one of the US's leading oil refiners. A joint venture between Marathon Oil (which owns 62%) and Ashland (38%), MAP operates seven refineries with the combined capacity to process 935,000 barrels of crude oil a day. MAP sells refined products at more than 6,000 Marathon- and Ashland-branded gas stations, and through retail subsidiary Speedway SuperAmerica, which has more than 2,400 outlets. Speedway SuperAmerica and Pilot Corporation have combined their travel center operations. MAP also holds stakes in more than 8,000 miles of pipeline.

**KEY COMPETITORS**
BP
ChevronTexaco
Exxon Mobil

## MARITZ INC.

1375 N. Highway Dr.
Fenton, MO 63099
Phone: 636-827-4000
Fax: 636-827-3312
Web: www.maritz.com

CEO: W. Stephen Maritz
CFO: James W. Kienker
HR: Terry L. Goring
Type: Private

2001 Sales: $1,318.0 million
1-Yr. Sales Change: (0.5%)
Employees: 6,200
FYE: March 31

Not only can Maritz send your employees on business trips, it can motivate them to go. With about 240 offices in North America and Europe, Maritz offers travel, employee motivation, and marketing services. Its performance improvement and incentive programs help client companies improve workforce quality and customer satisfaction. The company is also one of the nation's largest custom market research companies. In addition, TQ3 Maritz Travel Solutions co-owns, with TUI Business Travel and Internet Travel Group, TQ3 Travel Solutions, Europe's top travel firm and a leading global agency with 1,300 locations in more than 50 countries. Maritz, which is owned by the founding Maritz family, bought e-learning company Librix Learning in 2001.

**KEY COMPETITORS**
American Express
Carlson
J.D. Power

See pages 308–309 for a full profile of this company.

## MARK IV INDUSTRIES, INC.

501 John James Audubon Pkwy.
Amherst, NY 14226
Phone: 716-689-4972
Fax: 716-689-6098
Web: www.mark-iv.com

CEO: William P. Montague
CFO: Mark G. Barberio
HR: Michelle Acquilina
Type: Private

2001 Est. Sales: $2,000.0 mil.
1-Yr. Sales Change: 0.3%
Employees: 15,500
FYE: February 28

Mark IV Industries' engineered components and systems are on the mark when it comes to fluid-handling and power-steering uses. Mark IV primarily targets aftermarket (some 60% of sales) and OEM customers. Its automotive unit makes idlers, pulleys, belts, power-steering and air-conditioning hoses, manifolds, and water pumps. Mark IV's industrial unit makes circulating liquid temperature control systems used to monitor the temperature of injection molding machines. The company has sold its Dayco industrial product line, including units that make industrial power transmission belts and fluid transfer and hydraulic hoses, to Parker Hannifin. European private equity firm BC Partners owns the company.

**KEY COMPETITORS**
Dana
Dover
United Technologies

See pages 310–311 for a full profile of this company.

## THE MARMON GROUP, INC.

225 W. Washington St.
Chicago, IL 60606
Phone: 312-372-9500
Fax: 312-845-5305
Web: www.marmon.com

CEO: Robert A. Pritzker
CFO: Robert C. Gluth
HR: Larry Rist
Type: Private

2000 Sales: $6,785.6 million
1-Yr. Sales Change: 3.9%
Employees: 40,000
FYE: December 31

With more monikers than most, The Marmon Group monitors a melange of more than 100 autonomous manufacturing and service companies. Marmon's manufacturing units make medical products, mining equipment, industrial materials and components, consumer products, transportation equipment, building products, and water-treatment products. Services include marketing and distribution and consumer credit information. Overall, Marmon companies operate about 550 facilities in more than 50 countries. Chicago's Pritzker family (owners of the Hyatt hotel chain) owns The Marmon Group.

**KEY COMPETITORS**
GE
ITT Industries
TRW

 **See pages 312–313 for a full profile of this company.**


## MARS, INCORPORATED

6885 Elm St.
McLean, VA 22101
Phone: 703-821-4900
Fax: 703-448-9678
Web: www.mars.com

CEO: John Franklyn Mars
CFO: R. E. Barnes
HR: —
Type: Private

2000 Est. Sales: $15,000.0 mil.
1-Yr. Sales Change: 0.0%
Employees: 30,000
FYE: December 31

Mars is a private planet orbiting around chocolate, rice, and pet food. The #2 US candy maker (behind Hershey) makes global favorites, including M&M's, Snickers, and the Mars bar. Other products include 3 Musketeers, Dove, Milky Way, Skittles, Twix, and Starburst sweets; Combos and Kudos snacks; Uncle Ben's rice (the US #1 branded rice); and pet food under the names Pedigree, Sheba, and Whiskas. Mars also makes drink vending equipment and electronic automated payment systems. The Mars family (including siblings Forrest Mars Jr., president and CEO John Mars, and VP Jacqueline Badger Mars) owns the highly secretive firm — making the Mars family one of the richest in the country.

**KEY COMPETITORS**
Cadbury Schweppes
Hershey
Nestlé

 **See pages 314–315 for a full profile of this company.**


## THE MARTIN-BROWER COMPANY, L.L.C.

333 E. Butterfield Rd., Ste. 500
Lombard, IL 60148
Phone: 630-271-8300
Fax: 630-271-8680

CEO: Ray Guerin
CFO: Peter Swan
HR: Phil Menzel
Type: Private

2000 Est. Sales: $2,500.0 mil.
1-Yr. Sales Change: 4.2%
Employees: 2,200
FYE: June 30

Ronald McDonald is worth his weight in gold(en arches) to The Martin-Brower Company. Martin-Brower is a distributor of supplies (such as crew hats, first-aid kits, lightbulbs, and trash bags) to some of the McDonald's restaurants in the US and Canada. Martin-Brower makes regular deliveries to each store through a network of more than 20 distribution centers in North America. In addition, the company serves McDonald's through joint ventures in Brazil, Puerto Rico, Central America, and the Caribbean. Martin-Brower changed hands in 1998 when privately owned food and beverage distributor Reyes Holdings purchased the company from UK-based Sygen International (previously PIC International).

**KEY COMPETITORS**
Alliant Exchange
Golden State Foods
Keystone Foods

## MARTY FRANICH AUTO CENTER

550 Auto Center Dr.
Watsonville, CA 95076
Phone: 831-722-4181
Fax: 831-724-1853
Web: www.franichford.com

CEO: Steven "Rocky" Franich
CFO: —
HR: —
Type: Private

2000 Sales: $924.7 million
1-Yr. Sales Change: 7.6%
Employees: —
FYE: December 31

Fleet customers find smooth sailing at the Marty Franich Auto Center dealerships. Founded in 1948, the company consists of two full-service dealerships in Watsonville, California, that sell Chrysler, Dodge, Eagle, Ford, Jeep, Lincoln, Mercury, and Plymouth vehicles. The dealer also sells used vehicles, and it operates parts and service departments. The company makes almost 90% of its sales from fleet buyers. It also sells cars to rental outfits nationwide, including Hertz, Budget Rent-a-Car, and Avis Group. President and CEO Steven Franich, the son of founder Martin (Marty) Franich, heads the company.

**KEY COMPETITORS**
AutoNation
Prospect Motors

## MARY KAY INC.

16251 Dallas Pkwy.
Addison, TX 75001
Phone: 972-687-6300
Fax: 972-687-1609
Web: www.marykay.com

CEO: Richard Rogers
CFO: David Holl
HR: Darrell Overcash
Type: Private

2000 Sales: $1,200.0 million
1-Yr. Sales Change: 20.0%
Employees: 3,600
FYE: December 31

Mary Kay is in the pink (and in Avon's shadow) as the US's #2 direct seller of beauty products. It sells more than 200 products in eight product categories: facial skin care, cosmetics, fragrances, nutritional supplements, sun protection, nail care, body care, and men's skin care. Some 800,000 direct-sales consultants demonstrate Mary Kay products in the US (80% of sales) and about 35 other countries. Consultants vie for prizes such as the use of cars (including pink Cadillacs, first awarded in 1969). Mary Kay has a mostly female workforce, although it does employ some men (such as its chairman/CEO and CFO). Founder Mary Kay Ash passed away in November 2001; her family owns most of the company.

**KEY COMPETITORS**
Alticor
Avon
L'Oréal

 See pages 316–317 for a full profile of this company.

## MARYLAND STATE LOTTERY AGENCY

6776 Reisterstown Rd., Ste. 204
Baltimore, MD 21215
Phone: 410-318-6200
Fax: 410-764-4263
Web: www.msla.state.md.us

CEO: Buddy Roogow
CFO: Sandra Long
HR: Bobby Sinclair
Type: Government-owned

2001 Sales: $1,211.0 million
1-Yr. Sales Change: 3.1%
Employees: 150
FYE: June 30

The Maryland State Lottery Agency offers players a variety of ways to amass a fortune. Among its games of chance are scratch-offs bearing titles such as Grand Casino, Scratch Keno, Money Talks, and Festivus Maximus II. The agency's numbers games include Cash in Hand, Lotto, Pick 3, and Pick 4. Maryland State Lottery also participates in the seven-state The Big Game lottery. The agency, which was created in 1973, distributes about 55% of its revenue as prizes; the rest goes to state-funded programs, retailers, and operational expenses. Proceeds from lottery sales helped build Camden Yards, home of Major League Baseball's Baltimore Orioles.

**KEY COMPETITORS**
Multi-State Lottery
New Jersey Lottery
Pennsylvania Lottery

## MASHANTUCKET PEQUOT GAMING ENTERPRISE INC.

| | | |
|---|---|---|
| Rte. 2 | CEO: William Sherlock | 2000 Est. Sales: $1,300.0 mil. |
| Mashantucket, CT 06339 | CFO: John O'Brien | 1-Yr. Sales Change: 8.3% |
| Phone: 860-312-3000 | HR: Joanne Franks | Employees: — |
| Fax: 860-312-1599 | Type: Private | FYE: September 30 |
| Web: www.foxwoods.com | | |

The wealthiest tribe in the US, the Mashantucket Pequot Tribal Nation has seen its fortunes rise through Mashantucket Pequot Gaming Enterprise, the owner and operator of the Foxwoods Resort Casino in Mashantucket, Connecticut. Foxwoods is the world's largest casino, offering more than 5,800 slot machines and 350 gaming tables, as well as hotels, restaurants, lounges, and retail shops. Estimates of the casino's annual revenues exceed $1 billion; the state of Connecticut receives 25% of the take from all slot machines. The Pequots also own two golf courses, Fox Navigation (ferry service), the Pequot Pharmaceutical Network (mail-order and discount pharmaceuticals), and three Connecticut hotels.

**KEY COMPETITORS**
Connecticut Lottery
Mohegan Tribal Gaming
Trump Hotels & Casinos

 See pages 318–319 for a full profile of this company.


## MASSACHUSETTS INSTITUTE OF TECHNOLOGY

| | | |
|---|---|---|
| 77 Massachusetts Ave. | CEO: Charles M. Vest | 2000 Sales: $2,191.4 million |
| Cambridge, MA 02139 | CFO: Allan S. Bufferd | 1-Yr. Sales Change: 41.5% |
| Phone: 617-253-1000 | HR: Laura Avakian | Employees: 8,400 |
| Fax: 617-253-8000 | Type: School | FYE: June 30 |
| Web: web.mit.edu | | |

It's patently clear that the Massachusetts Institute of Technology (MIT) takes the prize. A leading research university, the school receives more than 300 patents a year (trailing only the University of California); Nobel Prizes have been awarded to 55 people associated with MIT. Blending that science and engineering acumen with a top business program, MIT graduates have started more than 4,000 companies — Hewlett-Packard and Intel to name just two. Research, much of it federally sponsored, accounts for more than half of the school's revenue. Tuition for MIT's 10,000 students runs about $26,000 a year. The faculty of the 26 academic departments includes 950 professors. Founded in 1865, MIT is privately endowed.


## MASSACHUSETTS MUTUAL LIFE INSURANCE COMPANY

| | | |
|---|---|---|
| 1295 State St. | CEO: Robert J. O'Connell | 2000 Sales: $15,340.4 million |
| Springfield, MA 01111 | CFO: Howard E. Gunton | 1-Yr. Sales Change: 23.1% |
| Phone: 413-788-4411 | HR: Susan A. Alfano | Employees: 8,000 |
| Fax: 413-744-6005 | Type: Mutual company | FYE: December 31 |
| Web: www.massmutual.com | | |

After flirting with the possibility of demutualizing, Massachusetts Mutual Life Insurance (MassMutual) has decided to stay the course. Founded in 1851, MassMutual sells individuals and small businesses a variety of life insurance and pension products through more than 1,300 offices in the US. Its Financial Services Group offers retirement plans for individuals and businesses, annuities, and trust services (through The MassMutual Trust Company). Other subsidiaries include OppenheimerFunds (mutual funds); David L. Babson & Co. (investor services); and Cornerstone Real Estate (real estate equities). Massachusetts Mutual Life also operates in Asia, Europe, and South America.

**KEY COMPETITORS**
New York Life
Northwestern Mutual
Prudential

 See pages 320–321 for a full profile of this company.

## MASSACHUSETTS STATE LOTTERY COMMISSION

| | | |
|---|---|---|
| 60 Columbian St. | CEO: Jay Mitchell | 2001 Sales: $3,935.9 million |
| Braintree, MA 02184 | CFO: Jeanette Maillet | 1-Yr. Sales Change: 5.9% |
| Phone: 781-849-5555 | HR: Deborah Keyes | Employees: 410 |
| Fax: 781-849-5509 | Type: Government-owned | FYE: June 30 |
| Web: www.masslottery.com | | |

For a lucky few, the Commonwealth creates uncommon wealth. The Massachusetts State Lottery Commission offers several numbers games (Mass Cash, Mass Millions, Megabucks) and scratch-off games (Draw Poker, Lifetime Cash, High Stakes). Massachusetts also participates in the seven-state Big Game lottery. State law requires that at least 45% of lottery proceeds must go to pay prizes, a maximum of 15% can be used for operating expenses, and the remainder must be distributed to individual cities and towns in Massachusetts. Created in 1971, the Massachusetts State Lottery Commission distributes revenue to the state's 351 cities and towns.

**KEY COMPETITORS**
Multi-State Lottery
New Hampshire Lottery
Vermont Lottery

## MASTERCARD INTERNATIONAL INCORPORATED

| | | |
|---|---|---|
| 2000 Purchase St. | CEO: Robert W. Selander | 2000 Sales: $1,571.2 million |
| Purchase, NY 10577 | CFO: Denise K. Fletcher | 1-Yr. Sales Change: 13.1% |
| Phone: 914-249-2000 | HR: Michael W. Michl | Employees: 3,100 |
| Fax: 914-249-4206 | Type: Private | FYE: December 31 |
| Web: www.mastercard.com | | |

Surpassing Visa in market share — now that would be priceless. MasterCard International is the US's #2 payment system and is owned by its more than 20,000 financial institution members worldwide. The company provides marketing, approval, and transaction processing services for its payment products, including branded MasterCard credit and debit and Maestro debit cards. It is also promoting Mondex chip-based smart cards (it owns 51% of Mondex). MasterCard also operates the Cirrus ATM network. To gain market share from Visa, the company plans to merge with Europay, its European counterpart; the combined entity will boast the world's largest debit card network but would still be #2 to Visa in credit cards.

**KEY COMPETITORS**
American Express
Morgan Stanley Dean Witter
Visa

 See pages 322–323 for a full profile of this company.

## MAYO FOUNDATION

| | | |
|---|---|---|
| 200 1st St. SW | CEO: Michael B. Wood | 2000 Sales: $3,709.7 million |
| Rochester, MN 55905 | CFO: David R. Ebel | 1-Yr. Sales Change: 34.9% |
| Phone: 507-284-2511 | HR: Marita Heller | Employees: 44,000 |
| Fax: 507-284-0161 | Type: Not-for-profit | FYE: December 31 |
| Web: www.mayo.edu | | |

If you're trying to lead a healthy life, don't hold the Mayo. The not-for-profit Mayo Foundation provides health care, most notably for difficult medical conditions, through its renowned Mayo Clinic in Rochester, Minnesota. The foundation also operates major facilities in Arizona and Jacksonville, as well as a network of 13 affiliated community hospitals and clinics in Iowa, Minnesota, and Wisconsin. The foundation also conducts research and trains physicians, nurses, and other health professionals. It dates back to a frontier practice launched by William Mayo in 1863.

**KEY COMPETITORS**
Ascension
Catholic Health Initiatives
Tenet Healthcare

 See pages 324–325 for a full profile of this company.

## MBM CORPORATION

| | | |
|---|---|---|
| 2641 Meadowbrook Rd. | CEO: Jerry L. Wordsworth | 2000 Sales: $2,700.0 million |
| Rocky Mount, NC 27801 | CFO: Jeff Kowalk | 1-Yr. Sales Change: 0.0% |
| Phone: 252-985-7200 | HR: Tim Ozment | Employees: 2,500 |
| Fax: 252-985-7241 | Type: Private | FYE: December 31 |

What's on the menu at your favorite restaurant? Just ask MBM Corporation, one of the leading privately owned food service distributors in the US. The company specializes in providing food to national restaurant chains such as Arby's, Burger King, Chick-fil-A, and Darden Restaurants (Red Lobster, Olive Garden, Bahama Breeze). MBM fills its customers' orders through its network of about 30 distribution centers across the US. J. R. Wordsworth founded the company nearly 50 years ago as a retail food distributor. MBM made the transition to its present role in restaurant food distribution after Wordsworth's children bought the business in the 1970s.

**KEY COMPETITORS**
Marriott International
McLane Foodservice
SYSCO


## MCCARTHY

| | | |
|---|---|---|
| 1341 N. Rock Hill Rd. | CEO: Michael D. Bolen | 2001 Sales: $1,205.0 million |
| St. Louis, MO 63124 | CFO: George F Scherer | 1-Yr. Sales Change: 28.2% |
| Phone: 314-968-3300 | HR: James Faust | Employees: 2,500 |
| Fax: 314-968-4642 | Type: Private | FYE: March 31 |
| Web: www.mccarthy.com | | |

A company that was in construction before Reconstruction, McCarthy is one of the oldest privately held builders in the US. The general contractor has projects worldwide and ranks among the top builders of health care facilities in the US. Contracts include heavy construction projects (bridges and water and waste-treatment plants), industrial projects (biopharmaceutical, food processing, and microelectronics facilities), commercial projects (retail stores and office buildings), and institutional projects (airports, schools, and prisons). McCarthy also offers consulting, project management, financing, and cost analysis services. Irish immigrant Timothy McCarthy founded the employee-owned company in 1864.

**KEY COMPETITORS**
DPR Construction
Skanska
Turner Corporation


## MCKEE FOODS CORPORATION

| | | |
|---|---|---|
| 10260 McKee Rd. | CEO: Jack McKee | 2001 Sales: $900.0 million |
| Collegedale, TN 37315 | CFO: Barry Patterson | 1-Yr. Sales Change: 4.0% |
| Phone: 423-238-7111 | HR: Eva L. Disbro | Employees: 6,000 |
| Fax: 423-238-7127 | Type: Private | FYE: June 30 |
| Web: www.mckeefoods.com | | |

When Little Debbie smiles up out of your lunch bag, you know you are loved. McKee Foods' Little Debbie is the US's leading brand of snack cake, named for and featuring the smiling face of a granddaughter of the company's founders. The company makes snack cakes, creme-filled cookies, crackers, and candy. McKee Foods also sells granola bars, fruit snacks, and cereals under its Sunbelt brand. Low prices and family packs of individually wrapped treats — both conducive to quick lunch packing — have driven sales. The company started in 1934 with founder O. D. McKee and his wife, Ruth, selling nickel cakes from the back seat of their car. McKee Foods is still owned and operated by the McKee family.

**KEY COMPETITORS**
Interstate Bakeries
Lance
Tasty Baking

## MCKINSEY & COMPANY

55 E. 52nd St.
New York, NY 10022
Phone: 212-446-7000
Fax: 212-446-8575
Web: www.mckinsey.com

CEO: Rajat Gupta
CFO: Donna Rosenwasser
HR: Jerome Vascellaro
Type: Private

2000 Sales: $3,400.0 million
1-Yr. Sales Change: 17.2%
Employees: 13,000
FYE: December 31

Focusing on the big picture has made McKinsey & Company a big success. It is one of the world's top management consulting firms with 84 offices in 43 countries. The company provides a full spectrum of consulting services (finance, technology management, strategy) primarily to private companies, but also to family-owned businesses and foreign governments. Recruiting the top graduates from business schools, it uses Darwinian "move up or get out" policies to weed out all but the best. McKinsey's reputation comes from a few basic ideals: The client's interests come first; be discreet; be honest; don't overextend yourself. Alumni include American Express chairman Harvey Golub and former CBS chief Michael Jordan.

**KEY COMPETITORS**
Accenture
Booz-Allen
Boston Consulting

 See pages 326–327 for a full profile of this company.


## MEDIANEWS GROUP, INC.

1560 Broadway, Ste. 2100
Denver, CO 80202
Phone: 303-563-6360
Fax: 303-894-9327
Web: www.medianewsgroup.com

CEO: William D. Singleton
CFO: Ronald A. Mayo
HR: Charles M. Kamen
Type: Private

2001 Sales: $853.2 million
1-Yr. Sales Change: (9.9%)
Employees: 11,200
FYE: June 30

MediaNews Group makes news of its own as one of the nation's Top 10 newspaper firms. The firm has almost 50 daily and 80 non-daily publications in 10 states, including *The Denver Post, The Salt Lake Tribune,* and the *Los Angeles Daily News.* MediaNews focuses on building newspaper clusters in specific geographic regions. It also operates Web sites for most of its daily papers and has expanded into radio (with stations in Texas and Alaska) and television (through the acquisition of KTVA in Anchorage, Alaska). The company is a venture of vice chairman and CEO Dean Singleton and chairman Richard Scudder, who began buying newspapers together in 1983.

**KEY COMPETITORS**
E. W. Scripps
Gannett
Tribune


## MEDLINE INDUSTRIES, INC.

1 Medline Place
Mundelein, IL 60060
Phone: 847-949-5500
Fax: 800-351-1512
Web: www.medline.com

CEO: Charles S. Mills
CFO: Bill Abington
HR: Joseph Becker
Type: Private

2000 Sales: $1,016.0 million
1-Yr. Sales Change: 12.3%
Employees: 3,277
FYE: December 31

Medline Industries, a private medical equipment distributor and manufacturer, goes toe-to-toe with the bigger guns, selling more than 100,000 products, such as furnishings for hospital rooms, exam equipment, housekeeping supplies, and specialty care products. The company manufactures about 70% of its products and then distributes them to such customers as hospitals, extended care facilities, and home health care providers. Marketing efforts are handled by Medline's some 600 sales representatives and 20 distribution centers. The company is owned by the Mills family, which founded Medline in 1910 as a manufacturer of nurses' gowns.

**KEY COMPETITORS**
Allegiance
Kimberly-Clark
Owens & Minor

## MEDSTAR HEALTH

5565 Sterrett Place, 5th Fl.
Columbia, MD 21044
Phone: 410-772-6500
Fax: 410-715-3905
Web: www.medstarhealth.org

CEO: John P. McDaniel
CFO: Steven C. Glass
HR: David Noe
Type: Not-for-profit

2001 Est. Sales: $1,990.0 mil.
1-Yr. Sales Change: 10.6%
Employees: 21,700
FYE: June 30

Whether you've been knocked out and are seeing stars or you're just plain sickly, MedStar Health can cater to you. The not-for-profit organization runs seven hospitals in Baltimore and Washington, DC. With more than 4,600 affiliated physicians, MedStar offers such services as acute care, rehabilitation, assisted living, hospice, long-term care, and emergency services. Its MedStar Physician Partners contracts with private physicians in the Baltimore/Washington, DC area. MedStar also manages an independent practice association, which includes both primary and specialty care physicians. After continued financial losses, Georgetown University sold a controlling interest in its hospital to MedStar.

**KEY COMPETITORS**
Ascension
Bon Secours Health
Johns Hopkins Medicine

## MEIJER, INC.

2929 Walker Ave. NW
Grand Rapids, MI 49544
Phone: 616-453-6711
Fax: 616-791-2572
Web: www.meijer.com

CEO: Jim McLean
CFO: Jim Walsh
HR: Wendell "Windy" Ray
Type: Private

2001 Est. Sales: $10,000.0 mil.
1-Yr. Sales Change: 5.3%
Employees: 80,000
FYE: January 31

Meijer (pronounced "Meyer") is the green giant of retailing in the Midwest. The company operates about 150 combination grocery and general merchandise stores; more than half are in Michigan, while the rest are in Illinois, Indiana, Kentucky, and Ohio. Its huge stores (which average 200,000 to 250,000 sq. ft. each, or about the size of four regular grocery stores) stock about 120,000 items, including Meijer private-label products. Customers can choose from about 40 departments, including hardware, apparel, toys, and electronics. Most stores also sell gasoline, offer banking services, and have multiple in-store restaurants. Founder Hendrik Meijer opened his first store in 1934; the company is still family-owned.

**KEY COMPETITORS**
Kroger
SUPERVALU
Wal-Mart

 See pages 328–329 for a full profile of this company.

## MEMORIAL HERMANN HEALTHCARE SYSTEM

7737 Southwest Fwy., Ste. 200
Houston, TX 77074
Phone: 713-448-5525
Fax: 713-448-5540
Web: www.mhcs.org

CEO: Dan S. Wilford
CFO: Carrol Aulbaugh
HR: Doug Veckstett
Type: Not-for-profit

1998 Sales: $1,003.2 million
1-Yr. Sales Change: (16.4%)
Employees: 12,000
FYE: June 30

Memorial Hermann Healthcare System is a "munster" of an organization. Houston's largest not-for-profit health care system includes about a dozen hospitals (one is a children's hospital), two long-term nursing facilities, and a retirement community. Through Memorial Hermann Regional Healthcare Services, the company is also affiliated with 16 community hospitals. Subsidiaries include home health care agency Memorial Hermann Home Health and physician practice company Memorial Hermann Health Network Providers. The company's Memorial Hermann Family Practice Residency Program is affiliated with the University of Texas-Houston Medical School. The organization was formed by the 1997 merger of two smaller systems.

**KEY COMPETITORS**
CHRISTUS Health
HCA
Tenet Healthcare

## MEMORIAL SLOAN-KETTERING CANCER CENTER

1275 York Ave.
New York, NY 10021
Phone: 212-639-2000
Fax: 212-639-3576
Web: www.mskcc.org

CEO: Harold Varmus
CFO: Michael P. Gutnick
HR: Michael Browne
Type: Not-for-profit

2000 Sales: $876.4 million
1-Yr. Sales Change: 10.9%
Employees: 7,296
FYE: December 31

Ranked as one of the nation's top cancer centers, Memorial Sloan-Kettering Cancer Center includes Memorial Hospital for pediatric and adult cancer care and the Sloan-Kettering Institute for cancer research activities. The center specializes in bone-marrow transplants and chemotherapy and offers programs in cancer prevention, treatment, research, and education. Memorial Sloan-Kettering offers inpatient and outpatient services to more than 10,000 patients every year. Other services include pain management, rehabilitation, and psychological programs.

**KEY COMPETITORS**
Johns Hopkins Medicine
New York City Health and
  Hospitals
University of Texas


## MEMPHIS LIGHT, GAS AND WATER DIVISION

220 S. Main St.
Memphis, TN 38103
Phone: 901-528-4011
Fax: 901-528-4758
Web: www.mlgw.com

CEO: Herman Morris Jr.
CFO: John McCullough
HR: Michael Magness
Type: Government-owned

2000 Sales: $1,160.0 million
1-Yr. Sales Change: 8.0%
Employees: 2,600
FYE: December 31

Memphis Light, Gas and Water Division (MLGW) helps lighten up the Memphis blues. The municipally owned utility provides electricity, water, and natural gas services for all of Shelby County, Tennessee, including the city of Memphis. It serves primarily residential and commercial customers. MLGW buys electricity from the Tennessee Valley Authority and distributes it to more than 409,000 customers. The company purchases natural gas on the spot market, transmits it through open access pipelines, and delivers it to 308,000 customers. Through its artesian water system, the company supplies water to nearly 250,000 customers. MLGW also plans to build a fiber-optic network in Memphis.

**KEY COMPETITORS**
AEP
American Water Works
Nashville Electric


## MENARD, INC.

4777 Menard Dr.
Eau Claire, WI 54703
Phone: 715-876-5911
Fax: 715-876-2868

CEO: John R. Menard
CFO: Earl R. Rasmussen
HR: Terri Jain
Type: Private

2001 Est. Sales: $5,000.0 mil.
1-Yr. Sales Change: 11.1%
Employees: 7,600
FYE: January 31

Menard thinks it knows what it takes to build a solid home and a solid business. The company is the nation's #3 home improvement retailer (behind The Home Depot and Lowe's), with more than 150 stores in Illinois, Indiana, Iowa, Michigan, Minnesota, Nebraska, North and South Dakota, and Wisconsin. Its supermarket-style stores are smaller than those of its rivals, although the company has been increasing the size. The stores sell home-improvement products such as paint, tools, and hardware, and unlike competitors, all have full-service lumberyards (most of them indoors). Menard is owned by president and CEO John Menard, who founded the company in 1972. He also owns an Indy race-car team.

**KEY COMPETITORS**
Home Depot
Lowe's
TruServ

 See pages 330–331 for a full profile of this company.

## MENASHA CORPORATION

1645 Bergstrom Rd.
Neenah, WI 54957
Phone: 920-751-1000
Fax: 920-751-1236
Web: www.menasha.com

CEO: Harold R. Smethills Jr.
CFO: Arthur Huge
HR: Linda Mingus
Type: Private

2000 Sales: $1,121.0 million
1-Yr. Sales Change: 13.1%
Employees: 6,046
FYE: December 31

Menasha has the whole package. Founded in 1849 as a woodenware business, the holding company now owns businesses that make packaging and paperboard, returnable material handling systems, product labels, and promotional materials. Each company is independently operated. The company's main subsidiaries are Menasha Packaging Company (corrugated packaging), ORBIS Corporation (returnable materials handling products), Poly Hi Solidur (polymers), and Promo Edge Company (printing). It also has investments in other manufacturing companies. Menasha operates nearly 70 facilities across the US and in seven other countries. Descendants of founder Elisha Smith own a majority of Menasha.

**KEY COMPETITORS**
Boise Cascade
Smurfit-Stone Container
Sonoco Products

## MERIDIAN AUTOMOTIVE SYSTEMS, INC.

550 Town Center Dr., Ste. 450
Dearborn, MI 48126
Phone: 313-336-4182
Fax: 313-253-3559
Web: www.meridianautosystems.com

CEO: Robert H. Barton
CFO: Richard Newsted
HR: Tom Eggebeen
Type: Private

1999 Sales: $1,200.0 million
1-Yr. Sales Change: 100.0%
Employees: 6,000
FYE: December 31

From bumper to bumper, Meridian Automotive Systems has the line on what it takes to keep a vehicle together. The auto parts company manufactures products that include headlamps, armrests, brake lights, and piston covers, as well as engine covers, body panels, and stamped bumpers. Meridian also has process development activities such as molding, painting and plating, rollforming, and stamping. The company controls about half of the SMC (systems, modules, and components) market in the US, and it has a 65% share of the heavy-truck SMC market. Meridian's major customers include Ford, General Motors, and DaimlerChysler. The company operates 30 plants in Asia, Europe, and North and South America.

**KEY COMPETITORS**
A.G. Simpson
Faurecia
Tower Automotive

## METALDYNE CORPORATION

47603 Halyard Dr.
Plymouth, MI 48170
Phone: 734-207-6200
Fax: 734-207-6500
Web: www.metaldyne.com

CEO: Timothy D. Leuliette
CFO: William M. Lowe
HR: Jim Strahley
Type: Private

2000 Sales: $1,650.2 million
1-Yr. Sales Change: (1.8%)
Employees: 11,600
FYE: December 31

Whether you're cruising down the highway or being towed, Metaldyne products may be involved. The metal-forming and -machining company's Chassis Group, Engine Group, and Transmission and Driveline Group manufacture automotive components for passenger cars and commercial vehicles. Products include components and assemblies for engines, noise and vibration control, transmissions, wheels, suspensions, axles, and drivelines. Metaldyne's Diversified Industrial Group subsidiary makes packaging and sealing products, towing systems, insulation facing, and cutting tools. Metaldyne, now part of Heartland Industrial Partners, was formed through the consolidation of MascoTech, Simpson Industries, and Global Metal Technologies.

**KEY COMPETITORS**
Dana
Delphi Automotive Systems
Visteon Corporation

## METROMEDIA COMPANY

| | | |
|---|---|---|
| 1 Meadowlands Plaza | CEO: John W. Kluge | 2000 Est. Sales: $1,500.0 mil. |
| East Rutherford, NJ 07073 | CFO: Robert A. Maresca | 1-Yr. Sales Change: (6.8%) |
| Phone: 201-531-8000 | HR: Jamie Smith-Wagner | Employees: 29,500 |
| Fax: 201-531-2804 | Type: Private | FYE: December 31 |
| Web: www.metromediarestaurants.com | | |

Do you want a side of fiber optics with your steak? One of the US's largest private companies, Metromedia owns or franchises some 1,000 Ponderosa, Bennigan's, Bonanza, and Steak and Ale restaurants worldwide. Through Metromedia International Group, it has interests in telecommunications ventures in Eastern Europe and the former Soviet Union. These include cable TV, wireless and land-based phone systems, radio stations, and toll-calling services. Metromedia also controls Metromedia Fiber Network, which operates fiber-optic networks in urban areas. Its Metromedia Energy is an energy broker and provider of long-distance telephone services. Founder and president John Kluge and partner Stuart Subotnick run Metromedia.

**KEY COMPETITORS**
Deutsche Telekom
Level 3 Communications
Outback Steakhouse

 See pages 332–333 for a full profile of this company.

## METROPOLITAN TRANSPORTATION AUTHORITY

| | | |
|---|---|---|
| 347 Madison Ave. | CEO: Marc V. Shaw | 2000 Sales: $4,033.0 million |
| New York, NY 10017 | CFO: Gary G. Caplan | 1-Yr. Sales Change: (27.9%) |
| Phone: 212-878-7000 | HR: Dave Knapp | Employees: 62,800 |
| Fax: 212-878-0186 | Type: Government-owned | FYE: December 31 |
| Web: www.mta.nyc.ny.us | | |

No Sigma Chi or Delta Delta Delta chapter has anything on New York City's Metropolitan Transportation Authority (MTA) — it rushes almost 8 million people on an average day. The largest public transportation system in the US, the MTA moves more than 2.1 billion passengers a year. The MTA runs buses in New York City's five boroughs, provides subway service to all but Staten Island, and operates the Staten Island Railway. It also offers bus and rail service to Connecticut and Long Island and maintains toll bridges and tunnels. The MTA has adopted subway-to-bus transfers and electronic fare and toll cards (MetroCard and E-ZPass, respectively).

**KEY COMPETITORS**
Coach USA
Laidlaw
Port Authority of NY & NJ

 See pages 334–335 for a full profile of this company.

## MICHAEL FOODS, INC.

| | | |
|---|---|---|
| 5353 Wayzata Blvd., Signal Bank Bldg., Ste. 324 | CEO: Gregg A. Ostrander | 2000 Sales: $1,080.6 million |
| Minneapolis, MN 55416 | CFO: John D. Reedy | 1-Yr. Sales Change: 2.6% |
| Phone: 952-546-1500 | HR: Ron Bergman | Employees: 4,100 |
| Fax: 952-546-3711 | Type: Private | FYE: December 31 |
| Web: www.michaelfoods.com | | |

For Michael Foods, the egg comes first (to answer that age-old riddle). The diversified food processor and distributor has four divisions, but eggs account for about 60% of sales. With the help of 14 million hens, Michael Foods is the largest US producer of long-shelf-life liquid eggs to industry and consumers. Its other divisions produce Kohler dairy-mix products and Northern Star refrigerated potato products and distribute refrigerated foods such as cheese, eggs, and butter. Customers include food processors, food service companies, and grocery stores. Growth has come from acquisitions and new value-added products. A group led by management, the Michael family, and two investment firms took the company private in 2001.

**KEY COMPETITORS**
Cal-Maine Foods
Kraft Foods
Primera Foods

## MICHIGAN AVENUE PARTNERS

4900 First Avenue
McCook, IL 60525
Phone: 708-485-9000
Fax: 800-338-9180

CEO: Michael W. Lynch
CFO: Dave Poremba
HR: Don Byrd
Type: Private

2000 Sales: $836.0 million
1-Yr. Sales Change: 51.2%
Employees: 2,116
FYE:

Michigan Avenue Partners is no lightweight in the aluminum industry. Originally founded as a commercial real estate developer, the buyout firm has invested in aluminum processors through its McCook Metals subsidiary to become North America's #2 aluminum plate processor (Alcoa is #1). The company has acquired rolling mill operations in Illinois, Indiana, and Alabama from Reynolds Metals and Canada-based Noranda. Boeing and Lockheed Martin use its products in jet fighters and booster rockets. Michigan Avenue Partners buys aluminum for processing into plate from other manufacturers, such as Reynolds.

**KEY COMPETITORS**
Alcan
Alcoa
Kaiser Aluminum


## MICHIGAN LOTTERY

101 E. Hillsdale
Lansing, MI 48909
Phone: 517-335-5756
Fax: 517-335-5644
Web: www.state.mi.us/milottery

CEO: James E. Kipp
CFO: Scott Matteson
HR: —
Type: Government-owned

2000 Sales: $1,694.8 million
1-Yr. Sales Change: (2.1%)
Employees: 200
FYE: December 31

Michigan's kids win in the Michigan Lottery, which has contributed some $9.8 billion to public education in the Great Lakes State since the lottery was started in 1972. The Michigan Lottery runs the Michigan Millions jackpot game, as well as daily numbers games and instant-win games such as 3 For The Money, Silver Dollars, and Cashword. About half of ticket sales are awarded in prizes, while more than 35% goes to the state's K-12 education fund. Retailers also get a small commission on ticket sales (about 7%). In addition, Michigan takes part in the multistate lottery, The Big Game, with Georgia, Illinois, Maryland, Massachusetts, New Jersey, and Virginia.

**KEY COMPETITORS**
Multi-State Lottery
Ohio Lottery
Hoosier Lottery


## MICRO ELECTRONICS, INC.

4119 Leap Rd.
Hilliard, OH 43026
Phone: 614-850-3000
Fax: 614-850-3001
Web: www.microelectronics.com

CEO: Dale Brown
CFO: James Koehler
HR: Deanna Lyon
Type: Private

2001 Sales: $916.0 million
1-Yr. Sales Change: 22.1%
Employees: 2,300
FYE: September 30

Micro Electronics is the parent of several technologically gifted children: its divisions. The company operates nearly 20 Micro Center computer retail stores in the US. The stores feature about 36,000 products in 700 different categories, which makes Micro Center the largest of Micro Electronics' divisions. Micro Electronics sells its own brands of notebook and desktop computers under the WinBook and PowerSpec names. MEI-Micro Center is the company's mail-order operation; training is provided through the Micro Center Computer Education unit. Micro Electronics is selling its corporate sales unit. The company is owned by founder and president John Baker and other private investors.

**KEY COMPETITORS**
Best Buy
Circuit City
CompUSA

 See pages 336–337 for a full profile of this company.

## MICRO WAREHOUSE, INC.

535 Connecticut Ave.
Norwalk, CT 06854
Phone: 203-899-4000
Fax: 203-899-4203
Web: www.warehouse.com

CEO: Jerome B. York
CFO: Laurie Schmalkuche
HR: Michelle Visosky
Type: Private

2000 Est. Sales: $2,600.0 mil.
1-Yr. Sales Change: 8.3%
Employees: 3,000
FYE: December 31

Do you count disks instead of sheep? Micro Warehouse lets you shop in the middle of the night. The company sells computer products through catalogs, the Internet, and telemarketers. Serving individual, corporate, education, and government customers the company distributes more than 120 million catalogs worldwide each year. Micro Warehouse offers more than 30,000 items, including computers, hardware, software, peripherals, and networking equipment. Most of the company's sales are in the US. An investor group including CEO Jerome York, Gary Wilson, and Freeman Spogli & Co. bought the company in early 2000.

**KEY COMPETITORS**
CDW Computer Centers
CompuCom
Insight Enterprises

 See pages 338–339 for a full profile of this company.


## MICRONPC, LLC

906 E. Karcher Rd.
Nampa, ID 83687
Phone: 208-898-3434
Fax: 208-898-3424
Web: www.micronpc.com

CEO: Michael S. Adkins
CFO: —
HR: —
Type: Private

2001 Sales: $810.0 million
1-Yr. Sales Change: (19.0%)
Employees: 1,000
FYE: August 31

MicronPC is a chip off the old Micron block. Once the personal computer division of Micron Electronics (now Interland), MicronPC manufactures desktop and notebook computers, and servers. The company also resells accessories such as Lexmark printers and Intel wireless LAN equipment (access points, PC cards). MicronPC has found success primarily in government markets but is focusing on growth in small and medium-sized business, education, and consumer markets. Gores Technology Group, a specialist in the acquisition and management of technology companies, bought MicronPC in 2001.

**KEY COMPETITORS**
Compaq
Dell Computer
Gateway


## MIDAMERICAN ENERGY HOLDINGS COMPANY

666 Grand Ave.
Des Moines, IA 50309
Phone: 515-242-4300
Fax: 515-281-2389
Web: www.midamerican.com

CEO: David L. Sokol
CFO: Patrick J. Goodman
HR: Maureen Sammon
Type: Private

2000 Sales: $5,103.1 million
1-Yr. Sales Change: 16.0%
Employees: 9,550
FYE: December 31

Starting out as an alternative energy producer, MidAmerican Energy Holdings has grown into a major utility holding company. Its MidAmerican Energy Company generates, transmits, and distributes electricity to about 670,000 customers and distributes natural gas to another 650,000 in the midwestern US; it also sells wholesale energy. Subsidiary Northern Electric serves about 1.5 million customers and about 600,000 gas customers in the UK. Subsidiary CalEnergy has global power projects and gas exploration operations. Majority-owned residential real estate brokerage HomeServices.Com operates in 12 states in the US. Warren Buffett's Berkshire Hathaway and other investors bought MidAmerican Energy Holdings in 2000.

**KEY COMPETITORS**
Alliant Energy
Scottish and Southern Energy
UtiliCorp

See pages 340–341 for a full profile of this company.

## MILLIKEN & COMPANY INC.

920 Milliken Rd.
Spartanburg, SC 29304
Phone: 864-503-2020
Fax: 864-503-2100
Web: www.milliken.com

CEO: Roger Milliken
CFO: John Lewis
HR: Tommy Hodge
Type: Private

2000 Est. Sales: $4,000.0 mil.
1-Yr. Sales Change: 14.3%
Employees: 20,000
FYE: November 30

Milliken & Company makes fabrics and chemicals used in products ranging from crayons to space suits. One of the world's largest textile companies, Milliken produces finished fabrics for uniforms, space suits, rugs, and carpets, as well as textiles for tennis balls, printer ribbons, and sails. The company also makes chemicals (used in plastics) and petroleum products. Milliken owns more than 1,300 patents and operates about 65 plants worldwide, including a large textile research center. The company has about 200 shareholders (most from the Milliken family), but brothers Roger and Gerrish Milliken control the company. Roger, who is known for his support of conservative causes, has led the company since 1947.

**KEY COMPETITORS**
Burlington Industries
DuPont
Shaw Industries

 See pages 342–343 for a full profile of this company.

## MINNESOTA MUTUAL COMPANIES, INC.

400 Robert St. North
St. Paul, MN 55101
Phone: 651-665-3500
Fax: 651-665-4488
Web: www.minnesotamutual.com

CEO: Robert L. Senkler
CFO: Gregory S. Strong
HR: Keith M. Campbell
Type: Private

2000 Sales: $2,000.0 million
1-Yr. Sales Change: 13.5%
Employees: —
FYE: December 31

With 10,000 lakes in their state, Minnesotans have learned to be careful. Minnesota Mutual's flagship Minnesota Life Insurance Company helps them take care, with individual and group life and disability insurance and annuities. Other business units include Advantus Capital Management, which provides asset management. Two other subsidiaries, Securian Holding and Securian Financial (offering advisory programs, mutual funds, and annuities), were created by the conversion of Minnesota Mutual Life into the mutual holding company Minnesota Mutual Companies.

**KEY COMPETITORS**
New York Life
Northwestern Mutual
Prudential

## MINYARD FOOD STORES, INC.

777 Freeport Pkwy.
Coppell, TX 75019
Phone: 972-393-8700
Fax: 972-462-9407
Web: www.minyards.com

CEO: Elizabeth Minyard
CFO: Mario J. LaForte
HR: Alan Vaughan
Type: Private

2001 Sales: $910.0 million
1-Yr. Sales Change: (9.0%)
Employees: 6,700
FYE: June 30

Everything's bigger in Texas, including regional grocery chains such as Minyard Food Stores. Its some 80 supermarkets are located primarily in the Dallas/Fort Worth area, where it has about a 10% market share. Almost half are conventional supermarkets that operate under the Minyard Food Stores name. The rest include Sack 'n Save warehouse stores (low-cost shopping with customers bagging their own groceries), and Carnival Food Stores, which stock more ethnic products. Minyard also owns 14 gas stations. The Minyard family started the company in 1932 with one East Dallas neighborhood grocery. It is among the largest US private companies owned and run by women: sisters Elizabeth Minyard and Gretchen Minyard Williams.

**KEY COMPETITORS**
Albertson's
Kroger
Randall's

## MODERN CONTINENTAL COMPANIES, INC.

600 Memorial Dr.
Cambridge, MA 02139
Phone: 617-864-6300
Fax: 617-864-8766
Web: www.moderncontinental.com

CEO: Lelio Marino
CFO: Peter Grela
HR: Edward Burns
Type: Private

2001 Sales: $1,118.0 million
1-Yr. Sales Change: 41.2%
Employees: 5,700
FYE: June 30

Modern Continental Companies is a modern concern with Old World values. Italian immigrant Lelio Marino founded the company in 1967 after he and co-worker Kenneth Anderson quit their jobs at a Boston construction firm. A heavy construction leader in New England, Modern Continental Companies focuses on highways, mass transit systems, and other infrastucture projects. Its most notable current job is on Boston's Central Artery Tunnel, "The Big Dig," due for completion in 2003. The company also develops residential, commercial, and marina projects; Marino's personal interests have led the company to dabble in health care, restaurant operation, organic farming, and tourism. Marino owns 75% of the company; Anderson, 25%.

**KEY COMPETITORS**
Bechtel
Granite Construction
Peter Kiewit Sons'


## MONTEFIORE MEDICAL CENTER

111 E. 210th St.
Bronx, NY 10467
Phone: 718-920-4321
Fax: 718-920-6321
Web: www.montefiore.com

CEO: Spencer Foreman
CFO: Joel A. Perlman
HR: Roberta Cash
Type: Not-for-profit

Sales: —
1-Yr. Sales Change: —
Employees: —
FYE: December 31

As the university hospital for the Albert Einstein College of Medicine, Montefiore Medical Center is a leading teaching and research center. More than a century old, the hospital serves residents of New York City (particularly the Bronx, where it is located) and southern Westchester County through more than 30 locations. It also offers skilled nursing care, home health care, psychiatric services, and a children's medical center. Specialties include cardiology, oncology, women's health, and AIDS research. The hospital has a partnership with Bentley Health Care, created by renowned oncologist Bernard Salick, to open cancer clinics in the Bronx, Manhattan, and Westchester County.

**KEY COMPETITORS**
Catholic Healthcare Network
New York City Health and
  Hospitals
Saint Vincent Catholic Medical
  Centers


## MORSE OPERATIONS, INC.

6363 NW 6th Way, Ste. 400
Fort Lauderdale, FL 33309
Phone: 954-351-0055
Fax: 954-771-6493
Web: www.edmorse.com

CEO: Edward J. Morse
CFO: Dennis MacInnes
HR: Betty Anne Beaver
Type: Private

Sales: —
1-Yr. Sales Change: —
Employees: —
FYE: December 31

Cars from Morse Operations (or similar enterprises by founder Ed Morse) have traveled America's roads for more than 50 years. The company owns 17 new-car dealerships in Florida and one in Alabama that sell over 20,000 cars annually, making it one of the largest auto megadealers in the nation. Most of the dealerships operate under the Ed Morse name. The company sells more than two dozen brands of cars. The dealerships also sell used cars and offer parts and service departments; the company operates a fleet sales division, too. Owner and CEO Ed Morse entered the automobile business in 1946 with a 20-car rental fleet. The company's Bayview Cadillac in Fort Lauderdale is the world's largest volume seller of Cadillacs.

**KEY COMPETITORS**
AutoNation
Holman Enterprises
United Auto Group

## MOTIVA ENTERPRISES LLC

| | | |
|---|---|---|
| 1100 Louisiana St. | CEO: Roger L. Ebert | 2000 Sales: $19,446.0 million |
| Houston, TX 77002 | CFO: William M. Kaparich | 1-Yr. Sales Change: 59.4% |
| Phone: 713-277-8000 | HR: Bruce Culpepper | Employees: 8,000 |
| Fax: 713-277-7856 | Type: Joint venture | FYE: December 31 |
| Web: www.equilonmotivaequiva.com | | |

Cost-savings is the motive behind Motiva Enterprises, which was formed in 1998 to combine the eastern and southeastern US refining and marketing businesses of Texaco, Shell Oil, and Saudi Aramco. The company operates four refineries with a total capacity of 825,000 barrels a day, and it sells fuel at about 13,000 Shell and Texaco gas stations. Motiva and sister company Equilon, which operates in the West and Midwest, together make up the #1 US gasoline retailer. ChevronTexaco and Saudi Aramco each own 35% of Motiva, and Shell owns 30%. In order to gain regulatory clearance to be acquired by Chevron, Texaco agreed in 2001 to sell its stakes in Equilon (to Shell) and Motiva (to Shell and Saudi Aramco).

**KEY COMPETITORS**
7-Eleven
BP
Exxon Mobil

See pages 344–345 for a full profile of this company.

## MSX INTERNATIONAL, INC.

| | | |
|---|---|---|
| 275 Rex Blvd. | CEO: Thomas T. Stallkamp | 2000 Sales: $1,035.2 million |
| Auburn Hills, MI 48326 | CFO: Frederick K. Minturn | 1-Yr. Sales Change: 36.2% |
| Phone: 248-299-1000 | HR: Paul Wagner | Employees: 14,000 |
| Fax: 248-844-4115 | Type: Private | FYE: December 31 |
| Web: www.msxi.com | | |

MSX International (MSXI) never tires of steering its clients into the driver's seat. The company provides engineering, business, and staffing services to clients that hail primarily from the auto industry. MSXI generates about 80% of its revenue by providing services to automotive companies such as DaimlerChrysler, Ford, and GM. Among its offerings are contract staffing, product design, training, document storage, Web development, marketing, and purchasing services. Although MSXI has concentrated heavily on the auto industry, the company wants to expand its presence in industries such as medicine, consumer products, and financial services. Citicorp owns more than 80% of the company.

**KEY COMPETITORS**
Adecco
CDI
Manpower

## MTD PRODUCTS INC.

| | | |
|---|---|---|
| 5965 Grafton Rd. | CEO: Curtis E. Moll | 2001 Est. Sales: $800.0 mil. |
| Valley City, OH 44280 | CFO: Ronald C. Houser | 1-Yr. Sales Change: 6.7% |
| Phone: 330-225-2600 | HR: Regis A. Dauk | Employees: 6,500 |
| Fax: 330-273-4617 | Type: Private | FYE: July 31 |
| Web: www.mtdproducts.com | | |

MTD Products wants to mow down its foes. The outdoor power equipment manufacturer makes walk-behind and tractor mowers, snow throwers, edgers, and tillers under the Cub Cadet, White Outdoor, Yard-Man, and Yard Machines brands. Its MTD Pro line is aimed at commercial users. MTD's Mechanical Systems division also makes transmission systems for the appliance industry. The company owns 53% of Shiloh Industries, which bought MTD's auto parts division in 1999. MTD is buying the Troy-Bilt tiller and mower business from Garden Way, which has filed for bankruptcy. MTD was formed in 1932 by German immigrants Theo Moll, Emil Jochum, and Erwin Gerhard as the Modern Tool and Die Company. The Moll family still owns MTD.

**KEY COMPETITORS**
Black & Decker
Deere
Toro

## MTS, INCORPORATED

2500 Del Monte St.
West Sacramento, CA 95691
Phone: 916-373-2500
Fax: 916-373-2535
Web: www.towerrecords.com

CEO: Michael T. Solomon
CFO: DeVaughn D. Searson
HR: Shauna Pompei
Type: Private

2001 Sales: $1,079.5 million
1-Yr. Sales Change: (1.9%)
Employees: 6,795
FYE: July 31

It can name that tune in three letters, but it's still not the winner. MTS, the #2 US specialty retailer of music (after Musicland), owns and franchises more than 170 stores in 18 countries around the world. Its Tower stores offer a wide selection of music, books, and videos. MTS also runs WOW! stores (a joint venture with electronics retailer The Good Guys) and publishes several free music magazines. International operations — including nearly 50 stores in Japan — account for more than 40% of sales. Founder and chairman Russell Solomon, a high-school dropout, and his son and CEO Michael, own 99% of MTS.

**KEY COMPETITORS**
Musicland
Trans World Entertainment
Virgin Group

 See pages 346–347 for a full profile of this company.

## MULTI-STATE LOTTERY ASSOCIATION

1701 48th St., Ste. 210
West Des Moines, IA 50266
Phone: 515-453-1400
Fax: 515-453-1420
Web: www.musl.com

CEO: Charles Strutt
CFO: J. Bret Toyne
HR: Doug Orr
Type: Association

1998 Est. Sales: $1,000.0 mil.
1-Yr. Sales Change: —
Employees: 9
FYE: June 30

It takes a lot of MUSL to produce some of the largest jackpots in the world. Made up of 22 member lotteries, the Multi-State Lottery Association (MUSL) operates the Powerball drawing, which has produced one of the world's biggest jackpot prizes — $295 million in 1998. Through MUSL, smaller states can combine their buying power to get large jackpots and drive lottery sales. The not-for-profit association, which pays out half of its ticket sales in prizes and uses the other half to help fund state legislature projects, also allows the states to share the cost of lottery operation. MUSL was founded in 1988 by six state lotteries. While Powerball is its most popular game, MUSL also offers Rolldown and Wild Card 2.

**KEY COMPETITORS**
Massachusetts State Lottery
New York State Lottery
Texas Lottery

## THE MUTUAL OF OMAHA COMPANIES

Mutual of Omaha Plaza
Omaha, NE 68175
Phone: 402-342-7600
Fax: 402-351-2775
Web: www.mutualofomaha.com

CEO: John W. Weekly
CFO: Tommie D. Thompson
HR: Rick Frederick
Type: Mutual company

2000 Sales: $4,240.4 million
1-Yr. Sales Change: 8.1%
Employees: —
FYE: December 31

The people at The Mutual of Omaha Companies want to protect human (and wild) life. Known for its *Mutual of Omaha's Wild Kingdom* nature show, the company provides individual health and accident coverage (via subsidiary Mutual of Omaha Insurance); its United of Omaha unit offers life insurance and annuities. The firm also offers personal property/casualty lines (homeowners, boat, auto, and flood coverage), brokerage services, and mutual funds. Offering products mainly through agent networks, Mutual of Omaha has moved to de-emphasize its traditional indemnity insurance in favor of developing managed care alternatives; it is also working to increase sales of its life insurance and annuities products.

**KEY COMPETITORS**
Aetna
CIGNA
Guardian Life

 See pages 348–349 for a full profile of this company.

## MUZAK LLC

| | | |
|---|---|---|
| 3318 Lakemont Boulevard | CEO: William A. Boyd | 2000 Sales: $192.1 million |
| Fort Mill, SC 29708 | CFO: Stephen P. Villa | 1-Yr. Sales Change: 47.8% |
| Phone: 803-396-3000 | HR: Frank Messana | Employees: 1,395 |
| Fax: 803-396-3077 | Type: Private | FYE: December 31 |
| Web: www.muzak.com | | |

The hills are alive with the sound of Muzak. The king of canned music, Muzak offers 60 music channels delivered via satellite (72% of business), local broadcast transmission, tapes, and CDs. The company counts retailers, grocery stores, hotels, office buildings, and factories among its 325,000 customers, and an estimated 100 million people hear Muzak tunes each day. In addition to providing music from genres such as classical, country, Latin, oldies, and contemporary, the company also sells, installs, and maintains such equipment as sound systems and intercoms. Investment firm ABRY Partners owns about 62% of the company; radio station giant Clear Channel, nearly 21%.

**KEY COMPETITORS**
DMX/AEI MUSIC
PlayNetwork
TM Century

 **See pages 350–351 for a full profile of this company.**


## NATIONAL AMUSEMENTS INC.

| | | |
|---|---|---|
| 200 Elm St. | CEO: Sumner M. Redstone | 1998 Est. Sales: $2,917.5 mil. |
| Dedham, MA 02026 | CFO: Jerome Magner | 1-Yr. Sales Change: 1,141.5% |
| Phone: 781-461-1600 | HR: Maureen Dixon | Employees: 6,000 |
| Fax: 781-461-1412 | Type: Private | FYE: December 31 |
| Web: www.national-amusements.com | | |

Media mogul Sumner Redstone puts the business in show business through National Amusements. What began as a humble operator of drive-in theaters has evolved into a powerhouse that controls about 68% of media giant Viacom. Redstone is chairman of Viacom, with holdings that span cable networks, video retailer Blockbuster (82%), Paramount Pictures, TV networks CBS and UPN, and publisher Simon & Schuster. True to its roots, National Amusements operates Showcase Cinemas and Multiplex Cinemas with about 1,400 screens across the US, the UK, and Latin America. The company is an equal partner in MovieTickets.com, the online ticketing service. Its other subsidiaries include WMS Industries and Midway Games.

**KEY COMPETITORS**
AOL Time Warner
Regal Cinemas
Walt Disney


## NATIONAL ASSOCIATION FOR STOCK CAR AUTO RACING

| | | |
|---|---|---|
| 1801 W. International Speedway Blvd. | CEO: Mike Helton | 2000 Est. Sales: $2,000.0 mil. |
| Daytona Beach, FL 32115 | CFO: Doris Rumery | 1-Yr. Sales Change: 33.3% |
| Phone: 386-253-0611 | HR: Starr Gsell | Employees: — |
| Fax: 386-252-8804 | Type: Private | FYE: December 31 |
| Web: www.nascar.com | | |

NASCAR: It's not just for rednecks anymore. The National Association for Stock Car Auto Racing is one of the fastest growing spectator sports in the US, appealing to all demographics, including women, who make up 40% of its audience. NASCAR runs more than 90 races each year in 25 states through three racing circuits: Busch Grand National, Craftsman Truck, and its signature Winston Cup Series. The Winston Cup Series, featuring popular drivers like Jeff Gordon and Dale Jarrett, alone draws more than 6 million race fans each year. NBC and FOX have taken note, paying $2.4 billion over six years for broadcast rights. NASCAR was founded in 1947 by Bill France and is still owned by the France family.

**KEY COMPETITORS**
CART
Indy Racing League
NFL

## NATIONAL ASSOCIATION OF SECURITIES DEALERS, INC.

| | | |
|---|---|---|
| 1735 K St. NW | CEO: Robert R. Glauber | 2000 Sales: $1,554.6 million |
| Washington, DC 20006 | CFO: — | 1-Yr. Sales Change: 32.1% |
| Phone: 202-728-8000 | HR: Diane E. Carter | Employees: 3,200 |
| Fax: 202-293-6260 | Type: Not-for-profit | FYE: December 31 |
| Web: www.nasd.com | | |

The National Association of Securities Dealers (NASD) is parent of the #2 and #3 US stock markets — the NASD Automated Quotations system (Nasdaq) and the American Stock Exchange (AMEX). Nasdaq is an electronic dealer exchange and lacks a physical trading floor; dealers set buy and sell prices, pocketing the difference. About 4,800 companies are listed on Nasdaq. AMEX offers an auction-based exchange of more than 600 companies. The NASD's other main subsidiary, NASD Regulation, oversees over-the-counter securities trading and disciplines traders. Virtually all US securities dealers are members. NASD plans to spin off Nasdaq as a for-profit exchange.

**KEY COMPETITORS**
Instinet
Island ECN
NYSE

 See pages 352–353 for a full profile of this company.

## NATIONAL BASKETBALL ASSOCIATION

| | | |
|---|---|---|
| Olympic Tower, 645 Fifth Ave. | CEO: David J. Stern | 2000 Sales: $2,164.0 million |
| New York, NY 10022 | CFO: Robert Criqui | 1-Yr. Sales Change: 126.5% |
| Phone: 212-407-8000 | HR: Patrica E. Swedin | Employees: — |
| Fax: 212-754-6414 | Type: Association | FYE: August 31 |
| Web: www.nba.com | | |

The NBA is about to be a slam-dunk again. The National Basketball Association will likely shake off its drastic drop in attendance and TV ratings, as well as on and off court image problems, now that superstar Michael Jordan has come out of retirement for the second time. Recent criticisms of the NBA have ranged from boring play to the seemingly endless supply of selfish and oft-arrested players. The 29-team league is divided into Eastern and Western Conferences and includes one Canadian team. The NBA also operates the Women's NBA (WNBA). The league rakes in millions in merchandising revenue and will soon cut a new 6-year $4 billion TV contract with Walt Disney's ABC and ESPN and AOL Time Warner's Turner Sports.

**KEY COMPETITORS**
Major League Baseball
NFL
NHL

 See pages 354–355 for a full profile of this company.

## NATIONAL DISTRIBUTING COMPANY, INC.

| | | |
|---|---|---|
| 1 National Dr. SW | CEO: Jay M. Davis | 2000 Est. Sales: $1,600.0 mil. |
| Atlanta, GA 30336 | CFO: John A. Carlos | 1-Yr. Sales Change: 6.7% |
| Phone: 404-696-9440 | HR: Bruce E. Carter | Employees: 2,500 |
| Fax: 404-691-0364 | Type: Private | FYE: December 31 |

Although National Distributing Company tries to be a wallflower, the beverages it sells often make it the life of the party. An intensely private company founded in the 1900s by Chris Carlos (joined by Alfred Davis in 1942), National Distributing is among the nation's top three wholesale wine, spirits, and beer vendors. The company distributes such brands as Jack Daniels whiskey, Jose Cuervo tequila, Korbel wine, and Smirnoff vodka. National Distributing operates in Colorado, Florida, Georgia, Maryland, New Mexico, South Carolina, Virginia, and Washington, DC. The Carlos and Davis families own and operate National Distributing.

**KEY COMPETITORS**
Georgia Crown Distributing
Southern Wine & Spirits
Sunbelt Beverage

## NATIONAL FOOTBALL LEAGUE

280 Park Ave.
New York, NY 10017
Phone: 212-450-2000
Fax: 212-681-7573
Web: www.nfl.com

CEO: Paul J. Tagliabue
CFO: Barbara A. Kaczynski
HR: John Buzzeo
Type: Not-for-profit

2001 Est. Sales: $4,000.0 mil.
1-Yr. Sales Change: 11.0%
Employees: 450
FYE: March 31

Football may be a game of inches, but it is also a multi-billion dollar business for the National Football League. Running America's most popular sport, the organization acts a trade association for its 31 franchises, promoting the game, licensing team logos, and negotiating media deals. The franchises operate as separate businesses but share much of the revenue generated through broadcasting and merchandising. The NFL scored a financial touchdown in 1998 when it signed an eight-year television contract worth $17.6 billion. It plans to reorganize its two conferences in 2002 when the new Houston Texans franchise joins the league. The NFL was founded as the American Professional Football Association in 1920.

**KEY COMPETITORS**
Major League Baseball
NASCAR
NBA

 See pages 356–357 for a full profile of this company.


## NATIONAL GEOGRAPHIC SOCIETY

1145 17th St. NW
Washington, DC 20036
Phone: 202-857-7000
Fax: 202-775-6141
Web: www.nationalgeographic.com

CEO: John M. Fahey Jr.
CFO: Christopher A. Liedel
HR: Robert E. Howell
Type: Not-for-profit

2000 Sales: $500.0 million
1-Yr. Sales Change: (16.7%)
Employees: 1,500
FYE: December 31

It's not your father's National Geographic Society anymore. Still publishing its flagship *National Geographic* magazine, the not-for-profit organization with 10 million members has expanded into an array of venues to enhance our knowledge of the big blue marble. For-profit subsidiary National Geographic Ventures is fortifying the organization's presence on television and the Web and in map-making and retail. The organization owns part of the National Geographic Channel, a cable channel it operates jointly with NBC and FOX. The National Geographic Society continues to support geographic expeditions (it has funded more than 7,000 treks) and sponsor exhibits, lectures, and education programs.

**KEY COMPETITORS**
Discovery Communications
Rand McNally
Time

 See pages 358–359 for a full profile of this company.


## NATIONAL GYPSUM COMPANY

2001 Rexford Rd.
Charlotte, NC 28211
Phone: 704-365-7300
Fax: 800-392-6421
Web: www.national-gypsum.com

CEO: Thomas C. Nelson
CFO: Bill Parmelle
HR: Nick Rodono
Type: Private

2000 Est. Sales: $1,510.0 mil.
1-Yr. Sales Change: 7.1%
Employees: 2,650
FYE:

National Gypsum Company (NGC) wallows in its walloping array of wall supplies. The company, a manufacturer of building and construction materials, specializes in gypsum wallboard produced under the Gold Bond and Durabase names. It also produces joint treatment compounds (ProForm), cement board (PermaBase), plaster, and framing systems. NGC markets its products to architects, contractors, do-it-yourselfers, and to the manufactured home industry. It also operates a facility that tests the acoustical, fire, and structural properties of building materials. Chairman Dick Spangler (the former president of the University of North Carolina) and his family (which includes son-in-law and CEO Thomas Nelson) own the company.

**KEY COMPETITORS**
Georgia-Pacific Corporation
Temple-Inland
USG

## NATIONAL HOCKEY LEAGUE

| | | |
|---|---|---|
| 1251 Avenue of the Americas, 47th Fl. | CEO: Gary B. Bettman | 2000 Sales: $1,697.2 million |
| New York, NY 10020 | CFO: Craig Harnett | 1-Yr. Sales Change: 15.0% |
| Phone: 212-789-2000 | HR: Janet A. Meyers | Employees: — |
| Fax: 212-789-2020 | Type: Association | FYE: June 30 |
| Web: www.nhl.com | | |

The National Hockey League (NHL) is the coolest game on earth — literally. It has seen its revenue increase steadily in the 1990s, benefiting from rule changes designed to make for more offensive-minded games. Thirty teams in the US and Canada are geographically aligned into the Eastern Conference (Atlantic, Northeast, and Southeast divisions) and Western Conference (Central, Northwest, and Pacific). Two expansion teams started play in the 2000-01 season (Columbus Blue Jackets, Minnesota Wild), which also began a new $600 million TV deal with ABC and ESPN secured by commissioner Gary Bettman. Founded in 1917, the NHL also oversees seven minor and semi-pro hockey leagues.

**KEY COMPETITORS**
Major League Baseball
NBA
NFL

 See pages 360–361 for a full profile of this company.


## NATIONAL LIFE INSURANCE CO.

| | | |
|---|---|---|
| 1 National Life Dr. | CEO: Patrick Welch | 2000 Sales: $1,056.0 million |
| Montpelier, VT 05604 | CFO: Bill Smith | 1-Yr. Sales Change: (2.5%) |
| Phone: 802-229-3333 | HR: Susan S. Chiapetta | Employees: — |
| Fax: 802-229-9281 | Type: Mutual company | FYE: December 31 |
| Web: natlifeinsco.com | | |

Founded in 1848, National Life Insurance is one of the oldest life insurance firms in the US. Through its subsidiaries, the company offers a full range of individual life insurance and annuity products and is shifting its status from that of an insurance outfit to that of a financial services company by increasing its investment services segment. Affiliates include Life Insurance Company of the Southwest (annuities) and the Sentinel Funds (investment products and services). National Life is a mutual company owned by its policyholders, but it is restructuring to become a public stock company.

**KEY COMPETITORS**
MetLife
New York Life
Prudential


## NATIONAL RAILROAD PASSENGER CORPORATION

| | | |
|---|---|---|
| 60 Massachusetts Ave. NE | CEO: George D. Warrington | 2000 Sales: $2,110.8 million |
| Washington, DC 20002 | CFO: Arlene R. Friner | 1-Yr. Sales Change: 3.4% |
| Phone: 202-906-3000 | HR: Lorraine A. Green | Employees: 25,000 |
| Fax: 202-906-3306 | Type: Government-owned | FYE: September 30 |
| Web: www.amtrak.com | | |

Fueled by government dollars, Amtrak keeps on chugging, hoping to operate under its own steam. The National Railroad Passenger Corporation, better known as Amtrak, carries 22.5 million passengers a year and operates over 22,000 miles of track in 45 US states. A for-profit company that has never been profitable, Amtrak is almost wholly owned by the US Department of Transportation and receives large subsidies (more than $360 million in 2000) from the federal government, which wants Amtrak to be self-sufficient. To do that by 2003, Amtrak has introduced its Acela high-speed service for the Boston-Washington, DC, commuter route and is carrying mail and other express cargo to boost revenues.

**KEY COMPETITORS**
AMR
Delta
Greyhound

See pages 362–363 for a full profile of this company.

## NATIONAL RURAL UTILITIES COOPERATIVE FINANCE CORPORATION

| | | |
|---|---|---|
| 2201 Cooperative Way | CEO: Sheldon C. Petersen | 2000 Sales: $1,021.0 million |
| Herndon, VA 20171 | CFO: Steven L. Lilly | 1-Yr. Sales Change: 29.1% |
| Phone: 703-709-6700 | HR: Melanie Smith | Employees: 186 |
| Fax: 703-709-6778 | Type: Cooperative | FYE: May 31 |
| Web: www.nrucfc.org | | |

Forget *Sesame Street* morals — try Wall Street money. Because cooperation alone only goes so far, the National Rural Utilities Cooperative Finance Corporation in 1969 set up the National Rural Electric Cooperative Association, a lobby representing more than 1,000 electric co-ops in 49 states. Owned by the electric and telecommunications cooperatives that make up its membership, the financial organization supplements government loans that traditionally fueled rural electric utilities. The organization sells commercial paper, medium-term notes, and collateral trust bonds to its members. The firm also offers short-term lines of credit and finances intermediate and long-term loans.

**KEY COMPETITORS**
AgFirst
FINOVA
GE

## NATIONWIDE

| | | |
|---|---|---|
| One Nationwide Plaza | CEO: William G. "Jerry" Jurgensen | 2000 Sales: $32,834.0 million |
| Columbus, OH 43215 | CFO: Robert A. Oakley | 1-Yr. Sales Change: 17.5% |
| Phone: 614-249-7111 | HR: Donna A. James | Employees: 35,000 |
| Fax: 614-249-7705 | Type: Mutual company | FYE: December 31 |
| Web: www.nationwide.com | | |

From coast to coast to coast to coast, Nationwide has got you covered. The mutual insurance company is a leading seller of property/casualty policies in the US, but it also offers life insurance and financial services, managed health care, and a variety of commercial insurance coverage. The company controls most of Nationwide Financial, through which it sells its life insurance and financial services in the US; other domestic affiliates include Farmland Insurance, GatesMcDonald, and Scottsdale Insurance. Nationwide operates in more than 35 countries and is expanding its international financial services.

**KEY COMPETITORS**
Allstate
Prudential
State Farm

 See pages 364–365 for a full profile of this company.

## NAVY EXCHANGE SERVICE COMMAND

| | | |
|---|---|---|
| 3280 Virginia Beach Blvd. | CEO: Steven Maas | 1999 Sales: $1,696.2 million |
| Virginia Beach, VA 23452 | CFO: Michael P. Good | 1-Yr. Sales Change: 2.1% |
| Phone: 757-463-6200 | HR: Craig Sinclair | Employees: 16,000 |
| Fax: 757-631-3659 | Type: Government-owned | FYE: January 31 |
| Web: www.navy-nex.com | | |

Before Old Navy, there was the Navy Exchange Service Command (NEXCOM). Active-duty military personnel, reservists, retirees, and their family members can shop at more than 110 NEXCOM retail stores (brand-name and private-label merchandise ranging from apparel to home electronics), about 185 NEXCOM Ships Stores (basic necessities), and its 100 Uniform Support Centers (the sole source of authorized uniforms). NEXCOM also runs about 40 Navy Lodges in the US and six foreign countries. NEXCOM receives tax dollars for its shipboard stores, but it is otherwise self-supporting. Most of the profits fund morale, welfare, and recreational programs for sailors.

**KEY COMPETITORS**
Kmart
Target
Wal-Mart

## NAVY FEDERAL CREDIT UNION

| | | |
|---|---|---|
| 820 Follin Ln. | CEO: Brian L. McDonnell | 2000 Sales: $1,015.8 million |
| Vienna, VA 22180 | CFO: Brady Cole | 1-Yr. Sales Change: 13.0% |
| Phone: 703-255-8000 | HR: Louise Foreman | Employees: — |
| Fax: 703-255-8741 | Type: Cooperative | FYE: December 31 |
| Web: www.navyfcu.org | | |

"Once a member always a member" promises Navy Federal Credit Union (NFCU). The policy undoubtedly helped the some 2 million members of NFCU become one of the nation's largest credit unions. Formed in 1933, Navy Federal Credit Union provides US Navy and Marine Corps personnel and their families with checking and savings accounts, mortgages, IRAs, and a variety of loans (including auto and student loans). Members (who can retain their credit union privileges even after discharge from the armed services) get access to Visa's PLUS Network and the Armed Forces Financial Network automated teller machines.

**KEY COMPETITORS**
Bank of America
U.S. Central Credit Union
USAA

## NESCO, INC.

| | | |
|---|---|---|
| 6140 Parkland Blvd. | CEO: Robert J. Tomsich | 2000 Sales: $1,200.0 million |
| Mayfield Heights, OH 44124 | CFO: Frank Rzicznek | 1-Yr. Sales Change: 9.1% |
| Phone: 440-461-6000 | HR: — | Employees: 10,250 |
| Fax: 440-449-3111 | Type: Private | FYE: December 31 |
| Web: www.nescoinc.com | | |

NESCO doesn't take diversification lightly. The holding company's operations include industrial equipment manufacturing, real estate investment, and staffing services. NESCO's material handling operations include Continental Conveyor (conveyor systems for the mining industry) and Goodman Conveyor (bulk conveyor equipment). The company's ACC Automation unit makes dip molding equipment for manufacturing everything from rubber gloves to condoms. Other subsidiaries include Wis-Con Total Power (small and mid-sized engines), Penn Union (electrical connectors), and NESCO Service Co. (staffing). Founder Robert Tomsich owns the company, which is not related to Oklahoma-based NESCO, a specialty contactor.

**KEY COMPETITORS**
FKI
Ingersoll-Rand
MAN

## NEW BALANCE ATHLETIC SHOE, INC.

| | | |
|---|---|---|
| Brighton Landing | CEO: James S. Davis | 2000 Sales: $1,100.0 million |
| Boston, MA 02135 | CFO: John Gardner | 1-Yr. Sales Change: 23.6% |
| Phone: 617-783-4000 | HR: Carol O'Donnell | Employees: 2,400 |
| Fax: 617-787-9355 | Type: Private | FYE: December 31 |
| Web: www.newbalance.com | | |

New Balance Athletic Shoe wins by doing it differently. Unlike rivals NIKE and adidas-Salomon, the company shuns celebrity endorsers; its lesser-known athletes reflect its emphasis on substance versus style. The approach attracts a loyal clientele of aging boomer jocks who are less fickle than the teens chased by other shoe firms. New Balance is known for its wide selection of shoe widths. In addition to men's and women's shoes for running, cross-training, basketball, tennis, hiking, and golf, the company offers fitness apparel and kid's shoes and owns leather boot maker Dunham. It was founded in 1906 to make arch supports; owner and CEO James Davis bought New Balance on the day of the Boston Marathon in 1972.

**KEY COMPETITORS**
adidas-Salomon
NIKE
Reebok

## NEW JERSEY STATE LOTTERY COMMISSION

Brunswick Avenue Circle
Lawrenceville, NJ 08648
Phone: 609-599-5800
Fax: 609-599-5935
Web: www.state.nj.us/lottery

CEO: Virginia E. Haines
CFO: William Jourdain
HR: Delores Matos
Type: Government-owned

2000 Sales: $1,800.0 million
1-Yr. Sales Change: 5.9%
Employees: 150
FYE: June 30

Tollbooths aren't the only state operation to throw your money at in New Jersey. The New Jersey State Lottery Commission offers the state's residents a variety of scratch-off and numbers games. Among its colorfully titled scratch-off games are For Every Dream, Spam, and Elvis. Its numbers games include Jersey Cash 5, Lotzee, Pick 3, Pick 4, and Pick 6. New Jersey also participates in The Big Game, a seven-state lottery. The New Jersey State Lottery Commission distributes nearly 55% of its revenue as prizes; about 40% goes to state programs. Since it was established in 1970, the commission has provided about $11 billion for state programs.

**KEY COMPETITORS**
Multi-State Lottery
New York State Lottery
Pennsylvania Lottery

## NEW UNITED MOTOR MANUFACTURING, INC.

45500 Fremont Blvd.
Fremont, CA 94538
Phone: 510-498-5500
Fax: 510-770-4160
Web: www.nummi.com

CEO: Kanji Ishii
CFO: Y. Toyoda
HR: Patricia Pineda
Type: Joint venture

Sales: —
1-Yr. Sales Change: —
Employees: —
FYE: December 31

What do you get when a Japanese production process meets a California lifestyle? New United Motor Manufacturing, Inc. (NUMMI), a 50-50 joint venture between General Motors (GM) and Toyota. NUMMI makes Tacoma pickup trucks and Corolla sedans for Toyota, and Chevrolet Prizm sedans (which may be discontinued and replaced by a next-generation model) for GM. The Tacoma pickup is made only at the NUMMI plant in Fremont, California. The plant's production is divided between Toyota (60%) and GM (40%), with general five-year production cycles for specific models. NUMMI can produce 240,000 cars and 150,000 pickups a year. Together GM and Toyota are researching alternative-fuel vehicles to meet strict emissions requirements.

**KEY COMPETITORS**
DaimlerChrysler
Ford
Nissan

 See pages 366–367 for a full profile of this company.

## NEW YORK CITY HEALTH AND HOSPITALS CORPORATION

125 Worth St., Ste. 510
New York, NY 10013
Phone: 212-788-3321
Fax: 212-788-0040
Web: www.ci.nyc.ny.us/html/hhc

CEO: Luis R. Marcos
CFO: Rick Langfelder
HR: Pamela S. Silverblatt
Type: Government-owned

2000 Sales: $4,100.0 million
1-Yr. Sales Change: (0.8%)
Employees: 33,500
FYE: June 30

New York City Health and Hospitals takes care of the Big Apple. As one of the largest municipal health service systems in the US, the organization runs 11 acute care hospitals, as well as community clinics, diagnostic and treatment centers, long-term care facilities, and a home health care agency. It also operates MetroPlus, an HMO. Medicaid restrictions and decade-old reimbursement rates have troubled the company financially, as has the burden of poverty-induced illnesses among its largely uninsured clientele. The publicly supported corporation has responded by cutting jobs, reducing patients' length of stay, and trimming unnecessary facilities.

**KEY COMPETITORS**
Catholic Healthcare Network
North Shore-Long Island
Jewish Health System
Saint Vincent Catholic Medical Centers

 See pages 368–369 for a full profile of this company.

## NEW YORK LIFE INSURANCE COMPANY

51 Madison Ave.
New York, NY 10010
Phone: 212-576-7000
Fax: 212-576-8145
Web: www.newyorklife.com

CEO: Seymour "Sy" Sternberg
CFO: Jay S. Calhoun
HR: Richard A. Hansen
Type: Mutual company

2000 Sales: $21,996.0 million
1-Yr. Sales Change: 8.8%
Employees: 11,800
FYE: December 31

Though not the only New York life insurance company, *the* New York Life Insurance Company is one of the US's top five providers of life insurance policies, annuities, mutual funds, and other investments. It also provides third-party asset management services to institutions and has an agreement with AARP to provide insurance to its members. Unlike its competitors, the company is not rushing to demutualize, claiming its war chest is large enough to fund its growth without selling stock. Outside the US, New York Life has operations in Asia (where the company is expanding) and South America.

**KEY COMPETITORS**
MetLife
Prudential
TIAA-CREF

 See pages 370–371 for a full profile of this company.


## NEW YORK STATE LOTTERY

One Broadway Center
Schenectady, NY 12301
Phone: 518-388-3300
Fax: 518-388-3368
Web: www.nylottery.org

CEO: Margaret R. DeFrancisco
CFO: Jerry Woitkoski
HR: Charlie Titus
Type: Government-owned

2001 Sales: $4,185.3 million
1-Yr. Sales Change: 13.9%
Employees: 350
FYE: March 31

When New Yorkers play the lottery, it's the schools that hit the jackpot. The New York State Lottery is one of the largest state-run lotteries in the US, raising more than $1 billion per year for state education coffers during most of the past decade. The lottery offers players instant-win games, as well as the multimillion-dollar jackpots of its lotto games. In addition, the New York lottery operates Quick Draw, a Keno-style game in which numbers are picked every five minutes. Started in 1967, the lottery sells tickets through more than 17,000 retailers and some 14,000 online terminals (maintained by GTECH Holdings). About 50% of sales are paid out as prizes; almost 40% goes to education programs.

**KEY COMPETITORS**
Connecticut Lottery
Multi-State Lottery
Pennsylvania Lottery

 See pages 372–373 for a full profile of this company.


## NEW YORK STOCK EXCHANGE, INC.

11 Wall St.
New York, NY 10005
Phone: 212-656-3000
Fax: 212-656-2126
Web: www.nyse.com

CEO: Richard A. Grasso
CFO: Keith R. Helsby
HR: Frank Z. Ashen
Type: Not-for-profit

2000 Sales: $815.3 million
1-Yr. Sales Change: 10.8%
Employees: —
FYE: December 31

It's not called the Big Board for nothing: The New York Stock Exchange (NYSE) is the world's premier stock market and the US's oldest and largest. The member-owned, not-for-profit group lists more than 3,000 companies, including most of the largest US corporations, and is actively recruiting foreign companies seeking to trade in the US. The NYSE is an auction exchange, meaning that stock prices are set largely by demand on a central trading floor. The stock exchange's predecessor was founded in 1792 and had become the NYSE by 1863. The NYSE has made plans to go public, but the process has been frequently stalled.

**KEY COMPETITORS**
Instinet
Island ECN
NASD

See pages 374–375 for a full profile of this company.

## NEW YORK UNIVERSITY

| | | |
|---|---|---|
| 70 Washington Sq. South | CEO: L. Jay Oliva | 2001 Sales: $1,691.6 million |
| New York, NY 10012 | CFO: Harold T. Read | 1-Yr. Sales Change: 9.4% |
| Phone: 212-998-1212 | HR: Karen Bradley | Employees: 13,000 |
| Fax: 212-995-4040 | Type: School | FYE: August 31 |
| Web: www.nyu.edu | | |

Students can shrug off their small town blues at New York University (NYU). Its setting and heritage have helped make it one of the most popular educational institutions. With some 50,000 students attending its 13 schools and colleges, NYU is among the largest private schools in the US. It is well regarded for its arts and humanities studies, and its law school and Leonard N. Stern School of Business are also among the best in the country. In addition to a Manhattan campus, NYU has branch campuses in Westchester and Rockland counties, New York. The school was started in 1831. Its alumni include Federal Reserve Chairman Alan Greenspan and film producer Ismail Merchant (*The Remains of the Day*).

## THE NEWARK GROUP

| | | |
|---|---|---|
| 20 Jackson Dr. | CEO: Fred G. von Zuben | 2001 Sales: $883.0 million |
| Cranford, NJ 07016 | CFO: Richard Cardone | 1-Yr. Sales Change: 2.2% |
| Phone: 908-276-4000 | HR: Carl R. Crook | Employees: 4,150 |
| Fax: 908-276-2888 | Type: Private | FYE: April 30 |
| Web: www.newarkgroup.com | | |

The Newark Group is proof that one man's trash is another man's treasure. The company, founded in 1912, is a major producer of paper products from recycled materials. Its recycled fibers division operates paper mills across the US and converts the 2.5 million tons of wastepaper it collects annually into several grades of paper and fiber products, including envelopes, corrugated cardboard, and newspaper. The paperboard division produces 1.3 million tons of paperboard per year from its 15 US mill sites. Recycled paperboard ends up in such products as books, puzzles, gameboards, and packaging. The company's brands include BreezeBoard (100% recycled paperboard), NewKote (boxboard), and Stress Relief (separator stock).

**KEY COMPETITORS**
Oji Paper
Smurfit-Stone Container
Weyerhaeuser

## NIKKEN GLOBAL INC.

| | | |
|---|---|---|
| 52 Discovery | CEO: Toshizo "Tom" Watanabe | 2000 Sales: $1,500.0 million |
| Irvine, CA 92618 | CFO: Kendall Cho | 1-Yr. Sales Change: 0.0% |
| Phone: 949-789-2000 | HR: Joann Kaplan | Employees: — |
| Fax: 800-669-8856 | Type: Private | FYE: December 31 |
| Web: www.nikken.com | | |

Nikken Global wants to attract you — and your friends and relatives — to buy and sell magnetic therapeutic devices through its global distribution network (think Amway). The company has pulled in independent distributors to sell its "wellness" products, such as pillows, sleep masks, support wraps, shoe inserts, and blankets. Nikken tugs at Fido and Fluffy, too, offering pet products such as blankets and vitamins as well as human nutritional supplements, jewelry, and skin care. The company does business in some 20 countries in the Asia-Pacific region, Europe, and North America. Nikken is owned by Isamu Masuda, who founded the company in Japan in 1975.

**KEY COMPETITORS**
BIOflex
Biomagnetics
Magnetherapy

## NORTH PACIFIC GROUP, INC.

815 NE Davis St.
Portland, OR 97232
Phone: 503-231-1166
Fax: 503-238-2641
Web: www.north-pacific.com

CEO: Thomas J. Tomjack
CFO: Christopher D. Cassard
HR: Karen Austin
Type: Private

2000 Sales: $1,200.0 million
1-Yr. Sales Change: 6.4%
Employees: 840
FYE: December 31

Paneling, poles, pilings, or pipes, North Pacific Group (NOR PAC) is building on the construction industry. The company is one of North America's largest wholesale distributors of building materials. Employee-owned since the 1986 retirement of its founder, Doug David, NOR PAC distributes wood, steel, agricultural, and food products. Wood products, which make up the majority of its business, include lumber, millwork, poles, and plain old logs. NOR PAC operates through 30 sales facilities and over 175 inventory locations, selling its products to furniture makers, retailers, and metal fabricators. Its more than 30 subsidiaries include Saxonville USA, Landmark Building Products, and Cascade Imperial Mills.

**KEY COMPETITORS**
Georgia-Pacific Group
Louisiana-Pacific
Weyerhaeuser

## NORTH SHORE-LONG ISLAND JEWISH HEALTH SYSTEM

145 Community Dr.
Great Neck, NY 11021
Phone: 516-465-8100
Fax: 516-465-8396
Web: www.nslij.com

CEO: Michael J. Dowling
CFO: Bob Shapiro
HR: Ronald Stone
Type: Not-for-profit

2000 Sales: $2,309.8 million
1-Yr. Sales Change: (0.9%)
Employees: 35,000
FYE: December 31

This hospital system has a scope that stretches long beyond Long Island. The product of a merger between the North Shore Health System and Long Island Jewish Medical Center, North Shore-Long Island Jewish Health System (NS-LIJ) runs 14 hospitals in Long Island and New York's outer boroughs; several of these are affiliated with regional medical schools (including New York University and the Albert Einstein College of Medicine). The system also has sports medicine, rehabilitation, and outpatient surgery centers and offers home care and hospice services. NS-LIJ is part of the Biomedical Research Alliance of New York, which conducts biomolecular and gene therapy research and conducts clinical cancer trials.

**KEY COMPETITORS**
Catholic Healthcare Network
New York City Health and
Hospitals
Saint Vincent Catholic Medical
Centers

## NORTHWESTERN MUTUAL

720 E. Wisconsin Ave.
Milwaukee, WI 53202
Phone: 414-271-1444
Fax: 414-299-7022
Web: www.northwesternmutual.com

CEO: Edward J. Zore
CFO: Gary E. Long
HR: Susan A. Lueger
Type: Mutual company

2000 Sales: $15,382.0 million
1-Yr. Sales Change: 9.2%
Employees: 3,900
FYE: December 31

The Quiet Company is raising its voice. Facing increased competition amid financial industry reform, Northwestern Mutual, which has long resisted change, is remaking itself to offer its nearly 3 million owner/policyholders wealth accumulation and management services in addition to traditional life, disability, and nonmedical health insurance products. Northwestern Mutual's 7,500 insurance agents target individuals and small businesses. Other lines of business include Midwestern investment bank Robert W. Baird & Co. and pension manager Frank Russell Company (known for the Russell 2000 stock index). The company has opened its own trust services subsidiary, Northwestern Mutual Trust.

**KEY COMPETITORS**
New York Life
Prudential
TIAA-CREF

 **See pages 376–377 for a full profile of this company.**

## NORTHWESTERN UNIVERSITY

| | | |
|---|---|---|
| 633 Clark St. | CEO: Henry S. Bienen | 2000 Sales: $875.3 million |
| Evanston, IL 60208 | CFO: Eugene S. Sunshine | 1-Yr. Sales Change: 11.9% |
| Phone: 847-491-3741 | HR: Guy E. Miller | Employees: 5,700 |
| Fax: 847-491-8406 | Type: School | FYE: August 31 |
| Web: www.nwu.edu | | |

The home of the blues is also home to the purple and white. With its main campus in the Chicago suburb of Evanston, Northwestern University serves its 17,500 students through 12 schools and colleges, including the McCormick School of Engineering and Applied Sciences and the Medill School of Journalism. Its Chicago campus houses the schools of law and medicine, as well as several hospitals of the McGaw Medical Center. Northwestern's J. L. Kellogg Graduate School of Management is among the top-ranked business schools in the US. The university also is home to numerous research centers and 19 intercollegiate athletic teams. Founded in 1851, Northwestern is the only private institution in the Big 10 conference.

 See pages 378–379 for a full profile of this company.

## NOVANT HEALTH, INC.

| | | |
|---|---|---|
| 3333 Silas Creek Pkwy. | CEO: Paul M. Wiles | 2000 Sales: $801.9 million |
| Winston-Salem, NC 27103 | CFO: Dean Swindle | 1-Yr. Sales Change: 4.9% |
| Phone: 336-718-5000 | HR: Mel Asbury | Employees: 12,000 |
| Fax: 336-718-9258 | Type: Not-for-profit | FYE: December 31 |
| Web: www.novanthealth.org | | |

Novant Health is a top private, not-for-profit health system in North Carolina. Formed in 1997 by a merger of Carolina Medicorp and Presbyterian Healthcare System, Novant serves more than 2 million people in about 18 counties across North and South Carolina and Virginia. The system includes about eight inpatient hospitals with nearly 2,000 beds, in addition to a women's health and wellness center, long-term-care facilities, and numerous outpatient offices. Novant Health also includes the for-profit PARTNERS National Health Plans of North Carolina, an HMO covering more than 300,000 members.

**KEY COMPETITORS**
Greenville Hospital System
Sentara Healthcare
Wake Forest University Baptist
  Medical Center

## NOVEON, INC.

| | | |
|---|---|---|
| 9911 Brecksville Rd. | CEO: Steven J. Demetriou | 2000 Sales: $1,168.0 million |
| Cleveland, OH 44141 | CFO: Michael D. Friday | 1-Yr. Sales Change: — |
| Phone: 216-447-5000 | HR: — | Employees: 3,221 |
| Fax: 216-447-5669 | Type: Private | FYE: December 31 |
| Web: www.noveoninc.com | | |

Polymers and additives add up to big business for Noveon. The specialty chemical maker, formerly the Performance Materials segment of what is now Goodrich Corp., was spun off as PMD Group in early 2001 and renamed Noveon that May. Its products include performance polymer systems and additives (colorants, fragrance enhancers) used in food and beverages, personal and home care products, and pharmaceuticals. Noveon's additives are also found in paints, coatings, water treatments, lubricants, and rubber. The company also manufactures post-chlorinated polyvinyl chloride (CPVC) resins and compounds, and thermoplastic polyurethanes (TPUs). It has operations worldwide. Noveon is owned by AEA Investors and DB Capital Partners.

**KEY COMPETITORS**
BASF AG
Dow Chemical
DuPont

## NRT INCORPORATED

339 Jefferson Rd.
Parsippany, NJ 07054
Phone: 973-240-5000
Fax: 973-240-5039
Web: www.nrtinc.com

CEO: Robert M. Becker
CFO: Daniel J. Happer
HR: Ross Anthony
Type: Private

2000 Est. Sales: $2,800.0 mil.
1-Yr. Sales Change: 7.7%
Employees: 37,000
FYE: December 31

NRT is Not a Realty Trust anymore. The #1 residential real estate company in the US began life in 1996 as National Realty Trust, established by real estate franchisor HFS (now Cendant) to own the nearly 400 real estate offices that came with the purchase of Coldwell Banker. Cendant and a subsidiary of Apollo Advisors restructured the trust into NRT to snap up successful independent realtors in hot metropolitan markets and rebrand them under Cendant's franchise names (Century 21, Coldwell Banker, and ERA). The realtor has more than 750 offices in about 25 markets. After a planned IPO was aborted due to a tumbling market, NRT remains controlled by Cendant and Apollo Advisors.

**KEY COMPETITORS**
Baird & Warner
Dewolfe
Kennedy-Wilson

## OCEAN SPRAY CRANBERRIES, INC.

1 Ocean Spray Dr.
Lakeville-Middleboro, MA 02349
Phone: 508-946-1000
Fax: 508-946-7704
Web: www.oceanspray.com

CEO: H. Robert Hawthorne
CFO: Timothy Chan
HR: John Soi
Type: Cooperative

2000 Est. Sales: $1,300.0 mil.
1-Yr. Sales Change: (4.4%)
Employees: 2,000
FYE: August 31

Ocean Spray Cranberries has transformed cranberries from turkey sidekick to the stuff of everyday beverages, cereal, and mixed drinks. Known for its blue-and-white wave logo, the company controls about 50% of the US cranberry drinks market. A marketing cooperative owned by more than 900 cranberry and citrus growers in the US and Canada, Ocean Spray has blended the cranberry with fruits from apples to tangerines in a line of juices. It also makes other cranberry products (sauce, snacks), grapefruit juice, and Ocean Spray Premium 100% juice drinks. Ocean Spray was started in 1912 as a cranberry sauce marketer and became a co-op in 1930. It has been bogged down in recent years by bumper harvests and low prices.

**KEY COMPETITORS**
National Grape Cooperative
Northland Cranberries
Tropicana Products

 See pages 380–381 for a full profile of this company.

## OGLETHORPE POWER CORPORATION

2100 E. Exchange Place
Tucker, GA 30085
Phone: 770-270-7600
Fax: 770-270-7676
Web: www.opc.com

CEO: Thomas A. Smith
CFO: Anne F. Appleby
HR: W. Clayton Robbins
Type: Cooperative

2000 Sales: $1,199.4 million
1-Yr. Sales Change: 2.0%
Employees: 160
FYE: December 31

Not-for-profit Oglethorpe Power Corporation is one of the largest electricity cooperatives in the US, with contracts to supply 39 member/owners (making up most of Georgia's retail electric suppliers) until 2025. Oglethorpe's member/owners, which also operate as not-for-profits, serve about 1.4 million residential, commercial, and industrial customers. Oglethorpe's generating capacity of more than 3,300 MW is derived mainly from coal-fired and nuclear facilities. Along with the generating plants Oglethorpe owns or leases, it has power contracts with other suppliers, which account for about 25% of its energy mix.

**KEY COMPETITORS**
MEAG Power
Southern Company
TVA

## OHIO FARMERS INSURANCE COMPANY

| | | |
|---|---|---|
| 1 Park Circle | CEO: Cary Blair | 2000 Est. Sales: $800.0 mil. |
| Westfield Center, OH 44251 | CFO: Robert Krisowaty | 1-Yr. Sales Change: (4.8%) |
| Phone: 330-887-0101 | HR: Debra Cummings | Employees: — |
| Fax: 330-887-0840 | Type: Private | FYE: December 31 |
| Web: www.westfield-cos.com | | |

Ohio Farmers Insurance has plowed beyond the crop and cattle biz. The 150-year-old company is chartered as a stock company without stockholders. Its affiliates — including Beacon Insurance, Old Guard Insurance, Westfield Insurance, and Westfield National — are known by the umbrella name Westfield Group. The company offers such standard personal lines as auto and homeowners insurance; its niche products include fidelity and surety bonds and specialty coverage for farmers, auto repair shops, and religious organizations. The company has opened Westfield Bank, offering personal and business banking services through a referral program involving independent insurance agents in northeastern Ohio.

**KEY COMPETITORS**
Allstate
Prudential
State Farm

## OHIO LOTTERY COMMISSION

| | | |
|---|---|---|
| 615 W. Superior Ave. | CEO: Dennis G. Kennedy | 2000 Sales: $2,155.8 million |
| Cleveland, OH 44113 | CFO: Gale W. Fisk | 1-Yr. Sales Change: 0.2% |
| Phone: 216-787-3200 | HR: Theresa DiPietro | Employees: 350 |
| Fax: 216-787-5215 | Type: Government-owned | FYE: June 30 |
| Web: www.ohiolottery.com | | |

The year was 1974 — Nixon resigned, an energy crisis gripped the nation, and Ray Stevens ignited a streaking sensation. But were residents of the Buckeye State paying attention? Maybe not — they had a brand new state lottery to play! Since selling its first lottery ticket that fateful year, the Ohio Lottery Commission has raised more than $9 billion for education in Ohio, the cause to which lottery proceeds are dedicated. The commission offers a variety of instant ticket games (Money Island, Cool Cat) and numbers games (Pick 3, Pick 4) for Ohioans' wagering pleasure. Facing slumping sales, in 2000 the Ohio Lottery Commission debuted numbers game Super Lotto Plus, which offered players better odds of winning.

**KEY COMPETITORS**
Michigan Lottery
Multi-State Lottery
Pennsylvania Lottery

## THE OHIO STATE UNIVERSITY

| | | |
|---|---|---|
| 1800 Cannon Dr. | CEO: William E. Kirwan | 2001 Sales: $1,660.9 million |
| Columbus, OH 43210 | CFO: William Shkurti | 1-Yr. Sales Change: 6.9% |
| Phone: 614-292-6446 | HR: Larry M. Lewellen | Employees: 32,000 |
| Fax: 614-292-2387 | Type: School | FYE: June 30 |
| Web: www.osu.edu | | |

Ohio State University (OSU) is Ohio's largest institution of higher learning, and its Columbus campus has the nation's second-largest single-campus enrollment (about 48,000 students), behind The University of Texas at Austin. OSU also boasts four regional campuses and two agricultural institutes. OSU's 4,600 faculty members offer instruction in more than 175 undergraduate programs, 120 master's degree programs, and more than 90 doctoral programs. Its colleges and schools range from the Austin E. Knowlton School of Architecture to the College of Medicine and Public Health to the Fisher College of Business. Prominent university alumni include author John Jakes and Olympian Jesse Owens.

 See pages 382–383 for a full profile of this company.

## OHIOHEALTH

3535 Olentangy River Rd.
Columbus, OH 43214
Phone: 614-566-5424
Fax: 614-447-8244
Web: www.ohiohealth.com

CEO: William W. Wilkins
CFO: John Kowalski
HR: John Boswell
Type: Not-for-profit

2000 Sales: $1,200.0 million
1-Yr. Sales Change: 27.1%
Employees: 15,000
FYE: June 30

With nearly 4,000 affiliated physicians in more than half of the state's 88 counties, not-for-profit OhioHealth aims to keep Buckeyes healthy. Established in 1984, the system operates eight acute-care hospitals and is affiliated with four more. Additional facilities include outpatient centers, long-term care facilities, rehabilitation centers, radiology and imaging centers, women's health centers, and sleep centers. Subsidiary HomeReach provides home health care and medical supply services. Its WorkHealth program offers workers' compensation care management and occupational rehabilitation services. OhioHealth's joint venture, OhioHealth Group, operates the HealthReach PPO.

**KEY COMPETITORS**
Catholic Health Initiatives
Catholic Healthcare Partners
Trinity Health


## OMNISOURCE CORPORATION

1610 N. Calhoun St.
Fort Wayne, IN 46808
Phone: 219-422-5541
Fax: 219-424-0307
Web: www.omnisource.com

CEO: Leonard I. Rifkin
CFO: Gary Rohrs
HR: Ben Eisbart
Type: Private

2001 Est. Sales: $820.0 mil.
1-Yr. Sales Change: (1.8%)
Employees: 1,400
FYE: September 30

OmniSource lives on scraps. Irving Rifkin founded the private, family-owned scrap-metal processor and trader in 1943 to supply scrap for WWII. OmniSource was a pioneer in adopting formal quality-control programs and in turning scrap into briquettes for foundry and steel-mill furnace use. Today the company rates as one of the largest scrap recycling firms in North America. Through a network of six brokerage offices, it tracks national and international scrap prices and activities. OmniSource operates 26 processing facilities, a secondary aluminum smelting plant, and a heavy-media separation facility. The founder's son, Leonard Rifkin, is chairman and CEO.

**KEY COMPETITORS**
Commercial Metals
David J. Joseph
Metal Management


## O'NEAL STEEL, INC.

744 41st St. N.
Birmingham, AL 35222
Phone: 205-599-8000
Fax: 205-599-8037
Web: www.onealsteel.com

CEO: Bill Jones
CFO: Don Freriks
HR: Shawn Smith
Type: Private

2000 Sales: $941.0 million
1-Yr. Sales Change: 0.0%
Employees: 2,950
FYE: December 31

O'Neal Steel has an angle on the steel industry. It is one of the leading private metals service companies in the US. O'Neal sells a full range of metal products — including angles, bars, beams, coil, pipe, plate, and sheet — made from aluminum, brass, bronze, and steel. It also offers such metal-processing services as cutting, punching, forming, bending, and machining. O'Neal operates about 40 plants in the US. Its Metalwest subsidiary has nine plants mostly in the Rocky Mountain region. Founded by Kirkman O'Neal in 1922 in Alabama, it has expanded largely through mergers and acquisitions. The company is still owned and run by the O'Neal family.

**KEY COMPETITORS**
Reliance Steel
Ryerson Tull
Worthington Industries

## OPUS CORPORATION

| | | |
|---|---|---|
| 10350 Bren Rd. West | CEO: Mark H. Rauenhorst | 2000 Sales: $1,400.0 million |
| Minnetonka, MN 55343 | CFO: Ron Schiferal | 1-Yr. Sales Change: 27.3% |
| Phone: 952-656-4444 | HR: Jan Maistrovich | Employees: 1,250 |
| Fax: 952-656-4529 | Type: Private | FYE: December 31 |
| Web: www.opuscorp.com | | |

What a piece of work is Opus. Founded in 1953 as Rauenhorst Construction Company, the commercial real estate development and management firm builds custom facilities (office buildings, warehouses, and malls) for purchase or lease and develops business parks. The company also offers architecture, engineering, construction, property management, and financing and leasing. Opus operates through five indepedent operating companies and has several subsidiaries that provide support functions. It has nearly 30 offices across the US. The Gerald Rauenhorst family owns the company.

**KEY COMPETITORS**
Brookfield Properties
Lincoln Property
Structure Tone


## OXFORD AUTOMOTIVE, INC.

| | | |
|---|---|---|
| 1250 Stephenson Hwy. | CEO: John W. Potter | 2001 Sales: $823.5 million |
| Troy, MI 48083 | CFO: Aurelian Bukatko | 1-Yr. Sales Change: 1.8% |
| Phone: 248-577-1400 | HR: Michael Hart | Employees: 7,400 |
| Fax: 248-577-3388 | Type: Private | FYE: March 31 |
| Web: www.oxauto.com | | |

Oxford Automotive, a supplier of metal car and truck components, is riding the sport utility vehicle (SUV) boom all the way to the bank. The company manufactures suspension and structural systems, leaf springs, and other components for the automotive manufacturing industry. A majority of those components roll out on SUVs, minivans, and light trucks made by such companies as GM, Ford, Renault, Peugeot, and DaimlerChrysler. The company's products can be found on Ford's F-Series pickups and on DaimlerChrysler's Ram pickups. European sales account for nearly 45% of Oxford's revenue. Chairman Selwyn Isakow owns about 56% of the company.

**KEY COMPETITORS**
Budd Company
Magna International
Tower Automotive


## PACIFIC MUTUAL HOLDING COMPANY

| | | |
|---|---|---|
| 700 Newport Center Dr. | CEO: Thomas C. Sutton | 2000 Sales: $4,417.0 million |
| Newport Beach, CA 92660 | CFO: Khanh T. Tran | 1-Yr. Sales Change: 42.9% |
| Phone: 949-219-3011 | HR: Anthony J. Bonno | Employees: 3,600 |
| Fax: 949-219-7614 | Type: Mutual company | FYE: December 31 |
| Web: www.pacificlife.com | | |

Life insurance is Pacific Mutual Holding's stock-in-trade. Pacific Mutual owns stock company Pacific LifeCorp, which, through its primary subsidiary Pacific Life Insurance, is the largest California-based life insurance outfit. Pacific Life offers fixed and variable life insurance policies, annuities, and pension plans; other subsidiaries manage health plans and provide real estate advice. Through Pacific Select Distributors, the company markets such investment products as annuities, mutual funds, and index funds. With operations both in the US and the UK, Pacific Mutual also owns almost a third of PIMCO Advisors, a major investment management firm majority owned by insurer Allianz.

**KEY COMPETITORS**
MetLife
New York Life
Prudential

See pages 384–385 for a full profile of this company.

## PARKDALE MILLS, INC.

P.O. Box 1787
Gastonia, NC 28053
Phone: 704-874-5000
Fax: 704-874-5176
Web: www.parkdalemills.com

CEO: Anderson D. Warlick
CFO: Greg Sellers
HR: Reid Baker
Type: Private

2001 Sales: $1,001.0 million
1-Yr. Sales Change: 0.1%
Employees: 3,650
FYE: September 30

Like that nice, soft-spun cotton in your undies? Thank Parkdale Mills. Parkdale, founded in 1916, is the largest independent yarn spinner in the US. The company manufactures cotton and cotton-polyester blend yarns and specializes in spun yarn that winds up in consumer goods such as sheets, towels, underwear, and hosiery. Parkdale has customers worldwide, including Jockey International, Lands' End, Fieldcrest Cannon, L.L. Bean, and Springmaid. The company operates and owns 66% of Parkdale America, a joint venture with polyester and nylon yarn maker Unifi. It also operates mills in Mexico through a joint venture with Burlington Industries. Chairman Duke Kimbrell owns about half of Parkdale.

**KEY COMPETITORS**
Avondale Incorporated
Guilford Mills
National Textiles

## PARSONS & WHITTEMORE, INCORPORATED

4 International Dr.
Rye Brook, NY 10573
Phone: 914-937-9009
Fax: 914-937-2259

CEO: Arthur L. Schwartz
CFO: Robert Masson
HR: Suzanne Henry
Type: Private

2001 Sales: $1,100.0 million
1-Yr. Sales Change: 5.3%
Employees: 2,500
FYE: March 31

Parsons & Whittemore is one of the world's largest producers of market pulp, the raw material used in papermaking. It is also a supplier of bleached kraft pulp, which is used to make paper bags, butcher wrap, newsprint, strong bond and ledger paper, and tissue. Parsons & Whittemore has pulp mills in Alabama and in Canada. It also produces newsprint through its Alabama River Newsprint joint venture with Canada's Abitibi-Consolidated, the world's largest newsprint maker. Chairman George Landegger and his family own the company. Landegger's father, Karl, came to the US from Austria in 1938 and bought Parsons & Whittemore, then a small pulp-trading firm founded in 1909.

**KEY COMPETITORS**
Pope & Talbot
Weyerhaeuser
Willamette

## PARSONS BRINCKERHOFF INC.

1 Penn Plaza
New York, NY 10119
Phone: 212-465-5000
Fax: 212-465-5096
Web: www.pbworld.com

CEO: Thomas J. O'Neill
CFO: Richard A. Schrader
HR: John J. Ryan
Type: Private

2001 Sales: $1,193.0 million
1-Yr. Sales Change: 10.2%
Employees: 9,289
FYE: October 31

After converting (and covering) the US, Parsons Brinckerhoff is spreading its word (and pavement) around the globe. As the top US transportation engineering firm, the company provides planning, design, management, and maintenance for construction projects. The company specializes in transit systems, tunnels, bridges, highways, and airports, as well as telecommunications, energy, and environmental projects. Founded in 1885 by William Barclay Parsons, the company designed New York City's first subway. Other projects have included San Francisco's rapid transit system and Boston's Central Artery/Tunnel. Employee-owned Parsons Brinckerhoff is expanding on its more than 250 offices in nearly 80 countries.

**KEY COMPETITORS**
HNTB Corporation
Louis Berger Group
URS

## PARSONS CORPORATION

100 W. Walnut St.
Pasadena, CA 91124
Phone: 626-440-2000
Fax: 626-440-2630
Web: www.parsons.com

CEO: James F. McNulty
CFO: Curtis A. Bower
HR: David R. Goodrich
Type: Private

2000 Sales: $2,400.0 million
1-Yr. Sales Change: 33.3%
Employees: 13,500
FYE: December 31

Almost evangelically, Parsons carries its message — and its engineering, procurement, and construction management services — worldwide. The company provides design, planning, and construction management through five operating groups: advanced technologies, communications, energy and chemicals, infrastructure and technology, and transportation. Among its many projects, Parsons has designed power plants; built dams, resorts, and shopping centers; and provided environmental services such as the cleanup of hazardous nuclear wastes. Parsons has also added improvements to airports and rail systems, bridges, and highways. Customers of the employee-owned company include government agencies and private industries.

**KEY COMPETITORS**
Bechtel
Bouygues
Fluor

 See pages 386–387 for a full profile of this company.


## PARTNERS HEALTHCARE SYSTEM, INC.

Prudential Tower, 800 Boylston St., Ste. 1150
Boston, MA 02199
Phone: 617-278-1000
Fax: 617-278-1049
Web: www.partners.org

CEO: Samuel O. Thier
CFO: Stanley J. Lukowski
HR: Dennis Colling
Type: Not-for-profit

2000 Sales: $3,316.6 million
1-Yr. Sales Change: 15.4%
Employees: 30,000
FYE: September 30

Partners HealthCare System runs Massachusetts' biggest hospital group. Formed in 1994 by Brigham and Women's Hospital and Massachusetts General Hospital, the not-for-profit organization offers primary and specialist care, acute-care hospitals, and other services. Affiliated institutions include the Harvard Medical School, Dana-Farber/Partners CancerCare (a collaboration between the Dana-Farber Cancer Institute and Partners hospitals), and Partners Community HealthCare (a physician network encompassing more than 1,000 practitioners). The organization also sponsors research programs and community health outreach programs.

**KEY COMPETITORS**
Baystate Health Systems
CareGroup
HCA


## P.C. RICHARD & SON

150 Price Pkwy.
Farmingdale, NY 11735
Phone: 631-843-4300
Fax: 631-843-4469
Web: www.pcrichard.com

CEO: Gary Richard
CFO: Tom Pohmer
HR: Bonni Richard
Type: Private

2001 Est. Sales: $880.0 mil.
1-Yr. Sales Change: 18.9%
Employees: 2,173
FYE: January 31

P.C. Richard & Son is out to beat The Wiz — and short out Circuit City, too. Founded in 1909 by Dutch immigrant milkman and jack-of-all-trades Peter Christiana Richard, the family-owned company has more than 40 stores in the New York City metropolitan area. Once a hardware store, P.C. Richard now gets about half of its sales from appliances (air conditioners, stoves, microwaves, vacuum cleaners), and it also sells home electronics (televisions, DVD players, VCRs, sound systems), and computers. The firm is operated by fourth-generation Richard family members. P.C. Richard attempted to go public in 1993 but withdrew its offering after a tepid response.

**KEY COMPETITORS**
Cablevision Electronics
 Investments
Circuit City
Sears

## PELLA CORPORATION

| | | |
|---|---|---|
| 102 Main St. | CEO: Gary Christenson | 2000 Sales: $910.0 million |
| Pella, IA 50219 | CFO: Herbert Liennenbrugger | 1-Yr. Sales Change: 1.1% |
| Phone: 641-628-1000 | HR: Karin Peterson | Employees: 6,300 |
| Fax: 641-628-6070 | Type: Private | FYE: November 30 |
| Web: www.pella.com | | |

Window and door maker Pella got out of a jamb by offering its products through retailers. Originally Pella focused on upscale homeowners, builders, and designers, marketing its products through a network of distribution centers and upscale Pella Window Stores retail outlets. The company expanded its market, allowing do-it-yourselfers to buy its ProLine windows and doors through building supply stores. Its products include sliding French and contemporary doors and awning, clad casement, and bay windows. Pella was founded in 1925 as Rolscreen Company (after its first product — a roll-up window screen). The descendants of founder Pete Kuyper own the company.

**KEY COMPETITORS**
Andersen Corporation
Atrium
JELD-WEN

## PENN MUTUAL LIFE INSURANCE CO.

| | | |
|---|---|---|
| 600 Dresher Rd. | CEO: Robert E. Chappell Jr. | 2000 Sales: $1,221.3 million |
| Horsham, PA 19044 | CFO: Nancy S. Brodie | 1-Yr. Sales Change: 9.6% |
| Phone: 215-956-8000 | HR: Michael A. Biondolillo | Employees: — |
| Fax: 215-956-8347 | Type: Mutual company | FYE: December 31 |
| Web: www.pennmutual.com | | |

Founded in 1847, Penn Mutual Life Insurance offers life insurance, annuities, and investment products. The company has five main subsidiaries, including Penn Insurance and Annuity and brokerages Janney Montgomery Scott and Hornor, Townsend & Kent. Penn sells its products to high-net-worth individuals, professionals, and small businesses. Products include term, whole life, universal life, variable universal life, and disability income insurance policies, as well as a full range of deferred and immediate annuity products. The company also provides trust services and asset management to individuals and institutions.

**KEY COMPETITORS**
Pacific Mutual
Provident Mutual
Union Central

## THE PENNSYLVANIA LOTTERY

| | | |
|---|---|---|
| 2850 Turnpike Industrial Dr. | CEO: Robert F. Mars III | 2000 Sales: $1,707.0 million |
| Middletown, PA 17057 | CFO: Larry P. Williams | 1-Yr. Sales Change: 2.3% |
| Phone: 717-986-4699 | HR: Sabrina Theiss | Employees: — |
| Fax: 717-986-4767 | Type: Government-owned | FYE: June 30 |
| Web: www.palottery.com | | |

Even if they don't become millionaires, senior citizens in Pennsylvania can still benefit from the state lottery. Established in 1971, Pennsylvania Lottery proceeds are dedicated to programs geared toward seniors (property-tax relief, rent rebates, reduced-cost transportation, co-pay prescriptions). Proceeds also fund more than 50 Area Agencies on Aging across Pennsylvania. State law mandates that at least 40% of lottery proceeds must be awarded in prizes, and at least 30% must be used for benefit programs. Pennsylvanians can choose from games ranging from traditional lottery game Super 6 Lotto to daily wagering game Big 4. Automated Wagering International operates the lottery's computer systems.

**KEY COMPETITORS**
New Jersey Lottery
New York State Lottery
Ohio Lottery

## THE PENNSYLVANIA STATE UNIVERSITY

| | | |
|---|---|---|
| 408 Old Main | CEO: Graham B. Spanier | 2001 Sales: $2,150.4 million |
| University Park, PA 16802 | CFO: Gary C. Schultz | 1-Yr. Sales Change: 9.1% |
| Phone: 814-865-4700 | HR: — | Employees: 27,112 |
| Fax: 814-865-7145 | Type: School | FYE: June 30 |
| Web: www.psu.edu | | |

Chartered in 1855 to apply scientific principles to farming, The Pennsylvania State University system is one of the largest in the US. Penn State has an enrollment of more than 80,000 students (about 15% are graduate students) and more than 4,500 faculty members. It offers 160 undergraduate and 150 graduate programs at 24 campuses. The school's largest campus, with just more than half of the undergraduate students, and its oldest is at University Park in central Pennsylvania. Other sites include the College of Medicine in Hershey and the Dickinson School of Law in Carlisle. Fisher-Price cofounder Herman Fisher, football great Roosevelt Grier, and former US Secretary of Defense William Perry attended Penn State.

## PENSION BENEFIT GUARANTY CORPORATION

| | | |
|---|---|---|
| 1200 K St. NW | CEO: David M. Strauss | 2000 Sales: $3,298.0 million |
| Washington, DC 20005 | CFO: N. Anthony Calhoun | 1-Yr. Sales Change: 106.1% |
| Phone: 202-326-4040 | HR: Sharon Barbee-Fletcher | Employees: — |
| Fax: 202-326-4042 | Type: Government agency | FYE: September 30 |
| Web: www.pbgc.gov | | |

Underfunded pension plans give the heebie-jeebies to PBGC, or Pension Benefit Guaranty Corporation. The government corporation was established to promote the growth of defined-benefit pension plans, provide payment of retirement benefits, and keep pension premiums as low as possible. It protects the pensions of more than 43 million workers and monitors employers to ensure that plans are adequately funded. The agency receives no tax funds; its income is generated by insurance premiums paid by employers (about $19 per employee), investments, and assets recovered from terminated plans. Pension Benefit Guaranty is empowered to take over a company's pension plan if the plan is in financial distress.

 See pages 388–389 for a full profile of this company.

## PENSKE CORPORATION

| | | |
|---|---|---|
| 13400 Outer Dr. West | CEO: Roger S. Penske | 2000 Sales: $10,000.0 million |
| Detroit, MI 48239 | CFO: J. Patrick Conroy | 1-Yr. Sales Change: 56.3% |
| Phone: 313-592-5000 | HR: Randall W. Johnson | Employees: 34,000 |
| Fax: 313-592-5256 | Type: Private | FYE: December 31 |
| Web: www.penske.com | | |

Penske, headed by race-car legend Roger Penske, seems to be on the right track as a diversified transportation firm. Closely held Penske has stakes in Penske Truck Leasing Company (79%-owned by GE Capital), the US's #2 truck-rental operation, after Ryder. Penske Automotive operates five car dealerships in California and owns nearly 60% of publicly traded United Auto Group, which runs about 120 franchise dealerships. Penske owns 15% of electronic fuel-injection system maker Diesel Technology (Robert Bosch owns the rest) but has sold its 49% stake in truck engine maker Detroit Diesel. The company operates its Penske Auto Centers in more than 630 Kmart stores. Roger Penske owns 59% of the company.

**KEY COMPETITORS**
AutoNation
Discount Tire
Ryder

 See pages 390–391 for a full profile of this company.

## PENSKE TRUCK LEASING

Rte. 10 Green Hills
Reading, PA 19607
Phone: 610-775-6000
Fax: 610-775-6432
Web: www.pensketruckleasing.com

CEO: Brian Hard
CFO: Frank Cocuzza
HR: John W. Kaisoglus
Type: Joint venture

2000 Sales: $3,477.0 million
1-Yr. Sales Change: 28.8%
Employees: 19,562
FYE: December 31

Penske Truck Leasing is positioning itself as a top player in commercial truck leasing. The company has expanded by buying Rollins Truck Leasing and ranks #2 in the industry behind rival Ryder. Penske Truck Leasing operates more than 200,000 vehicles from more than 900 locations in the US, Canada, Europe, Mexico, and South America. The company offers full-service leasing, contract maintenance, and commercial and consumer truck rental. It also provides global logistics, door-to-door delivery, and warehousing and distribution services. Founded in 1988, Penske Truck Leasing is a joint venture of GE Capital (79%) and Penske Corp.

**KEY COMPETITORS**
AMERCO
Ryder
UniGroup

## PEPPER CONSTRUCTION GROUP, LLC

643 N. Orleans St.
Chicago, IL 60610
Phone: 312-266-4700
Fax: 312-266-2792
Web: www.pepperconstruction.com

CEO: J. Stanley Pepper
CFO: Joel D. Thomason
HR: John Beasley
Type: Private

2001 Sales: $834.0 million
1-Yr. Sales Change: 15.4%
Employees: 1,250
FYE: September 30

Although Pepper Construction Group sprinkles buildings across the US, it mainly spices up the construction landscape in the US Midwest. A top general contractor and construction manager in the region, Pepper, through its subsidiaries, builds commercial buildings, hospitals, hotels, malls, and schools. Commercial, health care, and retail markets account for two-thirds of sales. The firm, which outsources its design and engineering tasks, can perform concrete, drywall, masonry, and millwork jobs and offers hazardous waste services through Pepper Environmental Technologies. The firm's regular clients include Marshall Field's and Northwestern University. Founded by Stanley Pepper in Chicago in 1927, the firm is owned and run by the founder's family.

**KEY COMPETITORS**
Bovis Lend Lease
Turner Corporation
Walsh Group

## PERDUE FARMS INCORPORATED

31149 Old Ocean City Rd.
Salisbury, MD 21804
Phone: 410-543-3000
Fax: 410-543-3292
Web: www.perdue.com

CEO: James A. Perdue
CFO: Michael Cooper
HR: Rob Heflin
Type: Private

2001 Sales: $2,700.0 million
1-Yr. Sales Change: 8.0%
Employees: 19,500
FYE: March 31

James Perdue makes Big Bird nervous. His family's company is one of the largest in the US poultry market, selling 46 million pounds of distinctly yellow chicken products and nearly 4 million pounds of turkey products each week. Vertically integrated, Perdue Farms hatches the eggs, grows the chickens, then slaughters, packs, and distributes the meat. Perdue is expanding its value-added chicken parts and food service products and has established a plant in China through a joint venture. It also processes grain and makes vegetable oils and pet food ingredients. Founded by Arthur Perdue (James' grandfather) in 1920, the company sells its products in the East, Midwest, and South, and it exports to more than 50 countries.

**KEY COMPETITORS**
ConAgra
Gold Kist
Tyson Foods

📖 See pages 392–393 for a full profile of this company.

## PETCO ANIMAL SUPPLIES, INC.

9125 Rehco Rd.
San Diego, CA 92121
Phone: 858-453-7845
Fax: 858-677-3095
Web: www.petco.com

CEO: Brian K. Devine
CFO: James M. Myers
HR: Janet D. Mitchell
Type: Private

2001 Sales: $1,151.2 million
1-Yr. Sales Change: 16.2%
Employees: 12,800
FYE: January 31

Petco Animal Supplies, the nation's #2 pet supply specialty retailer, is hounding PETsMART for top dog status. Petco operates more than 530 stores in about 40 states and Washington, DC. The company's 15,000-sq.-ft. superstores carry some 10,000 pet-related items, including premium cat and dog foods, collars, leashes, grooming products, toys, and animal habitats. The stores also offer grooming, obedience training, and veterinary services. Petco sells birds, fish, and reptiles, and it sponsors adoption programs for cats and dogs. The company markets products and services online through Petco.com. An investor group that includes Leonard Green & Partners bought Petco in 2000. Petco filed to go public in December 2001.

**KEY COMPETITORS**
Kroger
PETsMART
Wal-Mart

 See pages 394–395 for a full profile of this company.


## PETER KIEWIT SONS', INC.

Kiewit Plaza
Omaha, NE 68131
Phone: 402-342-2052
Fax: 402-271-2939
Web: www.kiewit.com

CEO: Kenneth E. Stinson
CFO: Michael J. Piechoski
HR: John B. Chapman
Type: Private

2000 Sales: $4,463.0 million
1-Yr. Sales Change: 11.2%
Employees: 11,146
FYE: December 31

Peter Kiewit Sons' doesn't peter out — it keeps building and building. The employee-owned construction firm is one of the largest general contractors in the US, with projects in 43 US states and Washington, DC, as well as in Canada and Puerto Rico. Kiewit specializes in heavy construction projects such as highways, commercial buildings, mining infrastructure, and waste-disposal systems. Government contracts account for more than 75% of its jobs. Level 3 Communications (a telecommunications business Kiewit divested in 1998) accounts for about 40% of sales. The company has expanded its construction services in the offshore drilling industry through its Kiewit Offshore Services unit.

**KEY COMPETITORS**
Bechtel
Fluor
Turner Corporation

 See pages 396–397 for a full profile of this company.


## PETRO STOPPING CENTERS, L.P.

6080 Surety Dr.
El Paso, TX 79905
Phone: 915-779-4711
Fax: 915-774-7382
Web: www.petrotruckstops.com

CEO: J. A. "Jack" Cardwell Sr.
CFO: David A. Appleby
HR: Walter Kalinowski
Type: Private

2000 Sales: $983.2 million
1-Yr. Sales Change: 36.6%
Employees: 4,186
FYE: December 31

Petro Stopping Centers is the center of attention for truckers who need a petro stop. The firm operates 57 truck stops (almost half of them franchised) in 32 states. Its truck stops sell Mobil-brand diesel fuel, gas, and travel merchandise such as food, toiletries, truck accessories, and electronics. (Fuel accounts for almost 80% of sales.) The centers also provide Petro:Lube facilities (preventive maintenance services), showers, laundry services, game rooms, and Iron Skillet restaurants (home-style cooking). Chairman and CEO Jack Cardwell, who founded the company in 1975, and his son, SVP Jim, own 52% of the company. Truck maker Volvo has a 29% stake.

**KEY COMPETITORS**
Flying J
Pilot
TravelCenters of America

## PILOT CORPORATION

5508 Lonas Rd.
Knoxville, TN 37909
Phone: 865-588-7487
Fax: 865-450-2800
Web: www.pilotcorp.com

CEO: James A. Haslam III
CFO: Jeffrey L. Cornish
HR: Mark A. Rowan
Type: Private

2000 Sales: $1,768.0 million
1-Yr. Sales Change: 34.8%
Employees: 7,209
FYE: December 31

Pilot has been known to offer a salve to those suffering from white-line fever. Catering to truckers and travelers alike, Pilot operates about 140 travel centers in 36 states (through a joint venture with Marathon Ashland Petroleum); each feature one or more national food chains, such as Subway, Dairy Queen, Wendy's, and Taco Bell. Pilot features fuel islands large enough to service several 18-wheelers at a time and private showers for its customers. Pilot also operates more than 65 convenience stores in Tennessee and Virginia. James Haslam II got Pilot off the ground in 1958 as a gas station that sold cigarettes and soft drinks; now his son, CEO James Haslam III, pilots the firm. The Haslam family owns the company.

**KEY COMPETITORS**
Flying J
Petro Stopping Centers
TravelCenters of America

## PLANET AUTOMOTIVE GROUP, INC.

2333 Ponce De Leon Blvd Ste. 600
Coral Gables, FL 33134
Phone: 305-774-7690
Fax: 305-774-7697
Web: www.planetautomotive.com

CEO: Alan Potamkin
CFO: David Yusko
HR: Andy Pfeifer
Type: Private

2000 Sales: $1,350.0 million
1-Yr. Sales Change: 3.4%
Employees: 1,600
FYE: December 31

Expect a lot of iron, glass, and rubber on the surface of Planet Automotive Group. Formerly Potamkin Manhattan, the company coalesced from a network of auto dealerships owned by the Potamkin family. The company's 20 dealerships operate primarily in Florida, but also in Illinois, Iowa, Massachusetts, New York, and Pennsylvania. It has grown through acquisitions of new- and used-car dealerships. The company's dealerships also offer parts and service departments. The late Victor Potamkin opened his first dealership in 1946, and his two sons, Robert and Alan, now run the company.

**KEY COMPETITORS**
AutoNation
Holman Enterprises
United Auto Group

## PLASTIPAK PACKAGING, INC.

9135 General Court
Plymouth, MI 48170
Phone: 734-455-3600
Fax: 734-354-7391
Web: www.plastipak.com

CEO: William C. Young
CFO: Mary E. Young
HR: Matt Leslie
Type: Private

2001 Sales: $812.0 million
1-Yr. Sales Change: 43.5%
Employees: 3,300
FYE: October 31

Plastipak Packaging likes to keep things bottled up. The company supplies plastic containers for products such as carbonated and noncarbonated beverages, cleaning products, distilled spirits, and processed juices. Plastipak makes high-density polyethylene (HDPE) resins and polyethylene terephthalate (PET) at its plants in the US and South America. In conjunction with Canada-based Husky Injection Molding Systems, Plastipak has pioneered a molding process, EXI-PAK, that allows products that were once confined to glass or metal containers to be packaged in plastic. Plastipak also licenses its technologies to manufacturers, including customers in Brazil, Germany, and New Zealand. The Young family owns and runs Plastipak.

**KEY COMPETITORS**
PolyOne
PVC Container
Silgan

## PLATINUM EQUITY HOLDINGS

| | | |
|---|---|---|
| 2049 Century Park East, Ste. 2700 | CEO: Tom T. Gores | 1999 Sales: $792.0 million |
| Los Angeles, CA 90067 | CFO: William Foltz | 1-Yr. Sales Change: 13.1% |
| Phone: 310-712-1850 | HR: Kathleen A. Wilkinson | Employees: 10,000 |
| Fax: 310-712-1848 | Type: Private | FYE: December 31 |
| Web: www.peh.com | | |

Platinum Equity Holdings knows "an oldie but a goodie" when it sees one. The information technology investment firm buys underperforming businesses, including units of large corporations. These companies, many of which are more than 20 years old, usually offer legacy products and services and have well-established customer bases and distribution operations. Platinum focuses on companies offering products and/or services in such sectors as call center and help desk operations, data communications and networking, information systems, and software. Platinum buys companies around the world and usually takes full ownership. Owned by CEO Tom Gores, the firm has operations in the US, Europe, Asia, and South America.

**KEY COMPETITORS**
Apollo Advisors
Clayton, Dubilier
KKR


## THE PORT AUTHORITY OF NEW YORK AND NEW JERSEY

| | | |
|---|---|---|
| 241 Erie St. | CEO: Ronald Shiftan | 2000 Sales: $2,648.3 million |
| Jersey City, NJ 07310 | CFO: Charles F. McClafferty | 1-Yr. Sales Change: 4.0% |
| Phone: 201-216-2924 | HR: Paul Segalini | Employees: 7,000 |
| Fax: — | Type: Government-owned | FYE: December 31 |
| Web: www.panynj.gov | | |

The Port Authority of New York and New Jersey operates tunnels, bridges, airports, shipping terminals, and other facilities in the two-state Port District, a 1,500-sq.-mi. region surrounding the Statue of Liberty. Rail subsidiary Port Authority Trans-Hudson (PATH), carries about 260,000 passengers daily. A self-supporting public agency, the Port Authority receives no tax money and relies on tolls, fees, and rents. Its facilities include the Holland and Lincoln tunnels, John F. Kennedy International Airport, and the World Trade Center, much of which was destroyed in a terrorist attack in 2001. Executive Director Neil Levin was killed in the attack, and 73 other Port Authority employees were listed as dead or missing.

**KEY COMPETITORS**
Coach USA
MTA
Amtrak

 See pages 398–399 for a full profile of this company.


## POWER AUTHORITY OF THE STATE OF NEW YORK

| | | |
|---|---|---|
| 123 Main St. | CEO: Joseph J. Seymour | 2000 Sales: $2,034.0 million |
| White Plains, NY 10601 | CFO: Michael H. Urbach | 1-Yr. Sales Change: 39.5% |
| Phone: 914-681-6200 | HR: Vincent C. Vesce | Employees: 1,531 |
| Fax: 212-468-6360 | Type: Government-owned | FYE: December 31 |
| Web: www.nypa.gov | | |

Even jaded Manhattanites get a charge out of the Power Authority of the State of New York (NYPA), which generates and transmits more than 20% of New York's electricity. The US's largest state-owned public power provider, NYPA operates 21 generating facilities that produce about 5,700 MW of electricity. It sells power to government agencies, utilities, companies, and neighboring states; customers include some of the biggest electricity users in the US, including the New York City government. NYPA receives no state money or tax credits; it finances projects through bond sales.

**KEY COMPETITORS**
Con Edison
Energy East
KeySpan Energy

## PRAIRIE FARMS DAIRY INC.

1100 N. Broadway St.
Carlinville, IL 62626
Phone: 217-854-2547
Fax: 217-854-6426
Web: www.prairiefarms.com

CEO: Leonard J. Southwell
CFO: Paul Benne
HR: Tom Weber
Type: Cooperative

2000 Sales: $1,046.0 million
1-Yr. Sales Change: 9.0%
Employees: 3,000
FYE: September 30

The bittersweet torture Prairie Farms Dairy inflicts upon the lactose intolerant! With about 800 members, Prairie Farms is one of the largest dairy cooperatives in the Midwest. It produces milk, butter, cottage cheese, sour cream, and orange juices, primarily under the Prairie Farms label. It also makes goodies such as ice cream, yogurt, sherbet, and dips. The company's products are sold in stores, schools, and to institutional clients in the Midwest. Subsidiary PFD Supply distributes food and paper products to fast-food restaurants, including Burger King and McDonald's.

**KEY COMPETITORS**
AMPI
Dairy Farmers of America
Land O'Lakes


## PREMCOR INC.

8182 Maryland Ave.
St. Louis, MO 63105
Phone: 314-854-9696
Fax: 314-854-1580
Web: www.premcor.com

CEO: William C. Rusnack
CFO: Ezra C. Hunt
HR: Paula Novak
Type: Private

2000 Sales: $7,301.7 million
1-Yr. Sales Change: 61.5%
Employees: 2,100
FYE: December 31

Premcor, all decked out in its refineries, has left its retail operations behind. One of the largest independent oil refiners in the US, Premcor produces gasoline, diesel, and aviation fuel. It owns a refinery in Texas, one in Illinois, and one in Ohio; the three have the combined capacity to process more than 490,000 barrels of crude oil per day. The company markets unbranded gasoline and other petroleum products wholesale to about 600 retail outlets through its own distribution networks. Blackstone Group controls about 80% of Premcor; Occidental Petroleum, about 18%. Premcor plans to sell a 2.4% stake in the company to the public.

**KEY COMPETITORS**
BP
Phillips Petroleum
Valero


## PRESBYTERIAN HEALTHCARE SERVICES

2501 Buena Vista SE
Albuquerque, NM 87125
Phone: 505-841-1234
Fax: 505-923-8539
Web: www.phs.org

CEO: James H. Hinton
CFO: Pete McCanna
HR: Rita Arthur
Type: Not-for-profit

2000 Sales: $1,000.0 million
1-Yr. Sales Change: 125.2%
Employees: 7,500
FYE: December 31

Established in the early 1900s as a sanatorium for tuberculosis patients, not-for-profit Presbyterian Healthcare Services (PHS) now cares for more than 400,000 New Mexicans. PHS's Presbyterian Health Plan serves individuals, spouses, and dependents, covering everything from preventive to emergency care. PHS hospitals offer small group plans for companies with fewer than 50 employees and group health plans with HMO and point-of-service options. Enrollees include the State of New Mexico, University of New Mexico, and Intel. Its network of 12 hospitals, community health centers, and clinics stretches from Cimarron to Ruidoso.

**KEY COMPETITORS**
Banner Health System
Catholic Health Initiatives
Triad Hospitals

## PRICEWATERHOUSECOOPERS

| | | |
|---|---|---|
| 1301 Avenue of the Americas | CEO: Samuel A. DiPiazza | 2001 Est. Sales: $24,000.0 mil. |
| New York, NY 10019 | CFO: Geoffrey E. Johnson | 1-Yr. Sales Change: 11.6% |
| Phone: 646-471-4000 | HR: Amy DiGeso | Employees: 160,000 |
| Fax: 646-394-1301 | Type: Partnership | FYE: June 30 |
| Web: www.pwcglobal.com | | |

Haven't these people heard of spacing? PricewaterhouseCoopers became the world's largest accounting firm, inching ahead of then-leader Andersen when Price Waterhouse merged with Coopers and Lybrand in 1998. Through offices in more than 150 countries, the firm provides services in six lines of business: Audit, Assurance and Business Advisory Services (financial, regulatory reporting, and technology issues); Business Process Outsourcing (accounting, internal audit); Corporate Finance and Recovery Services (business advisory); Global HR Solutions (human resource and insurance management services); Management Consulting Services; and Global Tax Services.

**KEY COMPETITORS**
Andersen
Ernst & Young
KPMG

 **See pages 400–401 for a full profile of this company.**


## PRIMUS, INC.

| | | |
|---|---|---|
| 3110 Kettering Blvd. | CEO: Richard W. Schwartz | 2001 Sales: $1,040.0 million |
| Dayton, OH 45439 | CFO: Jack W. Johnston | 1-Yr. Sales Change: 11.7% |
| Phone: 937-294-6878 | HR: — | Employees: 3,093 |
| Fax: 937-293-9591 | Type: Private | FYE: January 31 |
| Web: www.winholesale.com | | |

You Win some, you Win some more. So it goes for Primus, which invests in a collection of some 425 small wholesale distributors in about 40 states that sell plumbing, heating, air-conditioning, electrical, and other supplies to contractors and other customers. The companies are easily recognizable by their Win-prefixed names, such as Columbia Winnelson (plumbing products), Salt Lake Windustrial (pipes and valves), and Dayton Winfastener (specialty fasteners). Primus supports its companies, through units Dapsco and Distro, with bulk purchasing, warehousing, and data processing. Primus is owned mostly by heirs of the investors, including chairman Richard Schiewetz, who founded Primus in 1956.

**KEY COMPETITORS**
Ferguson Enterprises
Hughes Supply
W.W. Grainger


## PRINTPACK, INC.

| | | |
|---|---|---|
| 4335 Wendell Dr. | CEO: Dennis M. Love | 2001 Sales: $1,026.5 million |
| Atlanta, GA 30336 | CFO: R. Michael Hembree | 1-Yr. Sales Change: 13.2% |
| Phone: 404-691-5830 | HR: Nicklas D. Stucky | Employees: 3,800 |
| Fax: 404-699-7122 | Type: Private | FYE: June 30 |
| Web: www.printpack.com | | |

Printpack wraps its flexible packaging around salty snacks, confections, baked goods, cookies, crackers, and cereal, as well as tissues and paper towels. The company's packaging includes plastic film, aluminum foil, metallized films and paper with specialized coatings, and cast and blown monolayer and co-extruded films. Customers include Frito-Lay (14% of sales), Georgia Pacific, General Mills, and Quaker Oats. Printpack manufactures packaging materials at 17 plants in the US, Mexico, and the UK. The founding Love family owns and manages the company, which was started in 1956.

**KEY COMPETITORS**
Alcoa
Pechiney
Pliant Corporation

## PROSPECT MOTORS, INC.

645 North Hwy. 49 & 88
Jackson, CA 95642
Phone: 209-223-1740
Fax: 209-223-0395
Web: www.prospectmotors.com

CEO: William Halvorson
CFO: Steve McCarty
HR: Linda Hamilton
Type: Private

1998 Est. Sales: $1,200.0 mil.
1-Yr. Sales Change: 21.3%
Employees: 75
FYE: May 31

Your prospects for finding an American-made car are pretty good at Prospect Motors, one of the largest General Motors dealers in the US. Prospect sells new and used Buick, Cadillac, Chevrolet, Oldsmobile, Pontiac, and Toyota cars and trucks throughout California. The company also operates a body shop and parts and service departments and engages in auto leasing. Founded in 1970, the Halvorson family's Prospect has made its name by selling and leasing in bulk — mostly fleet sales and leases to car rental agencies in California and other western states. Prospect also owns Amador Motors dealerships in the California towns of Sutter Creek (Chrysler-Plymouth, Dodge, Jeep) and Jackson (Toyota).

**KEY COMPETITORS**
AutoNation
Penske Automotive
Tuttle-Click

## PROVENA HEALTH

9223 W. St. Francis Rd.
Frankfort, IL 60423
Phone: 815-469-4888
Fax: 815-469-4864
Web: www.provena.org

CEO: William Foley
CFO: William M. Wheeler
HR: Terry S. Solem
Type: Not-for-profit

2000 Sales: $869.0 million
1-Yr. Sales Change: 20.8%
Employees: 11,400
FYE: December 31

The offspring of a very holy union, Provena Health was created from the merger of Illinois Roman Catholic hospital groups, Franciscan Sisters Health Care (Frankfort), ServantCor (Kankakee), and Mercy Center for Health Care Services (Aurora), in an effort to stay competitive in an era of managed care. Provena has seven hospitals, 14 nursing homes, more than 40 clinics, six home health agencies, and its own PersonalCare HMO. It also has a hospice program, and its HealthCare Equipment unit sells a large selection of medical equipment. Provena is sponsored by Franciscan Sisters of the Sacred Heart, Servants of the Holy Heart of Mary, and Sisters of Mercy of the Americas.

**KEY COMPETITORS**
Advocate Health Care
BJC Health
Rush System for Health

## PROVIDENCE HEALTH SYSTEM

506 2nd Ave., Ste. 1200
Seattle, WA 98104
Phone: 206-464-3355
Fax: 206-464-3038
Web: www.providence.org

CEO: Henry G. Walker
CFO: Maurice M. Smith Jr.
HR: Sue Byington
Type: Not-for-profit

2000 Sales: $3,229.0 million
1-Yr. Sales Change: 7.6%
Employees: 32,238
FYE: December 31

Sisterhood is powerful in health care. The order of the Sisters of Providence runs not-for-profit Providence Health System in the Pacific Northwest (with outposts in Alaska and California). The system operates more than 20 acute care hospitals, as well as long-term-care and assisted-living facilities and primary care centers. In addition the company offers health plans, low-income housing, and home health, hospice, and community outreach services. The Sisters were founded in 1843 in Montreal; their work in the US began in 1856, when five members of the order established a mission in the then Washington Territory.

**KEY COMPETITORS**
Adventist Health
Legacy Health System
Tenet Healthcare

## PUBLIX SUPER MARKETS, INC.

| | | |
|---|---|---|
| 1936 George Jenkins Blvd. | CEO: Charles H. Jenkins Jr. | 2000 Sales: $14,724.2 million |
| Lakeland, FL 33815 | CFO: David P. Phillips | 1-Yr. Sales Change: 12.7% |
| Phone: 863-688-1188 | HR: James H. Rhodes II | Employees: 126,000 |
| Fax: 863-284-5532 | Type: Private | FYE: December 31 |
| Web: www.publix.com | | |

Shoppers at Publix shouldn't have to worry about being checked out — although with its share of gender and race discrimination lawsuits, they might wonder. Publix Super Markets is one of the nation's largest grocers and is the largest employee-owned supermarket chain. Most of its more than 650 stores are in Florida, but it also operates in Alabama, Georgia, and South Carolina. Publix produces some of its own deli, bakery, and dairy goods, and many stores offer fresh flowers, housewares, photo processing, and pharmaceutical services. It is planning a test run for PublixDirect (its online grocery and delivery service). Members of the founding Jenkins family control the employee-owned company.

**KEY COMPETITORS**
Albertson's
Wal-Mart
Winn-Dixie

 **See pages 402–403 for a full profile of this company.**

## PUERTO RICO ELECTRIC POWER AUTHORITY

| | | |
|---|---|---|
| Ave. Ponce De Leon 17 1/2 | CEO: Hector Rosario | 2000 Sales: $1,987.3 million |
| San Turce, PR 00909 | CFO: Luis Figueroa | 1-Yr. Sales Change: 29.9% |
| Phone: 787-289-3434 | HR: Ana Blanes | Employees: 10,200 |
| Fax: 787-289-4665 | Type: Government-owned | FYE: June 30 |
| Web: www.prepa.com | | |

No man is an island, but Puerto Rico Electric Power Authority (PREPA) stands alone on one. Founded in 1941, the government-owned utility is the sole electricity distributor for Puerto Rico, where it serves more than 1.3 million residential and business customers. PREPA has a generating capacity of nearly 4,400 MW, primarily from fuel oil at four steam plants and a combustion turbines plant. In order to keep up with increasing demand, the Puerto Rican government has allowed independent power producers to build cogeneration plants on the island to sell power to PREPA. The company is also refurbishing some of its own plants.

## PURDUE PHARMA L.P.

| | | |
|---|---|---|
| One Stamford Forum | CEO: Raymond R. Sackler | 2000 Sales: $1,200.0 million |
| Stamford, CT 06901 | CFO: Edward Mahony | 1-Yr. Sales Change: 47.8% |
| Phone: 203-588-8000 | HR: Patricia L. Leigh | Employees: 3,000 |
| Fax: 203-588-8850 | Type: Private | FYE: December 31 |
| Web: www.purduepharma.com | | |

Purdue Pharma's mantra could be "no pain, no gain." The pharmaceutical firm (formerly Purdue Frederick), known for over-the-counter medicines like Betadine (an antiseptic) and Senokot (a laxative), concentrates its research and development on pain management. Prescription drugs include pain relievers MS Contin, OxyContin, and Tramadol HCR. The company markets its own products as well as those of other manufacturers. Purdue Pharma also sponsors Partners Against Pain, an organization devoted to pain control. Founded in 1892, the company is part of a network of affiliates (including Mundipharma, Purdue Biopharma, and Napp Pharmaceuticals) with operations in Asia, Australia, North America, and Europe.

**KEY COMPETITORS**
Bayer AG
Elan Corporation
Johnson & Johnson

## PURITY WHOLESALE GROCERS, INC.

5400 Broken Sound Blvd. NW, Ste. 100
Boca Raton, FL 33487
Phone: 561-994-9360
Fax: 561-241-4628
Web: www.pwg-inc.com

CEO: Salvatore Ricciardi
CFO: Alan Rutner
HR: Karen McGrath
Type: Private

2001 Sales: $1,450.0 million
1-Yr. Sales Change: 11.5%
Employees: 440
FYE: June 30

Untainted by grocery retailing, Purity Wholesale Grocers (PWG) sticks to getting the goods to grocers. The company takes advantage of the discounts granted to large wholesalers and retailers (and of the promotional pricing offered in certain regions) by purchasing items and selling them to retailers not privy to those discounts. PWG moves groceries, health and beauty care items, pharmaceutical products, dairy foods, and dry goods to US grocery chains, drugstores, and convenience stores. PWG's marketing network is made up of 12 independently operated food distributors, marketers, and transportation firms. The company is owned by Jeff Levitetz, who founded PWG in 1982.

**KEY COMPETITORS**
Dot Foods
Nash Finch
Spartan Stores

## QUAD/GRAPHICS, INC.

W224 N3322 Duplainville Rd.
Pewaukee, WI 53072
Phone: 414-566-6000
Fax: —
Web: www.qg.com

CEO: Harry V. Quadracci
CFO: John C. Fowler
HR: Emmy M. LaBode
Type: Private

2000 Sales: $1,800.0 million
1-Yr. Sales Change: 20.0%
Employees: 14,000
FYE: December 31

Your mailbox may be filled with Quad/Graphics' handiwork. The largest privately held printer in the US, the company prints catalogs, magazines, books, direct mail, and other items. It offers a full range of services, including design, photography, desktop production, printing, binding, wrapping, and (through subsidiary Parcel/Direct) distribution and transportation. At some 22 facilities — six of which are in Wisconsin — the company prints catalogs for Bloomingdale's and Victoria's Secret, among others, as well as periodicals such as *People, Newsweek, National Geographic,* and *Sports Illustrated.* Founder and president Harry Quadracci and company employees own Quad/Graphics.

**KEY COMPETITORS**
Dai Nippon Printing
Quebecor World
R. R. Donnelley

 See pages 404–405 for a full profile of this company.

## QUALITY CHEKD DAIRIES, INC.

1733 Park St.
Naperville, IL 60563
Phone: 630-717-1110
Fax: 630-717-1126
Web: www.qchekd.com

CEO: Peter Horvath
CFO: Tom Bruce
HR: —
Type: Cooperative

2001 Sales: $2,500.0 million
1-Yr. Sales Change: —
Employees: 14
FYE: September 30

The founders of Quality Chekd Dairies were better dairymen than proofreaders. The non-profit cooperative provides marketing, purchasing, and training services to its some 40 member dairies and dairy product processors in the US, Mexico, El Salvador, and Colombia. Along with access to the co-op's marketing, accounting, and purchasing services, members can attend its COW TECH training programs. Quality Chekd also offers food quality and safety testing services through an independent lab. Most of its members are smaller regional dairies and processors, but they all enjoy the use of the red check mark logo, familiar to grocery shoppers.

**KEY COMPETITORS**
Dairy Farmers of America
Foremost Farms
MMPA

## QUALITY KING DISTRIBUTORS INC.

| | | |
|---|---|---|
| 2060 9th Ave. | CEO: Glenn Nussdorf | 2001 Sales: $2,400.0 million |
| Ronkonkoma, NY 11779 | CFO: Dennis Barkey | 1-Yr. Sales Change: 17.1% |
| Phone: 631-737-5555 | HR: Jane Midgal | Employees: 1,300 |
| Fax: 631-439-2388 | Type: Private | FYE: October 31 |
| Web: www.qkd.com | | |

Quality King Distributors rules a gargantuan gray market empire. It buys US name-brand products that have been exported to overseas markets, re-imports them, then sells them below suggested retail prices. The practice is deeply disliked by US manufacturers, but has been ruled legal by the Supreme Court. Quality King distributes groceries and hair, health, and beauty care products to pharmacy and grocery chains, grocery distributors, and wholesale clubs throughout the US. Bernard Nussdorf and his wife Ruth founded Quality King in 1960 in Queens, New York. The Nussdorf family still owns the company, which has transferred its pharmaceutical distribution business to affiliate QK Healthcare prior to spinning it off.

**KEY COMPETITORS**
Cardinal Health
McKesson

## QUALITY STORES, INC.

| | | |
|---|---|---|
| 455 E. Ellis Rd. | CEO: Peter D. Fitzsimmons | 2001 Sales: $1,126.0 million |
| Muskegon, MI 49443 | CFO: Thomas J. Reinebach | 1-Yr. Sales Change: 3.1% |
| Phone: 231-798-8787 | HR: Ted G. Britton | Employees: 5,900 |
| Fax: 231-798-8414 | Type: Private | FYE: January 31 |

If Old MacDonald had the help of Quality Stores, Inc. (QSI), he might have been able to handle more than a cow, a cat, a duck, and a hen. QSI operates more than 300 farming goods retail stores under six names in 31 states, although it is converting its stores to the Quality Farm & Country banner. The company was formed in 1999 by the merger of #2 farming goods retailer Central Tractor Farm & Country and #3 Quality Stores. QSI's stores sell tractor parts, fencing, animal supplies, and hardware. Burdened by debt and liquidity problems, QSI said it would close about 90 stores; it filed Chapter 11 bankruptcy in November 2001. The company is owned by QSI Holdings, an affiliate of investment firm J.W. Childs Associates. Chairman Jerry Horn owns about 10%.

**KEY COMPETITORS**
Agway
Tractor Supply
Wal-Mart

 See pages 406–407 for a full profile of this company.

## QUEXCO INCORPORATED

| | | |
|---|---|---|
| 2777 N. Stemmons Fwy. | CEO: Howard M. Meyers | 2001 Sales: $2,000.0 million |
| Dallas, TX 75207 | CFO: William Haberberger | 1-Yr. Sales Change: — |
| Phone: 214-688-4000 | HR: Shirley Crary | Employees: 7,000 |
| Fax: 214-630-5864 | Type: Private | FYE: December 31 |

Quexco gets the lead out and puts it back in. A leading secondary lead producer, this private holding company recycles scrapped lead acid batteries into refined lead and lead products. Quexco's RSR Corporation subsidiary is one of the largest lead smelters in the US, with operations in California, Indiana, New York, and Texas. Quexco also owns Eco-Bat Technologies plc, a UK-based battery recycler with operations in Europe and South Africa. The company's RSR Technologies subsidiary (formerly its R&D unit) offers technology and product development services to the metals industry. Chairman and CEO Howard Meyers, who also heads Bayou Steel Corporation, controls Quexco.

**KEY COMPETITORS**
Exide
Noranda
Renco

## QUIKTRIP CORPORATION

| | | |
|---|---|---|
| 901 N. Mingo Rd. | CEO: Chester Cadieux | 2001 Sales: $2,929.0 million |
| Tulsa, OK 74116 | CFO: Terry Carter | 1-Yr. Sales Change: 24.8% |
| Phone: 918-836-8551 | HR: Kim Owen | Employees: 6,045 |
| Fax: 918-834-4117 | Type: Private | FYE: April 30 |
| Web: www.quiktrip.com | | |

QuikTrip provides a quick fix for people on the go. QuikTrip (QT) owns and operates more than 350 gasoline and convenience stores in Georgia, Illinois, Iowa, Kansas, Missouri, Nebraska, Oklahoma, and its newest markets, Texas and Arizona. QT stores, which average 4,500 to 5,000 sq. ft., feature the company's own brand of gas, as well as brand-name beverages, tobacco, and candy, and QT's own Quick 'n Tasty and HOTZI lines of sandwiches. The company's FleetMaster program offers commercial trucking companies detailed reports showing drivers' product purchases, amounts spent, and odometer readings. QuikTrip was founded in 1958 by chairman, president, and CEO Chester Cadieux and partners.

**KEY COMPETITORS**
ChevronTexaco
Hale-Halsell
Phillips Petroleum

## RACETRAC PETROLEUM, INC.

| | | |
|---|---|---|
| 300 Technology Ct. | CEO: Carl E. Bolch Jr. | 2000 Sales: $2,811.0 million |
| Smyrna, GA 30082 | CFO: Robert J. Dumbacher | 1-Yr. Sales Change: 52.3% |
| Phone: 770-431-7600 | HR: Sue Jackson | Employees: 4,932 |
| Fax: 770-431-7612 | Type: Private | FYE: December 31 |
| Web: www.racetrac.com | | |

RaceTrac Petroleum hopes it is a popular pit stop for gasoline and snacks in the Southeast. The company operates about 500 company-owned and franchised gas stations and convenience stores in Alabama, Arkansas, Florida, Georgia, Kentucky, Louisiana, Mississippi, North Carolina, South Carolina, Tennessee, Texas, and Virginia under the RaceTrac and Raceway names. Carl Bolch founded RaceTrac in Missouri in 1934. His son, chairman and CEO Carl Bolch Jr., moved the company into high-volume gas stations with long, self-service islands that can serve many vehicles at once. RaceTrac's convenience stores also sell fresh deli food, rent videos, and offer some fast-food fare. The Bolch family owns the company.

**KEY COMPETITORS**
ChevronTexaco
Exxon Mobil
Motiva Enterprises

## RALEY'S INC.

| | | |
|---|---|---|
| 500 W. Capitol Ave. | CEO: Michael J. Teel | 2001 Sales: $3,000.0 million |
| West Sacramento, CA 95605 | CFO: William Anderson | 1-Yr. Sales Change: 5.3% |
| Phone: 916-373-3333 | HR: Dan Abfalter | Employees: 17,000 |
| Fax: 916-371-1323 | Type: Private | FYE: June 30 |
| Web: www.raleys.com | | |

Raley's has to stock plenty of fresh fruit and great wines — it sells to the people who produce them. The company operates about 150 supermarkets and larger-sized superstores, mostly in Northern California, but also in Nevada and New Mexico. In addition to its flagship Raley's Superstores, the company operates Bel Air Markets, Nob Hill Foods (an upscale Bay Area chain), and a discount warehouse chain, Food Source. Raley's stores typically offer groceries, natural foods, liquor, and pharmacies. Readers of *Consumer Reports* named Raley's the #1 supermarket chain in the US. Founded during the Depression by Tom Raley, the company is owned by Tom's daughter Joyce Raley Teel and is run by the family.

**KEY COMPETITORS**
Albertson's
Safeway
Save Mart Supermarkets

## RAND MCNALLY & COMPANY

8255 N. Central Park Ave.
Skokie, IL 60076
Phone: 847-329-8100
Fax: 847-329-6361
Web: www.randmcnally.com

CEO: Michael Hehir
CFO: —
HR: Mary Lynn Smedinghoff
Type: Private

2000 Est. Sales: $200.0 mil.
1-Yr. Sales Change: 11.7%
Employees: 1,000
FYE: December 31

The art of cartography is alive and well at mapmaker extraordinaire Rand McNally. The largest commercial mapmaker in the world, the company is famous for its flagship Rand McNally Road Atlas, but it also produces travel-related software (TripMaker, StreetFinder) and educational products. It makes mileage and routing software for the transportation industry and sells its wares online and through some 50,000 retail outlets (including nearly 30 of its own) across the US. The company is struggling to use its powerful brand name to compete online with rivals such as MapQuest.com and Maps.com. Founded in 1856, Rand McNally was owned by the McNally family until AEA Investors bought a controlling interest in 1997.

**KEY COMPETITORS**
AAA
MapQuest.com
Michelin

 See pages 408–409 for a full profile of this company.

## R. B. PAMPLIN CORP.

805 SW Broadway, Ste. 2400
Portland, OR 97205
Phone: 503-248-1133
Fax: 503-248-1175
Web: www.pamplin.org

CEO: Robert B. Pamplin Jr.
CFO: David Hastings
HR: —
Type: Private

2000 Sales: $890.0 million
1-Yr. Sales Change: 5.5%
Employees: 7,584
FYE: December 31

Founded by a man of the cloth, R. B. Pamplin casts a wide net. The family-owned conglomerate, started in 1957 by minister and company CEO Robert Pamplin Jr. (Robert Sr. is chairman), makes textiles, asphalt, and concrete. Its affiliates have interests ranging from entertainment to retail stores offering Christian products. The company's Mount Vernon Mills is one of the largest denim producers in the US. Affiliate Pamplin Broadcasting operates six radio stations in the northwestern US. The philanthropic Pamplin family has restored its ancestral antebellum plantation, creating Pamplin Historical Park in Virginia.

**KEY COMPETITORS**
Avondale Incorporated
Cone Mills
U.S. Concrete

## RECREATIONAL EQUIPMENT, INC.

6750 S. 228th St.
Kent, WA 98032
Phone: 253-395-3780
Fax: 253-395-4352
Web: www.rei.com

CEO: Dennis Madsen
CFO: Brad Johnson
HR: Glen Simmons
Type: Cooperative

2000 Sales: $698.3 million
1-Yr. Sales Change: 12.5%
Employees: 7,000
FYE: December 31

Outdoor gear and clothing from Recreational Equipment, Inc. (REI) outfits everyone from mountain climbers to mall walkers. One of the nation's largest consumer cooperatives, REI was formed by Lloyd and Mary Anderson and 21 mountaineers in 1938. Through about 60 stores in 24 states (and one in Tokyo, which it is closing), REI sells high-end gear, clothing, and footwear for camping, bicycling, climbing, paddling, and other outdoor activities. It also repairs gear, operates an adventure travel service, and markets online and via catalogs. REI donates to conservation and recreation groups, and it offers a gift registry. Its 1.8 million member-owners share REI's profits through an annual patronage refund.

**KEY COMPETITORS**
L.L. Bean
Lost Arrow
North Face

 See pages 410–411 for a full profile of this company.

## RED APPLE GROUP, INC.

| | | |
|---|---|---|
| 823 11th Ave. | CEO: John A. Catsimatidis | 2001 Sales: $1,100.0 million |
| New York, NY 10019 | CFO: Gary Pokrassa | 1-Yr. Sales Change: 10.0% |
| Phone: 212-956-5803 | HR: John Geldea | Employees: 3,117 |
| Fax: 212-262-4979 | Type: Private | FYE: February 28 |

Red Apple Group sells apples (and more) in the Big Apple. Most of the company's sales come from subsidiary United Refining, which processes 72,000 barrels of oil a day and distributes fuel to its more than 300 KwikFill/Red Apple gas stations/convenience stores in New York, Pennsylvania, and Ohio. In addition, Red Apple Group controls Gristede's Foods, a leading New York City supermarket chain. The group also has real estate operations. CEO John Catsimatidis owns Red Apple Group, which lost out to Russian oil giant LUKOIL in its 2000 bid to acquire East Coast gasoline retailer Getty Petroleum Marketing. Red Apple agreed to purchase regional gas retailer Country Fair (68 gas stations) in 2001.

**KEY COMPETITORS**
Getty Petroleum Marketing
A&P
Motiva Enterprises

## REGAL CINEMAS, INC.

| | | |
|---|---|---|
| 7132 Mike Campbell Dr. | CEO: Michael L. Campbell | 2000 Sales: $1,130.7 million |
| Knoxville, TN 37918 | CFO: Amy Miles | 1-Yr. Sales Change: 9.0% |
| Phone: 865-922-1123 | HR: Raymond L. Smith | Employees: 15,159 |
| Fax: 865-922-6739 | Type: Private | FYE: December 31 |
| Web: www.regalcinemas.com | | |

Regal Cinemas is the king of the world of movie theater chains. The company has more than 4,000 screens at about 350 theaters in 32 states. Regal operates mostly multiplex theaters in midsized urban and suburban locales. The company also operates a handful of IMAX 3-D theaters at select multiplexes. Regal Cinemas is owned by investment firms Kohlberg Kravis Roberts (KKR) and Hicks, Muse, Tate & Furst. Philip Anschutz, chairman of Qwest Communications, bought about $425 million of Regal's debt in 2000 and 2001, which is likely to leave him in control after a restructuring.

**KEY COMPETITORS**
AMC Entertainment
Carmike Cinemas
Loews Cineplex Entertainment

 See pages 412–413 for a full profile of this company.

## RENCO GROUP INC.

| | | |
|---|---|---|
| 30 Rockefeller Plaza | CEO: Ira L. Rennert | 2001 Sales: $2,150.0 million |
| New York, NY 10112 | CFO: Roger L. Fay | 1-Yr. Sales Change: (14.0%) |
| Phone: 212-541-6000 | HR: Justin W. D'Atri | Employees: 14,000 |
| Fax: 212-541-6197 | Type: Private | FYE: October 31 |

Renco Group is a holding company for a diverse bunch of businesses. Its AM General subsidiary makes the HUMVEE, an extra-wide all-terrain vehicle used by the military, and the HUMMER, the HUMVEE's civilian counterpart. Renco Steel and WCI Steel manufacture, fabricate, and distribute steel. Other Renco Group companies include Doe Run, the world's #2 smelter; coal miner Rencoal; and Consolidated Sewing Machine, which makes industrial sewing machines. Renco was established in 1980 and is owned by Ira Rennert, an industrialist and a former business consultant whose Long Island, New York, home is double the size of the White House and is said to include 29 bedrooms, 42 bathrooms, a 100-car garage, and an English pub.

**KEY COMPETITORS**
Oshkosh Truck
Singer
United States Steel

## REPUBLIC TECHNOLOGIES INTERNATIONAL, LLC

| | | |
|---|---|---|
| 3770 Embassy Pkwy. | CEO: Joseph F. Lapinsky | 2000 Sales: $1,265.4 million |
| Akron, OH 44333 | CFO: — | 1-Yr. Sales Change: 22.5% |
| Phone: 330-670-3000 | HR: John Willoughby | Employees: 3,889 |
| Fax: 330-670-3106 | Type: Private | FYE: December 31 |
| Web: www.republictech.com | | |

Republic Technologies International (RTI) is the US's largest producer of high-quality steel bars. The company's steel bars and wire rods are used to make automobiles, heavy equipment, and similar products. Customers — including DaimlerChrysler, Ford, GM, and their suppliers — turn RTI's steel into components such as bearings, crankshafts, and spark plug shells. The company has been trying to stem the flow of losses by shutting down outdated plants and shifting production to modern mills, but it's been forced to file for bankruptcy protection. Investment company Blackstone Management Associates owns 52% of RTI; Veritas Capital Management owns 16%; Kobe Steel and United States Steel combined own about 20%.

**KEY COMPETITORS**
AK Steel Holding Corporation
Nucor
United States Steel

## RETAIL BRAND ALLIANCE, INC.

| | | |
|---|---|---|
| 100 Phoenix Ave. | CEO: Claudio Del Vecchio | 2001 Sales: $1,000.0 million |
| Enfield, CT | CFO: Brian K. Baumann | 1-Yr. Sales Change: — |
| Phone: 860-741-0771 | HR: Susan Eyvazzadeh | Employees: 10,000 |
| Fax: 860-745-9714 | Type: Private | FYE: July 31 |

Given a food court and some seasonal kiosks, Retail Brand Alliance could open its own shopping malls. A holding company for upscale clothing retailers in the US, the Retail Brand Alliance boasts a portfolio that includes women's apparel chains Casual Corner, August Max, and Petite Sophisticate, with some 1,000 mostly mall-based shops in about 45 states; men's suits and women's clothing retailer Brooks Brothers; jewelry and accessories designer Carolee Designs; and women's sportswear designer Adrienne Vittadini. President and CEO Claudio Del Vecchio owns Retail Brand Alliance, which he acquired as the Casual Corner Group in 1997 from his father's company, Luxottica Group (operator of LensCrafters and Sunglass Hut).

**KEY COMPETITORS**
AnnTaylor
Federated
The Limited

## REYES HOLDINGS LLC

| | | |
|---|---|---|
| 225 E. Deer Path Rd., Ste. 270 | CEO: J. Christopher Reyes | 2001 Sales: $3,900.0 million |
| Lake Forest, IL 60045 | CFO: Dan Doheny | 1-Yr. Sales Change: 11.4% |
| Phone: 847-604-9966 | HR: — | Employees: 2,800 |
| Fax: 847-604-9965 | Type: Private | FYE: September 30 |

Closely held Reyes Holdings has a kingly grasp over two things that are often held closely together — food and beer. Reyes Holdings owns several wholesale food and beer companies, including The Martin-Brower Company, which distributes supplies to some of the McDonald's in the US and Canada through a network of 135 distribution centers. In addition, Martin-Brower serves McDonald's in Brazil, the Caribbean, Central America, and Puerto Rico. Reyes Holdings also counts Premium Distributors of Virginia, Chicago Beverage Systems, and California's Harbor Distributing among the wholesalers it owns. Reyes Holdings has closed Zema Foods, a Chicago produce distributor. Chairman Chris Reyes and VP David Reyes own the company.

**KEY COMPETITORS**
McLane Foodservice
SYSCO
U.S. Foodservice

## RICELAND FOODS, INC.

2120 S. Park Ave.
Stuttgart, AR 72160
Phone: 870-673-5500
Fax: 870-673-3366
Web: www.riceland.com

CEO: Richard E. Bell
CFO: Harry E. Loftis
HR: Linda Dobrovich
Type: Cooperative

1999 Sales: $812.6 million
1-Yr. Sales Change: 1.1%
Employees: 1,850
FYE: July 31

Riceland Foods is ingrained in the marketing and milling business. Started in 1921, the cooperative markets rice, soybeans, and wheat grown by its more than 8,000 member-owners in Arkansas, Louisiana, Mississippi, Missouri, and Texas. As one of the world's leading millers of rice, Riceland sells long grain, brown, wild, and flavored rice (under the Riceland name as well as private labels) to grocery, food service, and food manufacturing customers. The co-op also sells Chef-way oil and shortening products and processes soybeans, edible oils, and lecithin. Riceland markets its products throughout the US and internationally, mainly in the Caribbean, Mexico, the Middle East, South Africa, and Western Europe.

**KEY COMPETITORS**
American Rice
Mars
Riviana Foods

## RICH PRODUCTS CORPORATION

1150 Niagara St.
Buffalo, NY 14213
Phone: 716-878-8000
Fax: 716-878-8765
Web: www.richs.com

CEO: Robert E. Rich Jr.
CFO: Charles R. Trego
HR: Brian Townson
Type: Private

2000 Sales: $1,620.0 million
1-Yr. Sales Change: 6.9%
Employees: 7,000
FYE: December 31

Starting in 1945 with "the miracle cream from the soya bean," Rich Products has grown from a niche maker of soy-based whipped toppings and frozen desserts to a major US frozen foods manufacturer. Since the 1960s the company has developed new products, such as Coffee Rich (nondairy coffee creamer), and expanded through acquisitions to include frozen bakery and pizza doughs and ingredients for the food service and in-store bakery markets, plus SeaPak (seafood) and Byron's (barbecue). Rich Products markets some 2,300 products in about 70 countries. The company, owned and operated by the founding Rich family, also owns the Wichita Wranglers and Buffalo Bisons minor league baseball teams.

**KEY COMPETITORS**
ConAgra
Kraft Foods
Nestlé

## RITZ CAMERA CENTERS, INC.

6711 Ritz Way
Beltsville, MD 20705
Phone: 301-419-0000
Fax: 301-419-2995
Web: www.ritzcamera.com

CEO: David Ritz
CFO: Jay Sloan
HR: Alan MacDonald
Type: Private

2000 Sales: $1,305.0 million
1-Yr. Sales Change: 63.1%
Employees: 12,000
FYE: December 31

Ritz Camera Centers began as a one-man portrait studio and developed into the largest photographic chain in the US. The company has more than 1,000 stores nationwide offering one-hour photofinishing, digital imaging, cameras, film, and related products. Ritz Camera also sells binoculars and cellular phones, among other items. Some of its stores operate as The Camera Shop; the company sells online as well. Subsidiary Boater's World Marine Centers has more than 100 stores nationwide that offer gear and clothing for fishing, boating, and watersports. CEO David Ritz owns Ritz Camera, which was founded in 1918. Ritz's cousin, Chuck Wolf, owned Wolf Camera, the #2 photo chain in the US, which Ritz Camera acquired in 2001.

**KEY COMPETITORS**
Walgreen
Wal-Mart
West Marine

## RIVERWOOD INTERNATIONAL CORPORATION

| | | |
|---|---|---|
| 3350 Riverwood Pkwy., Ste. 1400 | CEO: Stephen M. Humphrey | 2000 Sales: $1,128.7 million |
| Atlanta, GA 30339 | CFO: Daniel Blount | 1-Yr. Sales Change: 1.4% |
| Phone: 770-644-3000 | HR: Robert H. Burg | Employees: 4,000 |
| Fax: 770-644-2962 | Type: Private | FYE: December 31 |
| Web: www.riverwood.com | | |

Riverwood International is a CUK above the rest. That's because it's one of only two major producers of coated unbleached kraft (CUK) paperboard for packaged goods. (Mead is the other.) The company makes CUK board for packaging beverages (carrierboard) and consumer products (folding cartons). Its products are used by companies such as Anheuser-Busch, Coca-Cola, and Nestlé. The company prints and cuts most of its carrierboard into beverage cartons and also makes and leases packaging machinery to its clients. Almost all of the cartonboard is sold to independent packagers. The company was taken private in 1995 by a group of investment firms. Clayton, Dubilier, & Rice and EXOR Group each own about 30% of the company.

**KEY COMPETITORS**
Mead
Smurfit-Stone Container
Sonoco Products

## THE ROBERT WOOD JOHNSON FOUNDATION

| | | |
|---|---|---|
| Rte. 1 and College Rd. East | CEO: Steven A. Schroeder | 2000 Sales: $929.6 million |
| Princeton, NJ 08543 | CFO: Rona Smyth Henry | 1-Yr. Sales Change: 43.8% |
| Phone: 609-452-8701 | HR: David L. Waldman | Employees: 150 |
| Fax: 609-452-1865 | Type: Foundation | FYE: December 31 |
| Web: www.rwjf.org | | |

The Robert Wood Johnson Foundation has its finger on the pulse of health care. The nation's largest charitable organization devoted exclusively to health care issues, the Johnson Foundation donates some $400 million each year to more than 800 programs that address four primary areas: access to health care, substance abuse, chronic care, and community health issues. The foundation annually supports about 2,300 programs spanning initiatives such as the gathering of health statistics, training, policy analysis, and public education. Johnson & Johnson heir Robert Wood Johnson started the organization in 1936; its endowment totals more than $8 billion in assets.

## THE ROCKEFELLER FOUNDATION

| | | |
|---|---|---|
| 420 Fifth Ave. | CEO: Gordon R. Conway | 2000 Sales: $126.7 million |
| New York, NY 10018 | CFO: Denise Gray-Felder | 1-Yr. Sales Change: (81.4%) |
| Phone: 212-869-8500 | HR: Robert Giacometti | Employees: 230 |
| Fax: 212-764-3468 | Type: Foundation | FYE: December 31 |
| Web: www.rockfound.org | | |

The Rockefeller Foundation — one of America's oldest private charitable organizations — supports grants, fellowships, and conferences that try to identify and alleviate need and suffering around the world. Its goals focus on agricultural policies and practices that ensure food in poor areas, creative cultural expression through the arts, employment opportunities for America's urban poor, and fair health care practices. Its cross theme of global inclusion seeks to ensure that the globalization process includes poor and disenfranchised populations around the world.

 See pages 414–415 for a full profile of this company.

## ROLL INTERNATIONAL CORPORATION

| | | |
|---|---|---|
| 11444 W. Olympic Blvd., 10th Fl. | CEO: Stewart A. Resnick | 2000 Est. Sales: $825.0 mil. |
| Los Angeles, CA 90064 | CFO: Robert A. Kors | 1-Yr. Sales Change: 17.9% |
| Phone: 310-966-5700 | HR: — | Employees: 5,100 |
| Fax: 310-914-4747 | Type: Private | FYE: December 31 |

Churning out collectible family heirlooms (or flea market fodder) is the primary business of Stewart and Lynda Resnick's Roll International. The centerpiece of the Resnicks' empire is The Franklin Mint, the world's largest collectibles company, with operations in about 15 countries. The Franklin Mint sells goods by mail order, through its Web site, and in company-owned and independent retail stores. It also operates The Franklin Mint Museum, which has displayed such authentic items as a Jacqueline Kennedy Onassis necklace and a Princess Diana gown. Other Roll operations include Paramount Farms (pistachios), Paramount Citrus (citrus products), and Teleflora (floral delivery service).

**KEY COMPETITORS**
Enesco Group
IOS Brands
Sun Growers

 See pages 416–417 for a full profile of this company.

## ROOMS TO GO

| | | |
|---|---|---|
| 11540 Hwy. 92 East | CEO: Jeffrey Seaman | 2000 Sales: $1,040.0 million |
| Seffner, FL 33584 | CFO: Lou Stein | 1-Yr. Sales Change: 20.9% |
| Phone: 813-623-5400 | HR: Linda Garcia | Employees: 4,834 |
| Fax: 813-620-1717 | Type: Private | FYE: December 31 |
| Web: www.roomstogo.com | | |

Need that sofa, recliner, table, and lamp in a hurry? Rooms To Go, with more than 70 stores in Florida, Georgia, North Carolina, South Carolina, Tennessee, and Texas, markets its limited selection of furniture to brand-conscious, time-pressed customers. It packages low- to moderately priced furniture and accessories and offers discounts for those willing to buy a roomful. Rooms To Go also operates a Rooms to Go Kids chain with about a dozen stores in the Southeast. Rooms To Go has opened stores in Japan and Puerto Rico. President and owner Jeffrey Seaman and his father, Morty, founded the firm in 1990 after selling Seaman Furniture Company.

**KEY COMPETITORS**
Havertys
J. C. Penney
Sears

## ROONEY BROTHERS COMPANY

| | | |
|---|---|---|
| 5601 S. 122nd East Ave. | CEO: Timothy P. Rooney | 2001 Sales: $1,053.0 million |
| Tulsa, OK 74146 | CFO: Jim Lawson | 1-Yr. Sales Change: 5.1% |
| Phone: 918-583-6900 | HR: Jackie Proffitt | Employees: 2,400 |
| Fax: 918-592-4334 | Type: Private | FYE: September 30 |

Film star Mickey isn't the only Rooney to have landed big contracts. Rooney Brothers, through its Manhattan Construction unit, builds hospitals, government buildings (George Bush Presidential Library in Texas), offices, highways, and sports arenas (Reliant Stadium in Houston). It offers construction manager, general contractor, and design/build services to its clients, located mainly in the southwestern and mid-Atlantic states. Rooney Brothers also makes construction materials, operates building supply stores, and manufactures electronics. Family-owned Rooney Brothers was organized in 1984 to acquire Manhattan Construction, which was founded by patriarch L. H. Rooney in 1896.

**KEY COMPETITORS**
Austin Industries
Hensel Phelps Construction
MA Mortenson

## ROSENBLUTH INTERNATIONAL

| | | |
|---|---|---|
| 2401 Walnut St. | CEO: Hal F. Rosenbluth | 2000 Sales: $5,500.0 million |
| Philadelphia, PA 19103 | CFO: Thomas Sukay | 1-Yr. Sales Change: 22.2% |
| Phone: 215-977-4000 | HR: Cecily Carel | Employees: 5,500 |
| Fax: 215-977-4028 | Type: Private | FYE: December 31 |
| Web: www.rosenbluth.com | | |

In the mood for a trip? Rosenbluth International will help you unravel the travel scene. A leading travel management company, Rosenbluth emphasizes services for corporate clients (ChevronTexaco, J.P. Morgan Chase, NIKE). With 1,300 locations worldwide, the company is known for staying abreast of evolving travel technology and offers its services with the aid of travel systems such as its Discount Analysis Containing Optimal Decision Algorithms (DACODA, maximizes savings on airlines tickets). Its biztravel.com offers business travelers Web-based travel services. Founded in 1892 by Marcus Rosenbluth, the company still is owned and operated by his family, including his great-grandson, chairman and CEO Hal Rosenbluth.

**KEY COMPETITORS**
American Express
Carlson Wagonlit
WorldTravel

 See pages 418–419 for a full profile of this company.

## ROSEN'S DIVERSIFIED, INC.

| | | |
|---|---|---|
| 1120 Lake Ave. | CEO: Thomas J. Rosen | 2001 Sales: $800.0 million |
| Fairmont, MN 56031 | CFO: Rob Hovde | 1-Yr. Sales Change: 14.3% |
| Phone: 507-238-4201 | HR: Dominick Driano | Employees: 2,000 |
| Fax: 507-238-9966 | Type: Private | FYE: September 30 |

Rosen's Diversified has the goods to make the grass greener for the cows it slaughters. The agricultural holding company has interests in meatpacking, including Long Prairie Packing and Skylark Meats, and in companies that distribute chemical fertilizers for farms. Its beef-slaughtering operations consist of meatpacking plants in three states, with the capacity to slaughter about 3,500 head of cattle a day. Rosen's Diversified processes meat for restaurants, government customers, and food manufacturers in the US. The company was founded in 1946 by brothers Elmer and Ludwig Rosen. CEO Thomas Rosen (the son of Elmer) and other family members share ownership of the company.

**KEY COMPETITORS**
Cargill
ConAgra
Farmland Industries

## ROSENTHAL AUTOMOTIVE COMPANIES

| | | |
|---|---|---|
| 1100 S. Glebe Rd. | CEO: Robert M. Rosenthal | 2000 Sales: $825.2 million |
| Arlington, VA 22204 | CFO: Donald B. Bavely | 1-Yr. Sales Change: 4.3% |
| Phone: 703-553-4300 | HR: Jeraldine Mendez | Employees: 1,625 |
| Fax: 703-553-8435 | Type: Private | FYE: December 31 |

A dealer of wheels in a city of wheeler-dealers, Rosenthal Automotive operates about 15 auto dealerships in the Washington, DC, area. Rosenthal's dealerships sell more than 20,000 new cars a year, including Chevrolets, Hondas, Jaguars, Mazdas, Nissans, Toyotas, Volkswagens, and Volvos. The company also sells used cars and has wholesale and fleet operations. Chairman and owner Robert Rosenthal founded Rosenthal Automotive in 1954 when he opened his first Chevrolet dealership in Arlington, Virginia. In 1997 Rosenthal joined other dealers in the Washington, DC, area to form Capital Automotive REIT, the first automotive-only real estate investment trust in the US. Rosenthal owns about 15% of Capital Automotive REIT.

**KEY COMPETITORS**
Brown Automotive
Jim Koons Automotive
Ourisman Automotive

## ROTARY INTERNATIONAL

| | | |
|---|---|---|
| 1 Rotary Center, 1560 Sherman Ave. | CEO: Frank J. Devlyn | 2000 Sales: $62.0 million |
| Evanston, IL 60201 | CFO: Ladd Waldo | 1-Yr. Sales Change: 0.0% |
| Phone: 847-866-3000 | HR: C. Engblom | Employees: 400 |
| Fax: 847-866-9732 | Type: Not-for-profit | FYE: June 30 |
| Web: www.rotary.org | | |

The members of service organization Rotary International strive to put "Service Above Self." The organization addresses issues such as AIDS, hunger, and illiteracy, and includes about 30,000 clubs across 163 countries with a membership of nearly 1.2 million (predominantly men, although women are its fastest-growing segment). Its not-for-profit Rotary Foundation invests $90 million a year in international education and humanitarian programs (funds are raised through voluntary contributions). Rotary International also sponsors Interact clubs for secondary school students, as well as a network of about 6,500 Rotaract clubs for members ages 18-30. It is governed by a 19-member board and maintains offices globally.

 See pages 420–421 for a full profile of this company.

## ROUNDY'S, INC.

| | | |
|---|---|---|
| 23000 Roundy Dr. | CEO: Gerald F. Lestina | 2000 Sales: $2,990.9 million |
| Pewaukee, WI 53072 | CFO: Robert D. Ranus | 1-Yr. Sales Change: 9.7% |
| Phone: 262-953-7999 | HR: Debra A. Lawson | Employees: 9,071 |
| Fax: 262-953-6580 | Type: Cooperative | FYE: December 31 |
| Web: www.roundys.com | | |

Roundy's rounds up name-brand and private-label goods and distributes them to about 800 warehouse and grocery stores in 14 states, mostly in the Midwest and South. The company is a wholesale cooperative with nearly 60 members, operating about 100 stores in Wisconsin and Illinois, and it services nearly 700 independent stores (about 45% of sales). In addition, Roundy's owns about 50 food outlets under such names as Orchard Foods, Park & Save, and Pick 'n Save. The Pick 'n Save chain (which also includes independents) is Wisconsin's #1 food retailer. Founded in 1872, Roundy's offers members and customers a host of support services. Co-op members own about 65% of the company; employees and other investors own the rest.

**KEY COMPETITORS**
Fleming Companies
A&P
SUPERVALU

 See pages 422–423 for a full profile of this company.

## ROYSTER-CLARK, INC.

| | | |
|---|---|---|
| 600 Fifth Ave., 25th Fl. | CEO: Francis P. Jenkins Jr. | 2000 Sales: $913.2 million |
| New York, NY 10020 | CFO: Walter R. Vance | 1-Yr. Sales Change: 27.7% |
| Phone: 212-332-2965 | HR: Ken W. Carter | Employees: 3,130 |
| Fax: 212-332-2473 | Type: Private | FYE: December 31 |
| Web: www.roysterclark.com | | |

Royster-Clark has been spreading it on thick for more than 125 years. The company makes fertilizer (nearly two-thirds of sales) and crop-protection products. It processes seed to sell under its own label and to leading seed companies. Operations include granulation, blending, and seed-processing plants, 400 retail farm supply centers, and a network of distribution terminals and warehouses. The company offers such agronomic services as crop management, custom blending and spreading, and soil sampling. Royster-Clark operates in the eastern, southern, and midwestern US.

**KEY COMPETITORS**
Agrium
Tractor Supply
Wilbur-Ellis

## RUDOLPH AND SLETTEN, INC.

| | | |
|---|---|---|
| 989 E. Hillsdale Blvd., Ste. 100 | CEO: Allen Rudolph | 2001 Sales: $852.0 million |
| Foster City, CA 94404 | CFO: Jim Evans | 1-Yr. Sales Change: 26.2% |
| Phone: 650-572-1919 | HR: Norma Adjmi | Employees: 1,200 |
| Fax: 650-577-1558 | Type: Private | FYE: June 30 |
| Web: www.rsconstruction.com | | |

Rudolph and Sletten builds on shaky ground in California, but the force is with it. The firm built Lucasfilm's Skywalker Ranch production facility and is a leading player in the Silicon Valley, where it raised corporate campuses for Apple Computer, Microsoft, and Sun Microsystems, among others. Acting as on-site general contractor or construction manager, the company specializes in projects for the health-care, high-tech research and manufacturing, biotechnology, and entertainment industries; it also takes on such unique projects as the Monterey Bay Aquarium. Onslow "Rudy" Rudolph, father of president Allen Ruldoph, founded the company in 1960 and was joined by Kenneth Sletten in 1962.

**KEY COMPETITORS**
Devcon Construction
DPR Construction
Webcor Builders

## RUSH SYSTEM FOR HEALTH

| | | |
|---|---|---|
| 1653 W. Congress Pkwy. | CEO: Leo M. Henikoff | 2000 Est. Sales: $1,400.0 mil. |
| Chicago, IL 60612 | CFO: James T. Frankenbach | 1-Yr. Sales Change: 0.0% |
| Phone: 312-942-5000 | HR: Mary K. Lambe | Employees: 8,896 |
| Fax: 312-942-5581 | Type: Not-for-profit | FYE: June 30 |
| Web: www.rush.edu | | |

In a rush for medical care? The medical centers, hospitals, and skilled nursing facilities that make up the Rush System for Health provide comprehensive health care in the Chicago area. Its cornerstone is the Rush-Presbyterian-St. Luke's Medical Center, which includes Rush Children's Hospital, the Johnston R. Bowman Health Center for the Elderly, and Rush University (which boasts a medical school and related colleges). Other operations include physician practice management subsidiary Aria Services for Physicians and physician/hospital organization Rush-Presbyterian-St. Luke's Health Associates. Rush, which traces its origins back to 1837, has been at its present location since 1875.

**KEY COMPETITORS**
Advocate Health Care
Covenant Ministries
Sisters of Mercy

## RUSSELL STOVER CANDIES INC.

| | | |
|---|---|---|
| 4900 Oaks St. | CEO: Thomas S. Ward | 2001 Sales: $471.0 million |
| Kansas City, MO 64112 | CFO: Dick Masinton | 1-Yr. Sales Change: (5.8%) |
| Phone: 816-842-9240 | HR: Robinn S. Weber | Employees: 5,200 |
| Fax: 816-842-5593 | Type: Private | FYE: February 28 |
| Web: www.russellstover.com | | |

For Russell Stover Candies, life is a box of chocolates. The largest US maker of boxed chocolates is protecting its sweet position. Faced with growing competition as Hershey and Mars invade the boxed-chocolate arena, it has countered with a chocolate bar by packaging its version of that popular campfire treat — the s'more (graham cracker, marshmallow, chocolate). It also sells bagged candy, but boxed treats — especially Whitman's Sampler and Pangburn's Millionaires — are its main business. For diabetics and others the company offers sugar-free candy, including a sugarless version of Millionaires. Founded by Russell Stover in 1923, the company is owned by the Ward family and led by brothers Tom and Scott Ward.

**KEY COMPETITORS**
Hershey
Mars
Nestlé

📖 See pages 424–425 for a full profile of this company.

## SACRAMENTO MUNICIPAL UTILITY DISTRICT

| | | |
|---|---|---|
| 6301 S St. | CEO: Jan E. Schori | 2000 Sales: $967.6 million |
| Sacramento, CA 95817 | CFO: Gail R. Hullibarger | 1-Yr. Sales Change: 24.8% |
| Phone: 916-452-3211 | HR: Shirley Lewis | Employees: 2,026 |
| Fax: 916-732-5835 | Type: Government-owned | FYE: December 31 |
| Web: www.smud.org | | |

Because it doesn't want its name to be mud, the Sacramento Municipal Utility District (SMUD) is powering up for competition. One of the largest locally owned electric utilities in the US, SMUD serves nearly 520,000 customers in California's Sacramento and Placer counties. It generates half of its electricity (its 1,200-MW capacity is derived primarily from hydroelectric and cogeneration power plants) and buys the rest. Having one of the US's largest solar energy distribution systems, it is a leader in advanced and renewable generation technology. In response to deregulation, SMUD is increasing its generation capacity and selling wholesale power, and it has increased rates after a spike in wholesale electricity costs.

**KEY COMPETITORS**
Edison International
Los Angeles Water and Power
PG&E

## SALVATION ARMY USA

| | | |
|---|---|---|
| 615 Slaters Ln. | CEO: John Busby | 2000 Sales: $1,803.0 million |
| Alexandria, VA 22313 | CFO: Don McDougald | 1-Yr. Sales Change: 5.6% |
| Phone: 703-684-5500 | HR: Myrtle V. Ryder | Employees: 45,096 |
| Fax: 703-684-3478 | Type: Not-for-profit | FYE: September 30 |
| Web: www.salvationarmyusa.org | | |

The largest civil army in the land, the Salvation Army is more than 3 million strong. Its programs assist alcoholics, drug addicts, the homeless, the handicapped, the elderly, prison inmates, people in crisis, and the unemployed through a range of services. These include day-care centers, programs for people with disabilities, substance abuse programs, and educational facilities for at-risk students. It also provides disaster relief in the US and abroad. The Salvation Army USA is a national unit of the Salvation Army, an international body based in London, which oversees Army activities in more than 100 countries.

 See pages 426–427 for a full profile of this company.

## SAMMONS ENTERPRISES, INC.

| | | |
|---|---|---|
| 5949 Sherry Ln., Ste. 1900 | CEO: Robert W. Korba | 2000 Sales: $1,934.0 million |
| Dallas, TX 75225 | CFO: Joseph A. Ethridge | 1-Yr. Sales Change: (3.3%) |
| Phone: 214-210-5000 | HR: Carol Cochran | Employees: 3,000 |
| Fax: 214-210-5099 | Type: Private | FYE: December 31 |

Sammons Enterprises summons its revenues from several sources. The diversified holding company's interests include insurance (Midland National Life Insurance and North American Company for Life and Health Insurance), water bottling (Mountain Valley Spring), industrial equipment distribution (Briggs-Weaver), and industrial trucks (Briggs Equipment). Briggs-Weaver ranks among the leading industrial supply distributors in the US. Sammons Enterprises also owns The Grove Park Inn Resort in Asheville, North Carolina. The late Charles Sammons, an orphan who became a billionaire philanthropist, founded the company in 1962. His estate still owns the company, and his widow, Elaine Sammons, serves as chairman.

**KEY COMPETITORS**
Nestlé
Prudential
W.W. Grainger

## S&P COMPANY

| | | |
|---|---|---|
| 100 Shoreline Hwy., Bldg. B, Ste. 395 | CEO: Bernard Orsi | 2001 Sales: $775.0 million |
| Mill Valley, CA 94941 | CFO: Harvey Rubinson | 1-Yr. Sales Change: (22.5%) |
| Phone: 415-332-0550 | HR: — | Employees: 300 |
| Fax: 415-332-0567 | Type: Private | FYE: June 30 |

After years of chugging along, S&P's days of brewing the blue ribbon are over. S&P owns Pabst Brewing, which had breweries in Pennsylvania and Texas. Pabst shut down its 115-year old Texas brewery in May 2001 and its Pennsylvania plant the following September. The company transferred production of its brands (Pabst Blue Ribbon, Pearl, Lone Star, Old Milwaukee, Schlitz, and Colt 45) to Miller Brewing. Pabst pays Miller to brew the beers, but retains ownership of the brands and markets the products. Once the #4 US brewer, Pabst struggled to compete with nation's top three brewing giants. The Kalmanovitz Charitable Trust (established by the late founder Paul Kalmanovitz) was granted ownership of the company in 2000.

**KEY COMPETITORS**
Adolph Coors
Anheuser-Busch
Miller Brewing

 See pages 428–429 for a full profile of this company.

## SANTA MONICA FORD CORPORATION

| | | |
|---|---|---|
| 1230 Santa Monica Blvd. | CEO: L. Wayne Harding | 2000 Est. Sales: $800.0 mil. |
| Santa Monica, CA 90404 | CFO: Dean Chow | 1-Yr. Sales Change: 6.7% |
| Phone: 310-451-1588 | HR: Ricky Berardy | Employees: — |
| Fax: 310-394-8115 | Type: Private | FYE: December 31 |

You can get a new car from Santa Monica Ford if the other Santa doesn't bring one. Santa Monica Ford is one of the top-selling Ford dealers in the US, selling about 24,000 vehicles a year. The dealership sells new and used Ford cars and trucks, with most of its business from fleet sales (mass quantities to corporate customers). Santa Monica Ford also operates a parts and service department. Established in 1948, Santa Monica Ford offers a customer satisfaction program that includes surveys, follow-up phone calls, and keep-in-touch letters. Chairman L. Wayne Harding owns the company.

**KEY COMPETITORS**
AutoNation
Galpin Motors
Tuttle-Click

## SAS INSTITUTE INC.

| | | |
|---|---|---|
| SAS Campus Dr. | CEO: James H. Goodnight | 2000 Sales: $1,120.0 million |
| Cary, NC 27513 | CFO: W. Greyson Quarles Jr. | 1-Yr. Sales Change: 9.8% |
| Phone: 919-677-8000 | HR: Jeff Chambers | Employees: 8,500 |
| Fax: 919-677-4444 | Type: Private | FYE: December 31 |
| Web: www.sas.com | | |

Don't even think about sassing SAS Institute's data crunching abilities. The world's largest privately held software specialist offers statistical analysis system (SAS) software, which lets users extract, manage, and analyze large volumes of data for influencing business decisions. SAS (pronounced "sass") also sells software tailored to specific industries — banking, manufacturing, and government — to ease such tasks as financial reporting and credit analysis. The company, which is mulling going public, leads the industry in employee retention (perks include on-site day care, putting greens, and meditation rooms). SAS is owned by co-founders James Goodnight (CEO, 67%) and John Sall (EVP, 33%).

**KEY COMPETITORS**
Cognos
Hyperion
Information Builders

See pages 430–431 for a full profile of this company.

## SAVE MART SUPERMARKETS

1800 Standiford Ave.
Modesto, CA 95350
Phone: 209-577-1600
Fax: 209-577-3857

CEO: Robert M. Piccinini
CFO: Ron Riesenbeck
HR: Mike Silveira
Type: Private

2001 Sales: $1,524.0 million
1-Yr. Sales Change: 3.8%
Employees: 7,200
FYE: March 31

Save Mart Supermarkets is one of the big wheels in the California grocery business. A sponsor of the NASCAR Dodge/Save Mart 350, the company has about 100 grocery stores in northern and central California. Its supermarkets and warehouse stores operate under the S-Mart, Save Mart Foods, and Food Maxx banners. The chain has been trying out different formats, including an upscale prototype with its own coffeehouse and expanded offerings of ethnic and organic foods and its popular private-label salad mix line, Fresh Favorites. Save Mart also owns distributor SMART Refrigerated Transport. CEO Bob Piccinini owns most of Save Mart, which was founded in 1952 by his father, Mike Piccinini, and uncle, Nick Tocco.

**KEY COMPETITORS**
Fred Meyer
Raley's
Safeway

## S.C. JOHNSON & SON, INC.

1525 Howe St.
Racine, WI 53403
Phone: 262-260-2000
Fax: 262-260-6004
Web: www.scjohnson.com

CEO: William D. Perez
CFO: W. Lee McCollum
HR: Gayle P. Kosterman
Type: Private

2001 Sales: $4,500.0 million
1-Yr. Sales Change: 7.1%
Employees: 9,500
FYE: June 30

S.C. Johnson & Son helped consumers move from the flyswatter to the spray can. The company is one of the world's largest makers of consumer chemical products. These include Drano-brand drain cleaner, Glade air freshener, Johnson floor wax, OFF! insect repellent, Pledge furniture polish, Windex window cleaner, and Ziploc plastic bags. The first to sell a water-based insecticide (Raid in 1956), the company operates in nearly 70 countries. The founder's great-grandson, chairman emeritus Samuel Johnson, and his immediate family own about 60% of S.C. Johnson; descendants of the founder's daughter own about 40%. The company has sold most of its personal care line and spun off its commercial products unit.

**KEY COMPETITORS**
Clorox
Procter & Gamble
Unilever

 See pages 432–433 for a full profile of this company.

## SC JOHNSON COMMERCIAL MARKETS, INC.

8310 16th St.
Sturtevant, WI 53177
Phone: 262-631-4001
Fax: 262-260-4282
Web: www.scjprofessional.com

CEO: Samuel Curtis "Curt" Johnson
CFO: Mike Bailey
HR: Jody Krueger
Type: Private

2001 Sales: $1,300.0 million
1-Yr. Sales Change: 0.0%
Employees: 3,600
FYE: June 30

Think of SC Johnson Commercial Markets as the industrial-strength version of S.C. Johnson & Son. Split off from the well-known private company in 1999, SC Johnson Commercial Markets consists of two main divisions: Johnson Wax Professional and Johnson Polymer. Johnson Wax Professional provides commercial hygiene, appearance, pest control, and food sanitation products and services to retailers, building service contractors, hospitality firms, and food service operators. Johnson Polymer produces acrylic polymers and resins used in printing, packaging, coatings, and adhesives. SC Johnson Commercial Markets has operations throughout the US and in more than 50 other countries. The Johnson family controls the company.

**KEY COMPETITORS**
Ecolab
Rentokil Initial
Unilever

## SCHNEIDER NATIONAL, INC.

| | | |
|---|---|---|
| 3101 S. Packerland Dr. | CEO: Donald J. Schneider | 2000 Sales: $3,089.0 million |
| Green Bay, WI 54306 | CFO: Tom Gannon | 1-Yr. Sales Change: 3.0% |
| Phone: 920-592-2000 | HR: Tim Fliss | Employees: 18,775 |
| Fax: 920-592-3063 | Type: Private | FYE: December 31 |
| Web: www.schneider.com | | |

Schneider National is the Big Daddy of trucking firms. With its signature bright-orange fleet of 14,000 trucks and more than 40,000 trailers, the company is the largest truckload carrier in the US. Known for using the latest technologies, the company links all its trucks by satellite to enhance scheduling and loading efficiency. Its Schneider Logistics division provides supply chain analysis that allows its US, Canadian, Mexican, and European clients to ship products more efficiently. Schneider National also provides expedited services for time-sensitive and high-security goods. Donald Schneider, whose father founded the company, owns and runs Schneider National.

**KEY COMPETITORS**
J. B. Hunt
Swift Transportation
Werner

 See pages 434–435 for a full profile of this company.


## SCHNUCK MARKETS, INC.

| | | |
|---|---|---|
| 11420 Lackland Rd. | CEO: Craig D. Schnuck | 2001 Sales: $1,969.0 million |
| St. Louis, MO 63146 | CFO: Todd R. Schnuck | 1-Yr. Sales Change: (6.2%) |
| Phone: 314-994-9900 | HR: William Jones | Employees: 16,000 |
| Fax: 314-994-4465 | Type: Private | FYE: October 31 |
| Web: www.schnucks.com | | |

If you'll meet me in St. Louis, chances are there'll be a Schnuck Market in sight. The region's largest (and the nation's 35th-largest) food chain, Schnuck Markets operates more than 95 stores, mostly in the St. Louis area, but also in other parts of Missouri and in Illinois and Indiana. All stores offer a full line of groceries, and most have pharmacies, video rental outlets, and florist shops. Although most stores operate under the Schnuck banner, the company also runs four Logli supermarkets in Illinois. Schnuck Markets also allows shoppers to purchase groceries via the Internet. Founded in 1939, the company is owned by the Schnuck family.

**KEY COMPETITORS**
Dierbergs Markets
Kroger
SUPERVALU


## SCHREIBER FOODS, INC.

| | | |
|---|---|---|
| 425 Pine St. | CEO: Larry Ferguson | 2000 Est. Sales: $1,300.0 mil. |
| Green Bay, WI 54301 | CFO: Brian Liddy | 1-Yr. Sales Change: 12.1% |
| Phone: 920-437-7601 | HR: Jeff Ottum | Employees: 3,000 |
| Fax: 920-437-1617 | Type: Private | FYE: September 30 |
| Web: www.sficorp.com | | |

If you order cheese on that burger, you might well get a taste of Schreiber Foods. The cheese processor is a major supplier of the cheese used on hamburgers by US fast-food restaurants. Schreiber also supplies process, natural, and substitute cheese to grocery stores, delis, schools, distributors, and food manufacturers. Its brands include American Heritage, Cache Valley, Cooper, and Clearfield. Subsidiary Green Bay Machinery makes equipment for slicing and wrapping cheese, and Schreiber's Arden International Kitchens unit makes frozen entrees. Schreiber International exports cheese worldwide. Founded in 1945, Schreiber opted in 1999 to transfer its ownership into an employee stock ownership plan.

**KEY COMPETITORS**
Dairy Farmers of America
Great Lakes Cheese
Kraft Foods

## SCHWAN'S SALES ENTERPRISES, INC.

115 W. College Dr.
Marshall, MN 56258
Phone: 507-532-3274
Fax: 507-537-8226
Web: www.schwans.com

CEO: M. Lenny Pippin
CFO: Don Miller
HR: Dave Paskach
Type: Private

2000 Est. Sales: $3,100.0 mil.
1-Yr. Sales Change: (7.5%)
Employees: 6,000
FYE: December 31

Frozen pizza is the flashy part of Schwan's Sales Enterprises. With pizza brands such as Tony's, Red Baron, and Freschetta, the company is the #2 frozen pizza maker in the US, behind Kraft Foods. Schwan's is also a top supplier to the institutional frozen pizza market and has operations in Europe. But pizza isn't the only slice in the company's revenue — its core business is a fleet of home-delivery trucks. Schwan's delivers casseroles, ice cream, and more than 300 other frozen foods to homes in the continental US. Schwan's has sold its Lyon Financial Services subsidiary. The family of late founder Marvin Schwan owns the company.

**KEY COMPETITORS**
Kraft Foods
SYSCO

See pages 436–437 for a full profile of this company.


## SCIENCE APPLICATIONS INTERNATIONAL CORPORATION

10260 Campus Point Dr.
San Diego, CA 92121
Phone: 858-546-6000
Fax: 858-546-6800
Web: www.saic.com

CEO: J. Robert Beyster
CFO: Thomas E. Darcy
HR: Bernard Theull
Type: Private

2001 Sales: $5,895.7 million
1-Yr. Sales Change: 6.6%
Employees: 41,500
FYE: January 31

It definitely pays to have a rich Big Brother or an Uncle Sam with deep pockets. Science Applications International Corporation (SAIC) derives about 55% of its sales from systems integration, R&D, and other services to the US government. SAIC has diversified into the commercial sector by providing services such as implementing plant management software for oil companies, installing and integrating telecommunications networks, and automating health care systems for HMOs. Its Telcordia Technologies subsidiary (formerly the research arm of the Baby Bells) supplies a variety of software and services to telecoms. Employees own about 80% of SAIC, which is the nation's largest employee-owned research and engineering company.

**KEY COMPETITORS**
EDS
IBM
Titan

See pages 438–439 for a full profile of this company.


## THE SCOULAR COMPANY

2027 Dodge St.
Omaha, NE 68102
Phone: 402-342-3500
Fax: 402-342-5568
Web: www.scoular.com

CEO: Randal L. Linville
CFO: John M. Heck
HR: Yvonne Lutz
Type: Private

2001 Sales: $2,098.0 million
1-Yr. Sales Change: 4.1%
Employees: 400
FYE: May 31

The people who grow the wheat aren't usually the ones who grind it. The Scoular Company handles the process that goes on between the two groups. The company is best known for grain marketing, trading more than 400 million bushels of grain and more than 1 million tons of grain byproducts (used for animal feed) annually throughout North America. Other divisions offer fish meal products for animal and aquaculture feeds, ingredients for food manufacturing, truck freight brokering, and livestock marketing. Founded in 1892 to run grain elevators, it still operates 11 elevators in Nebraska and South Dakota. The employee-owned company has facilities throughout the US, Mexico, and Canada.

**KEY COMPETITORS**
ADM
Cargill
Cenex Harvest States

## SEAGATE TECHNOLOGY, INC.

| | | |
|---|---|---|
| 920 Disc Dr. | CEO: Stephen J. Luczo | 2000 Sales: $6,448.0 million |
| Scotts Valley, CA 95067 | CFO: Charles C. Pope | 1-Yr. Sales Change: (5.2%) |
| Phone: 831-438-6550 | HR: — | Employees: 60,000 |
| Fax: 831-438-7205 | Type: Private | FYE: June 30 |
| Web: www.seagate.com | | |

Seagate Technology knows that if you want to survive in the storage market, you'd better have drive. The company is a leading independent maker of storage drives for computers. It makes disk and tape drives used in systems ranging from personal computers to high-end servers. Seagate, which sells primarily to manufacturers, also develops business intelligence software through its Crystal Decisions subsidiary and offers network storage products through its XIOtech subsidiary. It has used personnel cuts and facility consolidation to battle an industry slump brought on by falling PC prices. The company was taken private in a deal led by Silver Lake Partners and Texas Pacific Group in 2000.

**KEY COMPETITORS**
IBM
Maxtor
Western Digital

 See pages 440–441 for a full profile of this company.


## SEALY CORPORATION

| | | |
|---|---|---|
| Sealy Drive | CEO: Ronald L. Jones | 2000 Sales: $1,101.5 million |
| Trinity, NC 27370 | CFO: E. Lee Wyatt | 1-Yr. Sales Change: 11.8% |
| Phone: 336-861-3500 | HR: Jeffrey C. Claypool | Employees: 6,077 |
| Fax: 336-861-3501 | Type: Private | FYE: November 30 |
| Web: www.sealy.com | | |

Sealy can rest assured that it's North America's #1 bedding maker. The company makes mattresses and box springs and sells them at more than 7,000 stores; brands include Sealy, Barrett, and Stearns & Foster. Customers include sleep shops, furniture and department stores, warehouse clubs, and mass merchandisers as well as the hospitality industry. Sealy also licenses its name to makers of sofas, pillows, and other items. The US is Sealy's main market, but it has licensees and sales operations around the world. Sealy runs more than 30 factories in Argentina, Brazil, Canada, Mexico, Puerto Rico, and the US. Boston-based investment firm Bain Capital, along with company management, owns Sealy.

**KEY COMPETITORS**
Serta
Simmons
Spring Air

See pages 442–443 for a full profile of this company.


## SECURITY BENEFIT GROUP, INC.

| | | |
|---|---|---|
| 700 SW Harrison St. | CEO: Howard R. Fricke | 2000 Sales: $1,500.0 million |
| Topeka, KS 66636 | CFO: Donald Schepker | 1-Yr. Sales Change: (6.3%) |
| Phone: 785-431-3000 | HR: Craig Anderson | Employees: — |
| Fax: 785-431-5177 | Type: Private | FYE: December 31 |
| Web: www.securitybenefit.com | | |

Security Benefit Group is the largest life insurer in the Jayhawk State. The group operates through Security Benefit Life Insurance Company, which offers variable life insurance, annuities, mutual funds, and asset management services through about 16,500 sales representatives. Security Benefit is highlighting its asset management skills by opening several new funds. After more than 100 years as a mutual company, the company has made plans to convert to stock ownership but has not followed through on those plans. Security Benefit's roots go back to the Knights and Ladies of Security, a benefit society begun in 1892 in Topeka, Kansas.

**KEY COMPETITORS**
Aetna
American United Life
John Hancock Financial
 Services

## SEMATECH, INC.

2706 Montopolis Dr.
Austin, TX 78741
Phone: 512-356-3500
Fax: 512-356-3086
Web: www.sematech.org

CEO: Bob Helms
CFO: Stuart Clark
HR: Linda Cline
Type: Consortium

Sales: —
1-Yr. Sales Change: —
Employees: —
FYE: December 31

SEMATECH (from "semiconductor manufacturing technology") is more than just semi-technical. The not-for-profit research consortium, which is funded by members' dues, pursues advances in design, lithography, and other facets of production to improve chip manufacturing techniques. Employees from SEMATECH's members — Agere, Advanced Micro Devices, Conexant, Hewlett-Packard, Hynix, IBM, Infineon, Intel, Motorola, Philips, STMicroelectronics, Taiwan Semiconductor, and Texas Instruments — carry out research at the group's Texas site. The consortium, widely credited with restoring the US to global chip dominance, has lost some of its original US members in recent years as it has expanded internationally.

**KEY COMPETITORS**
MCC
SAIC
SRI International

 **See pages 444–445 for a full profile of this company.**

## SENTARA HEALTHCARE

6015 Poplar Hall Dr.
Norfolk, VA 23502
Phone: 757-455-7000
Fax: 757-455-7964
Web: www.sentara.com

CEO: David L. Bernd
CFO: Richard D. Hill
HR: John Gordon
Type: Not-for-profit

Sales: —
1-Yr. Sales Change: —
Employees: 14,000
FYE: April 30

Health care's a beach for Sentara Healthcare. The not-for-profit organization provides medical services for about 2 million residents of southeastern Virginia and northeastern North Carolina. The system includes hospitals, assisted-living centers, more than 30 primary care offices, an integrated outpatient health care campus, and a couple of fitness centers. Sentara's Optima Health Plan offers HMO coverage. The organization also provides home health services, ground and air medical transport, community health education programs, and mobile diagnostic vans.

**KEY COMPETITORS**
Bon Secours Health
Carilion Health System
Novant Health

## SENTRY INSURANCE, A MUTUAL COMPANY

1800 North Point Dr.
Stevens Point, WI 54481
Phone: 715-346-6000
Fax: 715-346-7516
Web: www.sentry-insurance.com

CEO: Dale R. Schuh
CFO: William J. Lohr
HR: Greg Mox
Type: Mutual company

2000 Sales: $1,716.0 million
1-Yr. Sales Change: 23.0%
Employees: 4,200
FYE: December 31

Vigilant for its policyholders, Sentry Insurance (of the famous Minuteman statue logo) offers a variety of insurance coverage, including life, group health, auto, and property/casualty insurance. The mutual company (owned by its policyholders) offers coverage through several subsidiaries. Sentry also provides specialized insurance to small and large businesses, including manufacturers and retailers. The company's Sentry Equity Services offers mutual fund services through its Sentry Fund. Sentry was founded in 1904 to provide insurance to members of the Wisconsin Retail Hardware Association.

**KEY COMPETITORS**
Allstate
Prudential
State Farm

## SERTA, INC.

| | | |
|---|---|---|
| 325 Spring Lake Dr. | CEO: Edward F. Lilly | 2000 Sales: $858.0 million |
| Itasca, IL 60143 | CFO: — | 1-Yr. Sales Change: 2.9% |
| Phone: 630-285-9350 | HR: — | Employees: 4,800 |
| Fax: 630-285-9330 | Type: Private | FYE: December 31 |
| Web: www.serta.com | | |

Serta, the #2 mattress manufacturer in the world (behind Sealy), hopes to keep the competition awake at night. It is the nation's #1 mattress supplier to hotels and motels; its Perfect Sleeper mattress line, which it has been selling since the 1930s, is the best-selling premium mattress in the US. Serta's top-of-the-line mattress collection is sold under the Perfect Night name. Founded in 1931 by 13 mattress makers who licensed the Serta name, the company is now owned by eight independent licensees; each licensee has separate marketing, manufacturing, and sales operations. The group has 27 factories in the US, four in Canada, and another 27 throughout Asia, Europe, the Middle East, and South America.

**KEY COMPETITORS**
Sealy
Simmons
Spring Air


## SERVICES GROUP OF AMERICA

| | | |
|---|---|---|
| 4025 Delridge Way SW, Ste. 500 | CEO: Thomas J. Stewart | 2001 Sales: $1,480.0 million |
| Seattle, WA 98106 | CFO: Peter Smith | 1-Yr. Sales Change: 23.1% |
| Phone: 206-933-5225 | HR: Lanett Draper | Employees: 3,300 |
| Fax: 206-933-5247 | Type: Private | FYE: January 31 |
| Web: www.fsafood.com | | |

Though it bears a rather vague company name, Services Group of America's operations are pretty specific. Its subsidiary, Food Services of America, is a food service distributor, supplying hospitals, schools, and restaurants in 15 western and midwestern states. Services Group also runs Development Services of America, a real estate developer, and Travel Services of America. The company sold Eagle Insurance Group to focus on food services. After being convicted of violating US election laws in 1998, owner and CEO Thomas Stewart paid $5 million in fines and was sentenced to home detention and community service. The company, formed in 1985, bought fast-food distributor McCabe's Quality Foods in January 2001.

**KEY COMPETITORS**
Alliant Exchange
SYSCO
U.S. Foodservice


## THE SF HOLDINGS GROUP, INC.

| | | |
|---|---|---|
| 373 Park Ave. S. | CEO: Dennis Mehiel | 2001 Sales: $1,316.7 million |
| New York, NY 10016 | CFO: Hans H. Heinsen | 1-Yr. Sales Change: 3.1% |
| Phone: 212-779-7448 | HR: Jeffery Seidman | Employees: 8,234 |
| Fax: 212-779-9562 | Type: Private | FYE: September 30 |

The words "Can I get that to go?" are like money in the bank for the SF Holdings Group. Through subsidiaries the company produces disposable paper and plastic cups, plates, cutlery, and food packaging sold under brand names such as Centerpiece, Hoffmaster, Lily, Preference, and Sweetheart. Its Sweetheart Cup subsidiary accounts for almost 75% of sales and primarily sells its wares to institutional food service customers such as restaurant chains, schools, theaters, and airlines. The Fonda Group, another subsidiary, also sells to institutional food service customers and to consumer markets, as well as through supermarkets and warehouse clubs. Chairman and CEO Dennis Mehiel controls SF Holdings.

**KEY COMPETITORS**
Dart Container
Huhtamäki
Solo Cup

## SHAMROCK FOODS COMPANY

2228 N. Black Canyon Hwy.
Phoenix, AZ 85009
Phone: 602-272-6721
Fax: 602-233-2791
Web: www.shamrockfoods.com

CEO: Norman McClelland
CFO: Philip Giltner
HR: Charlie Roberts
Type: Private

2001 Sales: $1,100.0 million
1-Yr. Sales Change: (6.5%)
Employees: 2,196
FYE: September 30

Milk does a business good, too. Thanks to that udder delight, Shamrock Foods has fortified itself from a tiny mom-and-pop dairy into a food processor and distributor serving supermarkets, convenience stores, restaurants, and institutional clients in Arizona, California, Colorado, Nevada, New Mexico, and Texas. Most of the company's business is dedicated to processing dairy products, including milk, cottage cheese, sour cream, and eggnog. Production of the company's ice cream is outsourced. Its products are sold under the Shamrock Farms and Sunland brands, as well as under private labels. Started in 1922, Shamrock Foods is owned and run by the founding McClelland family.

**KEY COMPETITORS**
Dairy Farmers of America
Dean Foods
Land O'Lakes

## SHEETZ, INC.

5700 Sixth Ave.
Altoona, PA 16602
Phone: 814-946-3611
Fax: 814-946-4375
Web: www.sheetz.com

CEO: Stanton R. Sheetz
CFO: Joseph S. Sheetz
HR: Phil Freeman
Type: Private

2001 Est. Sales: $1,900.0 mil.
1-Yr. Sales Change: 17.3%
Employees: 7,500
FYE: September 30

You might say Sheetz is to the convenience store business what Wal-Mart is to discount shopping. Noted for being exceptionally large (stores average 4,200 sq. ft., nearly twice the size of the average 7-Eleven), Sheetz stores sell groceries, fountain drinks, baked goods, and made-to-order sandwiches and salads, as well as discount gas and cigarettes. The company operates about 250 combination convenience stores and gas stations, mostly in small and mid-sized towns in Pennsylvania, but also in towns throughout Maryland, Ohio, Virginia, and West Virginia. Founded in 1952 by Bob Sheetz, the company is owned and run by the Sheetz family.

**KEY COMPETITORS**
7-Eleven
Uni-Marts
Wawa

## SIERRA PACIFIC INDUSTRIES

19794 Riverside Ave.
Anderson, CA 96007
Phone: 530-378-8000
Fax: 530-378-8109
Web: www.spi-ind.com

CEO: A.A. "Red" Emmerson
CFO: Mark Emmerson
HR: Ed Bond
Type: Private

2000 Est. Sales: $1,500.0 mil.
1-Yr. Sales Change: 3.4%
Employees: 3,600
FYE: December 31

Sierra Pacific Industries isn't your run-of-the-mill company. One of the largest US landowners, it manufactures millwork products and lumber in Northern California. Subsidiary Sierra Pacific Windows makes aluminum clad and wood patio doors and specialty windows. Protests in the 1980s against logging on public land prompted the company to begin buying its own forested areas; it now owns 1.5 million acres of California timberlands. The company, however, has announced plans to sell 30,000 to 50,000 acres of forestland to the US Forest Service for preservation. Sierra Pacific traces its roots to a company started in the late 1920s by R. H. "Curly" Emmerson, father of CEO Red Emmerson. The Emmerson family owns Sierra Pacific.

**KEY COMPETITORS**
Georgia-Pacific Group
Louisiana-Pacific
Weyerhaeuser

## SINCLAIR OIL CORPORATION

| | | |
|---|---|---|
| 550 E. South Temple | CEO: Robert E. Holding | 2000 Est. Sales: $1,900.0 mil. |
| Salt Lake City, UT 84102 | CFO: Charles Barlow | 1-Yr. Sales Change: 58.3% |
| Phone: 801-524-2700 | HR: Lowell Hardy | Employees: 6,500 |
| Fax: 801-526-3000 | Type: Private | FYE: December 31 |
| Web: www.sinclairoil.com | | |

Way out west, where fossils are found, brontosaur signs litter the ground. They belong to Sinclair Oil's more than 2,600 service stations and convenience stores in 22 western and midwestern US states. The company also operates three oil refineries, two pipelines (one jointly owned with Conoco), exploration operations, and a trucking fleet, all in the western half of the US. It owns the Grand America Hotel, the Little America hotel chain, and two ski resorts (Sun Valley in Idaho and Snowbasin in Utah). Snowbasin will be used in the 2002 Winter Olympics. The man behind all of this is Earl Holding, whose storied company, founded in 1916 by Harry Sinclair, was a central figure in the infamous Teapot Dome scandal.

**KEY COMPETITORS**
Exxon Mobil
Vail Resorts
Valero

## SINGER N.V.

| | | |
|---|---|---|
| 915 Broadway, 18th Fl. | CEO: Stephen H. Goodman | 1998 Sales: $1,263.9 million |
| New York, NY 10010 | CFO: — | 1-Yr. Sales Change: 19.4% |
| Phone: 917-534-5398 | HR: Terance Brogan | Employees: 18,000 |
| Fax: — | Type: Private | FYE: December 31 |
| Web: www.singerco.com | | |

Singer's name is on the lips of tailors throughout the world. Singer is the #1 global maker of consumer sewing machines. Singer's machines range from basic $99 models to computerized units priced at $4,500. Its zigzag sewing machine is its mainstay consumer product. Its products are sold in 150 countries through about 1,000 Singer retail outlets, more than 33,000 independent dealers and mass merchandisers, and a door-to-door sales force of 12,000. Singer emerged from Chapter 11 bankruptcy protection in September 2000 with creditors owning the company and a mandate to restructure operations and shed noncore businesses. Legally based in the Netherlands Antilles, the company's executive office is in New York City.

**KEY COMPETITORS**
Brother International
Electrolux AB
Hirsch

## SISTERS OF CHARITY OF LEAVENWORTH HEALTH SERVICES CORPORATION

| | | |
|---|---|---|
| Cantwell Hall, 4200 S. 4th St. | CEO: Bill Murray | 1999 Sales: $980.5 million |
| Leavenworth, KS 66048 | CFO: Mike Rowe | 1-Yr. Sales Change: 11.6% |
| Phone: 913-895-2800 | HR: Dennis "Mike" Groves | Employees: 10,000 |
| Fax: 913-895-2900 | Type: Not-for-profit | FYE: May 31 |
| Web: www.sclhsc.org | | |

In 1857 a group of Catholic sisters arrived in Kansas, then still a territory, and began teaching and tending the sick. A decade later they incorporated, establishing a foundation for what would eventually be the Sisters of Charity of Leavenworth Health Services. The not-for-profit health care organization operates about a dozen hospitals, clinics, and medical centers in California, Colorado, Kansas, and Montana. Its facilities provide health services to low-income and uninsured people. The organization added to its network with the purchase of Bethany Medical Center in Kansas City, Kansas, from hospital giant HCA; it then had to close the center due to financial woes.

**KEY COMPETITORS**
Health Midwest
Province Healthcare
Tenet Healthcare

## SISTERS OF MERCY HEALTH SYSTEM-ST. LOUIS

2039 N. Geyer Rd.
St. Louis, MO 63131
Phone: 314-965-6100
Fax: 314-957-0466
Web: www.smhs.com

CEO: Ronald B. Ashworth
CFO: James Jaacks
HR: Stephen Isenhower
Type: Not-for-profit

1999 Sales: $2,298.1 million
1-Yr. Sales Change: 5.9%
Employees: 26,000
FYE: June 30

Not to be confused with the goth rock band of the same name, Sisters of Mercy was founded by the Sisters of Mercy of the St. Louis Regional Community in 1986 to provide a range of health care and social services through its network of facilities in Arkansas, Illinois, Kansas, Louisiana, Mississippi, Missouri, Oklahoma, and Texas. Through nine regional units, the system runs about 20 acute-care hospitals; it also operates a psychiatric hospital, long-term care facilities, physician practices, and outpatient facilities. For-profit subsidiary Mercy Health Plans offers managed care health plans in Arkansas, Kansas, Missouri, and Texas. Sisters of Mercy also runs several charitable foundations.

**KEY COMPETITORS**
BJC Health
HCA
Tenet Healthcare


## SKADDEN, ARPS, SLATE, MEAGHER & FLOM LLP

4 Times Square
New York, NY 10036
Phone: 212-735-3000
Fax: 212-735-2000
Web: www.skadden.com

CEO: Robert C. Sheehan
CFO: Karl Duchek
HR: Laurel Henschel
Type: Partnership

2000 Sales: $1,154.0 million
1-Yr. Sales Change: 12.6%
Employees: 4,235
FYE: December 31

Have you heard about the law firm that sued the business information publisher for a profile that opened with a wickedly clever lawyer joke? Neither have we, and we'd like to keep it that way. Skadden, Arps, Slate, Meagher & Flom, the largest US law firm and one of the largest in the world, employs more than 1,600 attorneys in 22 offices around the world. Founded in 1948, the firm offers counsel for corporate dealings, litigation, and international concerns. Best known for its mergers and acquisitions practice, Skadden, Arps also has a strong presence in securities and bankruptcy.

**KEY COMPETITORS**
Baker & McKenzie
Clifford Chance
Wachtell, Lipton

See pages 446–447 for a full profile of this company.


## SKIDMORE OWINGS & MERRILL LLP

14 Wall St.
New York, NY 10005
Phone: 212-298-9300
Fax: 212-298-9500
Web: www.som.com

CEO: H. Guy Leibler
CFO: Joseph Dailey
HR: Barbara Schiola
Type: Partnership

2000 Est. Sales: $100.0 mil.
1-Yr. Sales Change: 0.0%
Employees: 900
FYE: September 30

Skidmore Owings & Merrill (SOM) prefers a skyline view. Some of the world's tallest buildings have been designed by the company, which ranks among the world's leading international architecture and engineering firms. The company has earned its fame with innovative modernist designs and such high-profile projects as the John Hancock Center and Sears Tower. It also provides graphics, interior design, and urban design and planning services. In recent years SOM has also pursued building renovations, other institutional projects (including airport additions and convention centers), and foreign commissions, particularly in Asia. The firm has offices in five major US cities, Hong Kong, and London.

**KEY COMPETITORS**
AECOM
Hellmuth, Obata + Kassabaum
Parsons Brinckerhoff

See pages 448–449 for a full profile of this company.

## SMITHSONIAN INSTITUTION

| | | |
|---|---|---|
| 1000 Jefferson Dr. SW | CEO: Lawrence Small | 1999 Sales: $869.6 million |
| Washington, DC 20560 | CFO: Rick R. Johnson | 1-Yr. Sales Change: 12.3% |
| Phone: 202-357-2700 | HR: Carolyn E. Jones | Employees: 6,400 |
| Fax: 202-786-2377 | Type: Not-for-profit | FYE: September 30 |
| Web: www.si.edu | | |

Your attic may be full of junk, but the junk in the nation's attic (better known as the Smithsonian Institution) is a lot more valuable. The world's largest museum, the Smithsonian houses more than 140 million pieces in 16 museums and galleries. More than 40 million people every year come view its exhibits on art, music, TV and film, science, history, and other subjects. Admission to its museums, most of which are located on the National Mall in Washington, DC (two are in New York City), is usually free. The Smithsonian also operates the National Zoo and a handful of research facilities. The federal government supplies nearly 50% of its operating revenue.

 See pages 450–451 for a full profile of this company.

## SOAVE ENTERPRISES L.L.C.

| | | |
|---|---|---|
| 3400 E. Lafayette St. | CEO: Anthony Soave | 2000 Sales: $878.0 million |
| Detroit, MI 48207 | CFO: Michael L. Piesko | 1-Yr. Sales Change: 8.8% |
| Phone: 313-567-7000 | HR: Marcia Moss | Employees: 1,835 |
| Fax: 313-567-0966 | Type: Private | FYE: December 31 |
| Web: www.soaveenterprises.com | | |

Soave Enterprises is suave enough to manage multiple lines of business. Most of Soave's subsidiaries, including Ferrous Processing & Trading, process steel and scrap metal. Other company endeavors include construction, transportation, real estate, beer distribution (Michigan), a hydroponic tomato farm, and auto dealerships (including Ford, Honda, and Porsche). Soave's Commuter Express provides shuttle services for the Detroit Metropolitan Airport and other Detroit-area businesses. The company has also formed joint venture Gemini Recycling Group (with David J. Joseph Co.) to process, transport, and sell scrap metal. The bulk of Soave's operations are in Michigan. Founder Anthony Soave owns the company.

**KEY COMPETITORS**
David J. Joseph
Steel Technologies
Tang Industries

## SOLO CUP COMPANY

| | | |
|---|---|---|
| 1700 Old Deerfield Rd. | CEO: Robert L. Hulseman | 2000 Sales: $833.0 million |
| Highland Park, IL 60035 | CFO: Ronald L. Whaley | 1-Yr. Sales Change: — |
| Phone: 847-831-4800 | HR: Michelle Root | Employees: 4,700 |
| Fax: 847-831-5849 | Type: Private | FYE: December 31 |
| Web: www.solocup.com | | |

Solo Cup's goodies are best enjoyed in the company of others. A leader in the disposable product market, the company manufactures plastic cups, plates, bowls, storage containers, cutlery, and drinking straws. In addition to mass-market retailers, Solo Cup's items are sold to end users, including restaurants, schools, hospitals, and coffee shops. The company has nearly 15 manufacturing facilities and about a dozen warehouses. Solo or at parties, the firm's goods are sold, soiled, and thrown out around the world. Leo J. Hulseman founded the Paper Container Manufacturing Company in 1936; it became Solo Cup in 1946, named for the cone-shaped paper cup that made it famous. His descendants own and operate the company.

**KEY COMPETITORS**
Dart Container
Huhtamäki
sf holdings

## SOUTH CAROLINA PUBLIC SERVICE AUTHORITY

1 Riverwood Dr.
Moncks Corner, SC 29461
Phone: 843-761-8000
Fax: 843-761-7060
Web: www.santeecooper.com

CEO: John H. Tiencken Jr.
CFO: Emily S. Brown
HR: Ronald H. Holmes
Type: Government-owned

2000 Sales: $862.4 million
1-Yr. Sales Change: 5.9%
Employees: 1,625
FYE: December 31

Someone's got to turn on those bright lights in the big city — and in the small cities, too. South Carolina Public Service Authority, known as Santee Cooper, provides electricity to 15 cooperatives and two municipalities that serve about 475,000 customers in South Carolina. It directly retails electricity to nearly 130,000 additional customers. One of the largest US state-owned utilities, Santee Cooper operates in all 46 counties in South Carolina and owns or has interests in hydroelectric, coal-fired, nuclear, and combustion turbine generating stations. The Santee Cooper Regional Water System treats and distributes water from Lake Moultrie for the Lake Moultrie Water Agency, which serves about 90,000 consumers.

**KEY COMPETITORS**
MEAG Power
SCANA
TVA

## SOUTHERN STATES COOPERATIVE, INCORPORATED

6606 W. Broad St.
Richmond, VA 23260
Phone: 804-281-1000
Fax: 804-281-1413
Web: www.southernstates-coop.com

CEO: Wayne A. Boutwell
CFO: Jonathan A. Hawkins
HR: Richard G. Sherman
Type: Cooperative

2001 Sales: $1,739.0 million
1-Yr. Sales Change: 12.4%
Employees: 5,700
FYE: June 30

Founded in 1923 to provide affordable, high-quality seed to Virginia farmers, Southern States Cooperative serves about 321,000 members, mainly in midwestern and southern states. The co-op offers its farmer-owners feed and fertilizer manufacturing, seed processing, grain marketing, and petroleum and propane services, as well as wholesale farm supplies. Its Southern States and GardenSouth stores (about 740 outlets) sell farm supplies, garden products, and fuel. Other services include GrowMaster Crop Services, sales financing, and an aquaculture program. Southern States Cooperative merged with Michigan Livestock Exchange in 1998 and purchased Agway Inc.'s consumer wholesale dealer business.

**KEY COMPETITORS**
ADM
Cenex Harvest States
Scoular

## SOUTHERN WINE & SPIRITS OF AMERICA, INC.

1600 NW 163rd St.
Miami, FL 33169
Phone: 305-625-4171
Fax: 305-625-4720
Web: www.southernwineandspirits.com

CEO: Harvey Chaplin
CFO: Steven Becker
HR: Mark Krauss
Type: Private

2000 Sales: $3,500.0 million
1-Yr. Sales Change: 12.9%
Employees: —
FYE: December 31

Fueled by alcohol and nicotine, Southern Wine & Spirits of America delivers market dominance. The firm is the #1 US distributor of wine and spirits, serving nine states. In addition to importing and distributing wine and spirits, it distributes imported brews, such as Grolsch and Steinlager; cigars, such as Don Diego and Montecristo; and nonalcoholic beverages, including Clamato and Rose's Lime Juice. It is entering new markets through acquisitions. Southern Wine & Spirits lobbied and stopped mail-order companies from shipping wine to Florida. Chairman and CEO Harvey Chaplin and his secretive family own more than 50% of the company.

**KEY COMPETITORS**
National Distributing
Sunbelt Beverage
Young's Market

## SOUTHWIRE COMPANY

1 Southwire Dr.
Carrollton, GA 30119
Phone: 770-832-4242
Fax: 770-832-4929
Web: www.southwire.com

CEO: Stuart Thorn
CFO: J. Guyton Cochran Jr.
HR: Mike Wiggins
Type: Private

2000 Sales: $1,500.0 million
1-Yr. Sales Change: 15.4%
Employees: 3,000
FYE: December 31

Southwire hopes everyone's cable-ready. One of the world's largest cable and wire manufacturers, Southwire makes building wire and cable, utility cable products, industrial power cable, telecommunications cable, copper and aluminum rods, and cord products. The company also provides engineering and machining and fabrication services. Southwire is buying General Cable Corporation's building wire assets; that acquisition will make the company North America's largest producer of building wire. Founded in 1950 by Roy Richards Sr. (the chairman's father), Southwire is owned by the Richards family.

**KEY COMPETITORS**
AFC Cable
Phelps Dodge
Superior TeleCom

## SPITZER MANAGEMENT, INC.

150 E. Bridge St.
Elyria, OH 44035
Phone: 440-323-4671
Fax: 440-323-3623
Web: www.spitzer.com

CEO: Alan Spitzer
CFO: —
HR: —
Type: Private

2000 Est. Sales: $850.0 mil.
1-Yr. Sales Change: 0.0%
Employees: 1,700
FYE: December 31

Pick a car, any car. Spitzer Management, with more than 30 franchises in Ohio, Pennsylvania, and Florida, sells almost every kind of car from A to V (Acura, Buick, Cadillac, Chevy, Chrysler, Dodge, Ford, GMC, Jeep, Lincoln, Mazda, Mercury, Mitsubishi, Oldsmobile, Plymouth, Pontiac, Toyota, and Volkswagen). Spitzer dealerships sell both new and used cars and offer parts and service departments. The company also has interests in real estate, the hotel business, and marinas and manages a golf course. Owner and CEO Alan Spitzer's statewide (Ohio) campaign to legalize gambling failed, ruining plans to build a casino on company-owned land. However, he plans to build homes and condos on the site.

**KEY COMPETITORS**
AutoNation
Ricart Automotive

## SPRINGS INDUSTRIES, INC.

205 N. White St.
Fort Mill, SC 29715
Phone: 803-547-1500
Fax: 803-547-1636
Web: www.springs.com

CEO: Crandall Close Bowles
CFO: Kenneth E. Kutcher
HR: Gracie P. Coleman
Type: Private

2000 Sales: $2,275.1 million
1-Yr. Sales Change: 2.5%
Employees: 18,200
FYE: December 31

Watch out — Springs Industries wants to cozy up in your bedroom. The company makes sheets, pillows, shower curtains, bedspreads, towels, and bath rugs under the Springmaid and Wamsutta brands. Springs also makes infant apparel, fabrics, and window blinds and hardware (Bali, Graber brands). The company makes private-label items for Wal-Mart and Target, and licensed brands such as Disney and John Deere. Springs sells through department stores, mass retailers, catalogs, and outlet stores. The Close family, descendants of co-founder Leroy Springs (whose great-great-granddaughter Crandall Close Bowles is CEO), owns about 55% of the company. She joined with Heartland Industrial Partners to take Springs private.

**KEY COMPETITORS**
Dan River
Pillowtex
WestPoint Stevens

 See pages 452–453 for a full profile of this company.

## SRI INTERNATIONAL

| | | |
|---|---|---|
| 333 Ravenswood Ave. | CEO: Curtis R. Carlson | 2000 Sales: $164.0 million |
| Menlo Park, CA 94025 | CFO: Thomas Furst | 1-Yr. Sales Change: 2.5% |
| Phone: 650-859-2000 | HR: Jeanie Tooker | Employees: 1,400 |
| Fax: 650-326-5512 | Type: Not-for-profit | FYE: December 31 |
| Web: www.sri.com | | |

SRI International is a not-for-profit think tank that works on solutions to the problems of its corporate and government clients. Units ponder advances in biotechnology, chemicals and energy, computer science, electronics, and education and public policy — and ways to commercialize those advances. Among SRI's clients are Visa, the National Cancer Institute, and the US Department of Defense. Subsidiaries include SRI Consulting (management consulting) and Sarnoff Corp. (electronics and biomedical technologies). SRI, funded through royalties and other investments, has spun off more than 20 firms. The organization was the Stanford Research Institute before becoming fully independent of Stanford University in 1970.

**KEY COMPETITORS**
PAREXEL
Quintiles Transnational
SAIC

 **See pages 454–455 for a full profile of this company.**

## SRP

| | | |
|---|---|---|
| 1521 N. Project Dr. | CEO: William P. Schrader | 2001 Sales: $3,026.8 million |
| Tempe, AZ 85281 | CFO: Mark B. Bonsall | 1-Yr. Sales Change: 68.4% |
| Phone: 602-236-5900 | HR: L.J. U'Ren | Employees: 4,096 |
| Fax: 602-236-2170 | Type: Government-owned | FYE: April 30 |
| Web: www.srpnet.com | | |

One of the US's largest publicly owned utilities, SRP (Salt River Project) provides Phoenix with two types of current: electric and water. Electricity comes from the Salt River Project Agricultural Improvement and Power District, which is a political subdivision of the State of Arizona. The District has a generating capacity of 6,200-MW and distributes power to more than 750,000 customers; its subsidiary New West Energy markets excess electricity and provides related services. Water comes from the Salt River Valley Water Users' Association, a private firm that delivers about 1 million acre-feet of water to residents and agricultural irrigators; it also operates canals, reservoirs, and wells in its service area.

**KEY COMPETITORS**
American States Water
Pinnacle West
UniSource Energy

## SSM HEALTH CARE SYSTEM INC.

| | | |
|---|---|---|
| 477 N. Lindbergh Blvd. | CEO: Sister Mary J. Ryan | 2000 Sales: $1,458.8 million |
| St. Louis, MO 63141 | CFO: Elizabeth Alhand | 1-Yr. Sales Change: 10.4% |
| Phone: 314-994-7800 | HR: Steven Barney | Employees: 20,500 |
| Fax: 314-994-7900 | Type: Not-for-profit | FYE: December 31 |
| Web: www.ssmhc.com | | |

The health care mission of SSM Health Care System began with five nuns who fled religious persecution in Germany in 1872 only to arrive in St. Louis in the midst of a smallpox epidemic. They formed their first hospital there in 1877 and later became pioneers in bringing health care to the rural frontier, founding the Oklahoma Territory's first hospital in 1898. Today the not-for-profit, sponsored by the Franciscan Sisters of Mary, owns and operates some 20 acute care hospitals with more than 5,000 licensed beds. The company also operates nursing homes and rehabilitation clinics, and offers home health and hospice care. SSM's facilities are located in Illinois, Missouri, Oklahoma, and Wisconsin.

**KEY COMPETITORS**
BJC Health
HCA
Tenet Healthcare

## STANFORD UNIVERSITY

857 Serra St.
Stanford, CA 94305
Phone: 650-723-2300
Fax: 650-725-0247
Web: www.stanford.edu

CEO: John Hennessy
CFO: Mariann Byerwalter
HR: John Cammidge
Type: School

2000 Sales: $1,957.3 million
1-Yr. Sales Change: 11.9%
Employees: —
FYE: August 31

Prospectors panning for gold in higher education can strike it rich at Stanford University. The school is one of the premier institutions in the US, boasting respected programs in business, engineering, law, and medicine. Its campus is home to more than 14,000 students as well as 1,600 faculty members. Stanford is also a top research university, with a host of laboratories and research centers investigating topics in science, genetics, and the humanities. A private institution, Stanford supports its activities through a nearly $9 billion endowment, one of the largest in the US. The university was founded in 1885 by Leland Stanford Sr. and his wife, Jane, in memory of their son, Leland Jr.

 See pages 456–457 for a full profile of this company.


## STAPLE COTTON COOPERATIVE ASSOCIATION

214 W. Market St.
Greenwood, MS 38935
Phone: 662-453-6231
Fax: 662-453-6274
Web: www.staplcotn.com

CEO: Woods E. Eastland
CFO: Mack L. Alford
HR: Eugene A. Stansel Jr.
Type: Cooperative

2000 Sales: $1,041.0 million
1-Yr. Sales Change: 22.5%
Employees: 230
FYE: August 31

Wear underwear? Chances are Staplcotn had a hand in it. Staple Cotton Cooperative Association, best known for its Staplcotn cotton marketing arm, serves nearly 12,000 member-owners in 48 states. Founded in 1921 by Mississippi cotton producer Oscar Bledsoe and 10 Delta growers, it sells about 3 million bales of cotton annually. Most of the yield is sold to the US textile industry to make men's knit underwear, T-shirts, sheets, towels, and denim. Customers include Fruit of the Loom and Levi Strauss & Co. The co-op's Stapldiscount subsidiary offers low-interest loans for equipment, buildings, and land. Staplcotn is represented worldwide by Amcot, which also represents three other US cotton co-ops.

**KEY COMPETITORS**
Calcot
Cargill
Plains Cotton


## STATE FARM INSURANCE COMPANIES

1 State Farm Plaza
Bloomington, IL 61710
Phone: 309-766-2311
Fax: 309-766-3621
Web: www.statefarm.com

CEO: Edward B. Rust Jr.
CFO: Roger S. Joslin
HR: Arlene Hogan
Type: Mutual company

2000 Sales: $47,863.1 million
1-Yr. Sales Change: 7.1%
Employees: 79,300
FYE: December 31

Like an enormous corporation, State Farm is everywhere. One of the US's largest personal lines property/casualty companies, State Farm Insurance Companies provide auto insurance, as well as homeowners, nonmedical health, and life insurance. The mutual now has a federal thrift charter and provides such banking services as deposit accounts, CDs, mortgages, and other loans nationwide through the Internet and telephone. State Farm operates throughout the US and Canada and has more than 16,000 agents. Since its founding, the group's companies have been run by only two families, the Mecherles (1922-54) and the Rusts (1954-present).

**KEY COMPETITORS**
Allstate
AIG
Liberty Mutual

 See pages 458–459 for a full profile of this company.

## STATE OF FLORIDA DEPARTMENT OF THE LOTTERY

250 Marriott Dr.
Tallahassee, FL 32301
Phone: 850-487-7777
Fax: 850-487-4541
Web: www.flalottery.com

CEO: David Griffin
CFO: David Faulkenberry
HR: Karen Doulding
Type: Government-owned

2000 Sales: $2,256.4 million
1-Yr. Sales Change: 3.6%
Employees: 650
FYE: June 30

No dimpled chads here — unless it's a grinning guy named Chad holding a winning ticket. The State of Florida Department of the Lottery runs instant-play scratch tickets and lotto games, including Florida Lotto (the big jackpot), Fantasy 5, and Cash 3. Lotto tickets are sold at thousands of retail outlets statewide. The Florida Lottery gives 38 cents of every dollar generated to Florida's Educational Enhancement Trust Fund, which provides funding for programs from pre-kindergarten up to the state university. The Florida Lottery pays out half of sales in prize money. Lottery officials have stepped up marketing efforts in hopes of reviving lagging sales.

**KEY COMPETITORS**
Florida Gaming
Georgia Lottery
Multi-State Lottery

## STATE UNIVERSITY OF NEW YORK

State University Plaza
Albany, NY 12246
Phone: 518-443-5555
Fax: 518-443-5321
Web: www.suny.edu

CEO: Thomas F. Egan
CFO: Brian T. Stenson
HR: Donna Amiraian
Type: School

2000 Sales: $5,076.3 million
1-Yr. Sales Change: 9.7%
Employees: —
FYE: June 30

SUNY days are ahead for many New Yorkers seeking higher education. With more than 373,000 students, the State University of New York (SUNY) is neck-and-neck with California State University in vying to be the largest university system in the US. SUNY maintains 64 campuses around New York State, including 13 university colleges and four university centers, 30 community colleges, five technical colleges, and two health centers. Its institutions offer more than 5,000 programs of study. State funding (about $1.7 billion) covers a third of its operating revenues, while tuition and fees account for 15%. Its research institutes claim some $800 million in federal and state grants and contracts.

 See pages 460–461 for a full profile of this company.

## STATER BROS. HOLDINGS INC.

21700 Barton Rd.
Colton, CA 92324
Phone: 909-783-5000
Fax: 909-783-3930
Web: www.staterbrosmarkets.org

CEO: Jack H. Brown
CFO: Phillip J. Smith
HR: Kathy Finazzo
Type: Private

2001 Sales: $2,573.9 million
1-Yr. Sales Change: 6.5%
Employees: 12,600
FYE: September 30

Although supermarket chain Stater Bros. Markets doesn't serve many movie stars (like rival Ralph's) or command national attention (like rivals Albertson's and Safeway), it is a star to the simple folk in Southern California. Stater Bros. Holdings has about 155 Stater Bros. Markets, located mostly in Riverside and San Bernardino counties. It also has stores in Kern, Los Angeles, Orange, and San Diego counties. In 1999 the company converted about 45 outlets it bought from Albertson's to the Stater Bros. Market name. It also has a 50% stake in milk and juice processor Santee Dairies. Stater Bros. is owned by La Cadena Investments, a general partnership consisting of Stater Bros. CEO Jack Brown and other company executives.

**KEY COMPETITORS**
Albertson's
Fred Meyer
Safeway

 See pages 462–463 for a full profile of this company.

## STEVEDORING SERVICES OF AMERICA INC.

| | | |
|---|---|---|
| 1131 SW Klickitat Way | CEO: Jon Hemingway | 2001 Est. Sales: $1,000.0 mil. |
| Seattle, WA 98134 | CFO: Charles Sadowski | 1-Yr. Sales Change: 5.3% |
| Phone: 206-623-0304 | HR: — | Employees: 6,000 |
| Fax: 206-623-0179 | Type: Private | FYE: January 31 |
| Web: www.ssofa.com | | |

Stevedoring is a romantic-sounding way to say heavy lifting, which Stevedoring Services of America (SSA) does a lot of. The largest terminal operator in the US, SSA loads and unloads ships at ports and terminals from Seattle to New Zealand. The company handles a variety of cargo including lumber, scrap metal, paper products, and cars. It also provides rail-yard services and warehousing, and it offers shipment tracking. SSA's Tideworks Technology division provides administrative and operational software and technology services for terminal operators. Founded in the 1880s, the firm has been owned by the Smith and Hemingway families since 1949; CEO Jon Hemingway is the third generation of his family to head the company.

**KEY COMPETITORS**
Evergreen Marine
Hutchison Whampoa
P&O


## STRATEGIC HOTEL CAPITAL LLC

| | | |
|---|---|---|
| 77 W. Wacker Dr., Ste 4600 | CEO: Laurence S. Geller | 2000 Sales: $1,000.0 million |
| Chicago, IL 60601 | CFO: — | 1-Yr. Sales Change: 16.2% |
| Phone: 312-658-5000 | HR: — | Employees: 47 |
| Fax: 312-658-5799 | Type: Private | FYE: December 31 |
| Web: www.shci.com | | |

Strategic Hotel Capital (SHC) strategically invests capital in hotels. The private investment group owns more than 30 hotel properties, which operate on a "fee for service" basis, in the US, Europe, and Mexico. Its affiliated brands include Four Seasons, Hilton, Marriott, and Ritz-Carlton, as well as trophy properties such as Manhattan's Marriott East Side and Essex House Westin and San Diego's Hyatt Regency. SHC has put up 10 of its properties for sale to reinvest in the global upscale hotel market. The company receives funding from Goldman Sachs and Prudential; CEO Laurence Geller also owns a stake in the company.

**KEY COMPETITORS**
Hilton
Marriott International
Starwood Hotels & Resorts


## THE STRUCTURE TONE ORGANIZATION

| | | |
|---|---|---|
| 15 East 26th St. | CEO: Anthony Carvette | 2001 Est. Sales: $2,100.0 mil. |
| New York, NY 10010 | CFO: Ray Froimowitz | 1-Yr. Sales Change: 5.0% |
| Phone: 212-481-6100 | HR: Tony Tursy | Employees: 1,600 |
| Fax: 212-685-9267 | Type: Private | FYE: October 31 |
| Web: www.structuretone.com | | |

Structured to set the right tone for its clients, The Structure Tone Organization (STO) develops corporate and commercial properties through its three construction management and general contracting firms. The first, Structure Tone, provides services in the US, Asia, and Europe; its clients include MetLife. Constructors & Associates, which was formed in 1977 and joined STO in 1987, builds for US clients such as AT&T Broadband. International builder Pavarini Construction began in 1896 and joined STO in 1996 and worked on projects such as The Chrysler Building East in New York City. STO was founded in 1971 by Lou Marino and Patrick Donaghy, whose family now owns the company.

**KEY COMPETITORS**
Bechtel
Skanska
Turner Corporation

## SUNBELT BEVERAGE CORPORATION

4601 Hollins Ferry Rd.
Baltimore, MD 21227
Phone: 410-536-5000
Fax: 410-536-5560
Web: www.charmer-sunbelt.com

CEO: Charles Merinoff
CFO: Gene Luciano
HR: Paul Puca
Type: Private

2001 Est. Sales: $910.0 mil.
1-Yr. Sales Change: 7.1%
Employees: 1,700
FYE: March 31

Sunbelt Beverage has become one of the biggest swigs in its business. A leading wine and spirits wholesaler in a rapidly consolidating industry, the company operates through four subsidiaries: Premier Beverage (Florida), Churchill Distributors (Maryland), Ben Arnold-Sunbelt Beverage (South Carolina), and Arizona Beverage Distribution. Division management bought Sunbelt Beverage from McKesson (drugs and sundries wholesaler) and took it private in 1988 with the backing of investment firm Weiss, Peck & Greer. Herman Merinoff, owner of New York-based wholesaler Charmer Industries, has a majority stake in Sunbelt Beverage.

**KEY COMPETITORS**
Glazer's Wholesale Drug
National Distributing
Southern Wine & Spirits

## SUNKIST GROWERS, INC.

14130 Riverside Dr.
Sherman Oaks, CA 91423
Phone: 818-986-4800
Fax: 818-379-7405
Web: www.sunkist.com

CEO: Jeffrey D. Gargiulo
CFO: H. B. "Bud" Flach
HR: John R. McGovern
Type: Cooperative

2000 Sales: $846.7 million
1-Yr. Sales Change: (1.8%)
Employees: —
FYE: October 31

Perhaps the US enterprise least susceptible to an outbreak of scurvy, Sunkist Growers is a cooperative owned by 6,500 citrus farmers in California and Arizona. Sunkist markets fresh oranges, lemons, grapefruit, and tangerines in the US and overseas. Fruit that doesn't meet fresh market standards is turned into juices, oils, and peels for use in food products. The Sunkist brand is one of the most recognized names in the US; through licensing agreements, the name appears on dozens of beverages and other products, from vitamins to fruit rolls, in more than 55 countries. Most of the company's sales come from US customers. Sunkist's biggest export customers are Japan, South Korea, and Hong Kong.

**KEY COMPETITORS**
Chiquita Brands
Dole
Fresh Del Monte Produce

 See pages 464–465 for a full profile of this company.

## SUNOCO LOGISTICS PARTNERS L.P.

1801 Market St.
Philadelphia, PA 19103
Phone: 215-977-3000
Fax: 215-977-3409

CEO: Deborah M. Fretz
CFO: Thomas W. Hofmann
HR: —
Type: Partnership

2000 Sales: $2,160.6 million
1-Yr. Sales Change: 80.5%
Employees: 1,170
FYE: December 31

Seeking to put some daylight between its operating units, Sunoco formed Sunoco Logistics Partners in 2001 to acquire, own and operate a large swath of its midstream and downstream assets. This includes over 3,600 miles of crude oil and refined product pipelines in Texas and Oklahoma, as well as about 35 terminals and other storage assets related to Sunoco's refining and marketing operations in the Midwest, Gulf Coast, and Eastern seaboard states. Sunoco Logistics Partners also purchases domestic crude and resells it to Sunoco's refining and marketing division. Sunoco subsidiary Sunoco Partners controls 80% of Sunoco Logistics Partners.

**KEY COMPETITORS**
Plains All American Pipeline
TEPPCO Partners
TransMontaigne

## SUTHERLAND LUMBER COMPANY, L.P.

| | | |
|---|---|---|
| 4000 Main St. | CEO: Steve Scott | 2000 Est. Sales: $825.0 mil. |
| Kansas City, MO 64111 | CFO: Steve Scott | 1-Yr. Sales Change: 3.1% |
| Phone: 816-756-3000 | HR: Shanna Wilson | Employees: 2,300 |
| Fax: 816-756-3594 | Type: Private | FYE: December 31 |
| Web: www.sutherlands.com | | |

Who says lumber can't be high tech? Sutherland Lumber operates about 70 lumber and home improvement stores in 15 mostly Southern states. Subsidiary Housemart.com offers more than 40,000 items online, fulfilling orders through four Oklahoma stores. Its stores range in size from 50,000 to 190,000 sq. ft. Sutherland sells lumber, paints, tools, and building packages for houses, sheds, garages, and farm buildings. In addition, the stores sell lawn and garden equipment, plumbing supplies, and materials for hobbies and crafts. The company, which is owned and operated by the Sutherland family, was founded in 1917 as an oilfield supplier. The family also has holdings in ranching, farmland, timber, and manufacturing.

**KEY COMPETITORS**
Ace Hardware
Home Depot
Lowe's


## SUTTER HEALTH

| | | |
|---|---|---|
| 2200 River Plaza | CEO: Van R. Johnson | 2000 Sales: $3,500.0 million |
| Sacramento, CA 95833 | CFO: Robert Reed | 1-Yr. Sales Change: 19.9% |
| Phone: 916-733-8800 | HR: Ken Buback | Employees: 35,000 |
| Fax: 916-286-6841 | Type: Not-for-profit | FYE: December 31 |
| Web: www.sutterhealth.org | | |

Sutter Health is one of the nation's largest not-for-profit health care systems. It was organized in 1996 through the merger of Sutter Health and California Healthcare System. Today the company caters to residents in more than 100 northern California communities. Its services are provided through the firm's approximately 5,000 affiliated doctors, from facilities of various types, including: acute care hospitals, home health/hospice networks, medical groups, occupational health services centers, and skilled nursing facilities. Sutter Health's network also boasts several research institutes.

**KEY COMPETITORS**
Adventist Health
Catholic Healthcare West
Tenet Healthcare


## SWAGELOK

| | | |
|---|---|---|
| 29500 Solon Rd. | CEO: William R. Cosgrove | 2000 Sales: $1,200.0 million |
| Solon, OH 44139 | CFO: Frank J. Roddy | 1-Yr. Sales Change: 14.3% |
| Phone: 440-248-4600 | HR: James L. Francis | Employees: 3,300 |
| Fax: 440-349-5970 | Type: Private | FYE: December 31 |
| Web: www.swagelok.com | | |

With sales partners worldwide, it's vital for Swagelok to speak many languages fluidly. The company makes fluid system components, which include plug, pinch, and radial diaphragm valves, sanitary fittings, welding systems, and 8,400 other products. Its products are used by bioprocessing and pharmaceuticals research companies and in the oil and gas, power, and semiconductor industries. Swagelok has 270 manufacturing, research, sales, and distribution facilities in about 40 countries. Founded in 1947 by Fred Lennon in his kitchen, the company requires all prospective sales people and their families to tour company facilities for two months before coming on board. The Lennon family still controls the company.

**KEY COMPETITORS**
CIRCOR International
ITT Industries
Tyco International

## SWIFTY SERVE CORPORATION

| | | |
|---|---|---|
| 1824 Hillandale Rd. | CEO: W. Clay Hamner | 2001 Sales: $1,100.0 million |
| Durham, NC 27705 | CFO: C. Alan Bentley | 1-Yr. Sales Change: 22.2% |
| Phone: 919-384-9888 | HR: Darrell Davis | Employees: 5,900 |
| Fax: 919-384-1578 | Type: Private | FYE: March 31 |

Swifty Serve can get you fueled up quick for that road trip. The convenience store operator provides gas, coffee, and other essentials through more than 600 stores in the Southeast under the names Country Cupboard, EZ Serve, Majic Mart, Sav-A-Ton, Sunshine Travel Centers, Swifty Serve, and Town Star. Co-CEOs W. Clay Hamner and Wayne Rogers (who played Trapper John in the TV series *M*A*S*H*) formed Swifty Serve in 1999 by combining the Swifty Mart and E-Z Serve chains. Hamner and Rogers (previously partners in The Pantry, a rival chain) own 29% of the company. Ownership of the other 71% is divided equally among investment firms Bay Harbour Management, Electra Fleming, and Halpern, Denny.

**KEY COMPETITORS**
7-Eleven
The Pantry
Racetrac Petroleum


## SWINERTON INCORPORATED

| | | |
|---|---|---|
| 580 California St., Ste. 1200 | CEO: James R. Gillette | 2000 Sales: $1,550.0 million |
| San Francisco, CA 94104 | CFO: Michael Re | 1-Yr. Sales Change: 34.8% |
| Phone: 415-421-2980 | HR: Paul Smolinski | Employees: 1,450 |
| Fax: 415-433-0943 | Type: Private | FYE: December 31 |
| Web: www.swinerton.com | | |

Swinerton is building up the West just as it helped rebuild San Francisco after the 1906 earthquake. The construction group, formerly Swinerton & Walberg, builds a diverse array of facilities, including resorts, subsidized housing, public schools, Hollywood soundstages, hospitals, and airport terminals. Swinerton offers general contracting through Harbison-Mahony-Higgins, Westwood Swinerton, and Swinerton Builders; it also provides engineering construction, property management, and project management and property assessment. The employee-owned company, which has been acquiring other contractors in the past decade to expand in the Northwest and Southwest, traces its family tree to 1888.

**KEY COMPETITORS**
Charles Pankow Builders
DPR Construction
Webcor Builders


## SYNNEX INFORMATION TECHNOLOGIES, INC.

| | | |
|---|---|---|
| 3797 Spinnaker Ct. | CEO: Robert Huang | 2000 Sales: $3,700.0 million |
| Fremont, CA 94538 | CFO: Richard Powers | 1-Yr. Sales Change: 23.5% |
| Phone: 510-656-3333 | HR: Rebecca Chou | Employees: 1,200 |
| Fax: 510-668-3777 | Type: Private | FYE: November 30 |
| Web: www.synnex.com | | |

Cynics might think one company can't be an electronics contract manufacturer and distributor at the same time, but SYNNEX proves them wrong. SYNNEX Information Technologies custom-builds electronics for PC makers such as Compaq, Hewlett-Packard, and IBM, as well as for systems integrators and resellers. The company makes and configures PCs, printed circuit boards (PCBs), and other electronics. SYNNEX also provides design, distribution, and support services; its online services include parts catalogs, configuration, and ordering. The company works closely with majority shareholder MiTAC International, a Taiwan-based computer and PCB manufacturer. SYNNEX (pronounced "Sin-nuks") was founded by CEO Robert Huang in 1980.

**KEY COMPETITORS**
Avnet
Sanmina-SCI
Solectron

## TAC WORLDWIDE COMPANIES

| | | |
|---|---|---|
| 109 Oak St. | CEO: Michael J. Iandoli | 2000 Sales: $1,100.0 million |
| Newton, MA 02164 | CFO: — | 1-Yr. Sales Change: 10.0% |
| Phone: 617-969-3100 | HR: — | Employees: 1,298 |
| Fax: 617-244-9849 | Type: Private | FYE: December 31 |
| Web: www.1tac.com | | |

TAC Worldwide wants to be a permanent fixture in the temporary staffing business. The company offers contract and temporary staffing services through 125 offices in all 50 states and more than 20 countries in Europe, North America, and Southeast Asia. TAC offers staffing in fields such as information technology, engineering, office support, and entertainment. Each year it places 50,000 contract and temporary employees with more than 6,500 companies. Chairman Salvatore Balsamo founded the company as Technical Aid Corporation in 1969. Balsamo and his family own TAC Worldwide.

**KEY COMPETITORS**
Adecco
Manpower
Randstad


## TANG INDUSTRIES, INC.

| | | |
|---|---|---|
| 3773 Howard Hughes Pkwy., Ste. 350N | CEO: Cyrus Tang | 2000 Est. Sales: $1,250.0 mil. |
| Las Vegas, NV 89109 | CFO: Kurt R. Swanson | 1-Yr. Sales Change: 1.6% |
| Phone: 702-734-3700 | HR: Vaughn Kuerschner | Employees: 3,700 |
| Fax: 702-734-6766 | Type: Private | FYE: December 31 |
| Web: www.tangindustries.com | | |

Although it's not a good source of Vitamin C, Tang Industries *is* a diversified holding company; its largest holding is National Material, a metal-fabricating and -distributing company that engages in steel stamping and recycles and trades aluminum and scrap metal. In a joint venture with Acme Steel, National Material operates a wide-steel-coil processing plant in Chicago. The firm also has steel operations in China. Tang Industries' holdings include real estate, manufacturer GF Office Furniture, and Curatek Pharmaceuticals, which specializes in niche markets overlooked by large drugmakers. The company was founded in 1964 by Chinese immigrant Cyrus Tang after he bought a small metal-stamping shop in Illinois.

**KEY COMPETITORS**
Commercial Metals
Ryerson Tull
Steelcase


## TAP PHARMACEUTICAL PRODUCTS INC.

| | | |
|---|---|---|
| 675 North Field Dr. | CEO: H. Thomas Watkins | 2000 Sales: $3,538.9 million |
| Lake Forest, IL 60045 | CFO: Kevin Dolan | 1-Yr. Sales Change: 20.9% |
| Phone: — | HR: Denise Kitchen | Employees: 2,500 |
| Fax: 800-830-6936 | Type: Joint venture | FYE: December 31 |
| Web: www.tap.com | | |

TAP Pharmaceutical Products taps into the drug industry's hottest trends. The 50-50 joint venture between Abbott Laboratories and Takeda Chemical Industries develops and sells drugs in the US and Canada. Products target cancer, gastroenterology, gynecology, and urology. Its Lupron treats endometriosis and prostate cancer; TAP agreed to pay a record-setting $875 million to settle criminal and civil charges over its pricing and marketing of the drug. It also markets gastric acid inhibitor Prevacid with Abbott. Drug candidates include fast-acting erectile dysfunction treatment Uprima. Although the therapy won European approval, TAP withdrew it from FDA consideration after questions arose over its efficacy and safety.

**KEY COMPETITORS**
AstraZeneca
Pfizer
PRAECIS PHARMACEUTICALS

## TAUBER OIL COMPANY

| | | |
|---|---|---|
| 55 Waugh Dr., Ste. 700 | CEO: David W. Tauber | 2001 Sales: $1,800.0 million |
| Houston, TX 77210 | CFO: Stephen E. Hamlin | 1-Yr. Sales Change: 80.0% |
| Phone: 713-869-8700 | HR: Debbie Moseley | Employees: 60 |
| Fax: 713-869-8069 | Type: Private | FYE: September 30 |
| Web: www.tauberoil.com | | |

No petrochemical product is taboo for oil refiner and marketer Tauber Oil. The company, which was founded by O. J. Tauber Sr. in 1953, markets refined petroleum products, natural gas, carbon black feedstocks, liquefied petroleum gases, chemicals, and petrochemicals (including benzene, styrene monomer, and methanol). The company is one of the US's leading suppliers of feedstocks for reforming and olefin cracking. Subsidiary Tauber Petrochemical was created in 1997 to beef up the company's international petrochemical business. Tauber maintains a fleet of more than 100 rail cars.

**KEY COMPETITORS**
Exxon Mobil
Lyondell Chemical
Valero

## TAYLOR CORPORATION

| | | |
|---|---|---|
| 1725 Roe Crest Dr. | CEO: Glen A. Taylor | 2000 Est. Sales: $1,310.0 mil. |
| North Mankato, MN 56003 | CFO: Bill Kozitza | 1-Yr. Sales Change: 0.8% |
| Phone: 507-625-2828 | HR: Deb Newman | Employees: 14,000 |
| Fax: 507-625-2988 | Type: Private | FYE: December 31 |
| Web: www.taylorcorp.com | | |

Taylor Corporation has an invitation to print just about everything but money. Founded in 1951 as Carlson Craft, the company is one of the largest specialty printers in the US. Taylor operates some 85 firms in Australia, Europe, and North America. The company's subsidiaries (such as catalog company Current) print business cards, envelopes, graduation announcements, greeting cards, labels, stationery, and wedding invitations. Other subsidiaries offer direct marketing, office supplies, and online sales of printed products. Taylor acquired American Pad and Paper's Creative Card division in 2000. Chairman and CEO Glen Taylor owns the company. He is also majority owner of the Minnesota Timberwolves.

**KEY COMPETITORS**
Hallmark
Quebecor World
R. R. Donnelley

## TEACHERS INSURANCE AND ANNUITY ASSOCIATION-COLLEGE RETIREMENT EQUITIES FUND

| | | |
|---|---|---|
| 730 3rd Ave. | CEO: John H. Biggs | 2000 Sales: $37,273.0 million |
| New York, NY 10017 | CFO: Richard L. Gibbs | 1-Yr. Sales Change: (3.6%) |
| Phone: 212-490-9000 | HR: Matina S. Horner | Employees: 5,000 |
| Fax: 212-916-4840 | Type: Not-for-profit | FYE: December 31 |
| Web: www.tiaa-cref.org | | |

It's punishment enough to write the name *once* on a blackboard. Teachers Insurance and Annuity Association-College Retirement Equities Fund (TIAA-CREF) is one of the US's largest, if not longest-named, private pension systems, providing for teachers and other academic staff members as well as non-academic investors. TIAA-CREF's core offerings include pension funds, annuities, and IRAs, while TIAA-CREF Enterprises offers tuition financing, education IRAs, and trust services (through TIAA-CREF Trust). Other products include life, health, and disability insurance and mutual funds.

**KEY COMPETITORS**
Charles Schwab
FMR
Vanguard Group

📖 See pages 466–467 for a full profile of this company.

## TEAM HEALTH, INC.

| | | |
|---|---|---|
| 1900 Winston Rd. | CEO: Lynn Massingale | 2000 Sales: $919.0 million |
| Knoxville, TN 37919 | CFO: David Jones | 1-Yr. Sales Change: 7.8% |
| Phone: 865-693-1000 | HR: Lisa Courtney | Employees: 1,804 |
| Fax: 865-539-8003 | Type: Private | FYE: |
| Web: www.teamhealth.com | | |

Team Health hopes to score some points with its outsourced physician services. It has contracts with more than 350 hospitals in about 30 states to provide medical staffing, management, administrative, and other support services. With some 2,000 physicians in its network, the firm specializes in emergency medicine, radiology, pediatrics, anesthesia, and hospitalists (hospital physicians who coordinate care during patients' stays with their primary physicians and other medical professionals). It operates through physician-managed regional affiliates. Team Health's AccessNurse unit offers health information and advice and occupational medicine programs. A group of emergency physicians founded Team Health in 1979.

**KEY COMPETITORS**
EmCare
PhyAmerica
RehabCare

## TENNESSEE VALLEY AUTHORITY

| | | |
|---|---|---|
| 400 W. Summit Hill Dr. | CEO: Oswald "Ike" Zeringue | 2001 Sales: $6,999.0 million |
| Knoxville, TN 37902 | CFO: David N. Smith | 1-Yr. Sales Change: 3.5% |
| Phone: 865-632-2101 | HR: John E. Long Jr. | Employees: — |
| Fax: — | Type: Government-owned | FYE: September 30 |
| Web: www.tva.gov | | |

A working monument to the New Deal, Tennessee Valley Authority (TVA) is the largest government-owned power producer in the US, with nearly 30,400 MW of generating capacity. Created by Congress in 1933, the federal corporation transmits electricity to 158 local distribution utilities (84% of sales), which serve 8.3 million consumers. TVA covers 80,000 sq. mi., serving nearly all of Tennessee and parts of Alabama, Georgia, Kentucky, Mississippi, North Carolina, and Virginia; it also manages the Tennessee River system. Because TVA is tax exempt, it's able to offer some of the lowest rates in the nation. The authority is preparing for deregulation and trying to cut its $25 billion debt.

 See pages 468–469 for a full profile of this company.

## THE TEXAS A&M UNIVERSITY SYSTEM

| | | |
|---|---|---|
| John B. Connally Bldg., 301 Tarrow, 3rd Fl. | CEO: Howard D. Graves | 2000 Sales: $2,619.8 million |
| College Station, TX 77840 | CFO: Tom D. Kale | 1-Yr. Sales Change: 46.2% |
| Phone: 979-458-6000 | HR: Patti Couger | Employees: 23,000 |
| Fax: 979-845-2490 | Type: School | FYE: August 31 |
| Web: tamusystem.tamu.edu | | |

Everything is bigger in Texas, even its universities. With more than 90,000 students at nine institutions, The Texas A&M University System ranks among the largest in the US. Its flagship school at College Station is well-known not only for its programs in engineering and agriculture, but also for its long-held traditions and school spirit. Other system institutions include Tarleton State University and Prairie View A&M. The system also runs eight state extension agencies and a health sciences center. Texas A&M was founded in 1876 as the Agricultural and Mechanical College of Texas. The A&M system was formed in 1948. It is funded in part by a $7.7 billion state endowment (shared with the University of Texas).

 See pages 470–471 for a full profile of this company.

## TEXAS HEALTH RESOURCES

| | | |
|---|---|---|
| 611 Ryan Plaza Dr., Ste. 900 | CEO: Douglas D. Hawthorne | 2000 Sales: $1,340.1 million |
| Arlington, TX 76011 | CFO: Ron Bourland | 1-Yr. Sales Change: 3.8% |
| Phone: 817-462-7900 | HR: Bonnie Bell | Employees: 16,000 |
| Fax: — | Type: Not-for-profit | FYE: December 31 |
| Web: www.texashealth.org | | |

This company is takin' care of Texas, with about 25 health care facilities in the Dallas/Fort Worth and North Texas region. Formed by the merger of Harris Methodist Health System, Presbyterian Healthcare System, and Arlington Memorial Hospital Foundation, the not-for-profit system includes acute-care hospitals, mental health centers, a retirement community and senior care centers, and home health services. Its network includes more than 4,000 physicians and more than 4,200 beds. Texas Health Resources sold its unprofitable St. Paul Medical Center to the University of Texas.

**KEY COMPETITORS**
Baylor Health
HCA
Triad Hospitals

## TEXAS LOTTERY COMMISSION

| | | |
|---|---|---|
| 611 E. Sixth St. | CEO: Linda Cloud | 2000 Sales: $3,939.9 million |
| Austin, TX 78701 | CFO: Bart Sanchez | 1-Yr. Sales Change: 24.8% |
| Phone: 512-344-5000 | HR: Jim Richardson | Employees: 335 |
| Fax: 512-344-5490 | Type: Government-owned | FYE: August 31 |
| Web: www.txlottery.org | | |

The eyes of Texas are watching the lotto jackpot. The Texas Lottery Commission oversees one of the country's largest state lotteries, which has pumped more than $7 billion into state coffers since it was created in 1991. About 55% of lottery sales are paid out in prize money, while more than 30% goes to the state's Foundation School Fund. The lottery offers four numbers games, including Lotto Texas, Pick 3, Cash 5, and Texas Two Step, and several instant-win games sold through retailers and vending machines around the state. Retailers such as grocery stores, gas stations, and liquor and convenience stores make a small commission on tickets they sell.

**KEY COMPETITORS**
Multi-State Lottery

 See pages 472–473 for a full profile of this company.

## TEXAS PACIFIC GROUP

| | | |
|---|---|---|
| 301 Commerce St., Ste. 3300 | CEO: David Bonderman | Sales: — |
| Fort Worth, TX 76102 | CFO: Jim O'Brien | 1-Yr. Sales Change: — |
| Phone: 817-871-4000 | HR: Jennifer Dixon | Employees: — |
| Fax: 817-871-4010 | Type: Partnership | FYE: December 31 |
| Web: www.texpac.com | | |

Yee-hah! Let's round us up some LBOs. Investment firm Texas Pacific Group has staked its claim on the buyout frontier with a reputation for scooping up and reforming troubled companies other firms wouldn't dare touch. Its holdings include Oxford Health Plans, Magellan Health Services, Ducati Motor, J. Crew, semiconductor maker ZiLOG, and airlines. Texas Pacific Group makes money not only from fund management fees but also from the increased values of holdings. With the US buyout frontier becoming increasingly settled and expensive, the company is heading overseas to invest in Europe. CEO David "Bondo" Bonderman is known for turning around Continental Airlines.

**KEY COMPETITORS**
Clayton, Dubilier
Hicks, Muse
KKR

 See pages 474–475 for a full profile of this company.

## TEXAS PETROCHEMICALS LP

| | | |
|---|---|---|
| 3 Riverway, Ste. 1500 | CEO: Bill Waycaster | 2001 Sales: $858.7 million |
| Houston, TX 77056 | CFO: Carl Stutt | 1-Yr. Sales Change: 15.3% |
| Phone: 713-627-7474 | HR: Jimmy Rhodes | Employees: 316 |
| Fax: 713-477-8762 | Type: Private | FYE: June 30 |
| Web: www.txpetrochem.com | | |

Texas Petrochemicals has kept motoring along thanks to the US Clean Air Act of 1990, which requires an oxygenate in gasoline in heavily populated areas. The company derives 58% of its sales from the production of MTBE, the predominate oxygenate used in US gasoline; however, it plans to reduce dependence on MTBE after several incidents of groundwater contamination. Other products include butadiene, butene-1, high-purity isobutylene, diisobutylene, and isobutylene concentrate, which are used in the manufacture of synthetic rubber, plastic resins, and lubricants. Texas Petrochemicals operates its own cogeneration power plant and sells the excess capacity. TPC Holdings owns the company, which was formed in 1968.

**KEY COMPETITORS**
Equistar Chemicals
Lyondell Chemical
Valero

## TIC HOLDINGS INC.

| | | |
|---|---|---|
| 2211 Elk River Rd. | CEO: Ron McKenzie | 2000 Sales: $998.0 million |
| Steamboat Springs, CO 80487 | CFO: Jim Kissane | 1-Yr. Sales Change: 34.0% |
| Phone: 970-879-2561 | HR: Barbara Judd | Employees: 6,000 |
| Fax: 970-879-6078 | Type: Private | FYE: December 31 |
| Web: www.tic-inc.com | | |

TIC Holdings doesn't flinch when it comes to constructing heavy industrial projects. Founded in 1974, the firm's services include civil engineering, heavy equipment erection, pipeline construction, and electrical installation. Its companies rank among leading building contractors in the US in the wastewater, petrochemical, power, refining, mining, and industrial process markets, as well as in the electrical and instrumentation and pulp and paper industries. Subsidiary Western Summit Constructors focuses on water and wastewater projects. California-based Granite Construction is selling its 30% stake back to the firm, which is otherwise employee-owned.

**KEY COMPETITORS**
Black & Veatch
Foster Wheeler
H. B. Zachry

## TISHMAN REALTY & CONSTRUCTION CO. INC.

| | | |
|---|---|---|
| 666 Fifth Ave. | CEO: John L. Tishman | 2001 Sales: $1,640.0 million |
| New York, NY 10103 | CFO: Larry Schwarzwalder | 1-Yr. Sales Change: 47.9% |
| Phone: 212-399-3600 | HR: Christine Smith | Employees: 920 |
| Fax: 212-397-1316 | Type: Private | FYE: June 30 |
| Web: www.tishman.com | | |

Tishman Realty & Construction is an immigrant success story writ large. The company builds office, hospitality, recreational, industrial, and other kinds of property for its own account and for other owners. The firm offers third-party developers a full menu of real estate design, construction, management, and financing services. High profile projects handled by the company (or its publicly owned predecessor) include Disney World's EPCOT Center, Madison Square Garden, the ill-fated World Trade Center, and Chicago's John Hancock Center. Chairman and CEO John Tishman and his family — scions of immigrant founder Julius Tishman, who began building tenements a century ago — own the company.

**KEY COMPETITORS**
CB Richard Ellis
Gilbane
Trammell Crow

 See pages 476–477 for a full profile of this company.

## TOPA EQUITIES, LTD.

| | | |
|---|---|---|
| 1800 Avenue of the Stars, Ste. 1400 | CEO: John E. Anderson | 2000 Sales: $865.0 million |
| Los Angeles, CA 90067 | CFO: Brenda Seuthe | 1-Yr. Sales Change: 11.5% |
| Phone: 310-203-9199 | HR: Virginia Flores | Employees: 1,600 |
| Fax: 310-557-1837 | Type: Private | FYE: December 31 |

Holding company Topa Equities casts a wide net. Owned by John Anderson, Topa has about 30 businesses involved in automobile dealerships (Silver Star Automotive), beer distribution, insurance, real estate, and more. Topa's beverage operations include Ace Beverage, Mission Beverages, and Paradise Beverages; the firm dominates the Hawaiian and Caribbean beer markets and serves California. Brands sold include all major US brews and leading US imports Corona, Guinness, Heineken, and Labatt, among others. Anderson started in 1956 as a distributor of Hamm's beer. UCLA's Anderson School of Business, to which Anderson donated $15 million, is named for him.

**KEY COMPETITORS**
Citigroup
Prospect Motors
Young's Market

## TOPCO ASSOCIATES, INC.

| | | |
|---|---|---|
| 7711 Gross Point Rd. | CEO: Steven K. Lauer | 2001 Est. Sales: $3,150.0 mil. |
| Skokie, IL 60077 | CFO: — | 1-Yr. Sales Change: (7.4%) |
| Phone: 847-676-3030 | HR: Dennis Pieper | Employees: 271 |
| Fax: 847-676-4949 | Type: Cooperative | FYE: March 31 |
| Web: www.topcoess.com | | |

Topco Associates is principally into private label procurement. Owned by about 30 companies (mostly supermarket operators), the private brand cooperative uses the combined number of its members to buy products cheaper than members could buy on their own. Topco markets more than 7,000 private-label items, including fresh meat, dairy and bakery goods, produce, general merchandise, health and beauty products, and pharmacy items. Topco's brands include Food Club, Pet Club, and a line of "Top" labels such as Top Crest. It also helps market items sold under members' own brand names. Formed to help grocers deal with WWII shortages, most of Topco's members are in the US.

**KEY COMPETITORS**
Shurfine International

 See pages 478–479 for a full profile of this company.

## TOWERS PERRIN

| | | |
|---|---|---|
| 335 Madison Ave. | CEO: Mark Mactas | 2000 Sales: $1,448.0 million |
| New York, NY 10017 | CFO: Mark L. Wilson | 1-Yr. Sales Change: 8.2% |
| Phone: 212-309-3400 | HR: Anne Donovan Bodnar | Employees: 8,919 |
| Fax: 212-309-0975 | Type: Private | FYE: December 31 |
| Web: www.towers.com | | |

Refusing to live in an ivory tower, this company aims to offer practical advice. One of the leading management consulting firms in the world, Towers Perrin offers such services as human resources and management consulting, employee benefits services, and consulting for the health care industry. Its Tillinghast-Towers Perrin unit focuses on risk management and actuarial services, while its Towers Perrin Reinsurance division serves clients primarily as a reinsurance intermediary. The firm, which has an extensive client roster that includes more than 700 of the *FORTUNE* 1000 companies, operates from 78 offices in 23 countries. Towers Perrin was founded by four partners in 1934 and is owned by more than 630 partners.

**KEY COMPETITORS**
Hewitt Associates
PricewaterhouseCoopers
Watson Wyatt

 See pages 480–481 for a full profile of this company.

## TRACINDA CORPORATION

| | | |
|---|---|---|
| 150 Rodeo Dr., Ste. 250 | CEO: Kirk Kerkorian | Sales: — |
| Beverly Hills, CA 90212 | CFO: Anthony L. Mandekic | 1-Yr. Sales Change: — |
| Phone: 310-271-0638 | HR: Anthony L. Mandekic | Employees: — |
| Fax: 310-271-3416 | Type: Private | FYE: December 31 |

Tracinda may be the majority owner of casino and hotel operator MGM Mirage and MGM, but its biggest show is owner Kirk Kerkorian, who has owned all or part of the studio three times (and hopes to sell it again). He bought it first in 1969 and sold it to — and bought it back from — Ted Turner. After selling to financier Giancarlo Parretti, Kerkorian bought MGM again when Credit Lyonnais auctioned the studio after Parretti defaulted. In 1996 Kerkorian and Lee Iacocca tried to take over Chrysler before it merged with Daimler-Benz; he is suing the carmaker, claiming the merger was really a takeover that jilted shareholders. He maintains a minority stake in DaimlerChrysler. Tracinda is named after Kerkorian's daughters, Tracy and Linda.

**KEY COMPETITORS**
Mandalay Resort Group
News Corp.
Warner Bros.

## TRADER JOE'S COMPANY

| | | |
|---|---|---|
| 800 S. Shamrock Ave. | CEO: Dan Bane | 2000 Est. Sales: $1,000.0 mil. |
| Monrovia, CA 91016 | CFO: Randy Scoville | 1-Yr. Sales Change: 5.3% |
| Phone: 626-599-3700 | HR: Carol Impara | Employees: — |
| Fax: 626-301-4431 | Type: Private | FYE: June 30 |
| Web: www.traderjoes.com | | |

When it comes to grocery chains, Trader Joe's isn't your average Joe. With more than 130 stores in 15 mostly West and East Coast states, the company offers upscale grocery fare such as health foods, organic produce, and nutritional supplements. To keep costs down, its stores have no service departments and average about 9,000 sq. ft. (and thus have a much more limited selection than typical supermarkets). The company's specialty is its line of more than 800 private-label products, including beverages, soup, snacks, and frozen items. Started by Joe Coulombe as a Los Angeles convenience store chain in 1958, the company was bought in 1979 by German billionaires Karl and Theo Albrecht, who also own the ALDI food chain.

**KEY COMPETITORS**
Safeway
Whole Foods
Wild Oats Markets

## TRAMMELL CROW RESIDENTIAL

| | | |
|---|---|---|
| 2859 Paces Ferry Rd. #1100 | CEO: J. Ronald Terwilliger | 2000 Est. Sales: $2,000.0 mil. |
| Atlanta, GA 30339 | CFO: Michael Collins | 1-Yr. Sales Change: 11.1% |
| Phone: 770-801-1600 | HR: Tim Swango | Employees: 4,000 |
| Fax: 770-801-5395 | Type: Private | FYE: December 31 |
| Web: www.tcresidential.com | | |

Trammell Crow Residential builds quite a nest. A builder and manager of upscale apartment complexes, the company operates regionally through some 30 national and divisional partners. These partners work with the company to handle the purchase, development, and building of multi-family projects. Trammell Crow Residential has more than 60,000 units; heaviest concentrations of properties are in the Southeast, the West Coast, and Texas. Trammell Crow Residential Services manages the complexes. The company split off from mammoth Trammell Crow Co. in 1977 but is still associated with the Crow family empire of real estate development firms.

**KEY COMPETITORS**
Gables Residential Trust
JPI
Lincoln Property

## TRANSAMMONIA, INC.

350 Park Ave.
New York, NY 10022
Phone: 212-223-3200
Fax: 212-759-1410

CEO: Ronald P. Stanton
CFO: Edward G. Weiner
HR: Marguerite Harrington
Type: Private

2000 Sales: $2,447.0 million
1-Yr. Sales Change: 65.3%
Employees: 218
FYE: December 31

Fertilizer, liquefied petroleum gas (LPG), and petrochemicals form the lifeblood of international trader Transammonia. The company trades, distributes, and transports these commodities around the world. Transammonia's fertilizer business includes ammonia, phosphates, and urea; the company is building an ammonia plant in Algeria in a joint venture with Germany's Firtzwerder. Transammonia's Sea-3 subsidiary imports propane from Algeria, the North Sea region, and Venezuela to its terminals in Newington, New Hampshire, and Tampa, Florida. The company's Trammochem unit trades in petrochemicals, specializing in aromatics, methanol, methyltertiary butyl ether (MTBE), and olefins. Trammo Gas trades in LPG.

**KEY COMPETITORS**
Cargill
ConAgra
Norsk Hydro

## TRAVELCENTERS OF AMERICA, INC.

24601 Center Ridge Rd., Ste. 200
Westlake, OH 44145
Phone: 440-808-9100
Fax: 440-808-3306
Web: www.tatravelcenters.com

CEO: Edwin P. Kuhn
CFO: James W. George
HR: Ivan Wagner
Type: Private

2000 Sales: $2,060.0 million
1-Yr. Sales Change: 41.6%
Employees: 10,635
FYE: December 31

TravelCenters of America is in the food, fuel, and relaxation business for the long haul. The company's network of about 160 interstate highway travel centers in 40 states is the nation's largest. Company-owned and franchised truck stops provide gas, fast-food and sit-down restaurants (Country Pride, Buckhorn, Mrs. B's), convenience stores, and lodging. With professional truck drivers accounting for most of the customers, some outlets also offer "trucker-only" services such as laundry and shower facilities, barbershops, telephone and TV rooms, and truck repair services. Investment group Oak Hill Capital Partners owns TravelCenters of America.

**KEY COMPETITORS**
Flying J
Petro Stopping Centers
Pilot

## TRINITY HEALTH

34605 12 Mile Rd.
Farmington Hills, MI 48331
Phone: 248-489-6000
Fax: 248-489-6836
Web: www.trinity-health.org

CEO: Judith C. Pelham
CFO: James H. Combes
HR: William Anderson
Type: Not-for-profit

2001 Sales: $4,500.0 million
1-Yr. Sales Change: 9.8%
Employees: 45,700
FYE: June 30

Trinity Health is really more of a duo than a trio; the not-for-profit company is the result of a coupling between Mercy Health Services and Holy Cross Health System. Trinity Health runs nearly 50 hospitals and more than 300 outpatient facilities, as well as long-term care facilities, home health agencies, and hospice programs, in seven states. Its subsidiary, Trinity Health Plans, operates the Care Choices HMO in some 22 Michigan counties. Trinity Health sold its majority stake in GNA, formerly its rehabilitation therapy subsidiary. Catholic Health Ministries sponsors the organization.

**KEY COMPETITORS**
Ascension
Detroit Medical Center
Triad Hospitals

## TRUMAN ARNOLD COMPANIES

701 S. Robison Rd.
Texarkana, TX 75501
Phone: 903-794-3835
Fax: 903-832-7226

CEO: Greg Arnold
CFO: Steve McMillen
HR: Denny Peterson
Type: Private

2001 Sales: $1,120.0 million
1-Yr. Sales Change: 72.3%
Employees: 400
FYE: September 30

Truman Arnold Companies (TAC) markets and distributes more than 2 billion gallons of petroleum a year. The company was founded by Texarkana, Texas, businessman Truman Arnold in 1964 as a branded petroleum jobber. The company sold its multi-state Road Runner branded convenience store chain in 1989. TAC's network of petroleum terminals, trucks, and aviation fixed based operation (FBO) facilities serves clients throughout North America. The company is still owned and operated by the Arnold family.

**KEY COMPETITORS**
Gulf Oil
Streicher Mobile Fueling
Sun Coast Resources

## THE TRUMP ORGANIZATION

725 Fifth Ave.
New York, NY 10022
Phone: 212-832-2000
Fax: 212-935-0141
Web: www.trumponline.com

CEO: Donald J. Trump
CFO: Allen Weisselberg
HR: Norma Foerderer
Type: Private

2000 Sales: $8,000.0 million
1-Yr. Sales Change: 14.3%
Employees: 22,000
FYE: December 31

Real estate developer Donald Trump continues to raise the roof (and rents) in New York City. Through the Trump Organization, The Donald can claim several pieces of prime real estate in the Big Apple, including Trump International Hotel and Tower, Trump Tower (26 floors of it, anyway), the Empire State Building (50% of the land), 40 Wall Street, and the General Motors Building (50%). Trump also owns 42% of publicly traded Trump Hotels & Casino Resorts, operater of three Atlantic City casinos (Trump Taj Mahal, Trump Plaza, and Trump Marina) and a riverboat casino in Indiana. Other holdings include a Florida resort and 50% of the Miss USA, Miss Teen USA, and Miss Universe beauty pageants.

**KEY COMPETITORS**
Lefrak Organization
MGM Mirage
Park Place Entertainment

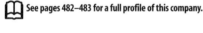 See pages 482–483 for a full profile of this company.

## TRUSERV CORPORATION

8600 W. Bryn Mawr Ave.
Chicago, IL 60631
Phone: 773-695-5000
Fax: 773-695-6516
Web: www.truserv.com

CEO: Pamela Lieberman
CFO: —
HR: Robert Ostrov
Type: Cooperative

2000 Sales: $3,993.6 million
1-Yr. Sales Change: (11.3%)
Employees: 4,300
FYE: December 31

TruServ trumps Ace Hardware as the largest member-owned hardware cooperative in the US. Formed by the merger of Cotter & Company (supplier to the True Value chain) and ServiStar Coast to Coast, the cooperative serves some 7,700 retail outlets, including its flagship True Value hardware stores. The company sells home improvement and garden supplies and also manufactures its own brand of paints and the necessary applicators. Its other chains include Grand Rental Station, C&S Choices, Home & Garden Showplace, and Taylor Rental Center. TruServ has streamlined its executive staff and announced plans to cut up to 10% of its workforce amid a loan default, revelations of accounting problems, and stores quitting the co-op.

**KEY COMPETITORS**
Ace Hardware
Home Depot
Lowe's

 See pages 484–485 for a full profile of this company.

## TRUSTMARK INSURANCE COMPANY

| | | |
|---|---|---|
| 400 Field Dr. | CEO: J. Grover Thomas Jr. | 2000 Sales: $1,322.1 million |
| Lake Forest, IL 60045 | CFO: Richard D. Batten | 1-Yr. Sales Change: 13.3% |
| Phone: 847-615-1500 | HR: Robert R. Worobow | Employees: 3,500 |
| Fax: 847-615-3910 | Type: Mutual company | FYE: December 31 |
| Web: www.trustmarkinsurance.com | | |

Trustmark Insurance was established in 1913 as the Brotherhood of All Railway Employees to provide disability coverage to railroad workers. Trustmark is licensed in all 50 states and covers more than 2.5 million people from all walks of life. Operations include group and individual health coverage (medical, dental, disability, and life insurance) and voluntary insurance products (specialty products through voluntary payroll deductions). Subsidiary Starmark markets health plans to small businesses. Other subsidiaries offer third-party administration and cost management of health care plans and combat health-care fraud. A mutual company, Trustmark's policyholders own the company.

**KEY COMPETITORS**
Blue Cross
CIGNA
Prudential


## TTC ILLINOIS, INC.

| | | |
|---|---|---|
| 50 Meadowview Center | CEO: Michael McCafferty | 2000 Sales: $809.0 million |
| Kankakee, IL 60901 | CFO: Don Ciaccio | 1-Yr. Sales Change: 22.6% |
| Phone: 815-935-8100 | HR: — | Employees: 26,000 |
| Fax: 815-936-3098 | Type: Private | FYE: December 31 |
| Web: www.ttcillinois.com | | |

TTC Illinois runs on people power, and lots of it. One of the largest professional employer organizations (PEO) in the US, the company specializes in providing personnel management services to clients in a variety of industries, including transportation, manufacturing, property management, and warehousing. The company frees its clients to focus on the bottom line by offering such administrative functions as payroll, insurance, workers' compensation, benefits, and records management. Former independent trucker James Hunt founded the company in 1990 and sold it to TTC employees in 1995.

**KEY COMPETITORS**
EPIX
Gevity HR
TeamStaff


## TTI, INC.

| | | |
|---|---|---|
| 2441 Northeast Pkwy. | CEO: Paul E. Andrews Jr. | 2001 Sales: $1,146.0 million |
| Fort Worth, TX 76106 | CFO: Nick M. Kypreos | 1-Yr. Sales Change: 20.0% |
| Phone: 817-740-9000 | HR: Dick Andrews | Employees: 1,720 |
| Fax: 817-740-1622 | Type: Private | FYE: March 31 |
| Web: www.ttiinc.com | | |

TTI is passionate about passives. Each year the company distributes more than 1.7 million electronic components, including passive components such as resistors and capacitors, and interconnects such as cables, sockets, and filter connectors. Suppliers of its 160,000 line items include 3M, Spectrum Control, Koninklijke Philips, and Vishay Intertechnology. TTI also offers services such as component packaging and supply chain management. TTI, which owner and CEO Paul Andrews founded in 1971 as a supplier to the military, serves manufacturers of aerospace and defense systems, computers, telecom equipment, medical devices, and industrial products. The company is expanding its presence in Europe.

**KEY COMPETITORS**
All American Semiconductor
Arrow Electronics
Smith & Associates

## TTX COMPANY

| | | |
|---|---|---|
| 101 N. Wacker Dr. | CEO: Andrew F. Reardon | 2000 Sales: $1,020.4 million |
| Chicago, IL 60606 | CFO: Thomas D. Marion | 1-Yr. Sales Change: 3.6% |
| Phone: 312-853-3223 | HR: Michelle Pomeroy | Employees: 1,614 |
| Fax: 312-984-3790 | Type: Private | FYE: December 31 |
| Web: www.ttx.com | | |

TTX keeps the railroad industry chugging by leasing railcars to railroad companies in the US. Rail companies generally prefer to rent railcars as needed rather than buy them because the cars are often switched and traded along the tracks. With 130,000 railcars, TTX's fleet includes cars designed to carry containers, autos, farm and construction equipment, and lumber and steel products. The company has distribution centers in Illinois and Washington and maintains its fleet through repair centers in 16 US states. TTX is owned by the largest railroads in the US, including #1 Union Pacific and #2 Burlington Northern Santa Fe.

**KEY COMPETITORS**
GATX
Greenbrier
XTRA

## TUFTS ASSOCIATED HEALTH PLANS, INC.

| | | |
|---|---|---|
| 333 Wyman St. | CEO: Harris A. Berman | 2000 Sales: $2,000.0 million |
| Waltham, MA 02454 | CFO: Richard Hallworth | 1-Yr. Sales Change: 0.0% |
| Phone: 781-466-9400 | HR: Sally Iadonisi | Employees: 3,000 |
| Fax: 781-466-8583 | Type: Not-for-profit | FYE: December 31 |
| Web: www.tufts-healthplan.com | | |

Managed health care headaches in New England have made times tough for Tufts. The not-for-profit company provides management, administrative, and marketing services for its affiliates and subsidiaries, including Tufts Associated Health Maintenance Organization (TAHMO), Total Health Plan, and Tufts Benefit Administrators. Its provider network serves more than 900,000 members. The company offers HMO, PPO, point-of-service, and other plans to its customers. State regulators placed the company's subsidiary Tufts Health Plan of New England (TNE) into receivership; the company responded by closing TNE, raising premiums, and cutting other costs.

**KEY COMPETITORS**
Blue Cross (MA)
ConnectiCare
Harvard Pilgrim

## TY INC.

| | | |
|---|---|---|
| 280 Chestnut Ave. | CEO: H. Ty Warner | 2000 Est. Sales: $800.0 mil. |
| Westmont, IL 60559 | CFO: Michael W. Kanzler | 1-Yr. Sales Change: (36.0%) |
| Phone: 630-920-1515 | HR: Diane Digangi | Employees: 1,000 |
| Fax: 630-920-1980 | Type: Private | FYE: December 31 |
| Web: www.ty.com | | |

Take some fabric, shape it like an animal, fill it with plastic pellets, and you too could own luxury hotels. That's the lesson taught by Ty Warner, sole owner of the firm behind Beanie Babies and their worldwide cult following. Since 1993 Ty has produced more than 325 different Beanie Babies, with colorful names such as Swoop the pterodactyl and Buzzie the bee, as well as hundreds of other Beanie toys. Beanies debut at about $6, but once "retired" they can fetch hundreds or thousands of dollars from collectors. Ty doesn't advertise, limits production, and sells Beanies only through small, specialty retailers. Beanie bucks enabled Warner to buy two Four Seasons hotels (in New York and California) in recent years.

**KEY COMPETITORS**
Applause
Hasbro
Play-By-Play

 See pages 486–487 for a full profile of this company.

## UIS, INC.

| | | |
|---|---|---|
| 15 Exchange Place, Ste. 1120 | CEO: Andrew E. Pietrini | 2000 Sales: $1,087.0 million |
| Jersey City, NJ 07302 | CFO: Joseph F. Arrigo | 1-Yr. Sales Change: 0.6% |
| Phone: 201-946-2600 | HR: Andrew E. Pietrini | Employees: 8,910 |
| Fax: 201-946-9325 | Type: Private | FYE: December 31 |

As the maker of those little heart-shaped candies with tiny messages of love, UIS is probably better known for its somewhat tougher products, namely its car parts. UIS' subsidiaries include Champion Laboratories (oil and fuel filters), Neapco (transmission parts), Wells Manufacturing (ignition and electrical components), Pioneer (auto specialty supplier). Other operations include New England Confectionery (Sweethearts, Necco wafers, Clark Bar) and Hurd Millwork (window and patio doors). Founder Harry Lebensfeld started the company in 1945 with the purchase of an Indiana desk maker. UIS is owned by a trust for Lebensfeld's only child (who is married to EVP Richard Pasculano) and her children.

**KEY COMPETITORS**
Dana
Delphi Automotive Systems
Federal-Mogul

## UJC OF NORTH AMERICA

| | | |
|---|---|---|
| 111 Eighth Ave., Ste. 11E | CEO: Stephen Solender | 2000 Est. Sales: $2,000.0 mil. |
| New York, NY 10016 | CFO: Robert Goldberg | 1-Yr. Sales Change: 0.0% |
| Phone: 212-284-6500 | HR: Lance Jacobs | Employees: 500 |
| Fax: 212-284-6835 | Type: Not-for-profit | FYE: June 30 |
| Web: www.ujc.org | | |

From supporting nursing homes in the US to helping emigres fleeing the former Soviet Union, UJC Federations of North America works to better Jewish life across the globe. One of the nation's leading not-for-profit organizations, UJC raises about $2 billion annually. It comprises three philanthropic outfits: the United Jewish Appeal, the Council for Jewish Federations, and the United Israel Appeal. The three operations bring more than 200 Jewish welfare and fund-raising agencies and organizations together under the auspices of the UJC. The United Jewish Appeal was founded in 1939 as a response to the previous year's infamous Kristallnacht, a coordinated attack on Jews in Germany and Austria.

## UNIFIED WESTERN GROCERS, INC.

| | | |
|---|---|---|
| 5200 Sheila St. | CEO: Alfred A. Plamann | 2001 Sales: $2,929.5 million |
| Commerce, CA 90040 | CFO: Richard J. Martin | 1-Yr. Sales Change: (4.5%) |
| Phone: 323-264-5200 | HR: Don Giltin | Employees: 4,200 |
| Fax: 323-265-4006 | Type: Cooperative | FYE: September 30 |
| Web: www.uwgrocers.com/ | | |

Unified Western Grocers guarantees that food and general merchandise reach about 3,700 mostly independent grocery stores in Arizona, California, Colorado, Hawaii, Nevada, Oregon, Utah, and Washington. The food wholesaler and cooperative supplies a full line of groceries, as well as its own bakery and dairy goods. In addition to name-brand items, its offerings include private labels Gingham, Springfield, and Western Family. The co-op also provides member support services such as store remodeling, financing, and insurance. Unified serves about 670 patrons, many of whom own shares in the company. It was formed in 1999 when Certified Grocers of California merged with United Grocers of Oregon.

**KEY COMPETITORS**
Fleming Companies
SUPERVALU
Topco Associates

 See pages 488–489 for a full profile of this company.

## UNIGROUP, INC.

| | | |
|---|---|---|
| One Premier Dr. | CEO: Robert J. Baer | 2000 Sales: $2,009.0 million |
| Fenton, MO 63026 | CFO: Donald Ellington | 1-Yr. Sales Change: 7.0% |
| Phone: 636-326-3100 | HR: Sherry Fagin | Employees: 1,871 |
| Fax: 636-326-1106 | Type: Private | FYE: December 31 |
| Web: www.unigroupinc.com | | |

Moving household goods has made many of UniGroup's companies household names. The moving service company transports household goods and other items in more than 100 countries through subsidiaries United Van Lines and Mayflower Transit. Its Trans Advantage unit sells and leases trucks and trailers and provides moving supplies, and its Vanliner Group offers property/casualty insurance to movers. Subsidiary UniGroup Worldwide offers relocation management and assistance around the globe. The company also provides corporate relocation services through Pinnacle Group Associates. Founded in 1987, UniGroup is owned by senior management and agents of United Van Lines and Mayflower Transit.

**KEY COMPETITORS**
Allied Worldwide
AMERCO
Atlas World

## UNIHEALTH FOUNDATION

| | | |
|---|---|---|
| 5959 Topanga Canyon Blvd., Ste. 390 | CEO: David R. Carpenter | Sales: — |
| Woodland Hills, CA 91367 | CFO: Katherine McNallen | 1-Yr. Sales Change: — |
| Phone: 818-888-4090 | HR: Paul Heredia | Employees: — |
| Fax: 818-888-4094 | Type: Foundation | FYE: September 30 |

UniHealth Foundation is what is left of what was once one of California's fastest-growing health systems. The not-for-profit foundation sold its eight hospitals to Catholic Healthcare West and its CliniShare home health services and ElderMed senior citizens care services to Trinity Care and used those assets to start a second life as a grant-making organization. The philanthropic foundation focuses on health education and access to ambulatory, acute care, and sub-acute care, as well as on other community-based programs and services.

## THE UNION CENTRAL LIFE INSURANCE COMPANY

| | | |
|---|---|---|
| 1876 Waycross Rd. | CEO: John H. Jacobs | 2000 Sales: $1,130.7 million |
| Cincinnati, OH 45240 | CFO: Stephen R. Hatcher | 1-Yr. Sales Change: (1.2%) |
| Phone: 513-595-2200 | HR: Stephen K. Johnston | Employees: — |
| Fax: 513-595-5418 | Type: Mutual company | FYE: December 31 |
| Web: www.unioncentral.com | | |

Next stop for insurance, Union Central. Union Central Life Insurance Company is a mutual life insurance company that operates in 50 states and the District of Columbia. The company offers a range of individual life and disability insurance, investment products, annuities, group retirement plans, and group insurance. Union Central also offers employee and executive benefit planning, estate planning, and retirement planning. Union Central's investments are mainly in bonds and collateralized mortgage obligations, of which mortgage investments accounted for about 20%. Union Central was founded in 1867.

**KEY COMPETITORS**
MetLife
New York Life
Prudential

## THE UNION LABOR LIFE INSURANCE COMPANY

111 Massachusetts Ave. NW
Washington, DC 20001
Phone: 202-682-0900
Fax: 202-682-7932
Web: www.ullico.com

CEO: Robert A. Georgine
CFO: John Grelle
HR: Rick Silas
Type: Private

2000 Sales: $885.7 million
1-Yr. Sales Change: 16.8%
Employees: —
FYE: December 31

This union is for life. Founded in 1925 by the American Federation of Labor to provide life insurance to union members, The Union Labor Life Insurance Company (ULLICO) has since grown into an insurance and financial services holding company. ULLICO serves organized employers, individual union members, and jointly managed trust funds through its subsidiaries. The company offers an array of products, including group life and health, property and casualty insurance, individual and direct-response marketing, third-party administration, and investment services. ULLICO also operates programs such as "J for Jobs," which uses jointly managed trust fund money to invest in union-built commercial real estate projects.

**KEY COMPETITORS**
MetLife
Nationwide
Prudential

## UNITED SPACE ALLIANCE

600 Gemini St.
Houston, TX 77058
Phone: 281-212-6000
Fax: 281-212-6177
Web: www.unitedspacealliance.com

CEO: Russell D. Turner
CFO: Bill Caple
HR: —
Type: Joint venture

2000 Est. Sales: $1,200.0 mil.
1-Yr. Sales Change: —
Employees: 4,066
FYE: December 31

USA! USA! United Space Alliance (USA) is a space-race heavyweight (each of the four Space Shuttles — Columbia, Discovery, Atlantis, and Endeavour — weighs 173,000 pounds). A joint venture between Lockheed Martin and Boeing, USA was established in 1996 to consolidate NASA's various Space Shuttle contracts under a single entity. As prime contractor, the company is involved in astronaut and flight controller training, flight software development, Shuttle payload integration, and vehicle processing, launch, and recovery operations. USA also provides training and operations planning for the International Space Station. Its main operations are at the Johnson Space Center (Texas) and Kennedy Space Center (Florida).

**KEY COMPETITORS**
EADS
Honeywell Aerospace
Northrop Grumman

## UNITED STATES POSTAL SERVICE

475 L'Enfant Plaza SW
Washington, DC 20260
Phone: 202-268-2500
Fax: 202-268-4860
Web: www.usps.gov

CEO: John E. "Jack" Potter
CFO: Richard J. Strasser Jr.
HR: Suzanne Medvidovich
Type: Government-owned

2001 Sales: $65,834.0 million
1-Yr. Sales Change: 2.0%
Employees: 797,795
FYE: September 30

No, the United States Postal Service (USPS) doesn't deliver your e-mail, but it is trying to find Internet opportunities. An independent government agency, the USPS delivers more than 200 billion pieces of mail a year (nearly half of the world's total), relying on postage and fees for income. Though it has a monopoly on delivering nonurgent letters, the USPS faces competition for services such as package delivery. Facing a decline in the volume of "snail mail" because of the Internet, the agency is pursuing e-commerce strategies such as express delivery and computerized postage. An 11-member board of governors, nine of whom are appointed by the president of the US, oversees the agency.

**KEY COMPETITORS**
DHL
FedEx
UPS

📖 See pages 490–491 for a full profile of this company.

## UNITED WAY OF AMERICA

701 N. Fairfax St.
Alexandria, VA 22314
Phone: 703-836-7100
Fax: 703-683-7840
Web: national.unitedway.org

CEO: Brian A. Gallagher
CFO: —
HR: Paul Springer
Type: Not-for-profit

2000 Sales: $3,910.0 million
1-Yr. Sales Change: 3.7%
Employees: 10,000
FYE: December 31

About 45,000 agencies benefit from the financial support they receive from United Way of America (UWA). A not-for-profit organization, UWA's 1,400 local organizations help to fund a range of endeavors, including the American Cancer Society, Big Brothers/Big Sisters, Catholic Charities, Girl Scouts and Boy Scouts, and the Salvation Army. During the fund-raising campaign that began in 1999, UWA raised nearly $3.8 billion (about 50% from employee contributions and more than 20% from corporations), and its administrative expenses average 10% of all funds raised. Each of the local organizations is an independent entity, and UWA supports them with services such as national advertising and research.

 See pages 492–493 for a full profile of this company.

## THE UNIVERSITY OF ALABAMA SYSTEM

401 Queen City Ave.
Tuscaloosa, AL 35401
Phone: 205-348-5122
Fax: 205-348-5915
Web: www.ua.edu

CEO: Thomas C. Meredith Jr.
CFO: JoAnne G. Jackson
HR: Charlotte Harris
Type: School

2000 Sales: $2,089.8 million
1-Yr. Sales Change: 5.9%
Employees: 20,000
FYE: September 30

Students in the Heart of Dixie can choose among three campuses overseen by the University of Alabama System. The flagship Tuscaloosa campus offers 275 degree programs to its more than 14,000 students. The University of Alabama at Birmingham offers about 140 degree programs and has an enrollment of more than 10,000 students; it is also home to the university's school of medicine and a 900-bed hospital. The system's Huntsville campus has more than 7,000 students enrolled in its five colleges and graduate school. Each campus offers bachelor's, master's, and Ph.D. degree programs. The University of Alabama was founded in Tuscaloosa in 1831 as the state's first public university.

## UNIVERSITY OF CALIFORNIA

1111 Franklin St.
Oakland, CA 94607
Phone: 510-987-0700
Fax: 510-987-0894
Web: www.ucop.edu

CEO: Richard C. Atkinson
CFO: Joseph P. Mullinix
HR: Lubbe Levin
Type: School

2001 Sales: $15,887.0 million
1-Yr. Sales Change: 13.1%
Employees: 108,827
FYE: June 30

Along with celebrities and smog, California boasts one of the nation's leading systems of higher education. The University of California (UC) offers areas of study in more than 150 disciplines. It has nearly 174,000 students at its nine undergraduate and graduate campuses (which include three law schools and five medical schools): Berkeley, Davis, Irvine, Los Angeles, Riverside, San Diego, San Francisco, Santa Barbara, and Santa Cruz. The university's 10th campus, UC Merced, is scheduled to open in 2004. UC also operates three US Department of Energy research labs in California and New Mexico. While no longer using affirmative action in its admissions process, UC is making efforts to boost minority enrollment.

 See pages 494–495 for a full profile of this company.

## THE UNIVERSITY OF CHICAGO

| | | |
|---|---|---|
| 5801 S. Ellis Ave. | CEO: Don M. Randel | 2000 Sales: $1,639.2 million |
| Chicago, IL 60637 | CFO: Patricia Woodworth | 1-Yr. Sales Change: 93.4% |
| Phone: 773-702-1234 | HR: G. Chris Keeley | Employees: 11,900 |
| Fax: 773-702-0809 | Type: School | FYE: June 30 |
| Web: www.uchicago.edu | | |

The University of Chicago ranks as one of the world's youngest and most esteemed universities. Boasting more than 70 Nobel Prize recipients (Enrico Fermi, Milton Friedman, Saul Bellow), the College of the university offers a common core curriculum based on the "Great Books." Undergraduates can major in more than 40 areas, not including business and engineering. Among the U of C's graduate divisions and professional schools are the University of Chicago Law School and Graduate School of Business, both of which are ranked in the top 10 by *U.S. News & World Report.* Founded in 1891 by John D. Rockefeller, the university has an endowment exceeding $3.8 billion. More than 12,000 students attend the U of C.

 See pages 496–497 for a full profile of this company.

## UNIVERSITY OF FLORIDA

| | | |
|---|---|---|
| 226 Tigert Hall | CEO: Charles E. Young | 2001 Sales: $2,781.9 million |
| Gainesville, FL 32611 | CFO: John P. Kruczek | 1-Yr. Sales Change: 130.2% |
| Phone: 352-392-3261 | HR: Larry T. Ellis | Employees: 23,500 |
| Fax: 352-392-6278 | Type: School | FYE: June 30 |
| Web: www.ufl.edu | | |

UF students know it's great to be a Florida Gator. Founded in 1853, the University of Florida is the state's oldest and largest university. The school is a major land-grant research university located on 2,000 acres 115 miles north of Orlando. It has more than 43,000 students, making it one of the nation's largest universities. Its 23 colleges and schools offer more than 100 undergraduate majors and nearly 200 graduate programs, including law, dentistry, pharmacy, medicine, and veterinary medicine. A founding member of the Southeastern Conference, the university fields athletic teams (the Florida Gators) that are typically nationally ranked.

## UNIVERSITY OF ILLINOIS

| | | |
|---|---|---|
| 352 Henry Administration Bldg., 506 S. Wright | CEO: James J. Stukel | 2000 Sales: $2,722.2 million |
| Urbana, IL 61801 | CFO: Craig S. Bazzani | 1-Yr. Sales Change: 6.1% |
| Phone: 217-333- 1920 | HR: Robert K. Todd | Employees: — |
| Fax: 217-337-3070 | Type: School | FYE: June 30 |
| Web: www.uillinois.edu | | |

The log cabins that used to dot the landscape in the Land of Lincoln have given way to the three campuses of the University of Illinois. Established as a land grant institution in 1867, the university has grown to include campuses in Chicago, Springfield, and Urbana-Champaign. Its more than 65,000 students (more than half of whom study at the Urbana-Champaign campus) can choose from academic fields ranging from business to fine arts to medicine. The Urbana-Champaign campus is the site of the National Center for Supercomputing Applications (which developed Mosaic, the basis for popular Internet browsers such as AOL Time Warner's Navigator), while the university's Springfield campus houses the Institute for Public Affairs.

## THE UNIVERSITY OF IOWA

249 IMU
Iowa City, IA 52242
Phone: 319-335-3500
Fax: 319-335-0860
Web: www.uiowa.edu

CEO: Mary Sue Coleman
CFO: Douglas K. True
HR: Robert S. Foldesi
Type: School

2000 Sales: $1,531.4 million
1-Yr. Sales Change: 0.0%
Employees: 16,006
FYE: June 30

The University of Iowa Hawkeyes see clearly from their perch as Iowa's largest university. Founded in 1847, the university has more than 28,000 students (more than 19,000 undergraduate and rest are graduate students) on its Iowa City campus. The university is home to 10 colleges spanning a variety of majors and disciplines, including distinguished programs in audiology, print making, creative writing, speech pathology, and nursing. Among the University of Iowa's distinguished alumni are John Irving, Flannery O'Connor, Gene Wilder, and Tennessee Williams.


## THE UNIVERSITY OF KENTUCKY

Administration Bldg., Room 104
Lexington, KY 40506
Phone: 859-257-9000
Fax: 859-323-1075
Web: www.uky.edu

CEO: Charles T. Wethington Jr.
CFO: Henry Clay Owen
HR: Telan Williamson Jr.
Type: School

2000 Sales: $1,304.9 million
1-Yr. Sales Change: 23.9%
Employees: 13,000
FYE: June 30

Bluegrass and basketball. Perennial basketball powerhouse The University of Kentucky (UK) serves about 31,000 students on its main campus at Lexington (as well as Lexington Community College) through 10 undergraduate colleges and graduate, medical, and law schools. It offers nearly 100 certified degree programs, such as agriculture, communications, dentistry, education, engineering, and fine arts. UK operates the Chandler Medical Center, which works with its nationally ranked colleges of medicine, nursing, and pharmacy. A public university and research institution, the school was founded in 1865 as the Agricultural and Mechanical College of the Kentucky University.


## UNIVERSITY OF MASSACHUSETTS

One Beacon St., 26th Fl.
Boston, MA 02108
Phone: 617-287-7000
Fax: 617-287-7044
Web: www.massachusetts.edu

CEO: William M. Bulger
CFO: Stephen W. Lenhardt
HR: Roy Milbury
Type: School

2000 Sales: $1,384.5 million
1-Yr. Sales Change: 17.9%
Employees: 11,256
FYE: June 30

The University of Massachusetts (UMass) has been expanding across the commonwealth since its founding in 1863. About 58,000 students attend UMass, a public school focusing on research. The university's flagship campus in Amherst offers bachelor's degrees in about 100 areas, master's in nearly 70, and doctorates in 50. UMass has gained recognition in areas of study such as chemical engineering and computer science. Its University of Massachusetts Medical School, in Worcester, has an affiliated teaching hospital and more than 600 students studying medicine, nursing, and biomedical sciences. Alumni include entertainer Bill Cosby, singer Natalie Cole, and former General Electric CEO Jack Welch.

## THE UNIVERSITY OF MICHIGAN

| | | |
|---|---|---|
| 3074 Fleming Administration Bldg. | CEO: Lee C. Bollinger | 2001 Sales: $2,696.3 million |
| Ann Arbor, MI 48109 | CFO: Robert A. Kasdin | 1-Yr. Sales Change: (41.5%) |
| Phone: 734-764-1817 | HR: Jackie R. McClain | Employees: — |
| Fax: 734-764-4546 | Type: School | FYE: June 30 |
| Web: www.umich.edu | | |

Michigan — it's shaped like a mitten, and higher education fits the state like a glove. The University of Michigan has been a leader in the state's education effort since its founding in 1817. With about 52,000 students and more than 5,000 faculty members scattered across three campuses (Ann Arbor, with about 37,000 students; Dearborn; and Flint), the university's diverse academic units span areas of study including architecture, dentistry, education, law, medicine, music, and social work. Notable alumni include Gerald Ford (the university is home to the Gerald R. Ford Library and the Ford School of Public Policy) and Arthur Miller.

## UNIVERSITY OF MINNESOTA

| | | |
|---|---|---|
| 234 Morrill Hall, 100 Church St. SE | CEO: Mark G. Yudof | 2001 Sales: $2,301.1 million |
| Minneapolis, MN 55455 | CFO: Richard H. Pfuntzenreuter | 1-Yr. Sales Change: (28.6%) |
| Phone: 612-625-5000 | HR: Carol Carrier | Employees: 30,823 |
| Fax: 612-625-3875 | Type: School | FYE: June 30 |
| Web: www.umn.edu | | |

The University of Minnesota — this place is a zoo! Gophers scurry about the university's Minneapolis-St. Paul campus, Bulldogs roam its campus in Duluth, Cougars prowl its Morris campus, and Golden Eagles soar across its campus in Crookston. Feeble mascot jokes aside, the land grant institution has been educating students since 1869. Its more than 58,000 students can choose academic fields ranging from education to engineering to public health. In 2000 the NCAA placed the university's basketball team on probation and eliminated five basketball scholarships as penalty for academic fraud uncovered in the basketball program.

## UNIVERSITY OF MISSOURI SYSTEM

| | | |
|---|---|---|
| 321 University Hall | CEO: Manuel T. Pacheco | 2001 Sales: $1,446.0 million |
| Columbia, MO 65211 | CFO: James E. Cofer | 1-Yr. Sales Change: 6.6% |
| Phone: 573-882-2121 | HR: R. Kenneth Hutchinson | Employees: 27,914 |
| Fax: 573-882-2721 | Type: School | FYE: June 30 |
| Web: www.system.missouri.edu | | |

"Show-Me" the education! The University of Missouri, founded in 1839 (it was the first publicly supported institution of higher education created in the Louisiana Territory), educates more than 56,000 students at four campuses and through a statewide extension program; some 24% of the students are in graduate or professional programs. Nicknamed "Mizzou," the university's cadre of campuses includes flagship UM-Columbia (home to about 23,300 students, 20 schools and colleges, and the University of Missouri Health Sciences Center), UM-Kansas City, UM-Rolla, and UM-St. Louis. Offering fields of study ranging from journalism to law to fine arts, the university has a more than 9,500-member faculty and research staff.

## THE UNIVERSITY OF NEBRASKA

| | | |
|---|---|---|
| 3835 Holdrege St. | CEO: L. Dennis Smith | 1999 Sales: $1,016.3 million |
| Lincoln, NE 68583 | CFO: David E. Lechner | 1-Yr. Sales Change: (18.6%) |
| Phone: 402-472-2111 | HR: John Russell | Employees: — |
| Fax: 402-472-2410 | Type: School | FYE: June 30 |
| Web: www.uneb.edu | | |

The University of Nebraska has sprouted four campuses out in the fields of the Cornhusker State. Founded in 1869, the state university system offers bachelor's, master's, and doctoral degrees in such programs as agriculture, business, education, and engineering at its campuses in Kearney, Lincoln, and Omaha. The university's Medical Center in Omaha trains doctors, performs research, and is affiliated with a 700-bed teaching hospital. The University of Nebraska also operates research and extension services across the state. More than 46,000 students attend classes in the university system, which is recovering from a severe 1997 enrollment drop caused by tighter admissions standards.

## THE UNIVERSITY OF PENNSYLVANIA

| | | |
|---|---|---|
| 3451 Walnut St. | CEO: Judith Rodin | 2000 Sales: $3,007.0 million |
| Philadelphia, PA 19104 | CFO: Craig Carnaroli | 1-Yr. Sales Change: 6.5% |
| Phone: 215-898-5000 | HR: John J. Heuer | Employees: — |
| Fax: 215-898-9659 | Type: School | FYE: June 30 |
| Web: www.upenn.edu | | |

When he wasn't founding our country or experimenting with lightning, Benjamin Franklin took the time to establish the University of Pennsylvania, the first university in the US. Since opening its doors to students in 1751, the Ivy League university has accumulated a notable list of accomplishments, including the creation of the first medical school in the US and the invention of the ENIAC computer. The university's nearly 22,000 students pursue their studies in four undergraduate schools and a dozen graduate and professional schools, including the renowned Wharton School and the Annenburg School for Communications. University president Judith Rodin became the first female to head an Ivy League university in 1994.

## UNIVERSITY OF PITTSBURGH OF THE COMMONWEALTH SYSTEM OF HIGHER EDUCATION

| | | |
|---|---|---|
| 4200 5th Ave. | CEO: Mark A. Nordenberg | 2000 Sales: $1,033.1 million |
| Pittsburgh, PA 15260 | CFO: Arthur Ramicone | 1-Yr. Sales Change: 5.0% |
| Phone: 412-624-4141 | HR: Ronald W. Frisch | Employees: — |
| Fax: 412-624-7282 | Type: School | FYE: June 30 |
| Web: www.pitt.edu | | |

Now this is a school that really needs a nickname. The University of Pittsburgh of the Commonwealth System of Higher Education (Whew! Pitt for short) has nearly 29,000 students spread across its five campuses. Its flagship Pittsburgh campus has more than 23,000 students. The Pitt Panthers pursue their studies in 16 schools and colleges, including arts and sciences, engineering, and business. Pitt also is affiliated with the UPMC Health System, which operates a network of hospitals and an insurance company, manages physicians' offices, and offers long-term care and in-home services. The university was founded in 1787 and has an endowment exceeding $1 billion.

## UNIVERSITY OF ROCHESTER

Administration Bldg.
Rochester, NY 14627
Phone: 585-275-2121
Fax: 585-275-0359
Web: www.rochester.edu

CEO: Thomas H. Jackson
CFO: Ronald J. Paprocki
HR: —
Type: School

2001 Sales: $1,418.7 million
1-Yr. Sales Change: 5.8%
Employees: 12,242
FYE: June 30

The buzz about the University of Rochester is music to some ears. The private, upstate New York institution is nationally recognized for its programs in medicine, engineering, and business, and its Eastman School of Music (founded by George Eastman, founder of Eastman Kodak) is one of the top music schools in the US. The university, which has an endowment of more than $1.2 billion, offers more than 175 bachelor's, master's, and doctoral degrees to its nearly 7,900 full- and part-time students. Undergraduate tuition runs more than $24,000. Founded as a Baptist-sponsored institution in 1850, the university is nonsectarian today.

## UNIVERSITY OF SOUTHERN CALIFORNIA

University Park
Los Angeles, CA 90089
Phone: 213-740-2311
Fax: 213-740-4749
Web: www.usc.edu

CEO: Steven B. Sample
CFO: Frank Arambula
HR: Dennis F. Dougherty
Type: School

2000 Sales: $1,185.8 million
1-Yr. Sales Change: 3.8%
Employees: 17,000
FYE: June 30

This Trojan horse, filled with more than 28,000 students, is more than welcome at the the University of Southern California (USC). Founded in 1880, the private university (home of the Trojans) grew up with the city of Los Angeles. It offers 76 undergraduate majors and 122 postgraduate degrees. Recognized for distinguished programs in business, engineering, film, law, medicine, public administration, and science, USC boasts two Los Angeles campuses and a string of research centers and health care facilities. The university also supports medical staffs at five Los Angeles hospitals. USC is the largest private employer in Los Angeles.

## UNIVERSITY OF TENNESSEE

800 Andy Holt Tower
Knoxville, TN 37996
Phone: 865-974-2225
Fax: 865-974-6435
Web: www.utenn.edu

CEO: J. Wade Gilley
CFO: Emerson H. Fly
HR: Alan Chesney
Type: School

2000 Sales: $1,696.1 million
1-Yr. Sales Change: 30.2%
Employees: 14,004
FYE: June 30

Home sweet home to nearly 43,000 students, the University of Tennessee (UT) includes a main campus in Knoxville (with about 28,500 students), three other campuses, and agriculture, space, and public-service institutes. UT's academic programs include business, engineering, law, pharmacy, medicine, and veterinary medicine. The school also operates the UT Medical Center in Knoxville. Founded in 1794 as Blount College, UT became the nation's first coeducational college when it admitted women for a few years in the early 1800s (it began admitting women again in 1892). Notable alumni include former Senate Majority Leader Howard Baker, Nobel Prize-winning economist James Buchanan, and author Cormac McCarthy.

## THE UNIVERSITY OF TEXAS SYSTEM

| | | |
|---|---|---|
| 601 Colorado St. | CEO: R. D. "Dan" Burck | 2000 Sales: $5,943.1 million |
| Austin, TX 78701 | CFO: Kerry L. Kennedy | 1-Yr. Sales Change: 43.9% |
| Phone: 512-499-4200 | HR: Gerald Schroeder | Employees: 79,430 |
| Fax: 512-499-4218 | Type: School | FYE: August 31 |
| Web: www.utsystem.edu | | |

These students are hooked on higher education. The University of Texas System runs nine universities throughout the longhorn state with a total enrollment of some 153,000 students, making it one of the largest university systems in the US. (Its flagship school in Austin, with 50,000 students, ranks as having the largest campus population in the nation.) UT also runs six health centers and four medical schools and receives more than $1 billion a year in research money. Its $10 billion endowment (managed by the University of Texas Investment Management Co.) is the third-largest in the country (after Harvard and Yale). Established in 1876, UT Austin opened in 1883. The UT System was formally organized in 1950.

 **See pages 498–499 for a full profile of this company.**


## UNIVERSITY OF VIRGINIA

| | | |
|---|---|---|
| 1404 University Ave. | CEO: John T. Casteen III | 2000 Sales: $1,287.8 million |
| Charlottesville, VA 22903 | CFO: Leonard W. Sandridge | 1-Yr. Sales Change: 5.6% |
| Phone: 434-924-0311 | HR: Thomas E. Gausvik | Employees: 11,608 |
| Fax: 434-982-4378 | Type: School | FYE: June 30 |
| Web: www.virginia.edu | | |

It says a lot that the University of Virginia (UVa) is Thomas Jefferson's proudest achievement. The nation's third president (as well as inventor, philosopher, and author, among other titles) founded the US's first nonreligious public university in 1819. With more than 18,500 students enrolled in its graduate and undergraduate schools, UVa is one of the most prestigious public universities in the US. *U.S. News & World Report* ranks the school as the nation's #1 public university in a tie with the University of California at Berkeley. UVa has been noted for its top-rated law program and English department and for its 150-year-old, student-enforced conduct code (the Honor System).


## UNIVERSITY OF WASHINGTON

| | | |
|---|---|---|
| 301 Gerberding Hall, Ste. 400 | CEO: Richard L. McCormick | 2000 Sales: $2,696.3 million |
| Seattle, WA 98195 | CFO: V'Ella Warren | 1-Yr. Sales Change: 9.8% |
| Phone: 206-543-2560 | HR: Elizabeth Coveney | Employees: 25,917 |
| Fax: 206-543-5651 | Type: School | FYE: June 30 |
| Web: www.washington.edu | | |

The University of Washington (UW) is Husky indeed, with more than 37,400 students enrolled at its main Seattle campus. Founded in 1861 as the Territorial University of Washington, UW (pronounced "U-dub" by those on campus) also has smaller branches in Tacoma and Bothell. The university maintains 16 schools and colleges for both undergraduate and graduate students (more than 70% of students on the main campus are undergrads). It also operates a health sciences center and an academic medical center, which includes the University of Washington Medical Center and Harborview Medical Center.

## THE UNIVERSITY OF WISCONSIN SYSTEM

Van Hise Hall, 1220 Linden Dr.
Madison, WI 53706
Phone: 608-262-2321
Fax: 608-262-3985
Web: www.uwsa.edu

CEO: Katharine C. Lyall
CFO: Deborah A. Durken
HR: George H. Brooks
Type: School

2000 Sales: $2,922.3 million
1-Yr. Sales Change: 14.2%
Employees: 23,981
FYE: June 30

Looking for something to do in Baraboo? You could always take some classes at UW Baraboo, one of The University of Wisconsin System's 26 campuses. The system, one of the largest in the nation, serves more than 155,000 students through 13 four-year and 13 two-year campuses. Its top school is the University of Wisconsin at Madison, which offers undergraduate, graduate, and doctoral degrees and regularly ranks as one of the top public schools in the US. It has more than 40,000 students and a nationally recognized graduate program in sociology. The system's other major campus is the University of Wisconsin at Milwaukee, with nearly 23,000 students.

 See pages 500–501 for a full profile of this company.

## UNIVERSITY SYSTEM OF MARYLAND

3300 Metzerott Rd.
Adelphi, MD 20783
Phone: 301-445-2740
Fax: 301-445-2761
Web: www.usmh.usmd.edu

CEO: Donald N. Langenberg
CFO: Joseph F. Vivona
HR: Donald Tynes
Type: School

2000 Sales: $2,291.5 million
1-Yr. Sales Change: (11.6%)
Employees: —
FYE: June 30

Maryland's nickname, "The Free State," doesn't apply to its system of higher education. The University System of Maryland (USM) has 11 public campuses and two research institutes that serve nearly 130,000 undergraduate and graduate students. The university system, formed in 1988, combined the former University of Maryland (dating to 1807 and including five campuses) with six other institutions. USM offers more than 600 academic programs, including bachelor's, master's, doctoral, and professional degrees. Its flagship campus at College Park was founded in 1856 and became a public land-grant university in 1865.

## U.S. CAN CORPORATION

700 East Butterfield Rd., Ste. 250
Lombard, IL 60148
Phone: 630-678-8000
Fax: 630-573-0715
Web: www.uscanco.com

CEO: Paul W. Jones
CFO: John L. Workman
HR: Roger B. Farley
Type: Private

2000 Sales: $809.5 million
1-Yr. Sales Change: 13.4%
Employees: 2,700
FYE: December 31

U.S. Can might not be an expert when it comes to carrying a tune, but it can carry lots of other stuff. The company makes steel and plastic nonbeverage containers in the US and Europe that hold everything from food to paint. Its aerosol containers, which account for the largest portion of sales, are used to package household, automotive, paint, hygiene, and industrial products. Besides standard containers the company offers custom and specialty products such as decorative tins, stampings, and collectible items like metal signs, as well as containers used to store chemicals. U.S. Can's approximately 7,000 customers include Gillette and Sherwin Williams. Private investment firm Berkshire Partners owns 77% of U.S. Can.

**KEY COMPETITORS**
Ball Corporation
Crown Cork & Seal
Silgan

## U.S. CENTRAL CREDIT UNION

| | | |
|---|---|---|
| 7300 College Blvd., Ste. 600 | CEO: Dan Kampen | 2000 Sales: $1,450.0 million |
| Overland Park, KS 66210 | CFO: Kathryn Brick | 1-Yr. Sales Change: 7.3% |
| Phone: 913-661-3800 | HR: Linda Pfingsten | Employees: 186 |
| Fax: 913-345-2628 | Type: Cooperative | FYE: December 31 |
| Web: www.uscentral.org | | |

Credit unions stand united in U.S. Central Credit Union, a cooperative "central bank" for a network of nearly 35 "corporate" (or regional) credit unions, which in turn represent a network of approximately 11,000 consumer credit unions nationwide. The cooperative performs a variety of liquidity and cash management functions, such as funds transfer, settlement services, risk management, and custody services. Subsidiary U.S. Central Capital Markets provides investment advisory services to the corporate credit unions, while majority-owned Corporate Network eCom offers Web-based banking and bill payment services to the network and its members.

**KEY COMPETITORS**
Concord EFS
EDS
Jack Henry

## USAA

| | | |
|---|---|---|
| 9800 Fredericksburg Rd., USAA Bldg. | CEO: Robert G. Davis | 2000 Sales: $8,551.0 million |
| San Antonio, TX 78288 | CFO: Joe Robles Jr. | 1-Yr. Sales Change: 2.8% |
| Phone: 210-498-2211 | HR: Elizabeth Conklyn | Employees: 22,000 |
| Fax: 210-498-9940 | Type: Mutual company | FYE: December 31 |
| Web: www.usaa.com | | |

USAA has a decidedly military bearing. The mutual insurance company serves more than 4 million customers, primarily military personnel and their families. Its products and services include property/casualty (sold only to military personnel) and life insurance, banking, discount brokerage, and investment management. USAA relies largely on technology and direct marketing to sell its products, reaching clients via the telephone and Internet. The company also has a large mail-order catalog business (computers, furniture, giftware, jewelry, and home and auto safety items), and it offers long-distance telephone services.

**KEY COMPETITORS**
MetLife
Nationwide
State Farm

 **See pages 502–503 for a full profile of this company.**

## VANDERBILT UNIVERSITY

| | | |
|---|---|---|
| 2201 West End Ave. | CEO: E. Gordon Gee | 2001 Sales: $1,418.9 million |
| Nashville, TN 37235 | CFO: Lauren J. Brisky | 1-Yr. Sales Change: 10.9% |
| Phone: 615-322-7311 | HR: Darlene Lewis | Employees: 15,427 |
| Fax: 615-343-3930 | Type: School | FYE: June 30 |
| Web: www.vanderbilt.edu | | |

The house that Cornelius built, private Vanderbilt University was founded in 1873 with a $1 million grant from industrialist Cornelius Vanderbilt. The university's endowment has grown to about $1.8 billion, and the campus today is a haven for more than 10,000 students and 1,900 full-time faculty. Vanderbilt has 10 schools and colleges; its Owen Graduate School of Management and its medical school rank near the top of national surveys. A major research university, Vanderbilt receives nearly $150 million a year in sponsored awards to fund its facilities. Chancellor Joe Wyatt retired in 2000; E. Gordon Gee, former president of Brown University, replaced him.

## THE VANGUARD GROUP, INC.

100 Vanguard Blvd.
Malvern, PA 19355
Phone: 610-648-6000
Fax: 610-669-6605
Web: www.vanguard.com

CEO: John J. Brennan
CFO: Ralph K. Packard
HR: Kathleen C. Gubanich
Type: Private

2000 Est. Sales: $1,600.0 mil.
1-Yr. Sales Change: 6.7%
Employees: 11,000
FYE: December 31

Just like Lord Nelson's flagship for which it was named, The Vanguard Group is in battle, hoping to torpedo rival FMR, the world's largest mutual fund company. Vanguard offers a wide variety of stocks, bonds, and mixed funds of US and foreign companies' securities. Its most popular products are index funds, which track the market and are generally a safe, long-term investment. Unlike other fund companies, Vanguard keeps costs low; the investor-owned company plows earnings back into its funds, rather than diverting them into fees or advertising. It also reduces costs on its actively managed funds by outsourcing management to other companies.

**KEY COMPETITORS**
Barclays
FMR
Mellon Financial

See pages 504–505 for a full profile of this company.


## VARTEC TELECOM, INC.

1600 Viceroy Dr.
Dallas, TX 75235
Phone: 214-424-1000
Fax: 214-424-1555
Web: www.vartec.com

CEO: Sherman Henderson
CFO: Gary Egger
HR: —
Type: Private

2000 Sales: $995.0 million
1-Yr. Sales Change: 3.6%
Employees: 1,276
FYE: December 31

Actors and comedians employed to promote 10-10 calling plans can thank VarTec Telecom, a leading provider of "dial-around" long-distance service, which helped pioneer the calling method. VarTec provides residential and business calling plans, as well as Internet access and 800-number service. The company was founded in 1989 by president Joe Mitchell and his wife, EVP Connie Mitchell, along with EVP Ray Atkinson. Holding company Telephone Electronics Corp. owns a majority stake in VarTec, which has agreed to merge with business telecom services reseller Lightyear Communications and to acquire Dallas-based long-distance retailer Excel Communications.

**KEY COMPETITORS**
AT&T
Sprint FON
WorldCom


## VENTURE INDUSTRIES

33662 James J. Pompo Dr.
Fraser, MI 48026
Phone: 810-294-1500
Fax: 810-296-8863
Web: www.ventureindustries.com

CEO: Larry J. Winget Sr.
CFO: James E. Butler Jr.
HR: Debra Wangurd
Type: Private

2000 Sales: $2,400.0 million
1-Yr. Sales Change: (2.0%)
Employees: 18,000
FYE: December 31

When it comes to plastic automotive components, Venture Industries is ready for uncharted territory. The company is a leading maker of injection-molded plastic components for automotive OEMs. Products include interior systems, cockpit modules, front-end systems, exterior trim, and closures and panels. Venture Industries also offers design, preproduction, engineering, assembly, tooling, and logistics services to most of the world's automakers. Customers include GM, Ford, DaimlerChrysler, BMW, Honda, and Volkswagen. The company offers engineering and technology services in Asia, Australia, Europe, and North America and continues to expand into new regions. CEO Larry Winget owns Venture Industries.

**KEY COMPETITORS**
DaimlerChrysler
Ford
General Motors

## VERIZON WIRELESS INC.

180 Washington Valley Rd.
Bedminster, NJ 07921
Phone: 908-306-7000
Fax: 908-306-6927
Web: www.verizonwireless.com

CEO: Dennis F. Strigl
CFO: Edward "Ted" Langston
HR: Marc C. Reed
Type: Joint venture

2000 Sales: $14,236.0 million
1-Yr. Sales Change: 85.9%
Employees: 38,000
FYE: December 31

Out ahead on the horizon, Verizon Wireless is the #1 mobile phone operator in the US. The company serves 29.4 million mobile phone customers nationwide. It is developing third-generation wireless services based on CDMA (code division multiple access) technology. Verizon Wireless began operations in 2000 when Bell Atlantic and Vodafone combined their US wireless assets, including their PrimeCo partnership. Verizon Wireless gained GTE's US wireless operations when Bell Atlantic bought GTE to form Verizon Communications. Verizon Communications owns 55% of the company, and Vodafone owns 45%. Plans for an IPO, which had been postponed in 2001, have been revived, but no timetable has been mentioned.

**KEY COMPETITORS**
AT&T Wireless
Cingular Wireless
Sprint PCS

## VERTIS INC.

250 W. Pratt St.
Baltimore, MD 21201
Phone: 410-528-9800
Fax: 410-528-9288
Web: www.vertisinc.com

CEO: Donald E. Roland
CFO: Dean D. Durbin
HR: Catherine S. Leggett
Type: Private

2000 Sales: $2,000.0 million
1-Yr. Sales Change: 11.1%
Employees: 10,000
FYE: December 31

Vertis helps retailers peddle their wares. The company (formerly Big Flower Holdings) is a leading provider of integrated marketing and advertising services through three operating units: TC Advertising, LTC Group, and Webcraft. TC Advertising is one of the nation's largest printers of TV listing guides and advertising circulars and inserts, and it offers newspaper circulation-building services. Vertis provides digital media production and other new media services, as well as strategic consulting, through LTC Group. Webcraft's offerings include promotional campaign creation, direct mail printing, and Internet integration. An investor group led by Thomas H. Lee Company and Evercore Partners owns Vertis.

**KEY COMPETITORS**
ACG Holdings
Harte-Hanks
Valassis

 **See pages 506–507 for a full profile of this company.**

## VIEWSONIC CORPORATION

381 Brea Canyon Rd.
Walnut, CA 91789
Phone: 909-444-8800
Fax: 909-468-1202
Web: www.viewsonic.com

CEO: James Chu
CFO: James Morlan
HR: Joanne Thielen
Type: Private

2000 Sales: $1,000.0 million
1-Yr. Sales Change: (3.8%)
Employees: 700
FYE: December 31

ViewSonic has a display for every occasion. The company makes color computer monitors, including the Professional series for high-end computer-aided design, desktop publishing, and graphic design; the Graphics line for graphics applications, home use, and small office automation; the value-priced E2 series for small business and personal use; and the A Series for replacing monitors included in bundled systems. ViewSonic, which purchased Nokia's display business and continues to offer Nokia branded monitors, also makes liquid crystal and plasma flat-panel displays and liquid crystal display projectors. CEO James Chu, who founded ViewSonic in 1987, advocates stock ownership for all employees.

**KEY COMPETITORS**
NEC
Samsung Electronics
Sony

## VIRGINIA STATE LOTTERY

900 E. Main St.
Richmond, VA 23219
Phone: 804-692-7000
Fax: 804-692-7102
Web: www.valottery.com

CEO: Penelope W. Kyle
CFO: Donna van Cleave
HR: —
Type: Government-owned

2001 Sales: $1,002.8 million
1-Yr. Sales Change: 3.1%
Employees: 300
FYE: June 30

For some Virginians taking a chance at the corner store involves more than choosing the least overcooked hot dog. The Virginia State Lottery operates several instant-win scratch-off games, as well as popular number games (Pick 3, Pick 4, and a six-number Lotto game). More than half of the money raised from ticket sales is paid out in prizes; about 35% goes to the state's general fund earmarked for public education. Unclaimed prize money, about $7 million a year, is used specifically to build or renovate schools. Virginia also participates in the seven-state Big Game lottery. Created in 1987, the Virginia State Lottery has collected more than $4 billion for the state.

**KEY COMPETITORS**
Kentucky Lottery
Maryland State Lottery
Multi-State Lottery

## VISA INTERNATIONAL

900 Metro Center Blvd.
Foster City, CA 94404
Phone: 650-432-3200
Fax: 650-432-3087
Web: www.visa.com

CEO: Malcolm Williamson
CFO: Ken Sommer
HR: Elizabeth Rounds
Type: Private

2000 Est. Sales: $3,000.0 mil.
1-Yr. Sales Change: 7.1%
Employees: 5,000
FYE: September 30

Paper or plastic? Visa International hopes you'll choose the latter. Visa operates the world's largest consumer payment system (ahead of MasterCard and American Express) with about 1 billion credit and other payment cards in circulation. The company is owned by 21,000 banks, each of which issues and markets its own Visa products in competition with the others. They all participate in the VisaNet payment system, which provides authorization, transaction processing, and settlement services for purchases from 21 million merchants worldwide. In addition to credit cards, Visa also provides its customers with debit cards, Internet payment systems, value-storing smart cards, and traveler's checks.

**KEY COMPETITORS**
American Express
MasterCard
Morgan Stanley Dean Witter

 See pages 508–509 for a full profile of this company.

## VOUGHT AIRCRAFT INDUSTRIES, INC.

9314 W. Jefferson Blvd.
Dallas, TX 75211
Phone: 972-946-2011
Fax: 972-946-3465
Web: www.voughtaircraft.com

CEO: Tom Risley
CFO: William J. McMillan
HR: Margo B. Parker
Type: Private

2000 Est. Sales: $1,000.0 mil.
1-Yr. Sales Change: —
Employees: 5,000
FYE: December 31

Vought Aircraft Industries is one of the world's largest aerostructures subcontractors. The company provides fuselage subassemblies (doors and fuselage panels), nacelles, thrust reversers, empennage structures, wings, and other components for both military and commercial aircraft manufacturers. It makes parts for almost all of Boeing's commercial fleet, ranging from the 737 to the 777. Other customers include Dassault Aviation, GE, Gulfstream, Lockheed Martin, NASA, and Raytheon. Vought subcontracts for programs that build military cargo planes (C-17), bombers (B-2), and fighters (F-14 and F/A-18). It also provides spare parts, maintenance, repair, and overhaul services. The Carlyle Group owns about 90% of Vought.

**KEY COMPETITORS**
CPI Aerostructures
Goodrich
LMI Aerospace

## VT INC.

| | | |
|---|---|---|
| 8500 Shawnee Mission Pkwy., Ste. 200 | CEO: Cecil Van Tuyl | 2000 Sales: $4,300.0 million |
| Merriam, KS 66202 | CFO: Robert J. Holcomb | 1-Yr. Sales Change: 19.4% |
| Phone: 913-432-6400 | HR: John A. Morford | Employees: 6,000 |
| Fax: 913-789-1039 | Type: Private | FYE: December 31 |
| Web: www.vanenterprises.com | | |

VT is in pursuit of the pole-position as one of the top five US car dealers. The company operates about 50 dealerships in 13 states, primarily Texas, Arizona, and Missouri; it sells about 104,000 new cars per year. It offers nearly 60 brands of new and used cars (and RVs) made by General Motors, Ford, Honda, Isuzu, and Nissan, among others. VT also engages in fleet sales and receives a significant portion of its revenue from back-shop operations such as parts and service and body shop sales. Founder and co-CEO Cecil Van Tuyl began his automotive empire in 1955. He owns the company with son and co-CEO Larry Van Tuyl.

**KEY COMPETITORS**
AutoNation
Hendrick Automotive
Jordan Automotive

## VULCAN NORTHWEST INC.

| | | |
|---|---|---|
| 110 110th Ave. NE, Ste. 550 | CEO: Jody Patton | Sales: — |
| Bellevue, WA 98004 | CFO: Joseph Franzi | 1-Yr. Sales Change: — |
| Phone: 425-453-1940 | HR: Pam Faber | Employees: — |
| Fax: 425-453-1985 | Type: Private | FYE: December 31 |
| Web: www.paulallen.com | | |

Even with all his Vulcan logic, could Spock invest like *this?* Brainy billionaire Paul Allen organizes his business and charitable ventures under Vulcan Northwest. Allen, who co-founded Microsoft with Bill Gates, promotes a "wired world" vision, in which everyone is united through interconnecting communications, entertainment, and information systems. Vulcan Northwest includes Allen's stake in Microsoft (about 5%), as well as holdings in dozens of companies providing computer, multimedia, or communications products and services, and six charitable organizations supporting the arts, medical research, and conservation. Allen also owns the NBA's Portland Trail Blazers and the NFL's Seattle Seahawks.

**KEY COMPETITORS**
Benchmark Capital
Draper Fisher Jurvetson
Kleiner Perkins

 See pages 510–511 for a full profile of this company.

## WAFFLE HOUSE INC.

| | | |
|---|---|---|
| 5986 Financial Dr. | CEO: Joe W. Rogers Jr. | 2001 Est. Sales: $625.0 mil. |
| Norcross, GA 30071 | CFO: T.J. Turner | 1-Yr. Sales Change: 7.8% |
| Phone: 770-729-5700 | HR: Ann Parker | Employees: 6,000 |
| Fax: 770-729-5999 | Type: Private | FYE: June 30 |
| Web: www.wafflehouse.com | | |

The pancake's crunchier cousin gets top billing at the Waffle House. The company owns or franchises about 1,300 restaurants, most of which are in the Southeast. If you need your waffle fix at 3 a.m., Waffle House is open 24 hours a day. The first of these roadside restaurants opened on Labor Day, 1955, and the menu has changed little since then. In addition to their namesake golden grids, the stores offer traditional coffee shop fare with a southern twang, including cheeseburgers, T-bone steaks, sandwiches, grits, and hash browns. The company has shied away from the media since a 1983 lawsuit alleged it was paying excessively low wages. Employee-owned Waffle House has also been the subject of several suits alleging race and gender bias.

**KEY COMPETITORS**
Advantica Restaurant Group
IHOP
Shoney's

 See pages 512–513 for a full profile of this company.

## WAKE FOREST UNIVERSITY BAPTIST MEDICAL CENTER

Medical Center Blvd.
Winston-Salem, NC 27157
Phone: 336-716-2011
Fax: 336-716-6841
Web: www.wfubmc.edu

CEO: Richard H. Dean
CFO: Douglas E. Nelson
HR: Kevin A. Myatt
Type: Not-for-profit

Sales: —
1-Yr. Sales Change: —
Employees: 9,600
FYE: June 30

Wake Forest University Baptist Medical Center is a bastion of health in the thick of tobacco country. The not-for-profit system is comprised of Wake Forest University School of Medicine (founded in 1902), the North Carolina Baptist Hospitals (founded in 1923, with facilities devoted to geriatrics, cancer, pediatrics, and more), and an affiliated regional system that includes community hospitals and primary care offices. The company also offers rehabilitation, skilled nursing, home health, and a unit devoted to coordinating special services for international patients. Wake Forest University Baptist Medical Center also operates QualChoice, an HMO.

**KEY COMPETITORS**
Greenville Hospital System
Novant Health
Sentara Healthcare

## WAKEFERN FOOD CORPORATION

600 York St.
Elizabeth, NJ 07207
Phone: 908-527-3300
Fax: 908-527-3397
Web: www.shoprite.com

CEO: Thomas Infusino
CFO: Ken Jasinkiewicz
HR: Ernie Bell
Type: Cooperative

2000 Sales: $5,800.0 million
1-Yr. Sales Change: 5.5%
Employees: 5,000
FYE: September 30

Started by seven men who each invested $1,000, Wakefern Food has grown into the largest supermarket cooperative in the US. The co-op is owned by more than 40 independent grocers who operate about 200 ShopRite supermarkets in Connecticut, Delaware, New Jersey (where it is a dominant chain), New York, and Pennsylvania. More than half of ShopRite stores offer pharmacies. In addition to name-brand and private-label products (ShopRite, Chef's Express, Reddington Farms), Wakefern supports its members with advertising, merchandising, insurance, and other services. Although the holdings of members range in size from one store to 32 (Big V Supermarkets), each member holds an equal voting share.

**KEY COMPETITORS**
C&S Wholesale
A&P
Pathmark

 See pages 514–515 for a full profile of this company.

## THE WALSH GROUP

929 W. Adams St.
Chicago, IL 60607
Phone: 312-563-5400
Fax: 312-563-5466
Web: www.walshgroup.com

CEO: Matthew M. Walsh
CFO: Larry Kibbon
HR: Rhonda Hardwick
Type: Private

2000 Sales: $1,304.0 million
1-Yr. Sales Change: 20.7%
Employees: 2,600
FYE: December 31

The Walsh Group erects walls, halls, malls, and more. Walsh provides design/build and construction services for industrial, public, and commercial projects throughout the US. Its undertakings have ranged from prisons to skyscrapers to shopping malls. The group consists of Walsh Construction Company of Chicago and Archer Western Contractors of Fort Lauderdale, Florida. Operating from 14 regional offices, Walsh provides complete project management services, from planning and demolition to general contracting and finance. It also renovates and restores buildings and provides interior construction and design services. The Walsh family owns the company, which was founded in 1898.

**KEY COMPETITORS**
Bechtel
McCarthy
Turner Corporation

## WARREN EQUITIES INC.

| | | |
|---|---|---|
| 27 Warren Way | CEO: Herbert Kaplan | 2001 Sales: $984.0 million |
| Providence, RI 02905 | CFO: John Dziedzic | 1-Yr. Sales Change: 23.5% |
| Phone: 401-781-9900 | HR: Thomas Palumbo | Employees: 2,200 |
| Fax: 401-461-7160 | Type: Private | FYE: May 31 |
| Web: www.warreneq.com | | |

Warren Equities fills car tanks and stomachs in the US Northeast. The holding company sells fuel and groceries from about 640 service stations and convenience stores from Maine to Virginia operating under the Xtra Mart brand. Warren's distribution companies supply those stores, as well as independent outlets, with gasoline and grocery and tobacco products. Other Warren companies trade and store petroleum, provide environmental testing services, and make promotional signs and clothing. Chairman and owner Warren Alpert founded the company in 1950 after Standard Oil awarded him a distributorship. His foundation gives annual grants to medical researchers; he has donated more than $20 million to Harvard Medical School.

**KEY COMPETITORS**
7-Eleven
Getty Petroleum Marketing
Wawa

## WASHINGTON GROUP INTERNATIONAL, INC.

| | | |
|---|---|---|
| Morrision Knudsen Plaza | CEO: Stephen G. Hanks | Sales: — |
| Boise, ID 83729 | CFO: George H. Juetten | 1-Yr. Sales Change: — |
| Phone: 208-386-5000 | HR: Larry L. Myers | Employees: 35,000 |
| Fax: 208-386-7186 | Type: Private | FYE: November 30 |
| Web: www.wgint.com | | |

Staying alive, Washington Group International, although under reorganization after filing for bankruptcy in 2001, remains one of the largest US construction and engineering firms. It provides design and construction services for projects such as bridges, highways, manufacturing plants, mining, nuclear facilities, pipelines, power facilities, and railroads; it also operates mines and provides environmental management services. The former Morrison Knudsen doubled in size with the acquisition of Raytheon's engineering and construction unit in 2000; the combined company changed its name to Washington Group International that year. However, the company believed the Raytheon transaction caused it to slide into bankruptcy.

**KEY COMPETITORS**
Bechtel
Fluor
Turner Corporation

## WASHINGTON UNIVERSITY IN ST. LOUIS

| | | |
|---|---|---|
| 1 Brookings Dr. | CEO: Mark Stephen Wrighton | 2000 Sales: $1,023.8 million |
| St. Louis, MO 63130 | CFO: Barbara Feiner | 1-Yr. Sales Change: (2.8%) |
| Phone: 314-935-5000 | HR: John Loya | Employees: 7,963 |
| Fax: 314-935-4259 | Type: School | FYE: June 30 |
| Web: www.wustl.edu | | |

Washington University in St. Louis is the gateway to higher education for more than 12,000 students. Founded in 1853, the private university is renowned for its academic programs in business, law, medical research, occupational therapy, physical therapy, and social work. Students can also explore fields of study such as architecture, art, and engineering. Faculty members include a US poet laureate, a Nobel prize winner, and a recipient of the National Medal of Arts. A leader in research, the university receives substantial research funding from the National Science Foundation and the National Institutes of Health.

## WATKINS ASSOCIATED INDUSTRIES

1958 Monroe Dr. NE
Atlanta, GA 30324
Phone: 404-872-3841
Fax: 404-872-2812

CEO: John Watkins
CFO: Richard Wuori
HR: Milton Eades
Type: Private

2000 Sales: $1,076.0 million
1-Yr. Sales Change: 9.6%
Employees: 10,000
FYE: December 31

A family business involved in trucking, seafood, and concrete may sound fishy, but the highly diversified Watkins Associated is on the up and up. Its Watkins Motor Lines (which makes up about 90% of sales) is a long-haul, less-than-truckload (LTL) carrier serving customers in the US, Canada, and Mexico. The trucking company operates some 2,800 tractors, 11,000 trailers, and 133 terminals. Its services include online tracking and expedited delivery. Watkins Associated's other activities include shrimp processing, real estate development (primarily apartment complexes and shopping centers), bridge building, and citrus growing. Bill Watkins founded the family-owned company in 1932 with a $300 pickup truck.

**KEY COMPETITORS**
CNF
Old Dominion
Roadway


## WAWA INC.

260 W. Baltimore Pike
Wawa, PA 19063
Phone: 610-358-8000
Fax: 610-358-8878
Web: www.wawa.com

CEO: Richard D. Wood Jr.
CFO: Edward Chambers
HR: Karen Casale
Type: Private

2000 Est. Sales: $1,500.0 mil.
1-Yr. Sales Change: 7.3%
Employees: 13,000
FYE: December 31

It's not baby talk — when folks say they need to go to the Wawa, they need groceries. Wawa runs more than 500 Wawa Food Markets in Delaware, Maryland, New Jersey, Pennsylvania, and Virginia. The stores are noted for their coffee and their salad and deli offerings, including hoagie sandwiches; about 50 outlets also sell gas. Unlike many convenience store chains, Wawa has its own dairy (which supplies the stores and about 1,000 hospitals, schools, and other institutions). The company opened its first store in 1964, but its roots go back to an iron foundry begun in 1803 by the Wood family; food operations began in 1902 when George Wood started a dairy in Wawa, Pennsylvania. The Wood family owns 52% of the company.

**KEY COMPETITORS**
7-Eleven
Sheetz
Uni-Marts


## WCI COMMUNITIES, INC.

24301 Walden Center Dr.
Bonita Springs, FL 34134
Phone: 941-947-2600
Fax: 941-498-8338
Web: www.wcicommunities.com

CEO: Alfred Hoffman Jr.
CFO: James P. Dietz
HR: S. Charles Mattoff
Type: Private

2000 Sales: $882.2 million
1-Yr. Sales Change: 29.5%
Employees: 2,600
FYE: December 31

Sunny climes and a generation of baby boomers nearing retirement may spell success for WCI Communities. The company develops palatial leisure and retirement communities on both the Atlantic and Gulf coasts in Florida. WCI builds luxury homes and residential towers, then adds amenities such as golf courses, marinas, tennis courts, and restaurants. The homebuilder also sells parcels of land in its communities to other developers for commercial and industrial use. WCI handles development, provides mortgage lending for homebuyers, and operates some of its communities' amenities. The company hopes to expand into suitable markets outside Florida.

**KEY COMPETITORS**
Lennar
Pulte Homes
Toll Brothers

## WEGMANS FOOD MARKETS, INC.

| | | |
|---|---|---|
| 1500 Brooks Ave. | CEO: Robert B. Wegman | 2000 Sales: $2,800.0 million |
| Rochester, NY 14603 | CFO: Jim Leo | 1-Yr. Sales Change: 4.9% |
| Phone: 716-328-2550 | HR: Gerald Pierce | Employees: 29,826 |
| Fax: 716-464-4664 | Type: Private | FYE: December 31 |
| Web: www.wegmans.com | | |

One name strikes fear in the hearts of supermarket owners in New York, Pennsylvania, and New Jersey: Wegmans. The supermarket chain owns about 60 stores, but the stores are hardly typical — they're much larger than most supermarkets (up to 120,000 sq. ft.), and they offer specialty shops such as huge in-store cafes, cheese shops with some 400 different varieties, and French-style pastry shops with exotic desserts. The company is also known for its gourmet cooking classes and an extensive employee-training program. In addition, Wegmans runs about 15 Chase-Pitkin Home & Garden home-improvement stores. Founded in 1916, the company is still owned by the family of founder John Wegman. His nephew, Robert Wegman, is CEO.

**KEY COMPETITORS**
Ahold USA
Penn Traffic
Safeway


## WESTCON GROUP, INC.

| | | |
|---|---|---|
| 520 White Plains Rd., Ste. 100 | CEO: Alan Marc Smith | 2001 Sales: $1,939.2 million |
| Tarrytown, NY 10591 | CFO: John P. O'Malley III | 1-Yr. Sales Change: 66.0% |
| Phone: 914-829-7000 | HR: — | Employees: 1,059 |
| Fax: 914-829-7137 | Type: Private | FYE: February 28 |
| Web: www.westcongroup.com | | |

Westcon Group is down with OPP — other people's products. The company's three divisions, Comstor, Westcon, and Voda One, resell networking equipment made by Cisco Systems (more than 65% of sales), Nortel Networks, Lucent, and other top manufacturers. Networking servers, switches, and routers; network security systems; and virtual private network systems top Westcon's product list. The company also provides support services, including training, network design, and logistical support. Chairman Thomas Dolan and EVP Philip Raffiani founded Westcon in 1985. South Africa-based networking company Datatec owns an 85% stake in the company.

**KEY COMPETITORS**
Ingram Micro
ScanSource
Tech Data


## WESTFARM FOODS

| | | |
|---|---|---|
| 635 Elliott Ave. | CEO: John E. Mueller | 2001 Sales: $1,116.2 million |
| Seattle, WA 98119 | CFO: Stephen Boyd | 1-Yr. Sales Change: 1.5% |
| Phone: 206-284-7220 | HR: John Lamantia | Employees: 1,300 |
| Fax: 206-281-3456 | Type: Cooperative | FYE: March 31 |
| Web: www.darigold.com | | |

Churning out golden dairy foods since 1918, WestFarm Foods (formerly Darigold) is one of the largest dairy cooperatives in the US. It is owned by about 850 dairy producers in Northern California, Idaho, Oregon, and Washington. With 12 processing plants and three Darigold Farm stores, the co-op makes, distributes, and markets butter, cheese, cultured products (cottage cheese, sour cream), dry milk, fluid milk, ice cream and frozen novelties, and juice under the Darigold name. Its Dairy Export subsidiary also owns about 80% of juice maker Olympic Foods and 30% of the Western Feed Division of Land O' Lakes. Affiliate and part-owner County Classic Dairies operates as Darigold Farms of Montana.

**KEY COMPETITORS**
Dairy Farmers of America
Land O'Lakes
Suiza Dairy Group

## WHITE CASTLE SYSTEM, INC.

555 W. Goodale St.
Columbus, OH 43215
Phone: 614-228-5781
Fax: 614-464-0596
Web: www.whitecastle.com

CEO: E. W. "Bill" Ingram III
CFO: William A. Blake
HR: Fred Gunderson
Type: Private

2000 Est. Sales: $400.0 mil.
1-Yr. Sales Change: 0.0%
Employees: 10,000
FYE: December 31

White Castle doesn't rook hamburger lovers out of a meal. White Castle System's little square hamburgers, known as Slyders, are steamed over a bed of onions and can be found at about 350 restaurants in 12 eastern and midwestern states. White Castle, founded in 1921, was the first fast-food hamburger chain; it still owns all of the White Castle restaurants. White Castle's PSB subsidiary makes metal products, including fixtures and cooking tools needed at the restaurants. PSB also makes lawn spreaders under the PrizeLAWN brand. Chairman E. W. Ingram III (grandson of co-founder E. W. Ingram) and his family own the company.

**KEY COMPETITORS**
Burger King
McDonald's
Wendy's

 **See pages 516–517 for a full profile of this company.**


## THE WHITING-TURNER CONTRACTING COMPANY

300 E. Joppa Rd.
Baltimore, MD 21286
Phone: 410-821-1100
Fax: 410-337-5770
Web: www.whiting-turner.com

CEO: Willard Hackerman
CFO: Charles Irish
HR: Edward Spaulding
Type: Private

2000 Sales: $1,646.0 million
1-Yr. Sales Change: 16.1%
Employees: 2,000
FYE: December 31

Whiting-Turner Contracting is a big fish in an ocean of builders. The employee-owned firm provides construction management, general contracting, and design-build services, primarily for large commercial, institutional, and infrastructure projects in the US. Although the company subcontracts about 85% of its volume, in-house activities include mechanical and electrical work, concrete forming, and foundation services. Projects span a wide range of facilities, including biotech clean rooms, schools, shopping centers, stadiums, and corporate headquarters for such clients as AT&T, General Motors, and the US Army. G. W. C. Whiting and LeBaron Turner founded the company in 1909 to build sewer lines.

**KEY COMPETITORS**
Bechtel
Fluor
Skanska


## WILBUR-ELLIS COMPANY

345 California St., 27th Fl.
San Francisco, CA 94104
Phone: 415-772-4000
Fax: 415-772-4011
Web: www.wilbur-ellis.com

CEO: Herbert B. Tully
CFO: Jim Crawford
HR: Ofelia Lee
Type: Private

2000 Sales: $1,131.0 million
1-Yr. Sales Change: (13.0%)
Employees: 2,000
FYE: December 31

Helpful hint: Don't stand downwind of the Wilbur-Ellis Company. A distributor for major chemical companies, Wilbur-Ellis sells animal feed, fertilizer, insecticides, seed, and machinery through outlets in North America. Subsidiary Connell Brothers exports and distributes chemicals and feed throughout the Pacific Rim. Additionally, Wilbur-Ellis provides consulting, pesticide spraying, and other agriculture-related services. It also owns Knox McDaniels, a supplier of vitamin and mineral premix products in the western US. Brayton Wilbur Sr. and Floyd Ellis founded the company in 1921 as a fish-oil supplier; it is still owned by the Wilbur family.

**KEY COMPETITORS**
Agrium
Agway
CF Industries

## WILLIAM BEAUMONT HOSPITAL

| | | |
|---|---|---|
| 3601 W. 13 Mile Rd. | CEO: Ted Wasson | 2000 Sales: $1,000.0 million |
| Royal Oak, MI 48073 | CFO: Dennis R. Herrick | 1-Yr. Sales Change: 14.3% |
| Phone: 248-551-5000 | HR: Wesley Kokko | Employees: 11,500 |
| Fax: 248-551-1555 | Type: Private | FYE: December 31 |
| Web: www.beaumont.edu | | |

Dr. William Beaumont was an army doctor on Mackinac Island, Michigan, in the 1820s when a French fur trapper stumbled in with a gunshot wound to the gut. The wound left a permanent hole, and Beaumont used the unique insight to undertake groundbreaking studies of the digestive system. Some 200 years later the frontier physician's name graces William Beaumont Hospital, which includes two teaching hospitals (more than 1,000 beds) in suburban Detroit, a rehabilitation center, five nursing homes, a home health care service, a research institute, and primary and specialty care clinics. The hospitals are affiliated with the University of Michigan Medical School, Wayne State University School of Medicine, and Oakland University.

**KEY COMPETITORS**
Detroit Medical Center
Henry Ford Health System
Trinity Health


## WILLIAMSON-DICKIE MANUFACTURING COMPANY

| | | |
|---|---|---|
| 509 W. Vickery Blvd. | CEO: Philip C. Williamson | 2000 Sales: $820.0 million |
| Fort Worth, TX 76104 | CFO: Britt Ingebritson | 1-Yr. Sales Change: 5.1% |
| Phone: 817-336-7201 | HR: Marett Cobb | Employees: 6,300 |
| Fax: 817-877-5027 | Type: Private | FYE: December 31 |
| Web: www.dickies.com | | |

Appreciated by the working class and the sophomore class alike, Williamson-Dickie Manufacturing Company makes Dickies-brand khaki pants, bib overalls, jeans, and women's and children's apparel. It also produces Workrite safety uniforms. Founded in 1922, the company's work clothes were originally tailored with the blue-collar set in mind, but in recent years the Dickie's look has also fallen into favor with fashionable teens. Williamson-Dickie's work clothes portfolio includes Dickies T-shirts, which are made extra long to prevent the display of "plumber's crack" by squatting workmen. Dickies products are sold worldwide through retailers and directly to businesses. The founding Williamson family owns the company.

**KEY COMPETITORS**
Carhartt
Levi Strauss
VF


## WINCO FOODS, INC.

| | | |
|---|---|---|
| 650 N. Armstrong Place | CEO: William D. Long | 2001 Sales: $1,300.0 million |
| Boise, ID 83704 | CFO: Gary R. Piva | 1-Yr. Sales Change: 12.1% |
| Phone: 208-377-0110 | HR: Roger Cochell | Employees: 5,300 |
| Fax: 208-377-0474 | Type: Private | FYE: March 31 |
| Web: www.wincofoods.com | | |

WinCo Foods isn't just big on self-service — it's giant. Inside the immense stores (most of which are 82,000 sq. ft.) of this supermarket chain, customers are asked to shop for food in bulk and bag their own groceries. The company's 30-plus stores also feature pizza shops, bakeries, health and beauty products, and organic foods. WinCo Foods, formerly known as Waremart Foods, was renamed as a shortened version of "winning company." The name is also an acronym for its states of operation, which include Washington, Idaho, Nevada, California, and Oregon. Founded in 1968, WinCo Foods formerly operated stores under the Cub Foods and Waremart names. Employees own about 80% of the company.

**KEY COMPETITORS**
Albertson's
Raley's
Safeway

## WINGATE PARTNERS

750 N. St. Paul St., Ste. 1200
Dallas, TX 75201
Phone: 214-720-1313
Fax: 214-871-8799
Web: www.wingatepartners.com

CEO: Frederick B. Hegi Jr.
CFO: Alna Evans
HR: Alna Evans
Type: Private

Sales: —
1-Yr. Sales Change: —
Employees: —
FYE: December 31

Wingate Partners gets by on more than a wing and a prayer, rescuing lackluster manufacturing, distribution, and service businesses. With three funds worth some $290 billion, the investment firm avoids banking, media, high-tech, real estate, and certain other companies, investing instead in companies that are underperforming or that are in industries in transition. Targets often have revenues between $100 million and $500 million and may or may not be profitable at the time of purchase. It will invest between $10 million and $20 million in a holding. Wingate's portfolio includes holdings in Kevco (manufactured-housing building products distributor) and auto parts distributor Pro Parts Xpress.

**KEY COMPETITORS**
AEA Investors
Clayton, Dubilier
Texas Pacific Group

 **See pages 518–519 for a full profile of this company.**

## WIRTZ CORPORATION

680 N. Lakeshore Dr., 19th Fl.
Chicago, IL 60611
Phone: 312-943-7000
Fax: 312-943-9017

CEO: William W. Wirtz
CFO: Max Mohler
HR: Cindy Krch
Type: Private

2001 Sales: $860.0 million
1-Yr. Sales Change: (2.3%)
Employees: 2,000
FYE: June 30

Wirtz does best on ice. It owns the Chicago Blackhawks hockey team and is partnered with Jerry Reinsdorf, majority owner of the Chicago Bulls basketball team, for ownership of the United Center, where the teams play. Wirtz owns liquor distributorships, including Judge & Dolph, the largest in Illinois, and Edison Liquor Co. The Wirtz family gave thousands of dollars to state lawmakers in 1999 to pass a law that protected liquor distributors by making it difficult for liquor producers to switch distributors. (The law later was declared unconstitutional.) The firm owns property in Wisconsin, Mississippi, Texas, Nevada, and Florida. Arthur Wirtz (father of CEO William Wirtz) founded the family-controlled empire in 1922.

**KEY COMPETITORS**
Detroit Red Wings
Johnson Brothers
Southern Wine & Spirits

## W.K. KELLOGG FOUNDATION

1 Michigan Ave. East
Battle Creek, MI 49017
Phone: 616-968-1611
Fax: 616-968-0413
Web: www.wkkf.org

CEO: William C. Richardson
CFO: La June Montgomery-Tally
HR: —
Type: Foundation

2001 Sales: $222.7 million
1-Yr. Sales Change: (19.6%)
Employees: 209
FYE: August 31

Charitable grants from W.K. Kellogg Foundation are gr-r-reat! Founded in 1930 by cereal industry pioneer Will Keith Kellogg, the foundation provides about $200 million in grants each year to programs focused on youth and education, as well as health issues. It also funds many rural development and agricultural projects and works to foster greater volunteerism. Most of its grants go to initiatives in the US, though it also makes grants in Latin America and Africa. The foundation's work is funded primarily from its nearly $6 billion trust. Kellogg donated $66 million in stock to the foundation's trust in 1934; the Kellogg Foundation now owns about one-third of the Kellogg Company.

 **See pages 520–521 for a full profile of this company.**

## WKI HOLDING COMPANY, INC.

One Pyrex Place
Elmira, NY 14902
Phone: 607-377-8000
Fax: 607-377-8946
Web: www.worldkitchen.com

CEO: Steven G. Lamb
CFO: Joseph W. McGarr
HR: Craig A. Saline
Type: Private

2000 Sales: $827.6 million
1-Yr. Sales Change: 34.0%
Employees: 5,200
FYE: December 31

WKI Holding has cooked up a kitchen kingpin. The holding company's World Kitchen subsidiary (formerly Corning Consumer Products) makes some of the most popular kitchenware and tableware in the US. Its brands — including Corelle, CorningWare, Pyrex, Revere, and Visions — have been used since 1915, when a Corning engineer's wife used a streetlamp glass shade experimentally to bake a cake. The company doubled its size with its 1999 purchases of houseware firms EKCO Group (Farberware, Baker's Secret) and General Housewares (Chicago Cutlery, OXO); it adopted the WKI Holding name in 2000. Buyout firm Kohlberg Kravis Roberts bought most of the company in 1998 from optical fiber and high-performance glass maker Corning.

**KEY COMPETITORS**
Newell Rubbermaid
SEB
Tupperware

## W. L. GORE & ASSOCIATES, INC.

555 Paper Mill Rd.
Newark, DE 19711
Phone: 302-738-4880
Fax: 302-738-7710
Web: www.gore.com

CEO: Robert W. Gore
CFO: Charles Carroll
HR: Sally Gore
Type: Private

2000 Sales: $1,350.0 million
1-Yr. Sales Change: 5.5%
Employees: 5,888
FYE: March 31

W. L. Gore and Associates would like you to take a deep breath. The company makes fluoropolymer products from its breathable, lightweight GORE-TEX fabric. Product uses range from clothing and shoes to hernia repair patches, guitar strings, dental floss, space suits, and sutures. In addition to its apparel (popular among hikers and hunters), W. L. Gore makes insulated wire and cable and air filters. The company is also known for its lattice management style: bosses are "sponsors," and employees are "associates" working under no fixed authority, and consensus determines objectives. Each office has no more than 200 workers. The Gore family owns 75% of the company; Gore associates own the rest.

**KEY COMPETITORS**
Belden
Burlington Industries
Malden Mills

 See pages 522–523 for a full profile of this company.

## WOLVERINE PACKING COMPANY

2535 Rivard St.
Detroit, MI 48207
Phone: 313-259-7500
Fax: 313-568-1909
Web: www.wolverinepacking.com

CEO: Alfred J. "Jim" Bonahoom
CFO: Brian Bartes
HR: Denise Goodrich
Type: Private

2000 Sales: $810.0 million
1-Yr. Sales Change: 44.6%
Employees: 250
FYE: December 31

If Mary lost her little lamb anywhere near Detroit, it probably ended up at Wolverine Packing. The wholesale meat packer and distributor is one of the largest lamb processors in the US. The company slaughters, processes, trims, and packs veal and lamb and sells frozen beef, pork, and poultry to the food service industry and retailers. Wolverine Packing also produces Halal meats (in accordance with Muslim dietary laws) and portion control and patty products, and markets its veal as Bonnie Maid Premium Veal. The company was founded in 1937 and has operations in Detroit's historic Eastern Market district. The family of the late Al Bonahoom, the company's founder, owns and operates Wolverine Packing.

**KEY COMPETITORS**
ConAgra
IBP
Rosen's Diversified

## WOODBRIDGE GROUP

2500 Meijer Dr.
Troy, MI 48084
Phone: 248-288-0100
Fax: 248-288-1640
Web: www.woodbridgegroup.com

CEO: T. Robert Beamish
CFO: Annie Brideau
HR: Grant Oliver
Type: Private

2000 Sales: $880.0 million
1-Yr. Sales Change: —
Employees: 5,000
FYE: December 31

Foam is where the heart is for Woodbridge Group. The company is a Tier II supplier of structural, seating, energy absorbing, and mechanical automotive foams. Products include foams for interior components that provide knee and lower-limb protection in the event of a collision. Additional foam applications include head restraints, armrests, rear seat bolsters, carpet padding, and acoustical foams. Woodbridge also offers assembly services and can assist its customers with product design and engineering. Co-founder and chairman T. Robert Beamish controls more than 75% of the company.

**KEY COMPETITORS**
Carpenter
Foamex
Lear

## WORLDTRAVEL BTI

1055 Lenox Blvd., Ste. 420
Atlanta, GA 30319
Phone: 404-841-6600
Fax: 404-814-2983
Web: www.worldtravel.com

CEO: Michael A. Buckman
CFO: Thomas Barham
HR: Nancy Pavey
Type: Private

2000 Sales: $3,800.0 million
1-Yr. Sales Change: 8.6%
Employees: 5,800
FYE: December 31

Instead of phoning home, E.T. could have called WorldTravel BTI. WorldTravel has grown from a small travel agency to #3 in the US (behind American Express and Carlson Wagonlit). Clients include many large US corporations such as PepsiCo, Deloitte Touche, and De Beers. WorldTravel has more than 1,600 ticketing locations and 45 affiliates across the US; through Business Travel International (BTI) it offers another 3,000 locations in more than 70 countries. Its WorldTravelNet offers personalized travel information and services, including real-time flight status, hotel rates, weather, and maps. Chairman John Fentener van Vlissingen owns a majority stake in the company through BCD Holdings.

**KEY COMPETITORS**
American Express
Carlson Wagonlit
Rosenbluth International

## YALE UNIVERSITY

451 College St.
New Haven, CT 06520
Phone: 203-432-4771
Fax: 203-432-7891
Web: www.yale.edu

CEO: Richard C. Levin
CFO: Robert L. Culver
HR: Katherine F. "Kitty" Matzkin
Type: School

2000 Sales: $1,263.7 million
1-Yr. Sales Change: 9.9%
Employees: 10,800
FYE: June 30

What do President George W. Bush, writer William F. Buckley Jr., and actress Meryl Streep have in common? They are all Yalies. Yale University is one of the nation's most prestigious private liberal arts institutions, as well as one of its oldest (founded in 1701). Its $10.1 billion endowment ranks second only to Harvard's in the US. Yale comprises an undergraduate college, a graduate school, and 10 professional schools. Programs of study include architecture, law, medicine, and drama. Its 12 residential colleges (a system borrowed from Oxford) serve as dormitory, dining hall, and social center. The school has more than 11,000 students and some 3,300 faculty members.

## YMCA OF THE USA

| | | |
|---|---|---|
| 101 N. Wacker Dr. | CEO: Kenneth Gladish | 2000 Sales: $3,907.3 million |
| Chicago, IL 60606 | CFO: Kate Spencer | 1-Yr. Sales Change: 11.6% |
| Phone: 312-977-0031 | HR: — | Employees: 25,000 |
| Fax: 312-977-9063 | Type: Not-for-profit | FYE: December 31 |
| Web: www.ymca.net | | |

If the Village People can be believed, it's fun to stay at the YMCA. One of the nation's largest not-for-profit community service organizations, YMCA of the USA assists the nearly 2,400 individual YMCAs across the country and represents them on both national and international levels. YMCAs serve more than 17 million people across the US. One of the largest child-care providers in the US, YMCAs also offer programs in areas such as aquatics, arts and humanities, health and fitness, and teen leadership. The first YMCA in the US was established in 1851 as an outgrowth of the YMCA movement launched by George Williams in the UK in 1844.

## YOUNG'S MARKET COMPANY, LLC

| | | |
|---|---|---|
| 2164 N. Batavia St. | CEO: Charles Andrews | 2001 Est. Sales: $1,300.0 mil. |
| Orange, CA 92865 | CFO: Dennis J. Hamann | 1-Yr. Sales Change: 18.2% |
| Phone: 714-283-4933 | HR: Naomi Buenaslor | Employees: 1,700 |
| Fax: 714-283-6175 | Type: Private | FYE: February 28 |
| Web: www.youngsmkt.com | | |

Although no longer young, Young's Market Company is in high spirits. Young's Market is one of the largest distributors of beer, wine, and distilled spirits in the US. It is a major supplier along the Pacific coast and operates in Hawaii through subsidiary Better Brands. The company distributes products for Bacardi and Brown-Forman, among others. An alliance with Sunbelt Beverage Corporation has created a larger distribution network for Young's. John Young founded the company in 1888, which at one time included grocery retailing and specialty food distribution. The Underwood family, relatives of the Youngs, bought Young's Market in 1990.

**KEY COMPETITORS**
Glazer's Wholesale Drug
Southern Wine & Spirits
Topa Equities

## THE YUCAIPA COMPANIES LLC

| | | |
|---|---|---|
| 9130 W. Sunset Blvd. | CEO: Ronald W. Burkle | Sales: — |
| Los Angeles, CA 90069 | CFO: — | 1-Yr. Sales Change: — |
| Phone: 310-789-7200 | HR: Marla Hunter | Employees: — |
| Fax: 310-884-2600 | Type: Private | FYE: December 31 |

The Yucaipa Companies has commitment problems. The investment vehicle of billionaire businessman Ron Burkle, the company made its name with grocery stores, having owned Jurgensen's, Falley's, and ABC Markets, among other chains. It now holds a 2% stake in Kroger. Yucaipa also owns 70% of Golden State Foods (one of McDonald's largest food suppliers) and 9% of food distributor Fleming. By the late 1990s the company was moving into cyberspace, with a 50% stake in e-commerce Web site CheckOut.com and other online investments. Yucaipa sold CheckOut.com in 2001 and bought 6% of retail giant Kmart. It also owns music and video distributor Alliance Entertainment and holds a minority stake in marketing firm Simon Worldwide.

**KEY COMPETITORS**
Ingram Entertainment
Keystone Foods
Wal-Mart

📖 See pages 524–525 for a full profile of this company.

# Hoover's Handbook of Private Companies

THE INDEXES

Massachusetts Mutual Life
Insurance Company **320-321**,
667
Minnesota Mutual Companies,
Inc. 677
New York Life Insurance
Company **370-371**, 688
Northwestern Mutual **376-377**,
690
Pacific Mutual Holding
Company **384-385**, 695
Penn Mutual Life Insurance
Co. 698
The Union Central Life
Insurance Company 753

**Multiline Insurance**

American United Life Insurance
Company 539
Amica Mutual Insurance
Company 540
Liberty Mutual Insurance
Companies **294-295**, 658
The Mutual of Omaha
Companies **348-349**, 680
National Life Insurance Co. 684
Nationwide **364-365**, 685
Ohio Farmers Insurance
Company 693
Sentry Insurance, A Mutual
Company 726
Trustmark Insurance
Company 750
The Union Labor Life Insurance
Company 754
USAA **502-503**, 763

**Property/Casualty Insurance**

American Family Insurance
Group **42-43**, 538
Kemper Insurance
Companies **268-269**, 650
State Farm Insurance
Companies **458-459**, 735

**Surety, Title & Miscellaneous
Insurance**

Federated Insurance
Companies 607
Pension Benefit Guaranty
Corporation **388-389**, 699

## LEISURE

**Gambling Resorts & Casinos**

Horseshoe Gaming Holding
Corp. 634
Mashantucket Pequot Gaming
Enterprise Inc. **318-319**, 667

**Gaming Activities**

California State Lottery
Commission 564
Connecticut Lottery
Corporation 581
Georgia Lottery
Corporation 615
Illinois Department of the
Lottery 638
Maryland State Lottery
Agency 666

Massachusetts State Lottery
Commission 668
Michigan Lottery 675
Multi-State Lottery
Association 680
New Jersey State Lottery
Commission 687
New York State
Lottery **372-373**, 688
Ohio Lottery Commission 693
The Pennsylvania Lottery 698
State of Florida Department of
the Lottery 736
Texas Lottery
Commission **472-473**, 744
Virginia State Lottery 766

**Lodging**

Hyatt Corporation **240-241**,
636
Strategic Hotel Capital LLC 737

**Miscellaneous Entertainment**

Feld Entertainment,
Inc. **188-189**, 608

**Professional Sports Teams
& Organizations**

The Edward J. DeBartolo
Corporation **172-173**, 602
The Green Bay Packers,
Inc. **210-211**, 621
Major League Baseball **306-307**,
663
National Association for Stock
Car Auto Racing 681
National Basketball
Association **354-355**, 682
National Football
League **356-357**, 683
National Hockey
League **360-361**, 684

**Restaurants**

Buffets, Inc. 562
Chick-fil-A Inc. **124-125**, 575
Doctor's Associates
Inc. **160-161**, 595
Domino's Inc. **162-163**, 595
Investors Management
Corp. 642
Waffle House Inc. **512-513**, 767
White Castle System,
Inc. **516-517**, 772

**Specialty Eateries & Catering
Services**

Delaware North Companies
Inc. 590

**Sporting Activities**

24 Hour Fitness Worldwide
Inc. 528
ClubCorp, Inc. **130-131**, 577

**Travel Agencies, Tour Operators
& Other Travel Services**

Carlson Wagonlit
Travel **108-109**, 567
Liberty Travel, Inc. **296-297**,
658
Maritz Inc. **308-309**, 664

Rosenbluth
International **418-419**, 717
WorldTravel BTI 776

## MANUFACTURING

**Diversified Machinery**

AMSTED Industries
Incorporated 540
Connell Limited
Partnership 581
NESCO, Inc. 686

**Fluid Control Equipment, Pumps,
Seals & Valves**

Colfax Corporation 578
Swagelok 739

**Glass & Clay Products**

Guardian Industries
Corp. **212-213**, 623

**Industrial Equipment & Products
Distribution**

CHEMCENTRAL
Corporation 573
Consolidated Electrical
Distributors Inc. 582
Graybar Electric Company,
Inc. **208-209**, 620

**Lighting & Other Fixtures**

Genlyte Thomas Group LLC 613

**Machine Tools, Components
& Accessories**

Harbour Group Industries,
Inc. 625

**Material Handling Machinery**

Crown Equipment
Corporation 586

**Packaging & Containers**

Dart Container
Corporation **150-151**, 588
Graham Packaging Company,
L. P. 620
Green Bay Packaging Inc. 621
Plastipak Packaging, Inc. 702
Printpack, Inc. 705
The SF Holdings Group,
Inc. 727
U.S. Can Corporation 762

**Paper & Paper Products**

Central National-Gottesman
Inc. 571
Menasha Corporation 673
The Newark Group 689
Parsons & Whittemore,
Incorporated 696
Riverwood International
Corporation 715

**Rubber & Plastic Products**

Woodbridge Group 776

**Textile Manufacturing**

Beaulieu Of America, LLC 552
Milliken & Company
Inc. **342-343**, 677
Parkdale Mills, Inc. 696
R. B. Pamplin Corp. 711

W. L. Gore & Associates,
Inc. **522-523**, 775
**Wire & Cable**
Jordan Industries, Inc. 647

# MATERIALS
# & CONSTRUCTION
**Engineering & Architectural
Services**
AECOM Technology
Corporation 531
Barton Malow Company 550
BE&K Inc. 552
Black & Veatch 556
CH2M Hill Companies, Ltd. 573
The Day & Zimmermann Group,
Inc. 589
Parsons Brinckerhoff Inc. 696
Skidmore Owings & Merrill
LLP **448-449**, 730
**Heavy Construction**
Austin Industries Inc. 547
Bechtel Group, Inc. **74-75**, 552
The Beck Group 553
Brasfield & Gorrie, LLC 560
Charles Pankow Builders,
Ltd. 573
Clark Enterprises, Inc. 576
Devcon Construction
Incorporated 592
Dick Corporation 593
Dillingham Construction
Corporation 593
DPR Construction, Inc. 597
Dunn Industries, Inc. 599
Fisher Development, Inc. 608
Gilbane, Inc. 615
H. B. Zachry Company 627
Hensel Phelps Construction
Co. 630
Hoffman Corporation 632
Hunt Construction Group 635
J. F. Shea Co., Inc. 643
J.S. Alberici Construction Co.,
Inc. 649
M. A. Mortenson Company 663
McCarthy 669
Modern Continental Companies,
Inc. 678
Parsons Corporation **386-387**,
697
Pepper Construction Group,
LLC 700
Peter Kiewit Sons',
Inc. **396-397**, 701
Rooney Brothers Company 716
Rudolph and Sletten, Inc. 719
The Structure Tone
Organization 737
Swinerton Incorporated 740
TIC Holdings Inc. 745
The Walsh Group 768
Washington Group
International, Inc. 769
The Whiting-Turner Contracting
Company 772

**Lumber, Wood Production
& Timber Operations**
Columbia Forest Products
Inc. 579
Lumbermens Merchandising
Corporation 662
Sierra Pacific Industries 728
**Miscellaneous Building Materials**
Andersen Corporation **50-51**,
541
G-I Holdings, Inc. 612
JELD-WEN, inc. 643
National Gypsum Company 683
Pella Corporation 698
**Plumbing & HVAC Equipment**
Kohler Co. **284-285**, 653

# MEDIA
**Information Collection
& Delivery Services**
The Associated Press **60-61**, 546
Bloomberg L.P. **80-81**, 556
**Media**
Cox Enterprises, Inc. **146-147**,
585
The Hearst
Corporation **228-229**, 629
National Amusements Inc. 681
**Motion Picture & Video
Production & Distribution**
DreamWorks SKG **166-167**,
597
Lucasfilm Ltd. **302-303**, 661
**Movie Theaters**
Cinemark USA, Inc. **126-127**,
575
Regal Cinemas, Inc. **412-413**,
712
**Publishing**
Advance Publications,
Inc. **32-33**, 530
Consumers Union of United
States, Inc. **138-139**, 582
Encyclopædia Britannica,
Inc. **176-177**, 603
Freedom Communications,
Inc. 611
Hallmark Cards, Inc. **216-217**,
625
International Data
Group **248-249**, 641
Johnson Publishing Company,
Inc. **258-259**, 646
Journal Communications
Inc. 648
Landmark Communications,
Inc. 655
MediaNews Group, Inc. 670
Rand McNally &
Company **408-409**, 711
**Television Production,
Programming & Distribution**
Harpo, Inc. **218-219**, 625

**TV Broadcasting**
Corporation for Public
Broadcasting **144-145**, 585
Discovery Communications,
Inc. **158-159**, 594
ESPN, Inc. 605

# METALS & MINING
**Coal**
AEI Resources, Inc. 531
**Diversified Mining & Metals**
Quexco Incorporated 709
**Metals & Alloys Distribution**
O'Neal Steel, Inc. 694
Tang Industries, Inc. 741
**Miscellaneous Mining & Metals
Processing**
Soave Enterprises L.L.C. 731
**Steel Production**
Earle M. Jorgensen
Company 601
OmniSource Corporation 694
Renco Group Inc. 712
Republic Technologies
International, LLC 713
Southwire Company 733

# REAL ESTATE
**Miscellaneous Real Estate
Services**
CB Richard Ellis Services,
Inc. **120-121**, 571
Colliers International Property
Consultants Inc. 578
Cushman & Wakefield Inc. 587
**Property Investment
& Management**
Berwind Group 554
Gale & Wentworth, L.L.C. 613
Helmsley Enterprises,
Inc. **230-231**, 629
JMB Realty Corporation 645
NRT Incorporated 692
Trammell Crow Residential 747
The Trump
Organization **482-483**, 749
**Real Estate Development**
The Irvine Company
Inc. **252-253**, 642
JPI 648
The Lefrak
Organization **290-291**, 656
Lincoln Property Company 659
Opus Corporation 695
Tishman Realty & Construction
Co. Inc. **476-477**, 745
WCI Communities, Inc. 770
**Residential Construction**
A. G. Spanos Companies 532
David Weekley Homes 588

## RETAIL

**Auto Parts Retail & Wholesale**
CARQUEST Corporation **112-113**, 569
Discount Tire Co. 594
General Parts, Inc. 613
Heafner Tire Group, Inc. 628
LDI, Ltd. 656
Les Schwab Tire Centers 657

**Building Materials & Gardening Supplies Retail & Wholesale**
84 Lumber Company **26-27**, 528
Ace Hardware Corporation **30-31**, 529
American Builders & Contractors Supply Co., Inc. 537
Builder Marts of America, Inc. 562
Builders FirstSource, Inc. 562
Do it Best Corp. 594
Lanoga Corporation 655
Menard, Inc. **330-331**, 672
North Pacific Group, Inc. 690
Primus, Inc. 705
Quality Stores, Inc. **406-407**, 709
Sutherland Lumber Company, L.P. 739
TruServ Corporation **484-485**, 749

**Clothing, Shoe & Accessory Retail & Wholesale**
American Retail Group Inc. 539
J. Crew Group, Inc. **254-255**, 642
L.L. Bean, Inc. **300-301**, 660
Retail Brand Alliance, Inc. 713

**Consumer Electronics & Appliance**
P.C. Richard & Son 697

**Convenience Stores & Gas Stations**
Clark Retail Group, Inc. 577
Cumberland Farms, Inc. 586
Flying J Inc. 609
Hale-Halsell Co. 624
Holiday Companies 633
Petro Stopping Centers, L.P. 701
Pilot Corporation 702
QuikTrip Corporation 710
RaceTrac Petroleum, Inc. 710
Sheetz, Inc. 728
Swifty Serve Corporation 740
TravelCenters of America, Inc. 748
Wawa Inc. 770

**Department Stores**
Belk, Inc. **76-77**, 553
Boscov's Department Stores 559

**Discount & Variety**
Army and Air Force Exchange Service **52-53**, 543

Navy Exchange Service Command 685

**Drug, Health & Beauty Products**
Alticor Inc. 536

**Grocery**
Bashas' Inc. 550
Big V Supermarkets, Inc. 554
Big Y Foods, Inc. 554
Brookshire Grocery Company 561
Demoulas Super Markets Inc. 591
Furrs Supermarkets, Inc. 612
Giant Eagle Inc. **198-199**, 615
The Golub Corporation 617
H. E. Butt Grocery Company **224-225**, 627
Houchens Industries Inc. 634
Hy-Vee, Inc. 636
IGA, INC. **242-243**, 638
Inserra Supermarkets, Inc. 640
Jitney-Jungle Stores of America, Inc. 644
K-VA-T Food Stores, Inc. 654
Meijer, Inc. **328-329**, 671
Minyard Food Stores, Inc. 677
Publix Super Markets, Inc. **402-403**, 707
Raley's Inc. 710
Save Mart Supermarkets 722
Schnuck Markets, Inc. 723
Stater Bros. Holdings Inc. **462-463**, 736
Trader Joe's Company 747
Wegmans Food Markets, Inc. 771
WinCo Foods, Inc. 773

**Home Furnishings & Housewares**
Abbey Carpet Company, Inc. 529
Carpet Co-op Association of America 568
Rooms To Go 716

## SPECIALTY RETAIL

**Auto Dealers & Distributors**
Asbury Automotive Group, Inc. 543
Bill Heard Enterprises 555
Brown Automotive Group Ltd. 561
Burt Automotive Network 563
David Wilson's Automotive Group 589
Don Massey Cadillac, Inc. 596
The Faulkner Organization 606
Gulf States Toyota, Inc. 624
Hendrick Automotive Group 630
The Herb Chambers Companies 631
Holman Enterprises 633
Jim Koons Automotive 644
JM Family Enterprises, Inc. **256-257**, 644
Jordan Automotive Group 647
Larry H. Miller Group 656

Marty Franich Auto Center 666
Morse Operations, Inc. 678
Planet Automotive Group, Inc. 702
Prospect Motors, Inc. 706
Rosenthal Automotive Companies 717
Santa Monica Ford Corporation 721
Spitzer Management, Inc. 733
VT Inc. 767

**Computer & Software**
Fry's Electronics, Inc. **196-197**, 612
Micro Electronics, Inc. **336-337**, 675
Micro Warehouse, Inc. **338-339**, 676

**Jewelry Retail & Wholesale**
M. Fabrikant & Sons 662

**Miscellaneous Retail**
DFS Group Limited **156-157**, 592
Petco Animal Supplies, Inc. **394-395**, 701
Ritz Camera Centers, Inc. 714
Roll International Corporation **416-417**, 716

**Music, Video, Book & Entertainment**
Anderson News Company 541
Baker & Taylor Corporation **68-69**, 548
Barnes & Noble College Bookstores, Inc. 549
Columbia House Company 579
Follett Corporation **192-193**, 609
Ingram Entertainment Holdings Inc. 639
Ingram Industries Inc. **244-245**, 639
MTS, Incorporated **346-347**, 680

**Office Products Retail & Distribution**
Gould Paper Corporation 619

**Sporting Goods**
Bass Pro Shops, Inc. 550
Dick's Sporting Goods, Inc. 593
Recreational Equipment, Inc. **410-411**, 711

**Toy & Hobby Retail & Wholesale**
Hobby Lobby Stores, Inc. 632
K-B Toys 649

## TELECOMMUNICATIONS

**Cable TV & Satellite Systems**
Intelsat, Ltd. 640

**Miscellaneous End-User Communications Services**
Concert Communications Company 580
VarTec Telecom, Inc. 764

Note: Page numbers in **boldface** indicate the company's profile.

## ALABAMA
**Birmingham**
BE&K Inc. 552
Brasfield & Gorrie, LLC 560
EBSCO Industries Inc. **170-171**, 601
O'Neal Steel, Inc. 694

**Tuscaloosa**
The University of Alabama System 755

## ALASKA
**Anchorage**
Arctic Slope Regional Corporation 542

## ARIZONA
**Chandler**
Bashas' Inc. 550

**Phoenix**
Shamrock Foods Company 728

**Scottsdale**
Discount Tire Co. 594

**Tempe**
SRP 734

## ARKANSAS
**Stuttgart**
Riceland Foods, Inc. 714

## CALIFORNIA
**Altadena**
Charles Pankow Builders, Ltd. 573

**Anderson**
Sierra Pacific Industries 728

**Artesia**
California Dairies Inc. 563

**Beverly Hills**
Tracinda Corporation 747

**Brea**
Earle M. Jorgensen Company 601

**Colton**
Stater Bros. Holdings Inc. **462-463**, 736

**Commerce**
Unified Western Grocers, Inc. **488-489**, 752

**El Segundo**
CB Richard Ellis Services, Inc. **120-121**, 571

**Foster City**
Rudolph and Sletten, Inc. 719
Visa International **508-509**, 766

**Fountain Valley**
Kingston Technology Company **272-273**, 651

**Fremont**
ASI Corp. 545
New United Motor Manufacturing, Inc. **366-367**, 687
SYNNEX Information Technologies, Inc. 740

**Glendale**
DreamWorks SKG **166-167**, 597

**Irvine**
Freedom Communications, Inc. 611
Golden State Foods **202-203**, 617
Nikken Global Inc. 689

**Jackson**
Prospect Motors, Inc. 706

**Livingston**
Foster Farms 610

**Long Beach**
California State University **98-99**, 564

**Los Angeles**
AECOM Technology Corporation 531
Gores Technology Group 619
Los Angeles Department of Water and Power 660
Platinum Equity Holdings 703
Roll International Corporation **416-417**, 716
Topa Equities, Ltd. 746
University of Southern California 760
The Yucaipa Companies LLC **524-525**, 777

**Menlo Park**
Knowledge Universe, Inc. **278-279**, 652
SRI International **454-455**, 734

**Mill Valley**
S&P Company **428-429**, 721

**Milpitas**
Devcon Construction Incorporated 592

**Modesto**
E. & J. Gallo Winery **168-169**, 600
Save Mart Supermarkets 722

**Monrovia**
Trader Joe's Company 747

**Newport Beach**
The Irvine Company Inc. **252-253**, 642
Pacific Mutual Holding Company **384-385**, 695

**Nicasio**
Lucasfilm Ltd. **302-303**, 661

**Oakland**
Crowley Maritime Corporation 585
Kaiser Foundation Health Plan, Inc. **266-267**, 649
University of California **494-495**, 755

**Orange**
David Wilson's Automotive Group 589
Young's Market Company, LLC 777

**Pasadena**
Parsons Corporation **386-387**, 697

**Pleasanton**
Dillingham Construction Corporation 593

**Redwood City**
DPR Construction, Inc. 597

**Roseville**
Adventist Health 530

**Sacramento**
AgAmerica, FCB 533
California Public Employees' Retirement System **96-97**, 563
California State Lottery Commission 564
Sacramento Municipal Utility District 720
Sutter Health 739

**San Diego**
Linsco/Private Ledger Corp. 659
Petco Animal Supplies, Inc. **394-395**, 701
Science Applications International Corporation **438-439**, 724

**San Francisco**
24 Hour Fitness Worldwide Inc. 528
Bechtel Group, Inc. **74-75**, 552
Catholic Healthcare West **118-119**, 570
Chemoil Corporation 574
Delta Dental Plan of California 591
DFS Group Limited **156-157**, 592
Fisher Development, Inc. 608
Levi Strauss & Co. **292-293**, 657
Swinerton Incorporated 740
Wilbur-Ellis Company 772

**San Jose**
Fry's Electronics, Inc. **196-197**, 612
MA Laboratories, Inc. 662

**Santa Ana**
GeoLogistics Corporation 614

**Santa Monica**
A-Mark Financial Corporation 536
Santa Monica Ford Corporation 721

## Scotts Valley
Seagate Technology,
Inc. **440-441**, 725

## Sherman Oaks
Sunkist Growers, Inc. **464-465**,
738

## South San Francisco
Core-Mark International,
Inc. 584

## Stanford
Stanford University **456-457**,
735

## Stockton
A. G. Spanos Companies 532

## Ventura
Kinko's, Inc. **274-275**, 651

## Walnut
J. F. Shea Co., Inc. 643
ViewSonic Corporation 765

## Watsonville
Marty Franich Auto Center 666

## West Sacramento
MTS, Incorporated **346-347**, 680
Raley's Inc. 710

## Westlake Village
Consolidated Electrical
Distributors Inc. 582

## Woodland Hills
UniHealth Foundation 753

# COLORADO
## Denver
Catholic Health
Initiatives **116-117**, 569
Duke Energy Field Services
Corporation 598
Leprino Foods Company 657
MediaNews Group, Inc. 670

## Englewood
Burt Automotive Network 563

## Greeley
Hensel Phelps Construction
Co. 630

## Greenwood Village
CH2M Hill Companies, Ltd. 573

## Steamboat Springs
TIC Holdings Inc. 745

# CONNECTICUT
## Bristol
ESPN, Inc. 605

## Cheshire
Bozzuto's Inc. 560

## Enfield
Retail Brand Alliance, Inc. 713

## Greenwich
Holberg Industries,
Inc. **236-237**, 633

## Mashantucket
Mashantucket Pequot Gaming
Enterprise Inc. **318-319**, 667

## Milford
Doctor's Associates
Inc. **160-161**, 595

## New Britain
Connecticut Lottery
Corporation 581

## New Haven
Yale University 776

## Norwalk
Applera Corporation 542
Micro Warehouse, Inc. **338-339**,
676

## Stamford
Asbury Automotive Group,
Inc. 543
Conair Corporation 580
Purdue Pharma L.P. 707

## West Hartford
Colt's Manufacturing Company,
Inc. **132-133**, 578

# DELAWARE
## Newark
W. L. Gore & Associates,
Inc. **522-523**, 775

# DISTRICT OF COLUMBIA
AARP **28-29**, 529
AFL-CIO **34-35**, 532
The American Red Cross **44-45**,
538
The Carlyle Group **110-111**, 567
Corporation for Public
Broadcasting **144-145**, 585
Federal Reserve
System **186-187**, 607
Intelsat, Ltd. 640
International Brotherhood of
Teamsters **246-247**, 641
National Association of Securities
Dealers, Inc. **352-353**, 682
National Geographic
Society **358-359**, 683
National Railroad Passenger
Corporation **362-363**, 684
Pension Benefit Guaranty
Corporation **388-389**, 699
Smithsonian
Institution **450-451**, 731
The Union Labor Life Insurance
Company 754
United States Postal
Service **490-491**, 754

# FLORIDA
## Boca Raton
Purity Wholesale Grocers,
Inc. 708

## Bonita Springs
Abbey Carpet Company, Inc. 529
WCI Communities, Inc. 770

## Coral Gables
Planet Automotive Group,
Inc. 702

## Daytona Beach
National Association for Stock
Car Auto Racing 681

## Deerfield Beach
JM Family Enterprises,
Inc. **256-257**, 644

## Fort Lauderdale
Morse Operations, Inc. 678

## Gainesville
University of Florida 756

## Heathrow
AAA 528

## Jacksonville
JEA 643

## Lakeland
BREED Technologies, Inc. 561
Publix Super Markets,
Inc. **402-403**, 707

## Miami
Southern Wine & Spirits of
America, Inc. 732

## Seffner
Rooms To Go 716

## Tallahassee
State of Florida Department of
the Lottery 736

## Tampa
EPIX Holdings Corporation 603

## Vero Beach
George E. Warren
Corporation 614

# GEORGIA
## Atlanta
American Cancer Society,
Inc. **40-41**, 537
Carpet Co-op Association of
America 568
Cerulean Companies, Inc. 572
Chick-fil-A Inc. **124-125**, 575
Cingular Wireless 576
Cox Enterprises, Inc. **146-147**,
585
Emory University 602
Georgia Lottery Corporation 615
Gold Kist Inc. **200-201**, 616
National Distributing Company,
Inc. 682
Printpack, Inc. 705
Riverwood International
Corporation 715
Trammell Crow Residential 747
Watkins Associated
Industries 770
WorldTravel BTI 776

**West Des Moines**
Hy-Vee, Inc. 636
Multi-State Lottery
Association 680

## KANSAS
**Kansas City**
Associated Wholesale Grocers,
Inc. **62-63**, 547
**Leavenworth**
Sisters of Charity of Leavenworth
Health Services
Corporation 729
**Merriam**
VT Inc. 767
**Overland Park**
U.S. Central Credit Union 763
**Topeka**
Security Benefit Group, Inc. 725
**Wichita**
Koch Industries, Inc. **280-281**,
653

## KENTUCKY
**Ashland**
AEI Resources, Inc. 531
**Bowling Green**
Houchens Industries Inc. 634
**Lexington**
The University of Kentucky 757
**Louisville**
Genlyte Thomas Group LLC 613

## LOUISIANA
**Baton Rouge**
Louisiana State University
System 661

## MAINE
**Freeport**
L.L. Bean, Inc. **300-301**, 660

## MARYLAND
**Adelphi**
University System of
Maryland 762
**Baltimore**
Crown Central Petroleum
Corporation 586
Johns Hopkins Medicine 645
The Johns Hopkins
University 646
Maryland State Lottery
Agency 666
Sunbelt Beverage
Corporation 738
Vertis Inc. **506-507**, 765
The Whiting-Turner Contracting
Company 772
**Beltsville**
Ritz Camera Centers, Inc. 714

**Bethesda**
The ASCII Group, Inc. 544
Clark Enterprises, Inc. 576
Discovery Communications,
Inc. **158-159**, 594
Goodwill Industries International,
Inc. 618
**Chevy Chase**
Chevy Chase Bank, F.S.B. 574
**Columbia**
MedStar Health 671
**Marriottsville**
Bon Secours Health System,
Inc. 557
**Salisbury**
Perdue Farms
Incorporated **392-393**, 700

## MASSACHUSETTS
**Boston**
Bain & Company **64-65**, 548
Blue Cross and Blue Shield of
Massachusetts, Inc. **84-85**, 557
The Boston Consulting
Group **94-95**, 559
Boston University 560
CareGroup, Inc. 566
Colliers International Property
Consultants Inc. 578
Connell Limited Partnership 581
FMR Corp. **190-191**, 609
International Data
Group **248-249**, 641
Liberty Mutual Insurance
Companies **294-295**, 658
New Balance Athletic Shoe,
Inc. 686
Partners HealthCare System,
Inc. 697
University of Massachusetts 757
**Braintree**
Massachusetts State Lottery
Commission 668
**Cambridge**
Arthur D. Little, Inc. **54-55**, 543
Harvard University **220-221**, 626
Massachusetts Institute of
Technology 667
Modern Continental Companies,
Inc. 678
**Canton**
Cumberland Farms, Inc. 586
**Chelsea**
Gulf Oil, L.P. 624
**Dedham**
National Amusements Inc. 681
**Framingham**
Bose Corporation **92-93**, 559
**Lakeville-Middleboro**
Ocean Spray Cranberries,
Inc. **380-381**, 692

**Newton**
TAC Worldwide Companies 741
**North Reading**
Converse Inc. **142-143**, 583
**Norwood**
Corporate Software & Technology,
Inc. 584
**Pittsfield**
K-B Toys 649
**Somerville**
The Herb Chambers
Companies 631
**Springfield**
Big Y Foods, Inc. 554
Massachusetts Mutual Life
Insurance Company **320-321**,
667
**Tewksbury**
Demoulas Super Markets
Inc. 591
**Waltham**
Global Companies LLC 616
Tufts Associated Health Plans,
Inc. 751
**Wellesley**
Harvard Pilgrim Health Care,
Inc. 626

## MICHIGAN
**Ada**
Alticor Inc. 536
**Ann Arbor**
Domino's Inc. **162-163**, 595
Flint Ink Corporation 608
The University of Michigan 758
**Auburn Hills**
Guardian Industries
Corp. **212-213**, 623
MSX International, Inc. 679
**Battle Creek**
W.K. Kellogg
Foundation **520-521**, 774
**Dearborn**
Meridian Automotive Systems,
Inc. 673
**Detroit**
Blue Cross Blue Shield of
Michigan **86-87**, 557
Detroit Medical Center 591
Henry Ford Health System 630
Penske Corporation **390-391**,
699
Soave Enterprises L.L.C. 731
Wolverine Packing Company 775
**Farmington Hills**
Trinity Health 748
**Fraser**
Venture Industries 764
**Grand Rapids**
Gordon Food Service 618
Meijer, Inc. **328-329**, 671

Note: Page numbers in **boldface** indicate the company's profile.

## SYMBOLS

*2000 HR Service Center Survey* (publications) 481
24 Hour Fitness Worldwide Inc. 258
24/7 Media (marketing). *See* 24/7 Real Media
24/7 Real Media 506
3 For The Money lottery game 675
3 Musketeers candy 314, 315, 665
*The 30-Second Seduction* (educational video) 139
3Com Corporation 137, 545, 662
3M. *See* Minnesota Mining and Manufacturing Company
40 Wall Street 482, 483
501 brand jeans 293
55 ALIVE/Mature Driving 29
7 UP soft drink 110, 232, 597, 634
7-Eleven, Inc. 728
800.com (online retailer) 511
84 Lumber Company **26-27**, 528

## A

AAA 528
AAL Bank and Trust 534
The A&B Group (starters and alternators) 152
A&E cable network 228, 229, 629
A&F. *See* Abercrombie & Fitch
A&P grocery stores 103, 198, 224, 592
A&W restaurants and root beer 597
Aardman Animations 166
Aaron, Roger S. 447
AARP **28-29**, 370, 529, 688
AB, A/S. *See* entry under primary company name
Abacus Concepts 430
Abbany, Zul 431
Abbey Carpet Company, Inc. 529
Abbott Laboratories 66, 741
ABC, Inc. 166, 218, 228, 229, 360, 605, 682, 684
ABC Markets 524, 777
ABC Supply 537
Abel, Gregory E. 341
Abercrombie & Fitch 254
Abex (aircraft parts) 304
Abfalter, Dan 710
Abinder, Susan 637
Abington, Bill 670
Abitibi-Consolidated 696
About.com 282
AboveNet Communications, Inc. 333
Abrams, Steve L. 323
Abramsom, Richard 455
ABRY Partners 350, 681
Academy Awards 166, 218, 302, 400, 597, 661
Accel Partners 282
Accenture 48, 286, 540

Access Blue (managed care plan) 84, 85, 558
Access Business Network 536
AccessAtlanta.com 146
AccessNurse 743
The Accident Fund Company 87
Accor Group (hotels and tourism) 106, 108, 567
Accuride Corporation 283
Ace Auto Parts 112
Ace Beverage 746
Ace glass products 212
Ace Hardware Corporation **30-31**, 212, 479, 484, 529, 565, 594, 623, 749
Ace Insurance Agency 30
Acela train service 362, 684
ACENET 30
Ackerman, Val 355
Acklands Ltd. (automotive after market products) 112
Acktion Corporation 112
Acme Markets 198
Acme Steel 741
Acone, Adam 361
Acosta, Alan 457
Acoustic Wave speakers 93
Acoustimass speakers 93
Acquilina, Michelle 311, 664
Act III (theaters) 282, 412
Actava Group 332
ACTIVENT fabrics 523
Acura car 138, 733
A.D. Makepeace Company 380
Adams, Barbara 611
Adams, Ed 179, 603
Adams, Jacob 542
Adams, John 220
Adams, John Quincy 220
Adams, J. Phillip 609
Adams, Pam 175
Adams, Richard C. 71
Adams, Staci 594
Adams Super Food Stores 560
Adamson, Terrence B. 359
Adaptec 137
adidas-Salomon AG 686
Adjemian, Vart K. 141
Adjmi, Norma 719
ADL. *See* Arthur D. Little, Inc.
ADM. *See* Archer Daniels Midland Company
Adolph Coors Company 428
AdOne Classified Network 32
AdSEND digital ad delivery 546
ADT Automotive 146
Advance Online (training) 279
Advance Publications, Inc. **32-33**, 530
Advanced Micro Devices, Inc. 444, 445, 662, 726
Advanced Polymer 164
Advanced Research Projects Agency 444
Advanced Research & Technology Institute 638
Advance/Newhouse Communications 158, 594

Advantage Foods (poultry processor) 392
Advantage Sales & Marketing 530
Advantages/ESM Ferolie 530
Advantica Restaurant Group 282
Advantus Capital Management 677
Adventist Health 530
*Adventure* (magazine) 358, 359
AEA Investors 408, 691, 711
Aeon (aluminum substrates) 440
AEP Industries 90
Aerospace Corporation 438
Aestix (e-commerce) 88
Aether Systems (wireless technology) 508
Aetna Heiwa Life 320
Aetna, Inc. 226, 370
Afable, Mark V. 43
Afable, Richard F. 115
AFC Enterprises, Inc. 124, 575
AFL-CIO **34-35**, 246, 492, 532, 754
Ag Processing Inc. **36-37**, 532
A.G. Spanos Companies 532
Ag States Agency 122, 123
AgAmerica, FCB 533
Agere Systems (microelectronics) 444, 445, 726
AgFirst Farm Credit Bank 534
AG/Fleming Northwest 546
Aggies of Texas A&M University 471
AGP. *See* Ag Processing Inc.
AGP Grain Cooperative 37
AgraTrade Financing, Inc. 200, 201
Agree hair products 432
AgrEvo 104
Agri International 200
AgriBank, FCB 534
AgriBioTech 264
Agribrands International 104
Agricultural and Mechanical College of Texas for Colored Youth 470, 743
Agricultural and Mechanical College of the Kentucky University 757
Agricultural Marketing Act (1929) 184
Agriliance, LLC 122, 123, 184, 185
AgriRecycle 392
Agri-Service Centers 123
Aguallo, Robert 97
Aguirre, DeeAnne 89, 558
Agway Energy Products LLC 38, 39
Agway Inc. **38-39**, 535
AHC Realty Corporation 31
A.H.C. Store Development Corporation 31
Ahold USA 479
AHS Blue Cross 174
Aid Association for Lutherans/Lutheran Brotherhood 534
Aidekman, Al 515
Aijala, Ainar D., Jr. 155
Air France Holidays 658
Air Line Pilots Association 34
Air Partners 474
Air Wisconsin Airlines Corporation 534

American Football League 88
American Forest Products 282
*American Graffiti* (movie) 302, 303
American Hardware Supply. *See* ServiStar Coast to Coast
American Heritage carpets 342
American Heritage cheese 723
American Hockey League 361
American Honda Motor Company 630
American Hospital Association Committee on Hospital Service 82
American Institute of Architects 448
American League baseball 306, 307, 663
American Management Systems 430
American Manufacturers Mutual Insurance Company 268
American Medical Association 82
American Medical Instruments, Inc. 313
American Motorists Insurance Company 268
American Pad and Paper 742
American Professional Football Association 211, 356, 683
American Protection Industries 416
American Protection Insurance 268
American Public Television 145
The American Red Cross **44-45**, 493, 538
American Retail Group, Inc. 539
American Rod & Gun 550
American Seaway Foods 198
American Society for the Control of Cancer 40
American Standard Insurance Company 42, 43
American Steel Foundaries 540
The American Stock Exchange, Inc. **46-47**, 352, 353, 374, 539, 682
American Stores 462
American Tobacco Company 598
American United Life Insurance Company 539
America's Cup (yacht racing) 250, 251
America's Tire Company 594
Ameridrives couplings 578
AmeriServ Food Company. *See* AmeriServe Food Distribution
AmeriServe Food Distribution 236, 633
AmeriSource Health Corporation. *See* AmerisourceBergen Corporation
AmerisourceBergen Corporation 466
AmeriState Mobile Medical Services 518
Ametex furniture 299, 659
AmEx. *See* American Express Company
AMEX. *See* The American Stock Exchange, Inc.

AMFM (radio station operator) 232, 350, 631
Amherst College 78
AMI Community Hospital (Santa Cruz, CA) 118
Amica Mutual Insurance Company 540
Amiraian, Donna 461, 736
*Amistad* (movie) 166, 167
Ammon, Donald R. 530
Ammon, Theodore 506
Amoco. *See* BP p.l.c.
Amory, Louis 65
Amphenol Corporation (cables and connectors) 283
AMPI. *See* Associated Milk Producers Inc.
Am-Safe, Inc. 313
Amstar Sugar Corporation 162
Amsted Industries Inc. 540
Amtrak. *See* National Railroad Passenger Corporation
Amundsen, Chris 492
Amway Corporation 536
*Amy & Isabelle* (movie) 219
Anacostia Museum and Center for African American History & Culture 450, 451
Anaheim Angels (baseball team) 307
Anapamu wine 169
Anbuma Group (steel tubing) 312
Anchor Blue Clothing 539
Andersen **48-49**, 66, 206, 286, 540, 620, 705
Andersen, Arthur 48
Andersen Consulting. *See* Accenture
Andersen Corporation **50-51**, 541
Andersen, Darl J. 550
Andersen, Fred 50
Andersen, Hans 50
Andersen, Herbert 50
Andersen, Sarah J. 51
Andersen Worldwide. *See* Andersen
Anderson & Cromwell 190
Anderson, Brian 141
Anderson, Charles 541
Anderson Copper and Brass Company 313
Anderson, Craig 725
Anderson, David R. (American Family Insurance) 43
Anderson, David (SEMATECH) 445
Anderson, Gary E. 165, 596
Anderson, Greg 471
Anderson Hickey (office furniture) 222
Anderson, John E. 746
Anderson, Kenneth 678
Anderson, Lloyd 410, 711
Anderson, Mary 410, 711
Anderson News Company 541
Anderson, Richard 177, 603
Anderson, R. John 293
Anderson School of Business 746
Anderson, Walter 33, 516
Anderson, William (Raley's) 710

Anderson, William (Trinity Health) 748
Andhurst brand 77
André champagne 169
The Andrew W. Mellon Foundation 541
Andrews, Charles 777
Andrews, Dick 750
Andrews, Duane P. 439
Andrews, Paul E., Jr. 750
Andronico's Markets 489
Andrus, Ethel 28
Andrus Foundation 28, 29
Anfinson's 406
Anheuser-Busch Companies, Inc. 72, 428, 553, 715
Animal Planet (cable channel) 158, 159, 594
Anixter International Inc. 180, 181
Ann J. Kellogg School 520
Ann Sacks art tiles 284, 285, 653
*The Annals of America* (books) 176, 177, 603
Annenberg, Walter 144, 492
The Annenberg/CPB Projects 144, 145
Annenburg School for Communication 759
Annexstad, Al 607
Annis, Rick 570
Anschutz, Philip F. 332, 412, 712
Anselmo L. Morvillo (printing) 404
Anson, Mark 97
Answer Products Inc. 656
Antares Capital Corporation 321
Anthem Insurance Companies, Inc. 82, 84, 226
Anthony, Barbara Cox 146
Anthony, Ross 692
Anthony's pasta 91
*Antz* (movie) 166, 167
AOL Time Warner Inc. 32, 33, 80, 248, 346, 356, 416, 510, 579, 682, 756
AP. *See* The Associated Press
AP Radio Network 60
AP WirePhoto network 60
Apallas, Yeoryios 429
Apax Partners &Company 332
APCOA/Standard Parking 236, 633
Apex Oil Company, Inc. 542, 586
Apex Orchards (almonds and pistachios) 416
Apollo Advisors 692
Apollo Management 577
Apple Computer, Inc. 430, 597, 719
Apple Market 62, 63, 488
Applebaum, Jay I. 519
Appleby, Anne F. 692
Appleby, David A. 701
Applera Corporation 542
Applied Biosystems 542
APS Holding 112
Apter, C. Victoria 467
APTN. *See* Associated Press Television Network
APW Limited 581
Aquarius Travel 418

Brookhaven Country Club
(Dallas) 130
Brookhaven National
Laboratories 438
Brookhaven Science Associates 70
Brooklyn College 128, 129
Brooklyn Rapid Transit 334
Brooklyn Staten Island Family
Health Network 369
Brooklyn-Port Authority Marine
Terminal 399
Brooks Brothers stores 713
Brooks, David 200
Brooks, George H. 501, 762
Brooks, Robert 210
Brookshire Grocery Company 561
Brookshire, Tim 561
Broome, Anne C. 495
Brose, Bryan 607
Brosnan, Timothy 307
Brotherhood of All Railway
Employees 750
Broughton, Joan 411
Brouillard, Jack C. 225, 627
Broun, Elizabeth 451
Brouse, John S. 235, 632
Brover, Barry 549
Brower, Paul G. 201
Brown Automotive Group Ltd. 561
Brown, Collin 257
Brown, Craig D. 72, 73
Brown, Dale 337, 675
Brown, Emily S. 732
Brown Fintube Company 281
Brown, Fleming & Murray
(accounting) 182
Brown, George 415
Brown, Gifford E. 165, 596
Brown, G. Michael "Mickey" 318
Brown, Harris, Stevens (real
estate) 230
Brown, Herbert G. 421
Brown, Jack H. 462, 463, 736
Brown, J. Frank 401
Brown, LaRay 369
Brown, Loren 109
Brown, Paul F. 609
Brown, Richard 629
Brown, Robert T. 461
Brown, Ron 386
Brown, Sandy J. 363
Brown, Stephen 107
Brown, Tina 32
Brown University 382, 763
Brown, Vincent P. 97, 563
Browne, Joe 357
Browne, Michael 672
Brown-Forman Corporation 320,
616, 777
Browning, John 132
Bruce, Ailsa Mellon 541
Bruce, Peter W. 377
Bruce, Tom 708
Bruckmann, Rosser, Sherill &
Company 644
Brune Reiseburo (travel
agency) 108
Brunner, Kim M. 459

Bruno's Supermarkets, Inc. 282,
644
Brunswick Building (Chicago) 449
Bryan, Lowell L. 327
Bryant, Dave 652
BT Group 580
Buback, Ken 739
Buchanan, James 760
Buck Consultants, Inc. 480
Buck, James E. 375
Buck, Peter 160, 161, 595
Buckcherry (performer) 167
Buckeye (potato chips) 90
Buckhorn restaurants 748
Buckley, William F., Jr. 776
Buckman, Michael A. 776
Buckner, William A. 105
Budget Rent-a-Car
Corporation 666
Budreau, Karen 249, 641
Buenaslor, Naomi 777
Bueti, Antonio 372
Buffalo Bills (football team) 357
Buffalo Bisons (baseball team) 714
Buffalo Sabres (hockey team) 361
Buffenbarger, R. Thomas 35
Bufferd, Allan S. 667
Buffets, Inc. 562
Buffett, Warren E. 340, 474, 510,
676
Bugs Burger Bug Killers 432
Buhler & Partners 73
Buhrmaster, Robert C. 262, 263,
647
Buick cars 596, 606, 706, 733
Builder Marts of America, Inc. 30,
212, 562, 623
Builders Emporium 406
Builders FirstSource, Inc. 562
Builder's Transport (trucking) 434
Building Materials Corporation of
America 612
Bukatko, Aurelian 695
Bulger, William M. 757
Bulldog office seating 277
Bullock, Lee W. 363
Bundy, McGeorge 194
Bundy, Steve 601
Bunge, Johann Peter Gottlieb 565
Bunnell, Ron 549
Bunshaft, Gordon 448
Bunting, W. Clark 159
Burch, Larry 345
Burck, R. D. 498, 499, 761
Burg, Robert H. 715
Burgdorf, Lawrence 436
Burger King Corporation 72, 124,
516, 669, 704
Burgo, Raymond 199
Burke, John P. 483
Burke, Sheila 451
Burkett, Charles L. 87
Burkett, Lawrence V. 321
The Burkhardt Company
(binders) 170
Burkhead, J. Gary 191
Burkle, Joe 462
Burkle, Ronald W. 462, 524, 525,
777

Burlington Industries, Inc. 696
Burlington Northern Santa Fe
Corporation 751
Burlwood wine 169
Burnell, Karen 542
Burnett, Leo 72
Burnham, Dick 632
Burnham, Lem 357
Burns, Edward 678
Burns, Stephanie 165
Burstein, Mark 135
Burt Automotive Network 563
Burton, James E. 97, 563
Busby, Elsie 427
Busby, John 427, 720
Buscarinio, Carolyn M. 371
Busch, David C. 423
Busch Grand National racing
circuit 681
Bush, George H. W. (former US
President) 110, 186, 567, 776
Bush, George W. (US
President) 110
Bushaw, Dewey P. 385
Business Express 418
Business Forum 338
Business Integration Group 587
*Business Travelers' Briefcase Atlas*
(book) 409
Business Travel International
(BTI) 776
*Business Week* (magazine) 378,
454
Bussells, Walter P. 643
Butcher, Ernesto L. 399
Butler, Bruce W. 85
Butler Capital 202, 406
Butler, James E., Jr. 764
Butler, Stephen G. 287
Butt, Charles C. 224, 225, 627
Butt, Florence 224
Butt, Howard, Jr. 224
Butt, Howard, Sr. 224
Butterbrodt, John 58
The Buttonwood Agreement
(1792) 374
*Buy Me That! A Kid's Survival
Guide to TV Advertising*
(educational video) 139
Buyers' Choice brands 423
Buzzeo, John 357, 683
BW Holdings 90, 558
BWP Distributor, Inc. 113
BX (Base Exchange) 52
Byers, Debbie 479
Byerwalter, Mariann 457, 735
Byfield Travel 308
Byington, Sue 706
Bykerk, Cecil D. 349
Bynum, Joseph R. 469
Byrd, Don 675
Byron's barbecue 714

**C**

C. Itoh & Company 242
C. Jespersen (accounting) 286
C&N (tour company) 106
CA One Services (airport food) 590
Cable Educational Network 158

Carpet One stores 568
CARQUEST Corporation **112-113**, 569, 613
Carr, J. Robert 29, 529
Carrefour SA 593
Carreras, Jose 251
Carrico, Stephen J. 630
Carrier, Carol 758
Carrington-Chase brand 442, 443
Carrion, Esperanza 205
Carroll, Charles 523, 775
Carroll, David M. 634
Carroll, Jim 149
Carroll, Matt 69
Carsey, Marcy 218
Carter, Bruce E. 682
Carter, Diane E. 353, 682
Carter, Jimmy 186
Carter, John 75
Carter, Ken W. 718
Carter, Mary Ann 115
Carter, Paul 610
Carter, Sandra J. 85
Carter, Stephen M. 576
Carter, Terry 710
Carter, Vince 251
Carter, William H. 91, 558
Cartographic and Information Services 408
Cartoonbank.com 33
Cartwright Williams (marketing) 73
Carusello, Mike 596
Caruso, Joseph A. 215
Carver 92
Carvette, Anthony 737
Carville, James 661
Casal, Carolina 204
Casale, Karen 770
Cascade Imperial Mills 690
Casein (glue) 90
Casey, Julianna 115
Casey, Katie 47, 539
Casey, Mary Beth 73
Cash and Carry warehouse stores 488
Cash Flurries lottery game 373
Cash in Hand lottery game 666
Cash, Roberta 678
Cash Saver stores 62, 63
Cashword lottery game 675
Cason, Marsden 143
Casper, Gerhard 456
Cassard, Christopher D. 690
Cassava chips 204
Cassutt, Mark 263
Casteen, John T., III 761
Castellani, Frederick C. 321
Castelli (office furniture) 222
Castle Computing 338
Castleberry, Michael 622
Casual Corner stores 713
Cataligent (consulting) 55
Catamount Dairy Holdings 38
Catelli pasta 91
Caterair International 110
Caterpillar Inc. 590, 600
Catholic Charities USA 492, 493, 755
Catholic Health Association 115

Catholic Healthcare Audit Network 116
Catholic Health Corporation of Omaha 116, 569
Catholic Health East **114-115**, 116, 569
Catholic Health Initiatives 114, **116-117**, 569
Catholic Health Ministries 748
Catholic Health System (Buffalo, NY) 115
Catholic Healthcare Network 570
Catholic Healthcare Partners 570
Catholic Healthcare West 56, **118-119**, 570, 753
Catholic Managed Care Consortium 115
Catholic Relief Services 56
Cathy, Dan T. 124, 125
Cathy, Donald M. 125
Cathy, S. Truett 124, 125, 575
Catsimatidis, John A. 712
Cauz, Jorge 177
Cavalier, Michael 127
Cavarra, Mary K. 245
Caxton-Iseman Capital 562
CB Richard Ellis Services, Inc. **120-121**, 571
CBRE Stewardship 121
CBS Telenoticias 80
CBS Television Network 80, 178, 218, 326, 356, 681
C. C. Butt Grocery 224
CC Industries 621
CCI/Triad Systems Corporation (computer systems) 333
CDnow 579
*CD-ROM WAREHOUSE* (catalogs) 338
Cearlock, Dennis B. 71
CEI Citicorp Holding 333
Celera Genomics 542
Celey, Floyd 318
Cenex Harvest States Cooperatives **122-123**, 184, 185, 288, 571, 572
Center for Biomedical Ethics 457
Center for Computer Research in Music and Acoustics 457
Center for Elephant Conservation 188
Center for Folklife Programs and Cultural Heritage 451
Center for Human Genetics 560
Center for Integrated Facilities Engineering 457
Center for International Legal Studies 194
Center for Space Physics 560
Center for the Study of Language and Information 457
Centerpiece paper products 727
Central Artery Tunnel (Boston) 678, 696
Central Farmers Fertilizer Company 572
Central Hockey League 361
Central Market 224, 225, 627
Central National-Gottesman Inc. 571

Central National Life Insurance Company 174
Central Pacific Railroad 384, 456
Central Tractor Farm & Country 406, 709
Centre Capital (investments) 350
Centric Group 178, 603
Centric Software, Inc. 283
Century 21 (real estate) 692
Century of Progress Exposition 448
Century Products 518
Cerestar 104
Cerro Corporation 312
Cerro Metal Products Company 313
Cerro Negro 386
Certified Grocers of California 488, 752
Cerulean Companies, Inc. 572
Cesar pet food 315
Cetec (audio equipment) 310
CF Industries, Inc. 572, 622
CFM International, Inc. 572
CGC. *See* ContiGroup Companies
CGI Equities 126
CGI Group 154
CH2M Hill Companies, Ltd. 573
Chait, Ben 198
Chalker, John R. 309
Chamberlain Group keyless entry systems 598
Chamberlain, Wilt 354
Chambers, Anne Cox 146
Chambers, Edward 770
Chambers, Herbert G. 631
Chambers, Jeff 431, 721
Champion Laboratories 752
Championship Auto Racing Teams 390
CHAMPUS 52, 174
Chan, Timothy 381, 692
Chancellor Media (radio) 232
Chandler, Gregg 572
Chandler, Jim 245
Chandler Medical Center 757
Chandran, Robert V. 574
Change Your Life TV 218
Channel, Karen 624
Channel One Network 460, 653
Chao, Elaine 492
Chaplin, Harvey 732
Chapman, Byrne W. 43
Chapman Hall Center for Children and the Laborartory Schools 497
Chapman, John B. 397, 701
Chapman, William 239, 636
Chappel Brothers 314
Chappell, Robert E. 698
Chappie pet food 315
Charles Pankow Builders, Ltd. 573
Charles, Saul 254
Charles Schwab Corporation 190
Charlesbank Equity Fund IV 628
Charlotte Hornets (basketball team) 355
Charlotte Sting (basketball team) 355
Charmer Industries, Inc. 738

DaimlerChrysler AG 390, 560, 563, 644, 649, 673, 679, 695, 706, 713, 747, 764. *See also* Chrysler Corporation
Dairy Export 771
Dairy Farmers of America 58, 90, **148-149**, 288, 587, 588, 654
Dairy Queen 702
Dairylea Cooperative Inc. 588
Dairyman's Cooperative Creamery Association 288
Dairymen 58
Daisy Kingdom home furnishings 453
Dakin stuffed animals 486
Dallas Cowboys (football team) 357
Dallas Mavericks (basketball team) 355
Dallas Stars (hockey team) 361
Daly, Ann 167
Daly, William 361
D'Amato, Anthony 90
D'Amour, Charles 479
D'Amour, Donald H. 554
D'Amour, Gerald 554
D'Amour, Paul 554
Dana auto parts 112, 113, 569
Dana-Farber Cancer Institute 697
D'Angelo Law Library 497
Daniel, D. Ronald 221
Daniel, Ronald 326
Daniel, William D. 639
D'Aniello, Daniel A. (Baker & Taylor) 69
D'Aniello, Daniel A. (Carlyle Group) 110, 111
Daniels, Randy A. 461
Danish Creamery Association 563
Danly Die Set 581
Dan's (food stores) 545
Dapsco 705
Darbelnet, Robert L. 528
D'Arcy Masius Benton & Bowles 72, 73, 551
Darcy, Thomas E. 439, 724
D'Arcy, William 72
Darden Restaurants, Inc. 669
Darigold Farm stores 771
Darling, Bruce B. 495
Darman, Richard 110, 567
Dart Container Corporation **150-151**, 588
Dart Energy 150
Dart, Kenneth B. 150, 151, 588
Dart, Robert C. 150, 151
Dart, Tom 150
Dart, William A. 150, 151
Dart, William F. 150
*Darwin Magazine* 249
Dassault Aviation 766
Data Broadcasting Corporation 350
*Data CommWAREHOUSE* (catalogs) 338
Data Insight 430
DataFlash memory 273
Datatec 771
D'Atri, Justin W. 712
Datz, Linda 655
Daugherty, Arthur 234
Daugherty, Tim R. 185

Daughters of Charity National Health System 56, 116, 544
Daughters of Charity, Province of the West 118, 119
Dauk, Regis A. 679
Dauska, Walter J. 621
Davco, Inc. (engine accessories) 391
Davel Communications Group, Inc. 181
Davenport, Lynn E. 173, 602
Davenport, Margaret 617
*David and Lisa* (movie) 219
David, Doug 690
David J. Johnson Company 731
David L. Babson & Company, Inc. 320, 321, 667
The David Leadbetter Golf Academy 251
David Sarnoff Research Center 454
David Weekley Homes 589
David Wilson's Automotive Group 589
Davidowski, Ronald 597
Davids Ltd. 243
Davidson, H. Clint, Jr. 598
Davidson, Sheila K. 371
Davidson, William 212, 213, 623
Davis, Alfred 682
Davis, Andy 615
Davis, Angela 552
Davis, Darrell 740
Davis, Jacob 292
Davis, James S. (New Balance Athletic Shoe) 686
Davis, Jay M. 682
Davis, J. B. 652
Davis, Jim (SAS Institute) 431
Davis, Jocelyn 29, 529
Davis, Joseph D. 253
Davis, Leonard 28
Davis, Nancy 659
Davis, Richard 408
Davis, Robert G. (USAA) 503, 763
Davis, Robert T. (United States Postal Service) 491
Davis Vision, Inc. 235
Davisson, Bill 622
Dawson, Chuck 443
Day & Zimmermann, Inc. 589
Day, Randy 393
Dayco Industrial Power Transmission 310, 664
DaySpring (greeting cards) 216, 217
*Dayton* (Ohio) *Daily News* 146
Dayton Engineering Laboratories 152
Dayton Winfastener 705
DB Capital Partners 691
DDB Needham Worldwide (advertising) 372
De Beers (diamonds) 776
de Goya y Lucientes, Francisco José 204
De Luca (entree maker) 392
De Luca, Michael 167
de Marillac, Louise (Saint) 56
de Munnik, Hans 287
De Paul, Vincent (Saint) 56

De Santi, Dan 247
Dean, Donna J. 415
Dean Foods Company 148, 288
Dean, Hilton 183, 605
Dean, Lloyd H. 119, 570
Dean, Richard H. 768
DeBartolo, Edward J. 172
DeBartolo, Edward J., Jr. 172, 602
DeBartolo Entertainment 172
DeBiasi, Glenn 535
DeBruce Grain, Inc. 589
DeBruce, Paul 589
DeCanniere, Dan 631
DeCarlo, Anthony J. 662
Decker, Harold 44, 45, 538
Decker, Michael B. 519
DeCota, William R. 399
Dedman, Robert H., Jr. 131, 577
Dedman, Robert H., Sr. 130, 131
*Deep Impact* (movie) 166, 167
Deep Woods OFF repellents 433
Deering Harvester 342
Deering, William 342
DeFabis, Mike 62
Defender handgun 578
DeFrancisco, Margaret R. 372, 373, 688
Defratus, Kellie 597
DeGiovanni, Frank F. 195
DeGregorio, Bob 289
Del Monte Foods Company 474, 475
Del Moro, Robert J. 413
Del Vecchio, Claudio 713
Del Webb (developer) 643
Delaney, Dennis 245, 639
Delano, Harley J. 489
DeLany, Clarence 48
Delaware North Companies Inc. 590
Delchamps stores 644
Delco Remy International, Inc. **152-153**, 590
Deliberto, Robert 109
Deli-Fast Foods 623
Dell Computer Corporation 338
Deloitte Touche Tohmatsu **154-155**, 206, 590, 620, 776
Deloitte, William 154
Delta Air Lines, Inc. 94
Delta Center arena 656
Delta Dental Plan of California 591
Delta faucets 298
Delta Woodside 342
DeLuca, Carmela 161, 595
DeLuca, Frederick A. 160, 161, 595
DeMarco, Frederick L. 145
DeMarco, John 313
DeMartino, Frank A. 387
Demetrion, James T. 451
Demetriou, Steven J. 691
Demorest, Harry L. 579
Demoulas, George 591
Demoulas, Mike 591
Demoulas Super Markets Inc. 591
Dempsey, Jack 242
Denaro, Robert P. 409
Denbury Resources Inc. (oil and gas) 475

Lewin, Dennis 357
Lewis, Daniel C. 89
Lewis, Darlene 763
Lewis, Henrietta 432
Lewis, John L. (AFL-CIO) 34
Lewis, John (Milliken) 343, 677
Lewis, Lemuel E. 655
Lewis, Shirley 720
Lewis, Thomas C. 427
Lewis, Wendy 307, 663
Lexington Community College 757
Lexington Furniture 298, 299, 659
LexisNexis Group (databases) 80
Lexmark International, Inc. 676
Lexus automobiles 256, 589, 631, 644, 656
Ley, Mark 253, 642
LFE (hydraulic equipment) 310
LHC, Inc. 261
Liakopulos, Nick 243
Liang, Christine 545
Liang, Marcel 545
Libbey-Owens-Ford 212
Liberatore, Jorinne 597
Liberty Financial Companies, Inc. 658
Liberty Media Group 158, 232, 594
Liberty Mutual Insurance Companies 294-295, 658
Liberty Northwest Insurance Corporation 294, 295
Liberty ships 266
Liberty Travel, Inc. 296-297, 658
Liberty Wanger Asset Management 294
Library and Information Commission 79
Library at Northwestern University (Evanston, IL) 449
Libris 2000 (library automation) 69
Librix Learning 308, 664
Liddy, Brian 723
Liebentritt, Donald J. 181
Lieberman, Pamela Forbes 484, 485, 749
Liebgott, Robert 485
Liedel, Christopher A. 359, 683
Liennenbrugger, Herbert 698
Life Care Centers of America 658
Life Insurance Company of the Southwest 684
Life Partners Group (insurance) 232
Lifeboat Matey (prepublication services) 506
Lifecast.com 130
LifeStyle Furnishings International Ltd. 298-299, 659
Lifestyle music systems 93
Lifetime Cash lottery game 668
Lifetime Entertainment Services 228, 229, 629
Light House stores 577
Lightfoot, Angela 431
Lightfoot, H. Harrison 463
Lightning Print 244
Lightning Source (on-demand printing) 244, 245
Lightolier lighting fixtures 613
Lightstyle juice products 381

Lightyear Communications 764
Liles, Bob 611
Lillian August funiture 299
Lilly, Edward F. 727
Lilly, Steven L. 685
Lily paper products 727
LIN Broadcasting (cellular) 332
LIN Holdings (TV stations) 333
Lin, Maya 276, 652
Linares, Nora 472
Lincoln, Bob 551
Lincoln Building (New York City) 231
Lincoln car 633, 647, 666, 733
Lincoln Center for the Performing Arts, Library-Museum (New York City) 449
Lincoln Medical and Mental Health Center (New York City) 369
Lincoln, Murray 364
Lincoln Property Company 659
Lincoln Tunnel 398, 399, 703
Lind, David R. 121
Lindahl, Dennis 633
Lindburg, Arthur 178
Lindenmeyr family 574
Lindgren, Tim 241
Lindman, Joanne O'Rourke 45
Lindner, Carl H. 518
Lindner, Richard G. 576
Lindquist, Gern 30
Lindsay, James W. 36
Lineage furniture 298
Ling, Robert M., Jr. 489
Lin's (food stores) 545
Linsco/Private Ledger Corporation 659
LinuxWorld Conference & Expo 249
Linville, Randal L. 724
The Lion King (movie) 166
Lipoff, Deborah 409
Lipp, Marie 582
Lips, Barbara Woodward 324
Lipstein, Steven H. 555
Lipton 530
Lipton, Marty 446
Liquitint dye 343
Liria, Peter, Jr. 175
Lisbon University 449
Listi, Frank 203
Litchfield Luxury Theatres 412
Litho-Krome (lithography) 217
Litner, Jon 361
Little America hotel chain 729
Little & Walker 54
Little, Arthur D. 54
Little Caesar pizza 162, 657
Little Debbie snack food 669
Little, Royal 54
Little, Vincent 422
Littlejohn & Levy 565
Littwin, Lawrence 472
Litzsinger, Richard 192
Litzsinger, R. Mark 193
Liuzzi, R. C. 572
Livingston Cellars wine 169
Livingston, John T. 477
L.J. Melody & Company 120, 121, 571

L.L. Bean, Inc. 254, 300-301, 660, 696
L.L. Distribution Systems 236
L.L. Kids (catalog) 300
Lloyd, Donald 545
Lloyd, Emily 135
Lloyd, James T. 363
Lloyd's of London 480
LMC (savings and loan) 268
LMR (record label) 290
Lobinsky, James J. 403
Local Initiatives Support 194
Locke, John 176
Lockets medicated lozenges 315
Lockhart, Eugene 322
Lockhart, James 388
Lockheed Martin Corporation 110, 675, 754, 766
Locomotion 229
Loebbaka, Charles R. 379
Loeffler, Tom 499
Lofgren, Christopher B. 435
Loftis, Harry E. 714
Lofton, Kevin 117
Logli supermarkets 723
Lohr, William J. 726
Lomar Distributing 636
Lombardi, Francis J. 399
Lombardi, Paul V. 599
Lombardi, Vince 210, 621
Lombardini (small engines) 310
Lonczak, William 373
London School of Economics 134
Lone Star beer 428, 721
Long, Bruce C. 215
Long, Gary E. 377, 690
Long Island Jewish Medical Center 690
The Long Island Rail Road Company 334, 335
Long, John E., Jr. 469, 743
Long Prairie Packing 717
Long, Sandra 666
Long, William D. 773
The Longaberger Company 660
Longaberger, Dave 660
Longaberger, Tami 660
Longhorns of the University of Texas System 761
Longo Toyota auto dealership 390
Longshore, George F. 115, 569
Long-Term Capital Management 186
Long-term Equity Anticipation Securities 47
Look Good . . . Feel Better cancer patient support 41
Loomis, Fargo & Company 518
Looney Tunes 424
Loose Change lottery game 373
Lopez, George 491
Lopez, Julia I. 415
Lopez, Lucille 591
Lopez, Nancy 251
Lopez, Victor 241
Lorentz, Norman E. 491
Lorton, Donald E. 566
Los Alamos National Laboratory 438, 494, 495

Los Angeles Clippers (basketball team) 355
Los Angeles Convention Center 576
Los Angeles County Department of Water and Power 660
*Los Angeles Daily News* 670
Los Angeles Dodgers (baseball team) 307
Los Angeles Kings (hockey team) 361
Los Angeles Lakers (basketball team) 355
Los Angeles Olympic Organizing Committee 108
Los Angeles Sparks (basketball team) 355
Loser, Ugo 65
Loss Prevention Services 31
Lotman, Herbert 650
Lottes, Art E., III 112, 113, 569
Lotto lottery game 766
Lotto Texas lottery game 472, 473, 744
Lotus Development 136
Lotzee lottery game 687
Louis-Dreyfus, Julia 378
Louisiana Downs (racetrack) 172, 173
Louisiana State University System 661
Lourdes Health System 115
Love, Dennis M. 705
Love, Janet 593
Lovelett, Steve 645
Lovell, Richard 109
Lovett, Michael 245
Lovins, Harriet 625
Lovstad, John 534
Lowe, William M. 673
Lowe's Companies, Inc. 26, 30, 330, 484, 529, 672
Lowe's Food Stores 535
Lowman, Don 481
Lown, Andy D. 347
Loworn, Holly 597
Lowrey, F. A. 534
Loya, John 769
Loyal pet food 315
Loyola University of Chicago 661
Lozano, Joe J. 627
LS&CO. *See* Levi Strauss & Company
LSI Logic Corporation 444
LSU Agricultural and Mechanical College 661
LTC Group 506, 765
The LTV Corporation 110, 388
Lubetkin, Roy S. 39
Lübmann, Hartwick 287
Lubrizol 466
Lucas Digital 302
Lucas, George W., Jr. 302, 303, 661
Lucasfilm Ltd. 196, **302-303**, 661, 719
Lucent Technologies Inc. 74, 208, 589, 771
Lucente, Francie 572
Luciani, Alfred J. 318

Luciano, Gene 738
Lucius, Charles E. 71
Luck, Oliver 357
Lucky 7s lottery game 373
Lucky supermarkets 462
Luczo, Stephen J. 440, 441, 725
Ludeman, Christopher R. 121
Ludgate, Alan 165
Ludgate Office Complex (London) 449
Ludington, Callaway 179
Lueger, Susan A. 377, 690
Luft, Robert 281
Lugo, Miguel 205, 619
Luker Inc. 200, 201
OAO LUKOIL 712
Lukowski, Stanley J. 697
Lumbermen's Building Centers 655
Lumbermens Life Agency 650
Lumbermens Merchandising Corporation 662
Lumbermens Mutual Casualty Company 268, 269
Lumpkins, Robert L. 105, 566
Lund, Constance E. 539
Lundin, John 127
Lundy Packing Company 140
Lupinacci, Vince 464
Lupron drug 741
Lurie, Robert 180
Luse, Robert 587
Lussier, Marcel 478
Lussier, Rose M. 534
Lustig, Rick 139, 582
Lutheran Brotherhood 534
Lutheran Health Systems 549
Lutnick, Howard W. 565
Lutz, Yvonne 724
Luxor (furniture) 170, 171
Luxottica (sunglasses) 713
LVMH Moët Hennessy Louis Vuitton SA 156, 592
Lyall, Katharine C. 501, 762
Lyall, Lynn 536
Lybrand, Ross Bros. & Montgomery 400
Lybrand, William 400
Lycos, Inc. 190
Lykes Brothers 464
Lyman, Gregory A. 521
Lyman, Ray 454
Lynch, John H. (Knoll) 276
Lynch, John T. (Towers Perrin) 480
Lynch, Mary 575
Lynch, Michael W. 675
Lynch, Peter 190, 504
Lyon, Deanna 675
Lyon Financial Services 436, 724
Lyon, Wayne B. 298, 299
Lyondell Chemical Company 604
Lyons, Charlotte 259
Lyons, James E., Sr. 99
Lyons, William M. 537
Lytle, Walter 247

**M**

M. Fabrikant & Sons 662
*M\*A\*S\*H* (movie and TV show) 740

M-16 guns 133
Ma, Abraham 662
MA Laboratories, Inc. 662
M. A. Mortenson Companies, Inc. 663
Maack, Robert G. 425
Maas, Steven 685
Mabe, Donald W. 201
Mabry, Rodney H. 499
Mac Direct 338
Mac Publications 248
Mac Store 338
*Mac SystemsWAREHOUSE* (catalogs) 338
MacAndrews & Forbes Holdings Inc. **304-305**, 663
Macari, Emma Espino 129
MacArthur Foundation 414
MacCarthy, Mark 509
MacDonald, Alan 714
MacDonald, Halsted & Laybourne 66
MacDonald, Laurie 167
MacDonnell, Robert I. 283
Macey's (food stores) 545
Macfarquhar, Colin 176
MacFood Services 650
Macht, Patricia K. 97
MacInnes, Dennis 678
Macintosh computer 336, 337, 338, 430
Mack, Chuck 247
Mack, David S. 335
Mack, Russell 317
MacKay Shields LLC 370, 371
MacKinnon, Ian A. 505
Macleod-Stedman (hardware distributor) 484
Macmanus, Christopher 117
MacManus Group (advertising) 551
MacManus, John & Adams (advertising) 72
MacManus, Theodore 72
MacMillan, John 104
MacMillan, Whitney 104
Macnee, Walter M. 323
*MacNeil/Lehrer NewsHour* 144
Macomber, John D. 408
Macrides, Foster G. 586
Mactas, Mark 481, 746
*MacUser* (magazine) 248, 338
*MacWAREHOUSE* (catalogs) 338
MACWORLD Expo 248, 249
*Macworld* (magazine) 248, 249
Macy's department stores 156
Madden, John 30, 251
Madden, Nicole 27
Madden, Richard H. 145
Maddocks, David 143
Maddox, Elton 141
Maddrey, Erwin 342
Madia, William J. 71
Madison Dairy Produce 288
Madison Female Academy Building 500
Madison Square Advisors LLC 371
Madison Square Garden 476, 745
Madison Studio brand 77
Madsen, Dean 545

Michael, J. Christopher 547
Michaels, Paul S. 315
Michaels Stores, Inc. 632
Michaelson, Michael W. 283
Compagnie Générales des
Établissements Michelin
(tires) 594, 628
Michigan Avenue Partners 674
Michigan Blues 86
Michigan Community Health
Project 520
Michigan International
Speedway 390
Michigan Livestock Exchange 732
Michigan Lottery 675
Michigan Society for Group
Hospitalization 86
Michigan State Medical Society 86
Michl, Michael W. 323, 668
Mickey's brand beer 428
Micro Center stores 336, 337, 675
Micro D (computer wholesaler) 244
Micro Electronics, Inc. **336-337,**
675
Micro Warehouse, Inc. 136,
**338-339,** 676
MicroAire Surgical Instruments,
Inc. 313
Micron Electronics, Inc. See
Interland, Inc.
Micron Technology, Inc. 264, 444
MicronPC 136, 137, 676
Microsoft Corporation 48, 78, 134,
136, 137, 166, 176, 272, 312, 337,
353, 492, 508, 510, 545, 555, 584,
662, 719, 767
MicroStrategy Inc. 400
*MicroWAREHOUSE* (catalogs) 338
Mid-Am. See Dairy Farmers of
America
Mid-America Dairymen 58, 90, 148
MidAmerican Energy Holdings
Company **340-341,** 396, 676
Midas International (mufflers) 237
Mid-Continent Distributor 616
Middleton, Joe 293
Midgal, Jane 709
*Midland* (Michigan) *Daily
News* 229
Midland National Life
Insurance 720
Mid-Mountain Foods 654
Midway Games 681
Midwest Agri-Commodities 538
Midwest Manufacturing and
Distributing 331
Midwest Select (hospital
network) 116
Mies van der Rohe, Ludwig 276
Mighty Ducks of Anaheim (hockey
team) 361
Mignon restaurants 106
Mikaliunas, Richard A. 47
Milbank, Jeremiah 90
Milberg, John E. 385
Milberger, Patrick A. 277
Milbury, Roy 757
Miles, Amy 413, 712
Miles, Dan 109

Miles, Lisa 568
Milhous, Paul 506
Milhous, Robert 506
Military Honor and Decency Act
(1996) 52
Military Service Company 170, 171
Milk Marketing 58, 148
Milken, Lowell 278, 279, 652
Milken, Michael 154, 278, 279, 282,
304, 652
Milky Way 314, 315, 665
Millad clarifying agents 342, 343
Millennium Chemicals, Inc. 604
Millennium Millions lottery
game 372
Miller, Arthur 758
Miller Brewing Company 428, 721
Miller, Bruce L. 377
Miller, Coleen 445
Miller, Don 437, 724
Miller, Edward D., Jr. 645
Miller, Frank, III 648
Miller, Guy E. 379, 691
Miller, James E. 321
Miller, Kirk E. 267
Miller, Larry H. 656
Miller, Lynn C. 385
Miller, Richard G. (Parsons) 387
Miller, Richard P., Jr. (State
University of New York) 461
Miller, Robert 156, 592
Miller, Toni 550
Miller/Howard Consulting
Group 480
Miller's Outpost 539
Milligan, Patricia 481
Milliken & Company Inc. **342-343,**
677
Milliken, Gerrish 342, 677
Milliken, Roger 343, 677
Milliken, Seth 342
Millionaires candy 424, 425, 719
Millitron dye 342
Mills, Charles (Hunt
Consolidated) 635
Mills, Charles S. (Medline
Industries) 670
Milne Fruit Products 380
Milton Bradley games 417
Milwaukee Brewers (baseball
team) 306, 307
Milwaukee Bucks (basketball
team) 355
*Milwaukee Journal Sentinel* 648
Mind/Body Medical Institute 566
Mini Chopper convenience
stores 617
Minigus, Linda 673
MiniScribe (disk drives) 400
Minit Mart 577
Minnaugh, Mark 199, 615
Minnesota Cooperative Creameries
Association 288
Minnesota Linseed Oil 122
Minnesota Lynx (basketball
team) 355
Minnesota Mining and
Manufacturing Company 522, 750

Minnesota Mutual Companies,
Inc. 677
Minnesota Timberwolves (basketball
team) 355, 742
Minnesota Twins (baseball
team) 307
Minnesota Valley Canning 72
Minnesota Vikings (football
team) 357, 498
Minnesota Wild (hockey team) 360,
361, 663, 684
Grupo Minsa S.A. de C.V.
(flour) 232, 333
Minturn, Frederick K. 679
Minute Maid 512, 620
Minyard, Elizabeth 677
Minyard Food Stores 677
Miramax Films 228, 229
Miramontes, Lou 287
Mirante, Arthur, II 587
Mirrer, Louise 129
Misenhimer, Holly 563
Miss USA/Universe pageants 482,
483, 749
Mission Beverages 746
Mission Hills Country Club
(California) 130, 131, 577
Missouri Portland Cement 104
*Mister Roger's Neighborhood* 144
MIT. See Massachusetts Institute of
Technology
MiTAC International 740
Mitchell, A. Joe, Jr. 764
Mitchell, Connie 764
Mitchell, Janet D. 395, 701
Mitchell, Jay 668
Mitchell, Lee Roy 126, 127, 575
Mitchell, Pat 145
Mitchell, Robert W. 245, 639
Mitchell, Roger 286
Mitchell, Tandy 127
Mitchell, Tom 440
Mitchell, W. E. 253
Mitsubishi Corporation 606, 647,
733
Mitsubishi Estate 587
Mitsui Group 122, 123, 571
Mizeur, Dave 638
M.L. Stern & Company, Ltd.
(broker) 384, 385
MML Bay State Life Insurance
Company 321
MML Investors Services, Inc. 321
Mobil Corporation. See Exxon Mobil
Corporation
Mobouck, Patrick C. 153
Moccio, Anthony J. 554
*MODE* (magazine) 611
Modern Continental Companies,
Inc. 678
Modern Maid appliances 618
*Modern Maturity* (magazine) 28,
29, 529
Modern Products 222
Modern Tool and Die Company 679
Modie, Christine M. 321
Moe, Don 253
Moeller, Joseph W. 281
Mogensen, Dennis 265, 648

Neher, Pat 253
Neighborhood Entertainment theater chain 412
The Neiman Marcus Group 630
Neiman Marcus Travel Services 107
Nekura 364
Nelson, Christian 424
Nelson, Curtis C. 107
Nelson, Douglas E. 768
Nelson, Marilyn Carlson 106, 107, 567
Nelson, Maurice S., Jr. 601
Nelson, Ronald L. 167, 597
Nelson, Thomas C. 29, 683
Nelson, William H. 641
Nemacolin Woodlands resort 26
Nemeth, Ken 63
Neomediam plumbing products 284, 653
NESCO, Inc. 686
Nestlé Purina PetCare 626
Nestlé SA 264
Nestlé USA 254, 474, 715
Nestler (office furniture) 222
Nestor Levy, Susan E. 57
Netchvolodoff, Alexander V. 147
Netcon 74
Netscape Communications 248, 456
Netscape Navigator Web browser 756
*Netscape World: The Web* (magazine) 248
NetSuite Development 191
Network Solutions, Inc. (Internet domain registrar) 438
*Network World* (magazine) 249
Neuhaus, Solomon 32
Nevarez, Miguel A. 499
New Balance Athletic Shoe, Inc. 686
*New Car Buying Guide* (book) 139
*The New Ebony Cookbook* (book) 258, 259
New England Cable News 229
New England Confectionery 752
New England Frozen Foods 102
New England Patriots (football team) 357
New Jersey Devils (hockey team) 361
New Jersey Nets (basketball team) 355
New Jersey State Lottery Commission 687
New Millennium World Atlas Deluxe Edition (software) 409
New Orleans Saints (football team) 357
New United Motor Manufacturing, Inc. **366-367**, 687
New West Energy 734
New World Communications Group 304
New World Television 304
New York Blue Shield 174
New York City Board of Higher Education 128
New York City Building 449

New York City Community College 128
New York City Health and Hospitals Corporation **368-369**, 687
New York City Technical College 128, 129
New York City Transit Authority 334, 335
New York Condensed Milk 90
New York Curb Market Association 46
*The New Yorker* (magazine) 32, 33
New York Federal Reserve Bank 186
New York Giants (football team) 356, 357
New York Helmsley hotel 231
New York International Airport 398
New York Islanders (hockey team) 361
New York Jets (football team) 357
New York Knicks (basketball team) 355
New York Liberty (basketball team) 355
New York Life Insurance Company 28, **370-371**, 688
New York Life, L.P. 350
New York Metropolitan Museum of Art 204
New York Mets (baseball team) 307
*New York Morning Journal* 228
New York-New Jersey Port 398
New York Palace hotel 230
*New York Post* 486
New York Public Library 134
New York Racket store 76, 553
New York Rangers (hockey team) 361
New York State Institute of Applied Arts and Sciences 128
New York State Lottery **372-373**, 688
New York Stock Exchange, Inc. 46, 142, 352, **374-375**, 688
New York Supreme Court 368
The New York Times Company 32, 46
New York Transportation Infrastruture Bond Act 334
New York University 689, 690
*New York World* 228
New York Yankees (baseball team) 250, 307
The Newark Group 689
Newark International Airport 399
Newbridge partnerships 474
Newby, D. M. 315
NewCap Insurance Company, Limited 115, 116
Newcourt Financial 208
Newhouse Broadcasting 33
Newhouse, Donald E. 32, 33, 61, 530
Newhouse, Samuel I. 32
Newhouse, Samuel I., Jr. 32, 33, 530
NewKote boxboard 689
Newland Communities 96
Newlin, David B. 533

Newman, Deb 742
NewMedia 176
Newport City housing development 290, 656
Newport Pacific Management, Inc. 294, 295
Newport, Tom 568
The News Corporation Limited 228, 304
NewSouth Communications 283
Newspaper Association of America 60
Newspaper Industry Communication Center 60, 61
Newsted, Richard 673
*Newsweek* (magazine) 176, 404, 708
Nexant (energy consulting) 74
NEXCOM Ships Stores 685
Nexstar Financial Corporation 282, 283, 653
Nextera Enterprises, Inc. 278, 279, 652
NFL. *See* National Football League
Nibblebox (animation) 278
NICC. *See* Newspaper Industry Communication Center
Nichols, Jean 545
Nichols, Ken L. 31
Nichols, Rodney P. 664
Nicholson, Bruce J. 534
Nicholson, Pam 179
Nick Bollettieri Tennis Academy 251
Nickelodean cable network 218
Nicklaus, Jack 130, 382
NicoDerm CQ drug 40
Niekamp, Randy 586
Nielsen Dillingham (contractor) 593
Night Train wine 169
Nightingale, Florence 56
NIKE, Inc. 418, 686, 717
Nikken Global Inc. 689
Nikon Corporation 137
Nilles, Richard 271
Nirvana (music group) 166
Nissan Motor Company, Ltd. 561, 563, 717, 767
Nitschke, Ray 210, 621
Nixon, Richard M. 58, 600
NK brand grains 622
NL Industries 583
n-LIGHTEN optical transmitter 522
Nob Hill Foods 710
Nobel Educational Dynamics 278
Nobel Learning Communities 278, 279, 652
Nobel prize 40, 128, 134, 196, 324, 378, 456, 496, 560, 667, 756, 760, 769
Nobles, Cy S. 281
Noe, David 671
Nokia Corporation 765
Nolan, Frances 467
Nolan, John 491
Noland, Joseph J. 427
None Such brands 90
NOR PAC 690

Pontiac vehicle 256, 561, 606, 706, 733
Poole, Robert M. 359
POP.com (Web site) 166
Pope, Charles C. 441, 725
Pope, Darryl L. 261
Popeye cartoon character 242
Popeye's Chicken & Biscuits restaurants 124, 575
Popko, Kathleen 115
Pople, John 378
Popular Club Plan (catalog sales) 254
*Popular Mechanics* (magazine) 229
Population Council 79, 194
Porcelain Steel Building (construction) 516
Poremba, Dave 675
PORK PACT 36
Dr.ING.h.c.F.Porsche AG 630, 631, 731
The Port Authority of New York and New Jersey **398-399**, 703
The Port Authority Trans-Hudson System (PATH) 398, 399, 703
Port Newark/Elizabeth Marine Terminal 399
Porter, Arthur T. 591
Porter, Joe 198
Porter, M. R. 484
Porter, Townsend H., Jr. 441
Portland Children's Museum 79
Portland Fire (basketball team) 355
Portland State University 520
Portland Trail Blazers (basketball team) 355, 510, 511, 767
Portman, John 240
Post Exchange (PX) 52
Postal Reorganization Act (1970) 490
Postal Service. *See* United States Postal Service
Posturepedic mattress 442
Pot o' Gold lottery game 373, 473
Potamkin, Alan 702
Potamkin, Robert 702
Potamkin, Victor 702
Potter, John E. (US Postal Service) 490, 491, 754
Potter, John W. (Oxford Automotive) 695
Potter, Kent 574
Poughkeepsie Savings Bank 640
Powell, Colin 110, 128
Powell, Jerome H. 111
Powell, Lura J. 71
Power Authority of the State of New York 703
Power Investments (engines) 152
*Powerball - The Game Show* (TV show) 581
Powerball Lottery 372, 581, 680
PowerBridge Group 340
PowerOne Media 32
Powers, Larry K. 613
Powers, Richard 740
PowerSpec PC computers 336, 337, 675
Powerstreet online brokerage 190

PPG Industries, Inc. 212
PRADCO (fishing tackle) 170, 171
Prairie Farms Dairy Inc. 704
*A Prairie Home Companion* (radio program) 144
Prairie View A&M University 470, 471, 743
Prasetio, John 49
Pratt, Steven H. 57
Prausa, John W. 455
Praver, Mitch 359
PRECLUDE dura substitute 523
Preference paper products 727
Preferred Financial Group 226, 227
Preferred HealthAlliance 348
Preferred Provider Organization of Michigan 86, 87, 557
Premcor Inc. 340, 704
Premier Bedding 442
Premier Beverage 738
Premier Foodservice Distributors of America 479
Premier (health care) 115
Premiere Cinemas 412
Premium Distributors 713
Premium Standard Farms (pork) 140, 583
PREPA. *See* Puerto Rico Electric Power Authority
Pre-Paid Legal Services Inc. 154
Presby, J. Thomas 155
Presbyterian Healthcare Services (New Mexico) 704
Presbyterian Healthcare System (North Carolina) 691
Presbyterian Healthcare System (Texas) 744
The Presbyterian Hospital (New York City) 44, 134
Presidential Medal of Freedom 258
Presidential Plaza apartments (New Jersey) 291
Presley, Elvis 416, 424
Presley, Greg 644
Press, Jonathan 355
Press, Terry 167
Presta, Kelly 509
Prestige carpets 342
Preston, Forrest 658
Preston, William 69
Prevacid drug 741
Price Chopper warehouse stores 62, 63, 547, 617
Price Mart stores 62, 63
Price, Samuel 400
Price, William 474
PricewaterhouseCoopers 48, 154, 182, 206, 286, **400-401**, 540, 620, 705
*Pride in Performance-Keep It Going* (book) 657
Priest, Patricia 553
Priestly, Kay G. 49, 540
PRIMEA power assemblies 523
PrimeCo (telecom) 765
PRIMEDIA, Inc. (publishing) 282, 283, 460, 653
PRIMESTAR (satellite TV) 92
Primus, Inc. 705

Prince, Jack 289
*The Prince of Egypt* (movie) 166, 167
Prince pasta 90, 91
Princeton University 378
Printpack, Inc. 705
Prior Energy Corporation 637
PRISTYNE UX filter media 523
Pritzker, A. N. 240, 312
Pritzker and Pritzker (law firm) 312
Pritzker, Bob 240
Pritzker, Donald 240
Pritzker, Jay 240, 312, 482
Pritzker, Nicholas 240, 312
Pritzker, Nicholas J. 241
Pritzker, Penny S. 241
Pritzker, Robert 312
Pritzker, Robert A. 313, 665
Pritzker School of Medicine 497
Pritzker, Thomas J. 240, 241, 636
Private Brands (soup stock) 122
Private Health Care Systems 214
Private Ledger. *See* Linsco/Private Ledger Corporation
PrizeLAWN lawn spreaders 516, 772
Prizm car 366, 367, 687
Pro & Son's, Inc. 489
Pro Line windows and doors 698
Pro Parts Xpress (auto parts) 518, 519, 774
Proagro 36
The Procter & Gamble Company 72, 106, 304, 432, 551, 620
Proctor, Deborah A. 57
Proctor, Georganne 75, 552
Producers Creamery Company 148
Production Response Systems 506
Productivity Point International 278, 279
Pro-Fac Cooperative (vegetables) 38
Professional Audio 310
Proffer, Lanny M. 359
Proffitt, Jackie 716
Proffitt's stores 76
ProForm compound 683
ProForm fitness equipment 637
ProGold (corn sweeteners) 538
Prograft Medical 522
Progressive Baker 105
Progressive Grocers 62
Project RISE 246
Pro-Lawn (turf care) 38
Promo Edge Company (printing) 673
Propeller office tables 277
Pro-Pet (pet foods) 38, 622
Prosise, Robert 171
ProSource 236
ProSource Wholesale Floorcoverings 568
Prospect Motors Inc. 706
Protection Services Industries 655
Protective Closures 310
Proven Value auto products 112
Provena Health 706

Tricamo, Frank 63, 547
TRICARE (government health care
contracts) 52
TRICON Global Restaurants,
Inc. 124, 162, 236, 575, 595
Trill pet food 315
Trinity Care 753
Trinity Church (New York City) 134
Trinity College of Art and
Sciences 598
Trinity Health 748
Trinity Industries 598
Tripifoods, Inc. 243
*TripMaker* (software) 408, 711
Trites, Dennis L. 101
Triton Energy 232
Triton TBS 123
Triumph Packaging 618
Trofholz, Donald 213
Trojans of the University of
Southern California 760
Tropicana juice 380
Trosino, Vincent J. 459
Troy-Bilt tillers 679
Truck-Lite 390, 391
True, Douglas K. 757
True Value hardware 30, 212, 484,
485, 749
Truess, Jim 622
Truett's Grill 124
Truitt, Gary R. 235
Truman Arnold Companies 749
Trumka, Richard L. 35, 532
Trump, Donald J. 230, 372, 482,
483, 629, 749
Trump, Ivana 482
The Trump Organization **482-483**,
749
Trupo, Mary 419
TruServ Corporation 30, **484-485**,
529, 562, 594, 749
*Trust Betrayed: Inside the AARP*
(book) 28
Trustees of the California State
University. *See* (Trustees of the)
California State University
Trustmark Insurance Company 750
Tru-Tec Services, Inc. 281
TRW Inc. 152, 386
Tsai, Gerry 190
TTC Illinois, Inc. 750
TTI, Inc. 750
TTX Company 751
Tu, John 272, 273, 651
Tubi Speciali Auto (air-conditioning
hoses) 310
Tuccillo, Dan 323
Tucker, Albert 120
Tucker, Lynch, & Coldwell 120
Tucker Rocky Distributing 656
*Tucker: The Man and His Dream*
(movie) 303
*Tuesdays with Morrie* (movie) 218,
219, 625
Tufts Associated Health Plans,
Inc. 751
Tufts University 566
TUI Business Travel 308, 664
Tully, Herbert B. 772
Tunes lozenges 315

Turley, James 183
Turley, Robert 393
Turnbull, Andrew B. 210
Turner Entertainment
Company 417
Turner Foods 270
Turner Home Entertainment 188
Turner, Jana L. 121
Turner, Jim 597
Turner, LeBaron 772
Turner, Robert Edward "Ted" 747
Turner, Roger 513
Turner, Russell D. 754
Turner Sports 682
Turner, T. J. 513, 767
Turning Leaf wines 168, 169, 600
Turquands Barton Mayhew
(accounting) 182
Tursy, Tony 737
Tuxedo Fruit 464
TVA. *See* Tennessee Valley Authority
*TV Guide* 144
Twentieth Century Fox 417
Twin Fair stores 328
Twix candy 314, 315, 665
Two Trees Inn 318, 319
Ty Inc. **486-487**, 751
Tyco International Ltd. 146
Tyler Rubber Company 142
Tynes, Donald 762
Tyson Foods, Inc. 200, 616
Tzagournis, Manuel 383

**U**

UAL Corporation 94, 630
UAW. *See* United Auto Workers
UBS PaineWebber 290
UCLA. *See* University of California
Los Angeles
Udow, Marianne 87
Ueberroth, Heidi 355
Ueberroth, Peter 108, 278
Ugeux, Georges 375
UIS, Inc. 752
UJC of North America 752
Ukrop's Super Markets 479
Ullman, Myron, III 156
Ulsamer, James S. 69
Ultra Mart stores 422
UltraLeather 452
Ultra-Light Arms 132
UltraSuede 452
Umansky, David J. 451
UMass. *See* University of
Massachusetts
Unanue & Sons 204
Unanue, Andy 205
Unanue, Anthony 204
Unanue, Charles 204
Unanue, Francisco J. 204, 205
Unanue, Joseph A. 204, 205, 619
Unanue, Prudencio 204
Uncle Ben's Rice 314, 315, 665
*Undeclared* (TV show) 166, 167,
597
Underwood family 777
Underwood, John R. 211
UNext (online training) 278, 279,
496

Unhjem, Michael B. 83
UNICEF 79
Unifi 696
Unified Western Grocers,
Inc. **488-489**, 752
Uniform Federal Fund-Raising
Program (1957) 492
Uniform Support Centers 685
UniGroup, Inc. 753
Uni-Group office panels 222
UniHealth Foundation 118, 753
Unilever 100, 530
Unilloyd (company) 574
The Union Central Life Insurance
Company 753
Union College of Law 378
The Union Labor Life Insurance
Company 754
Union Oil Company 184
Union Pacific Corporation 751
Union Tank Car Company 313
Union Theological Seminary 134
Uniroyal Goodrich Tire
Company 594
Unison Capital Corporation,
Inc. 261
United Airlines. *See* UAL
Corporation
United Artists Theatre Circuit
(movie chain) 412
United Asset Management
Corporation 414
United Auto Group, Inc. 390, 391,
699
United Auto Workers 35, 222, 366
United Biscuits (UK) 232, 333
United Building Centers 655
United Center arena 774
United Chair (office furniture) 222
United Community Funds and
Councils 492
United Concordia Companies,
Inc. 234, 235
United Defense Industries 110, 567
United Express airline 534
United Farm Workers 168
United Food and Commercial
Workers Union 402
United Grocers of Oregon 488, 752
United Harvest 123, 571
United Israel Appeal 752
United Jewish Appeal 752
United Medical Service 174
United Mine Workers 234
United Mutual Fire Insurance
Company 294
United Mutual Life Insurance 539
United Nations 414, 420, 482
United Negro College Fund 78, 79
United of Omaha Life Insurance
Company 349, 680
United Parcel Service, Inc. 34, 246,
404, 490, 641
United Press International 60, 228
United Refining 712
United Services Automobile
Association. *See* USAA
United Space Alliance 754
United States Army Automobile
Insurance Association 502

Waldron, Maureen 581
Walgreen Company 639
Walker Brothers Grocery 488
Walker, Edward V. 363
Walker, Henry G. 706
Walker, Kenneth L. 443
Walker, Mark 652
Walker, Robert C. 63, 547
Walker, Samuel 132
Walker, William 54
*Walking With Dinosaurs* (TV show) 158, 594
Walkush, J. P. 439
Wall, James H. 155, 590
Wall, John T. 353
*The Wall Street Journal* 80
Wallace, Eugene C. 566
Wallach, Abraham 483
Wallach, Dan 27, 528
Wallach, Kenneth L. 571
Waller, Jeffrey M. 433
Wallsten, Lloyd 143
Wal-Mart Stores, Inc. 102, 103, 168, 198, 236, 260, 346, 394, 452, 486, 565, 595, 632, 633, 644, 646, 733
Walsh, Bill 173
The Walsh Group 768
Walsh, Jim 329, 671
Walsh, Matthew M. 768
Walsh, Tim 610
The Walt Disney Company 32, 166, 176, 228, 229, 296, 360, 452, 476, 524, 597, 605, 682, 733, 745
Walt Disney Internet Group 492, 524
Walter Industries, Inc. (builders) 282, 283
WALTERMART SUPERMARKETS 243
Walters, Paul F. 391
Waltham pet food 315
Walton, Bill R. 77
Walton, R. Keith 135
Walton, Robert D. 97
Walton, Sam 198, 260
Wamsutta home furnishings 452, 453
Wanek, Ron 544
Wanek, Todd 544
Wang, Caden 157, 592
Wangurd, Debra 764
WAPE-FM (Jacksonville) 147
Warburg Pincus 276, 652
Ward, Jim 303
Ward, Louis 424
Ward Paper Box Company 424
Ward, Scott H. 424, 425, 719
Ward, Thomas S. 424, 425, 719
Warden, Gail L. 630
Warehouse.com 338
Waremart Foods 773
Warga, Thomas J. 371
Warlick, Anderson D. 696
Warm Wishes greeting cards 216
The Warnaco Group, Inc. 100
Warner Brothers 278, 350, 417
Warner Communications. *See* AOL Time Warner Inc.

Warner, H. Ty 487, 751
Warner, John H., Jr. 439
Warner, Tim 127
Warner, Ty 486
*Warning: Dieting May Be Hazardous To Your Health* (educational video) 139
Warren, David P. 353
Warren Electric 578
Warren Equities Inc. 769
Warren, George E. 614
Warren, V'Ella 761
Warrin, Catherine 554
Warrington, George D. 362, 363, 684
Warshauer, Myron 236, 237
Washington Capitals (hockey team) 361
The Washington Companies. *See* Washington Group International, Inc.
Washington Counsel (lobbying) 182
Washington Group International, Inc. 769
Washington Mystics (basketball team) 355
The Washington Post Company 176
Washington Redskins (football team) 357
Washington University in St. Louis 769
Washington University Medical Center 555
Washington Wizards (basketball team) 354, 355
Wasilov, Alex 419
Wassall PLC 282
Wasson, Ted 773
Waste Control Specialties 583
Watanabe, Toshizo "Tom" 689
Water Pik Technologies 71
Waterhouse, Edwin 400
Waterman office products 262
Watkins Associated Industries 770
Watkins, Bill (Watkins Associated Industries) 770
Watkins, H. Thomas 741
Watkins, John 770
Watkins, William D. (Seagate) 440, 441
Watsmann, Judy 291, 656
Watson, Anthony L. 628
Watterson, Scott R. 637
Watts, Howard 115
Wausau 364
Wausau Commercial Insurance Market 295
Wauth, Ed 644
Wave radio 92, 93, 559
Waverly furniture 299
Wavtrace (wireless access equipment) 511
Wawa Inc. 770
Wax, Charles J. 53, 543
WAXN-TV (Charlotte, NC) 147
Waycaster, Bill 745
Wayne Foods 140
Wayne State University 591

Wayne State University School of Medicine 773
WBAB-FM (Long Island, NY) 147
WBAL-TV (Baltimore) 228
WBLI-FM (Long Island, NY) 147
WBTS-FM (Atlanta) 147
WCI Communities, Inc. 770
WCI Steel 712
WDUV-FM (Tampa, FL) 147
We Care Hair salons 160
WealthBuilder annuities 617
Weather Channel 655
Weatheringon, Carman 177
Weaver, H. Pratt 480
Webauction.com 338
Webb, Del 643
Webber, Henry 497
Webcraft 506, 765
Weber, Arnold R. 379
Weber, Paul 642
Weber, Robinn S. 425, 719
Weber, Tom 704
WEBS. *See* World Equity Benchmark Shares
Webster, Bill 549
Webvan 266
*The Wedding* (movie) 219
WeddingChannel.com 305, 663
WEDR-FM (Miami) 147
Weed, Joe K. 171
Weeker, J. T. 491
Weekley, David 588
Weekly, John W. 349, 680
Wegman, John 771
Wegman, Robert B. 771
Wegmans Food Markets, Inc. 771
Wehrli, Cary 536
Weider fitness equipment 637
Weimer, Linda 501
Weinbach, Lawrence A. 48
Weinberg Collge of Arts and Sciences 379
Weinberg, Richard A. 612
Weinberger, Alan D. 544
Weinberger, Carlyle 544
Weiner, Edward G. 748
Weiner, Steven 455
Weinshilboum, Richard M. 325
Weinstein, David C. 191
Weis, Gerald R. "Gary" 580
Weis Markets 479
Weiss, Douglas A. 145
Weiss, Louis 514
Weiss, Peck & Greer 738
Weisselberg, Allen 483, 749
Weisser, Alberto 565
Weissman, Jerry 174
Weizenbaum, Morris 198
Welch, John F., Jr. "Jack" 757
Welch, Patrick 684
Welch's juice 577
Wellcraft boats 614
Weller, H. S. 348
Welles, Judith 389
Wellington Management Group 504
Wellmark Health Networks 226
WellPoint Health Networks 82, 572
Wells Fargo & Company 110, 518

# HOOVER'S MEANS BUSINESS